Formulas and Equations

$m = \dfrac{y_2 - y_1}{x_2 - x_1}$ Slope of a line

$ax + b = 0$ Linear equation

$y = mx + b$ Slope–intercept form

$y = m(x - x_1) + y_1$ Point–slope form

$x = h$ Vertical line

$y = b$ Horizontal line

$d = rt$ Distance, rate, and time

$s = 16t^2$ Distance for a falling object

$a^2 - b^2 = (a - b)(a + b)$ Difference of two squares

$(a + b)^2 = a^2 + 2ab + b^2$
$(a - b)^2 = a^2 - 2ab + b^2$ Square of a binomial

$x = -\dfrac{b}{2a}$ Vertex formula (x-coordinate)

$y = a(x - h)^2 + k$ Vertex form

$ax^2 + bx + c = 0$ Quadratic equation

$x = \dfrac{-b \pm \sqrt{b^2 - 4ac}}{2a}$ Quadratic formula

$(x - h)^2 + (y - k)^2 = r^2$ Equation of a circle

$d = \sqrt{(x_2 - x_1)^2 + (y_2 - y_1)^2}$ Distance between two points

Geometry

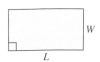

Rectangle
$A = LW$
$P = 2L + 2W$

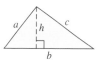

Triangle
$A = \frac{1}{2}bh$
$P = a + b + c$

Pythagorean Theorem
$c^2 = a^2 + b^2$

Circle
$C = 2\pi r$
$A = \pi r^2$

Rectangular (Parallelepiped) Box
$V = LWH$
$S = 2LW + 2LH + 2WH$

Cylinder
$V = \pi r^2 h$
$S = 2\pi rh + 2\pi r^2$

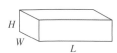

Sphere
$V = \frac{4}{3}\pi r^3$
$S = 4\pi r^2$

Cone
$V = \frac{1}{3}\pi r^2 h$
$S = \pi r^2 + \pi r\sqrt{r^2 + h^2}$

Annotated Instructor's Edition

Intermediate Algebra

with Applications and Visualization

Second Edition

Gary K. Rockswold

Minnesota State University, Mankato

Terry A. Krieger

Winona State University

PEARSON

Addison
Wesley

Boston • San Francisco • New York • London • Toronto
Sydney • Tokyo • Singapore • Madrid • Mexico City
Munich • Paris • Cape Town • Hong Kong • Montreal

Publisher	Greg Tobin
Editor in Chief	Maureen O'Connor
Acquisitions Editor	Jennifer Crum
Project Editor	Lauren Morse
Editorial Assistant	Marcia Emerson
Managing Editor	Ron Hampton
Production Supervisor	Kathleen A. Manley
Production Services	Kathy Diamond
Photo Researcher	Beth Anderson
Compositor	Nesbitt Graphics, Inc.
Media Producer	Lynne Blaszak
Software Development	Chris Tragasz and Kathleen Bowler
Marketing Manager	Dona Kenly
Marketing Coordinator	Lindsay Skay
Prepress Supervisor	Caroline Fell
Manufacturing Buyer	Evelyn Beaton
Design Supervisor	Dennis Schaefer
Cover Designer	Andrea Menza
Cover Photograph	Art Wolfe/Photo Researchers, Inc.

To

Palmer and Betty Rockswold
Reuben and Marlene Krieger

Photo Credits

p. 1: Lester Lefkowitz/Corbis; p. 3: NASA; p. 73: Beth Anderson;
p. 144: PhotoDisc Blue; p. 216: Corbis RF; p. 300: Digital Vision; p. 374: Digital
Vision; p. 461: PhotoDisc; p. 493: Sara Anderson; p. 529: Digital Vision;
p. 599: Digital Vision; p. 669: Digital Vision; p. 707: PhotoDisc

Library of Congress Cataloging-in-Publication Data

Rockswold, Gary K.
   Intermediate algebra with applications and visualization—2nd ed. / Gary K.
Rockswold, Terry A. Krieger.
     p. cm.
   Rev. ed. cf: Intermediate algebra through modeling and visualization, c2002.
   Includes bibliographical references and index.
   ISBN 0-321-15892-X
   1. Algebra. I. Krieger, Terry A. II. Rockswold, Gary K. Intermediate algebra
through modeling and visualization. III. Title.

QA152.3.R65 2005
512.9—dc22   2003069048

(Annotated Instructor's Edition: ISBN 0-321-15893-8)

3 4 5 6 7 8 9 10—RRDW—08 07 06 05

CONTENTS

7   Radical Expressions and Functions   461

8   Quadratic Functions and Equations   529

9 Exponential and Logarithmic Functions   599

10 Conic Sections   669

LIST OF APPLICATIONS

PREFACE

Intermediate Algebra with Applications and Visualization, Second Edition, offers an innovative approach to the intermediate algebra curriculum that allows students to gain both skills and understanding. This textbook not only demonstrates the relevance of mathematics, but it also prepares students for future courses. The early introduction of functions and graphs allows instructors to use applications and visualization to present mathematical concepts. Real data, graphs, and tables play an important role in the course, giving meaning to the numbers and equations that students encounter. This approach increases student interest, motivation, and the likelihood for success.

 ## Approach

In *Intermediate Algebra with Applications and Visualization,* Second Edition, mathematical concepts are often introduced by moving from the concrete to the abstract. Relevant applications underscore mathematical concepts. This text includes a diverse collection of unique, up-to-date applications that answer the commonly asked question: "When will I ever use this?" Applications, visualization, and the Rule of Four allow greater access to mathematics for students having different learning styles. However, the primary purpose of this text is to teach mathematical concepts and skills. Building skills is an objective of every section. Standard mathematical definitions, theorems, symbolism, and rigor are maintained.

A comprehensive curriculum is presented with a balanced and flexible approach that is essential for today's intermediate algebra courses. Instructors have the flexibility to strike their own balance with regard to emphasis on skills, rule of four, applications, and graphing calculator technology. With this approach to the Rule of Four (verbal, graphical, numerical, and symbolic methods), instructors can easily emphasize one rule more than another to meet their students' needs. This flexibility also extends to applications and graphing calculator use. The text contains numerous practical applications, including modeling of real-world data with functions. Instructors have the freedom to integrate graphing calculators throughout the course. However, graphing calculator use is optional.

 ## Changes Incorporated in the Second Edition

This edition contains several important changes resulting from numerous comments and suggestions made by instructors, students, and reviewers. Eight new sections were added to increase both the breadth and depth of topics discussed. Increased emphasis is given to problem solving, formulas from geometry, graphing equations by hand, polynomial equations, parabolas, complex fractions, linear programming, and inverse functions. More than 100 new examples were added to help guide students in their learning of mathematical skills and concepts. Approximately 2000 new exercises were added to allow instructors greater flexibility when making assignments that meet their students' needs. Many of these new exercises emphasize basic skills needed for future mathematics courses. The extensive exercise sets are carefully graded with several levels of difficulty.

Organization

The text consists of 11 chapters and 58 sections. The order of these chapters is slightly different in this edition. First, the chapter covering quadratic functions and equations is now located after the chapter covering radical expressions and functions. However, in this edition, Chapter 8, Quadratic Functions and Equations, can be taught directly after Chapter 5, Polynomial Expressions and Functions. Second, the chapter covering exponential and logarithmic functions now occurs before the chapter covering conic sections.

Chapter 1: Real Numbers and Algebra
This chapter reviews several topics from beginning algebra, including numbers, operations on numbers, and integer exponents. Formulas are introduced, and the xy-plane is used to plot and visualize data.

Chapter 2: Linear Functions and Models
Basic concepts about functions, along with their verbal, symbolic, graphical, and numerical representations, are discussed in this chapter. It features linear functions, linear models, slope, and lines. The applications presented make concepts, such as slope, more concrete and relevant to students.

Chapter 3: Linear Equations and Inequalities
This chapter covers solving linear equations and inequalities. Symbolic, graphical, and numerical techniques for solving equations and inequalities are presented. Many of the concepts presented in this chapter are used to solve equations and inequalities in subsequent chapters. Applications promote student learning and understanding. Compound inequalities and absolute value inequalities are included.

Chapter 4: Systems of Linear Equations
The concepts presented in Chapter 3 are extended to systems of linear equations and inequalities. Emphasis is given to systems involving two equations in two variables. Linear programming, matrix methods, and determinants are included at the end of the chapter.

Chapter 5: Polynomial Expressions and Functions
Polynomials and polynomial functions are introduced, and an extensive discussion of factoring is included. This chapter extends to polynomials many of the techniques introduced in Chapters 2 and 3. Functions, applications, and real-world data continue to underlie many of the discussions. Students also learn to solve polynomial equations by applying their knowledge of factoring.

Chapter 6: Rational Expressions and Functions
Rational expressions and functions are introduced in this chapter. Arithmetic operations on rational expressions are included. Applications occur throughout, along with a special section on proportions and variation.

Chapter 7: Radical Expressions and Functions
Radical notation and some basic functions, such as the square root and cube root functions, are discussed. Presentation of properties of rational exponents is delayed until this chapter so that students can immediately apply them. Additional material on simplifying radical expressions is included. The chapter concludes with a section on complex numbers.

Chapter 8: Quadratic Functions and Equations

Quadratic functions and their graphs are discussed early in this chapter so that students may use these concepts to understand solutions to quadratic equations. Additional material on graphs of quadratic functions was added. The connection between x-intercepts, zeros of a quadratic function, and solutions to a quadratic equation is made. Methods for solving quadratic equations are discussed extensively. Except for the topic of complex solutions to quadratic equations, this chapter can be taught immediately after Chapter 5, Polynomial Expressions and Functions.

Chapter 9: Exponential and Logarithmic Functions

This chapter begins with a section on composite and inverse functions. Logarithms, properties of logarithms, exponential and logarithmic functions, and exponential and logarithmic equations are covered in this chapter. Linear growth and exponential growth are compared, enabling students to grasp the fundamental difference between these two types of growth. The chapter contains many applications.

Chapter 10: Conic Sections

This chapter introduces parabolas, circles, ellipses, and hyperbolas. It concludes with a section on solving nonlinear systems of equations and inequalities.

Chapter 11: Sequences and Series

This chapter introduces the basic concepts of both sequences and series, concentrating on arithmetic and geometric sequences and series. Both graphical and symbolic representations of sequences are discussed, along with applications and models. The chapter concludes with the binomial theorem.

 Features

Applications and Models

Interesting, straightforward applications are a strength of this textbook, helping students become more effective problem solvers. Applications are intuitive and not overly technical so that they can be introduced in a minimum of class time. Current data are utilized to create meaningful mathematical models, exposing students to a wealth of actual uses of mathematics. A unique feature of this text is that the applications are woven into both the discussions and the exercises. Students can more easily learn how to solve applications when they are discussed within the text. (See pages 94, 108, and 173.)

Putting It All Together

This helpful feature occurs at the end of each section to summarize techniques and reinforce the mathematical concepts presented in the section. It is given in an easy-to-follow grid format. (See pages 34, 83, and 174.)

Section Exercise Sets

The exercise sets are the heart of any mathematics text, and this textbook includes a wide variety of exercises that are instructive for student learning. Each exercise set contains exercises involving basic concepts, skill-building, and applications. In addition, many exercises ask students to read and interpret graphs. Writing About Mathematics exercises are also included at the end of every exercise set. The exercise sets are carefully graded and categorized by topic, making it easier for instructors to select appropriate assignments. (See pages 98, 127, and 154.)

Checking Basic Concepts

After every two sections, this feature presents a brief set of exercises that students can use for review purposes or group activities. These exercises require 10–20 minutes to complete and can be used during class if time permits. (See pages 132, 324, and 417.)

Making Connections

This feature occurs throughout the text and helps students relate previously learned concepts to new concepts. (See pages 43, 76, and 186.)

Critical Thinking

One or more Critical Thinking exercises are included in most sections. They pose questions that can be used for either classroom discussion or homework assignments. These exercises typically ask students to extend a mathematical concept beyond what has already been discussed. (See pages 26, 482, and 546.)

Technology Notes

Occurring throughout the text, Technology Notes offer students guidance, suggestions, and cautions on the use of the graphing calculator. (See pages 123, 150, and 466.)

Group Activities: Working with Real Data

This feature occurs after selected sections (1 or 2 per chapter) and provides an opportunity for students to work collaboratively on a problem that involves real-world data. Most activities can be completed with limited use of class time. (See pages 116, 314, and 488.)

Chapter and Section Introductions

Many intermediate algebra students have little or no understanding of what mathematics is about. Chapter and section introductions present and explain some of the reasons for studying mathematics. They provide insights into the relevance of mathematics to many aspects of real life. (See pages 50, 73, and 300.)

Chapter Summaries

Chapter summaries are presented in an easy-to-read grid format for students to use in reviewing the important topics in the chapter. (See pages 63, 202, and 363.)

Chapter Review Exercises

Chapter Review Exercises contain both skill-building exercises, which are keyed to the appropriate sections within the chapter, and application exercises, which stress the practical relevance of mathematical concepts. The Chapter Review Exercises stress techniques for solving problems and provide students with the review necessary to pass a chapter test successfully. (See pages 136, 205, and 590.)

Chapter Tests

A test is provided in the end-of-chapter review material so that students can apply their knowledge and practice their skills. (See pages 70, 141, and 210.)

Extended and Discovery Exercises

These exercises occur at the end of each chapter and are usually more complex than the Review Exercises, requiring extension or discovery of a topic presented in the chapter. They can be utilized for either collaborative learning or extra homework assignments. (See pages 71, 142, and 371.)

Cumulative Review Exercises

This new feature appears after every three chapters. These exercise sets allow students to review skills and concepts related to more than one chapter. (See pages 212, 458, and 665.)

Graphing Calculator Icons and Calculator Helps

In this edition, the icon is used to denote an exercise that requires students to have access to *graphing* calculators. This feature allows instructors to easily make assignments for students who do not have graphing calculators. However, exercises without an icon can often be completed with or without the aid of technology. Calculator Helps are found in the margin, and refer students to the Appendix, Using the Graphing Calculator, that gives actual keystrokes for the TI-83, TI-83 Plus, and TI-84 Plus graphing calculators. (See pages 58, 62, and 152.)

Sources

For the numerous applications that appear throughout the text, genuine sources are cited to help establish the practical applications of mathematics. (See pages 101, 300, and 378.) In addition, a comprehensive bibliography appears at the end of the text.

Supplements for the Student

Student's Solutions Manual (0-321-20589-8)

This manual, written by co-author Terry Krieger, contains solutions to the odd-numbered exercises for each section (excluding Writing About Mathematics and Group Activity exercises) and solutions to all Checking Basic Concepts exercises, Chapter Review Exercises, and Chapter Test questions.

InterAct Math® Tutorial Software (0-321-20583-9)

This interactive tutorial software provides algorithmically generated practice exercises correlated at the objective level to the content of the text. Every exercise in the program is accompanied by an example and a guided solution designed to involve students in the solution process. Selected problems also include a video clip to provide additional instruction and help students visualize concepts. The software recognizes common student errors and provides appropriate feedback; it also tracks student activity and scores and can generate printed summaries of students' progress.

MathXL®

MathXL® is an online homework, tutorial, and assessment system that uses algorithmically generated exercises correlated to every objective of your textbook. Students can take chapter tests and receive personalized study plans based on their test results. The study plan diagnoses weaknesses and links students to areas they need to study and retest. Students can work unlimited practice exercises that provide tutorial instruction, and they can also access animations and video clips directly from selected exercises.

Videotapes (0-321-20585-5)

Created specifically to accompany *Intermediate Algebra with Applications and Visualization,* Second Edition, these videotapes cover every section of every chapter, and the lecturers present examples that are taken directly from the textbook. Each video segment includes a "stop the tape" feature that encourages students to pause the video, work through the example presented on their own, and then resume play to watch the video instructor go over the solution.

Digital Video Tutor (0-321-20584-7)

This supplement provides the entire set of videotapes for this textbook in digital format on CD-ROM, making it easy and convenient for students to watch video segments displayed on a computer, either at home or on campus. Available for student purchase with the text at minimal cost, the Digital Video Tutor is ideal for distance learning and supplemental instruction.

Addison-Wesley Math Tutor Center

The Addison-Wesley Math Tutor Center is staffed by qualified mathematics instructors who provide students with tutoring on examples and odd-numbered exercises from their textbooks. Tutoring is provided via toll-free telephone, fax, or e-mail, and White Board technology allows tutors and students to see problems actually being worked while they "talk" in real time over the Internet during their tutoring sessions. The Math Tutor Center is accessed through a registration number that may be bundled free with a new textbook or purchased separately with a used textbook.

MyMathLab

Ideal for lecture-based, lab-based, and online courses, MyMathLab provides students and instructors with a centralized point of access to the wide variety of multimedia resources available with their Addison-Wesley textbook. The pages of the textbook are loaded into MyMathLab, and as students work through a section of the online text, they can link directly to supplementary resources (such as tutorial software, interactive animations, and video clips) that provide instruction, exploration, and practice beyond that offered in the printed textbook. MyMathLab generates personalized study plans for students and offers them unlimited practice exercises for areas in which they need improvement.

Supplements for the Instructor

Annotated Instructor's Edition (0-321-15893-8)

The Annotated Instructor's Edition contains Teaching Tips and provides answers to every exercise in the textbook except the Writing About Mathematics exercises. Answers that do not fit on the same page as the exercises themselves are supplied in the Instructor's Answers at the back of the textbook.

Instructor's Solutions Manual (0-321-20588-X)

This manual provides solutions to all section-level exercises (excluding Writing About Mathematics exercises), Critical Thinking exercises, Checking Basic Concepts exercises, Chapter Review Exercises, Extended and Discovery Exercises, Group Activity exercises, and Chapter Test questions.

Adjunct Support Manual (0-321-26184-4)

This manual includes resources designed to help both new and adjunct faculty with course preparation and classroom management. It offers helpful teaching tips and additional exercises for selected content.

Printed Test Bank and Instructor's Resource Guide (0-321-20587-1)

The Printed Test Bank portion of this manual contains

- three free-response test forms per chapter, one of which (Form C) places stronger emphasis on applications and graphing calculator technology than the other test forms;
- one multiple-choice test form per chapter; and
- one free-response and one multiple-choice final exam.

The Resource Guide portion of this manual contains

- four sets of cumulative review exercises that cover Chapters 1–3, 1–6, 1–9, and 1–11;
- transparency masters consisting of tables, figures, and examples from the text;
- notes for presenting graphing calculator topics, as well as supplemental activities.

TestGen with QuizMaster (0-321-20580-4)

TestGen enables instructors to build, edit, print, and administer tests by using a computerized bank of questions developed to cover all the objectives of the textbook. Instructors can modify test bank questions or add new questions by using the built-in question editor, which allows users to create graphs, import graphics, insert math notation, and insert variable numbers or text. Tests can be printed or administered online via the Web or other network. TestGen comes packaged with QuizMaster, which allows students to take tests on a local area network. The software is available on a dual-platform Windows/Macintosh CD-ROM.

MathXL®

MathXL® is an online homework, tutorial, and assessment system that uses algorithmically generated exercises correlated to every objective of your textbook. Instructors can assign tests and homework provided by Addison-Wesley or create and customize their own tests and homework assignments. Instructors can also track their students' results and tutorial work in an online gradebook.

MyMathLab

Ideal for lecture-based, lab-based, and online courses, MyMathLab provides students and instructors with a centralized point of access to the wide variety of multimedia resources available with their Addison-Wesley textbook. The pages of the textbook are loaded into MyMathLab, and as students work through a section of the online text, they can link directly to supplementary resources (such as tutorial software, interactive animations, and video clips) that provide instruction, exploration, and practice beyond that offered in the printed textbook. MyMathLab generates personalized study plans for students and offers them unlimited practice exercises for areas in which they need improvement. Instructors can use MyMathLab to create, edit, and assign homework and tests and track all student work in an online gradebook. Extensive course-management capabilities, including a host of communication tools for course participants, are provided to create a user-friendly and interactive online learning environment.

 ## Acknowledgments

Many individuals contributed to the development of this textbook. We thank the following reviewers, whose comments and suggestions were invaluable in preparing *Intermediate Algebra with Applications and Visualization*, Second Edition.

Jerry Allison, *Black Hawk College*
Mary Lou Baker, *Columbia State Community College*

Duane Bollenbacher, *Bluffton College*
Debra Bryant, *Tennessee Technological University*
Michael Butler, *College of the Redwoods*
James A. Cochran, *Kirkwood Community College*
Joseph Ediger, *Portland State University*
Robert A. Farinelli, *Community College of Allegheny-Boyce Campus*
Linda H. Fitzpatrick, *Western Kentucky University*
William Fox, *Francis Marion University*
Deborah O. Garrison, *Valencia Community College*
Margaret Gorlin, *Middlesex County College*
Peter A. Johnson, *Eastern Connecticut State University*
Jennifer R. Lawhon, *Valencia Community College*
Janna Liberant, *Rockland Community College*
Elizabeth A. Mefford, *Walters State Community College*
Michelle Merriweather, *Southern Connecticut State University*
Donna Mills, *Frederick Community College*
Faith Peters, *Miami-Dade Community College*
Debra Pharo, *Northwestern Michigan College*
Larry Pontaski, *Pueblo Community College*
Polina Sabinin, *Wentworth Institute of Technology*
Damon Scott, *Francis Marion University*
Jack C. Sharp, *Floyd College*
Terry Shell, *Santa Rosa Junior College*
Katherine R. Struve, *Columbus State Community College*
Brian Sucevic, *Valencia Community College*
Marjorie Szoke, *Valencia Community College*
John Thoo, *Yuba College*
David Wasilewski, *Luzerne County Community College*
Fred Worth, *Henderson State University*

Elina Niemelä and Janis Cimperman deserve special credit for their help with accuracy checking. Without the excellent cooperation from the professional staff at Addison-Wesley Publishing Company, this project would have been impossible. Thanks go to Greg Tobin and Maureen O'Connor for giving their support. Particular recognition is due Jennifer Crum and Lauren Morse, who gave essential advice and assistance. The outstanding contributions of Kathy Manley, Joe Vetere, Dennis Schaefer, Dona Kenly, Lindsay Skay, Marcia Emerson, and Lynne Blaszak are greatly appreciated. Special thanks go to Kathy Diamond, who was instrumental in the success of this project. Thanks go to Wendy Rockswold and Carrie Krieger, who not only proofread the manuscript, but also gave invaluable encouragement and support. We also thank the many students and instructors who used the previous edition of this textbook. Their suggestions were insightful and helpful. Please feel free to send us your comments and questions at either of the following e-mail addresses: *gary.rockswold@mnsu.edu* or *tkrieger@mcleodusa.net*. Your opinion is important to us.

Gary K. Rockswold
Terry A. Krieger

WALKTHROUGH

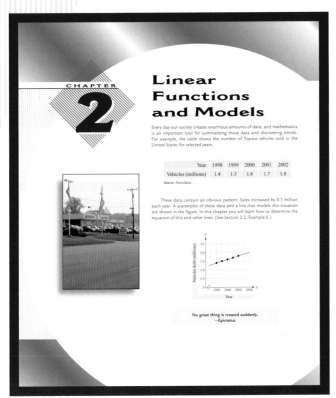

CHAPTER

2

Linear Functions and Models

Every day our society creates enormous amounts of data, and mathematics is an important tool for summarizing those data and discovering trends. For example, the table shows the number of Toyota vehicles sold in the United States for selected years.

Year	1998	1999	2000	2001	2002
Vehicles (millions)	1.4	1.5	1.6	1.7	1.8

Source: Autodata.

These data contain an obvious pattern: Sales increased by 0.1 million each year. A scatterplot of these data and a line that models this situation are shown in the figure. In this chapter you will learn how to determine the equation of this and other lines. (See Section 2.2, Example 6.)

No great thing is created suddenly.
—Epictetus

◆ Chapter Openers

Each chapter opener describes an application to motivate students by giving them insight into the relevance of that chapter's central mathematical concepts.

Rule of Four

Throughout the text, concepts are presented by means of verbal, graphical, numerical, and symbolic representations to support multiple learning styles and methods of problem solving. This textbook provides a flexible approach to the Rule of Four that lets instructors easily emphasize whichever method(s) they prefer.

REPRESENTATIONS OF A FUNCTION

A function f forms a relation between inputs x and outputs y that can be represented verbally, numerically, symbolically, and graphically. Functions can also be represented with diagrams. We begin by considering a function f that converts yards to feet.

VERBAL REPRESENTATION (WORDS) To convert x yards to y feet we must multiply x by 3. Therefore, if function f computes the number of feet in x yards, a **verbal representation** of f is "Multiply the input x in yards by 3 to obtain the output y in feet."

NUMERICAL REPRESENTATION (TABLE OF VALUES) A function f that converts yards to feet is shown in Table 2.1, where $y = f(x)$.
A *table of values* is called a **numerical representation** of a function. Many times it is impossible to list all valid inputs x in a table. On the one hand, if a table does not contain every x-input, it is a *partial* numerical representation. On the other hand, a *complete* numerical representation includes *all* valid inputs. Table 2.1 is a partial numerical representation of f because many valid inputs, such as $x = 10$ or $x = 5.3$, are not shown in it. Note that for each valid input x there is exactly one output y. For a function, inputs are not listed more than once in a table.

SYMBOLIC REPRESENTATION (FORMULA) A *formula* provides a **symbolic representation** of a function. The computation performed by f to convert x yards to y feet is expressed by $y = 3x$. A formula for f is $f(x) = 3x$, where $y = f(x)$. We say that function f is *defined by* or *given by* $f(x) = 3x$. Thus $f(2) = 3 \cdot 2 = 6$.

GRAPHICAL REPRESENTATION (GRAPH) A **graphical representation**, or **graph**, visually associates an x-input with a y-output. The ordered pairs

$$(1, 3), (2, 6), (3, 9), (4, 12), (5, 15), (6, 18), \text{ and } (7, 21)$$

from Table 2.1 are plotted in Figure 2.2(a) on the next page. This scatterplot suggests a line for the graph f. For each real number x there is exactly one real number y determined by $y = 3x$. If we restrict inputs to $x \geq 0$ and plot all ordered pairs $(x, 3x)$, then a line with no breaks will appear, as shown in Figure 2.2(b).

Walkthrough

Applications and Models

Both the exposition and the exercises contain unique applications that model real-world data. Examples often begin with concrete applications that are used to derive the abstract mathematical concepts—an approach that motivates students by illustrating the relevance of the math from the very start. Application headings in the exercise sets call out the real-world topics presented, and sources of data are cited throughout.

Graphing Calculator Technology

Graphing calculator use is optional, but for instructors who want to integrate graphing calculators, this textbook thoroughly and seamlessly integrates graphing technology without sacrificing traditional algebraic skills. Students can solve problems using multiple methods, learning to evaluate graphing calculator techniques against other problem-solving methods.

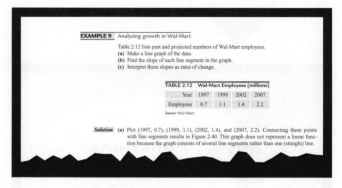

EXAMPLE 9 Analyzing growth in Wal-Mart

Table 2.12 lists past and projected numbers of Wal-Mart employees.
(a) Make a line graph of the data.
(b) Find the slope of each line segment in the graph.
(c) Interpret these slopes as rates of change.

TABLE 2.12 Wal-Mart Employees (millions)

Year	1997	1999	2002	2007
Employees	0.7	1.1	1.4	2.2

Source: Wal-Mart.

Solution (a) Plot (1997, 0.7), (1999, 1.1), (2002, 1.4), and (2007, 2.2). Connecting these points with line segments results in Figure 2.40. This graph does not represent a linear function because the graph consists of several line segments rather than one (straight) line.

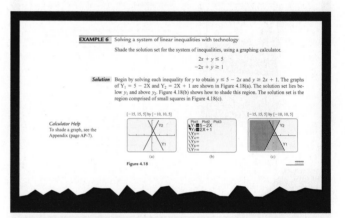

EXAMPLE 6 Solving a system of linear inequalities with technology

Shade the solution set for the system of inequalities, using a graphing calculator.

$$2x + y \le 5$$
$$-2x + y \ge 1$$

Solution Begin by solving each inequality for y to obtain $y \le 5 - 2x$ and $y \ge 2x + 1$. The graphs of $Y_1 = 5 - 2X$ and $Y_2 = 2X + 1$ are shown in Figure 4.18(a). The solution set lies below y_1 and above y_2. Figure 4.18(b) shows how to shade this region. The solution set is the region comprised of small squares in Figure 4.18(c).

Calculator Help
To shade a graph, see the Appendix (page AP-7).

Figure 4.18

Making Connections

 This feature occurs throughout and helps students see how topics are interrelated. It also helps motivate students by calling out connections between mathematical concepts.

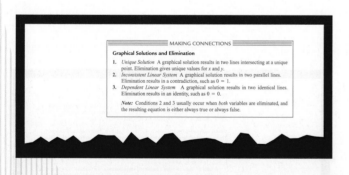

MAKING CONNECTIONS

Graphical Solutions and Elimination

1. *Unique Solution* A graphical solution results in two lines intersecting at a unique point. Elimination gives unique values for x and y.
2. *Inconsistent Linear System* A graphical solution results in two parallel lines. Elimination results in a contradiction, such as 0 = 1.
3. *Dependent Linear System* A graphical solution results in two identical lines. Elimination results in an identity, such as 0 = 0.

Note: Conditions 2 and 3 usually occur when *both* variables are eliminated, and the resulting equation is either always true or always false.

Critical Thinking

The Critical Thinking feature appears in most sections and poses a question that can be used for either classroom discussion or homework. Critical Thinking questions typically ask students to extend a mathematical concept beyond what has already been discussed in the text.

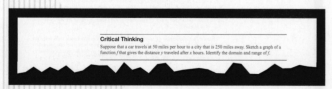

Critical Thinking

Suppose that a car travels at 50 miles per hour to a city that is 250 miles away. Sketch a graph of a function f that gives the distance y traveled after x hours. Identify the domain and range of f.

Technology Notes

 Occurring throughout, Technology Notes offer students guidance and suggestions for using the graphing calculator to solve problems and explore concepts.

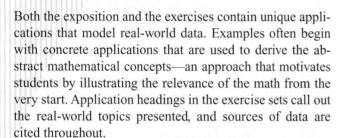

Technology Note: *Shading of Linear Inequalities*

When shading the solution set for a linear inequality, graphing calculators often show solid lines even if a line should be dashed. For example, the graphs for $y < 5 - 2x$ and $y \le 5 - 2x$ are identical on some graphing calculators.

Walkthrough

Putting It All Together

This helpful feature occurs at the end of each section to summarize techniques and reinforce concepts. These unique summaries give students a consistent, visual study aid for every section of the textbook.

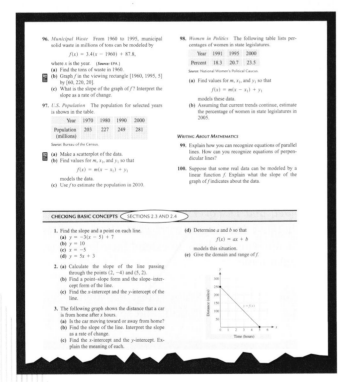

Section Exercise Sets

Each exercise set contains a wide variety of problems involving basic concepts, skill-building, and applications, and many exercises ask students to read and interpret graphs. Exercise sets are carefully graded and categorized according to the topics within sections, making it easier for instructors to select appropriate assignments. Each set concludes with Writing About Mathematics exercises to help students verbalize and synthesize concepts.

Checking Basic Concepts

Provided after every two sections, Checking Basic Concepts can be used for review or for group activities. These brief exercise sets require 10–20 minutes to complete and can be used during class if time permits.

Group Activities: Working with Real Data

Group Activities (1–2 per chapter) ask students to work collaboratively to solve a problem involving real data. Most activities can be completed with limited use of class time.

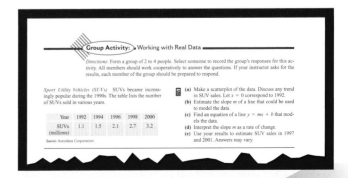

Walkthrough

For Extra Help

Found at the beginning of each exercise set, these boxes direct students to the various supplementary resources available to them for extra help and practice.

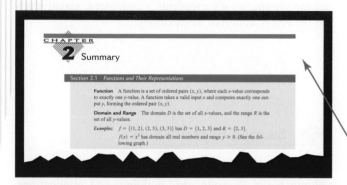

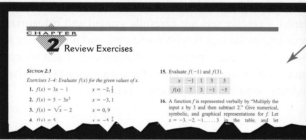

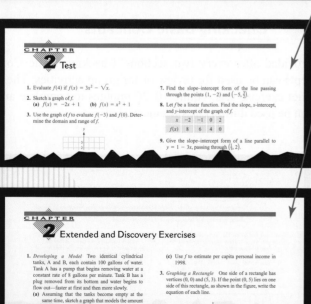

End-of-Chapter Material

The end-of-chapter material includes the following features to ensure that students have ample opportunities to practice skills, synthesize concepts, and explore material in greater depth:

- A *Chapter Summary* to present the key concepts from each section

- Extensive *Chapter Review Exercises* that include both skill-building exercises and applications, and stress different problem-solving techniques

- The *Chapter Test* to give students a chance to apply their knowledge and practice their skills

- *Extended and Discovery Exercises,* which are ideal for collaborative learning or extra-credit homework assignments, allowing students to extend their knowledge of a particular topic

- *Cumulative Review Exercises* presented after every three chapters that stress both skills and concepts

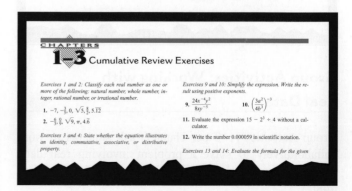

Real Numbers and Algebra

"Why do I need to learn math?" This question is commonly asked by students across the country. A look at history provides some reasons for studying mathematics.

All of us have ancestors who were unable to perform even basic arithmetic. They did not lack intelligence—rather, they lacked education. In about A.D. 400, Saint Augustine declared that people who could add and subtract were in conspiracy with the devil. One hundred years ago many Americans were educated in rural schools, where it was common for school boards to have difficulty finding teachers who could multiply and divide. In the 1940s and 1950s, many mathematics teachers had no training beyond algebra. Today, knowledge of algebra, trigonometry, and calculus is essential for many occupations.

Mathematics opens doors in our society. Without mathematical skills, opportunities are lost. Most vocations and professions require a higher level of mathematical understanding than in the past. Seldom are the mathematical expectations of employees lowered, as the workplace becomes more technical—not less. Mathematics is the *language of technology*. The Department of Education cites mathematics as a key to achievement in our society. Students with a solid mathematics background earned, on average, 38 percent more per hour than their peers without such a background.

Decisions in high school or college to avoid mathematics classes have lifelong ramifications that affect vocations, incomes, and lifestyles. Switching majors to escape taking mathematics may prevent you from pursuing your dreams. Like reading and writing, mathematics is a necessary component for you to reach your full potential.

What skills will be needed in society during the next 50 years? Although no one can answer this question with certainty, history demonstrates that the importance of mathematics will not diminish, but will likely increase.

**It is not enough to have a good mind; the
main thing is to use it well.
—René Descartes**

Sources: A. Toffler and H. Toffler, *Creating a New Civilization; USA Today.*

TEACHING TIP

Use this introduction to stress the
importance of learning math.

1.1   DESCRIBING DATA WITH SETS OF NUMBERS

**Natural and Whole Numbers · Integers and Rational Numbers ·
Real Numbers · Properties of Real Numbers**

INTRODUCTION

The need for numbers has existed in nearly every society. Numbers first occurred in the measurement of time, currency, goods, and land. As the complexity of a society increased, so did its numbers. One tribe that lived near New Guinea counted only to 6. Any number higher than 6 was referred to as "many." This number system met the needs of that society. However, a highly technical society could not function with so few numbers.   (**Source:** *Historical Topics for the Mathematics Classroom, Thirty-first Yearbook,* NCTM.)

In this section we discuss numbers that are vital to our technological society. We also show how different types of data can be described with sets of numbers.

NATURAL AND WHOLE NUMBERS

One important set of numbers found in most societies is the set of **natural numbers**. These numbers comprise the counting numbers and may be expressed as

$$N = \{1, 2, 3, 4, 5, 6, \ldots\}.$$

Set braces, { }, are used to enclose the elements of a set. Because there are infinitely many natural numbers, three dots show that the list continues in the same pattern without end. A second set of numbers, called the **whole numbers**, is given by

$$W = \{0, 1, 2, 3, 4, 5, \ldots\}.$$

TEACHING TIP

Discuss reasons why we need numbers other than the natural numbers.

Natural numbers and whole numbers can be used when data are not broken into fractional parts. For example, Table 1.1 lists the number of bachelor's degrees awarded during selected academic years. Note that either natural numbers or whole numbers are appropriate to describe the data because a fraction of a degree cannot be awarded.

TABLE 1.1   Bachelor's Degrees Awarded

Year	1969–1970	1979–1980	1989–1990	1999–2000
Degrees	792,317	929,417	1,051,344	1,185,000

Source: Department of Education.

EXAMPLE 1   Describing image resolution

The screens for computer terminals or graphing calculators are made up of tiny squares called *pixels*. A rectangular screen on a graphing calculator might be 95 pixels across and 63 pixels high, whereas a computer terminal could be 2048 by 2048 pixels. Figure 1.1 shows a graphing calculator screen. Fractional parts of a pixel do not occur. As a result, natural numbers are appropriate to describe them.

(a) Find the number of pixels in a graphing calculator screen that is 95 by 63 pixels.

(b) The photograph in Figure 1.2 shows an image of Jupiter and two of its moons, Io and Europa, taken by *Voyager 1*. This photograph is 820 by 540 pixels. How many pixels are there?

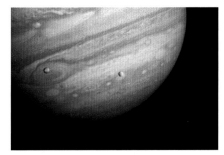

TEACHING TIP

It is not necessary for students to understand pixels in this course.

```
95*63
                5985
820*540
              442800
```

Figure 1.1

Figure 1.2 Jupiter and Two Moons
Source: NASA.

Solution   (a) There are $95 \times 63 = 5985$ pixels. (See Figure 1.1.)

(b) There are $820 \times 540 = 442{,}800$ pixels.

INTEGERS AND RATIONAL NUMBERS

The set of **integers** is given by

$$I = \{\dots, -3, -2, -1, 0, 1, 2, 3, \dots\}.$$

The integers include both the natural numbers and the whole numbers. During the eighteenth century, negative numbers were not readily accepted by all mathematicians. Such numbers did not seem to have real meaning. However, today when a person opens a personal checking account for the first time, negative numbers quickly take on meaning. There is a difference between a positive and a negative balance.

A **rational number** is any number that can be expressed as the ratio of two integers $\frac{p}{q}$, where $q \neq 0$ because we cannot divide by 0. Rational numbers can be written as fractions and include all integers. Some examples of rational numbers are

$$\frac{8}{1}, \quad \frac{2}{3}, \quad -\frac{3}{5}, \quad -\frac{7}{2}, \quad \frac{22}{7}, \quad 1.2, \quad \text{and} \quad 0.$$

Note that 1.2 and 0 are both rational numbers because they can be written as $\frac{12}{10}$ and $\frac{0}{1}$.

Rational numbers may be expressed in decimal form that either *repeats* or *terminates*. The fraction $\frac{1}{3}$ may be expressed as $0.\overline{3}$, a repeating decimal, and the fraction $\frac{1}{4}$ may be expressed as 0.25, a terminating decimal. The overbar indicates that $0.\overline{3} = 0.3333333\dots$

Integers and rational numbers are used to describe things such as temperature. Table 1.2 on the next page lists equivalent temperatures in both degrees Fahrenheit and degrees Celsius. Note that both positive and negative numbers are used to describe temperature.

TABLE 1.2   Fahrenheit and Celsius Temperature

°F	°C	Observation
−89	−67.$\overline{2}$	Alcohol freezes
−40	−40	Mercury freezes
0	−17.$\overline{7}$	Snow and salt mixture freezes
32	0	Water freezes
100	37.$\overline{7}$	A very warm day
212	100	Water boils

EXAMPLE 2   Classifying numbers

Classify each real number as one or more of the following: natural number, whole number, integer, or rational number.

(a) $\dfrac{6}{3}$ (b) -1 (c) 0 (d) $-\dfrac{11}{3}$

Solution   (a) Because $\frac{6}{3} = 2$, the number $\frac{6}{3}$ is a natural number, a whole number, an integer, and a rational number.

(b) The number -1 is an integer and a rational number but not a natural or a whole number.

(c) The number 0 is a whole number, an integer, and a rational number but not a natural number.

(d) The fraction $-\frac{11}{3}$ is a rational number as it is the ratio of two integers. However, it is not a natural number, a whole number, or an integer.

REAL NUMBERS

Real numbers can be represented by decimal numbers. Every fraction has a decimal form, so real numbers include rational numbers. However, some real numbers cannot be expressed by fractions. They are called **irrational numbers**. The numbers $\sqrt{2}$, $\sqrt{15}$, and π are examples of irrational numbers. They can be expressed by decimals but not by decimals that either repeat or terminate. Examples of real numbers include

$$2, \quad -10, \quad 151\tfrac{1}{4}, \quad -131.37, \quad \tfrac{1}{3}, \quad -\sqrt{5}, \quad \text{and} \quad \sqrt{11}.$$

Any real number may be approximated by a terminating decimal. We use the symbol $\approx$, which means **approximately equal**, to denote an approximation. Each of the following real numbers has been approximated to three *decimal places*.

Calculator Help
To evaluate π and square roots, see the Appendix (page AP-1).

$$\pi \approx 3.142, \quad \frac{2}{3} \approx 0.667, \quad \sqrt{200} \approx 14.142$$

Figure 1.3 shows the relationships among the different sets of numbers. Note that each real number is either a rational number or an irrational number but not both. The natural numbers, whole numbers, and integers are contained in the set of rational numbers.

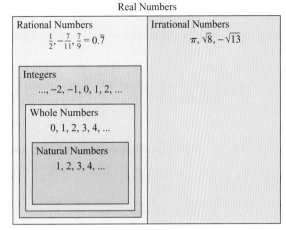

Figure 1.3   The Set of Real Numbers

EXAMPLE 3   Classifying numbers

Classify each real number as one or more of the following: a natural number, an integer, a rational number, or an irrational number.

$$5, \quad -1.2, \quad \frac{13}{7}, \quad -\sqrt{7}, \quad -12, \quad \sqrt{16}$$

Solution   Natural numbers: 5 and $\sqrt{16} = 4$

Integers: 5, -12, and $\sqrt{16} = 4$

Rational numbers: 5, -1.2, $\frac{13}{7}$, -12, and $\sqrt{16} = 4$

Irrational number: $-\sqrt{7}$

Even though a data set may contain only integers, decimals are often needed to describe it. One common way to do so is to find the **average**. To calculate the average of a set of numbers, we find their sum and divide by the number of numbers in the set.

EXAMPLE 4   Analyzing test scores

A student obtains the following test scores: 81, 96, 79, and 82.
(a) Find the student's average test score.
(b) Is this average a natural, a rational, an irrational, or a real number?

Solution   **(a)** To find the average, we find the sum of the 4 test scores and then divide by 4:

$$\frac{81 + 96 + 79 + 82}{4} = \frac{338}{4} = 84.5.$$

(b) The average of these 4 test scores is both a rational number *and* a real number but is neither a natural number nor an irrational number.

PROPERTIES OF REAL NUMBERS

Several properties of real numbers are used in algebra. They are the identity properties, the commutative properties, the associative properties, and the distributive properties.

IDENTITY PROPERTIES   The **identity property of 0** states that, if 0 is added to any real number a, the result is a. The number 0 is called the **additive identity**. For example,

$$-3 + 0 = -3 \quad \text{and} \quad 0 + 18 = 18.$$

The **identity property of 1** states that, if any number a is multiplied by 1, the result is a. The number 1 is called the **multiplicative identity**. Examples include

$$-7 \cdot 1 = -7 \quad \text{and} \quad 1 \cdot 9 = 9.$$

We can summarize these results as follows.

IDENTITY PROPERTIES
For any real number a, $$a + 0 = 0 + a = a$$ and $$a \cdot 1 = 1 \cdot a = a.$$

COMMUTATIVE PROPERTIES   The **commutative property for addition** states that two numbers, a and b, can be added in any order and the result is the same. That is, $a + b = b + a$. For example, if a person is paid \$5 and then \$7 or paid \$7 and then \$5, the result is the same. Either way the person is paid a total of

$$5 + 7 = 7 + 5 = \$12.$$

There is also a **commutative property for multiplication**. It states that two numbers, a and b, can be multiplied in any order and the result is the same. That is, $a \cdot b = b \cdot a$. For example, 3 groups of 5 people or 5 groups of 3 people both contain

$$3 \cdot 5 = 5 \cdot 3 = 15 \text{ people.}$$

We can summarize these results as follows.

COMMUTATIVE PROPERTIES
For any real numbers a and b, $$a + b = b + a$$ and $$a \cdot b = b \cdot a.$$

ASSOCIATIVE PROPERTIES   The commutative properties allow us to reverse the order of two numbers when we add or multiply. The associative properties allow us to change how numbers are grouped. For example, we may add the numbers 3, 4, and 5 as follows.

$$(3 + 4) + 5 = 7 + 5 = 12$$
$$3 + (4 + 5) = 3 + 9 = 12$$

In either case we obtain the same answer, which is the result of the **associative property for addition**. Note that we did not change the order of the numbers; rather we only changed how the numbers were grouped. There is also an **associative property for multiplication**, which is illustrated as follows.

$$(3 \cdot 4) \cdot 5 = 12 \cdot 5 = 60$$
$$3 \cdot (4 \cdot 5) = 3 \cdot 20 = 60$$

We can summarize these results as follows.

ASSOCIATIVE PROPERTIES

For any real numbers a, b, and c,

$$(a + b) + c = a + (b + c)$$

and

$$(a \cdot b) \cdot c = a \cdot (b \cdot c).$$

Note: Sometimes we omit the multiplication dot. Thus $a \cdot b = ab$ and $5 \cdot x = 5x$.

EXAMPLE 5   Identifying properties of real numbers

State the property of real numbers that justifies each statement.
(a) $4 \cdot (3x) = (4 \cdot 3)x$ **(b)** $(1 \cdot 5) \cdot 4 = 5 \cdot 4$ **(c)** $5 + ab = ab + 5$

Solution   **(a)** This equation illustrates the associative property for multiplication, with the grouping of the numbers changed. That is, $4 \cdot (3x) = (4 \cdot 3)x = 12x$.
(b) This equation illustrates the identity property of 1 because $1 \cdot 5 = 5$.
(c) This equation illustrates the commutative property of addition; the order of the terms 5 and ab changed.

DISTRIBUTIVE PROPERTIES   The **distributive properties** are used frequently in algebra to simplify expressions. An example of a distributive property is

$$3(6 + 5) = 3 \cdot 6 + 3 \cdot 5.$$

It is important to multiply the 3 by both the 6 and 5–not just the 6. This distributive property is valid when addition is replaced by subtraction. For example,

$$3(6 - 5) = 3 \cdot 6 - 3 \cdot 5.$$

We can summarize these results as follows.

TEACHING TIP

Emphasize the distributive properties. Have students simplify
$-(2 - x)$ and $-4(2x - 3)$.

DISTRIBUTIVE PROPERTIES

For any real numbers a, b, and c,

$$a(b + c) = ab + ac$$

and

$$a(b - c) = ab - ac.$$

Note: Because multiplication is commutative, the distributive properties may be written as

$$(b + c)a = ba + ca \quad \text{and} \quad (b - c)a = ba - ca.$$

EXAMPLE 6   Applying the distributive properties

Apply a distributive property to each expression.
(a) $5(4 + x)$ **(b)** $10 - (1 + a)$ **(c)** $9x - 5x$ **(d)** $5x + 2x - 3x$

Solution   **(a)** $5(4 + x) = 5 \cdot 4 + 5 \cdot x = 20 + 5x$
(b) $10 - (1 + a) = 10 - 1(1 + a) = 10 - (1 \cdot 1) - (1 \cdot a) = 9 - a$
(c) $9x - 5x = (9 - 5)x = 4x$
(d) Because each term contains an x, apply the distributive property to all three terms:

$$5x + 2x - 3x = (5 + 2 - 3)x = 4x.$$

PUTTING IT ALL TOGETHER

Data and numbers play a central role in a diverse, technological society. Because of the variety of data, it has been necessary to develop different sets of numbers. Without numbers, data could be described qualitatively but not quantitatively. For example, we might say that the day seems hot, but we would not be able to give an actual number for the temperature. The following table summarizes some of the sets of numbers.

Concept	Comments	Examples
Natural Numbers	Sometimes referred to as the *counting numbers*	$1, 2, 3, 4, 5, \ldots$
Whole Numbers	Includes the natural numbers	$0, 1, 2, 3, 4, \ldots$
Integers	Includes the natural numbers and the whole numbers	$\ldots, -2, -1, 0, 1, 2, \ldots$
Rational Numbers	Includes integers and all fractions $\frac{p}{q}$, where p and $q \neq 0$ are integers, and all repeating and terminating decimals	$\frac{1}{2}, -3, \frac{128}{6}, -0.335, 0,$ $0.25 = \frac{1}{4}, \quad \text{and} \quad 0.\overline{3} = \frac{1}{3}$

Concept	Comments	Examples
Irrational Numbers	Includes real numbers that cannot be expressed *exactly* by a fraction	$-\pi,\ \sqrt{2},$ and $\sqrt{7}$
Real Numbers	Any number that can be expressed in decimal form, including the rational numbers and the irrational numbers	$\pi,\ \sqrt{3},\ -\dfrac{4}{7},\ 0,\ -10,$ $0.\overline{6}=\dfrac{2}{3},3,$ and $\sqrt{15}$

TEACHING TIP

Putting It All Together occurs at the end of each section. Point out to students that it provides a summary of important topics discussed in the section.

The real numbers have several important properties, which are summarized in the following table.

Property	Definition	Examples
Identity (0 and 1)	The identity for addition is 0 and the identity for multiplication is 1. For any real number a, $a+0=a$ and $a\cdot 1=a$.	$5+0=5$ and $5\cdot 1=5$
Commutative	For any real numbers a and b, $a+b=b+a$ and $a\cdot b=b\cdot a$.	$4+6=6+4$ and $4\cdot 6=6\cdot 4$
Associative	For any real numbers a, b, and c, $(a+b)+c=a+(b+c)$ and $(a\cdot b)\cdot c=a\cdot(b\cdot c)$.	$(3+4)+5=3+(4+5)$ and $(3\cdot 4)\cdot 5=3\cdot(4\cdot 5)$
Distributive	For any real numbers a, b, and c, $a(b+c)=ab+ac$ and $a(b-c)=ab-ac$.	$5(x+2)=5x+10,$ $5(x-2)=5x-10,$ and $5x+4x=(5+4)x=9x$

1.1 EXERCISES

FOR EXTRA HELP

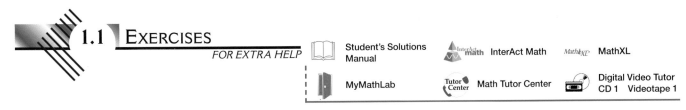

Student's Solutions Manual   InterAct Math   MathXL

MyMathLab   Math Tutor Center   Digital Video Tutor CD 1 Videotape 1

CONCEPTS

$N=\{1,2,3,\ldots\};\ W=\{0,1,2,\ldots\}$

1. Which numbers are in the set of natural numbers and which are in the set of whole numbers?

2. Which numbers are in the set of integers? Give an example of an integer that is not a natural number.
$I=\{\ldots,-2,-1,0,1,2,\ldots\};\ -5$

3. Which numbers are in the set of rational numbers? Give an example. $\dfrac{p}{q}$ where p and $q\neq 0$ are integers; $\tfrac{3}{4}$

4. Which numbers are in the set of real numbers? If a number is a real number but not a rational number, what type of number must it be? Give an example of a real number that is not a rational number.
Any number that can be expressed as a decimal; irrational; $\sqrt{2}$

5. Give an example of the commutative property for addition. $3+2=2+3$

6. Give an example of the commutative property for multiplication. $4 \cdot 3 = 3 \cdot 4$

7. Why is the number 1 called the multiplicative identity? $1 \cdot a = a$, for any real number a

8. Why is the number 0 called the additive identity? $0 + a = a$, for any real number a

9. Give an example of the associative property for multiplication. $2 \cdot (3 \cdot 4) = (2 \cdot 3) \cdot 4$

10. Give an example of a distributive property.

$$2(3 + 4) = 2 \cdot 3 + 2 \cdot 4$$

CLASSIFYING NUMBERS

Exercises 11–18: Classify the number as one or more of the following: natural number, integer, rational number, or real number.

11. 14,531 (Number of Subway franchises in 2000)
Natural, integer, rational, and real

12. -14.5 (Percent change in the number of unhealthy days in Los Angeles from 1995 to 1996)   Rational and real

13. $\frac{89}{3687}$ (Fraction of 18- to 19-year-old males who are married in the U.S.)   Rational and real

14. 4 (Pounds of garbage the average person produces each day)   Natural, integer, rational, and real

15. 7.5 (Average number of gallons of water a person uses each minute while taking a shower)   Rational and real

16. 2.62 (Average number of people per household in 2000)   Rational and real

17. $90\sqrt{2}$ (Distance in feet from home plate to second base in baseball)   Real

18. -71 (Wind chill when the temperature is $-30°F$ and the wind speed is 40 miles per hour)   Integer, rational, and real

Exercises 19–24: Classify each real number as one or more of the following: natural number, whole number, integer, rational number, or irrational number. *

19. $-5, 6, \frac{1}{7}, \sqrt{7}, 0.2$ **20.** $-3, \frac{2}{9}, \sqrt{9}, -1.37$

21. $\frac{3}{1}, -\frac{5}{8}, \sqrt{5}, 0.\overline{45}, \pi$ **22.** $0, \frac{50}{10}, -\frac{23}{27}, 0.\overline{6}, -\sqrt{3}$

23. $-2, \frac{1}{2}, \sqrt{9}, 0.\overline{26}$ **24.** $\sqrt{4}, \sqrt{6}, \frac{4}{2}, 0.26$

Exercises 25–30: For the measured quantity, state the set of numbers that is most appropriate to describe it. Choose from the natural numbers, integers, or rational numbers. Explain your answer.

25. Shoe sizes
Rational

26. Populations of states
Natural

27. Gallons of gasoline   **28.** Speed limits   Natural
Rational

29. Temperatures given in a winter weather forecast in Montana   Integers

30. Number of compact discs sold   Natural

PROPERTIES OF REAL NUMBERS

Exercises 31–44: State whether the equation is the result of an identity, a commutative, an associative, or a distributive property.

31. $b + 0 = b$ Identity   **32.** $1 \cdot 5 = 5$ Identity

33. $4 + a = a + 4$ Commutative

34. $(5 + 1) + 8 = 5 + (1 + 8)$ Associative

35. $8(9x - 3) = 8 \cdot 9x - 8 \cdot 3$ Distributive

36. $4(3 + 5a) = 4 \cdot 3 + 4 \cdot 5a$ Distributive

37. $4 \cdot (10 \cdot 6) = (4 \cdot 10) \cdot 6$ Associative

38. $x \cdot 5 = 5x$ Commutative

39. $3 \cdot (6 \cdot 2) = (6 \cdot 2) \cdot 3$ Commutative

40. $bac = abc$ Commutative

41. $4(x - 3) = (x - 3)4$ Commutative

42. $4 \cdot (5x) = 20x$ Associative

43. $5(x - 3) - 2(x - 3) = 3(x - 3)$ Distributive

44. $4 - (a - b) = 4 - a + b$ Distributive

Exercises 45–52: Use a commutative property to write an equivalent expression.

45. $4 + a$ $a + 4$ **46.** ba ab

47. $a \cdot \frac{1}{3}$ $\frac{1}{3}a$ **48.** $100 + x$ $x + 100$

49. $1 + x$ $x + 1$ **50.** $b \cdot 5$ $5b$

51. yx xy **52.** $b + a$ $a + b$

Exercises 53–60: Use an associative property to write an equivalent expression.

53. $4 + (5 + b)$
$(4 + 5) + b = 9 + b$

54. $(x + 2) + 3$
$x + (2 + 3) = x + 5$

55. $5(10x)$
$(5 \cdot 10)x = 50x$

56. $(a \cdot 5) \cdot 4$
$a(5 \cdot 4) = a \cdot 20$

57. $(x + y) + z$
$x + (y + z)$

58. $-3(4x)$
$(-3 \cdot 4) \cdot x = -12x$

*Answers on page IA-1

59. $(x \cdot 3)4$
$x \cdot (3 \cdot 4) = x \cdot 12$

60. $(a + 6) + 5$
$a + (6 + 5) = a + 11$

Exercises 61–82: Use a distributive property to write an equivalent expression.

61. $4(x + y)$
$4x + 4y$

62. $-3(a + 5)$
$-3a - 15$

63. $(x - 7)5$
$5x - 35$

64. $(11 + b)a$
$11a + ba$

65. $-(x + 1)$
$-x - 1$

66. $-(a - 2)$
$-a + 2$

67. $ax - ay$
$a(x - y)$

68. $4a + 4b$
$4(a + b)$

69. $12 + 3x$
$3(4 + x)$

70. $2 - 4x$
$2(1 - 2x)$

71. $3x + 7x$
$(3 + 7)x = 10x$

72. $\frac{1}{2}z + \frac{3}{2}z$ $\left(\frac{1}{2} + \frac{3}{2}\right)z = 2z$

73. $8t - 2t$ $(8 - 2)t = 6t$

74. $y - \frac{2}{3}y$ $\left(1 - \frac{2}{3}\right)y = \frac{1}{3}y$

75. $x - \frac{3}{4}x$ $\left(1 - \frac{3}{4}\right)x = \frac{1}{4}x$

76. $13r - 6r$ $(13 - 6)r = 7r$

77. $3 - (1 - 2z)$
$3 - 1 + 2z = 2 + 2z$

78. $5 - (1 - 4y)$
$5 - 1 + 4y = 4 + 4y$

79. $3z + 4z + z$ $8z$

80. $5z + 4z + 2z$ $11z$

81. $10t - t - 4t$ $5t$

82. $20t - 2t - t$ $17t$

Exercises 83–88: Use a distributive property to evaluate the expression two different ways.

83. $7(11 - 3)$ 56

84. $(5 + 9)12$ 168

85. $13(16 + 23)$ 507

86. $4(12 - 8)$ 16

87. $5(19 - 7)$ 60

88. $(8 + 12)9$ 180

Exercises 89–94: Calculate the average of the list of numbers. Classify the result as a natural number, an integer, or a rational number.

89. $3, 4, 5, 8$
5, natural, integer, and rational

90. $5, 8, 10, 23, 9$
11, natural, integer, and rational

91. $45, 33, 52$ $43.\overline{3}$, rational

92. $3.2, 7.5, 8.1, 12.8, 13.4$ 9, natural, integer, and rational

93. $121.5, 45.7, 99.3, 45.9$ 78.1, rational

94. $99.88, 39.11, 85.67, 23.86, 19.11$ 53.526, rational

Exercises 95–100: Use properties of real numbers to evaluate the expression mentally.

95. $8 + 3 + 2 + 7$ 20

96. $52 + 103 + 48 + 97$ 300

97. $\frac{2}{9} \cdot 8 \cdot 9 \cdot \frac{3}{8}$ 6

98. $\frac{1}{2} \cdot \frac{1}{3} \cdot \frac{1}{4} \cdot 2 \cdot 3 \cdot 4$ 1

99. $4 \cdot 16 - 4 \cdot 6$ 40

100. $7 \cdot 12 + 7 \cdot 3 + 7 \cdot 5$ 140

APPLICATIONS

101. *Digital Images* If an image downloaded from the Internet is 240 pixels across by 360 pixels high and a different image is 360 pixels across by 240 pixels high, how do the total numbers of pixels in the images compare? What property of real numbers does this result illustrate? Both 86,400; commutative

102. *Digital Images* The dimensions of digital images on the Internet can vary greatly in size. Calculate the number of pixels in each image.
(a) 760 by 480 pixels 364,800
(b) 64 by 128 pixels 8192

103. *Higher Education* The following table lists the total higher education enrollment for selected years.

Year	1997	1998	1999	2000
Students (millions)	14.5	14.6	14.9	15.1

Source: Department of Education.

(a) What was the enrollment in 1999? 14.9 million
(b) Mentally estimate the average enrollment for this 4-year period. About 14.8 million
(c) Calculate the average enrollment. Is your estimate from part (b) in reasonable agreement with your calculated result? 14.775 million; yes

104. *Federal Budget* The following table lists the spending by the federal government for selected years.

Year	1997	1998	1999	2000	2001
Budget ($ trillions)	1.6	1.7	1.7	1.8	1.9

Source: Office of Management and Budget.

(a) What was the budget in 1999? $1.7 trillion
(b) Mentally estimate the average budget for this 5-year period. About $1.7 trillion
(c) Calculate the average budget. Is your estimate from part (b) in reasonable agreement with your calculated result? $1.74 trillion; yes

105. *Earnings* Earning $120 one day and $80 the next day is equivalent to earning $80 the first day and $120 the second day. What property of real numbers is illustrated? Commutative property for addition

106. *Geometry* The area A of a rectangle equals the product of its length L and width W. What property states that either formula, $A = LW$ or $A = WL$, is correct? Commutative property for multiplication

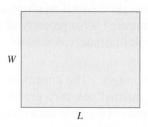

W

L

WRITING ABOUT MATHEMATICS

107. Is subtraction either commutative or associative? Explain, using examples.

108. Is division either commutative or associative? Explain, using examples.

Group Activity: Working with Real Data

Directions: Form a group of 2 to 4 people. Select someone to record the group's responses for this activity. All members of the group should work cooperatively to answer the questions. If your instructor asks for your results, each member of the group should be prepared to respond.

1. *New Windchill Factor* Before November 1, 2001, the windchill factor was based on wind speeds taken 33 feet above ground level. Today wind speeds are measured 5 feet above the ground, which corresponds to the typical height of a person's face. The following table lists the current windchill factor for different wind speeds when the temperature is $0°F$.

Windchill Temperatures at $0°F$

Wind Speed (mph)	0	5	10	15
Windchill ($°F$)	0	−11	−16	−19

Wind Speed (mph)	20	25	30
Windchill ($°F$)	−22	−24	−26

Source: National Weather Service.

(a) Find the windchill factor when the wind speed is 20 miles per hour and the temperature is $0°F$. −22°F

(b) For each 5-mile-per-hour increase in the wind speed, does the windchill factor decrease by the same amount? Explain. No, the amount of decrease gets smaller.

(c) Estimate the windchill factor when the wind speed is 40 miles per hour. Explain your reasoning.

(d) Look up the true value for part (c) on the Internet. −29°F

2. *New Windchill Factor* The following table lists the current windchill factor for different temperatures when the wind speed is 15 miles per hour.

Windchill Temperatures with a 15-mph Wind

Temperature ($°F$)	−30	−20	−10	0
Windchill ($°F$)	−58	−45	−32	−19

Temperature ($°F$)	10	20	30
Windchill ($°F$)	−7	6	19

Source: National Weather Service.

(a) Find the windchill factor when the temperature is $-20°F$ and the wind speed is 15 miles per hour. −45°F

(b) Is the windchill factor always a fixed number of degrees less than the actual temperature? Explain. No, the amount subtracted depends on the actual temperature.

(c) Estimate the windchill factor when the temperature is $-40°F$. Explain your reasoning.

(d) Look up the true value for part (c) on the Internet. −71°F

2.(c) About −71°F; answers may vary.

1.(c) About −29°F; answers may vary.

1.2 OPERATIONS ON REAL NUMBERS

The Real Number Line · Arithmetic Operations · Data and Number Sense

INTRODUCTION

Real numbers are used to describe data. To obtain information from data we frequently perform operations on real numbers. For example, exams are often assigned a score between 0 and 100. This step reduces each exam to a number or *data point*. We might obtain more information about the exams by calculating the average score. To do so we perform the arithmetic operations of addition and division.

In this section we discuss operations on real numbers and provide examples of where these computations occur in real life.

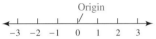

Figure 1.4 The Number Line

THE REAL NUMBER LINE

You can visualize the real number system by using a number line, as shown in Figure 1.4. Each real number corresponds to a point on the number line. The point associated with the real number 0 is called the **origin**.

If a real number a is located to the left of a real number b on the number line, we say that a is **less than** b and write $a < b$. Similarly, if a real number a is located to the right of a real number b, we say that a is **greater than** b and write $a > b$. Thus $-3 < 2$ because -3 is located to the left of 2, and $2 > -3$ because 2 is located to the right of -3. If $a > 0$, then a is a **positive number**, and if $a < 0$, then a is a **negative number**.

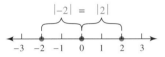

Figure 1.5

The **absolute value** of a real number a, written $|a|$, is equal to its distance from the origin on the number line. Distance may be either a positive number or zero, but it cannot be a negative number. As the points corresponding to 2 and -2 are both 2 units from the origin, $|2| = 2$ and $|-2| = 2$, as shown in Figure 1.5. The absolute value of a real number is *never* negative.

EXAMPLE 1 Finding the absolute value of a real number

Find the absolute value of each real number.
(a) 9.12
(b) $-\pi$
(c) $-a$, if a is a positive number
(d) a, if a is a negative number

Solution **(a)** $|9.12| = 9.12$
(b) $|-\pi| = \pi$ because $\pi \approx 3.14$ is a positive number.
(c) If a is positive, $-a$ is negative and $|-a| = a$.
(d) If a is negative, $-a$ is positive. Thus $a < 0$ implies that $|a| = -a$. For example, if we let $a = -5$, then $|-5| = -(-5) = 5$.

TEACHING TIP

This definition of absolute value may need additional explanation when $a < 0$.

From Example 1 note that

$$|a| = a \qquad \text{if } a > 0 \text{ or } a = 0, \text{ and}$$
$$|a| = -a \qquad \text{if } a < 0.$$

ARITHMETIC OPERATIONS

The four arithmetic operations are addition, subtraction, multiplication, and division.

ADDITION AND SUBTRACTION OF REAL NUMBERS   In an addition problem, the two numbers added are called **addends**, and the answer is called the **sum**. In the addition problem $3 + 5 = 8$, the numbers 3 and 5 are the addends and 8 is the sum.

The **additive inverse** or **opposite** of a real number a is $-a$. For example, the additive inverse of 5 is -5 and the additive inverse of -1.6 is 1.6. When we add opposites, the result is 0. That is, $a + (-a) = 0$ for every real number a.

EXAMPLE 2   Finding additive inverses

Find the additive inverse or opposite of each number or expression. Then find the sum of the number or expression and its opposite.

(a) 10,961   (b) π (c) $-\dfrac{3}{4}$ (d) $6x - 2$

Solution   (a) The opposite of 10,961 is $-10,961$. Their sum is $10{,}961 + (-10{,}961) = 0$.
(b) The opposite of π is $-\pi$. Their sum is $\pi + (-\pi) = 0$.
(c) The opposite of $-\frac{3}{4}$ is $\frac{3}{4}$. Their sum is $-\frac{3}{4} + \frac{3}{4} = 0$.
(d) The opposite of $6x - 2$ is $-(6x - 2) = -6x + 2$. Their sum is

$$6x - 2 + (-6x) + 2 = 6x + (-6x) - 2 + 2 = 0.$$

When you add real numbers, it may be helpful to think of money. A positive number represents being paid an amount of money, whereas a negative number indicates a debt owed. The sum

$$8 + (-6) = 2$$

would represent being paid \$8 and owing \$6, resulting in \$2 being left over. Similarly,

$$-7 + (-5) = -12$$

would represent owing \$7 and owing \$5, resulting in a debt of \$12.

To add two real numbers we may use the following rules.

ADDITION OF REAL NUMBERS

To add two numbers that are either *both positive* or *both negative*, add their absolute values. Their sum has the same sign as the two numbers.

To add two numbers with *opposite signs*, find the absolute value of each number. Subtract the smaller absolute value from the larger. The sum has the same sign as the number with the larger absolute value. If the two numbers are opposites, their sum is 0.

The next example illustrates addition of real numbers.

EXAMPLE 3   Adding real numbers

Evaluate each expression.

(a) $-3 + (-5)$ **(b)** $-4 + 7$ **(c)** $8.4 + (-9.5)$

Solution   **(a)** The addends are both negative, so we add the absolute values $|-3|$ and $|-5|$ to obtain 8. As the signs of the addends are both negative, the answer is -8. That is, $-3 + (-5) = -8$. If we owe \$3 and then owe an additional \$5, the total amount owed is \$8.

(b) The addends have opposite signs, so we subtract their absolute values to obtain 3. The answer is positive because $|7|$ is greater than $|-4|$. That is, $-4 + 7 = 3$. If we owe \$4 and are paid \$7, the result is that we have \$3 to keep.

(c) $8.4 + (-9.5) = -1.1$ because $|-9.5|$ is 1.1 more than $|8.4|$. If we are paid \$8.40 and owe \$9.50, we still owe \$1.10.

TEACHING TIP

You may need to review addition of real numbers by doing a few examples similar to Example 3. Remind students that, if the signs are *different*, they should start by finding the *difference* of their absolute values.

Addition of positive and negative numbers occurs at banks if we let deposits be represented by positive numbers and withdrawals be represented by negative numbers.

EXAMPLE 4   Balancing a checking account

The initial balance in a checking account is \$157. Find the final balance if the following represents a list of withdrawals and deposits: $-55, -19, 123, -98$.

Solution   We find the sum.

$$157 + (-55) + (-19) + 123 + (-98) = 102 + (-19) + 123 + (-98)$$
$$= 83 + 123 + (-98)$$
$$= 206 + (-98)$$
$$= 108$$

The final balance is \$108. This result may be supported by evaluating the expression with a calculator. See Figure 1.6, where the sum has been calculated two different ways. Instead of adding the opposite of a number, we can also subtract.

```
157+(-55)+(-19)+
123+(-98)
               108
157-55-19+123-98
               108
```

Figure 1.6

TEACHING TIP

Students often confuse the negation key with the subtraction key.

Technology Note: *Subtraction and Negation*

On graphing calculators, two different keys typically represent subtraction and negation. In the first calculation in Figure 1.6, we used the negation key, and in the second calculation, we used the subtraction key.

The answer to a subtraction problem is called the **difference**. When you're subtracting two real numbers, it sometimes helps to change the subtraction problem to an addition problem.

SUBTRACTION OF REAL NUMBERS

For any real numbers a and b,

$$a - b = a + (-b).$$

To subtract b from a, add a and the opposite of b.

EXAMPLE 5   Subtracting real numbers

Evaluate each expression.

(a) $-12 - 7$ **(b)** $-5.1 - (-10.6)$ **(c)** $\dfrac{1}{2} - \left(-\dfrac{2}{3}\right)$ **(d)** $3t - 7t$

TEACHING TIP

After a few examples, students can simplify $3t - 7t$ to $-4t$ without writing the step for the distributive property.

Solution   **(a)** $-12 - 7 = -12 + (-7) = -19$

(b) $-5.1 - (-10.6) = -5.1 + 10.6 = 5.5$

(c) $\dfrac{1}{2} - \left(-\dfrac{2}{3}\right) = \dfrac{1}{2} + \dfrac{2}{3} = \dfrac{3}{6} + \dfrac{4}{6} = \dfrac{7}{6}$

(d) $3t - 7t = (3 - 7)t = -4t$

MULTIPLICATION AND DIVISION OF REAL NUMBERS   In a multiplication problem, the two numbers multiplied are called the **factors**, and the answer is called the **product**. In the problem $3 \cdot 5 = 15$, the numbers 3 and 5 are factors and 15 is the product. The **multiplicative inverse** or **reciprocal** of a nonzero number a is $\frac{1}{a}$. The product of a nonzero number a and its reciprocal is $a \cdot \frac{1}{a} = 1$. For example, the reciprocal of -5 is $-\frac{1}{5}$ because $-5 \cdot -\frac{1}{5} = 1$, and the reciprocal of $\frac{2}{3}$ is $\frac{3}{2}$ because $\frac{2}{3} \cdot \frac{3}{2} = 1$. To multiply positive or negative numbers we may use the following rules.

MULTIPLICATION OF REAL NUMBERS

The product of two numbers with *like* signs is positive. The product of two numbers with *unlike* signs is negative.

EXAMPLE 6   Multiplying real numbers

Evaluate each expression.

(a) $-11 \cdot 8$ **(b)** $\dfrac{3}{5} \cdot \dfrac{4}{7}$ **(c)** $-1.2(-10)$ **(d)** $(1.2)(5)(-7)$

Solution   **(a)** The product is negative because the factors -11 and 8 have unlike signs. Thus $-11 \cdot 8 = -88$.

(b) The product is positive because both factors are positive. Thus $\dfrac{3}{5} \cdot \dfrac{4}{7} = \dfrac{3 \cdot 4}{5 \cdot 7} = \dfrac{12}{35}$.

(c) As both factors are negative, the product is positive. Thus $-1.2(-10) = 12$.

(d) $(1.2)(5)(-7) = (6)(-7) = -42$

In the division problem $20 \div 4 = 5$, the number 20 is the **dividend**, 4 is the **divisor**, and 5 is the **quotient**. This division problem can be written as $\frac{20}{4} = 5$. Division of real numbers can be defined in terms of multiplication and reciprocals.

	DIVISION OF REAL NUMBERS

For real numbers a and b, with $b \neq 0$,

$$\frac{a}{b} = a \cdot \frac{1}{b}.$$

That is, to divide a by b, multiply a by the reciprocal of b.

The expression $b \neq 0$ is read "b **not equal to** 0."

EXAMPLE 7 Dividing real numbers

Evaluate each expression.

(a) $-12 \div \frac{1}{2}$ **(b)** $\dfrac{\frac{2}{3}}{-7}$ **(c)** $\dfrac{-4}{-24}$ **(d)** $6 \div 0$

Solution **(a)** $-12 \div \frac{1}{2} = -12 \cdot \frac{2}{1} = -24$

(b) $\dfrac{\frac{2}{3}}{-7} = \frac{2}{3} \div (-7) = \frac{2}{3} \cdot \left(-\frac{1}{7}\right) = -\frac{2}{21}$

(c) $\dfrac{-4}{-24} = -4 \cdot \left(-\frac{1}{24}\right) = \frac{4}{24} = \frac{1}{6}$

(d) $6 \div 0 = \frac{6}{0}$ is undefined because division by 0 is not possible.

Many calculators have the capability to perform arithmetic on fractions and express the answer as either a decimal or a fraction. The next example illustrates this capability.

EXAMPLE 8 Performing arithmetic operations with technology

Use a calculator to evaluate each expression as a decimal and as a fraction.

(a) $\frac{1}{3} + \frac{2}{5} - \frac{4}{9}$ **(b)** $\left(\frac{4}{9} \cdot \frac{3}{8}\right) \div \frac{2}{3}$

Solution **(a)** From Figure 1.7,

$$\frac{1}{3} + \frac{2}{5} - \frac{4}{9} = 0.2\overline{8}, \quad \text{or} \quad \frac{13}{45}.$$

In Figure 1.7, the second calculation uses the "Frac" feature. This feature converts the answer to a fraction, rather than to a decimal.

Note: Generally it is a good idea to put parentheses around fractions when you are using a calculator.

```
(1/3)+(2/5)-(4/9
)
          .2888888889
(1/3)+(2/5)-(4/9
)▶Frac
               13/45
```

Figure 1.7

(b) From Figure 1.8,

$$\left(\frac{4}{9} \cdot \frac{3}{8}\right) \div \frac{2}{3} = 0.25, \quad \text{or} \quad \frac{1}{4}.$$

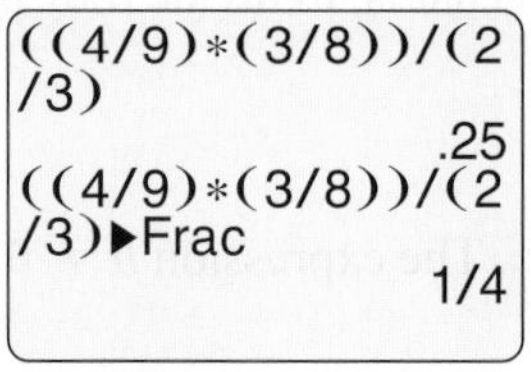

```
((4/9)*(3/8))/(2
/3)
                .25
((4/9)*(3/8))/(2
/3)▶Frac
               1/4
```

Figure 1.8

Calculator Help
To express answers as fractions, see the Appendix (page AP-2).

TEACHING TIP

Students may use different reasons to arrive at similar conclusions in this subsection.

DATA AND NUMBER SENSE

In everyday life we commonly make approximations involving a variety of data. To make estimations we often use arithmetic operations on real numbers. Sometimes we have to ask ourselves if a result looks reasonable.

EXAMPLE 9   Determining a reasonable answer

Table 1.3 lists the number of endangered species reported for selected years. Determine mentally which of the following values represents the average number of endangered species from 1998 to 2001: 920, 949, or 972. Explain your reasoning.

TABLE 1.3   Endangered Species

Year	1998	1999	2000	2001
Species	924	939	961	972

Source: Fish and Wildlife Service.

Solution   The average value would lie between the maximum and minimum numbers of endangered species. The value of 920 is less than the smallest value in Table 1.3 and 972 is equal to the largest value in the table. The only reasonable choice is 949 because it is located in the middle of the four data items.

EXAMPLE 10   Determining a reasonable answer

It is 2823 miles from New York to Los Angeles. Determine mentally which of the following would best estimate the number of hours of driving time required to travel this distance in a car: 50, 100, or 120 hours.

Solution   Speed equals distance divided by time. Dividing by 100 is easy, so start by dividing 100 hours into 2800 miles. The average speed would be $\frac{2800}{100} = 28$ miles per hour, which is too slow for most drivers. A more reasonable choice is 50 hours because then the average speed would be double, or about 56 miles per hour.

EXAMPLE 11 Estimating a numeric value

Table 1.4 lists the number of subscribers of cellular telephones in selected years. Estimate the number of subscribers in 1998.

TABLE 1.4   Cellular Phone Subscribers

Year	1994	1995	1996	1997	1998
Subscribers (millions)	24.1	33.8	44.0	55.3	?

Source: Cellular Telecommunications Industry Association.

Solution The data show that the number of subscribers has increased each year by about 10 or 11 million. A reasonable estimate might be $55 + 11 = 66$ million. Estimates may vary slightly.

PUTTING IT ALL TOGETHER

The number line may be used to visualize the set of real numbers. Each real number corresponds to a point on the number line. To obtain information from data we often perform arithmetic operations on those data. There are four basic arithmetic operations: addition, subtraction, multiplication, and division. The absolute value of a real number a cannot be a negative number and is equal to the distance between a and the origin on the number line. The following table summarizes some of the information presented in this section.

Operation	Definition	Examples
Absolute Value of a Real Number	For any real number a, $\lvert a \rvert = a$ if $a > 0$ or $a = 0$, and $\lvert a \rvert = -a$ if $a < 0$.	$\lvert -5 \rvert = 5$, $\lvert 3.7 \rvert = 3.7$, and $\lvert -4 + 4 \rvert = 0$
Addition of Real Numbers	See the highlighted box: Addition of Real Numbers on page 14.	$3 + (-6) = -3$, $-2 + (-10) = -12$, $-1 + 3 = 2$, and $18 + 11 = 29$
Subtraction of Real Numbers	We can transform a subtraction problem into an addition problem: $$a - b = a + (-b).$$	$4 - 6 = 4 + (-6) = -2$, $-7 - (-8) = -7 + 8 = 1$, $-8 - 5 = -8 + (-5) = -13$, and $9 - (-1) = 9 + 1 = 10$
Multiplication of Real Numbers	The product of two numbers with *like* signs is positive. The product of two numbers with *unlike* signs is negative.	$3 \cdot 5 = 15$ and $-4(-7) = 28$ $-8 \cdot 7 = -56$ and $5(-11) = -55$
Division of Real Numbers	For real numbers a and b with $b \neq 0$, $$\frac{a}{b} = a \cdot \frac{1}{b}.$$	$-3 \div \frac{3}{4} = -3 \cdot \frac{4}{3} = -4$ and $\frac{5}{2} \div \left(-\frac{7}{4}\right) = \frac{5}{2}\left(-\frac{4}{7}\right) = -\frac{10}{7}$

1.2 EXERCISES

FOR EXTRA HELP

 Student's Solutions Manual

 InterAct Math

MathXL

 MyMathLab

 Math Tutor Center

 Digital Video Tutor CD 1   Videotape 1

CONCEPTS

1. If $a > b$, then a is located to the _____ of b on the number line.   right

2. If $a < 0$, then a is located to the _____ of the origin on the number line.   left

3. The product of two negative numbers is a _____ number.   positive

4. The sum of two negative numbers is a $\overset{\text{negative}}{\text{_____}}$ number.

5. The quotient of a positive number and a negative number is a _____ number.   negative

6. If $a < 0$ and $b > 0$, then $a - b$ is a $\overset{\text{negative}}{\text{_____}}$ number.

7. The additive inverse of a is _____. $-a$

8. The multiplicative inverse, or reciprocal, of $\frac{a}{b}$ is _____. $\frac{b}{a}$ for $a \neq 0$

THE REAL NUMBER LINE AND ABSOLUTE VALUE

Exercises 9–14: Plot each number on a number line. Be sure to include an appropriate scale. *

9. $0, 4, -3, 1.5$

10. $10, 20, -5, -15$

11. $100, 300, -200, 50$

12. $-0.4, 0.2, 0.5, -0.1, 0$

13. $-\frac{3}{2}, \pi, \frac{1}{3}, 2$

14. $-2, -\frac{1}{2}, 1, \frac{7}{3}$

Exercises 15–22: Evaluate the absolute value.

15. $|-6.1|$ 6.1

16. $|17|$ 17

17. $|8 - 11|$ 3

18. $|2 \cdot 8 - 23|$ 7

19. $|x|$, where $x > 0$ x

20. $|x|$, where $x < 0$ $-x$

21. $|x - y|$, where $x > 0$ and $y < 0$ $x - y$

22. $|x + y|$, where $x < 0$ and $y < 0$ $-(x + y)$

Exercises 23–28: State whether only positive numbers are typically used to measure the given quantity or whether both positive and negative numbers are used. Explain your reasoning.

23. Area   Positive

24. Distance   Positive

25. Temperature   Both

26. A person's net worth   Both

27. Gas mileage of a car   Positive

28. Elevation relative to sea level   Both

ARITHMETIC OPERATIONS

Exercises 29–40: Find the additive inverse, or opposite, of the number or expression.

29. 56 -56

30. $-\frac{5}{7}$ $\frac{5}{7}$

31. -6.9 6.9

32. 12.8 -12.8

33. $-\pi + 2$ $\pi - 2$

34. $a + b$ $-a - b$

35. $a - b$ $-a + b$

36. $-x + 3$ $x - 3$

37. $-(x - y)$ $x - y$

38. $-1 - x$ $1 + x$

39. $z - (2 - z)$ $-2z + 2$

40. $2z - (1 + 2z)$ 1

Exercises 41–52: Find the multiplicative inverse, or reciprocal, of the number or expression.

41. 3 $\frac{1}{3}$

42. $\frac{3}{8}$ $\frac{8}{3}$

43. $-\frac{2}{3}$ $-\frac{3}{2}$

44. 1.5 $\frac{2}{3} = 0.\overline{6}$

45. π $\frac{1}{\pi}$

46. $-\frac{x}{y}$ $-\frac{y}{x}$

47. $a + 3$ $\frac{1}{a + 3}$

48. $x - 1$ $\frac{1}{x - 1}$

49. $-\frac{2a}{b}$ $-\frac{b}{2a}$

50. $-\frac{2b}{3a}$ $-\frac{3a}{2b}$

51. $\frac{1}{x - 7}$ $x - 7$

52. $\frac{3}{x + y}$ $\frac{x + y}{3}$

Exercises 53–82: Perform the following arithmetic operations and simplify.

53. $4 + (-6)$ -2

54. $-10 + 14$ 4

55. $-7.4 + (-9.2)$ -16.6

56. $-8.4 - 10.3$ -18.7

57. $-\frac{3}{4} - \left(-\frac{1}{4}\right)$ $-\frac{2}{4} = -\frac{1}{2}$

58. $\frac{1}{5} - \left(-\frac{3}{10}\right)$ $\frac{5}{10} = \frac{1}{2}$

59. $-9 + 1 + (-2) + 5$ -5

60. $-5 + 7 - (-2) + 3$ 7

*Answers on page IA-1

61. $-6 \cdot -12$ 72

62. $-(8 \cdot -4)$ 32

63. $-\frac{1}{2} \cdot \frac{5}{7} \cdot \frac{1}{3}$ $-\frac{5}{42}$

64. $-\frac{6}{7} \cdot -\frac{5}{3}$ $\frac{30}{21} = \frac{10}{7}$

65. $-\frac{1}{2} \div -\frac{3}{4}$ $\frac{4}{6} = \frac{2}{3}$

66. $-5 \div \frac{4}{5}$ $-\frac{25}{4}$

67. $\frac{3}{4} \div (-2)$ $-\frac{3}{8}$

68. $-\frac{4}{5} \div \frac{7}{10}$ $-\frac{40}{35} = -\frac{8}{7}$

69. $-\frac{8}{2}$ -4

70. $-\frac{45}{9}$ -5

71. $-25 \div -5$ 5

72. $8 \div 0$ Undefined

73. $\frac{1}{0}$ Undefined

74. $\frac{0}{7}$ 0

75. $-4 \cdot 7 \cdot (-5)$ 140

76. $-2 \cdot -6 \cdot 6 \cdot -1$ -72

77. $6 \cdot \frac{2}{3} \cdot 3 \cdot \left(-\frac{1}{6}\right)$ -2

78. $\left(\frac{4}{5} \cdot \frac{5}{8}\right) \div \frac{1}{2}$ 1

79. $4x - 9x$ $-5x$

80. $\frac{1}{2}x - \frac{3}{4}x$ $-\frac{1}{4}x$

81. $z - 4z + 2z$ $-z$

82. $5z - 3z - 6z$ $-4z$

Exercises 83–90: Use a calculator to evaluate the expression.

83. $-23.1 + 45.7 - (-34.6)$ 57.2

84. $102 - (-341) + (-112)$ 331

85. $\frac{1}{2} + \frac{2}{3} - \frac{5}{7}$ $\frac{19}{42}$

86. $-\frac{8}{13} + \frac{1}{2} - \frac{2}{5}$ $-\frac{67}{130}$

87. $-\frac{3}{4} \cdot \frac{4}{5} \div \frac{5}{3}$ $-\frac{9}{25}$

88. $\left(\frac{3}{4} \div (-11)\right) - \frac{2}{5}$ $-\frac{103}{220}$

89. $\frac{1}{2}\left(\frac{4}{11} + \frac{2}{5}\right)$ $\frac{21}{55}$

90. $-\frac{5}{13} + \left(\frac{3}{5} \div \frac{2}{17}\right)$ $\frac{613}{130}$

DATA AND NUMBER SENSE

Exercises 91–96: Mentally estimate the average of the list of numbers. Check your estimate by calculating the average.

91. $9, 5, 15, -9$ 5

92. $12, 8, 27, -7$ 10

93. $-2, 12, 7, -17$ 0

94. $45, 55, 65, 35$ 50

95. $101, 99, -42, 82$ 60

96. $-4, 2, 5, -8, 5, 24$ 4

Exercises 97–104: Mentally evaluate the expression.

97. $-2 + 8 + 3 + 2 - 11$ 0

98. $-22 + 43 - 78 + 7$ -50

99. $103 - 44 + 97 - 56$ 100

100. $10 + 11 + 12 - 11 - 11 - 11$ 0

101. $\frac{1}{5} \cdot \frac{2}{3} \cdot \frac{1}{7} \cdot \frac{1}{9} \cdot 5 \cdot \frac{3}{2} \cdot 7 \cdot 9$ 1

102. $\frac{1}{2} \cdot \frac{1}{3} \cdot \frac{1}{4} \cdot (-4) \cdot (-3) \cdot (-2)$ -1

103. $\left(\frac{1}{2} - \frac{1}{3}\right) + \left(\frac{1}{3} - \frac{1}{4}\right) + \left(\frac{1}{4} - \frac{1}{5}\right) + \left(\frac{1}{5} - \frac{1}{6}\right)$ $\frac{2}{6} = \frac{1}{3}$

104. $\frac{1}{2} \div \frac{1}{3} \cdot \frac{1}{3} \div \frac{1}{4} \cdot \frac{1}{4} \div \frac{1}{5} \cdot \frac{1}{5}$ $\frac{1}{2}$

APPLICATIONS

105. *Buying a Computer* An advertisement for a computer states that it costs $202 down and $98.99 per month for 24 months. Mentally estimate which of the following represents the cost of the computer if it is purchased under these terms: $2600, $3200, or $3800. Explain your reasoning. Find the actual cost. $2600; $2577.76; answers may vary.

106. *Leasing a Car* To lease a car costs $1497 down and $249 per month for 36 months. Mentally estimate the cost of the lease. Find the actual cost. $10,500; $10,461; answers may vary.

107. *Amway Sales* The following table lists worldwide retail sales for Amway products.

Year	1988	1990	1992
Sales ($ billions)	1.8	2.1	3.9

Year	1994	1996	1998
Sales ($ billions)	5.3	6.8	5.7

Source: Amway.

107.(b) $4.6 billion; average of 1992 and 1994 sales

(a) What were Amway sales in 1994? $5.3 billion

(b) Estimate sales in 1993. Explain how you arrived at your estimate and compare it to the actual value of $4.5 billion.

(c) Estimate sales in 1997. Actual sales were $7.0 billion in 1997. Discuss the difficulty of obtaining an accurate estimate from only the data given in the table. $6.25 billion; answers may vary.

108. *Injuries at Work*   The following table lists the rate of injury cases per 100 full-time workers in private industry.   108.(a) 7.5; average of 1992 and 1998 rates
5.85; average of 1999 and 2001 rates

Year	1992	1998	1999	2001
Rate	8.3	6.7	6.3	5.4

Source: Bureau of Labor Statistics.

(a) Estimate the injury rates in 1995 and 2000. Explain how you obtained your estimates.
(b) Which estimate do you think is more accurate? Explain your reasoning.   5.85; answers may vary.

109. *Cybercrimes*   The number of reported hacking incidents for U.S. business computer systems has risen dramatically in recent years. The following table lists reported hacking incidents.

Year	1998	1999	2000	2001	2002
Rate	3734	9859	21,756	52,658	82,094

Source: Carnegie Mellon University.

(a) Has the number of hacking incidents increased by a fixed number each year? Explain.   No
(b) What was the average number of hacking incidents over this 5-year period?   34,020.2
(c) If current trends continue, estimate the number of hacking incidents for 2003. Then discuss any difficulties that you may have encountered in making this estimate.   120,000; answers may vary.

110. *Cigarette Consumption*   Although smoking in the United States has declined since 1980, it has continued to grow globally. The following table lists the global cigarette consumption.

Year	1950	1960	1970	1980	1990	2000
Cigarettes (trillions)	1.7	2.2	3.1	4.4	5.4	5.5

Source: Department of Agriculture.

(a) In 1960 the world population was 3 billion people. How many cigarettes were consumed per person?   About 733
(b) In 2000 the world population was 6 billion people. How many cigarettes were consumed per person?   About 917

4.9 trillion; average of 1980 and 1990 values

(c) Estimate cigarette consumption in 1985. Explain your reasoning.
(d) Is cigarette consumption likely to increase or decrease between 2000 and 2010? Explain your reasoning.   Answers may vary.

111. *Cable Modems*   Cable modems provided by the cable TV industry give high-speed access to the Internet. The following table lists the number of cable modem subscribers for selected years.

Year	1999	2000	2001	2002
Subscribers (millions)	1.0	2.0	3.0	4.3

Source: Yankee Group.

(a) Discuss any trends in cable modem subscribers from 1999 through 2002.   They are increasing.
(b) Estimate the number of subscribers in 2003. Explain your reasoning.   About 5.5 million; answers may vary.

112. *Digital Subscriber Lines*   Local phone companies provide digital subscriber lines (DSL) for high-speed Internet access. This technology competes directly with cable modem service provided by cable TV companies. The following table lists the number of digital subscriber lines for selected years.

Year	1999	2000	2001	2002
DSL users (millions)	0.3	0.7	1.5	2.7

Source: Yankee Group.

(a) Discuss any trends in DSL from 1999 through 2002.   DSL use is increasing.
(b) Estimate the number of subscribers in 2003. Explain your reasoning.   About 4–5 million; answers may vary.

WRITING ABOUT MATHEMATICS

113. Suppose that $a \neq b$. Explain how a number line can be used to determine whether a is greater than b or whether a is less than b. Give an example of each situation.

114. Explain why a positive number times a negative number is a negative number.

CHECKING BASIC CONCEPTS SECTIONS 1.1 AND 1.2

1. Identify each number as one or more of the following: a natural number, an integer, a rational number, or a real number.
   (a) -9 **(b)** $\frac{8}{4}$ **(c)** $\sqrt{5}$ **(d)** 0.5

2. Identify the property of real numbers that each equation illustrates. Write the property, using variables.
   (a) $3 + 4 = 4 + 3$ Commutative; $a + b = b + a$
   (b) $-5 \cdot (4 \cdot 8) = (-5 \cdot 4) \cdot 8$
   (c) $4(5 + 2) = 4 \cdot 5 + 4 \cdot 2$
   (d) $4x - (5 - x) = 4x - 5 + x$ Distributive; $a(b - c) = ab - ac$ with $a = -1$

1.(a) Integer, rational, real (b) Natural, integer, rational, real (c) Real (d) Rational, real
2.(b) Associative; $a \cdot (b \cdot c) = (a \cdot b) \cdot c$
 (c) Distributive; $a(b + c) = ab + ac$

3. Evaluate each expression.
   (a) $-3 + 4 + (-5)$ -4
   (b) $5.1 \cdot (-4) \cdot 2$ -40.8
   (c) $-\frac{2}{3} \cdot \left(\frac{1}{4} \div \frac{2}{5}\right)$ $-\frac{5}{12}$

4. A small lake covers 200 acres, has an average depth of 15 feet, and contains about 2 billion gallons of water. Estimate the number of gallons in a lake that covers 600 acres and has an average depth of 30 feet.   About 12 billion gallons

TEACHING TIP

Consider having the class break into groups of 2 to 4 and work some of these problems. Walk around the room, answer questions, and listen to how students discuss mathematics. It is an eye-opening experience.

1.3 INTEGER EXPONENTS

Bases and Positive Exponents · Zero and Negative Exponents · Product, Quotient, and Power Rules · Order of Operations · Scientific Notation

TEACHING TIP

Exponents are an important topic. You may want to spend two class periods on this section.

INTRODUCTION

Technology has brought with it the need for both small and large numbers. The size of an average virus is 5 millionths of a centimeter, whereas the distance to the nearest star, Alpha Centauri, is 25 trillion miles. To represent such numbers we often use exponents. In this section we discuss properties of integer exponents and some of their applications.   (***Source:*** C. Ronan, *The Natural History of the Universe.*)

BASES AND POSITIVE EXPONENTS

The area of a square that is 8 inches on a side is given by the expression

$$\underbrace{8 \cdot 8}_{2 \text{ factors}} = 8^2 = 64 \text{ square inches.}$$

The expression 8^2 is an **exponential expression** with **base** 8 and **exponent** 2. Exponential expressions occur frequently in a variety of applications. For example, suppose that an investment doubles its initial value 3 times. Then its final value is

$$\underbrace{2 \cdot 2 \cdot 2}_{3 \text{ factors}} = 2^3 = 8$$

times larger than its original value. Table 1.5 on the next page contains examples of exponential expressions.

TABLE 1.5

Expression	Base	Exponent
$2 \cdot 2 \cdot 2 = 2^3$	2	3
$6 \cdot 6 \cdot 6 \cdot 6 = 6^4$	6	4
$7 = 7^1$	7	1
$0.5 \cdot 0.5 = 0.5^2$	0.5	2
$x \cdot x \cdot x = x^3$	x	3

Read 0.5^2 as "0.5 squared," 2^3 as "2 cubed," and 6^4 as "6 to the fourth power." The terms *squared* and *cubed* come from geometry. If the length of a side of a square is 4, then its area is

$$4 \cdot 4 = 4^2 = 16$$

square units, as illustrated in Figure 1.9. Similarly, if the length of an edge (side) of a cube is 4, then its volume is

$$4 \cdot 4 \cdot 4 = 4^3 = 64$$

cubic units, as shown in Figure 1.10.

4

4

4

4

4

4 Squared

4 Cubed

Figure 1.9

Figure 1.10

EXAMPLE 1   **Writing numbers in exponential notation**

Using the given base, write each number as an exponential expression. Check your results with a calculator.
(a) 10,000   (base 10)
(b) 27   (base 3)
(c) 32   (base 2)

Solution   **(a)** $10,000 = 10 \cdot 10 \cdot 10 \cdot 10 = 10^4$
(b) $27 = 3 \cdot 3 \cdot 3 = 3^3$
(c) $32 = 2 \cdot 2 \cdot 2 \cdot 2 \cdot 2 = 2^5$

These values are supported in Figure 1.11, where we evaluated exponential expressions with a calculator, using the $\boxed{\land}$ key.

Calculator Help
To calculate exponential expressions, see the Appendix (page AP-1).

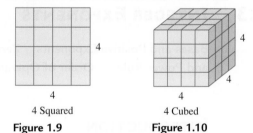

```
10^4
              10000
3^3
                 27
2^5
                 32
```

Figure 1.11

Computer memory is often measured in bytes. A *byte* is capable of storing one letter of the alphabet. For example, the word "math" requires four bytes to store in a computer. Bytes of computer memory are often manufactured in amounts equal to powers of 2, as illustrated in the next example.

EXAMPLE 2 Using exponents to analyze computer memory

In computer technology, 1 K (kilobyte) of memory is equal to 2^{10} bytes, and 1 MB (megabyte) of memory is equal to 2^{20} bytes. Determine whether 1 K of memory is equal to 1000 bytes and whether 1 MB is equal to 1,000,000 bytes. (**Source:** D. Horn, *Basic Electronics Theory*.)

Solution Figure 1.12 shows that $2^{10} = 1024$ and that $2^{20} = 1,048,576$. Thus 1 K represents slightly more than 1000 bytes and 1 MB is more than 1,000,000 bytes.

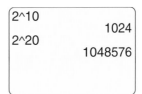

Figure 1.12

ZERO AND NEGATIVE EXPONENTS

Exponents can be defined for any integer. If a is any nonzero real number, we define

$$a^0 = 1.$$

For example, $3^0 = 1$ and $\left(\frac{1}{7}\right)^0 = 1$. We can also define a^{-n}, where n is a positive integer, as

$$a^{-n} = \frac{1}{a^n}.$$

Thus $5^{-4} = \frac{1}{5^4}$ and $y^{-2} = \frac{1}{y^2}$.

Using these definitions, we obtain

$$\frac{1}{a^{-n}} = \frac{1}{\dfrac{1}{a^n}} = \frac{a^n}{1} = a^n.$$

Thus $\frac{1}{2^{-5}} = 2^5$ and $\frac{1}{x^{-2}} = x^2$. If a and b are nonzero numbers, then

$$\frac{a^{-n}}{b^{-m}} = \frac{\dfrac{1}{a^n}}{\dfrac{1}{b^m}} = \frac{1}{a^n} \cdot \frac{b^m}{1} = \frac{b^m}{a^n}.$$

Thus $\frac{4^{-3}}{z^{-2}} = \frac{z^2}{4^3}$. This discussion leads to the following properties for integer exponents.

TEACHING TIP

Many instructors have students use properties 3–5 to change negative exponents to positive exponents before simplifying.

INTEGER EXPONENTS

Let a and b be nonzero real numbers and m and n be positive integers. Then

1. $a^n = a \cdot a \cdot a \cdot \cdots \cdot a$ (n factors of a).

2. $a^0 = 1$.   (*Note:* 0^0 is undefined.)

3. $a^{-n} = \dfrac{1}{a^n}$ and $\dfrac{1}{a^{-n}} = a^n$.

4. $\dfrac{a^{-n}}{b^{-m}} = \dfrac{b^m}{a^n}$.

5. $\left(\dfrac{a}{b}\right)^{-n} = \left(\dfrac{b}{a}\right)^n$.

EXAMPLE 3   **Evaluating expressions**

Evaluate each expression.

(a) 3^{-4} **(b)** $\dfrac{1}{2^{-3}}$ **(c)** $\left(\dfrac{5}{7}\right)^{-2}$ **(d)** $\dfrac{1}{(xy)^{-1}}$ **(e)** $\dfrac{2^{-2}}{3t^{-3}}$

Solution   **(a)** $3^{-4} = \dfrac{1}{3^4} = \dfrac{1}{3 \cdot 3 \cdot 3 \cdot 3} = \dfrac{1}{81}$ **(b)** $\dfrac{1}{2^{-3}} = 2^3 = 2 \cdot 2 \cdot 2 = 8$

(c) $\left(\dfrac{5}{7}\right)^{-2} = \left(\dfrac{7}{5}\right)^2 = \dfrac{7}{5} \cdot \dfrac{7}{5} = \dfrac{49}{25}$ **(d)** $\dfrac{1}{(xy)^{-1}} = (xy)^1 = xy$

$\underline{\hspace{2cm}}$ Base is xy.

(e) Note that only t and not $3t$ is raised to the power of -3.

$$\frac{2^{-2}}{3t^{-3}} = \frac{t^3}{3(2^2)} = \frac{t^3}{3 \cdot 4} = \frac{t^3}{12}$$

$\underline{\hspace{2cm}}$ Base is t.

Powers of 10 are important because they are used in mathematics to express numbers that are either small or large in absolute value. Table 1.6 may be used to simplify powers of 10. Note that, if the power decreases by 1, the result decreases by a factor of $\frac{1}{10}$.

TEACHING TIP

Complete Table 1.6 in class for powers of 2. Use the table to justify why $2^0 = 1$.

Critical Thinking

Use Table 1.6 to explain why it is reasonable for 10^0 to equal 1.

In the second row, each value can be obtained by dividing the value to the left by 10. Hence $10^0 = 10 \div 10 = 1$.

TABLE 1.6   Powers of Ten

Power of 10	10^3	10^2	10^1	10^0	10^{-1}	10^{-2}	10^{-3}
Value	1000	100	10	1	$\dfrac{1}{10}$	$\dfrac{1}{100}$	$\dfrac{1}{1000}$

PRODUCT, QUOTIENT, AND POWER RULES

We can calculate products and quotients of exponential expressions *provided their bases are the same*. For example,

$$3^2 \cdot 3^3 = \underbrace{(3 \cdot 3)}_{2 \text{ factors}} \cdot \underbrace{(3 \cdot 3 \cdot 3)}_{3 \text{ factors}} = 3^5. \qquad 2 + 3 = 5$$

This expression has a total of $2 + 3 = 5$ factors of 3, so the result is 3^5. To multiply exponential expressions with like bases, add exponents. Thus

$$x^3 \cdot x^4 = \underbrace{(x \cdot x \cdot x)}_{3 \text{ factors}} \cdot \underbrace{(x \cdot x \cdot x \cdot x)}_{4 \text{ factors}} = x^7. \qquad 3 + 4 = 7$$

TEACHING TIP

Time spent on exponents is time well spent. Many students continue to have difficulty with exponents in college algebra and calculus.

THE PRODUCT RULE

For any nonzero number a and integers m and n,

$$a^m \cdot a^n = a^{m+n}.$$

Note that the product rule holds for negative exponents. For example,

$$10^5 \cdot 10^{-2} = 10^{5+(-2)} = 10^3.$$

EXAMPLE 4   Using the product rule

Multiply and simplify. Use positive exponents.

(a) $10^2 \cdot 10^4$ **(b)** $7^3 \cdot 7^{-4}$ **(c)** $x^3 \cdot x^{-2} \cdot x^4$ **(d)** $3y^2 \cdot 2y^{-4}$

Solution   **(a)** $10^2 \cdot 10^4 = 10^{2+4} = 10^6 = 1{,}000{,}000$ Add exponents.

(b) $7^3 \cdot 7^{-4} = 7^{3+(-4)} = 7^{-1} = \dfrac{1}{7}$

(c) $x^3 \cdot x^{-2} \cdot x^4 = x^{3+(-2)+4} = x^5$

(d) $3y^2 \cdot 2y^{-4} = 3 \cdot 2 \cdot y^2 \cdot y^{-4} = 6y^{2+(-4)} = 6y^{-2} = \dfrac{6}{y^2}$

Note that 6 is *not* raised to the power of -2 in the expression $6y^{-2}$.

Consider division of exponential expressions. Here

$$\frac{6^5}{6^3} = \frac{6 \cdot 6 \cdot 6 \cdot 6 \cdot 6}{6 \cdot 6 \cdot 6} = \frac{6}{6} \cdot \frac{6}{6} \cdot \frac{6}{6} \cdot 6 \cdot 6 = 1 \cdot 1 \cdot 1 \cdot 6 \cdot 6 = 6^2. \qquad 5 - 3 = 2$$

Because there are two more 6s in the numerator, the result is $6^{5-3} = 6^2$. Thus, to divide exponential expressions with like bases, subtract exponents.

THE QUOTIENT RULE

For any nonzero number a and integers m and n,

$$\frac{a^m}{a^n} = a^{m-n}.$$

Note that the quotient rule holds for negative exponents. For example,

$$\frac{2^{-6}}{2^{-4}} = 2^{-6-(-4)} = 2^{-2} = \frac{1}{2^2}.$$

However, you may want to evaluate this quotient as

$$\frac{2^{-6}}{2^{-4}} = \frac{2^4}{2^6} = \frac{1}{2^2}.$$

Note: The quotient rule can also be used to justify that $a^0 = 1$. For example, $\frac{3^2}{3^2} = \frac{9}{9} = 1$ and by the quotient rule $\frac{3^2}{3^2} = 3^{2-2} = 3^0$. Thus $3^0 = 1$.

EXAMPLE 5   **Using the quotient rule**

Simplify each expression. Use positive exponents.

(a) $\dfrac{10^4}{10^6}$ (b) $\dfrac{x^5}{x^2}$ (c) $\dfrac{15x^2y^3}{5x^4y}$ (d) $\dfrac{3a^{-2}b^5}{9a^4b^{-3}}$

Solution   (a) $\dfrac{10^4}{10^6} = 10^{4-6} = 10^{-2} = \dfrac{1}{10^2} = \dfrac{1}{100}$ Subtract exponents.

(b) $\dfrac{x^5}{x^2} = x^{5-2} = x^3$

(c) $\dfrac{15x^2y^3}{5x^4y} = \dfrac{15}{5} \cdot \dfrac{x^2}{x^4} \cdot \dfrac{y^3}{y^1} = 3 \cdot x^{(2-4)}y^{(3-1)} = 3x^{-2}y^2 = \dfrac{3y^2}{x^2}$

(d) $\dfrac{3a^{-2}b^5}{9a^4b^{-3}} = \dfrac{3b^5b^3}{9a^4a^2} = \dfrac{b^8}{3a^6}$

How should we evaluate $(4^3)^2$? To answer this question consider

$$(4^3)^2 = 4^3 \cdot 4^3 = 4^{3+3} = 4^6. \qquad 3 \cdot 2 = 6$$

Similarly,

$$(x^4)^3 = x^4 \cdot x^4 \cdot x^4 = x^{4+4+4} = x^{12}. \qquad 4 \cdot 3 = 12$$

These results suggest that, to raise a power to a power, multiply the exponents.

RAISING POWERS TO POWERS

For any real number a and integers m and n,

$$(a^m)^n = a^{mn}.$$

EXAMPLE 6   **Raising powers to powers**

Simplify each expression. Use positive exponents.

(a) $(5^2)^3$ (b) $(2^4)^{-2}$ (c) $(b^{-7})^5$ (d) $\dfrac{(x^3)^{-2}}{(x^{-5})^2}$

Solution   (a) $(5^2)^3 = 5^{2 \cdot 3} = 5^6 = 15{,}625$ Multiply exponents.

(b) $(2^4)^{-2} = 2^{4(-2)} = 2^{-8} = \dfrac{1}{2^8} = \dfrac{1}{256}$

(c) $(b^{-7})^5 = b^{-7\cdot5} = b^{-35} = \dfrac{1}{b^{35}}$

(d) $\dfrac{(x^3)^{-2}}{(x^{-5})^2} = \dfrac{x^{-6}}{x^{-10}} = \dfrac{x^{10}}{x^6} = x^4$

How can we simplify the expression $(2x)^3$? Consider

$$(2x)^3 = 2x \cdot 2x \cdot 2x = (2 \cdot 2 \cdot 2) \cdot (x \cdot x \cdot x) = 2^3 x^3.$$

This result suggests that, to cube a product, cube each factor.

RAISING PRODUCTS TO POWERS

For any real numbers a and b and integer n,

$$(ab)^n = a^n b^n.$$

EXAMPLE 7   Raising products to powers

Simplify each expression. Use positive exponents.

(a) $(6y)^2$ **(b)** $(x^2y)^{-2}$ **(c)** $(2xy^3)^4$ **(d)** $\dfrac{(2a^2b^{-3})^2}{4(ab^3)^3}$

Solution   **(a)** $(6y)^2 = 6^2 y^2 = 36y^2$ Base is $6y$.

(b) $(x^2y)^{-2} = \dfrac{1}{(x^2y)^2} = \dfrac{1}{(x^2)^2 y^2} = \dfrac{1}{x^4 y^2}$

(c) $(2xy^3)^4 = 2^4 x^4 (y^3)^4 = 16x^4 y^{12}$

(d) $\dfrac{(2a^2b^{-3})^2}{4(ab^3)^3} = \dfrac{2^2 a^4 b^{-6}}{4a^3 b^9} = \dfrac{4a^4}{4a^3 b^9 b^6} = \dfrac{a}{b^{15}}$

The expression $\left(\dfrac{a}{b}\right)^3$ can be simplified as

$$\left(\dfrac{a}{b}\right)^3 = \dfrac{a}{b} \cdot \dfrac{a}{b} \cdot \dfrac{a}{b} = \dfrac{a^3}{b^3}.$$

This result suggests the following rule.

RAISING QUOTIENTS TO POWERS

For nonzero numbers a and b and any integer n,

$$\left(\dfrac{a}{b}\right)^n = \dfrac{a^n}{b^n}, \qquad b \neq 0.$$

EXAMPLE 8   Raising quotients to powers

Simplify each expression. Use positive exponents.

(a) $\left(\dfrac{3}{x}\right)^3$ **(b)** $\left(\dfrac{1}{2^3}\right)^{-2}$ **(c)** $\left(\dfrac{3x^{-3}}{y^2}\right)^4$ **(d)** $\left(\dfrac{3x^2}{4y^2z}\right)^3$

Solution **(a)** $\left(\dfrac{3}{x}\right)^3 = \dfrac{3^3}{x^3} = \dfrac{27}{x^3}$

(b) $\left(\dfrac{1}{2^3}\right)^{-2} = \left(\dfrac{2^3}{1}\right)^2 = \dfrac{(2^3)^2}{1^2} = 2^6 = 64$

(c) $\left(\dfrac{3x^{-3}}{y^2}\right)^4 = \dfrac{3^4(x^{-3})^4}{(y^2)^4} = \dfrac{81x^{-12}}{y^8} = \dfrac{81}{x^{12}y^8}$

(d) $\left(\dfrac{3x^2}{4y^2z}\right)^3 = \dfrac{3^3x^6}{4^3y^6z^3} = \dfrac{27x^6}{64y^6z^3}$

EXAMPLE 9   Simplifying expressions

Write each expression using positive exponents. Simplify the result completely.

(a) $\left(\dfrac{x^2y^{-3}}{3z^{-4}}\right)^{-2}$ **(b)** $\dfrac{(rt^3)^{-3}}{(r^2t^3)^{-2}}$

Solution **(a)** $\left(\dfrac{x^2y^{-3}}{3z^{-4}}\right)^{-2} = \left(\dfrac{3z^{-4}}{x^2y^{-3}}\right)^2$

$= \left(\dfrac{3y^3}{x^2z^4}\right)^2$

$= \dfrac{9y^6}{x^4z^8}$

(b) $\dfrac{(rt^3)^{-3}}{(r^2t^3)^{-2}} = \dfrac{(r^2t^3)^2}{(rt^3)^3}$

$= \dfrac{r^4t^6}{r^3t^9}$

$= \dfrac{r}{t^3}$

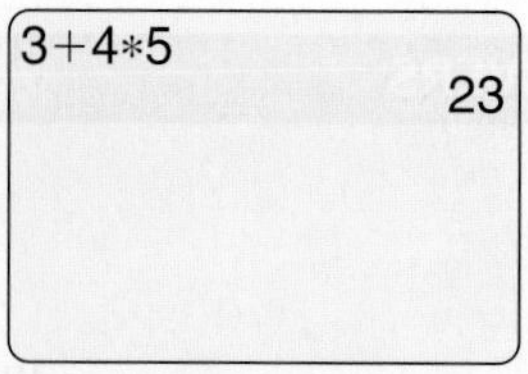

`3+4*5`
`          23`

ORDER OF OPERATIONS

When we evaluate the expression $3 + 4 \cdot 5$, is the result 35 or 23? Figure 1.13 shows that a calculator gives a result of 23. This is because multiplication is performed before addition.

Because it is important that we evaluate arithmetic expressions consistently, the following rules are used. (Two people should evaluate the same expression the same way.)

Figure 1.13

ORDER OF OPERATIONS

Use the following order of operations. First, perform all calculations within parentheses and absolute values, or above and below the fraction bar.

1. Evaluate all exponential expressions. Do any negations *after* evaluating exponents.
2. Do all multiplication and division from *left to right*.
3. Do all addition and subtraction from *left to right*.

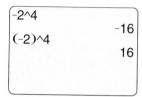

Figure 1.14

Be sure to evaluate exponents before performing negation. For example,

$$-2^4 = -(2 \cdot 2 \cdot 2 \cdot 2) = -16, \quad \text{but} \quad (-2)^4 = (-2)(-2)(-2)(-2) = 16.$$

These results are supported by Figure 1.14.

EXAMPLE 10 Evaluating arithmetic expressions

Evaluate each expression. Use a calculator to support your results.

(a) $5 - 3 \cdot 2 - (4 + 5)$ **(b)** $-3^2 + \dfrac{5 + 7}{2 + 1}$ **(c)** $4^3 - 5(2 - 6 \cdot 2)$

Solution **(a)**
$$
\begin{aligned}
5 - 3 \cdot 2 - (4 + 5) &= 5 - 3 \cdot 2 - 9 \\
&= 5 - 6 - 9 \\
&= -1 - 9 \\
&= -10
\end{aligned}
$$

(b) Assume that both the numerator and the denominator of a fraction have parentheses around them.

$$
\begin{aligned}
-3^2 + \frac{5 + 7}{2 + 1} &= -3^2 + \frac{(5 + 7)}{(2 + 1)} \\
&= -3^2 + \frac{12}{3} \\
&= -9 + \frac{12}{3} \\
&= -9 + 4 \\
&= -5
\end{aligned}
$$

(c)
$$
\begin{aligned}
4^3 - 5(2 - 6 \cdot 2) &= 4^3 - 5(2 - 12) \\
&= 4^3 - 5(-10) \\
&= 64 - 5(-10) \\
&= 64 + 50 \\
&= 114
\end{aligned}
$$

Figure 1.15

These results are supported by Figure 1.15.

SCIENTIFIC NOTATION

Calculator Help
To display numbers in scientific notation, see the Appendix (page AP-2).

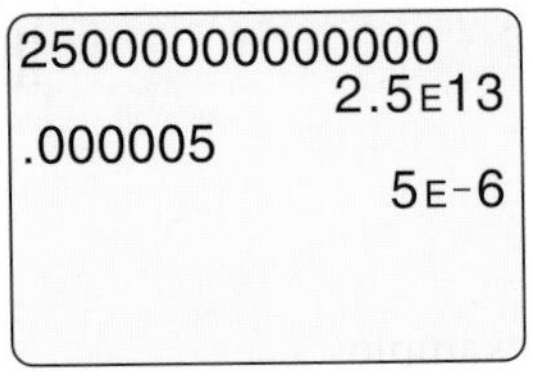

```
25000000000000
            2.5E13
.000005
            5E-6
```

Figure 1.16

Numbers that are large or small in absolute value occur frequently in applications. For simplicity these numbers are often expressed in scientific notation. As mentioned in the introduction to the section, the distance to the nearest star is 25 trillion miles. This number can be expressed in scientific notation as

$$25{,}000{,}000{,}000{,}000 = 2.5 \times 10^{13}.$$

In contrast, a typical virus is about 5 millionths of a centimeter in diameter. In scientific notation this number can be written as

$$0.000005 = 5 \times 10^{-6}.$$

A calculator set in *scientific mode* expresses these numbers in scientific notation, as illustrated in Figure 1.16. The letter E denotes a power of 10. That is, $2.5\text{E}13 = 2.5 \times 10^{13}$ and $5\text{E}-6 = 5 \times 10^{-6}$.

SCIENTIFIC NOTATION

A real number a is in **scientific notation** when a is written as $b \times 10^n$, where $1 \le |b| < 10$ and n is an integer.

Use the following steps to express a positive number a in scientific notation.

WRITING A POSITIVE NUMBER IN SCIENTIFIC NOTATION

1. Move the decimal point in a number a until it represents a number b such that $1 \le b < 10$.
2. Count the number of decimal places that the decimal point was moved. Let this positive integer be n.
3. If the decimal point was moved to the left, then $a = b \times 10^n$.
   If the decimal point was moved to the right, then $a = b \times 10^{-n}$.

Note: The scientific notation for a negative number a is the additive inverse of the scientific notation of $|a|$. For example, $5200 = 5.2 \times 10^3$, so $-5200 = -5.2 \times 10^3$.

Table 1.7 shows the values of some important powers of 10.

TABLE 1.7   Important Powers of 10

Number	10^{-3}	10^{-2}	10^{-1}	10^3	10^6	10^9	10^{12}
Value	Thousandth	Hundredth	Tenth	Thousand	Million	Billion	Trillion

---

EXAMPLE 11   Writing a number in scientific notation

Express each number in scientific notation.
(a) 360,000   (Dots in 1 square inch of some types of laser print)
(b) 0.00000538   (Time in seconds for light to travel 1 mile)
(c) 10,000,000,000   (Estimated world population in 2050)

TEACHING TIP

Students often have difficulty with scientific notation when the exponent of 10 is negative. Do other examples like Example 11.

Solution **(a)** Move the assumed decimal point in 360,000 *five places* to the *left* to obtain 3.6.

$$3.6\,0\,0\,0\,0.$$

The scientific notation for 360,000 is 3.6×10^5.

(b) Move the decimal point in 0.00000538 *six places* to the *right* to obtain 5.38.

$$0.0\,0\,0\,0\,0\,5.38$$

The scientific notation for 0.00000538 is 5.38×10^{-6}.

(c) Move the decimal point in 10,000,000,000 *ten places* to the *left* to obtain 1.

$$1.\overline{0\,0\,0\,0\,0\,0\,0\,0\,0\,0}.$$

The scientific notation for 10,000,000,000 is 1×10^{10}. Note that positive powers of 10 indicate a large number, whereas negative powers of 10 indicate a small number.

In the next example we convert numbers from scientific form to **standard form**.

EXAMPLE 12   Writing a number in standard form

Write the number in standard form.
(a) 2×10^8 (Number of years for the sun to orbit in the Milky Way)
(b) 2.1×10^{-2} (Fraction of deaths worldwide caused by lung cancer in 1997)

Solution **(a)** Because the exponent of 10 is *positive*, move the assumed decimal point in 2 to the *right* 8 places to obtain 200,000,000.

(b) Because the exponent of 10 is *negative*, move the decimal point in 2.1 to the *left* 2 places to obtain 0.021.

Arithmetic can be performed on expressions in scientific notation. For example, multiplication of the expressions 8×10^4 and 4×10^2 may be done by hand.

$$
\begin{aligned}
(8 \times 10^4) \cdot (4 \times 10^2) &= (8 \cdot 4) \times (10^4 \cdot 10^2) && \text{Properties of real numbers} \\
&= 32 \times 10^6 && \text{Add exponents and simplify.} \\
&= (3.2 \times 10^1)(10^6) && \text{Write in scientific notation.} \\
&= 3.2 \times 10^7 && \text{Add exponents.}
\end{aligned}
$$

Division may be performed as follows.

$$
\begin{aligned}
\frac{8 \times 10^4}{4 \times 10^2} &= \frac{8}{4} \times \frac{10^4}{10^2} && \text{Property of fractions} \\
&= 2 \times 10^2 && \text{Subtract exponents.}
\end{aligned}
$$

Calculator Help
To enter numbers in scientific notation, see the Appendix (page AP-3).

The next example illustrates how scientific notation is used in applications.

EXAMPLE 13   Analyzing the federal debt

In 2001, the federal debt held by the public was 3.17 trillion dollars, and the population of the United States was 281 million. Approximate the national debt per person.

Solution   In scientific notation 3.17 trillion equals 3.17×10^{12} and 281 million equals 281×10^{6}, or 2.81×10^{8}. The per person debt held by the public is given by

$$\frac{3.17 \times 10^{12}}{2.81 \times 10^{8}} \approx \$11{,}281.$$

Figure 1.17 supports this result.

```
(3.17*10^12)/(2.
81*10^8)
          11281.13879
```

Figure 1.17

Answers will vary. For example, a 19-year-old would be about $19 \times 365 \times 24 \times 60 \times 60 \approx 6 \times 10^{8} = 600{,}000{,}000$ seconds old.

Critical Thinking

Estimate the number of seconds that you have been alive.

1.3   PUTTING IT ALL TOGETHER

The following table summarizes important properties of exponents, where a and b are nonzero real numbers and m and n are integers.

Property	Definition	Examples
Bases and Exponents	In the expression a^{n}, a is the base and n is the exponent. *Note:* 0^{0} is undefined.	$3^{4} = 3 \cdot 3 \cdot 3 \cdot 3 = 81,\quad 7^{0} = 1,$ $2^{-3} = \dfrac{1}{2^{3}} = \dfrac{1}{2 \cdot 2 \cdot 2} = \dfrac{1}{8},$ and $-3^{2} = -9$
The Product Rule	$a^{m} \cdot a^{n} = a^{m+n}$	$8^{4} \cdot 8^{2} = 8^{4+2} = 8^{6}$ and $5^{6} \cdot 5^{-3} = 5^{6+(-3)} = 5^{3}$
The Quotient Rule	$\dfrac{a^{m}}{a^{n}} = a^{m-n}$	$\dfrac{6^{7}}{6^{4}} = 6^{7-4} = 6^{3}$ and $\dfrac{7^{-4}}{7^{-2}} = 7^{(-4-(-2))} = 7^{-2} = \dfrac{1}{7^{2}}$
The Power Rules	1. $(a^{m})^{n} = a^{mn}$ 2. $(ab)^{n} = a^{n}b^{n}$ 3. $\left(\dfrac{a}{b}\right)^{n} = \dfrac{a^{n}}{b^{n}}$	1. $(2^{2})^{3} = 2^{6}$ 2. $(3y)^{4} = 3^{4}y^{4}$ 3. $\left(\dfrac{x^{2}}{y}\right)^{4} = \dfrac{x^{8}}{y^{4}}$

Property	Definition	Examples
Quotients and Negative Exponents	**1.** $\dfrac{1}{a^{-n}} = a^{n}$ **2.** $\dfrac{a^{-n}}{b^{-m}} = \dfrac{b^{m}}{a^{n}}$ **3.** $\left(\dfrac{a}{b}\right)^{-n} = \left(\dfrac{b}{a}\right)^{n}$	**1.** $\dfrac{1}{x^{-2}} = x^{2}$ **2.** $\dfrac{z^{-3}}{y^{-5}} = \dfrac{y^{5}}{z^{3}}$ **3.** $\left(\dfrac{4}{t}\right)^{-2} = \left(\dfrac{t}{4}\right)^{2} = \dfrac{t^{2}}{4^{2}}$
Scientific Notation	A positive number a is in scientific notation when a is written as $b \times 10^{n}$, where $1 \le b < 10$ and n is an integer.	$52{,}600 = 5.26 \times 10^{4}$ and $0.0068 = 6.8 \times 10^{-3}$

1.3 EXERCISES

FOR EXTRA HELP

📖 Student's Solutions Manual

InterAct Math

MathXL

🚪 MyMathLab

📞 Math Tutor Center

Digital Video Tutor
CD 1   Videotape 1

CONCEPTS

1. Identify the base and the exponent in the expression 8^{3}. Base: 8; exponent: 3

2. Evaluate 97^{0} and 2^{-1}. $1, \frac{1}{2}$

3. Write 7 cubed, using symbols. 7^{3}

4. Write 5 squared, using symbols. 5^{2}

5. Are the expressions 2^{3} and 3^{2} equal? Explain your answer. No. $2^{3} = 8$ and $3^{2} = 9$

6. Are the expressions -4^{2} and $(-4)^{2}$ equal? Explain your answer. No. $-4^{2} = -16$ and $(-4)^{2} = 16$

7. $7^{-n} = $ _____ $\frac{1}{7^{n}}$

8. $6^{m} \cdot 6^{n} = $ _____ 6^{m+n}

9. $\dfrac{5^{m}}{5^{n}} = $ _____ 5^{m-n}

10. $(3x)^{k} = $ _____ $3^{k}x^{k}$

11. $(2^{m})^{k} = $ _____ 2^{mk}

12. $\left(\dfrac{x}{y}\right)^{m} = $ _____ $\dfrac{x^{m}}{y^{m}}$

13. $\dfrac{1}{x^{-n}} = $ _____ x^{n}

14. $\dfrac{a^{-n}}{b^{-m}} = $ _____ $\dfrac{b^{m}}{a^{n}}$

15. $\left(\dfrac{y}{z}\right)^{-n} = $ _____ $\left(\dfrac{z}{y}\right)^{n}$ or $\dfrac{z^{n}}{y^{n}}$

16. $5 \times 10^{2} = $ _____   500

PROPERTIES OF EXPONENTS

Exercises 17–22: (Refer to Example 1.) Write the number as an exponential expression, using the base shown. Check your result with a calculator.

17. 8   (base 2) 2^{3}

18. 1000   (base 10) 10^{3}

19. 256   (base 4) 4^{4}

20. $\frac{1}{16}$ (base 2) 2^{-4}

21. 1   (base 6) 6^{0}

22. $\frac{1}{125}$ (base 5) 5^{-3}

Exercises 23–36: Evaluate the expression.

23. 4^{2} 16

24. 2^{-3} $\frac{1}{8}$

25. -3^{4} -81

26. $(-3)^{4}$ 81

27. 5^{0} 1

28. $\left(-\dfrac{2}{3}\right)^{-3}$ $-\frac{27}{8}$

29. $\left(\dfrac{2}{3}\right)^{3}$ $\frac{8}{27}$

30. $\dfrac{1}{4^{-2}}$ 16

31. $\left(-\dfrac{1}{2}\right)^4$ $\frac{1}{16}$ **32.** $\left(-\dfrac{3}{4}\right)^3$ $-\frac{27}{64}$

33. $\left(-\dfrac{3}{5}\right)^{-2}$ $\frac{25}{9}$ **34.** $\dfrac{3^{-2}}{2^{-4}}$ $\frac{16}{9}$

35. $\dfrac{4^{-3}}{5^{-2}}$ $\frac{25}{64}$ **36.** $\left(\dfrac{1}{2}\right)^{-4}$ 16

Exercises 37–42: Use the product rule and positive exponents to simplify the expression.

37. (a) $3^5 \cdot 3^{-3}$ $3^2 = 9$ **(b)** $x^2 x^5$ x^7 41. (b) $\dfrac{8}{ab^3}$

38. (a) $10^{-5} \cdot 10^2$ $\frac{1}{10^3} = \frac{1}{1000}$ **(b)** $y^4 y^{-3}$ y

39. (a) $(-3x^{-2})(5x^5)$ $-15x^3$ **(b)** $(ab)(a^2 b^{-3})$ $\frac{a^3}{b^2}$

40. (a) $6z^2(-z^3)$ $-6z^5$ **(b)** $(a^2 b^{-3})(2ab^3)$ $2a^3$

41. (a) $5^{-2} \cdot 5^3 \cdot 2^{-4} \cdot 2^3$ $\frac{5}{2}$ **(b)** $2a^3 \cdot b^2 \cdot 4a^{-4} \cdot b^{-5}$

42. (a) $2^{-3} \cdot 3^4 \cdot 3^{-2} \cdot 2^5$ **(b)** $3x^{-4} \cdot 2x^2 \cdot 5y^4 \cdot y^{-3}$ $\frac{30y}{x^2}$

$2^2 \cdot 3^2 = 36$

Exercises 43–48: Use the quotient rule and other properties of exponents to simplify the expression. Use positive exponents to write your answer.

43. (a) $\dfrac{4^3}{4^2}$ 4 **(b)** $\dfrac{10^{-3}}{10^{-5}}$ $10^2 = 100$

44. (a) $\dfrac{5^4}{5^{-7}}$ $5^{11} = 48,828,125$ **(b)** $\dfrac{6^{-5}}{6}$ $\frac{1}{6^6} = \frac{1}{46,656}$

45. (a) $\dfrac{b^{-3}}{b^2}$ $\frac{1}{b^5}$ **(b)** $\dfrac{24x^3}{6x}$ $4x^2$

46. (a) $\dfrac{x^0}{x^{-5}}$ x^5 **(b)** $\dfrac{10x^5}{5x^{-3}}$ $2x^8$

47. (a) $\dfrac{12a^2 b^3}{18a^4 b^2}$ $\frac{2b}{3a^2}$ **(b)** $\dfrac{21x^{-3} y^4}{7x^4 y^{-2}}$ $\frac{3y^6}{x^7}$

48. (a) $\dfrac{-6x^7 y^3}{3x^2 y^{-5}}$ $-2x^5 y^8$ **(b)** $\dfrac{32x^3 y}{-24x^5 y^{-3}}$ $-\frac{4y^4}{3x^2}$

Exercises 49–54: Use the power rules to simplify the expression. Use positive exponents to write your answer.

49. (a) $(3^2)^4$ $3^8 = 6561$ **(b)** $(x^3)^{-2}$ $\frac{1}{x^6}$

50. (a) $(-2^2)^3$ $-2^6 = -64$ **(b)** $(xy)^3$ $x^3 y^3$

51. (a) $(4y^2)^3$ $64y^6$ **(b)** $(-2xy^3)^{-4}$ $\frac{1}{16x^4 y^{12}}$

52. (a) $(-2a^2)^3$ $-8a^6$ **(b)** $(a^{-1} b^5)^{-2}$ $\frac{a^2}{b^{10}}$

53. (a) $\left(\dfrac{4}{x}\right)^3$ $\frac{64}{x^3}$ **(b)** $\left(\dfrac{2x}{z^4}\right)^{-5}$ $\frac{z^{20}}{32x^5}$

54. (a) $\left(\dfrac{-3}{x^3}\right)^2$ $\frac{9}{x^6}$ **(b)** $\left(\dfrac{2xy}{3z^5}\right)^{-1}$ $\frac{3z^5}{2xy}$

Exercises 55–82: Use rules of exponents to simplify the expression. Use positive exponents to write your answer.

55. $\dfrac{12m^2 n^{-5}}{8mn^{-2}}$ $\frac{3m}{2n^3}$ **56.** $\dfrac{15m^{-1} n}{5m^{-2} n^3}$ $\frac{3m}{n^2}$

57. $\dfrac{4r^3 t^2}{2r^{-1} t^{-3}}$ $2r^4 t^5$ **58.** $\dfrac{44r^5 t^2}{11r^2 t^5}$ $\frac{4r^3}{t^3}$

59. $\dfrac{ab^{-2} c^3}{a^2 bc^4}$ $\frac{1}{ab^3 c}$ **60.** $\dfrac{r^3 s^{-3} t^3}{r^{-1} s t^6}$ $\frac{r^4}{s^4 t^3}$

61. $(2x^3 y^{-2})^{-2}$ $\frac{y^4}{4x^6}$ **62.** $(4x^{-4} y)^2$ $\frac{16y^2}{x^8}$

63. $\dfrac{(b^2)^3}{(b^{-1})^2}$ b^8 **64.** $\dfrac{(a^3)^{-1}}{(a^{-3})^{-2}}$ $\frac{1}{a^9}$

65. $\dfrac{(-3ab^2)^3}{(a^2 b)^2}$ $-\frac{27b^4}{a}$ **66.** $\dfrac{(-2ab)^3}{(ab)^2}$ $-8ab$

67. $\dfrac{(-m^2 n^{-1})^{-2}}{(mn)^{-1}}$ $\frac{n^3}{m^3}$ **68.** $\dfrac{(-mn^4)^{-1}}{(m^2 n)^{-3}}$ $-\frac{m^5}{n}$

69. $\left(\dfrac{2a^3}{6b}\right)^4$ $\frac{a^{12}}{81b^4}$ **70.** $\left(\dfrac{-3a^2}{9b^3}\right)^4$ $\frac{a^8}{81b^{12}}$

71. $\left(\dfrac{t^{-3}}{t^{-4}}\right)^2$ t^2 **72.** $\left(\dfrac{r^{-2}}{2r^{-1}}\right)^{-4}$ $16r^4$

73. $\dfrac{8x^{-3} y^{-2}}{4x^{-2} y^{-4}}$ $\frac{2y^2}{x}$ **74.** $\dfrac{6x^{-1} y^{-1}}{9x^{-2} y^3}$ $\frac{2x}{3y^4}$

75. $\left(\dfrac{2t}{-r^2}\right)^{-3}$ $-\frac{r^6}{8t^3}$ **76.** $\left(\dfrac{t^2}{3r}\right)^{-1}$ $\frac{3r}{t^2}$

77. $\dfrac{(r^2 t^2)^{-2}}{(r^3 t)^{-1}}$ $\frac{1}{rt^3}$ **78.** $\dfrac{(2rt)^2}{(rt^4)^{-2}}$ $4r^4 t^{10}$

79. $\dfrac{4x^{-2} y^3}{(2x^{-1} y)^2}$ y **80.** $\dfrac{(ab)^3}{a^4 b^{-4}}$ $\frac{b^7}{a}$

81. $\left(\dfrac{-15r^2 t}{3r^{-3} t^4}\right)^3$ $-\frac{125r^{15}}{t^9}$ **82.** $\left(\dfrac{4(xy)^2}{(2xy^{-2})^3}\right)^{-2}$ $\frac{4x^2}{y^{16}}$

ORDER OF OPERATIONS

Exercises 83–102: (Refer to Example 10.) Evaluate each expression.

83. $4 + 5 \cdot 6$ 34 **84.** $4 - 5 - 9$ -10

85. $2(4 + (-8))$ -8 **86.** $500 - 10^3$ -500

87. $5 \cdot 2^3$ 40

88. $\frac{4+8}{2} - \frac{6+1}{3}$ $\frac{11}{3}$

89. $\frac{-2^4 - 3^2}{4} + \frac{1+2}{4}$ $-\frac{11}{2}$

90. $\frac{(-4^2 + 1)}{\frac{2}{3}}$ $-\frac{45}{2}$

91. $\frac{1 - 2 \cdot 4^2}{5^{-1}}$ -155

92. $6 \div 4 \div 2$ $\frac{3}{4}$

93. $4 + 6 - 3 \cdot 5 \div 3$ 5

94. $-3(25 - 2 \cdot 5^2) \div 5$ 15

95. $\frac{-3^2 + 3}{3}$ -2

96. $\frac{2 \cdot 4 - 7}{7}$ $\frac{1}{7}$

97. $1 + 5^2 - (-5)^2$ 1

98. $1 - 3 \cdot 4^3$ -191

99. $|7 - 2^2 \cdot 3|$ 5

100. $\frac{4^2 - |5 - (-6)|}{-2^2}$ $-\frac{5}{4}$

101. $\sqrt{4^2 + 3^2}$ 5

102. $\sqrt{13^2 - 12^2}$ 5

SCIENTIFIC NOTATION

Exercises 103–110: Write the number in scientific notation.

103. 2,391,000   (U.S. deaths in 1999) 2.391×10^6

104. 118,000   (New York City AIDS cases in 2000) 1.18×10^5

105. 26.9 billion   (Dollars spent on health care in 1960) 2.69×10^{10}

106. 1.2 trillion   (Dollars spent on health care in 1999) 1.2×10^{12}

107. 0.051   (Fraction of the population expected to spend time in prison) 5.1×10^{-2}

108. 0.156   (Fraction of people without health insurance) 1.56×10^{-1}

109. 0.000001   (Approximate wavelength of light in meters) 1.0×10^{-6}

110. 0.00258   (Fraction of people who died from heart disease in 1998) 2.58×10^{-3}

Exercises 111–118: Write the number in standard form.

111. 5×10^5 500,000

112. -7.85×10^3 -7850

113. 9.3×10^6 9,300,000

114. 2.961×10^2 296.1

115. -6×10^{-3} -0.006

116. 4.1×10^{-2} 0.041

117. 5.876×10^{-5} 0.00005876

118. 9.9×10^{-1} 0.99

Exercises 119–124: Evaluate the expression. Write your answer in both scientific notation and standard form.

119. $(2 \times 10^4)(3 \times 10^2)$ 6×10^6; 6,000,000

120. $(5 \times 10^{-4})(4 \times 10^6)$ 2×10^3; 2000

121. $(4 \times 10^{-4})(2 \times 10^{-2})$ 8×10^{-6}; 0.000008

122. $\frac{6 \times 10^4}{2 \times 10^2}$ 3×10^2; 300

123. $\frac{6.2 \times 10^3}{3.1 \times 10^{-2}}$ 2×10^5; 200,000

124. $\frac{2 \times 10^{-2}}{8 \times 10^{-5}}$ 2.5×10^2; 250

APPLICATIONS

125. *GPS Clocks*   The Global Positioning System (GPS) is made up of 24 satellites that allow individuals with a GPS receiver to pinpoint their positions on Earth. Every 1024 weeks the clocks in the GPS satellites reset to zero. The first time this resetting occurred was on August 21, 1999.   (*Source:* Associated Press.)
   (a) Find an exponent k so that $2^k = 1024$. $k = 10$
   (b) Estimate the number of years in 1024 weeks. $\frac{1024}{52} \approx 20$ years

126. *Foreign Currency*   During May 1999, one dollar was equivalent to 1818 Italian lira.   (*Source:* Lipper.)
   (a) Write 1818 in scientific notation. 1.818×10^3
   (b) At that time 1,000,000 lira was equivalent to about how many dollars?   About $550

127. *Volume*   If the sides of a cube have length a, then its volume is $V = a^3$. Find the volume of a cube with sides of length $2a$. $V = (2a)^3 = 8a^3$

128. *Area*   If the sides of a square have length a, then its area is $A = a^2$. Find the area of a square with sides of length $3a$. $A = (3a)^2 = 9a^2$

129. *Area*   Find the area of the square. $A = (3ab)^2 = 9a^2b^2$

3*ab*

3*ab*

130. *Volume*   Find the volume of the cube shown.

$V = (4xy)^3 = 64x^3y^3$

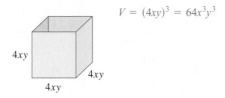

4*xy*

4*xy*

4*xy*

131. *Calculating Interest*   If P dollars are deposited in a savings account paying 5% annual interest, the amount A in the account after x years is given by the formula $A = P(1.05)^x$. Find A for the given values of P and x.
(a) $P = \$500; x = 2$ years $A = \$551.25$
(b) $P = \$1000, x = 4$ years $A = \$1215.51$

132. *Calculating Interest*   If P dollars are deposited in a savings account paying r percent annual interest, then the amount A in the account after x years is given by the formula $A = P(1 + \frac{r}{100})^x$. Find A for the given values of P, r, and x.
(a) $P = \$200, r = 10\%, x = 7$ years $A = \$389.74$
(b) $P = \$1500, r = 8\%, x = 15$ years $A = \$4758.25$

133. *Astronomy*   Light travels at 186,000 miles per second. The distance that light travels in 1 year is called a *light-year*.   About 5.866×10^{12} mi
(a) Calculate the number of miles in 1 light-year. Write your answer in scientific notation.
(b) Express your answer from part (a) in standard notation.   5,866,000,000,000
(c) Except for the sun, the nearest star is Alpha Centauri. Its distance from Earth is about 4.27 light-years. How many miles is this?   About 2.5×10^{13}
(d) If a rocket flew at 50,000 miles per hour, how many years would it take to reach Alpha Centauri?   About 57,000 yr

134. *Movie Box Office*   The *Star Wars* prequel *Episode I: The Phantom Menace* had a record-breaking first day, grossing $28,500,000.
(a) Write this number in scientific notation. 2.85×10^7

(b) If the average cost of a ticket was $6, estimate the number of people that attended the movie on its first day.   About 4,750,000

135. *Federal Debt*   (Refer to Example 13.) In 1990, the federal debt held by the public was $2.19 trillion, and the population of the United States was 249 million. Approximate the national debt per person.   About $8795 per person

136. *Federal Debt*   In 1980, the federal debt held by the public was $710 billion, and the debt per person was $3127. Approximate the population of the United States in 1980.   About 227 million

137. *Computer Memory*   (Refer to Example 2.) If a computer has 256 MB of memory, how many bytes is this? Express your answer in standard form. $256 \times 2^{20} = 268,435,456$ bytes

138. *Computer Memory*   One gigabyte of computer memory equals 2^{30} bytes. Write the number of bytes in 1 gigabyte, using standard notation.   1,073,741,824 bytes

139. *World Population*   The following table lists populations of selected countries in 1996 and their projected populations in 2025. Rewrite the table, expressing each population in scientific notation.*

Country	1996	2025
China	1,255,100,000	1,480,000,000
Germany	82,400,000	80,900,000
India	975,800,000	1,330,200,000
Mexico	95,800,000	130,200,000
United States	265,000,000	332,500,000

Source: United Nations Population Fund.

140. *World Population*   If current trends continue, world population P in billions may be modeled by the equation $P = 6(1.014)^x$, where x is in years and $x = 0$ corresponds to the year 2000. Estimate the world population in 2010 and 2025. (***Source:*** United Nations Population Fund.)   6.9 billion; 8.5 billion

WRITING ABOUT MATHEMATICS

141. A student evaluates three expressions:

$$-4^2 \quad \text{as} \quad 16; \quad 6 + 4 \cdot 2 \quad \text{as} \quad 20; \quad \text{and}$$
$$20 \div 4 \div 2 \quad \text{as} \quad 10.$$

Correct the errors and explain the mistakes.

142. Give the product and quotient rules for exponents and an example of each.

*Answer on page IA-1

Group Activity: Working with Real Data

Directions: Form a group of 2 to 4 people. Select someone to record the group's responses for this activity. All members of the group should work cooperatively to answer the questions. If your instructor asks for your results, each member of the group should be prepared to respond.

1. *Walk to the Moon* The distance to the moon is about 2.37×10^5 miles. Walking at 4 miles per hour, estimate the number of hours it would take to travel this distance. How many years is this? 59,250 hr; 6.76 yr

2. *Salary* Suppose that for full-time work a person earns 1¢ for the first week, 2¢ for the second week, 4¢ for the third week, 8¢ for the fourth week, and so on for 1 year.
   (a) Discuss whether you think this pay scale would be a good deal. It would be a good deal.
   (b) Estimate how much this person would make the last week of a 52-week year.
   2^{52-1} cents, or about $22.5 trillion

1.4 VARIABLES, EQUATIONS, AND FORMULAS

**Basic Concepts · Modeling Data · Square Roots and Cube Roots
Tables and Calculators (Optional)**

INTRODUCTION

Most of the mathematics that people have discovered throughout the ages can be derived only by using pencil and paper, not from science and measured data. However, one of the amazing aspects of mathematics is that it can be used in countless applications that improve our quality of life. Without mathematics, we would not have compact disc players, cars, warm buildings, or accurate weather forecasts. Mathematics can even be used to predict the increase in sea level if the polar ice caps were to melt. (See Exercise 1 in the Chapter 1 Extended and Discovery Exercises.) In this section we introduce some of the mathematical concepts that are used to model our world.

BASIC CONCEPTS

Suppose that we want to calculate the distance traveled by a car moving at a constant speed of 30 miles per hour. One method would be to make a table of values, as shown in Table 1.8.

TEACHING TIP

Point out that many times formulas are found by looking for patterns in tables of numbers.

TABLE 1.8

1-hour increase

Elapsed time (hours)	1	2	3	4	5	6
Distance (miles)	30	60	90	120	150	180

30-mile increase

Note that for each 1-hour increase the distance increases by 30 miles. Many times it is not possible to list all relevant values in a table. Instead, we use *variables* to describe data. For example, we might let elapsed time be represented by the variable t and let distance be represented by the variable d. If $t = 2$, then $d = 60$; if $t = 5$, then $d = 150$. In this example, the value of d is always equal to the value of t multiplied by 30. We can *model* this situation by using the *equation* or *formula* $d = 30t$. The values for distance in Table 1.8 can be calculated by letting $t = 1, 2, 3, 4, 5, 6$ in this formula.

A **variable** is a symbol, such as x, y, or t, used to represent any unknown number or quantity. An **algebraic expression** consists of numbers, variables, arithmetic symbols $(+, -, \times, \div)$, and grouping symbols, such as parentheses, brackets, and square roots. Examples of algebraic expressions include

$$6, \quad x + 2, \quad 4(t - 5) + 1, \quad \sqrt{x + 1}, \quad \text{and} \quad LW. \qquad \text{Expressions}$$

An **equation** is a statement that two algebraic expressions are equal. Examples of equations include

$$3 + 6 = 9, \quad x + 1 = 4, \quad d = 30t, \quad \text{and} \quad x + y = 20. \qquad \text{Equations}$$

The first equation contains only constants, the second equation contains one variable, and both the third and fourth equations contain two variables. A **formula** is an equation that can calculate one quantity by using a known value of another quantity. (Formulas can also contain known values of more than one quantity.) Formulas show relationships between variables. The formula $y = \frac{x}{3}$ computes the number of yards in x feet. If $x = 15$, then $y = \frac{15}{3} = 5$. That is, in 15 feet there are 5 yards.

EXAMPLE 1   Writing and using a formula

If a car travels at a constant speed of 70 miles per hour, write a formula that calculates the distance d that the car travels in t hours. Evaluate your formula when $t = 1.5$ and interpret the result.

Solution   Traveling at 70 miles per hour, the car will travel a distance of $d = 70t$ miles in t hours. Evaluating this formula at $t = 1.5$ results in

$$d = 70(1.5) = 105.$$

After 1.5 hours the car has traveled 105 miles.

EXAMPLE 2   Writing formulas

Write a formula that does each of the following.
(a) Finds the circumference C of a circle with radius r
(b) Calculates the pay P for working H hours at $9 per hour
(c) Converts Q quarts to C cups

Solution   (a) The circumference of a circle is $C = 2\pi r$, where $\pi \approx 3.14$.
(b) Pay equals the product of the hourly wage and the hours worked. Thus $P = 9H$.
(c) There are 4 cups in each quart, so $C = 4Q$.

EXAMPLE 3   Evaluating formulas from geometry

Evaluate each formula for the given value(s) of the variable(s). See Figure 1.18.
(a) $A = \pi r^2$, $r = 4$ Area of a circle
(b) $P = 2L + 2W$, $L = 8$ and $W = 4$ Perimeter of a rectangle
(c) $V = s^3$, $s = 3$ Volume of a cube

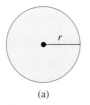

(a)

(b)

(c)

Figure 1.18

Solution   **(a)** $A = \pi(4)^2 = \pi(16) = 16\pi$ Let $r = 4$.
(b) $P = 2(8) + 2(4) = 16 + 8 = 24$ Let $L = 8$ and $W = 4$.
(c) $V = 3^3 = 3 \cdot 3 \cdot 3 = 27$ Let $s = 3$.

MODELING DATA

Faster moving automobiles require more distance to stop. For example, at 60 miles per hour it takes more than twice the distance to stop than it does at 30 miles per hour. Highway engineers have developed formulas to estimate the braking distance of a car.

EXAMPLE 4   Calculating braking distance

The braking distances in feet for a car traveling on wet, level pavement are shown in Table 1.9. Distances have been rounded to the nearest foot.

TEACHING TIP

The distances in Table 1.9 are usually upper bounds for stopping distances. Many cars can stop in less distance.

TABLE 1.9

Speed (mph)	10	20	30	40	50	60	70
Distance (feet)	11	44	100	178	278	400	544

Source: L. Haefner, *Introduction to Transportation Systems.*

(a) If a car doubles its speed, what happens to the braking distance?
(b) If the speed is represented by the variable x and the braking distance by the variable d, then the braking distance may be calculated by the formula $d = \frac{x^2}{9}$. Verify the distance values in Table 1.9 for $x = 10, 30, 60$.
(c) Calculate the braking distance for a car traveling at 90 miles per hour. If a football field is 300 feet long, how many football field lengths does this braking distance represent?

Solution   **(a)** When the speed increases from 10 to 20 miles per hour, the stopping distance increases by a factor of $\frac{44}{11} = 4$. Similarly, if the speed doubles from 30 to 60 miles per hour, the distance increases by a factor of $\frac{400}{100} = 4$. Thus it appears that, if the speed of a car doubles, the braking distance quadruples.

Critical Thinking

Write a formula that calculates the time T for a bike rider to travel 100 miles moving at x miles per hour. Test your formula for different values of x.

$$T = \frac{100}{x}$$

(b) Let $x = 10, 30, 60$ in the formula $d = \frac{x^2}{9}$. Then

$$d = \frac{10^2}{9} = \frac{100}{9} \approx 11 \text{ feet,}$$

$$d = \frac{30^2}{9} = \frac{900}{9} = 100 \text{ feet, and}$$

$$d = \frac{60^2}{9} = \frac{3600}{9} = 400 \text{ feet.}$$

These values agree with the values in Table 1.9.

(c) If $x = 90$, then $d = \frac{90^2}{9} = 900$ feet. At 90 miles per hour the braking distance equals three football fields stretched end to end.

In the next example we find a formula that models a data table.

EXAMPLE 5   Finding a formula

The data in Table 1.10 can be modeled by the formula $y = ax$. Find a.

Solution Each value of y is 3 times the corresponding value of x, so $a = 3$. We can also find a symbolically. If $x = 1$, then $y = 3$. We can substitute these values into the equation.

TABLE 1.10

x	y
1	3
2	6
3	9
4	12
5	15

$$
\begin{array}{ll}
y = ax & \text{Given equation} \\
3 = a \cdot 1 & \text{Let } x = 1 \text{ and } y = 3. \\
3 = a & a \cdot 1 = a
\end{array}
$$

Thus $a = 3$. The formula $y = 3x$ models the data in Table 1.10.

SQUARE ROOTS AND CUBE ROOTS

The number b is a **square root** of a number a if $b^2 = a$. For example, one square root of 9 is 3 because $3^2 = 9$. The other square root of 9 is -3 because $(-3)^2 = 9$. We use the symbol $\sqrt{9}$ to denote the *positive* or **principal square root** of 9. That is, $\sqrt{9} = 3$. The following are examples of how to evaluate the square root symbol. A calculator is sometimes needed to approximate square roots.

$$\sqrt{16} = 4, \quad -\sqrt{100} = -10, \quad \sqrt{3} \approx 1.732, \quad \pm\sqrt{4} = \pm 2$$

The symbol "$\pm$" is read "plus or minus." Note that ± 2 represents the numbers 2 or -2.

The number b is a **cube root** of a number a if $b^3 = a$. The cube root of 8 is 2 because $2^3 = 8$, which may be written as $\sqrt[3]{8} = 2$. Similarly, $\sqrt[3]{-27} = -3$ because $(-3)^3 = -27$. Each real number has *exactly one* real cube root.

EXAMPLE 6   Finding square roots and cube roots

Evaluate each expression.

(a) $\sqrt{3^2 + 4^2}$ **(b)** $\sqrt[3]{64}$ **(c)** $\sqrt[3]{-2^3 - 19}$

Solution **(a)** $\sqrt{3^2 + 4^2} = \sqrt{9 + 16} = \sqrt{25} = 5$. *Note:* $\sqrt{3^2 + 4^2} \neq \sqrt{3^2} + \sqrt{4^2} = 3 + 4 = 7$.

Calculator Help
To calculate square roots and cube roots, see the Appendix (page AP-1).

(b) $\sqrt[3]{64} = 4$ because $4 \cdot 4 \cdot 4 = 64$.

(c) $\sqrt[3]{-2^3 - 19} = \sqrt[3]{-8 - 19} = \sqrt[3]{-27} = -3$ because $(-3)(-3)(-3) = -27$.

EXAMPLE 7   Finding lengths of sides

Find the length of a side s for each geometric shape.
(a) A square with area 100 square feet
(b) A cube with volume 125 cubic inches

Solution   **(a)** The area of a square is $A = s^2$. Thus $s = \sqrt{100} = 10$ feet because $10^2 = 100$.

(b) The volume of a cube is $V = s^3$. Thus $s = \sqrt[3]{125} = 5$ inches because $5^3 = 125$.

≡ MAKING CONNECTIONS ≡

Square Roots and Cube Roots

The square root of a negative number is not a real number. However, the cube root of a negative number is a real number. For example, $\sqrt{-8}$ is not a real number, whereas $\sqrt[3]{-8} = -2$ is a real number.

Roots of numbers often occur in biology, as illustrated in the next example.

EXAMPLE 8   Analyzing the walking speed of animals

When smaller animals walk, they tend to take faster, shorter steps, whereas larger animals tend to take slower, longer steps. For example, a hyena is about 0.8 meter high at the shoulder and takes roughly 1 step per second when walking, whereas an elephant 3 meters high at the shoulder takes 1 step every 2 seconds. If an animal is h meters high at the shoulder, then the frequency F in steps per second while it is walking can be estimated with the formula $F = \frac{0.87}{\sqrt{h}}$. The value of F is referred to as the animal's *stepping frequency*.   (**Source:** C. Pennycuick, *Newton Rules Biology*.)

(a) A Thomson's gazelle is about 0.6 meter high at the shoulder. Estimate its stepping frequency.
(b) A giraffe is about 2.7 meters high at the shoulder. Estimate its stepping frequency.
(c) What happens to the stepping frequency as h increases?

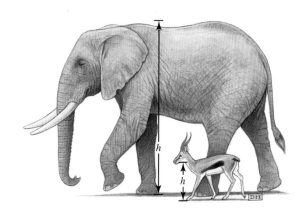

Solution   (a) $F = \frac{0.87}{\sqrt{0.6}} \approx 1.12$. A Thomson's gazelle takes about 1.12 steps per second when walking.

(b) $F = \frac{0.87}{\sqrt{2.7}} \approx 0.53$. A giraffe takes roughly half a step per second when walking, or 1 step every 2 seconds.

(c) As h increases, the denominator of $\frac{0.87}{\sqrt{h}}$ also increases, so the ratio becomes smaller. Thus, as h increases, the stepping frequency decreases.

TABLES AND CALCULATORS (OPTIONAL)

Many calculators are able to generate tables. To generate a table, we specify the formula, the starting x-value (TblStart), and the increment (Δ Tbl) between x-values. The calculator generates the required table automatically, as demonstrated in the next example.

EXAMPLE 9   Using the table feature

Make a table for $y = \frac{x^2}{9}$, starting at $x = 10$ and incrementing by 10. Compare this table to Table 1.9 in Example 4.

Solution   In Figure 1.19 the desired table is generated. Note that, if values are rounded to the nearest foot, the values in Figure 1.19(c) agree with those in Table 1.9.

Calculator Help
To display a table of values, see the Appendix (page AP-3).

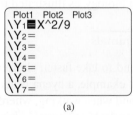
(a)

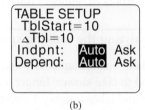
(b)

(c)

Figure 1.19

PUTTING IT ALL TOGETHER

The following table summarizes some of the important topics discussed in this section.

Concept	Comments	Examples
Variable	Represents an unknown quantity	x, y, z, A, V
Algebraic Expression	Consists of numbers, variables, operation symbols, and grouping symbols	$2x - 8$ $3 - (5y + 6)$ s^3 $2L + 2W$

Concept	Comments	Examples	
Equation	A statement that two algebraic expressions are equal—always contains an equals sign	$5x = 10$ $y = 2x + 1$ $n + 5 = 3 - n$ $z^2 + 1 = 17$	
Formula	An equation used to calculate one quantity, using known values of other quantities—shows relationships between variables	$A = \pi r^2$ $C = 2\pi r$ $V = s^3$ $P = 2L + 2W$ $A = \dfrac{1}{2}bh$	Area of a circle Circumference of a circle Volume of a cube Perimeter of a square Area of a triangle
Square Root	The *positive* or *principal square root* of a is written $\sqrt{a}$. The square root of a negative number is not a real number	$\sqrt{25} = 5$ $\pm\sqrt{100} = \pm10$ $-\sqrt{16} = -4$	
Cube Root	The cube root of a is written $\sqrt[3]{a}$	$\sqrt[3]{-8} = -2$ because $(-2)^3 = -8$. $\sqrt[3]{64} = 4$ because $4^3 = 64$.	

1.4 EXERCISES

FOR EXTRA HELP

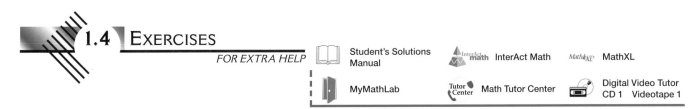

Student's Solutions Manual   InterAct Math   MathXL

MyMathLab   Math Tutor Center   Digital Video Tutor CD 1   Videotape 1

CONCEPTS

1. A(n) _____ is a symbol used to represent an unknown number or quantity.   variable

2. A(n) _____ is a statement that says two algebraic expressions are equal.   equation

3. An equation always contains a(n) _____ sign.   equals

4. A(n) _____ is an equation that can be used to calculate one quantity by using known values of another quantity.   formula

5. Identify the variables in the equation
$$x^2 + y^2 = 9.$$ x and y

6. Give an example of an equation containing no variables. $3 + 7 = 10$

7. Give an example of an equation containing one variable. $3x = 15$

8. Give an example of an equation containing two variables. $3y + x = 5$

9. $\sqrt{9} = \underline{\quad 3 \quad}$ 10. $\sqrt[3]{-8} = \underline{\quad -2 \quad}$

11. If $b > 0$, then $\sqrt{b^2} = \underline{\quad b \quad}$.

12. $\sqrt[3]{b^3} = \underline{\quad b \quad}$

WRITING FORMULAS

Exercises 13–20: Write a formula that does the following.

13. Converts x miles to y feet $y = 5280x$

14. Converts x quarts to y gallons $y = \frac{x}{4}$

15. Finds the area A of a square with a side of length s $A = s^2$

16. Finds the surface area A of a cube with a side of length s $A = 6s^2$

17. Determines the number of seconds y in x hours $y = 3600x$

18. Determines the gas mileage G of a car that travels m miles on g gallons of gas $G = \frac{m}{g}$

19. Determines the area A of a triangle with base b and height h $A = \frac{1}{2}bh$

20. Determines the perimeter P of a square with side s $P = 4s$

USING DATA, VARIABLES, AND FORMULAS

Exercises 21–38: Evaluate the formula for the given value(s) of the variable(s).

21. $y = 5x$ $x = 6$ $y = 30$

22. $y = \frac{x}{10}$ $x = 30$ $y = 3$

23. $y = x + 5$ $x = -3.1$ $y = 1.9$

24. $d = 5 - 4t$ $t = -1.5$ $d = 11$

25. $d = t^2 + 1$ $t = -3$ $d = 10$

26. $z = 3k^2 - \frac{3}{4}$ $k = \frac{1}{4}$ $z = -\frac{9}{16}$

27. $z = \sqrt{2k}$ $k = 18$ $z = 6$

28. $y = \sqrt{5 - x}$ $x = 1$ $y = 2$

29. $y = -\frac{1}{2}\sqrt[3]{x}$ $x = \frac{1}{8}$ $y = -\frac{1}{4}$

30. $M = \sqrt[3]{1 - p}$ $p = 65$ $M = -4$

31. $N = 3h^3 - 1$ $h = \frac{1}{3}$ $N = -\frac{8}{9}$

32. $S = 1 - \frac{1}{2}w^3$ $w = -2$ $S = 5$

33. $P = |5 - w|$ $w = 4.7$ $P = 0.3$

34. $D = |2t - 5|$ $t = 2.5$ $D = 0$

35. $A = \frac{1}{2}bh$ $b = 3,\ h = 6$ $A = 9$

36. $P = 2L + 2W$ $L = 9,\ W = 7$ $P = 32$

37. $V = \pi r^2 h$ $r = \frac{1}{2},\ h = 5$ $V = \frac{5}{4}\pi$

38. $S = 2\pi r(r + h)$ $r = 2,\ h = 8$ $S = 40\pi$

Exercises 39–42: Select the formula that best models the data in the table.

39.

x	1	2	3	4	5	(ii)
y	2	4	6	8	10	

(i) $y = x + 2$, (ii) $y = 2x$, (iii) $y = 4x - 2$

40.

x	-2	-1	0	1	2	(i)
y	4	1	0	1	4	

(i) $y = x^2$, (ii) $y = x + 6$, (iii) $y = 2x$

41.

x	-4	-2	0	2	4	(iii)
y	4	2	0	2	4	

(i) $y = x^2$, (ii) $y = x$, (iii) $y = |x|$

42.

x	-27	-1	0	8	64	(i)
y	-3	-1	0	2	4	

(i) $y = \sqrt[3]{x}$, (ii) $y = \frac{x}{4}$, (iii) $y = \sqrt{x}$

Exercises 43–46: (Refer to Example 5.) Find a value of the variable a so that the equation models the data.

43. $y = ax$

x	-2	-1	0	1	2	-3
y	6	3	0	-3	-6	

44. $y = ax$

x	-10	-5	5	10	15	1.5
y	-15	-7.5	7.5	15	22.5	

45. $d = t - a$

t	0	1	2	3	4	2
d	-2	-1	0	1	2	

46. $N = aw^2$

w	0	2	4	6	8	-1
N	0	-4	-16	-36	-64	

Exercises 47–52: Complete the table for each x-value, using the formula.

47. $y = 2.5x - 0.5$

x	0	2	4	6	8
y	-0.5	4.5	9.5	14.5	19.5

48. $y = \frac{1}{2}x^2$

x	0	2	4	6	8
y	0	2	8	18	32

49. $y = |5x|$

x	−3	−1	1	3
y	15	5	5	15

50. $y = \sqrt{x + 2}$

x	−2	−1	2	7
y	0	1	2	3

51. $y = \sqrt[3]{x} - 2$

x	−1	0	1	8
y	−3	−2	−1	0

52. $y = x^3 - 4x$

x	−2	0	1	2
y	0	0	−3	0

APPLICATIONS

53. *Modeling Motion*   The following table lists the distance y traveled by a car in t hours. Find an equation that models these data. $y = 60t$

Elapsed time (hours)	1	2	3	4
Distance (miles)	60	120	180	240

54. *Braking Distance*   (Refer to Example 4.) The braking distance d for a car on *dry,* level pavement traveling at x miles per hour is given by $d = \frac{x^2}{12}$.   (*Source:* L. Haefner.)

(a) Make a table of braking distances for speeds of 10 to 70 miles per hour in increments of 10 miles per hour.*

(b) What is the braking distance for a car traveling at 40 miles per hour? $133.\overline{3}$ ft

(c) What happens to the braking distance when the speed doubles?   It quadruples.

(d) At 60 miles per hour how much farther does it take the car to stop on wet pavement than on dry pavement?   100 ft

$\left(\textit{Hint}: \text{For wet pavement } d = \frac{x^2}{9}.\right)$

55. *Diving and Water Pressure*   The world's record for descending below the surface of the ocean on a sin-

gle breath is in excess of 400 feet by Francisco Ferreras. During his descent his heart rate slows from 60 beats per minute on the surface to 4 beats per minute at 400 feet. He is able to hold his breath for 7 minutes. These dives are dangerous because of the extreme water pressure. The water pressure P in pounds per square inch at a depth of x feet can be calculated with the formula $P = 0.445x$.   178 psi

(a) Calculate the water pressure at a depth of 400 feet.

(b) The world's deepest diving mammals are sperm whales, which can dive to a depth of 7000 feet. Calculate the water pressure at this depth.
(*Source:* G. Carr, *Mechanics of Sport.*)   3115 psi

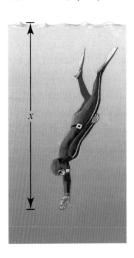

56. *Bicycle Speed Records*   The fastest speed attained on a bicycle is 223.3 feet per second. This speed was attained by the bicyclist following a pace vehicle. The bicyclist thus experienced less wind resistance and was carried along by the draft or "suction" created by the pace vehicle. The formula $M = \frac{15}{22}x$ converts feet per second to miles per hour. Find the speed of this record in miles per hour.   (*Source:* G. Carr.)   152.25 mph

57. *Wing Span and Weight*   A bird's weight W is frequently related to the length L of its wing span. For one species of bird the formula $W = 1.1L^3$ could be used to predict a bird's weight W in kilograms for a wing span of L meters.   (*Source:* C. Pennycuick.)

(a) If a bird has a wing span of 0.75 meter, estimate its weight.   About 0.464 kg

(b) If a bird has a wing span of 1.5 meters, estimate its weight.   About 3.7125 kg

(c) If the wing span of a bird doubles, what happens to its weight?   It increases by 8 times.

*Answer on page IA-1

58. *Wing Span and Weight*   (Refer to the preceding exercise.) The formula $L = \sqrt[3]{16W}$ relates the weight W of one species of bird in pounds to its wing span L in feet.

   (a) Estimate the wing span L associated with $W = 5$ pounds. $\sqrt[3]{80} \approx 4.3$ ft

   (b) Does a doubling of the weight W double the wing span? Explain.   No, it increases by a factor of $\sqrt[3]{2}$.

59. *Stepping Frequency*   (Refer to Example 8.) The formula $F = \dfrac{0.87}{\sqrt{h}}$ gives the stepping frequency F of an animal with a shoulder height h. Suppose that an animal has four times the shoulder height of another animal. How do their stepping frequencies compare?
The taller animal has half the stepping frequency of the other.

60. *Birds*   The surface area of a bird's wings S is frequently related to its weight W. For one species of bird, the formula $S = 0.11\sqrt[3]{W^2}$ could be used to predict the surface area S in square meters of a bird's wings for a weight W in kilograms.   (*Source:* C. Pennycuick.)

   (a) If a bird weighs 0.5 kilogram, estimate the area of its wings.   About 0.069 m²

   (b) If a bird's weight doubles, does the area of its wings also double?   No

61. *Escape Velocity*   To escape the gravity of a planet or a moon, a spacecraft must reach the *escape velocity*, which we denote E. The larger the planet or moon, the greater the escape velocity is. But for a spacecraft simply to attain a circular orbit, a slower velocity C is necessary. The relationship between E and C is modeled by $E = \sqrt{2}C$. Use this formula to approximate the missing values in the following table. (*Source:* H. Karttunen, *Fundamental Astronomy.*)

Planet	Venus	Earth	Moon	Mars
C (mph)	16,260	17,706	3790	8050
E (mph)	22,995	25,040	5360	11,384

Source: M. Zeilik, *Introductory Astronomy and Astrophysics.*

62. *Escape Velocity*   (Refer to the preceding exercise.) The escape velocity for the largest planet in our solar system, Jupiter, is 136,000 miles per hour. Calculate the velocity necessary for a circular orbit around Jupiter. (*Source:* M. Zeilik.)   96,167 mph

63. *Escape Velocity*   (Refer to Exercise 61.) The speed necessary for a circular orbit around Saturn is 57,000 miles per hour. Find the escape velocity for Saturn. (*Source:* M. Zeilik.)   80,610 mph

64. *Animals and Trotting Speeds*   (Refer to Example 8.) The relationship between the shoulder height h and an animal's stepping frequency F in steps per second while *trotting* is given by the formula $F = \dfrac{1.84}{\sqrt{h}}$.
(*Source:* C. Pennycuick.)

   (a) Estimate the stepping frequency for a trotting buffalo that is 1.5 meters high at the shoulders.   1.5 steps per second

   (b) Discuss what happens to an animal's stepping frequency while trotting as its shoulder height increases.   It will decrease.

65. *Pulse Rate in Animals*   According to one model, the rate at which an animal's heart beats varies with its weight. Smaller animals tend to have faster pulses, whereas larger animals tend to have slower pulses. The pulse rate of an animal can be modeled by the equation $N = \dfrac{885}{\sqrt{W}}$, where N is the number of beats per minute and W is the animal's weight in pounds.
(*Source:* C. Pennycuick.)

   (a) Estimate the pulse for a 25-pound dog.   177 bpm

   (b) Estimate the pulse for a 1600-pound elephant.   22 bpm

66. *Pulse Rate in Animals*   (Refer to the preceding exercise.) Suppose that an animal has half the pulse rate of another animal. How do the weights of these animals compare?   The larger animal is 4 times heavier.

67. *Area of an Equilateral Triangle*   An equilateral triangle has three sides equal in length. Its area A is given by $A = \dfrac{\sqrt{3}}{4}s^2$, where s is the length of a side, as shown in the accompanying figure. Calculate the areas for the given values of s.

   (a) $s = 2$ feet $\sqrt{3} \approx 1.73$ ft²

   (b) $s = 4$ meters $4\sqrt{3} \approx 6.93$ m²

68. *Equilateral Triangle*   (Refer to the preceding exercise.) What happens to the area of an equilateral triangle if the length of a side triples?   Increases by 9 times

69. *Circumference of a Circle*   The circumference C of a circle is given by $C = 2\pi r$, where r is the radius. Calculate the circumference of each circle with the given radius.

   (a) $r = 14$ inches $28\pi \approx 88$ in.

   (b) $r = 1.3$ miles $2.6\pi \approx 8.2$ mi

70. *Area of a Circle*   The area A of a circle is given by $A = \pi r^2$, where r is the radius. Calculate the area of each circle with the given radius.
  (a) $r = 12$ inches $144\pi \approx 452 \text{ in}^2$
  (b) $r = 6$ feet $36\pi \approx 113 \text{ ft}^2$

Exercises 71–74: Find the length of a side s for each geometric shape.

71. A square with an area of 81 square inches   9 in.

72. A square with an area of 121 square meters   11 m

73. A cube with a volume of 27 cubic meters   3 m

74. A cube with a volume of 64 cubic feet   4 ft

75. *Inline Skating*   During a strenuous skating workout, an athlete can burn 336 calories in 40 minutes. (*Source: Runner's World.*)
  (a) Write a formula that calculates the calories C burned from skating 40 minutes a day for x days. $C = 336x$
  (b) How many calories could be burned in 30 days?   10,080

76. *Inline Skating*   (Refer to the preceding exercise.) If a person loses 1 pound for every 3500 calories burned, write a formula that gives the number of pounds P lost in x days from skating 40 minutes per day. How many pounds could be lost in 100 days? $P = \frac{336}{3500}x$; 9.6

WRITING ABOUT MATHEMATICS

77. Explain the difference between an algebraic expression and an equation.

78. Give an example of a formula that models an application and identify each variable. Explain how to use the formula.

CHECKING BASIC CONCEPTS   SECTIONS 1.3 AND 1.4

1. Evaluate each expression.
  (a) 2^4 16
  (b) $3^{-2} \cdot 2^0$ $\frac{1}{9}$
  (c) $\dfrac{2^4}{2^2 \cdot 2^{-3}}$ 32
  (d) $x^3 \cdot x^{-4} \cdot x^2$ x
  (e) $\left(\dfrac{2x^3}{y^{-4}}\right)^2$ $4x^6y^8$

2. Evaluate each expression.
  (a) $4 + 5 \cdot (-2)$ -6
  (b) $\dfrac{1+3}{-4+3}$ -4
  (c) $2^3 - 5(2 - 3 \cdot 4)$ 58

3. Express each number in scientific notation.
  (a) 103,000 1.03×10^5
  (b) 0.000523 5.23×10^{-4}
  (c) 6.7 6.7×10^0

4. Express each number in standard form.
  (a) 5.43×10^6 5,430,000
  (b) 9.8×10^{-3} 0.0098

5. *Indoor Air Pollution*   Ventilation is an effective method for removing indoor air pollution. The formula $y = 900x$ calculates the cubic feet per hour of air that should be circulated in a classroom containing x people. Make a table showing the ventilation necessary for classes containing 10, 20, 30, and 40 people. How much ventilation is necessary per person? (*Source: American Society of Heating, Refrigerating, and Air-Conditioning Engineers, ASHRAE.*) *
  900 ft^3/hr per person

  *Answer on page IA-1

1.5   INTRODUCTION TO GRAPHING

**Relations · The Cartesian Coordinate System · Scatterplots and Line Graphs ·
The Viewing Rectangle (Optional) · Graphing with Calculators (Optional)**

INTRODUCTION

Computers, the Internet, and other types of electronic communication are creating large amounts of data. The challenge for society is to use these data to solve important problems and create new knowledge. Before conclusions can be drawn, data must be analyzed. A powerful tool in this step is visualization. Pictures and graphs are capable of communicating large quantities of information in short periods of time. A full page of computer graphics typically contains a hundred times more information than a page of text.

  The map in Figure 1.20 shows the average date of the first 32°F temperature in autumn. Imagine trying to describe this map by using *only* words. In this section we discuss how graphs are used to visualize data.   (***Source:*** J. Williams, *The Weather Almanac 1995.*)

TEACHING TIP

Ask students for other examples
where a visual format is easier to
understand than a written format.

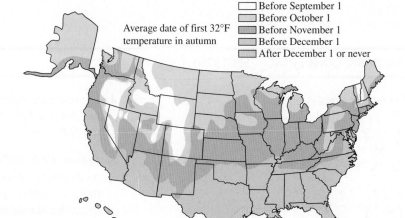

Average date of first 32°F
temperature in autumn

☐ Before September 1
▨ Before October 1
▨ Before November 1
▨ Before December 1
▨ After December 1 or never

Figure 1.20

RELATIONS

Table 1.11 lists monthly average wind speeds in miles per hour for San Francisco. In this table January corresponds to 1, February to 2, and so on, until December is represented by 12. For example, in April the average wind speed is 12 miles per hour.

TABLE 1.11   Average Wind Speeds in San Francisco

Month	1	2	3	4	5	6	7	8	9	10	11	12
Wind Speed (mph)	7	9	11	12	13	14	14	13	11	9	8	7

Source: J. Williams, *The Weather Almanac 1995.*

If we let x be the month and y be the wind speed, then the **ordered pair** (x, y) represents the average wind speed y during month x. For example, the ordered pair $(2, 9)$ indicates that in February the average wind speed is 9 miles per hour, whereas the ordered pair $(9, 11)$ indicates that the average wind speed in September is 11 miles per hour. *Order is important* in an ordered pair.

The data in Table 1.11 establish a *relation*; that is, each month is associated with a wind speed in an ordered pair (month, wind speed). This relation can be represented by a set S, which contains 12 ordered pairs:

$$S = \{(1, 7), (2, 9), (3, 11), (4, 12), (5, 13), (6, 14),$$
$$(7, 14), (8, 13), (9, 11), (10, 9), (11, 8), (12, 7)\}.$$

	RELATION

A **relation** is a set of ordered pairs.

If we denote the ordered pairs in a relation (x, y), then the set of all x-values is called the **domain** of the relation and the set of all y-values is called the **range**. In Table 1.11 the domain is

$$D = \{1, 2, 3, 4, 5, 6, 7, 8, 9, 10, 11, 12\},$$

which corresponds to the 12 months. The range is

$$R = \{7, 8, 9, 11, 12, 13, 14\},$$

which corresponds to the monthly average wind speeds. Note that an average wind speed of 14 miles per hour occurs more than once in Table 1.11, but it is listed only once in the range set R. The same is true for the values 7, 9, 11, and 13.

EXAMPLE 1   Finding the domain and range of a relation

Find the domain and range for the relation given by

$$S = \{(-1, 5), (0, 1), (2, 4), (4, 2), (5, 1)\}.$$

Solution   The domain D is determined by the first element in each ordered pair, or

$$D = \{-1, 0, 2, 4, 5\}.$$

The range R is determined by the second element in each ordered pair, or

$$R = \{1, 2, 4, 5\}.$$

EXAMPLE 2   Finding the domain and range of a relation

Table 1.12 lists the average cost of tuition and fees at public colleges from 1997 through 2000. Express this table as a relation S. Identify the domain and range of S.

TABLE 1.12 Tuition and Fees at Public Colleges

Year	1997	1998	1999	2000
Cost	$3111	$3247	$3356	$3510

Source: The College Board.

Solution   Let the year be the first element in the ordered pair and the cost of tuition be the second element. Then relation S is given by the following set of ordered pairs.

$$S = \{(1997, 3111), (1998, 3247), (1999, 3356), (2000, 3510)\}$$

The domain of S is

$$D = \{1997, 1998, 1999, 2000\}$$

and the range of S is

$$R = \{3111, 3247, 3356, 3510\}.$$

It is possible for a relation to contain infinitely many ordered pairs. For example, let the equation $y = 2x$ define a relation S, where x is any real number. Then S contains infinitely many ordered pairs of the form $(x, 2x)$, such as $(-2, -4)$, $(3, 6)$, and $(0.1, 0.2)$.

EXAMPLE 3   Analyzing a relation

The equation $T = 6 - 2x$ identifies a relation between x and T. Give four ordered pairs in this relation.

Solution   One way to determine four ordered pairs is to give x four different values. For example, when $x = 1$, $T = 6 - 2(1) = 4$. Thus the ordered pair $(1, 4)$ belongs to this relation. Table 1.13 lists this ordered pair along with three additional ordered pairs: $(2, 2)$, $(3, 0)$, and $(4, -2)$.

TABLE 1.13

x	T
1	4
2	2
3	0
4	-2

THE CARTESIAN COORDINATE SYSTEM

We can use the **Cartesian coordinate system**, or *xy-plane*, to visualize or *graph* a relation. The horizontal axis is the *x*-axis and the vertical axis is the *y*-axis. The axes intersect at the **origin** and determine four regions called **quadrants**. They are numbered I, II, III, and IV counterclockwise, as illustrated in Figure 1.21. We can plot the ordered pair (x, y) by using the *x*-axis and the *y*-axis. For example, the point $(1, 2)$ is located in quadrant I, 1 unit to the right of the origin and 2 units above the *x*-axis, as shown in Figure 1.22.

TEACHING TIP

The *xy*-plane is used to graph relations. Relations are a generalization of functions, which we introduce in the next section.

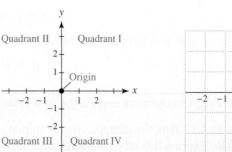

Figure 1.21 The *xy*-plane   **Figure 1.22** Plotting a Point

Similarly, the ordered pair $(-2, 3)$ is located in quadrant II, $(-3, -3)$ is in quadrant III, and $(3, -2)$ is in quadrant IV. See Figure 1.23. A point lying on a coordinate axis does not belong to any quadrant. The point $(-2, 0)$ is located on the *x*-axis, whereas the point $(0, -2)$ lies on the *y*-axis.

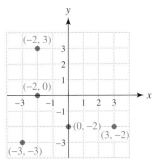

Figure 1.23 Plotting Points

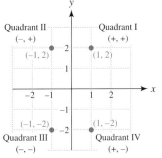

Figure 1.24

For any point (x, y), we can determine the quadrant in which it is located. For example, the point $(1, 2)$ lies in quadrant I because both x and y are positive, whereas $(-1, -2)$ lies in quadrant III because both x and y are negative. The point $(-1, 2)$ lies in quadrant II where x is negative and y is positive, and $(1, -2)$ lies in quadrant IV where x is positive and y is negative. These concepts are illustrated in Figure 1.24, where $(+, +)$ indicates that $x > 0$ and $y > 0$ for any point (x, y) in quadrant I. Other quadrants and ordered pairs can be interpreted similarly.

EXAMPLE 4   **Plotting points**

Plot the data listed in Table 1.14. State the quadrant containing each point or the axis on which each point lies.

TABLE 1.14

x	-3	0	1	4
y	1	4	-2	3

Solution   We plot the points $(-3, 1)$, $(0, 4)$, $(1, -2)$, and $(4, 3)$ in the xy-plane, as shown in Figure 1.25. The point $(-3, 1)$ is in quadrant II, $(1, -2)$ is in quadrant IV, and $(4, 3)$ is in quadrant I. The point $(0, 4)$ lies on the y-axis and does not belong to any quadrant.

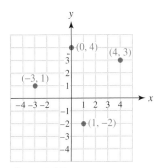

Figure 1.25

EXAMPLE 5   **Graphing points given an equation**

Evaluate $y = x^2 + 1$ for $x = -2, -1, 0, 1,$ and 2. Plot the resulting ordered pairs.

Solution   Start by evaluating the formula $y = x^2 + 1$ for each x-value.

$$x = -2: \qquad y = (-2)^2 + 1 = 5$$
$$x = -1: \qquad y = (-1)^2 + 1 = 2$$
$$x = 0: \qquad y = 0^2 + 1 = 1$$
$$x = 1: \qquad y = 1^2 + 1 = 2$$
$$x = 2: \qquad y = 2^2 + 1 = 5$$

The points $(-2, 5)$, $(-1, 2)$, $(0, 1)$, $(1, 2)$, and $(2, 5)$ are plotted in Figure 1.26.

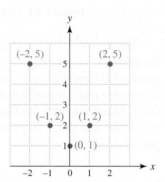

Figure 1.26

TEACHING TIP

Try plotting points for $y = 2x$ and $y = 1 - x$.

EXAMPLE 6   Determining the domain and range

Use the graph to determine the domain and range of the relation.

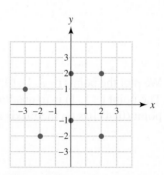

Figure 1.27

Solution   The relation shown in Figure 1.27 includes the points $(-3, 1)$, $(-2, -2)$, $(0, 2)$, $(0, -1)$, $(2, 2)$, and $(2, -2)$. The domain of this relation consists of the x-values of these ordered pairs, or $D = \{-3, -2, 0, 2\}$. The range of this relation consists of the y-values of these ordered pairs, or $R = \{-2, -1, 1, 2\}$.

SCATTERPLOTS AND LINE GRAPHS

If distinct points are plotted in the xy-plane, the resulting graph is called a **scatterplot**. Figure 1.27 is an example. A scatterplot of a different relation is shown in Figure 1.28, where the points $(1, 2)$, $(2, 4)$, $(3, 5)$, $(4, 6)$, $(5, 4)$, and $(6, 3)$ have been plotted. Its domain is $D = \{1, 2, 3, 4, 5, 6\}$, and its range is $R = \{2, 3, 4, 5, 6\}$.

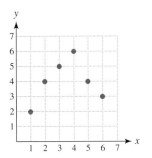

Figure 1.28 A Scatterplot

The next example illustrates how to make a scatterplot from real data.

EXAMPLE 7   *Making a scatterplot of gasoline prices*

Table 1.15 lists the average price of a gallon of gasoline for selected years. Make a scatterplot of these data.

TABLE 1.15   Average Prices of Gasoline

Year	1955	1965	1975	1985	1995
Price (per gallon)	29¢	31¢	57¢	120¢	121¢

Source: Department of Energy.

Solution   Plot the points (1955, 29), (1965, 31), (1975, 57), (1985, 120), and (1995, 121). The *x*-values vary from 1955 to 1995, so we label the *x*-axis from 1955 to 1995. The *y*-values vary from 29 to 121, so we label the *y*-axis from 0 to 150. (Note that labels on the *x*- and *y*-axes may vary.) Figure 1.29 shows these points as plotted and labeled. Note that the double hash marks // on the *x*-axis indicate that there is a break in the scale, which starts at 0 and then jumps to 1955.

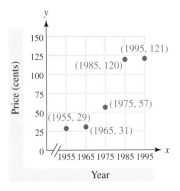

Figure 1.29 Price of Gasoline

Sometimes it is helpful to connect the data points in a scatterplot with straight line segments. This type of graph emphasizes changes in the data and is called a **line graph**.

EXAMPLE 8 | Interpreting a line graph

The line graph shown in Figure 1.30 depicts the total number of all types of college degrees awarded in millions for selected years.   (***Source:*** Department of Education.)

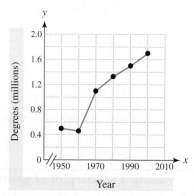

Figure 1.30 College Graduates

(a) Did the number of graduates ever decrease during this time period? Explain.
(b) Approximate the number of college graduates in the year 1970.
(c) Determine the 10-year period when the increase in the number of college graduates was greatest. What was this increase?

Solution (a) Yes, the number decreased slightly between 1950 and 1960. For this time period, the line segment slopes slightly downward from left to right.
(b) In 1970, about 1.1 million degrees were awarded.
(c) The greatest increase corresponds to the line segment that slopes upward most from left to right. This increase occurred between 1960 and 1970 and was about $1.1 - 0.5 = 0.6$ million graduates.

Critical Thinking

Answers will vary. Consider a bar graph or histogram.

Discuss ways that the following list of test scores could be visualized.
Test Scores: 10, 10, 8, 7, 6, 6, 10, 5, 8, 6

THE VIEWING RECTANGLE (OPTIONAL)

Graphing calculators provide several features beyond those found on scientific calculators. Graphing calculators have additional keys that can be used to create tables, scatterplots, and graphs.

The **viewing rectangle**, or **window**, on a graphing calculator is similar to the viewfinder in a camera. A camera cannot take a picture of an entire scene. The camera must be centered on some object and can photograph only a portion of the available scenery. A camera can capture different views of the same scene by zooming in and out, as can graphing calculators. The xy-plane is infinite, but the calculator screen can show only a finite, rectangular region of the xy-plane. The viewing rectangle must be specified by setting minimum and maximum values for both the x- and y-axes before a graph can be drawn.

We use the following terminology regarding the size of a viewing rectangle. **Xmin** is the minimum x-value along the x-axis, and **Xmax** is the maximum x-value. Similarly, **Ymin** is the minimum y-value along the y-axis, and **Ymax** is the maximum y-value. Most graphs show an x-scale and a y-scale with tick marks on the respective axes. Sometimes the distance between consecutive tick marks is 1 unit, but at other times it might be 5 or 10 units. The distance represented by consecutive tick marks on the x-axis is called **Xscl**, and the distance represented by consecutive tick marks on the y-axis is called **Yscl** (see Figure 1.31). This information about the viewing rectangle can be written as [Xmin, Xmax, Xscl] by [Ymin, Ymax, Yscl]. For example, [−10, 10, 1] by [−10, 10, 1] means that Xmin = −10, Xmax = 10, Xscl = 1, Ymin = −10, Ymax = 10, and Yscl = 1. This setting is referred to as the **standard viewing rectangle**. The window in Figure 1.31 is [−3, 3, 1] by [−3, 3, 1].

TEACHING TIP

Spend some time having students learn how to set a window. Be sure to explain what [−10, 10, 1] by [−10, 10, 1] means.

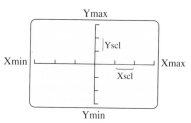

Figure 1.31

EXAMPLE 9 Setting the viewing rectangle

Show the viewing rectangle [−2, 3, 0.5] by [−100, 200, 50] on your calculator.

Solution The window setting and viewing rectangle are displayed in Figure 1.32. Note that in Figure 1.32(b) there are 6 tick marks on the positive x-axis because its length is 3 units and the distance between consecutive tick marks is 0.5 unit.

Calculator Help

To set a viewing rectangle, see the Appendix (page AP-4).

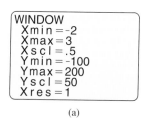

(a)

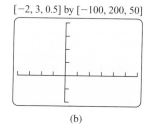

(b)

Figure 1.32

GRAPHING WITH CALCULATORS (OPTIONAL)

Many graphing calculators have the capability to create scatterplots and line graphs. The next example illustrates how to make a scatterplot with a graphing calculator.

EXAMPLE 10   Making a scatterplot with a graphing calculator

Plot the points $(-2, -2)$, $(-1, 3)$, $(1, 2)$, and $(2, -3)$ in $[-4, 4, 1]$ by $[-4, 4, 1]$.

Solution   We entered the points $(-2, -2)$, $(-1, 3)$, $(1, 2)$, and $(2, -3)$ shown in Figure 1.33(a), using the STAT EDIT feature. The variable L1 represents the list of x-values, and the variable L2 represents the list of y-values. In Figure 1.33(b) we set the graphing calculator to make a scatterplot with the STATPLOT feature, and in Figure 1.33(c) the points have been plotted. If you have a different model of calculator you may need to consult your owner's manual.

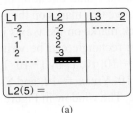   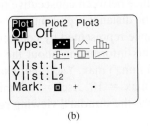   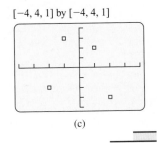

(a)   (b)   (c)

Figure 1.33

In the next example, a graphing calculator is used to create a line graph of sales of cordless telephones.

EXAMPLE 11   Making a line graph with a graphing calculator

Table 1.16 lists numbers of cordless telephones sold for selected years from 1987 through 2000. Make a line graph of these sales in an appropriate viewing rectangle. Then interpret the line graph.

TABLE 1.16   Cordless Phone Sales

Year	1987	1990	1993	1996	2000
Phones (millions)	6.2	9.9	18.7	22.8	33.3

Source: Cellular Telecommunications Industry Association.

Solution   Plot the points $(1987, 6.2)$, $(1990, 9.9)$, $(1993, 18.7)$, $(1996, 22.8)$, and $(2000, 33.3)$. The x-values vary from 1987 to 2000, and the y-values vary between 6.2 and 33.3. We select the viewing rectangle $[1985, 2002, 5]$ by $[0, 40, 10]$, although other viewing rectangles are possible. The viewing rectangle should be large enough to show all five data points without being too large. A line graph can be created by selecting this option on the graphing calculator.

Calculator Help

To make a line graph, see the Appendix (page AP-4).

Figures 1.34(a) and 1.34(b) show the data entries and plotting scheme. Figure 1.34(c) shows the resulting graph. It reveals that sales have increased dramatically during this time period.

TEACHING TIP

Students tend to have difficulty choosing an appropriate window. Explain how the window used in Example 11 was found.

[1985, 2002, 5] by [0, 40, 10]

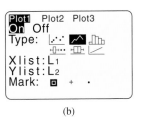

(a)   (b)

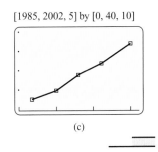

(c)

Figure 1.34

PUTTING IT ALL TOGETHER

Graphs are frequently used in mathematics, science, and business as a way to summarize and understand data better. The *xy*-plane is commonly used to visualize relations.

Concept	Explanation	Example
Relation	A set of ordered pairs	$S = \{(1, 2), (-2, 3), (4, 2)\}$
Domain and Range	If a relation consists of a set of ordered pairs (x, y), then the set of x-values is the domain and the set of y-values is the range.	If $S = \{(1, 2), (-2, 3), (4, 2)\}$, then $D = \{-2, 1, 4\}$ and $R = \{2, 3\}$.
Scatterplot	A scatterplot results when individual points are plotted in the *xy*-plane.	
Line Graph	A line graph is similar to a scatterplot except that line segments are drawn between consecutive points.	

1.5 EXERCISES

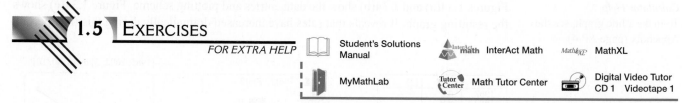

FOR EXTRA HELP

Student's Solutions Manual	InterAct Math
MyMathLab	MathXL
	Math Tutor Center
	Digital Video Tutor CD 1 Videotape 1

CONCEPTS

1. What is a relation?   A set of ordered pairs (x, y)

2. What are the domain and range of a relation?
Domain: set of all x-values; Range: set of all y-values

3. Sketch the xy-plane and identify each of the following: the x-axis, the y-axis, the origin, and the four quadrants. *

4. Sketch an example of a scatterplot and a line graph. *

RELATIONS AND THE RECTANGULAR COORDINATE SYSTEM

Exercises 5–10: Identify the domain and range of the relation S.   7. $D = \{-2, -1, 0, 1, 2\}; R = \{0, 1, 2, 3\}$

5. $S = \{(1, 2), (3, -4), (5, 6)\}$
   $D = \{1, 3, 5\}; R = \{-4, 2, 6\}$
6. $S = \{(0, 4), (0, 6), (3, -1), (4, 0)\}$
   $D = \{0, 3, 4\}; R = \{-1, 0, 4, 6\}$
7. $S = \{(-2, 3), (-1, 2), (0, 1), (1, 0), (2, 1)\}$
8. $S = \left\{\left(\frac{1}{2}, -\frac{3}{4}\right), \left(-\frac{5}{8}, \frac{4}{7}\right), \left(\frac{1}{2}, \frac{3}{4}\right), \left(\frac{8}{7}, \frac{3}{4}\right)\right\}$ $D = \left\{-\frac{5}{8}, \frac{1}{2}, \frac{8}{7}\right\};$
   $R = \left\{-\frac{3}{4}, \frac{4}{7}, \frac{3}{4}\right\}$
9. $S = \{(41, 67), (87, 53), (41, 88), (96, 24)\}$
   $D = \{41, 87, 96\}; R = \{24, 53, 67, 88\}$
10. $S = \{(-1.2, -1.1), (0.8, 2.5), (1.5, -0.6)\}$
   $D = \{-1.2, 0.8, 1.5\}; R = \{-1.1, -0.6, 2.5\}$

*Exercises 11–14: Express the relation S in the table as a set of ordered pairs. Then identify the domain and range of S. *

11.
x	1	3	5	7	9
y	3	7	11	15	19

12.
x	−2.1	−1.5	0.7	1.3	2.9
y	9.6	7.4	3.3	−2.0	−8.8

13. U.S. unemployment rate in percent

x	1996	1997	1998	1999	2000	2001
y	5.5	4.9	4.5	4.2	4.0	4.2

Source: Department of Labor.

14. U.S. population in millions

x	1800	1840	1880	1920	1960	2000
y	5	17	50	106	179	281

Source: Bureau of the Census.

*Exercises 15–20: Express the relation shown in the graph as a set of ordered pairs. Identify the domain and range. *

15.   **16.**

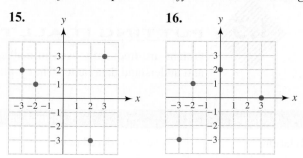

17.   **18.**

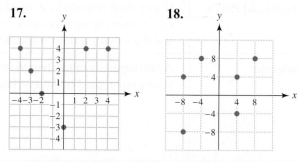

19. Billions of dollars spent on military personnel in the United States; answers may vary slightly. (*Source:* Department of Defense.)

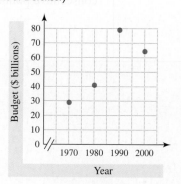

*Answers on pages IA-1–IA-2

20. Cases of tetanus in the United States; answers may vary slightly.   (***Source:*** Department of Health and Human Services.)

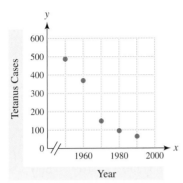

Exercises 21–24: Plot the points in the table in the xy-plane. State the quadrant containing each point or the axis on which each point lies. *

21.

x	1	−3	0	−1
y	2	0	−2	3

22.

x	2	−4	−2	0
y	6	−4	0	−5

23.

x	10	−30	50	−20
y	50	20	−25	−25

24.

x	0.2	0.4	0.6	0.8
y	3	1	−1	−3

Exercises 25–30: (Refer to Example 3.) Find four ordered pairs that belong to the relation determined by the given equation. Answers may vary. *

25. $y = 4x$ **26.** $y = 3x + 5$

27. $A = 4 - t^2$ **28.** $R = 3t^2$

29. $z = \dfrac{1}{r^2 + 1}$ **30.** $z = \dfrac{2}{5 - r}$

SCATTERPLOTS AND LINE GRAPHS

Exercises 31–34: Complete the following. *
  (a) *Find the domain and range of the relation.*
  (b) *Determine the minimum and maximum of the x-values; of the y-values.*
  (c) *Label appropriate scales on the x- and y-axes.*
  (d) *Make a scatterplot of the data by hand.*

31. $\{(0, 2), (-3, 4), (-2, -4), (1, -3), (0, 0)\}$

32. $\{(1, 1), (3, 0), (-4, -4), (5, -2), (0, 3)\}$

33. $\{(10, 50), (-30, 40), (20, -50), (30, 20)\}$

34. $\{(5, 15), (25, 20), (10, 10), (-10, 30), (-20, -10)\}$

Exercises 35–38: Make a line graph from the ordered pairs. *

35. $(0, 2), (1, 4), (2, 5), (4, 4), (5, 2)$

36. $(-2, 4), (-1, 1), (0, 0), (1, 1), (2, 4)$

37. $(4, 4), (8, -4), (12, 8), (16, 0), (20, -8)$

38. $(10, 20), (20, 30), (30, 40), (40, 60), (50, 30)$

Exercises 39–42: Make a line graph from the table of data. *

39.

x	0	1	2	3
y	−2	−1	0	3

40.

x	−2	−1	0	1	2
y	0	3	4	3	0

41.

x	0	1	2	3
y	−3	0	3	0

42.

x	0	1	4	9
y	0	1	2	3

Exercises 43–48: (Refer to Example 5.) Evaluate the formula for x = −2, −1, 0, 1, and 2. Plot the resulting ordered pairs. *

43. $y = 3x$ **44.** $y = -2x$

45. $y = -x + 2$ **46.** $y = 2x + 4$

47. $y = x^2 - 1$ **48.** $y = \frac{1}{2}x^2$

*Answers on pages IA-2–IA-3

GRAPHING CALCULATORS

Exercises 49–54: *Show the given viewing rectangle on your graphing calculator. Predict the number of tick marks on the positive x-axis and the positive y-axis.**

49. Standard viewing rectangle   10; 10

50. $[-12, 12, 2]$ by $[-8, 8, 2]$ 6; 4

51. $[0, 100, 10]$ by $[-50, 50, 10]$ 10; 5

52. $[-30, 30, 5]$ by $[-20, 20, 5]$ 6; 4

53. $[1980, 1995, 1]$ by $[12000, 16000, 1000]$ 15; 4

54. $[1900, 1990, 10]$ by $[1700, 2800, 100]$ 9; 11

56. $S = \{(-5, 1), (-3, 2), (-1, 3), (1, -2), (4, -3)\}$

Exercises 55–58: *Express the relation shown in the graph as a set of ordered pairs.*

55. $[-3, 3, 1]$ by $[-2, 2, 1]$ **56.** $[-6, 6, 1]$ by $[-4, 4, 1]$

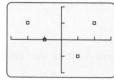   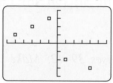

55. $S = \{(-2, 1), (-1, 0), (1, -1), (2, 1)\}$

57. $[-5, 5, 1]$ by $[-3, 3, 1]$ **58.** $[1900, 2000, 20]$ by $[0, 500, 100]$

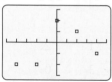   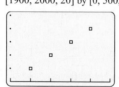

57. $S = \{(-4, -2), (-2, -2), (0, 2), (2, 1), (4, -1)\}$
58. $S = \{(1920, 100), (1940, 200), (1960, 300), (1980, 400)\}$

Exercises 59–64: *Use your calculator to make a scatterplot of the relation after determining an appropriate viewing rectangle.**

59. $\{(4, 3), (-2, 1), (-3, -3), (5, -2)\}$

60. $\{(5, 5), (2, 0), (-2, 7), (2, -8), (-1, -5)\}$

61. $\{(20, 40), (-25, -15), (-20, 25), (15, -25)\}$

62. $\{(-13, 12), (3, 10), (-15, -4), (12, -9)\}$

63. $\{(100, -100), (50, 200), (-150, -140), (-30, 80)\}$

64. $\{(-125, 75), (45, 65), (-53, -67), (150, -80)\}$

APPLICATIONS

Exercises 65–70: *Graphing Real Data   Each table contains real data.**

(a) *Make a line graph of the data.*
(b) *Comment on any trends in the data.*

65. Head Start participation y in thousands during year x

x	1970	1980	1990	2000
y	480	380	540	860

Source: Department of Health and Human Services.

66. Sales y of CDs in millions during year x

x	1988	1990	1992	1994	2000
y	150	290	410	660	1273

Source: Recording Industry Association of America.

67. Welfare beneficiaries y in millions during year x

x	1991	1993	1995	1997	1999
y	12.6	14.1	13.7	10.9	7.0

Source: Administration for Children and Families.

68. Medicaid recipients y in millions during year x

x	1975	1981	1990	1996	1998
y	3.6	3.4	3.2	4.3	4.0

Source: Health Care Financing Administration.

69. Projected Asian-American population y in millions during year x

x	1998	2000	2002	2004
y	10.5	11.2	12.0	12.8

Source: Bureau of the Census.

70. Internet usage in millions of users y during year x

x	1989	1991	1993	1995	2001
y	1.6	7.5	20.1	49.6	125

Source: The Internet Society.

WRITING ABOUT MATHEMATICS

71. Explain how the domain and range of a relation can be used to determine an appropriate viewing rectangle for a scatterplot.

72. Explain the difference between a scatterplot and a line graph. Give an example of each.

*Answers on pages IA-3–IA-4

CHECKING BASIC CONCEPTS SECTION 1.5

1. State the domain and range of the relation
   $S = \{(-5, 3), (1, 4), (2, 3), (1, -1)\}$.
   $D = \{-5, 1, 2\}; R = \{-1, 3, 4\}$

2. Plot the following points in the xy-plane. State the quadrant containing each point or the axis on which each point lies. *
   (a) $(1, 4)$
   (b) $(0, -3)$
   (c) $(2, -2)$
   (d) $(-2, 3)$

3. Evaluate $y = 2 - x^2$ for $x = -2, -1, 0, 1$, and 2. Plot the resulting ordered pairs. *

4. The following table lists the number of people in millions living below the poverty level for selected years. Make a line graph of these data. Comment on any trends in the data. *
   Decreased, started to increase, then decreased.

Year	1960	1970	1980	1990	2000
Number	40	25	29	34	31

Source: Bureau of the Census.

*Answers on page IA-4

CHAPTER 1 Summary

Section 1.1 *Describing Data with Sets of Numbers*

Sets of Numbers

Natural Numbers	$N = \{1, 2, 3, 4, \ldots\}$
Whole Numbers	$W = \{0, 1, 2, 3, \ldots\}$
Integers	$I = \{\ldots, -2, -1, 0, 1, 2, \ldots\}$
Rational Numbers	Can be written as $\frac{p}{q}$, where p and $q \neq 0$ are integers; includes repeating and terminating decimals

Examples: $\dfrac{1}{2}, -3, 6, \sqrt{9}, 0.\overline{7}, 0.123$

Irrational Numbers A real number that is not rational

Examples: $\pi, \sqrt{11}, -\sqrt{3}$

Real Numbers Any number that can be written in decimal form

Examples: $-\dfrac{2}{3}, 0, 12.6, \sqrt{11}, \pi$

Properties of Real Numbers

Identity Properties

$$a + 0 = a \qquad\qquad a \cdot 1 = a$$

Commutative Properties

$$a + b = b + a \qquad\qquad a \cdot b = b \cdot a$$

Associative Properties

$$(a + b) + c = a + (b + c) \qquad (a \cdot b) \cdot c = a \cdot (b \cdot c)$$

Distributive Properties

$$a(b + c) = ab + ac \qquad\qquad a(b - c) = ab - ac$$

Section 1.2   *Operations on Real Numbers*

Real Number Line   The number line is used to graph real numbers.

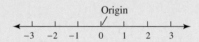

Origin

$-3 \quad -2 \quad -1 \quad 0 \quad 1 \quad 2 \quad 3$

Absolute Value $|a|$ equals a if $a > 0$ or $a = 0$, and $-a$ if $a < 0$.

Examples: $|-4| = 4$, $|7| = 7$, and $|\pi - 7| = 7 - \pi$ because $7 > \pi$

Operations on Real Numbers

Addition   *Examples:* $-3 + 4 = 1$, $3 + (-4) = -1$, and
$$-3 + (-4) = -7$$

Subtraction   Use $a - b = a + (-b)$.

Examples: $-5 - 6 = -5 + (-6) = -11$ and
$$4 - (-3) = 4 + 3 = 7$$

Multiplication   The product of two numbers with like signs is positive. The product of two numbers with unlike signs is negative.

Examples: $3 \cdot (-4) = -12$ and $-5 \cdot (-6) = 30$

Division   Use $\dfrac{a}{b} = a \cdot \dfrac{1}{b}$.

Examples: $\dfrac{1}{2} \div -\dfrac{4}{5} = \dfrac{1}{2} \cdot -\dfrac{5}{4} = -\dfrac{5}{8}$ and

$$-\dfrac{3}{2} \div 6 = -\dfrac{3}{2} \cdot \dfrac{1}{6} = -\dfrac{3}{12} = -\dfrac{1}{4}$$

Section 1.3   *Integer Exponents*

Exponential Expression

$$\text{Base} \rightarrow 6^2 \leftarrow \text{Exponent}$$

Integer Exponents Let n be a positive integer and a be a nonzero number.

$$a^n = a \cdot a \cdot a \cdot \cdots \cdot a \quad (n \text{ factors of } a)$$

$$a^0 = 1 \text{ (Note: } 0^0 \text{ is undefined.)}$$

$$a^{-n} = \frac{1}{a^n}$$

Examples: $4^3 = 4 \cdot 4 \cdot 4 = 64, 5^0 = 1,$ and $2^{-3} = \frac{1}{2^3}$

Properties of Exponents

Product Rule $\quad a^m \cdot a^n = a^{m+n}$

$\qquad$ *Example:* $z^3 \cdot z^5 = z^8$

Quotient Rule $\quad \dfrac{a^m}{a^n} = a^{m-n}$

$\qquad$ *Example:* $\dfrac{x^5}{x^7} = x^{-2} = \dfrac{1}{x^2}$

Power Rules $\quad (a^m)^n = a^{mn}, (ab)^n = a^n b^n,$ and $\left(\dfrac{a}{b}\right)^n = \dfrac{a^n}{b^n}$

$\qquad$ *Examples:* $(5^2)^3 = 5^6, (2x)^3 = 8x^3,$ and $\left(\dfrac{2x}{y}\right)^3 = \dfrac{8x^3}{y^3}$

Negative Exponents $\quad \dfrac{1}{a^{-n}} = a^n, \dfrac{a^{-n}}{b^{-m}} = \dfrac{b^m}{a^n},$ and $\left(\dfrac{a}{b}\right)^{-n} = \left(\dfrac{b}{a}\right)^n$

$\qquad$ *Examples:* $\dfrac{1}{2^{-3}} = 2^3, \dfrac{x^{-4}}{y^{-3}} = \dfrac{y^3}{x^4},$ and $\left(\dfrac{2}{5}\right)^{-4} = \left(\dfrac{5}{2}\right)^4$

Order of Operations

Use the following order of operations. First, perform all calculations within parentheses and absolute values, or above and below the fraction bar.
1. Evaluate all exponential expressions. Do any negation *after* evaluating exponents.
2. Do all multiplication and division from *left to right*.
3. Do all addition and subtraction from *left to right*.

Example: $-2^4 - 2 \cdot 3 = -16 - 2 \cdot 3 = -16 - 6 = -22$

Scientific Notation A number a written as $b \times 10^n$, where $1 \le |b| < 10$ and n is an integer.

Examples: $23,400 = 2.34 \times 10^4$ and $0.0034 = 3.4 \times 10^{-3}$

Section 1.4 *Variables, Equations, and Formulas*

Terminology

Variable $\qquad\qquad$ Symbol that represents an unknown quantity

$\qquad\qquad\qquad$ *Examples:* $x, y, z, A,$ and T

Algebraic Expression	Consists of numbers, variables, operation symbols, and grouping symbols
	Examples: $3z$, $(x - y)^3$, $4a + 3b$, 5, and $|x - 2|$
Equation	A statement that two algebraic expressions are equal
	Examples: $2 + 4 = 6$, $2x = 8$, and $x^2 + 2 = 10$
Formula	An equation used to calculate one quantity by using known values of other quantities
	Examples: $P = 2W + 2L$ and $A = \pi r^2$

Square Root   The number b is a square root of a number a if $b^2 = a$.

Example: The square roots of 36 are 6 and -6.

Principal Square Root   The positive square root of a number, denoted $\sqrt{a}$.

Examples: $\sqrt{4} = 2$, $\sqrt{100} = 10$, and $\sqrt{81} = 9$

Cube Root   The number b is a cube root of a number a if $b^3 = a$.

Examples: $\sqrt[3]{8} = 2$, $\sqrt[3]{-27} = -3$, and $\sqrt[3]{64} = 4$

Section 1.5   *Introduction to Graphing*

Relation   A set of ordered pairs

Example: $S = \{(-2, 3), (0, 3), (1, 2)\}$

Domain and Range   In a relation consisting of ordered pairs (x, y), the set of x-values is the domain and the set of y-values is the range.

Example: For $S = \{(-2, 3), (0, 3), (1, 2)\}$, $D = \{-2, 0, 1\}$ and $R = \{2, 3\}$.

The Cartesian Coordinate System (*xy*-plane)

Points	Plotted as (x, y) ordered pairs
Four Quadrants	I, II, III, and IV; the axes do not lie in a quadrant.
	Note: The point $(1, 0)$ does not lie in a quadrant.

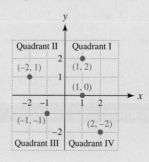

Scatterplots and Line Graphs

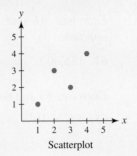

Scatterplot

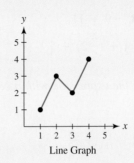

Line Graph

CHAPTER 1 Review Exercises

SECTION 1.1

Exercises 1 and 2: Classify each real number as one or more of the following: natural number, whole number, integer, rational number, or irrational number.*

1. $-2, 9, \frac{2}{5}, \sqrt{11}, \pi, 2.68$

2. $\frac{6}{2}, -\frac{2}{7}, \sqrt{6}, 0.\overline{3}, \frac{0}{4}$

Exercises 3–8: State whether the equation illustrates an identity, commutative, associative, or distributive property.

3. $a \cdot 1 = a$ Identity   **4.** $4 \cdot x = x \cdot 4$ Commutative

5. $(a + 1) + 4 = a + (1 + 4)$ Associative

6. $a(b + 2) = a \cdot b + a \cdot 2$ Distributive

7. $3(t + 2) - r(t + 2) = (3 - r)(t + 2)$ Distributive

8. $4x + 8x = 12x$ Distributive

9. Use identity properties to simplify the expression $1 \cdot (a + 0)$. a

10. Use a commutative property to write $x \cdot \frac{1}{4}$ as an equivalent expression. $\frac{1}{4}x$

11. Use an associative property to write $8(10x)$ as an equivalent expression. $(8 \cdot 10)x = 80x$

12. Use a distributive property to write $5z - 3z$ as an equivalent expression. $(5 - 3)z = 2z$

Exercises 13 and 14: Evaluate the expression two different ways by applying a distributive property.

13. $5(8 + 11)$ 95   **14.** $3(9 - 5)$ 12

Exercises 15 and 16: Calculate the average of the list of numbers.

15. $6, 9, 3, 11, 5, 20$ 9

16. $3.2, 6.8, 6.1, 10.8, 1.7$ 5.72

Exercises 17–20: Use properties of real numbers to evaluate the expression mentally.

17. $12 + 23 + (-2) + 7$ 40

18. $\frac{3}{2} \cdot \frac{2}{5} \cdot \frac{5}{7} \cdot \frac{7}{3}$ 1

19. $5 \cdot 23 + 5 \cdot 7$ 150   **20.** $45 - 34 + 55 - 66$ 0

SECTION 1.2

21. Plot the numbers $-3, 0, 2,$ and $\frac{7}{2}$ on a number line.*

22. Evaluate the expression $\left| -7.2 + 4 \right|$.   3.2

23. Find the additive inverse of $-\frac{2}{3}$. $\frac{2}{3}$

24. Find the multiplicative inverse of $\frac{4}{5}$. $\frac{5}{4}$

25. Find the opposite of $-2x + 3$. $2x - 3$

26. Find the reciprocal of $-\dfrac{1}{a + b}$. $-(a + b) = -a - b$

*Answers on page IA-4

Exercises 27–30: Evaluate the expression without a calculator.

27. $-5 + (-7) + 8$ -4 **28.** $-9 + 11$ 2

29. $-12 - (-8)$ -4 **30.** $\frac{1}{2} + (-2) + \frac{3}{4}$ $-\frac{3}{4}$

Exercises 31 and 32: Evaluate the expression with a calculator.

31. $\frac{2}{3} \div (-4) - \frac{1}{3}$ $-\frac{1}{2}$ **32.** $-\frac{7}{11} + \dfrac{\frac{1}{5}}{\frac{2}{9}}$ $\frac{29}{110}$

SECTION 1.3

33. Identify the base and the exponent in the expression 4^{-2}.   Base: 4; exponent: -2

34. Use a calculator to determine whether 3^{π} and π^3 are equal. $3^{\pi} \approx 31.54$; $\pi^3 \approx 31.01$; not equal

Exercises 35–38: Evaluate the expression.

35. -2^4 -16 **36.** $(-2)^4$ 16

37. 9^0 1 **38.** $\left(\frac{2}{3}\right)^{-3}$ $\frac{27}{8}$

Exercises 39–54: Simplify the expression. Write the result using positive exponents.

39. $4^3 \cdot 4^{-5}$ $\frac{1}{4^2} = \frac{1}{16}$ **40.** $10^4 \cdot 10^{-2}$ $10^2 = 100$

41. $x^7 x^{-2}$ x^5 **42.** $\dfrac{3^4}{3^{-7}}$ 3^{11}

43. $\dfrac{5a^{-4}}{10a^2}$ $\frac{1}{2a^6}$ **44.** $\dfrac{15a^4 b^3}{3a^2 b^6}$ $\frac{5a^2}{b^3}$

45. $(2^2)^4$ 2^8 **46.** $(x^{-3})^5$ $\frac{1}{x^{15}}$

47. $(4x^{-2}y^3)^2$ $\frac{16y^6}{x^4}$ **48.** $(4a)^5$ $4^5 a^5 = 1024a^5$

49. $\left(\dfrac{5x^3}{3z^4}\right)^3$ $\frac{125x^9}{27z^{12}}$ **50.** $\left(\dfrac{-3x^4 y^3}{z}\right)^{-2}$ $\frac{z^2}{9x^8 y^6}$

51. $\left(\dfrac{3a^{-4}}{4b^{-7}}\right)^2$ $\frac{9b^{14}}{16a^8}$ **52.** $\left(\dfrac{3m^2 n^{-4}}{9m^3 n}\right)^{-1}$ $3mn^5$

53. $\left(\dfrac{rt}{2r^3 t^{-1}}\right)^{-3}$ $\frac{8r^6}{t^6}$ **54.** $\left(\dfrac{3r^2}{4t^{-3}}\right)^2$ $\frac{9r^4 t^6}{16}$

Exercises 55–60: Evaluate each expression by hand.

55. $2 + 3 \cdot 9$ 29 **56.** $4 - 1 - 6$ -3

57. $5 \cdot 2^3$ 40 **58.** $\frac{2 + 4}{2} + \frac{3 - 1}{3}$ $\frac{11}{3}$

59. $20 \div 4 \div 2$ $\frac{5}{2}$ **60.** $\dfrac{3^3 - 2^4}{4 - 3}$ 11

Exercises 61 and 62: Write the number in scientific notation.

61. $186,000$ 1.86×10^5 **62.** 0.00034 3.4×10^{-4}

Exercises 63 and 64: Write the number in standard form.

63. 4.5×10^4 $45,000$ **64.** 9.23×10^{-3} 0.00923

SECTION 1.4

Exercises 65 and 66: Write a formula for the following.

65. Converting x feet to y inches $y = 12x$

66. Finding the total area A of 6 circles all with radius r
   $A = 6\pi r^2$

Exercises 67–72: Evaluate the formula for the given value(s) of the variable(s).

67. $y = 12x$ $x = 3$ $y = 36$

68. $d = \sqrt{t - 3}$ $t = 67$ $d = 8$

69. $N = h^2 - \frac{3}{4}$ $h = \frac{3}{2}$ $N = \frac{3}{2}$

70. $P = w^3 - 2$ $w = -2$ $P = -10$

71. $A = \frac{1}{2}bh$ $b = 4, h = 5$ $A = 10$

72. $V = a^2 b$ $a = 3, b = 3$ $V = 27$

73. Select the formula that best models the data in the table.

x	1	2	3	4	5
y	-1	1	3	5	7

(i) $y = x - 2$,   (ii) $y = 3x - 4$,
(iii) $y = 2x - 3$ (iii)

74. Find a value for a so that $y = ax$ models the data.

x	-2	0	2	4	6
y	-3	0	3	6	9

$a = \frac{3}{2}$

SECTION 1.5

75. Identify the domain and range of the relation
$S = \{(-1, 1), (2, 3), (3, -6), (3, 7)\}$.
   $D = \{-1, 2, 3\}; R = \{-6, 1, 3, 7\}$

$S = \{(-8, 4), (-4, -4), (4, 0), (8, 4)\}$
$D = \{-8, -4, 4, 8\}, R = \{-4, 0, 4\}$

76. Express the relation shown in the graph as a set of ordered pairs. Identify the domain and range.

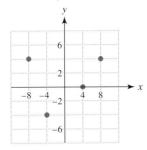

Exercises 77–80: Evaluate the formula for $x = -2$, $-1, 0, 1,$ and 2. Plot the resulting ordered pairs. *

77. $y = -3x$

78. $y = \frac{1}{2}x - 1$

79. $y = x^2$

80. $y = \dfrac{5}{x^2 + 1}$

Exercises 81 and 82: Plot the points in the table. State the quadrant containing each point or the axis on which the point lies. *

81.

x	-2	-1	0	2
y	2	-3	1	-1

82.

x	-15	-5	10	20
y	-5	0	20	-10

Exercises 83 and 84: Show the viewing rectangle on your graphing calculator. Predict the number of tick marks on the positive x-axis and the positive y-axis. *

83. $[-9, 9, 1]$ by $[-6, 6, 3]$ 9; 2

84. $[-20, 20, 5]$ by $[-12, 12, 4]$ 4; 3

Exercises 85 and 86: Make a scatterplot of the relation. Identify the domain and range. *

85. $\{(0, 4), (-1, 2), (3, 3), (4, -1), (2, 0)\}$

86. $\{(-10, 10), (50, 20), (-20, -30), (45, -25)\}$

APPLICATIONS

87. *Mayors' Salaries*   The following table lists the four highest mayors' salaries in 2001.

City	Chicago	New York	Houston	Detroit
Salary	$170,000	$165,000	$160,500	$157,300

Source: U.S. Conference of Mayors.

(a) Mentally estimate which of the following represents the average salary: $141,500, $163,200, or $168,750. $163,200

(b) Check your estimate by calculating the actual average. $163,200

88. *Calculating Interest*   If P dollars are deposited in a savings account paying 1% annual interest, then the amount A in the account after t years is given by the formula $A = P(1.01)^t$. Find A for the given values of P and t.

(a) $P = \$2500, t = 1$ year $2525

(b) $P = \$800, t = 2$ years $816.08

89. *Speed of Earth*   Earth orbits the sun in a nearly circular orbit with a radius of 93,000,000 miles.

(a) Calculate the distance in miles traveled by Earth in 1 year. Write your answer in scientific notation. (*Hint:* The circumference of a circle is given by $C = 2\pi r$.) 5.8×10^8 mi

(b) Estimate the speed of Earth around the sun in miles per hour.   66,700 mph

90. *Modeling Motion*   The following table lists the distance in miles traveled by a car for various elapsed times. Find an equation that models these data.

Elapsed Time (hr)	2	4	6	8
Distance (mi)	80	160	240	320

$d = 40t$

91. *Heart Beat in Animals*   The rate N at which an animal's heart beats varies with its weight. This relation can be modeled by the equation $N = \frac{885}{\sqrt{W}}$, where N is in beats per minute and W is the animal's weight in pounds. Estimate the pulse for a 16-pound cat and a 144-pound person.   (*Source:* C. Pennycuick, *Newton Rules Biology*.)   221 bpm; 74 bpm

92. *Graphing Real Data*   The following data show the poverty threshold y for a single person from 1960 through 2000. Make a line graph and comment on any trends in the data. *   The threshold has increased.

x	1960	1970	1980	1990	2000
y	$1490	$1954	$4190	$6652	$8794

Source: Bureau of the Census.

93. *Area*   Find the area of a square whose sides have length $4ab$. $A = (4ab)^2 = 16a^2b^2$

94. *Volume*   Find the volume of a cube whose sides have length $5z$. $V = (5z)^3 = 125z^3$

*Answers on pages IA-4–IA-5

CHAPTER

1 Test

1. Natural: $\sqrt{9}$ Rational: $-5, \frac{2}{3}, \sqrt{9}, -1.83$
   Whole: $\sqrt{9}$
   Integer: $-5, \sqrt{9}$ Irrational: $-\frac{1}{\sqrt{5}}, \pi$

11. $S = \{(-30, 20), (-20, 20), (-10, 10), (10, 30), (20, 10), (30, -20)\}$
    $D = \{-30, -20, -10, 10, 20, 30\}$
    $R = \{-20, 10, 20, 30\}$

1. Classify each real number as one or more of the following: natural number, whole number, integer, rational number, or irrational number.

$$-5, \frac{2}{3}, -\frac{1}{\sqrt{5}}, \sqrt{9}, \pi, -1.83$$

2. State whether each equation illustrates an identity, commutative, associative, or distributive property.
   (a) $a + 0 = a$ Identity
   (b) $4(12x) = 48x$ Associative
   (c) $5(2 + 3x) = 5(3x + 2)$ Commutative
   (d) $a(x - y) = ax - ay$ Distributive

3. Calculate the average of the list of numbers: 34, 15, 96, 11, 0   31.2

4. Plot the numbers $-1.5, 0, 3,$ and $\frac{3}{2}$ on a number line. *

5. Evaluate the expression $\left|\frac{1}{2} + \frac{2}{3} - \frac{8}{3}\right|$. $\frac{3}{2}$

6. Find the multiplicative inverse of $-\frac{5}{4}$. $-\frac{4}{5}$

7. Evaluate each expression.

   (a) $-\frac{1}{2} + \frac{2}{3} \div 3$ $-\frac{5}{18}$

   (b) $-4 + \dfrac{\frac{2}{3}}{-\frac{1}{4}}$ $-\frac{20}{3}$

   (c) $5 - 2 \cdot 5^2 \div 5$ -5

8. Evaluate each expression.
   (a) 5^{-2} $\frac{1}{25}$ (b) π^0 1
   (c) $\left(-\frac{2}{5}\right)^4$ $\frac{16}{625}$

9. Simplify each expression. Use positive exponents to write the result.
   (a) $x^6 \cdot x^{-4} \cdot y^3$ x^2y^3 (b) $\dfrac{16x^{-2}y^8}{6xy^{-7}}$ $\dfrac{8y^{15}}{3x^3}$

   (c) $(2yz^{-2})^3$ $\dfrac{8y^3}{z^6}$ (d) $\left(\dfrac{15x^4}{10xy^{-2}}\right)^{-2}$ $\dfrac{4}{9x^6y^4}$

10. Write 5.2×10^{-4} in standard form.   0.00052

11. Express the relation shown in the graph as a set of ordered pairs. Identify the domain and range.

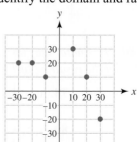

12. Make a scatterplot of the data. Write an equation that models the data. * $y = 1.25x$

x	1	2	3	4
y	1.25	2.50	3.75	5.00

13. Use your calculator to make a scatterplot of the relation S after determining an appropriate viewing rectangle. *

$S = \{(-15, 5), (10, 20), (-10, 15), (0, 0), (5, 35)\}$

14. *Temperature*   The formula $C = \frac{5}{9}(F - 32)$ can be used to convert degrees Fahrenheit, F, to degrees Celsius, C. If the outside temperature is 5°F, find the equivalent temperature in Celsius. $-15°C$

15. *Alcohol Consumption*   In 1994, about 211 million people in the United States were age 14 or over. They consumed, on average, 2.21 gallons of alcohol per person. Use scientific notation to estimate the total gallons of alcohol consumed by this age group. (*Source:* Department of Health and Human Services.) 4.6631×10^8 gal

16. *Radius of a Circle*   If a circle has an area of A square units, its radius r is given by $r = \sqrt{\frac{A}{\pi}}$. Find the radius of a circle with an area of 25 square feet. Approximate this radius to the nearest hundredth of a foot. $\sqrt{\frac{25}{\pi}} \approx 2.82$ ft

*Answers on page IA-5

Extended and Discovery Exercises

$$3. \ y = \frac{0.455W}{(0.0254H)^2} \approx \frac{705W}{H^2}$$

1. *Global Warming* If the global climate were to warm significantly as a result of the greenhouse effect or other climatic change, the Arctic ice cap would start to melt. This ice cap contains an estimated 680,000 cubic miles of water. More than 200 million people currently live on land that is less than 3 feet above sea level. In the United States several large cities have low average elevations. Three examples are Boston (14 feet), New Orleans (4 feet), and San Diego (13 feet). In this exercise you are to estimate the rise in sea level if this cap were to melt and determine whether this event would have a significant impact on people.

  (a) The surface area of a sphere is given by the formula $4\pi r^2$, where r is its radius. Although the shape of the earth is not exactly spherical, it has an average radius of 3960 miles. Estimate the surface area of the earth. $1.97 \times 10^8 \, \text{mi}^2$

  (b) Oceans cover approximately 71% of the total surface area of the earth. How many square miles of the earth's surface are covered by oceans? $1.40 \times 10^8 \, \text{mi}^2$

  (c) Approximate the potential rise in sea level by dividing the total volume of the water from the ice cap by the surface area of the oceans. Convert your answer from miles to feet. 25.7 ft

  (d) Discuss the implications of your calculation. How would cities such as Boston, New Orleans, and San Diego be affected? They would be flooded.

  (e) The Antarctic ice cap contains 6,300,000 cubic miles of water. Estimate how much sea level would rise if this ice cap melted. (***Source:*** Department of the Interior, Geological Survey.) 238 ft

2. *Injuries at Work* The following table lists the injuries per 100 full-time workers in private industry.

Year	1992	1995	1998	2001
Injuries	8.3	7.3	6.4	5.4

Source: Bureau of Labor Statistics.

Explain your reasoning for each of the following.

  (a) Make a scatterplot of the data. Discuss how the injury rate has changed over this period of time. *

  (b) Estimate the injury rate in 1989. About 9.3

  (c) Assuming that trends continue, estimate the injury rate in 2004. About 4.4

  (d) Would it be valid to try to estimate when the accident rate will reach 0? Explain. No, the apparent trend cannot continue. There will always be injuries of this type.

3. *Body Mass Index* Many studies have tried to find a recommended relationship between a person's height and weight. The following steps may be used to compute the body mass index (BMI). Federal guidelines suggest that $19 \leq \text{BMI} \leq 25$ is desirable. (***Source:*** Associated Press.)

Step 1: Multiply a person's weight W in pounds by 0.455.

Step 2: Multiply a person's height H in inches by 0.0254.

Step 3: Square the result in Step 2.

Step 4: Divide the answer in Step 1 by the answer in Step 3.

The result is the person's BMI.

Write a formula to calculate the BMI given the height H and weight W of a person. Let y represent the BMI.

Exercises 4–6: Body Mass Index (Refer to the previous exercise.) Compute the BMI for each individual.

4. 119 pounds, 5 feet 9 inches (Steffi Graf, tennis player) (***Source:*** J. Monroe, *Steffi Graf*). 17.6

5. 153 pounds, 5 feet 10 inches (Jackie Joyner-Kersee, track and field athlete) (***Source:*** M. Goldstein and J. Larson, *Jackie Joyner-Kersee Superwoman.*) 22.0

6. 300 pounds, 7 feet 1 inch (Shaquille O'Neal, professional basketball player) (***Source:*** The Topps Company, Inc.) 29.3

*Answer on page IA-5

Exercises 7–10: Modeling Data with Formulas *Find values for a and b so that the formula models the data in the table.*

7. $y = ax + b$ $a = -\frac{3}{2}, b = \frac{1}{2}$

x	−3	−1	1	3
y	5	2	−1	−4

8. $y = a\sqrt{x} + b$ $a = -2, b = 3$

x	1	4	9	16
y	1	−1	−3	−5

9. $y = ax^2 + bx$ $a = \frac{1}{2}, b = \frac{1}{2}$

x	1	2	3	4
y	1	3	6	10

10. $y = b(a^x)$ $a = 2, b = 3$

x	0	1	2	3
y	3	6	12	24

Linear Functions and Models

Every day our society creates enormous amounts of data, and mathematics is an important tool for summarizing those data and discovering trends. For example, the table shows the number of Toyota vehicles sold in the United States for selected years.

Year	1998	1999	2000	2001	2002
Vehicles (millions)	1.4	1.5	1.6	1.7	1.8

Source: Autodata.

These data contain an obvious pattern: Sales increased by 0.1 million each year. A scatterplot of these data and a line that models this situation are shown in the figure. In this chapter you will learn how to determine the equation of this and other lines. (See Section 2.2, Example 6.)

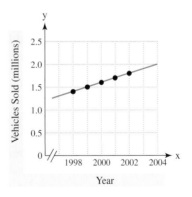

No great thing is created suddenly.
—Epictetus

2.1   FUNCTIONS AND THEIR REPRESENTATIONS

Basic Concepts · Representations of a Function · Definition of a Function · Identifying a Function · Tables, Graphs, and Calculators (Optional)

INTRODUCTION

TEACHING TIP

Functions are essential in mathematics. You may want to spend two days on this section.

In Chapter 1 we showed how to use numbers to describe data. For example, instead of simply saying that it is *hot* outside, we might use the number 102°F to describe the temperature. We also showed that data can be modeled with formulas and graphs. Formulas and graphs are sometimes used to represent functions, which are important in mathematics. In this section we introduce functions and their representations.

BASIC CONCEPTS

Functions are used to calculate many important quantities. For example, suppose that a person works for $7 per hour. Then we could use a function f to calculate the amount of money someone earned after working x hours simply by multiplying the *input x* by 7. The result y is called the *output*. This concept is shown visually in the following diagram.

For each valid input x, a function computes *exactly one* output y, which may be represented by the ordered pair (x, y). If the input is 5 hours, f outputs $7 \cdot 5 = \$35$; if the input is 8 hours, f outputs $7 \cdot 8 = \$56$. These results can be represented by the ordered pairs $(5, 35)$ and $(8, 56)$. Sometimes an input may not be valid. For example, if $x = -3$, there is no reasonable output because a person cannot work -3 hours.

We say that *y is a function of x* because the output y is determined by and *depends* on the input x. As a result, y is called the *dependent variable* and x is the *independent variable*. To emphasize that y is a function of x, we use the notation $y = f(x)$. The symbol $f(x)$ does not represent multiplication of a variable f and a variable x. The notation $y = f(x)$ is called *function notation*, is read "y equals f of x," and means that function f with input x produces output y. For example, if $x = 3$ hours, $y = f(3) = \$21$.

FUNCTION NOTATION

The notation $y = f(x)$ is called **function notation**. The **input** is x, the **output** is y, and the *name* of the function is f.

$$\underset{\text{Output} \quad \text{Input}}{y = f(x)}$$

Name

The variable y is called the **dependent variable** and the variable x is called the **independent variable**. The expression $f(4) = 28$ is read "f of 4 equals 28" and indicates that f outputs 28 when the input is 4. A function computes *exactly one* output for each valid input. The letters f, g, and h are often used to denote names of functions.

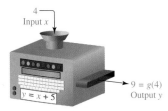

Figure 2.1 Function Machine

Functions can be used to compute a variety of quantities. For example, suppose that a boy has a sister that is exactly 5 years older than he is. If the age of the boy is x, then a function g can calculate the age of his sister by adding 5 to x. Thus $g(4) = 4 + 5 = 9$, $g(10) = 10 + 5 = 15$, and in general $g(x) = x + 5$. That is, function g adds 5 to every input x to obtain the output $y = g(x)$.

Functions can be represented by an input–output machine, as illustrated in Figure 2.1. This machine represents function g and receives input $x = 4$, adds 5 to this value, and then outputs $g(4) = 4 + 5 = 9$.

REPRESENTATIONS OF A FUNCTION

A function f forms a relation between inputs x and outputs y that can be represented verbally, numerically, symbolically, and graphically. Functions can also be represented with diagrams. We begin by considering a function f that converts yards to feet.

VERBAL REPRESENTATION (WORDS)   To convert x yards to y feet we must multiply x by 3. Therefore, if function f computes the number of feet in x yards, a **verbal representation** of f is "Multiply the input x in yards by 3 to obtain the output y in feet."

NUMERICAL REPRESENTATION (TABLE OF VALUES)   A function f that converts yards to feet is shown in Table 2.1, where $y = f(x)$.

TABLE 2.1

x (yards)	y (feet)
1	3
2	6
3	9
4	12
5	15
6	18
7	21

A *table of values* is called a **numerical representation** of a function. Many times it is impossible to list all valid inputs x in a table. On the one hand, if a table does not contain every x-input, it is a *partial* numerical representation. On the other hand, a *complete* numerical representation includes *all* valid inputs. Table 2.1 is a partial numerical representation of f because many valid inputs, such as $x = 10$ or $x = 5.3$, are not shown in it. Note that for each valid input x there is exactly one output y. For a function, inputs are not listed more than once in a table.

SYMBOLIC REPRESENTATION (FORMULA)   A *formula* provides a **symbolic representation** of a function. The computation performed by f to convert x yards to y feet is expressed by $y = 3x$. A formula for f is $f(x) = 3x$, where $y = f(x)$. We say that function f is *defined by* or *given by* $f(x) = 3x$. Thus $f(2) = 3 \cdot 2 = 6$.

GRAPHICAL REPRESENTATION (GRAPH)   A **graphical representation**, or **graph**, visually associates an x-input with a y-output. The ordered pairs

$$(1, 3), (2, 6), (3, 9), (4, 12), (5, 15), (6, 18), \text{ and } (7, 21)$$

from Table 2.1 are plotted in Figure 2.2(a) on the next page. This scatterplot suggests a line for the graph f. For each real number x there is exactly one real number y determined by $y = 3x$. If we restrict inputs to $x \geq 0$ and plot all ordered pairs $(x, 3x)$, then a line with no breaks will appear, as shown in Figure 2.2(b).

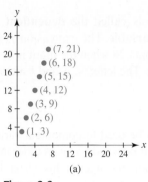

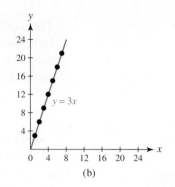

Figure 2.2

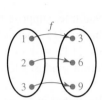

(a) Function

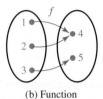

(b) Function

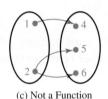

(c) Not a Function

Figure 2.3

═══ MAKING CONNECTIONS ═══

Functions, Points, and Graphs

If $f(a) = b$, then the point (a, b) lies on the graph of f. Conversely, if the point (a, b) lies on the graph of f, then $f(a) = b$. Thus each point on the graph of f can be written in the form $(a, f(a))$.

DIAGRAMMATIC REPRESENTATION (DIAGRAM)   Functions may be represented by **diagrams**. Figure 2.3(a) is a diagram of a function, where an arrow is used to identify the output y associated with input x. For example, input 2 results in output 6, which is written in function notation as $f(2) = 6$. That is, 2 yards are equivalent to 6 feet. Figure 2.3(b) shows a function f even though $f(1) = 4$ and $f(2) = 4$. Although two inputs for f have the same output, each valid input has exactly one output. In contrast, Figure 2.3(c) shows a relation that is not a function because input 2 results in two different outputs, 5 and 6.

═══ MAKING CONNECTIONS ═══

Four Representations of a Function

Symbolic Representation $f(x) = x + 1$

Numerical Representation   *Graphical Representation*

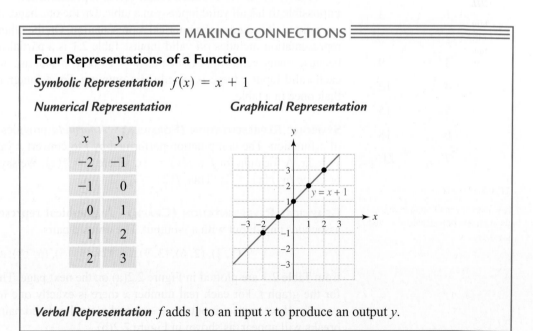

Verbal Representation f adds 1 to an input x to produce an output y.

EXAMPLE 1   Calculating sales tax

Let a function f compute a sales tax of 7% on a purchase of x dollars. Use the given representation to evaluate $f(2)$.

(a) ***Verbal Representation***   Multiply a purchase of x dollars by 0.07 to obtain a sales tax of y dollars.

(b) ***Numerical Representation***   Shown in Table 2.2

(c) ***Symbolic Representation*** $f(x) = 0.07x$

(d) ***Graphical Representation***   Shown in Figure 2.4

(e) ***Diagrammatic Representation***   Shown in Figure 2.5

TABLE 2.2

x	$f(x)$
$1.00	$0.07
$2.00	$0.14
$3.00	$0.21
$4.00	$0.28

Figure 2.4 Sales Tax of 7%

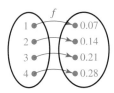

Figure 2.5

Solution

(a) Multiply the input 2 by 0.07 to obtain 0.14. The sales tax on $2.00 is $0.14.

(b) From Table 2.2, $f(2) = \$0.14$.

(c) Because $f(x) = 0.07x, f(2) = 0.07(2) = \mathbf{0.14}$, or $0.14.

(d) To evaluate $f(2)$ with a graph, first find 2 on the x-axis. Then move vertically upward until you reach the graph of f. The point on the graph may be estimated as $(\mathbf{2, 0.14})$, meaning that $f(\mathbf{2}) = \mathbf{0.14}$ (see Figure 2.6).

TEACHING TIP

Spend time on Example 1(d). Students often have difficulty evaluating a function when they use a graph rather than a formula.

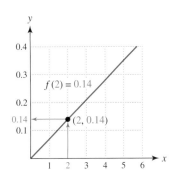

Figure 2.6

(e) In Figure 2.5, follow the arrow from **2** to **0.14**. Thus $f(2) = 0.14$.

EXAMPLE 2   Evaluating symbolic representations (formulas)

Evaluate each function f at the given value of x.
(a) $f(x) = 3x - 7$ $x = -2$
(b) $f(x) = \dfrac{x}{x + 2}$ $x = 0.5$
(c) $f(x) = \sqrt{x - 1}$ $x = 10$

Solution   (a) $f(-2) = 3(-2) - 7 = -6 - 7 = -13$
(b) $f(0.5) = \dfrac{0.5}{0.5 + 2} = \dfrac{0.5}{2.5} = 0.2$
(c) $f(10) = \sqrt{10 - 1} = \sqrt{9} = 3$

There are many examples of functions. For instance, if we know the radius r of a circle, we can calculate its circumference by using $C(r) = 2\pi r$. The next example illustrates how functions are used in applications.

EXAMPLE 3   Computing crutch length

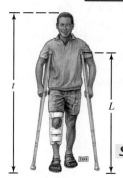

People who sustain leg injuries often require crutches. A proper crutch length can be estimated without using trial and error. The function L, given by $L(t) = 0.72t + 2$, outputs an appropriate crutch length in inches for a person t inches tall.   (*Source: Journal of the American Physical Therapy Association.*)
(a) Find $L(60)$ and interpret the result.
(b) If one person is 70 inches tall and another person is 71 inches tall, what should be the difference in their crutch lengths?

Solution   (a) $L(60) = 0.72(60) + 2 = 45.2$. Thus a person 60 inches tall needs crutches that are about 45.2 inches long.
(b) From the formula, $L(t) = 0.72t + 2$, we can see that each 1-inch increase in t results in a 0.72-inch increase in L. For example,

$$L(71) - L(70) = 53.12 - 52.4 = 0.72.$$

DEFINITION OF A FUNCTION

A function is a fundamental concept in mathematics. Its definition should allow for all representations of a function. *A function receives an input x and produces exactly one output y,* which can be expressed as an ordered pair:

$$(x, y).$$

Input $\nearrow$ $\nwarrow$ Output

A relation is a set of ordered pairs, and a function is a special type of relation.

FUNCTION
A **function** f is a set of ordered pairs (x, y), where each x-value corresponds to exactly one y-value.

The **domain** of f is the set of all x-values, and the **range** of f is the set of all y-values. For example, a function f that converts 1, 2, 3, and 4 yards to feet could be expressed as

$$f = \{(1, 3), (2, 6), (3, 9), (4, 12)\}.$$

The domain of f is $D = \{1, 2, 3, 4\}$, and the range of f is $R = \{3, 6, 9, 12\}$.

═══════════════ MAKING CONNECTIONS ═══════════════

Relations and Functions

A relation can be thought of as a set of input–output pairs. A function is a special type of relation whereby each input results in exactly one output.

EXAMPLE 4 Computing average income

The function f computes the average 1998 individual income in dollars by educational attainment. This function is defined by $f(N) = 16{,}124$, $f(H) = 22{,}895$, $f(B) = 40{,}478$, and $f(M) = 51{,}183$, where N denotes no diploma, H a high school diploma, B a bachelor's degree, and M a master's degree.   (*Source:* Bureau of the Census.)
(a) Write f as a set of ordered pairs.
(b) Give the domain and range of f.
(c) Discuss the relationship between education and income.

Solution (a) $f = \{(N, 16124), (H, 22895), (B, 40478), (M, 51183)\}$.
(b) The domain of function f is $D = \{N, H, B, M\}$, and the range of function f is $R = \{16124, 22895, 40478, 51183\}$.
(c) Education pays—the greater the educational attainment the greater are annual earnings.

EXAMPLE 5 Finding the domain and range graphically

Use the graphs of f shown in Figures 2.7 and 2.8 to determine each function's domain and range.
(a)   (b)

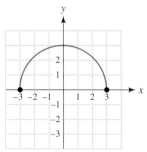

Figure 2.7

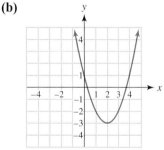

Figure 2.8

Solution (a) The domain is the set of all x-values that correspond to points on the graph of f. Figure 2.9 on the next page shows that the domain D includes all x-values satisfying $-3 \le x \le 3$. (Recall that the symbol $\le$ is read "*less than or equal to.*") Because the graph is a semicircle with no breaks, the domain includes all real numbers between

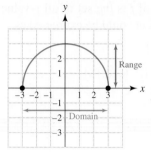

Figure 2.9

−3 and 3. The range R is the set of y-values that correspond to points on the graph of f. Thus R includes all y-values satisfying $0 \le y \le 3$.

(b) The arrows on the ends of the graph indicate that the graph extends indefinitely left and right, as well as upward. Thus D includes all real numbers. The smallest y-value on the graph is $y = -3$, which occurs when $x = 2$. Thus the range is $y \ge -3$. (Recall that the symbol $\ge$ is read "*greater than or equal to*.")

Critical Thinking

Suppose that a car travels at 50 miles per hour to a city that is 250 miles away. Sketch a graph of a function f that gives the distance y traveled after x hours. Identify the domain and range of f.

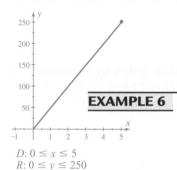

$D: 0 \le x \le 5$
$R: 0 \le y \le 250$

Again, the domain of a function is the set of all valid inputs. To determine the domain of a function from a formula, we must determine x-values for which the formula is defined. This concept is demonstrated in the next example.

EXAMPLE 6   Finding the domain of a function

Use $f(x)$ to find the domain of f.

(a) $f(x) = 5x$ **(b)** $f(x) = \dfrac{1}{x - 2}$ **(c)** $f(x) = \sqrt{x}$

Solution   **(a)** Because we can always multiply a real number x by 5, function f is defined for all real numbers. Thus the domain includes all real numbers.

(b) Because we cannot divide by 0, input $x = 2$ is not valid. The expression is defined for all other values of x. Thus the domain includes all real numbers except 2, or $x \ne 2$.

(c) Because square roots of negative numbers are not real numbers, the inputs for f cannot be negative. The domain of f includes all nonnegative numbers, or $x \ge 0$.

IDENTIFYING A FUNCTION

Recall that for a function each valid input x produces exactly one output y. In the next three examples we demonstrate techniques for identifying a function.

EXAMPLE 7   Determining whether a set of ordered pairs is a function

The set S of ordered pairs (x, y) represents the monthly average temperature y in degrees Fahrenheit for the month x in Washington, D.C. Determine whether S is a function.

$S = \{$(January, 33), (February, 37), (March, 45), (April, 53), (May, 66), (June, 73),
(July, 77), (August, 77), (September, 70), (October, 51), (November, 48),
(December, 37)$\}$

(**Source:** A. Miller and J. Thompson, *Elements of Meteorology*.)

Solution   The input x is the month and the output y is the monthly average temperature. The set S *is* a function because each month x is paired with exactly one monthly average temperature y. Note that, even though an average temperature of $37°$F occurs in both February and December, S is nonetheless a function.

EXAMPLE 8   Determining whether a table of values represents a function

Determine whether Table 2.3 represents a function.

TABLE 2.3

x	y
1	−4
2	8
3	2
1	5
4	−6

Solution   The table does not represent a function because input $x = 1$ produces two outputs: -4 and 5. That is, the following two ordered pairs both belong to this relation.

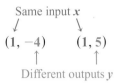

VERTICAL LINE TEST   To determine whether a graph represents a function, we must be convinced that it is impossible for an input x to have two or more outputs y. If two distinct points have the same x-coordinate on a graph, then the graph cannot represent a function. For example, the ordered pairs $(-1, 1)$ and $(-1, -1)$ could not lie on the graph of a function because input -1 results in *two* outputs: 1 and -1. When the points $(-1, 1)$ and $(-1, -1)$ are plotted, they lie on the same vertical line, as shown in Figure 2.10(a). A graph passing through these points intersects the vertical line twice, as illustrated in Figure 2.10(b).

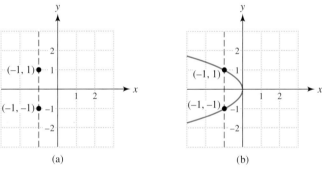

Figure 2.10

To determine whether a graph represents a function, visualize vertical lines moving across the xy-plane. If each vertical line intersects the graph *at most once*, then it is a graph of a function. This test is called the **vertical line test**. Note that the graph in Figure 2.10(b) fails the vertical line test and therefore does not represent a function.

VERTICAL LINE TEST

If every vertical line intersects a graph at no more than one point, then the graph represents a function.

EXAMPLE 9   Determining whether a graph represents a function

Determine whether the graphs shown in Figures 2.11 and 2.12 on the next page represent functions.

(a)

Figure 2.11

(b)

Figure 2.12

Solution **(a)** Any vertical line will cross the graph at most once, as depicted in Figure 2.13. Therefore the graph *does* represent a function.

(b) The graph *does not* represent a function because some vertical lines can intersect the graph twice, as shown in Figure 2.14.

Figure 2.13 Passes Vertical Line Test

Figure 2.14 Fails Vertical Line Test

Tables, Graphs, and Calculators (Optional)

TEACHING TIP

Calculator use is *optional* in this text.

We can use graphing calculators to create graphs and tables, usually more efficiently and reliably than pencil-and-paper techniques. However, a graphing calculator uses the same techniques that we might use to sketch a graph. For example, one way to sketch a graph of $y = 2x - 1$ is first to make a table of values, as shown in Table 2.4.

We can plot these points in the xy-plane, as shown in Figure 2.15. Next we might connect the points, as shown in Figure 2.16.

TABLE 2.4

x	y
−1	−3
0	−1
1	1
2	3

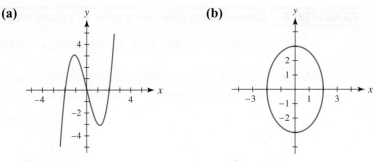

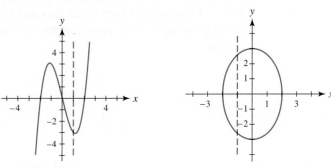

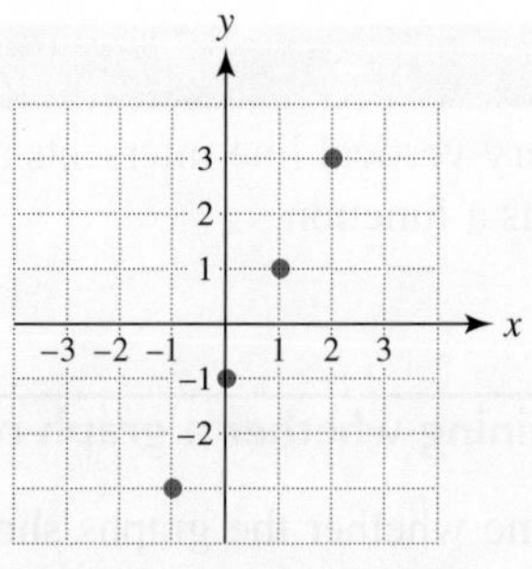

Figure 2.15 Plotting Points

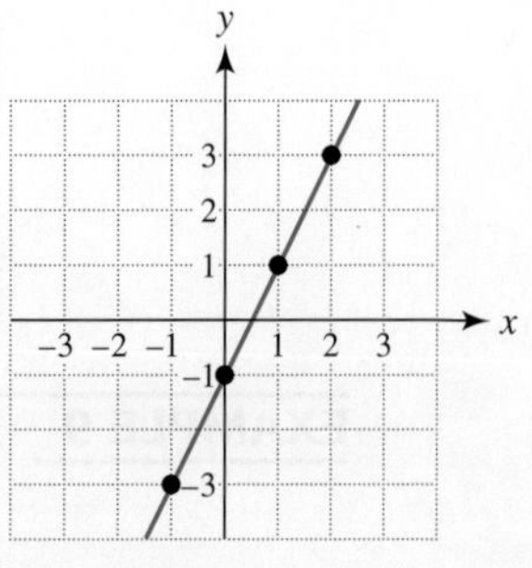

Figure 2.16 Graphing a Line

In a similar manner a graphing calculator plots numerous points and connects them to make a graph. To create a similar graph with a graphing calculator, we enter the formula $Y_1 = 2X - 1$, set an appropriate viewing rectangle, and graph as shown in Figure 2.17(a) and (b). A table of values can also be generated as illustrated in Figure 2.17(c).

Calculator Help

To make a graph, see the Appendix (page AP-5). To make a table, see the Appendix (page AP-3).

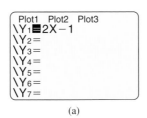

(a)

$[-10, 10, 1]$ by $[-10, 10, 1]$

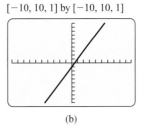

(b)

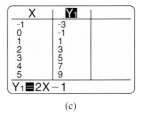

(c)

Figure 2.17

PUTTING IT ALL TOGETHER

One important concept in mathematics is that of a function. A function calculates exactly one output for each valid input and produces input–output ordered pairs in the form (x, y). A function typically computes something, such as area, speed, or sales tax. The following table summarizes some concepts related to functions.

Concept	Explanation	Examples
Function	A set of ordered pairs (x, y), where each x-value corresponds to exactly one y-value	$f = \{(1, 3), (2, 3), (3, 1)\}$ $f(x) = 2x$ A graph of $y = x + 2$ A table of values for $y = 4x$
Independent Variable	The *input* variable for a function	*Function* *Independent Variable* $f(x) = 2x$ x $A(r) = \pi r^2$ r $V(s) = s^3$ s
Dependent Variable	The *output* variable of a function. There is exactly one output for each valid input.	*Function* *Dependent Variable* $y = f(x)$ y $T = F(r)$ T $V = g(r)$ V
Domain and Range of a Function	The domain is the set of all valid inputs. The range is the set of all outputs.	For $S = \{(-1, 0), (3, 4), (5, 0)\}$, $D = \{-1, 3, 5\}$ and $R = \{0, 4\}$. The domain of $f(x) = \frac{1}{x}$ includes all real numbers except 0, or $x \neq 0$.

continued on next page

continued from previous page

Concept	Explanation	Examples
Vertical Line Test	If every vertical line intersects a graph in no more than one point, the graph represents a function.	This graph does *not* pass this test and thus does not represent a function. ![graph showing a sideways parabola with a dashed vertical line, axes labeled y and x]

A function can be represented verbally, symbolically, numerically, and graphically. The following table summarizes these four representations.

Type of Representation	Explanation	Comments
Verbal	Precise word description of what is computed	May be oral or written Must be stated *precisely*
Symbolic	Mathematical formula	Efficient and concise way of representing a function (e.g., $f(x) = 2x - 3$)
Numerical	List of specific inputs and their outputs	May be in the form of a table or an explicit set of ordered pairs
Graphical, diagrammatic	Shows inputs and outputs visually	No words, formulas, or tables Many types of graphs and diagrams are possible.

2.1 EXERCISES

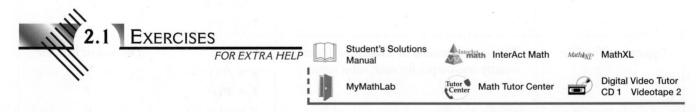

FOR EXTRA HELP

Student's Solutions Manual

InterAct Math

MathXL

MyMathLab

Math Tutor Center

Digital Video Tutor
CD 1   Videotape 2

CONCEPTS

1. The notation $y = f(x)$ is called _____ notation.   function

2. The notation $y = f(x)$ is read _____.   y equals f of x

3. The notation $f(x) = x^2 + 1$ is called a _____ representation of a function.   symbolic

4. A table of values is a _____ representation of a function.   numerical

5. The set of valid inputs for a function is called the _____.   domain

6. The set of outputs for a function is called the _____. range

7. A function computes _____ output for each valid input. one

8. What is the vertical line test used for?
To identify graphs of functions

9. Name four types of representations for a function.
Verbal, numerical, symbolic, and graphical or diagrammatic

10. If $f(3) = 4$, then the point _____ is on the graph of f. If $(3, 6)$ is on the graph of f, then $f(_) = $ _____. (3, 4); 3; 6

Exercises 11–14: Determine whether the phrase describes a function.

11. Calculating the square of a number Yes

12. Determining your age to the nearest whole number Yes

13. Listing the students who passed a given math exam No

14. Listing the children of parent x No

REPRESENTING AND EVALUATING FUNCTIONS

Exercises 15–24: Evaluate $f(x)$ at the given values of x.

15. $f(x) = 4x - 2$ $x = -1, 0$ $-6; -2$

16. $f(x) = 5 - 3x$ $x = -4, 2$ $17; -1$

17. $f(x) = \sqrt{x}$ $x = 0, \frac{9}{4}$ $0; \frac{3}{2}$

18. $f(x) = \sqrt[3]{x}$ $x = -1, 27$ $-1; 3$

19. $f(x) = x^2$ $x = -5, \frac{3}{2}$ $25; \frac{9}{4}$

20. $f(x) = x^3$ $x = -2, 0.1$ $-8; 0.001$

21. $f(x) = 3$ $x = -8, \frac{7}{3}$ $3; 3$

22. $f(x) = x^2 + 5$ $x = -\frac{1}{2}, 6$ $\frac{21}{4}; 41$

23. $f(x) = \dfrac{2}{x + 1}$ $x = -5, 4$ $-\frac{1}{2}; \frac{2}{5}$

24. $f(x) = \dfrac{x}{x - 4}$ $x = -3, 1$ $\frac{3}{7}; -\frac{1}{3}$

Exercises 25–30: Do the following.

(a) Write a formula for the function described.
(b) Evaluate the function for input 10 and interpret the results.

25. Function I computes the number of inches in x yards.
(a) $I(x) = 36x$ (b) $I(10) = 360$

26. Function M computes the number of miles in x feet.
(a) $M(x) = \frac{x}{5280}$ (b) $M(10) = \frac{10}{5280} \approx 0.0019$

27. Function A computes the area of a circle with radius r.
(a) $A(r) = \pi r^2$ (b) $A(10) = 100\pi \approx 314.2$

28. Function C computes the circumference of a circle with radius r. (a) $C(r) = 2\pi r$ (b) $C(10) = 20\pi \approx 62.8$

29. Function A computes the square feet in x acres. (*Hint:* There are 43,560 square feet in one acre.)
(a) $A(x) = 43,560x$ (b) $A(10) = 435,600$

30. Function K computes the number of kilograms in x pounds. (*Hint:* There are about 2.2 pounds in one kilogram.)   (a) $K(x) = \frac{x}{2.2}$ (b) $K(10) = \frac{10}{2.2} = 4.\overline{54}$

*Exercises 31–40: Sketch a graph of f.**

31. $f(x) = -x + 3$ **32.** $f(x) = -2x + 1$

33. $f(x) = 2x$ **34.** $f(x) = \frac{1}{2}x - 2$

35. $f(x) = 4 - x$ **36.** $f(x) = 6 - 3x$

37. $f(x) = x^2$ **38.** $f(x) = \sqrt{x}$

39. $f(x) = \sqrt{x + 1}$ **40.** $f(x) = \frac{1}{2}x^2 - 1$

Exercises 41–46: Use the graph of f to evaluate the given expressions.

41. $f(0)$ and $f(2)$ 3; −1   **42.** $f(-2)$ and $f(2)$ −2; 0

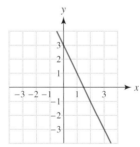 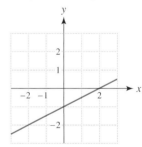

43. $f(-2)$ and $f(1)$ 0; 2   **44.** $f(-1)$ and $f(0)$ 1; 0

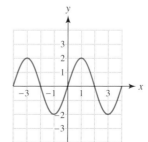 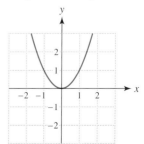

*Answers on pages IA-5–IA-6

45. $f(1)$ and $f(2)$ $-4; -3$ **46.** $f(-1)$ and $f(4)$ $3; 2$

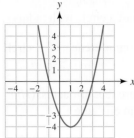

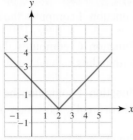

Exercises 47 and 48: Use the table to evaluate the given expression.

47. $f(0)$ and $f(2)$ $5.5; 3.7$

x	0	1	2	3	4
$f(x)$	5.5	4.3	3.7	2.5	1.9

48. $f(-10)$ and $f(5)$ $23; -33$

x	-10	-5	0	5	10
$f(x)$	23	96	-45	-33	23

Exercises 49 and 50: Use the diagram to evaluate $f(1990)$. Interpret your answer.

49. The function f computes average fuel efficiency of new U.S. passenger cars in miles per gallon during year x.   (***Source:*** Department of Transportation.) 26.9

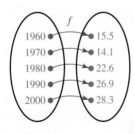

In 1990 the fuel efficiency was 26.9 mpg.

50. The function f computes average cost of tuition at public colleges and universities during academic year x.
(***Source:*** The College Board.) $\$1809$

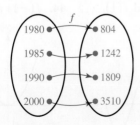

In 1990 average cost of tuition was $\$1809$.

Exercises 51–54: Express the verbal representation for the function f numerically, symbolically, and graphically.

57. Divide the input x by 3 to obtain the output y.

Let $x = -3, -2, -1, \ldots, 3$ for the numerical representation (table), and let $-3 \le x \le 3$ for the graph. *

51. Add 5 to the input x to obtain the output y. $y = x + 5$

52. Square the input x to obtain the output y. $y = x^2$

53. Multiply the input x by 5 and then subtract 2 to obtain the output y. $y = 5x - 2$

54. Divide the input x by 2 and then add 3 to obtain the output y. $y = \frac{x}{2} + 3$

55. Subtract $\frac{1}{2}$ from the input x to obtain the output y.

Exercises 55–58: Give a verbal representation for $f(x)$.

55. $f(x) = x - \frac{1}{2}$ **56.** $f(x) = \frac{3}{4}x$

57. $f(x) = \dfrac{x}{3}$ **58.** $f(x) = x^2 + 1$

56. Multiply the input x by $\frac{3}{4}$ to obtain the output y.

59. *Cost of Driving*   In 2000, the average cost of driving a new car in the United States was about 50 cents per mile. Symbolically, graphically, and numerically represent a function f that computes the cost in dollars of driving x miles. For the numerical representation (table) let $x = 10, 20, 30, \ldots, 70$.   (***Source:*** Associated Press.) $f(x) = 0.50x;$*

58. Square the input x and then add 1 to obtain the output y.

60. *Federal Income Taxes*   In 2001, the lowest U.S. income tax rate was 15 percent. Symbolically, graphically, and numerically represent a function f that computes the tax on a taxable income of x dollars. For the numerical representation (table) let $x = 1000, 2000, 3000, \ldots, 7000$, and for the graphical representation let $0 \le x \le 30,000$.   (***Source:*** Internal Revenue Service.)
$f(x) = 0.15x;$*

61. *Home Prices*   The median price P of a single-family home in thousands of dollars from 1980 to 1990 can be approximated by $P(x) = 3.421(x - 1980) + 61$, where x is the year. Evaluate $P(1986)$ and interpret the result. $81.526;$ in 1986, the median price was $\$81,526$.

62. *Motorcycles*   The number of Harley-Davidson motorcycles manufactured in thousands between 1985 and 1995 can be approximated by the formula $N(x) = 6.409(x - 1985) + 30.3$, where x is the year. Evaluate $N(1990)$ and interpret the result.
$62.345;$ in 1990, 62,345 motorcycles were manufactured.

Exercises 63–66: Do the following.

(**a**) *Use the graph of f to estimate $f(-1)$.*
(**b**) *Use the formula to evaluate $f(-1)$.*

63. $f(x) = 3x + 1$ -2 **64.** $f(x) = 1 - x$ 2

65. $f(x) = 0.5x^2$ 0.5 **66.** $f(x) = \frac{5}{2}$ $\frac{5}{2}$

*Answers on pages IA-6–IA-7

IDENTIFYING DOMAINS AND RANGES

Exercises 67–74: Use the graph of f to estimate its domain and range.

67.

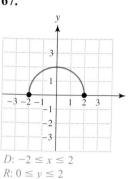

D: $-2 \le x \le 2$
R: $0 \le y \le 2$

68.

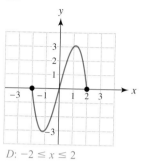

D: $-2 \le x \le 2$
R: $-3 \le y \le 3$

69.

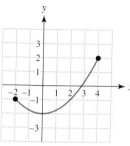

D: $-2 \le x \le 4$
R: $-2 \le y \le 2$

70.

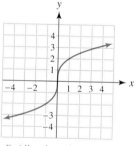

D: All real numbers
R: All real numbers

71.

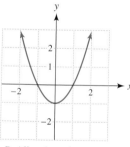

D: All real numbers
R: $y \ge -1$

72.

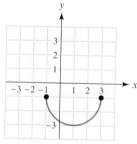

D: $-1 \le x \le 3$
R: $-3 \le y \le -1$

73.

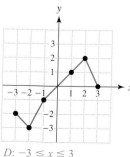

D: $-3 \le x \le 3$
R: $-3 \le y \le 2$

74.

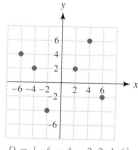

D = $\{-6, -4, -2, 2, 4, 6\}$
R = $\{-4, -2, 2, 4, 6\}$

Exercises 75 and 76: Use the diagram to find the domain and range of f.

75.

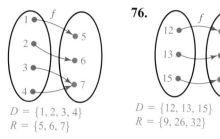

D = $\{1, 2, 3, 4\}$
R = $\{5, 6, 7\}$

76.

D = $\{12, 13, 15\}$
R = $\{9, 26, 32\}$

Exercises 77–86: Find the domain.

77. $f(x) = 10x$
All real numbers

78. $f(x) = 5 - x$
All real numbers

79. $f(x) = x^2 - 3$
All real numbers

80. $f(x) = \frac{1}{2}x^2$ All real numbers

81. $f(x) = \dfrac{3}{x - 5}$ $x \ne 5$

82. $f(x) = \dfrac{x}{x + 1}$ $x \ne -1$

83. $f(x) = \dfrac{2x}{x^2 + 1}$
All real numbers

84. $f(x) = \dfrac{6}{1 - x}$ $x \ne 1$

85. $f(x) = \sqrt{x - 1}$
$x \ge 1$

86. $f(x) = |x|$ All real numbers

87. *Accidental Deaths*   The function f computes the number of accidental deaths y per 100,000 people during year x.   (*Source:* Department of Health and Human Services.)   (b) D = $\{1910, 1930, 1950, 1970, 1990, 2000\}$
R = $\{35.5, 36.9, 56.2, 60.3, 80.5, 84.4\}$

$f = \{(1910, 84.4), (1930, 80.5), (1950, 60.3),$
$(1970, 56.2), (1990, 36.9), (2000, 35.5)\}$

(a) Evaluate $f(1950)$ and interpret the result.   60.3
(b) Identify the domain and range of f.
(c) Describe the trend in accidental deaths from 1910 through 2000.   Decreased

88. *Motor Vehicle Registrations*   The following table lists motor vehicle registrations y in millions during year x. Let $y = f(x)$.

x	1920	1940	1960	1980	2000
$f(x)$	9	32	74	156	216

Source: American Automobile Manufacturers Association.

(a) Evaluate $f(1940)$ and interpret the result.   32
(b) Identify the domain and range of f.
(c) Represent f with a diagram.*
(b) D = $\{1920, 1940, 1960, 1980, 2000\}$
R = $\{9, 32, 74, 156, 216\}$

IDENTIFYING A FUNCTION

89. *Average Precipitation*   The table lists the monthly average precipitation P in Las Vegas, Nevada, where

*Answer on page IA-7

$x = 1$ corresponds to January and $x = 12$ corresponds to December.

x (month)	1	2	3	4	5	6
P (inches)	0.5	0.4	0.4	0.2	0.2	0.1

x (month)	7	8	9	10	11	12
P (inches)	0.4	0.5	0.3	0.2	0.4	0.3

Source: J. Williams.

(a) Determine the value of P during May.   0.2
(b) Is P a function of x? Explain.
(c) If $P = 0.4$, find x.   2, 3, 7, 11
   (b) Yes. Each month has one average amount of precipitation.

90. *Wind Speeds*   The table lists the monthly average wind speed W in Louisville, Kentucky, where $x = 1$ corresponds to January and $x = 12$ corresponds to December.

x (month)	1	2	3	4	5	6
W (mph)	10.4	12.7	10.4	10.4	8.1	8.1

x (month)	7	8	9	10	11	12
W (mph)	6.9	6.9	6.9	8.1	9.2	9.2

Source: J. Williams.

(a) Determine the month with the highest average wind speed.   February
(b) Is W a function of x? Explain.
(c) If $W = 6.9$, find x.   7, 8, 9

   (b) Yes. Each month has exactly one average wind speed.

Exercises 91–94: Determine whether the diagram could represent a function.

91.   No

92.   Yes
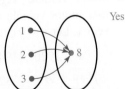

93.   Yes
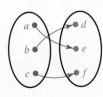

94.   No
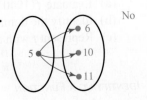

Exercises 95–104: Determine whether the graph represents a function. If it does, identify the domain and range.

95.
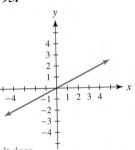
It does.
D: All real numbers
R: All real numbers

96.
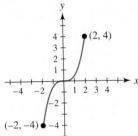
It does.
D: $-2 \le x \le 2$
R: $-4 \le y \le 4$

97.
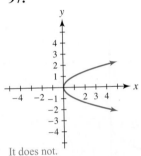
It does not.

98.
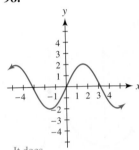
It does.
D: All real numbers
R: $-2 \le y \le 2$

99.
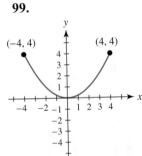
It does.
D: $-4 \le x \le 4$
R: $0 \le y \le 4$

100.
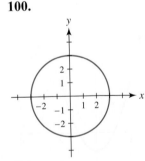
It does not.

101.
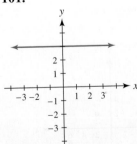
It does.
D: All real numbers
R: $y = 3$

102.
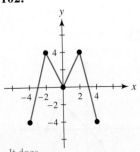
It does.
D: $-4 \le x \le 4$
R: $-4 \le y \le 4$

103. It does not.

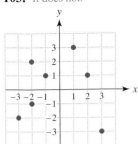

104. It does.
$D = \{-6, -4, -2, 0, 2, 4, 6\}$
$R = \{-6, -4, -2, 2, 4, 6\}$

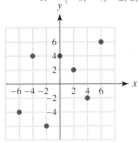

108. S is given by the table. It does.

x	-3	-2	-1
y	10	10	10

WRITING ABOUT MATHEMATICS

109. Give an example of a function. Identify the domain and range of your function.

110. Explain in your own words what a function is. How is a function different from a relation?

111. Explain how to evaluate a function by using a graph. Give an example.

112. Give one difficulty that may occur when you use a table of values to evaluate a function.

Exercises 105–108: Determine whether S defines a function.

105. $S = \{(1, 2), (4, 5), (7, 8), (5, 4), (2, 2)\}$ It does.

106. $S = \{(4, 7), (-2, 1), (3, 8), (4, 9)\}$ It does not.

107. S is given by the table.   It does not.

x	5	10	5
y	2	1	0

2.2 LINEAR FUNCTIONS

Basic Concepts · Representations of Linear Functions · Modeling Data with Linear Functions

INTRODUCTION

In applied mathematics, functions are used to model real-world phenomena, such as electricity, weather, and the economy. Because there are so many different applications of mathematics, a wide assortment of functions have been created. In fact, new functions are invented every day for use in business, education, and government. In this section we discuss an important type of function called a *linear function*.

BASIC CONCEPTS

Suppose that the air conditioner is turned on when the temperature inside a house is 80°F. The resulting temperatures are listed in Table 2.5 for various elapsed times. Note that for each 1-hour increase in elapsed time, the temperature decreases by 2°F.

TABLE 2.5   House Temperature

			1-hour increase			
Elapsed Time (hours)	0	1	2	3	4	5
Temperature (°F)	80	78	76	74	72	70
			2°F decrease			

A scatterplot is shown in Figure 2.18, which suggests that a line models these data.

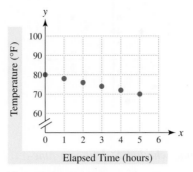

Calculator Help

To make a scatterplot, see the
Appendix (page AP-4).

Figure 2.18 Temperature in a Home

Over this 5-hour period, the air conditioner lowers the temperature by $2°F$ for each hour that it runs. The temperature is found by multiplying the elapsed time x by -2 and adding the initial temperature of $80°F$. This situation is modeled by $f(x) = -2x + 80$. For example,

$$f(2.5) = -2(2.5) + 80 = 75$$

means that the temperature is $75°F$ after the air conditioner has run for 2.5 hours. A graph of $f(x) = -2x + 80$, where $0 \leq x \leq 5$, is shown in Figure 2.19. We call f a *linear function* because its graph is a *line*. If a function is *not* a linear function, then it is a **nonlinear function.**

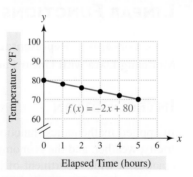

Figure 2.19 A Linear Function

TEACHING TIP

Ask students whether
$f(x) = 2x + 3x$ represents a
linear function.

LINEAR FUNCTION

A function f defined by $f(x) = ax + b$, where a and b are constants, is a **linear function**.

For $f(x) = -2x + 80$, we have $a = -2$ and $b = 80$. The constant a represents the rate at which the air conditioner cools the building, and the constant b represents the initial temperature.

In general, a linear function defined by $f(x) = ax + b$ changes by a units for each unit increase in x. This *rate of change* is an increase if $a > 0$ and a decrease if $a < 0$. For example, if new carpet costs \$20 per square yard, then the linear function defined by $C(x) = 20x$

gives the cost of installing x square yards of carpet. The value of $a = 20$ gives the cost (rate of change) for each additional square yard of carpet. For function C, the value of b is 0 because it cost \$0 to buy 0 square yards of carpet.

Note: If f is a linear function, then $f(0) = a(0) + b = b$. Thus b can be found by evaluating $f(x)$ at $x = 0$.

EXAMPLE 1   **Identifying linear functions**

Determine whether f is a linear function. If f is a linear function, find values for a and b so that $f(x) = ax + b$.

(a) $f(x) = 4 - 3x$ (b) $f(x) = 8$ (c) $f(x) = 2x^2 + 8$

Solution   (a) Let $a = -3$ and $b = 4$. Then $f(x) = -3x + 4$, and f is a linear function.
(b) Let $a = 0$ and $b = 8$. Then $f(x) = 0x + 8$, and f is a linear function.
(c) Function f is not linear because its formula contains x^2. The formula for a linear function cannot contain an x with an exponent other than 1.

EXAMPLE 2   **Determining linear functions**

Use each table of values to determine whether $f(x)$ could represent a linear function. If f could be linear, write a formula for f in the form $f(x) = ax + b$.

(a)

x	0	1	2	3
$f(x)$	10	15	20	25

(b)

x	-2	0	2	4
$f(x)$	4	2	0	-2

(c)

x	0	1	2	3
$f(x)$	1	2	4	7

Solution   (a) For each unit increase in x, $f(x)$ increases by 5 units so $f(x)$ could be linear with $a = 5$. Because $f(0) = 10$, $b = 10$. Thus $f(x) = 5x + 10$.
(b) For each 2-unit increase in x, $f(x)$ decreases by 2 units, or equivalently, each unit increase in x results in a 1-unit decrease in $f(x)$, so $f(x)$ could be linear with $a = -1$. Because $f(0) = 2$, $b = 2$. Thus $f(x) = -x + 2$.
(c) Each unit increase in x does not result in a constant change in $f(x)$. Thus $f(x)$ does not represent a linear function.

REPRESENTATIONS OF LINEAR FUNCTIONS

The graph of a linear function is a line. To graph a linear function f we usually start by making a table of values and then plot two or more points. We can then sketch the graph of f by drawing a line through these points, as demonstrated in the next example.

EXAMPLE 3   Graphing a linear function by hand

Sketch a graph of $f(x) = x - 1$.

Solution   Begin by making a table of values containing at least three points. Pick convenient values of x, such as $x = -1, 0, 1$.

$$f(-1) = -1 - 1 = -2$$
$$f(0) = 0 - 1 = -1$$
$$f(1) = 1 - 1 = 0$$

Display the results, as shown in Table 2.6.

Plot the points $(-1, -2)$, $(0, -1)$, and $(1, 0)$. Then sketch a line through the points to obtain the graph of f. A graph of a line results when *infinitely* many points are plotted, as shown in Figure 2.20.

TABLE 2.6

x	y
-1	-2
0	-1
1	0

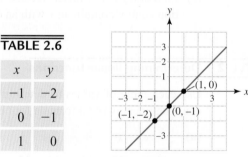

Figure 2.20

Critical Thinking

Two points determine a line. Why is it a good idea to plot at least three points when graphing a linear function by hand?

A third point will verify that the first two points have been plotted correctly.

EXAMPLE 4   Representing a linear function

A linear function is given by $f(x) = -3x + 2$.
(a) Give a verbal representation of f.
(b) Make a numerical representation (table) of f by letting $x = -1, 0, 1$.
(c) Plot the points in the table from part (b). Then sketch a graph of f.

TABLE 2.7

x	$f(x)$
-1	5
0	2
1	-1

Solution   **(a)** *Verbal Representation*   Multiply the input x by -3 and then add 2 to obtain the output.
(b) *Numerical Representation*   Evaluate $f(x) = -3x + 2$ at $x = -1, 0, 1$, which results in Table 2.7.
(c) *Graphical Representation*   To make a graph of f by hand, plot the points $(-1, 5)$, $(0, 2)$, and $(1, -1)$ from Table 2.7. Then draw a line passing through these points, as shown in Figure 2.21.

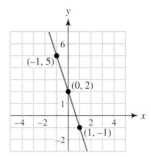

Figure 2.21

In the next example a graphing calculator is used to create a graph and table of a linear function.

EXAMPLE 5 Using a graphing calculator

Give numerical and graphical representations of $f(x) = \frac{1}{2}x - 2$.

Solution *Numerical Representation*   To make a numerical representation, construct the table for $Y_1 = .5X - 2$, starting at $x = -3$ and incrementing by 1, as shown in Figure 2.22(a). (Other tables are possible.)

Graphical Representation   Graph Y_1 in the standard viewing rectangle, as shown in Figure 2.22(b). (Other viewing rectangles may be used.)

Calculator Help
To make a table, see the Appendix (page AP-3). To make a graph, see the Appendix (page AP-5).

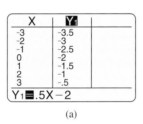

(a)

$[-10, 10, 1]$ by $[-10, 10, 1]$

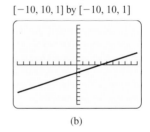

(b)

Figure 2.22

MAKING CONNECTIONS

Mathematics in Newspapers

Think of the mathematics that you see in newspapers. Often percentages are described *verbally*, numbers are displayed in *tables*, and data are shown in *graphs*. Seldom are *formulas* given, which is an important reason not to study only symbolic representations.

MODELING DATA WITH LINEAR FUNCTIONS

A distinguishing feature of a linear function is that each time the input x increases by 1 unit, the output $f(x) = ax + b$ always changes by an amount equal to a. For example, the number of doctors in the private sector from 1970 to 2000 can be modeled by

$$f(x) = 15{,}260x - 2{,}973{,}000,$$

where x is the year. The value $a = 15{,}260$ indicates that the number of doctors has increased, on average, by 15,260 each year.   (**Source:** American Medical Association.)

The following are other examples of quantities that are modeled by linear functions. Try to determine the value of the constant a.

- The wages earned by an individual working x hours at \$8 per hour
- The distance traveled by light in x seconds if the speed of light is 186,000 miles per second
- The cost of tuition and fees when registering for x credits if each credit costs \$80 and the fees are fixed at \$50

When we are modeling data with a linear function defined by $f(x) = ax + b$, the following concepts are helpful to determine a and b.

MODELING DATA WITH A LINEAR FUNCTION

The formula $f(x) = ax + b$ may be interpreted as follows.

$$f(x) = \quad ax \quad + \quad b$$

$$\text{(New amount)} = \text{(Change)} + \text{(Fixed amount)}$$

When x represents time, *change* equals (rate of change) $\times$ (time).

$$f(x) = \quad a \quad \times \quad x \quad + \quad b$$

$$\text{(Future amount)} = \text{(Rate of change)} \times \text{(Time)} + \text{(Initial amount)}$$

These concepts are applied in the next three examples.

EXAMPLE 6   Modeling car sales

Table 2.8 shows numbers of Toyota vehicles sold in the United States. (Refer to the introduction to this chapter.)

TABLE 2.8   Toyota Vehicles Sold (millions)

Year	1998	1999	2000	2001	2002
Vehicles	1.4	1.5	1.6	1.7	1.8

Source: Autodata.

(a) What were the sales in 1998?
(b) What was the annual increase in sales?

(c) Find a linear function *f* that models this data. Let *x* = 0 correspond to 1998, *x* = 1 to 1999, and so on.

(d) Use *f* to predict sales in 2004.

Solution **(a)** In 1998, 1.4 million vehicles were sold.

(b) Sales have increased by 0.1 million (100,000) vehicles per year. Because this rate of change is the same each year, we can model the data *exactly* with a linear function.

(c) Initial sales in 1998 (*x* = 0) were 1.4 million vehicles, and each year sales increased by 0.1 million vehicles. Thus

$$f(x) \quad = \quad 0.1 \quad \times \quad x \quad + \quad 1.4$$
$$(\text{Future sales}) = (\text{Rate of change in sales}) \times (\text{Time}) + (\text{Initial sales}),$$

or $f(x) = 0.1x + 1.4$.

(d) Because *x* = 6 corresponds to 2004, evaluate $f(6)$.

$$f(6) = 0.1(6) + 1.4 = 2 \text{ million vehicles}$$

In the next example we model tuition and fees.

EXAMPLE 7   Modeling the cost of tuition and fees

Suppose that tuition costs $80 per credit and that student fees are fixed at $50. Give symbolic, numerical, and graphical representations for a linear function that models tuition and fees.

Solution **Symbolic Representation**   Total cost is found by multiplying $80 (rate or cost per credit) by the number of credits *x* and then adding the fixed fees (fixed amount) of $50. Thus $f(x) = 80x + 50$.

Numerical Representation   Table 2.9 lists tuition and fees for 4, 8, 12, and 16 credits. (Other values are also possible.) For example, $f(4) = 80(4) + 50 = 370$, so the cost of 4 credits is $370.

Graphical Representation   Start by plotting the points from Table 2.9. Then sketch a line that passes through these points, as shown in Figure 2.23.

Calculator Help
To make a scatterplot, see the Appendix (page AP-4).

TABLE 2.9   Tuition

Credits	Cost
4	$370
8	$690
12	$1010
16	$1330

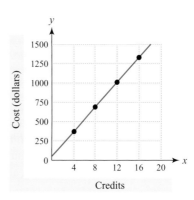

Figure 2.23 Tuition

In the next example we consider a simple linear function that models the speed of a car.

EXAMPLE 8   Modeling with a constant function

A car travels on a freeway with its speed recorded at regular intervals, as listed in Table 2.10.

TABLE 2.10   Speed of a Car

Elapsed Time (hours)	0	1	2	3	4
Speed (miles per hour)	70	70	70	70	70

(a) Discuss the speed of the car during this time interval.
(b) Find a formula for a function f that models these data.
(c) Sketch a graph of f together with the data.

Solution (a) The speed of the car appears to be constant at 70 miles per hour.
(b) Because the speed is constant, the rate of change is 0. Thus

TEACHING TIP

Emphasize that the change is 0 for
a constant function.

$$f(x) \quad = \quad 0x \quad + \quad 70$$
$$\text{(Future speed)} = \text{(Change in speed)} + \text{(Initial speed)}$$

and $f(x) = 70$.
(c) Because $y = f(x)$, graph $y = 70$ with the data points

$$(0, 70), (1, 70), (2, 70), (3, 70), \text{ and } (4, 70)$$

to obtain Figure 2.24.

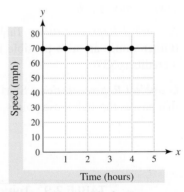

Figure 2.24 Speed of a Car

The function defined by $f(x) = 70$ is an example of a *constant function*. A **constant function** *is a linear function* with $a = 0$ and can be written as $f(x) = b$. Regardless of the input, a constant function always outputs the same value, b. Its graph is a horizontal line. The following are two applications of constant functions.

- A thermostat calculates a constant function regardless of the weather outside by maintaining a set temperature.
- A cruise control in a car calculates a constant function by maintaining a fixed speed, regardless of the type of road or terrain.

2.2 PUTTING IT ALL TOGETHER

A linear function is a relatively simple function used to model real data. A clear understanding of linear functions is essential to the understanding of functions in general.

Concept	Explanation	Examples
Linear Function	Can be represented by $f(x) = ax + b$	$f(x) = 2x - 6$, $a = 2$ and $b = -6$ $f(x) = 10$, $a = 0$ and $b = 10$
Constant Function	Can be represented by $f(x) = b$	$f(x) = -7$, $b = -7$ $f(x) = 22$, $b = 22$
Rate of Change for a Linear Function	The output of a linear function changes by a constant amount for each unit increase in the input.	$f(x) = -3x + 8$ decreases 3 units for each unit increase in x. $f(x) = 5$ neither increases nor decreases. The rate of change is 0.

The following table summarizes symbolic, verbal, numerical, and graphical representations of a linear function.

Type of Representation	Comments	Example
Symbolic	Mathematical formula in the form $f(x) = ax + b$	$f(x) = 2x + 1$, where $a = 2$ and $b = 1$
Verbal	Multiply the input x by a and add b.	Multiply the input x by 2 and add 1 to obtain the output.
Numerical (table of values)	For each unit increase in x in the table, the output of $f(x) = ax + b$ changes by an amount equal to a.	1-unit increase $\begin{array}{c\|ccc} x & 0 & 1 & 2 \\ \hline f(x) & 1 & 3 & 5 \end{array}$ 2-unit increase
Graphical	The graph of a linear function is a line. Plot at least 3 points and then sketch the line.	$y = 2x + 1$

2.2 EXERCISES

FOR EXTRA HELP

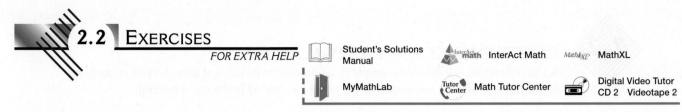

Student's Solutions Manual

InterAct Math

MathXL

MyMathLab

Math Tutor Center

Digital Video Tutor
CD 2   Videotape 2

CONCEPTS

1. The formula for a linear function is given by $f(x) =$ _____. $ax + b$

2. The formula for a constant function is given by $f(x) =$ _____. b

3. The graph of a linear function is a _____.   line

4. The graph of a constant function is a _____.
   horizontal line

5. If $f(x) = 7x + 5$, each time x increases by 1 unit, $f(x)$ increases by _____ units.   7

6. If $f(x) = 5$, each time x increases by 1 unit, $f(x)$ increases by _____ units.   0

IDENTIFYING LINEAR FUNCTIONS

Exercises 7–14: Determine whether f is a linear function. If f is linear, give values for a and b so that f may be expressed as $f(x) = ax + b$.

7. Linear: $a = \frac{1}{2}$, $b = -6$

7. $f(x) = \frac{1}{2}x - 6$

8. $f(x) = x$ Linear: $a = 1$, $b = 0$

9. $f(x) = \frac{5}{2} - x^2$
   Nonlinear

10. $f(x) = \sqrt{x} + 3$
    Nonlinear

11. $f(x) = -9$
    Linear: $a = 0$, $b = -9$

12. $f(x) = 1.5 - 7.3x$
    Linear: $a = -7.3$, $b = 1.5$

13. $f(x) = -9x$
    Linear: $a = -9$, $b = 0$

14. $f(x) = \dfrac{1}{x}$ Nonlinear

Exercises 15–18: Determine whether the graph represents a linear function.

15. It does.

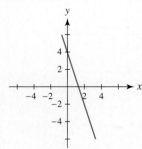

16. It does not.

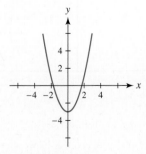

17. It does not.

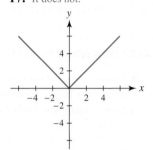

18. It does.

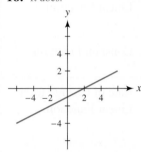

Exercises 19–26: (Refer to Example 2.) Use the table to determine whether $f(x)$ could represent a linear function. If it could, write $f(x)$ in the form $f(x) = ax + b$.

19. Yes; $f(x) = 3x - 6$

x	0	1	2	3
$f(x)$	-6	-3	0	3

20. Yes; $f(x) = 2x - 2$

x	0	2	4	6
$f(x)$	-2	2	6	10

21. Yes; $f(x) = \frac{3}{2}x + 3$

x	-2	0	2	4
$f(x)$	0	3	6	9

22. No

x	0	3	6	9
$f(x)$	8	4	2	1

23. No

x	-2	-1	0	1
$f(x)$	-5	0	20	40

24. Yes; $f(x) = -3x$

x	-2	-1	0	1
$f(x)$	6	3	0	-3

25. Yes; $f(x) = 2x - 2$

x	1	2	3	4
$f(x)$	0	2	4	6

26.

x	1	2	3	4
$f(x)$	0	1	3	7

No

EVALUATING LINEAR FUNCTIONS

Exercises 27–32: Evaluate $f(x)$ at the given values of x.

27. $f(x) = 4x$ $x = -4, 5$ $-16; 20$

28. $f(x) = -2x + 1$ $x = -2, 3$ $5; -5$

29. $f(x) = 5 - x$ $x = -\frac{2}{3}, 3$ $\frac{17}{3}; 2$

30. $f(x) = \frac{1}{2}x - \frac{1}{4}$ $x = 0, \frac{1}{2}$ $-\frac{1}{4}; 0$

31. $f(x) = -22$ $x = -\frac{3}{4}, 13$ $-22; -22$

32. $f(x) = 9x - 7$ $x = -1.2, 2.8$ $-17.8; 18.2$

Exercises 33–38: Use the graph of f to evaluate the given expressions.

33. $f(-1)$ and $f(0)$ $-2; 0$ **34.** $f(-2)$ and $f(2)$ $4; 0$

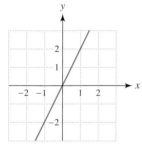

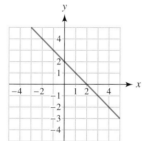

35. $f(-2)$ and $f(4)$ $-1; -4$ **36.** $f(0)$ and $f(3)$ $-1; 1$

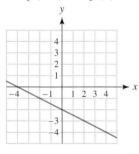

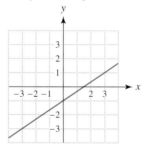

37. $f(-3)$ and $f(1)$ $1; 1$ **38.** $f(1.5)$ and $f(0.5\pi)$ $-2; -2$

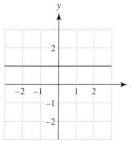

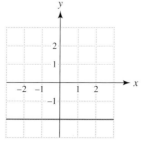

Exercises 39–42: Use the verbal description to write a formula for $f(x)$. Then evaluate $f(3)$.

39. Multiply the input by 6. $f(x) = 6x; 18$

40. Multiply the input by -3 and add 7. $f(x) = -3x + 7; -2$

41. Divide the input by 6 and subtract $\frac{1}{2}$. $f(x) = \frac{x}{6} - \frac{1}{2}; 0$

42. Output 8.7 for every input. $f(x) = 8.7; 8.7$

REPRESENTING LINEAR FUNCTIONS

Exercises 43–46: Match $f(x)$ with its graph (a.–d.).

43. $f(x) = 3x$ d.   **44.** $f(x) = -2x$ c.

45. $f(x) = x - 2$ b.   **46.** $f(x) = 2x + 1$ a.

a.   **b.**

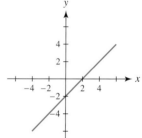

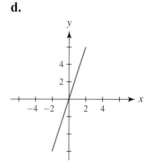

c.   **d.**

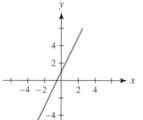

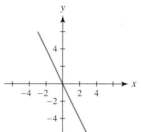

Exercises 47–56: Sketch a graph of $y = f(x)$.*

47. $f(x) = 2$ **48.** $f(x) = -1$

49. $f(x) = 2x$ **50.** $f(x) = -\frac{1}{2}x$

51. $f(x) = x + 1$ **52.** $f(x) = x - 2$

53. $f(x) = 3x - 3$ **54.** $f(x) = -2x + 1$

55. $f(x) = 3 - x$ **56.** $f(x) = \frac{1}{4}x + 2$

Exercises 57–62: Write a symbolic representation (formula) for a linear function f that calculates the following.

57. The number of pounds in x ounces $f(x) = \frac{1}{16}x$

*Answers on page IA-7

58. The number of dimes in x dollars $f(x) = 10x$

59. The distance traveled by a car moving at 65 miles per hour for t hours $f(t) = 65t$

60. The long-distance phone bill *in dollars* for calling t minutes at 10 cents per minute and a fixed fee of $4.95 $f(t) = 0.10t + 4.95$

61. The total number of hours in a day during day x $f(x) = 24$

62. The cost of downhill skiing x times with a $500 season pass $f(x) = 500$

Modeling

Exercises 63–66: Match the situation with the graph (a.–d.) that models it best, where x-values represent time from 1990 to 2000.

63. The cost of college tuition. b.

64. The cost of 1 megabyte of computer memory. d.

65. The distance between Chicago and Denver. c.

66. The total distance traveled by a satellite orbiting Earth a.

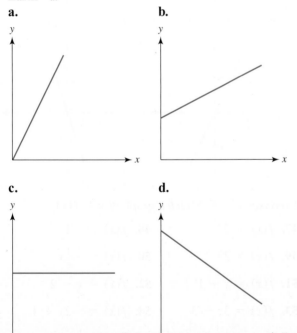

a.

b.

c.

d.

Applications

67. *Thermostat* Let $y = f(x)$ describe the temperature y of a room that is kept at $70°F$ for x hours.

(a) Represent f symbolically and graphically over a 24-hour period for $0 \le x \le 24$. $f(x) = 70;$*

(b) Construct a table of f for $x = 0, 4, 8, 12, \ldots, 24$.*

(c) What type of function is f? Constant

68. *Cruise Control* Let $y = f(x)$ describe the speed y of an automobile after x minutes if the cruise control is set at 60 miles per hour.

(a) Represent f symbolically and graphically over a 15-minute period for $0 \le x \le 15$. $f(x) = 60;$*

(b) Construct a table of f for $x = 0, 1, 2, \ldots, 6$.*

(c) What type of function is f? Constant

69. *Distance* A car is initially 50 miles south of the Minnesota–Iowa border traveling south on Interstate 35. Distances D between the car and the border are recorded in the table for various elapsed times t. Find a linear function given by $D(t) = at + b$ that models these data. $D(t) = 60t + 50$

t (hours)	0	2	3	5
D (miles)	50	170	230	350

70. *Estimating the Weight of a Bass* Sometimes the weight of a fish can be estimated by measuring its length. The table lists typical weights of bass having various lengths.

Length (inches)	12	14	16	18	20	22
Weight (pounds)	1.0	1.7	2.5	3.6	5.0	6.6

Source: Minnesota Department of Natural Resources.

(a) Let x be the length and y be the weight. Make a line graph of the data.*

(b) Could the data be modeled accurately with a linear function? Explain your answer.
No. The graph does not form a straight line.

71. *Solid Waste* In 1960, the average American disposed of 2.7 pounds of garbage per day, whereas in 2003 this amount was 4.3 pounds per day. (*Source: Environmental Protection Agency.*)

(a) Find a linear function f that calculates the amount of garbage disposed of by a person in 1960 after x days. Find $f(60)$ and interpret the result.

(b) Repeat part (a) for 2003 with a linear function g.

(a) $f(x) = 2.7x$; 162 (b) $g(x) = 4.3x$; 258

72. *Rain Forests* Rain forests are defined as forests that grow in regions receiving more than 70 inches of rain

*Answers on pages IA-7–IA-8

per year. The world is losing an estimated 49 million acres of rain forest each year. (**Source:** *New York Times Almanac.*)

(a) Find a linear function *f* that calculates the acres of rain forest in millions lost in *x* years. $f(x) = -49x$

(b) Evaluate $f(7)$ and interpret the result.
−343; in 7 years the world loses 343 million acres of rain forest.

73. *Age in the United States* The median age of the population for each year *x* between 1820 and 1995 can be approximated by

$$f(x) = 0.09x - 147.1$$

(**Source:** Bureau of the Census.)

(a) Graph *f* in the viewing rectangle

[1820, 1995, 20] by [0, 40, 10].
Median age is increasing.
Discuss any trends shown in the graph.*

(b) Construct the table for *f* starting at $x = 1820$, incrementing by 20. Use the table to evaluate $f(1900)$ and interpret the result.* $f(1900) = 23.9$

(c) The value of *a* in the formula for $f(x)$ is 0.09. Interpret this value.
Each year the median age increased by 0.09 year, on average.

74. *Temperature and Volume* If a sample of a gas, such as helium, is heated, it will expand. The expression $V(T) = 0.147T + 40$ calculates the volume *V* in cubic inches of a sample of gas at temperature *T* in degrees Celsius.   (a) 40 in³; The volume is 40 in³ at 0°C.

(a) Evaluate $V(0)$ and interpret the result.

(b) If the temperature increases by 10°C, by how much does the volume increase?   1.47 in³

(c) What is the volume of the gas when the temperature is 100°C?   54.7 in³

75. *Temperature and Volume* (Refer to the preceding exercise.) A sample of gas at 0°C has a volume *V* of 137 cubic centimeters, which increases in volume by 0.5 cubic centimeter for every 1°C increase in temperature *T*.   (a) $V(T) = 0.5T + 137$

(a) Write a formula $V(T) = aT + b$ that gives the volume of the gas at temperature *T*.

(b) Find the volume of the gas when $T = 50°C$.
162 cm³

76. *Cost* To make a music video it costs $750 to rent a studio plus $5 for each copy produced.

(a) Write a formula $C(x) = ax + b$ that calculates the cost of producing *x* videos. $C(x) = 5x + 750$

(b) Find the cost of producing 2500 videos. $13,250

77. *Baseball* The table shows the average length of a major league baseball game in minutes for various years.

Year	2000	2001	2002
Length (minutes)	180	176	172

Source: Elias Sports Bureau.

(a) What was the average length of a baseball game in 2000?   180 minutes

(b) By how many minutes did the average length change each year?   Decreased by 4 minutes

(c) Find a linear function *f* that models these data. Let $x = 0$ correspond to 2000. $f(x) = -4x + 180$

(d) Use *f* to predict the average length of a game in 2004.   164 minutes

78. *Wal-Mart Sales* The table shows Wal-Mart's share as a percentage of overall U.S. retail sales for various years. (This percentage excludes restaurants and motor vehicles.)

Year	1998	1999	2000	2001	2002
Share (%)	6	6.5	7	7.5	8

Source: Commerce Department, Wal-Mart.

(a) What was Wal-Mart's share of the market in 1998?   6%

(b) By how much (percent) did Wal-Mart's share increase each year?   0.5%

(c) Find a linear function *f* that models these data. Let $x = 0$ correspond to 1998. $f(x) = 0.5x + 6$

(d) Use *f* to predict Wal-Mart's share in 2005.   9.5%

79. *Weight Lifting* Lifting weights can increase a person's muscle mass. Each additional pound of muscle burns an extra 40 calories per day. Write a linear function that models the number of calories burned each day by *x* pounds of muscle. By burning an extra 3500 calories a person can lose 1 pound of fat. How many pounds of muscle are needed to burn the equivalent of 1 pound of fat in 30 days? (**Source:** *Runner's World.*) $f(x) = 40x$; about 2.92 lb

80. *Number of Doctors* The number *N* of doctors in the private sector from 1970 to 2000 can be approximated by $N(t) = 15,260t + 333,200$, where *t* is the year and $t = 0$ corresponds to 1970.*

(a) Evaluate $N(0)$ and $N(30)$ and interpret each result.

(b) Explain what the numbers 15,260 and 333,200 represent in the formula.

*Answers on page IA-8

81. Explain how you can determine whether a function is linear by using its

   (a) symbolic representation,

   (b) graphical representation, and

   (c) numerical representation.

82. Describe one way to determine whether a set of data points can be modeled by a linear function.

CHECKING BASIC CONCEPTS   SECTIONS 2.1 AND 2.2

1. Find a formula and sketch a graph for a function that squares the input x and then subtracts 1 from the result. $f(x) = x^2 - 1$*
   2.(a) $D: -3 \le x \le 3; R: -4 \le y \le 4$

2. Use the accompanying graph to do the following.

   (a) Find the domain and range of f.

   (b) Evaluate $f(0)$ and $f(2)$. 0; 4

   (c) Is f a linear function? Explain.
       No. The graph is not a line.

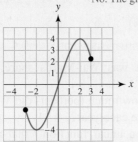

3. Determine whether f is a linear function.

   (a) $f(x) = 4x - 2$ Yes

   (b) $f(x) = 2\sqrt{x} - 5$ No

   (c) $f(x) = -7$ Yes

   (d) $f(x) = 9 - 2x + 5x$ Yes

4. Graph $f(x) = 4 - 3x$. Evaluate $f(-2)$.*   10

5. Find a formula for a linear function that models the data. $f(x) = \frac{1}{2}x - 1$

x	0	1	2	3	4
$f(x)$	-1	$-\frac{1}{2}$	0	$\frac{1}{2}$	1

6. The median age in the United States from 1970 to 2000 can be approximated by

$$f(x) = 0.264x + 27.7,$$

where $x = 0$ corresponds to 1970, $x = 1$ to 1971, and so on.*

   (a) Evaluate $f(20)$ and interpret the result.

   (b) Explain the meaning of the numbers 0.264 and 27.7.

TEACHING TIP

Consider having the class break into groups of 2 to 4 and work some of these problems. Walk around the room, answer questions, and listen to how students discuss mathematics. It is an eye-opening experience.

*Answers on page IA-8

2.3   **THE SLOPE OF A LINE**

Slope · Slope–Intercept Form of a Line · Interpreting Slope in Applications

INTRODUCTION

Figure 2.25 shows some graphs of lines, where the x-axis represents time.

Which graph might represent the total amount of water flowing from a faucet?

Which graph might represent the height of a young adult who has stopped growing?

Which graph might represent the amount of gas in your car's tank while you are driving?

To answer these questions, you probably used the concept of slope. In mathematics, slope is a real number that measures the "tilt" of a line in the xy-plane. We assume throughout the text that lines are always straight. In this section we discuss how slope relates to the graph of a linear function and how to interpret slope.

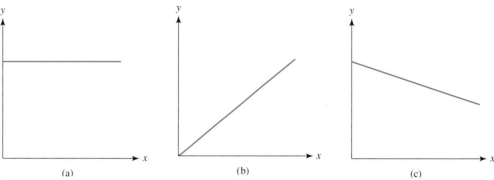

(a)   (b)   (c)

Figure 2.25

SLOPE

The graph shown in Figure 2.26 illustrates the cost of buying x gallons of gasoline. The graph tilts upward from left to right, which indicates that the cost increases as the number of gallons purchased increases. Note that for every 2 gallons purchased the cost increases by \$3. We say that the graph *rises* 3 units for every 2 units of *run*. The ratio $\frac{\text{rise}}{\text{run}}$ equals the *slope* of the line. The slope of this line is $\frac{3}{2}$, or 1.5. That is, for every unit of run along the x-axis the graph rises 1.5 units. A slope of 1.5 indicates that gasoline costs \$1.50 per gallon.

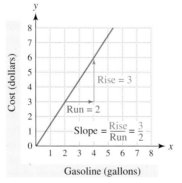

Figure 2.26 Cost of Gasoline

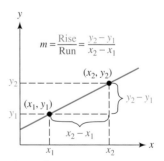

Figure 2.27

A more general case is shown in Figure 2.27 where a line passes through the points (x_1, y_1) and (x_2, y_2). The **rise** or *change in y* is $y_2 - y_1$, and the **run** or *change in x* is $x_2 - x_1$. The slope m is given by $m = \frac{\text{rise}}{\text{run}} = \frac{y_2 - y_1}{x_2 - x_1}$. The expression x_1 has a **subscript** of 1 and is read "x sub one" or "x one." Thus x_1 and x_2 denote two different x-values. Similar comments can be made about y_1 and y_2.

SLOPE

The **slope** m of the line passing through the points (x_1, y_1) and (x_2, y_2) is

$$m = \frac{y_2 - y_1}{x_2 - x_1},$$

where $x_1 \neq x_2$. That is, slope equals rise over run.

Note: *Change in x* is sometimes denoted Δx and equals $x_2 - x_1$. The expression Δx is read "delta x." Similarly, *change in y* is sometimes denoted Δy and equals $y_2 - y_1$. Using this notation, we can express slope as $m = \frac{\Delta y}{\Delta x} = \frac{y_2 - y_1}{x_2 - x_1}$.

EXAMPLE 1   Calculating the slope of a line

Find the slope of the line passing through the points $(-4, 1)$ and $(2, 4)$. Plot these points and graph the line. Interpret the slope.

Solution   Begin by letting $(x_1, y_1) = (-4, 1)$ and $(x_2, y_2) = (2, 4)$. The slope is

$$m = \frac{y_2 - y_1}{x_2 - x_1} = \frac{4 - 1}{2 - (-4)} = \frac{3}{6} = \frac{1}{2}.$$

A graph of the line passing through these two points is shown in Figure 2.28. A slope of $\frac{1}{2}$ indicates that the line rises 1 unit for every 2 units of run. This slope is equivalent to 3 units of rise for every 6 units of run.

TEACHING TIP

Students should realize that 3 units of rise for 6 units of run, 1 unit of rise for 2 units of run, or $\frac{1}{2}$ unit of rise for 1 unit of run are all equivalent.

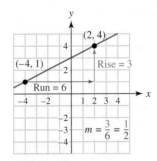

Figure 2.28

We would get the same slope in Example 1 if we let $(x_1, y_1) = (2, 4)$ and $(x_2, y_2) = (-4, 1)$. In this case the calculation would be

$$m = \frac{y_2 - y_1}{x_2 - x_1} = \frac{1 - 4}{-4 - 2} = \frac{-3}{-6} = \frac{1}{2}.$$

If a line has **positive slope**, the line *rises* from left to right. In Figure 2.29 the rise is 2 units for each unit of run, so the slope is 2. If a line has **negative slope**, the line *falls* from left to right. In Figure 2.30 the line *falls* 1 unit for every 2 units of run, so the slope is $-\frac{1}{2}$.

Slope 0 indicates that a line is horizontal, as shown in Figure 2.31. If (x_1, y_1) and (x_2, y_2) are two points on a vertical line, $x_1 = x_2$. In Figure 2.32 the run is $x_2 - x_1 = 0$, so a vertical line has **undefined slope**.

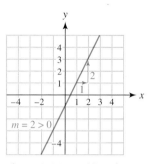

Figure 2.29 Positive Slope

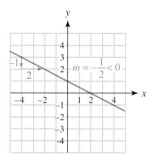

Figure 2.30 Negative Slope

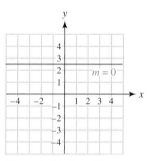

Figure 2.31 Zero Slope

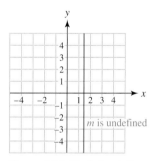

Figure 2.32 Undefined Slope

EXAMPLE 2   Sketching a line with a given slope

Sketch a line passing through the point $(0, 4)$ and having slope $-\frac{2}{3}$.

Solution   Start by plotting the point $(0, 4)$. Because $m = \frac{\text{change in } y}{\text{change in } x}$, a slope of $-\frac{2}{3}$ indicates that the y-values *decrease* 2 units each time the x-values increase by 3 units. That is, the line *falls* 2 units for every 3-unit increase in the run. The line passes through $(0, 4)$, so a 2-unit decrease in y and a 3-unit increase in x results in the line passing through the point $(0 + 3, 4 - 2)$ or $(3, 2)$, as shown in Figure 2.33.

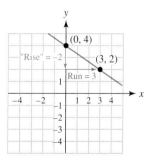

Figure 2.33

SLOPE–INTERCEPT FORM OF A LINE

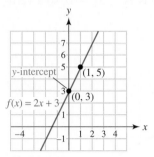

Figure 2.34

Because $f(0) = 3$ and $f(1) = 5$, the graph of $f(x) = 2x + 3$ is a line that passes through $(0, 3)$ and $(1, 5)$, as shown in Figure 2.34. Therefore the slope of this line is

$$m = \frac{5 - 3}{1 - 0} = 2.$$

Note that slope 2 equals the coefficient of x in the formula $f(x) = 2x + 3$. In general, if $f(x) = ax + b$, the slope of the graph of f is $m = a$. For example, the graph of $f(x) = 6x - 5$ has slope $m = 6$, and the graph of $f(x) = -\frac{4}{5}x + 1$ has slope $m = -\frac{4}{5}$.

The point $(0, 3)$ lies on the graph of $f(x) = 2x + 3$ and is located on the y-axis. The y-value of 3 is called the *y-intercept*. A **y-intercept** is the y-coordinate of a point where a graph intersects the y-axis. To find a y-intercept let $x = 0$ in $f(x)$. If $f(x) = ax + b$, then

$$f(0) = a(0) + b = b.$$

Thus if $f(x) = -4x + 7$, the y-intercept is 7, and if $f(x) = \frac{1}{2}x - 8$, the y-intercept is -8.

Because $y = f(x)$, any linear function may be represented by $y = mx + b$, where m is the slope and b is the y-intercept. The form $y = mx + b$ is called the *slope–intercept form* of a line.

SLOPE–INTERCEPT FORM

The line with slope m and y-intercept b is given by

$$y = mx + b,$$

the **slope–intercept form** of a line.

EXAMPLE 3   Graphing lines

Identify the slope and y-intercept for the three lines $y = \frac{1}{2}x - 2$, $y = \frac{1}{2}x$, and $y = \frac{1}{2}x + 2$. Graph and compare the lines.

Solution   The graph of $y = \frac{1}{2}x - 2$ has slope $\frac{1}{2}$ and y-intercept -2. This line passes through the point $(0, -2)$ and rises 1 unit for each 2 units of run (see Figure 2.35). The graph of $y = \frac{1}{2}x$ has slope $\frac{1}{2}$ and y-intercept 0, and the graph of $y = \frac{1}{2}x + 2$ has slope $\frac{1}{2}$ and y-intercept 2. These lines are parallel, and the vertical distance between them always equals 2.

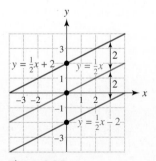

Figure 2.35

EXAMPLE 4   Sketching a line

Sketch a line with slope -2 and y-intercept 3. Write its slope–intercept form.

Solution   For the y-intercept of 3, plot the point $(0, 3)$. Because the slope is -2, each **1**-unit increase in x results in a **2**-unit decrease in y. Thus the line passes through the point $(0 + 1, 3 - 2)$ or $(1, 1)$. The slope–intercept form of this line is $y = -2x + 3$. See Figure 2.36.

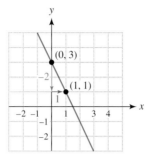

Figure 2.36

EXAMPLE 5   Using a graph to write the slope–intercept form

For each graph shown in Figures 2.37 and 2.38, write the slope–intercept form of the line.

(a)

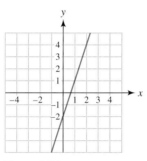

Figure 2.37

(b)

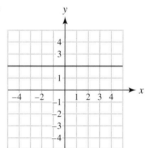

Figure 2.38

Solution   **(a)** The graph passes through $(0, -2)$, so the y-intercept is -2. Because the graph rises 3 units for each unit increase in x, the slope is 3. The slope–intercept form is $y = 3x - 2$.
   (b) The graph passes through $(0, 2)$, so the y-intercept is 2. Because the graph is a horizontal line, its slope is 0. The slope–intercept form is $y = 0x + 2$, or more simply, $y = 2$.

EXAMPLE 6   Finding the slope–intercept form

The points listed in Table 2.11 all lie on a line.
(a) Find the missing value in the table.
(b) Write the slope–intercept form of the line.

TABLE 2.11

x	-1	0	2
y	1	?	10

Solution   (a) The line passes through $(-1, 1)$ and $(2, 10)$ so its slope is

$$m = \frac{10 - 1}{2 - (-1)} = \frac{9}{3} = 3.$$

For each unit increase in x, y increases by 3. When x increases from -1 to 0, y increases from 1 to $1 + 3 = 4$. Therefore the missing value is 4.

(b) Because the line passes through the point $(0, 4)$, its y-intercept is 4. The slope–intercept form is $y = 3x + 4$.

INTERPRETING SLOPE IN APPLICATIONS

TEACHING TIP

Be sure to do an example where slope is interpreted in a physical situation. Consider Example 7.

When a linear function is used to model physical quantities, the slope of its graph provides certain information. Slope can be interpreted as a **rate of change** of a quantity, which we illustrate in the next three examples.

EXAMPLE 7   Interpreting slope

The distance y in miles that an athlete riding a bicycle is from home after x hours is shown in Figure 2.39.
(a) Find the y-intercept. What does the y-intercept represent?
(b) The graph passes through the point $(2, 6)$. Discuss the meaning of this point.
(c) Find the slope–intercept form of this line. Interpret the slope as a rate of change.

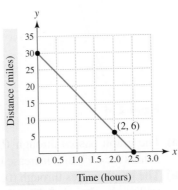

Figure 2.39 Distance from Home

Solution   (a) From the graph, the y-intercept is 30, which indicates that the athlete is initially 30 miles from home.
(b) The point $(2, 6)$ means that after 2 hours the athlete is 6 miles from home.
(c) The line passes through the points $(0, 30)$ and $(2, 6)$. Thus its slope is

$$m = \frac{6 - 30}{2 - 0} = -12,$$

and the slope–intercept form is $y = -12x + 30$. A slope of -12 indicates that the athlete is traveling at 12 miles per hour *toward* home. The negative sign indicates that the distance between the athlete and home is *decreasing*.

EXAMPLE 8   Interpreting slope

If a sample of a gas is heated, it will expand. The expression $V(t) = 0.183t + 50$ gives the volume V of a sample of helium in cubic inches at a temperature of t degrees Celsius.
(a) Find the slope of the graph of V.
(b) Interpret the slope as a rate of change.

Solution   (a) The slope of the graph of $V(t) = 0.183t + 50$ is $m = 0.183$.
(b) A slope of $m = 0.183$ means that the sample of helium increases in volume by 0.183 cubic inch for each $1°C$ increase in temperature.

EXAMPLE 9   Analyzing growth in Wal-Mart

Table 2.12 lists past and projected numbers of Wal-Mart employees.
(a) Make a line graph of the data.
(b) Find the slope of each line segment in the graph.
(c) Interpret these slopes as rates of change.

TABLE 2.12	Wal-Mart Employees (millions)			
Year	1997	1999	2002	2007
Employees	0.7	1.1	1.4	2.2

Source: Wal-Mart.

Solution   (a) Plot (1997, 0.7), (1999, 1.1), (2002, 1.4), and (2007, 2.2). Connecting these points with line segments results in Figure 2.40. This graph does not represent a linear function because the graph consists of several line segments rather than one (straight) line.

Critical Thinking

An athlete runs away from home at 10 miles per hour for 30 minutes and then jogs back home at 5 miles per hour. Sketch a graph that shows the distance between the athlete and home.

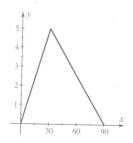

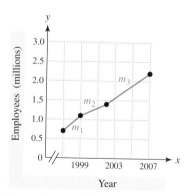

Figure 2.40 Wal-Mart Employees

(b) The slopes of the line segments are

$$m_1 = \frac{1.1 - 0.7}{1999 - 1997} = 0.2, \quad m_2 = \frac{1.4 - 1.1}{2002 - 1999} = 0.1, \quad \text{and}$$

$$m_3 = \frac{2.2 - 1.4}{2007 - 2002} = 0.16.$$

(c) Slope $m_1 = 0.2$ means that, on average, the number of Wal-Mart employees increased by 0.2 million (or 200,000) per year between 1997 and 1999. Slopes m_2 and m_3 can be interpreted similarly.

2.3 PUTTING IT ALL TOGETHER

The graph of a linear function is a line. The "tilt" of a line is called the slope and equals rise over run. A positive slope indicates that the line *rises* from left to right, whereas a negative slope indicates that the line *falls* from left to right. A horizontal line has slope 0 and a vertical line has undefined slope. The slope of the graph of $f(x) = ax + b$ is $m = a$ and its y-intercept is b. When a linear function is being used to model physical quantities, slope indicates a rate of change in the quantity. The following table summarizes some basic concepts of slope and the slope–intercept form.

Concept	Explanation	Example
Slope	The slope of the line passing through the points (x_1, y_1) and (x_2, y_2) is given by $$m = \frac{\text{rise}}{\text{run}} = \frac{y_2 - y_1}{x_2 - x_1}.$$	The slope of the line passing through $(-2, 3)$ and $(1, 5)$ is $$m = \frac{5 - 3}{1 - (-2)} = \frac{2}{3}.$$ If the x-values increase by 3 units, the y-values increase by 2 units.
Slope–Intercept Form for a Line $y = mx + b$	The slope equals m, and the y-intercept equals b.	If $y = \frac{1}{2}x + 1$, then the slope is $\frac{1}{2}$ and the y-intercept is 1.
Slope as a Rate of Change	The slope of the graph of a linear function indicates the rate at which a quantity is either increasing or decreasing.	From 1981 to 2000 average public college tuition and fees can be modeled by $$f(x) = 136x + 772,$$ where $x = 1$ corresponds to 1981. The slope of the graph of f is $m = 136$ and indicates that, on average, tuition and fees increased by \$136 per year between 1981 and 2000.

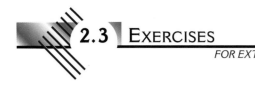

2.3 EXERCISES

FOR EXTRA HELP

Student's Solutions Manual

InterAct Math

MathXL

MyMathLab

Math Tutor Center

Digital Video Tutor
CD 2   Videotape 2

SLOPE

Exercises 1–6: Use the concept of rise over run to find the slope of the line.

1. 2

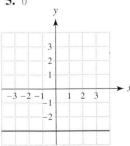

2. −1

3. −$\frac{2}{3}$

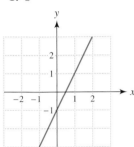

4. Undefined

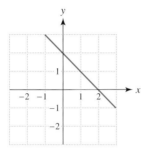

5. 0

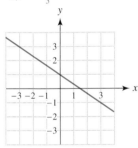

6. $\frac{1}{2}$

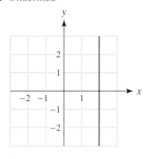

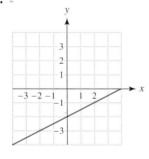

Exercises 7–20: Find the slope of the line passing through the two points.

7. $(1, 2), (2, 4)$ 2

8. $(-3, 2), (2, -3)$ −1

9. $(2, 1), (-1, 3)$ −$\frac{2}{3}$

10. $\left(-\frac{3}{5}, -\frac{4}{5}\right), \left(\frac{4}{5}, \frac{3}{5}\right)$ 1

11. $(-3, 6), (4, 6)$ 0

12. $(-3, 5), (-5, 5)$ 0

13. $\left(\frac{1}{2}, -\frac{2}{7}\right), \left(\frac{1}{2}, \frac{13}{17}\right)$ Undefined

14. $(-1, 6), (-1, -4)$ Undefined

15. $\left(\frac{1}{3}, -\frac{4}{3}\right), \left(\frac{1}{6}, \frac{1}{3}\right)$ −10

16. $\left(-\frac{1}{2}, \frac{3}{2}\right), \left(2, \frac{1}{2}\right)$ −$\frac{2}{5}$

17. $(1989, 10), (1999, 16)$ $\frac{3}{5}$

18. $(1950, 6.1), (2000, 10.6)$ 0.09

19. $(2.1, 3.6), (-1.2, 4.3)$ $-0.\overline{21}$

20. $(12, -34), (14, 64)$ 49

*Exercises 21–28: Sketch a line passing through the given point with slope m.**

21. $(0, -2), \ m = 3$

22. $(0, 1), \ m = -1$

23. $(0, 4), \ m = -\frac{1}{2}$

24. $(0, -3), \ m = \frac{2}{3}$

25. $(-1, 1), \ m = -2$

26. $(2, 1), \ m = \frac{1}{2}$

27. $(2, -3), \ m = \frac{1}{2}$

28. $(-2, 3), \ m = -\frac{3}{5}$

SLOPE–INTERCEPT FORM

Exercises 29–38: Do the following.

  (a) *Find the slope and y-intercept of the line.*
  (b) *Graph the equation.**

29. $y = x + 2$ (a) 1; 2

30. $y = x - 2$ (a) 1; −2

31. $y = -3x + 2$ (a) −3; 2

32. $y = \frac{1}{2}x - 1$ (a) $\frac{1}{2}$; −1

33. $y = \frac{1}{3}x$ (a) $\frac{1}{3}$; 0

34. $y = -2x$ (a) −2; 0

35. $y = 2$ (a) 0; 2

36. $y = -3$ (a) 0; −3

37. $y = -x + 3$ (a) −1; 3

38. $y = \frac{2}{3}x - 2$ (a) $\frac{2}{3}$; −2

*Answers on pages IA-8–IA-9

Exercises 39–44: Use the graph to express the line in slope–intercept form.

39. $y = -x + 4$

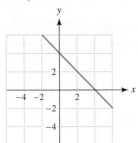

40. $y = -2x + 2$

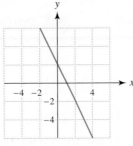

41. $y = 2$

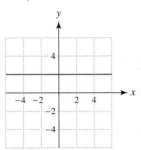

42. $y = \frac{1}{2}x - 1$

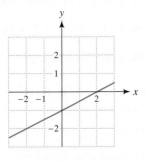

43. $y = x - 2$

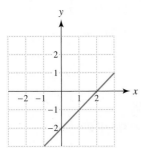

44. $y = -\frac{2}{3}x + 1$

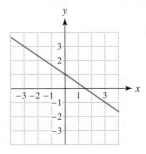

Exercises 45–48: Write the slope–intercept form for a line satisfying the following conditions.

45. Slope 3, y-intercept -5 $y = 3x - 5$

46. Slope $-\frac{2}{3}$, y-intercept 7 $y = -\frac{2}{3}x + 7$

47. Passing through $(1, 0)$ and $\left(0, -\frac{3}{2}\right)$ $y = \frac{3}{2}x - \frac{3}{2}$

48. Passing through $(0, 4)$ and $(-2, 0)$ $y = 2x + 4$

Exercises 49–52: Let f be a linear function. Use the table to find the slope and y-intercept of the graph of f.

49.

x	0	1	2	3
$f(x)$	-2	0	2	4

2; −2

50.

x	-1	0	1	2
$f(x)$	5	10	15	20

5; 10

51.

x	-2	-1	1	2
$f(x)$	18	11	-3	-10

−7; 4

52.

x	-4	-2	2	4
$f(x)$	6	3	-3	-6

$-\frac{3}{2}$; 0

Exercises 53–56: Let $f(x)$ represent a linear function.

(a) *Find the missing value in the table.*
(b) *Write the slope–intercept form for f.*

53.

x	0	1	2
$f(x)$	-1	1	?

(a) 3
(b) $f(x) = 2x - 1$

54.

x	1	2	3
$f(x)$	12	8	?

(a) 4
(b) $f(x) = -4x + 16$

55.

x	-2	0	4
$f(x)$	2	?	11

(a) 5
(b) $f(x) = \frac{3}{2}x + 5$

56.

x	0	5	20
$f(x)$	?	10	40

(a) 0
(b) $f(x) = 2x$

INTERPRETING SLOPE

Exercises 57–60: **Modeling**   *Choose the graph (a.–d.) that models the situation best.*

57. Money that a person earns after x hours, working for $10 per hour   c.

58. Total acres of rain forests in the world during the past 20 years   d.

59. World population from 1980 to 2000   b.

60. Square miles of land in Nevada from 1950 to 2000   a.

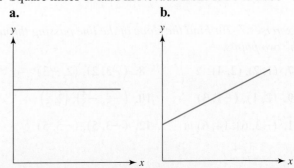

c.

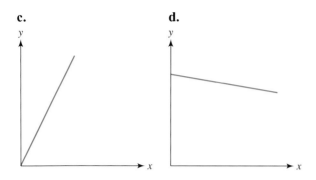

d.

Exercises 61–64: Modeling   The line graph represents the gallons of water in a small swimming pool after x hours. Assume that a pump at the pool can either add water to or remove water from the pool. *

(a) *Estimate the slope of each line segment.*
(b) *Interpret each slope as a rate of change.*
(c) *Describe what happened to the amount of water in the pool.*

61.

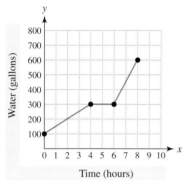

62.

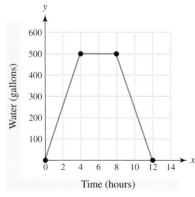

63.

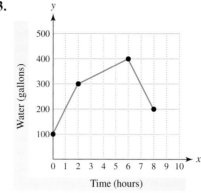

64.

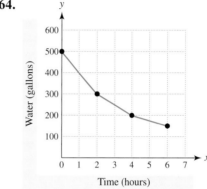

Exercises 65–68: Modeling Distance   An individual is driving a car along a straight road. The graph shows the distance that the driver is from home after x hours. *

(a) *Find the slope of each line segment in the graph.*
(b) *Interpret each slope as a rate of change.*
(c) *Describe both the motion and location of the car.*

65.

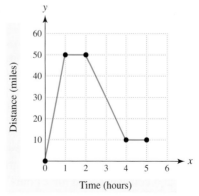

66.

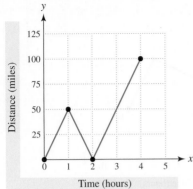

67.

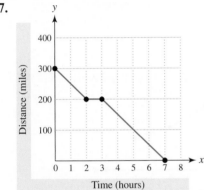

68.

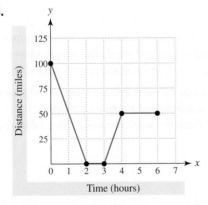

Exercises 69–72: Sketching a Model   *Sketch a graph that models the given situation.* *

69. The distance that a bicycle rider is from home if the rider is initially 20 miles away from home and arrives home after riding at a constant speed for 2 hours

70. The distance that an athlete is from home if the athlete runs away from home at 8 miles per hour for 30 minutes and then walks back home at 4 miles per hour

71. The distance that a person is from home if this individual drives to a mall, stays 2 hours, and then drives home, assuming that the distance to the mall is 20 miles and that the trip takes 30 minutes

72. The amount of water in a 10,000-gallon swimming pool that is filled at the rate of 1000 gallons per hour, left full for 10 hours, and then drained at the rate of 2000 gallons per hour

APPLICATIONS   73.(d) The number of children born to older mothers is increasing by about 4000 each year.

73. *Older Mothers*   The number of children in thousands born to mothers 40 years old or older is modeled by $f(x) = 4x - 7910$, where x is the year with $1990 \le x \le 2000$.   (*Source:* National Center for Health Statistics.)
  (a) Estimate the number of children born to older mothers in 1993.   62 thousand
   (b) Graph f. Describe the graph. *   Increasing
  (c) What is the slope of the graph of f?   4
  (d) Interpret the slope as a rate of change.

74. *Number of Radio Stations*   The number of radio stations on the air from 1950 to 1995 may be modeled by

$$f(x) = 214.2x - 415,368,$$

where x is the year.   (*Source:* National Association of Broadcasters.)   8748
  (a) How many radio stations were on the air in 1980?
  (b) What is the slope of the graph of f?   214.2
  (c) Interpret the slope as a rate of change.
  The number of radio stations increased by about 214 stations per year.

75. *Commercial Banks*   From 1987 to 2000 the number N of federally insured banks could be approximated by

$$N(t) = -416t + 13,723,$$

where t is the year and $t = 0$ corresponds to 1987.
  (a) How many federally insured banks were there in 2000?   8315
  (b) What is the slope of the graph of N? Interpret this slope as a rate of change.*
  (c) What is the y-intercept of the graph of N? Interpret this intercept.*

76. *Population Density*   From 1900 to 2000 the population density D of the United States in people per square mile could be approximated by

$$D(t) = 0.581t + 21.5,$$

where t is the year and $t = 0$ corresponds to 1900.

*Answers on page IA-10

(a) Find population density in 1900 and 2000.
21.5; 79.6

(b) What is the slope of the graph of *D*? Interpret this slope as a rate of change.*

(c) What is the *y*-intercept of the graph of *D*? Interpret this intercept.*

77. *Cost of Carpet*   The graph shows the cost of buying *x* square yards of carpet. Find the slope of this graph and interpret the result.

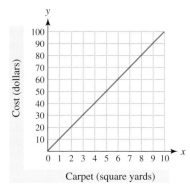

Carpet (square yards)

$m = 10$; The carpet costs $10 per square yard.

78. *Cost of Removing Snow*   The graph shows the cost of removing *x* tons of snow. Find the slope of this graph and interpret the result.

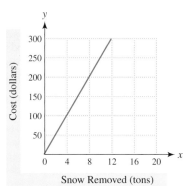

Snow Removed (tons)

$m = 25$; Snow removal costs $25 per ton.

79. *Filling a Swimming Pool*   A 20,000-gallon swimming pool is being filled at a constant rate. Over a 5-hour period the water in the pool increases from $\frac{1}{4}$ full to $\frac{5}{8}$ full. At what rate is water entering the pool?   1500 gallons per hour

80. *Speed of an Airplane*   An airplane on a 1200-mile trip is flying at a constant rate. Over a 2-hour period

the location of the plane changes from covering $\frac{1}{3}$ of the distance to covering $\frac{7}{8}$ of the distance. What is the speed of the airplane?   325 mph

81. *Two-Cycle Engines*   Two-cycle engines used in snowmobiles, jet skis, chain saws, and outboard motors require a mixture of gas and oil to run properly. For certain engines the amount of oil in pints that should be added to *x* gallons of gasoline is computed by $f(x) = \frac{4}{25}x$.   (*Source:* Johnson Outboard Motor Company.)

(a) How many pints of oil should be added to 6 gallons of gasoline? $\frac{24}{25} = 0.96$ pint

(b) Graph *f* for $0 \le x \le 25$.*

(c) What is the slope of the graph of *f*? $\frac{4}{25} = 0.16$

(d) Interpret the slope as a rate of change.
0.16 pint of oil should be added per gallon of gasoline.

82. *Fat Grams*   Some slices of pizza contain 10 grams of fat.

(a) Find a formula $f(x)$ that calculates the number of fat grams in *x* slices of pizza. $f(x) = 10x$

(b) Graph *f* for $0 \le x \le 6$.*

(c) What is the slope of the graph of *f*?   10

(d) Interpret the slope as a rate of change.
The total amount of fat increases at a rate of 10g of fat per slice of pizza.

83. *U.S. Average Family Income*   In 1990, the average family income was about $37,000, and in 2000 it was about $57,000.   (*Source:* Department of the Treasury.)

(a) Let $x = 0$ represent 1990, $x = 1$ represent 1991, and so on. Find values for *a* and *b* so that $f(x) = ax + b$ models the data. $a = 2000$; $b = 37,000$

(b) Estimate the average family income in 1995.
$47,000

84. *Minimum Wage*   In 1980, the minimum wage was about $3.10 per hour, and in 1999 it was $5.15. (*Source:* Department of Labor.)

(a) Let $x = 0$ represent 1980, $x = 1$ represent 1981, until $x = 19$ represents 1999. Find values for *a* and *b* so that $f(x) = ax + b$ models the data.

(b) If this trend continued, what should have been the minimum wage in 2003?   About $5.58
84. (a) $a \approx 0.108$; $b = 3.1$

WRITING ABOUT MATHEMATICS

85. Describe the information that the slope *m* of a line gives. Be as complete as possible.

86. Could one line have two different slope–intercept forms? Explain your answer.

*Answers on page IA-10

Group Activity: Working with Real Data

Directions: Form a group of 2 to 4 people. Select someone to record the group's responses for this activity. All members should work cooperatively to answer the questions. If your instructor asks for the results, each member of the group should be prepared to respond.

Sport Utility Vehicles (SUVs) SUVs became increasingly popular during the 1990s. The table lists the number of SUVs sold in various years.

Year	1992	1994	1996	1998	2000
SUVs (millions)	1.1	1.5	2.1	2.7	3.2

Source: Autodata Corporation.

(d) SUV sales increased by 0.27 million/yr.
(e) 1997: 2.45 million; 2001: 3.53 million

   (a) Make a scatterplot of the data. Discuss any trend in SUV sales. Let $x = 0$ correspond to 1992.*
(b) Estimate the slope m of a line that could be used to model the data. $m = 0.27$; answers may vary.
(c) Find an equation of a line $y = mx + b$ that models the data. $y = 0.27x + 1.1$; answers may vary.
(d) Interpret the slope m as a rate of change.
(e) Use your results to estimate SUV sales in 1997 and 2001. Answers may vary.

*Answers on page IA-11

2.4 EQUATIONS OF LINES AND LINEAR MODELS

Point–Slope Form · Horizontal and Vertical Lines · Parallel and Perpendicular Lines

INTRODUCTION

In 1999, there were approximately 100 million Internet users in the United States, and this number grew to about 144 million in 2002. This growth is illustrated in Figure 2.41, where the line passes through the points (1999, 100) and (2002, 144). In this section we discuss how to find the equation of the line that models these data. To do so we need to discuss the *point–slope form* of a line.

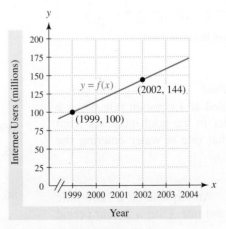

Figure 2.41 U.S. Internet Users

POINT–SLOPE FORM

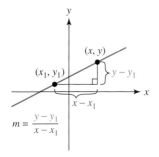

Figure 2.42

If we know the slope m and y-intercept b of a line, we can write its slope–intercept form, $y = mx + b$. The slope–intercept form is an example of an **equation of a line**. The point–slope form is a different form of the equation of a line.

Suppose that a (nonvertical) line with slope m passes through the point (x_1, y_1). If (x, y) is a different point on this line, then $m = \dfrac{y - y_1}{x - x_1}$ (see Figure 2.42).

We can use this slope formula to find the point–slope form.

$$m = \frac{y - y_1}{x - x_1} \qquad \text{Slope formula}$$

$$m(x - x_1) = y - y_1 \qquad \text{Multiply each side by } (x - x_1).$$

$$y - y_1 = m(x - x_1) \qquad \text{Rewrite the equation.}$$

$$y = m(x - x_1) + y_1 \qquad \text{Add } y_1 \text{ to each side.}$$

The equation $y - y_1 = m(x - x_1)$ is traditionally called the *point–slope form*. We think of y as being a function of x, written $y = f(x)$, so the equivalent form $y = m(x - x_1) + y_1$ is also referred to as the point–slope form.

|||||||| **POINT–SLOPE FORM**

The line with slope m passing through the point (x_1, y_1) is given by

$$y = m(x - x_1) + y_1,$$

or equivalently,

$$y - y_1 = m(x - x_1),$$

the **point–slope form** of a line. ||||||||

EXAMPLE 1   Using the point–slope form

Find the point–slope form of a line passing through the point $(1, 2)$ with slope -3. Does the point $(2, -1)$ lie on this line?

Solution   Let $m = -3$ and $(x_1, y_1) = (1, 2)$ in the point–slope form.

$$y = m(x - x_1) + y_1 \qquad \text{Point–slope form}$$

$$y = -3(x - 1) + 2 \qquad \text{Substitute.}$$

To determine whether the point $(2, -1)$ lies on the line, substitute 2 for x and -1 for y in the equation.

$$-1 \overset{?}{=} -3(2 - 1) + 2 \qquad \text{Let } x = 2 \text{ and } y = -1.$$

$$-1 \overset{?}{=} -3 + 2 \qquad \text{Simplify.}$$

$$-1 = -1 \qquad \text{The point satisfies the equation.}$$

The point $(2, -1)$ lies on the line because it satisfies the point–slope form.

We can use the point–slope form to find the equation of a line passing through two points.

EXAMPLE 2 Finding the equation of a line

Use the point–slope form to find an equation of the line passing through $(-2, 3)$ and $(6, -1)$.

Solution Before we can apply the point–slope form, we must find the slope.

$$m = \frac{y_2 - y_1}{x_2 - x_1} \qquad \text{Slope formula}$$

$$= \frac{-1 - 3}{6 - (-2)} \qquad \text{Substitute.}$$

$$= -\frac{1}{2} \qquad \text{Simplify.}$$

We can use either $(-2, 3)$ or $(6, -1)$ for (x_1, y_1) in the point–slope form. If we choose $(-2, 3)$, the point–slope form becomes the following.

$$y = m(x - x_1) + y_1 \qquad \text{Point–slope form}$$

$$y = -\frac{1}{2}(x - (-2)) + 3 \qquad \text{Let } x_1 = -2 \text{ and } y_1 = 3.$$

$$y = -\frac{1}{2}(x + 2) + 3 \qquad \text{Simplify.}$$

If we choose $(6, -1)$, the point–slope form with $x_1 = 6$ and $y_1 = -1$ becomes

$$y = -\frac{1}{2}(x - 6) - 1.$$

Note that, although the two point–slope forms are different, they are equivalent equations because their graphs are identical.

Example 2 illustrates the fact that the point–slope form *is not* unique for a given line. However, the slope–intercept form *is* unique because each line has a unique slope and a unique y-intercept. If we simplify both point–slope forms in Example 2, they reduce to the same slope–intercept form.

TEACHING TIP

Emphasize that the slope–intercept form is unique but that the point–slope form is not.

$$y = -\frac{1}{2}(x + 2) + 3 \qquad y = -\frac{1}{2}(x - 6) - 1 \qquad \text{Point–slope forms}$$

$$y = -\frac{1}{2}x - 1 + 3 \qquad y = -\frac{1}{2}x + 3 - 1 \qquad \text{Distributive property}$$

$$y = -\frac{1}{2}x + 2 \qquad y = -\frac{1}{2}x + 2 \qquad \text{Identical slope–intercept forms}$$

In the next example we model the data presented in the introduction to this section.

EXAMPLE 3   Modeling growth in Internet usage

In 1999, there were approximately 100 million Internet users in the United States, and this number grew to about 144 million in 2002 (see Figure 2.41).
(a) Find values for m, x_1, and y_1, so that $f(x) = m(x - x_1) + y_1$ models these data.
(b) Interpret m as a rate of change.
(c) Use f to estimate Internet usage in 2003.

Solution **(a)** The slope of the line passing through (1999, 100) and (2002, 144) is

$$m = \frac{144 - 100}{2002 - 1999} = \frac{44}{3}.$$

Thus, by choosing the point (**1999**, **100**) for the point–slope form, we can write

$$f(x) = \frac{44}{3}(x - 1999) + 100.$$

(b) Slope $m = \frac{44}{3} \approx 14.7$ indicates that the number of Internet users is increasing by about 14.7 million users per year.
(c) $f(2003) = \frac{44}{3}(2003 - 1999) + 100 \approx 159$ million.

═ MAKING CONNECTIONS ═

Modeling and the Dependent Variable x.

From Example 3, $f(x) = \frac{44}{3}(x - 1999) + 100$ models the number of Internet users in the United States. In this formula x represented the actual year. We could also model Internet users with $g(x) = \frac{44}{3}x + 100$, where $x = 0$ corresponds to 1999, $x = 1$ to 2000, and so on. Then to estimate the Internet users in 2003, we let $x = 4$.

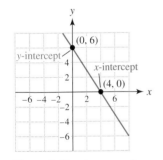

Figure 2.43 *x*-intercept 4;
y-intercept 6

If a line intersects the *y*-axis at the point (0, 6), the *y*-intercept is 6. Similarly, if the line intersects the *x*-axis at the point (4, 0), the *x-intercept* is 4. This line and its intercepts are illustrated in Figure 2.43. The *x*-coordinate of a point where a graph intersects the *x*-axis is called the **x-intercept**. The next example interprets intercepts in a physical situation.

EXAMPLE 4   Modeling water in a pool

A small swimming pool containing 6000 gallons of water is emptied by a pump removing 1200 gallons per hour.
(a) How long did it take to empty the pool?
(b) Sketch a linear function f that models the amount of water in the pool after x hours.
(c) Identify the *x*-intercept and the *y*-intercept. Interpret each intercept.
(d) Find the slope–intercept form of the line in the graph. Interpret the slope as a rate of change.
(e) What are the domain and range of f?

Solution   (a) The time needed to empty the pool was $\frac{6000}{1200} = 5$ hours.

(b) Initially the pool contained 6000 gallons, and after 5 hours the pool was empty. Therefore the graph of f is a line passing through the points $(0, 6000)$ and $(5, 0)$, as shown in Figure 2.44.

(c) The x-intercept is 5, which means that after 5 hours the pool is empty. The y-intercept of 6000 means that initially (when $x = 0$) the pool contained 6000 gallons of water.

(d) To find the equation of the line shown in Figure 2.44, we first find the slope of the line passing through the points $(0, 6000)$ and $(5, 0)$.

$$
\begin{aligned}
m &= \frac{y_2 - y_1}{x_2 - x_1} && \text{Slope formula} \\[4pt]
&= \frac{0 - 6000}{5 - 0} && \text{Substitute.} \\[4pt]
&= -1200 && \text{Simplify.}
\end{aligned}
$$

The slope is -1200 and the y-intercept is 6000, so the slope–intercept form is

$$y = -1200x + 6000.$$

A slope of -1200 indicates that the pump *removed* water at the rate of 1200 gallons per hour.

(e) The domain is $D: 0 \leq x \leq 5$, and the range is $R: 0 \leq y \leq 6000$.

Critical Thinking

Can the graph of a function have more than one y-intercept? Explain. Can the graph of a function have more than one x-intercept? Explain.

No, it would not pass the vertical line test.
Yes, the graph could pass the vertical line test.

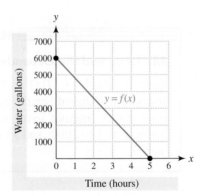

Figure 2.44 Water in a Pool

In the next example we introduce a way to model linear data by hand.

EXAMPLE 5   Modeling linear data by hand

Find a line $y = mx + b$ that models the data in Table 2.13.

TEACHING TIP

In this text, students can learn the basics of modeling data even if they do not use calculators. Try Example 5.

TABLE 2.13

x	10	20	30	40	50
y	15	24	30	39	45

Solution **STEP 1:** *Carefully make a scatterplot of the data* Be sure to label properly the x- and y-axes. For these data we can label each axis from 0 to 60 and have each hash mark represent 10 units. A scatterplot of the data is shown in Figure 2.45(a).

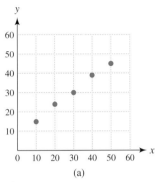
(a)

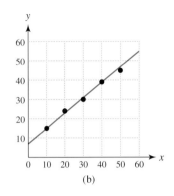
(b)

Figure 2.45

STEP 2: *Sketch a line that models the data* You may want to use a ruler for this step. In Figure 2.45(b) a line is drawn that passes through the first and fourth data points. Your line may be slightly different. Note that the line does not have to pass through any of the data points.

STEP 3: *Choose two points on the line and find the equation of the line* The line in Figure 2.45(b) passes through $(10, 15)$ and $(40, 39)$. Therefore its slope is

$$m = \frac{39 - 15}{40 - 10} = \frac{24}{30} = \frac{4}{5}.$$

The equation of the line is

$$y = \frac{4}{5}(x - 10) + 15 \quad \text{or} \quad y = \frac{4}{5}x + 7.$$

Note that answers may vary because the data are not exactly linear. ___

≡ MAKING CONNECTIONS ≡

Modeling, Lines, and Linear Functions

If a set of data is modeled by $y = mx + b$, then the data are also modeled by the linear function defined by $f(x) = mx + b$ because $y = f(x)$. In Example 5 the data set is modeled by $y = \frac{4}{5}x + 7$, so it is also modeled by $f(x) = \frac{4}{5}x + 7$.

HORIZONTAL AND VERTICAL LINES

The graph of a constant function is a horizontal line. For example, the graph of $f(x) = 3$ is a horizontal line with y-intercept 3, as shown in Figure 2.46 on the next page. Its equation may be expressed as $y = 3$, so every point on the line has a y-coordinate of 3. In general, the equation $y = b$ represents a horizontal line with y-intercept b, as shown in Figure 2.47 on the next page.

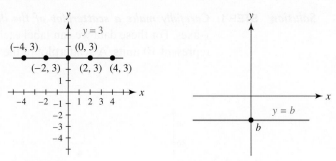

Figure 2.46   **Figure 2.47**

A vertical line cannot be represented by a function because different points on a vertical line have the same x-coordinate. The equation of the vertical line depicted in Figure 2.48 is $x = 3$. In general, the equation of a vertical line with x-intercept h is $x = h$, as shown in Figure 2.49.

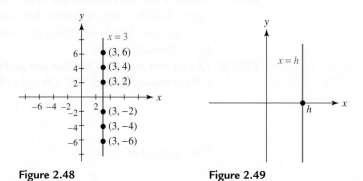

Figure 2.48   **Figure 2.49**

EQUATIONS OF HORIZONTAL AND VERTICAL LINES

The equation of a horizontal line with y-intercept b is $y = b$.

The equation of a vertical line with x-intercept h is $x = h$.

EXAMPLE 6   Finding equations of horizontal and vertical lines

Find equations of the vertical and horizontal lines that pass through the point $(-3, 4)$. Graph these two lines.

Solution   The x-coordinate of the point $(-3, 4)$ is -3. The vertical line $x = -3$ passes through *every* point in the xy-plane with an x-coordinate of -3, including the point $(-3, 4)$.

Similarly, the horizontal line $y = 4$ passes through *every* point with a y-coordinate of 4, including the point $(-3, 4)$. The lines $x = -3$ and $y = 4$ are graphed in Figure 2.50.

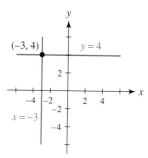

Figure 2.50

Calculator Help

To graph a vertical line, see the
Appendix (page AP-6).

Technology Note: *Graphing Vertical Lines*

The equation of a vertical line is $x = h$ and cannot be expressed on a graphing calculator in the
form "$Y_1 = $". Some graphing calculators graph a vertical line by accessing the DRAW menu.
The accompanying figure shows a calculator graph of Figure 2.50.

TEACHING TIP

Students are not required to know
how to graph vertical lines with a
calculator, but many students are
interested in how to do so.

$[-6, 6, 1]$ by $[-6, 6, 1]$

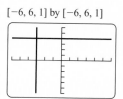

PARALLEL AND PERPENDICULAR LINES

Slope is important when we are determining whether two lines are parallel. For example, the
lines $y = 2x$ and $y = 2x + 1$ are parallel because they both have slope 2.

PARALLEL LINES

Two lines with the same slope are parallel.

Two nonvertical parallel lines have the same slope.

EXAMPLE 7 Finding parallel lines

Find the slope–intercept form of a line parallel to $y = -2x + 5$, passing through $(-4, 3)$.

Solution Because the line $y = -2x + 5$ has slope -2, any parallel line also has slope -2. The line
passing through $(-4, 3)$ with slope -2 is determined as follows.

$$y = -2(x + 4) + 3 \qquad \text{Point–slope form}$$
$$y = -2x - 8 + 3 \qquad \text{Distributive property}$$
$$y = -2x - 5 \qquad \text{Slope–intercept form}$$

Figure 2.51 shows three pairs of perpendicular lines with their slopes labeled. Note in Figures 2.51(a) and 2.51(b) that the product $m_1 m_2$ equals -1. That is,

$$m_1 m_2 = 1 \cdot (-1) = -1 \quad \text{and} \quad m_1 m_2 = 2 \cdot \left(-\frac{1}{2}\right) = -1.$$

A more general situation for the slopes of two perpendicular lines is shown in Figure 2.51(c), where

$$m_1 m_2 = m_1 \cdot \left(-\frac{1}{m_1}\right) = -1.$$

That is, if two nonvertical lines are perpendicular, then the product of their slopes is -1.

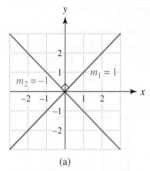
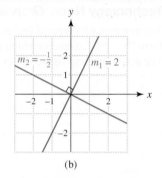
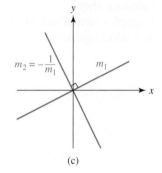

     (a)   (b)   (c)

Figure 2.51 Perpendicular Lines

These results are summarized in the following box.

PERPENDICULAR LINES

Two lines with nonzero slopes m_1 and m_2 are perpendicular if $m_1 m_2 = -1$.

If two lines have slopes m_1 and m_2 such that $m_1 \cdot m_2 = -1$, then they are perpendicular.

Table 2.14 shows examples of slopes m_1 and m_2 that result in perpendicular lines because $m_1 m_2 = -1$. Note that m_1 and m_2 are negative reciprocals of each other; that is, $m_2 = -\frac{1}{m_1}$ and $m_1 = -\frac{1}{m_2}$.

Table 2.14   Slopes of Perpendicular Lines

m_1	1	$-\frac{1}{2}$	-4	$\frac{2}{3}$	$\frac{3}{4}$	0.25
m_2	-1	2	$\frac{1}{4}$	$-\frac{3}{2}$	$-\frac{4}{3}$	-4
$m_1 m_2$	-1	-1	-1	-1	-1	-1

EXAMPLE 8   Finding perpendicular lines

Find the slope–intercept form of the line perpendicular to $y = -\frac{1}{2}x + 1$, passing through the point (3, 2). Graph the lines.

Solution   The line $y = -\frac{1}{2}x + 1$ has slope $m_1 = -\frac{1}{2}$. The slope of a perpendicular line is $m_2 = 2$ because

$$m_1 \cdot m_2 = -\frac{1}{2} \cdot 2 = -1.$$

The slope–intercept form of a line having slope **2** and passing through **(3, 2)** can be found as follows.

$$y = 2(x - 3) + 2 \qquad \text{Point–slope form}$$
$$y = 2x - 6 + 2 \qquad \text{Distributive property}$$
$$y = 2x - 4 \qquad \text{Slope–intercept form}$$

A graph of these perpendicular lines is shown in Figure 2.52.

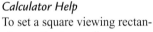

Figure 2.52

Technology Note: *Square Viewing Rectangles*

The accompanying figure shows a square viewing rectangle, in which the perpendicular lines from Example 8 intersect at 90°. Try graphing the two perpendicular lines in Example 8 by using the viewing rectangle $[-6, 6, 1]$ by $[-10, 10, 1]$. Do the lines appear perpendicular? For many graphing calculators a square viewing rectangle results when the distance along the y-axis is about $\frac{2}{3}$ the distance along the x-axis. On some graphing calculators you can create a square viewing rectangle automatically by using the ZOOM menu.

Calculator Help

To set a square viewing rectangle, see the Appendix (page AP-6).

TEACHING TIP

For lines to look perpendicular on a graphing calculator screen, a square window must be used. On many graphing calculators a menu can be used to set a square window.

$[-6, 6, 1]$ by $[-4, 4, 1]$

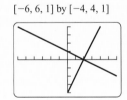

EXAMPLE 9   Equations of perpendicular lines

Find the slope–intercept form of each line shown in Figure 2.53. Verify that the two lines are perpendicular.

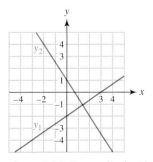

Figure 2.53 Perpendicular Lines

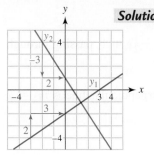

Figure 2.54

Solution In Figure 2.54, the graph of y_1 has slope $m_1 = \frac{2}{3}$ because the line rises 2 units for every 3 units of run. Its y-intercept is -2, and its slope–intercept form is $y_1 = \frac{2}{3}x - 2$. The graph of y_2 has slope $m_2 = -\frac{3}{2}$ because the line falls 3 units for every 2 units of run. Its y-intercept is 1, and its slope–intercept form is $y = -\frac{3}{2}x + 1$. To be perpendicular, the product of their slopes must equal -1; that is,

$$m_1 \cdot m_2 = \frac{2}{3} \cdot \left(-\frac{3}{2}\right) = -1.$$

2.4 PUTTING IT ALL TOGETHER

The following table shows important forms of an equation of a line.

Concept	Comments	Example
Point–Slope Form $y = m(x - x_1) + y_1$ or $y - y_1 = m(x - x_1)$	Used to find an equation of a line, given two points or one point and the slope	Given two points $(1, 2)$ and $(3, 5)$, first compute $$m = \frac{5 - 2}{3 - 1} = \frac{3}{2}.$$ An equation of this line is $$y = \frac{3}{2}(x - 1) + 2.$$
Slope–Intercept Form $y = mx + b$	A unique equation for a line, determined by the slope m and the y-intercept b	An equation of the line with slope $m = 3$ and y-intercept $b = -5$ is $$y = 3x - 5.$$

The graph of a linear function f is a line. Therefore linear functions can be represented by

$$f(x) = mx + b \quad \text{or} \quad f(x) = m(x - x_1) + y_1.$$

The following table summarizes the important concepts involved with special types of lines.

Concept	Equation(s)	Example
Horizontal Line	$y = b$, where b is a constant	A horizontal line with y-intercept 5 has the equation $y = 5$.
Vertical Line	$x = h$, where h is a constant	A vertical line with x-intercept -3 has the equation $x = -3$.
Parallel Lines	$y = m_1 x + b_1$ and $y = m_2 x + b_2$, where $m_1 = m_2$	The lines $y = 2x - 1$ and $y = 2x + 5$ are parallel because both have slope 2.
Perpendicular Lines	$y = m_1 x + b_1$ and $y = m_2 x + b_2$, where $m_1 m_2 = -1$	The lines $y = 3x - 5$ and $y = -\frac{1}{3}x + 2$ are perpendicular because $m_1 m_2 = 3\left(-\frac{1}{3}\right) = -1$.

2.4   EXERCISES

FOR EXTRA HELP

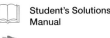 Student's Solutions Manual

 InterAct Math

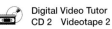 MathXL

 MyMathLab

 Math Tutor Center

Digital Video Tutor
CD 2   Videotape 2

CONCEPTS

1. How many lines are determined by two distinct points? 1

2. How many lines are determined by a point and a slope? 1

3. Give the slope–intercept form of a line. $y = mx + b$

4. Give the point–slope form of a line.
$y = m(x - x_1) + y_1$ or $y - y_1 = m(x - x_1)$

5. Give an equation of a horizontal line with y-intercept b. $y = b$

6. Give an equation of a vertical line with x-intercept h.
$x = h$

7. If two parallel lines have slopes m_1 and m_2, what can be said about m_1 and m_2? $m_1 = m_2$

8. If two perpendicular lines have slopes m_1 and m_2, then $m_1 \cdot m_2 = $ _____. -1

9. Give an equation of a line that is parallel to the line $y = -\frac{3}{4}x + 1$. $y = -\frac{3}{4}x - 3$; answers may vary.

10. Give an equation of a line that is perpendicular to the line $y = -\frac{3}{4}x$. $y = \frac{4}{3}x + 2$; answers may vary.

11. Give an equation of a line that is perpendicular to the x-axis. $x = 1$; answers may vary.

12. Give an equation of a line that is perpendicular to the y-axis. $y = -5$; answers may vary.

Exercises 13–18: Match the equation with its graph (a.–f.), where m and b are constants.

13. $y = mx + b$, $m > 0$ and $b \neq 0$ d.

14. $y = mx + b$, $m < 0$ and $b \neq 0$ b.

15. $y = mx$, $m < 0$ a.   **16.** $y = b$ c.

17. $y = mx$, $m > 0$ f.   **18.** $x = h$ e.

a.

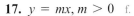

b.

c.

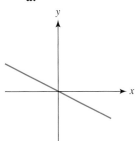

d.

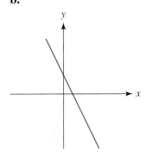

e.

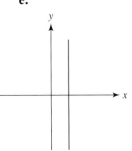

f.

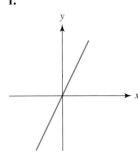

Exercises 19–22: Determine whether the given point lies on the line.

19. $(-3, 4)$ $y = -\frac{2}{3}x + 2$ Yes

20. $(4, 2)$ $y = \frac{1}{4}x - 1$ No

21. $(-4, 3)$ $y = \frac{1}{2}(x + 4) + 2$ No

22. $(1, -13)$ $y = 3(x - 5) - 1$ Yes

EQUATIONS OF LINES

Exercises 23–26: Use the labeled point and the slope to find the slope–intercept form of the line.

23. $y = -\frac{3}{4}x - \frac{1}{4}$

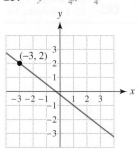

24. $y = \frac{1}{4}x - \frac{11}{4}$

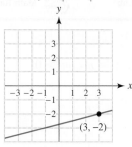

25. $y = \frac{1}{3}x + \frac{8}{3}$

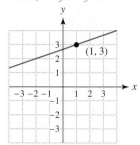

26. $y = -\frac{1}{4}x - \frac{11}{4}$

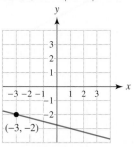

Exercises 27–36: Find a point–slope form of the line satisfying the given conditions.

27. Slope -2, passing through $(2, -3)$
$y = -2(x - 2) - 3$

28. Slope $\frac{1}{2}$, passing through $(-4, 1)$ $y = \frac{1}{2}(x + 4) + 1$

29. Slope 1.3, passing through $(1990, 25)$
$y = 1.3(x - 1990) + 25$

30. Slope 45, passing through $(1999, 103)$
$y = 45(x - 1999) + 103$

31. Passing through $(1, 3)$ and $(-5, -1)$
$y = \frac{2}{3}(x - 1) + 3$ or $y = \frac{2}{3}(x + 5) - 1$

32. Passing through $(-2, 4)$ and $(3, -1)$
$y = -(x + 2) + 4$ or $y = -(x - 3) - 1$

33. Passing through $(1980, 5)$ and $(2000, 45)$
$y = 2(x - 1980) + 5$ or $y = 2(x - 2000) + 45$

34. Passing through $(1990, 50)$ and $(2000, -10)$
$y = -6(x - 1990) + 50$ or $y = -6(x - 2000) - 10$

35. Passing through $(6, 0)$ and $(0, 4)$
$y = -\frac{2}{3}(x - 6) + 0$ or $y = -\frac{2}{3}(x - 0) + 4$

36. Passing through $(1980, 16)$ and $(2000, 66)$
$y = \frac{5}{2}(x - 1980) + 16$ or $y = \frac{5}{2}(x - 2000) + 66$

Exercises 37–42: Write the equation in slope–intercept form.

37. $y = 2(x - 1) - 2$ $y = 2x - 4$

38. $y = -3(x + 2) + 5$ $y = -3x - 1$

39. $y = \frac{1}{2}(x + 4) + 1$ $y = \frac{1}{2}x + 3$

40. $y = -\frac{2}{3}(x - 3) - 6$ $y = -\frac{2}{3}x - 4$

41. $y = 22(x - 1.5) - 10$ $y = 22x - 43$

42. $y = -30(x + 3) + 106$ $y = -30x + 16$

Exercises 43–52: Find the slope–intercept form of the line satisfying the given conditions.

43. Slope $-\frac{1}{3}$, passing through $(0, -5)$ $y = -\frac{1}{3}x - 5$

44. Slope 5, passing through $(-1, 4)$ $y = 5x + 9$

45. Passing through $(3, -2)$ and $(2, -1)$ $y = -x + 1$

46. Passing through $(8, 3)$ and $(-7, 3)$ $y = 3$

47. x-intercept 2, y-intercept $-\frac{2}{3}$ $y = \frac{1}{3}x - \frac{2}{3}$

48. x-intercept -3, y-intercept 4 $y = \frac{4}{3}x + 4$

49. Parallel to $y = 4x - 2$, passing through $(1, 3)$
$y = 4x - 1$

50. Parallel to $y = -\frac{2}{3}x$, passing through $(0, -10)$
$y = -\frac{2}{3}x - 10$

51. Perpendicular to $y = -\frac{1}{3}x + 4$, passing through $(-3, 5)$ $y = 3x + 14$

52. Perpendicular to $y = \frac{3}{4}(x - 2) + 1$, passing through $(-2, -3)$ $y = -\frac{4}{3}x - \frac{17}{3}$

Exercises 53–58: (Refer to Example 8.) Do the following.

(a) *Find the slope–intercept form of the line perpendicular to the given line, passing through the given point.*

(b) *Graph the two lines.**

53. $y = \frac{1}{2}x$, $(0, 2)$
(a) $y = -2x + 2$

54. $y = -3x$, $(0, -3)$ (a) $y = \frac{1}{3}x - 3$

55. $y = -2x + 1$, $(-1, 2)$ (a) $y = \frac{1}{2}x + \frac{5}{2}$

56. $y = \frac{2}{3}x + 2$, $(-1, 0)$ (a) $y = -\frac{3}{2}x - \frac{3}{2}$

57. $y = -\frac{1}{3}x + 2$, $(1, 1)$ (a) $y = 3x - 2$

58. $y = -\frac{4}{3}x + 2$, $(1, -1)$ (a) $y = \frac{3}{4}x - \frac{7}{4}$

*Answers on page IA-11

60.(a) $y_1 = \frac{1}{3}x + 1$; $y_2 = -3x + 1$ (b) $m_1m_2 = \frac{1}{3}(-3) = -1$

Exercises 59–62: (Refer to Example 9.) Do the following.

(a) *Find the slope–intercept form of each line.*

(b) *Verify that the two lines are perpendicular.*

59.(a) $y_1 = 2x$; $y_2 = -\frac{1}{2}x$

59. (b) $m_1m_2 = 2\left(-\frac{1}{2}\right) = -1$ **60.**

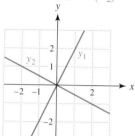

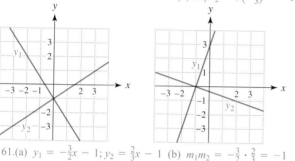

62.(a) $y_1 = 3x + 3$; $y_2 = -\frac{1}{3}x - \frac{1}{3}$

61. **62.** (b) $m_1m_2 = 3\left(-\frac{1}{3}\right) = -1$

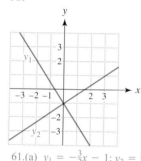

61.(a) $y_1 = -\frac{3}{2}x - 1$; $y_2 = \frac{2}{3}x - 1$ (b) $m_1m_2 = -\frac{3}{2} \cdot \frac{2}{3} = -1$

Exercises 63–70: Find an equation of a line satisfying the given conditions.

63. Vertical, passing through $(-1, 6)$ $x = -1$

64. Vertical, passing through $(2, -7)$ $x = 2$

65. Horizontal, passing through $\left(\frac{3}{4}, -\frac{5}{6}\right)$ $y = -\frac{5}{6}$

66. Horizontal, passing through $(5.1, 6.2)$ $y = 6.2$

67. Perpendicular to $y = \frac{1}{2}$, passing through $(4, -9)$ $x = 4$

68. Perpendicular to $x = 2$, passing through $(3, 4)$ $y = 4$

69. Parallel to $x = 4$, passing through $\left(-\frac{2}{3}, \frac{1}{2}\right)$ $x = -\frac{2}{3}$

70. Parallel to $y = -2.1$, passing through $(7.6, 3.5)$ $y = 3.5$

Exercises 71–74: Decide whether the points in the table lie on a line. If they do, find the slope–intercept form of the line.   Yes; $y = 4x - 8$

71.

x	1	2	3	4
y	-4	0	4	8

72.   No

x	-1	0	1	2
y	8	5	4	1

73.   No

x	-3	0	3	6
y	4	8	14	18

74.   Yes; $y = \frac{3}{2}x - 3$

x	-2	2	4	6
y	-6	0	3	6

GRAPHICAL INTERPRETATION

75. *Distance and Speed*   A person is driving a car along a straight road. The graph shows the distance y in miles that the driver is from home after x hours.

(a) Is the person traveling toward or away from home?   Away

(b) The graph passes through $(1, 35)$ and $(3, 95)$. Discuss the meaning of these points.

(c) Find the slope–intercept form of the line. Interpret the slope as a rate of change.

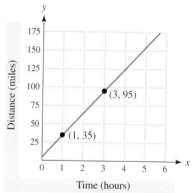

(b) After 1 hour the person is 35 miles from home. After 3 hours the person is 95 miles from home. (c) $y = 30x + 5$; the person is traveling at 30 mph.

76. *Water Flow*   The graph on the next page shows the amount of water y in an 80-gallon tank after x minutes have elapsed.

(a) Is water entering or leaving the tank? How much water is in the tank after 3 minutes?   Leaving; 50 gal

(b) Find the x- and y-intercepts. Explain their meanings. x-int: 8; y-int: 80; the tank is empty after 8 min and has 80 gal initially.

(c) Find a slope–intercept form of the line. Interpret the slope as a rate of change.

(d) Let $y = f(x)$. What are the domain and range of f?

(c) $y = -10x + 80$; water is leaving the tank at 10 gallons per minute.

(d) D: $0 \le x \le 8$

  R: $0 \le y \le 80$

78.(b) Zero tons of rock would have no cost.
78.(d) The cost of the rock is $24 per ton.

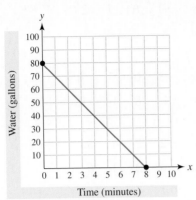

Time (minutes)

77.(a) Two acres have 100 people and 4 acres have 200 people, on average.
77.(b) A zero-acre parcel has no people.

77. U.S. Population Density   The graph illustrates the average number of people living on parcels of land of various sizes in 1960.

(a) The graph passes through the points (2, 100) and (4, 200). Discuss the meaning of these points.

(b) Explain why it is reasonable for the graph to pass through the point (0, 0).

(c) Find the slope–intercept form of the line. $y = 50x$

(d) Interpret the slope as a rate of change.

(e) Write the equation of this line as a linear function P that outputs the average number of people living on x acres of land. $P(x) = 50x$

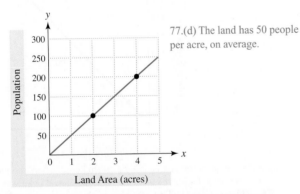

Land Area (acres)

77.(d) The land has 50 people per acre, on average.

78. (a) Two tons of rock cost $48, and five tons of rock cost $120.

78. Cost of Rock   The graph at the top of the next column shows the cost of purchasing landscape rock.

(a) The graph passes through the points (2, 48) and (5, 120). Discuss the meaning of these points.

(b) Explain why it is reasonable for the graph to pass through the point (0, 0).

(c) Find the slope–intercept form of the line. $y = 24x$

(d) Interpret the slope as a rate of change.

(e) Write the equation of this line as a linear function C that outputs the cost of x tons of landscape rock. $C(x) = 24x$

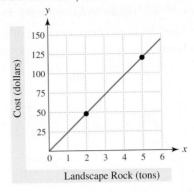

Landscape Rock (tons)

APPLICATIONS

79. Projected Cost of College   The projected annual cost of the average private college or university is shown in the table. This cost includes tuition, fees, room, and board.

Year	2003	2007
Cost	$25,000	$37,000

Source: Cerulli Associates.

$y = 3000x - 5,984,000$

(a) Find the slope–intercept form of a line that passes through these two data points.

(b) Interpret the slope as a rate of change.

(c) Estimate the annual cost of private college in 2005. $31,000

(b) The cost is increasing by $3000 per year.

80. Western Population   In 1950 the western region of the United States had a population of 20 million, and in 2000 it was 63 million.   (**Source:** Bureau of the Census.)

(a) Find a function f defined by

$$f(x) = mx + b, \quad f(x) = 0.86x - 1657$$

which models this population during year x.

(b) Use f to estimate this population in 1960 and 2010.
1960: 28.6 million; 2010: 71.6 million

(c) Estimate this population in 1900 and discuss your result. -23 million; this answer has no meaning.

Exercises 81–84: Modeling Data   *Determine* $f(x) = mx + b$ *so that* f *models the data, where* x *is the year. Then use* $f(x)$ *to make the estimate asked for.*

81. Projected Chicken Consumption   In 2005 the average American will eat 57 pounds of chicken and in 2010 this amount will increase to 60 pounds. Estimate chicken consumption in 2008.   (**Source:** Department of Agriculture.) $f(x) = 0.6x - 1146$; 58.8 lb

82. *Internet* In 2000 the average American spent 9 hours per week on the Internet and in 2002 this time increased to 11 hours per week. Estimate the time spent on the Internet in 2005. (*Source:* UCLA Center for Communication Policy.) $f(x) = x - 1991$; 14 hr per week

83. *Life Expectancy* The life expectancy for a baby born in 1900 was 48 years and in 2000 it was 77 years. Estimate the life expectancy in 1970.
(*Source:* Bureau of the Census.) $f(x) = 0.29x - 503$; 68.3 yr

84. *HIV Infections* In 1994 about 22,000 Americans became infected with HIV. In 1999 this number was about 15,000. Estimate the number of infections in 1996. (*Source:* Centers for Disease Control and Prevention.) $f(x) = -1400x + 2,813,600$; 19,200

Exercises 85–88: Modeling Data (Refer to Example 5.) *Find the slope–intercept form of a line that models the data. Because the data are not exactly linear, answers may vary slightly.*

85. $y = 4x - 3$

x	1	2	3	4
y	1	4	10	13

86. $y = -2x + 5$

x	1	3	5	7
y	3	0	-5	-10

87. $y = -3.5x + 11.5$

x	1	2	3	4	5
y	8	3	0	-1	-6

88. $y = 1.375x - 8.75$

x	10	20	30	40	50
y	5	20	30	50	60

Exercises 89–92: Modeling Data (Refer to Example 5.) *Find the slope–intercept form of a line that models the data. The data may not be exactly linear, so answers may vary.*

89. Toyota Vehicles Sold (millions) $y = 0.1x - 198.4$

x	1998	1999	2000	2001	2002
y	1.4	1.5	1.6	1.7	1.8

Source: Autodata.

90. Projected Basic Cable Costs (dollars) $y = x - 1991.75$

x	2001	2003	2006
y	9.25	11.25	14.25

Source: Morgan Stanley.

91. Worldwide Cigarette Consumption (trillions)

x	1950	1960	1970	1980	1990
y	1.7	2.2	3.1	4.4	5.4

Source: Department of Agriculture. $y = 0.09x - 173.8$

92. Projected Online Betting Losses ($ billions)

x	2002	2003	2004	2005	2006
y	4.0	6.1	8.3	10.4	12.6

Source: Christiansen Capital Advisors. $y = 2.15x - 4300.3$

93. *Cost of Driving* The cost of driving a car includes both fixed costs and mileage costs. Assume that it costs $189.20 per month for insurance and car payments and it costs $0.30 per mile for gasoline, oil, and routine maintenance.
(a) Find values for a and b so that $f(x) = ax + b$ models the monthly cost of driving the car x miles. $a = 0.30, b = 189.20$
(b) What does the y-intercept on the graph of f represent? The fixed cost of owning the car.

94. *HIV Infection Rates* In 1999, there were an estimated 24 million HIV infections worldwide, with an annual infection rate of 5.4 million.
(*Source:* Centers for Disease Control and Prevention.)
(a) Find values for m, x_1, and y_1 so that $f(x) = m(x - x_1) + y_1$ models the number of HIV infections in year x.
(b) Estimate the number of HIV infections in 2003.
(a) $m = 5.4$; $x_1 = 1999$; $y_1 = 24$ (b) 45.6 million

95. *State and Federal Inmates* From 1988 to 1995, state and federal prison inmates in thousands can be modeled by
$$f(x) = 70(x - 1988) + 628,$$
where x is the year. (*Source:* Department of Justice.)
(a) Find the number of inmates in 1988. 628,000
(b) Graph f in the viewing rectangle [1988, 1995, 1] by [600, 1200, 100].*
(c) What is the slope of the graph of f? Interpret the slope as a rate of change.
70; the number of inmates is increasing by 70,000 per year.

*Answers on page IA-11

96. *Municipal Waste*   From 1960 to 1995, municipal solid waste in millions of tons can be modeled by

$$f(x) = 3.4(x - 1960) + 87.8,$$

where x is the year.   (*Source:* EPA.)

(a) Find the tons of waste in 1960.   87.8 million tons

(b) Graph f in the viewing rectangle [1960, 1995, 5] by [60, 220, 20]. *

(c) What is the slope of the graph of f? Interpret the slope as a rate of change.
     3.4; solid waste is increasing by 3.4 million tons per year.

97. *U.S. Population*   The population for selected years is shown in the table.

Year	1970	1980	1990	2000
Population (millions)	203	227	249	281

Source: Bureau of the Census.

(a) Make a scatterplot of the data. *

(b) Find values for m, x_1, and y_1 so that

$$f(x) = m(x - x_1) + y_1$$

models the data.   (b) $m = 2.6$; $x_1 = 1970$; $y_1 = 203$; answers may vary.

(c) Use f to estimate the population in 2010.
     307 million; answers may vary.

98. *Women in Politics*   The following table lists percentages of women in state legislatures.

Year	1991	1995	2000
Percent	18.3	20.7	23.5

Source: National Women's Political Caucus.
   (a) $m = 0.6$; $x_1 = 1991$; $y_1 = 18.3$;   answers may vary.

(a) Find values for m, x_1, and y_1 so that

$$f(x) = m(x - x_1) + y_1$$

models these data.

(b) Assuming that current trends continue, estimate the percentage of women in state legislatures in 2005.   26.7; answers may vary.

WRITING ABOUT MATHEMATICS

99. Explain how you can recognize equations of parallel lines. How can you recognize equations of perpendicular lines?

100. Suppose that some real data can be modeled by a linear function f. Explain what the slope of the graph of f indicates about the data.

CHECKING BASIC CONCEPTS   SECTIONS 2.3 AND 2.4

1. Find the slope and a point on each line.
  (a) $y = -3(x - 5) + 7$ $m = -3$; (5, 7); answers may vary.
  (b) $y = 10$ $m = 0$; (1, 10); answers may vary.
  (c) $x = -5$ m is undefined; (−5, 0); answers may vary.
  (d) $y = 5x + 3$ $m = 5$; (0, 3); answers may vary.

2. (a) Calculate the slope of the line passing through the points $(2, -4)$ and $(5, 2)$.   2
  (b) Find a point–slope form and the slope–intercept form of the line.
  (c) Find the x-intercept and the y-intercept of the line. x-int: 4; y-int: −8

  (b) $y = 2(x - 2) - 4$ or $y = 2(x - 5) + 2$; $y = 2x - 8$

3. The following graph shows the distance that a car is from home after x hours.   Toward home
  (a) Is the car moving toward or away from home?
  (b) Find the slope of the line. Interpret the slope as a rate of change.
  (c) Find the x-intercept and the y-intercept. Explain the meaning of each.

(d) Determine a and b so that

$$f(x) = ax + b$$

models this situation. $a = -50, b = 250$

(e) Give the domain and range of f.
     $D: 0 \le x \le 5$; $R: 0 \le y \le 250$

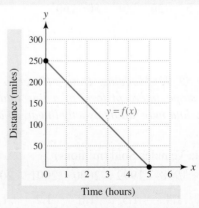

(b) −50; the car is moving toward home at 50 mph.

(c) x-int: 5, after 5 hours the driver is home; y-int: 250, the driver is initially 250 miles from home.

4. Find the equation of a vertical line and the equation of a horizontal line passing through $(-2, 5)$.

$x = -2; y = 5$

5. Find equations of lines that are perpendicular and parallel to $y = -\frac{1}{2}x + 3$, passing through $(2, -4)$. $y = 2x - 8; y = -\frac{1}{2}x - 3$

2 Summary

Section 2.1 Functions and Their Representations

Function   A function is a set of ordered pairs (x, y), where each x-value corresponds to exactly one y-value. A function takes a valid input x and computes exactly one output y, forming the ordered pair (x, y).

Domain and Range   The domain D is the set of all x-values, and the range R is the set of all y-values.

Examples: $f = \{(1, 2), (2, 3), (3, 3)\}$ has $D = \{1, 2, 3\}$ and $R = \{2, 3\}$.

$f(x) = x^2$ has domain all real numbers and range $y \geq 0$. (See the following graph.)

Function Notation $y = f(x)$ and is read "y equals f of x."

Example: $f(x) = \frac{2x}{x - 1}$ implies that $f(3) = \frac{2 \cdot 3}{3 - 1} = \frac{6}{2} = 3$.

Function Representations   A function can be represented symbolically, numerically, graphically, or verbally.

Symbolic Representation $f(x) = x^2$

Numerical Representation

x	y
-2	4
-1	1
0	0
1	1
2	4

Graphical Representation

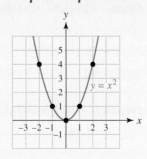

Verbal Representation f computes the square of the input x.

Vertical Line Test   If every vertical line intersects a graph at most once, then the graph represents a function.

Section 2.2   *Linear Functions*

Linear Function   A linear function can be represented by $f(x) = ax + b$. Its graph is a (straight) line. For each unit increase in x, $f(x)$ changes by an amount equal to a.

Example: $f(x) = 2x - 1$ represents a linear function with $a = 2$ and $b = -1$.

Numerical Representation

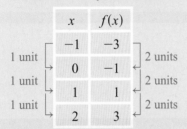

Graphical Representation

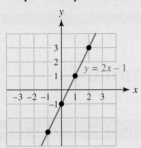

Each 1-unit increase in x results in a 2-unit increase in $f(x)$.

Modeling Data with Linear Functions   When data have a constant rate of change, they can be modeled by $f(x) = ax + b$. The constant a represents the rate of change, and the constant b represents the initial amount or the value when $x = 0$. That is,

$$f(x) = (\textbf{constant rate of change})x + (\textbf{initial amount}).$$

Example: In the following table, the y-values decrease by 3 units for each unit increase in x. Also, when $x = 0$, $y = 4$. Thus the data are modeled by $f(x) = -3x + 4$.

x	-2	-1	0	1	2
y	10	7	4	1	-2

Section 2.3   *The Slope of a Line*

Slope   The slope m of the line passing through the points (x_1, y_1) and (x_2, y_2) is

$$m = \frac{\text{rise}}{\text{run}} = \frac{y_2 - y_1}{x_2 - x_1},$$

where $x_1 \neq x_2$.

Example: The slope of the line connecting $(-2, 3)$ and $(4, 0)$ is

$$m = \frac{0 - 3}{4 - (-2)} = \frac{-3}{6} = -\frac{1}{2}.$$

Slope–Intercept Form   The equation $y = mx + b$ gives the slope m and y-intercept b of a line.

Example: The graph of $y = -\frac{1}{2}x + 1$ has slope $-\frac{1}{2}$ and y-intercept 1.

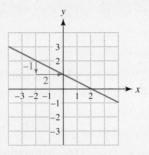

x	-2	0	2	4
y	2	1	0	-1

y decreases by 1 unit for each 2-unit increase in x.

Slope as a Rate of Change   The slope of the graph of a linear function indicates how fast the function is increasing or decreasing.

Example: If $V(t) = 10t$ models the volume of water in a tank in gallons after t minutes, water is *entering* the tank at 10 gallons per minute.

Section 2.4   *Equations of Lines and Linear Models*

Point–Slope Form

$$y = m(x - x_1) + y_1 \quad \text{or} \quad y - y_1 = m(x - x_1),$$

where m is the slope and (x_1, y_1) is a point on the line.

Example: The point–slope form of the line with slope **4** passing through $(2, -3)$ is

$$y = 4(x - 2) - 3.$$

Equations of Horizontal and Vertical Lines

$$y = b \qquad \text{(horizontal)}$$
$$x = h \qquad \text{(vertical)}$$

Example: The equation of the horizontal line passing through $(2, 3)$ is $y = 3$. The equation of the vertical line passing through $(2, 3)$ is $x = 2$.

Parallel Lines

Two lines with the same slope are parallel.

Two nonvertical parallel lines have the same slope.

Example: The lines $y = 2x - 1$ and $y = 2x + 3$ are parallel with slope **2**.

Perpendicular Lines   Two lines with nonzero slopes m_1 and m_2 are perpendicular if $m_1 m_2 = -1$. If two lines have slopes m_1 and m_2 such that $m_1 \cdot m_2 = -1$, then they are perpendicular.

Example: The lines $y = 2x - 1$ and $y = -\frac{1}{2}x + 3$ are perpendicular because the product of their slopes equals -1. That is, $2\left(-\frac{1}{2}\right) = -1$.

CHAPTER 2 Review Exercises

SECTION 2.1

Exercises 1–4: Evaluate f(x) for the given values of x.

1. $f(x) = 3x - 1$ $x = -2, \frac{1}{3}$ $-7; 0$

2. $f(x) = 5 - 3x^2$ $x = -3, 1$ $-22; 2$

3. $f(x) = \sqrt{x} - 2$ $x = 0, 9$ $-2; 1$

4. $f(x) = 5$ $x = -5, \frac{7}{5}$ $5; 5$

Exercises 5 and 6: Do the following.

  (a) *Write a symbolic representation (formula) for the function described.*

  (b) *Evaluate the function for the input 5 and interpret the result.*

5. Function P computes the number of pints in q quarts.
  (a) $P(q) = 2q$ (b) $P(5) = 10$; there are 10 pints in 5 quarts.

6. Function f computes 3 less than 4 times a number x.
  (a) $f(x) = 4x - 3$ (b) $f(5) = 17$; three less than four times 5 is 17.

7. If $f(3) = -2$, then the point _____ lies on the graph of f. $(3, -2)$

8. If $(4, -6)$ lies on the graph of f, then $f(\underline{\quad}) =$ _____. $4; -6$

Exercises 9–12:* Sketch a graph of f.

9. $f(x) = -2x$ **10.** $f(x) = \frac{1}{2}x - \frac{3}{2}$

11. $f(x) = x^2 - 1$ **12.** $f(x) = \sqrt{x + 1}$

Exercises 13 and 14: Use the graph of f to evaluate the given expressions.

13. $f(0)$ and $f(-3)$ $1; 4$ **14.** $f(-2)$ and $f(1)$ $1; -2$

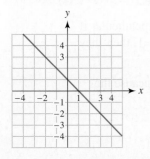
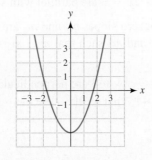

15. Evaluate $f(-1)$ and $f(3)$. $7; -1$

x	-1	1	3	5
$f(x)$	7	3	-1	-5

16. A function f is represented verbally by "Multiply the input x by 3 and then subtract 2." Give numerical, symbolic, and graphical representations for f. Let $x = -3, -2, -1, \ldots, 3$ in the table, and let $-3 \le x \le 3$ for the graph.
  Numerical:* Symbolic: $f(x) = 3x - 2$ Graphical:*

Exercises 17 and 18: Use the graph of f to estimate its domain and range.

17.   D: All real numbers   **18.**   D: $-4 \le x \le 4$
      R: $y \le 4$ R: $-4 \le y \le 0$

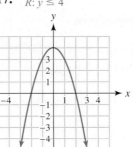
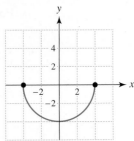

Exercises 19 and 20: Determine whether the graph represents a function.

19.   Yes   **20.**   No

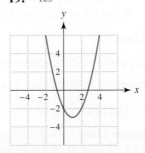
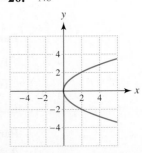

Exercises 21 and 22: Find the domain and range of S. Then state whether S defines a function.

21. $S = \{(-3, 4), (-1, 4), (2, 3), (4, -1)\}$
  $D = \{-3, -1, 2, 4\}, R = \{-1, 3, 4\}$; yes

22. $S = \{(-1, 5), (0, 3), (1, -2), (-1, 2), (2, 4)\}$
  $D = \{-1, 0, 1, 2\}, R = \{-2, 2, 3, 4, 5\}$; no   *Answers on page IA-11

Exercises 23–26: Find the domain.

All real numbers

23. $f(x) = -3x + 7$ **24.** $f(x) = \sqrt{x}$ $x \geq 0$

25. $f(x) = \frac{3}{x}$ $x \neq 0$ **26.** $f(x) = x^2 + 2$ All real numbers

SECTION 2.2

Exercises 27 and 28: Determine whether the graph represents a linear function.

27. No

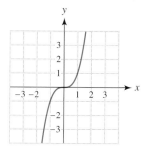

28. Yes

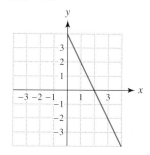

Exercises 29–32: Determine whether f is a linear function. If f is linear, give values for a and b so that f may be expressed as $f(x) = ax + b$.   29. Yes; $a = -4, b = 5$

29. $f(x) = -4x + 5$ **30.** $f(x) = 7 - x$ Yes; $a = -1, b = 7$

31. $f(x) = \sqrt{x}$ No   **32.** $f(x) = 6$ Yes; $a = 0, b = 6$

Exercises 33 and 34: Use the table to determine whether $f(x)$ could represent a linear function. If it could, write the formula for f in the form $f(x) = ax + b$.

33.

x	0	2	4	6
$f(x)$	−3	0	3	6

Yes; $f(x) = \frac{3}{2}x - 3$

34.

x	−1	0	1	2
$f(x)$	−5	0	10	15

No

35. Evaluate $f(x) = \frac{1}{2}x + 3$ at $x = -4$. 1

36. Use the graph to evaluate $f(-2)$ and $f(1)$.

$f(-2) = -3; f(1) = 0$

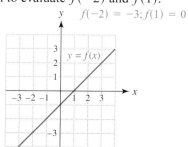

Exercises 37–40: Sketch a graph of $y = f(x)$.*

37. $f(x) = x + 1$ **38.** $f(x) = 1 - 2x$

39. $f(x) = -\frac{1}{3}x$ **40.** $f(x) = -1$

SECTION 2.3

Exercises 41–44: Determine the slope of the line in the graph.

41. −2

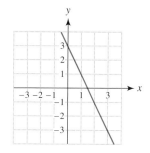

42. 0

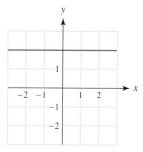

43. $\frac{1}{3}$

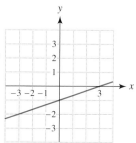

44. Undefined

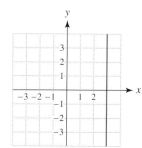

Exercises 45–48: Calculate the slope of the line passing through the given points.

45. $(-1, 2), (3, 8)$ $\frac{3}{2}$ **46.** $\left(-3, \frac{5}{2}\right), \left(1, -\frac{1}{2}\right)$ $-\frac{3}{4}$

47. $(3, -4), (5, -4)$ 0   **48.** $(-2, 6), (-2, 8)$ Undefined

49. Sketch a line passing through $(1, 2)$ with slope $m = -\frac{1}{2}$.*

50. Find the slope and y-intercept of the line $y = -\frac{2}{3}x$. Graph the line.* $-\frac{2}{3}; 0$

51. Use the graph to express the line in slope–intercept form.

$y = -3x + 1$

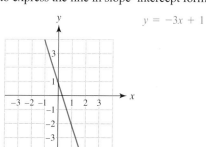

*Answers on page IA-12

52. Write the slope–intercept form of a line passing through $(0, 2)$ and $(-1, 0)$. $\ y = 2x + 2$

53. Let f be a linear function. Use the table to find the slope and y-intercept of the graph of f. $\ -1; 1$

x	-2	0	3
$f(x)$	3	1	-2

54. The line graph represents the gallons of water in a small swimming pool after x hours.*
   (a) Estimate the slope of each line segment.
   (b) Interpret each slope as a rate of change.
   (c) Describe what happens to the amount of water in the pool.

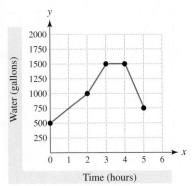
Time (hours)

55. *Sketching a Model*   A distance runner starts at home and runs at a constant speed. After 1.5 hours she is 12 miles from home. She then turns around and runs home at the same speed. Sketch a graph that shows the distance that the runner is from home after x hours.*

56. Let $f(x) = \frac{1}{2}x - 2$.
   (a) Find the slope and y-intercept of the graph of f.   (a) $\frac{1}{2}; -2$
   (b) Sketch a graph of f.*

SECTION 2.4

57. Determine whether the point $(2, 1)$ lies on the graph of $y = \frac{3}{2}x - 2$.   Yes, it does.

58. Let f be a linear function. Find the slope, x-intercept, and y-intercept of the graph of f. $-2; 2; 4$

x	-1	0	1	2
$f(x)$	6	4	2	0

Exercises 59–62: Write the slope–intercept form of a line satisfying the given conditions.

59. x-intercept 2, y-intercept -3 $y = \frac{3}{2}x - 3$

60. Passing through $(-1, 4)$ and $(2, -2)$ $y = -2x + 2$

61. Parallel to $y = 4x - 3$, passing through $\left(-\frac{3}{5}, \frac{1}{5}\right)$

62. Perpendicular to $y = \frac{1}{2}x$, passing through $(-1, 1)$
   $y = -2x - 1$
   61. $y = 4x + \frac{13}{5}$

Exercises 63 and 64: Find the slope–intercept form of the line.

63. $y = -x + 2$

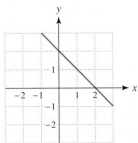

64. $y = 2x - 3$

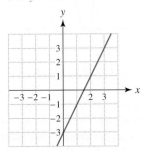

Exercises 65 and 66: Determine whether the given point lies on the line.

65. $(2, -1)$ $\qquad$ $y = -2(x - 1) + 3$ No

66. $\left(4, -\frac{5}{2}\right)$ $\qquad$ $y = \frac{1}{4}(x + 2) - 4$ Yes

Exercises 67 and 68: Find an equation of a line satisfying the given conditions.

67. Vertical, passing through $(-4, 14)$ $x = -4$

68. Horizontal, passing through $\left(\frac{11}{13}, -\frac{7}{13}\right)$ $y = -\frac{7}{13}$

Exercises 69 and 70: Decide whether the points in the table lie on a line. If they do, find the slope–intercept form of the line.

69.

x	1	2	3	4
y	6	7	8	7

They don't.

70.

x	-2	0	2	4
y	1	5	9	13

They do;
$y = 2x + 5$

*Answers on page IA-12

APPLICATIONS

71. *U.S. Population* The following line graph shows the population of the United States in millions.*
(a) Find the slope of each line segment.
(b) Interpret each slope as a rate of change.

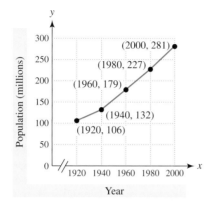

72. *Flow Rates* A water tank has an inlet pipe with a flow rate of 10 gallons per minute and an outlet pipe with a flow rate of 6 gallons per minute. A pipe can be either completely closed or open. The following graph shows the number of gallons of water in the tank after x minutes. Interpret the graph.*

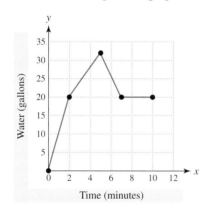

73. *Age at First Marriage* The median age at the first marriage for men from 1890 to 1960 can be modeled by $f(x) = -0.0492x + 119.1$, where x is the year.
(*Source:* National Center of Health Statistics.)
(a) Find the median age in 1910. About 25.1
(b) Graph f in [1885, 1965, 10] by [22, 26, 1]. What happened to the median age during this time period?* Decreased
(c) What is the slope of the graph of f? Interpret the slope as a rate of change.
−0.0492; the median age decreased by about 0.0492 year per year.

74. *Marriages* From 1980 to 1997 the number of U.S. marriages in millions could be modeled by the formula $f(x) = 2.4$, where x is the year. 2.4 million
(a) Estimate the number of marriages in 1991.
(b) What information does f give about the number of marriages during this time period?
The number of marriages each year did not change.

75. *Fat Grams* One cup of whole milk contains 8 grams of fat.
(a) Give a formula for $f(x)$ that calculates the number of fat grams in x cups of milk. $f(x) = 8x$
(b) What is the slope of the graph of f? 8
(c) Interpret the slope as a rate of change.
The total fat increases at a rate of 8g per cup.

76. *Birth Rate* The U.S. birth rate per 1000 people from 1990 through 1997 is shown in the table.

Year	1990	1991	1992	1993
Birth Rate	16.7	16.3	16.0	15.7

Year	1994	1995	1996	1997
Birth Rate	15.3	14.8	14.7	14.5

Source: Bureau of the Census.

(a) Make a scatterplot of the data.*
(b) Model the data with $f(x) = mx + b$, where x is the year. Answers may vary. $f(x) = -0.31x + 633.6$
(c) Use f to estimate the birth rate in 2000.
About 13.6 per 1000 people; answers may vary.

77. *Unhealthy Air Quality* The Environmental Protection Agency (EPA) monitors air quality in U.S. cities. The function f, represented by the following table, gives the annual number of days with unhealthy air quality in Los Angeles, California, from 1995 through 1999. (b) $D = \{1995, 1996, 1997, 1998, 1999\}$, $R = \{27, 56, 60, 94, 113\}$

x	1995	1996	1997	1998	1999
$f(x)$	113	94	60	56	27

Source: Environmental Protection Agency.
(a) 113; in 1995, there were 113 unhealthy days.
(a) Find $f(1995)$ and interpret your result.
(b) Identify the domain and range of f.
(c) Discuss the trend of air pollution in Los Angeles.
The number of unhealthy days is decreasing.

*Answers on page IA-12

78. *Temperature Scales*   The following table shows equivalent temperatures in degrees Celsius and degrees Fahrenheit.   (b) $f(x) = \frac{9}{5}x + 32$; a 1°C change equals a $\frac{9}{5}$°F change.

°C	−40	0	15	35	100
°F	−40	32	59	95	212

    (a) Plot the data. Let the *x*-axis correspond to the Celsius temperature and the *y*-axis correspond to the Fahrenheit temperature. What type of relation exists between the data?   Linear*

(b) Find $f(x) = ax + b$ so that f receives the Celsius temperature *x* as input and outputs the corresponding Fahrenheit temperature. Interpret the slope of the graph of *f*.

(c) If the temperature is 20°C, what is this temperature in degrees Fahrenheit?   68°F

79. *Graphical Model*   A 500-gallon water tank is initially full and then emptied at a constant rate of 50 gallons per minute. Ten minutes after the tank is empty, it is filled by a pump that outputs 25 gallons per minute. Sketch a graph that depicts the amount of water in the tank after *x* minutes.*

80. *HIV Infections*   In 2000, there were about 875,000 AIDS cases in the United States, with an annual infection rate of 25,000.   (*Source:* Centers for Disease Control and Prevention.)   (a) $f(x) = 25,000(x − 2000) + 875,000$

(a) Assuming that this trend continues, find $f(x) = m(x − x_1) + y_1$ so that f models the number of AIDS cases during year *x*.

(b) Find $f(2004)$ and interpret the result.
975,000; total (cumulative) number of U.S. AIDS cases reported in 2004

Exercises 81–86: Modeling   Match the situation to the graph (a.–f.) that models it best.

81. The total federal debt *y* from 1985 to 1990.   b.

82. The distance *y* from New York City to Seattle, Washington, during year *x*.   e.

83. The amount of money *y* earned working for *x* hours at a fixed hourly rate.   a.

84. The sales of 8-millimeter movie projectors from 1970 to 1990.   d.

85. The yearly average temperature *y* in degrees Celsius at the South Pole for year *x*.   f.

86. The height above sea level of a rocket launched from a submarine during the first minute of the rocket's flight.   c.

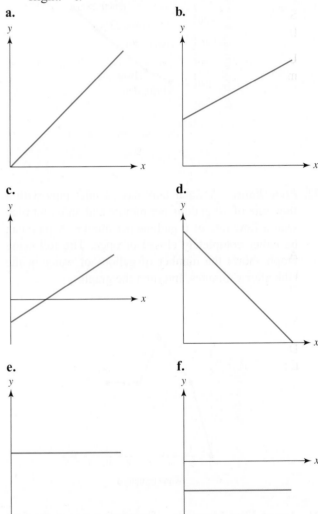

Test

1. Evaluate $f(4)$ if $f(x) = 3x^2 - \sqrt{x}$. 46

2. Sketch a graph of f.*
   (a) $f(x) = -2x + 1$ **(b)** $f(x) = x^2 + 1$

3. Use the graph of f to evaluate $f(-3)$ and $f(0)$. Determine the domain and range of f. 0; −3

   D: $-3 \leq x \leq 3$;
   R: $-3 \leq y \leq 0$

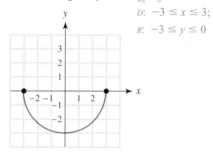

4. A function f is represented verbally by "Square the input x and then subtract 5." Give symbolic, numerical, and graphical representations of f. Let $x = -3, -2, -1, \ldots, 3$ in the numerical representation (table) and let $-3 \leq x \leq 3$ for the graph. $f(x) = x^2 - 5$;*

5. Determine whether the graph represents a function. Explain your reasoning. No, it fails the vertical line test.

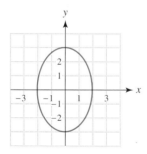

6. Determine the slope of the line shown in the graph. $-\frac{1}{2}$

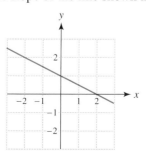

12.(b) From 1970 to 1980 beneficiaries increased by 0.4 million/yr. From 1980 to 1990 there was no change. From 1990 to 2000 beneficiaries decreased by 0.4 million/yr; answers may vary slightly.

7. Find the slope–intercept form of the line passing through the points $(1, -2)$ and $\left(-5, \frac{3}{2}\right)$. $y = -\frac{7}{12}x - \frac{17}{12}$

8. Let f be a linear function. Find the slope, x-intercept, and y-intercept of the graph of f. −2; 2; 4

x	−2	−1	0	2
$f(x)$	8	6	4	0

9. Give the slope–intercept form of a line parallel to $y = 1 - 3x$, passing through $\left(\frac{1}{3}, 2\right)$. $y = -3x + 3$

10. Find the slope–intercept form for the line shown in the graph. Then find the equation of a line that passes through the origin and is perpendicular to the given line. $y = \frac{2}{3}x - 2$; $y = -\frac{3}{2}x$

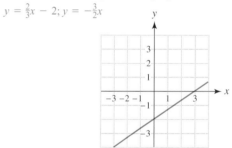

11. Find an equation of a vertical line passing through the point $\left(\frac{2}{3}, -\frac{1}{7}\right)$. $x = \frac{2}{3}$

12. *Modeling* The line graph shows the number of welfare beneficiaries in millions for selected years. (*Source:* Administration for Children and Families.)
    (a) Find the slope of each line segment.
    (b) Interpret each slope as a rate of change.

    (a) $m_1 = 0.4$, $m_2 = 0$, $m_3 = -0.4$

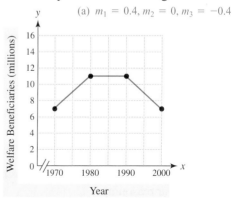

*Answers on page IA-13

13. *Distance from Home*   Starting at home, a driver travels away from home on a straight highway for 2 hours at 60 miles per hour, stops for 1 hour, and then drives home at 40 miles per hour. Sketch a graph that shows the distance between the driver and home.*

 14. *Memorial Day Travelers*   The table shows the number of travelers on Memorial Day for selected years.

Year	1990	1992	1994
Travelers (millions)	24.8	27.0	29.2

Year	1996	1998	2000
Travelers (millions)	30.3	32.0	34.4

Source: American Automobile Association.

(a) Make a scatterplot of the data.*

(b) Find values for m, x_1, and y_1 so that $f(x) = m(x - x_1) + y_1$ models these data.

(c) Use f to estimate the number of travelers in 2002.
About 36.3 million

(b) $m = 0.96$, $x_1 = 1990$, $y_1 = 24.8$; answers may vary.

CHAPTER

2 Extended and Discovery Exercises

1.(b) Tank B; it flows faster at first, so it empties the first half of the tank faster than a pump removing water at a constant rate.

1. *Developing a Model*   Two identical cylindrical tanks, A and B, each contain 100 gallons of water. Tank A has a pump that begins removing water at a constant rate of 8 gallons per minute. Tank B has a plug removed from its bottom and water begins to flow out—faster at first and then more slowly.

   (a) Assuming that the tanks become empty at the same time, sketch a graph that models the amount of water in each tank. Explain your graphs.*

   (b) Which tank is half empty first? Explain.

2. *Modeling Real Data*   Per capita personal incomes in the United States from 1990 through 2000 are listed in the following table.

Year	1990	1991	1992	1993
Income	$18,666	$19,091	$20,105	$20,800

Year	1994	1995	1996	2000
Income	$21,809	$23,359	$24,436	$29,676

Source: Department of Commerce.

   (a) Make a scatterplot of the data.*

   (b) Find a function f that models the data. Explain your reasoning.
   $f(x) = 1100(x - 1990) + 18,000$; answers may vary.

   (c) Use f to estimate per capita personal income in 1998.   About $26,800; answers may vary slightly.

3. *Graphing a Rectangle*   One side of a rectangle has vertices $(0, 0)$ and $(5, 3)$. If the point $(0, 5)$ lies on one side of this rectangle, as shown in the figure, write the equation of each line.

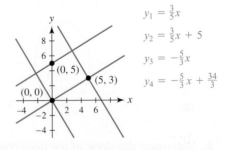

$y_1 = \frac{3}{5}x$

$y_2 = \frac{3}{5}x + 5$

$y_3 = -\frac{5}{3}x$

$y_4 = -\frac{5}{3}x + \frac{34}{3}$

*Exercises 4–6: (Refer to Exercise 3.) Graph the rectangle that satisfies the given conditions. Write the equation of each line.**

4. Vertices $(0, 0)$, $(2, 2)$, and $(1, 3)$

5. Vertices $(1, 1)$, $(5, 1)$, and $(1, 5)$

6. Vertices $(4, 0)$, $(0, 4)$, $(0, -4)$, and $(-4, 0)$

*Answers on page IA-13

7. *Remaining Life Expectancy* The table lists the average *remaining* life expectancy E in years for females at age x.

x (year)	0	10	20	30	40
E (year)	72.3	69.9	60.1	50.4	40.9

x (year)	50	60	70	80
E (year)	31.6	23.1	15.5	9.2

Source: Department of Health and Human Services.

(a) Make a line graph of the data.*

(b) Assume that the graph represents a function f. Calculate the slopes of each line segment and interpret each slope as a rate of change.*

(c) Determine the life expectancy (not the remaining life expectancy) of a 20-year-old woman. What is the life expectancy of a 70-year-old woman? Discuss reasons why these two expectancies are not equal.   80.1 yr, 85.5 yr; a 70-year-old has lived through much of the risk that a 20-year-old must still live through.

8. *Weight of a Small Fish* The figure shows a graph of a function f that models the weight in milligrams of a small fish, *Lebistes reticulatus*, during the first 14 weeks of its life. (*Source:* D. Brown and P. Rothery, *Models in Biology*.)   (a) 7 mg, 105 mg, 158 mg; answers may vary.

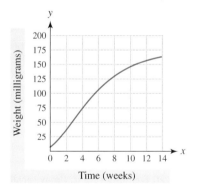

Time (weeks)

(b) 16.3 mg/wk, 8.8 mg/wk

(a) Estimate the weight of the fish when it hatches, at 6 weeks, and at 12 weeks.

(b) If (x_1, y_1) and (x_2, y_2) are points on the graph of a function, the *average rate of change of f from x_1 to x_2* is given by $\frac{y_2 - y_1}{x_2 - x_1}$. Approximate the average rates of change of f from hatching to 6 weeks and from 6 weeks to 12 weeks.

(c) Interpret these rates of change.

(d) During which time period does the fish gain weight the fastest?   The first 6 weeks

(c) The fish gains, on average, 16.3 mg/wk during the first 6 wk and 8.8 mg/wk during the second 6 wk.

9. *Interpreting Carbon Dioxide Levels* Carbon dioxide gas is a greenhouse gas that may cause Earth's climate to warm. Plants absorb carbon dioxide during daylight and release carbon dioxide at night. The burning of fossil fuels, such as gasoline, produces carbon dioxide. At Mauna Loa, Hawaii, atmospheric carbon dioxide levels in parts per million have been measured regularly since 1958. The accompanying figure shows a graph of the carbon dioxide levels between 1960 and 2000. (*Source:* A. Nilsson, *Greenhouse Earth.*)

(a) What is the overall trend in the carbon dioxide levels?   They are increasing.

(b) Discuss what happens to the carbon dioxide levels each year.   They oscillate.

(c) Give an explanation for the shape of this graph.

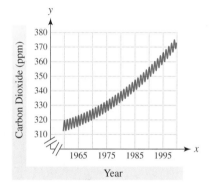

Year

10. *Carbon Dioxide in Alaska* (Refer to Exercise 9.) The atmospheric carbon dioxide levels at Barrow, Alaska, in parts per million from 1970 to 2000 are shown in the accompanying figure.
(*Source:* M. Zeilik, S. Gregory, and D. Smith, *Introductory Astronomy and Astrophysics.*)   Increasing, as in Hawaii, but oscillations are larger.

(a) Compare this graph with the graph in Exercise 9.

(b) Discuss possible reasons for their similarities and differences.

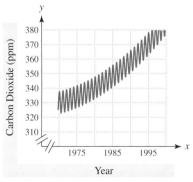

Year

9. (c) Seasonal changes in plant growth affect the carbon dioxide levels slightly due to photosynthesis.

10. (b) The climate in Alaska is more extreme, so the seasonal changes in plant growth are more dramatic. Both increase overall due to the use of fossil fuels and other factors. *Answers on page IA-13

Linear Equations and Inequalities

In this chapter we solve equations both symbolically and visually. A graph contains approximately the same amount of information as a page of text. However, many people find the information in a graph easier to absorb. The reason is that much of the human brain is devoted to processing visual information. The accompanying table lists the approximate age in years of several forms of communication. Note that eyesight has had a considerably longer time to evolve than other forms.

Form of Communication	Age (years)
Eyesight	500,000,000
Oral communication	50,000
Written words	5000
Printed books	500
Television	60
Scientific visualization	20

Say it, I'll forget. Demonstrate it, I may recall.
But if I'm involved, I'll understand.
—Old Chinese Proverb

Sources: M. Friedhoff and W. Benzon, *The Second Computer Revolution: Visualization*;
G. Nielson and B. Shriver, Editors, *Visualization in Scientific Computing.*

3.1 LINEAR EQUATIONS

Equations · Symbolic Solutions · Numerical and Graphical Solutions · Intercepts of a Line

INTRODUCTION

A primary objective of mathematics is solving equations. Billions of dollars are spent each year to solve equations that hold the answers for creating better products. The ability to solve equations has resulted in televisions, CD players, satellites, fiber optics, CAT scans, computers, and accurate weather forecasts. In this section we discuss linear equations and their applications.

EQUATIONS

TEACHING TIP

Emphasize that, after finding a linear function with $a \neq 0$, the student can form a linear equation by setting the formula equal to a number. This step can help explain how equations occur in applications.

In Chapter 2 we discussed modeling data with *linear* functions. Linear functions can also be used to solve time and distance problems. For example, suppose $f(x) = 50x + 100$ models the distance in miles that a car is from the Texas border after x hours. We could use $f(x)$ to determine when the car is 300 miles from the border by solving the equation

$$50x + 100 = 300.$$

This is an example of a *linear equation* in one variable.

LINEAR EQUATION IN ONE VARIABLE

A **linear equation** in one variable is an equation that can be written in the form

$$ax + b = 0,$$

where $a \neq 0$.

TEACHING TIP

Use Figure 3.1 to explain visually why a linear equation has one solution.

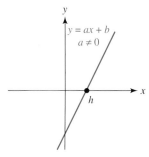

Figure 3.1

Examples of linear equations include

$$2x - 1 = 0, \quad -5x = 10 + x, \quad \text{and} \quad 3x + 8 = 2.$$

Although the second and third equations do not appear to be in the form $ax + b = 0$, they can be transformed by using properties of algebra, which we discuss later in this section.

To *solve* an equation means to find all values for a variable that make the equation a true statement. Such values are called **solutions**, and the set of all solutions is called the **solution set**. For example, substituting **2** for x in the equation $3x - 1 = 5$ results in $3(\mathbf{2}) - 1 = 5$, which is a true statement. The value 2 *satisfies* the equation $3x - 1 = 5$ and is the only solution. The solution set is $\{2\}$. Two equations are *equivalent* if they have the same solution set.

Because every linear equation can be written in the form $ax + b = 0$ with $a \neq 0$, linear equations have one solution. To understand this condition visually, consider the graph of $y = ax + b$ shown in Figure 3.1. Its graph is a line with a nonzero slope that cannot be horizontal. The equation of the x-axis is $y = 0$, so a solution to the linear equation $ax + b = 0$ with $a \neq 0$ corresponds to the x-intercept h of the line $y = ax + b$. Because this line intersects the x-axis once, the equation $ax + b = 0$ has one solution.

═══ MAKING CONNECTIONS ═══

Linear Functions and Equations

A linear function can be written as $f(x) = ax + b$.

A linear equation can be written as $ax + b = 0$ with $a \neq 0$.

SYMBOLIC SOLUTIONS

Linear equations can be solved symbolically. *One advantage of a symbolic method is that the solution is always exact.* To solve an equation symbolically, we write a sequence of equivalent equations, using algebraic properties. For example, to solve $3x - 5 = 0$, we might add 5 to each side of the equation and then divide each side by 3 to obtain $x = \frac{5}{3}$.

$$3x - 5 = 0 \qquad \text{Given equation}$$
$$3x - 5 + 5 = 0 + 5 \qquad \text{Add 5 to each side.}$$
$$3x = 5 \qquad \text{Simplify.}$$
$$\frac{3x}{3} = \frac{5}{3} \qquad \text{Divide each side by 3.}$$
$$x = \frac{5}{3} \qquad \text{Simplify.}$$

The solution is $\frac{5}{3}$.

Adding 5 to each side is an example of the *addition property of equality* and dividing each side by 3 is an example of the *multiplication property of equality*. Note that dividing each side by 3 is equivalent to multiplying each side by $\frac{1}{3}$.

PROPERTIES OF EQUALITY

Addition Property of Equality

If a, b, and c are real numbers, then
$$a = b \quad \text{is equivalent to} \quad a + c = b + c.$$

Multiplication Property of Equality

If a, b, and c are real numbers with $c \neq 0$, then
$$a = b \quad \text{is equivalent to} \quad ac = bc.$$

TEACHING TIP

Point out that, to solve an equation, the same action must be applied to each side of the equation.

The addition property states that an equivalent equation results if the same number is added to (or subtracted from) each side of an equation. Similarly, the multiplication property states that an equivalent equation results if each side of an equation is multiplied (or divided) by the same nonzero number.

EXAMPLE 1   Solving a linear equation symbolically

Solve $2 - \frac{1}{2}x = 1$.

Solution   To solve an equation, we write a sequence of equivalent equations by applying the properties of equality.

$$2 - \frac{1}{2}x = 1 \qquad \text{Given equation}$$

$$-2 + 2 - \frac{1}{2}x = 1 + (-2) \qquad \text{Add } -2 \text{ to each side.}$$

$$-\frac{1}{2}x = -1 \qquad \text{Simplify.}$$

$$-2\left(-\frac{1}{2}x\right) = -1(-2) \qquad \text{Multiply each side by } -2, \text{ the reciprocal of } -\frac{1}{2}.$$

$$x = 2 \qquad \text{Simplify.}$$

The solution is 2.

In the next example we use the distributive property to solve a linear equation.

EXAMPLE 2   Solving a linear equation symbolically

Solve $2(x - 1) = 4 - \frac{1}{2}(4 + x)$. Check your answer.

Solution   We begin by applying the distributive property.

TEACHING TIP

Emphasize the correct use of the distributive property in Example 2. For example, students often forget to multiply both of the terms in $(x - 1)$ by 2.

$$2(x - 1) = 4 - \frac{1}{2}(4 + x) \qquad \text{Given equation}$$

$$2x - 2 = 4 - 2 - \frac{1}{2}x \qquad \text{Distributive property}$$

$$2x - 2 = 2 - \frac{1}{2}x \qquad \text{Simplify.}$$

Next, we transpose (or move) the constant terms to the right and the x-terms to the left.

$$2x - 2 + 2 = 2 - \frac{1}{2}x + 2 \qquad \text{Add 2 to each side.}$$

$$2x = 4 - \frac{1}{2}x \qquad \text{Simplify.}$$

$$2x + \frac{1}{2}x = 4 - \frac{1}{2}x + \frac{1}{2}x \qquad \text{Add } \frac{1}{2}x \text{ to each side.}$$

$$\frac{5}{2}x = 4 \qquad \text{Simplify.}$$

Finally, we multiply by $\frac{2}{5}$, which is the reciprocal of $\frac{5}{2}$.

$$\frac{2}{5} \cdot \frac{5}{2}x = 4 \cdot \frac{2}{5} \qquad \text{Multiply by } \frac{2}{5}.$$

$$x = \frac{8}{5} = 1.6 \qquad \text{Simplify.}$$

The solution is $\frac{8}{5}$.

To check our answer, we substitute $x = \frac{8}{5}$ into the *given* equation.

$$2(x - 1) = 4 - \frac{1}{2}(4 + x) \qquad \text{Given equation}$$

$$2\left(\frac{8}{5} - 1\right) \overset{?}{=} 4 - \frac{1}{2}\left(4 + \frac{8}{5}\right) \qquad \text{Let } x = \frac{8}{5}.$$

$$\frac{16}{5} - 2 \overset{?}{=} 4 - 2 - \frac{4}{5} \qquad \text{Distributive property}$$

$$\frac{6}{5} = \frac{6}{5} \qquad \text{It checks.}$$

Critical Thinking

When you are checking an answer, why is it important to substitute the answer into the *given* equation?

The answer must satisfy the given equation. A different equation could have an error in it.

The equation in Example 2 contained a fraction. Sometimes it is easier to avoid working with fractions. To clear an equation of fractions we can multiply each side by a common denominator.

EXAMPLE 3   Solving equations with fractions or decimals

Solve each equation.

(a) $\frac{1}{3}(2z - 3) - \frac{1}{2}z = -2$ **(b)** $0.4t + 0.3 = 0.75 - 0.05t$

Solution   **(a)** The least common denominator of $\frac{1}{3}$ and $\frac{1}{2}$ is 6, so multiply each side by 6.

$$\frac{1}{3}(2z - 3) - \frac{1}{2}z = -2 \qquad \text{Given equation}$$

$$6\left(\frac{1}{3}(2z - 3) - \frac{1}{2}z\right) = 6(-2) \qquad \text{Multiply each side by 6.}$$

$$2(2z - 3) - 3z = -12 \qquad \text{Distributive property}$$

$$4z - 6 - 3z = -12 \qquad \text{Distributive property}$$

$$z - 6 = -12 \qquad \text{Combine terms.}$$

$$z = -6 \qquad \text{Add 6 to each side.}$$

The solution is -6.

(b) The decimals 0.4, 0.75, 0.3, and 0.05 can be written as $\frac{4}{10}$, $\frac{75}{100}$, $\frac{3}{10}$, and $\frac{5}{100}$. A common denominator is 100, so multiply each side by 100.

$$0.4t + 0.3 = 0.75 - 0.05t \qquad \text{Given equation}$$

$$100(0.4t + 0.3) = 100(0.75 - 0.05t) \qquad \text{Multiply each side by 100.}$$

$$40t + 30 = 75 - 5t \qquad \text{Distributive property}$$

$$45t + 30 = 75 \qquad \text{Add } 5t \text{ to each side.}$$

$$45t = 45 \qquad \text{Subtract 30 from each side.}$$

$$t = 1 \qquad \text{Divide each side by 45.}$$

The solution is 1.

In the next example, we model some real data with a linear function and then use this function to make an estimate.

EXAMPLE 4   Modeling LCD screens

Flat screens or LCD (liquid crystal display) screens are becoming increasingly popular. In 2002 about 30 million LCD screens were manufactured and this number is expected to increase to 90 million in 2006.
(a) Find a linear function that models these data.
(b) Estimate the year when 105 million LCD screens might be manufactured.

Solution   (a) The graph of this linear function must pass through (2002, 30) and (2006, 90). Its slope is

$$m = \frac{90 - 30}{2006 - 2002} = \frac{60}{4} = 15.$$

Using the point (2002, 30) in the point–slope form gives

$$f(x) = 15(x - 2002) + 30.$$

(b) We must solve the equation $f(x) = 105$.

$15(x - 2002) + 30 = 105$	Equation to be solved
$15(x - 2002) = 75$	Subtract 30 from each side.
$x - 2002 = 5$	Divide each side by 15.
$x = 2007$	Add 2002 to each side.

In 2007, 105 million LCD screens might be manufactured.

TEACHING TIP

Although numerical solutions may appear to be "trivial," many students gain a better understanding of what it means to solve an equation by looking at a numerical solution.

NUMERICAL AND GRAPHICAL SOLUTIONS

Linear equations can also be solved numerically (with a table) and graphically. The disadvantage of using a table or graph is that the solution is often an estimate, rather than exact. These two methods are demonstrated in the next example.

EXAMPLE 5   Solving equations numerically and graphically

Solve $2 - \frac{1}{2}x = 1$ numerically and graphically.

Solution   *Numerical Solution*   Begin by constructing a table for the expression $2 - \frac{1}{2}x$, as shown in Table 3.1. This expression equals 1 when $x = 2$. That is, the solution to $2 - \frac{1}{2}x = 1$ is 2.

X	Y₁	
0	2	
1	1.5	
2	1	
3	.5	
4	0	
5	-.5	
6	-1	
Y₁◼2−(1/2)X		

TABLE 3.1   A Numerical Solution

x	0	1	2	3	4	5	6
$2 - \frac{1}{2}x$	2	1.5	1	0.5	0	−0.5	−1

Figure 3.2 A Numerical Solution

In Figure 3.2 a calculator has been used to create the same table.

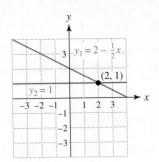

Figure 3.3 Graphical
Solution

Graphical Solution   One way to find a graphical solution is to let y_1 equal the left side of the equation, to let y_2 equal the right side of the equation, and then to graph $y_1 = 2 - \frac{1}{2}x$ and $y_2 = 1$, as shown in Figure 3.3. The graphs intersect at the point $(2, 1)$. We are seeking an x-value that satisfies $2 - \frac{1}{2}x = 1$, so 2 is the solution. Note that the y-value in the ordered pair $(2, 1)$ is 1. This value is ignored because the given equation contains only the variable x. As a result, the solution is *not* 1.

Technology Note: *Finding a Numerical Solution*

Even though the solution to Example 2 is the decimal number 1.6, it is possible to find it numerically. Let

$$Y_1 = 2(X - 1) \quad \text{and} \quad Y_2 = 4 - (1/2)(4 + X)$$

and start incrementing by 1. There is no value where $y_1 = y_2$, as shown in the left-hand figure. However, note that when $x = 1$, $y_1 < y_2$ and when $x = 2$, $y_1 > y_2$. This change indicates that there is a solution between $x = 1$ and $x = 2$. When x is incremented by 0.1, $y_1 = y_2$ when $x = 1.6$, as shown in the right-hand figure.

X	Y₁	Y₂
-2	-6	3
-1	-4	2.5
0	-2	2
1	**0**	**1.5**
2	2	1
3	4	.5
4	6	0

X=1

X	Y₁	Y₂
1.3	.6	1.35
1.4	.8	1.3
1.5	1	1.25
1.6	**1.2**	**1.2**
1.7	1.4	1.15
1.8	1.6	1.1
1.9	1.8	1.05

X=1.6

Many times a graphical solution is an *approximate* solution because it depends on how accurately a graph can be read. To verify that a graphical solution is exact, check it by substituting it in the given equation, as is done in the next two examples.

EXAMPLE 6   Solving a linear equation graphically

Figure 3.4 shows graphs of $y_1 = 2x + 1$ and $y_2 = -x + 4$. Use the graph to solve the equation $2x + 1 = -x + 4$. Check your answer.

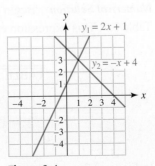

Figure 3.4

Solution   The graphs of y_1 and y_2 intersect at the point (1, 3). Therefore 1 is the solution. We can check this solution by substituting $x = 1$ in the equation.

$$2x + 1 = -x + 4 \qquad \text{Given equation}$$
$$2(1) + 1 \overset{?}{=} -1 + 4 \qquad \text{Let } x = 1.$$
$$3 = 3 \qquad \text{The answer checks.}$$

EXAMPLE 7   **Solving a linear equation graphically**

Solve $3(1 - x) = 2$ graphically.

Solution   We begin by graphing $Y_1 = 3(1 - X)$ and $Y_2 = 2$, as shown in Figure 3.5. Their graphs intersect near the point (0.3333, 2). Because $\frac{1}{3} = 0.\overline{3}$, the solution appears to be $\frac{1}{3}$. Note that this graphical solution is *approximate*. We can verify our result as follows.

TEACHING TIP

Graphical solutions are usually found by setting the left side of the equation equal to y_1, setting the right side of the equation equal to y_2, and then finding the point of intersection.

$$3(1 - x) = 2 \qquad \text{Given equation}$$
$$3\left(1 - \frac{1}{3}\right) \overset{?}{=} 2 \qquad \text{Substitute } x = \tfrac{1}{3}.$$
$$2 = 2 \qquad \text{It checks.}$$

Calculator Help
To find a point of intersection, see the Appendix (page AP-7).

$[-6, 6, 1]$ by $[-4, 4, 1]$

Intersection
X=.33333333 Y=2

Figure 3.5

Technology can be helpful when we are solving an equation that is complicated. In the next example, we solve an application graphically.

EXAMPLE 8   **Solving a linear equation graphically**

From 1985 to 1990, sales of compact discs in millions in the United States can be modeled by $y_1 = 51.6(x - 1985) + 9.1$, and sales of vinyl LP records in millions can be modeled by $y_2 = -31.9(x - 1985) + 167.7$. Estimate graphically the year x when sales of LP records and compact discs were equal. Interpret the slopes of the graphs of y_1 and y_2 as rates of change.   (***Source:*** Recording Industry Association of America.)

Solution   Let $Y_1 = 51.6(X - 1985) + 9.1$ and $Y_2 = -31.9 (X - 1985) + 167.7$, as shown in Figure 3.6(a) on the next page. Their graphs intersect near (1986.9, 107.1), as shown in Figure 3.6(b). An x-value of 1986.9 corresponds to the year that CD and LP record sales were equal. A y-value of 107.1 represents the number (in millions) of each that were sold. Rounded to the nearest million and year, CD and LP record sales were both 107 million in 1987.

The slope of the graph of y_1 is 51.6. This slope indicates that sales of CDs from 1985 to 1990 were *increasing*, on average, by 51.6 million per year. In contrast, sales of vinyl LP records were *decreasing*, on average, by 31.9 million per year.

Calculator Help
To find a point of intersection, see the Appendix (page AP-7).

[1984, 1991, 1] by [0, 350, 50]

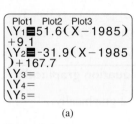
(a)

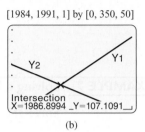
(b)

Figure 3.6

INTERCEPTS OF A LINE

Equations of lines can be written in slope–intercept form or point–slope form. A third form for the equation of a line is called *standard form*, which is defined as follows.

STANDARD FORM OF A LINE

An equation for a line is in **standard form** when it is written as
$$ax + by = c,$$
where a, b, and c are constants with a and b not both 0.

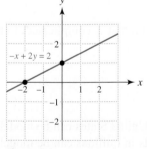

Figure 3.7

Examples of lines in standard form include
$$3x - 7y = -2, \quad -5x - 6y = 0, \quad 2y = 5, \quad \text{and} \quad x + y = 4.$$

To graph a line in standard form, we often start by locating the x- and y-intercepts. For example, the graph of $-x + 2y = 2$ is shown in Figure 3.7. All points on the x-axis have a y-coordinate of 0. To find the x-intercept, we let $y = 0$ in the equation $-x + 2y = 2$ and then solve for x to obtain -2. Note that the graph intersects the x-axis at $(-2, 0)$. Similarly, all points on the y-axis have an x-coordinate of 0. To find the y-intercept, we let $x = 0$ in the equation $-x + 2y = 2$ and then solve for y to obtain 1. Note that the graph intersects the y-axis at the point $(0, 1)$. This discussion is summarized by the following.

FINDING INTERCEPTS

To find the x-intercept of a line, let $y = 0$ in its equation and solve for x.

To find the y-intercept of a line, let $x = 0$ in its equation and solve for y.

Note: In some texts intercepts are defined to be points rather than real numbers. In this case the x-intercept in Figure 3.7 is $(-2, 0)$ and the y-intercept is $(0, 1)$.

EXAMPLE 9   Finding intercepts of a line in standard form

Let the equation of a line be $3x - 2y = 6$.
(a) Find the x- and y-intercepts.
(b) Graph the line.
(c) Solve the equation for y to obtain the slope–intercept form.

Solution   (a) ***x-intercept:***   Let $y = 0$ in $3x - 2y = 6$ to obtain $3x = 6$, or $x = 2$. The x-intercept is 2.

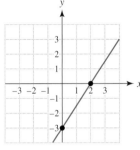

y

y-intercept: Let $x = 0$ in $3x - 2y = 6$ to obtain $-2y = 6$, or $y = -3$. The y-intercept is -3.
(b) Sketch a line passing through $(2, 0)$ and $(0, -3)$, as shown in Figure 3.8.
(c) To solve for y, start by subtracting $3x$ from each side.

Figure 3.8

$$3x - 2y = 6 \qquad \text{Given equation.}$$

$$-2y = -3x + 6 \qquad \text{Subtract } 3x \text{ from each side.}$$

$$-\frac{1}{2}(-2y) = -\frac{1}{2}(-3x + 6) \qquad \text{Multiply each side by } -\frac{1}{2}.$$

$$y = \frac{3}{2}x - 3 \qquad \text{Distributive property}$$

The slope–intercept form of the line is $y = \frac{3}{2}x - 3$.

3.1   PUTTING IT ALL TOGETHER

The following table summarizes some important topics related to linear equations.

Concept	Explanation	Examples
Linear Equations	Can be written as $ax + b = 0$, where $a \neq 0$; has *one solution*	$3x - 4 = 0$, $2(x + 3) = -2$, and $2x = \frac{2}{3} - 5x$
Solution Set	The set of all solutions	The solution set for $x - 4 = 0$ is $\{4\}$ because 4 is the only solution to the equation.
Addition Property of Equality	$a = b$ is equivalent to $a + c = b + c$.	If 2 is added to each side of $x - 2 = 1$, the equation becomes $x = 3$.
Multiplication Property of Equality	$a = b$ is equivalent to $ac = bc$ for $c \neq 0$.	If each side of $\frac{1}{2}x = 3$ is multiplied by 2, the resulting equation is $x = 6$.
Standard Form for a Line	$ax + by = c$, where a, b, and c are constants with a and b not both zero	$3x + 5y = 10$, $-2x + y = 0$, $3y = 18$, and $x = 4$
Finding intercepts	To find the x-intercept, let $y = 0$ and solve for x. To find the y-intercept, let $x = 0$ and solve for y.	Let $2x + 4y = 8$. x-intercept: $2x + 4(0) = 8$, or $x = 4$ y-intercept: $2(0) + 4y = 8$, or $y = 2$

continued on next page

continued from previous page

Linear equations can be solved symbolically, graphically, and numerically. Symbolic solutions to linear equations are *always exact*, whereas graphical and numerical solutions are *sometimes approximate*. The following illustrates how to solve the equation $2x - 1 = 3$ with each method.

Symbolic Solution	***Graphical Solution***	***Numerical Solution***

$$2x - 1 = 3$$
$$2x = 4$$
$$x = 2$$

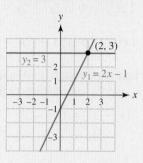

x	0	1	2	3
$2x - 1$	-1	1	3	5

Because $2x - 1$ equals 3 when $x = 2$ the solution to $2x - 1 = 3$ is 2.

The solution is 2.

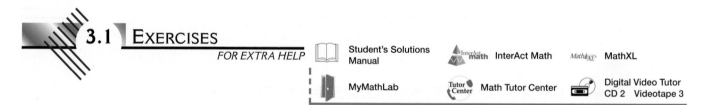

3.1 EXERCISES

FOR EXTRA HELP

Student's Solutions Manual   InterAct Math   MathXL

MyMathLab   Math Tutor Center   Digital Video Tutor CD 2   Videotape 3

CONCEPTS

1. Give the general form of a linear equation.
   $ax + b = 0, a \neq 0$

2. How many solutions does a linear equation have?
   One

3. Is 1 the solution for $4x - 1 = 3x$?   Yes

4. Are $3x = 6$ and $x = 2$ equivalent equations?   Yes

5. What symbol must occur in every equation?
   An equals sign ($=$)

6. Name three methods for solving a linear equation.
   Numerical, graphical, symbolic

7. If a graphical solution to a linear equation results in the point of intersection $(3, 4)$, then the solution is _____.   3

8. The standard form for the equation of a line is _____. $ax + by = c, a$ and b not both 0

9. The addition property of equality states that $a = b$ is equivalent to _____. $a + c = b + c$

10. The multiplication property of equality states that $a = b$ is equivalent to _____. $ac = bc,$ for $c \neq 0$

Exercises 11–16: Decide whether the given value for the variable is a solution to the equation.

11. $x - 6 = -2$ $x = 5$ No

12. $-\frac{1}{2}x + 1 = \frac{1}{3}x - \frac{2}{3}$ $x = 2$ Yes

13. $3(2t + 3) = \frac{13}{3} - t$ $t = -\frac{2}{3}$ Yes

14. $t - 1 = 2 - (t + 1)$ $t = 2$ No

15. $-(2z - 3) + 2z = 1 - z$ $z = -2$ Yes

16. $-\frac{1}{3}(4 - z) + \frac{2}{5}(z + 1) = -\frac{1}{5}$ $z = 1$ Yes

SYMBOLIC SOLUTIONS

Exercises 17–46: Solve the equation symbolically.

17. $3x - 7 = 8$ 5   18. $5 - 2x = -2$ $\frac{7}{2}$

19. $2x = 8 - \frac{1}{2}x$ $\frac{16}{5}$ 20. $-7 = 3.5x$ -2

21. $3x - 1 = 11(1 - x)$ $\frac{6}{7}$

22. $4 - 3x = -5(1 + 2x)$ $-\frac{9}{7}$

23. $x + 4 = 2 - \frac{1}{3}x$ $-\frac{3}{2}$

24. $2x - 5 = 6 - \frac{5}{2}x$ $\frac{22}{9}$ **25.** $2(x - 1) = 5 - 2x$ $\frac{7}{4}$

26. $-(x - 4) = 4(x + 1) + 3(x - 2)$ $\frac{3}{4}$

27. $\dfrac{2x + 1}{3} = \dfrac{2x - 1}{2}$ $\frac{5}{2}$ **28.** $\dfrac{3 - 4x}{5} = \dfrac{3x - 1}{2}$ $\frac{11}{23}$

29. $4.2x - 6.2 = 1 - 1.1x$ $\frac{72}{53} \approx 1.36$

30. $8.4 - 2.1x = 1.4x$ 2.4 **31.** $\frac{1}{2}x - \frac{3}{2} = 4$ 11

32. $5 - \frac{1}{3}x = x - 3$ 6

33. $4(x - 1980) + 6 = 18$ 1983

34. $-5(x - 1900) - 55 = 145$ 1860

35. $2(y - 3) + 5(1 - 2y) = 4y + 1$ $-\frac{1}{6}$

36. $4(y + 1) - (3 - 5y) = -2(y - 2)$ $\frac{3}{11}$

37. $-3(2 - 3z) + 2z = 1 - 3z$ $\frac{1}{2}$

38. $-\big(5 - (z + 1)\big) = 9 - \big(5 - (2z - 3)\big)$ -5

39. $\frac{2}{3}(t - 3) + \frac{1}{2}t = 5$ 6 **40.** $\frac{1}{5}t + \frac{3}{10} = 2 - \frac{1}{2}t$ $\frac{17}{7}$

41. $\dfrac{3k}{4} - \dfrac{2k}{3} = \dfrac{1}{6}$ 2

42. $\dfrac{k + 1}{3} - \dfrac{1}{2} = \dfrac{3k - 3}{6}$ 2

43. $0.2(n - 2) + 0.4n = 0.05$ 0.75

44. $0.15(n + 1) = 0.1n + 1$ 17

45. $0.7y - 0.8(y - 1) = 2$ -12

46. $0.2y + 0.3(5 - 2y) = -0.2y$ 7.5

NUMERICAL SOLUTIONS

Exercises 47–50: Complete the table. Then use the table to solve the equation.

47. $-4x + 8 = 0$ 2

x	1	2	3	4	5
$-4x + 8$	4	0	-4	-8	-12

48. $3x + 2 = 5$ 1

x	-2	-1	0	1	2
$3x + 2$	-4	-1	2	5	8

49. $4 - 2x = x + 7$ -1

x	-2	-1	0	1	2
$4 - 2x$	8	6	4	2	0
$x + 7$	5	6	7	8	9

50. $3(x - 1) = -2(1 - x)$ 1

x	-2	-1	0	1	2
$3(x - 1)$	-9	-6	-3	0	3
$-2(1 - x)$	-6	-4	-2	0	2

Exercises 51–56: Solve the linear equation numerically.

51. $x - 3 = 7$ 10 **52.** $2x + 1 = 11$ 5

53. $2y - \frac{1}{2} = \frac{3}{2}$ 1 **54.** $7 - 4y = -5$ 3

55. $3(z - 1) + 1.5 = 2z$ 1.5

56. $-3z - 6 = z + 2$ -2

GRAPHICAL SOLUTIONS

Exercises 57–60: A linear equation is solved graphically by letting y_1 equal the left side of the equation and y_2 equal the right side of the equation. Find the solution. Check your answer.

57. -2

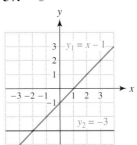

58. 1

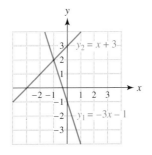

59. -1

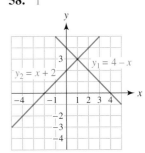

60. -2

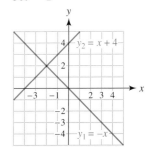

Exercises 61–68: Solve the equation graphically. Check your answer.

61. $5 - 2x = 7$ –1   **62.** $-2x + 3 = -7$ 5

63. $2x - (x + 2) = -2$ 0

64. $x + 1 = 3 - x$ 1   **65.** $3(x + 2) + 1 = x + 1$ –3

66. $x + 5 = 2x + 2$ 3

 67. $5(x - 1990) + 15 = 100$ 2007

 68. $10(x - 1985) - 20 = 55$ 1992.5

SOLVING LINEAR EQUATIONS BY MORE THAN ONE METHOD

Exercises 69–72: Solve the equation (a) numerically, (b) graphically, and (c) symbolically.

Do your answers agree?

69. $2x - 1 = 13$ 7

70. $9 - x = 3x + 1$ 2

 71. $3x - 5 - (x + 1) = 0$ 3

 72. $\frac{1}{2}x - 1 = \frac{5 - x}{2}$ 3.5

APPLICATIONS

73. *Broadway Revenue* Record Broadway ticket revenues were recorded for the 1999 season. These ticket revenues in millions of dollars have grown at a constant rate during the past decade and may be modeled by

$$f(x) = 32.8(x - 1999) + 588,$$

where x is the year. (*Source:* The League of American Theatres and Producers, Inc.)   (a) $456.8 million, $588 million
   (a) Estimate ticket revenues in 1995 and 1999.
   (b) Estimate the year when they were $424 million.
   1994

74. *Centenarians* In 1990 there were 37,306 centenarians, people aged 100 or older, in the United States. The number of centenarians is estimated to increase by 8260 per year. (*Source:* Bureau of the Census.)
   (a) Find values for m, x_1, and y_1 so that the formula $f(x) = m(x - x_1) + y_1$ models the number of centenarians during year x. $m = 8260, x_1 = 1990, y_1 = 37,306$
   (b) Estimate the year when there will be 450,000 centenarians. $x \approx 2040$

75. *State and Federal Inmates* From 1988 to 1995 the number of state and federal prison inmates in thou-

sands can be modeled by $f(x) = 70x - 138,532$ during year x. (*Source:* Department of Justice.)
   (a) Determine symbolically the year when there were 908 thousand inmates. 1992
   (b) Solve part (a) numerically. 1992
   (c) Solve part (a) graphically. 1992

76. *U.S. Government Costs* From 1960 to 1990 the cost (in 1960 dollars) to administer social and economic programs rose from $1.9 billion to $16 billion. This cost in billions of dollars can be modeled by $f(x) = 0.47x - 919.3$, where x is the year. (*Source:* Center for the Study of American Business.)
   (a) Estimate symbolically when the cost was $6.6 billion. 1970
   (b) Solve part (a) numerically. 1970
   (c) Solve part (a) graphically. 1970

77. *Car Sales* In 1998 Toyota sold 1.4 million vehicles. This number increased to 1.8 million in 2002. (*Source:* Autodata.)   (a) $f(x) = 0.1x - 198.4$
   (a) Find a linear function that models the data.
   (b) Determine the year when Toyota sold 1.7 million vehicles by solving a linear equation. 2001
   (c) Predict the year when Toyota may sell 2 million vehicles. 2004

78. *Injured at Work* In 1992 private industry reported 8.3 injuries per 100 full-time workers. By 2002 this number decreased to 5.4. (*Source:* Department of Labor.)
   (a) Find a linear function that models the data.
   (b) Estimate the year when the reported injuries equaled 6 per 100 full-time workers. 2000
   (a) $f(x) = -0.29x + 585.98$

79. *U.S. Population Density* In 1900 there were, on average, 22 people per square mile in the United States. By 2000 the population density had increased to 80 people per square mile. (*Source:* Bureau of the Census.)
   (a) Find a linear function that models the data.
   (b) Determine the year when the population density was 51 people per square mile. 1950
   (a) $f(x) = 0.58x - 1080$

80. *CD and LP Record Sales* (Refer to Example 8.) From 1985 to 1990, sales of CDs (compact discs) in the United States can be modeled by the equation $y_1 = 51.6(x - 1985) + 9.1$, and sales of LPs (vinyl records) can be modeled by $y_2 = -31.9(x - 1985) + 167.7$. All sales are in millions. Determine symbolically the year when sales of CDs and LPs were about equal. Late 1986

81. Explain each of the following terms: linear equation, solution, solution set, and equivalent equations. Give an example of each.

82. Explain how to solve the equation $ax + b = 0$ symbolically and graphically. Use both methods to solve the equation $5x + 10 = 0$.

Group Activity: Working with Real Data

Directions: Form a group of 2 to 4 people. Select someone to record the group's responses for this activity. All members of the group should work cooperatively to answer the questions. If your instructor asks for your results, each member of the group should be prepared to respond.

(a) Soccer participation is increasing.   (b) $f(x) = 0.15(x - 1980) + 0.9$; answers may vary.

U.S. Youth Soccer   Soccer has become an increasingly popular sport for young people in the United States. The table lists organized soccer participation for youths under the age of 19.

Year	1980	1986	1992	1998
Number (millions)	0.9	1.5	2.3	3.6

Source: Soccer Industry Council of America.

 (a) Make a scatterplot of the data. Discuss any trend in soccer participation.*

(b) Find a linear function f given by

$$f(x) = m(x - x_1) + y_1$$

that models the data.

(c) Interpret m as a rate of change.

(d) Estimate the year when participation was 2 million.

(e) If trends continue, predict the year when participation may reach 5 million.

2007; answers may vary.

(c) The number of participants in youth soccer is increasing at a rate of about 0.15 million, or 150,000, per year; answers may vary.   (d) 1987; answers may vary.

*Answer on page IA-14

 **3.2   INTRODUCTION TO PROBLEM SOLVING**

Solving a Formula for a Variable · Steps for Solving a Problem · Percentages

INTRODUCTION

Problem-solving skills are essential because every day we must solve problems—both small and large—for survival. A logical approach to a problem is often helpful, which is especially true in mathematics. In this section we discuss steps that can be used to solve mathematical problems, which often involve formulas. We begin the section by discussing how to solve a formula for a variable.

SOLVING A FORMULA FOR A VARIABLE

W

L

Figure 3.9 $P = 2W + 2L$

The perimeter P of a rectangle with width W and length L is given by $P = 2W + 2L$, as illustrated in Figure 3.9.

Suppose that we know the perimeter P and length L of this rectangle. Even though the formula is written to calculate P, we can still use it to find the width W. This technique is demonstrated in the next example.

EXAMPLE 1 Finding the width of a rectangle

A rectangle has a perimeter of 80 inches and a length of 23 inches.
(a) Write a formula to find the width W of a rectangle with known perimeter P and length L.
(b) Use the formula to find W.

Solution **(a)** We must solve $P = 2W + 2L$ for W.

$$P = 2W + 2L \qquad \text{Given formula}$$

$$P - 2L = 2W \qquad \text{Subtract } 2L.$$

$$\frac{1}{2}(P - 2L) = \frac{1}{2}(2W) \qquad \text{Multiply by } \tfrac{1}{2}.$$

$$\frac{P}{2} - L = W \qquad \text{Distributive property}$$

The required formula is $W = \frac{P}{2} - L$.
(b) Substitute $P = 80$ and $L = 23$ into this formula. The width is

$$W = \frac{80}{2} - 23 = 17 \text{ inches.} \qquad \rule{1cm}{0.4pt}$$

In the next example we use a formula that converts degrees Fahrenheit to degrees Celsius to find a formula that converts degrees Celsius to degrees Fahrenheit.

EXAMPLE 2 Converting temperature

The formula $C = \frac{5}{9}(F - 32)$ can be used to convert degrees Fahrenheit to degrees Celsius.
(a) Use this formula to convert $212°\,$F to an equivalent Celsius temperature.
(b) Solve the formula for F to obtain a formula that can convert degrees Celsius to degrees Fahrenheit. Interpret the slope of the graph of F.
(c) Use this new formula to convert $25°$C to an equivalent Fahrenheit temperature.

Solution **(a)** $C = \frac{5}{9}(212 - 32) = \frac{5}{9}(180) = 100°\text{C}$

(b)

$$C = \frac{5}{9}(F - 212) \qquad \text{Given formula}$$

$$\frac{9}{5}C = \frac{9}{5} \cdot \frac{5}{9}(F - 32) \qquad \text{Multiply by } \tfrac{9}{5}.$$

$$\frac{9}{5}C = F - 32 \qquad \text{Simplify.}$$

$$\frac{9}{5}C + 32 = F \qquad \text{Add 32.}$$

The required formula is $F = \frac{9}{5}C + 32$. The slope of the graph of F is $m = \frac{9}{5}$, which indicates that a $1°$ increase in Celsius temperature is equivalent to a $\frac{9°}{5}$ increase in Fahrenheit temperature.
(c) Substitute 25 for C in this formula.

$$F = \frac{9}{5}(25) + 32 = 77°\text{F} \qquad \rule{1cm}{0.4pt}$$

Sometimes an equation of two variables can be used to determine the formula for a function. To do so, we must let one variable be the dependent variable and the other variable be the independent variable. For example,

$$2x - 5y = 10$$

is the equation of a line written in standard form. Solving this equation for y gives the following result.

$$-5y = -2x + 10 \qquad \text{Subtract } 2x.$$

$$-\frac{1}{5}(-5y) = -\frac{1}{5}(-2x + 10) \qquad \text{Multiply by } -\frac{1}{5}.$$

$$y = \frac{2}{5}x - 2 \qquad \text{Distributive property}$$

If y is the dependent variable, x is the independent variable, and $y = f(x)$, then

$$f(x) = \frac{2}{5}x - 2$$

defines a function f whose graph is the line determined by $2x - 5y = 10$.
This process is demonstrated further in the next example.

EXAMPLE 3   Writing a function

TEACHING TIP

This example shows how to solve for a variable and how to write the result in function notation.

Solve each equation for y and write a formula for a function f defined by $y = f(x)$.
(a) $4(x - 2y) = -3x$
(b) $\dfrac{x + y}{2} - 5 = 20$

Solution   **(a)** Begin by applying the distributive property.

$$4(x - 2y) = -3x \qquad \text{Given formula}$$

$$4x - 8y = -3x \qquad \text{Distributive property}$$

$$-8y = -7x \qquad \text{Subtract } 4x.$$

$$y = \frac{7}{8}x \qquad \text{Divide by } -8.$$

Thus $f(x) = \frac{7}{8}x$.
(b) Begin by adding 5 to each side.

$$\frac{x + y}{2} - 5 = 20 \qquad \text{Given formula}$$

$$\frac{x + y}{2} = 25 \qquad \text{Add 5.}$$

$$\frac{2(x + y)}{2} = 2(25) \qquad \text{Multiply by 2.}$$

$$x + y = 50 \qquad \text{Simplify.}$$

$$y = 50 - x \qquad \text{Subtract } x.$$

Thus $f(x) = 50 - x$.

STEPS FOR SOLVING A PROBLEM

Solving problems in mathematics can be challenging, especially when formulas and equations are not given to us. In these situations we have to write them, but to do so, we need a strategy. The following steps are often a helpful strategy. They are based on George Polya's (1888–1985) four-step process for problem solving.

STEPS FOR SOLVING A PROBLEM
STEP 1: Read the problem carefully to be sure that you understand it. (You may need to read the problem more than once.). Assign a variable to what you are being asked to find. If necessary, write other quantities in terms of this variable.
STEP 2: Write an equation that relates the quantities described in the problem. You may need to sketch a diagram, make a chart, or refer to known formulas.
STEP 3: Solve the equation and determine the solution.
STEP 4: Look back and check your answer. Does it seem reasonable? Did you find the required information?

In the next example we apply these steps to a word problem involving unknown numbers.

EXAMPLE 4   Solving a number problem

The sum of three consecutive *even* integers is 108. Find the three numbers.

Solution   **STEP 1:** *Start by assigning a variable to an unknown quantity.*

$$n: \text{ smallest of the three integers}$$

Next, write the other two numbers in terms of n.

$$n + 2: \text{ next consecutive } \textit{even} \text{ integer}$$

$$n + 4: \text{ largest of the three even integers}$$

STEP 2: *Write an equation that relates these unknown quantities.* As the sum of these three even integers is 108, the needed equation is

$$n + (n + 2) + (n + 4) = 108.$$

STEP 3: *Solve the equation in STEP 2.*

$n + (n + 2) + (n + 4) = 108$	Equation to be solved
$(n + n + n) + (2 + 4) = 108$	Commutative and associative properties
$3n + 6 = 108$	Combine like terms.
$3n = 102$	Subtract 6 from each side.
$n = 34$	Divide each side by 3.

The smallest of the three numbers is 34, so the three numbers are 34, 36, and 38.

STEP 4: *Check your answer.* The sum of these three even integers is

$$34 + 36 + 38 = 108.$$

The answer checks.

In the next example we apply this procedure to find the dimensions of a room.

EXAMPLE 5   Solving a geometry problem

The length of a rectangular room is 2 feet more than its width. If the perimeter of the room is 80 feet, find the width and length of the room.

Solution   **STEP 1:** *Start by assigning a variable to an unknown quantity.*

$$x\text{: width of the room}$$
$$x + 2\text{: length of the room}$$

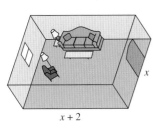

See Figure 3.10.

Figure 3.10

STEP 2: *Write an equation that relates these unknown quantities.* The perimeter is the distance around the room and equals 80 feet. Thus

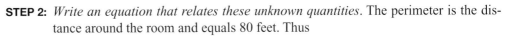

$$x + (x + 2) + x + (x + 2) = 80,$$

which simplifies to

$$4x + 4 = 80.$$

STEP 3: *Solve the equation in STEP 2.*

$4x + 4 = 80$	Equation to be solved
$4x = 76$	Subtract 4 from each side.
$\dfrac{4x}{4} = \dfrac{76}{4}$	Divide each side by 4.
$x = 19$	Simplify.

The width is 19 feet and the length is 21 feet.

STEP 4: *Check your answer.* The perimeter of the room is

$$19 + 21 + 19 + 21 = 80 \text{ feet.}$$

The answer checks.

Many times we are called upon to solve a mixture problem. Such problems may involve a mixture of acid solutions or a mixture of investments. In the next example an athlete jogs at two different speeds, and mathematics is used to determine how much time is spent jogging at each speed.

EXAMPLE 6   Solving a "mixture" problem

An athlete begins jogging at 8 miles per hour and then jogs at 7 miles per hour, traveling 10.9 miles in 1.5 hours. How long did the athlete jog at each speed?

Solution   **STEP 1:** *Start by assigning a variable to an unknown quantity.* Let t represent the time spent jogging at 8 miles per hour. Because total time spent jogging is 1.5 hours, the time spent jogging at 7 miles per hour must be $1.5 - t$.

STEP 2: *Write an equation that relates these unknown quantities.* A table is often helpful in solving a mixture problem. As shown in Table 3.2 on the next page, the distance that the athlete jogs at 8 miles per hour is $8t$ because distance equals rate times time ($d = rt$). The distance traveled at 7 miles per hour is $7(1.5 - t)$, and the total distance traveled is 10.9 miles. From the third column, we can write the equation, consisting of three terms, as

$$8t + 7(1.5 - t) = 10.9.$$

TABLE 3.2

	Speed	Time	Distance
First Part	8	t	$8t$
Second Part	7	$1.5 - t$	$7(1.5 - t)$
Total		1.5	10.9

STEP 3: *Solve the equation in STEP 2.*

$8t + 7(1.5 - t) = 10.9$	Equation to be solved
$8t + 10.5 - 7t = 10.9$	Distributive property
$t + 10.5 = 10.9$	Combine like terms.
$t = 0.4$	Subtract 10.5 from each side.

The athlete jogged 0.4 hour at 8 miles per hour and $1.5 - 0.4 = 1.1$ hours at 7 miles per hour.

STEP 4: *Check your answer.* Start by calculating the distance traveled at each speed.

$8 \cdot 0.4 = 3.2$ miles	Distance at 8 mph
$7 \cdot 1.1 = 7.7$ miles	Distance at 7 mph

The total distance jogged is $3.2 + 7.7 = 10.9$ miles. The answer checks.

PERCENTAGES

Applications involving percentages often make use of linear equations. Taking P percent of x is given by Px, where P is written in decimal form. For example, to calculate 35% of x, we compute $0.35x$. As a result, 35% of $150 is $0.35(150) = 52.5$, or $52.50.

EXAMPLE 7 Analyzing smoking data

In 1998, an estimated 27.7% of Americans aged 12 and older, or 60 million people, were cigarette smokers. Use these data to estimate the number of Americans that are aged 12 and older. (*Source:* Department of Health and Human Services.)

Solution Let x be the number of Americans aged 12 and older. Then 27.7% of x equals 60 million, so we must solve the equation

TEACHING TIP

You may want to review how to convert percentages to decimals.

$$0.277x = 60.$$

To solve this equation, we divide both sides by 0.277.

$$\frac{0.277x}{0.277} = \frac{60}{0.277}$$

$$x \approx 216.6 \quad \text{Approximate}$$

In 1998, approximately 216.6 million Americans were aged 12 and older.

Note: The word *of* often indicates multiplication when working with percentages.

In chemistry acids are frequently mixed. In the next example, percentages are used to determine how to mix an acid solution with a prescribed concentration.

EXAMPLE 8 Mixing acid

A chemist mixes 2 liters of 20% sulfuric acid with another sample of 60% sulfuric acid to obtain a sample of 50% sulfuric acid. How much of the 60% sulfuric acid was used? See Figure 3.11.

Figure 3.11 Mixing acid

Solution **STEP 1:** Assign a variable x as follows.

$$x: \text{liters of 60\% sulfuric acid}$$

$$x + 2: \text{liters of 50\% sulfuric acid}$$

STEP 2: Table 3.3 can be used to organize our calculations. The total amount of pure sulfuric acid in the 20% and 60% samples must equal the amount of pure sulfuric acid in the final 50% acid solution.

TABLE 3.3 Mixing Acid

Concentration (as a decimal)	Solution Amount (liters)	Pure Acid (liters)
0.20 (20%)	2	0.20(2)
0.60 (60%)	x	$0.60x$
0.50 (50%)	$x + 2$	$0.50(x + 2)$

From the third column, we can write the equation

$$0.20(2) \quad + \quad 0.60x \quad = \quad 0.50(x + 2).$$

(Pure acid in 20% solution) + (Pure acid in 60% solution) = (Pure acid in 50% solution)

STEP 3: Solve the equation in STEP 2.

$0.20(2) + 0.60x = 0.50(x + 2)$	Equation to be solved
$2(2) + 6x = 5(x + 2)$	Multiply by 10.
$4 + 6x = 5x + 10$	Distributive property
$x = 6$	Subtract $5x$ and 4 from each side.

Six liters of the 60% acid solution should be added to the 2 liters of 20% acid solution.

STEP 4: If 6 liters of 60% acid solution are added to 2 liters of 20% solution, then there will be 8 liters of acid solution containing

$$0.60(6) + 0.20(2) = 4 \text{ liters}$$

of pure acid. This mixture represents a $\frac{4}{8} = 0.50$, or 50% mixture. The answer checks.

3.2 PUTTING IT ALL TOGETHER

When solving an application problem we often find it helpful to follow the *Steps for Solving a Problem* discussed on page 160. Be sure to read the problem carefully and check your answer. Many times a graph, diagram, or chart is useful. The following table summarizes some other important concepts from this section.

Concept	Explanation	Examples
Writing a Function	If possible, solve an equation for a variable. Express the result in function notation.	$5x + y = 10$ $y = -5x + 10$ If $y = f(x)$, then $f(x) = -5x + 10$.
Changing a Percentage to a Decimal	Move the decimal point two places to the left.	$73\% = 0.73$, $5.3\% = 0.053$, and $125\% = 1.25$
Percent Problems	To find $P\%$ of a quantity Q, change $P\%$ to a decimal and multiply by Q.	To find 45% of $200, calculate $0.45 \times 200 = \$90$.

3.2 EXERCISES

FOR EXTRA HELP

Student's Solutions Manual

 InterAct Math

 MathXL

MyMathLab

Math Tutor Center

Digital Video Tutor
CD 2   Videotape 3

CONCEPTS

1. If we solve $2y = x$ for y, we obtain $y = $ _____. $\frac{x}{2}$

2. If $y = 4x - 7$ and $y = f(x)$, then $f(x) = $_____.
$4x - 7$

3. If a rectangle has width W and length L, then its perimeter is $P = $ _____. $2W + 2L$

4. The first step in solving an application is to _____.
read the problem carefully

SOLVING FOR A VARIABLE

Exercises 5–12: Solve the equation for the given variable.

5. $4x + 3y = 12$; y
$y = -\frac{4}{3}x + 4$

6. $6x - 3y = 6$; y
$y = 2x - 2$

7. $5(2x - 3y) = 2x$; x
$x = \frac{15}{8}y$

8. $-2(2x + y) = 3y$; x
$x = -\frac{5}{4}y$

9. $S = 6ab$; b $b = \frac{S}{6a}$

10. $S = 2\pi rh$; r $r = \frac{S}{2\pi h}$

11. $\dfrac{r + t}{2} = 7$; t
$t = 14 - r$

12. $\dfrac{2 + a + b}{3} = 8$; a
$a = 22 - b$

Exercises 13–18: Solve the equation for y. Let $y = f(x)$ and write a formula for $f(x)$.

13. $-3x + y = 8$
$f(x) = 3x + 8$

14. $2x - 5y = 10$ $f(x) = \frac{2}{5}x - 2$

15. $4x = 2\pi y$ $f(x) = \frac{2x}{\pi}$

16. $\dfrac{x}{2} = \dfrac{y}{3}$ $f(x) = \frac{3x}{2}$

17. $\dfrac{3y}{8} = x$ $f(x) = \frac{8x}{3}$

18. $\dfrac{3x + 2y}{4} = 3$ $f(x) = -\frac{3}{2}x + 6$

WRITING AND SOLVING EQUATIONS

Exercises 19–28: Do the following.

   (a) *Translate the sentence into an equation, using the variable x.*

   (b) *Solve the resulting equation.*

19. The sum of a number and 2 is 12. (a) $x + 2 = 12$ (b) 10

20. Twice a number plus 7 equals 9. (a) $2x + 7 = 9$ (b) 1

21. A number divided by 5 equals the number increased by 1. (a) $\frac{x}{5} = x + 1$ (b) $-\frac{5}{4}$

22. 25 times a number is 125. (a) $25x = 125$ (b) 5

23. If a number is increased by 5 and then divided by 2, the result equals 7. (a) $\frac{x + 5}{2} = 7$ (b) 9

24. A number subtracted from 8 is 5. (a) $8 - x = 5$ (b) 3

25. The quotient of a number and 2 is 17. (a) $\frac{x}{2} = 17$ (b) 34

26. The product of 5 and a number equals 95.
(a) $5x = 95$ (b) 19

27. The sum of three consecutive integers is 30.
(a) $x + (x + 1) + (x + 2) = 30$ (b) 9

28. A rectangle that is 5 inches longer than it is wide has a perimeter of 60 inches.
(a) $2x + 2(x + 5) = 60$ (b) 12.5

APPLICATIONS

29. *Perimeter of a Rectangle*   (Refer to Example 1.) A rectangle has a perimeter of 86 feet and a width of 19 feet.

   (a) Write a formula to find the length L of a rectangle with perimeter P and width W. $L = \frac{P}{2} - W$

   (b) Use the formula to find L.   24 feet

30. *Perimeter of a Triangle*   The perimeter P of a triangle with sides a, b, and c is $P = a + b + c$.

   (a) Solve this formula for a. $a = P - b - c$

   (b) Use the formula to find a if $b = 5$, $c = 7$, and $P = 15$.   3

31. *Area of a Cylinder*   The area A of the side of a cylinder with height h and radius r is $A = 2\pi rh$.

Solve this formula for h.

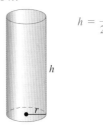

$h = \frac{A}{2\pi r}$

32. *Volume of a Cylinder*   The volume V of a cylinder with height h and radius r is $V = \pi r^2 h$. Solve this formula for h. $h = \frac{V}{\pi r^2}$

33. *Temperature*   (Refer to Example 2.) Solve the formula $F = \frac{9}{5}C + 32$ for C. $C = \frac{5}{9}(F - 32)$

34. *Area of a Parallelogram*   The area A of a parallelogram with base b and height h is $A = bh$. Solve this formula for b.

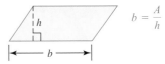

$b = \frac{A}{h}$

35. *Area of a Triangle*   The area A of a triangle with base b and height h is $A = \frac{1}{2}bh$. Solve this formula for h.

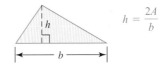

$h = \frac{2A}{b}$

36. *Volume of a Box*   The volume V of a box with length L, width W, and height H is $V = WLH$. Solve this formula for L.

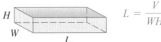

$L = \frac{V}{WH}$

37. *Number Problem*   (Refer to Example 4.) The sum of three consecutive integers is 135. Find the three integers.   44, 45, 46

38. *Number Problem*   Are there three consecutive *even integers* whose sum is 82? If so, find the three integers.   No

39. *Number Problem*   Twice the sum of three consecutive *odd integers* is 150. Find the three integers.
23, 25, 27

40. *Number Problem*   Ten plus twice the sum of two consecutive integers is 196. Find the two integers.
46, 47

41. *Geometry*   Find the value of x if the perimeter of the room is 48 feet.   8 ft

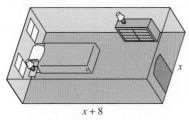

$x + 8$

42. *Fencing*   Three identical pens for dogs are to be enclosed with 120 feet of fence, as illustrated in the accompanying figure. If the length of each pen is twice its width plus 2 feet, find the dimensions of each pen.   8 ft by 18 ft

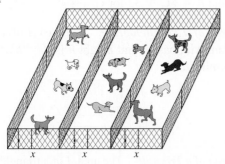

x x x

43. *Distance and Time*   A train 100 miles west of St. Louis, Missouri, is traveling east at 60 miles per hour. How long will it take for the train to be 410 miles east of St. Louis?   8.5 hr

44. *Distance and Time*   (Refer to Example 6.) At first an athlete jogs at 6 miles per hour and then jogs at 5 miles per hour, traveling 7 miles in 1.3 hours. How long did the athlete jog at each speed?
0.5 hr at 6 mph; 0.8 hr at 5 mph

45. *Chemical Mixture*   (Refer to Example 8.) A chemist mixes 3 liters of 30% sulfuric acid with a sample of 80% sulfuric acid to obtain a sample of 60% sulfuric acid. How much of the 80% sulfuric acid was used?   4.5 L

46. *Antifreeze Mixture*   A radiator holds 4 gallons of fluid. If it is full with a 20% solution, how much fluid should be drained and replaced with a 70% antifreeze mixture to result in a 50% mixture of antifreeze?   2.4 gal

47. *Loan Interest*   A student takes out two student loans, one at 6% annual interest and the other at 4% annual interest. The total amount of the two loans is $5000, and the total interest after 1 year is $244. Find the amount of each loan. $2200 at 6%; $2800 at 4%

48. *Angles in a Triangle*   The sum of the degree measures of the angles in a triangle equals 180°. Find the measure of x in the triangle shown.   50°

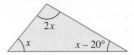

$2x$
x $x - 20°$

49. *Classroom Ventilation*   Ventilation is an effective method for removing indoor air pollutants. A classroom should have a ventilation rate of 900 cubic feet of air per hour for each person in the classroom. (*Source:* ASHRAE.)

(a) What ventilation rate should a classroom containing 40 people have?   36,000 ft³/hr

(b) If a classroom ventilation system moves 60,000 cubic feet of air per hour, determine the maximum number of people that should be in the classroom.   66 people

50. *Lead Poisoning*   According to the EPA, the maximum amount of lead that can be ingested by a person without becoming ill is 36.5 milligrams per year. (*Source:* N. Nemerow and A. Dasgupta, *Industrial and Hazardous Waste Treatment.*)

(a) Write an expression that gives the maximum amount of lead in milligrams that can be "safely" ingested over x years.   36.5x

(b) Under these guidelines what is the minimum number of years that the consumption of 500 milligrams should be spread over?   About 13.7 yr

51. *Wal-Mart Stores*   In 2007 the number of Wal-Mart employees is expected to be 2.2 million, a 57% increase over the number of employees in 2002. How many Wal-Mart employees were there in 2002?
About 1.4 million

52. *Airline Fares*   In 2002 the average one-way fare paid by American Express clients on domestic routes was $282, an 8.44% decrease from 2001. Find the average one-way fare paid in 2001.   About $308

53. *Meeting a Future Mate*   According to a survey, about 32% of adult Americans believe that they will meet their mates on the Internet during this century. In this survey 480 respondents held this belief. Determine the number of people participating in the survey. (*Source: Men's Health*.)   1500 people

54. *Union Membership*   In 1998, 6.9 million, or 37.5%, of all government workers were unionized. How many government workers were there in 1998? (*Source: Department of Labor*.)   18.4 million

55. *Cancer and Heart Disease*   About 550,000 people died from cancer in the United States during 2000. Heart disease accounted for 29.1% more deaths than cancer. What is the total number of people who died from heart disease or cancer during 2000?   (*Source: National Center for Health Statistics*.)   About 1,260,000

56. *Grades*   To receive an A in a college course a student must average 90 percent correct on four exams of 100 points each and on a final exam of 200 points. If a student scores 83, 87, 94, and 91 on the 100-point exams, what minimum score on the final exam is necessary for the student to receive an A?   92.5% or 185

WRITING ABOUT MATHEMATICS

57. A student solves the following equation for y. What is the student's mistake?

$$\frac{x + 2y}{2} = 5$$
$$x + y \overset{?}{=} 5$$
$$y \overset{?}{=} 5 - x$$

58. Explain how to find $P\%$ of a quantity Q. Give an example.

CHECKING BASIC CONCEPTS   SECTIONS 3.1 AND 3.2

1. How many solutions does a linear equation have?   1

2. Solve $\frac{1}{2}z - (1 - 2z) = \frac{2}{3}z$. $\frac{6}{11}$

3. Solve $2(3x + 4) + 3 = -1$
   (a) symbolically, -2
   (b) graphically, and -2
   (c) numerically. -2
   Do your answers agree?   Yes

4. At first an athlete jogs at 10 miles per hour and then jogs at 8 miles per hour, traveling 10.2 miles in 1.2 hours. How long did the athlete jog at each speed?   0.3 hr at 10 mph; 0.9 hr at 8 mph

---

3.3 LINEAR INEQUALITIES

Basic Concepts · Symbolic Solutions · Numerical and Graphical Solutions · An Application

INTRODUCTION

On a freeway, the speed limit might be 75 miles per hour. A driver traveling x miles per hour is obeying the speed limit if $x \leq 75$ and breaking the speed limit if $x > 75$. A speed of $x = 75$ represents the boundary between obeying the speed limit and breaking it. A posted speed limit, or *boundary*, allows drivers to easily determine whether they are speeding.

Solving linear inequalities is closely related to solving linear equations because equality is the boundary between *greater than* and *less than*. In this section we discuss techniques needed to solve linear inequalities.

BASIC CONCEPTS

An **inequality** results whenever the equals sign in an equation is replaced with any one of the symbols $<$, $\leq$, $>$, or $\geq$. Examples of linear equations include

$$2x + 1 = 0, \quad 1 - x = 6, \quad \text{and} \quad 5x + 1 = 3 - 2x,$$

and, therefore, examples of linear inequalities include

$$2x + 1 < 0, \quad 1 - x \geq 6, \quad \text{and} \quad 5x + 1 \leq 3 - 2x.$$

A **solution** to an inequality is a value of the variable that makes the statement true. The set of all solutions is called the **solution set**. Two inequalities are *equivalent* if they have the same solution set. Inequalities frequently have *infinitely many solutions*. For example, the solution set to the inequality $x - 5 > 0$ includes all real numbers greater than 5, which can be written as $x > 5$. Using **set-builder notation**, we can write the solution set as $\{x \mid x > 5\}$. This expression is read as "the set of all real numbers x such that x is greater than 5." The vertical line $\mid$ in set-builder notation is read "such that." To summarize, then, we have the following.

Inequality	*Set-Builder Notation*	*Meaning*
$t \leq 3$	$\{t \mid t \leq 3\}$	The set of all real numbers t such that t is less than or equal to 3.
$z < 8$	$\{z \mid z < 8\}$	The set of all real numbers z such that z is less than 8.

Next we more formally define a linear inequality in one variable.

LINEAR INEQUALITY IN ONE VARIABLE

A **linear inequality** in one variable is an inequality that can be written in the form

$$ax + b > 0,$$

where $a \neq 0$. (The symbol $>$ may be replaced with $\geq$, $<$, or $\leq$.)

Note: The variable in a linear equation or a linear inequality never has a power other than 1. Thus expressions such as x^2, x^3, or $\sqrt{x}$ do not occur.

TEACHING TIP

Emphasize the relation among linear functions, equations, and inequalities by discussing Making Connections. Give an example.

MAKING CONNECTIONS

Linear Functions, Equations, and Inequalities

A *linear function* is given by $f(x) = ax + b$, a *linear equation* by $ax + b = 0$, and a *linear inequality* by $ax + b > 0$. A linear equation (with $a \neq 0$) has one solution. A linear inequality has infinitely many solutions.

To understand linear inequalities better, suppose that it costs a student \$100 to make a large batch of candy. If the student sells bags of this candy for \$5 each, then the profit y is $y = 5x - 100$, where x represents the number of bags sold. The graph of y is a line with slope 5 and y-intercept -100, as shown in Figure 3.12.

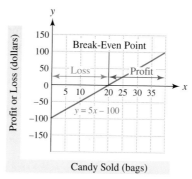

Figure 3.12 Candy Profit

Because the *x*-intercept is 20, the student will *break even* when $5x - 100 = 0$, or when 20 bags of candy are sold. (The **break-even point** occurs when the *revenue* from selling the candy equals the *cost* of making the candy.) Note that the student incurs a *loss* when the line is below the *x*-axis, or when $5x - 100 < 0$. This situation corresponds to selling less than 20 bags, or $x < 20$. A profit occurs when the graph is above the *x*-axis, or when $5x - 100 > 0$. This situation corresponds to selling more than 20 bags, or $x > 20$. Selling $x = 20$ bags of candy represents the *boundary* between loss and profit.

These concepts for the solution set for a linear inequality are summarized as follows.

 **SOLUTION SET FOR A LINEAR INEQUALITY**

The solution set for a linear inequality $ax + b > 0$ with $a \neq 0$ is either $\{x \mid x < k\}$ or $\{x \mid x > k\}$, where *k* is the solution to $ax + b = 0$. Note that *k* corresponds to the *x*-intercept for the graph of the line $y = ax + b$. Similar statements can be made for the symbols $<$, $\leq$, or $\geq$.

SYMBOLIC SOLUTIONS

The inequality $3 < 5$ is equivalent to $3 + 1 < 5 + 1$. That is, we can add the same number to each side of an inequality. This is an example of one property of inequalities. The following properties are used to solve inequalities.

PROPERTIES OF INEQUALITIES

Let *a*, *b*, and *c* be real numbers.

1. $a < b$ and $a + c < b + c$ are equivalent.
   (The same number may be added to or subtracted from each side of an inequality.)
2. If $c > 0$, then $a < b$ and $ac < bc$ are equivalent.
   (Each side of an inequality may be multiplied or divided by the same positive number.)
3. If $c < 0$, then $a < b$ and $ac > bc$ are equivalent.
   (Each side of an inequality may be multiplied or divided by the same negative number provided the inequality symbol is reversed.)

Similar properties exist for the $\leq$ and $\geq$ symbols.

When applying Property 2 or 3, we need to determine whether the inequality symbol should be reversed. For example, if each side of the inequality $3 < 5$ is multiplied by the *positive* number 2, we obtain

$$2 \cdot 3 < 2 \cdot 5 \quad \text{or} \quad 6 < 10,$$

which is a true statement. However, if each side of the inequality $3 < 5$ is multiplied by the *negative* number -2, we obtain

$$-2 \cdot 3 > -2 \cdot 5 \quad \text{or} \quad -6 > -10,$$

$\uparrow$
Reverse inequality symbol.

which is a true statement because the inequality symbol is reversed from $<$ to $>$.

To solve an inequality we apply properties of inequalities to find a simpler, equivalent inequality, as illustrated in the next example.

EXAMPLE 1   Solving linear inequalities symbolically

Solve each inequality.

(a) $2x - 1 > 4$ **(b)** $\frac{1}{2}(z - 3) - (2 - z) \le 1$

Solution   **(a)** Begin by adding 1 to each side of the inequality.

$2x - 1 > 4$	Given inequality
$2x - 1 + 1 > 4 + 1$	Add 1 to each side.
$2x > 5$	Simplify.
$\dfrac{2x}{2} > \dfrac{5}{2}$	Divide by 2; do *not* reverse inequality symbol because $2 > 0$.
$x > \dfrac{5}{2}$	Simplify.

The solution set is $\left\{ x \mid x > \frac{5}{2} \right\}$.

(b) To clear fractions multiply each term by 2.

$\dfrac{1}{2}(z - 3) - (2 - z) \le 1$	Given inequality
$(z - 3) - 2(2 - z) \le 2$	Multiply by 2; do *not* reverse inequality symbol because $2 > 0$.
$z - 3 - 4 + 2z \le 2$	Distributive property
$3z - 7 \le 2$	Combine like terms.
$3z - 7 + 7 \le 2 + 7$	Add 7 to each side.
$3z \le 9$	Simplify.
$z \le 3$	Divide by 3; do *not* reverse inequality symbol because $3 > 0$.

The solution set is $\{ z \mid z \le 3 \}$.

In the next example we use Property 3 of inequalities.

EXAMPLE 2 Solving linear inequalities

Solve each inequality.

(a) $5 - 3x \le x - 3$ (b) $\dfrac{2t - 3}{5} \ge \dfrac{t + 1}{3} + 3t$

Solution (a) Begin by subtracting 5 from each side of the inequality.

$5 - 3x \le x - 3$	Given inequality
$5 - 3x - 5 \le x - 3 - 5$	Subtract 5 from each side.
$-3x \le x - 8$	Simplify.
$-3x - x \le x - 8 - x$	Subtract x from each side.
$-4x \le -8$	Simplify.

Next divide each side by -4. As we are dividing by a *negative* number, Property 3 requires reversing the inequality by changing $\le$ to $\ge$.

$\dfrac{-4x}{-4} \ge \dfrac{-8}{-4}$	Divide by -4; reverse the inequality because $-4 < 0$.
$x \ge 2$	Simplify.

The solution set is $\{x \mid x \ge 2\}$.

(b) To clear fractions multiply each term by 15.

$\dfrac{2t - 3}{5} \ge \dfrac{t + 1}{3} + 3t$	Given inequality
$15 \cdot \left(\dfrac{2t - 3}{5}\right) \ge 15 \cdot \left(\dfrac{t + 1}{3}\right) + 15 \cdot 3t$	Multiply each term by 15; do not reverse the inequality symbol because $15 > 0$.
$3(2t - 3) \ge 5(t + 1) + 45t$	Simplify: $\frac{15}{5} = 3$ and $\frac{15}{3} = 5$
$6t - 9 \ge 5t + 5 + 45t$	Distributive property
$6t - 9 + 9 \ge 50t + 5 + 9$	Add 9 to each side.
$6t \ge 50t + 14$	Simplify.
$6t - 50t \ge 50t - 50t + 14$	Subtract $50t$ from each side.
$-44t \ge 14$	Simplify.
$t \le \dfrac{14}{-44}$	Divide by -44; reverse the inequality symbol because $-44 < 0$.
$t \le -\dfrac{7}{22}$	Reduce.

The solution set is $\left\{t \mid t \le -\frac{7}{22}\right\}$.

NUMERICAL AND GRAPHICAL SOLUTIONS

In Section 3.1 we solved linear equations with symbolic, numerical, and graphical methods. We can also use these methods to solve linear inequalities.

EXAMPLE 3   Solving linear inequalities numerically

Use Table 3.4 to find the solution set for each equation or inequality.
(a) $-\frac{1}{2}x + 1 = 0$ (b) $-\frac{1}{2}x + 1 > 0$ (c) $-\frac{1}{2}x + 1 < 0$

TABLE 3.4

x	-1	0	1	2	3	4	5
$-\frac{1}{2}x + 1$	$\frac{3}{2}$	1	$\frac{1}{2}$	0	$-\frac{1}{2}$	-1	$-\frac{3}{2}$

Solution   (a) The expression $-\frac{1}{2}x + 1$ equals 0 when $x = 2$. Thus the solution set is $\{x \mid x = 2\}$.

(b) The expression $-\frac{1}{2}x + 1$ is positive when $x < 2$. Thus the solution set is $\{x \mid x < 2\}$.

(c) The expression $-\frac{1}{2}x + 1$ is negative when $x > 2$. Thus the solution set is $\{x \mid x > 2\}$.

EXAMPLE 4   Solving linear inequalities graphically

Use Figure 3.13 to find the solution set for each equation or inequality.

(a) $-\frac{1}{2}x + 1 = 0$ (b) $-\frac{1}{2}x + 1 > 0$ (c) $-\frac{1}{2}x + 1 < 0$

Solution   (a) The graph of $y = -\frac{1}{2}x + 1$ in Figure 3.13 crosses the x-axis at $x = 2$. Thus the solution set to $-\frac{1}{2}x + 1 = 0$ is $\{x \mid x = 2\}$.

(b) The graph is above the x-axis when $x < 2$. Thus the solution set to $-\frac{1}{2}x + 1 > 0$ is $\{x \mid x < 2\}$.

(c) The graph is below the x-axis when $x > 2$. Thus the solution set to $-\frac{1}{2}x + 1 < 0$ is $\{x \mid x > 2\}$.

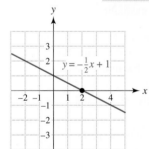

Figure 3.13

TEACHING TIP

Note how the solutions to each part of Example 4 are related.

Note: Numerical and graphical solutions can sometimes be difficult to find if the x-value that determines equality is not an integer. Symbolic methods work well in such situations.

Sometimes linear inequalities are written in the form $y_1 < y_2, y_1 \leq y_2, y_1 > y_2$, or $y_1 \geq y_2$, where both y_1 and y_2 contain variables. These types of inequalities can also be solved graphically or numerically.

Figure 3.14 shows the distances that two cars are from Chicago, Illinois, after x hours while traveling in the same direction on a freeway. The distance for Car 1 is denoted y_1, and the distance for Car 2 is denoted y_2.

TEACHING TIP

Spend some time explaining Figure 3.14. Solving inequalities graphically will require a few examples before students understand the concept.

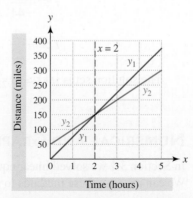

Figure 3.14   Distances of Two Cars

When $x = 2$ hours, $y_1 = y_2$ and both cars are 150 miles from Chicago. To the left of the dashed vertical line $x = 2$, the graph of y_1 is below the graph of y_2, so Car 1 is closer to Chicago than Car 2. Thus

$$y_1 < y_2 \quad \text{when} \quad x < 2.$$

To the right of the dashed vertical line $x = 2$, the graph of y_1 is above the graph of y_2, so Car 1 is farther from Chicago than Car 2. Thus

$$y_1 > y_2 \quad \text{when} \quad x > 2.$$

EXAMPLE 5 Solving an inequality graphically

Solve $5 - 3x \leq x - 3$.

Solution The graphs of $y_1 = 5 - 3x$ and $y_2 = x - 3$ intersect at the point $(2, -1)$, as shown in Figure 3.15. Equality, or $y_1 = y_2$, occurs when $x = 2$ and the graph of y_1 is below the graph of y_2 when $x > 2$. Thus $5 - 3x \leq x - 3$ is satisfied when $x \geq 2$. The solution set is $\{x \mid x \geq 2\}$. Figure 3.16 shows the same graph generated with a graphing calculator.

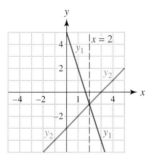

Figure 3.15

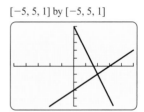

$[-5, 5, 1]$ by $[-5, 5, 1]$

Figure 3.16

Critical Thinking

Use the results from Example 5 to write the solution set for $5 - 3x \geq x - 3$. $\{x \mid x \leq 2\}$

AN APPLICATION

In the lower atmosphere, the air generally becomes colder as the altitude increases. One mile above Earth's surface the temperature is about $29°F$ colder than the ground-level temperature. As the air temperature cools, the chance of clouds forming increases. In the next example we estimate the altitudes at which clouds will not form.

EXAMPLE 6 Finding the altitude of clouds

If ground temperature is $90°F$, the temperature T above Earth's surface is modeled by $T(x) = 90 - 29x$, where x is the altitude in miles. Suppose that clouds will form only if the temperature is $53°F$ or colder. (*Source:* A. Miller and R. Anthes, *Meteorology.*)
(a) Determine symbolically the altitudes at which there are no clouds.
(b) Give graphical support for your answer.

Solution   **(a)** *Symbolic Solution*   Clouds will not form at altitudes at which the temperature is greater than 53°F. Thus we must solve the inequality $T(x) > 53$.

$$90 - 29x > 53 \qquad \text{Inequality to be solved}$$

$$90 - 29x - \mathbf{90} > 53 - \mathbf{90} \qquad \text{Subtract 90 from each side.}$$

$$-29x > -37 \qquad \text{Simplify.}$$

$$\frac{-29x}{-29} < \frac{-37}{-29} \qquad \text{Divide by } -29; \text{ reverse inequality.}$$

$$x < \frac{37}{29} \qquad \text{Simplify.}$$

The result, $\frac{37}{29} \approx 1.28$, indicates that clouds will not form below about 1.28 miles. Note that models are usually not exact, so rounding values is appropriate.

(b) *Graphical Solution*   Graph $Y_1 = 90 - 29X$ and $Y_2 = 53$. In Figure 3.17 their graphs intersect near the point (1.28, 53). The graph of y_1 is above the graph of y_2 when $x < 1.28$.

Calculator Help
To find a point of intersection, see the Appendix (page AP-7).

[0, 2, 1] by [0, 100, 10]

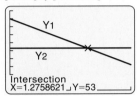

Intersection
X=1.2758621 ␣Y=53

Figure 3.17

We may substitute x-values from the solution set into the inequality and check them. If they do not check, then our solution set is incorrect. We may also check the solution set graphically.

Critical Thinking

A linear equation has one solution that can be checked by substituting it into the given equation. A linear inequality has infinitely many solutions. Discuss ways that the solution set for a linear inequality could be checked.

3.3   PUTTING IT ALL TOGETHER

The following table summarizes some important topics related to linear inequalities.

Concept	Explanation	Examples
Linear Inequalities in One Variable	Can be written as $$ax + b > 0,$$ where $a \neq 0$ and $>$ may be replaced by $<$, $\leq$, or $\geq$; has infinitely many solutions	$3x - 4 > 0$, $-(x - 5) < 2$, $2x \geq 5 - x$, and $4 - 2(x + 1) \leq 7x - 1$
Set-Builder Notation	Used to express sets of real numbers	$\{x \mid x > 4\}$ represents the set of real numbers x such that x is greater than 4.
Properties of Inequalities	See the box on page 169. Be sure to note Property 3: When multiplying or dividing by a negative number, *reverse* the inequality symbol.	*Property 1*: $x - 3 \geq 2$ is equivalent to $x \geq 5$. *Property 2*: $2x \leq 6$ is equivalent to $x \leq 3$. *Property 3*: $-3x < 6$ is equivalent to $x > -2$.

Linear inequalities can be solved symbolically, graphically, or numerically. Each method is used as follows to solve the inequality $2x - 4 > 0$.

Symbolic Solution	**Graphical Solution**	**Numerical Solution**

$$2x - 4 > 0$$
$$2x > 4$$
$$x > 2$$

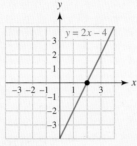

x	$2x - 4$
0	-4
1	-2
2	0
3	2
4	4

The graph of $y = 2x - 4$ is above the x-axis when $x > 2$.

The values of $2x - 4$ are greater than 0 when $x > 2$.

 **3.3** EXERCISES

FOR EXTRA HELP

📖 Student's Solutions Manual   InterAct Math   MathXL

🚪 MyMathLab   Math Tutor Center   Digital Video Tutor CD 2 Videotape 3

CONCEPTS

1. Give an example of a linear inequality.
   $3x + 2 < 5$; answers may vary.

2. Can a linear inequality have infinitely many solutions? Explain. Yes; consider $x + 2 > 2$.

3. Are $2x > 6$ and $x > 3$ equivalent inequalities? Explain. Yes; they have the same solution set.

4. Are $-4x < 8$ and $x < -2$ equivalent inequalities? Explain. No; $-4x < 8$ is equivalent to $x > -2$.

5. Give one difference between an equation and an inequality. An equation has an equals sign, whereas an inequality has an inequality symbol.

6. Name three methods for solving a linear inequality. Numerical, graphical, symbolic

Exercises 7–10: Decide whether the given value for the variable is a solution to the inequality.

7. $x - 5 \leq 3$ $x = 2$ Yes

8. $\frac{3}{2}x - \frac{1}{2} \geq 1 - x$ $x = -2$ No

9. $2t - 3 > 5t - (2t + 1)$ $t = 5$ No

10. $2(z - 1) < 3(z + 1)$ $z = \pi$ Yes

SYMBOLIC SOLUTIONS

Exercises 11–34: Solve the inequality symbolically.

11. $x + 3 \leq 5$ $\{x \mid x \leq 2\}$ 12. $x - 5 \geq -3$ $\{x \mid x \geq 2\}$

13. $\frac{1}{4}x > 9$ $\{x \mid x > 36\}$ 14. $14 < -3.5x$ $\{x \mid x < -4\}$

15. $4x - 2 \geq \frac{5}{2}$ $\{x \mid x \geq \frac{9}{8}\}$ 16. $4 - 3x \leq -\frac{2}{3}$ $\{x \mid x \geq \frac{14}{9}\}$

17. $x - \frac{3}{2} < 7 - \frac{1}{2}x$ 18. $4x - 6 > 12 - 10x$
$\{x \mid x > \frac{9}{7}\}$

19. $\frac{5}{2}(2x - 3) < 6 - 2x$ $\{x \mid x < \frac{27}{14}\}$ 17. $\{x \mid x < \frac{17}{3}\}$

20. $1 - \left(\frac{3}{2}x - 4\right) > \frac{1}{2}(x + 1)$ $\{x \mid x < \frac{9}{4}\}$

21. $\frac{3x - 2}{2} \leq \frac{x - 4}{5}$ 22. $\frac{5 - 2x}{2} \geq \frac{2x + 1}{4}$
$\{x \mid x \leq \frac{2}{13}\}$ $\{x \mid x \leq \frac{3}{2}\}$

23. $3(x - 2000) + 15 < 45$ $\{x \mid x < 2010\}$

24. $-2(x - 1990) + 75 > 25$ $\{x \mid x < 2015\}$

25. $0.4x - 0.7 < 1.3$ $\{x \mid x < 5\}$

26. $-0.3(x - 5) + 0.2 > 2$ $\{x \mid x < -1\}$

27. $\frac{4}{5}x - \frac{1}{5} \geq -5$ 28. $\frac{3x}{4} - \frac{1}{2} \leq \frac{1}{4}(2x + 1)$
$\{x \mid x \geq -6\}$ $\{x \mid x \leq 3\}$

29. $-\frac{1}{3}(z-3) - \frac{1}{4} \geq \frac{1}{4}(5-z)$ $\{z \mid z \leq -6\}$

30. $2(3-2z) - (1-z) \leq 4z - (1+z)$ $\{z \mid z \geq 1\}$

31. $\frac{3}{4}(2t-5) \leq \frac{1}{2}(4t-6) + 1$ $\{t \mid t \geq -\frac{7}{2}\}$

32. $\frac{5}{6}x + (3-x) \geq \frac{x-3}{3}$ $\{x \mid x \leq 8\}$

33. $\frac{1}{2}\left(4 - (x+3)\right) + 4 > -\frac{1}{3}\left(2x - (1-x)\right)$
$\{x \mid x > -\frac{25}{3}\}$

34. $\frac{x - (2-3x)}{2} < \frac{1 - (4-5x)}{6}$ $\{x \mid x < \frac{3}{7}\}$

NUMERICAL SOLUTIONS

Exercises 35 and 36: Complete the table. Then use the table to solve the inequality.

35. $-2x + 6 \leq 0$ $\{x \mid x \geq 3\}$

x	1	2	3	4	5
$-2x + 6$	4	2	0	-2	-4

36. $3x - 1 < 8$ $\{x \mid x < 3\}$

x	0	1	2	3	4
$3x - 1$	-1	2	5	8	11

Exercises 37–40: Solve the inequality numerically.

37. $x - 3 > 0$ $\{x \mid x > 3\}$ **38.** $2x < 0$ $\{x \mid x < 0\}$

39. $2x - 1 \geq 3$ $\{x \mid x \geq 2\}$ **40.** $2 - 3x \leq -4$ $\{x \mid x \geq 2\}$

GRAPHICAL SOLUTIONS

Exercises 41–44: Use the graph of y_1 to solve each equation or inequality.

    (a) $y_1 = 0$ *(b)* $y_1 < 0$ *(c)* $y_1 > 0$

41.

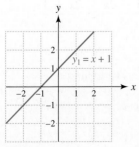

(a) $\{x \mid x = -1\}$
(b) $\{x \mid x < -1\}$
(c) $\{x \mid x > -1\}$

42.

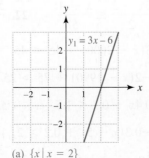

(a) $\{x \mid x = 2\}$
(b) $\{x \mid x < 2\}$
(c) $\{x \mid x > 2\}$

43.

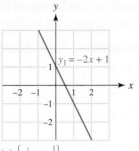

(a) $\{x \mid x = \frac{1}{2}\}$
(b) $\{x \mid x > \frac{1}{2}\}$
(c) $\{x \mid x < \frac{1}{2}\}$

44.

(a) $\{x \mid x = 0\}$
(b) $\{x \mid x > 0\}$
(c) $\{x \mid x < 0\}$

Exercises 45–48: Use the graph to solve the inequality.

45. $y_1 \leq y_2$ $\{x \mid x \geq 1\}$ **46.** $y_2 > y_1$ $\{x \mid x < 2\}$

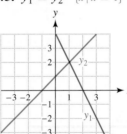
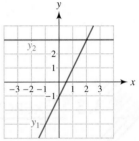

47. $y_1 > y_2$ $\{x \mid x > 2\}$ **48.** $y_1 \leq y_2$ $\{x \mid x \geq -2\}$

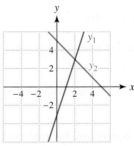
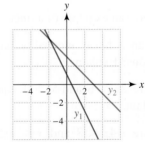

49.(a) Car 1; the slope of the line for Car 1 is greater than the slope of the line for Car 2.   (b) 5 hr; 400 mi.

49. ***Distance Between Cars***   Car 1 and Car 2 are traveling in the same direction. Their distances in miles north of St. Louis, Missouri, after x hours are shown in the following graph, where $0 \leq x \leq 8$.
  (a) Which car is traveling faster? Explain.
  (b) How many hours elapse before the two cars are the same distance from St. Louis? How far are they from St. Louis when this equality occurs?
  (c) During what time interval is Car 2 farther from St. Louis than Car 1? $0 \leq x < 5$

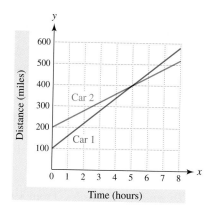

50. Use the following graph to solve each inequality.
(a) $f(x) > g(x)$ {$x\,|\,x > 10$}
(b) $f(x) \le g(x)$ {$x\,|\,x \le 10$}

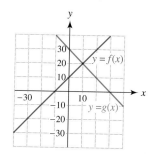

Exercises 51–62: Solve the inequality graphically.

51. $x - 1 < 0$ {$x\,|\,x < 1$} **52.** $4 - 2x \le 0$ {$x\,|\,x \ge 2$}

53. $2x \ge 0$ {$x\,|\,x \ge 0$} **54.** $3x + 6 > 0$ {$x\,|\,x > -2$}

55. $4 - 2x \le 8$
{$x\,|\,x \ge -2$} **56.** $-2x + 3 < -3$ {$x\,|\,x > 3$}

57. $x - (2x + 4) > 0$ **58.** $2x + 1 \ge 3x - 4$ {$x\,|\,x \le 5$}
{$x\,|\,x < -4$}

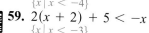 **59.** $2(x + 2) + 5 < -x$
{$x\,|\,x < -3$}

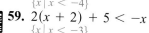 **60.** $\dfrac{x + 5}{3} \ge \dfrac{1 - x}{2}$ {$x\,|\,x \ge -1.4$}

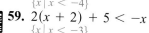 **61.** $25(x - 1995) + 100 \le 0$ {$x\,|\,x \le 1991$}

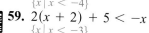 **62.** $5(x - 1980) - 20 > 50$ {$x\,|\,x > 1994$}

SOLVING LINEAR INEQUALITIES BY MORE THAN ONE METHOD

Exercises 63–66: Solve the inequality (a) numerically, (b) graphically, and (c) symbolically.

63. $5x - 2 < 8$
{$x\,|\,x < 2$} **64.** $2x - 4 - 3(x + 3) \le 0$
{$x\,|\,x \ge -13$}

65. $3x - 3 \ge 2x$
{$x\,|\,x \ge 3$} **66.** $x - 1 > \dfrac{4 - x}{2}$
{$x\,|\,x > 2$}

INEQUALITIES AND FUNCTIONS

Exercises 67–72: Solve each equation or inequality for the given $f(x)$.

67. $f(x) = x - 5$ **68.** $f(x) = 4x$
(a) $f(x) = 7$ {$x\,|\,x = 12$} (a) $f(x) = -2$ {$x\,|\,x = -\frac{1}{2}$}
(b) $f(x) > 7$ {$x\,|\,x > 12$} (b) $f(x) < -2$ {$x\,|\,x < -\frac{1}{2}$}

69. $f(x) = 4 - 3x$
(a) $f(x) \ge 11$ {$x\,|\,x \le -\frac{7}{3}$}
(b) $f(x) \le 11$ {$x\,|\,x \ge -\frac{7}{3}$}

70. $f(x) = 9 - 3x$
(a) $f(x) < 0$ {$x\,|\,x > 3$}
(b) $f(x) > 0$ {$x\,|\,x < 3$}

71. $f(x) = 3(x + 7) + 1$
(a) $f(x) \le -5$ {$x\,|\,x \le -9$}
(b) $f(x) \ge -5$ {$x\,|\,x \ge -9$}

72. $f(x) = -2(4 - 3x)$
(a) $f(x) > 16$ {$x\,|\,x > 4$}
(b) $f(x) < 16$ {$x\,|\,x < 4$}

APPLICATIONS

73. *Federal Debt*   The line graph shows the total federal debt in trillions of dollars from 1940 through 2000. Estimate the years when the deficit was less than $1 trillion dollars. 1980 or before

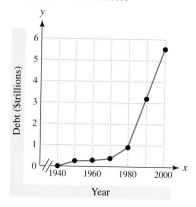

74. *Interest*   The graph on the next page shows the annual interest y on a loan of x dollars with an interest rate of 10%. Determine the loan amounts that result in the following.
(a) An annual interest equal to $100 $1000
(b) An annual interest of more than $100
(c) An annual interest of $100 or less $1000 or less
(b) More than $1000

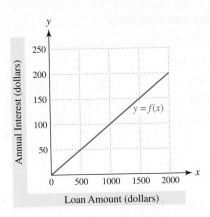

Loan Amount (dollars)

75. *Profit*   A band buys 500 blank CDs and records their music on them. They sell the CDs to earn a profit. Refer to the graph to answer the following questions.

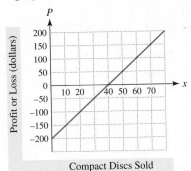

Compact Discs Sold

(a) How much did the band pay for the blank CDs? $200
(b) How much did the band charge for their recorded CDs? $5 each
(c) Write an equation that gives the profit P from selling x CDs. $P = 5x - 200$
(d) Determine the break-even point. $x = 40$ CDs
(e) When will the band make a profit? $x > 40$ CDs

76. *Average Temperature*   On March 1 the average high temperature in Minnesota is about 21°F. On March 30 this average increases to about 46°F. Use a linear function to estimate the days in March when the average high temperature is 31°F or less.   March 13 or before

77. *Geometry*   Find values for x so that the perimeter of the figure is less than 50 feet. $x < 10$ ft

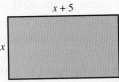

$x + 5$

x

78. *Geometry*   A rectangle is twice as long as it is wide. If the rectangle is to have a perimeter of 36 inches or less, what values for the width are possible?   6 in. or less

79. *Distance and Time*   Two cars are traveling in the same direction along a freeway. After x hours, the first car's distance in miles from a rest stop is given by $y_1 = 70x$ and the second car's distance in miles is given by $y_2 = 60x + 35$.   (a) First car: 70 mph; second car: 60 mph
(a) What is the speed of each car?
(b) When are the cars the same distance from the rest stop?   When $x = 3.5$ hr
(c) At what times is the first car farther from the rest stop than the second? Assume that $x \geq 0$.   Elapsed times after 3.5 hr

80. *Sales of CDs and LP Records*   From 1985 to 1990 sales of CDs, in millions, in the United States can be modeled by

$$y_1 = 51.6(x - 1985) + 9.1,$$

and sales of vinyl LP records, in millions, can be modeled by

$$y_2 = -31.9(x - 1985) + 167.7.$$

(a) Graph y_1 and y_2 in the viewing rectangle given by [1984, 1991, 1] by [0, 350, 50].*
(b) Estimate the years when CD sales were greater than or equal to LP record sales.   1987 or after
(c) Solve part (b) symbolically.   1987 or after

81. *Altitude and Temperature*   (Refer to Example 6.) If the temperature on the ground is 60°F, the air temperature x miles high is given by $T(x) = 60 - 29x$. Determine the altitudes at which the air temperature is greater than 0°F.   (*Source:* A. Miller.)   Below about 2.07 mi

82. *Altitude and Dew Point*   If the dew point on the ground is 70°F, then the dew point x miles high is given by $D(x) = 70 - 5.8x$.   (*Source:* A. Miller.)

(a) For each 1-mile increase in altitude, how much does the dew point change?   Decreases 5.8°F
(b) Determine the altitudes at which the dew point is greater than 30°F.   Below about 6.9 mi

83. *AIDS Research*   AIDS research funding in 1994 was $1.3 billion and in 2000 it was $1.8 billion. Use a linear function to estimate the years in which AIDS funding was greater than or equal to $1.55 billion.   (*Source:* National Institutes of Health.)   1997 or after

84. *Hepatitis C Research*   The hepatitis C virus (HCV) can live in a person for years without any symptoms after the individual was initially infected, possibly by a tainted blood transfusion. An estimated 4 million Americans have HCV, and some 10,000 people die from it each year. From 1994 to 2000 research fund-

*Answer on page IA-14

ing for hepatitis C in millions of dollars may be modeled by $f(x) = 4.43(x - 1994) + 7$, where x is the year. Determine when this funding was less than or equal to $20.3 million. (*Source:* National Institutes of Health.)   1997 or before

85. *Size and Weight of a Fish*   If a bass has a length of x inches, where $20 \le x \le 25$, its weight W in pounds can be estimated by $W(x) = 0.96x - 14.4$.
   (a) What length of bass is likely to weigh 6.7 pounds?   About 22 in.
   (b) What lengths of bass are likely to weigh less than 6.7 pounds?   Less than 22 in.

86. *Distant Galaxies*   In the late 1920s the famous observational astronomer Edwin P. Hubble (1889–1953) determined both the distance to several galaxies and the velocity at which they were receding from Earth. The graph shows four galaxies with their distances x in light-years from Earth and velocities y in miles per second that they are moving away from Earth.
   (a) The farther the galaxy is from Earth, the faster it is receding from Earth.

(*Source:* A. Sharov and I. Novikov, *Edwin Hubble, The Discoverer of the Big Bang Universe.*)

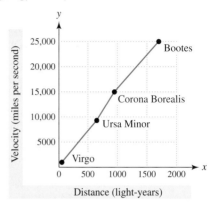

   (a) What relationship exists between distance and velocity of a galaxy?
   (b) A galaxy is determined to be receding at more than 12,500 miles per second. What can be said about its distance from Earth?
        It is more than 800 light-years from Earth.

WRITING ABOUT MATHEMATICS

87. Explain the following terms and give an example of each.
   (a) Linear function
   (b) Linear equation
   (c) Linear inequality

88. Suppose that a student says that a linear equation and a linear inequality can be solved symbolically in exactly the same way. How would you respond?

Group Activity: Working with Real Data

Directions: Form a group of 2 to 4 people. Select someone to record the group's responses for this activity. All members of the group should work cooperatively to answer the questions. If your instructor asks for your results, each member of the group should be prepared to respond.

1. *Born Outside the United States*   The foreign-born portion of the population increased from 4.7% in 1970 to 10.4% in 2000. This increase could be modeled by a linear function. Use these data to estimate the year when this percentage was 7%. (*Source:* Bureau of the Census.)   1982

2. When do you expect the foreign-born population to be 12%?   About 2008 or 2009

3. What does your model say about the foreign-born population in 1940 and in 2500? Are your answers reasonable? What do these results say about your model?
   −1%; 105.4%; no; it is not accurate for years that are not near 1970 or 2000.

3.4   COMPOUND INEQUALITIES

Basic Concepts · Symbolic Solutions and Number Lines ·
Numerical and Graphical Solutions · Interval Notation

INTRODUCTION

A person weighing 143 pounds and needing to purchase a life vest for white-water rafting is not likely to find one designed exactly for this weight. Life vests are manufactured to support a range of body weights. A vest approved for weights between 100 and 160 pounds might be appropriate for this person. In other words, if a person's weight is w, this life vest is safe if $w \geq 100$ *and* $w \leq 160$. This example illustrates the concept of a *compound inequality*.

BASIC CONCEPTS

A **compound inequality** consists of two inequalities joined by the words *and* or *or*. The following are two examples of compound inequalities.

$$2x \geq -3 \quad \text{and} \quad 2x < 5$$
$$x + 2 \geq 3 \quad \text{or} \quad x - 1 < -5$$

If a compound inequality contains the word *and*, a solution must satisfy *both* inequalities. For example, 1 is a solution to the first compound inequality because

$$2(1) \geq -3 \quad \text{and} \quad 2(1) < 5$$
$$\text{True} \qquad\qquad \text{True}$$

are both true statements.

If a compound inequality contains the word *or*, a solution must satisfy *at least one* of the two inequalities. Thus 5 is a solution to the second compound inequality, because the first statement is true.

$$5 + 2 \geq 3 \quad \text{or} \quad 5 - 1 < -5$$
$$\text{True} \qquad\qquad \text{False}$$

Note that 5 does not need to satisfy the second statement for this compound inequality to be true.

EXAMPLE 1   Determining solutions to compound inequalities

Determine whether the given x-values are solutions to the compound inequalities.
(a) $x + 1 < 9$ and $2x - 1 > 8$ $x = 5, -5$
(b) $5 - 2x \leq -4$ or $5 - 2x \geq 4$ $x = 2, -3$

Solution   **(a)** Substitute $x = 5$ in the given compound inequality.

$$5 + 1 < 9 \quad \text{and} \quad 2(5) - 1 > 8$$
$$\text{True} \qquad\qquad\quad \text{True}$$

Both inequalities are true, so 5 is a solution.
Now substitute $x = -5$.

$$-5 + 1 < 9 \quad \text{and} \quad 2(-5) - 1 > 8$$
$$\text{True} \qquad\qquad\quad \text{False}$$

To be a solution both inequalities must be true, so -5 is not a solution.

(b) Substitute $x = 2$ into the given compound inequality.

$$5 - 2(2) \le -4 \quad \text{or} \quad 5 - 2(2) \ge 4$$
False   False

Neither inequality is true, so 2 is not a solution.
Now substitute $x = -3$.

$$5 - 2(-3) \le -4 \quad \text{or} \quad 5 - 2(-3) \ge 4$$
False   True

At least one of the two inequalities is true, so -3 is a solution.

SYMBOLIC SOLUTIONS AND NUMBER LINES

We can use a number line to graph solutions to compound inequalities, such as

$$x \le 6 \quad \text{and} \quad x > -4.$$

The solution set for $x \le 6$ is shaded to the left of 6, with a bracket placed at $x = 6$, as shown in Figure 3.18. The solution set for $x > -4$ can be shown by shading a different number line to the right of -4 and placing a left parenthesis at -4. Because the inequalities are connected by *and*, the solution set consists of all numbers that are shaded on *both* number lines. The final number line represents the **intersection** of the two solution sets. That is, the solution set includes real numbers where the graphs "overlap."

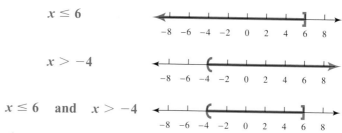

Figure 3.18

1. No numbers satisfy *both* inequalities.

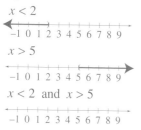

2. Every real number is either greater than 2 or less than 5.

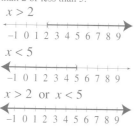

Note: A bracket, either [or], is used when an inequality contains $\le$ or $\ge$. A parenthesis, either (or), is used when an inequality contains $<$ or $>$. This notation makes clear whether an endpoint is included in the inequality.

Critical Thinking

Graph the following inequalities and discuss your results.

1. $x < 2$ and $x > 5$
2. $x > 2$ or $x < 5$

In the next example we use a number line to help solve a compound inequality.

EXAMPLE 2 Solving a compound inequality containing "and"

Solve $2x + 4 > 8$ and $5 - x < 9$. Graph the solution.

Solution   First solve each linear inequality separately.

$$2x + 4 > 8 \quad \text{and} \quad 5 - x < 9$$
$$2x > 4 \quad \text{and} \quad -x < 4$$
$$x > 2 \quad \text{and} \quad x > -4$$

Graph the two inequalities on two different number lines. On a third number line, shade solutions that appear on both of the first two number lines. As shown in Figure 3.19, the solution set is $\{x \mid x > 2\}$.

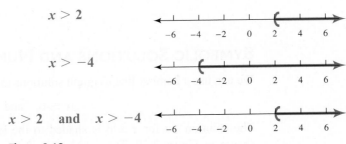

$x > 2$

$x > -4$

$x > 2 \quad \text{and} \quad x > -4$

Figure 3.19

Sometimes a compound inequality containing the word *and* can be combined into a three-part inequality. For example, rather than writing

$$x > 5 \quad \text{and} \quad x \leq 10,$$

we could write the **three-part inequality**

$$5 < x \leq 10.$$

This three-part inequality is represented by the number line shown in Figure 3.20.

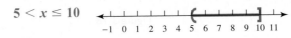

$5 < x \leq 10$

Figure 3.20

EXAMPLE 3   Solving three-part inequalities

Solve each inequality.

(a) $4 < t + 2 \leq 8$ (b) $-3 \leq 3z \leq 6$ (c) $-\dfrac{5}{2} < \dfrac{1 - m}{2} < 4$

Solution   (a) To solve a three-part inequality, isolate the variable by applying properties of inequalities to each part of the inequality.

$$4 < t + 2 \leq 8 \qquad \text{Given three-part inequality}$$
$$4 - 2 < t + 2 - 2 \leq 8 - 2 \qquad \text{Subtract 2 from each part.}$$
$$2 < t \leq 6 \qquad \text{Simplify each part.}$$

The solution set is $\{t \mid 2 < t \leq 6\}$.

(b) To simplify, divide each part by 3.

$$-3 \le 3z \le 6 \qquad \text{Given three-part inequality}$$

$$\frac{-3}{3} \le \frac{3z}{3} \le \frac{6}{3} \qquad \text{Divide each part by 3.}$$

$$-1 \le z \le 2 \qquad \text{Simplify each part.}$$

The solution set is $\{z \mid -1 \le z \le 2\}$.

(c) Multiply each part by 2 to clear fractions.

$$-\frac{5}{2} < \frac{1 - m}{2} < 4 \qquad \text{Given three-part inequality}$$

$$2 \cdot \left(-\frac{5}{2}\right) < 2 \cdot \left(\frac{1 - m}{2}\right) < 2 \cdot 4 \qquad \text{Multiply each part by 2.}$$

$$-5 < 1 - m < 8 \qquad \text{Simplify each part.}$$

$$-5 - 1 < 1 - m - 1 < 8 - 1 \qquad \text{Subtract 1 from each part.}$$

$$-6 < -m < 7 \qquad \text{Simplify each part.}$$

$$-1 \cdot (-6) > -1 \cdot (-m) > -1 \cdot 7 \qquad \begin{array}{l}\text{Multiply each part by } -1; \\ \textit{reverse} \text{ inequality symbols.}\end{array}$$

$$6 > m > -7 \qquad \text{Simplify each part.}$$

$$-7 < m < 6 \qquad \text{Rewrite inequality.}$$

The solution set is $\{m \mid -7 < m < 6\}$.

Note: Either $6 > m > -7$ or $-7 < m < 6$ is a correct way to write a three-part inequality. *However*, we usually write the smaller number on the left side and the larger number on the right side.

Three-part inequalities occur frequently in applications. In the next example we find altitudes at which the air temperature is within a certain range.

EXAMPLE 4   Solving a three-part inequality

Air temperature is colder at higher altitudes. If the ground-level temperature is $80°\,\text{F}$, the air temperature x miles above Earth's surface can be modeled by $T(x) = 80 - 29x$. Find the altitudes at which the air temperature ranges from $22°\text{F}$ to $-7°\text{F}$. (***Source:*** A. Miller and R. Anthes, *Meteorology.*)

Solution   We write and solve the three-part inequality $-7 \le T(x) \le 22$.

$$-7 \le 80 - 29x \le 22 \qquad \text{Substitute for } T(x).$$

$$-87 \le -29x \le -58 \qquad \text{Subtract 80 from each part.}$$

$$\frac{-87}{-29} \ge x \ge \frac{-58}{-29} \qquad \text{Divide by } -29; \textit{reverse} \text{ inequality symbols.}$$

$$3 \ge x \ge 2 \qquad \text{Simplify.}$$

$$2 \le x \le 3 \qquad \text{Rewrite inequality.}$$

The air temperature ranges from $22°\text{F}$ to $-7°\text{F}$ for altitudes between 2 and 3 miles.

We can also solve compound inequalities containing the word *or*. To write the solution to such an inequality we sometimes use *union* notation. For any two sets A and B, the **union** of A and B, denoted $A \cup B$, is defined by

$$A \cup B = \{x \mid x \text{ is an element of } A \text{ or an element of } B\}.$$

If the solution to an inequality is $\{x \mid x < 1\}$ or $\{x \mid x \geq 3\}$, then it can also be written as

$$\{x \mid x < 1\} \cup \{x \mid x \geq 3\}.$$

That is, we can replace the word *or* with the $\cup$ symbol.

EXAMPLE 5   Solving a compound inequality with "or"

Solve $x + 2 < -1$ or $x + 2 > 1$.

Solution   We first solve each linear inequality.

$$x + 2 < -1 \quad \text{or} \quad x + 2 > 1 \qquad \text{Given compound inequality}$$
$$x < -3 \quad \text{or} \quad x > -1 \qquad \text{Subtract 2.}$$

We can graph the simplified inequalities on different number lines, as shown in Figure 3.21. A solution must satisfy at least one of the two inequalities. Thus the solution set for the compound inequality results from taking the *union* of the first two number lines. We can write the solution, using set-builder notation, as $\{x \mid x < -3\} \cup \{x \mid x > -1\}$ or $\{x \mid x < -3 \text{ or } x > -1\}$.

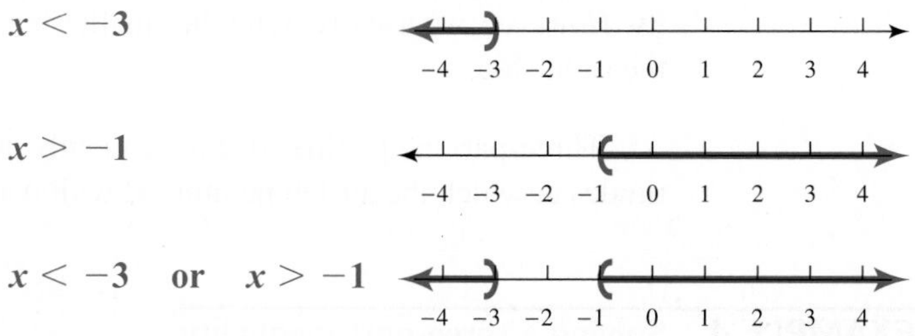

$x < -3$

$x > -1$

$x < -3$ or $x > -1$

Figure 3.21

Critical Thinking

Carbon dioxide is emitted when human beings breathe. In one study of college students, the amount of carbon dioxide exhaled in grams per hour was measured during both lectures and exams. The average amount exhaled during lectures L satisfied $25.33 \leq L \leq 28.17$, whereas the average amount exhaled during exams E satisfied $36.58 \leq E \leq 40.92$. What do these results indicate? Explain. (***Source:*** T. Wang, *ASHRAE Trans.*)

Students exhale more carbon dioxide during an exam than they do during a lecture. This increase may be caused by anxiety during examinations.

═══════════════ MAKING CONNECTIONS ═══════════════

Writing Three-Part Inequalities

The inequality $-2 < x < 1$ means that $x > -2$ *and* $x < 1$. A three-part inequality should *not* be used when *or* connects a compound inequality. Writing $x < -2$ or $x > 1$ as $1 < x < -2$ is incorrect because it states that x must be both greater than 1 *and* less than -2. It is impossible for any value of x to satisfy this statement.

NUMERICAL AND GRAPHICAL SOLUTIONS

Compound inequalities can also be solved graphically and numerically, as illustrated in the next example.

EXAMPLE 6 Solving a compound inequality numerically and graphically

Calculator Help
To find a point of intersection, see the Appendix (page AP-7).

Tuition at private colleges and universities from 1980 to 1997 can be modeled by $f(x) = 575(x - 1980) + 3600$. Estimate when the average tuition was between \$8200 and \$10,500.

Solution **Numerical Solution** Let $Y_1 = 575(X - 1980) + 3600$. Make a table of values, as shown in Figure 3.22(a). In 1988, the average tuition was \$8200 and in 1992 it was \$10,500. Therefore from 1988 to 1992 the average tuition ranged from \$8200 to \$10,500.

Graphical Solution Let $Y_1 = 575(X - 1980) + 3600$, $Y_2 = 8200$, and $Y_3 = 10,500$. We must find x-values so that $y_2 \le y_1 \le y_3$. Figures 3.22(b) and (c) show that y_1 is between y_2 and y_3 when $1988 \le x \le 1992$.

[1980, 1997, 1] by [3000, 12000, 3000]   [1980, 1997, 1] by [3000, 12000, 3000]

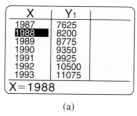

(a)

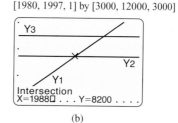

(b)

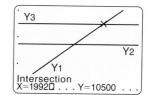

(c)

Figure 3.22

INTERVAL NOTATION

The solution set in Example 4 was $\{x \mid 2 \le x \le 3\}$. This solution set can be graphed on a number line, as shown in Figure 3.23.

TEACHING TIP

Spend some time on interval notation. Students many times find this concept difficult.

Figure 3.23

A convenient notation for number line graphs is called **interval notation**. Instead of drawing the entire number line as in Figure 3.23, the solution set can be expressed as [2, 3] in interval notation. Because the solution set includes the endpoints 2 and 3, brackets are used. A solution set that includes all real numbers satisfying $-2 < x < 3$ can be expressed as $(-2, 3)$. Parentheses indicate that the endpoints are *not* included. The interval $0 \le x < 4$ is represented by $[0, 4)$.

Table 3.5 on the next page provides some examples of interval notation. The symbol ∞ refers to infinity, and it does not represent a real number. The interval $(5, \infty)$ represents $x > 5$, which has no maximum x-value, so ∞ is used for the right endpoint. The symbol $-\infty$ may be used similarly and denotes "negative infinity."

TABLE 3.5   Interval Notation

Inequality	Interval Notation	Number Line Graph
$-1 < x < 3$	$(-1, 3)$	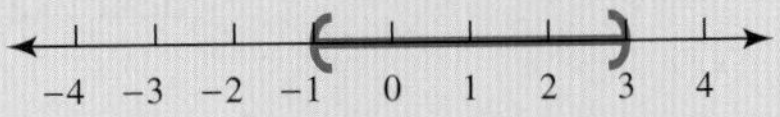
$-3 < x \leq 2$	$(-3, 2]$	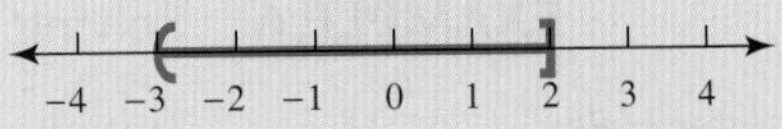
$-2 \leq x \leq 2$	$[-2, 2]$	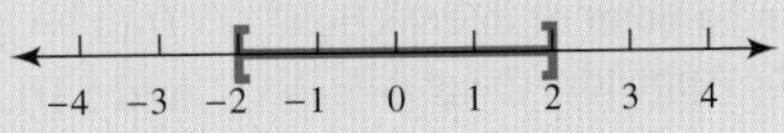
$x < -1$ or $x > 2$	$(-\infty, -1) \cup (2, \infty)$ ($\cup$ is the union symbol.)	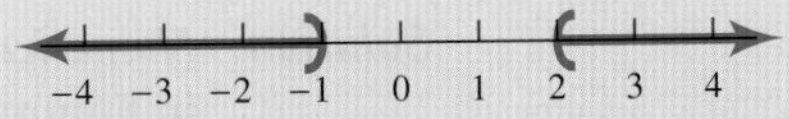
$x > -1$	$(-1, \infty)$	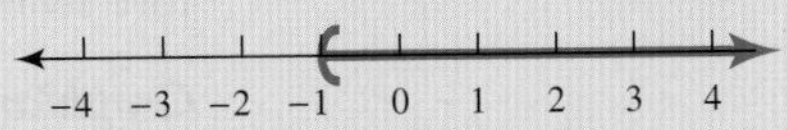
$x \leq 2$	$(-\infty, 2]$	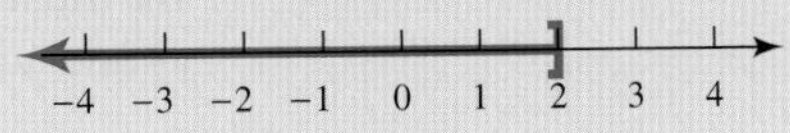

=== MAKING CONNECTIONS ===

Points and Intervals

The expression (1, 2) may represent a point in the xy-plane or the interval $1 < x < 2$. To alleviate confusion, phrases such as "the point (1, 2)" or "the interval (1, 2)" are used.

EXAMPLE 7   Writing inequalities in interval notation

Write each expression in interval notation.
(a) $-2 \leq x < 5$ (b) $x \geq 3$ (c) $x < -5$ or $x \geq 2$
(d) $x > 0$ and $x \leq 3$ (e) $\{x \mid x \leq 1 \text{ or } x \geq 3\}$

Solution (a) $[-2, 5)$ (b) $[3, \infty)$ (c) $(-\infty, -5) \cup [2, \infty)$
(d) $(0, 3]$ (e) $(-\infty, 1] \cup [3, \infty)$

EXAMPLE 8   Solving an inequality

Solve $2x + 1 \leq -1$ or $2x + 1 \geq 3$. Write the solution in interval notation.

Solution First solve each inequality.

$$2x + 1 \leq -1 \quad \text{or} \quad 2x + 1 \geq 3 \qquad \text{Given compound inequality}$$
$$2x \leq -2 \quad \text{or} \quad 2x \geq 2 \qquad \text{Subtract 1.}$$
$$x \leq -1 \quad \text{or} \quad x \geq 1 \qquad \text{Divide by 2.}$$

The solution set may be written as $(-\infty, -1] \cup [1, \infty)$.

3.4 PUTTING IT ALL TOGETHER

The following table summarizes some important topics related to compound inequalities.

Concept	Explanation	Examples
Compound Inequality	Two inequalities joined by *and* or *or*.	$x < -1$ or $x > 2$; $2x \geq 10$ and $x + 2 < 6$
Three-Part Inequality	Can be used to write some types of compound inequalities	$x > -2$ and $x \leq 3$ is equivalent to $-2 < x \leq 3$.
Interval Notation	Notation used to write sets of real numbers rather than using number lines or inequalities	$-2 \leq z \leq 4$ is equivalent to $[-2, 4]$. $x < 4$ is equivalent to $(-\infty, 4)$. $x \leq -2$ or $x > 0$ is equivalent to $(-\infty, -2] \cup (0, \infty)$.

The following table lists basic strategies for solving compound inequalities.

Type of Inequality	Method to Solve Inequality
Solving a Compound Inequality with *and*	**STEP 1:** First solve each inequality individually. **STEP 2:** The solution set includes values that satisfy *both* inequalities from Step 1.
Solving a Compound Inequality with *or*	**STEP 1:** First solve each inequality individually. **STEP 2:** The solution set includes values that satisfy *at least one* of the inequalities from Step 1.
Solving a Three-Part Inequality	Work on all three parts at the same time. Be sure to perform the same step on each part. Continue until the variable is isolated in the middle.

3.4 EXERCISES

FOR EXTRA HELP

📖 Student's Solutions Manual   InterAct math InterAct Math   MathXL MathXL

🚪 MyMathLab   Tutor Center Math Tutor Center   📼 Digital Video Tutor CD 2 Videotape 3

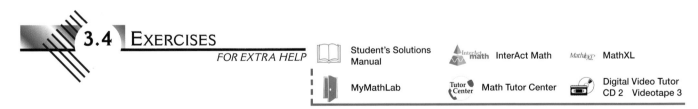

CONCEPTS

1. Give an example of a compound inequality containing the word *and*. $x > 1$ and $x \leq 7$; answers may vary.

2. Give an example of a compound inequality containing the word *or*. $x \leq 3$ or $x > 5$; answers may vary.

3. Is 1 a solution of the compound inequality $x > 3$ and $x \leq 5$?   No

4. Is 1 a solution of the compound inequality $x < 3$ or $x \geq 5$?   Yes

5. Is the compound inequality $x \geq -5$ and $x \leq 5$ equivalent to $-5 \leq x \leq 5$?   Yes

6. Name three methods for solving a compound inequality.   Numerical, graphical, symbolic

Exercises 7–12: Determine whether the given values of x are solutions to the compound inequality.

7. $x - 1 < 5$ and $2x > 3$ $x = 2, x = 6$
Yes, no

8. $2x + 1 \geq 4$ and $1 - x \leq 3$ $x = -2, x = 3$
No, yes

9. $3x < -5$ or $2x \geq 3$ $x = 0, x = 3$
No, yes

10. $x + 1 \leq -4$ or $x + 1 \geq 4$ $x = -5, x = 2$
Yes, no

11. $2 - x > -5$ and $2 - x \leq 4$ $x = -3, x = 0$
No, yes

12. $x + 5 \geq 6$ or $3x \leq 3$ $x = -1, x = 1$
Yes, yes

INTERVAL NOTATION

Exercises 13–32: Write the inequality in interval notation.

13. $2 \leq x \leq 10$ $[2, 10]$ **14.** $-1 < x < 5$ $(-1, 5)$

15. $5 < x \leq 8$ $(5, 8]$ **16.** $-\frac{1}{2} \leq x \leq \frac{5}{6}$ $\left[-\frac{1}{2}, \frac{5}{6}\right]$

17. $x < 4$ $(-\infty, 4)$ **18.** $x \leq -3$ $(-\infty, -3]$

19. $x > -2$ $(-2, \infty)$ **20.** $x \geq 6$ $[6, \infty)$

21. $x \leq -2$ or $x \geq 4$ **22.** $x \leq -1$ or $x > 6$
$(-\infty, -2] \cup [4, \infty)$ $(-\infty, -1] \cup (6, \infty)$

23. $x < 1$ or $x \geq 5$ **24.** $x < -3$ or $x > 3$
$(-\infty, 1) \cup [5, \infty)$ $(-\infty, -3) \cup (3, \infty)$

25. $(-3, 5]$

26. $[2, \infty)$

27. $(-\infty, -2)$

28. $[-4, 4]$

29. $\{x \mid x < 4\}$ $(-\infty, 4)$ **30.** $\{x \mid -1 \leq x < 4\}$ $[-1, 4)$

31. $\{x \mid x < 1$ or $x > 2\}$ **32.** $\{x \mid -\infty < x < \infty\}$
$(-\infty, 1) \cup (2, \infty)$ $(-\infty, \infty)$

SYMBOLIC SOLUTIONS

Exercises 33–40: Solve the compound inequality. Graph the solution set, using a number line.

33. $x \leq 3$ and $x \geq -1$ **34.** $x \geq 5$ and $x > 6$
$\{x \mid -1 \leq x \leq 3\}$ $\{x \mid x > 6\}$

35. $2x < 5$ and $2x > -4$ $\{x \mid -2 < x < 2.5\}$

36. $2x + 1 < 3$ and $x - 1 \geq -5$ $\{x \mid -4 \leq x < 1\}$

37. $x \leq -1$ or $x \geq 2$ $\{x \mid x \leq -1$ or $x \geq 2\}$

38. $2x \leq -6$ or $x \geq 6$ $\{x \mid x \leq -3$ or $x \geq 6\}$

39. $5 - x > 1$ or $x + 3 \geq -1$ All real numbers

40. $1 - 2x > 3$ or $2x - 4 \geq 4$ $\{x \mid x < -1$ or $x \geq 4\}$

Exercises 41–50: Solve the compound inequality. Write your answer in interval notation.

41. $x - 3 \leq 4$ and $x + 5 \geq -1$ $[-6, 7]$

42. $2z \geq -10$ and $z < 8$ $[-5, 8)$

43. $3t - 1 > -1$ and $2t - \frac{1}{2} > 6$ $\left(\frac{13}{4}, \infty\right)$

44. $2(x + 1) < 8$ and $-2(x - 4) > -2$ $(-\infty, 3)$

45. $x - 4 \geq -3$ or $x - 4 \leq 3$ $(-\infty, \infty)$

46. $1 - 3n \geq 6$ or $1 - 3n \leq -4$ $\left(-\infty, -\frac{5}{3}\right] \cup \left[\frac{5}{3}, \infty\right)$

47. $-x < 1$ or $5x + 1 < -10$ $\left(-\infty, -\frac{11}{5}\right) \cup (-1, \infty)$

48. $7x - 6 > 0$ or $-\frac{1}{2}x \leq 6$ $[-12, \infty)$

49. $1 - 7x < -48$ and $3x + 1 \leq -9$ No solutions

50. $3x - 4 \leq 8$ or $4x - 1 \leq 13$ $(-\infty, 4]$

Exercises 51–72: Solve the three-part inequality. Write your answer in interval notation.   53. $\left[-\frac{1}{4}, \frac{11}{8}\right)$

51. $-2 \leq t + 4 < 5$ **52.** $5 < t - 7 < 10$
$[-6, 1)$ $(12, 17)$

53. $-\frac{5}{8} \leq y - \frac{3}{8} < 1$ **54.** $-\frac{1}{2} < y - \frac{3}{2} < \frac{1}{2}$ $(1, 2)$

55. $-27 \leq 3x \leq 9$ $[-9, 3]$ **56.** $-4 < 2y < 22$ $(-2, 11)$

57. $\frac{1}{2} < -2y \leq 8$ $\left[-4, -\frac{1}{4}\right)$ **58.** $-16 \leq -4x \leq 8$ $[-2, 4]$

59. $-4 < 5z + 1 \leq 6$ **60.** $-3 \leq 3z + 6 < 9$ $[-3, 1)$
$(-1, 1]$

61. $3 \leq 4 - n \leq 6$ **62.** $-1 < 3 - n \leq 1$ $[2, 4)$
$[-2, 1]$

63. $-1 < 2z - 1 < 3$ **64.** $2 \leq 4z + 5 \leq 6$ $\left[-\frac{3}{4}, \frac{1}{4}\right]$
$(0, 2)$

65. $-2 \leq 5 - \frac{1}{3}m < 2$ **66.** $-\frac{3}{2} < 4 - 2m < \frac{7}{2}$ $\left(\frac{1}{4}, \frac{11}{4}\right)$
$(9, 21]$

67. $100 \leq 10(5x - 2) \leq 200$ $\left[\frac{12}{5}, \frac{22}{5}\right]$

68. $-15 < 5(x - 1990) < 30$ $(1987, 1996)$

69. $-3 < \dfrac{3z + 1}{4} < 1$ **70.** $-3 < \dfrac{z - 1}{2} < 5$ $(-5, 11)$
$\left(-\frac{13}{3}, 1\right)$

71. $-\dfrac{5}{2} \le \dfrac{2 - m}{4} \le \dfrac{1}{2}$ **72.** $\dfrac{4}{5} \le \dfrac{4 - 2m}{10} \le 2$
[0, 12]   [−8, −2]

NUMERICAL AND GRAPHICAL SOLUTIONS

Exercises 73–76: Use the table to solve the three-part inequality. Write your answer in interval notation.

73. $-3 \le 3x \le 6$ [−1, 2] **74.** $-5 \le 2x - 1 \le 1$ [−2, 1]

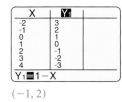

75. $-1 < 1 - x < 2$ **76.** $-2 \le -2x < 4$ (−2, 1]

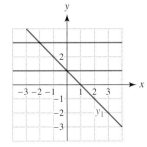

(−1, 2)

Exercises 77–80: Use the graph to solve the compound inequality. Write your answer in interval notation.

77. $-2 \le y_1 \le 2$ [−3, 1] **78.** $1 \le y_1 < 3$ (−2, 0]

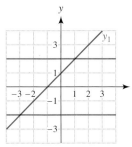

79. $y_1 < -2$ or $y_1 > 2$ **80.** $y_1 \le -2$ or $y_1 \ge 4$

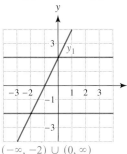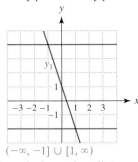

(−∞, −2) ∪ (0, ∞)   (−∞, −1] ∪ [1, ∞)

81. *Distance* The function f gives the distance y in miles between a car and the city of Omaha, Nebraska, after x hours, where $0 \le x \le 6$. The graphs of f and the horizontal lines $y = 100$ and $y = 200$ are shown in the following figure.

(a) Is the car moving toward or away from Omaha? Explain. Toward because distance is decreasing

(b) Determine the times when the car is 100 miles or 200 miles from Omaha. 4 hr, 2 hr

(c) When is the car from 100 to 200 miles from Omaha? From 2 to 4 hr

(d) When is the car's distance from Omaha greater than or equal to 200 miles? During the first 2 hr

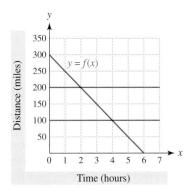

82. Use the following figure to solve each equation or inequality. Assume that the domains of $y_1, y_2,$ and y_3 are $0 \le x \le 5$.

(a) $y_1 = y_2$ 1
(b) $y_2 = y_3$ 3
(c) $y_1 \le y_2 \le y_3$ $\{x \mid 1 \le x \le 3\}$
(d) $y_2 < y_3$ $\{x \mid 0 \le x < 3\}$

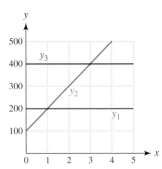

Exercises 83–86: (Refer to Example 6.) Solve the compound inequality numerically or graphically. Write your answer in interval notation.

83. $-2 \le 2x - 4 \le 4$ [1, 4]

84. $-1 \le 1 - x \le 3$ [−2, 2]

85. $x + 1 < -1$ or $x + 1 > 1$ (−∞, −2) ∪ (0, ∞)

86. $2x - 1 < -3$ or $2x - 1 > 5$ (−∞, −1) ∪ (3, ∞)

97.(a) [6, 9]; the car is from 470 to 680 mi from the rest stop for times between 6 and 9 hr.

USING MORE THAN ONE METHOD

Exercises 87–90: Solve the compound inequality symbolically, graphically, and numerically. Write the solution set in interval notation.

87. $4 \le 5x - 1 \le 14$ [1, 3]

88. $-4 < 2x < 4$ $(-2, 2)$

89. $4 - x \ge 1$ or $4 - x < 3$ $(-\infty, \infty)$

90. $x + 3 \ge -2$ or $x + 3 \le 1$ $(-\infty, \infty)$

APPLICATIONS

91. *Educational Attainment*   The line graph shows the percentage of the population that completed 4 years or more of college for selected years. Estimate the years when this percentage ranged from 6% to 17%. (*Source:* Bureau of the Census.)   From 1950 to 1980

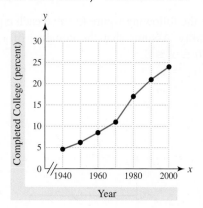

92. *School Enrollment*   The line graph shows the school enrollment in millions from kindergarten through university level. Estimate the years when the enrollment was from 57 to 65 million students. (*Source:* Department of Education.)   From 1970 to 1995

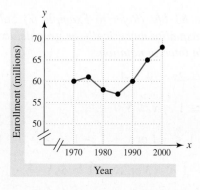

93. *Medicare Costs*   Based on current trends, future Medicare costs in billions of dollars may be modeled by $f(x) = 18x - 35{,}750$, where $1995 \le x \le 2007$. Estimate the years when Medicare costs will be from 250 to 340 billion dollars.   (*Source:* Office of Management and Budget.)   From 2000 to 2005

94. *Median Home Prices*   The median price P of a single-family home from 1980 to 1991 may be modeled by $P(x) = 3400(x - 1980) + 61{,}000$, where x is the year. Determine the years when the median price ranged from \$78,000 to \$95,000.   (*Source:* Department of Commerce.)   From 1985 to 1990

95. *Geometry*   For what values of x is the perimeter of the rectangle from 40 to 60 feet?   From $5.\overline{6}$ to 9 ft

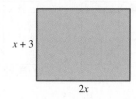

96. *Geometry*   A rectangle is three times as long as it is wide. If the rectangle is to have a perimeter from 100 to 160 inches, what values for the width are possible?   From 12.5 to 20 in.

97. *Distance and Time*   A car's distance in miles from a rest stop is given by $f(x) = 70x + 50$, where x is time in hours.
   (a) Construct a table for f for $x = 4, 5, 6, \ldots, 10$ and use the table to solve the inequality $470 \le f(x) \le 680$. Explain what your result means. *(See top of page.)
   (b) Solve the inequality in part (a) symbolically.   [6, 9]

98. *Altitude and Temperature*   If the air temperature at ground level is $70°F$, the air temperature x miles high is given by $T(x) = 70 - 29x$. Determine the altitudes at which the air temperature is from $26.5°F$ to $-2.5°F$.   (*Source:* A. Miller and R. Anthes, *Meteorology*.)
From 1.5 to 2.5 miles

99. *Temperature Scales*   The formula

$$F = \frac{9}{5}C + 32$$

may be used to convert Celsius temperatures to Fahrenheit temperatures. The greatest temperature ranges on Earth are recorded in Siberia where the temperature has varied from $-90°F$ to $98°F$. Find this temperature range in degrees Celsius.
$-67.\overline{7}°C$ to $36.\overline{6}°C$

*Answer on page IA-14

100. *Temperature Scales*   The formula

$$C = \frac{5}{9}(F - 32)$$

may be used to convert Fahrenheit temperatures to Celsius temperatures. If the Celsius temperature ranged from 5°C to 20°C, use this formula to find the corresponding temperature range in degrees Fahrenheit.   41°F to 68°F

WRITING ABOUT MATHEMATICS

101. Suppose that the solution set for a compound inequality can be written as $x < -3$ or $x > 2$. A student writes it as $2 < x < -3$. Is the student's three-part inequality correct? Explain your answer.

102. How can you determine whether an x-value is a solution to a compound inequality connected by the word *and*? Give an example. Repeat the question for a compound inequality connected by the word *or*.

CHECKING BASIC CONCEPTS   SECTIONS 3.3 AND 3.4

1. Solve the linear inequality $4 - 3x < \frac{1}{2}x$. $\left\{x \mid x > \frac{8}{7}\right\}$

2. Use the graph to solve each equation or inequality.

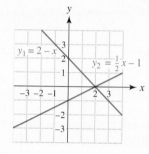

(a) $\frac{1}{2}x - 1 = 2 - x$ $\{x \mid x = 2\}$

(b) $\frac{1}{2}x - 1 < 2 - x$ $\{x \mid x < 2\}$

(c) $\frac{1}{2}x - 1 \geq 2 - x$ $\{x \mid x \geq 2\}$

3. (a) Is 3 a solution of the compound inequality $x + 2 < 4$ or $2x - 1 \geq 3$?   Yes

(b) Is 3 a solution of the compound inequality $x + 2 < 4$ and $2x - 1 \geq 3$?   No

4. Solve the following compound inequalities. Write your answers in interval notation.

(a) $-5 \leq 2x + 1 \leq 3$ $[-3, 1]$

(b) $1 - x \leq -2$ or $1 - x > 2$ $(-\infty, -1) \cup [3, \infty)$

(c) $-2 < \dfrac{4 - 3x}{2} \leq 6$ $\left[-\frac{8}{3}, \frac{8}{3}\right)$

3.5   ABSOLUTE VALUE EQUATIONS AND INEQUALITIES

Basic Concepts · Absolute Value Equations · Absolute Value Inequalities

INTRODUCTION

Monthly average temperatures can vary greatly from one month to another, whereas yearly average temperatures remain fairly constant from one year to the next. In Boston, Massachusetts, the yearly average temperature is 50°F, but monthly average temperatures can vary from 28°F to 72°F. Because 50°F − 28°F = 22°F and 72°F − 50°F = 22°F, the monthly average temperatures are always within 22°F of the yearly average temperature of 50°F. If T represents a monthly average temperature, we can model this situation by using the absolute value inequality

$$|T - 50| \leq 22.$$

The absolute value is necessary because a monthly average temperature T can be either greater than or less than $50°F$ by as much as $22°F$. In this section we discuss how to solve absolute value equations and inequalities. (***Source:*** A. Miller and J. Thompson, *Elements of Meteorology*.)

BASIC CONCEPTS

TABLE 3.6

x	$|x|$
-2	2
-1	1
0	0
1	1
2	2

In Chapter 1 we discussed the absolute value of a number. We can define a function called the **absolute value function** given by $f(x) = |x|$. To graph $y = |x|$, we begin by making a table of values, as shown in Table 3.6.

Next we plot these points and then sketch the graph shown in Figure 3.24. Note that the graph is V-shaped.

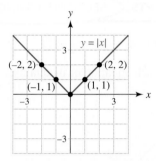

Figure 3.24 Absolute Value

Because the input for $f(x) = |x|$ can be any real number, the domain of the absolute value function is all real numbers, which can be written in interval notation as $(-\infty, \infty)$. The graph of the absolute value function shows that the output y (range) is any real number greater than or equal to 0. That is, the output from $f(x) = |x|$ can never be negative. In interval notation the range can be expressed as $[0, \infty)$.

ABSOLUTE VALUE EQUATIONS

An equation that contains an absolute value is called an **absolute value equation**. Examples include

$$|x| = 2, \quad |2x - 1| = 5, \quad \text{and} \quad |5 - 3x| - 3 = 1.$$

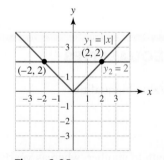

Figure 3.25

Consider the absolute value equation $|x| = 2$. This equation has *two* solutions: 2 and -2 because $|2| = 2$ and $|-2| = 2$. We can also demonstrate this result with a table of values or a graph. Refer back to Table 3.6: $|x| = 2$ when $x = -2$ or $x = 2$. In Figure 3.25 the graph of $y_1 = |x|$ intersects the graph of $y_2 = 2$ at the points $(-2, 2)$ and $(2, 2)$. The x-values at these points of intersection correspond to the solutions -2 and 2.

We generalize this discussion in the following manner.

SOLVING $|x| = k$

1. If $k > 0$, then $|x| = k$ is equivalent to $x = k$ or $x = -k$.
2. If $k = 0$, then $|x| = k$ is equivalent to $x = 0$.
3. If $k < 0$, then $|x| = k$ has no solutions.

EXAMPLE 1   Solving absolute value equations

Solve each equation.
(a) $|x| = 20$ **(b)** $|x| = -5$

Solution   **(a)** The solutions are -20 and 20.
(b) There are no solutions because $|x|$ is never negative.

We can solve other absolute value equations similarly.

EXAMPLE 2   Solving an absolute value equation

Solve $|2x - 5| = 3$.

Solution   If $|2x - 5| = 3$, then either $2x - 5 = 3$ or $2x - 5 = -3$. Solve each equation separately.

$2x - 5 = 3$ or	$2x - 5 = -3$	Equations to be solved
$2x = 8$ or	$2x = 2$	Add 5.
$x = 4$ or	$x = 1$	Divide by 2.

The solutions are 1 and 4.

A table of values can be used to solve the equation $|2x - 5| = 3$ from Example 2. Table 3.7 shows that $|2x - 5| = 3$ when $x = 1$ or $x = 4$.

TABLE 3.7

x	0	1	2	3	4	5	6
$|2x - 5|$	5	3	1	1	3	5	7

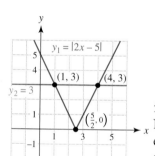

Figure 3.26

This equation can also be solved by graphing $y_1 = |2x - 5|$ and $y_2 = 3$. To graph y_1, first plot some of the points from Table 3.7. Its graph is V-shaped, as shown in Figure 3.26. Note that the x-coordinate of the "point" or vertex of the V can be found by solving the equation $2x - 5 = 0$ to obtain $\frac{5}{2}$. The graph of y_1 intersects the graph of y_2 at the points $(1, 3)$ and $(4, 3)$, giving the solutions 1 and 4, so the graphical solutions agree with the numerical and symbolic solutions.

This discussion leads to the following result.

ABSOLUTE VALUE EQUATIONS

Let $k > 0$ be a positive number. Then

$$|ax + b| = k$$

is equivalent to

$$ax + b = k \quad \text{or} \quad ax + b = -k.$$

EXAMPLE 3   Solving absolute value equations

Solve.
(a) $|5 - x| - 2 = 8$ **(b)** $\left|\frac{1}{2}(x - 6)\right| = \frac{3}{4}$

Solution (a) Start by adding 2 to each side to obtain

$$|5 - x| = 10.$$

This equation is satisfied by the solution from either of the following equations.

$5 - x = 10$ or $5 - x = -10$		Equations to be solved
$-x = 5$ or $-x = -15$		Subtract 5.
$x = -5$ or $x = 15$		Multiply by -1.

The solutions are -5 and 15.

(b) This equation is satisfied by the solution from either of the following equations. To begin solving, multiply by 4 to clear fractions.

$\frac{1}{2}(x - 6) = \frac{3}{4}$ or $\frac{1}{2}(x - 6) = -\frac{3}{4}$	Equations to be solved
$2(x - 6) = 3$ or $2(x - 6) = -3$	Multiply by 4.
$2x - 12 = 3$ or $2x - 12 = -3$	Distributive property
$2x = 15$ or $2x = 9$	Add 12.
$x = \frac{15}{2}$ or $x = \frac{9}{2}$	Divide by 2.

The solutions are $\frac{9}{2}$ and $\frac{15}{2}$.

The next example illustrates absolute value equations that have either 0 or 1 solution.

EXAMPLE 4   Solving absolute value equations

Solve.
(a) $|2x - 1| = -2$ (b) $|4 - 2x| = 0$

Solution (a) Because an absolute value can never be negative, the expression $|2x - 1|$ is always greater than or equal to 0. There are no solutions. Figure 3.27 shows that the graph of $y_1 = |2x - 1|$ never intersects the graph of $y_2 = -2$.

(b) If $|y| = 0$, then $y = 0$. Thus the given equation is satisfied when $4 - 2x = 0$ or when $x = 2$. The solution is 2.

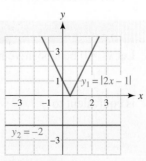

Figure 3.27

Sometimes an absolute value equation can have an absolute value on each side of the equation. An example would be $|2x| = |x - 3|$. In this situation either $2x = x - 3$ (the two expressions are equal), or $2x = -(x - 3)$ (the two expressions are opposites). These concepts are summarized as follows.

▥	**SOLVING** $|ax + b| = |cx + d|$

Let a, b, c, and d be constants. Then $|ax + b| = |cx + d|$ is equivalent to

$$ax + b = cx + d \quad \text{or} \quad ax + b = -(cx + d).$$

EXAMPLE 5   Solving absolute value equations

Solve $|2x| = |x - 3|$.

Solution   Solve the following compound equality.

$$2x = x - 3 \quad \text{or} \quad 2x = -(x - 3)$$
$$x = -3 \quad \text{or} \quad 2x = -x + 3$$
$$3x = 3$$
$$x = 1$$

The solutions are -3 and 1.

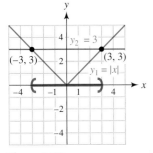

Figure 3.28

The solution set to Example 5 is shown graphically in Figure 3.28. Note that the graphs of $y_1 = |2x|$ and $y_2 = |x - 3|$ are V-shaped and intersect at the points $(-3, 6)$ and $(1, 2)$. Thus the solutions are -3 and 1.

ABSOLUTE VALUE INEQUALITIES

As with other inequalities, we can solve absolute value inequalities graphically. For example, to solve $|x| < 3$, let $y_1 = |x|$ and $y_2 = 3$ (see Figure 3.29). Their graphs intersect at the points $(-3, 3)$ and $(3, 3)$. The graph of y_1 is below the graph of y_2 for x-values between, but not including, $x = -3$ and $x = 3$. The solution set is $\{x \mid -3 < x < 3\}$ and is shaded on the x-axis.

Other absolute value inequalities can be solved graphically in a similar way. In Figure 3.30 the solutions to $|2x - 1| = 3$ are -1 and 2. The V-shaped graph of $y_1 = |2x - 1|$ is below the horizontal line $y_2 = 3$ when $-1 < x < 2$. Thus $|2x - 1| < 3$ whenever $-1 < x < 2$. The solution set is shaded on the x-axis.

Figure 3.29

TEACHING TIP

Take time to explain Figure 3.30 and Figure 3.31 on the next page. Emphasize that, if the student finds the points of intersection, he or she can write the solution to the inequality easily.

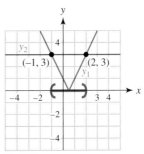

Figure 3.30

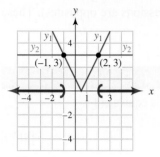

Figure 3.31

In Figure 3.31 the V-shaped graph of $y_1 = |2x - 1|$ is above the horizontal line $y_2 = 3$ both to the left of -1 and to the right of 2. That is, $|2x - 1| > 3$ whenever $x < -1$ or $x > 2$. The solution set is shaded on the x-axis.

This discussion is summarized as follows.

ABSOLUTE VALUE INEQUALITIES

Let the solutions to $|ax + b| = k$ be c and d, where $c < d$ and $k > 0$.

1. $|ax + b| < k$ is equivalent to $c < x < d$.
2. $|ax + b| > k$ is equivalent to $x < c$ or $x > d$.

Similar statements can be made for inequalities involving $\leq$ or $\geq$.

═══ MAKING CONNECTIONS ═══

Graphs of $y = |ax + b|$

The graph of $y = |ax + b|$, $a \neq 0$, is V-shaped and intersects a horizontal line above the x-axis twice. This graph can be used to help visualize the solution to either $|ax + b| < k$ or $|ax + b| > k$.

EXAMPLE 6   Solving absolute value equations and inequalities

Solve each absolute value equation and inequality.
(a) $|2 - 3x| = 4$ **(b)** $|2 - 3x| < 4$ **(c)** $|2 - 3x| > 4$

Solution   **(a)** Solve the given equation.

$$2 - 3x = 4 \quad \text{or} \quad 2 - 3x = -4 \qquad \text{Equations to be solved}$$

$$-3x = 2 \quad \text{or} \quad -3x = -6 \qquad \text{Subtract 2.}$$

$$x = -\frac{2}{3} \quad \text{or} \quad x = 2 \qquad \text{Divide by } -3.$$

The solutions are $-\frac{2}{3}$ and 2.

(b) Solutions to $|2 - 3x| < 4$ include x-values between, but not including, $-\frac{2}{3}$ and 2. Thus the solution set is $\{x \mid -\frac{2}{3} < x < 2\}$, or in interval notation, $\left(-\frac{2}{3}, 2\right)$.

(c) Solutions to $|2 - 3x| > 4$ include x-values to the left of $x = -\frac{2}{3}$ or to the right of $x = 2$. Thus the solution set is $\{x \mid x < -\frac{2}{3} \text{ or } x > 2\}$, or in interval notation, $\left(-\infty, -\frac{2}{3}\right) \cup (2, \infty)$.

EXAMPLE 7   Solving an absolute value inequality

Solve $\left|\frac{2x - 5}{3}\right| > 3$. Write the solution set in interval notation.

Solution Start by solving $\left|\frac{2x-5}{3}\right| = 3$ as follows.

$$\frac{2x-5}{3} = 3 \quad \text{or} \quad \frac{2x-5}{3} = -3 \qquad \text{Equations to be solved}$$

$$2x - 5 = 9 \quad \text{or} \quad 2x - 5 = -9 \qquad \text{Multiply by 3.}$$

$$2x = 14 \quad \text{or} \quad 2x = -4 \qquad \text{Add 5.}$$

$$x = 7 \quad \text{or} \quad x = -2 \qquad \text{Divide by 2.}$$

Because the inequality symbol is $>$, the solution set is $x < -2$ or $x > 7$, which can be written in interval notation as $(-\infty, -2) \cup (7, \infty)$.

EXAMPLE 8   **Modeling temperature in Boston**

In the introduction to this section we discussed how the inequality $\left|T - 50\right| \le 22$ models the range for the monthly average temperatures T in Boston, Massachusetts.
(a) Solve this inequality and interpret the result.
(b) Give graphical support for part (a).

Solution **(a)** *Symbolic Solution*   Start by solving $\left|T - 50\right| = 22$.

$$T - 50 = 22 \quad \text{or} \quad T - 50 = -22 \qquad \text{Equations to be solved}$$

$$T = 72 \quad \text{or} \quad T = 28 \qquad \text{Add 50 to both sides.}$$

Thus the solution set to $\left|T - 50\right| \le 22$ is $\{T \mid 28 \le T \le 72\}$. Monthly average temperatures in Boston vary from $28°F$ to $72°F$.

(b) *Graphical Solution*   The graphs of $y_1 = \left|x - 50\right|$ and $y_2 = 22$ intersect at the points $(28, 22)$ and $(72, 22)$, as shown in Figures 3.32(a) and (b), respectively. The V-shaped graph of y_1 intersects the horizontal graph of y_2, or is below it, when $28 \le x \le 72$. Thus the solution set is $\{T \mid 28 \le T \le 72\}$. This result agrees with the symbolic result.

Calculator Help
To graph an absolute value, see the Appendix (page AP-7).

[0, 100, 10] by [0, 70, 10]

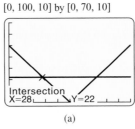

(a)

[0, 100, 10] by [0, 70, 10]

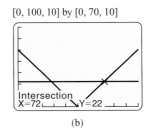

(b)

Figure 3.32

---

1. The solution set includes all real numbers because an absolute value is always greater than -3. An absolute value is always nonnegative.
2. There are no solutions because an absolute value is never less than 0.

Critical Thinking

Find the solution set for the following inequalities. Discuss your results.

1. $\left|2x - 5\right| > -3$
2. $\left|2x - 5\right| < -3$

3.5   PUTTING IT ALL TOGETHER

The absolute value function is given by $f(x) = |x|$, and its graph is V-shaped. Its domain (set of valid inputs) includes all real numbers, and its range (outputs) includes all nonnegative real numbers. The following table summarizes methods for solving absolute value equations and inequalities involving $<$ and $>$ symbols. Inequalities containing $\leq$ and $\geq$ symbols are solved similarly.

Problem	Symbolic Solution	Graphical Solution
$|ax + b| = k, k > 0$	Solve the equations $$ax + b = k$$ and $$ax + b = -k.$$	Graph $y_1 = |ax + b|$ and $y_2 = k$. Find the x-values of the two points of intersection.
$|ax + b| < k, k > 0$	If the solutions to $$|ax + b| = k$$ are c and d, $c < d$, then the solutions to $$|ax + b| < k$$ satisfy $$c < x < d.$$	Graph $y_1 = |ax + b|$ and $y_2 = k$. Find the x-values of the two points of intersection. The solutions are between these x-values on the number line, where the graph of y_1 lies below the graph of y_2.
$|ax + b| > k, k > 0$	If the solutions to $$|ax + b| = k$$ are c and d, $c < d$, then the solutions to $$|ax + b| > k$$ satisfy $$x < c \quad \text{or} \quad x > d.$$	Graph $y_1 = |ax + b|$ and $y_2 = k$. Find the x-values of the two points of intersection. The solutions are outside these x-values on the number line, where the graph of y_1 is above the graph of y_2.

3.5   EXERCISES

FOR EXTRA HELP

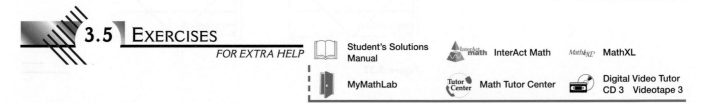

CONCEPTS

1. Give an example of an absolute value equation.
   $|3x + 2| = 6$; answers may vary.

2. Give an example of an absolute value inequality.
   $|2x - 1| \leq 17$; answers may vary.

3. Is -3 a solution to $|x| = 3$?   Yes

4. Is -4 a solution to $|x| > 3$?   Yes

5. Is $|x| = 5$ equivalent to $x = -5$ or $x = 5$?   Yes

6. Is $|x| < 3$ equivalent to $x < -3$ or $x > 3$? Explain.
   No, it is equivalent to $-3 < x < 3$.

Exercises 7–12: Determine whether the given values of x are solutions to the absolute value equation or inequality.

7. $|2x - 5| = 1$ $\quad x = -3, x = 3$ No, yes

8. $|5 - 6x| = 1$ $\quad x = 1, x = 0$ Yes, no

9. $|7 - 4x| \leq 5$ $\quad x = -2, x = 2$ No, yes

10. $|2 + x| < 2$ $\quad x = -4, x = -1$ No, yes

11. $|7x + 4| > -1$ $\quad x = -\frac{4}{7}, x = 2$ Yes, yes

12. $|12x + 3| \geq 3$ $\quad x = -\frac{1}{4}, x = 2$ No, yes

Exercises 13 and 14: Use the graph of y_1 to solve the equation.

13. $y_1 = 2$ 0, 4

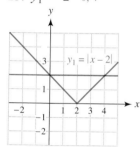

14. $y_1 = 3$ −2, 1

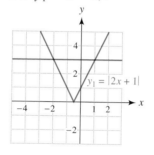

SYMBOLIC SOLUTIONS

Exercises 15–38: Solve the absolute value equation.

15. $|x| = 7$ −7, 7

16. $|x| = 4$ −4, 4

17. $|x| = 0$ 0

18. $|x| = -6$ No solutions

19. $|4x| = 9$ $-\frac{9}{4}, \frac{9}{4}$

20. $|-3x| = 7$ $-\frac{7}{3}, \frac{7}{3}$

21. $|-2x| - 6 = 2$ −4, 4

22. $|5x| + 1 = 5$ $-\frac{4}{5}, \frac{4}{5}$

23. $|2x + 1| = 11$ −6, 5

24. $|1 - 3x| = 4$ $-1, \frac{5}{3}$

25. $|-2x + 3| + 3 = 4$ 1, 2

26. $|6x + 2| - 2 = 6$ $-\frac{5}{3}, 1$

27. $|\frac{1}{2}x - 1| = 5$ −8, 12

28. $|6 - \frac{3}{4}x| = 3$ 4, 12

29. $|2x - 6| = -7$ No solutions

30. $|1 - \frac{2}{3}x| + 2 = 0$ No solutions

31. $|\frac{2}{3}z - 1| - 3 = 8$ −15, 18

32. $|1 - 2z| + 5 = 10$ −2, 3

33. $|z - 1| = |2z|$ $-1, \frac{1}{3}$

34. $|2z + 3| = |2 - z|$ $-5, -\frac{1}{3}$

35. $|3t + 1| = |2t - 4|$ $-5, \frac{3}{5}$

36. $|\frac{1}{2}t - 1| = |3 - \frac{3}{2}t|$ 2

37. $|\frac{1}{4}x| = |3 + \frac{1}{4}x|$ −6

38. $|2x - 1| = |2x + 2|$ $-\frac{1}{4}$

Exercises 39–42: Solve the absolute value equation and inequalities.

39. **(a)** $|2x| = 8$ −4, 4
(b) $|2x| < 8$ $\{x \mid -4 < x < 4\}$
(c) $|2x| > 8$ $\{x \mid x < -4 \text{ or } x > 4\}$

40. **(a)** $|3x - 9| = 6$ 1, 5
(b) $|3x - 9| \leq 6$ $\{x \mid 1 \leq x \leq 5\}$
(c) $|3x - 9| \geq 6$ $\{x \mid x \leq 1 \text{ or } x \geq 5\}$

41. **(a)** $|5 - 4x| = 3$ $\frac{1}{2}, 2$
(b) $|5 - 4x| \leq 3$ $\{x \mid \frac{1}{2} \leq x \leq 2\}$
(c) $|5 - 4x| \geq 3$ $\{x \mid x \leq \frac{1}{2} \text{ or } x \geq 2\}$

42. **(a)** $\left|\dfrac{x - 5}{2}\right| = 2$ 1, 9

(b) $\left|\dfrac{x - 5}{2}\right| < 2$ $\{x \mid 1 < x < 9\}$

(c) $\left|\dfrac{x - 5}{2}\right| > 2$ $\{x \mid x < 1 \text{ or } x > 9\}$

Exercises 43–74: Solve the absolute value inequality. Write your answer in interval notation. 54. $(-\infty, -2) \cup \left(-\frac{6}{5}, \infty\right)$

43. $|x| \leq 3$ $[-3, 3]$

44. $|x| < 2$ $(-2, 2)$

45. $|k| > 4$ $(-\infty, -4) \cup (4, \infty)$

46. $|k| \geq 5$ $(-\infty, -5] \cup [5, \infty)$

47. $|t| \leq -3$ No solutions

48. $|t| < -1$ No solutions

49. $|z| > 0$ $(-\infty, 0) \cup (0, \infty)$

50. $|2z| \geq 0$ $(-\infty, \infty)$

51. $|2x| > 7$

52. $|-12x| < 30$ $\left(-\frac{5}{2}, \frac{5}{2}\right)$

53. $|-4x + 4| < 16$ $(-3, 5)$

54. $|-5x - 8| > 2$

55. $2|x + 5| \geq 8$ $(-\infty, -9] \cup [-1, \infty)$

56. $-3|x - 1| \geq -9$ $[-2, 4]$

57. $|8 - 6x| - 1 \leq 2$ $\left[\frac{5}{6}, \frac{11}{6}\right]$

58. $4 - \left|\dfrac{2x}{3}\right| < -7$

59. $5 + \left|\dfrac{2 - x}{3}\right| \leq 9$ $[-10, 14]$

60. $\left|\dfrac{x + 3}{5}\right| \leq 12$ $[-63, 57]$

61. $|2x - 1| \leq -3$ No solutions

62. $|x + 6| \geq -5$ $(-\infty, \infty)$

63. $|x + 1| - 1 > -3$ $(-\infty, \infty)$

64. $-2|1 - 7x| \geq 2$ No solutions

65. $|2z - 4| \leq -1$ No solutions

66. $|4 - z| \leq 0$ 4

51. $\left(-\infty, -\frac{7}{2}\right) \cup \left(\frac{7}{2}, \infty\right)$ 58. $\left(-\infty, -\frac{33}{2}\right) \cup \left(\frac{33}{2}, \infty\right)$

67. $|3z - 1| > -3$
$(-\infty, \infty)$

68. $|2z| \geq -2$ $(-\infty, \infty)$

69. $\left|\dfrac{2 - t}{3}\right| \geq 5$
$(-\infty, -13] \cup [17, \infty)$

70. $\left|\dfrac{2t + 3}{5}\right| \geq 7$
$(-\infty, -19] \cup [16, \infty)$

71. $|t - 1| \leq 0.1$
$[0.9, 1.1]$

72. $|t - 2| \leq 0.01$
$[1.99, 2.01]$

73. $|b - 10| > 0.5$
$(-\infty, 9.5) \cup (10.5, \infty)$

74. $|b - 25| \geq 1$
$(-\infty, 24] \cup [26, \infty)$

NUMERICAL AND GRAPHICAL SOLUTIONS

Exercises 75 and 76: Use the table of $y = |ax + b|$ to solve each equation or inequality. Write your answers in interval notation for parts (b) and (c).

75. (a) $y = 2$ $\;^{-1, 3}$ **(b)** $y < 2$ $\;^{(-1, 3)}$ **(c)** $y > 2$ $\;^{(-\infty, -1) \cup (3, \infty)}$

x	-2	-1	0	1	2	3	4
y	3	2	1	0	1	2	3

76. (a) $y = 6$ $\;^{-6, 18}$ **(b)** $y \leq 6$ $\;^{[-6, 18]}$ **(c)** $y \geq 6$ $\;^{(-\infty, -6] \cup [18, \infty)}$

x	-12	-6	0	6	12	18	24
y	9	6	3	0	3	6	9

Exercises 77 and 78: Use the graph of y_1 to solve each equation or inequality. Write your answers in interval notation for parts (b) and (c).

77. (a) $y_1 = 1$ $\;^{-1, 0}$ **(b)** $y_1 \leq 1$ $\;^{[-1, 0]}$ **(c)** $y_1 \geq 1$ $\;^{(-\infty, -1] \cup [0, \infty)}$

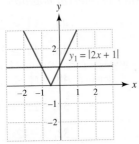

78. (a) $y_1 = 3$ $\;^{-2, 4}$ **(b)** $y_1 < 3$ $\;^{(-2, 4)}$ **(c)** $y_1 > 3$ $\;^{(-\infty, -2) \cup (4, \infty)}$

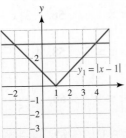

Exercises 79–88: Solve the inequality graphically. Write your answer in interval notation.

79. $|x| \geq 1$ $\;^{(-\infty, -1] \cup [1, \infty)}$

80. $|x| < 2$ $(-2, 2)$

81. $|x - 1| \leq 3$ $\;[-2, 4]$

82. $|x + 5| \geq 2$
$(-\infty, -7] \cup [-3, \infty)$

83. $|4 - 2x| > 2$
$(-\infty, 1) \cup (3, \infty)$

84. $|1.5x - 3| \geq 6$
$(-\infty, -2] \cup [6, \infty)$

 85. $|10 - 3x| < 4$
$(2, 4.\overline{6})$

 86. $|7 - 4x| \leq 2.5$ $\;[1.125, 2.375]$

 87. $|8.1 - x| > -2$
$(-\infty, \infty)$

 88. $\left|\dfrac{5x - 9}{2}\right| \leq -1$
No solutions

USING MORE THAN ONE METHOD

Exercises 89–92: Solve the absolute value inequality

   (a) *symbolically,*
   (b) *graphically, and*
   (c) *numerically.*

Write your answer in set-builder notation.

89. $|3x| \leq 9$
$\{x \mid -3 \leq x \leq 3\}$

90. $|5 - x| \geq 3$
$\{x \mid x \leq 2 \text{ or } x \geq 8\}$

91. $|2x - 5| > 1$
$\{x \mid x < 2 \text{ or } x > 3\}$

92. $|-8 - 4x| < 6$
$\{x \mid -3.5 < x < -0.5\}$

APPLICATIONS

*Exercises 93–96: **Average Temperatures** (Refer to Example 8.) The given inequality models the range for the monthly average temperatures T in degrees Fahrenheit at the location specified.*

   (a) *Solve the inequality.*
   (b) *Give a possible interpretation of the inequality.*

93. $|T - 43| \leq 24$, Marquette, Michigan

94. $|T - 62| \leq 19$, Memphis, Tennessee

95. $|T - 10| \leq 36$, Chesterfield, Canada

96. $|T - 61.5| \leq 12.5$, Buenos Aires, Argentina
(a) $\{T \mid 49 \leq T \leq 74\}$ (b) Monthly average temperatures vary from 49°F to 74°F.

97. Highest Elevations The table lists the highest elevation in each continent.

93.(a) $\{T \mid 19 \leq T \leq 67\}$
(b) Monthly average temperatures vary from 19°F to 67°F.
94.(a) $\{T \mid 43 \leq T \leq 81\}$
(b) Monthly average temperatures vary from 43°F to 81°F.
95.(a) $\{T \mid -26 \leq T \leq 46\}$
(b) Monthly average temperatures vary from -26°F to 46°F.

Continent	Elevation (feet)
Asia	29,028
S. America	22,834
N. America	20,320
Africa	19,340
Europe	18,510
Antarctica	16,066
Australia	7,310

Source: National Geographic   About 19,058 ft

   (a) Calculate the average A of these elevations.

(b) Which continents have their highest elevations within 1000 feet of A? Africa and Europe

(c) Which continents have their highest elevations within 5000 feet of A?
South America, North America, Africa, Europe, and Antarctica

98. *Distance* Suppose that two cars, both traveling at a constant speed of 60 miles per hour, approach each other on a straight highway.

(a) If they are initially 4 miles apart, sketch a graph of the distance between the cars after x minutes, where $0 \le x \le 4$. (*Hint:* 60 miles per hour = 1 mile per minute)* $|-2x + 4| = 2$

(b) Write an absolute value equation whose solution gives the times when the cars were 2 miles apart.

(c) Solve your equation from part (b).   1, 3

99. *Error in Measurements* Products are often manufactured to be a given size or shape to within a certain tolerance. For instance, if an aluminum can is supposed to have a diameter of 2.5 inches, either 2.501 inches or 2.499 inches might be acceptable. If the maximum error in the diameter of the can is restricted to 0.002 inch, an acceptable diameter d must satisfy the absolute value inequality

$$|d - 2.5| \le 0.002.$$

Solve this inequality for d and interpret the result.

100. *Error in Measurements* (Refer to the preceding exercise.) Suppose that a person can operate a stopwatch accurately to within 0.02 second. If a runner's time in the 400-meter dash is recorded as 51.57 seconds, within what range of values could the true time fall?   From 51.55 to 51.59 sec

99. $\{d \mid 2.498 \le d \le 2.502\}$ The diameter can vary from 2.498 to 2.502 in.

101. *Relative Error* If a quantity is measured to be x and the actual value is t, then the relative error in the measurement is $\left|\frac{x - t}{t}\right|$. If the true measurement is $t = 20$ and you want the relative error to be less than 0.05 (5%), what values for x are possible?
Values between 19 and 21, exclusively

102. *Relative Error* (Refer to the preceding exercise.) The volume V of a box is 50 cubic inches. How accurately must you measure the volume of the box for the relative error to be less than 3%?
Within 1.5 cubic inches—that is, between 48.5 and 51.5 cubic inches

WRITING ABOUT MATHEMATICS

103. If $a \ne 0$, how many solutions are there to the equation $|ax + b| = k$ when
(a) $k > 0$, **(b)** $k = 0$, and **(c)** $k < 0$?
Explain each answer.

104. Suppose that you know two solutions to the equation $|ax + b| = k$. How can you use these solutions to solve the inequalities $|ax + b| < k$ and $|ax + b| > k$? Give an example.

CHECKING BASIC CONCEPTS   **SECTION 3.5**

Write your answers in interval notation whenever possible.

1. Solve $\left|\frac{3}{4}x - 1\right| - 3 = 5$. $-\frac{28}{3}, 12$

2. Solve the absolute value equation and inequalities.
(a) $|3x - 6| = 8$ **(b)** $|3x - 6| < 8$ $\left(-\frac{2}{3}, \frac{14}{3}\right)$
(c) $|3x - 6| > 8$ $\left(-\infty, -\frac{2}{3}\right) \cup \left(\frac{14}{3}, \infty\right)$

3. Solve the inequality $|-2(3 - x)| < 6$. Then solve $|-2(3 - x)| \ge 6$. $(0, 6)$ and $(-\infty, 0] \cup [6, \infty)$

2.(a) $-\frac{2}{3}, \frac{14}{3}$

4. Use the graph to solve the equation and inequalities.

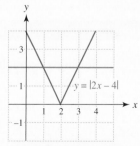

$y = |2x - 4|$

1, 3

(a) $|2x - 4| = 2$ **(b)** $|2x - 4| \le 2$ $[1, 3]$
(c) $|2x - 4| \ge 2$ $(-\infty, 1] \cup [3, \infty)$

*Answer on page IA-14

CHAPTER 3 Summary

Linear Equations in One Variable Can be written as $ax + b = 0$, where $a \neq 0$. Linear equations have *one* solution.

Examples: $3x - 5 = 0$ and $x + 2 = 1 - 3x$

Symbolic, Graphical, and Numerical Solutions Linear equations can be solved with these methods.

Example: Solve $3x - 1 = 2$.

Symbolic Solution

$$3x - 1 = 2$$
$$3x = 3$$
$$x = 1$$

Numerical Solution

x	$3x - 1$
0	-1
1	2
2	5
3	8

$3x - 1 = 2$ when $x = 1$.

Graphical Solution

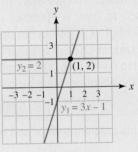

Solution is 1.

Lines

Standard Form $ax + by = c$, where a, b, and c are constants with a and b not both 0.

Finding x-intercepts Let $y = 0$ and solve for x.

Finding y-intercepts Let $x = 0$ and solve for y.

Example: $3x - 4y = 24$

$3x - 4(0) = 24$ implies $x = 8$; x-intercept is 8.

$3(0) - 4y = 24$ implies $y = -6$; y-intercept is -6.

Solving a Formula for a Variable Use properties of algebra to solve for a specified variable.

Example: Solve $N = \frac{a + b}{2}$ for b.

$$2N = a + b \qquad \text{Multiply by 2.}$$
$$2N - a = b \qquad \text{Subtract } a.$$

Steps for Solving a Problem

STEP 1: Read the problem carefully and be sure that you understand it. (You may need to read the problem more than once.) Assign a variable to what you are being asked to find. If necessary, write other quantities in terms of this variable.

STEP 2: Write an equation that relates the quantities described in the problem. You may need to sketch a diagram, make a chart, or refer to known formulas.

STEP 3: Solve the equation and determine the solution.

STEP 4: Look back and check your answer. Does it seem reasonable? Did you find the required information?

Section 3.3 *Linear Inequality*

Linear Inequality in One Variable   Can be written as $ax + b > 0$, where $a \neq 0$. (The symbol $>$ can be replaced with $<$, $\leq$, or $\geq$.) Linear inequalities have *infinitely many* solutions.

Examples: $3x - 5 < 0, x + 2 \geq 1 - 3x$

Symbolic, Numerical, and Graphical Solutions   Linear inequalities can be solved with these methods.

Example: Solve $4 - 2x \geq 0$.

Symbolic Solution	*Numerical Solution*	*Graphical Solution*

Symbolic Solution

$$4 - 2x \geq 0$$
$$-2x \geq -4$$
$$x \leq 2$$

Reverse inequality

Numerical Solution

x	$4 - 2x$
0	4
1	2
2	0
3	-2
4	-4

Graphical Solution

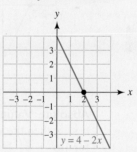

$4 - 2x \geq 0$ when $x \leq 2$ Graph is above the x-axis for $x \leq 2$.

Section 3.4 *Compound Inequality*

Compound Inequality   Two inequalities connected by *and* or *or*.

Examples: For $x + 1 < 3$ *or* $x + 1 > 6$, a solution satisfies *at least* one of the inequalities.

For $2x + 1 < 3$ *and* $1 - x > 6$, a solution satisfies *both* inequalities.

Three-Part Inequality   A compound inequality in the form $x > a$ *and* $x < b$ can be written as $a < x < b$.

Example: $1 \leq x < 7$ means $x \geq 1$ *and* $x < 7$.

Interval Notation   Can be used to identify intervals on the real number line.

Examples: $-2 < x \le 3$ is equivalent to $(-2, 3]$.

  $x < 5$ is equivalent to $(-\infty, 5)$.

  Real numbers are denoted $(-\infty, \infty)$.

Section 3.5   *Absolute Value Equations and Inequalities*

Absolute Value Equations   The graph of $y = |ax + b|$, $a \ne 0$, is V-shaped and intersects the horizontal line $y = k$ twice if $k > 0$. In this case there are two solutions to the equation $|ax + b| = k$ determined by $ax + b = k$ or $ax + b = -k$.

Example: The equation $|2x - 1| = 5$ has two solutions.

Symbolic Solution

$$2x - 1 = 5 \quad \text{or} \quad 2x - 1 = -5$$
$$2x = 6 \quad \text{or} \quad 2x = -4 \qquad \text{Add 1.}$$
$$x = 3 \quad \text{or} \quad x = -2 \qquad \text{Divide by 2.}$$

Graphical Solution

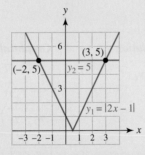

Numerical Solution

x	-3	-2	-1	0	1	2	3
$|2x - 1|$	7	5	3	1	1	3	5

The solutions are -2 and 3.

Absolute Value Inequalities   If the solutions to $|ax + b| = k$ are c and d with $c < d$, then the solution set for $|ax + b| < k$ is $\{x \mid c < x < d\}$, and the solution set for $|ax + b| > k$ is $\{x \mid x < c \text{ or } x > d\}$.

Example: The solutions to the equation $|2x - 1| = 5$ are -2 and 3, so the solution set for $|2x - 1| < 5$ is $\{x \mid -2 < x < 3\}$, and the solution set for $|2x - 1| > 5$ is $\{x \mid x < -2 \text{ or } x > 3\}$.

CHAPTER 3 Review Exercises

SECTION 3.1

Exercises 1 and 2: Complete the table and then use the table to solve the equation.

1. $3x - 6 = 0$ 2

x	0	1	2	3	4
$3x - 6$	-6	-3	0	3	6

2. $5 - 2x = 3$ 1

x	-1	0	1	2	3
$5 - 2x$	7	5	3	1	-1

3. Decide whether $-\frac{2}{3}$ is a solution to the linear equation $\frac{1}{2}z - 2(2z + 3) = 4z - 1$.   Yes.

4. Use the graph to solve the equation $y_1 = y_2$.   1

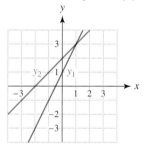

5. Solve $5 - 2x = -1 + x$ graphically.   2

6. Solve $4x - 3 = 5 + 2x$ graphically or numerically.   4

Exercises 7–16: Solve the equation.

7. $2x - 7 = 21$ 14

8. $1 - 7x = -\frac{5}{2}$ $\frac{1}{2}$

9. $-2(4x - 1) = 1 - x$ $\frac{1}{7}$

10. $-\frac{3}{4}(x - 1) + 5 = 6$ $-\frac{1}{3}$

11. $\frac{x - 4}{3} = 2$ 10

12. $\frac{2x - 3}{2} = \frac{x + 3}{5}$ $\frac{21}{8}$

13. $-2(z - 1960) + 32 = 8$ 1972

14. $5 - (3 - 2z) + 4 = 5(2z - 3) - (3z - 2)$ $\frac{19}{5}$

15. $\frac{2}{3}\left(\frac{t - 3}{2}\right) + 4 = \frac{1}{3}t - (1 - t)$ 4

16. $0.3r - 0.12(r - 1) = 0.4r + 2.1$ -9

SECTION 3.2

Exercises 17–22: Solve the equation for the given variable.

17. $5x - 4y = 20; y$ $y = \frac{5}{4}x - 5$

18. $-\frac{1}{3}x + \frac{1}{2}y = 1; y$ $y = \frac{2}{3}x + 2$

19. $2a + 3b = a; a$ $a = -3b$

20. $4m - 5n = 6m + 2n; n$ $n = -\frac{2}{7}m$

21. $A = \frac{1}{2}h(a + b); b$ $b = \frac{2A}{h} - a$

22. $V = \frac{1}{3}\pi r^2 h; h$ $h = \frac{3V}{\pi r^2}$

Exercises 23–26: Solve the equation for y. Let $y = f(x)$ and write a formula for $f(x)$.

23. $\frac{1}{2}x - \frac{3}{4}y = 2$ $f(x) = \frac{2}{3}x - \frac{8}{3}$

24. $3x + 4y = 10 - y$ $f(x) = -\frac{3}{5}x + 2$

25. $-7(x - 4y) = y + 1$ $f(x) = \frac{7}{27}x + \frac{1}{27}$

26. $\frac{y}{x} = 3$ $f(x) = 3x$

Exercises 27 and 28: Translate the sentence into an equation and then solve the equation.

27. The sum of twice x and 25 is 19.
$2x + 25 = 19; -3$

28. If 5 is subtracted from twice x, it equals x plus 1.
$2x - 5 = x + 1; 6$

SECTION 3.3

29. Use the table to solve $f(x) < 5$, where $f(x)$ represents a linear function. $\{x \mid x > -1\}$

x	-2	-1	0	1	2
$f(x)$	7	5	3	1	-1

30. Solve $2(3 - x) + 4 < 0$. $\{x \mid x > 5\}$

31. Solve the inequality $y_1 \geq y_2$, using the graph.

$\{x \mid x \geq 2\}$

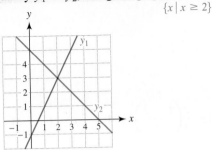

32. Solve $5 - 4x \leq -2$. $\{x \mid x \geq 1.75\}$

Exercises 33–40: Solve the inequality symbolically.

33. $-2x + 1 \leq 3$
$\{x \mid x \geq -1\}$

34. $x - 5 \geq 2x + 3$
$\{x \mid x \leq -8\}$

35. $\dfrac{3x - 1}{4} > \dfrac{1}{2}$
$\{x \mid x > 1\}$

36. $-3.2(x - 2) < 1.6x$
$\{x \mid x > \frac{4}{3}\}$

37. $\dfrac{2}{5}t - (5 - t) + 3 > 2\left(\dfrac{3 - t}{5}\right)$ $\{t \mid t > \frac{16}{9}\}$

38. $\dfrac{2(3x - 5)}{5} - 3 \geq \dfrac{2 - x}{3} + 2$ $\{x \mid x \geq 5\}$

39. $0.05t - 0.15 \leq 0.03 - 0.75(t - 2)$ $\{t \mid t \leq 2.1\}$

40. $0.6z - 1.55(z + 5) < 1 - 0.35(2z - 1)$
$\{z \mid z > -36.4\}$

SECTION 3.4

Use interval notation whenever possible for the remaining exercises.

*Exercises 41–44: Solve the compound inequality. Graph the solution set on a number line.**

41. $x + 1 \leq 3$ and $x + 1 \geq -1$ $[-2, 2]$

42. $2x + 7 < 5$ and $-2x \geq 6$ $(-\infty, -3]$

43. $5x - 1 \leq 3$ or $1 - x < -1$ $\left(-\infty, \frac{4}{5}\right] \cup (2, \infty)$

44. $3x + 1 > -1$ or $3x + 1 < 10$ $(-\infty, \infty)$

45. Use the table to solve $-2 \leq 2x + 2 \leq 4$. $[-2, 1]$

x	-3	-2	-1	0	1	2	3
$2x + 2$	-4	-2	0	2	4	6	8

46. Use the following figure to solve each equation and inequality.
(a) $y_1 = y_2$ -4
(b) $y_2 = y_3$ 2

(c) $y_1 \leq y_2 \leq y_3$ $[-4, 2]$
(d) $y_2 < y_3$ $(-\infty, 2)$

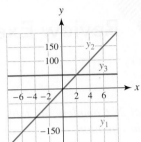

47. The graphs of y_1 and y_2 are shown in the following figure. Solve each equation and inequality.
(a) $y_1 = y_2$ 2
(b) $y_1 < y_2$ $(2, \infty)$
(c) $y_1 > y_2$ $(-\infty, 2)$

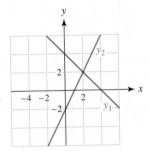

48. The graphs of three linear functions f, g, and h are shown in the following figure. Solve each equation and inequality.
(a) $f(x) = g(x)$ 4
(b) $g(x) = h(x)$ 2
(c) $f(x) < g(x) < h(x)$ $(2, 4)$

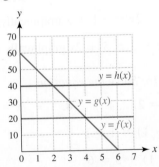

Exercises 49–54: Write the inequality in interval notation.

49. $-3 \leq x \leq \frac{2}{3}$ $\left[-3, \frac{2}{3}\right]$

50. $-6 < x \leq 45$ $(-6, 45]$

51. $x < \frac{7}{2}$ $\left(-\infty, \frac{7}{2}\right)$

52. $x \geq 1.8$ $[1.8, \infty)$

53. $x > -3$ and $x < 4$
$(-3, 4)$

54. $x < 4$ or $x > 10$
$(-\infty, 4) \cup (10, \infty)$

*Answers on page IA-14

Exercises 55–60: Solve the three-part inequality. Write the solution set in interval notation.

55. $-4 < x + 1 < 6$ (−5, 5)

56. $20 \le 2x + 4 \le 60$ [8, 28]

57. $-3 < 4 - \frac{1}{3}x < 7$ (−9, 21)

58. $2 \le \frac{1}{2}x - 2 \le 12$ [8, 28]

59. $-3 \le \dfrac{4 - 5x}{3} - 2 < 3$ $\left(-\frac{11}{5}, \frac{7}{5}\right]$

60. $30 \le \dfrac{2x - 6}{5} - 4 < 50$ [88, 138)

SECTION 3.5

Exercises 61–64: Determine whether the given values of x are solutions to the absolute value equation or inequality.

61. $|12x - 24| = 24$ $x = -3; x = 2$ No, no

62. $|5 - 3x| > 3$ $x = \frac{4}{3}; x = 0$ No, yes

63. $|3x - 6| \le 6$ $x = -3; x = 4$ No, yes

64. $|2 + 3x| + 4 < 11$ $x = -3; x = \frac{2}{3}$ No, yes

65. Use the accompanying table to solve the equation and inequalities.
  (a) $y_1 = 2$ **(b)** $y_1 < 2$ **(c)** $y_1 > 2$

X	Y1
-1	3
0	2
1	1
2	0
3	1
4	2
5	3
Y1■abs(2−X)	

(a) 0, 4
(b) (0, 4)
(c) $(-\infty, 0) \cup (4, \infty)$

66. Use the graph of $y = |2x + 2|$ to solve the equation and inequalities.
  (a) $|2x + 2| = 4$ −3, 1
  (b) $|2x + 2| \le 4$ [−3, 1]
  (c) $|2x + 2| \ge 4$ $(-\infty, -3] \cup [1, \infty)$

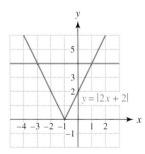

Exercises 67–72: Solve the absolute value equation.

67. $|x| = 22$ −22, 22

68. $|2x - 9| = 7$ 1, 8

69. $\left|4 - \frac{1}{2}x\right| = 17$ −26, 42

70. $\frac{1}{3}|3x - 1| + 1 = 9$ $-\frac{23}{3}, \frac{25}{3}$

71. $|2x - 5| = |5 - 3x|$ 0, 2

72. $|-3 + 3x| = |-2x + 6|$ $-3, \frac{9}{5}$

Exercises 73 and 74: Solve each absolute value equation and inequality.

73. **(a)** $|x + 1| = 7$ −8, 6
  (b) $|x + 1| \le 7$ [−8, 6]
  (c) $|x + 1| \ge 7$ $(-\infty, -8] \cup [6, \infty)$

74. **(a)** $|1 - 2x| = 6$ $-\frac{5}{2}, \frac{7}{2}$
  (b) $|1 - 2x| \le 6$ $\left[-\frac{5}{2}, \frac{7}{2}\right]$
  (c) $|1 - 2x| \ge 6$
    $\left(-\infty, -\frac{5}{2}\right] \cup \left[\frac{7}{2}, \infty\right)$

Exercises 75–82: Solve the absolute value inequality.

75. $|x| > 3$
  $(-\infty, -3) \cup (3, \infty)$

76. $|-5x| < 20$ (−4, 4)

77. $|4x - 2| \le 14$
  [−3, 4]

78. $\left|1 - \frac{4}{5}x\right| \ge 3$ $\left(-\infty, -\frac{5}{2}\right] \cup [5, \infty)$

79. $|t - 4.5| \le 0.1$
  [4.4, 4.6]

80. $-2|13t - 5| \ge -4$ $\left[\frac{3}{13}, \frac{7}{13}\right]$

81. $|5 - 4x| > -5$
  $(-\infty, \infty)$

82. $|2t - 3| \le 0$ $\frac{3}{2}$

Exercises 83 and 84: Solve the inequality graphically.

83. $|2x| \ge 3$
  $(-\infty, -1.5] \cup [1.5, \infty)$

84. $\left|\frac{1}{2}x - 1\right| \le 2$ [−2, 6]

APPLICATIONS

85. *Loan Interest* A student takes out two loans, one at 5% and the other at 7% annual interest. The total amount for both loans is $7700, and the total interest after one year is $469. Find the amount of each loan.
$3500 at 5%; $4200 at 7%

86. *Distance and Time* At first an athlete runs at 8 miles per hour and then runs at 10 miles per hour, traveling 12.8 miles in 1.4 hours. How long did the athlete run at each speed? 0.6 hr at 8 mph; 0.8 hr at 10 mph

87. *Expensive Homes* A typical 2200-square-foot house in Honolulu costs $415,000, which is only 54% of the cost of the same house in San Francisco. (San Francisco has the most expensive housing in the United States.) How much would this Honolulu house cost if it were in San Francisco? (*Source:* Runzheimer International.)   About $769,000

88. *Nightclub Fires* The number of reported nightclub fires has dropped from 1369 in 1980 to 498 in 1999.
  (a) Find $f(x) = ax + b$ so that f models these data.
  (b) Use $f(x)$ to estimate the number of nightclub fires in 1988.   About 1006; answers may vary slightly.
  (a) $f(x) = -45.84x + 92{,}136$ (approximate)

89. *Distance Between Bicyclists*   The following graph shows the distance between two bicyclists traveling toward each other along a straight road after x hours.

(a) After how long did the bicycle riders meet?   3 hr

(b) When were they 20 miles apart?   2 hr and 4 hr

(c) Find the times when they were less than 20 miles apart.   Between 2 and 4 hr, exclusively

(d) Estimate the sum of the speeds of the two bicyclists.   20 mph

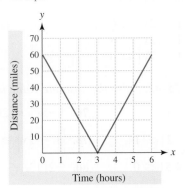

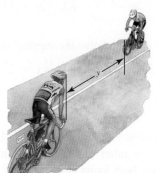

90. *Interest*   As shown in the following graph, the function f computes the annual interest y on a loan of x dollars with an interest rate of 15%. Determine the loan amounts that result in the following.

(a) An annual interest equal to $300 $2000

(b) An annual interest of more than $300   More than $2000

(c) An annual interest of less than $300   Less than $2000

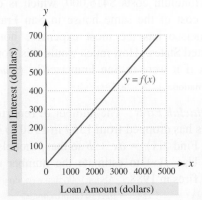

91. (a) Car 1; its graph has the steeper slope

91. *Distance*   Two cars, Car 1 and Car 2, are traveling in the same direction on a straight highway. Their distances in miles north of Austin, Texas, after x hours are shown in the following graph.

(a) Which car is traveling faster? Explain.

(b) How many hours elapse before the two cars are the same distance from Austin? How far are they from Austin?   3 hr; 200 mi

(c) During what time interval is Car 1 closer to Austin than Car 2?   Before $x = 3$ hr

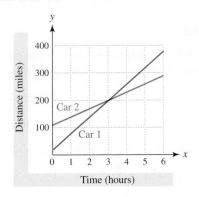

92. *School Bus Deaths*   The line graph shows the number of deaths occurring from school bus crashes. For which years were there more than 10 deaths?
(*Source:* National Center for Statistics and Analysis.)

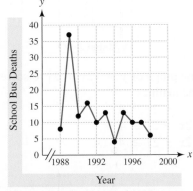

1989, 1990, 1991, 1993, and 1995

93. *Age in the United States*   The median age of the population for each year x between 1820 and 1995 can be approximated by

$$f(x) = 0.09x - 147.1.$$

(*Source:* Bureau of the Census.)

(a) Interpret the slope of the graph of f as a rate of change.   Median age is increasing at 0.09 yr/yr

(b) Estimate when the median age was 23 years.   1890

94. *Women Officers*   The number of women officers in the Marine Corps from 1960 to 1997 may be modeled by $f(x) = 17.7x - 34{,}636$, where x represents the year. Estimate the years when the number of women officers was from 490 to 670.   (*Source:* Department of Defense.)   Approximately from 1985 to 1995

95. *Weight of a Fish*   If a walleye has a length of x inches, where $30 \leq x \leq 35$, its weight W in pounds can be estimated by $W(x) = 1.11x - 23.3$.   (*Source:* Minnesota Department of Natural Resources.)
   (a) What length of walleye is likely to weigh 12 pounds?   About 31.8 in.
   (b) What lengths of walleye are likely to weigh less than 12 pounds?   Lengths less than 31.8 in.

96. *Air Temperature*   Suppose that the air temperature at ground level is $60°F$ and that the air cools $29°F$ for each one-mile increase in altitude.
   (a) Write $T(x) = ax + b$ so that T gives the temperature at an altitude of x miles. $T(x) = -29x + 60$
   (b) Estimate the altitudes at which the air temperature is from $40°F$ to $20°F$.   Approximately from 0.69 to 1.38 mi

97. *Distance and Time*   A car is 200 miles west of Rapid City, South Dakota, traveling east at 70 miles per hour. How long will it take for the car to be 395 miles east of Rapid City?   8.5 hr

98. *Geometry*   A rectangle is 5 feet longer than twice its width. If the rectangle has a perimeter of 88 feet, what are the dimensions of the rectangle?   13 ft by 31 ft

99. *Temperature Scales*   The formula
$$F = \frac{9}{5}C + 32$$
may be used to convert Fahrenheit temperature to Celsius temperature. The temperature range at Houghton Lake, Michigan, has varied between $-48°F$ and $107°F$. Find this temperature range in Celsius. $-44.\overline{4}°C$ to $41.\overline{6}°C$

100. *Error in Measurements*   A square garden is being fenced along its 160-foot perimeter. If the length L of the fence must be within 1 foot of the garden's perimeter, write an absolute value inequality that gives acceptable values for L. Solve your inequality.

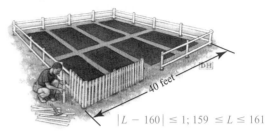

40 feet

$|L - 160| \leq 1$; $159 \leq L \leq 161$

101. *Average Precipitation*   The average rainfall in Houston, Texas, is 3.9 inches per month. Each month's average A is within 1.7 inches of 3.9 inches. (*Source:* J. Williams, *The Weather Almanac 1995*.)
   (a) Write an absolute value inequality that models this situation. $|A - 3.9| \leq 1.7$
   (b) Solve the inequality. $2.2 \leq A \leq 5.6$

102. *Relative Error*   If a quantity is measured to be T and the actual value is A, then the relative error in this measurement is $\left|\frac{T-A}{A}\right|$. If $A = 35$ and the relative error is to be less than 0.08 (8%), what values for T are possible?   Values between 32.2 and 37.8

CHAPTER

3 Test

1. Solve $3 - 5x = 18$. Check your answer. -3

2. Use the accompanying graph to solve each equation and inequality. Write your answers for parts (b) and (c) in interval notation.
   (a) $y_1 = y_2$ (b) $y_1 \geq y_2$ (c) $y_1 \leq y_2$ $[2, \infty)$
      2                  $(-\infty, 2]$

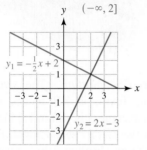

3. Solve $4 - 2x = 1 + x$ graphically.   1

4. Solve $-\frac{2}{3}(3x - 2) + 1 = x$ symbolically. $\frac{7}{9}$

5. Translate the following sentence into an equation and then solve the equation for x. "If 2 is added to 5 times x, it equals x minus 4." $2 + 5x = x - 4; -\frac{3}{2}$

Exercises 6 and 7: Solve the inequality. Write your answer in interval notation.

6. $-\frac{5}{2}x + \frac{1}{2} \leq 2$ $\left[-\frac{3}{5}, \infty\right)$ 7. $3.1(3 - x) < 2.9x$
                                                   $(1.55, \infty)$

8. Graph the solution set to the compound inequality on a number line. *
   $$2x + 6 < 2 \text{ and } -3x \geq 3$$

9. Use the table to solve the compound inequality $-3x < -3$ or $-3x > 6$. Write your answer in interval notation. $(-\infty, -2) \cup (1, \infty)$

x	-3	-2	-1	0	1	2	3
$-3x$	9	6	3	0	-3	-6	-9

10. Use the following figure to solve the equations and inequalities. Write your answers for parts (c) and (d) in interval notation.
    (a) $y_1 = y_2$ -5 (b) $y_2 = y_3$ 5
    (c) $y_1 \leq y_2 \leq y_3$ (d) $y_2 < y_3$ $(-\infty, 5)$
        $[-5, 5]$

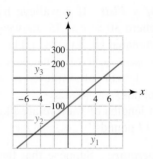

11. Solve the compound inequality
    $$-2 < 2 + \frac{1}{2}x < 2$$
    and write the solution set in interval notation. $(-8, 0)$

12. Solve the equation $\left|2 - \frac{1}{3}x\right| = 6$. $-12, 24$

13. Solve the equation and inequalities. Write your answers for parts (b) and (c) in interval notation.
    (a) $|1 - 5x| = 3$ $-\frac{2}{5}, \frac{4}{5}$
    (b) $|1 - 5x| \leq 3$ $\left[-\frac{2}{5}, \frac{4}{5}\right]$
    (c) $|1 - 5x| \geq 3$ $\left(-\infty, -\frac{2}{5}\right] \cup \left[\frac{4}{5}, \infty\right)$

14. *Sport Drinks*   The following graph shows a relationship between the calories in an 8-ounce serving of a sport drink and the corresponding grams of carbohydrates. Estimate the number of calories x in 8 ounces of a sport drink with the following grams of carbohydrates.   (*Source: Runner's World.*)
    (a) 16 grams of carbohydrates   64 calories
    (b) More than 16 grams of carbohydrates   More than 64 calories
    (c) Less than 16 grams of carbohydrates   Less than 64 calories
    (d) Interpret the slope of the graph.
        (d) Each gram of carbohydrates corresponds to 4 calories.

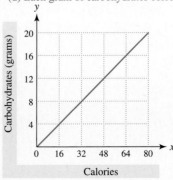

*Answers on page IA-14

15. *Drinking Fluids and Exercise* To determine the number of ounces of fluid that a person should drink in a day, divide his or her weight in pounds by 2 and then add 0.4 ounce for every minute of exercise.
   (a) Write a function that gives the fluid requirements for a person weighing 150 pounds and exercising *x* minutes a day. $f(x) = 0.4x + 75$
   (b) If a 150-pound runner needs 89 ounces of fluid each day, determine the runner's daily minutes of exercise.   35 min

16. *Solving a Formula* Solve the formula $d = \frac{1}{2}gt^2$ for *g*.

17. *Loan Interest* A student takes out two loans, one at 4% and the other at 6% annual interest. The total amount for both loans is $5000, and the total interest after one year is $230. Find the amount of each loan.
   $3500 at 4%; $1500 at 6%

16. $g = \dfrac{2d}{t^2}$

CHAPTER

3

2.(a) At some altitudes the air temperature is likely to reach the dew point.
   (b) Clouds will form at much lower altitudes than usual, and fog may develop.

Extended and Discovery Exercises

3.(b) The relationship appears to be linear. If the number of megabytes doubles, the number of seconds should also double.
   (c) $y \approx 47.9x - 0.1691$; each additional MB of memory can record approximately 47.9 sec of music.

1. *Clouds and Temperature* If the air temperature is greater than the dew point, clouds do not form. If the air temperature cools to the dew point, fog or clouds may appear. Suppose that the Fahrenheit temperature *x* miles high is given by $T(x) = 90 - 29x$ and that the dew point *x* miles high is given by $D(x) = 70 - 5.8x$. (**Source:** A. Miller.)
   (a) Find the temperature and dew point at ground level.   90°F; 70°F
   (b) At what altitude are the air temperature and dew point equal?   Approximately 0.86 mi
   (c) Determine the altitudes at which clouds do not form.   Below 0.86 mi
   (d) Determine the altitudes at which clouds may form.   Above 0.86 mi

2. *Critical Thinking* (Refer to Exercise 1.) For each 1-mile increase in altitude, the air temperature decreases 29°F, whereas the dew point decreases 5.8°F. At ground level the dew point is usually less than the air temperature. However, if the air temperature reaches the dew point, fog or clouds may form.
   (a) Discuss why clouds are likely to form at some altitude in the sky.
   (b) Suppose that the dew point is slightly less than the air temperature near the ground. How does that affect the altitude at which clouds form?

3. *Recording Music* A compact disc (CD) can hold approximately 600 million bytes. One *byte* is capable of storing one letter of the alphabet. For example, the

word "function" requires 8 bytes to store in computer memory. One million bytes is commonly referred to as a *megabyte* (MB). Recording music requires an enormous amount of memory. The accompanying table lists the megabytes *x* needed to record *y* seconds (sec) of music.

x (MB)	0.129	0.231	0.415	0.491
y (sec)	6.010	10.74	19.27	22.83

x (MB)	0.667	1.030	1.160	1.260
y (sec)	31.00	49.00	55.25	60.18

Source: Gateway 2000 System CD.

   (a) Make a scatterplot of the data. *
   (b) What type of relationship seems to exist between *x* and *y*? Why does this relationship seem reasonable?
   (c) Find the slope–intercept form of a line that models the data. Interpret the slope of this line as a rate of change. Answers may vary.
   (d) Check your answer in part (c) by graphing the line and data in the same graph. *
   (e) Write a linear equation whose solution gives the megabytes needed to record 120 seconds of music.
   (f) Solve the equation in part (e) graphically or symbolically.   About 2.5 MB   (e) $47.9x - 0.1691 = 120$

4. *Early Cellular Phone Growth* Cellular phone use has grown dramatically in the United States. When there were 25,000 customers in New York City, the in-

vestment cost per cellular site was $12 million. (A cellular site would include such things as a relay tower to transmit signals between cellular phones.) When the number of customers rose to 100,000, the investment cost per cellular site rose to $96 million. Although cost usually decreases with additional customers, such was not the case for early cellular technology. Instead, cost increased as a result of having to purchase expensive real estate and establish communications links among a large number of cellular sites. The relationship between cellular sites and investment cost per site was approximately linear.
(*Source:* M. Paetsch, *Mobile Communications in the US and Europe.*)

(a) Find values for m, x_1, and y_1 so that the formula $f(x) = m(x - x_1) + y_1$ models the cost per cellular site in millions of dollars when there were x customers. $m = 0.00112, x_1 = 25,000, y_1 = 12$

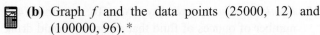
(b) Graph f and the data points (25000, 12) and (100000, 96). *

(c) Write an inequality whose solution set gives the numbers of customers when the investment cost per cellular site was between $28.8 million and $51.2 million. $28.8 \leq 0.00112(x - 25,000) + 12 \leq 51.2$

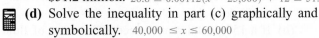
(d) Solve the inequality in part (c) graphically and symbolically. $40,000 \leq x \leq 60,000$

5. *Comparing Ages*   The age of the Universe is about 20 billion years, whereas the age of Earth is about 4.5 billion years. The earliest evidence of dinosaurs dates back 200 million years, whereas the earliest evidence for *Homo sapiens* dates back 300,000 years. If the age of the Universe is condensed into 1 year, determine the approximate times when Earth, the dinosaurs, and *Homo sapiens* first appeared.
Earth: Day 282.88, or about October 10; Dinosaurs: Day 361.35, or about December 28; Homo sapiens: Day 364.9945, or about 8 min before the end of the year. Note that January 1 corresponds to Day 0.

CHAPTERS
1–3 Cumulative Review Exercises

1. Natural: $\frac{8}{2}$; Whole: 0, $\frac{8}{2}$; Integer: -7, 0, $\frac{8}{2}$; Rational: -7, $-\frac{3}{5}$, 0, $\frac{8}{2}$, $5.\overline{12}$; Irrational: $\sqrt{5}$

Exercises 1 and 2: Classify each real number as one or more of the following: natural number, whole number, integer, rational number, or irrational number.

1. -7, $-\frac{3}{5}$, 0, $\sqrt{5}$, $\frac{8}{2}$, $5.\overline{12}$

2. $-\frac{6}{3}$, $\frac{0}{9}$, $\sqrt{9}$, π, $4.\overline{6}$

Exercises 3 and 4: State whether the equation illustrates an identity, commutative, associative, or distributive property.

3. $8x - 2x = 6x$ Distributive

4. $(6 + z) + 3 = 6 + (z + 3)$ Associative

Exercises 5 and 6: Use properties of real numbers to evaluate the expression mentally.

5. $11 + 26 + (-1) + 14$ 50

6. $7 \cdot 98$ 686

7. Plot the numbers -4, $-\frac{5}{2}$, 0, and 3 on a number line. *

8. Find the opposite of $-5y - 4$. $5y + 4$

Exercises 9 and 10: Simplify the expression. Write the result using positive exponents.

9. $\dfrac{24x^{-4}y^2}{8xy^{-5}}$ $\dfrac{3y^7}{x^5}$

10. $\left(\dfrac{3a^2}{4b^3}\right)^{-3}$ $\dfrac{64b^9}{27a^6}$

11. Evaluate the expression $15 - 2^3 \div 4$ without a calculator.   13

12. Write the number 0.000059 in scientific notation.
5.9×10^{-5}

Exercises 13 and 14: Evaluate the formula for the given value of the variable.

13. $J = \sqrt{38 - t}$ $t = 13$ 5

14. $r = 3 - z^3$ $z = -3$ 30

15. Select the formula that best models the data in the table.

x	-2	-1	0	1	2
y	7	5	3	1	-1

(i) $y = 2x + 11$ (ii) $y = -2x + 3$ (ii)
(iii) $y = x - 5$

2. Natural: $\sqrt{9}$; Whole: $\frac{0}{9}$, $\sqrt{9}$; Integer: $-\frac{6}{3}$, $\frac{0}{9}$, $\sqrt{9}$; Rational: $-\frac{6}{3}$, $\frac{0}{9}$, $\sqrt{9}$, $4.\overline{6}$; Irrational: π

*Answers on page IA-14

16. Identify the domain and range of the relation $S = \{(-2, 4), (0, 2), (1, 4), (3, 0)\}$.
$D = \{-2, 0, 1, 3\}$ $R = \{0, 2, 4\}$

Exercises 17 and 18: Evaluate the given formula for $x = -2, -1, 0, 1,$ and 2. Plot the resulting ordered pairs. *

17. $y = -2x + 1$ $(-2, 5), (-1, 3), (0, 1), (1, -1), (2, -3)$

18. $y = \dfrac{x^3 + 4}{2}$ $(-2, -2), \left(-1, \dfrac{3}{2}\right), (0, 2), \left(1, \dfrac{5}{2}\right), (2, 6)$

19. Sketch the graph of $f(x) = x^2 - 3$ by hand. *

20. Find the domain of $f(x) = \dfrac{4}{x}$. $x \neq 0$

Exercises 21 and 22: Use the graph or table to evaluate $f(0)$ and $f(-2)$.

21. $2, -2$

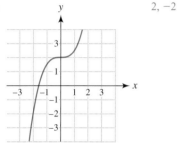

22. $2, -4$

x	-2	-1	0	1	2
$f(x)$	-4	-1	2	5	8

Exercises 23 and 24: Determine whether f is a linear function. If f is linear, give values for a and b so that f may be expressed as $f(x) = ax + b$.

23. $f(x) = 11 - 3x$ Yes; $a = -3, b = 11$

24. $f(x) = \sqrt{x} + 2$ No.

25. Use the table to write the formula for $f(x) = ax + b$.

x	-2	-1	0	1	2
$f(x)$	-5	-1	3	7	11

$f(x) = 4x + 3$

26. Sketch a graph of $f(x) = 3$. *

27. Find the slope and the y-intercept of the graph of $f(x) = 5x - 4$. $5; -4$

28. Calculate the slope of the line passing through the points $(3, -2)$ and $(-1, 6)$. -2

29. Sketch a line passing through the point $(1, 3)$ with slope $m = 2$. *

30. Use the graph to express the equation of the line in slope–intercept form. $y = -\frac{1}{2}x - 1$

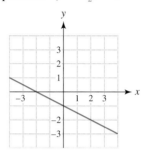

31. Let f be a linear function. Find the slope, x-intercept, and y-intercept of the graph of f. $3; -1; 3$

x	-2	-1	0	1	2
$f(x)$	-3	0	3	6	9

32. Write the equation of the vertical line that passes through the point $(5, 7)$. $x = 5$

Exercises 33 and 34: Write the slope–intercept equation for a line satisfying the given conditions.

33. Parallel to $y = 3x - 4$, passing through $(2, 1)$
$y = 3x - 5$

34. Perpendicular to $y = -x - 5$, passing through the point $(-3, 0)$ $y = x + 3$

35. Determine whether $\frac{8}{5}$ is a solution to the equation $\frac{1}{2}x - 4(x - 1) = \frac{1}{4}x - 2$.   Yes

36. Use the graph to solve the equation $y_1 = y_2$.   1

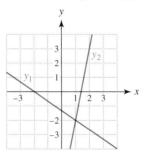

Exercises 37 and 38: Solve the equation.

37. $\frac{3}{4}(x - 2) + 4 = 2$ $-\frac{2}{3}$

38. $\frac{2}{3}\left(\dfrac{t - 7}{4}\right) - 2 = \frac{1}{3}t - (2t + 3)$ $\frac{1}{11}$

39. Use the table to solve $y < 2$, where y represents a linear function. Write the solution set in set-builder notation.

x	-2	-1	0	1	2
y	12	7	2	-3	-8

$\{x \mid x > 0\}$

40. Use the graph to solve the inequality $y_1 \leq y_2$. Write the solution set in interval notation. $(-\infty, -3]$

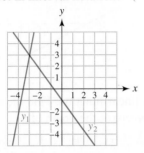

Exercises 41 and 42: Solve the inequality symbolically. Write the solution set in interval notation.

$(-\infty, 0]$

41. $\dfrac{4x - 9}{6} > \dfrac{1}{2}$ $(3, \infty)$ **42.** $\dfrac{2}{3}z - 2 \leq \dfrac{1}{4}z - (2z + 2)$

Exercises 43 and 44: Solve the compound inequality. Graph the solution set on a number line. *

43. $x + 2 > 1$ and $2x - 1 \leq 9$ $(-1, 5]$

44. $4x + 7 < 1$ or $3x + 2 \geq 11$ $\left(-\infty, -\dfrac{3}{2}\right) \cup [3, \infty)$

Exercises 45 and 46: Solve the three-part inequality. Write the solution set in interval notation.

45. $-7 \leq 2x - 3 \leq 5$ **46.** $-8 \leq -\dfrac{1}{2}x - 3 \leq 5$
$[-2, 4]$ $[-16, 10]$

47. Use the graph to solve the equation and inequalities.
   (a) $y_1 = 2$ $-3, 1$
   (b) $y_1 \leq 2$ $[-3, 1]$
   (c) $y_1 \geq 2$ $(-\infty, -3] \cup [1, \infty)$

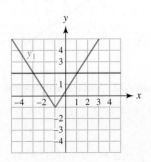

48. Solve the absolute value equation $\left|\dfrac{2}{3}x - 4\right| = 8$. $-6, 18$

Exercises 49 and 50: Solve the absolute value inequality. Write the solution set in interval notation.

49. $|3x + 5| > 13$ **50.** $-3|2t - 11| \geq -9$
$(-\infty, -6) \cup \left(\dfrac{8}{3}, \infty\right)$ $[4, 7]$

APPLICATIONS

51. *Calculating Interest*   If P dollars are deposited in a savings account paying 5% annual interest, then the amount A in the account after t years is given by the formula $A = P(1.05)^t$. Find A for the given values of P and t. Round your answer to the nearest cent.
   (a) $P = \$4300, t = 10$ years $\$7004.25$
   (b) $P = \$11,000, t = 6$ years $\$14,741.05$

52. *Modeling Motion*   The table lists the distance d in miles traveled by a car for various elapsed times t in hours. Find an equation that models these data.

Elapsed Time (hours)	3	5	7	9
Distance (miles)	195	325	455	585

$d = 65t$

53. *Sodium Content*   Some types of diet soda contain 120 milligrams of sodium per 12-ounce can.
   (a) Give a formula for $f(x)$ that calculates the number of milligrams of sodium in x ounces of this type of diet soda. $f(x) = 10x$
   (b) What is the slope of the graph of f? 10
   (c) Interpret the slope as a rate of change.
   The soda contains 10 mg of sodium per ounce.

54. *Graphical Model*   A 150-liter aquarium is initially empty. A small hose attached to a faucet begins to fill the aquarium at a constant rate of 5 liters per minute. After 10 minutes, the faucet is turned off for 15 minutes and the small hose is replaced by a larger hose that can fill the aquarium at a rate of 10 liters per minute. The faucet is turned back on until the aquarium is full. Sketch a graph that depicts the amount of water in the aquarium after x minutes. *

55. *Distance*   A motorcyclist and a bicyclist are traveling toward each other on a straight road. Their distances in miles south of Euclid, Ohio, after x hours are shown in the following graph.
   (a) Is the bicyclist traveling toward or away from Euclid? Explain.   Away; distance is increasing.
   (b) How many hours will elapse before they are the same distance from Euclid?   3 hours

*Answers on page IA-15

(c) During what time period is the motorcyclist farther away from Euclid than the bicyclist?

From 0 to 3 hours

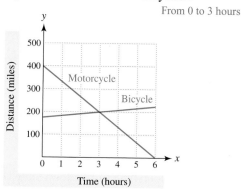

56. *Women Officers*   The number of women officers in the Marine Corps from 1960 to 1997 may be modeled by $f(x) = 17.7(x - 1960) + 56$, where x represents the year. Estimate the years in which the number of women officers was from 410 to 605.

(*Source:* Department of Defense.)   From 1980 to 1991

Systems of Linear Equations

In 1940, a physicist named John Atanasoff at Iowa State University needed to solve 29 equations with 29 variables simultaneously. This task was too difficult to do by hand, so he and a graduate student invented the first fully electronic digital computer. Thus the desire to solve a mathematical problem led to one of the most important inventions of the twentieth century. Today people can solve thousands of equations with thousands of variables. Solutions to such equations have resulted in better airplanes, cars, electronic devices, weather forecasts, and medical equipment.

Equations are also widely used in biology. The following table contains the weight W, neck size N, and chest size C for three black bears. Suppose that park rangers find a bear with a neck size of 22 inches and a chest size of 38 inches. Can they use the data in the table to estimate the bear's weight? Using systems of linear equations, they can answer this question.

W (pounds)	N (inches)	C (inches)
80	16	26
344	28	45
416	31	54
?	22	38

Education is what survives when what has been learned has been forgotten.
—B. F. Skinner

Sources: A. Tucker, *Fundamentals of Computing*; M. Triola, *Elementary Statistics*; Minitab, Inc.

TEACHING TIP

Use this introduction to explain how a real-life example can lead to a system of linear equations.

4.1 SYSTEMS OF LINEAR EQUATIONS IN TWO VARIABLES

Basic Concepts · Graphical and Numerical Solutions · Types of Linear Systems

INTRODUCTION

Many formulas involve more than one variable. For example, to calculate the heat index we need to know both the air temperature and the humidity. To calculate monthly car payments we need the loan amount, interest rate, and duration of the loan. Other applications involve large numbers of variables. To design new aircraft it is necessary to solve equations containing thousands of variables. In this section we consider systems of equations containing only two linear equations in two variables. However, the concepts discussed in this section are used to solve larger systems of equations.

BASIC CONCEPTS

Each year, more and more people buy music subscriptions through the Internet. These subscriptions provide unlimited access to a large assortment of music through a person's computer. Researchers project that a combined total of $400 million will be spent in 2004 and 2005 on music subscriptions, with an expected $200 million increase from 2004 to 2005. (*Source:* Jupiter Research.)

To determine the amount spent each year, we can let x be the amount spent in 2005 and y be the amount spent in 2004 where both amounts are in millions of dollars. Then the given information is described by the following *system of equations*.

$$x + y = 400 \qquad \text{The total is \$400 million.}$$
$$x - y = 200 \qquad \text{The difference is \$200 million.}$$

Each equation contains two variables, x and y. These two equations form a **system of two linear equations in two variables**. An ordered pair (x, y) is a **solution** to a system of equations if the values for x and y satisfy *both* equations. Any system of two linear equations in two variables can be written in **standard form** as

$$ax + by = c$$
$$dx + ey = k,$$

where a, b, c, d, e, and k are constants.

EXAMPLE 1 Testing for solutions

Determine which ordered pair is a solution to the system of equations: $(0, 3)$ or $(-1, 2)$.

$$-x + 4y = 9$$
$$3x - 3y = -9$$

Solution For $(\mathbf{0}, \mathbf{3})$ to be a solution, the values of $x = 0$ and $y = 3$ must satisfy *both* equations.

$$-\mathbf{0} + 4(\mathbf{3}) \stackrel{?}{=} 9 \qquad \text{False}$$
$$3(\mathbf{0}) - 3(\mathbf{3}) \stackrel{?}{=} -9 \qquad \text{True}$$

Because $(0, 3)$ does not satisfy *both* equations, $(0, 3)$ is *not* a solution. To test $(-1, 2)$, substitute $x = -1$ and $y = 2$ in each equation.

$$-(-1) + 4(2) \stackrel{?}{=} 9 \qquad \text{True}$$
$$3(-1) - 3(2) \stackrel{?}{=} -9 \qquad \text{True}$$

Both equations are true, so $(-1, 2)$ is a solution.

GRAPHICAL AND NUMERICAL SOLUTIONS

Graphical, numerical, and symbolic techniques can be used to solve systems of equations. In this section we focus on graphical and numerical techniques and delay discussion of symbolic techniques until the next section. In the next example we solve the system of equations presented earlier, which modeled spending on music subscriptions.

EXAMPLE 2   Solving a system of equations graphically

Solve the system of equations

$$x + y = 400$$
$$x - y = 200$$

graphically. Interpret the solution.

Solution   Start by solving the first equation for y.

$$x + y = 400 \qquad\qquad \text{First equation}$$
$$y = -x + 400 \qquad\qquad \text{Subtract } x.$$

Now solve the second equation for y.

$$x - y = 200 \qquad\qquad \text{Second equation}$$
$$-y = -x + 200 \qquad\qquad \text{Subtract } x.$$
$$y = x - 200 \qquad\qquad \text{Multiply by } -1.$$

The graph of $y_1 = -x + 400$ has slope -1, x-intercept 400, and y-intercept 400, and the graph of $y_2 = x - 200$ has slope 1, x-intercept 200, and y-intercept -200. See Figure 4.1. Because x and y represent sales, we graph these lines only in the first quadrant. Their graphs intersect at the point $(300, 100)$. (Note that $x = 300$ and $y = 100$ satisfy both of the given equations.) Thus $300 million is projected to be spent in 2005 on music subscriptions, and $100 million is expected to be spent in 2004.

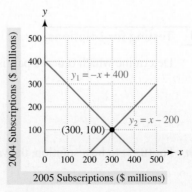

Figure 4.1

TEACHING TIP

Even though numerical solutions are not particularly efficient, they are important because they help many students understand what it means to solve a system of equations.

A numerical solution can be found to the equations in Example 2 by making a table of values for $y_1 = -x + 400$ and $y_2 = x - 200$. Table 4.1 shows that, when $x = 300$, both expressions equal 100. Thus the solution is (300, 100). This type of numerical solution is based on trial and error. If the solution is not a "nice" integer, finding the solution numerically may be difficult or even *impossible*. However, the important mathematical concept to remember is that you are looking for an x-value where $y_1 = y_2$.

TABLE 4.1 A Numerical Solution

x	100	200	300	400
$y_1 = -x + 400$	300	200	100	0
$y_2 = x - 200$	−100	0	100	200

X	Y1	Y2
100	300	-100
200	200	0
300	100	100
400	0	200
500	-100	300
600	-200	400
700	-300	500
X=300		

Figure 4.2

In Figure 4.2 a calculator was used to create a table similar to Table 4.1.

EXAMPLE 3 Solving a system of equations graphically

Solve the system of equations

$$\begin{aligned} 2x - 3y &= 6 \\ 4x + y &= 5 \end{aligned}$$

graphically. Check your answer.

Solution Solve the first equation for y.

$$\begin{aligned} 2x - 3y &= 6 && \text{First equation} \\ -3y &= -2x + 6 && \text{Subtract } 2x \text{ from each side.} \\ \frac{-3y}{-3} &= \frac{-2x}{-3} + \frac{6}{-3} && \text{Divide each term by } -3. \\ y &= \frac{2}{3}x - 2 && \text{Simplify.} \end{aligned}$$

Next, solve the second equation for y.

$$\begin{aligned} 4x + y &= 5 && \text{Second equation} \\ y &= -4x + 5 && \text{Subtract } 4x \text{ from each side.} \end{aligned}$$

Graph $y_1 = \frac{2}{3}x - 2$ and $y_2 = -4x + 5$, as shown in Figure 4.3(a) on the next page. (A similar calculator graph is shown in Figure 4.3(b).) Their graphs appear to intersect at $(1.5, -1)$. To be certain, check this answer.

$$\begin{aligned} 2x - 3y &= 6 && \text{First equation} \\ 2(1.5) - 3(-1) &\stackrel{?}{=} 6 && \text{Let } x = 1.5 \text{ and } y = -1. \\ 6 &= 6 && \text{The answer checks.} \end{aligned}$$

Now substitute these values in the second equation. (It is essential to check *both* equations.)

$$\begin{aligned} 4x + y &= 5 && \text{Second equation} \\ 4(1.5) + (-1) &\stackrel{?}{=} 5 && \text{Let } x = 1.5 \text{ and } y = -1. \\ 5 &= 5 && \text{The answer checks.} \end{aligned}$$

TEACHING TIP

Point out to students that it is important to check a graphical solution to determine whether it is exact or approximate.

Calculator Help

To find a point of intersection, see the Appendix (page AP-7).

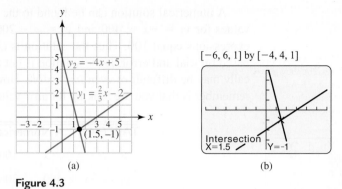

Figure 4.3

TYPES OF LINEAR SYSTEMS

A system of linear equations that has at least one solution is a **consistent system**; otherwise, it is an **inconsistent system**. A system of linear equations in two variables can be represented graphically by two lines in the xy-plane. Three different situations involving two lines are illustrated in Figure 4.4. In Figure 4.4(a) the lines intersect at a single point, which represents a *unique solution*. In this case the equations of the lines are called **independent equations**. In Figure 4.4(b) the two lines are identical, which occurs when the two equations are equivalent. For example, the equations $x + y = 1$ and $2x + 2y = 2$ are equivalent. If we divide each side of the second equation by 2 we obtain the first equation. As a result, their graphs are identical and every point on the line represents a solution. Thus there are infinitely many solutions, and the equations are called **dependent equations**. Finally, in Figure 4.4(c) the lines are parallel and do not intersect. There are no solutions, so the system is inconsistent.

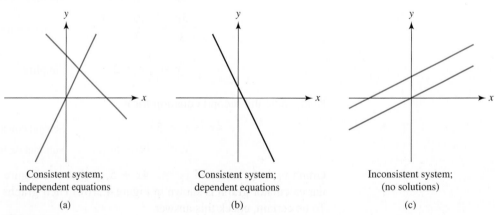

Consistent system; independent equations

(a)

Consistent system; dependent equations

(b)

Inconsistent system; (no solutions)

(c)

Figure 4.4

In the next three examples we illustrate each of these situations.

EXAMPLE 4   Solving a linear system with a unique solution

Suppose that two groups of students go to a football game. The first group buys 3 tickets and 3 soft drinks for $15, and the second group buys 4 tickets and 2 soft drinks for $16. Find the price of a ticket and the price of a soft drink graphically.

Solution Let x be the cost of a ticket and y be the cost of a soft drink. Then $3x + 3y = 15$ represents 3 tickets and 3 soft drinks costing \$15 and $4x + 2y = 16$ represents 4 tickets and 2 soft drinks costing \$16. This information can be written as a system of equations.

$$3x + 3y = 15$$
$$4x + 2y = 16$$

To find a solution graphically, we begin by solving each equation for y.

$$3x + 3y = 15 \qquad\qquad 4x + 2y = 16$$
$$3y = -3x + 15 \qquad\qquad 2y = -4x + 16$$
$$y = -x + 5 \qquad\qquad y = -2x + 8$$

The graphs of $y_1 = -x + 5$ and $y_2 = -2x + 8$ are shown in Figure 4.5 intersecting at the point $(3, 2)$. Thus the cost of a ticket is \$3 and the cost of a soft drink is \$2. Note that 3 tickets and 3 soft drinks cost \$15 and that 4 tickets and 2 soft drinks cost \$16, so our solution is correct.

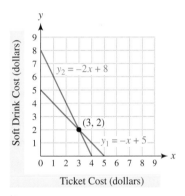

Figure 4.5

EXAMPLE 5 Solving a dependent linear system

Now suppose that two groups of students go to a different football game. The first group buys 4 tickets and 2 soft drinks for \$16, and the second group buys 2 tickets and 1 soft drink for \$8. If possible, find the price of a ticket and the price of a soft drink graphically.

Solution Let x be the cost of a ticket and y be the cost of a soft drink. Then this situation can be modeled by the following system of equations.

$$4x + 2y = 16$$
$$2x + \ y = 8$$

Solve each equation for y.

$$4x + 2y = 16 \qquad\qquad 2x + y = 8$$
$$2y = -4x + 16 \qquad\qquad y = -2x + 8$$
$$y = -2x + 8$$

Both equations simplify to the *same* slope–intercept form and thus the lines are identical, as shown in Figure 4.6 on the next page.

The system is consistent because there is at least one solution. The equations are dependent because not enough information is available to determine a unique solution. Note that the second group bought half what the first group bought and paid half as much. As a result, the two equations contain essentially the same information and are *equivalent*. Thus there are infinitely many solutions because every point on the line is a solution. For example, a ticket could cost $3 and a soft drink could cost $2, or a ticket could cost $2 and a soft drink could cost $4. The solution set can be expressed in set-builder notation as $\{(x, y) \mid 2x + y = 8\}$.

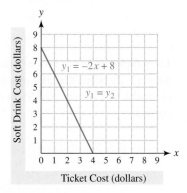

Figure 4.6

TEACHING TIP

Have students use Figure 4.6 to identify several solutions to Example 5.

The tables for y_1 and y_2 would be identical. If the system of two equations is dependent, there are infinitely many solutions.

Critical Thinking

Suppose that a system of two linear equations with two variables is dependent. If you try to solve this system numerically by using a table, how could you recognize that the equations are indeed dependent? Explain your answer.

EXAMPLE 6   Recognizing an inconsistent linear system

Now suppose that two groups of students go to a concert. The first group buys 4 tickets and 2 soft drinks for $20, and the second group buys 2 tickets and 1 soft drink for $12. If possible, find the price of a ticket and the price of a soft drink graphically.

Solution   Let x be the cost of a ticket and y be the cost of a soft drink. Then the following system models the data.

$$4x + 2y = 20$$
$$2x + y = 12$$

Solving for y, we can write each equation in slope–intercept form.

$$y = -2x + 10$$
$$y = -2x + 12$$

Their graphs are parallel lines with slope -2 and different y-intercepts. Thus they do not intersect (see Figure 4.7). The linear system is *inconsistent* because there are no solutions. Note that the second group purchased half what the first group purchased. If pricing had been consistent, the second group would have paid half, or $10, instead of $12. *Inconsistent pricing* resulted in an *inconsistent linear system*.

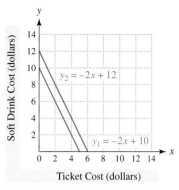

Figure 4.7

Critical Thinking

How would a table of values appear when you are solving an inconsistent system of equations?

The difference between two *y*-values for a given *x*-value would be a nonzero constant.

We can summarize these results as follows.

A SYSTEM OF TWO LINEAR EQUATIONS WITH TWO VARIABLES

A system involving two linear equations and two variables can have no solutions, one solution, or infinitely many solutions. Its graph consists of two lines.

1. If the two lines are parallel, the system is inconsistent and there are no solutions.
2. If the lines intersect at a single point, there is one solution. The system is consistent and the equations are independent.
3. If the lines are identical, the equations are *dependent* and there are infinitely many solutions. The system is consistent.

EXAMPLE 7   Finding an athlete's running speeds

An athlete jogs at a faster pace for 30 minutes and then jogs at a slower pace for 90 minutes. The first pace is 4 miles per hour faster than the second pace, and the athlete covers a total distance of 15 miles.

(a) Write a linear system whose solution gives the athlete's running speeds.

(b) Solve the resulting system graphically and numerically.

Solution   **(a)** Let x be the faster speed of the runner and y be the slower speed. The athlete runs $\frac{1}{2}$ hour at x miles per hour and $\frac{3}{2}$ hours at y miles per hour. Rate times time equals distance and the total distance traveled is 15 miles, so

$$\frac{1}{2}x + \frac{3}{2}y = 15.$$

Because the first pace is 4 miles per hour faster than the second pace,

$$x - y = 4.$$

Thus we need to solve the linear system of equations.

$$\frac{1}{2}x + \frac{3}{2}y = 15 \qquad \text{First equation}$$

$$x - \quad y = \quad 4 \qquad \text{Second equation}$$

(b) We begin by multiplying by 2 to clear fractions and then solve for y.

$$x + 3y = 30 \qquad \text{Multiply first equation by 2.}$$

$$3y = -x + 30 \qquad \text{Subtract } x.$$

$$y = -\frac{x}{3} + 10 \qquad \text{Divide by 3.}$$

Solving the second equation for y gives

$$y = x - 4.$$

We graph $Y_1 = -X/3 + 10$ and $Y_2 = X - 4$, as shown in Figure 4.8(a). The graphs intersect at the point $(10.5, 6.5)$. Thus the athlete ran at 10.5 miles per hour and then slowed to 6.5 miles per hour. A numerical solution is shown in Figure 4.8(b). To find this solution, we set the increment for x-values to 0.5.

[0, 20, 5] by [0, 20, 5]

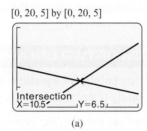
(a)

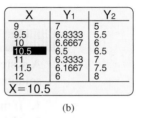
(b)

Figure 4.8

PUTTING IT ALL TOGETHER

A system of two linear equations in two variables may be written in standard form as

$$ax + by = c$$
$$dx + ey = k,$$

where a, b, c, d, e, and k are all constants. Linear systems in two variables may be solved graphically or numerically by first solving each equation for y and then graphing or constructing a table to find any solutions. The following table summarizes the types of systems of equations and the number of solutions that may be encountered.

System	Solution	Graph
Consistent, with a Unique Solution $$x + y = 3$$ $$x - y = 1$$ Equations are Independent	There is one solution: $x = 2$ and $y = 1$. This solution may be written as the ordered pair $(2, 1)$. *Check:* $$2 + 1 = 3 \quad \text{True}$$ $$2 - 1 = 1 \quad \text{True}$$	Graph $y_1 = 3 - x$ and $y_2 = x - 1$. Their graphs intersect at $(2, 1)$.

System	Solution	Graph
Consistent, with Infinitely Many Solutions $$x + y = 1$$ $$2x + 2y = 2$$ Equations are Dependent	There are infinitely many solutions, such as $(2, -1)$ and $(0, 1)$. *Solution Set:* $$\{(x, y) \mid x + y = 1\}$$	Graph $y_1 = 1 - x$ and $y_2 = (-2x + 2)/2$. The graphs are identical. 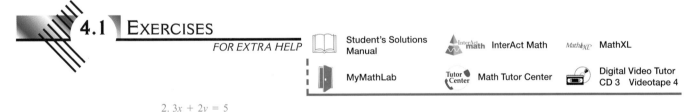
Inconsistent $$x + y = 1$$ $$x + y = 2$$	There are no solutions.	Graph $y_1 = 1 - x$ and $y_2 = 2 - x$. The lines are parallel with slope -1 and do not intersect.

4.1 EXERCISES

FOR EXTRA HELP

Student's Solutions Manual   InterAct Math   MathXL

MyMathLab   Math Tutor Center   Digital Video Tutor CD 3   Videotape 4

CONCEPTS

2. $3x + 2y = 5$
$2x - y = 0$; answers may vary.

1. Can a system of linear equations have exactly two solutions? Explain.   No; two lines cannot have exactly two points of intersection.

2. Give an example of a system of linear equations.

3. Name two ways to solve a system of linear equations.   Numerically and graphically

4. If a graphical solution consists of two distinct, intersecting lines, what does this result indicate about the number of solutions?   There is one solution.

5. If the graphical solution consists of two parallel lines, what does this result indicate about the number of solutions?   There are no solutions.

6. How many solutions does a dependent linear system have? How can you recognize a dependent linear system graphically?   There are infinitely many solutions because the two lines are identical.

Exercises 7–10: (Refer to Example 1.) Decide which of the ordered pairs is a solution for the linear system of equations.

7. $(1, -2), (4, 4)$
$2x - y = 4$
$3x + y = 1$ $(1, -2)$

8. $(-3, -1), (3, 1)$
$x - 3y = 0$
$3x + y = 10$ $(3, 1)$

9. $(4, 6), \left(-1, \frac{13}{3}\right)$
$$x - 3y = -14$$
$$4x + 3y = 9 \quad \left(-1, \frac{13}{3}\right)$$

10. $(4, 0), (3, 5)$
$$5x - 4y = 20$$
$$-x + 4y = -4 \quad (4, 0)$$

GRAPHICAL SOLUTIONS

Exercises 11–14: A system of two linear equations has been solved graphically. Use the graph to find any possible solutions.

11. $(3, 1)$

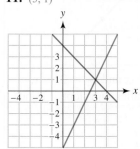

12. $(2, -1)$

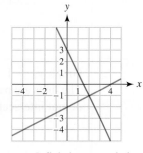

13. No solutions

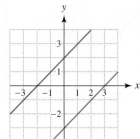

14. Infinitely many solutions satisfy $\{(x, y) \mid x + y = 2\}$.

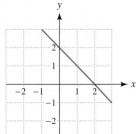

Exercises 15–32: Solve the system of equations. Determine whether the system is consistent or inconsistent. If the system is consistent state whether the equations are dependent or independent.

15. $-x + y = 1$
$\;\;\;\; x + y = 3$
$(1, 2)$; consistent; independent

16. $x + y = 2$
$\;\;\;\; x - y = 2$
$(2, 0)$; consistent; independent

17. $\;\; 2x + y = 5$
$-2x + y = -3$
$(2, 1)$; consistent; independent

18. $x + 2y = 3$
$2x - y = 1$
$(1, 1)$; consistent; independent

19. $\;\; x + \;\; y = 3$
$2x + 2y = 6$
$\{(x, y) \mid x + y = 3\}$; consistent; dependent

20. $\;\;\;\; x - y = 1$
$-x + y = 3$ No solutions; inconsistent

21. $3x - y = 0$
$2x + y = 5$
$(1, 3)$; consistent; independent

22. $-2x - y = -3$
$\;\;\;\; x + y = 2$
$(1, 1)$; consistent; independent

23. $-2x + y = 3$
$\;\;\; 4x - 2y = 2$
No solutions; inconsistent

24. $2x + 4y = 2$
$-x - 2y = -1$

24. $\{(x, y) \mid x + 2y = 1\};$ consistent; dependent

25. $x + y = 6$
$x - y = 2$
$(4, 2)$; consistent; independent

26. $x + y = 9$
$x - y = 3$
$(6, 3)$; consistent; independent

27. $\;\; x - \;\; y = 4$
$2x - 2y = 4$
No solutions; inconsistent

28. $2x + \;\; y = 5$
$4x + 2y = 10$

28. $\{(x, y) \mid 2x + y = 5\};$ consistent; dependent

29. $\;\; 6x - 4y = -2$
$-3x + 2y = 1$

30. $\;\; 4x - 3y = 3$
$-8x + 6y = 1$
No solutions; inconsistent

29. $\{(x, y) \mid -3x + 2y = 1\};$ consistent; dependent

31. $4x + 3y = 2$
$5x + 2y = 6$
$(2, -2)$; consistent; independent

32. $-3x + 2y = 4$
$\;\; 4x - \;\; y = 3$
$(2, 5)$; consistent; independent

Exercises 33–36: Solve the system of equations.

33. $2x + 2y = 4$
$\;\; x - 3y = -2 \quad (1, 1)$

34. $6x - \;\; y = 3$
$\;\; x - 2y = -5 \quad (1, 3)$

35. $-\frac{1}{2}x - \frac{1}{2}y = \frac{3}{2}$
$\;\;\; x - \frac{1}{2}y = 3 \quad (1, -4)$

36. $\frac{1}{2}x + \frac{1}{8}y = 1$
$-\frac{1}{2}x + \frac{5}{6}y = -1 \quad (2, 0)$

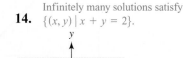 *Exercises 37–44: Use technology to solve the system of equations.*

37. $\frac{1}{4}x + \frac{1}{2}y = \frac{3}{20}$
$\frac{1}{8}x - \;\; y = -\frac{3}{10} \quad (0, 0.3)$

38. $\frac{1}{2}x - \frac{3}{8}y = \frac{1}{8} \quad (0.75, 0.\overline{6})$
$\frac{1}{3}x - \frac{1}{2}y = -\frac{1}{12}$

39. $0.1x + 0.2y = 0.25$
$0.7x - 0.3y = 0.9$
$(1.5, 0.5)$

40. $2.3x + 4.3y = 5.63$
$1.1x - 3.6y = 0.43$
$(1.7, 0.4)$

41. $0.1x + 0.2y = 50$
$0.3x - 0.1y = 10$
$(100, 200)$

42. $\;\;\; 0.5x + 0.2y = 14$
$-0.1x + 0.4y = 6$
$(20, 20)$

43. $\;\;\;\; x - 2y = 5$
$-2x + 4y = -2$
No solutions

44. $3x + 4y = 5$
$6x + 8y = 10$
Infinitely many solutions: $\{(x, y) \mid 3x + 4y = 5\}$

NUMERICAL SOLUTIONS

Exercises 45–48: A system of two linear equations has been solved numerically. Find any possible solutions.

45. $y_1 = 5 - x,$
$y_2 = 2x - 1 \quad (2, 3)$

X	Y₁	Y₂
0	5	-1
1	4	1
2	3	3
3	2	5
4	1	7
5	0	9
6	-1	11

X=0

46. $y_1 = 1 - 2x,$
$y_2 = -1 - 3x \quad (-2, 5)$

X	Y₁	Y₂
-6	13	17
-5	11	14
-4	9	11
-3	7	8
-2	5	5
-1	3	2
0	1	-1

X=-6

58.(a) $x +\quad y = 2$ $\qquad$ (b) 40 mph for 1.5 hr
$\quad$ $40x + 60y = 90$ $\qquad$ 60 mph for 0.5 hr

47. $y_1 = 2 - x,$
$\quad y_2 = x$ $\quad$ (1, 1)

X	Y₁	Y₂
0	2	0
1	1	1
2	0	2
3	-1	3
4	-2	4
5	-3	5
6	-4	6
X=0		

48. $y_1 = 2x - 1,$
$\quad y_2 = -3 + 2x$ $\quad$ No solutions

X	Y₁	Y₂
0	-1	-3
1	1	-1
2	3	1
3	5	3
4	7	5
5	9	7
6	11	9
X=0		

Exercises 49–54: Solve the system of linear equations numerically.

49. $x + y = 3$
$\quad x - y = 7$ $\quad$ (5, -2)

50. $2x + y = 3$
$\quad 3x - y = 7$ $\quad$ (2, -1)

51. $3x + 2y = \quad 5$
$\quad -x -\quad y = -5$
$\quad$ (-5, 10)

52. $2x + 3y = 3.5$
$\quad 3x + 2y = 6.5$
$\quad$ (2.5, -0.5)

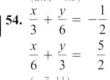 **53.** $0.5x - 0.1y = \quad 0.1$
$\quad 0.1x - 0.3y = -0.4$
$\quad$ (0.5, 1.5)

54. $\dfrac{x}{3} + \dfrac{y}{6} = -\dfrac{1}{2}$

$\dfrac{x}{6} + \dfrac{y}{3} = \dfrac{5}{2}$
$\quad$ (-7, 11)

WRITING AND SOLVING EQUATIONS

Exercises 55–62: Do the following.

(a) *Write a system of linear equations that models the situation.*

(b) *Solve the resulting system.*

55. The sum of two numbers is 18, and their difference is 6. Find the two numbers. $\quad$ (a) $x + y = 18$ $\quad$ (b) 12, 6
$\qquad\qquad x - y = \quad 6$

56. Twice a number minus a second number equals 5. The sum of the two numbers is 16. Find the two numbers.

57. An athlete ran for part of an hour at 6 miles per hour and for the rest of the hour at 8 miles per hour. The total distance traveled was 7 miles. How long did the athlete run at each speed? $\quad$ (b) $\frac{1}{2}$ hr at 6 mph; $\frac{1}{2}$ hr at 8 mph

58. A car was driven for 2 hours, part of the time at 40 miles per hour and the rest of the time at 60 miles per hour. The total distance traveled was 90 miles. How long did the car travel at each speed?

59. The perimeter of a rectangle is 76 inches. The rectangle's length is 4 inches longer than its width. Find the dimensions of this rectangle. $\quad$ (a) $2x + 2y = 76$
(b) 21 in. by 17 in. $\qquad\qquad x - \quad y = 4$

60. An isosceles triangle has a perimeter of 100 inches. The triangle's longest side is 10 inches longer than either of the other two sides. Find the length of each

56.(a) $2x - y = \quad 5$
$\qquad x + y = 16$ $\quad$ (b) 7, 9

57.(a) $x +\quad y = 1$
$\qquad 6x + 8y = 7$

60.(a) $x + 2y = 100$ $\quad$ (b) 40, 30, and 30 in.
$\qquad x - \quad y = 10$

side of the triangle. (*Hint:* An isosceles triangle has two sides with equal measure.)

61. The largest angle in an isosceles triangle is 60° larger than either of the other two angles. Find the measure of each angle. (*Hint:* An isosceles triangle has two angles with equal measure.) $\quad$ (a) $x + 2y = 180$
(b) 100°, 40°, 40° $\qquad\qquad x - \quad y = \quad 60$

62. If 2 boxes of popcorn and 3 soft drinks cost $7 and 3 boxes of popcorn and 2 soft drinks cost $8, find the price of a box of popcorn and the price of a soft drink. $\quad$ (a) $2x + 3y = 7$ $\quad$ (b) Popcorn: $2; soft drink: $1
$\qquad\qquad 3x + 2y = 8$

APPLICATIONS

63. *Online Consumer Sales* In 2002, $40 billion were spent on travel and computer hardware online. The amount spent on computer hardware was one-third the amount spent on travel. Find the amount spent on travel and the amount spent on computer hardware. (*Source:* Comscore Networks.)
$30 billion on travel; $10 billion on hardware

64. *Home Runs* In 1998, Mark McGwire and Sammy Sosa hit a total of 136 home runs. McGwire hit 4 more home runs than Sosa. How many home runs did each player hit? McGwire hit 70, and Sosa hit 66.

65. *NCAA Basketball* Kentucky and UCLA have appeared in the NCAA Division I men's basketball tournament 80 times, with Kentucky appearing 8 more times than UCLA. How many times has each team appeared in this tournament? (*Source:* NCAA.)
UCLA 36 times; Kentucky 44 times

66. *Student Loans* A student takes out two loans totaling $4000 to help pay for college expenses. One loan is at 10% annual interest, and the other is at 5% annual interest. The first-year interest is $250. Find the amount of each loan.
$3000 at 5%; $1000 at 10%

WRITING ABOUT MATHEMATICS

67. Discuss the types of systems of linear equations having two variables. Explain how you can recognize each type graphically.

68. Given

$$ax + by = c$$
$$dx + ey = k,$$

explain how to solve this linear system graphically. Demonstrate your method with an example.

4.2   THE SUBSTITUTION AND ELIMINATION METHODS

The Substitution Method · Identities and Contradictions ·
The Elimination Method · Models and Applications

INTRODUCTION

The ability to solve systems of equations has resulted in the development of CAT scans, satellites, computers, compact discs, and accurate weather forecasts. In the preceding section we showed how to solve a system of two linear equations in two variables, using graphical and numerical methods. In this section we demonstrate how to solve these systems symbolically.

THE SUBSTITUTION METHOD

To apply the **substitution method**, we begin by solving an equation for one of its variables. Then we substitute the result into the other equation. For example, consider the following system of equations.

$$2x + y = 5$$
$$3x - 2y = 4$$

It is convenient to solve the first equation for y to obtain $y = 5 - 2x$. Now substitute $(5 - 2x)$ for y in the second equation,

$$3x - 2(y) = 4 \qquad \text{Second equation}$$
$$3x - 2(5 - 2x) = 4, \qquad \text{Substitute.}$$

to obtain a linear equation in one variable.

$$3x - 2(5 - 2x) = 4$$
$$3x - 10 + 4x = 4 \qquad \text{Distributive property}$$
$$7x - 10 = 4 \qquad \text{Combine like terms.}$$
$$7x = 14 \qquad \text{Add 10 to each side.}$$
$$x = 2 \qquad \text{Divide each side by 7.}$$

TEACHING TIP

This section concentrates on symbolic solutions of linear systems. Graphical and numerical support may be demonstrated if desired.

To determine y substitute 2 for x in $y = 5 - 2x$ to obtain

$$y = 5 - 2(2) = 1.$$

The solution is $(2, 1)$.

Note: When using substitution, you may begin by solving for either variable in either equation. The same result is obtained regardless of which equation is used. However, it is often simpler to solve for a variable with a coefficient of 1 because there is less likelihood of encountering fractions.

EXAMPLE 1   Solving systems with substitution

Solve each system of equations.

(a) $y = 2x$
       $x + y = 21$

(b) $2x + y = -1$
     $2x - y = -3$

(c) $-3x + 2y = 3$
     $2x - 4y = -6$

Solution (a) The first equation is already solved for y, so we substitute $2x$ for y in the second equation.

$$
\begin{aligned}
x + \ \ y &= 21 && \text{Second equation} \\
x + 2x &= 21 && \text{Let } y = 2x. \\
3x &= 21 && \text{Add like terms.} \\
x &= \ \ 7 && \text{Divide by 3.}
\end{aligned}
$$

Substituting 7 for x in $y = 2x$ gives $y = 14$. The solution is $(7, 14)$.

(b) We start by solving for y in the first equation because its coefficient is 1.

$$
\begin{aligned}
2x + y &= -1 && \text{First equation} \\
y &= -2x - 1 && \text{Subtract } 2x.
\end{aligned}
$$

Now we substitute $(-2x - 1)$ for y in the second equation.

$$
\begin{aligned}
2x - y &= -3 && \text{Second equation} \\
2x - (-2x - 1) &= -3 && \text{Let } y = (-2x - 1). \\
2x + 2x + 1 &= -3 && \text{Distributive property} \\
4x &= -4 && \text{Subtract 1; combine like terms.} \\
x &= -1 && \text{Divide by 4.}
\end{aligned}
$$

Substituting -1 for x in $y = -2x - 1$ gives $y = 1$. The solution is $(-1, 1)$.

(c) Neither of the variables has a coefficient of 1. We start by solving for x in the second equation, but we could solve for the other variable.

$$
\begin{aligned}
2x - 4y &= -6 && \text{Second equation} \\
2x &= 4y - 6 && \text{Add } 4y. \\
x &= 2y - 3 && \text{Divide by 2.}
\end{aligned}
$$

Substitute $(2y - 3)$ for x in the first equation.

$$
\begin{aligned}
-3x + 2y &= 3 && \text{First equation} \\
-3(2y - 3) + 2y &= 3 && \text{Let } x = (2y - 3). \\
-6y + 9 + 2y &= 3 && \text{Distributive property} \\
-4y + 9 &= 3 && \text{Combine like terms.} \\
-4y &= -6 && \text{Subtract 9.} \\
y &= \frac{3}{2} && \text{Divide by } -4.
\end{aligned}
$$

Substituting $\frac{3}{2}$ for y in $x = 2y - 3$ gives $x = 0$. The solution is $\left(0, \frac{3}{2}\right)$.

Note: Do not stop after solving for the first variable. You must also solve for the second variable. Remember that a solution to a system of equations consists of an ordered pair, not a single number.

EXAMPLE 2   Finding per capita income

In 2000, the average of the per capita (or per person) incomes for Massachusetts and Maine was $32,000. The per capita income in Massachusetts exceeded the per capita income in Maine by $12,000. Find the 2000 per capita income for each state.

Solution   Let x be the per capita income in Massachusetts and y be the per capita income in Maine. The following system of equations models the data.

$$\frac{x + y}{2} = 32{,}000 \qquad \text{Their average is \$32,000.}$$

$$x - y = 12{,}000 \qquad \text{Their difference is \$12,000.}$$

Begin by solving the second equation for x.

$$x = y + 12{,}000.$$

Substitute $(y + \mathbf{12{,}000})$ into the first equation for x and solve for y.

$$\frac{(y + \mathbf{12{,}000}) + y}{2} = 32{,}000$$

$$(y + 12{,}000) + y = 64{,}000 \qquad \text{Multiply each side by 2.}$$

$$2y + 12{,}000 = 64{,}000 \qquad \text{Combine like terms.}$$

$$2y = 52{,}000 \qquad \text{Subtract 12,000 from each side.}$$

$$y = 26{,}000 \qquad \text{Divide each side by 2.}$$

Substituting for y in $x = y + 12{,}000$ yields $x = 38{,}000$. Thus, in 2000, the per capita income in Massachusetts was \$38,000, and in Maine it was \$26,000.

IDENTITIES AND CONTRADICTIONS

Before describing a second symbolic method to solve a system of linear equations, we need to discuss identities and contradictions. An **identity** is an equation that is always true regardless of the values of any variables. For example, $x + x = 2x$ is an identity, because it is true for all real numbers x. A **contradiction** is an equation that is always false, regardless of the values of any variables. For example, $x = x + 1$ is a contradiction because no real number x can be equal to itself plus 1. If an equation is true for some, but not all, values of any variables, then it is called a **conditional equation**. The equation $x + 1 = 4$ is conditional because 3 is the only solution. Thus far, we have only discussed conditional equations.

EXAMPLE 3   Determining identities and contradictions

Determine whether each equation is an identity, contradiction, or conditional equation.
(a) $0 = 1$ **(b)** $5 = 5$ **(c)** $2x = 6$ **(d)** $2(z - 1) + z = 3z + 2$

Solution   **(a)** The equation $0 = 1$ is always false. It is a contradiction.
(b) The equation $5 = 5$ is always true. It is an identity.
(c) The equation $2x = 6$ is true only when $x = 3$. It is a conditional equation.
(d) Simplify the equation to obtain the following.

$$2(z - 1) + z = 3z + 2 \qquad \text{Given equation}$$

$$2z - 2 + z = 3z + 2 \qquad \text{Distributive property}$$

$$3z - 2 = 3z + 2 \qquad \text{Combine like terms.}$$

$$-2 = 2 \qquad \text{Subtract } 3z \text{ from each side.}$$

Because $-2 = 2$ is a contradiction, the given equation is a contradiction.

THE ELIMINATION METHOD

The **elimination** (or addition) **method** is a second way to solve linear systems symbolically. This method is based on the property that "equals added to equals are equal." That is, if

$$a = b \quad \text{and} \quad c = d,$$

then

$$a + c = b + d.$$

The goal of this method is to obtain an equation from which one of the two variables has been eliminated. This task is sometimes accomplished by either adding or subtracting two equations. This method is demonstrated in the next example.

EXAMPLE 4   Applying the elimination method

Solve each system of equations.
(a) $x + y = 3$ **(b)** $4x + 3y = \quad 0$
$\quad\quad x - y = 1$ $\quad\quad\;\; 4x - 2y = -20$

Solution   **(a)** If we add the two equations, the y-variable will be eliminated.

$$
\begin{array}{r}
x + \;\; y = 3 \\
\underline{x - \;\; y = 1} \\
2x + 0y = 4 \quad \text{or} \quad x = 2
\end{array}
\quad \text{Add equations and solve.}
$$

To find the value of y, we substitute $x = 2$ in either equation.

$$
\begin{array}{ll}
x + y = 3 & \text{First equation} \\
2 + y = 3 & \text{Let } x = 2. \\
\quad\;\; y = 1 & \text{Subtract 2.}
\end{array}
$$

The solution is $(2, 1)$.
(b) If we subtract the equations, the x-variable will be eliminated.

$$
\begin{array}{r}
4x + 3y = \quad 0 \\
\underline{4x - 2y = -20} \\
0x + 5y = \quad 20 \quad \text{or} \quad y = 4
\end{array}
\quad \text{Subtract equations and solve.}
$$

To find the value of x, we substitute $y = 4$ in either equation.

$$
\begin{array}{ll}
4x + 3y = \quad 0 & \text{First equation} \\
4x + 3(4) = \quad 0 & \text{Let } y = 4. \\
\quad\quad\;\; 4x = -12 & \text{Subtract 12.} \\
\quad\quad\;\;\; x = \quad -3 & \text{Divide by 4.}
\end{array}
$$

The solution is $(-3, 4)$.

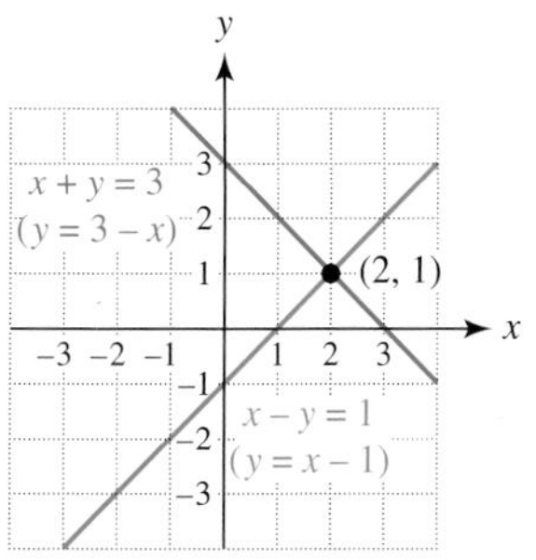

Figure 4.9

Our solutions to the systems of equations can be supported graphically. For example, if we graph the equations in Example 4(a), they intersect at the point (2, 1), as shown in Figure 4.9.

In the next example, the coordinates of the solution are fractions.

EXAMPLE 5   Applying the elimination method

Solve the following system by using elimination.

$$2x - y = 4$$
$$x + y = 1$$

Solution   Note that adding the two equations eliminates the variable y.

$$2x - \ y = 4$$
$$\underline{x + \ y = 1}$$
$$3x + 0y = 5 \quad \text{or} \quad x = \frac{5}{3} \qquad \text{Add the two equations and solve for } x.$$

Substituting $x = \frac{5}{3}$ in the second equation gives

$$\frac{5}{3} + y = 1 \quad \text{or} \quad y = -\frac{2}{3}.$$

The solution is $\left(\frac{5}{3}, -\frac{2}{3}\right)$.

In the next example, we use multiplication before we add the two equations.

EXAMPLE 6   Multiplying before applying elimination

Solve the system of equations.

$$x + \frac{1}{2}y = \ 1$$
$$-3x + 2y = 11$$

Solution   Neither variable can be eliminated by simply adding or subtracting the given equations. However, if we multiply each side of the first equation by -4, we eliminate fractions and then addition of the two equations eliminates the y-variable.

$$-4x - 2y = \ -4 \qquad \text{Multiply first equation by } -4.$$
$$\underline{-3x + 2y = \ \ 11}$$
$$-7x + 0y = \ \ 7 \quad \text{or} \quad x = -1 \qquad \text{Add equations and solve.}$$

To find the value of y, substitute $x = -1$ in the second equation.

$$-3x + 2y = 11 \qquad \text{Second equation}$$
$$-3(-1) + 2y = 11 \qquad \text{Let } x = -1.$$
$$2y = \ \ 8 \qquad \text{Subtract 3 from each side.}$$
$$y = \ \ 4 \qquad \text{Divide each side by 2.}$$

The solution is $(-1, 4)$.

═══════════════════ MAKING CONNECTIONS ═══════════════════

Substitution and Elimination

Substitution and elimination are two symbolic methods that accomplish the *same* task: solving a system of linear equations. Be aware that one method may be easier to perform than the other, depending on the system of equations to be solved.

EXAMPLE 7   Multiplying before applying elimination

Solve the following system by using elimination.

$$3x - 2y = 11$$
$$2x + 3y = 3$$

Solution   If we add or subtract these equations, neither variable will be eliminated. However, if we multiply the first equation by 3 and multiply the second equation by 2, we can eliminate y.

$9x - 6y = 33$	Multiply first equation by 3.
$\underline{4x + 6y = 6}$	Multiply second equation by 2.
$13x + 0y = 39$ or $x = 3$	Add the equations and solve.

Substituting $x = 3$ in $3x - 2y = 11$ gives

$$3(3) - 2y = 11 \quad \text{or} \quad y = -1.$$

The solution is $(3, -1)$.

Note: In Example 7 we could have multiplied the first equation by 2 and the second equation by -3. Adding the resulting equations would have eliminated the variable x.

EXAMPLE 8   Recognizing an inconsistent system

Use elimination to solve the following system.

$$3x - 4y = 5$$
$$-6x + 8y = 9$$

Solution   If we multiply the first equation by 2 and add, we obtain the following result.

$6x - 8y = 10$	Multiply first equation by 2.
$\underline{-6x + 8y = 9}$	
$0 = 19$	Adding the two equations gives a false result.

$[-6, 6, 1]$ by $[-4, 4, 1]$

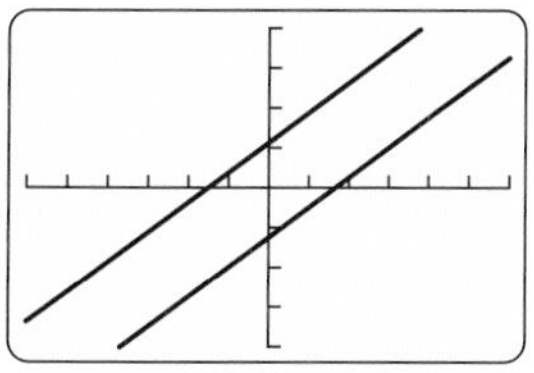

Figure 4.10

The statement $0 = 19$ is a contradiction, which tells us that the system has no solutions. If we solve each equation for y and graph, we obtain two parallel lines with slope $\frac{3}{4}$ that never intersect. This result is shown in Figure 4.10, where the equations are graphed as $Y_1 = (3X - 5)/4$ and $Y_2 = (6X + 9)/8$.

EXAMPLE 9   Recognizing dependent equations

Use elimination to solve the following system.

$$3x - 6y = 3$$
$$x - 2y = 1$$

Solution   If we multiply the second equation by -3 and add, we obtain the following.

$$3x - 6y = 3$$
$$\underline{-3x + 6y = -3} \qquad \text{Multiply second equation by } -3.$$
$$0 = 0 \qquad \text{Adding the two equations gives a true result.}$$

The statement $0 = 0$ is an identity, so the two equations are equivalent. If an ordered pair (x, y) satisfies the first equation, it also satisfies the second equation. Thus the solution set may be expressed as $\{(x, y) \mid x - 2y = 1\}$. For example, $(1, 0)$ and $(5, 2)$ are both solutions.

TEACHING TIP

Point out that Making Connections also applies to the method of substitution.

═══ MAKING CONNECTIONS ═══

Graphical Solutions and Elimination

1. *Unique Solution* A graphical solution results in two lines intersecting at a unique point. Elimination gives unique values for x and y.
2. *Inconsistent Linear System* A graphical solution results in two parallel lines. Elimination results in a contradiction, such as $0 = 1$.
3. *Dependent Linear System* A graphical solution results in two identical lines. Elimination results in an identity, such as $0 = 0$.

Note: Conditions 2 and 3 usually occur when *both* variables are eliminated, and the resulting equation is either always true or always false.

MODELS AND APPLICATIONS

Linear systems are often used in applications. In the next example we use a linear system to determine the cost of tuition.

EXAMPLE 10 Modeling tuition

A student is attempting to graduate on schedule by taking 14 credits of day classes at one college and 4 credits of night classes at a different college. A credit for day classes costs $20 more than a credit for night classes. If the student's total tuition is $2440, how much does each type of credit cost?

Solution   Let x be the cost of a credit for day classes and y be the cost of a credit for night classes. Then the data can be represented by the following system of equations.

$$x - y = 20 \qquad \text{Day credits cost \$20 more than night credits.}$$
$$14x + 4y = 2440 \qquad \text{The total cost is \$2440 for 14 credits during the day and 4 credits at night.}$$

To solve this system we multiply the first equation by 4 and then add the equations.

$$4x - 4y = 80 \qquad \text{Multiply by 4.}$$
$$\underline{14x + 4y = 2440}$$
$$18x + 0y = 2520 \quad \text{or} \quad x = 140 \qquad \text{Add and solve for } x.$$

Because $x = 140$ and $x - y = 20$, $y = 120$. Thus a credit for day classes costs $140 and a credit for night classes costs $120.

EXAMPLE 11   Modeling river travel

A boat travels 150 miles upstream in 10 hours, and the return trip takes 6 hours. Find the speed of the boat and the speed of the current.

Solution   Let x be the speed of the boat and y be the speed of the river current. The boat travels 150 miles upstream in 10 hours. Thus the speed of the boat *against* the current is $\frac{150}{10} = 15$ miles per hour, or $x - y = 15$. Similarly the boat travels 150 miles downstream in 6 hours. Thus the speed of the boat *with* the current is $\frac{150}{6} = 25$ miles per hour, or $x + y = 25$. We represent these data with the following equations.

TEACHING TIP

The solution to Example 11 is based on first finding the average speed of the boat in each direction.

$$x + y = 25$$
$$\underline{x - y = 15}$$
$$2x + 0y = 40 \quad \text{or} \quad x = 20 \qquad \text{Add equations and solve.}$$

Substituting $x = 20$ in $x + y = 25$ gives $y = 5$. The boat can travel 20 miles per hour in still water and the speed of the current is 5 miles per hour.

EXAMPLE 12   Burning calories while exercising

During strenuous exercise, an athlete can burn 12 calories per minute running and 10 calories per minute on a bicycle. In a 60-minute workout, an athlete burns 644 calories. How long did the athlete spend running and bicycling?

Solution   Let x be the time spent running and y be the time spent bicycling. Because the workout is 60 minutes long, we write $x + y = 60$. The number of calories burned running equals $12x$, and the number of calories burned bicycling equals $10y$. The total number of calories burned equals 644 so the system is as follows.

$$x + y = 60 \qquad \text{Total workout is 60 minutes.}$$
$$12x + 10y = 644 \qquad \text{Total calories equal 644.}$$

To solve this system we can multiply the first equation by -10 and add the equations to eliminate the y-variable.

$$-10x - 10y = -600 \qquad \text{Multiply first equation by } -10.$$
$$\underline{12x + 10y = 644}$$
$$2x + 0y = 44 \quad \text{or} \quad x = 22 \qquad \text{Add equations and solve.}$$

Substituting $x = 22$ in $x + y = 60$ gives $y = 38$. The athlete spent 22 minutes running and 38 minutes bicycling.

EXAMPLE 13 Mixing antifreeze

A mixture of water and antifreeze in a car is currently 20% antifreeze. If the radiator holds 5 gallons of fluid and this mixture should be 40% antifreeze, how many gallons of radiator fluid should be drained and replaced with a mixture containing 90% antifreeze?

Solution Let x be the gallons of 20% antifreeze that should remain in the radiator and y be the gallons of 90% antifreeze that should be added to the radiator. The radiator holds 5 gallons of fluid, so $x + y = 5$. The final solution in the radiator should contain 5 gallons of 40% solution or $5(0.4) = 2$ gallons of (pure) antifreeze. Thus the antifreeze in the 20% solution plus the antifreeze in the 90% solution must equal 2 gallons. That is, $0.2x + 0.9y = 2$. Table 4.2 summarizes this situation.

TABLE 4.2 Mixing Antifreeze

	20% Solution	90% Solution	40% Solution
Radiator Fluid (gallons)	x	y	5
Pure Antifreeze (gallons)	$0.2x$	$0.9y$	2

The resulting system to be solved is

$$x + y = 5$$
$$0.2x + 0.9y = 2.$$

Multiply the first equation by 2 and the second equation by -10. Then adding the resulting equations eliminates the x-variable.

$$
\begin{array}{r}
2x + 2y = 10 \\
-2x - 9y = -20 \\
\hline
0x - 7y = -10 \quad \text{or} \quad y = \dfrac{10}{7}
\end{array}
$$

Thus, $\frac{10}{7}$ gallons of fluid should be drained from the radiator and replaced with $\frac{10}{7}$ gallons of 90% antifreeze solution.

4.2 PUTTING IT ALL TOGETHER

Two symbolic methods for solving a system of linear equations are substitution and elimination. Symbolic methods are often superior to graphical and numerical methods because they give exact answers, whereas graphical and numerical methods can give approximate answers. The following table presents a summary of substitution and elimination.

Concept	Explanation
Substitution Method	**1.** Solve for a convenient variable such as y in the first equation. $$x + y = 3 \quad \text{or} \quad y = 3 - x$$ $$2x - y = 0$$ **2.** Substitute $(3 - x)$ in the second equation for y. Solve the equation for x. $$2x - (3 - x) = 0 \quad \text{or} \quad x = 1.$$ **3.** Substitute $x = 1$ in one of the given equations and find y. $$1 + y = 3 \quad \text{or} \quad y = 2.$$ **4.** The solution is $(1, 2)$. Check your answer.
Elimination Method	**1.** Multiply the first equation by -2 so that the coefficients of x in the two equations are additive inverses. $$x + 2y = 1 \quad \text{or} \quad -2x - 4y = -2$$ $$2x - 3y = 9 \qquad\qquad 2x - 3y = 9$$ **2.** Eliminate x by adding the two equations. $$-2x - 4y = -2$$ $$\underline{2x - 3y = 9}$$ $$0x - 7y = 7 \quad \text{or} \quad y = -1$$ **3.** Substitute $y = -1$ in one of the given equations and solve for x. $$x + 2(-1) = 1 \quad \text{or} \quad x = 3.$$ **4.** The solution is $(3, -1)$. Check your answer.

4.2 EXERCISES

FOR EXTRA HELP

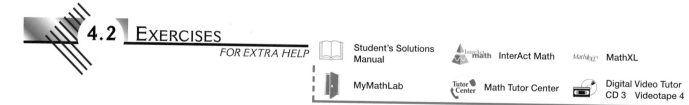

Student's Solutions Manual   InterAct Math   MathXL

MyMathLab   Math Tutor Center   Digital Video Tutor   CD 3   Videotape 4

CONCEPTS

1. Name two symbolic methods for solving a linear system.
Substitution and elimination

2. Are different solutions obtained when the same system of equations is solved symbolically, graphically, and numerically? Explain.
No; all methods produce the same solution. However, graphical and numerical answers are sometimes rounded.

3. When using elimination, how can you recognize an inconsistent system of equations?
Elimination yields a contradiction.

4. When using elimination, how can you recognize a dependent system of equations? Elimination yields an identity.

5. When you use substitution to solve

$$3x + y = 4$$
$$5x - 7y = -2,$$

what is a good first step? *Solve the first equation for y.*

6. When you are using elimination to solve

$$2x - 5y = 4$$
$$x + 3y = 11,$$

what is a good first step? *Multiply the second equation by −2.*

SUBSTITUTION METHOD

Exercises 7–10: Solve the system of linear equations by using substitution.

7. $y = 2x$
$3x + y = 5$ (1, 2)

8. $y = x + 1$
$x + 2y = 8$ (2, 3)

9. $x = 2y - 1$
$x + 5y = 20$ (5, 3)

10. $x = 3y$
$-x + 2y = 4$ (−12, −4)

Exercises 11 and 12: Use substitution to solve the system of equations. Then use the graph to support your answer.

11. $x - 2y = 0$
$3x + y = 7$ (2, 1)

12. $2x + 3y = 8$
$3x - 2y = -14$ (−2, 4)

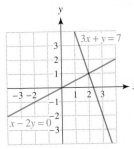
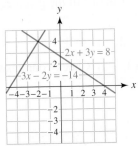

Exercises 13–18: Solve the system of equations by using substitution. Then solve the system graphically.

13. $y = 3x$
$x + y = 4$ (1, 3)

14. $x = \frac{1}{2}y$
$2x + y = 4$ (1, 2)

15. $x + y = 2$
$2x - y = 1$ (1, 1)

16. $x - y = 2$
$x + 2y = -1$ (1, −1)

17. $2x + 3y = 6$
$x - 2y = -4$ (0, 2)

18. $2x - y = 2$
$3x + 2y = 10$ (2, 2)

Exercises 19–30: Solve the system of equations by using substitution.

19. $2x - 5y = -1$
$-x + 3y = 0$
(−3, −1)

20. $5x + 10y = -5$
$-10x + 5y = 60$
(−5, 2)

21. $x - y = 1$
$2x + 6y = -2$ $\left(\frac{1}{2}, -\frac{1}{2}\right)$

22. $4x - y = -4$
$-2x + 5y = 29$ $\left(\frac{1}{2}, 6\right)$

23. $\frac{1}{2}x - \frac{1}{2}y = 1$
$2x - y = 6$ (4, 2)

24. $\frac{3}{4}x + \frac{1}{2}y = 5$
$x - 2y = 12$ (8, −2)

25. $\frac{1}{6}x - \frac{1}{3}y = -1$
$\frac{1}{3}x + \frac{5}{6}y = 7$ (6, 6)

26. $\frac{3}{5}x - \frac{1}{10}y = 4$
$\frac{2}{5}x + \frac{1}{10}y = 6$ (10, 20)

27. $\frac{1}{2}x + \frac{2}{3}y = -2$
$\frac{1}{4}x - \frac{1}{3}y = 3$ (4, −6)

28. $\frac{1}{5}x - \frac{1}{10}y = \frac{7}{40}$
$\frac{1}{4}x - \frac{1}{5}y = \frac{11}{40}$ $\left(\frac{1}{2}, -\frac{3}{4}\right)$

29. $0.1x + 0.4y = 1.3$
$0.3x - 0.2y = 1.1$
(5, 2)

30. $1.5x - 4.1y = -1.6$
$2.7x - 0.1y = 0.76$
(0.3, 0.5)

31. The following system is dependent.

$$x - y = 5$$
$$2x - 2y = 10$$

Solve this system by using substitution. Explain how you can recognize a dependent system when you are using substitution. *For $x = y + 5$, the result is 10 = 10, which is an identity.*

32. The following system is inconsistent.

$$-x + 2y = 5$$
$$2x - 4y = 10$$

Solve this system by using substitution. Explain how you can recognize an inconsistent system when you are using substitution. *For $x = 2y - 5$, the result is −10 = 10, which is a contradiction.*

ELIMINATION METHOD

Exercises 33 and 34: Use elimination to solve the system of equations. Then use the graph to support your answer.

33. $x - y = 5$
$x + y = 9$ (7, 2)

34. $3x - 2y = 9$
$5x + 2y = 7$ (2, −1.5)

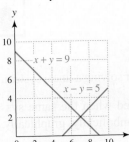
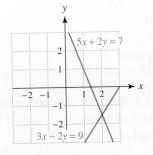

Exercises 35–38: Use elimination to solve the system of equations. Then solve the system graphically.

35. $x + y = 3$
$x - y = 1$ (2, 1)

36. $2x - y = 3$
$x + 2y = -1$ (1, −1)

37. $4x - y = 4$
$x + 2y = 1$ (1, 0)

38. $x - y = 1$
$x + 4y = 6$ (2, 1)

Exercises 39–50: Use elimination to solve the system.

39. $2x + y = 4$
$2x - y = -2$ $\left(\frac{1}{2}, 3\right)$

40. $2x + 3y = -6$
$2x - y = 4$ $\left(\frac{3}{4}, -\frac{5}{2}\right)$

41. $6x - 4y = 12$
$3x + 5y = -6$ $\left(\frac{6}{7}, -\frac{12}{7}\right)$

42. $-5x - 4y = -8$
$x - 4y = 10$ $\left(3, -\frac{7}{4}\right)$

43. $2x - 4y = 5$
$-x + 2y = 9$
Inconsistent: no solutions

44. $x - 3y = 5$
$2x - 6y = 1$
Inconsistent: no solutions

45. $2x + y = 2$
$4x + 2y = 4$
Dependent: $\{(x, y) \mid 2x + y = 2\}$

46. $\frac{1}{2}x + \frac{1}{7}y = 2$
$7x + 2y = 28$
Dependent: $\{(x, y) \mid 7x + 2y = 28\}$

47. $2x + 4y = -22$
$75x + 15y = -120$
$\left(-\frac{5}{9}, -\frac{47}{9}\right)$

48. $-3x + 20y = 67$
$2x + 5y = 47$ (11, 5)

49. $0.3x + 0.2y = 0.8$
$0.4x + 0.3y = 1.1$
(2, 1)

50. $1.2x + 4.3y = 1.7$
$2.4x - 1.5y = 1.38$
(0.7, 0.2)

Exercises 51–66: Solve the system of equations.

51. $2x + 3y = 7$
$2x - y = -13$ (−4, 5)

52. $2x - 3y = -25$
$x + 3y = 10$ (−5, 5)

53. $3u - 5v = 4$
$5u + v = 2$ $\left(\frac{1}{2}, -\frac{1}{2}\right)$

54. $4u - 3v = -2$
$-8u + 9v = 5$ $\left(-\frac{1}{4}, \frac{1}{3}\right)$

55. $2r - 3t = 7$
$-4r + 6t = -14$
Dependent: $\{(r, t) \mid 2r - 3t = 7\}$

56. $r - t = 10$
$-2r + 2t = -20$
Dependent: $\{(r, t) \mid r - t = 10\}$

57. $m - n = 5$
$m - n = 7$
Inconsistent: no solutions

58. $6m + 9n = 4$
$-4m - 6n = 2$
Inconsistent: no solutions

59. $2x - 3y = 2$
$3x - 5y = 4$ (−2, −2)

60. $x + 3y = \frac{5}{4}$
$-2x - 7y = -\frac{11}{4}$ $\left(\frac{1}{2}, \frac{1}{4}\right)$

61. $0.1x - 0.3y = -5$
$0.5x + 1.1y = 27$
(10, 20)

62. $0.6x - 0.2y = 1.8$
$-0.1x - 0.5y = 1.3$
(2, −3)

63. $\frac{1}{2}y - \frac{1}{2}z = -1$
$\frac{3}{4}y - \frac{1}{2}z = 1$ (8, 10)

64. $\frac{3}{4}y + \frac{1}{4}z = 13$
$-\frac{1}{4}y + \frac{1}{4}z = -3$ (16, 4)

65. $\frac{1}{5}x - \frac{2}{5}y = -\frac{3}{5}$
$x - y = 1$ (5, 4)

66. $\frac{1}{10}x - \frac{1}{5}y = 2$
$-\frac{1}{5}x + \frac{1}{10}y = -1.9$ (6, −7)

USING MORE THAN ONE METHOD

Exercises 67–72: Solve the system of equations graphically, numerically, and symbolically.

67. $x - y = 4$
$x + y = 6$ (5, 1)

68. $2x - y = 7$
$3x + y = 3$ (2, −3)

69. $5x + 2y = 9$
$3x - y = 1$ (1, 2)

70. $-x + 4y = 17$
$3x + 6y = 21$ (−1, 4)

71. $3x - 2y = 8.5$
$2x + 4y = 3$
(2.5, −0.5)

72. $-x - 3y = 1.8$
$2x - 5y = 0.8$
(−0.6, −0.4)

APPLICATIONS

73. *Burning Fat Calories* Two athletes engage in a strenuous 40-minute workout on a stair climber. The heavier athlete burns 58 more fat calories than the lighter athlete. Together they burn a total of 290 fat calories. How many fat calories did each athlete burn? If 1 fat gram equals 9 fat calories, how many fat grams did each athlete burn? (*Source: Runner's World.*) The heavier athlete burned 174 fat cal or about 19.3 fat g. The lighter athlete burned 116 fat cal or about 12.9 fat g.

74. *Burning Calories* During strenuous exercise, an athlete can burn 10 calories per minute on a rowing machine, whereas on a stair climber the athlete can burn 11.5 calories per minute. In a 60-minute workout an athlete burns 633 calories by using both exercise machines. How many minutes did the athlete spend on each type of workout equipment? (*Source: Runner's World.*) Rowing machine: 38 min; stair climber: 22 min

75. *Mixing Antifreeze* A mixture of water and antifreeze in a car is 10% antifreeze. In colder climates this mixture should contain 50% antifreeze. If the radiator contains 4 gallons of fluid, how many gallons of radiator fluid should be drained and replaced with a mixture containing 80% antifreeze? $\frac{16}{7}$ gal

76. *Mixing Acid* Determine the milliliters of 10% sulfuric acid and the milliliters of 25% sulfuric acid that should be mixed to obtain 20 milliliters of 18% sulfuric acid. $9.\overline{3}$ mL of 10% acid and $10.\overline{6}$ mL of 25% acid

77. *Hotel Rooms* The revenue from renting 50 hotel rooms is $4945. If premium rooms cost $115 and regular rooms cost $80, find the number of each type of room rented. 27 premium rooms; 23 regular rooms

78. *Coins* A sample of dimes and quarters totals $18. If there are 111 coins in all, how many of each type of coin are there? 65 dimes; 46 quarters

79. *Supplementary Angles*   The larger of two supplementary angles is 30° more than twice the smaller angle. Find the angles. (*Hint:* Supplementary angles sum to 180°.)   50° and 130°

80. *Per Capita Income*   In 2000, the average of the per capita incomes for Alaska and Arizona was $28,000. The per capita income in Alaska exceeded the per capita income in Arizona by $4000. Find the per capita income for each state. (*Source:* Bureau of Economic Analysis.)   Alaska: $30,000; Arizona: $26,000

81. *Airplane Speed*   A plane flies 2400 miles from Orlando, Florida, to Los Angeles, California, against the jet stream in 4 hours and 10 minutes. Then the plane flies back to Orlando with the jet stream in 3 hours and 45 minutes. Find the speed of the plane with the no wind and the speed of the jet stream.
Plane: 608 mph; jet stream: 32 mph

82. *Airplane Speed*   An airplane flies with the wind and travels 3000 miles in 5 hours. The return trip into the wind requires 6 hours. Find the speed of the wind and of the airplane in no wind.
Airplane: 550 mph; wind: 50 mph

83. *Boat Speed*   A boat travels downstream 150 miles in 5 hours. The return trip takes 7 hours and 30 minutes. Find the speed of the boat without a current and the speed of the current.   Boat: 25 mph; current: 5 mph

84. *River Current*   A tugboat can push a barge 165 miles upstream in 33 hours. The same tugboat and barge can make the return trip downstream in 15 hours. Determine the speed of the current and the speed of the tugboat when there is no current.
Current: 3 mph; tugboat: 8 mph

85. *Student Loans*   A student takes out two loans to help pay for college. One loan is at 8% simple interest, and the other is at 9% simple interest. The total amount borrowed is $3500, and the interest after 1 year for both loans is $294. Find the amount of each loan.
$2100 at 8% and $1400 at 9%

86. *Student Loans*   A student takes out two loans totaling $5000 at 4% and 6% interest. The total interest after one year is $254. Find the amount of each loan.
$2300 at 4%; $2700 at 6%

87. *College Tuition*   A student takes 12 credits of day classes and 6 credits of night classes. A credit for day classes costs $30 more than a credit for night classes. If the student's total tuition is $1800, how much does each type of credit cost?   Day: $110; night: $80

88. *Computer Sales*   Sales of personal computers are expected to increase in the twenty-first century. In 2000 and 2001, a combined total of 264 million personal computers were sold worldwide, with 12.9% more computers sold in 2001 than in 2000. How many personal computers were sold in 2000, and how many were sold in 2001? Round your answers to the nearest million.   (*Source:* International Data Corporation.)
About 124 million in 2000 and about 140 million in 2001.

89. *Geometry*   A basketball court has a perimeter of 296 feet. Its length is 44 feet greater than its width. Set up a system of two linear equations whose solution gives the length and width of the court. Solve the system
(a) symbolically, $2x + 2y = 296$
(b) graphically, and $x - y = 44$
(c) numerically.   (a)–(c) Length = 96 ft and width = 52 ft

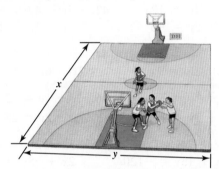

90. *Concert Tickets*   Tickets for a concert sold for $55 and $40. If 2000 tickets were sold for total receipts of $90,500, find how many of each type of ticket were sold   (a)–(c) 700 tickets at $55; 1300 tickets at $40
(a) symbolically,
(b) graphically, and
(c) numerically.

91. *Roof Trusses*   Linear systems are used in the design of roof trusses for houses and other types of buildings (see the accompanying figures). One of the simplest types of roof trusses is an equilateral triangle. If a 200-pound force is applied to the peak of the truss, the weights W_1 and W_2 exerted on each rafter are determined by the following system of equations. Solve this system.   Approximately 115.5 lb on each rafter

$$W_1 - W_2 = 0$$
$$\frac{\sqrt{3}}{2}(W_1 + W_2) = 200$$

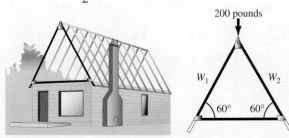

92. *Roof Trusses* (Refer to Exercise 91.) The weights W_1 and W_2 exerted on each rafter for the roof truss shown in the accompanying figure are determined by the following system of equations. Solve the system and interpret the result.

$$W_1 + \sqrt{2}W_2 = 300$$
$$\sqrt{3}W_1 - \sqrt{2}W_2 = 0$$

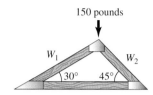

150 pounds

W_1 W_2

30°   45°

The weights exerted on the rafters are $W_1 \approx 109.8$ lb and $W_2 \approx 134.5$ lb.

WRITING ABOUT MATHEMATICS

93. Explain what it means for a linear system to be inconsistent. Give an example.

94. Describe two possible ways that you could use elimination to solve the following system of linear equations. (Do not actually solve the system.)

$$ax - y = c$$
$$x + dy = e$$

CHECKING BASIC CONCEPTS   SECTIONS 4.1 AND 4.2

1. Solve the system of linear equations

$$2x - y = 5$$
$$-x + 3y = 0$$

  (a) graphically and

  (b) numerically.

  Do your answers agree?   (3, 1); yes

2. Use substitution to solve the system of equations.

$$4x - 3y = -1$$
$$x + 4y = 14$$

(2, 3)

3. Use elimination to solve the system of equations. Is the system dependent? Is it inconsistent?

$$4x - 3y = -17$$
$$-6x + 2y = 23 \quad \left(-\tfrac{7}{2}, 1\right); \text{ no; no}$$

4. *Complementary Angles* The smaller of two complementary angles is 40° less than the larger angle.

  (a) Write a system of linear equations whose solution gives the measure of each angle. (*Hint:* Complementary angles sum to 90°.)

  (b) Solve the system and interpret the result.

    (a) $x + y = 90$ (b) (65, 25); the smaller angle is 25°
       $x - y = 40$ and the larger angle is 65°.

4.3 SYSTEMS OF LINEAR INEQUALITIES

Solving Linear Inequalities in Two Variables · Solving Systems of Linear Inequalities

INTRODUCTION

People often walk or jog in an effort to increase their heart rates and get in better shape. During strenuous exercise, older people should maintain lower heart rates than younger people. A person cannot maintain precisely one heart rate, so a range of heart rates is recommended by health professionals. For aerobic fitness, a 50-year-old's heart rate might be between 120 and 140 beats per minute, whereas a 20-year-old's heart rate might be between 140 and 160. Systems of linear inequalities can be used to model these situations.

SOLVING LINEAR INEQUALITIES IN TWO VARIABLES

Suppose that candy costs \$2 per pound and that peanuts cost \$1 per pound. The total cost C of buying x pounds of candy and y pounds of peanuts is given by

$$C = 2x + y.$$

If we only have \$5 to spend, the inequality

$$2x + y \leq 5$$

must be satisfied. To determine the different weight combinations of candy and peanuts that could be bought, we could use the graph shown in Figure 4.11. Points located on the line $2x + y = 5$ represent weight combinations resulting in a \$5 purchase. For example, the point $(2, 1)$ satisfies the equation $2x + y = 5$ and represents buying 2 pounds of candy and 1 pound of peanuts for \$5. Ordered pairs (x, y) located in the shaded region below the line represent purchases of less than \$5. The point $(1, 2)$ lies in the shaded region and represents buying 1 pound of candy and 2 pounds of peanuts for \$4. Note that, if we substitute $x = 1$ and $y = 2$ in the inequality, we obtain

$$2(1) + (2) \leq 5,$$

which is a true statement.

TEACHING TIP

In Figure 4.11, explain how points located below the line represent purchases less than \$5, points on the line represent purchases of \$5, and points above the line represent purchases more than \$5.

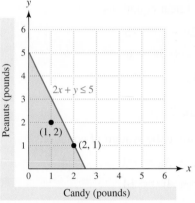

Figure 4.11 Purchases of Candy and Peanuts

When the equals sign in a linear equation of two variables is replaced with $<, \leq, >,$ or $\geq$, a **linear inequality in two variables** results. Examples include

$$2x + y \leq 5, \quad y \geq x - 5, \quad \text{and} \quad \frac{1}{2}x - \frac{3}{5}y < 8.$$

EXAMPLE 1   Solving linear inequalities

Shade the solution set for each inequality.
(a) $x > 1$ **(b)** $y \leq 2x - 1$ **(c)** $x - 2y < 4$

Solution **(a)** Begin by graphing the vertical line $x = 1$ with a dashed line because equality is *not* included. The solution set includes all points with x-values greater than 1, so shade the region to the right of this line, as shown in Figure 4.12(a).

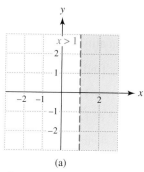

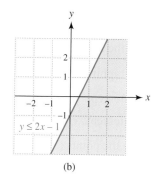

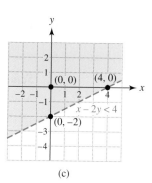

(a)   (b)   (c)

Figure 4.12

(b) Start by graphing $y = 2x - 1$ with a solid line because equality *is* included. The inequality sign is $\leq$, so the solution set includes all points on or below this line, as shown in Figure 4.12(b).

(c) Start by finding the intercepts for the line $x - 2y = 4$.

x-intercept: $y = 0$ implies $x - 2(0) = 4$ or $x = 4$

y-intercept: $x = 0$ implies $0 - 2y = 4$ or $y = -2$

Plot the points $(4, 0)$ and $(0, -2)$ and sketch a dashed line, as shown in Figure 4.12(c). To determine whether to shade above or below this line, substitute a *test point* in the inequality. For example, if we pick the test point $(0, 0)$ and then substitute $x = 0$ and $y = 0$ in the given equality, we find the following result.

$$x + 2y < 4 \qquad \text{Given inequality}$$
$$0 + 2(0) < 4 \qquad \text{Let } x = 0 \text{ and } y = 0.$$
$$0 < 4 \qquad \text{A true statement}$$

Because this substitution results in a true statement, shade the region *containing* $(0, 0)$, which is located above the dashed line.

The following steps can be used to graph a linear inequality in two variables.

SOLVING A LINEAR INEQUALITY GRAPHICALLY

1. Replace the inequality symbol with an equals sign.
2. Graph the resulting line. Use a solid line if the inequality symbol is $\leq$ or $\geq$ and a dashed line if it is $<$ or $>$.
3. **(a)** If the inequality is in the form $x \leq k$ or $x < k$ (where k is a constant) shade to the *left* of the vertical line. If the inequality is in the form $x \geq k$ or $x > k$, shade to the *right* of the vertical line.
   (b) If the inequality is in the form $y \leq mx + b$ or $y < mx + b$, shade *below* this line. If the inequality is in the form $y \geq mx + b$ or $y > mx + b$, shade *above* this line.
   (c) If you are uncertain as to which region to shade, choose a **test point** that is *not* on the line. Substitute it in the given inequality. If the test point makes the inequality true, then shade the region containing the test point. Otherwise, shade on the other side of the line.

<u>**EXAMPLE 2**</u>   Solving a linear inequality graphically

Shade the solution set for the linear inequality $4x - 3y < 12$.

Solution   Start graphing the line $4x - 3y = 12$ by finding its intercepts.

x-intercept: $y = 0$ implies $4x - 3(0) = 12$ or $x = 3$

y-intercept: $x = 0$ implies $4(0) - 3y = 12$ or $y = -4$

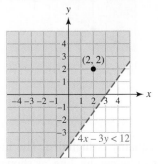

Figure 4.13

Locate the points $(3, 0)$ and $(0, -4)$ and sketch a dashed line. Any point not on this line can be used for a test point. We use the test point $(2, 2)$.

$$4x - 3y < 12 \qquad \text{Given inequality}$$
$$4(2) - 3(2) < 12 \qquad \text{Let } x = 2 \text{ and } y = 2.$$
$$2 < 12 \qquad \text{A true statement}$$

Thus shade the region containing the point $(2, 2)$, as shown in Figure 4.13.

SOLVING SYSTEMS OF LINEAR INEQUALITIES

A **system of linear inequalities** results when the equals signs in a system of linear equations are replaced with $<, \leq, >$, or $\geq$. The system of linear equations

$$x + y = 4$$
$$y = x$$

becomes a system of linear inequalities when it is written as

$$x + y \leq 4$$
$$y \geq x.$$

A solution to a system of inequalities must satisfy *both* inequalities. For example, the ordered pair $(1, 2)$ is a solution to this system because substituting $x = 1$ and $y = 2$ makes both inequalities true.

$$1 + 2 \leq 4 \qquad \text{True}$$
$$2 \geq 1 \qquad \text{True}$$

The solution set for $x + y \leq 4$ consists of points lying on the line $x + y = 4$ and all points below the line. This region is shaded in Figure 4.14(a). Similarly, the solutions to $y \geq x$ include the line $y = x$ and all points above it. This region is shaded in Figure 4.14(b).

TEACHING TIP

Use Figure 4.14 to emphasize that points satisfying a system of linear inequalities must be located in both shaded regions. Ask students to locate a point that satisfies one inequality but not the other.

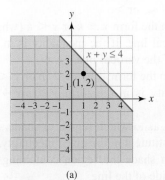

(a)

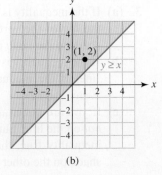

(b)

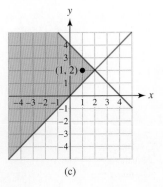

(c)

Figure 4.14

For a point (x, y) to be a solution to the *system* of linear inequalities, it must be located in both shaded regions shown in Figures 4.14(a) and 4.14(b). The *intersection* of the shaded regions is shown in Figure 4.14(c). Note that the point $(1, 2)$ is located in each shaded region shown in Figures 4.14(a) and 4.14(b). Therefore the point $(1, 2)$ is located in the shaded region shown in Figure 4.14(c) and is a solution of the system of linear inequalities.

EXAMPLE 3   Solving a system of linear inequalities

Shade the solution set for each system of inequalities.

(a) $x \le -1$ (b) $y < 2x$ (c) $2x - y < 2$
     $y \ge 2$ $x + y > 3$ $x + 2y \ge 6$

Solution (a) Graph the vertical line $x = -1$ and the horizontal line $y = 2$ as solid lines. The solution set is to the left of the line $x = -1$ and above the line $y = 2$. This region is shaded in Figure 4.15(a). The test point $(-2, 3)$ satisfies both inequalities and lies in the shaded region.

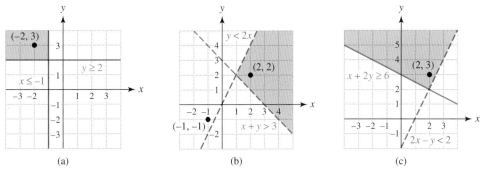

(a)   (b)   (c)

Figure 4.15

(b) Graph $y = 2x$ and $x + y = 3$ as dashed lines. These two lines divide the xy-plane into four regions. The test point $(-1, -1)$ does not satisfy both inequalities, so do not shade the region containing it. However, the point $(2, 2)$ does satisfy both inequalities. To verify this fact substitute $x = 2$ and $y = 2$ in each inequality.

$$2 < 2(2) \qquad \text{True}$$
$$2 + 2 > 3 \qquad \text{True}$$

Thus shade the region shown in Figure 4.15(b).

(c) Graph $2x - y = 2$ and $x + 2y = 6$ as dashed and solid lines, respectively. The test point $(2, 3)$ satisfies *both* inequalities, so shade the region containing it, as shown in Figure 4.15(c).

Critical Thinking

Yes. The point $(2, 2)$ satisfies *both* inequalities. No. The point $(2, 2)$ does *not* satisfy $2x - y < 2$.

Is the point where the two lines intersect in Figure 4.14(c) part of the solution set? Why or why not? Repeat this question for Figure 4.15(c).

EXAMPLE 4   Solving a linear inequality graphically

Shade the solution set for the system of linear inequalities.

$$x + 3y < 3$$
$$2x - y < 2$$

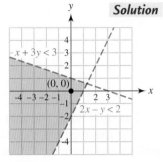

Figure 4.16

Solution   Begin by graphing the dashed lines $x + 3y = 3$ and $2x - y = 2$. Because the test point $(0, 0)$ satisfies both of the given inequalities, shade the region containing the origin, as shown in Figure 4.16.

Note: Finding a test point that satisfies a system of linear inequalities may require trial and error. You may need to pick one test point from each of the four regions determined by the two lines.

In the next example we demonstrate how systems of inequalities can model the situation discussed in the introduction to this section.

EXAMPLE 5   Modeling target heart rates

When exercising, people often try to maintain target heart rates that are percentages of their maximum heart rates. A person's maximum heart rate (MHR) is MHR $= 220 - A$, where A represents age and the MHR is in beats per minute. The shaded region shown in Figure 4.17 represents target heart rates for aerobic fitness for various ages.   (*Source:* Hebb Industries, Inc.)

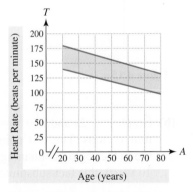

Figure 4.17   Target Heart Rates

(a) Estimate the range R of heart rates that are acceptable for someone 40 years old.
(b) By choosing two points on each line in Figure 4.17 and applying the point–slope form, we can show that the equations for these lines are approximately

$$T = -0.8A + 196 \qquad \text{Upper line}$$

and

$$T = -0.7A + 154, \qquad \text{Lower line}$$

where A represents age and T represents the target heart rate. Write a system of inequalities whose solution set is the shaded region, including the two lines.
(c) Use Figure 4.17 to determine whether $(30, 150)$ is a solution. Then verify your answer by using the system of inequalities.

Solution   (a) Figure 4.17 reveals that, when $A = 40$, target heart rates T are approximately $125 \le T \le 165$ beats per minute.

(b) The region lies below the upper line, above the lower line, and includes both lines. Therefore this region is modeled by

$$T \le -0.8A + 196$$
$$T \ge -0.7A + 154.$$

(c) Figure 4.17 shows that the point representing a 30-year-old person with a heart rate of 150 beats per minute lies in the shaded region, so $(30, 150)$ is a solution. This result can be verified by substituting $A = 30$ and $T = 150$ in the system.

$$150 \le -0.8(30) + 196 = 172 \qquad \text{True}$$
$$150 \ge -0.7(30) + 154 = 133 \qquad \text{True}$$

No solutions lie in both shaded regions.

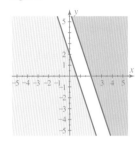

Critical Thinking

Graph the solution set to the following system and discuss your results.

$$3x + y \ge 6$$
$$3x + y \le 2$$

EXAMPLE 6   Solving a system of linear inequalities with technology

Shade the solution set for the system of inequalities, using a graphing calculator.

$$2x + y \le 5$$
$$-2x + y \ge 1$$

Solution   Begin by solving each inequality for y to obtain $y \le 5 - 2x$ and $y \ge 2x + 1$. The graphs of $Y_1 = 5 - 2X$ and $Y_2 = 2X + 1$ are shown in Figure 4.18(a). The solution set lies below y_1 and above y_2. Figure 4.18(b) shows how to shade this region. The solution set is the region comprised of small squares in Figure 4.18(c).

Calculator Help
To shade a graph, see the Appendix (page AP-7).

$[-15, 15, 5]$ by $[-10, 10, 5]$

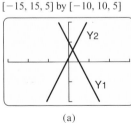

(a)

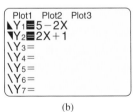

(b)

$[-15, 15, 5]$ by $[-10, 10, 5]$

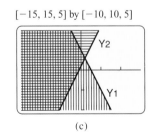

(c)

Figure 4.18

Technology Note: *Shading of Linear Inequalities*

When shading the solution set for a linear inequality, graphing calculators often show solid lines even if a line should be dashed. For example, the graphs for $y < 5 - 2x$ and $y \le 5 - 2x$ are identical on some graphing calculators.

4.3 PUTTING IT ALL TOGETHER

In this section we presented systems of linear inequalities in two variables. These systems usually have infinitely many solutions and can be represented by a shaded region in the *xy*-plane. The following table summarizes these concepts.

Concept	Explanation	Examples
Linear Inequality in Two Variables	$ax + by > c$, where a, b, and c are constants. ($>$ may be replaced with $<$, $\leq$, and $\geq$.)	$y \geq 5$, $x - y < -10$, and $6x - 7y \leq 22$
System of Linear Inequalities in Two Variables	Two linear inequalities where a solution must satisfy *both* inequalities	$x + y < 11$ and $x - y \geq 4$ $(8, 2)$ is a solution because $x = 8$ and $y = 2$ make *both* inequalities true.
Solution Set to a System of Linear Inequalities	Set of all solutions; typically a region in the *xy*-plane	$y \leq 5 - x$ (below $y = 5 - x$) and $y < 2x - 3$ (below $y = 2x - 3$) Use a dashed line for $<$ or $>$. Use a solid line for $\leq$ or $\geq$. Test points are helpful also. ![Graph showing shaded region with $y_1 \leq 5 - x$ and $y_2 < 2x - 3$, point $(3, -2)$]

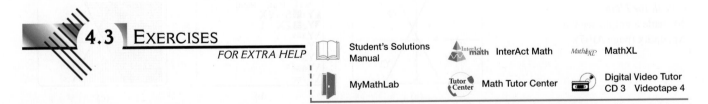

4.3 EXERCISES

FOR EXTRA HELP

Student's Solutions Manual   InterAct Math   MathXL

MyMathLab   Math Tutor Center   Digital Video Tutor CD 3 Videotape 4

CONCEPTS

1. If a system of inequalities contains two inequalities, how many of the inequalities must a solution satisfy?
   Two

2. Can a system of linear inequalities have infinitely many solutions? Explain.
   Yes; many points may satisfy a system of inequalities.

3. Does $(3, 1)$ satisfy $5x - 2y > 8$?   Yes

4. Does $(3, 4)$ satisfy the following system of inequalities?
   No
   $$x - 2y \geq -8$$
   $$2x - y < 1$$

5. When you are graphing the solution set to $y \leq x$, the boundary should be a (dashed/solid) line.   solid

6. When you are graphing the solution set to $2x - y > 2$, the boundary should be a (<u>dashed</u>/solid) line.   dashed

LINEAR INEQUALITIES

Exercises 7–24: Shade the solution set in the xy-plane.*

7. $x > 2$

8. $x \leq -1$

9. $y \leq 1$

10. $y > 0$

11. $y < -2x$

12. $y < 2x$

13. $y \geq x + 1$

14. $y \geq x - 2$

15. $y \geq 3x$

16. $y \leq 1 - x$

17. $y < 3x - 2$

18. $x + y > 3$

19. $2x - y \leq 4$

20. $4x + 2y < 8$

21. $-x + 3y > 3$

22. $-2x + y \leq 0$

23. $5x - 2y \leq -10$

24. $-3x + 2y < 6$

SYSTEMS OF INEQUALITIES

Exercises 25–42: Shade the solution set in the xy-plane.*

25. $x \geq 2$
  $y \leq 1$

26. $x < 3$
  $y > -2$

27. $x \leq 2$
  $y > -x$

28. $y \geq 2$
  $y \geq x$

29. $x \geq y$
  $y \leq 3$

30. $y > x + 1$
  $y < 2$

31. $y \geq x$
  $x \leq -2y$

32. $y > x - 1$
  $x > y - 2$

33. $\frac{1}{2}x + y \leq 1$
  $x - \frac{1}{3}y < 1$

34. $2x - y > 3$
  $y \leq x + 2$

35. $x \geq 1 + 2y$
  $y \leq 1 - x$

36. $4x + y \leq 4$
  $x - 3y \leq 3$

37. $\frac{1}{2}x - y \geq 1$
  $x - \frac{1}{3}y \geq 1$

38. $2x + y > 4$
  $x - y > 1$

39. $3x < 6 - 2y$
  $2y \geq 2 - 2x$

40. $-4x + 6y > 12$
  $2x - 4y < 8$

41. $\frac{1}{2}x - \frac{1}{2}y > 4$
  $-x - \frac{1}{3}y < 1$

42. $-\frac{2}{3}x + \frac{1}{6}y \geq \frac{4}{3}$
  $-\frac{1}{4}x - \frac{1}{3}y \geq 1$

Exercises 43–46: Match the inequality or system of inequalities with its graph (a.–d.).

43. $x + y \geq 2$ b.

44. $y \leq x + 1$ d.
  $y \geq x - 3$

45. $y \leq \frac{1}{2}x$ a.

46. $y \geq x + 1$ c.
  $y \leq 5$

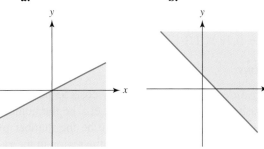

a.   b.

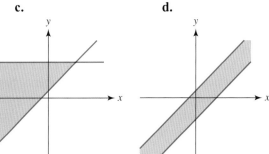

c.   d.

Exercises 47–50: Use the graph to write the inequality or system of inequalities.

47. $y \geq 2$

48. $y \leq -2x + 4$

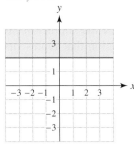
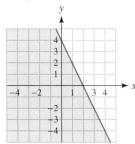

49. $y \geq x$
  $x \geq -2$

50. $y > x$
  $y < -x + 4$

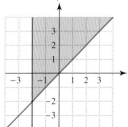
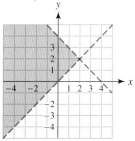

*Answers on page IA-15–IA-17

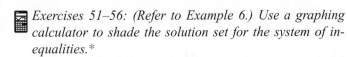

Exercises 51–56: (Refer to Example 6.) Use a graphing calculator to shade the solution set for the system of inequalities. *

51. $y \le 5$
$y \ge -3$

52. $y \ge -x$
$y \le x + 1$

53. $x + 2y \ge 8$
$6x - 3y \ge 10$

54. $y \ge 2.1x - 3.5$
$y \le 2.1x - 1.7$

55. $0.9x + 1.7y \le 3.2$
$1.9x - 0.7y \le 1.3$

56. $21x \ge 31y - 51$
$5x - 17y \le 18$

APPLICATIONS

57. *Candy Sales*   Suppose that candy costs $3 per pound and cashews cost $5 per pound. Let *x* be the number of pounds of candy bought and *y* be the number of pounds of cashews bought. Graph the region in the *xy*-plane that represents all possible weight combinations of candy and cashews that cost *less than* $15. *

58. *Tickets and Popcorn*   At a movie theater, tickets cost $8 and a bag of popcorn costs $4. Let *x* be the number of tickets bought and *y* be the number of bags of popcorn bought. Graph the region in the *xy*-plane that represents all possible combinations of tickets and bags of popcorn that cost $32 or less. *

59. *Retail Sales*   A small business manufactures compact disc players and radios. Because every CD player contains a radio, the business must make at least as many radios as compact disc players. The business can make at most a total of 40 compact disc players and radios per day. Let *x* be the number of compact disc players manufactured and *y* be the number of radios manufactured. Graph the region that represents all possible combinations of compact disc players and radios that can be manufactured in one day. *

60. *Retail Sales*   A small business can manufacture at most 40 large crates and 30 small crates per day. Let *x* be the number of large crates manufactured per day and *y* be the number of small crates manufactured per day. Graph the region in the *xy*-plane that represents all possible combinations of large and small crates that can be manufactured. *

61. *Target Heart Rate*   (Refer to Example 5.) The following graph shows target heart rates for general health and weight loss for a person *x* years old. These heart rates should be maintained for longer periods of time than the times specified for aerobic fitness.
  (a) What range of heart rates is recommended for someone 30 years old?   About 105 to 134 bpm

(b) The upper line has a slope of −0.6 and passes through the point (20, 140), and the lower line has a slope of −0.5 and passes through the point (20, 110). Write a system of inequalities whose solution set lies in the shaded region in the graph.

$$y \le -0.6(x - 20) + 140$$
$$y \ge -0.5(x - 20) + 110$$

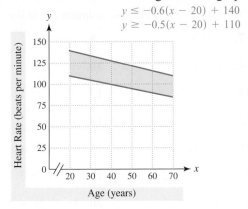

62. *Deserts, Grasslands, and Forests*   Two factors that have a critical effect on plant growth are temperature and precipitation. If a region has too little precipitation, it will be a desert. Forests tend to grow in regions where trees can exist at relatively low temperatures and rainfall is sufficient. At other levels of precipitation and temperature, grasslands may prevail. The following figure illustrates the relationship between forests, grasslands, and deserts as suggested by average annual temperature *T* in degrees Fahrenheit and precipitation *P* in inches.   (*Source:* A. Miller and J. Thompson, *Elements of Meteorology.*)

(a) Determine a system of linear inequalities that describes where grasslands are likely to occur.

(b) Bismarck, North Dakota, has an average annual temperature of 40°F and precipitation of 15 inches. According to the graph, what type of plant growth would you expect near Bismarck? Do these values satisfy the system of inequalities from part (a)?   Grasslands; yes

(a) $7P - 5T \le -70$
$35P - 3T \ge 140$

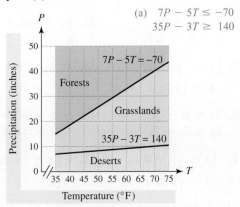

*Exercises 63–66: **Weight and Height**   The following figure shows a weight and height graph. The weight w is listed in pounds, and the height h in inches. The shaded area is the recommended region.*   (**Source:** Department of Agriculture.)

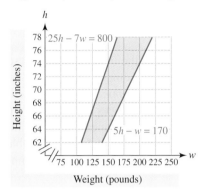

63. What does this graph indicate about an individual weighing 125 pounds with a height of 70 inches?
The person weighs less than recommended.

64. For a person 74 inches tall, use the graph to estimate the recommended weight range.   150 to 200 lb

65. Use the graph to find a system of linear inequalities that describes the recommended region. $25h - 7w \leq 800$
$5h - w \geq 170$

66. Explain why inequalities, rather than equalities, are more appropriate for describing recommended weight and height combinations.
People differ in body build, which makes a range of values more appropriate.

WRITING ABOUT MATHEMATICS

67. A student changes the following system of linear inequalities

$$2x - y \geq 6 \qquad\qquad y \geq 2x - 6$$
$$x - y \leq 4 \qquad \text{to} \qquad y \leq x - 4.$$

The student tests the point $(-2, -8)$, which satisfies the second system but not the first. Explain the student's errors.

68. Explain how a system of linear inequalities with two variables can have no solutions. Give an example to illustrate your answer.

Group Activity: Working with Real Data

Directions: Form a group of 2 to 4 people. Select someone to record the group's responses for this activity. All members of the group should work cooperatively to answer the questions. If your instructor asks for your results, each member of the group should be prepared to respond.

1. *CD Sales*   In 1987, compact disc (CD) sales accounted for 12% of all recorded music sales. By 1997, such sales had increased to 70%. (**Source:** Recording Industry Association of America.)

   (a) Set up a linear system to find values for *a* and *b* so that the graph of $y_1 = ax + b$ passes through the points (1987, 12) and (1997, 70). (*Hint:* To obtain the first equation, let $x = 1987$ and $y_1 = 12$ in $y_1 = ax + b$. To obtain the second equation, let $x = 1997$ and $y_1 = 70$.)

   (b) Have one member of the group solve the system symbolically, a second member solve it graphically, and a third member solve it numerically. If the group consists of only two members, solve it symbolically and graphically. How do your answers compare?
   1.(a) $1987a + b = 12$ (b) $a = 5.8, b = -11,512.6$
   $1997a + b = 70$ They are the same.

2. *Cassette Sales*   In 1987, cassette tape sales accounted for 63% of all recorded music sales. By 1997, such sales had decreased to 18%. (**Source:** Recording Industry Association of America.)

   (a) Set up a linear system to find values for *c* and *d* so that the graph of $y_2 = cx + d$ passes through the points (1987, 63) and (1997, 18).

   (b) Have one member of the group solve the system symbolically, a second member solve it graphically, and a third member solve it numerically. If the group consists of only two members, solve it symbolically and graphically. How do your answers compare?
   2.(a) $1987c + d = 63$ (b) $c = -4.5, d = 9004.5$
   $1997c + d = 18$ They are the same.

3. *Recorded Music Sales*   Estimate the year when CDs and cassette tapes had equal market shares. When were CD sales greater than cassette tape sales?
They were equal in 1992; after 1992

4.4   INTRODUCTION TO LINEAR PROGRAMMING

Basic Concepts · Region of Feasible Solutions · Solving Linear Programming Problems

INTRODUCTION

During World War II large numbers of troops were at the front. Keeping these soldiers supplied with equipment and food was an essential, but complex task. To solve this logistics problem, a new type of mathematics called *linear programming* was invented. Today, linear programming is important to business and the social sciences because it is a procedure that can be used to optimize quantities such as cost and profit. Linear programming applications frequently contain thousands of variables. In this section, we focus on problems involving only two variables. However, the concepts discussed in this section are important to your understanding of larger problems.

BASIC CONCEPTS

Suppose that a small business sells candy for $3 per pound and fresh ground coffee for $5 per pound. All inventory is sold by the end of the day. The revenue R collected in dollars is given by

$$R = 3x + 5y,$$

where x is the pounds of candy sold and y is the pounds of coffee sold. For example, if the business sells **80** pounds of candy and **40** pounds of coffee during a day, then its revenue is

$$R = 3(80) + 5(40) = \$440.$$

The function $R = 3x + 5y$ is called an **objective function**.

Suppose also that the company cannot package more than 150 pounds of candy and coffee per day. Then the inequality

$$x + y \le 150$$

represents a **constraint** on the objective function, which limits the company's revenue for any one day.

A goal of this business might be to maximize

$$R = 3x + 5y,$$

subject to the constraints

$$x + y \le 150$$
$$x \ge 0, \ y \ge 0.$$

Note that the constraints $x \ge 0$ and $y \ge 0$ are included because the number of pounds of candy or coffee cannot be negative. The problem that we have described is called a *linear programming problem*. Before learning how to solve a linear programming problem, we need to discuss the set of *feasible solutions*.

REGION OF FEASIBLE SOLUTIONS

The constraints for a linear programming problem consist of linear inequalities. These inequalities are satisfied by some points in the xy-plane but not by others. The set of solutions to these constraints is called the **feasible solutions**. For example, the region of feasible solutions to the constraints for the business just described is shaded in Figure 4.19.

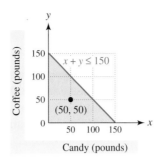

Figure 4.19 Constraints on Sales

The point (50, 50) lies in the shaded region and represents the small business selling 50 pounds of candy and 50 pounds of coffee. In the next example, we shade the region of feasible solutions to a set of constraints.

EXAMPLE 1 Finding the region of feasible solutions

Shade the region of feasible solutions to the following constraints.

$$x + 2y \leq 30$$
$$2x + y \leq 30$$
$$x \geq 0, \ y \geq 0$$

Solution The feasible solutions are the ordered pairs (x, y) that satisfy all four inequalities. They lie below the lines $x + 2y = 30$ and $2x + y = 30$ and above the line $y = 0$ and to the right of $x = 0$, as shown in Figure 4.20. Note that the inequalities $x \geq 0$ and $y \geq 0$ restrict the feasible solutions to quadrant I.

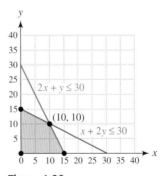

Figure 4.20

SOLVING LINEAR PROGRAMMING PROBLEMS

A **linear programming problem** consists of an *objective function* and a system of linear inequalities called *constraints*. The solution set for the system of linear inequalities is called the *region of feasible solutions*. The objective function describes a quantity that is to be optimized. The **optimal value** to a linear programming problem often results in maximum revenue or minimum cost.

When the system of constraints has only two variables, the boundary of the region of feasible solutions often consists of line segments intersecting at points called *vertices* (plural of **vertex**.) To solve a linear programming problem we use the *fundamental theorem of linear programming*.

▌▌▌▌	**FUNDAMENTAL THEOREM OF LINEAR PROGRAMMING**

If the optimal value for a linear programming problem exists, then it occurs at a vertex of the region of feasible solutions.

The fundamental theorem of linear programming is used to solve the following linear programming problem.

EXAMPLE 2   Maximizing an objective function

Maximize the objective function $R = 2x + 3y$ subject to

$$x + 2y \le 30$$
$$2x + y \le 30$$
$$x \ge 0, \ y \ge 0.$$

Solution   The region of feasible solutions is shaded in Figure 4.20, previously shown. Note that the vertices on the boundary of feasible solutions are $(0, 0)$, $(15, 0)$, $(10, 10)$, and $(0, 15)$. To find the maximum value of R, substitute each vertex in the formula for R, as shown in Table 4.3. The maximum value of R is 50 when $x = 10$ and $y = 10$.

TEACHING TIP

Any point in the region of feasible solutions is a solution. However, the *optimal* solution occurs at a vertex. This fact reduces the search from infinitely many points to a finite number of points.

TABLE 4.3

Vertex	$R = 2x + 3y$	
$(0, 0)$	$2(0) + 3(0) = 0$	
$(15, 0)$	$2(15) + 3(0) = 30$	
$(10, 10)$	$2(10) + 3(10) = 50$	← Maximum R
$(0, 15)$	$2(0) + 3(15) = 45$	

The following steps are helpful in solving linear programming word problems.

▌▌▌▌	**STEPS FOR SOLVING A LINEAR PROGRAMMING WORD PROBLEM**

STEP 1: Read the problem carefully. Consider making a table to display the information given.

STEP 2: Write the objective function and all the constraints.

STEP 3: Sketch a graph of the region of feasible solutions. Identify all vertices or corner points.

STEP 4: Evaluate the objective function at each vertex. A maximum (or a minimum) occurs at a vertex.

Note: If the region is unbounded, a maximum (or minimum) may not exist.

EXAMPLE 3 Minimizing the cost of vitamins

A breeder is mixing two different vitamins, Brand X and Brand Y, into pet food. Each serving of pet food should contain at least 60 units of vitamin A and 30 units of vitamin C. Brand X costs 80 cents per ounce and Brand Y costs 50 cents per ounce. Each ounce of Brand X contains 15 units of vitamin A and 10 units of vitamin C, whereas each ounce of Brand Y contains 20 units of vitamin A and 5 units of vitamin C. Determine how much of each brand of vitamin should be mixed to produce a minimum cost per serving.

Solution **STEP 1:** Begin by listing the information, as illustrated in Table 4.4.

Table 4.4

Brand	Amount	Vitamin A	Vitamin C	Cost
X	x	15	10	80 cents
Y	y	20	5	50 cents
Minimum		60	30	

STEP 2: If x ounces of Brand X are purchased at 80 cents per ounce and if y ounces of Brand Y are purchased at 50 cents per ounce, then the total cost C is given by $C = 80x + 50y$. Because each ounce of Brand X contains 15 units of vitamin A and each ounce of Brand Y contains 20 units of vitamin A, the total number of units of vitamin A is $15x + 20y$. If each serving of pet food must contain at least 60 units of vitamin A, the constraint is $15x + 20y \geq 60$. Similarly, because each serving requires at least 30 units of vitamin C, $10x + 5y \geq 30$. The linear programming problem then becomes the following.

Minimize: $C = 80x + 50y$ Cost (in cents)

Subject to: $15x + 20y \geq 60$ Vitamin A

$10x + 5y \geq 30$ Vitamin C

$x \geq 0, \ y \geq 0$

STEP 3: The region containing the feasible solutions is shown in Figure 4.21.

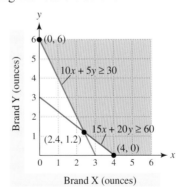

Figure 4.21

Note: To determine the vertex (2.4, 1.2) solve the system of equations

$$15x + 20y = 60$$
$$10x + 5y = 30$$

by using elimination.

STEP 4: The vertices for this region are $(0, 6)$, $(2.4, 1.2)$, and $(4, 0)$. Evaluate the objective function C at each vertex, as shown in Table 4.5.

TABLE 4.5

Vertex	$C = 80x + 50y$	
$(0, 6)$	$80(0) + 50(6) = 300$	
$(2.4, 1.2)$	$80(2.4) + 50(1.2) = 252$	← Minimum cost (cents)
$(4, 0)$	$80(4) + 50(0) = 320$	

The minimum cost occurs when 2.4 ounces of Brand X and 1.2 ounces of Brand Y are mixed, at a cost of \$2.52 per serving.

4.4　PUTTING IT ALL TOGETHER

The following table summarizes the basic concept of linear programming.

Concept	Comments	Example
Linear Programming	In a linear programming problem, the maximum or minimum of an objective function is found, subject to a set of constraints. If a solution exists, it occurs at a vertex in the region of feasible solutions.	Maximize the objective function $$R = x + 2y,$$ subject to the following constraints. $$3x + 2y \le 15$$ $$2x + 3y \le 15$$ $$x \ge 0, \ y \ge 0$$ The vertices are $(0, 0)$, $(5, 0)$, $(3, 3)$, and $(0, 5)$. The maximum, $R = 10$, occurs at vertex $(0, 5)$, and the minimum, $R = 0$, occurs at $(0, 0)$.

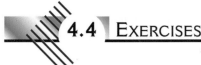

4.4 EXERCISES

FOR EXTRA HELP

 Student's Solutions Manual

 InterAct Math

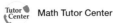 MathXL

MyMathLab

Math Tutor Center

Digital Video Tutor
CD 3   Videotape 4

CONCEPTS

1. A procedure used in business to optimize quantities such as cost and profit is called_____.
   linear programming

2. In linear programming, the function to be optimized is called the_____ function.   *objective*

3. The region in the *xy*-plane that satisfies the constraints is called the region of_____.
   feasible solutions

4. In linear programming, the constraints typically consist of a system of_____.   *linear inequalities*

5. If the optimal value for a linear programming problem exists, then it occurs at a_____ of the region of feasible solutions.   *vertex*

6. To find the optimal value in a linear programming problem, substitute each vertex in the_____ function.
   objective

REGIONS OF FEASIBLE SOLUTIONS

Exercises 7–20: Shade the region of feasible solutions for the following constraints. *

7. $x + y \leq 3$
   $x \geq 0, y \geq 0$

8. $2x + y \leq 4$
   $x \geq 0, y \geq 0$

9. $4x + 3y \leq 12$
   $x \geq 0, y \geq 0$

10. $5x + 3y \leq 15$
    $x \geq 0, y \geq 0$

11. $x \leq 5$
    $y \leq 2$
    $x \geq 0, y \geq 0$

12. $x \leq 3$
    $y \leq 4$
    $x \geq 1, y \geq 1$

13. $x + y \leq 5$
    $x + y \geq 2$
    $x \geq 0, y \geq 0$

14. $2x + y \leq 6$
    $x + y \geq 3$
    $x \geq 0, y \geq 0$

15. $3x + 2y \leq 6$
    $2x + 3y \leq 6$
    $x \geq 0, y \geq 0$

16. $5x + 3y \leq 30$
    $3x + 5y \leq 30$
    $x \geq 0, y \geq 0$

17. $x + y \leq 3$
    $x + 3y \geq 3$
    $x \geq 0, y \geq 0$

18. $3x + y \geq 6$
    $x + 2y \geq 6$
    $x \geq 0, y \geq 0$

19. $x + 2y \geq 4$
    $3x + 2y \geq 6$
    $x \geq 0, y \geq 0$

20. $4x + 3y \geq 12$
    $3x + 4y \geq 12$
    $x \geq 0, y \geq 0$

LINEAR PROGRAMMING

Exercises 21–24: Find the maximum of R on the region of feasible solutions.

21. $R = 4x + 5y$ *R = 31*

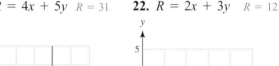

22. $R = 2x + 3y$ *R = 12*

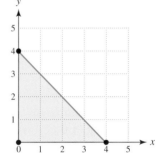

23. $R = x + 3y$ *R = 15*

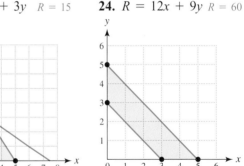

24. $R = 12x + 9y$ *R = 60*

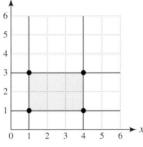

Exercises 25–28: Use the figures in Exercises 21–24 to complete Exercises 25–28, respectively, to minimize C.

25. $C = 2x + 3y$ *C = 5*

26. $C = 3x + y$ *C = 0*

27. $C = 5x + y$ *C = 2*

28. $C = 2x + 7y$ *C = 6*

Exercises 29–36: Maximize the objective function R, subject to the given constraints.

29. $R = 3x + 5y$
    $x + y \leq 150$
    $x \geq 0, y \geq 0$ *R = 750*

30. $R = 6x + 5y$
    $x + y \leq 8$
    $x \geq 0, y \geq 0$ *R = 48*

*Answers on page IA-17–IA-18

31. $R = 3x + 2y$
$2x + y \leq 6$
$x \geq 0, y \geq 0$ *R = 12*

32. $R = x + 3y$
$x + 2y \leq 4$
$x \geq 0, y \geq 0$ *R = 6*

33. $R = 12x + 9y$
$3x + y \leq 6$
$x + 3y \leq 6$
$x \geq 0, y \geq 0$ *R = 31.5*

34. $R = 10x + 30y$
$x + 3y \leq 12$
$3x + y \leq 12$
$x \geq 0, y \geq 0$ *R = 120*

35. $R = 4x + 5y$
$x + y \geq 2$
$x + 2y \leq 4$
$x \geq 0, y \geq 0$ *R = 16*

36. $R = 3x + 7y$
$x + y \geq 1$
$3x + y \leq 3$
$x \geq 0, y \geq 0$ *R = 21*

Exercises 37–42: Minimize the objective function C, subject to the given constraints.

37. $C = x + 2y$
$x \leq 3, y \leq 2$
$x \geq 0, y \geq 0$ *C = 0*

38. $C = 3x + y$
$x \leq 5, y \leq 3$
$x \geq 1, y \geq 1$ *C = 4*

39. $C = 8x + 15y$
$x + y \geq 4$
$x \geq 0, y \geq 0$ *C = 32*

40. $C = x + 2y$
$3x + 4y \geq 12$
$x \geq 0, y \geq 0$ *C = 4*

41. $C = 30x + 40y$
$2x + y \leq 6$
$x + y \geq 2$
$x \geq 0, y \geq 0$ *C = 60*

42. $C = 50x + 70y$
$2x + 3y \leq 6$
$x + y \geq 1$
$x \geq 0, y \geq 0$ *C = 50*

APPLICATIONS

Exercises 43–48: Use linear programming to solve the problem.

43. *Maximizing Revenue* A small business sells candy for $4 per pound and coffee for $6 per pound. The business can package and sell at most a total of 100 pounds of candy and coffee per day, but at least 20 pounds of candy must be sold each day. Determine how many pounds of candy and coffee need to be sold each day to maximize revenue. 20 lb candy; 80 lb coffee

44. *Minimizing Cost* It costs a business $20 to make one compact disc player and $10 to make one radio. Each week the company must make a combined total of at least 50 compact disc players and radios. At least as many compact disc players as radios must be manufac-

tured. Determine how many compact disc players and radios should be made to minimize weekly costs. 25 CD players; 25 radios

45. *Vitamin Cost* A pet owner is mixing two different vitamins, Brand X and Brand Y, into pet food. Brand X costs 90 cents per ounce and Brand Y costs 60 cents per ounce. Each serving is a mixture of the two brands and should contain at least 40 units of vitamin A and 30 units of vitamin C. Each ounce of Brand X contains 20 units of vitamin A and 10 units of vitamin C, whereas each ounce of Brand Y contains 10 units of vitamin A and 10 units of vitamin C. Determine how much of each brand of vitamin should be mixed to produce a minimum cost per serving. 1 ounce Brand X; 2 ounces Brand Y

46. *Pet Food Cost* A pet owner is buying two brands of food, X and Y, for his animals. Each serving of the mixture of the two foods should contain at least 60 grams of protein and 40 grams of fat. Brand X costs 75 cents per unit and Brand Y costs 50 cents per unit. Each unit of Brand X contains 20 grams of protein and 10 grams of fat, whereas each unit of Brand Y contains 10 grams of protein and 10 grams of fat. Determine how much of each brand should be bought to obtain a minimum cost per serving. 2 units Brand X; 2 units Brand Y

47. *Raising Animals* A breeder can raise no more than 50 hamsters and mice but no more than 20 hamsters. If she sells the hamsters for $15 each and the mice for $10 each, find the maximum revenue produced. $600

48. *Maximizing Profit* A business manufactures two parts, X and Y. Machines A and B are needed to make each part. To make part X, machine A is needed 3 hours and machine B is needed 1 hour. To make part Y, machine A is needed 1 hour and machine B is needed 2 hours. Machine A is available 60 hours per week and machine B is available 50 hours per week. The profit from part X is $300 and the profit from part Y is $250. How many parts of each type should be made to maximize weekly profit? 14 of part X; 18 of part Y

WRITING ABOUT MATHEMATICS

49. Give the steps for solving a linear programming word problem.

50. Is the vertex that gives the optimal solution always unique? Could there be more than one vertex that gives the optimal solution? Explain your reasoning.

CHECKING BASIC CONCEPTS   SECTIONS 4.3 AND 4.4

1. Write an inequality that describes the shaded region in the graph. $y \le -2x + 3$

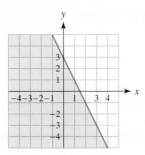

2. Graph the solution set for the linear system of inequalities. Use a test point to check your graph.*

$$2x + 3y \le 6$$
$$x + 2y \ge 4$$

3. Use linear programming to find the maximum of $R = 3x + 2y$, subject to the constraints $R = 12$

$$3x + 2y \le 12$$
$$4x + 4y \le 20$$
$$x \ge 0, \ y \ge 0.$$

*Answers on page IA-18

4.5   SYSTEMS OF LINEAR EQUATIONS IN THREE VARIABLES

Basic Concepts · **Solving Linear Systems with Substitution and Elimination** · **Modeling Data**

INTRODUCTION

In Sections 4.1 and 4.2, we described how to solve systems of linear equations in two variables. In applications linear systems commonly have many variables. Large linear systems are used in the design of electrical circuits, bridges, and ships. They also are used in business, economics, and psychology. Because of the enormous amount of work needed to solve large systems, technology is usually used to find approximate solutions. In this section we discuss symbolic methods for finding solutions of linear systems with three variables. These methods provide the basis for understanding how technology is able to solve large linear systems.

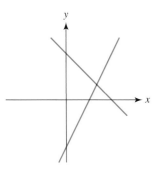

Figure 4.22

BASIC CONCEPTS

When we solve a linear system in two variables, we can express a solution as an ordered pair (x, y). A linear equation in two variables can be represented graphically by a line. A system of two linear equations with a unique solution can be represented graphically by two lines intersecting at a point, as shown in Figure 4.22.

When solving linear systems in three variables, we often use the variables x, y, and z. A solution is expressed as an **ordered triple** (x, y, z), rather than an ordered pair (x, y). For example, if the ordered triple $(1, 2, 3)$ is a solution, $x = 1$, $y = 2$, and $z = 3$ satisfy each equation. A linear equation in three variables can be represented by a flat plane in space. If the solution is unique, we can represent a linear system of three equations in three variables graphically by three planes intersecting at a single point, as illustrated in Figure 4.23.

Figure 4.23

Critical Thinking

The following figure of three planes in space represents a system of three linear equations in three variables. How many solutions are there? Explain.

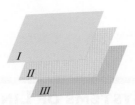

The next example shows how to determine whether an ordered triple is a solution.

EXAMPLE 1   **Checking for solutions to a system of three equations**

Determine whether $(4, 2, -1)$ or $(-1, 0, 3)$ is a solution.

$$2x - 3y + z = 1$$
$$x - 2y + 2z = 5$$
$$2y + z = 3$$

Solution   To check $(4, 2, -1)$, substitute $x = 4$, $y = 2$, and $z = -1$ in each equation.

$$2(4) - 3(2) + (-1) \stackrel{?}{=} 1 \qquad \text{True}$$
$$4 - 2(2) + 2(-1) \stackrel{?}{=} 5 \qquad \text{False}$$
$$2(2) + (-1) \stackrel{?}{=} 3 \qquad \text{True}$$

The ordered triple $(4, 2, -1)$ does not satisfy all three equations, so it is not a solution. Next, substitute $x = -1$, $y = 0$, and $z = 3$.

$$2(-1) - 3(0) + 3 \stackrel{?}{=} 1 \qquad \text{True}$$
$$-1 - 2(0) + 2(3) \stackrel{?}{=} 5 \qquad \text{True}$$
$$2(0) + 3 \stackrel{?}{=} 3 \qquad \text{True}$$

The ordered triple $(-1, 0, 3)$ satisfies all three equations, so it is a solution.　———

In the next example we show how a linear system involving three equations and three variables can be used to model a real-world situation. We solve this system of equations in Example 6.

EXAMPLE 2   Modeling real data with a linear system

The Bureau of Land Management studies antelope populations in Wyoming. It monitors the number of adult antelope, the number of fawns each spring, and the severity of the winter. The first two columns of Table 4.6 contain counts of fawns and adults for three representative winters. The third column shows the severity of each winter. The severity of the winter is measured from 1 to 5, with 1 being mild and 5 being severe.

TABLE 4.6

Fawns (F)	Adults (A)	Winter (W)
405	870	3
414	848	2
272	684	5
?	750	4

We want to use the data in the first three rows of the table to estimate the number of fawns F in the fourth row when the number of adults is 750 and the severity of the winter is 4. To do so, we use the formula

$$F = a + bA + cW,$$

where a, b, and c are constants. Write a system of linear equations whose solution gives appropriate values for a, b, and c.

Solution   From the first row in the table, we know that, when $F = 405$, $A = 870$, and $W = 3$, the formula

$$F = a + bA + cW$$

becomes

$$405 = a + b(870) + c(3).$$

Similarly, $F = 414$, $A = 848$, and $W = 2$ gives

$$414 = a + b(848) + c(2),$$

and $F = 272$, $A = 684$, and $W = 5$ yields

$$272 = a + b(684) + c(5).$$

To find values for a, b, and c we can solve the following system of linear equations.

$$405 = a + 870b + 3c$$
$$414 = a + 848b + 2c$$
$$272 = a + 684b + 5c$$

We can also write these equations as a linear system in the following form.

$$a + 870b + 3c = 405$$
$$a + 848b + 2c = 414$$
$$a + 684b + 5c = 272$$

Finding values for a, b, and c will allow us to use the formula $F = a + bA + cW$ to predict the number of fawns F when the number of adults A is 750 and the severity of the winter W is 4 (see Example 6).

Hunting, predators, and food supply; the number of variables would
increase.

Critical Thinking

The model presented in Example 2 considers only two variables that might affect the fawn population. What other factors might be included in the model? If we included these factors, what would happen to the number of variables in the model?

Linear systems of two equations can have no solutions, one solution, or infinitely many solutions. The same is true for larger linear systems. In this section we focus on linear systems having one solution.

SOLVING LINEAR SYSTEMS WITH SUBSTITUTION AND ELIMINATION

When solving systems of linear equations with more than two variables, we usually use both substitution and elimination. However, in the next example we use only substitution to solve a particular type of linear system in three variables.

EXAMPLE 3   Using substitution to solve a linear system of equations

TEACHING TIP

Rather than having students apply too many concepts at once, Example 3 allows students to focus on basic substitution.

Solve the following system.

$$2x - y + z = 7$$
$$3y - z = 1$$
$$z = 2$$

Solution   Note that the last equation gives us the value of z immediately. We can substitute $z = 2$ into the second equation and determine y.

$3y - z = 1$	Second equation
$3y - 2 = 1$	Substitute $z = 2$.
$3y = 3$	Add 2 to each side.
$y = 1$	Divide each side by 3.

Knowing that $y = 1$ and $z = 2$ allows us to find x by using the first equation.

$2x - y + z = 7$	First equation
$2x - 1 + 2 = 7$	Let $y = 1$ and $z = 2$.
$2x = 6$	Simplify and subtract 1.
$x = 3$	Divide each side by 2.

Thus $x = 3, y = 1$, and $z = 2$ and the solution is (**3, 1, 2**).

In the next example we use elimination and substitution to solve a system of linear equations. This four-step method is summarized in Putting It All Together at the end of this section.

EXAMPLE 4   Solving a linear system in three variables

TEACHING TIP

To help students understand the
method emphasize the four steps
presented in Examples 4 and 5.

Solve the following system.

$$
\begin{aligned}
x - y + 2z &= 6 \\
2x + y - 2z &= -3 \\
-x - 2y + 3z &= 7
\end{aligned}
$$

Solution   **STEP 1**   We begin by eliminating the variable x from the second and third equations. To eliminate x from the second equation we multiply the first equation by -2 and then add it to the second equation. To eliminate x from the third equation we add the first and third equations.

$\begin{aligned}-2x + 2y - 4z &= -12 \quad \text{First equation times } -2\\ \underline{2x + y - 2z = -3} \quad \text{Second equation}\\ 3y - 6z = -15 \quad \text{Add.}\end{aligned}$	$\begin{aligned}x - y + 2z &= 6 \quad \text{First equation}\\ \underline{-x - 2y + 3z = 7} \quad \text{Third equation}\\ -3y + 5z = 13 \quad \text{Add.}\end{aligned}$

STEP 2   Take the two resulting equations from Step 1 and eliminate either variable. Here we add the two equations to eliminate the variable y.

$$
\begin{aligned}
3y - 6z &= -15 \\
\underline{-3y + 5z} &= \underline{13} \\
-z &= -2 \quad \text{Add the equations.} \\
z &= 2 \quad \text{Multiply by } -1.
\end{aligned}
$$

STEP 3   Now we can use substitution to find the values of x and y. We let $z = 2$ in either equation used in Step 2 to find y.

$$
\begin{aligned}
3y - 6z &= -15 \\
3y - 6(2) &= -15 \quad \text{Substitute } z = 2. \\
3y - 12 &= -15 \quad \text{Multiply.} \\
3y &= -3 \quad \text{Add 12.} \\
y &= -1 \quad \text{Divide by 3.}
\end{aligned}
$$

STEP 4   Finally, we substitute $y = -1$ and $z = 2$ into any of the given equations to find x.

$$
\begin{aligned}
x - y + 2z &= 6 \quad \text{First given equation} \\
x - (-1) + 2(2) &= 6 \quad \text{Let } y = -1 \text{ and } z = 2. \\
x + 1 + 4 &= 6 \quad \text{Simplify.} \\
x &= 1 \quad \text{Subtract 5.}
\end{aligned}
$$

The solution is $(1, -1, 2)$. Check this solution.

In the next example we determine the price of tickets at a play.

EXAMPLE 5   Finding ticket prices

One thousand tickets were sold for a play, which generated $3800 in revenue. The prices of the tickets were $3 for children, $4 for students, and $5 for adults. There were 100 fewer student tickets sold than adult tickets. Find the number of each type of ticket sold.

Solution   Let x be the number of tickets sold to children, y be the number of tickets sold to students, and z be the number of tickets sold to adults. The total number of tickets sold was 1000, so

$$x + y + z = 1000.$$

Each child's ticket costs \$3, so the revenue generated from selling x tickets would be $3x$. Similarly, the revenue generated from students would be $4y$, and the revenue from adults would be $5z$. Total ticket sales were \$3800, so

$$3x + 4y + 5z = 3800.$$

The equation $z - y = 100$ or $y - z = -100$ must also be satisfied, as 100 fewer tickets were sold to students than adults.

To find the price of a ticket we need to solve the following system of linear equations.

$$\begin{aligned} x + \ y + \ z &= \ 1000 \\ 3x + 4y + 5z &= \ 3800 \\ y - \ z &= -100 \end{aligned}$$

STEP 1   We begin by eliminating the variable x from the second equation. To do so, we multiply the first equation by 3 and subtract the second equation.

$3x + 3y + 3z = \ 3000$	First given equation times 3
$3x + 4y + 5z = \ 3800$	Second equation
$\overline{ -y - 2z = -800}$	Subtract.

STEP 2   We then use the resulting equation from Step 1 and the third equation to eliminate y.

$-y - 2z = -800$	Equation from Step 1
$y - \ z = -100$	Third given equation
$\overline{ -3z = -900}$	Add the equations.
$z = 300$	Divide by -3.

STEP 3   To find y we can substitute $z = 300$ in the third equation.

$y - \ z = -100$	Third given equation
$y - 300 = -100$	Let $z = 300$.
$y = 200$	Add 300.

STEP 4   Finally, we substitute $y = 200$ and $z = 300$ in the first equation.

$x + y + z = 1000$	First given equation
$x + 200 + 300 = 1000$	Let $y = 200$ and $z = 300$.
$x = 500$	Subtract 500.

Thus 500 tickets were sold to children, 200 to students, and 300 to adults.

MODELING DATA

In the next example we solve the system of equations that we developed to model the data in Example 2.

EXAMPLE 6 Predicting fawns in the spring

Solve the following linear system for a, b, and c. Then use

$$F = a + bA + cW$$

to predict the number of fawns when the number of adults is 750 and the severity of the winter is 4.

$$a + 870b + 3c = 405$$
$$a + 848b + 2c = 414$$
$$a + 684b + 5c = 272$$

Solution **STEP 1** We begin by eliminating the variable a from the second and third equations. To do so, we subtract the second and third equations from the first equation.

$a + 870b + 3c = 405$	First equation		$a + 870b + 3c = 405$	First equation
$a + 848b + 2c = 414$	Second equation		$a + 684b + 5c = 272$	Third equation
$\overline{22b + c = -9}$	Subtract.		$\overline{186b - 2c = 133}$	Subtract.

STEP 2 We use the two resulting equations from Step 1 to eliminate c. To do so we multiply $22b + c = -9$ by 2 and add it to the other equation.

$$44b + 2c = -18 \quad \text{Twice } (22b + c = -9)$$
$$\underline{186b - 2c = 133}$$
$$230b = 115 \quad \text{Add the equations.}$$
$$b = 0.5 \quad \text{Divide by 230.}$$

STEP 3 To find c we substitute $b = 0.5$ in either equation used in Step 2.

$$44b + 2c = -18$$
$$44(0.5) + 2c = -18 \quad \text{Let } b = 0.5.$$
$$22 + 2c = -18 \quad \text{Multiply.}$$
$$2c = -40 \quad \text{Subtract 22.}$$
$$c = -20 \quad \text{Divide by 2.}$$

STEP 4 Finally, we substitute $b = 0.5$ and $c = -20$ in any of the given equations to find a.

$$a + 870b + 3c = 405 \quad \text{First given equation}$$
$$a + 870(0.5) + 3(-20) = 405 \quad \text{Let } b = 0.5 \text{ and } c = -20.$$
$$a + 435 - 60 = 405 \quad \text{Multiply.}$$
$$a = 30 \quad \text{Solve for } a.$$

The solution is $a = 30$, $b = 0.5$, and $c = -20$. Thus we may write

$$F = a + bA + cW$$
$$= 30 + 0.5A - 20W.$$

If there are 750 adults and the winter has a severity of 4, this model predicts

$$F = 30 + 0.5(750) - 20(4)$$
$$= 325 \text{ fawns.}$$

As the number of adults increases, so does the number of fawns. However, as the severity of the winter increases, the number of fawns decreases.

Critical Thinking

Give reasons why the coefficient for A is positive and the coefficient for W is negative in the formula

$$F = 30 + 0.5A - 20W.$$

 4.5 **PUTTING IT ALL TOGETHER**

In this section we discussed how to solve a system of three linear equations in three variables. Systems of linear equations can have no solutions, one solution, or infinitely many solutions. Our discussion focused on systems that have only one solution. The following table summarizes some of the important concepts presented in this section.

Concept	Explanation
System of Linear Equations in Three Variables	The following is a system of three linear equations in three variables. $$\begin{aligned} x - 2y + z &= 0 \\ -x + y + z &= 4 \\ -y + 4z &= 10 \end{aligned}$$
Solution to a Linear System in Three Variables	The solution to a linear system in three variables is an ordered triple, expressed as (x, y, z). The solution to the preceding system is $(1, 2, 3)$ because substituting $x = 1$, $y = 2$, and $z = 3$ in each equation results in a true statement. $\begin{aligned} (1) - 2(2) + (3) &= 0 \quad \text{True} \\ -(1) + (2) + (3) &= 4 \quad \text{True} \\ -(2) + 4(3) &= 10 \quad \text{True} \end{aligned}$
Solving a Linear System with Substitution and Elimination	Refer to Example 4. **STEP 1** Eliminate one variable, such as x, from two of the equations. **STEP 2** Use the two resulting equations in two variables to eliminate one of the variables, such as y. Solve for the remaining variable z. **STEP 3** Substitute z in one of the two equations from Step 2. Solve for the unknown variable y. **STEP 4** Substitute values for y and z in one of the given equations and find x. The solution is (x, y, z).

4.5 | EXERCISES

FOR EXTRA HELP

 Student's Solutions Manual

 InterAct Math

Mathᴸₓₚ MathXL

MyMathLab

Tutor Center Math Tutor Center

Digital Video Tutor
CD 3   Videotape 5

2. $x + y + z = 5$
    $2x - 3y + z = 7$
    $x + 2y - 4z = 2$
    Answers may vary.

CONCEPTS

1. Can a system of three linear equations and three variables have two solutions? Explain.
No; three planes cannot intersect at exactly 2 points.

2. Give an example of a system of three linear equations in three variables.

3. Does the ordered triple (1, 2, 3) satisfy the equation $x + y + z = 6$? Yes

4. Does (3, 4) represent a solution to the equation $x + y + z = 7$? Explain.
No; a solution must be an ordered triple.

5. To solve for two variables, how many equations do you usually need? Two

6. To solve for three variables, how many equations do you usually need? Three

SOLVING LINEAR SYSTEMS

Exercises 7–10: Determine which ordered triple is a solution to the linear system.

7. (1, 2, 3), (0, 2, 4)
$x + y + z = 6$
$x - y - z = -4$
$-x - y + z = 0$
(1, 2, 3)

8. (−1, 0, 2), (0, 4, 4)
$2x + y - 3z = -8$
$x - 3y + 2z = -4$
$3x - 2y + z = -4$
(0, 4, 4)

9. (1, 0, 3), (−1, 1, 2)
$3x - 2y + z = -3$
$-x + 3y - 2z = 0$
$x + 4y + 2z = 7$
(−1, 1, 2)

10. $\left(\frac{1}{2}, \frac{3}{2}, -\frac{1}{2}\right)$, (−1, 0, −2)
$x + 3y - 4z = 7$
$-x + 5y + 3z = \frac{11}{2}$
$3x - 2y - 7z = 2$
$\left(\frac{1}{2}, \frac{3}{2}, -\frac{1}{2}\right)$

Exercises 11–16: (Refer to Example 3.) Use substitution to solve the system of linear equations. Check your solution.

11. $x + y - z = 1$
$2y + z = -1$
$z = 1$
(3, −1, 1)

12. $2x + y - 3z = 1$
$y + 4z = 0$
$z = -1$
(−3, 4, −1)

13. $-x - 3y + z = -2$
$2y + 3z = 3$
$z = 2$
$\left(\frac{17}{2}, -\frac{3}{2}, 2\right)$

14. $3x + 2y - 3z = -4$
$-y + 2z = 4$
$z = 0$
$\left(\frac{4}{3}, -4, 0\right)$

15. $a - b + 2c = 3$
$-3b + c = 4$
$c = -2$
(5, −2, −2)

16. $5a + 2b - 3c = 10$
$5b - 2c = -4$
$c = 3$
$\left(\frac{91}{25}, \frac{2}{5}, 3\right)$

Exercises 17–34: (Refer to Example 4.) Use elimination and substitution to solve the system of linear equations.

17. $x + y - z = 11$
$-x + 2y + 3z = -1$
$2z = 4$
(11, 2, 2)

18. $x + 2y - 3z = -7$
$-2x + y + z = -1$
$3z = 9$
(2, 0, 3)

19. $x + y - z = -2$
$-x + z = 1$
$y + 2z = 3$
(1, −1, 2)

20. $x + y - 3z = 11$
$-2x + y + 2z = 1$
$-3y + 3z = -21$
(0, 5, −2)

21. $x + y - 2z = -7$
$y + z = -1$
$-y + 3z = 9$
(0, −3, 2)

22. $2x + 3y + z = 5$
$y + 2z = 4$
$-2y + z = 2$
$\left(\frac{3}{2}, 0, 2\right)$

23. $x + 2y + 2z = 1$
$x + y + z = 0$
$-x - 2y + 3z = -11$
(−1, 3, −2)

24. $x + y - z = 0$
$x - 3y + z = -2$
$x - y + 3z = 8$
(1, 2, 3)

25. $x + y + z = 5$
$y + z = 6$
$x + z = 3$
(−1, 2, 4)

26. $x + y + z = 0$
$x - y - z = 6$
$-x + y - z = 4$
(3, 2, −5)

27. $x + 2y + 3z = 24$
$-x + y + 2z = 1$
$x + y - 2z = 9$
(8, 5, 2)

28. $5x - 15y + z = 22$
$-10x + 12y - 2z = -8$
$4x - 2y - 3z = 9$
(−1, −2, −3)

29. $2x + y + z = 3$
$2x - y - z = 9$
$x + y - z = 0$
(3, −3, 0)

30. $x + 3y + z = -8$
$x - 2y = 11$
$2y - z = -16$
(1, −5, 6)

31. $2x + 6y - 2z = 47$
$2x + y + 3z = -28$
$-x + y + z = -\frac{7}{2}$
$\left(-\frac{3}{2}, 5, -10\right)$

32. $x + y + 2z = 23$
$3x - y + 3z = 8$
$2x + 2y + z = 13$
(−6, 7, 11)

33. $x + 3y - 4z = \frac{13}{2}$
$-2x + 3y - z = \frac{1}{2}$
$3x + z = 4$
$\left(\frac{3}{2}, 1, -\frac{1}{2}\right)$

34. $x - 2y + z = \frac{9}{2}$
$4x - y + 3z = 9$
$x + 2y = -\frac{3}{2}$
$\left(\frac{1}{2}, -1, 2\right)$

APPLICATIONS

35.(a) $x + 2y + 4z = 10$
$x + 4y + 6z = 15$
$3y + 2z = 6$

35. *Finding Costs*   The accompanying table shows the costs of purchasing different combinations of hamburgers, fries, and soft drinks.

Hamburgers	Fries	Soft Drinks	Total Cost
1	2	4	$10
1	4	6	$15
0	3	2	$6

 (a) Let x be the cost of a hamburger, y the cost of fries, and z be the cost of a soft drink. Write a system of three linear equations that represents the data in the table.

 (b) Solve the system of linear equations and interpret your answer. (2, 1, 1.5); a hamburger costs $2, fries $1, and a soft drink $1.50.

36. *Cost of CDs*   The accompanying table shows the total cost of purchasing various combinations of differently priced CDs. The types of CDs are labeled A, B, and C.

A	B	C	Total Cost
1	1	1	$37
3	2	1	$69
1	1	4	$82

(a) $x + y + z = 37$
$3x + 2y + z = 69$
$x + y + 4z = 82$

(b) (10, 12, 15)
Type A costs $10,
Type B costs $12, and
Type C costs $15.

 (a) Let x be the cost of a CD of type A, y be the cost of a CD of type B, and z be the cost of a CD of type C. Write a system of three linear equations that represents the data in the table.

 (b) Solve this linear system of equations and interpret your answer.

37. *Geometry*   The largest angle in a triangle is $55°$ more than the smallest angle. The sum of the measures of the two smaller angles is $10°$ more than the measure of the largest angle.

 (a) Let $x, y,$ and z be the measures of the three angles from largest to smallest. Write a system of three linear equations whose solution gives the measure of each angle. (*Hint:* The sum of the measures of the angles equals $180°$.) See p. 269.

 (b) Solve the system by using elimination and substitution. $x = 85°, y = 65°,$ and $z = 30°$

 (c) Check your solution. These values check.

38. *Geometry*   The perimeter of a triangle is 90 inches. The longest side is 20 inches longer than the shortest side and 10 inches longer than the remaining side.

39.(a) $N + P + K = 80$
$N + P - K = 8$
$9P - K = 0$

40.(a) $x + y + z = 100$
$x + y = 80$
$x - z = 34$

 (a) Let $x, y,$ and z be the lengths of the three sides from largest to smallest. Write a system of three linear equations whose solution gives the lengths of each side. See p. 269.

 (b) Solve the system by using elimination and substitution. $x = 40$ in., $y = 30$ in., and $z = 20$ in.

 (c) Check your solution. These values check.

39. *Mixture Problem*   One type of lawn fertilizer consists of a mixture of nitrogen, N, phosphorus, P, and potassium, K. An 80-pound sample contains 8 more pounds of nitrogen and phosphorus than potassium. There is 9 times as much potassium as phosphorus.

 (a) Write a system of three equations whose solution gives the amount of nitrogen, phosphorus, and potassium in this sample.

 (b) Solve the system of equations.
(40, 4, 36); 40 lb nitrogen, 4 lb phosphorus, 36 lb potassium

40. *Business Production*   A business has three machines that manufacture containers. Together they make 100 containers per day, whereas the two fastest machines can make 80 containers per day. The fastest machine makes 34 more containers per day than the slowest machine.

 (a) Let $x, y,$ and z be the number of containers that the machines make from fastest to slowest. Write a system of three equations whose solution gives the number of containers each machine can make.

 (b) Solve the system of equations.
(54, 26, 20); the machines make 54, 26, and 20 containers, respectively, per day.

41. *Predicting Fawns*   (Refer to Examples 2 and 6.) The accompanying table shows counts for fawns and adult deer and the severity of the winter. These data may be modeled by the equation $F = a + bA + cW$.

Fawns (F)	Adults (A)	Winter (W)
525	600	4
365	400	2
805	900	5
?	500	3

 (a) Use the first three rows to write a system of three linear equations in three variables whose solution gives values for $a, b,$ and c. See p. 269.

 (b) Solve this system of linear equations. See p. 269.

 (c) Predict the number of fawns when there are 500 adults and the winter has severity 3. 445 fawns

42. *Predicting Home Prices*   Selling prices of homes can depend on several factors such as size and age. The accompanying table shows the selling price for three homes. In this table, price P is given in thousands of dollars, age A in years, and home size S in thousands of square feet. These data may be modeled by the equation $P = a + bA + cS$.

Price (P)	Age (A)	Size (S)
190	20	2
320	5	3
50	40	1

$a + 20b + 2c = 190$
$a + 5b + 3c = 320$
$a + 40b + c = 50$

(a) Write a system of linear equations whose solution gives a, b, and c.

(b) Solve this system of linear equations.

(c) Predict the price of a home that is 10 years old and has 2500 square feet. $260,000

43. *Investment Mixture*   A sum of $30,000 was invested in three mutual funds. In one year the first fund grew by 8%, the second by 10%, and the third by 15%. Total earnings were $3550. The amount invested in the third fund was $2000 less than the combined amount invested in the other two funds. Use a linear system of equations to determine the amount invested in each fund.

$7500 at 8%, $8500 at 10%, and $14,000 at 15%

44. *Football Tickets*   A total of 2500 tickets were sold at a football game. Prices were $2 for children, $3 for students, and $5 for adults. Twice as many tickets were sold to students as children and ticket revenues were $7250. Use a system of linear equations to determine how many of each type of ticket were sold.

750 to children, 1500 to students, and 250 to adults

WRITING ABOUT MATHEMATICS

45. In the previous section we solved problems with two variables; to obtain a unique solution we needed two linear equations. In this section we solved problems with three variables; to obtain a unique solution we needed three equations. Try to generalize these results. In the design of aircraft, problems commonly involve 100,000 variables. How many equations are required to solve such problems? Can such problems be solved by hand? If not, how are such problems solved? Explain your answers.

46. In Exercise 42 the price of a home was estimated by its age and size. What other factors might affect the price of a home? Explain how these factors might affect the number of variables and equations in the linear system.

37.(a) $x + y + z = 180$
$x - z = 55$
$x - y - z = -10$

38.(a) $x + y + z = 90$
$x - z = 20$
$x - y = 10$

41.(a) $a + 600b + 4c = 525$
$a + 400b + 2c = 365$
$a + 900b + 5c = 805$

41.(b) $a = 5$, $b = 1$, and $c = -20$
$F = 5 + A - 20W$

Group Activity: Working with Real Data

Directions: Form a group of 2 to 4 people. Select someone to record the group's responses for this activity. All of the members of the group should work cooperatively to answer the questions. If your instructor asks for your results, each member of the group should be prepared to respond.

CEO Salaries   In 2002, hourly wages for the top three CEOs (chief executive officers) of U.S. corporations were calculated, based on working 14 hours per day for 365 days. Together the three CEOs made $44,000 per hour. The top CEO earned $2,000 more per hour than the combined hourly wages of the next two top CEOs, and the top CEO earned $7,000 more per hour than the next top CEO. (*Source: USA Today*, March 31, 2003.)

(a) Let x, y, and z be the hourly wages in *thousands* of dollars for the top CEOs from highest to lowest. Write a system of equations whose solution gives these hourly wages.

(b) Solve the system. Interpret the answer.

(c) The average American worker earned $16.23 per hour in 2002. How many hours does the average American work to earn an amount equal to one hour of work by the top CEO in 2002?
About 1417 hr

(a) $x + y + z = 44$
$x - y - z = 2$
$x - y = 7$

(b) (23, 16, 5); the top CEO made $23,000/hr, the 2nd CEO made $16,000/hr, and the 3rd CEO made $5000/hr.

4.6   MATRIX SOLUTIONS OF LINEAR SYSTEMS

Representing Systems of Linear Equations with Matrices · Gaussian Elimination · Using Technology to Solve Systems of Linear Equations (Optional)

INTRODUCTION

Suppose that the size of a bear's head and its overall length are known. Can its weight be estimated from these variables? Can a bear's weight be estimated if its neck size and chest size are known? In this section we show that systems of linear equations can be used to make such estimates.

In the previous section we solved systems of three linear equations in three variables by using elimination and substitution. In real life, systems of equations often contain thousands of variables. To solve a large system of equations, we need an efficient method. Long before the invention of the computer, Carl Fredrich Gauss (1777–1855) developed a method called *Gaussian elimination* to solve systems of linear equations. Even though it was developed more than 150 years ago, it is still used today in modern computers and calculators. In this section we introduce this method.

REPRESENTING SYSTEMS OF LINEAR EQUATIONS WITH MATRICES

Arrays of numbers are used frequently in many different real-world situations. Spreadsheets often make use of arrays. A **matrix** is a rectangular array of numbers. Each number in a matrix is called an **element**. The following are examples of *matrices* (plural of matrix), with their dimensions written below them.

$$\begin{bmatrix} 2 & 0 \\ 3 & 1 \end{bmatrix} \quad \begin{bmatrix} -1.2 & 5 & 0 \\ 1 & 0 & 1 \\ 4 & -5 & 7 \end{bmatrix} \quad \begin{bmatrix} 3 & -6 & 0 & \sqrt{3} \\ 1 & 4 & 0 & 9 \\ -3 & 1 & 1 & 18 \\ -10 & -4 & 5 & -1 \end{bmatrix} \quad \begin{bmatrix} 4 & 2 \\ 0 & 1 \\ 1 & 0 \end{bmatrix} \quad \begin{bmatrix} 1 & 5 & -1 \\ 3 & 4 & 2 \end{bmatrix}$$

$$2 \times 2 \qquad\qquad 3 \times 3 \qquad\qquad\qquad\qquad 4 \times 4 \qquad\qquad\qquad 3 \times 2 \qquad\qquad 2 \times 3$$

$$\text{rows} \times \text{columns}$$

The dimension of a matrix is stated much like the dimensions of a rectangular room. We might say that a room is n feet long and m feet wide. Similarly, the **dimension of a matrix** is $n \times m$ (n by m), if it has n rows and m columns. For example, the last matrix in the preceding group has a dimension of 2×3 because it has 2 rows and 3 columns. If the number of rows and columns are equal, the matrix is a **square matrix**. The first three matrices in that group are square matrices.

Matrices can be used to represent a system of linear equations. For example, if we have the system of equations

$$\begin{aligned} 3x - y + 2z &= 7 \\ x - 2y + z &= 0 \\ 2x + 5y - 7z &= -9, \end{aligned}$$

we can represent the system with the following **augmented matrix**. Note how the coefficients of the variables were placed in the matrix. A vertical line is positioned in the matrix where the equals signs occur in the system of equations. The rows and columns are labeled, and the **main diagonal** of the augmented matrix is circled. The matrix has dimension 3×4.

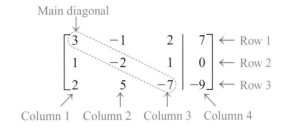

Main diagonal

$$\left[\begin{array}{ccc|c} 3 & -1 & 2 & 7 \\ 1 & -2 & 1 & 0 \\ 2 & 5 & -7 & -9 \end{array}\right] \begin{array}{l} \leftarrow \text{Row 1} \\ \leftarrow \text{Row 2} \\ \leftarrow \text{Row 3} \end{array}$$

Column 1   Column 2   Column 3   Column 4

EXAMPLE 1   Representing a linear system

Represent each linear system with an augmented matrix. State the dimension of the matrix.

(a) $\begin{aligned} x - 2y &= 9 \\ 6x + 7y &= 16 \end{aligned}$ **(b)** $\begin{aligned} x - 3y + 7z &= 4 \\ 2x + 5y - z &= 15 \\ 2x + y &= 8 \end{aligned}$

Solution   **(a)** This system can be represented by the following 2×3 matrix.

$$\left[\begin{array}{cc|c} 1 & -2 & 9 \\ 6 & 7 & 16 \end{array}\right]$$

(b) This system has three equations in three variables and can be represented by the following 3×4 matrix.

$$\left[\begin{array}{ccc|c} 1 & -3 & 7 & 4 \\ 2 & 5 & -1 & 15 \\ 2 & 1 & 0 & 8 \end{array}\right]$$

GAUSSIAN ELIMINATION

A convenient matrix form for representing a system of linear equations is **reduced row–echelon form**. The following matrices are examples of reduced row–echelon form. Note that there are 1s on the main diagonal with 0s above and below the 1s.

$$\left[\begin{array}{cc|c} 1 & 0 & 3 \\ 0 & 1 & -2 \end{array}\right] \qquad \left[\begin{array}{ccc|c} 1 & 0 & 0 & 3 \\ 0 & 1 & 0 & 1 \\ 0 & 0 & 1 & -1 \end{array}\right] \qquad \left[\begin{array}{ccc|c} 1 & 0 & 0 & 8 \\ 0 & 1 & 0 & 2 \\ 0 & 0 & 1 & 3 \end{array}\right]$$

If an augmented matrix representing a linear system is in reduced row–echelon form, we can usually determine the solution easily.

EXAMPLE 2   Determining a solution from reduced row–echelon form

Each matrix represents a system of linear equations. Find the solution.

(a) $\left[\begin{array}{ccc|c} 1 & 0 & 0 & 2 \\ 0 & 1 & 0 & -3 \\ 0 & 0 & 1 & 5 \end{array}\right]$ **(b)** $\left[\begin{array}{cc|c} 1 & 0 & 10 \\ 0 & 1 & -4 \end{array}\right]$

Solution   (a) The top row represents $1x + 0y + 0z = 2$ or $x = 2$. The second and third rows tell us that $y = -3$ and $z = 5$. The solution is $(2, -3, 5)$.

(b) The system involves two equations in two variables. The solution is $(10, -4)$.

We can use a numerical method called **Gaussian elimination** to solve a linear system. It makes use of the following matrix row transformations.

MATRIX ROW TRANSFORMATIONS

For any augmented matrix representing a system of linear equations, the following row transformations result in an equivalent system of linear equations.

1. Any two rows may be interchanged.
2. The elements of any row may be multiplied by a nonzero constant.
3. Any row may be changed by adding to (or subtracting from) its elements a multiple of the corresponding elements of another row.

Gaussian elimination can be used to transform an augmented matrix into reduced row–echelon form. Its objective is to use these matrix row transformations to obtain a matrix that has the following reduced row–echelon form, where (a, b) represents the solution.

$$\begin{bmatrix} 1 & 0 & | & a \\ 0 & 1 & | & b \end{bmatrix}$$

This method is illustrated in the next example.

EXAMPLE 3   Transforming a matrix into reduced row–echelon form

Use Gaussian elimination to transform the augmented matrix of the linear system into reduced row–echelon form. Find the solution.

$$x + y = 5$$
$$-x + y = 1$$

Solution   Both the linear system and the augmented matrix are shown.

Linear System   **Augmented Matrix**

$$x + y = 5$$
$$-x + y = 1$$

$$\begin{bmatrix} 1 & 1 & | & 5 \\ -1 & 1 & | & 1 \end{bmatrix}$$

First, we want to obtain a 0 in the second row, where the -1 is highlighted. To do so, we add row 1 to row 2 and place the result in row 2. This step is denoted $R_2 + R_1$ and eliminates the x-variable from the second equation.

$$x + \ y = 5$$
$$2y = 6$$ $R_2 + R_1 \rightarrow$ $\begin{bmatrix} 1 & 1 & | & 5 \\ 0 & 2 & | & 6 \end{bmatrix}$

To obtain a 1 where the 2 in the second row is located, we divide the second row by 2, denoted $\frac{R_2}{2}$.

$$
\begin{aligned}
x + y &= 5 \\
y &= 3
\end{aligned}
\qquad
\frac{R_2}{2} \rightarrow
\begin{bmatrix}
1 & 1 & 5 \\
0 & 1 & 3
\end{bmatrix}
$$

Next, we need to obtain a 0 where the 1 is highlighted. We do so by subtracting row 2 from row 1 and placing the result in row 1, denoted $R_1 - R_2$.

$$
\begin{aligned}
x &= 2 \\
y &= 3
\end{aligned}
\qquad
R_1 - R_2 \rightarrow
\begin{bmatrix}
1 & 0 & 2 \\
0 & 1 & 3
\end{bmatrix}
$$

This matrix is in reduced row–echelon form. The solution is (2, 3).

In the next example, we use Gaussian elimination to solve a system with three linear equations and three variables. To do so we transform the matrix into the following reduced row–echelon form, where (a, b, c) represents the solution.

$$
\begin{bmatrix}
1 & 0 & 0 & a \\
0 & 1 & 0 & b \\
0 & 0 & 1 & c
\end{bmatrix}
$$

Several calculations are involved in transforming the system to reduced row–echelon form.

EXAMPLE 4   Transforming a matrix to reduced row–echelon form

Use Gaussian elimination to transform the augmented matrix of the linear system into reduced row–echelon form. Find the solution.

$$
\begin{aligned}
x + y + 2z &= 1 \\
-x + + z &= -2 \\
2x + y + 5z &= -1
\end{aligned}
$$

Solution   The linear system and the augmented matrix are both shown.

Linear System	*Augmented Matrix*

$$
\begin{aligned}
x + y + 2z &= 1 \\
-x + + z &= -2 \\
2x + y + 5z &= -1
\end{aligned}
\qquad
\begin{bmatrix}
1 & 1 & 2 & 1 \\
-1 & 0 & 1 & -2 \\
2 & 1 & 5 & -1
\end{bmatrix}
$$

First, we want to put 0s in the second and third rows, where the -1 and 2 are highlighted. To obtain a 0 in the first position of the second row we add row 1 to row 2 and place the result in row 2, denoted $R_2 + R_1$. To obtain a 0 in the first position of the third row we subtract 2 times row 1 from row 3 and place the result in row 3, denoted $R_3 - 2R_1$. Row 1 does not change. These steps eliminate the x-variable from the second and third equations.

$$
\begin{aligned}
x + y + 2z &= 1 \\
y + 3z &= -1 \\
-y + z &= -3
\end{aligned}
\qquad
\begin{aligned}
& \\
R_2 + R_1 &\rightarrow \\
R_3 - 2R_1 &\rightarrow
\end{aligned}
\begin{bmatrix}
1 & 1 & 2 & 1 \\
0 & 1 & 3 & -1 \\
0 & -1 & 1 & -3
\end{bmatrix}
$$

To eliminate the y-variable in row 1, we subtract row 2 from row 1. To eliminate the y-variable from row 3, we add row 2 to row 3.

$$\begin{aligned} x \quad\;\; - \;\; z &= 2 \\ y + 3z &= -1 \\ 4z &= -4 \end{aligned} \qquad \begin{matrix} R_1 - R_2 \to \\ \\ R_3 + R_2 \to \end{matrix} \begin{bmatrix} 1 & 0 & -1 & 2 \\ 0 & 1 & 3 & -1 \\ 0 & 0 & 4 & -4 \end{bmatrix}$$

To obtain a 1 in row 3, where the highlighted 4 is located, we divide row 3 by 4.

$$\begin{aligned} x \quad\;\; - \;\; z &= 2 \\ y + 3z &= -1 \\ z &= -1 \end{aligned} \qquad \begin{matrix} \\ \\ \dfrac{R_3}{4} \to \end{matrix} \begin{bmatrix} 1 & 0 & -1 & 2 \\ 0 & 1 & 3 & -1 \\ 0 & 0 & 1 & -1 \end{bmatrix}$$

To transform the matrix into reduced row–echelon form, we need to put 0s in the highlighted locations. To do so we first add row 3 to row 1 and then subtract 3 times row 3 from row 2.

$$\begin{aligned} x &= 1 \\ y &= 2 \\ z &= -1 \end{aligned} \qquad \begin{matrix} R_1 + R_3 \to \\ R_2 - 3R_3 \to \\ \\ \end{matrix} \begin{bmatrix} 1 & 0 & 0 & 1 \\ 0 & 1 & 0 & 2 \\ 0 & 0 & 1 & -1 \end{bmatrix}$$

This matrix is now in reduced row–echelon form. The solution is $(1, 2, -1)$.

Critical Thinking

An *inconsistent* system of linear equations has no solutions, and a *dependent* system of linear equations has infinitely many solutions. Suppose that an augmented matrix row reduces to either of the following matrices. Explain what each matrix indicates about the given system of linear equations.

The first matrix represents an inconsistent system and the second matrix represents a dependent system.

$$\begin{bmatrix} 1 & 0 & 0 & 2 \\ 0 & 1 & 0 & 3 \\ 0 & 0 & 0 & 1 \end{bmatrix} \qquad \begin{bmatrix} 1 & 0 & 0 & 2 \\ 0 & 1 & 2 & 3 \\ 0 & 0 & 0 & 0 \end{bmatrix}$$

In the next example we find the amounts invested in three different mutual funds.

EXAMPLE 5   Determining investment amounts

A total of \$8000 was invested in three mutual funds that grew at a rate of 5%, 10%, and 20% over 1 year. After 1 year, the combined value of the three funds had grown by \$1200. Five times as much money was invested at 20% as at 10%. Find the amount invested in each fund.

Solution   Let x be the amount invested at 5%, y be the amount invested at 10%, and z be the amount invested at 20%. The total amount invested was \$8000, so

$$x + y + z = 8000.$$

The growth in the first mutual fund, paying 5% of x, is given by $0.05x$. Similarly, the growths in the other mutual funds are given by $0.10y$ and $0.20z$. As the total growth was \$1200, we can write

$$0.05x + 0.10y + 0.20z = 1200.$$

Multiplying this equation by 20 to eliminate decimals results in

$$x + 2y + 4z = 24{,}000.$$

Five times as much was invested at 20% as at 10%, so $z = 5y$, which can be written as $5y - z = 0$.

These three equations can be written as a system of linear equations and as an augmented matrix.

Linear System		*Augmented Matrix*

$$\begin{aligned} x + y + z &= 8{,}000 \\ x + 2y + 4z &= 24{,}000 \\ 5y - z &= \phantom{24{,}00}0 \end{aligned} \qquad \left[\begin{array}{ccc|c} 1 & 1 & 1 & 8{,}000 \\ 1 & 2 & 4 & 24{,}000 \\ 0 & 5 & -1 & 0 \end{array}\right]$$

A 0 can be obtained in the highlighted positions by subtracting row 1 from row 2.

$$\begin{aligned} x + y + z &= 8{,}000 \\ y + 3z &= 16{,}000 \\ 5y - z &= \phantom{24{,}00}0 \end{aligned} \quad R_2 - R_1 \rightarrow \quad \left[\begin{array}{ccc|c} 1 & 1 & 1 & 8{,}000 \\ 0 & 1 & 3 & 16{,}000 \\ 0 & 5 & -1 & 0 \end{array}\right]$$

Zeros can be obtained in the highlighted position by subtracting row 2 from row 1 and by subtracting 5 times row 2 from row 3.

$$\begin{aligned} x - z &= -8{,}000 \\ y + 3z &= 16{,}000 \\ -16z &= -80{,}000 \end{aligned} \quad \begin{aligned} R_1 - R_2 &\rightarrow \\ \\ R_3 - 5R_2 &\rightarrow \end{aligned} \quad \left[\begin{array}{ccc|c} 1 & 0 & -2 & -8{,}000 \\ 0 & 1 & 3 & 16{,}000 \\ 0 & 0 & -16 & -80{,}000 \end{array}\right]$$

To obtain a 1 in the highlighted position, divide row 3 by -16.

$$\begin{aligned} x - 2z &= -8{,}000 \\ y + 3z &= 16{,}000 \\ z &= 5{,}000 \end{aligned} \qquad \dfrac{R_3}{-16} \rightarrow \quad \left[\begin{array}{ccc|c} 1 & 0 & -2 & -8{,}000 \\ 0 & 1 & 3 & 16{,}000 \\ 0 & 0 & 1 & 5{,}000 \end{array}\right]$$

To obtain a 0 in each of the highlighted positions, add twice row 3 to row 1 and subtract three times row 3 from row 2.

$$\begin{aligned} x &= 2{,}000 \\ y &= 1{,}000 \\ z &= 5{,}000 \end{aligned} \quad \begin{aligned} R_1 + 2R_3 &\rightarrow \\ R_2 - 3R_3 &\rightarrow \\ \end{aligned} \quad \left[\begin{array}{ccc|c} 1 & 0 & 0 & 2{,}000 \\ 0 & 1 & 0 & 1{,}000 \\ 0 & 0 & 1 & 5{,}000 \end{array}\right]$$

Thus $2000 was invested at 5%, $1000 at 10%, and $5000 at 20%. ═════

USING TECHNOLOGY TO SOLVE SYSTEMS OF LINEAR EQUATIONS (OPTIONAL)

Examples 4 and 5 involve performing a lot of arithmetic. Trying to solve a large system of equations by hand is an enormous—if not impossible—task. In the real world, people use technology to solve large systems. Many types of graphing calculators can solve systems of linear equations.

In the next example we solve the linear systems from Examples 3 and 4 with a graphing calculator.

EXAMPLE 6   Using technology

Use a graphing calculator to solve the following systems of equations.

(a) $x + y = 5$
       $-x + y = 1$

(b) $x + y + 2z = 1$
       $-x + \quad z = -2$
       $2x + y + 5z = -1$

Solution (a) Enter the 2×3 augmented matrix from Example 3 in a graphing calculator, as shown in Figure 4.24(a). Then transform the matrix into reduced row–echelon form (rref), as shown in Figure 4.24(b). The solution is $(2, 3)$.

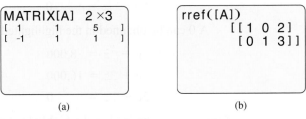

| (a) | (b) |

Figure 4.24

(b) Enter the 3×4 augmented matrix from Example 4 in a graphing calculator, as shown in Figure 4.25(a). (The fourth column of A can be seen by scrolling right.) Then transform the matrix into reduced row–echelon form (rref), as shown in Figure 4.25(b). The solution is $(1, 2, -1)$.

Calculator Help

To enter a matrix and put it in reduced row–echelon form, see the Appendix (pages AP-8 and AP-9).

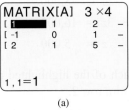
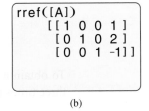

| (a) | (b) |

Figure 4.25

In the next example we use technology to solve an application.

EXAMPLE 7   Modeling the weight of male bears

The data shown in Table 4.7 give the weight W, head length H, and overall length L of three bears. These data can be modeled with the equation $W = a + bH + cL$, where a, b, and c are constants that we need to determine. (**Sources:** M. Triola, *Elementary Statistics*; Minitab, Inc.)

TABLE 4.7

W (pound)	H (inches)	L (inches)
362	16	72
300	14	68
147	11	52

(a) Set up a system of equations whose solution gives values for constants a, b, and c.

(b) Solve the system.

(c) Predict the weight of a bear with head length $H = 13$ inches and overall length $L = 65$ inches.

Solution (a) Substitute each row of the data in the equation $W = a + bH + cL$.

$$362 = a + b(16) + c(72)$$
$$300 = a + b(14) + c(68)$$
$$147 = a + b(11) + c(52)$$

Rewrite this system as

$$a + 16b + 72c = 362$$
$$a + 14b + 68c = 300$$
$$a + 11b + 52c = 147$$

and represent it as the augmented matrix

$$A = \begin{bmatrix} 1 & 16 & 72 & 362 \\ 1 & 14 & 68 & 300 \\ 1 & 11 & 52 & 147 \end{bmatrix}.$$

(b) Enter A in a graphing calculator and put it in reduced row–echelon form, as shown in Figures 4.26(a) and (b), respectively. The solution is $a = -374$, $b = 19$, and $c = 6$.

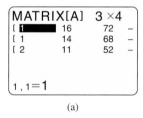
(a)

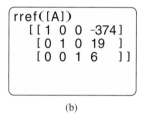
(b)

Figure 4.26

(c) For $W = a + bH + cL$, use

$$W = -374 + 19H + 6L$$

to predict the weight of a bear with head length $H = 13$ and overall length $L = 65$. Thus

$$W = -374 + 19(13) + 6(65)$$
$$= 263 \text{ pounds.}$$

PUTTING IT ALL TOGETHER

A matrix is a rectangular array of numbers. An augmented matrix may be used to represent a system of linear equations. One common method for solving a system of linear equations is Gaussian elimination. Matrix row operations may be used to transform an augmented

continued on next page

continued from previous page

matrix to reduced row–echelon form. Technology can be used to solve systems of linear equations efficiently. The following table summarizes augmented matrices and reduced row–echelon form.

Concept	Explanation
Augmented Matrix	A linear system can be represented by an augmented matrix. The following matrix has dimension 3×4. *Linear System* · *Augmented Matrix* $\begin{array}{rl} x + 2y - z = & 6 \\ -2x + y - z = & 7 \\ 2x + 3z = & -11 \end{array}$ $\quad \left[\begin{array}{ccc|c} 1 & 2 & -1 & 6 \\ -2 & 1 & -1 & 7 \\ 2 & 0 & 3 & -11 \end{array}\right]$
Reduced Row–Echelon Form	The following augmented matrix is in reduced row–echelon form, which results from transforming the preceding system to reduced row–echelon form. There are 1s along the main diagonal and 0s elsewhere in the first three columns. The solution to the linear system is $(-1, 2, -3)$. $\left[\begin{array}{ccc|c} 1 & 0 & 0 & -1 \\ 0 & 1 & 0 & 2 \\ 0 & 0 & 1 & -3 \end{array}\right]$

17. $\begin{aligned} x - y + 2z &= 6 \\ 2x + y - 2z &= 1 \\ -x + 2y - z &= 3 \end{aligned}$ 18. $\begin{aligned} 3x - y + 2z &= -1 \\ 2x - 2y + 2z &= 4 \\ x + 7y - 2z &= 2 \end{aligned}$

4.6 EXERCISES

FOR EXTRA HELP

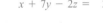

Student's Solutions Manual   InterAct Math InterAct Math $Math_{XL}$ MathXL

MyMathLab   Tutor Center Math Tutor Center   Digital Video Tutor CD 4   Videotape 5

2. $\begin{bmatrix} 2 & 1 & 3 \\ 0 & -4 & 2 \end{bmatrix}$; 2×3; answers may vary.

CONCEPTS

1. What is a matrix?   A rectangular array of numbers.

2. Give an example of a matrix and state its dimension.

3. Give an example of an augmented matrix and state its dimension. $\begin{bmatrix} 1 & 3 & 10 \\ 2 & -6 & 4 \end{bmatrix}$; 2×3; answers may vary.

4. If an augmented matrix is used to solve a system of three linear equations in three variables, what will be its dimension? 3×4

5. Give an example of a matrix in reduced row–echelon form. $\begin{bmatrix} 1 & 0 & -3 \\ 0 & 1 & 5 \end{bmatrix}$; answers may vary.

6. Identify the elements on the main diagonal in the augmented matrix $4, 2, -3$
$$\begin{bmatrix} 4 & -6 & -1 & 3 \\ 6 & 2 & -2 & 9 \\ 7 & 5 & -3 & 1 \end{bmatrix}.$$

DIMENSIONS OF MATRICES AND AUGMENTED MATRICES

Exercises 7–10: State the dimension of the matrix.

7. $\begin{bmatrix} 3 & -3 & 7 \\ 2 & 6 & -2 \\ 4 & 2 & 5 \end{bmatrix}$.   8. $\begin{bmatrix} -2 & 3 & 0 \\ 1 & -8 & 4 \end{bmatrix}$
3×3 2×3

1. $\begin{bmatrix} 1 & -3 & | & 1 \\ -1 & 3 & | & -1 \end{bmatrix}$ 12. $\begin{bmatrix} 4 & 2 & | & -5 \\ 5 & 8 & | & 2 \end{bmatrix}$ 13. $\begin{bmatrix} 2 & -1 & 2 & | & -4 \\ 1 & -2 & 0 & | & 2 \\ -1 & 1 & -2 & | & -6 \end{bmatrix}$ 14. $\begin{bmatrix} 3 & -2 & 1 & | & 5 \\ -1 & 0 & 2 & | & -4 \\ 1 & -2 & 1 & | & -1 \end{bmatrix}$

4.6   Matrix Solutions of Linear Systems   **279**

9. $\begin{bmatrix} 1 & 7 \\ 0 & 2 \\ 2 & -5 \end{bmatrix}$ 3×2 10. $\begin{bmatrix} 4 & 2 & -3 & -1 \\ 4 & -3 & 2 & -7 \\ 14 & 6 & 4 & 0 \end{bmatrix}$ 3×4

Exercises 11–14: Represent the linear system as an augmented matrix.

11. $\begin{aligned} x - 3y &= 1 \\ -x + 3y &= -1 \end{aligned}$ 12. $\begin{aligned} 4x + 2y &= -5 \\ 5x + 8y &= 2 \end{aligned}$

13. $\begin{aligned} 2x - y + 2z &= -4 \\ x - 2y &= 2 \\ -x + y - 2z &= -6 \end{aligned}$ 14. $\begin{aligned} 3x - 2y + z &= 5 \\ -x + 2z &= -4 \\ x - 2y + z &= -1 \end{aligned}$

Exercises 15–20: Write the system of linear equations that the augmented matrix represents. Use the variables x, y, and z.

15. $x + 2y = -6$ $\quad$ 16. $x - 5y = 7$
$\quad 5x - y = 4$ $\qquad\quad -3y = 6$

15. $\begin{bmatrix} 1 & 2 & | & -6 \\ 5 & -1 & | & 4 \end{bmatrix}$ 16. $\begin{bmatrix} 1 & -5 & | & 7 \\ 0 & -3 & | & 6 \end{bmatrix}$

17. $\begin{bmatrix} 1 & -1 & 2 & | & 6 \\ 2 & 1 & -2 & | & 1 \\ -1 & 2 & -1 & | & 3 \end{bmatrix}$ 18. $\begin{bmatrix} 3 & -1 & 2 & | & -1 \\ 2 & -2 & 2 & | & 4 \\ 1 & 7 & -2 & | & 2 \end{bmatrix}$

See p. 278. $\qquad\qquad$ See p. 278.

19. $\begin{bmatrix} 1 & 0 & 0 & | & 4 \\ 0 & 1 & 0 & | & -2 \\ 0 & 0 & 1 & | & 7 \end{bmatrix}$ 20. $\begin{bmatrix} 1 & 0 & 0 & | & 6 \\ 0 & 1 & 0 & | & -2 \\ 0 & 0 & 1 & | & 4 \end{bmatrix}$

20. $x = 6$, $y = -2$, $z = 4$

19. $x = 4$, $y = -2$, $z = 7$

GAUSSIAN ELIMINATION

Exercises 21–38: Use Gaussian elimination to find the solution. Write the solution as an ordered pair or ordered triple and check the solution.

21. $\begin{aligned} x + y &= 4 \\ x + 3y &= 10 \end{aligned}$ $(1, 3)$ 22. $\begin{aligned} x - 3y &= -7 \\ 2x + y &= 0 \end{aligned}$ $(-1, 2)$

23. $\begin{aligned} 2x + 3y &= 3 \\ -2x + 2y &= 7 \end{aligned}$ $\left(-\frac{3}{2}, 2\right)$ 24. $\begin{aligned} x + 3y &= -14 \\ 2x + 5y &= -24 \end{aligned}$ $(-2, -4)$

25. $\begin{aligned} x - y &= 5 \\ x + 3y &= -1 \end{aligned}$ $\left(\frac{7}{2}, -\frac{3}{2}\right)$ 26. $\begin{aligned} x + 4y &= 1 \\ 3x - 2y &= 10 \end{aligned}$ $\left(3, -\frac{1}{2}\right)$

27. $\begin{aligned} 4x - 8y &= -10 \\ x + y &= 2 \end{aligned}$ $\left(\frac{1}{2}, \frac{3}{2}\right)$ 28. $\begin{aligned} x - 7y &= -16 \\ 4x + 10y &= 50 \end{aligned}$ $(5, 3)$

29. $\begin{aligned} x + y + z &= 6 \\ 2y - z &= 1 \\ y + z &= 5 \end{aligned}$ $(1, 2, 3)$ 30. $\begin{aligned} x + y + z &= 3 \\ x + y - z &= 2 \\ y + z &= 2 \end{aligned}$ $\left(1, \frac{3}{2}, \frac{1}{2}\right)$

31. $\begin{aligned} x + 2y + 3z &= 6 \\ -x + 3y + 4z &= 0 \\ x + y - 2z &= -6 \end{aligned}$ $(3, -3, 3)$ 32. $\begin{aligned} 2x - 4y + 2z &= 10 \\ -x + 3y - 4z &= -19 \\ 2x - y - 6z &= -28 \end{aligned}$ $(-3, -2, 4)$

33. $\begin{aligned} x + y + z &= 0 \\ 2x + y + 2z &= -1 \\ x + y &= 0 \end{aligned}$ $(-1, 1, 0)$ 34. $\begin{aligned} x + y - 2z &= 5 \\ x + 2y - 2z &= 4 \\ -x - y + z &= -4 \end{aligned}$ $(4, -1, -1)$

35. $\begin{aligned} x + y + z &= 3 \\ -x - z &= -2 \\ x + y + 2z &= 4 \end{aligned}$ $(1, 1, 1)$ 36. $\begin{aligned} x + 2y - z &= 3 \\ -x - y + z &= 0 \\ x + 2y &= 5 \end{aligned}$ $(-1, 3, 2)$

37. $\begin{aligned} x + 2y + z &= 3 \\ 2x + y - z &= -6 \\ -x - y + 2z &= 5 \end{aligned}$ $(-3, 2, 2)$ 38. $\begin{aligned} x + y + z &= -3 \\ x - y - z &= -1 \\ -2x + y + 4z &= 4 \end{aligned}$ $\left(-2, -\frac{4}{3}, \frac{1}{3}\right)$

Exercises 39–48: Technology   Use a graphing calculator to solve the system of linear equations.

39. $\begin{aligned} x + 4y &= 13 \\ 5x - 3y &= -50 \end{aligned}$ $(-7, 5)$ 40. $\begin{aligned} 9x - 11y &= 7 \\ 5x + 6y &= 16 \end{aligned}$ $(2, 1)$

41. $\begin{aligned} 2x - y + 3z &= 9 \\ -4x + 5y + 2z &= 12 \\ 2x + 7z &= 23 \end{aligned}$ $(1, 2, 3)$ 42. $\begin{aligned} 3x - 2y + 4z &= 29 \\ 2x + 3y - 7z &= -14 \\ 5x - y + 11z &= 59 \end{aligned}$ $(5, -1, 3)$

43. $\begin{aligned} 6x + 2y + z &= 4 \\ -2x + 4y + z &= -3 \\ 2x - 8y &= -2 \end{aligned}$ $(1, 0.5, -3)$ 44. $\begin{aligned} -x - 9y + 2z &= -28.5 \\ 2x - y + 4z &= -17 \\ x - y + 8z &= -9 \end{aligned}$ $(-7, 4, 0.25)$

45. $\begin{aligned} 4x + 3y + 12z &= -9.25 \\ 15y + 8z &= -4.75 + x \\ 7z &= -5.5 - 6y \end{aligned}$ $(0.5, 0.25, -1)$

46. $\begin{aligned} 5x + 4y &= 13.3 + z \\ 7y + 9z &= 16.9 - x \\ x - 3y + 4z &= -4.1 \end{aligned}$ $(1.1, 2, 0.2)$

47. $\begin{aligned} 1.2x - 0.9y + 2.7z &= 5.37 \\ 3.1x - 5.1y + 7.2z &= 14.81 \\ 1.8y + 6.38 &= 3.6z - 0.2x \end{aligned}$ $(0.5, -0.2, 1.7)$

48. $\begin{aligned} 11x + 13y - 17z &= 380 \\ 5x - 14y - 19z &= 24 \\ -21y + 46z &= -676 + 7x \end{aligned}$ $(8, 12, -8)$

Exercises 49–54: (Refer to the Critical Thinking box in this section.) Row-reduce the matrix associated with the given system to determine whether the system of linear equations is inconsistent or dependent.

49. $\begin{aligned} x + 2y &= 4 \\ -2x - 4y &= -8 \end{aligned}$ Dependent   50. $\begin{aligned} x - 5y &= 4 \\ -2x + 10y &= 8 \end{aligned}$ Inconsistent

51. $\begin{aligned} x + y + z &= 3 \\ x + y - z &= 1 \\ x + y &= 3 \end{aligned}$ Inconsistent   52. $\begin{aligned} x + y + z &= 5 \\ x - y - z &= 8 \\ 2x + 2y + 2z &= 6 \end{aligned}$ Inconsistent

53. $x + 2y + 3z = 14$
$2x - 3y - 2z = -10$
$3x - y + z = 4$
Dependent

54. $x + 2y + 3z = 6$
$-x + 3y + 4z = 6$
$5y + 7z = 12$
Dependent

APPLICATIONS

55. *Weight of a Bear* Use the results of Example 7 to estimate the weight of a bear with a head length of 12 inches and an overall length of 60 inches. 214 lb

56. *Weight of a Bear* (Refer to Example 7.) Head length and overall length are not the only variables that can be used to estimate the weight of a bear. The data in the accompanying table list the weight W, neck size N, and chest size C of three bears. These data can be modeled by $W = a + bN + cC$. (*Sources:* M. Triola, *Elementary Statistics*; Minitab, Inc.)

W (pounds)	N (inches)	C (inches)
80	16	26
344	28	45
416	31	54

(a) Set up a system of equations whose solution gives values for the constants a, b, and c.

(b) Solve this system. Round each value to the nearest tenth. $a \approx -272.9, b \approx 19.8,$ and $c \approx 1.4$

(c) Predict the weight of a bear with neck size $N = 22$ inches and chest size $C = 38$ inches. About 216 lb

57. *Garbage and Household Size* A larger household produces more garbage, on average, than a smaller household. If we know the amount of metal M and plastic P waste produced each week, we can estimate the household size H from $H = a + bM + cP$. The table contains representative data for three households. (*Source:* M. Triola, *Elementary Statistics*.)

H (people)	M (pounds)	P (pounds)
3	2.00	1.40
2	1.50	0.65
6	4.00	3.40

(a) Set up a system of equations whose solution gives values for the constants a, b, and c.

(b) Solve this system with a graphing calculator. $a = 0.6, b = 0.5,$ and $c = 1$

56.(a) $a + 16b + 26c = 80$
$a + 28b + 45c = 344$
$a + 31b + 54c = 416$

57.(a) $a + 2b + 1.4c = 3$
$a + 1.5b + 0.65c = 2$
$a + 4b + 3.4c = 6$

(c) Predict the size of a household that produces 3 pounds of metal waste and 2 pounds of plastic waste each week. $4.1 \approx 4$ people

58. *Old Faithful Geyser* In Yellowstone National Park, Old Faithful Geyser has been a favorite attraction for decades. Although this geyser erupts about every 80 minutes, this time interval varies, as do the duration and height of the eruptions. The accompanying table shows the height H, duration D, and time interval T for three eruptions. (*Source:* National Park Service.)

H (feet)	D (seconds)	T (minutes)
160	276	94
125	203	84
140	245	79

(a) Assume that these data can be modeled by $H = a + bD + cT$. Set up a system of equations whose solution gives values for the constants a, b, and c.

(b) Solve this system by using a graphing calculator. Round each value to the nearest thousandth.

(c) Use this equation to estimate H when $D = 220$ and $T = 81$. About 131 ft

58.(a) $a + 276b + 94c = 160$
$a + 203b + 84c = 125$
$a + 245b + 79c = 140$

(b) $a \approx 0.828, b \approx 0.414,$ and $c \approx 0.478$

H

59. *Jogging Speeds* A runner in preparation for a marathon jogs at 5, 6, and 8 miles per hour. The runner travels a total distance of 12.5 miles in 2 hours and jogs the same length of time at 5 miles per hour and at 8 miles per hour. How long did the runner jog at each speed? $\frac{1}{2}$ hr at 5 mph, 1 hr at 6 mph, and $\frac{1}{2}$ hr at 8 mph

60. *Mixture Problem* Three different types of candy that cost $2, $3, and $4 per pound are to be mixed to

produce a 5-pound bag of candy that costs $14.50. If there are to be equal amounts of the $3-per-pound candy and the $4-per-pound candy, how much of each type of candy should be included in the mixture?
2 lb of $2 candy, 1.5 lb of $3 candy, and 1.5 lb of $4 candy

61. *Interest and Investments* (Refer to Example 5.) A total of $3000 is invested at 5%, 8%, and 12% annual interest. The interest earned after 1 year equals $285. The amount invested at 12% is triple the amount invested at 5%. Find the amount invested at each interest rate. *$500 at 5%, $1000 at 8%, and $1500 at 12%*

62. *Geometry* The measure of the largest angle in a triangle is twice the measure of the smallest angle. The remaining angle is 10° less than the largest angle. Find the measure of each angle. *76°, 66°, and 38°*

WRITING ABOUT MATHEMATICS

63. Explain what the dimension of a matrix means. What is the difference between a matrix that has dimension 3×4 and one that has dimension 4×3?

64. Discuss the advantages of using technology to transform an augmented matrix to reduced row–echelon form. Are there any disadvantages? Explain.

CHECKING BASIC CONCEPTS 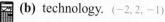 SECTIONS 4.5 AND 4.6

1. Determine which ordered triple is the solution to the system of equations. $(5, -4, 0)$, $(1, 3, -1)$
   (1, 3, −1)
$$x - y + 7z = -9$$
$$2x - 2y + 5z = -9$$
$$-x + 3y - 2z = 10$$

2. Solve the system of equations by using elimination and substitution. *(1, 2, 3)*
$$x - y + z = 2$$
$$2x - 3y + z = -1$$
$$-x + y + z = 4$$

3. Use an augmented matrix to represent the system of equations. Solve the system using
   (a) Gaussian elimination.
   (b) technology. *(−2, 2, −1)*
$$x + 2y + z = 1$$
$$x + y + z = -1$$
$$y + z = 1$$

4.7 DETERMINANTS

Calculation of Determinants · Area of Regions · Cramer's Rule

INTRODUCTION

Surveyors commonly calculate the areas of parcels of land. To do so they frequently divide the land into triangular regions. When the coordinates of the vertices of a triangle are known, determinants may be used to find the area of the triangle. A determinant is a real number that can be calculated for any square matrix. In this section we use determinants to find areas and to solve systems of linear equations.

CALCULATION OF DETERMINANTS

The concept of determinants originated with the Japanese mathematician Seki Kowa (1642–1708), who used them to solve systems of linear equations. Later, Gottfried Leibniz (1646–1716) formally described determinants and also used them to solve systems of linear equations. (**Source:** *Historical Topics for the Mathematical Classroom*, NCTM.)

We begin by defining a determinant of a 2×2 matrix.

DETERMINANT OF A 2 × 2 MATRIX

The **determinant** of

$$A = \begin{bmatrix} a & b \\ c & d \end{bmatrix}$$

is a *real number* defined by

$$\det A = ad - cb.$$

EXAMPLE 1 Calculating determinants

Find det A for each 2×2 matrix.

(a) $A = \begin{bmatrix} 1 & 2 \\ 3 & 4 \end{bmatrix}$ **(b)** $A = \begin{bmatrix} -1 & -3 \\ 2 & -8 \end{bmatrix}$

Solution **(a)** The determinant is calculated as follows.

$$\det A = \det \begin{bmatrix} 1 & 2 \\ 3 & 4 \end{bmatrix} = (1)(4) - (3)(2) = -2$$

(b) Similarly,

$$\det A = \det \begin{bmatrix} -1 & -3 \\ 2 & -8 \end{bmatrix} = (-1)(-8) - (2)(-3) = 14.$$

We can use determinants of 2×2 matrices to find determinants of 3×3 matrices. This method is called **expansion of a determinant by minors**.

DETERMINANT OF A 3 × 3 MATRIX

$$\det A = \det \begin{bmatrix} a_1 & b_1 & c_1 \\ a_2 & b_2 & c_2 \\ a_3 & b_3 & c_3 \end{bmatrix}$$

$$= a_1 \cdot \det \begin{bmatrix} b_2 & c_2 \\ b_3 & c_3 \end{bmatrix} - a_2 \cdot \det \begin{bmatrix} b_1 & c_1 \\ b_3 & c_3 \end{bmatrix} + a_3 \cdot \det \begin{bmatrix} b_1 & c_1 \\ b_2 & c_2 \end{bmatrix}$$

TEACHING TIP

Emphasize that a determinant is a real number, not a matrix.

The 2×2 matrices in this equation are called **minors**.

EXAMPLE 2   Calculating 3 × 3 determinants

Evaluate det A.

(a) $A = \begin{bmatrix} 2 & 1 & -1 \\ -1 & 3 & 2 \\ 4 & -3 & -5 \end{bmatrix}$ (b) $A = \begin{bmatrix} 5 & -2 & 4 \\ 0 & 2 & 1 \\ -1 & 4 & -4 \end{bmatrix}$

Solution   (a) We evaluate the determinant as follows.

$$\det \begin{bmatrix} 2 & 1 & -1 \\ -1 & 3 & 2 \\ 4 & -3 & -5 \end{bmatrix} = 2 \cdot \det \begin{bmatrix} 3 & 2 \\ -3 & -5 \end{bmatrix} - (-1) \cdot \det \begin{bmatrix} 1 & -1 \\ -3 & -5 \end{bmatrix}$$

$$+ 4 \cdot \det \begin{bmatrix} 1 & -1 \\ 3 & 2 \end{bmatrix}$$

$$= 2(-9) + 1(-8) + 4(5)$$

$$= -6$$

(b) We evaluate the determinant as follows.

$$\det \begin{bmatrix} 5 & -2 & 4 \\ 0 & 2 & 1 \\ -1 & 4 & -4 \end{bmatrix} = 5 \cdot \det \begin{bmatrix} 2 & 1 \\ 4 & -4 \end{bmatrix} - (0) \cdot \det \begin{bmatrix} -2 & 4 \\ 4 & -4 \end{bmatrix}$$

$$+ (-1) \cdot \det \begin{bmatrix} -2 & 4 \\ 2 & 1 \end{bmatrix}$$

$$= 5(-12) - 0(-8) + (-1)(-10)$$

$$= -50$$

Many graphing calculators can evaluate the determinant of a matrix, as illustrated in the next example, where we evaluate the determinants from Example 2.

EXAMPLE 3   Using technology to find determinants

Find each determinant of A, using a graphing calculator.

(a) $A = \begin{bmatrix} 2 & 1 & -1 \\ -1 & 3 & 2 \\ 4 & -3 & -5 \end{bmatrix}$ (b) $A = \begin{bmatrix} 5 & -2 & 4 \\ 0 & 2 & 1 \\ -1 & 4 & -4 \end{bmatrix}$

Solution   (a) Begin by entering the matrix and then evaluate the determinant, as shown in Figure 4.27. The result is det $A = -6$, which agrees with our earlier calculation.

Calculator Help
To find a determinant, see the Appendix (page AP-9).

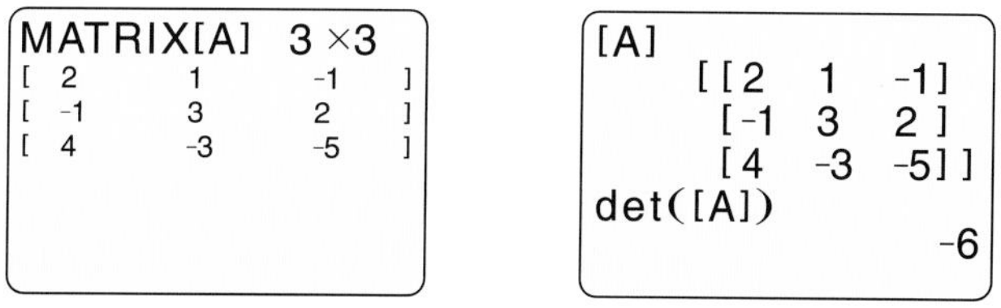

```
MATRIX[A]  3 ×3
[ 2        1        -1      ]
[ -1       3         2      ]
[ 4       -3        -5      ]
```
(a)

```
[A]
    [[2   1   -1]
     [-1  3    2 ]
     [4  -3  -5]]
det([A])
                -6
```
(b)

Figure 4.27

(b) The determinant of A evaluates to -50 (see Figure 4.28).

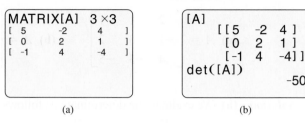

(a)   (b)

Figure 4.28

AREA OF REGIONS

A determinant may be used to find the area of a triangle. For example, if a triangle has vertices (a_1, a_2), (b_1, b_2), and (c_1, c_2), its area equals the absolute value of D, where

$$D = \frac{1}{2}\det\begin{bmatrix} a_1 & b_1 & c_1 \\ a_2 & b_2 & c_2 \\ 1 & 1 & 1 \end{bmatrix}.$$

If the vertices are entered in the columns of D counterclockwise, D will be positive. (**Source:** W. Taylor, *The Geometry of Computer Graphics.*)

EXAMPLE 4 Computing the area of a triangular parcel of land

A triangular parcel of land is shown in Figure 4.29. If all units are miles, find the area of the parcel of land by using a determinant.

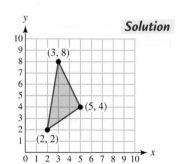

Figure 4.29

Solution The vertices of the triangular parcel of land are $(2, 2)$, $(5, 4)$, and $(3, 8)$. The area of the triangle is

$$D = \frac{1}{2}\det\begin{bmatrix} 2 & 5 & 3 \\ 2 & 4 & 8 \\ 1 & 1 & 1 \end{bmatrix} = \frac{1}{2} \cdot 16 = 8.$$

The area of the triangle is 8 square miles.

Critical Thinking

Suppose that you are given three distinct vertices and $D = 0$. What must be true about the three points? The points are colinear; they all lie on the same line.

CRAMER'S RULE

Determinants were developed independently by Gabriel Cramer (1704–1752). His work was published in 1750 and provided a method called **Cramer's rule** for solving systems of linear equations.

CRAMER'S RULE FOR LINEAR SYSTEMS IN TWO VARIABLES

The solution to the system of linear equations

$$a_1x + b_1y = c_1$$
$$a_2x + b_2y = c_2$$

is given by $x = \frac{E}{D}$ and $y = \frac{F}{D}$, where

$$E = \det\begin{bmatrix} c_1 & b_1 \\ c_2 & b_2 \end{bmatrix}, \quad F = \det\begin{bmatrix} a_1 & c_1 \\ a_2 & c_2 \end{bmatrix}, \quad \text{and} \quad D = \det\begin{bmatrix} a_1 & b_1 \\ a_2 & b_2 \end{bmatrix} \neq 0.$$

Note: If $D = 0$, the system has either no solutions or infinitely many solutions.

EXAMPLE 5 Using Cramer's rule

Use Cramer's rule to solve the following linear systems.
(a) $3x - 4y = 18$ **(b)** $-4x + 9y = -24$
     $7x + 5y = -1$ $6x + 17y = -25$

Solution **(a)** $E = \det\begin{bmatrix} c_1 & b_1 \\ c_2 & b_2 \end{bmatrix} = \det\begin{bmatrix} 18 & -4 \\ -1 & 5 \end{bmatrix} = (18)(5) - (-1)(-4) = 86$

$F = \det\begin{bmatrix} a_1 & c_1 \\ a_2 & c_2 \end{bmatrix} = \det\begin{bmatrix} 3 & 18 \\ 7 & -1 \end{bmatrix} = (3)(-1) - (7)(18) = -129$

$D = \det\begin{bmatrix} a_1 & b_1 \\ a_2 & b_2 \end{bmatrix} = \det\begin{bmatrix} 3 & -4 \\ 7 & 5 \end{bmatrix} = (3)(5) - (7)(-4) = 43$

Because $x = \frac{E}{D} = \frac{86}{43} = 2$ and $y = \frac{F}{D} = \frac{-129}{43} = -3$, the solution is $(2, -3)$.

(b) $E = \det\begin{bmatrix} c_1 & b_1 \\ c_2 & b_2 \end{bmatrix} = \det\begin{bmatrix} -24 & 9 \\ -25 & 17 \end{bmatrix} = (-24)(17) - (-25)(9) = -183$

$F = \det\begin{bmatrix} a_1 & c_1 \\ a_2 & c_2 \end{bmatrix} = \det\begin{bmatrix} -4 & -24 \\ 6 & -25 \end{bmatrix} = (-4)(-25) - (6)(-24) = 244$

$D = \det\begin{bmatrix} a_1 & b_1 \\ a_2 & b_2 \end{bmatrix} = \det\begin{bmatrix} -4 & 9 \\ 6 & 17 \end{bmatrix} = (-4)(17) - (6)(9) = -122$

Because $x = \frac{E}{D} = \frac{-183}{-122} = 1.5$ and $y = \frac{F}{D} = \frac{244}{-122} = -2$, the solution is $(1.5, -2)$.

Cramer's rule can be applied to systems that have any number of linear equations. Cramer's rule for three linear equations is discussed in the Extended and Discovery Exercises at the end of this chapter.

USING CRAMER'S RULE IN APPLICATIONS In applications, equations with hundreds of variables are routinely solved. Such systems of equations could be solved with Cramer's rule.

However, using Cramer's rule and the expansion of a determinant with minors to solve a linear system of equations with n variables requires at least

$$1 \cdot 2 \cdot 3 \cdot 4 \cdot \cdots \cdot n \cdot (n + 1)$$

multiplication operations. To solve a linear system involving only 25 variables would require about

$$1 \cdot 2 \cdot 3 \cdot 4 \cdot \cdots \cdot 25 \cdot 26 \approx 4 \times 10^{26}$$

multiplication operations. Supercomputers can perform about 1 trillion (1×10^{12}) multiplication operations per second. This would take about

$$\frac{4 \times 10^{26}}{1 \times 10^{12}} = 4 \times 10^{14} \text{ seconds.}$$

With $60 \times 60 \times 24 \times 365 = 31{,}536{,}000$ seconds in a year, 4×10^{14} seconds equals

$$\frac{4 \times 10^{14}}{31{,}536{,}000} \approx 12{,}700{,}000 \text{ years!}$$

Modern software packages do *not* use Cramer's rule for three or more variables.

4.7 PUTTING IT ALL TOGETHER

The determinant of a square matrix A is a real number, denoted det A. Cramer's rule is a method that uses determinants to solve systems of linear equations. The following table summarizes important topics from this section.

Concept	Explanation
Determinant of a 2 × 2 Matrix	The determinant of a 2×2 matrix A is given by $$\det A = \det \begin{bmatrix} a & b \\ c & d \end{bmatrix} = ad - cb.$$
Determinant of a 3 × 3 Matrix	The determinant of a 3×3 matrix A is given by $$\det A = \det \begin{bmatrix} a_1 & b_1 & c_1 \\ a_2 & b_2 & c_2 \\ a_3 & b_3 & c_3 \end{bmatrix}$$ $$= a_1 \cdot \det \begin{bmatrix} b_2 & c_2 \\ b_3 & c_3 \end{bmatrix} - a_2 \cdot \det \begin{bmatrix} b_1 & c_1 \\ b_3 & c_3 \end{bmatrix}$$ $$+ a_3 \cdot \det \begin{bmatrix} b_1 & c_1 \\ b_2 & c_2 \end{bmatrix}$$

Concept	Explanation
Area of a Triangle	If a triangle has vertices (a_1, a_2), (b_1, b_2), and (c_1, c_2), its area equals the absolute value of D, where $$D = \frac{1}{2}\det\begin{bmatrix} a_1 & b_1 & c_1 \\ a_2 & b_2 & c_2 \\ 1 & 1 & 1 \end{bmatrix}.$$
Cramer's Rule for Linear Systems in Two Variables	The solution to the linear system $$a_1 x + b_1 y = c_1$$ $$a_2 x + b_2 y = c_2$$ is given by $x = \frac{E}{D}$ and $y = \frac{F}{D}$, where $$E = \det\begin{bmatrix} c_1 & b_1 \\ c_2 & b_2 \end{bmatrix}, \quad F = \det\begin{bmatrix} a_1 & c_1 \\ a_2 & c_2 \end{bmatrix}, \quad \text{and}$$ $$D = \det\begin{bmatrix} a_1 & b_1 \\ a_2 & b_2 \end{bmatrix} \neq 0.$$ ***Note:*** If $D = 0$, then the system has either no solutions or infinitely many solutions.

4.7 EXERCISES

FOR EXTRA HELP

Student's Solutions Manual   InterAct Math   MathXL
MyMathLab   Math Tutor Center   Digital Video Tutor CD 4   Videotape 5

CALCULATING DETERMINANTS

Exercises 1–16: Evaluate det A by hand where A is the given matrix.

1. $\begin{bmatrix} 1 & -2 \\ 3 & -8 \end{bmatrix}$ -2

2. $\begin{bmatrix} 5 & -1 \\ 3 & 7 \end{bmatrix}$ 38

3. $\begin{bmatrix} -3 & 7 \\ 8 & -1 \end{bmatrix}$ -53

4. $\begin{bmatrix} 0 & -7 \\ -3 & 1 \end{bmatrix}$ -21

5. $\begin{bmatrix} 23 & 4 \\ 6 & -13 \end{bmatrix}$ -323

6. $\begin{bmatrix} 44 & -51 \\ -9 & 32 \end{bmatrix}$ 949

7. $\begin{bmatrix} 1 & -1 & 2 \\ 0 & 1 & -3 \\ 0 & -4 & 7 \end{bmatrix}$ -5

8. $\begin{bmatrix} 2 & -1 & -5 \\ -1 & 4 & -2 \\ 0 & 1 & 4 \end{bmatrix}$ 37

9. $\begin{bmatrix} 2 & -1 & 0 \\ 1 & -2 & 6 \\ 0 & 1 & 8 \end{bmatrix}$ -36

10. $\begin{bmatrix} 0 & 1 & -4 \\ 3 & -6 & 10 \\ 4 & -2 & 7 \end{bmatrix}$ -53

11. $\begin{bmatrix} -1 & 3 & 5 \\ 3 & -3 & 5 \\ 2 & -3 & 7 \end{bmatrix}$ -42

12. $\begin{bmatrix} 6 & -1 & 9 \\ 7 & 0 & -3 \\ 2 & 5 & -1 \end{bmatrix}$ 404

13. $\begin{bmatrix} 5 & 0 & 0 \\ 0 & -2 & 0 \\ 0 & 0 & 5 \end{bmatrix}$ -50

14. $\begin{bmatrix} 1 & 2 & 3 \\ 2 & 4 & 6 \\ 3 & 6 & 9 \end{bmatrix}$ 0

15. $\begin{bmatrix} 0 & 2 & -3 \\ 0 & 3 & -9 \\ 0 & 5 & 9 \end{bmatrix}$ 0

16. $\begin{bmatrix} 3 & -1 & 2 \\ 0 & 5 & 7 \\ 0 & 0 & -1 \end{bmatrix}$ -15

Exercises 17–20: Use technology to calculate det A, where A is the given matrix.

17. $\begin{bmatrix} 2 & -5 & 13 \\ 10 & 15 & -10 \\ 17 & -19 & 22 \end{bmatrix}$ −3555

18. $\begin{bmatrix} 1.6 & 3.1 & 5.7 \\ 2.1 & 6.7 & 8.1 \\ -0.4 & -0.8 & -3.1 \end{bmatrix}$ −7.027

19. $\begin{bmatrix} 17 & 0 & 4 \\ -9 & 14 & 1.5 \\ 13 & 67 & -11 \end{bmatrix}$ −7466.5

20. $\begin{bmatrix} 121 & 45 & -56 \\ -45 & 87 & 32 \\ -14 & -34 & 67 \end{bmatrix}$ 798,584

CALCULATING AREA

Exercises 21–26: Find the area of the figure by using a determinant. Assume that units are feet.

21. 15 ft²

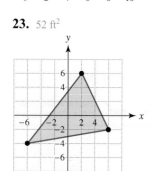

22. 48 ft²

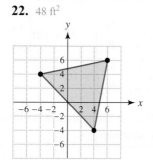

23. 52 ft²

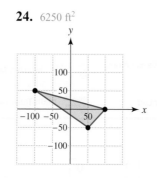

24. 6250 ft²

25. 25.5 ft²

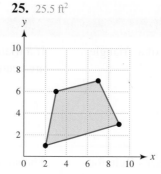

26. 90 ft²

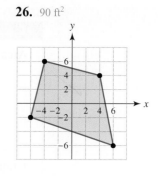

CRAMER'S RULE

Exercises 27–32: Solve the system of equations by using Cramer's rule.

27. $5x + 3y = 4$
$6x - 4y = 20$
$(2, -2)$

28. $-5x + 4y = -5$
$4x + 4y = -32$
$(-3, -5)$

29. $7x - 5y = -3$
$-4x + 6y = -8$
$\left(-\frac{29}{11}, -\frac{34}{11}\right)$

30. $-4x - 9y = -17$
$8x + 4y = 9$
$\left(\frac{13}{56}, \frac{25}{14}\right)$

31. $8x = 3y - 61$
$-x = 4y - 23$
$(-5, 7)$

32. $15y = -188 - 22x$
$23y = -173 - 16x$
$\left(-\frac{13}{2}, -3\right)$

WRITING ABOUT MATHEMATICS

33. Suppose that the first column of a 3×3 matrix A is all 0s. What is the value of det A? Give an example and explain your answer.

34. Estimate how long it might take a supercomputer to solve a linear system of equations with 15 variables, using Cramer's rule and expansion of determinant by minors. Explain your calculations. (*Hint:* See the discussion at the end of this section.)

CHECKING BASIC CONCEPTS   SECTION 4.7

1. Evaluate det A.

(a) $A = \begin{bmatrix} -3 & 4 \\ -2 & 3 \end{bmatrix}$ −1

(b) $A = \begin{bmatrix} 1 & -2 & 3 \\ 5 & 1 & 1 \\ 0 & 2 & -1 \end{bmatrix}$ 17

2. Use Cramer's rule to solve the system of equations. $(-4, 6)$

$$2x - y = -14$$
$$3x - 4y = -36$$

3. Find the area of a triangle with vertices $(-1, 2), (5, 6),$ and $(2, -3)$. 21 units²

CHAPTER

4 Summary

Section 4.1   *Systems of Linear Equations in Two Variables*

Systems of Linear Equations in Two Variables

$$ax + by = c$$
$$dx + ey = k$$

Systems of linear equations in two variables can have 0, 1, or infinitely many solutions. A solution is an ordered pair (x, y).

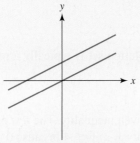

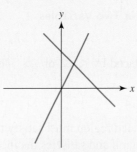

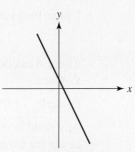

Inconsistent System;   Consistent System;   Consistent System;
(No Solutions)   Independent Equations   Dependent Equations

Example: $x + y = 4$
$\quad\quad\quad\quad\ x - y = 2$

The solution is (3, 1) because it satisfies *both* equations.

Graphical and Numerical Solutions   Systems of linear equations can be solved both graphically and numerically.

Example: $2x + y = 4$
$\quad\quad\quad\quad\ x + y = 3$

Graph and table $y_1 = 4 - 2x$ and $y_2 = 3 - x$. The solution is (1, 2).

Graphical Solution

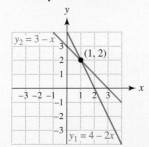

Numerical Solution

x	$4 - 2x$	$3 - x$
0	4	3
1	2	2
2	0	1
3	-2	0

Section 4.2   *The Substitution and Elimination Methods*

Two symbolic methods for solving systems of linear equations are *substitution* and *elimination*.

Substitution	**Elimination**
$x + y = 5$ or $y = 5 - x$	$x + y = 5$
$x - y = -3$	$x - y = -3$
	$\overline{2x + 0y = 2}$ Add the equations.

Substituting in the second equation, $x - (5 - x) = -3$, yields $x = 1$ and $y = 4$.

Thus $x = 1$ and $y = 4$.

Section 4.3   *Systems of Linear Inequalities*

Linear Inequalities in Two Variables

$$ax + by > c,$$

where > can be replaced by <, ≤, or ≥ . The solution set is typically a region in the *xy*-plane.

Example: $x + y \le 4$

Any point in the shaded region must satisfy the given inequality. The *test point*, $(0, 0)$, lies in the shaded region and satisfies the inequality $x + y \le 4$ because $0 + 0 \le 4$.

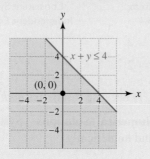

Systems of Linear Inequalities in Two Variables

$$ax + by > c$$
$$dx + ey > k,$$

where > can be replaced by <, ≤, or ≥ .

Example: $x + y \le 2$
$$y \ge x$$

The test point $(-2, 1)$ satisfies both inequalities so shade that region.

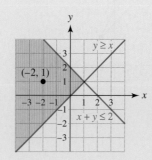

Section 4.4   *Introduction to Linear Programming*

Linear Programming Problem   A linear programming problem consists of an *objective function* to be minimized or maximized (optimized) and a system of linear inequalities called *constraints*. The solution set to the constraints is called the *region of feasible solutions*.

Fundamental Theorem of Linear Programming   If the optimal value for a linear programming problem exists, then it occurs at a *vertex* of the region of feasible solutions.

Example: The maximum of $R = 2x + 3y$ must occur at one of the vertices $(0, 0)$, $(0, 4.5)$, $(3, 3)$, and $(4.5, 0)$.

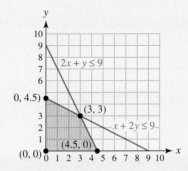

Vertex	$R = 2x + 3y$
$(0, 0)$	$2(0) + 3(0) = 0$
$(0, 4.5)$	$2(0) + 3(4.5) = 13.5$
$(3, 3)$	$2(3) + 3(3) = 15$ ⟵
$(4.5, 0)$	$2(4.5) + 3(0) = 9$

Maximum of $R = 15$ occurs at vertex $(3, 3)$.

Section 4.5   *Systems of Linear Equations in Three Variables*

Solution to a System of Linear Equations in Three Variables   An ordered triple (x, y, z) that satisfies *every* equation.

Example:
$$x - y + 2z = 3$$
$$2x - y + z = 5$$
$$x + y + z = 6$$

The solution is $(3, 2, 1)$ because these values for (x, y, z) satisfy all three equations.

$$3 - 2 + 2(1) = 3 \quad \text{True}$$
$$2(3) - 2 + 1 = 5 \quad \text{True}$$
$$1 + 2 + 3 = 6 \quad \text{True}$$

Elimination and Substitution   Systems of linear equations in three variables can be solved by elimination and substitution, using the following steps.

STEP 1   Eliminate one variable, such as x, from two of the given equations.

STEP 2   Use the two resulting equations with two variables to eliminate one of the variables, such as y. Solve for the remaining variable z.

STEP 3   Substitute z in one of the two equations from STEP 2. Solve for the unknown variable y.

STEP 4   Substitute values for y and z in one of the given equations. Then find x. The solution is (x, y, z).

Section 4.6   *Matrix Solutions of Linear Systems*

Matrix   A rectangular array of numbers is a matrix. If a matrix has n rows and m columns, it has dimension $n \times m$.

Example: Matrix $A = \begin{bmatrix} 3 & -1 & 7 \\ 0 & 6 & -2 \end{bmatrix}$ has dimension 2×3.

Augmented Matrix   Any linear system can be represented with an augmented matrix.

Linear System

$$4x - 3y = 5$$
$$x + 2y = 4$$

Augmented Matrix

$$\left[\begin{array}{cc|c} 4 & -3 & 5 \\ 1 & 2 & 4 \end{array} \right]$$

Gaussian Elimination   A numerical method that uses matrix row transformations to tranform a matrix into reduced row–echelon form from which the solution can be found.

Example: The matrix $\left[\begin{array}{cc|c} 4 & -3 & 5 \\ 1 & 2 & 4 \end{array} \right]$ reduces to $\left[\begin{array}{cc|c} 1 & 0 & 2 \\ 0 & 1 & 1 \end{array} \right]$.

The solution to the system is $(2, 1)$.

Section 4.7   *Determinants*

Determinant for a 2 × 2 Matrix   A determinant is a *real number*. The determinant of a 2×2 matrix is

$$\det A = \det \begin{bmatrix} a & b \\ c & d \end{bmatrix} = ad - cb.$$

Example: $\det \begin{bmatrix} 2 & 3 \\ 4 & 5 \end{bmatrix} = (2)(5) - (4)(3) = -2$

Determinant for a 3 × 3 Matrix

$$\det A = \det \begin{bmatrix} a_1 & b_1 & c_1 \\ a_2 & b_2 & c_2 \\ a_3 & b_3 & c_3 \end{bmatrix}$$

$$= a_1 \cdot \det \begin{bmatrix} b_2 & c_2 \\ b_3 & c_3 \end{bmatrix} - a_2 \cdot \det \begin{bmatrix} b_1 & c_1 \\ b_3 & c_3 \end{bmatrix} + a_3 \cdot \det \begin{bmatrix} b_1 & c_1 \\ b_2 & c_2 \end{bmatrix}$$

Example: $\det \begin{bmatrix} 2 & 3 & 2 \\ 3 & 7 & -3 \\ 0 & 0 & -1 \end{bmatrix} = 2 \det \begin{bmatrix} 7 & -3 \\ 0 & -1 \end{bmatrix} - 3 \det \begin{bmatrix} 3 & 2 \\ 0 & -1 \end{bmatrix} + 0$

$$= 2(-7) - 3(-3) = -5$$

Cramer's rule uses determinants to solve linear systems of equations. Determinants can also be used to find areas of triangles. See Putting It All Together for Section 4.7.

Review Exercises

SECTION 4.1

Exercises 1 and 2: Decide if either ordered pair is a solution.

1. $(2, -1), (3, 2)$ (3, 2)

$$3x - 2y = 5$$
$$-2x + 4y = 2$$

2. $(4, -3), (-1, 2)$ (4, −3)

$$x - 5y = 19$$
$$4x + 3y = 7$$

3. A system of linear equations has been solved graphically. Use the graph to find any solutions. Check your answer. (−1, −3)

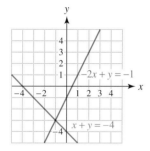

4. Use the table to solve (3.5, 8.5)

$$3x - y = 2$$
$$-x + y = 5.$$

Check your answer.

x	2	2.5	3	3.5	4
$3x - 2$	4	5.5	7	8.5	10
$x + 5$	7	7.5	8	8.5	9

Exercises 5–8: Solve the system of equations graphically. Determine whether the system is consistent or inconsistent. If the system is consistent, state whether the equations are dependent or independent.

5. $x + y = 6$

$x - y = -4$

(1, 5); consistent; independent

6. $x - y = -2$

$-2x + 2y = 4$

$\{(x, y) \mid x - y = -2\}$; consistent; dependent

7. $4x + 2y = 1$

$2x + y = 5$

No solutions; inconsistent

8. $x - 3y = 5$

$x + 5y = -3$

(2, −1); consistent; independent

Exercises 9 and 10: Solve the system of linear equations numerically.

9. $3x + y = 7$

$6x + y = 16$

(3, −2)

10. $4x + 2y = -6$ (−2, 1)

$3x - y = -7$

Exercises 11 and 12: Complete the following.

(a) *Write a system that models the situation.*

(b) *Solve the resulting system graphically.*

11. The sum of two numbers is 25 and their difference is 10. Find the two numbers. (a) $x + y = 25$ (b) (17.5, 7.5)

$x - y = 10$

12. Three times a number minus two times another number equals 19. The sum of the two numbers is 18. Find the two numbers. (a) $3x - 2y = 19$ (b) (11, 7)

$x + y = 18$

SECTION 4.2

Exercises 13–16: Use substitution to solve the system of equations.

13. $2x + 5y = -1$

$x + 2y = -1$

(−3, 1)

14. $3x + y = 6$ (2, 0)

$4x + 5y = 8$

15. $2x - 3y = -8$

$4x + 2y = 0$

(−1, 2)

16. $5x + 3y = -1$

$3x - 5y = -21$

(−2, 3)

Exercises 17–20: Use elimination to solve the system of equations, if possible.

17. $3x + y = 4$

$2x - y = -2$

$\left(\frac{2}{5}, \frac{14}{5}\right)$

18. $2x + 3y = -13$

$3x - 2y = 0$

(−2, −3)

19. $3x - y = 5$

$-6x + 2y = -10$

$\{(x, y) \mid 3x - y = 5\}$

20. $8x - 6y = 7$

$-4x + 3y = 11$

No solutions

SECTION 4.3

Exercises 21–28: Shade the solution set in the xy-plane. *

21. $y \geq 2$

22. $y < 2x - 3$

*Answers on page IA-18

23. $2x - y \le 4$

24. $-x + 3y > 3$

25. $y - x \ge 1$
      $y \le 2$

26. $-x + y \le 3$
      $3x + 2y \ge 6$

27. $y > x - 1$
      $y < 4 - 3x$

28. $x + y \ge 5$
      $2x - 3 < 6$

Exercises 29 and 30: Use the graph to write the system of inequalities.

29. $x > 1$
      $y < -1$

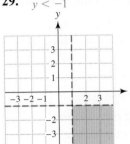

30. $y \le -x + 4$
      $y \ge 2x + 1$

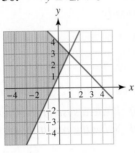

SECTION 4.4

31. Find the maximum of $R = 7x + 8y$ in the shaded region of feasible solutions. $R = 31$

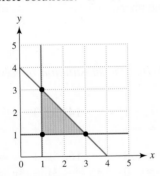

32. Use the figure from Exercise 31 to find the minimum of $C = x + 2y$. $C = 3$

Exercises 33 and 34: Maximize the objective function R subject to the given constraints.

33. $R = 2x + y$ $R = 6$
      $x + y \le 3$
      $x + y \ge 1$
      $x \ge 0, y \ge 0$

34. $R = 6x + 9y$ $R = 45$
      $3x + y \le 12$
      $x + 3y \le 12$
      $x \ge 0, y \ge 0$

SECTION 4.5

35. Is $(3, -4, 5)$ a solution for $x + y + z = 4$?   Yes

36. Decide whether either ordered triple is a solution: $(1, -1, 2), (1, 0, 5)$. $(1, -1, 2)$
      $2x - 3y + z = 7$
      $-x - y + 3z = 6$
      $3x - 2y + z = 7$

41. $\begin{bmatrix} 1 & 1 & 1 & | & -6 \\ 1 & 2 & 1 & | & -8 \\ 0 & 1 & 1 & | & -5 \end{bmatrix}$; $(-1, -2, -3)$

Exercises 37–40: Use elimination and substitution to solve the system of linear equations.

37. $x - y - 2z = -11$ $(-4, 3, 2)$
      $-x + 2y + 3z = 16$
      $3z = 6$

38. $x + y = 4$ $(-1, 5, -3)$
      $-2x + y + 3z = -2$
      $x - 2y + 5z = -26$

39. $2x - y = -5$ $(-1, 3, 2)$
      $x + 2y + z = 7$
      $-2x + y + z = 7$

40. $2x + 3y + z = 6$ $(1, 1, 1)$
      $-x + 2y + 2z = 3$
      $x + y + 2z = 4$

42. $\begin{bmatrix} 1 & 1 & 1 & | & -3 \\ -1 & 1 & 0 & | & 5 \\ 0 & 1 & 1 & | & -1 \end{bmatrix}$; $(-2, 3, -4)$

43. $\begin{bmatrix} 1 & 2 & -1 & | & 1 \\ -1 & 1 & -2 & | & 5 \\ 0 & 2 & 1 & | & 10 \end{bmatrix}$; $(-5, 4, 2)$

SECTION 4.6

Exercises 41–44: Write the system of linear equations as an augmented matrix. Then use Gaussian elimination to solve the system, writing the solution as an ordered triple. Check your solution.

41. $x + y + z = -6$
      $x + 2y + z = -8$
      $y + z = -5$

42. $x + y + z = -3$
      $-x + y = 5$
      $y + z = -1$

43. $x + 2y - z = 1$
      $-x + y - 2z = 5$
      $2y + z = 10$

44. $2x + 2y - 2z = -14$
      $-2x - 3y + 2z = 12$
      $x + y - 4z = -22$

44. $\begin{bmatrix} 2 & 2 & -2 & | & -14 \\ -2 & -3 & 2 & | & 12 \\ 1 & 1 & -4 & | & -22 \end{bmatrix}$; $(-4, 2, 5)$

*Exercises 45 and 46: **Technology**   Use a graphing calculator to solve the system of linear equations.*

45. $3x - 2y + 6z = -17$ $(-7, 4, 2)$
      $-2x - y + 5z = 20$
      $4y + 7z = 30$

46. $19x - 13y - 7z = 7.4$ $(5.4, 2.1, 9.7)$
      $22x + 33y - 8z = 110.5$
      $10x - 56y + 9z = 23.7$

SECTION 4.7

65.(a) $m + 3c + 5b = 14$
$m + 2c + 4b = 11$
$c + 3b = 5$

Exercises 47–50: Evaluate det A, where A is the given matrix.

47. $\begin{bmatrix} 6 & -5 \\ -4 & 2 \end{bmatrix}$ −8   **48.** $\begin{bmatrix} 0 & -6 \\ 5 & 9 \end{bmatrix}$ 30

49. $\begin{bmatrix} 3 & -5 & -3 \\ 1 & 4 & 7 \\ 0 & -3 & 1 \end{bmatrix}$ 89   **50.** $\begin{bmatrix} -2 & -1 & -7 \\ 2 & 1 & -3 \\ 3 & -5 & 8 \end{bmatrix}$ 130

Exercises 51 and 52: Use technology to calculate det A, where A is the given matrix.

51. $\begin{bmatrix} 22 & -45 & 3 \\ 15 & -12 & -93 \\ 5 & 81 & -21 \end{bmatrix}$ **52.** $\begin{bmatrix} 0.5 & -7.3 & 9.6 \\ 0.1 & 3.1 & 9.2 \\ -0.5 & -1.9 & 5.4 \end{bmatrix}$
181,845   67.688

Exercises 53 and 54: Find the area of the triangle by using a determinant. Assume that the units are feet.

53. 46 ft²   **54.** 128 ft²

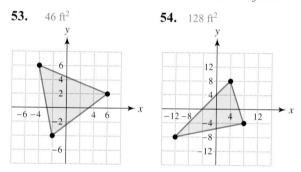

Exercises 55–58: Use Cramer's rule to solve the system.

55. $7x + 6y = 8$
$5x - 8y = 18$
$(2, -1)$

56. $-2x + 5y = 25$
$3x + 4y = -3$
$(-5, 3)$

57. $3x - 6y = 1.5$
$7x - 5y = 8$
$\left(\frac{3}{2}, \frac{1}{2}\right)$

58. $-5x + 4y = -47$
$6x - 7y = 63$
$(7, -3)$

APPLICATIONS

59. *Pedestrian Fatalities* Forty-seven percent of pedestrian fatalities occur on Friday and Saturday nights. The combined total of pedestrian fatalities in 1988 and 1998 was 12,090. There were 1650 more fatalities in 1988 than in 1998. Find the number of pedestrian fatalities during each year. (*Source:* National Highway Traffic Safety Administration.) 6870 in 1988; 5220 in 1998

60. *Burning Calories* During strenuous exercise, an athlete burns 11.5 calories per minute on a stair

climber and 9 calories per minute on a stationary bicycle. In a 30-minute workout the athlete burns 290 calories. How many minutes were spent on each type of workout equipment? (*Source: Runner's World.*)
Stair climber: 8 min; bicycle: 22 min

61. *Linear Programming* A business makes shirts and pants, which require both cutting and sewing. A shirt requires 20 minutes of cutting and 10 minutes of sewing, whereas a pair of pants requires 10 minutes of cutting and 20 minutes of sewing. The machine that sews is available for 480 minutes per day, and the machine that cuts is available 360 minutes per day. The profit from a shirt is $20 and the profit from a pair of pants is $25. How many shirts and how many pairs of pants should be made to maximize daily profit? What is the maximum profit? 8 shirts; 20 pants; $660

62. *Mixing Antifreeze* A car radiator should contain 4 gallons of fluid that is 40% antifreeze. An auto mechanic has a 30% solution of antifreeze and a 55% solution of antifreeze. If the car radiator is empty, how many gallons of each solution should be added?
30% solution: 2.4 gal; 55% solution: 1.6 gal

63. *Boat Speed* A boat travels 18 miles down a river in 1 hour. The return trip against the current takes 1.5 hours. Find the average speed of the boat and the average speed of the current. Boat: 15 mph; current: 3 mph

64. *Tickets* Tickets for a football game sold for $8 and $12. If 480 tickets were sold for total receipts of $4620, how many of each type of ticket were sold?
$8 tickets: 285; $12 tickets: 195

65. *Determining Costs* The accompanying table shows the costs for purchasing different combinations of malts, cones, and ice cream bars.

Malts	Cones	Bars	Total Cost
1	3	5	$14
1	2	4	$11
0	1	3	$5

(a) Let m be the cost of a malt, c the cost of a cone, and b the cost of an ice cream bar. Write a system of three linear equations that represents the data in the table.

(b) Solve this system. Malts: $3; cones: $2; bars: $1

66. *Geometry* The largest angle in a triangle is 20° more than the sum of the two smaller angles. The measure of the largest angle is 85° more than the smallest angle. Find the measure of each angle in the triangle.
100°, 65°, and 15°

67. *Mixture Problem*   Three different types of candy that cost \$1.50, \$2.00, and \$2.50 per pound are to be mixed to produce 12 pounds of candy worth \$26.00. If there is to be 2 pounds more of the \$2.50 candy than the \$2.00 candy, how much of each type of candy should be used in the mixture?
2 lb of \$1.50 candy, 4 lb of \$2 candy, and 6 lb of \$2.50 candy

68. *Estimating the Chest Size of a Bear*   The accompanying table shows the chest size C, weight W, and overall length L of three bears. These data can be modeled with the formula $C = a + bW + cL$.

(*Sources:* M. Triola, *Elementary Statistics*; Minitab, Inc.)

(a) $a + 202b + 63c = 40$
$a + 365b + 70c = 50$
$a + 446b + 77c = 55$

C (inches)	W (pounds)	L (inches)
40	202	63
50	365	70
55	446	77

(a) Set up a system of linear equations whose solution gives values for the constants a, b, and c.

(b) Solve this system. Round each value to the nearest thousandth. $a \approx 27.134$, $b \approx 0.061$, and $c \approx 0.009$

(c) Predict the chest size of a bear weighing 300 pounds and having a length of 68 inches.
About 46 in.

CHAPTER

4 Test

Exercises 1 and 2: Solve the system of equations graphically. Determine whether the system is consistent or inconsistent. If the system is consistent state whether the equations are dependent or independent.

1. $2x + y = 7$
$3x - 2y = 7$
(3, 1); consistent; independent

2. $8x - 4y = 3$
$-4x + 2y = 6$
No solutions; inconsistent

3. Solve the system of equations using substitution.
$(-3, 1)$
$$2x + 5y = -1$$
$$3x + 2y = -7$$

4. The difference of two numbers is 34. The first number is twice the second number.
(a) Write a system of linear equations that models the situation. $x - y = 34$
$x - 2y = 0$
(b) Solve the system using elimination.   (68, 34)

5. Shade the solution set in the xy-plane. Use a test point to check your graph.*
$$-2x + y \geq 3$$
$$x - 2y < -3$$

6. Use elimination and substitution to solve the system of linear equations. $(-4, 2, -5)$
$$x + 3y \qquad = 2$$
$$-2x + y + z = 5$$
$$y + z = -3$$

7. Use the graph to write the system of inequalities.
$y \leq x + 2$
$y \geq 3x - 1$

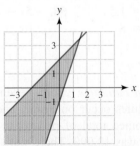

8. Consider the system of linear equations.

8. (a) $\begin{bmatrix} 1 & 1 & 1 & | & 2 \\ 1 & -1 & -1 & | & 3 \\ 2 & 2 & 1 & | & 6 \end{bmatrix}$

$x + y + z = 2$
$x - y - z = 3$
$2x + 2y + z = 6$

*Answer on page IA-18

(a) Write the system of linear equations as an augmented matrix.

(b) Use Gaussian elimination to solve the system, writing the solution as an ordered triple. $\left(\frac{5}{2}, \frac{3}{2}, -2\right)$

9. Evaluate det A if $A = \begin{bmatrix} 3 & 2 & -1 \\ 6 & 2 & -6 \\ 0 & 8 & -3 \end{bmatrix}$. 114

10. Solve the system of linear equations with Cramer's rule. $\left(-\frac{47}{2}, -\frac{83}{2}\right)$

$$5x - 3y = 7$$
$$-4x + 2y = 11$$

11. *College Tuition* In 2000, the average cost of private tuition, including room and board, was $12,636 more than public tuition. Private tuition was 4.6 times higher than public tuition. (*Source:* Department of Education.)

(a) Write a system of linear equations that models the situation.

(b) Solve the system and interpret the solution.

11. (a) $x - y = 12{,}636$
$x - 4.6y = 0$

11. (b) Approximately $(16146, 3510)$; private tuition was $16,146, and public tuition was $3510.

12. *Burning Calories* An athlete burns 12 calories per minute while running and 9 calories per minute on a rowing machine. During a one-hour workout, the athlete burns 669 calories. How many minutes were spent on each type of exercise?
Running: 43 min; rowing: 17 min

13. *Airplane Speed* An airplane travels 600 miles into the wind in 2.5 hours. The return trip with the wind takes 2 hours. Find the average speed of the airplane and the average wind speed.
Airplane: 270 mph; wind: 30 mph

14. *Geometry* The largest angle in a triangle is 50° more than the smallest angle. The sum of the measures of the smaller two angles is 10° more than the largest angle. Find the measure of each angle in the triangle. 85°, 60°, and 35°

15. *Linear Programming* Maximize $R = x + 2y$ subject to $R = 4$

$$x \geq 0, y \geq 0$$
$$2x + 3y \leq 6.$$

CHAPTER 4 Extended and Discovery Exercises

CRAMER'S RULE

Exercises 1–6: Cramer's rule can be applied to systems of three equations with three variables. For the system of equations

$$a_1x + b_1y + c_1z = d_1$$
$$a_2x + b_2y + c_2z = d_2$$
$$a_3x + b_3y + c_3z = d_3,$$

the solution can be written as follows.

$$D = \det \begin{bmatrix} a_1 & b_1 & c_1 \\ a_2 & b_2 & c_2 \\ a_3 & b_3 & c_3 \end{bmatrix}, \quad E = \det \begin{bmatrix} d_1 & b_1 & c_1 \\ d_2 & b_2 & c_2 \\ d_3 & b_3 & c_3 \end{bmatrix}$$

$$F = \det \begin{bmatrix} a_1 & d_1 & c_1 \\ a_2 & d_2 & c_2 \\ a_3 & d_3 & c_3 \end{bmatrix}, \quad G = \det \begin{bmatrix} a_1 & b_1 & d_1 \\ a_2 & b_2 & d_2 \\ a_3 & b_3 & d_3 \end{bmatrix}$$

If $D \neq 0$, a unique solution exists and is given by

$$x = \frac{E}{D}, \quad y = \frac{F}{D}, \quad z = \frac{G}{D}.$$

Use Cramer's rule to solve the equations.

1. $x + y + z = 6$
$2x + y + 2z = 9$
$y + 3z = 9$
$(1, 3, 2)$

2. $y + z = 1$
$2x - y - z = -1$
$x + y - z = 3$
$(0, 2, -1)$

3. $x + z = 2$
$x + y = 0$
$y + 2z = 1$
$(1, -1, 1)$

4. $x + y + 2z = 1$
$-x - 2y - 3z = -2$
$y - 3z = 5$
$(1, 2, -1)$

5. $x + 2z = 7$
$-x + y + z = 5$
$2x - y + 2z = 6$
$(-1, 0, 4)$

6. $x + 2y + 3z = -1$
$2x - 3y - z = 12$
$x + 4y - 2z = -12$
$(2, -3, 1)$

7.(c) $x = 8, y = 12, z = 9$; the traffic flow in the x-direction is 8 cars/min. Other values can be interpreted similarly.

298   **CHAPTER 4**   Systems of Linear Equations

ANALYSIS OF TRAFFIC FLOW

Exercises 7 and 8: Mathematics is frequently used to analyze traffic for timing of traffic lights. The following figure shows three one-way streets with intersections A, B, and C. The average number of cars traveling on certain portions of the streets is given in cars per minute. The variables x, y, and z represent unknown traffic flows that need to be determined. The number of vehicles entering an intersection must equal the number of vehicles exiting an intersection.

(a) *Verify that the accompanying system of linear equations describes the traffic flow at each of the three intersections.*

(b) *Express the system using an augmented matrix.*

(c) *Solve the system and interpret your solution.*

7. A: $8 + 12 = y + x$
    B: $z + 4 = 8 + 5$
    C: $y + 6 = z + 9$

(b) $\begin{bmatrix} 1 & 1 & 0 & | & 20 \\ 0 & 0 & 1 & | & 9 \\ 0 & 1 & -1 & | & 3 \end{bmatrix}$

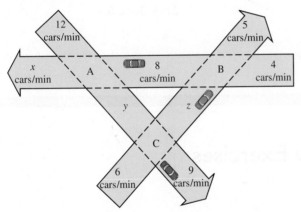

(c) $x = 6, y = 3, z = 5$; the traffic flow in the x-direction is 6 cars/min. Other values can be interpreted similarly.

8. A: $6 + 3 = y + x$
    B: $z + 10 = 6 + 9$
    C: $y + 7 = z + 5$

(b) $\begin{bmatrix} 1 & 1 & 0 & | & 9 \\ 0 & 0 & 1 & | & 5 \\ 0 & 1 & -1 & | & -2 \end{bmatrix}$

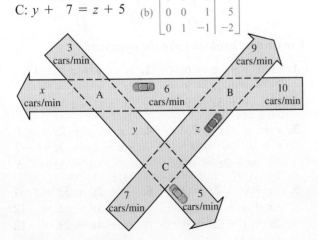

7 & 8.(a) The traffic flow into intersection A is $8 + 12$ cars/min, whereas the traffic flow out it $y + x$ cars/min. They must be equal so $8 + 12 = y + x$. Other equations can be interpreted similarly.

MATRICES AND ROAD MAPS

Exercises 9–12: **Adjacency Matrix**   *A matrix A can be used to represent a map showing distances between cities. Let a_{ij} denote the number in row i and column j of a matrix A. Now consider the following map illustrating freeway distances in miles between four cities. Each city has been assigned a number. For example, there is a direct route from Denver, Colorado (city 1), to Colorado Springs, Colorado (city 2), of approximately 60 miles. Therefore $a_{12} = 60$ in the accompanying matrix A. (Note that a_{12} is the number in row 1 and column 2.) The distance from Colorado Springs to Denver is also 60 miles, so $a_{21} = 60$. As there is no direct freeway connection between Las Vegas, Nevada (city 4), and Colorado Springs (city 2), we let $a_{24} = a_{42} = *$. The matrix A is called an* **adjacency matrix.**   (*Source:* S. Baase, *Computer Algorithms: Introduction to Design and Analysis.*)

9. Denver is city 1 and Las Vegas is city 4, so we use $a_{14} = 760$ mi or $a_{41} = 760$ mi.

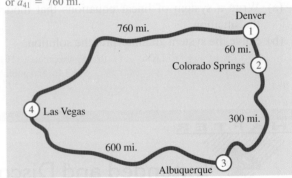

$A = \begin{bmatrix} 0 & 60 & * & 760 \\ 60 & 0 & 300 & * \\ * & 300 & 0 & 600 \\ 760 & * & 600 & 0 \end{bmatrix}$

9. Explain how to use A to find the freeway distance from Denver to Las Vegas.

10. Explain how to use A to find the freeway distance from Denver to Albuquerque.
    $a_{12} + a_{23} = 60 + 300 = 360$ mi

11. If a map shows 20 cities, what would be the dimension of the adjacency matrix? How many elements would there be in this matrix?
    20×20; 400

12. Why are there only zeros on the main diagonal of A?
    The elements on the main diagonal represent the distance from a city to itself, which is always 0.

Exercises 13 and 14: (Refer to Exercises 9–12.) Determine an adjacency matrix A for the road map.

13.

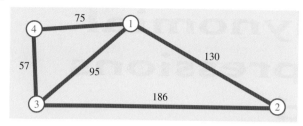

14.

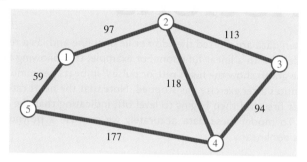

Exercises 15 and 16: (Refer to Exercises 9–12.) Sketch a road map represented by the adjacency matrix A. Is your answer unique? * No

15. $A = \begin{bmatrix} 0 & 30 & 20 & 5 \\ 30 & 0 & 15 & * \\ 20 & 15 & 0 & 25 \\ 5 & * & 25 & 0 \end{bmatrix}$

13. $\begin{bmatrix} 0 & 130 & 95 & 75 \\ 130 & 0 & 186 & * \\ 95 & 186 & 0 & 57 \\ 75 & * & 57 & 0 \end{bmatrix}$

14. $\begin{bmatrix} 0 & 97 & * & * & 59 \\ 97 & 0 & 113 & 118 & * \\ * & 113 & 0 & 94 & * \\ * & 118 & 94 & 0 & 177 \\ 59 & * & * & 177 & 0 \end{bmatrix}$

16. $A = \begin{bmatrix} 0 & 5 & * & 13 & 20 \\ 5 & 0 & 5 & * & * \\ * & 5 & 0 & 13 & * \\ 13 & * & 13 & 0 & 10 \\ 20 & * & * & 10 & 0 \end{bmatrix}$ No

SOLVING AN EQUATION IN FOUR VARIABLES

17. *Weight of a Bear*   In Section 4.6 we estimated the weight of a bear by using two variables. We may be able to make more accurate estimates by using three variables. The accompanying table shows the weight W, neck size N, overall length L, and chest size C for four bears. (**Sources:** M. Triola, *Elementary Statistics*; Minitab, Inc.)

W (pounds)	N (inches)	L (inches)	C (inches)
125	19	57.5	32
316	26	65	42
436	30	72	48
514	30.5	75	54

(a) We can model these data with the equation $W = a + bN + cL + dC$, where a, b, c, and d are constants. To do so, represent a system of linear equations by a 4×5 augmented matrix whose solution gives values for a, b, c, and d.

(b) Solve the system with a graphing calculator. Round each value to the nearest thousandth.

(c) Predict the weight of a bear with $N = 24$, $L = 63$, and $C = 39$. Interpret the result.

17. (a) $\begin{bmatrix} 1 & 19 & 57.5 & 32 & | & 125 \\ 1 & 26 & 65 & 42 & | & 316 \\ 1 & 30 & 72 & 48 & | & 436 \\ 1 & 30.5 & 75 & 54 & | & 514 \end{bmatrix}$

(b) $a \approx -552.272$
$b \approx 8.733$
$c \approx 2.859$
$d \approx 10.843$

(c) About 260 lb; a bear with a 24-in. neck, 63-in. length, and 39-in. chest weighs approximately 260 lb.

Polynomial Expressions and Functions

Many times when data are plotted they do not lie on a line and, as a result, cannot be modeled with a linear function. For example, the following table of data and line graph show the heart rate or pulse P in beats per minute of an athlete t minutes after exercise has stopped. Note that the heart rate decreases faster at first and then begins to level off, indicating that the data are nonlinear. To model these data accurately we can use a polynomial function that is nonlinear.

Time (minutes)	0	2	4	6	8
Heart Rate (beats per minute)	200	150	115	90	80

Source: V. Thomas, *Science and Sport.*

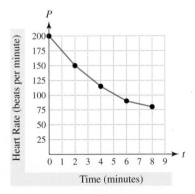

The struggle is what teaches us.
—Sue Grafton

5.1 POLYNOMIAL FUNCTIONS

Monomials and Polynomials · **Addition and Subtraction of Polynomials** · **Polynomial Functions** · **Evaluating Polynomials** · **Applications and Models**

INTRODUCTION

Many quantities in applications cannot be modeled with linear functions and equations. If data points do not lie on a line, we say that the data are *nonlinear*. For example, a scatterplot of the *cumulative* number of AIDS deaths from 1981 through 2000 is shown in Figure 5.1. Polynomials are often used to model nonlinear data such as these. Before modeling nonlinear data, we must first discuss basic concepts of monomials and polynomials. (*Source:* U.S. Department of Health and Human Services.)

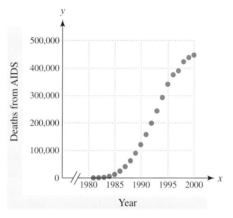

Figure 5.1 U.S. AIDS Deaths

MONOMIALS AND POLYNOMIALS

A **term** is a number, a variable, or a *product* of numbers and variables raised to powers. Examples of terms include

$$-15, \quad y, \quad x^4, \quad 3x^3z, \quad x^{-1/2}y^{-2}, \quad \text{and} \quad 6x^{-1}y^3.$$

If the variables in a term have only *nonnegative integer* exponents, the term is called a **monomial**. Examples of monomials include

$$-4, \quad 5y, \quad x^2, \quad 5x^2z^6, \quad -xy^7, \quad \text{and} \quad 6xy^3.$$

Note: Although a monomial can have a negative sign, it cannot contain any addition or subtraction signs. Also, a monomial cannot have division by a variable.

EXAMPLE 1 Identifying monomials

Determine whether the expression is a monomial.

(a) $-8x^3y^5$ **(b)** xy^{-1} **(c)** $9 + x^2$ **(d)** $\dfrac{2}{x}$

Solution **(a)** The expression $-8x^3y^5$ represents a monomial because it is a product of the number -8 and the variables x and y, which have the nonnegative integer exponents 3 and 5, respectively.

(b) The expression xy^{-1} is not a monomial because y has a negative exponent.

(c) The expression $9 + x^2$ is not a monomial because it is the sum of two monomials, 9 and x^2.

(d) This expression is not a monomial because it involves division by a variable. Note also that $\frac{2}{x} = 2x^{-1}$, which has a negative exponent.

Monomials occur in applications involving geometry, as illustrated in the next example.

EXAMPLE 2 Writing monomials

Write a monomial that represents the volume of a cube with sides of length x. Make a sketch of your result.

Solution The volume of a rectangular box equals the product of its length, width, and height. For a cube, all sides have the same length. If this length is x, its volume is given by $x \cdot x \cdot x = x^3$. See Figure 5.2.

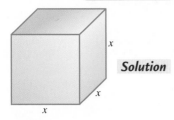

Figure 5.2 Volume: x^3

Critical Thinking

Write a monomial that represents the volume of four identical cubes with sides of length y.

$4y^3$

The **degree of a monomial** equals the sum of the exponents of the variables. A constant term has degree 0, unless the term is 0 (which has an undefined degree). The numeric constant in a monomial is called its **coefficient**. Table 5.1 shows the degree and coefficient of several monomials.

TABLE 5.1

Monomial	64	$4x^2y^3$	$-5x^2$	xy^3
Degree	0	5	2	4
Coefficient	64	4	-5	1

A **polynomial** is either a monomial or a sum of monomials. Examples of polynomials include

TEACHING TIP

Explain that terms are separated by addition ($+$) or subtraction ($-$) symbols.

$$5x^4z^2, \quad 9x^4 - 5, \quad 4x^2 + 5xy - y^2, \quad \text{and} \quad 4 - y^2 + 5y^4 + y^5$$

   1 term   2 terms   3 terms   4 terms

Polynomials containing one variable are called **polynomials of one variable**. The second and fourth polynomials shown are examples of polynomials of one variable. The **leading coefficient** of a polynomial of one variable is the coefficient of the monomial with highest degree. The **degree of a polynomial** equals the degree of the monomial with highest degree. Table 5.2 shows several polynomials of one variable along with their degrees and leading coefficients. A polynomial of degree 1 is a **linear polynomial**, a polynomial of degree 2 is a **quadratic polynomial**, and a polynomial of degree 3 is a **cubic polynomial**.

TABLE 5.2

Polynomial	Degree	Leading Coefficient	Type
-98	0	-98	Constant
$2x - 7$	1	2	Linear
$-5z + 9z^2 + 7$	2	9	Quadratic
$-2x^3 + 4x^2 + x - 1$	3	-2	Cubic
$7 - x + 4x^2 + x^5$	5	1	Fifth degree

ADDITION AND SUBTRACTION OF POLYNOMIALS

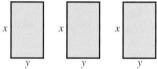

Figure 5.3 Total Area: $3xy$

Suppose that we have 3 rectangles of the same dimension having length x and width y, as shown in Figure 5.3. The total area is given by

$$xy + xy + xy.$$

This area is equivalent to 3 times xy, which can be expressed as $3xy$. In symbols we write

$$xy + xy + xy = 3xy.$$

We can add these three terms because they are *like terms*. If two terms contain the same variables raised to the same powers, we call them **like terms**. We can add or subtract *like* terms, but not *unlike* terms. For example, if one cube has sides of length x, and another cube has sides of length y, their respective volumes are x^3 and y^3. The total volume of the two cubes equals

$$x^3 + y^3,$$

but we cannot combine these terms into one term because they are unlike terms. However, the distributive property can be used to simplify

$$x^3 + 3x^3 = (1 + 3)x^3 = 4x^3$$

TEACHING TIP

Emphasize that only like terms can be combined. Give several examples of like terms.

because x^3 and $3x^3$ are like terms. To add or subtract monomials we simply combine like terms, as illustrated in the next example.

EXAMPLE 3   Adding and subtracting monomials

Simplify each expression by combining like terms.
(a) $8x^2 - 4x^2 + x^3$ **(b)** $9x - 6xy^2 + 2xy^2 + 4x$ **(c)** $5ab^2 - 4a^2 - ab^2 + a^2$

Solution **(a)** The terms $8x^2$ and $-4x^2$ are like terms, so they can be combined.

$$8x^2 - 4x^2 + x^3 = (8 - 4)x^2 + x^3 \qquad \text{Combine like terms.}$$
$$= 4x^2 + x^3 \qquad \text{Subtract.}$$

However, $4x^2$ and x^3 are unlike terms and cannot be combined.
(b) The terms $9x$ and $4x$ can be combined, as can $-6xy^2$ and $2xy^2$.

$$9x - 6xy^2 + 2xy^2 + 4x = 9x + 4x - 6xy^2 + 2xy^2 \qquad \text{Commutative property}$$
$$= (9 + 4)x + (-6 + 2)xy^2 \qquad \text{Combine like terms.}$$
$$= 13x - 4xy^2 \qquad \text{Add.}$$

(c) The terms $5ab^2$ and $-ab^2$ are like terms, as are $-4a^2$ and a^2, so they can be combined.

$$\begin{aligned} 5ab^2 - 4a^2 - ab^2 + a^2 &= 5ab^2 - 1ab^2 - 4a^2 + 1a^2 \quad \text{Commutative property}\\ &= (5-1)ab^2 + (-4+1)a^2 \quad \text{Combine like terms.}\\ &= 4ab^2 - 3a^2 \quad \text{Simplify.} \end{aligned}$$

To add two polynomials we combine like terms, as in the next example.

EXAMPLE 4   Adding polynomials

Simplify each expression.
(a) $(2x^2 - 3x + 7) + (3x^2 + 4x - 2)$ (b) $(z^3 + 4z + 8) + (4z^2 - z + 6)$

Solution (a) $\begin{aligned}(2x^2 - 3x + 7) + (3x^2 + 4x - 2) &= 2x^2 + 3x^2 - 3x + 4x + 7 - 2\\ &= (2+3)x^2 + (-3+4)x + (7-2)\\ &= 5x^2 + x + 5\end{aligned}$

(b) $\begin{aligned}(z^3 + 4z + 8) + (4z^2 - z + 6) &= z^3 + 4z^2 + 4z - z + 8 + 6\\ &= z^3 + 4z^2 + (4-1)z + (8+6)\\ &= z^3 + 4z^2 + 3z + 14\end{aligned}$

We can also add polynomials vertically, as in the next example.

EXAMPLE 5   Adding polynomials vertically

Find the sum.
(a) $(3x^2 - 5xy - 7y^2) + (xy + 4y^2 - x^2)$ (b) $(3x^3 - 2x + 7) + (x^3 + 5x^2 - 9)$

Solution (a) Polynomials can be added vertically by placing like terms in the same columns and then adding.

$$\begin{array}{r} 3x^2 - 5xy - 7y^2\\ -x^2 + xy + 4y^2\\ \hline 2x^2 - 4xy - 3y^2 \end{array} \quad \text{Add each column.}$$

(b) Note that the first polynomial does not contain an x^2-term and that the second polynomial does not contain an x-term. When you are adding vertically, leave a blank for a missing term.

$$\begin{array}{r} 3x^3 -2x + 7\\ x^3 + 5x^2 -9\\ \hline 4x^3 + 5x^2 - 2x - 2 \end{array} \quad \text{Add each column.}$$

Recall that to subtract integers we add the first integer and the *additive inverse* or *opposite* of the second integer. For example, to evaluate $3 - 5$ we perform the following operations.

$$\begin{aligned} 3 - 5 &= 3 + (-5) \quad \text{Add the opposite.}\\ &= -2 \quad \text{Simplify.} \end{aligned}$$

Similarly, to subtract two polynomials we add the first polynomial and the opposite of the second polynomial. To find the **opposite of a polynomial**, we negate each term. Table 5.3 shows three polynomials and their opposites.

TABLE 5.3

Polynomial	Opposite
$9 - x$	$-9 + x$
$5x^2 + 4x - 1$	$-5x^2 - 4x + 1$
$-x^4 + 5x^3 - x^2 + 5x - 1$	$x^4 - 5x^3 + x^2 - 5x + 1$

EXAMPLE 6   Subtracting polynomials

Simplify.
(a) $(y^5 + 3y^3) - (-y^4 + 2y^3)$ **(b)** $(5x^3 + 9x^2 - 6) - (5x^3 - 4x^2 - 7)$

Solution   **(a)** The opposite of $(-y^4 + 2y^3)$ is $(y^4 - 2y^3)$.

$$(y^5 + 3y^3) - (-y^4 + 2y^3) = (y^5 + 3y^3) + (y^4 - 2y^3)$$
$$= y^5 + y^4 + (3 - 2)y^3$$
$$= y^5 + y^4 + y^3$$

(b) The opposite of $(5x^3 - 4x^2 - 7)$ is $(-5x^3 + 4x^2 + 7)$

$$(5x^3 + 9x^2 - 6) - (5x^3 - 4x^2 - 7) = (5x^3 + 9x^2 - 6) + (-5x^3 + 4x^2 + 7)$$
$$= (5 - 5)x^3 + (9 + 4)x^2 + (-6 + 7)$$
$$= 0x^3 + 13x^2 + 1$$
$$= 13x^2 + 1$$

The following summarizes addition and subtraction of polynomials.

Critical Thinking

Is the sum of two quadratic polynomials always a quadratic polynomial? Explain.

No; consider
$(2x^2 + x) + (1 - 2x^2) = x + 1.$

ADDITION, SUBTRACTION, AND OPPOSITES OF POLYNOMIALS
1. To *add* two polynomials, combine like terms.
2. To *subtract* two polynomials, add the first polynomial and the opposite of the second polynomial.
3. The *opposite* of a polynomial is found by changing the sign of every term.

POLYNOMIAL FUNCTIONS

The following expressions are examples of polynomials of one variable.

$$1 - 5x, \quad 3x^2 - 5x + 1, \quad \text{and} \quad x^3 + 5$$

As a result, we say that the following are *symbolic representations* of polynomial functions of one variable.

$$f(x) = 1 - 5x, \quad g(x) = 3x^2 - 5x + 1, \quad \text{and} \quad h(x) = x^3 + 5$$

Function f is a *linear function* because it has degree 1, function g is a *quadratic function* because it has degree 2, and function h is a *cubic function* because it has degree 3.

EXAMPLE 7   Identifying polynomial functions

Determine whether $f(x)$ represents a polynomial function. If possible, identify the type of polynomial function and its degree.

(a) $f(x) = 5x^3 - x + 10$ (b) $f(x) = x^{-2.5} + 1$

(c) $f(x) = 1 - 2x$ (d) $f(x) = \dfrac{3}{x - 1}$

Solution (a) The expression $5x^3 - x + 10$ is a cubic polynomial, so $f(x)$ represents a cubic polynomial function. It has degree 3.

(b) $f(x)$ does not represent a polynomial function because the variables in a polynomial must have *nonnegative integer* exponents.

(c) $f(x) = 1 - 2x$ represents a polynomial function that is linear. It has degree 1.

(d) $f(x)$ does not represent a polynomial function because $\dfrac{3}{x - 1}$ is not a polynomial.

EVALUATING POLYNOMIALS

Frequently, monomials and polynomials represent formulas that can be evaluated. This situation is illustrated in the next example.

EXAMPLE 8   Writing and evaluating a polynomial

Write a polynomial that represents the total volume of two identical boxes having square bases. Make a sketch to illustrate your formula. Find the total volume of the boxes if each base is 11 inches on a side and the height of each box is 5 inches.

Solution Let b be the length of the base and h be the height of a side. The volume of one box is b^2h, as illustrated in Figure 5.4, and the volume of two boxes is $2b^2h$. To calculate their total volumes let $b = 11$ and $h = 5$ in the expression $2b^2h$. Then

$$2 \cdot 11^2 \cdot 5 = 1210 \text{ cubic inches.}$$

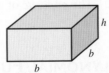

Figure 5.4 Volume: b^2h

EXAMPLE 9   Evaluating a polynomial function graphically and symbolically

A graph of $f(x) = 4x - x^3$ is shown in Figure 5.5. Evaluate $f(-1)$ graphically and check your result symbolically.

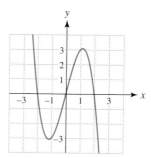

Figure 5.5

Solution *Graphical Evaluation*   To calculate $f(-1)$ graphically find -1 on the x-axis and move down until the graph of f is reached. Then move horizontally to the y-axis, as shown in Figure 5.6. Thus, when $x = -1$, $y = -3$ and $f(-1) = -3$.

Symbolic Evaluation   Evaluation of $f(x) = 4x - x^3$ is performed as follows.

$$f(-1) = 4(-1) - (-1)^3$$
$$= -4 - (-1)$$
$$= -3$$

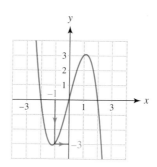

Figure 5.6 $f(-1) = -3$

EXAMPLE 10   Evaluating a polynomial function symbolically

Evaluate $f(x)$ at the given value of x.
(a) $f(x) = -3x^4 - 2,$ $x = 2$ **(b)** $f(x) = -2x^3 - 4x^2 + 5,$ $x = -3$

Solution   **(a)** Be sure to evaluate exponents before multiplying.

$$f(2) = -3(2)^4 - 2 = -3 \cdot 16 - 2 = -50$$

(b) $f(-3) = -2(-3)^3 - 4(-3)^2 + 5 = -2(-27) - 4(9) + 5 = 23$

APPLICATIONS AND MODELS

Polynomials may be used to model a wide variety of data. A scatterplot of the cumulative number of reported AIDS cases in thousands from 1984 to 1994 is shown in Figure 5.7 on the next page. In this graph $x = 4$ corresponds to 1984, $x = 5$ to 1985, and so on until $x = 14$ represents 1994. These data can be modeled with a quadratic function, as shown in Figure

5.8, where $f(x) = 4.1x^2 - 25x + 46$ is graphed with the data. Note that $f(x)$ was found by using a graphing calculator.   (*Source:* Department of Health and Human Services.)

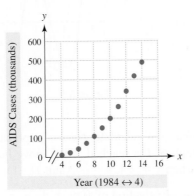

Figure 5.7   AIDS Cases (1984–1994)

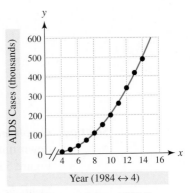

Figure 5.8   Modeling AIDS Cases

EXAMPLE 11   Modeling AIDS cases in the United States

Use $f(x) = 4.1x^2 - 25x + 46$ to model the number of AIDS cases.
(a) Estimate the number of AIDS cases reported by 1987. Compare it to the actual value of 71.4 thousand.
(b) By 1997, the total number of AIDS cases reported was 631 thousand. What estimate does $f(x)$ give? Discuss your result.

Solution   **(a)** The value $x = 7$ corresponds to 1987, so we evaluate $f(7)$, which gives

$$f(7) = 4.1(7)^2 - 25(7) + 46 = 71.9.$$

This model estimates that a cumulative total of 71.9 thousand AIDS cases were reported by 1987. This result compares favorably to the actual value of 71.4 thousand cases.

(b) To estimate the number in 1997, we evaluate $f(17)$ because $x = 17$ corresponds to 1997, obtaining

$$f(17) = 4.1(17)^2 - 25(17) + 46 = 805.9.$$

This result is considerably more than the actual value of 631 thousand. The reason is that f models data only from 1984 through 1994. After 1994, f gives estimates that are too large because the growth in AIDS cases has slowed in recent years.

A well-conditioned athlete's heart rate can reach 200 beats per minute during strenuous physical activity. Upon quitting, a typical heart rate decreases rapidly at first and then more gradually after a few minutes, as illustrated in the next example.

EXAMPLE 12   Modeling heart rate of an athlete

The polynomial $P(t) = 1.875t^2 - 30t + 200$ models a typical athlete's heart rate (or pulse P) in beats per minute (bpm) t minutes after exercise has stopped, where $0 \le t \le 8$.
(*Source:* V. Thomas, *Science and Sport.*)

(a) What is the initial heart rate when the athlete stops exercising?

(b) What is the heart rate after 8 minutes?

(c) A graph of P is shown in Figure 5.9. Interpret this graph.

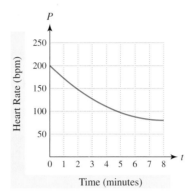

Figure 5.9

Solution **(a)** To find the initial heart rate evaluate $P(t)$ at $t = 0$, or

$$P(0) = 1.875(0)^2 - 30(0) + 200 = 200.$$

When the athlete stops exercising, the heart rate is 200 beats per minute. (This result agrees with the graph.)

(b) $P(8) = 1.875(8)^2 - 30(8) + 200 = 80$ beats per minute.

(c) The heart rate does not drop at a constant rate; rather, it drops rapidly at first and then gradually begins to level off.

PUTTING IT ALL TOGETHER

In this section we introduced monomials, polynomials, and polynomial functions. A monomial is a number or a product of numbers and variables, where each variable has a *nonnegative integer* exponent. A polynomial is a monomial or a sum of monomials. The formula for a polynomial function can be represented by a polynomial. To add polynomials we combine like terms. To subtract polynomials we add the first polynomial to the opposite of the second polynomial. Examples are given in the following table.

Concept	Examples
Addition of Polynomials	$(-3x^2 + 2x - 7) + (4x^2 - x + 1) = -3x^2 + 4x^2 + 2x - x - 7 + 1$ $= (-3 + 4)x^2 + (2 - 1)x + (-7 + 1)$ $= x^2 + x - 6$ $(x^4 + 8x^3 - 7x) + (5x^4 - 3x) = x^4 + 5x^4 + 8x^3 - 7x - 3x$ $= (1 + 5)x^4 + 8x^3 + (-7 - 3)x$ $= 6x^4 + 8x^3 - 10x$

continued on next page

continued from previous page

Opposite of a Polynomial	The opposite of $5x^3 + 2x^2 - 3x + 6$ is $-5x^3 - 2x^2 + 3x - 6$.
	The opposite of $-6x^6 + 4x^4 - 8x^2 - 17$ is $6x^6 - 4x^4 + 8x^2 + 17$.
Subtraction of Polynomials	$(5x^2 - 6x + 1) - (-5x^2 + 3x - 5) = (5x^2 - 6x + 1) + (5x^2 - 3x + 5)$
	$\qquad\qquad\qquad\qquad\quad = (5 + 5)x^2 + (-6 - 3)x + (1 + 5)$
	$\qquad\qquad\qquad\qquad\quad = 10x^2 - 9x + 6$
	$(x^4 - 6x^2 + 5x) - (x^4 - 5x + 7) = (x^4 - 6x^2 + 5x) + (-x^4 + 5x - 7)$
	$\qquad\qquad\qquad\qquad\quad = (1 - 1)x^4 - 6x^2 + (5 + 5)x - 7$
	$\qquad\qquad\qquad\qquad\quad = -6x^2 + 10x - 7$
Polynomial Functions	The following represent polynomial functions.
	$f(x) = 3$ $\qquad$ Degree $= 0$ $\qquad$ Constant
	$f(x) = 5x - 3$ $\qquad$ Degree $= 1$ $\qquad$ Linear
	$f(x) = x^2 - 2x - 1$ $\qquad$ Degree $= 2$ $\qquad$ Quadratic
	$f(x) = 3x^3 + 2x^2 - 6$ $\qquad$ Degree $= 3$ $\qquad$ Cubic
Evaluating a Polynomial Function	To evaluate $f(x) = -4x^2 + 3x - 1$ at $x = 2$, substitute 2 for x.
	$f(2) = -4(2)^2 + 3(2) - 1 = -16 + 6 - 1 = -11$

5.1 EXERCISES

FOR EXTRA HELP

📖 Student's Solutions Manual

🚪 MyMathLab

InterАct math InterAct Math

Tutor Center Math Tutor Center

MathXP MathXL

📼 Digital Video Tutor
CD 4   Videotape 6

CONCEPTS

1. Give an example of a monomial. $3x^2$; answers may vary.

2. What are the degree and leading coefficient of the polynomial $3x^2 - x^3 + 1$? $3; -1$

3. Are $-5x^3y$ and $6xy^3$ like terms? Explain.
No; the powers must match for each variable.

4. Give an example of a polynomial that has 3 terms and is degree 4. $x^4 - 3x + 5$; answers may vary.

5. Does the opposite of $x^2 + 1$ equal $-x^2 + 1$? Explain.
No; the opposite is $-x^2 - 1$.

6. Evaluate $4x^3y$ when $x = 2$ and $y = 3$.   96

7. When you evaluate a polynomial function for a value of x, can you calculate two answers? Explain.
No; a function has only one output for each input.

8. Could the graph of a polynomial function be a line? Explain.   Yes, if the polynomial is linear.

MONOMIALS AND POLYNOMIALS

Exercises 9–16: Determine whether the expression is a monomial.

9. x^4 Yes

10. x^{-4} No

11. $2x^2y + y^2$ No

12. $5 - \sqrt{x}$ No

13. $-4x^3y^3$ Yes

14. xy Yes

15. $\dfrac{3}{x - 2}$ No

16. $\pi x^4 y^2 z$ Yes

Exercises 17–22: Write a monomial that represents the described quantity.

17. The area of a square with sides equal to x x^2

18. The circumference of a circle with diameter d πd

19. The area of a circle with radius r πr^2

20. The area of three congruent triangles with base b and height h $\frac{3}{2}bh$

21. The number of members in a marching band that has x rows with y people in each row xy

22. The revenue from selling w items for z dollars each
wz

Exercises 23–28: Identify the degree and coefficient of the monomial.

23. $3x^7$ $7; 3$

24. $-5y^3$ $3; -5$

25. $-3x^2y^5$ $7; -3$

26. xy^5 $6; 1$

27. $-x^3y^3$ $6; -1$

28. $\sqrt{2}xy$ $2; \sqrt{2}$

Exercises 29–34: Identify the degree and leading coefficient of the polynomial. **31.** $3; -\frac{2}{5}$

29. $5x^2 - 4x + \frac{3}{4}$ $2; 5$

30. $-9y^4 + y^2 + 5$ $4; -9$

31. $5 - x + 3x^2 - \frac{2}{5}x^3$

32. $7x + 4x^4 - \frac{4}{3}x^3$ $4; 4$

33. $8x^4 + 3x^3 - 4x + x^5$ $5; 1$

34. $5x^2 - x^3 + 7x^4 + 10$ $4; 7$

Exercises 35–46: Combine like terms whenever possible.

35. $x^2 + 4x^2$ $5x^2$

36. $-3z + 5z$ $2z$

37. $6y^4 - 3y^4$ $3y^4$

38. $9xy - 7xy$ $2xy$

39. $5x^2y + 8xy^2$ Not possible

40. $5x + 4y$ Not possible

41. $9x^2 - x + 4x - 6x^2$ $3x^2 + 3x$

42. $-xy^2 - \frac{1}{2}xy^2$ $-\frac{3}{2}xy^2$

43. $x^2 + 9xy - y^2 + 4x^2 + y^2$ $5x^2 + 9xy$

44. $6xy + 4x - 6xy$ $4x$

45. $4x + 7x^3y^7 - \frac{1}{2}x^3y^7 + 9x - \frac{3}{2}x^3y^7$ $5x^3y^7 + 13x$

46. $19x^3 + x^2 - 3x^3 + x - 4x^2 + 1$ $16x^3 - 3x^2 + x + 1$

Exercises 47–54: Add the polynomials.

47. $(3x + 1) + (-x + 1)$ $2x + 2$

48. $(5y^3 + y) + (12y^3 - 5y)$ $17y^3 - 4y$

49. $(x^2 - 2x + 15) + (-3x^2 + 5x - 7)$ $-2x^2 + 3x + 8$

50. $(3x^3 - 4x + 3) + (5x^2 + 4x + 12)$ $3x^3 + 5x^2 + 15$

51. $(4x) + (1 - 4.5x)$ $-0.5x + 1$

52. $(y^5 + y) + (5 - y + \frac{1}{3}y^2)$ $y^5 + \frac{1}{3}y^2 + 5$

53. $(x^4 - 3x^2 - 4) + (-8x^4 + x^2 - \frac{1}{2})$ $-7x^4 - 2x^2 - \frac{9}{2}$

54. $(3z + z^4 + 2) + (-3z^4 - 5 + z^2)$
$-2z^4 + z^2 + 3z - 3$

Exercises 55–60: Find the opposite of the polynomial.

55. $6x^5$ $-6x^5$

56. $-5y^7$ $5y^7$

57. $19x^5 - 5x^3 + 3x$
$-19x^5 + 5x^3 - 3x$

58. $-x^2 - x - 5$ $x^2 + x + 5$

59. $-7z^4 + z^2 - 8$
$7z^4 - z^2 + 8$

60. $6 - 4x + 5x^2 - \frac{1}{10}x^3$
$-6 + 4x - 5x^2 + \frac{1}{10}x^3$

Exercises 61–68: Subtract the polynomials.

61. $(5x - 3) - (2x + 4)$ $3x - 7$

62. $(10x + 5) - (-6x - 4)$ $16x + 9$

63. $(x^2 - 3x + 1) - (-5x^2 + 2x - 4)$ $6x^2 - 5x + 5$

64. $(-x^2 + x - 5) - (x^2 - x + 5)$ $-2x^2 + 2x - 10$

65. $3(4x^4 + 2x^2 - 9) - 4(x^4 - 2x^2 - 5)$
$8x^4 + 14x^2 - 7$

66. $2(8x^3 + 5x^2 - 3x + 1) - 5(-5x^3 + 6x - 11)$
$41x^3 + 10x^2 - 36x + 57$

67. $4(x^4 - 1) - (4x^4 + 3x + 7)$ $-3x - 11$

68. $(5x^4 - 6x^3 + x^2 + 5) - (x^3 + 11x^2 + 9x - 3)$
$5x^4 - 7x^3 - 10x^2 - 9x + 8$

Exercises 69–76: Determine whether $f(x)$ represents a polynomial function. If possible, identify the degree and type of polynomial function.

69. $f(x) = x^4 + 5x^2 - 6$ Yes; 4; fourth degree

70. $f(x) = 5x^3$
Yes; 3; cubic

71. $f(x) = x^{-2}$ No

72. $f(x) = |x|$ No

73. $f(x) = \dfrac{1}{x^2 + 1}$ No

74. $f(x) = 5x - 7$
Yes; 1; linear

75. $f(x) = \frac{1}{3} + 3x - x^2$
Yes; 2; quadratic

76. $f(x) = x + 3x^{-2} + 6$ No

EVALUATING POLYNOMIALS

Exercises 77–82: Evaluate the polynomial at the given value(s) of the variable(s).

77. $-4x^2$ $\quad x = 2$ -16

78. $-2y^3$ $\quad y = -3$ 54

79. $2x^2y$ $\quad x = 2, y = 3$ 24

80. $-xy^3$ $\quad x = 4, y = -1$ 4

81. $a^2b - ab^2$ $\quad a = -3, b = 4$ 84

82. $3a^3 + 2b^3$ $\quad a = -2, b = 3$ 30

Exercises 83–86: Use the graph of f to evaluate both expressions.

83. $f(1)$ and $f(-2)$ $-1; 2$ **84.** $f(0)$ and $f(2)$ $-2; 4$

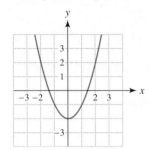
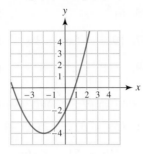

85. $f(-1)$ and $f(2)$ $-4; 2$ **86.** $f(-1)$ and $f(0)$ $-1; 2$

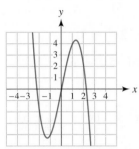
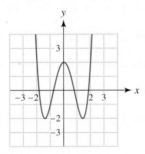

Exercises 87–100: Evaluate f(x) at the given x-value.

87. $f(x) = 3x^2$ $x = -2$ 12

88. $f(x) = x^2 - 2x$ $x = 3$ 3

89. $f(x) = 5 - 4x$ $x = -\frac{1}{2}$ 7

90. $f(x) = x^2 + 4x - 5$ $x = -3$ -8

91. $f(x) = 0.5x^4 - 0.3x^3 + 5$ $x = -1$ 5.8

92. $f(x) = 6 - 2x + x^3$ $x = 0$ 6

93. $f(x) = -x^3$ $x = -1$ 1

94. $f(x) = 3 - 2x$ $x = \frac{3}{10}$ 2.4

95. $f(x) = -x^2 - 3x$ $x = -3$ 0

96. $f(x) = 2x^3 - 4x + 1$ $x = 1$ -1

97. $f(x) = 1 - 2x + x^2$ $x = 2.4$ 1.96

98. $f(x) = 4x^2 - 20x + 25$ $x = 1.8$ 1.96

99. $f(x) = x^5 - 5$ $x = -1$ -6

100. $f(x) = 1.2x^4 - 5.7x + 3$ $x = \frac{3}{2}$ 0.525

APPLICATIONS

101. *Women on the Run*   The number of women participating in the New York marathon has increased dramatically in recent years. The polynomial function $f(x) = 8.87x^2 + 232x + 769$ models the number of women running each year from 1978 through 1998, where $x = 0$ corresponds to 1978, $x = 10$ to 1988, and $x = 20$ to 1998. See the accompanying figure.   (*Source: Runner's World.*)

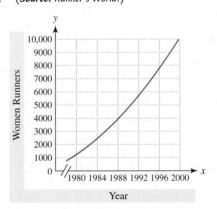

(a) Use the graph to estimate the number of women running in 1980 and in 1995.   1250; 7250

(b) Answer part (a), using the polynomial. How do your answers compare with your answers in part (a)?   1268; 7276; they are similar.

(c) Use the polynomial to find the increase in women runners from 1978 to 1998.   8188

102. *A PC for All?*   Worldwide sales of personal computers have climbed as prices have continued to drop. The polynomial function $f(x) = 0.7868x^2 + 12x + 79.5$ models the number of computers sold during year x, where $x = 0$ corresponds to 1997, $x = 1$ to 1998, and so on. Estimate the number of personal computers sold in 2003, using both the graph and the polynomial.   (*Source: International Data Corporation.*)   About 180 million

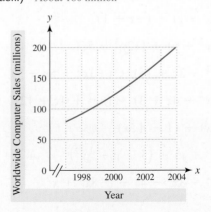

103. *Geometry*   A house has 8-foot-high ceilings. Three rooms are x feet by y feet and two rooms are x feet by z feet. Write a polynomial that gives the total volume of the five rooms. Find their total volume if $x = 10$ feet, $y = 12$ feet, and $z = 7$ feet.
$24xy + 16xz$; 4000 ft³

104. *U.S. AIDS Deaths*   The scatterplot shows the cumulative number of reported AIDS deaths. In this graph $x = 4$ corresponds to 1984, $x = 5$ to 1985, and so on until $x = 14$ corresponds to 1994. The data may be modeled by $f(x) = 2.4x^2 - 14x + 23$, where the output is in thousands of deaths.

(b) 478.6 thousand, which is too high; AIDS deaths did not continue to rise as rapidly as the model predicts.

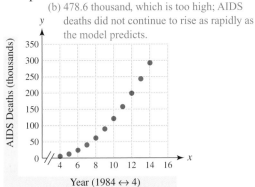

Year (1984 ↔ 4)

123 thousand, which is close to the actual value.

(a) Use $f(x)$ to estimate the cumulative total of AIDS deaths in 1990. Compare it with the actual value of 121.6 thousand.

(b) In 1997 the cumulative number of AIDS deaths was 390 thousand. What estimate does $f(x)$ give? Discuss your result.

105. *Squares and Circles*   Write a polynomial that gives the sum of the areas of a square with sides of length x and a circle with radius x. Find the combined area when $x = 10$ inches.
$x^2 + \pi x^2$; $100 + 100\pi \approx 414.2$ in²

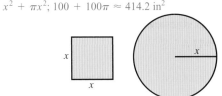

106. *Spheres*   Write a monomial that gives the volume of 9 spheres with radius y. Find the combined volumes when $y = 3$ feet. (*Hint*: The volume of a sphere with radius r is $\frac{4}{3}\pi r^3$.) $12\pi y^3$; 1017.9 ft³

107. *Heart Rate*   (Refer to Example 12.) Make a table of $f(t) = 1.875t^2 - 30t + 200$, starting at $t = 3$ and incrementing by 1. When was the athlete's heart rate between 80 and 110, inclusive? *   From 4 to 8 min

108. *Ocean Temperatures*   The polynomial function

$$f(x) = -0.064x^3 + 0.56x^2 + 2.9x + 61$$

models the ocean temperature in degrees Fahrenheit at Naples, Florida. In this formula $x = 1$ corresponds to January, $x = 2$ to February, and so on. (*Source:* J. Williams.)   (a) About 77.5° F

(a) What is the average ocean temperature in April?

(b) Use the graph of f to estimate when the maximum ocean temperature occurs. What is this maximum?   Late July; about 87° F

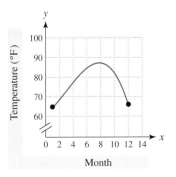

Month

109. *Microsoft Stocks*   If a person had bought $2500 of Microsoft stock in 1986, it would have been worth about $1.2 million in 1999. The following table shows the cost of this stock (adjusted for splits) in various years.

Year	1986	1994	1999
Cost ($)	0.19	20	90

Source: USA Today.
(i) $f(x)$ is the best, which can be determined from a table of values.

Which of the following polynomials models the data best, where $x = 6$ corresponds to 1986, $x = 14$ to 1994, and $x = 19$ to 1999? Explain how you made your decision.

(i) $f(x) = 0.886x^2 - 15.25x + 59.79$
(ii) $g(x) = 0.882x^2 - 15.4x + 60.15$

110. *SUV Sales*   Sales of sport utility vehicles (SUVs) increased dramatically between 1991 and 1999. In 1991 about 1 million SUVs were sold, and in 1999 3.2 million were sold. Growth in sales could be modeled by a linear function f.

(*Source:* Autodata Corporation.) $a = 0.275$ and $b = -546.525$

(a) Find values for a and b so that $f(x) = ax + b$ models the data. (*Hint:* The graph of f should pass through the points (1991, 1) and (1999, 3.2).)

(b) Estimate the number of SUVs sold in 1995.
2.1 million

*Answers on page IA-19

WRITING ABOUT MATHEMATICS

111. Discuss how to subtract two polynomials. Demonstrate your method with an example.

112. Explain the difference between a monomial and a polynomial. Give examples of each and an example that is neither a monomial nor a polynomial.

113. If a polynomial function has degree 1, what can be said about its graph? If a polynomial function has degree greater than 1, what can be said about its graph?

114. Explain how to evaluate a function graphically. Use your method to evaluate $f(x) = x^2$ at $x = -2$.

Group Activity: Working with Real Data

Directions: Form a group of 2 to 4 people. Select someone to record the group's responses for this activity. All members of the group should work cooperatively to answer the questions. If your instructor asks for the results, each member of the group should be prepared to respond.

Women in College The table shows the number of women attending 4-year institutions of higher education.

(a) $f(1983) = 3.8; f(1993) = 4.7; f(2003) = 5.2$

Year	1983	1993	2003
Women (millions)	3.8	4.7	5.2

Source: National Center for Education Statistics.

(b) $f(2010) = 5.312$; probably not, because this date is relatively far in the future.

(a) Verify that these data are modeled by

$$f(x) = -0.002x^2 + 8.042x - 8078.908,$$

where x is the year.

(c) Yes; estimating between data points is generally more reliable.
(d) No; in 1958, women attended college as they will in 2062.

(b) Make a table of $f(x)$, starting at $x = 2004$ and incrementing by 1. What does this model predict will happen in 2010? Is this model accurate that far into the future? Explain.*

(c) Would $f(x)$ be more accurate predicting the number of women attending college in 2001 than in 2010? Explain.

(d) The x-intercept on the graph of $f(x)$ are approximately 1958 and 2062. Do these x-intercepts have meaning in this model? Explain.

*Answers on page IA-19

5.2   MULTIPLICATION OF POLYNOMIALS

Review of Basic Properties · Multiplying Polynomials · Some Special Products

INTRODUCTION

The study of polynomials dates back to Babylonian civilization in about 1800–1600 B.C. Much later, Gottfried Leibniz (1646–1716) was the first to generalize polynomial functions of degree n. Many eighteenth century mathematicians devoted their entire careers to the study of polynomials. Their studies included multiplying and factoring polynomials. Both skills are used to solve equations. In this section we discuss the basics of polynomial multiplication. (*Sources: Historical Topics for the Mathematics Classroom, Thirty-first Yearbook*, NCTM; L. Motz and J. Weaver, *The Story of Mathematics*.)

REVIEW OF BASIC PROPERTIES

Distributive properties are used frequently in the multiplication of polynomials. For all real numbers a, b, and c

$$a(b + c) = ab + ac \quad \text{and}$$
$$a(b - c) = ab - ac.$$

In the next example we use these distributive properties to multiply expressions.

TEACHING TIP

Ask students to apply the distributive property to $-1(4 - 2z)$ and $-(2x + 1)$.

EXAMPLE 1   Using distributive properties

Multiply.
(a) $4(5 + x)$ **(b)** $-3(x - 4y)$ **(c)** $(2x - 5)(6)$

Solution   **(a)** $4(5 + x) = 4 \cdot 5 + 4 \cdot x = 20 + 4x$

(b) $-3(x - 4y) = -3 \cdot x - (-3) \cdot (4y) = -3x + 12y$

(c) $(2x - 5)(6) = 2x \cdot 6 - 5 \cdot 6 = 12x - 30$

You can visualize the solution in part (a) of Example 1 by using areas of rectangles. If a rectangle has width 4 and length $5 + x$, its area is $20 + 4x$, as shown in Figure 5.10.

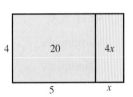

Figure 5.10   Area: $20 + 4x$

In Section 1.3 we discussed several properties of exponents. The following three properties of exponents are frequently used in the multiplication of polynomials.

TEACHING TIP

Spend some time reviewing properties of exponents. Many students forget how to apply properties of exponents.

PROPERTIES OF EXPONENTS

For any nonzero numbers a and b and integers m and n,

$$a^m \cdot a^n = a^{m+n}, \quad (a^m)^n = a^{mn}, \quad \text{and} \quad (ab)^n = a^n b^n.$$

We use these three properties to simplify expressions in the next two examples.

EXAMPLE 2   Multiplying powers of variables

Multiply each expression.
(a) $-2x^3 \cdot 4x^5$ **(b)** $(3xy^3)(4x^2y^2)$ **(c)** $6y^3(2y - y^2)$ **(d)** $-mn(m^2 - n)$

Solution   **(a)** $-2x^3 \cdot 4x^5 = (-2)(4)x^3x^5 = -8x^{3+5} = -8x^8$
(b) $(3xy^3)(4x^2y^2) = (3)(4)xx^2y^3y^2 = 12x^{1+2}y^{3+2} = 12x^3y^5$

Note: We cannot simplify $12x^3y^5$ further because x^3 and y^5 have different bases.

(c) $6y^3(2y - y^2) = 6y^3 \cdot 2y - 6y^3 \cdot y^2 = 12y^4 - 6y^5$

(d) $-mn(m^2 - n) = -mn \cdot m^2 + mn \cdot n = -m^3n + mn^2$ _____

EXAMPLE 3   Using properties of exponents

Simplify.
(a) $(x^2)^5$ **(b)** $(2x)^3$ **(c)** $(5x^3)^2$ **(d)** $(-mn^3)^2$

Solution   **(a)** $(x^2)^5 = x^{2\cdot5} = x^{10}$ **(b)** $(2x)^3 = 2^3x^3 = 8x^3$
(c) $(5x^3)^2 = 5^2(x^3)^2 = 25x^6$
(d) $(-mn^3)^2 = (-m)^2(n^3)^2 = m^2n^6$ _____

MULTIPLYING POLYNOMIALS

A polynomial with one term is a **monomial**, with two terms a **binomial**, and with three terms a **trinomial**. Examples are shown in Table 5.4.

TABLE 5.4

Monomials	$2x^2$	$-3x^4y$	9
Binomials	$3x - 1$	$2x^3 - x$	$x^2 + 5$
Trinomials	$x^2 - 3x + 5$	$5x^2 - 2x + 10$	$2x^3 - x^2 - 2$

In the next example we multiply two binomials, using both geometric and symbolic techniques.

EXAMPLE 4   Multiplying binomials

Multiply $(x + 1)(x + 3)$
(a) geometrically and
(b) symbolically.

Solution   **(a)** To multiply $(x + 1)(x + 3)$ geometrically, draw a rectangle $x + 1$ wide and $x + 3$ long, as shown in Figure 5.11(a). The area of the rectangle equals the product $(x + 1)(x + 3)$. This large rectangle can be divided into four smaller rectangles as shown in Figure 5.11(b). The sum of the areas of these four smaller rectangles equals the area of the large rectangle. The smaller rectangles have areas of x^2, x, $3x$, and 3. Thus

$$(x + 1)(x + 3) = x^2 + x + 3x + 3$$
$$= x^2 + 4x + 3.$$

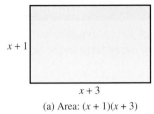
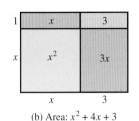

(a) Area: $(x + 1)(x + 3)$ (b) Area: $x^2 + 4x + 3$

Figure 5.11

(b) To multiply $(x + 1)(x + 3)$ symbolically we apply the distributive property.

$$(x + 1)(x + 3) = (x + 1)(x) + (x + 1)(3)$$
$$= x \cdot x + 1 \cdot x + x \cdot 3 + 1 \cdot 3$$
$$= x^2 + x + 3x + 3$$
$$= x^2 + 4x + 3$$

We can give graphical and numerical support to our result in Example 4 by letting $Y_1 = (X + 1)(X + 3)$ and $Y_2 = X^2 + 4X + 3$. The graphs of y_1 and y_2 appear to be identical in Figures 5.12(a) and 5.12(b). Figure 5.12(c) shows that $y_1 = y_2$ for each value of x in the table.

$[-6, 6, 1]$ by $[-4, 4, 1]$ $[-6, 6, 1]$ by $[-4, 4, 1]$

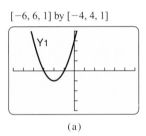
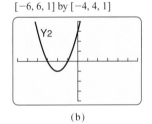

X	Y₁	Y₂
-3	0	0
-2	-1	-1
-1	0	0
0	3	3
1	8	8
2	15	15
3	24	24
X=-3		

(a)   (b)   (c)

Figure 5.12

To multiply $(x + 1)$ by $(x + 3)$ we multiplied every term in $x + 1$ by every term in $x + 3$. That is,

$$(x + 1)(x + 3) = x^2 + 3x + x + 3$$
$$= x^2 + 4x + 3.$$

Note: This process of multiplying binomials is sometimes called *FOIL*. You may use it to remind yourself to multiply the first terms (F), outside terms (O), inside terms (I), and last terms (L).

Multiply the *First terms* to obtain x^2. $(x + 1)(x + 3)$

Multiply the *Outside terms* to obtain $3x$. $(x + 1)(x + 3)$

Multiply the *Inside terms* to obtain x. $(x + 1)(x + 3)$

Multiply the *Last terms* to obtain 3. $(x + 1)(x + 3)$

The following method summarizes how to multiply two polynomials in general.

TEACHING TIP

Point out that this method is a general method that works for multiplying *any* two polynomials.

MULTIPLICATION OF POLYNOMIALS

The product of two polynomials may be found by multiplying every term in the first polynomial by every term in the second polynomial.

EXAMPLE 5 Multiplying polynomials

Multiply each binomial.
(a) $(2x - 1)(x + 2)$ **(b)** $(1 - 3x)(2 - 4x)$ **(c)** $(x^2 + 1)(5x - 3)$

Solution **(a)** $(2x - 1)(x + 2) = 2x \cdot x + 2x \cdot 2 - 1 \cdot x - 1 \cdot 2$
$$= 2x^2 + 4x - x - 2$$
$$= 2x^2 + 3x - 2$$
(b) $(1 - 3x)(2 - 4x) = 1 \cdot 2 - 1 \cdot 4x - 3x \cdot 2 + 3x \cdot 4x$
$$= 2 - 4x - 6x + 12x^2$$
$$= 2 - 10x + 12x^2$$
(c) $(x^2 + 1)(5x - 3) = x^2 \cdot 5x - x^2 \cdot 3 + 1 \cdot 5x - 1 \cdot 3$
$$= 5x^3 - 3x^2 + 5x - 3$$

EXAMPLE 6 Multiplying polynomials

Multiply each expression.
(a) $3x(x^2 + 5x - 4)$ **(b)** $-x^2(x^4 - 2x + 5)$ **(c)** $(x + 2)(x^2 + 4x - 3)$

Solution **(a)** $3x(x^2 + 5x - 4) = 3x \cdot x^2 + 3x \cdot 5x - 3x \cdot 4$
$$= 3x^3 + 15x^2 - 12x$$
(b) $-x^2(x^4 - 2x + 5) = -x^2 \cdot x^4 + x^2 \cdot 2x - x^2 \cdot 5$
$$= -x^6 + 2x^3 - 5x^2$$
(c) $(x + 2)(x^2 + 4x - 3) = x \cdot x^2 + x \cdot 4x - x \cdot 3 + 2 \cdot x^2 + 2 \cdot 4x - 2 \cdot 3$
$$= x^3 + 4x^2 - 3x + 2x^2 + 8x - 6$$
$$= x^3 + 6x^2 + 5x - 6$$

EXAMPLE 7 Multiplying polynomials

Multiply each expression.
(a) $2ab^3(a^2 - 2ab + 3b^2)$ **(b)** $4m(mn^2 + 3m)(m^2n - 4n)$

Solution **(a)** Multiply each term in the second polynomial by $2ab^3$.

$$2ab^3(a^2 - 2ab + 3b^2) = 2ab^3 \cdot a^2 - 2ab^3 \cdot 2ab + 2ab^3 \cdot 3b^2$$
$$= 2a^3b^3 - 4a^2b^4 + 6ab^5$$

(b) Start by multiplying every term in $(mn^2 + 3m)$ by $4m$.

$$4m(mn^2 + 3m)(m^2n - 4n) = (4m \cdot mn^2 + 4m \cdot 3m)(m^2n - 4n)$$

$$= (4m^2n^2 + 12m^2)(m^2n - 4n)$$

$$= 4m^2n^2 \cdot m^2n - 4m^2n^2 \cdot 4n + 12m^2 \cdot m^2n - 12m^2 \cdot 4n$$

$$= 4m^4n^3 - 16m^2n^3 + 12m^4n - 48m^2n$$

Sometimes it is convenient to multiply polynomials vertically. After multiplying, always place like terms in their respective columns. Leave blanks for missing terms.

EXAMPLE 8   Multiplying polynomials vertically

Multiply $(3x - 4y)(2x^2 + xy - 4y^2)$.

Solution   Start by stacking the polynomials as follows. Note that unlike terms can be multiplied but not added.

$$
\begin{array}{r}
2x^2 + xy - 4y^2 \\
3x - 4y \\
\hline
-8x^2y - 4xy^2 + 16y^3 \\
6x^3 + 3x^2y - 12xy^2 \\
\hline
6x^3 - 5x^2y - 16xy^2 + 16y^3
\end{array}
$$

Multiply first row by $-4y$.
Multiply first row by $3x$.
Add columns.

SOME SPECIAL PRODUCTS

The following special product often occurs in mathematics.

$$(a + b)(a - b) = a \cdot a - a \cdot b + b \cdot a - b \cdot b$$
$$= a^2 - ab + ba - b^2$$
$$= a^2 - b^2$$

That is, the product of a sum and difference equals the difference of their squares.

PRODUCT OF A SUM AND DIFFERENCE

For any real numbers a and b,

$$(a + b)(a - b) = a^2 - b^2.$$

EXAMPLE 9   Finding the product of a sum and difference

Multiply.
(a) $(x + 3)(x - 3)$ **(b)** $(5 - 4x^2)(5 + 4x^2)$

TEACHING TIP

Point out that if students do not recognize the product of a sum and difference, they can still multiply the expression by using either FOIL or the general method presented earlier.

Solution **(a)** If we let $a = x$ and $b = 3$, we can apply the rule

$$(a + b)(a - b) = a^2 - b^2.$$

Thus

$$(x + 3)(x - 3) = (x)^2 - (3)^2$$
$$= x^2 - 9.$$

(b) Because $(a - b)(a + b) = a^2 - b^2$, we can multiply as follows.

$$(5 - 4x^2)(5 + 4x^2) = (5)^2 - (4x^2)^2$$
$$= 25 - 16x^4$$

EXAMPLE 10 Finding the product of sums and differences

Multiply each expression.
(a) $4rt(r - 4t)(r + 4t)$ **(b)** $(2z + 5k^4)(2z - 5k^4)$

Solution **(a)** Start by finding the product of the difference and sum and then simplify.

$$4rt(r - 4t)(r + 4t) = 4rt(r^2 - 16t^2)$$
$$= 4rt \cdot r^2 - 4rt \cdot 16t^2$$
$$= 4r^3t - 64rt^3$$

(b) $(2z + 5k^4)(2z - 5k^4) = (2z)^2 - (5k^4)^2$
$$= 4z^2 - 25k^8$$

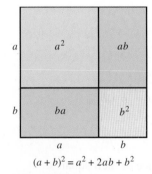

$(a + b)^2 = a^2 + 2ab + b^2$

Figure 5.13

Two other special products involve *squaring a binomial:*

$$(a + b)^2 = (a + b)(a + b)$$
$$= a^2 + ab + ba + b^2$$
$$= a^2 + 2ab + b^2$$

and

$$(a - b)^2 = (a - b)(a - b)$$
$$= a^2 - ab - ba + b^2$$
$$= a^2 - 2ab + b^2.$$

The first product is illustrated geometrically in Figure 5.13, where each side of a square has length $(a + b)$. The area of the square is

$$(a + b)(a + b) = (a + b)^2.$$

This area can also be computed by adding the area of the four small rectangles.

$$a^2 + ab + ba + b^2 = a^2 + 2ab + b^2$$

Thus $(a + b)^2 = a^2 + 2ab + b^2$. *To obtain the middle term, multiply the two terms in the binomial and double the result.*

SQUARE OF A BINOMIAL
For any real numbers a and b,
$(a + b)^2 = a^2 + 2ab + b^2$ and $(a - b)^2 = a^2 - 2ab + b^2.$

EXAMPLE 11 Squaring a binomial

Multiply.
(a) $(x + 5)^2$ **(b)** $(3 - 2x)^2$ **(c)** $(2m^3 + 4n)^2$ **(d)** $\big((2z - 3) + k\big)\big((2z - 3) - k\big)$

Solution **(a)** If we let $a = x$ and $b = 5$, we can apply the formula

$$(a + b)^2 = a^2 + 2ab + b^2.$$

TEACHING TIP

Work several problems like those in Example 11. Students tend to forget the middle term when they square a binomial. See Critical Thinking.

Thus

$$(x + 5)^2 = (x)^2 + 2(x)(5) + (5)^2 \qquad \text{To find the middle term, multiply}$$
$$= x^2 + 10x + 25 \qquad\qquad a \text{ and } b \text{ and double the result.}$$

(b) Applying the formula $(a - b)^2 = a^2 - 2ab + b^2$, we find

$$(3 - 2x)^2 = (3)^2 - 2(3)(2x) + (2x)^2$$
$$= 9 - 12x + 4x^2$$

(c) $(2m^3 + 4n)^2 = (2m^3)^2 + 2(2m^3)(4n) + (4n)^2$
$$= 4m^6 + 16m^3n + 16n^2$$

(d) If $a = 2z - 3$ and $b = k$, we can use $(a + b)(a - b) = a^2 - b^2$.

$$\big((2z - 3) + k\big)\big((2z - 3) - k\big) = (2z - 3)^2 - k^2$$
$$= (2z)^2 - 2(2z)(3) + (3)^2 - k^2$$
$$= 4z^2 - 12z + 9 - k^2$$

Critical Thinking

Suppose that a student is convinced that the expressions

$$(x + 3)^2 \quad \text{and} \quad x^2 + 9$$

are equivalent. How could you convince the student that $(x + 3)^2 \neq x^2 + 9$? Explain your answer.

Note: If you forget these special products, you can still use techniques learned earlier to multiply the polynomials in Examples 9–11. For example,

$$(3 - 2x)^2 = (3 - 2x)(3 - 2x)$$
$$= 3 \cdot 3 - 3 \cdot 2x - 2x \cdot 3 + 2x \cdot 2x$$
$$= 9 - 6x - 6x + 4x^2$$
$$= 9 - 12x + 4x^2.$$

If you let $x = 1$, the two expressions are not equal. Answers may vary.

PUTTING IT ALL TOGETHER

The following table summarizes some important concepts in this section.

Concept	Explanation	Examples
Distributive Properties	For all real numbers a, b, and c, $a(b + c) = ab + ac$ and $a(b - c) = ab - ac.$	$4(3 + a) = 12 + 4a$, $5(x - 1) = 5x - 5$, and $-(b - 5) = -1(b - 5) = -b + 5$

continued on next page

continued from previous page

Multiplying Polynomials	The product of two polynomials may be found by multiplying every term in the first polynomial by every term in the second polynomial.	$(2x + 3)(x - 7) = 2x \cdot x - 2x \cdot 7 + 3 \cdot x - 3 \cdot 7$ $= 2x^2 - 14x + 3x - 21$ $= 2x^2 - 11x - 21$
Properties of Exponents	For nonzero numbers a and b and integers m and n $a^m \cdot a^n = a^{m+n}$, $(a^m)^n = a^{mn}$, and $(ab)^n = a^n b^n$.	$5^2 \cdot 5^6 = 5^8$, $(2^3)^2 = 2^6$, $(5y^4)^2 = 25y^8$, $(a^2 b^3)^4 = a^8 b^{12}$, and $(-4rt^3)^2 = 16r^2 t^6$
Special Products of Binomials	Product of a sum and difference $(a + b)(a - b) = a^2 - b^2$ Squares of binomials $(a + b)^2 = a^2 + 2ab + b^2$ $(a - b)^2 = a^2 - 2ab + b^2$	$(x + 2)(x - 2) = x^2 - 4$, $(7y - 6z^2)(7y + 6z^2) = 49y^2 - 36z^4$, $(x + 4)^2 = x^2 + 8x + 16$, $(x - 4)^2 = x^2 - 8x + 16$, and $(2m - 3n^2)^2 = 4m^2 - 12mn^2 + 9n^4$

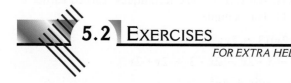

5.2 EXERCISES

FOR EXTRA HELP

CONCEPTS

1. The equation $5(x - 4) = 5x - 20$ illustrates what property?   Distributive

2. Give an example of a monomial, a binomial, and a trinomial. $3x, 2x - 7, x^2 - 3x + 1$; answers may vary.

3. Simplify the expression $x^3 \cdot x^5$. x^8

4. Simplify $(2x)^3$ and $(x^2)^3$. $8x^3$; x^6

5. $(a + b)(a - b) = $ _____. $a^2 - b^2$

6. $(a + b)^2 = $ _____. $a^2 + 2ab + b^2$

MULTIPLYING POLYNOMIALS

Exercises 7–14: Multiply the monomials.

7. $x^4 \cdot x^8$ x^{12}

8. $2x \cdot 4x^3$ $8x^4$

9. $-5y^7 \cdot 4y$ $-20y^8$

10. $3xy^2 \cdot 6x^3 y^2$ $18x^4 y^4$

11. $(-xy)(4x^3 y^5)$ $-4x^4 y^6$

12. $(4z^3)(-5z^2)$ $-20z^5$

13. $(5y^2 z)(4x^2 y z^5)$ $20x^2 y^3 z^6$

14. $x^2(-xy^2)$ $-x^3 y^2$

Exercises 15–26: Multiply.

15. $5(y + 2)$ $5y + 10$

16. $4(y - 7)$ $4y - 28$

17. $-2(5x + 9)$ $-10x - 18$

18. $-3x(5 + x)$ $-15x - 3x^2$

19. $-6y(y - 3)$ $-6y^2 + 18y$

20. $(2y - 5)8y^3$ $16y^4 - 40y^3$

21. $(9 - 4x)3x$ $27x - 12x^2$

22. $-(5 - x^2)$ $-5 + x^2$

23. $-ab(a^2 - b^2)$ $-a^3 b + ab^3$

24. $a^2 b^2(1 - 4ab)$ $a^2 b^2 - 4a^3 b^3$

25. $-5m(n^3 + m)$ $-5mn^3 - 5m^2$

26. $7n(3n - 2m^2)$ $21n^2 - 14m^2 n$

Exercises 27–30: Use the figure to write the product. Find the area of the rectangle if x = 5 inches.

27. $(x + 1)(x + 2)$

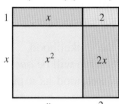

$x^2 + 3x + 2$; 42 in^2

28. $(x + 3)(x + 4)$

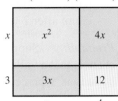

$x^2 + 7x + 12$; 72 in^2

29. $(2x + 1)(x + 1)$

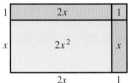

$2x^2 + 3x + 1$; 66 in^2

30. $(2x + 4)(3x + 2)$

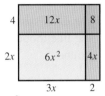

$6x^2 + 16x + 8$; 238 in^2

Exercises 31–34: (Refer to Example 4.) Multiply geometrically and symbolically.

31. $(x + 5)(x + 6)$
$x^2 + 11x + 30$

32. $(x + 1)(x + 4)$
$x^2 + 5x + 4$

33. $(2x + 1)(2x + 1)$
$4x^2 + 4x + 1$

34. $(x + 3)(2x + 4)$
$2x^2 + 10x + 12$

Exercises 35–40: Determine whether the equation is an identity. (Hint: If it is an identity, the equation must be true for all x-values.)

35. $(x - 2)^2 = x^2 - 4$ No

36. $(x + 4)^2 = x^2 + 16$ No

37. $(x + 3)(x - 2) = x^2 + x - 6$ Yes

38. $(5x - 1)^2 = 25x^2 - 10x + 1$ Yes

39. $2z(3z + 1) = 6z^2 + 1$ No

40. $-(z^2 + 4z) = -z^2 + 4z$ No

Exercises 41–58: Multiply the binomials.

41. $(x + 5)(x + 10)$
$x^2 + 15x + 50$

42. $(x - 5)(x - 10)$
$x^2 - 15x + 50$

43. $(x - 3)(x - 4)$
$x^2 - 7x + 12$

44. $(x + 3)(x + 4)$
$x^2 + 7x + 12$

45. $(2z - 1)(z + 2)$
$2z^2 + 3z - 2$

46. $(2z + 1)(z - 2)$
$2z^2 - 3z - 2$

47. $(y + 3)(y - 4)$
$y^2 - y - 12$

48. $(2y + 1)(5y + 1)$
$10y^2 + 7y + 1$

49. $(4x - 3)(4 - 9x)$
$-36x^2 + 43x - 12$

50. $(1 - x)(1 + 2x)$
$-2x^2 + x + 1$

51. $(-2z + 3)(z - 2)$
$-2z^2 + 7z - 6$

52. $(z - 2)(4z + 3)$
$4z^2 - 5z - 6$

53. $\left(z - \frac{1}{2}\right)\left(z + \frac{1}{4}\right)$
$z^2 - \frac{1}{4}z - \frac{1}{8}$

54. $\left(z - \frac{1}{3}\right)\left(z - \frac{1}{6}\right)$
$z^2 - \frac{1}{2}z + \frac{1}{18}$

55. $(x^2 + 1)(2x^2 - 1)$
$2x^4 + x^2 - 1$

56. $(x^2 - 2)(x^2 + 4)$
$x^4 + 2x^2 - 8$

57. $(x + y)(x - 2y)$
$x^2 - xy - 2y^2$

58. $(x^2 + y^2)(x - y)$
$x^3 - x^2y + xy^2 - y^3$

Exercises 59–72: Multiply the polynomials.

59. $4x(x^2 - 2x - 3)$
$4x^3 - 8x^2 - 12x$

60. $2x(3 - x + x^2)$
$2x^3 - 2x^2 + 6x$

61. $-x(x^4 - 3x^2 + 1)$
$-x^5 + 3x^3 - x$

62. $-3m^2(4m^3 + m^2 - 2m)$
$-12m^5 - 3m^4 + 6m^3$

63. $(2n^2 - 4n + 1)(3n^2)$ $6n^4 - 12n^3 + 3n^2$

64. $(x - y + 5)(xy)$ $x^2y - xy^2 + 5xy$

65. $(x + 1)(x^2 + 2x - 3)$ $x^3 + 3x^2 - x - 3$

66. $(2x - 1)(3x^2 - x + 6)$ $6x^3 - 5x^2 + 13x - 6$

67. $z(2 + z)(1 - z - z^2)$ $-z^4 - 3z^3 - z^2 + 2z$

68. $z^2(1 - z)(2 + z)$
$-z^4 - z^3 + 2z^2$

69. $2ab^2(2a^2 - ab + 3b^2)$
$4a^3b^2 - 2a^2b^3 + 6ab^4$

70. $2n(mn^2 + 2n)(3m^2n - 3n)$
$6m^3n^4 + 12m^2n^3 - 6mn^4 - 12n^3$

71. $(2r - 4t)(3r^2 + rt - t^2)$ $6r^3 - 10r^2t - 6rt^2 + 4t^3$

72. $-2(x - y)(x^2 + xy + y^2)$ $-2x^3 + 2y^3$

Exercises 73–82: Simplify the expression, using properties of exponents.

73. $(2^3)^2$ $2^6 = 64$

74. $(x^3)^5$ x^{15}

75. $2(z^3)^6$ $2z^{18}$

76. $(5y)^3$ $125y^3$

77. $(-5x)^2$ $25x^2$

78. $(2y)^4$ $16y^4$

79. $(-2xy^2)^3$ $-8x^3y^6$

80. $(3x^2y^3)^4$ $81x^8y^{12}$

81. $(-4a^2b^3)^2$ $16a^4b^6$

82. $-(5r^3t)^2$ $-25r^6t^2$

Exercises 83–110: Multiply the expressions.

83. $(x - 3)(x + 3)$
$x^2 - 9$

84. $(x + 5)(x - 5)$
$x^2 - 25$

85. $(3 - 2x)(3 + 2x)$
$9 - 4x^2$

86. $(4 - 5x)(4 + 5x)$
$16 - 25x^2$

87. $(x - y)(x + y)$
$x^2 - y^2$

88. $(2x + 2y)(2x - 2y)$
$4x^2 - 4y^2$

89. $(x + 2)^2$
$x^2 + 4x + 4$

90. $(y + 5)^2$ $y^2 + 10y + 25$

91. $(2x + 1)^2$
$4x^2 + 4x + 1$

92. $(3x + 5)^2$
$9x^2 + 30x + 25$

93. $(x - 1)^2$
$x^2 - 2x + 1$

94. $(x - 7)^2$
$x^2 - 14x + 49$

95. $(3x - 2)^2$
$9x^2 - 12x + 4$

96. $(6x - 5)^2$
$36x^2 - 60x + 25$

97. $3x(x + 1)(x - 1)$
$3x^3 - 3x$

98. $-4x(3x - 5)^2$
$-36x^3 + 120x^2 - 100x$

99. $3rt(t - 2r)(t + 2r)$ $3rt^3 - 12r^3t$

100. $5r^2t^2(t - 4)(t + 4)$ $5r^2t^4 - 80r^2t^2$

101. $(a^2 + 2b^2)(a^2 - 2b^2)$ $a^4 - 4b^4$

102. $(2a + 5b^4)(2a - 5b^4)$ $4a^2 - 25b^8$

103. $(3m^3 + 5n^2)^2$ **104.** $(6m + 4n^2)^2$
$9m^6 + 30m^3n^2 + 25n^4$ $36m^2 + 48mn^2 + 16n^4$

105. $(x^3 - 2y^3)^2$ **106.** $(6m - n^4)^2$
$x^6 - 4x^3y^3 + 4y^6$ $36m^2 - 12mn^4 + n^8$

107. $\big((x - 3) + y\big)\big((x - 3) - y\big)$ $x^2 - 6x - y^2 + 9$

108. $\big((2m - 1) + n\big)\big((2m - 1) - n\big)$
$4m^2 - 4m - n^2 + 1$

109. $\big(r - (t + 2)\big)\big(r + (t + 2)\big)$ $r^2 + t^2 - 4t - 4$

110. $\big(y - (z + 1)\big)\big(y + (z + 1)\big)$ $y^2 - z^2 - 2z - 1$

AREA

Exercises 111–114: Express the shaded area in terms of x. Find the area if $x = 20$ feet.

111. $x(x + 4)$; 480 ft²   **112.** $\frac{1}{2}(x + 1)(x - 1)$; 199.5 ft²

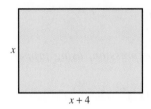
x
$x + 4$

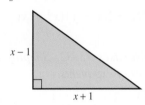
$x - 1$
$x + 1$

113. $(x + 3)^2$; 529 ft²   **114.** $\pi(2x + 1)^2$; $1681\pi \approx 5281$ ft²

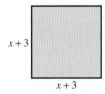
$x + 3$
$x + 3$

$2x + 1$

APPLICATIONS

115. *Interest*   If the annual interest rate r is expressed as a decimal and N dollars are deposited into an account, then the amount in the account after two years is $N(1 + r)^2$.

(a) Multiply this expression. $Nr^2 + 2Nr + N$

(b) Let $r = 0.10$ and $N = 200$. Use both the given expression and the expression you obtained in part (a) to find the amount of money in the account after 2 years. Do your answers agree?
$242; the answers agree.

116. *Probability*   Suppose that the likelihood, or chance, that a volleyball player's serve will be *out* of bounds is x percent. Then the likelihood as a percentage that two consecutive serves are *in* bounds is given by $100(1 - \frac{x}{100})^2$.

(a) Multiply this expression. $\frac{1}{100}x^2 - 2x + 100$

(b) Let $x = 25$. Use both the given expression and the expression you obtained in part (a) to find the likelihood that two consecutive serves are in bounds.   56.25%

117. *Numbers*   Write a polynomial that represents the product of two consecutive integers, where x is the smaller integer. $x(x + 1) = x^2 + x$

118. *Revenue*   Write a polynomial that represents the revenue received from selling $2y + 1$ items at a price of x dollars each. $x(2y + 1) = 2xy + x$

119. *Rectangular Pen*   A rectangular pen has a perimeter of 100 feet. If x represents its width, write a polynomial that gives the area of the pen in terms of x.
$x(50 - x) = 50x - x^2$

120. *Numbers*   Find an expression that represents the product of the sum and difference of two numbers. Let the two numbers be x and y.
$(x + y)(x - y) = x^2 - y^2$

WRITING ABOUT MATHEMATICS

121. Suppose that a student insists that

$$(x + 5)(x + 5)$$

equals $x^2 + 25$. Explain how you could convince the student otherwise.

122. Explain how to multiply two polynomials. Give an example of how your method works. Does your method give the correct result for any two polynomials?

CHECKING BASIC CONCEPTS   SECTIONS 5.1 AND 5.2

1. Combine like terms.
(a) $8x^2 + 4x - 5x^2 + 3x$ $3x^2 + 7x$
(b) $(5x^2 - 3x + 2) - (3x^2 - 5x^3 + 1)$
$5x^3 + 2x^2 - 3x + 1$

2. Write a polynomial that represents the revenue from ticket sales if $x + 120$ tickets are sold for x dollars each. Evaluate the polynomial for $x = 10$ and interpret the result. $x(x + 120)$; 1300; when tickets cost $10 each, the revenue will be $1300.

3. An athlete's heart rate t minutes after exercise is stopped is modeled by

$$f(t) = 2t^2 - 25t + 160,$$

where $0 \le t \le 6$.

(a) What was the initial heart rate when exercise stopped? 160 bpm

(b) What was the heart rate after 4 minutes of rest? 92 bpm

4. Multiply the expressions.

(a) $-5(x - 6)$ $-5x + 30$

(b) $4x^3(3x^2 - 5x)$ $12x^5 - 20x^4$

(c) $(2x - 1)(x + 3)$ $2x^2 + 5x - 3$

5. Multiply the following special products.

(a) $(5x - 6)(5x + 6)$ $25x^2 - 36$

(b) $(3x - 4)^2$ $9x^2 - 24x + 16$

6. Make a sketch of a rectangle whose area illustrates the fact that

$$(x + 2)(x + 4) = x^2 + 6x + 8.^*$$

*Answer on page IA-19

5.3 FACTORING POLYNOMIALS

Common Factors · Factoring and Equations · Factoring by Grouping

INTRODUCTION

If a golf ball is hit upward with a velocity of 88 feet per second, or 60 miles per hour, its height h in feet above the ground after t seconds is modeled by $h(t) = 88t - 16t^2$. To estimate when the ball strikes the ground, we can solve the *polynomial equation*

$$88t - 16t^2 = 0.$$

One method for solving this equation is by factoring (see Example 6). In this section we discuss factoring and how it is used to solve equations.

TEACHING TIP

Point out that one of the main reasons for factoring expressions is to solve equations.

COMMON FACTORS

When factoring a polynomial, we first look for factors that are common to each term in an expression. By applying a distributive property, we can write a polynomial as two factors. For example, each term in $2x^2 + 4x$ contains a factor of $2x$.

$$2x^2 = 2x \cdot x$$

$$4x = 2x \cdot 2$$

Thus the polynomial $2x^2 + 4x$ can be factored as follows.

$$2x^2 + 4x = 2x(x + 2)$$

EXAMPLE 1   Finding common factors

Factor.
(a) $4x^2 + 5x$ **(b)** $12x^3 - 4x^2$ **(c)** $6z^3 - 2z^2 + 4z$ **(d)** $4x^3y^2 + x^2y^3$

Solution   **(a)** Both $4x^2$ and $5x$ contain a common factor of x. That is,

$$4x^2 = x \cdot 4x \quad \text{and} \quad 5x = x \cdot 5.$$

Thus $4x^2 + 5x = x(4x + 5)$.
(b) Both $12x^3$ and $4x^2$ contain a common factor of $4x^2$. That is,

$$12x^3 = 4x^2 \cdot 3x \quad \text{and} \quad 4x^2 = 4x^2 \cdot 1.$$

Thus $12x^3 + 4x^2 = 4x^2(3x + 1)$.
(c) Each of the terms $6z^3$, $2z^2$, and $4z$ contains a common factor of $2z$. That is,

$$6z^3 = 2z \cdot 3z^2 \quad 2z^2 = 2z \cdot z, \quad \text{and} \quad 4z = 2z \cdot 2.$$

Thus $6z^3 - 2z^2 + 4z = 2z(3z^2 - z + 2)$.
(d) Both $4x^3y^2$ and x^2y^3 contain a common factor of x^2y^2. That is,

$$4x^3y^2 = x^2y^2 \cdot 4x \quad \text{and} \quad x^2y^3 = x^2y^2 \cdot y.$$

Thus $4x^3y^2 + x^2y^3 = x^2y^2(4x + y)$.

Many times we factor out the *greatest common factor*. For example, the polynomial $15x^4 - 5x^2$ has a common factor of $5x$. We could write this polynomial as

$$15x^4 - 5x^2 = 5x(3x^3 - x).$$

However, we can also factor out $5x^2$ to obtain

$$15x^4 - 5x^2 = 5x^2(3x^2 - 1).$$

Because $5x^2$ is the common factor with the highest degree and largest coefficient, we say that $5x^2$ is the **greatest common factor** (GCF) of $15x^4 - 5x^2$.

EXAMPLE 2   Factoring greatest common factors

Factor.
(a) $24x^5 + 12x^3 - 6x^2$ **(b)** $6m^3n^2 - 3mn^2 + 9m$ **(c)** $-9x^3 + 6x^2 - 3x$

Solution   **(a)** The GCF of $24x^5$, $12x^3$, and $6x^2$ is $6x^2$.

$$24x^5 = 6x^2 \cdot 4x^3, \quad 12x^3 = 6x^2 \cdot 2x, \quad \text{and} \quad 6x^2 = 6x^2 \cdot 1$$

Thus $24x^5 + 12x^3 - 6x^2 = 6x^2(4x^3 + 2x - 1)$.
(b) The GCF of $6m^3n^2$, $3mn^2$, and $9m$ is $3m$.

$$6m^3n^2 = 3m \cdot 2m^2n^2, \quad 3mn^2 = 3m \cdot n^2, \quad \text{and} \quad 9m = 3m \cdot 3$$

Thus $6m^3n^2 - 3mn^2 + 9m = 3m(2m^2n^2 - n^2 + 3)$.
(c) Rather than factoring out $3x$, we can also factor out $-3x$ and make the leading coefficient of the remaining expression positive.

$$-9x^3 = -3x \cdot 3x^2, \quad 6x^2 = -3x \cdot -2x, \quad \text{and} \quad -3x = -3x \cdot 1$$

Thus $-9x^3 + 6x^2 - 3x = -3x(3x^2 - 2x + 1)$.

FACTORING AND EQUATIONS

To solve equations by using factoring, we use the **zero-product property**. It states that, if the product of two numbers is 0, then at least one of the numbers must equal 0.

TEACHING TIP

Emphasize that to use the zero-product property one side of the equation must equal 0.

ZERO-PRODUCT PROPERTY

For all real numbers a and b, if $ab = 0$, then $a = 0$ or $b = 0$ (or both).

Note: The zero-product property works only for 0. If $ab = 1$, then it does *not* follow that $a = 1$ or $b = 1$. For example, $a = \frac{1}{3}$ and $b = 3$ also satisfy the equation $ab = 1$.

Sometimes factoring needs to be performed on an equation before the zero-product property can be applied. For example, the left side of the equation

$$2x^2 + 4x = 0$$

may be factored to obtain

$$2x(x + 2) = 0.$$

Note that $2x$ times $(x + 2)$ equals 0. By the zero-product property, we must have either

$$2x = 0 \quad \text{or} \quad x + 2 = 0.$$

Solving each equation for x gives

$$x = 0 \quad \text{or} \quad x = -2.$$

The x-values of 0 and -2 are called **zeros** of the polynomial $2x^2 + 4x$ because, when they are substituted in $2x^2 + 4x$, the result is 0.

EXAMPLE 3   Applying the zero-product property

Solve.
(a) $x(x - 1) = 0$ **(b)** $2x(x + 3) = 0$ **(c)** $(2x - 1)(3x + 2) = 0$

Solution   **(a)** The expression $x(x - 1)$ is the product of x and $(x - 1)$. By the zero-product property, either $x = 0$ or $x - 1 = 0$. The solutions are 0 and 1.

(b)
$$2x(x + 3) = 0 \qquad \text{Given equation}$$
$$2x = 0 \quad \text{or} \quad x + 3 = 0 \qquad \text{Zero-product property}$$
$$x = 0 \quad \text{or} \quad x = -3 \qquad \text{Solve each equation.}$$

The solutions are 0 and -3.

(c)
$$(2x - 1)(3x + 2) = 0 \qquad \text{Given equation}$$
$$2x - 1 = 0 \quad \text{or} \quad 3x + 2 = 0 \qquad \text{Zero-product property}$$
$$2x = 1 \quad \text{or} \quad 3x = -2 \qquad \text{Add 1; Subtract 2.}$$
$$x = \frac{1}{2} \quad \text{or} \quad x = -\frac{2}{3} \qquad \text{Divide by 2; divide by 3.}$$

The solutions are $\frac{1}{2}$ and $-\frac{2}{3}$.

EXAMPLE 4   Solving polynomial equations with factoring

Solve each polynomial equation.

(a) $x^2 - x = 0$ **(b)** $4x^2 = 16x$ **(c)** $2x^3 + 2x = 0$

Solution   **(a)** We begin by factoring out the greatest common factor x.

$$x^2 - x = 0 \qquad \text{Given equation}$$
$$x(x - 1) = 0 \qquad \text{Factor out } x.$$
$$x = 0 \quad \text{or} \quad x - 1 = 0 \qquad \text{Zero-product property}$$
$$x = 0 \quad \text{or} \quad x = 1 \qquad \text{Solve.}$$

The solutions are 0 and 1.

(b) Write the equation so that there is a 0 on its right side before applying the zero-product property.

$$4x^2 = 16x \qquad \text{Given equation}$$
$$4x^2 - 16x = 0 \qquad \text{Subtract } 16x \text{ from each side.}$$
$$4x(x - 4) = 0 \qquad \text{Factor out } 4x.$$
$$4x = 0 \quad \text{or} \quad x - 4 = 0 \qquad \text{Zero-product property}$$
$$x = 0 \quad \text{or} \quad x = 4 \qquad \text{Solve.}$$

The solutions are 0 and 4.

(c) Start by factoring out the GCF of $2x$.

$$2x^3 + 2x = 0 \qquad \text{Given equation}$$
$$2x(x^2 + 1) = 0 \qquad \text{Factor out } 2x.$$
$$2x = 0 \quad \text{or} \quad x^2 + 1 = 0 \qquad \text{Zero-product property}$$
$$x = 0 \quad \text{or} \quad x^2 = -1 \qquad \text{Solve.}$$

Because $x^2 \geq 0$ for any x, it follows that no real number can satisfy $x^2 = -1$. The only solution is 0.

In addition to solving equations symbolically, we can also solve them graphically. For example, the solutions to $x^2 - 2x = 0$ can be found by graphing $y = x^2 - 2x$, as shown in Figure 5.14. This graph can be created by plotting the points found in Table 5.5 and then connecting them with a smooth curve. The curve is a ∪-shaped graph called a *parabola* with x-intercepts 0 and 2. These x-intercepts correspond to the solutions to the equation.

TABLE 5.5

$y = x^2 - 2x$

x	y
-1	3
0	0
1	-1
2	0
3	3

Numerical Solution

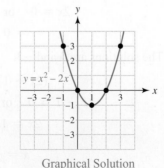

Graphical Solution

Figure 5.14

$$x^2 - 2x = 0$$
$$x(x - 2) = 0$$
$$x = 0 \quad \text{or} \quad x - 2 = 0$$
$$x = 0 \quad \text{or} \quad x = 2$$

Symbolic Solution

Note: Table 5.5 can be thought of as a numerical solution. The x-values of 0 and 2 are solutions to $x^2 - 2x = 0$. They are also zeros of $x^2 - 2x$ and x-intercepts for the graph of $y = x^2 - 2x$.

These concepts are generalized in the following.

≡ MAKING CONNECTIONS ≡

Zeros, x-Intercepts, and Solutions

The following statements are *equivalent*, where k is a real number and $P(x)$ is a polynomial.

1. A *zero* of a polynomial $P(x)$ is k.
2. An *x-intercept* on the graph of $y = P(x)$ is k.
3. A *solution* to the equation $P(x) = 0$ is k.

In the next example we solve an equation graphically and symbolically.

EXAMPLE 5   Solving an equation

Solve the equation $4x - x^2 = 0$ graphically and symbolically.

Solution   *Graphical Solution*   Make a table of values for $y = 4x - x^2$. Plot the points given in Table 5.6 and sketch a curve through them, as shown in Figure 5.15. The curve is a ∩-shaped graph, or parabola, with x-intercepts 0 and 4, which are the solutions to the given equation.

TABLE 5.6

x	y
-1	-5
0	0
1	3
2	4
3	3
4	0
5	-5

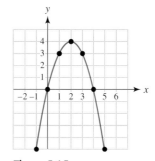

Figure 5.15

Symbolic Solution   Start by factoring the left side of the equation.

$$4x - x^2 = 0 \qquad \text{Given equation}$$
$$x(4 - x) = 0 \qquad \text{Factor out } x.$$
$$x = 0 \quad \text{or} \quad 4 - x = 0 \qquad \text{Zero-product property}$$
$$x = 0 \quad \text{or} \quad x = 4 \qquad \text{Solve each equation.}$$

Note that the graphical solutions agree with the symbolic solutions.

GRAPH OF $y = ax^2 + bx + c$

The graph of $y = ax^2 + bx + c$ is a **parabola**. It is a U-shaped graph if $a > 0$ and a ∩-shaped graph if $a < 0$. This graph can have zero, one, or two x-intercepts.

Technology Note: *Locating x-intercepts*

Many calculators have the capability to locate an x-intercept or zero. This method is illustrated in the accompanying figures, where the solution 2 to the equation $x^2 - 4 = 0$ is found.

Calculator Help

To find an x-intercept or zero, see the Appendix (page AP-10).

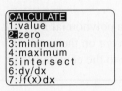

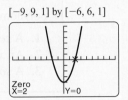

$[-9, 9, 1]$ by $[-6, 6, 1]$

In the next example we use factoring to estimate when a golf ball strikes the ground.

EXAMPLE 6 Modeling the flight of a golf ball

If a golf ball is hit upward at 88 feet per second, or 60 miles per hour, its height h in feet after t seconds is modeled by $h(t) = 88t - 16t^2$.
(a) Use factoring to determine when the golf ball strikes the ground.
(b) Solve part (a) graphically and numerically.

Solution **(a)** *Symbolic Solution* The golf ball strikes the ground when its height is 0.

$$88t - 16t^2 = 0 \qquad h(t) = 0$$

$$8t(11 - 2t) = 0 \qquad \text{Factor out } 8t.$$

$$8t = 0 \quad \text{or} \quad 11 - 2t = 0 \qquad \text{Zero-product property}$$

$$t = 0 \quad \text{or} \quad t = \frac{11}{2} \qquad \text{Solve for } t.$$

The ball strikes the ground after $\frac{11}{2}$, or 5.5 seconds. The solution of $t = 0$ is not used in this problem because it corresponds to the time that the ball is hit.

(b) *Graphical and Numerical Solutions* Graph $Y_1 = 88X - 16X^2$. Using a graphing calculator to find an x-intercept (or zero) yields the solution, 5.5. See Figure 5.16(a). Numerical support is shown in Figure 5.16(b), where $y_1 = 0$ when $x = 5.5$.

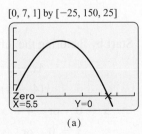

$[0, 7, 1]$ by $[-25, 150, 25]$

(a)

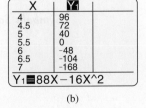

(b)

Figure 5.16

FACTORING BY GROUPING

Factoring by grouping is a technique that makes use of the associative and distributive properties. The next example illustrates the first step in this factoring technique.

EXAMPLE 7 Factoring out binomials

Factor.
(a) $2x(x + 1) + 3(x + 1)$ (b) $2x^2(3x - 2) - x(3x - 2)$

Solution (a) Both terms in the expression $2x(x + 1) + 3(x + 1)$ contain the binomial $(x + 1)$. Therefore the distributive property can be used to factor out this expression.
$$2x(x + 1) + 3(x + 1) = (2x + 3)(x + 1)$$

(b) Both terms in the expression $2x^2(3x - 2) - x(3x - 2)$ contain the binomial $(3x - 2)$. Therefore the distributive property can be used to factor this expression.
$$2x^2(3x - 2) - x(3x - 2) = (2x^2 - x)(3x - 2)$$

Now consider the polynomial
$$3t^3 + 6t^2 + 2t + 4.$$

We can factor this polynomial by first grouping it into two binomials.

$(3t^3 + 6t^2) + (2t + 4)$ Associative property

$3t^2(t + 2) + 2(t + 2)$ Factor out common factors.

$(3t^2 + 2)(t + 2)$ Factor out $(t + 2)$.

The following steps summarize factoring by grouping.

FACTORING BY GROUPING

STEP 1 Use parentheses to group the terms into binomials with common factors. Begin by writing the expression with a plus sign between the binomials.

STEP 2 Factor out the common factor in each binomial.

STEP 3 Factor out the common binomial. If there is no common binomial, try a different grouping.

EXAMPLE 8 Factoring by grouping

Factor each polynomial.
(a) $x^3 - 2x^2 + 3x - 6$ (b) $12x^3 - 9x^2 - 8x + 6$ (c) $2x - 2y + ax - ay$

Solution (a) $x^3 - 2x^2 + 3x - 6 = (x^3 - 2x^2) + (3x - 6)$ Group terms.

$= x^2(x - 2) + 3(x - 2)$ Factor out x^2 and 3.

$= (x^2 + 3)(x - 2)$ Factor out $x - 2$.

(b) $12x^3 - 9x^2 - 8x + 6 = (12x^3 - 9x^2) + (-8x + 6)$ Write with a plus sign between binomials.

$= 3x^2(4x - 3) - 2(4x - 3)$ Factor out $3x^2$ and -2.

$= (3x^2 - 2)(4x - 3)$ Factor out $4x - 3$.

(c) $2x - 2y + ax - ay = (2x - 2y) + (ax - ay)$ Group terms.
$$= 2(x - y) + a(x - y)$$ Factor out 2 and a.
$$= (2 + a)(x - y)$$ Factor out $x - y$.

5.3 PUTTING IT ALL TOGETHER

There are several different ways to solve an equation, including the use of symbolic, graphical, and numerical techniques. Factoring may be used to solve an equation symbolically. The following table summarizes topics covered in this section.

Concept	Explanation	Examples
Greatest Common Factor (GCF)	We can sometimes factor the greatest common factor out of a polynomial.	$3x^4 - 9x^3 + 12x^2 = 3x^2(x^2 - 3x + 4)$ The terms in $(x^2 - 3x + 4)$ have no obvious common factor, so $3x^2$ is called the *greatest common factor* of $3x^4 - 9x^3 + 12x^2$.
Zero-Product Property	If the product of two numbers is 0, then at least one of the numbers equals 0.	$xy = 0$ implies that $x = 0$ or $y = 0$. $x(2x + 1) = 0$ implies that $x = 0$ or $2x + 1 = 0$.
Factoring and Equations	Factoring may be used to solve equations.	$$6x^2 - 9x = 0$$ $$3x(2x - 3) = 0$$ $$3x = 0 \quad \text{or} \quad 2x - 3 = 0$$ $$x = 0 \quad \text{or} \quad x = \frac{3}{2}$$
Factoring by Grouping	Factoring by grouping is a method that can be used to factor four terms into a product of two binomials. It involves the associative and distributive properties.	$$4x^3 + 6x^2 + 10x + 15 = (4x^3 + 6x^2) + (10x + 15)$$ $$= 2x^2(2x + 3) + 5(2x + 3)$$ $$= (2x^2 + 5)(2x + 3)$$
Zeros, x-Intercepts, and Solutions	An x-intercept on the graph of $y = P(x)$ corresponds to a zero of $P(x)$ and to a solution to $P(x) = 0$.	*(graph of $y = x^2 - x$)* x-Intercepts: 0, 1 Zeros of $x^2 - x$: 0, 1 Solutions to $x^2 - x = 0$: 0, 1

5.3 EXERCISES

FOR EXTRA HELP

 Student's Solutions Manual

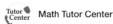 InterAct Math

 MathXL

 MyMathLab

Math Tutor Center

Digital Video Tutor
CD 4 Videotape 6

CONCEPTS

1. Give one reason for factoring expressions in mathematics.   To solve equations

2. If $x(x - 3) = 0$, what can be said about x or $(x - 3)$? What property did you use?
Either $x = 0$ or $x - 3 = 0$; zero-product property

3. Is $2x$ a common factor of $(4x^3 - 12x^2)$? Explain.
Yes, because $2x$ is a factor of each term.

4. Is $2x$ the greatest common factor (GCF) of $(4x^3 - 12x^2)$? Explain.
No, because $4x^2$ is the greatest common factor.

5. If $ab = 2$, does it follow that either $a = 2$ or $b = 2$? Explain.   No, because $\frac{1}{2}(4) = 2$ and $\frac{1}{2} \neq 2$ and $4 \neq 2$.

6. If $xy = 0$, does it follow that either $x = 0$ or $y = 0$? Explain.   Yes, by the zero-product property

FACTORING AND EQUATIONS

Exercises 7–34: Factor out the greatest common factor.

7. $10x - 15$ $5(2x - 3)$

8. $32 - 16x$ $16(2 - x)$

9. $4x + 6y$ $2(2x + 3y)$

10. $50a + 20b$ $10(5a + 2b)$

11. $9r - 15t$ $3(3r - 5t)$

12. $16m - 24n$ $8(2m - 3n)$

13. $2x^3 - 5x$ $x(2x^2 - 5)$

14. $3y - 9y^2$ $3y(1 - 3y)$

15. $8a^3 + 10a$
$2a(4a^2 + 5)$

16. $20b^3 + 25b^2$
$5b^2(4b + 5)$

17. $6r^3 - 18r^5$
$6r^3(1 - 3r^2)$

18. $7n^2 - 21n^4$
$7n^2(1 - 3n^2)$

19. $8x^3 - 4x^2 + 16x$
$4x(2x^2 - x + 4)$

20. $5x^3 - x^2 + 4x$
$x(5x^2 - x + 4)$

21. $9n^4 - 6n^2 + 3n$
$3n(3n^3 - 2n + 1)$

22. $5n^4 + 10n^2 - 25n$
$5n(n^3 + 2n - 5)$

23. $6t^6 - 4t^4 + 2t^2$
$2t^2(3t^4 - 2t^2 + 1)$

24. $15t^6 + 25t^4 - 20t^2$
$5t^2(3t^4 + 5t^2 - 4)$

25. $5x^2y^2 - 15x^2y^3$
$5x^2y^2(1 - 3y)$

26. $21xy + 14x^3y^3$
$7xy(3 + 2x^2y^2)$

27. $6a^3b^2 - 15a^2b^3$
$3a^2b^2(2a - 5b)$

28. $45a^2b + 30a^3b^2$
$15a^2b(3 + 2ab)$

29. $18mn^2 + 12m^2n^3$
$6mn^2(3 + 2mn)$

30. $24m^2n^3 - 36m^3n^2$
$12m^2n^2(2n - 3m)$

31. $15x^2y + 10xy - 25x^2y^2$ $5xy(3x + 2 - 5xy)$

32. $14a^3b^2 - 21a^2b^2 + 35a^2b$ $7a^2b(2ab - 3b + 5)$

33. $4a^2 - 2ab + 6ab^2$
$2a(2a - b + 3b^2)$

34. $5a^2 + 10a^2b^2 - 15ab$
$5a(a + 2ab^2 - 3b)$

Exercises 35–40: (Refer to Example 2(c).) Factor out the negative of the greatest common factor.

35. $-2x^2 + 4x - 6$
$-2(x^2 - 2x + 3)$

36. $-7x^5 - 21x^3 - 14x^2$
$-7x^2(x^3 + 3x + 2)$

37. $-8z^4 - 16z^3$
$-8z^3(z + 2)$

38. $-8z^5 - 24z^4$
$-8z^4(z + 3)$

39. $-4m^2n^3 - 6mn^2 - 8mn$ $-2mn(2mn^2 + 3n + 4)$

40. $-13m^4n^4 - 13m^3n^3 + 26m^2n^2$
$-13m^2n^2(m^2n^2 + mn - 2)$

Exercises 41–50: Use the zero-product property to solve the equation.

41. $mn = 0$
$m = 0$ or $n = 0$

42. $xyz = 0$
$x = 0$ or $y = 0$ or $z = 0$

43. $3z(z + 4) = 0$
$z = 0$ or $z = -4$

44. $2z(z - 1) = 0$
$z = 0$ or $z = 1$

45. $(r - 1)(r + 3) = 0$
$r = 1$ or $r = -3$

46. $(2r + 3)(r - 5) = 0$
$r = -\frac{3}{2}$ or $r = 5$

47. $(x + 2)(3x - 1) = 0$ $x = -2$ or $x = \frac{1}{3}$

48. $(4y - 3)(2y + 1) = 0$ $y = \frac{3}{4}$ or $y = -\frac{1}{2}$

49. $3x(y - 6) = 0$
$x = 0$ or $y = 6$

50. $7m(3n + 1) = 0$
$m = 0$ or $n = -\frac{1}{3}$

Exercises 51–56: Use the graph of $y = P(x)$ to do the following.

(a) Find the x-intercepts.

(b) Solve the equation $P(x) = 0$.

(c) What are the zeros of $P(x)$?

51.
(a) $-3, 0$
(b) $-3, 0$
(c) $-3, 0$

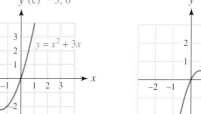

$y = x^2 + 3x$

52.
(a) $0, 1$
(b) $0, 1$
(c) $0, 1$

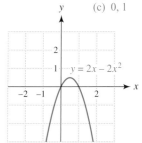

$y = 2x - 2x^2$

53.
(a) 0, 2
(b) 0, 2
(c) 0, 2

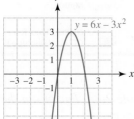

54.
(a) −2, 0
(b) −2, 0
(c) −2, 0

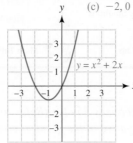

55.
(a) −1, 1
(b) −1, 1
(c) −1, 1

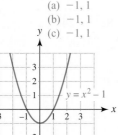

56.
(a) −2, 2
(b) −2, 2
(c) −2, 2

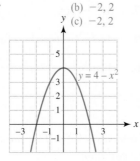

79. $x^3 + 3x^2 + 2x + 6$ $(x + 3)(x^2 + 2)$

80. $4x^3 + 3x^2 + 8x + 6$ $(4x + 3)(x^2 + 2)$

81. $6x^3 - 4x^2 + 9x - 6$ $(3x - 2)(2x^2 + 3)$

82. $x^3 - 3x^2 - 5x + 15$ $(x - 3)(x^2 - 5)$

83. $2x^3 - 3x^2 + 2x - 3$ $(x^2 + 1)(2x - 3)$

84. $8x^3 - 2x^2 + 12x - 3$ $(2x^2 + 3)(4x - 1)$

85. $x^3 - 7x^2 - 3x + 21$ $(x^2 - 3)(x - 7)$

86. $6x^3 - 15x^2 - 4x + 10$ $(3x^2 - 2)(2x - 5)$

87. $3x^3 - 15x^2 + 5x - 25$ $(x - 5)(3x^2 + 5)$

88. $2x^4 - x^3 + 4x - 2$ **89.** $xy + x + 3y + 3$
$(2x - 1)(x^3 + 2)$ $(y + 1)(x + 3)$

90. $ax + bx - ay - by$ **91.** $ab - 3a + 2b - 6$
$(a + b)(x - y)$ $(a + 2)(b - 3)$

92. $2ax - 6bx - ay + 3by$ $(2x - y)(a - 3b)$

Applications

93. *Flight of a Golf Ball*   (Refer to Example 6.) If a golf ball is hit upward at a velocity of 128 feet per second (about 87 mph), its height h in feet above the ground can be modeled by

$$h(t) = -16t^2 + 128t,$$

where t is in seconds.
(a) Use factoring to determine when the golf ball strikes the ground.   After 8 sec
(b) Use the graph of $y = h(t)$ to estimate when the golf ball strikes the ground.   After 8 sec

Exercises 57–62: Solve the equation graphically. Check your answer.

57. $x^2 - 2x = 0$ 0, 2   **58.** $x^2 + x = 0$ −1, 0

59. $x - x^2 = 0$ 0, 1   **60.** $3x - x^2 = 0$ 0, 3

61. $x^2 + 4x = 0$ −4, 0   **62.** $x^2 - 4x = 0$ 0, 4

Exercises 63–74: Solve the equation.

63. $x^2 - x = 0$ 0, 1   **64.** $4x - 2x^2 = 0$ 0, 2

65. $5x^2 - x = 0$ $0, \frac{1}{5}$ **66.** $4x^2 + 3x = 0$ $0, -\frac{3}{4}$

67. $10x^2 + 5x = 0$ $-\frac{1}{2}, 0$ **68.** $6x - 12x^2 = 0$ $0, \frac{1}{2}$

69. $15x^2 = 10x$ $0, \frac{2}{3}$ **70.** $4x = 8x^2$ $0, \frac{1}{2}$

71. $25x = 10x^2$ $0, \frac{5}{2}$ **72.** $34x^2 = 51x$ $0, \frac{3}{2}$

73. $32x^4 - 16x^3 = 0$ **74.** $45x^4 - 30x^3 = 0$ $0, \frac{2}{3}$
$0, \frac{1}{2}$

Factoring by Grouping

Exercises 75–92: Factor the polynomial.

75. $2x(x + 2) + 4(x + 2)$ $(2x + 4)(x + 2)$

76. $5(x - 1) - 2x(x - 1)$ $(5 - 2x)(x - 1)$

77. $(x - 5)x^2 - (x - 5)x$ $(x - 5)(x^2 - x)$

78. $7x(x - 1) - 3(x - 1)$ $(7x - 3)(x - 1)$

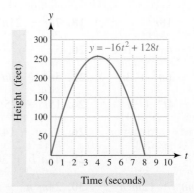

(c) Make a table of h, starting at $t = 3$ and incrementing by 1. Does the table support your answer in part (a)? *   Yes
(d) Use the table and graph of h to determine the maximum height of the golf ball. At what value of t did this occur?   256 ft; 4 sec

*Answer on page IA-19

94. *Flight of a Golf Ball* The height in feet reached by a golf ball after t seconds is given by

$$h(t) = -16t^2 + 96t.$$

After how many seconds does the golf ball strike the ground? After 6 sec

95. *Geometry* The area of a rectangle with width y and length 8 is $A = 8y$. A circle with radius y has area $A = \pi y^2$. For what positive value of y are these two areas equal? $\frac{8}{\pi}$

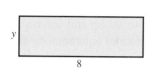 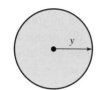

96. *U.S. AIDS Cases* The cumulative number of AIDS cases in thousands can be modeled by the function $f(x) = 4.1x^2 - 25x + 46$, where $x = 4$ corresponds to 1984, $x = 5$ to 1985, and so on. Estimate either graphically or numerically when the cumulative number of AIDS cases first reached 500 thousand. 1994

97. *Space Shuttle* Approximate altitudes y in feet reached by the space shuttle *Endeavour*, t seconds after liftoff, are shown in the table.

t (seconds)	20	30	40
y (feet)	4500	10,000	18,000

t (seconds)	50	60
y (feet)	28,000	40,000

Source: NASA.

The function models the data quite well.

(a) The function $f(t) = 11t^2 + 6t$ models the data, where $y = f(t)$. Make a table of f, starting at $t = 20$ and incrementing by 10. Comment on how well f models the data. *

97.(c) $-\frac{6}{11}$, 0; the shuttle is on the ground at time $t = 0$; the value $t = -\frac{6}{11}$ has no physical meaning.

(b) Predict the altitude reached by the shuttle 70 seconds after liftoff. Round your answer to the nearest thousand feet. About 54,000 ft

(c) Solve the equation $11t^2 + 6t = 0$. Do your results have any physical meaning? Explain.

98. *Average Temperature* Suppose that the monthly average temperatures T in degrees Fahrenheit for a city are given by $T(x) = 24x - 2x^2$, where $x = 1$ corresponds to January, $x = 2$ to February, and so on.

(a) What is the monthly average temperature in October? $40°$F

(b) Use factoring to solve the equation $24x - 2x^2 = 0$. Do your results have any physical meaning?

(c) Support your results in part (b) either graphically or numerically.

99. *Area* Suppose that the area of a rectangular room is 216 square feet. Is it possible to determine the dimensions of the room from this information? Explain. No; there are many possibilities, such as 9×24 and 8×27.

100. *Area* Suppose that the area of a rectangular room is $4x^2 + 8x$ square feet. If the length of the room is $4x$, is it possible to determine the width of the room in terms of x? Explain. Yes; the width is $x + 2$.

WRITING ABOUT MATHEMATICS

101. A student solves the following equation *incorrectly* by factoring.

$$x^2 - 5x \overset{?}{=} 1$$
$$x(x - 5) \overset{?}{=} 1$$
$$x \overset{?}{=} 1 \quad \text{or} \quad x - 5 \overset{?}{=} 1$$
$$x \overset{?}{=} 1 \quad \text{or} \quad x \overset{?}{=} 6$$

What is the student's mistake? Explain.

102. Explain how you would solve the equation $ax^2 + bx = 0$ symbolically and graphically.

98.(b),(c) $x = 0$ or $x = 12$; both correspond to December when the monthly average temperature is $0°$F.

*Answer on page IA-19

5.4 FACTORING TRINOMIALS

Factoring $x^2 + bx + c$ · Factoring Trinomials by Grouping · Factoring Trinomials with FOIL · Factoring with Graphs and Tables

INTRODUCTION

Items usually sell better at a lower price. At a higher price fewer items are sold, but more money is made on each item. For example, suppose that, if concert tickets are priced at $100 no one will buy a ticket, but for each $1 reduction in price 100 additional tickets will be sold. If the promoters of the concert need to gross $240,000 from ticket sales, what ticket price accomplishes this goal? To solve this problem we need to set up and solve a polynomial equation. In this section we describe how to solve polynomial equations by factoring trinomials in the form $x^2 + bx + c$ and $ax^2 + bx + c$.

FACTORING $x^2 + bx + c$

The product $(x + 3)(x + 4)$ can be found as follows.

$$(x + 3)(x + 4) = x^2 + 4x + 3x + 12$$
$$= x^2 + 7x + 12$$

The middle term $7x$ is found by calculating the sum $4x + 3x$, and the last term is found by calculating the product $3 \cdot 4 = 12$

When we factor polynomials, we are *reversing* the process of multiplication. To factor $x^2 + 7x + 12$ we must find m and n that satisfy

$$x^2 + 7x + 12 = (x + m)(x + n).$$

Because

$$(x + m)(x + n) = x^2 + (m + n)x + mn,$$

it follows that $mn = 12$ and $m + n = 7$. To determine m and n we list factors of 12 and their sum, as shown in Table 5.7.

TABLE 5.7   Factor Pairs for 12

Factors	1, 12	2, 6	3, 4
Sum	9	8	7

Because $3 \cdot 4 = 12$ and $3 + 4 = 7$, we can write the factored form as

$$x^2 + 7x + 12 = (x + 3)(x + 4).$$

This result can always be checked by multiplying the two binomials.

$$(x + 3)(x + 4) = x^2 + 7x + 12$$

$$\begin{array}{c} 3x \\ +4x \\ \hline 7x \end{array} \quad \longleftarrow \text{ The middle term checks.}$$

FACTORING $x^2 + bx + c$

To factor the trinomial $x^2 + bx + c$, find integers m and n that satisfy

$$m \cdot n = c \quad \text{and} \quad m + n = b.$$

Then $x^2 + bx + c = (x + m)(x + n)$.

EXAMPLE 1   Factoring the form $x^2 + bx + c$

Factor each trinomial.
(a) $x^2 + 10x + 16$ **(b)** $x^2 - 5x - 24$ **(c)** $x^2 + 7x - 30$

Solution   **(a)** We need to find a factor pair for 16 whose sum is 10. From Table 5.8 the required factor pair is $m = 2$ and $n = 8$. Thus

$$x^2 + 10x + 16 = (x + 2)(x + 8).$$

TABLE 5.8   **Factor Pairs for 16**

Factors	1, 16	2, 8	4, 4
Sum	17	10	8

(b) Factors of -24 whose sum equals -5 are **3** and **-8**. Thus

$$x^2 - 5x - 24 = (x + 3)(x - 8).$$

(c) Factors of -30 whose sum equals 7 are **-3** and **10**. Thus

$$x^2 + 7x - 30 = (x - 3)(x + 10).$$

EXAMPLE 2   Removing common factors first

Factor completely.
(a) $3x^2 + 15x + 18$ **(b)** $5x^3 + 5x^2 - 60x$

Solution   **(a)** If we first factor out the common factor of 3, the resulting trinomial is easier to factor.

$$3x^2 + 15x + 18 = 3(x^2 + 5x + 6)$$

TEACHING TIP

Remind students to "keep" the common factor of 3 because it is part of the complete factored form.

Now we find m and n such that $mn = 6$ and $m + n = 5$. These numbers are 2 and 3.

$$3x^2 + 15x + 18 = 3(x^2 + 5x + 6)$$
$$= 3(x + 2)(x + 3)$$

(b) First, we factor out the common factor of $5x$. Then we factor the resulting trinomial.

$$5x^3 + 5x^2 - 60x = 5x(x^2 + x - 12)$$
$$= 5x(x - 3)(x + 4)$$

Factoring may be used to solve the problem presented in the introduction to this section. To do so we let x be the number of dollars that the price of a ticket is reduced below \$100. Then $100 - x$ represents the price of a ticket. For each \$1 reduction in price, 100 additional tickets will be sold, so the number of tickets sold is given by $100x$. Because the number of tickets sold times the price of each ticket equals the total sales, we need to solve the equation

$$100x(100 - x) = 240,000$$

to determine when gross sales will reach \$240,000. Note that we cannot immediately apply the zero-product property to this equation because the product of $100x$ and $(100 - x)$ does not equal 0.

EXAMPLE 3   **Determining ticket cost**

Solve the equation $100x(100 - x) = 240,000$ symbolically. What should be the price of the tickets and how many tickets will be sold? Support your answer graphically.

Solution   **Symbolic Solution**   Begin by applying the distributive property.

$100x(100 - x) = 240,000$	Given equation
$10,000x - 100x^2 = 240,000$	Distributive property
$-100x^2 + 10,000x - 240,000 = 0$	Subtract 240,000.
$x^2 - 100x + 2400 = 0$	Divide each term by -100.
$(x - 40)(x - 60) = 0$	Factor.
$x = 40 \quad \text{or} \quad x = 60$	Solve.

If $x = 40$, the price is $100 - 40 = \$60$ per ticket. If $x = 60$, the price is $100 - 60 = \$40$. If $x = 40$, then $100 \cdot 40 = 4000$ tickets are sold at \$60 each. If $x = 60$, then $100 \cdot 60 = 6000$ tickets are sold at \$40 each. In either case, tickets sales are \$240,000.

Graphical Solution   To provide graphical support let $Y_1 = 100X(100 - X)$ and $Y_2 = 240000$. Their graphs intersect in Figure 5.17 at $x = 40$ and $x = 60$, which agrees with the symbolic solution. These graphs also illustrate how revenue increases to a maximum value and then decreases as the price of the tickets continues to increase from \$0 to \$100.

Calculator Help

To find a point of intersection, see the Appendix (page AP-7).

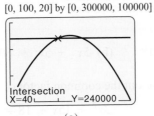

[0, 100, 20] by [0, 300000, 100000]   (a)   [0, 100, 20] by [0, 300000, 100000]   (b)

Intersection X=40 Y=240000   Intersection X=60 Y=240000

Figure 5.17

Critical Thinking

In Example 3 what price will maximize the revenue received from ticket sales? (*Hint:* Graph $y = 100x(100 - x)$.)

\$50 per ticket

FACTORING TRINOMIALS BY GROUPING

In this subsection we use grouping to factor trinomials in the form $ax^2 + bx + c$ with $a \neq 1$. For example, one way to factor $3x^2 + 14x + 8$ is to find two numbers m and n such that $mn = 3 \cdot 8 = 24$ and $m + n = 14$. Because $2 \cdot 12 = 24$ and $2 + 12 = 14$, $m = 2$ and $n = 12$. Using grouping, we can now factor this trinomial.

$3x^2 + 14x + 8 = 3x^2 + 2x + 12x + 8$	Write $14x$ as $2x + 12x$.
$= (3x^2 + 2x) + (12x + 8)$	Associative property
$= x(3x + 2) + 4(3x + 2)$	Distributive property
$= (x + 4)(3x + 2)$	Distributive property

FACTORING $ax^2 + bx + c$ BY GROUPING

To factor $ax^2 + bx + c$ perform the following steps. (Assume that a, b, and c have no factor in common.)

1. Find numbers m and n such that $mn = ac$ and $m + n = b$. This step may require trial and error.
2. Write the trinomial as $ax^2 + mx + nx + c$.
3. Use grouping to factor this expression as two binomials.

EXAMPLE 4   Factoring $ax^2 + bx + c$ by grouping

Factor each trinomial.
  (a) $3x^2 + 17x + 10$ **(b)** $12y^2 + 5y - 3$ **(c)** $6r^2 - 19r + 10$

Solution   **(a)** In this trinomial $a = 3$, $b = 17$, and $c = 10$. Because $mn = ac$ and $m + n = b$, the numbers m and n satisfy $mn = 30$ and $m + n = 17$. Thus $m = \mathbf{2}$ and $n = \mathbf{15}$.

$$
\begin{aligned}
3x^2 + 17x + 10 &= 3x^2 + \mathbf{2}x + \mathbf{15}x + 10 &&\text{Write } 17x \text{ as } 2x + 15x. \\
&= (3x^2 + 2x) + (15x + 10) &&\text{Associative property} \\
&= x(3x + 2) + 5(3x + 2) &&\text{Factor out } x \text{ and } 5. \\
&= (x + 5)(3x + 2) &&\text{Distributive property}
\end{aligned}
$$

(b) In this trinomial $a = 12$, $b = 5$, and $c = -3$. Because $mn = ac$ and $m + n = b$, the numbers m and n satisfy $mn = -36$ and $m + n = 5$. Thus $m = 9$ and $n = -4$.

$$
\begin{aligned}
12y^2 + 5y - 3 &= 12y^2 + 9y - 4y - 3 &&\text{Write } 5y \text{ as } 9y - 4y. \\
&= (12y^2 + 9y) + (-4y - 3) &&\text{Associative property} \\
&= 3y(4y + 3) - 1(4y + 3) &&\text{Factor out } 3y \text{ and } -1. \\
&= (3y - 1)(4y + 3) &&\text{Distributive property}
\end{aligned}
$$

(c) In this trinomial $a = 6$, $b = -19$, and $c = 10$. Because $mn = ac$ and $m + n = b$, the numbers m and n satisfy $mn = 60$ and $m + n = -19$. Thus $m = -4$ and $n = -15$.

$$
\begin{aligned}
6r^2 - 19r + 10 &= 6r^2 - 4r - 15r + 10 &&\text{Write } -19r \text{ as } -4r - 15r. \\
&= (6r^2 - 4r) + (-15r + 10) &&\text{Associative property} \\
&= 2r(3r - 2) - 5(3r - 2) &&\text{Factor out } 2r \text{ and } -5. \\
&= (2r - 5)(3r - 2) &&\text{Distributive property}
\end{aligned}
$$

FACTORING TRINOMIALS WITH FOIL

An alternative to factoring trinomials by grouping is to use FOIL in reverse. For example, the factors of $3x^2 + 7x + 2$ are two binomials.

$$3x^2 + 7x + 2 \stackrel{?}{=} (\underline{\quad} + \underline{\quad})(\underline{\quad} + \underline{\quad})$$

The expressions to be placed in the four blanks are yet to be found. By the FOIL method, we know that the product of the first terms is $3x^2$. Because $3x^2 = 3x \cdot x$, we can write

$$3x^2 + 7x + 2 \stackrel{?}{=} (\underline{\ 3x\ } + \underline{\quad})(\underline{\ x\ } + \underline{\quad}).$$

The product of the last terms in each binomial must equal 2. Because $2 = 1 \cdot 2$, we can put the 1 and 2 in the blanks, but we must be sure to place them correctly so that the product of the *outside terms* plus the product of the *inside terms* equals $7x$.

$$(3x + 1)(x + 2) = 3x^2 + 7x + 2$$

$$\underline{}\,1x\,\underline{}$$
$$+6x$$
$$\overline{7x} \quad \longleftarrow \text{ Middle term checks.}$$

If we had interchanged the 1 and 2, we would have obtained an incorrect result.

$$(3x + 2)(x + 1) = 3x^2 + 5x + 2$$

$$2x$$
$$+3x$$
$$\overline{5x} \quad \longleftarrow \text{ Middle term is } not \; 7x.$$

In the next example we factor expressions of the form $ax^2 + bx + c$, where $a \neq 1$. In this situation, we may need to *guess and check* or use *trial and error* a few times before finding the correct factors.

EXAMPLE 5   Factoring the form $ax^2 + bx + c$

Factor each trinomial.
(a) $2x^2 + 9x + 4$ **(b)** $6x^2 - x - 2$ **(c)** $4x^3 - 14x^2 + 6x$

Solution   **(a)** The factors of $2x^2$ are $2x$ and x, so we begin by writing

$$2x^2 + 9x + 4 \stackrel{?}{=} (2x + \underline{})(x + \underline{}).$$

The factors of the last term, 4, are either 1 and 4 or 2 and 2. Selecting the factors 2 and 2 results in a middle term of $6x$ rather than $9x$.

$$(2x + 2)(x + 2) = 2x^2 + 6x + 4$$

$$2x$$
$$+4x$$
$$\overline{6x} \quad \longleftarrow \text{ Middle term is } not \; 9x.$$

Next we try the factors 1 and 4.

$$(2x + 4)(x + 1) = 2x^2 + 6x + 4$$

$$4x$$
$$+2x$$
$$\overline{6x} \quad \longleftarrow \text{ Middle term is } not \; 9x.$$

Again we obtain the wrong middle term. By interchanging the 1 and 4, we find the correct factorization.

$$(2x + 1)(x + 4) = 2x^2 + 9x + 4$$

$$1x$$
$$+8x$$
$$\overline{9x} \quad \longleftarrow \text{ Middle term is } 9x.$$

Note: If a trinomial does not have any common factors, then its binomial factors will not have any common factors either. Thus $(2x + 2)$ and $(2x + 4)$ cannot be factors of $2x^2 + 9x + 4$ in the above example. These factors can be eliminated without checking.

(b) The factors of $6x^2$ are either $2x$ and $3x$ or $6x$ and x. The factors of -2 are either -1 and 2 or 1 and -2. To obtain a middle term of $-x$ we use the following factors.

$$(3x - 2)(2x + 1) = 6x^2 - x - 2$$

$$-4x$$
$$+3x$$
$$-x \qquad \longleftarrow \quad \text{It checks.}$$

To find the correct factorization we may need to guess and check a few times.

(c) Each term contains a common factor of $2x$, so we do the following step first.

$$4x^3 - 14x^2 + 6x = 2x(2x^2 - 7x + 3)$$

Next we factor $2x^2 - 7x + 3$. The factors of $2x^2$ are $2x$ and x. Because the middle term is negative, we use -1 and -3 for factors of 3.

$$4x^3 - 14x^2 + 6x = 2x(2x^2 - 7x + 3)$$
$$= 2x(2x - 1)(x - 3)$$

EXAMPLE 6   **Estimating passing distance**

A car traveling 48 miles per hour accelerates at a constant rate to pass a car in front of it. A no-passing zone begins 2000 feet away. The distance traveled in feet by the car after t seconds is modeled by $d(t) = 3t^2 + 70t$. How long does it take for the car to reach the no-passing zone?

Solution   We must determine the time when $d(t) = 2000$.

$$3t^2 + 70t = 2000 \qquad \text{Equation to be solved}$$
$$3t^2 + 70t - 2000 = 0 \qquad \text{Subtract 2000.}$$
$$(3t - 50)(t + 40) = 0 \qquad \text{Factor.}$$
$$3t - 50 = 0 \quad \text{or} \quad t + 40 = 0 \qquad \text{Zero-product property}$$
$$t = \frac{50}{3} \quad \text{or} \quad t = -40 \qquad \text{Solve.}$$

The car reaches the no-passing zone after $\frac{50}{3} \approx 16.7$ seconds. (The solution $t = -40$ has no physical meaning in this problem.)

Critical Thinking

Can every trinomial be factored with the methods discussed in this section? Try to factor the following trinomials and then make a conjecture.

$$x^2 + 2x + 2, \quad x^2 - x + 1, \quad \text{and} \quad 2x^2 + x + 2 \qquad \text{No}$$

FACTORING WITH GRAPHS AND TABLES

Polynomials can also be factored graphically. One way to do so is to use a graph of the polynomial to find its zeros. A number p is a *zero* if a value of 0 results when p is substituted in the polynomial. For example, both -2 and 2 are zeros of $x^2 - 4$ because

$$(-2)^2 - 4 = 0 \quad \text{and} \quad (2)^2 - 4 = 0.$$

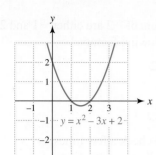

Figure 5.18

Now consider the trinomial $x^2 - 3x + 2$, whose graph is shown in Figure 5.18. Its x-intercepts or zeros are 1 and 2, and this trinomial factors as

$$x^2 - 3x + 2 = (x - 1)(x - 2).$$

We generalize these concepts as follows.

FACTORING WITH A GRAPH OR A TABLE OF VALUES

To factor the trinomial $x^2 + bx + c$, either graph or make a table of $y = x^2 + bx + c$. If the zeros of the trinomial are p and q, then the trinomial can be factored as

$$x^2 + bx + c = (x - p)(x - q).$$

If the trinomial $ax^2 + bx + c$ has zeros p and q, then it may be factored as

$$ax^2 + bx + c = a(x - p)(x - q).$$

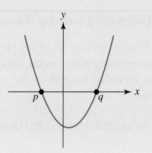

EXAMPLE 7 Factoring with technology

Factor each trinomial graphically or numerically.
(a) $x^2 - 2x - 24$ **(b)** $2x^2 - 51x + 220$

Solution **(a)** Graph $Y_1 = X^2 - 2X - 24$. The zeros of the trinomial are -4 and 6, as shown in Figure 5.19. Thus the trinomial factors as follows.

$$x^2 - 2x - 24 = \big(x - (-4)\big)(x - 6)$$
$$= (x + 4)(x - 6)$$

$[-9.4, 9.4, 1]$ by $[-30, 30, 5]$

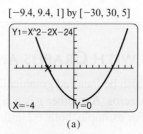

$[-9.4, 9.4, 1]$ by $[-30, 30, 5]$

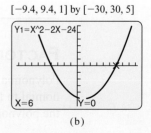

(a)   (b)

Figure 5.19

(b) Construct a table for $Y_1 = 2X^2 - 51X + 220$. Figure 5.20 reveals that the zeros are 5.5 and 20. The leading coefficient of $2x^2 - 51x + 220$ is 2, so we factor this expression as follows.

$$2x^2 - 51x + 220 = 2(x - 5.5)(x - 20)$$
$$= (2x - 11)(x - 20)$$

X	Y1
4	48
4.5	31
5	15
5.5	0
6	-14
6.5	-27
7	-39

$Y_1 = 2X^2 - 51X + 220$

(a)

X	Y1
18.5	-39
19	-27
19.5	-14
20	0
20.5	15
21	31
21.5	48

$Y_1 = 2X^2 - 51X + 220$

(b)

Figure 5.20

5.4 PUTTING IT ALL TOGETHER

Equations of the form $ax^2 + bx + c = 0$ occur in applications. One way to solve such equations is to factor the trinomial $ax^2 + bx + c$. This factorization may be done symbolically, graphically, or numerically. The following table includes an explanation and examples of each technique. To factor by grouping, see the box on page 339.

Technique	Explanation	Example
Symbolic Factoring	To factor $x^2 + bx + c$ find two factors of c whose sum is b.	To factor $x^2 - 3x - 4$ find two factors of -4 whose sum is -3. These factors are 1 and -4. $x^2 - 3x - 4 = (x + 1)(x - 4).$ It checks. $\longrightarrow -3x$
	To factor $ax^2 + bx + c$ find factors of ax^2 and c so that the middle term is bx. Grouping can also be used.	To factor $2x^2 + 3x - 2$ find factors of $2x^2$ and -2 so that the middle term is $3x$. $2x^2 + 3x - 2 = (2x - 1)(x + 2).$ It checks. $\longrightarrow 3x$

continued on next page

continued from previous page

Graphical Factoring	If p and q are zeros of $ax^2 + bx + c$, then the expression factors as $a(x - p)(x - q)$.	To factor $x^2 - 3x - 4$ ($a = 1$), graph $y = x^2 - 3x - 4$. The zeros are -1 and 4, and it follows that $$x^2 - 3x - 4 = (x + 1)(x - 4).$$ 
Numerical Factoring	If p and q are zeros of $ax^2 + bx + c$, then the expression factors as $a(x - p)(x - q)$.	To factor $2x^2 + 3x - 2$ make a table for $Y_1 = 2X^2 + 3X - 2$. The zeros are 0.5 and -2, so $$2x^2 + 3x - 2 = 2(x - 0.5)(x + 2)$$ $$= (2x - 1)(x + 2).$$ 	X	Y₁
-2	0
-1.5	-2
-1	-3
-.5	-3
0	-2
.5	0
1	3	 Y₁ ≡ 2X^2 + 3X − 2

5.4 | EXERCISES

FOR EXTRA HELP

📖 Student's Solutions Manual   🖥 InterAct Math   MathXL

🚪 MyMathLab   📞 Math Tutor Center   📼 Digital Video Tutor CD 4 Videotape 6

CONCEPTS

1. What is a trinomial? Give an example.
   A polynomial with three terms: $x^2 - x + 1$; answers may vary.
2. Name two methods for factoring $ax^2 + bx + c$.
   Symbolic and graphical; answers may vary.
3. The trinomial $3x^2 - x - 3$ is written in the form $ax^2 + bx + c$. Identify a, b, and c.
   $a = 3, b = -1, c = -3$
4. If you factor the trinomial $x^2 + 3x + 2$, do you obtain $(x + 1)(x + 2)$? Explain.   Yes; it checks, using FOIL.
5. Suppose that the graph of $y = x^2 + bx + c$ has x-intercepts -3 and 1. Factor $x^2 + bx + c$.
   $(x + 3)(x - 1)$
6. The graph of $y = 6x^2 - 15x + 6$ has x-intercepts $\frac{1}{2}$ and 2. Factor $6x^2 - 15x + 6$.
   $(6x - 3)(x - 2)$ or $3(2x - 1)(x - 2)$

FACTORING TRINOMIALS

Exercises 7–14: Determine whether the factors of the trinomial are the given binomials.

7. $x^2 + 5x + 6$ $(x + 2)(x + 3)$ Yes
8. $x^2 - 13x + 30$ $(x - 10)(x - 3)$ Yes
9. $x^2 - x - 20$ $(x + 5)(x - 4)$ No
10. $x^2 + 3x - 28$ $(x + 4)(x - 7)$ No
11. $6z^2 - 11z + 4$ $(2z - 1)(3z - 4)$ Yes
12. $4z^2 - 19z + 12$ $(2z - 4)(2z - 3)$ No
13. $10m^2 - 21m + 10$ $(5m + 2)(2m - 5)$ No

14. $12n^2 + 5n - 2$ $\quad (3n + 2)(4n - 1)$ Yes

Exercises 15–70: Factor completely.

15. $x^2 + 7x + 10$
$(x + 2)(x + 5)$

16. $x^2 + 3x - 10$
$(x - 2)(x + 5)$

17. $x^2 + 8x + 12$
$(x + 2)(x + 6)$

18. $x^2 - 8x + 12$
$(x - 6)(x - 2)$

19. $x^2 - 13x + 36$
$(x - 9)(x - 4)$

20. $x^2 + 11x + 24$
$(x + 3)(x + 8)$

21. $x^2 - 7x - 8$
$(x - 8)(x + 1)$

22. $x^2 - 21x - 100$
$(x - 25)(x + 4)$

23. $z^2 + z - 72$
$(z - 8)(z + 9)$

24. $z^2 + 6z - 55$
$(z - 5)(z + 11)$

25. $t^2 - 15t + 56$
$(t - 8)(t - 7)$

26. $t^2 - 14t + 40$
$(t - 10)(t - 4)$

27. $y^2 - 18y + 72$
$(y - 12)(y - 6)$

28. $y^2 - 15y + 54$
$(y - 9)(y - 6)$

29. $m^2 - 18m - 40$
$(m - 20)(m + 2)$

30. $m^2 - 22m - 75$
$(m - 25)(m + 3)$

31. $n^2 - 20n - 300$
$(n - 30)(n + 10)$

32. $n^2 - 13n - 30$
$(n - 15)(n + 2)$

33. $2x^2 + 7x + 3$
$(x + 3)(2x + 1)$

34. $2x^2 - 5x - 3$
$(x - 3)(2x + 1)$

35. $6x^2 - x - 2$
$(2x + 1)(3x - 2)$

36. $10x^2 + 3x - 1$
$(2x + 1)(5x - 1)$

37. $4z^2 + 19z + 12$
$(z + 4)(4z + 3)$

38. $4z^2 + 17z + 4$
$(z + 4)(4z + 1)$

39. $6t^2 - 17t + 12$
$(2t - 3)(3t - 4)$

40. $6t^2 - 13t + 6$
$(2t - 3)(3t - 2)$

41. $10y^2 + 13y - 3$
$(2y + 3)(5y - 1)$

42. $10y^2 + 23y - 5$
$(2y + 5)(5y - 1)$

43. $6m^2 - m - 12$
$(2m - 3)(3m + 4)$

44. $20m^2 - m - 12$
$(4m + 3)(5m - 4)$

45. $42n^2 + 5n - 25$
$(6n + 5)(7n - 5)$

46. $42n^2 + 65n + 25$
$(6n + 5)(7n + 5)$

47. $1 + x - 2x^2$
$(1 - x)(1 + 2x)$

48. $3 - 5x - 2x^2$
$(3 + x)(1 - 2x)$

49. $20 + 7x - 6x^2$
$(5 - 2x)(4 + 3x)$

50. $4 + 13x - 12x^2$
$(4 - 3x)(1 + 4x)$

51. $5y^2 + 5y - 30$
$5(y - 2)(y + 3)$

52. $3y^2 - 27y + 24$
$3(y - 8)(y - 1)$

53. $2z^2 + 12z + 16$
$2(z + 2)(z + 4)$

54. $4z^2 + 32z + 60$
$4(z + 3)(z + 5)$

55. $z^3 + 9z^2 + 14z$
$z(z + 2)(z + 7)$

56. $z^3 + 7z^2 + 12z$
$z(z + 3)(z + 4)$

57. $t^3 - 10t^2 + 21t$
$t(t - 7)(t - 3)$

58. $t^3 - 11t^2 + 24t$
$t(t - 8)(t - 3)$

59. $m^4 + 6m^3 + 5m^2$
$m^2(m + 1)(m + 5)$

60. $m^4 - m^3 - 2m^2$
$m^2(m - 2)(m + 1)$

61. $5x^3 + x^2 - 6x$
$x(x - 1)(5x + 6)$

62. $2x^3 + 8x^2 - 24x$
$2x(x - 2)(x + 6)$

63. $6x^3 + 21x^2 + 9x$
$3x(x + 3)(2x + 1)$

64. $12x^3 - 8x^2 - 20x$
$4x(x + 1)(3x - 5)$

65. $2x^3 - 14x^2 + 20x$
$2x(x - 5)(x - 2)$

66. $7x^3 + 35x^2 + 42x$
$7x(x + 2)(x + 3)$

67. $60z^3 + 230z^2 - 40z$
$10z(z + 4)(6z - 1)$

68. $24z^3 + 8z^2 - 80z$
$8z(z + 2)(3z - 5)$

69. $4x^4 + 10x^3 - 6x^2$
$2x^2(x + 3)(2x - 1)$

70. $30x^4 + 3x^3 - 9x^2$
$3x^2(2x - 1)(5x + 3)$

FACTORING WITH GRAPHS AND TABLES

Exercises 71–76: Factor the expression by using the graph of $y = f(x)$, where $f(x)$ is the given expression. Check your answer by multiplying.

71. $x^2 - 6x + 8$

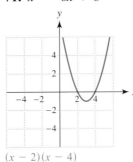

$(x - 2)(x - 4)$

72. $x^2 - x - 6$

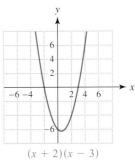

$(x + 2)(x - 3)$

73. $2x^2 - 2x - 4$

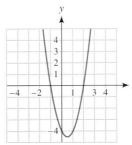

$2(x + 1)(x - 2)$

74. $3x^2 + 3x - 18$

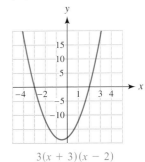

$3(x + 3)(x - 2)$

75. $2 + x - x^2$

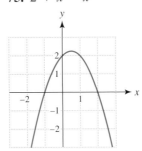

$-(x - 2)(x + 1)$

76. $3 - 2x - x^2$

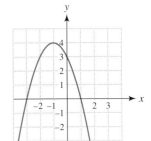

$-(x - 1)(x + 3)$

Exercises 77–80: Use the table to factor the expression completely. Check your answer by multiplying.

77. $x^2 - 3x - 4$

X	Y1
-2	6
-1	0
0	-4
1	-6
2	-6
3	-4
4	0

Y1≣X^2−3X−4

$(x + 1)(x - 4)$

78. $x^2 - 40x + 300$

X	Y1
-10	800
0	300
10	0
20	-100
30	0
40	300
50	800

Y1≣X^2−40X+300

$(x - 10)(x - 30)$

79. $2x^2 - 2x - 4$

X	Y₁
-3	20
-2	8
-1	0
0	-4
1	-4
2	0
3	8

$Y_1 = 2X^2 - 2X - 4$

$2(x + 1)(x - 2)$

80. $3x^2 - 18x + 24$

X	Y₁
0	24
1	9
2	0
3	-3
4	0
5	9
6	24

$Y_1 = 3X^2 - 18X + 24$

$3(x - 2)(x - 4)$

Exercises 81–90: Factor the expression graphically or numerically.

81. $x^2 + 3x - 10$
$(x - 2)(x + 5)$

82. $x^2 + 7x + 12$
$(x + 3)(x + 4)$

83. $x^2 - 3x - 28$
$(x - 7)(x + 4)$

84. $x^2 - 25x + 100$
$(x - 20)(x - 5)$

85. $2x^2 - 14x + 20$
$2(x - 5)(x - 2)$

86. $12x^2 - 6x - 6$
$6(x - 1)(2x + 1)$

87. $5x^2 - 30x - 200$
$5(x - 10)(x + 4)$

88. $12x^2 - 30x + 12$
$6(x - 2)(2x - 1)$

89. $8x^2 - 44x + 20$
$4(x - 5)(2x - 1)$

90. $20x^2 + 3x - 9$
$20\left(x - \frac{3}{5}\right)\left(x + \frac{3}{4}\right) = (5x - 3)(4x + 3)$

APPLICATIONS

91. *Ticket Prices*   (Refer to Example 3.) If tickets are sold for \$35, 1200 tickets are expected to be sold. For each \$1 reduction in ticket price, an additional 100 tickets will be sold.
   (a) Write an expression that gives the revenue from ticket sales when ticket prices are reduced by x dollars. $(35 - x)(1200 + 100x)$
   (b) Determine the ticket prices that result in sales of \$54,000.   \$20 or \$27

92. *Ticket Prices*   One airline ticket costs \$295. For each additional ticket sold to a group of up to 30 people, the price of all the tickets is reduced by \$5. For example, 2 tickets cost 2 · \$290 = \$580 and 3 tickets cost 3 · \$285 = \$855.
   (a) Write a polynomial that gives the cost of buying x tickets. $300x - 5x^2$
   (b) What is the cost of 20 tickets?   \$4000

(c) How many tickets were sold if the total cost is \$2500?   10

93. *Area of a Rectangle*   A rectangle has an area of 91 square feet. Its length is 6 feet more than its width. Find the dimensions of the rectangle.   7 ft by 13 ft

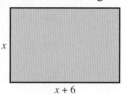

x

$x + 6$

94. *Area of a Triangle*   The base of a triangle is 2 inches less than its height. If the area of the triangle is 60 square inches, finds its height.   12 in.

95. *Numbers*   Find two consecutive integers whose product is 132.   11 and 12

96. *Passing Distances*   (Refer to Example 6.) The distance traveled in feet by a car passing another car after t seconds is given by $2t^2 + 88t$.
   (a) Use factoring to determine how long it takes for the car to travel 600 feet.   6 sec
   (b) Solve part (a) either graphically or numerically.   6 sec

WRITING ABOUT MATHEMATICS

97. A student factors each trinomial into the given pair of binomials.
   (i) $x^2 - 5x - 6$ $(x - 1)(x + 6)$
   (ii) $10x^2 - 11x - 6$ $(5x - 3)(2x + 2)$
   (iii) $12x^2 + 13x + 3$ $(6x + 1)(2x + 3)$
   Explain the error that the student is making.

98. Suppose that a graph of $y = x^2 + bx + c$ intersects the x-axis twice at p and q. Explain how you could use the graph to factor $x^2 + bx + c$.

CHECKING BASIC CONCEPTS   SECTIONS 5.3 AND 5.4

1. Factor out the greatest common factor.
   (a) $3x^2 - 6x$ **(b)** $16x^3 - 8x^2 + 4x$
   $3x(x - 2)$ $4x(4x^2 - 2x + 1)$

2. Use factoring to solve each equation.
   (a) $x^2 - 2x = 0$ **(b)** $9x^2 = 81x$
   0, 2   0, 9

3. Factor each trinomial. (a) $(x - 2)(x + 5)$
   (a) $x^2 + 3x - 10$ **(b)** $x^2 - 3x - 10$ $(x - 5)(x + 2)$
   (c) $8x^2 + 14x + 3$ $(2x + 3)(4x + 1)$

4. Solve $x^2 + 3x + 2 = 0$. $-1, -2$

5. A baseball is thrown upward at 64 feet per second or approximately 44 miles per hour. Its height above the ground after t seconds is given by

$$h(t) = -16t^2 + 64t + 8.$$

Determine when the baseball is 56 feet above the ground.   After 1 sec and 3 sec

5.5   SPECIAL TYPES OF FACTORING

Difference of Two Squares · **Perfect Square Trinomials** · **Sum and Difference of Two Cubes**

INTRODUCTION

Some polynomials can be factored with special methods. These factoring techniques are used in other mathematics courses to solve equations and simplify expressions. In this section we discuss these methods.

DIFFERENCE OF TWO SQUARES

When we factor polynomials, we are *reversing* the process of multiplying polynomials. In Section 5.2 we discussed the equation

$$(a - b)(a + b) = a^2 - b^2.$$

We can use this equation to factor a difference of two squares. For example, if we want to factor $x^2 - 25$, we can substitute x for a and **5** for b in

$$a^2 - b^2 = (a - b)(a + b)$$

to get

$$x^2 - 5^2 = (x - 5)(x + 5).$$

TEACHING TIP

Emphasize that the sum of two squares cannot be factored (without complex numbers.)

DIFFERENCE OF TWO SQUARES

For any real numbers a and b,

$$a^2 - b^2 = (a - b)(a + b).$$

Note: The sum of two squares *cannot* be factored (using real numbers). For example, $x^2 + y^2$ cannot be factored, whereas $x^2 - y^2$ can be factored. It is important to remember that $x^2 + y^2 \neq (x + y)^2$.

EXAMPLE 1   Factoring the difference of two squares

Factor each polynomial, if possible.
(a) $9x^2 - 64$ **(b)** $4x^2 + 9y^2$ **(c)** $9x^4 - y^6$ **(d)** $4a^3 - 4a$

Solution   **(a)** Note that $9x^2 = (3x)^2$ and $64 = 8^2$.

$$9x^2 - 64 = (3x)^2 - (8)^2$$
$$= (3x - 8)(3x + 8)$$

(b) Because $4x^2 + 9y^2$ is the *sum* of two squares, it *cannot* be factored. Note, however, that the expression $4x^2 - 9y^2$ *can* be factored as follows.

$$4x^2 - 9y^2 = (2x)^2 - (3y)^2$$
$$= (2x - 3y)(2x + 3y)$$

(c) If we let $a^2 = 9x^4$ and $b^2 = y^6$, then $a = 3x^2$ and $b = y^3$. Thus

$$9x^4 - y^6 = (3x^2)^2 - (y^3)^2$$
$$= (3x^2 - y^3)(3x^2 + y^3)$$

(d) Start by factoring out the common factor of $4a$.

$$4a^3 - 4a = 4a(a^2 - 1)$$
$$= 4a(a - 1)(a + 1)$$

EXAMPLE 2 Applying the difference of two squares

Factor each expression.
(a) $(n + 1)^2 - 9$ **(b)** $x^4 - y^4$ **(c)** $6r^2 - 24t^4$ **(d)** $x^3 + 3x^2 - 4x - 12$

Solution **(a)** Use $a^2 - b^2 = (a - b)(a + b)$, with $a = n + 1$ and $b = 3$.

$$(n + 1)^2 - 9 = (n + 1)^2 - 3^2 \qquad 9 = 3^2$$
$$= \big((n + 1) - 3\big)\big((n + 1) + 3\big) \qquad \text{Difference of squares}$$
$$= (n - 2)(n + 4) \qquad \text{Combine terms.}$$

(b) Use $a^2 - b^2 = (a - b)(a + b)$, with $a = x^2$ and $b = y^2$.

$$x^4 - y^4 = (x^2)^2 - (y^2)^2 \qquad \text{Write as squares.}$$
$$= (x^2 - y^2)(x^2 + y^2) \qquad \text{Difference of squares}$$
$$= (x - y)(x + y)(x^2 + y^2) \qquad \text{Difference of squares}$$

(c) Start by factoring out the common factor of 6.

$$6r^2 - 24t^4 = 6(r^2 - 4t^4) \qquad \text{Factor out 6.}$$
$$= 6\big(r^2 - (2t^2)^2\big) \qquad \text{Write as squares.}$$
$$= 6(r - 2t^2)(r + 2t^2) \qquad \text{Difference of squares}$$

(d) Start factoring by using *grouping* and then factor the difference of squares.

$$x^3 + 3x^2 - 4x - 12 = (x^3 + 3x^2) + (-4x - 12) \qquad \text{Associative property}$$
$$= x^2(x + 3) - 4(x + 3) \qquad \text{Factor out } x^2 \text{ and } -4.$$
$$= (x^2 - 4)(x + 3) \qquad \text{Distributive property}$$
$$= (x - 2)(x + 2)(x + 3) \qquad \text{Difference of squares}$$

PERFECT SQUARE TRINOMIALS

In Section 5.2 we also showed how to expand $(a + b)^2$ and $(a - b)^2$.

$$(a + b)^2 = a^2 + 2ab + b^2 \quad \text{and} \quad (a - b)^2 = a^2 - 2ab + b^2$$

The expressions $a^2 + 2ab + b^2$ and $a^2 - 2ab + b^2$ are called **perfect square trinomials**. If we can recognize a perfect square trinomial, we can use these formulas to factor it.

PERFECT SQUARE TRINOMIALS

For any real numbers a and b,

$$a^2 + 2ab + b^2 = (a + b)^2 \quad \text{and}$$
$$a^2 - 2ab + b^2 = (a - b)^2.$$

EXAMPLE 3   Factoring perfect square trinomials

Factor.
(a) $x^2 + 6x + 9$ **(b)** $81x^2 - 72x + 16$

Solution   **(a)** Let $a^2 = x^2$ and $b^2 = 3^2$. To be a perfect square trinomial the middle term must equal $2ab$.

$$2ab = 2(x)(3) = 6x,$$

which equals the given middle term. Thus $a^2 + 2ab + b^2 = (a + b)^2$ implies

$$x^2 + 6x + 9 = (x + 3)^2.$$

(b) Let $a^2 = (9x)^2$ and $b^2 = 4^2$. To be a perfect square trinomial the middle term must equal $2ab$.

$$2ab = 2(9x)(4) = 72x,$$

which equals the given middle term. Thus $a^2 - 2ab + b^2 = (a - b)^2$ implies

$$81x^2 - 72x + 16 = (9x - 4)^2.$$

EXAMPLE 4   Factoring perfect square trinomials

Factor each expression.
(a) $4x^2 + 4xy + y^2$ **(b)** $9r^2 - 12rt + 4t^2$ **(c)** $25a^3 + 10a^2b + ab^2$

Solution   **(a)** Let $a^2 = (2x)^2$ and $b^2 = y^2$. To be a perfect square trinomial the middle term must equal $2ab$.

$$2ab = 2(2x)(y) = 4xy,$$

which equals the given middle term. Thus $a^2 + 2ab + b^2 = (a + b)^2$ implies

$$4x^2 + 4xy + y^2 = (2x + y)^2.$$

(b) Let $a^2 = (3r)^2$ and $b^2 = (2t)^2$. To be a perfect square trinomial the middle term must equal $2ab$.

$$2ab = 2(3r)(2t) = 12rt,$$

which equals the given middle term. Thus $a^2 - 2ab + b^2 = (a - b)^2$ implies

$$9r^2 - 12rt + 4t^2 = (3r - 2t)^2.$$

(c) Start by factoring out the common factor of a. Then factor the resulting perfect square trinomial.

$$25a^3 + 10a^2b + ab^2 = a(25a^2 + 10ab + b^2)$$
$$= a(5a + b)^2$$

═══════ MAKING CONNECTIONS ═══════

Special Factoring and General Techniques

If you do not recognize a polynomial as being either the difference of two squares or a trinomial perfect square, then you can factor the polynomial by using the methods discussed in earlier sections.

SUM AND DIFFERENCE OF TWO CUBES

The sum or difference of two cubes may be factored. This fact is justified by the following two equations.

$$(a + b)(a^2 - ab + b^2) = a^3 + b^3 \quad \text{and}$$
$$(a - b)(a^2 + ab + b^2) = a^3 - b^3$$

These equations can be verified by multiplying the left side to obtain the right side. For example,

$$(a + b)(a^2 - ab + b^2) = a \cdot a^2 - a \cdot ab + a \cdot b^2 + b \cdot a^2 - b \cdot ab + b \cdot b^2$$
$$= a^3 - a^2b + ab^2 + a^2b - ab^2 + b^3$$
$$= a^3 + b^3.$$

SUM AND DIFFERENCE OF TWO CUBES

For any real numbers a and b,

$$a^3 + b^3 = (a + b)(a^2 - ab + b^2) \quad \text{and}$$
$$a^3 - b^3 = (a - b)(a^2 + ab + b^2).$$

EXAMPLE 5   Factoring the sum and difference of two cubes

Factor each polynomial.
(a) $x^3 + 8$ **(b)** $27x^3 - 64y^3$

Solution **(a)** Because $x^3 = (x)^3$ and $8 = 2^3$, we let $a = x$, $b = 2$, and factor. Substituting in
$$a^3 + b^3 = (a + b)(a^2 - ab + b^2)$$
gives
$$x^3 + 2^3 = (x + 2)(x^2 - x \cdot 2 + 2^2)$$
$$= (x + 2)(x^2 - 2x + 4).$$

Note that the quadratic factor does not factor further.
(b) Here, $27x^3 = (3x)^3$ and $64y^3 = (4y)^3$, so
$$27x^3 - 64y^3 = (3x)^3 - (4y)^3.$$

Substituting $a = 3x$ and $b = 4y$ in
$$a^3 - b^3 = (a - b)(a^2 + ab + b^2)$$

gives

$$(3x)^3 - (4y)^3 = (3x - 4y)\big((3x)^2 + 3x \cdot 4y + (4y)^2\big)$$
$$= (3x - 4y)(9x^2 + 12xy + 16y^2).$$

EXAMPLE 6   Factoring the sum and difference of two cubes

Factor each expression.
(a) $x^6 + 8y^3$ **(b)** $27p^9 - 8q^6$

Solution   **(a)** Let $a^3 = (x^2)^3$ and $b^3 = (2y)^3$. Then $a^3 + b^3 = (a + b)(a^2 - ab + b^2)$ implies

$$x^6 + 8y^3 = (x^2 + 2y)(x^4 - 2x^2y + 4y^2).$$

(b) Let $a^3 = (3p^3)^3$ and $b^3 = (2q^2)^3$. Then $a^3 - b^3 = (a - b)(a^2 + ab + b^2)$ implies

$$27p^9 - 8q^6 = (3p^3 - 2q^2)(9p^6 + 6p^3q^2 + 4q^4).$$

5.5   PUTTING IT ALL TOGETHER

In this section we presented three special types of factoring, which are summarized in the
following table.

Type of Factoring	Description	Example
The Difference of Two Squares	To factor the difference of two squares use $$a^2 - b^2 = (a - b)(a + b).$$ *Note:* $a^2 + b^2$ cannot be factored.	$25x^2 - 16 = (5x - 4)(5x + 4)$ $(a = 5x, b = 4)$ $4x^2 + y^2$ cannot be factored.
A Perfect Square Trinomial	To factor a perfect square trinomial use $$a^2 + 2ab + b^2 = (a + b)^2 \text{ or}$$ $$a^2 - 2ab + b^2 = (a - b)^2.$$	$x^2 + 4x + 4 = (x + 2)^2$ $(a = x, b = 2)$ $16x^2 - 24x + 9 = (4x - 3)^2$ $(a = 4x, b = 3)$ Be sure to check the middle term.
The Sum and Difference of Two Cubes	The sum and difference of two cubes can be factored as $$a^3 + b^3 = (a + b)$$ $$\cdot (a^2 - ab + b^2) \text{ or}$$ $$a^3 - b^3 = (a - b)$$ $$\cdot (a^2 + ab + b^2).$$	$x^3 + 8y^3 = (x + 2y)\big(x^2 - x \cdot 2y + (2y)^2\big)$ $= (x + 2y)(x^2 - 2xy + 4y^2)$ $(a = x, b = 2y)$ $125x^3 - 64 = (5x - 4)\big((5x)^2 + 5x \cdot 4 + 4^2\big)$ $= (5x - 4)(25x^2 + 20x + 16)$ $(a = 5x, b = 4)$

5.5 EXERCISES

FOR EXTRA HELP

 Student's Solutions Manual

 InterAct Math

 MathXL

MyMathLab

Math Tutor Center

Digital Video Tutor
CD 5   Videotape 6

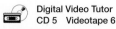

CONCEPTS

1. Give an example of a difference of two squares.
$x^2 - 9$; answers may vary.

2. Give an example of a perfect square trinomial.
$x^2 - 8x + 16$; answers may vary.

3. Give an example of the sum of two cubes.
$x^3 + 8$; answers may vary.

4. Factor $a^2 - b^2$. $(a - b)(a + b)$

5. Factor $a^2 + 2ab + b^2$. $(a + b)^2$

6. Factor $a^3 - b^3$. $(a - b)(a^2 + ab + b^2)$

DIFFERENCE OF TWO SQUARES

Exercises 7–10: Determine whether the expression represents a difference of two squares. Factor the expression.

7. $x^2 - 25$
Yes; $(x - 5)(x + 5)$

8. $16x^2 - 100$
Yes; $(4x - 10)(4x + 10)$

9. $x^3 + y^3$
No; $(x + y)(x^2 - xy + y^2)$

10. $9x^2 + 36y^2$
No; $9(x^2 + 4y^2)$

Exercises 11–36: Factor the expression completely, if possible.

11. $x^2 - 36$
$(x - 6)(x + 6)$

12. $y^2 - 144$
$(y - 12)(y + 12)$

13. $25 - z^2$
$(5 - z)(5 + z)$

14. $36 - y^2$
$(6 - y)(6 + y)$

15. $4z^2 + 25$
Cannot be factored

16. $9z^2 + 64$
Cannot be factored

17. $36x^2 - 100$
$4(3x - 5)(3x + 5)$

18. $4y^2 - 64$
$4(y - 4)(y + 4)$

19. $49a^2 - 64b^2$
$(7a - 8b)(7a + 8b)$

20. $9x^2 - 4y^2$
$(3x - 2y)(3x + 2y)$

21. $64z^2 - 25z^4$
$z^2(8 - 5z)(8 + 5z)$

22. $64z^4 - 49z^2$
$z^2(8z - 7)(8z + 7)$

23. $5x^3 - 125x$
$5x(x - 5)(x + 5)$

24. $100x^3 - x$
$x(10x - 1)(10x + 1)$

25. $4r^4 + t^6$
Cannot be factored

26. $9t^4 - 25r^6$
$(3t^2 - 5r^3)(3t^2 + 5r^3)$

27. $16t^4 - r^2$
$(4t^2 - r)(4t^2 + r)$

28. $t^4 + 9r^2$
Cannot be factored

29. $(x + 1)^2 - 25$
$(x - 4)(x + 6)$

30. $(x - 2)^2 - 9$
$(x - 5)(x + 1)$

31. $100 - (n - 4)^2$
$(14 - n)(6 + n)$

32. $81 - (n + 3)^2$
$(6 - n)(12 + n)$

33. $y^4 - 16$
$(y - 2)(y + 2)(y^2 + 4)$

34. $16z^4 - 1$
$(2z - 1)(2z + 1)(4z^2 + 1)$

35. $16x^4 - y^4$
$(2x - y)(2x + y)(4x^2 + y^2)$

36. $r^4 - 81t^4$
$(r - 3t)(r + 3t)(r^2 + 9t^2)$

Exercises 37–40: Use grouping to help factor the expression.

37. $x^3 + x^2 - x - 1$
$(x - 1)(x + 1)^2$

38. $x^3 + x^2 - 9x - 9$
$(x - 3)(x + 3)(x + 1)$

39. $4x^3 - 8x^2 - x + 2$
$(2x - 1)(2x + 1)(x - 2)$

40. $9x^3 - 18x^2 - 16x + 32$
$(3x - 4)(3x + 4)(x - 2)$

PERFECT SQUARE TRINOMIALS

Exercises 41–48: Determine whether the trinomial is a perfect square. If it is, factor it.

41. $x^2 + x + 16$ No

42. $4x^2 - 2x + 25$ No

43. $x^2 + 8x + 16$
Yes; $(x + 4)^2$

44. $x^2 - 4x + 4$
Yes; $(x - 2)^2$

45. $4z^2 - 4z + 1$
Yes; $(2z - 1)^2$

46. $9z^2 + 6z + 4$ No

47. $16t^2 - 12t + 9$ No

48. $4t^2 + 12t + 9$
Yes; $(2t + 3)^2$

Exercises 49–66: Factor the expression.

49. $x^2 + 2x + 1$
$(x + 1)^2$

50. $x^2 - 6x + 9$
$(x - 3)^2$

51. $4x^2 + 20x + 25$
$(2x + 5)^2$

52. $x^2 + 10x + 25$
$(x + 5)^2$

53. $x^2 - 12x + 36$
$(x - 6)^2$

54. $x^2 + 20x + 100$
$(x + 10)^2$

55. $36z^2 + 12z + 1$
$(6z + 1)^2$

56. $9z^2 - 24z + 16$
$(3z - 4)^2$

57. $4y^4 + 4y^3 + y^2$
$y^2(2y + 1)^2$

58. $16z^4 - 24z^3 + 9z^2$
$z^2(4z - 3)^2$

59. $9z^3 - 6z^2 + z$
$z(3z - 1)^2$

60. $49y^2 + 42y + 9$
$(7y + 3)^2$

61. $9x^2 + 6xy + y^2$
$(3x + y)^2$

62. $25x^2 + 30xy + 9y^2$
$(5x + 3y)^2$

63. $49a^2 - 28ab + 4b^2$
$(7a - 2b)^2$

64. $64a^2 - 16ab + b^2$
$(8a - b)^2$

65. $4x^4 - 4x^3y + x^2y^2$
$x^2(2x - y)^2$

66. $4x^3y + 12x^2y^2 + 9xy^3$
$xy(2x + 3y)^2$

SUM AND DIFFERENCE OF TWO CUBES

Exercises 67–84: Factor the expression.

67. $x^3 - 8$
$(x - 2)(x^2 + 2x + 4)$

68. $x^3 + 8$
$(x + 2)(x^2 - 2x + 4)$

69. $y^3 + z^3$
$(y + z)(y^2 - yz + z^2)$

70. $y^3 - z^3$
$(y - z)(y^2 + yz + z^2)$

71. $27x^3 - 8$
$(3x - 2)(9x^2 + 6x + 4)$

72. $64 - y^3$
$(4 - y)(16 + 4y + y^2)$

73. $64z^3 + 27t^3$
$(4z + 3t)(16z^2 - 12zt + 9t^2)$

74. $125t^3 - 64r^3$
$(5t - 4r)(25t^2 + 20tr + 16r^2)$

75. $8x^4 + 125x$
$x(2x + 5)(4x^2 - 10x + 25)$

76. $x^3y^2 + 8y^5$
$y^2(x + 2y)(x^2 - 2xy + 4y^2)$

77. $27y - 8x^3y$
$y(3 - 2x)(9 + 6x + 4x^2)$

78. $x^3y^3 + 1$
$(xy + 1)(x^2y^2 - xy + 1)$

79. $z^6 - 27y^3$
$(z^2 - 3y)(z^4 + 3z^2y + 9y^2)$

80. $z^6 + 27y^3$
$(z^2 + 3y)(z^4 - 3z^2y + 9y^2)$

81. $125z^6 + 8y^9$
$(5z^2 + 2y^3)(25z^4 - 10z^2y^3 + 4y^6)$

82. $125z^6 - 8y^9$
$(5z^2 - 2y^3)(25z^4 + 10z^2y^3 + 4y^6)$

83. $5m^6 + 40n^3$
$5(m^2 + 2n)(m^4 - 2m^2n + 4n^2)$

84. $10m^9 - 270n^6$
$10(m^3 - 3n^2)(m^6 + 3m^3n^2 + 9n^4)$

GENERAL FACTORING

Exercises 85–118: Factor the expression completely.

85. $25x^2 - 64$
$(5x - 8)(5x + 8)$

86. $25x^2 - 30x + 9$
$(5x - 3)^2$

87. $x^3 + 27$
$(x + 3)(x^2 - 3x + 9)$

88. $4 - 16y^2$
$4(1 - 2y)(1 + 2y)$

89. $64x^2 + 16x + 1$
$(8x + 1)^2$

90. $2x^2 - 5x + 3$
$(x - 1)(2x - 3)$

91. $3x^2 + 14x + 8$
$(x + 4)(3x + 2)$

92. $125x^3 - 1$
$(5x - 1)(25x^2 + 5x + 1)$

93. $x^4 + 8x$
$x(x + 2)(x^2 - 2x + 4)$

94. $2x^3 - 12x^2 + 18x$
$2x(x - 3)^2$

95. $64x^3 + 8y^3$
$8(2x + y)(4x^2 - 2xy + y^2)$

96. $54 - 16x^3$
$2(3 - 2x)(9 + 6x + 4x^2)$

97. $2r^2 - 8t^2$
$2(r - 2t)(r + 2t)$

98. $a^3 - ab^2$
$a(a - b)(a + b)$

99. $a^3 + 4a^2b + 4ab^2$
$a(a + 2b)^2$

100. $8r^4 + rt^3$
$r(2r + t)(4r^2 - 2rt + t^2)$

101. $x^2 - 3x + 2$
$(x - 2)(x - 1)$

102. $x^2 + 4x - 5$
$(x + 5)(x - 1)$

103. $4z^2 - 25$
$(2z - 5)(2z + 5)$

104. $(z + 1)^2 - 49$
$(z - 6)(z + 8)$

105. $x^4 + 16x^3 + 64x^2$
$x^2(x + 8)^2$

106. $4x^2 - 12xy + 9y^2$
$(2x - 3y)^2$

107. $z^3 - 1$
$(z - 1)(z^2 + z + 1)$

108. $8z^3 + 1$
$(2z + 1)(4z^2 - 2z + 1)$

109. $3t^2 - 5t - 8$
$(t + 1)(3t - 8)$

110. $15t^2 - 11t + 2$
$(3t - 1)(5t - 2)$

111. $7a^3 + 20a^2 - 3a$
$a(a + 3)(7a - 1)$

112. $b^3 - b^2 - 2b$
$b(b - 2)(b + 1)$

113. $x^6 - y^6$
$(x + y)(x - y)(x^2 + xy + y^2)(x^2 - xy + y^2)$

114. $a^8 - b^8$

115. $100x^2 - 1$
$(10x - 1)(10x + 1)$

116. $4x^2 + 28x + 49$
$(2x + 7)^2$

117. $p^3q^3 - 27$
$(pq - 3)(p^2q^2 + 3pq + 9)$

118. $a^2b^2 - c^2d^2$
$(ab - cd)(ab + cd)$

WRITING ABOUT MATHEMATICS

119. Explain how factoring $x^3 + y^3$ and $x^3 - y^3$ are similar.

120. Can $x^2 - y^2$ be factored? Can $x^2 + y^2$ be factored? Explain your answers.

114. $(a + b)(a - b)(a^2 + b^2)(a^4 + b^4)$

Group Activity: Working with Real Data

Directions: Form a group of 2 to 4 people. Select someone to record the group's responses for this activity. All members of the group should work cooperatively to answer the questions. If your instructor asks for your results, each member of the group should be prepared to respond.

Exercises 1–6: Geometric Factoring The polynomial $x^2 + 4x + 3$ can be factored by grouping.

When the rectangle is a square, the trinomial is a perfect square trinomial; see Exercises 3 and 4.

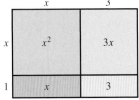

$$x^2 + 4x + 3 = x^2 + x + 3x + 3$$
$$= (x^2 + x) + (3x + 3)$$
$$= x(x + 1) + 3(x + 1)$$
$$= (x + 3)(x + 1)$$

This factorization is represented geometrically in the accompanying figure. Note that the outside dimensions of the large rectangle are $x + 3$ by $x + 1$ and therefore its area is $(x + 3)(x + 1)$. This area equals the sum of the four smaller rectangles inside the large rectangle. Thus

$$(x + 3)(x + 1) = x^2 + x + 3x + 3 = x^2 + 4x + 3.$$

Factor the following expressions geometrically. If the rectangle turns out to be a square, what can you say about the trinomial?

1. $x^2 + 3x + 2$
$(x + 1)(x + 2)$

2. $x^2 + 6x + 5$
$(x + 1)(x + 5)$

3. $4x^2 + 4x + 1$
$(2x + 1)^2$

4. $x^2 + 6x + 9$ $(x + 3)^2$

5. $6x^2 + 29x + 20$
$(x + 4)(6x + 5)$

6. $8x^2 + 59x + 21$
$(x + 7)(8x + 3)$

5.6   POLYNOMIAL EQUATIONS

**Quadratic Equations · Higher Degree Equations ·
Equations in Quadratic Form · Applications**

INTRODUCTION

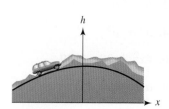

Figure 5.21

Polynomials are used to solve many important problems. One example is found in highway construction where the elevations of hills and valleys are modeled by quadratic polynomials.   (*Source:* F. Mannering and W. Kilareski, *Principles of Highway Engineering and Traffic Analysis.*)
The quadratic polynomial

$$h(x) = -0.0001x^2 + 100$$

could model the height of a hill, where $x = 0$ corresponds to the peak or crest of the hill, as illustrated in Figure 5.21. To determine any locations where the height of the hill is 75 feet, we can solve the quadratic equation

$$-0.0001x^2 + 100 = 75.$$

QUADRATIC EQUATIONS

Any *quadratic equation* can be written as $ax^2 + bx + c = 0$, where a, b, and c are constants, with $a \neq 0$. Quadratic equations can sometimes be solved by factoring and then applying the zero-product property. They can also be solved graphically. These techniques are demonstrated in the next two examples.

EXAMPLE 1   Solving a quadratic equation

Solve $x^2 - 4 = 0$ symbolically and graphically.

Solution   *Symbolic Solution*   Start by factoring the left side of the equation.

$$x^2 - 4 = 0 \qquad \text{Given equation}$$
$$(x - 2)(x + 2) = 0 \qquad \text{Difference of squares}$$
$$x - 2 = 0 \quad \text{or} \quad x + 2 = 0 \qquad \text{Zero-product property}$$
$$x = 2 \quad \text{or} \quad x = -2 \qquad \text{Solve each equation.}$$

The solutions are -2 and 2.

Graphical Solution   Start by making Table 5.9. Plot these points and connect them with a smooth curve called a parabola, as shown in Figure 5.22. The x-intercepts or zeros are -2 and 2, which are also the solutions to the equation.

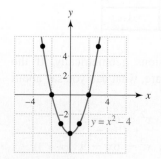

Figure 5.22

TABLE 5.9 $y = x^2 - 4$

x	-3	-2	-1	0	1	2	3
y	5	0	-3	-4	-3	0	5

EXAMPLE 2   Solving quadratic equations

Solve each equation.
(a) $4x^2 - 20x + 25 = 0$ **(b)** $3x^2 + 11x = 20$ **(c)** $x^2 + 25 = 0$

Solution   **(a)** Start by factoring the left side, which is a perfect square trinomial.

$$4x^2 - 20x + 25 = 0 \qquad \text{Given equation}$$
$$(2x - 5)(2x - 5) = 0 \qquad \text{Factor.}$$
$$2x - 5 = 0 \qquad \text{Zero-product property}$$
$$x = \frac{5}{2} \qquad \text{Solve.}$$

The only solution is $\frac{5}{2}$.

(b) Start by subtracting 20 from each side to obtain a 0 on the right side.

$$3x^2 + 11x = 20 \qquad \text{Given equation}$$
$$3x^2 + 11x - 20 = 0 \qquad \text{Subtract 20.}$$
$$(x + 5)(3x - 4) = 0 \qquad \text{Factor.}$$
$$x + 5 = 0 \quad \text{or} \quad 3x - 4 = 0 \qquad \text{Zero-product property}$$
$$x = -5 \quad \text{or} \quad x = \frac{4}{3} \qquad \text{Solve.}$$

The solutions are -5 and $\frac{4}{3}$.

(c) $x^2 + 25 = 0$ implies that $x^2 = -25$, which has no solutions because $x^2 \geq 0$ for all real numbers.

TEACHING TIP

Emphasize that use of the zero-product property requires that one side of the equation equal 0.

─────── MAKING CONNECTIONS ───────

Quadratic Equations and Solutions

Example 2 demonstrates that a quadratic equation can have 0, 1, or 2 solutions. The following graphs illustrate graphically how these quadratic equations have 0, 1, or 2 solutions.

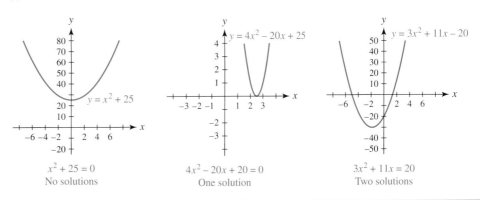

$x^2 + 25 = 0$	$4x^2 - 20x + 20 = 0$	$3x^2 + 11x = 20$
No solutions	One solution	Two solutions

EXAMPLE 3   Determining highway elevations

Solve the equation $-0.0001x^2 + 100 = 75$, which is discussed in the introduction to this section. See Figure 5.21 there.

Solution   Start by subtracting 75 from each side. Then multiply each side by $-10,000$ to clear fractions.

$$-0.0001x^2 + 100 = 75 \qquad \text{Given equation}$$
$$-0.0001x^2 + 25 = 0 \qquad \text{Subtract 75.}$$
$$-10,000(-0.0001x^2 + 25) = -10,000(0) \qquad \text{Multiply by } -10,000.$$
$$x^2 - 250,000 = 0 \qquad \text{Distributive property}$$
$$(x - 500)(x + 500) = 0 \qquad \text{Difference of squares}$$
$$x - 500 = 0 \quad \text{or} \quad x + 500 = 0 \qquad \text{Zero-product property}$$
$$x = 500 \quad \text{or} \quad x = -500 \qquad \text{Solve each equation.}$$

Thus the highway elevation is 75 feet high a distance of 500 feet on either side of the crest of the hill.

HIGHER DEGREE EQUATIONS

Using the techniques of factoring that we discussed in earlier sections, we can solve equations that involve higher degree polynomials. They can have more than two solutions.

EXAMPLE 4   Solving higher degree equations

Solve each equation.
(a) $x^3 = 4x$ **(b)** $2x^3 + 2x^2 - 12x = 0$ **(c)** $x^3 - 5x^2 - x + 5 = 0$

Solution   **(a)** Start by subtracting $4x$ from each side to obtain a 0 on the right side. (Do *not* divide each side by x because the solution $x = 0$ will be lost.)

$$x^3 = 4x \qquad \text{Given equation}$$
$$x^3 - 4x = 0 \qquad \text{Subtract } 4x.$$
$$x(x^2 - 4) = 0 \qquad \text{Factor out } x.$$
$$x(x - 2)(x + 2) = 0 \qquad \text{Difference of squares}$$
$$x = 0 \quad \text{or} \quad x - 2 = 0 \quad \text{or} \quad x + 2 = 0 \qquad \text{Zero-product property}$$
$$x = 0 \quad \text{or} \quad x = 2 \quad \text{or} \quad x = -2 \qquad \text{Solve each equation.}$$

The solutions are $-2, 0,$ and 2.
(b) Start by factoring out the common factor $2x$.

$$2x^3 + 2x^2 - 12x = 0 \qquad \text{Given equation}$$
$$2x(x^2 + x - 6) = 0 \qquad \text{Factor out } 2x.$$
$$2x(x + 3)(x - 2) = 0 \qquad \text{Factor trinomial.}$$
$$2x = 0 \quad \text{or} \quad x + 3 = 0 \quad \text{or} \quad x - 2 = 0 \qquad \text{Zero-product property}$$
$$x = 0 \quad \text{or} \quad x = -3 \quad \text{or} \quad x = 2 \qquad \text{Solve each equation.}$$

The solutions are $-3, 0,$ and 2.

TEACHING TIP

Example 4(b) asks students to first factor out a monomial and then factor a trinomial.

(c) To solve this equation use *grouping*.

$$x^3 - 5x^2 - x + 5 = 0 \qquad \text{Given equation}$$
$$(x^3 - 5x^2) + (-x + 5) = 0 \qquad \text{Associative property}$$
$$x^2(x - 5) - 1(x - 5) = 0 \qquad \text{Factor out } x^2 \text{ and } -1.$$
$$(x^2 - 1)(x - 5) = 0 \qquad \text{Distributive property}$$
$$(x - 1)(x + 1)(x - 5) = 0 \qquad \text{Difference of squares}$$
$$x - 1 = 0 \quad \text{or} \quad x + 1 = 0 \quad \text{or} \quad x - 5 = 0 \qquad \text{Zero-product property}$$
$$x = 1 \quad \text{or} \quad x = -1 \quad \text{or} \quad x = 5 \qquad \text{Solve each equation.}$$

The solutions are -1, 1, and 5.

The next example demonstrates how an equation can be solved symbolically, graphically, and numerically with the aid of a graphing calculator.

EXAMPLE 5 Solving a polynomial equation

Solve $16x^4 - 64x^3 + 64x^2 = 0$ symbolically, graphically, and numerically.

Solution **Symbolic Solution** Begin by factoring out the common factor $16x^2$.

$$16x^4 - 64x^3 + 64x^2 = 0 \qquad \text{Given equation}$$
$$16x^2(x^2 - 4x + 4) = 0 \qquad \text{Factor out } 16x^2.$$
$$16x^2(x - 2)^2 = 0 \qquad \text{Perfect square trinomial}$$

Solving results in

$$16x^2 = 0 \quad \text{or} \quad (x - 2) = 0 \qquad \text{Zero-product property}$$
$$x = 0 \quad \text{or} \quad x = 2. \qquad \text{Solve.}$$

Graphical Solution Graph $Y_1 = 16X^4 - 64X^3 + 64X^2$, as shown in Figures 5.23(a) and 5.23(b). Solutions to $y_1 = 0$ occur when $x = 0$ and $x = 2$.

Numerical Solution Construct the table for $Y_1 = 16X^4 - 64X^3 + 64X^2$, as shown in Figure 5.23(c). Solutions occur at $x = 0$ and $x = 2$.

$[-4.7, 4.7, 1]$ by $[-100, 100, 25]$ $[-4.7, 4.7, 1]$ by $[-100, 100, 25]$

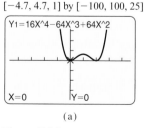
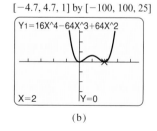
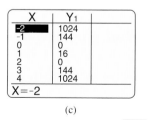

(a)   (b)   (c)

Figure 5.23

EQUATIONS IN QUADRATIC FORM

Sometimes equations do not appear to be quadratic, but they can be solved by using factoring techniques that we have already applied to quadratic equations. In these situations we often factor more than once, as demonstrated in the next example.

EXAMPLE 6   Solving equations in quadratic form

Solve each equation.
(a) $x^4 - 81 = 0$ **(b)** $x^4 - 5x^2 + 4 = 0$

Solution   **(a)** To solve this equation use the difference of squares twice.

$$(x^2)^2 - 9^2 = 0 \qquad \text{Rewrite given equation.}$$
$$(x^2 - 9)(x^2 + 9) = 0 \qquad \text{Difference of squares}$$
$$(x - 3)(x + 3)(x^2 + 9) = 0 \qquad \text{Difference of squares}$$
$$x - 3 = 0 \quad \text{or} \quad x + 3 = 0 \quad \text{or} \quad x^2 + 9 = 0 \qquad \text{Zero-product property}$$
$$x = 3 \quad \text{or} \quad x = -3 \quad \text{or} \quad x^2 = -9 \qquad \text{Solve each equation.}$$

The solutions are -3 and 3 because $x^2 = -9$ has no real number solutions.
(b) To solve this equation start by factoring the trinomial.

$$x^4 - 5x^2 + 4 = 0 \qquad \text{Given equation}$$
$$(x^2 - 4)(x^2 - 1) = 0 \qquad \text{Factor.}$$
$$(x - 2)(x + 2)(x - 1)(x + 1) = 0 \qquad \text{Difference of squares}$$
$$x = 2 \quad \text{or} \quad x = -2 \quad \text{or} \quad x = 1 \quad \text{or} \quad x = -1 \qquad \text{Solve.}$$

The solutions are $-2, -1, 1,$ and 2.

Note: To factor the equation in Example 6(a), it may be helpful to let $z = x^2$ and $z^2 = x^4$. Then the given equation becomes $z^2 - 81 = 0$, which factors to $(z - 9)(z + 9) = 0$. Substituting $z = x^2$ gives the factored equation $(x^2 - 9)(x^2 + 9) = 0$. Similar comments can be made for Example 6(b).

APPLICATIONS

Many times applications involving geometry make use of quadratic equations. In the next example we solve a quadratic equation to find the dimensions of a picture.

EXAMPLE 7   Finding the dimensions of a picture

A frame surrounding a picture is 3 inches wide. The picture inside the frame is 5 inches wider than it is high. If the overall area of the picture and frame is 336 square inches, find the dimensions of the picture inside the frame.

Solution   Let x be the height of the picture and $x + 5$ be its width. The dimensions of the picture and frame, in inches, are illustrated in Figure 5.24.

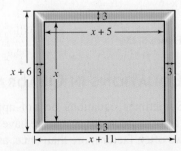

Figure 5.24

The overall area is given by $(x + 6)(x + 11)$, which equals 336 square inches.

$$(x + 6)(x + 11) = 336 \qquad \text{Equation to solve}$$
$$x^2 + 17x + 66 = 336 \qquad \text{Multiply binomials.}$$
$$x^2 + 17x - 270 = 0 \qquad \text{Subtract 336.}$$
$$(x - 10)(x + 27) = 0 \qquad \text{Factor.}$$
$$x = 10 \quad \text{or} \quad x = -27 \qquad \text{Zero-product property}$$

The only valid solution for x is 10 inches. Because the width is 5 inches more than the height, the dimensions are 10 inches by 15 inches.

Highway engineers often use quadratic functions to calculate stopping distances for cars. The faster a car is traveling, the farther it takes for the car to stop. The stopping distance for a car can be used to estimate its speed, as demonstrated in the next example. (***Source:*** F. Mannering.)

EXAMPLE 8   Finding the speed of a car

On wet, level pavement highway engineers sometimes estimate stopping distance d in feet for a car traveling at x miles per hour by

$$d(x) = \frac{1}{9}x^2 + \frac{11}{3}x.$$

Use this formula to approximate the speed of a car that takes 180 feet to stop.

Solution   We need to solve the equation $d(x) = 180$. Start by multiplying by 9 to clear fractions.

$$\frac{1}{9}x^2 + \frac{11}{3}x = 180 \qquad \text{Equation to be solved}$$

$$9\left(\frac{1}{9}x^2 + \frac{11}{3}x\right) = 9 \cdot 180 \qquad \text{Multiply by 9.}$$

$$x^2 + 33x = 1620 \qquad \text{Distributive property}$$
$$x^2 + 33x - 1620 = 0 \qquad \text{Subtract 1620.}$$
$$(x - 27)(x + 60) = 0 \qquad \text{Factor.}$$
$$x = 27 \quad \text{or} \quad x = -60 \qquad \text{Zero-product property}$$

The speed of the car is 27 miles per hour.

Note: To factor $x^2 + 33x - 1620$ we found values for m and n such that $mn = -1620$ and $m + n = 33$, which required some trial and error.

5.6   PUTTING IT ALL TOGETHER

The following is a typical strategy for solving a polynomial equation. When you have finished, be sure to check your answers.

1. If necessary, rewrite the equation so that a 0 appears on one side of the equation.
2. Factor out any common factors.

continued on next page

continued from previous page

3. Factor the remaining polynomial, using the techniques presented in this chapter.
4. Apply the *zero-product* property.
5. Solve each resulting equation.

The following table summarizes how to solve three types of higher degree polynomial equations.

Concept	Explanation	Example
Higher Degree Equations	Factor out common factors; then use the techniques for factoring.	$2x^3 - 32x = 0$ $2x(x^2 - 16) = 0$ $2x(x - 4)(x + 4) = 0$ $x = 0$ or $x = 4$ or $x = -4$
Equations in Quadratic Form	Factor these forms as $ax^2 + bx + c$.	$x^4 - 13x^2 + 36 = 0$ $(x^2 - 4)(x^2 - 9) = 0$ $(x - 2)(x + 2)(x - 3)(x + 3) = 0$ $x = 2$ or $x = -2$ or $x = 3$ or $x = -3$
Solving by Grouping	Use grouping to help factor a cubic expression having four terms. Apply the distributive property.	$x^3 - 7x^2 - 16x + 112 = 0$ $(x^3 - 7x^2) + (-16x + 112) = 0$ $x^2(x - 7) - 16(x - 7) = 0$ $(x^2 - 16)(x - 7) = 0$ $(x - 4)(x + 4)(x - 7) = 0$ $x = 4$ or $x = -4$ or $x = 7$

5.6 EXERCISES

FOR EXTRA HELP

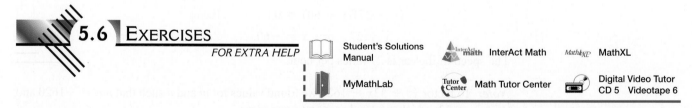

Student's Solutions Manual   InterAct Math   MathXL

MyMathLab   Math Tutor Center   Digital Video Tutor CD 5   Videotape 6

CONCEPTS

1. Give one reason why factoring is important in mathematics.   Solving polynomial equations

2. Factoring a polynomial is the *reverse* of _____ polynomials.   multiplying

3. When you are solving $x^2 = 16$ by factoring, what is a good first step?   Subtract 16 from each side.

4. To solve $x^2 - 3x - 3 = 1$ could you start by factoring the left side of the equation? Explain.
   No; the right side is not 0.

5. What is the solution to $(x - 1)^2 = 0$?   1

6. Does the equation $x^2 + 4 = 0$ have any real number solutions? Explain.   No; it implies that $x^2 = -4$.

SOLVING QUADRATIC EQUATIONS

Exercises 7–12: Solve the equation graphically. Then solve the equation symbolically.

7. $x^2 - 1 = 0$ $-1, 1$ 8. $x^2 - 9 = 0$ $-3, 3$

9. $\frac{1}{4}x^2 - 1 = 0$ $\quad -2, 2$ **10.** $\frac{1}{16}x^2 - 1 = 0$ $\quad -4, 4$

11. $x^2 - x - 2 = 0$ $\quad -1, 2$ **12.** $x^2 - x - 6 = 0$ $\quad -2, 3$

Exercises 13–24: Solve the quadratic equation.

13. $2x^2 = 32$ $\quad -4, 4$ **14.** $4x^2 = 64$ $\quad -4, 4$

15. $z^2 + 14z + 49 = 0$ $\quad -7$ **16.** $z^2 + 64 = 16z$ $\quad 8$

17. $9t^2 + 1 = 6t$ $\quad \frac{1}{3}$ **18.** $49t^2 + 28t + 4 = 0$ $\quad -\frac{2}{7}$

19. $15n^2 = 7n + 2$ $\quad -\frac{1}{5}, \frac{2}{3}$ **20.** $7n^2 + 57n + 8 = 0$ $\quad -8, -\frac{1}{7}$

21. $24m^2 + 23m = 12$ $\quad -\frac{4}{3}, \frac{3}{8}$ **22.** $11m^2 = 31m + 6$ $\quad -\frac{2}{11}, 3$

23. $x^2 + 12 = 0$ No solutions **24.** $2x^2 + 3 = 0$ No solutions

Exercises 25–28: Use the graph to solve the equation. Then solve the equation by factoring.

25. $x^2 + x - 6 = 0$ $\quad -3, 2$ **26.** $x^2 - 2x - 3 = 0$ $\quad -1, 3$

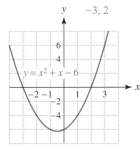 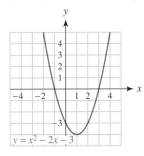

27. $2x^2 - 4x - 16 = 0$ $\quad -2, 4$ **28.** $2x^2 + 3x - 2 = 0$ $\quad -2, \frac{1}{2}$

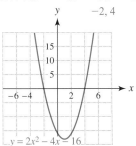 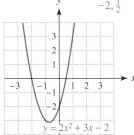

Exercises 29–32: The graph of the quadratic expression $y = ax^2 + bx + c$ is $\cap$-shaped when $a < 0$. If possible, sketch a graph of a quadratic expression with $a < 0$ that satisfies the condition.

29. No*

30. One x-intercept*

31. Two*

32. Three x-intercepts Not possible

HIGHER DEGREE EQUATIONS

Exercises 33–44: Solve the equation.

33. $z^3 = 9z$ $\quad -3, 0, 3$ **34.** $2z^3 + 8z = 0$ $\quad 0$

35. $x^3 + x = 0$ $\quad 0$ **36.** $x^3 = x$ $\quad -1, 0, 1$

37. $2x^3 - 6x^2 = 20x$ $\quad -2, 0, 5$ **38.** $3x^3 + 15x^2 + 12x = 0$ $\quad -4, -1, 0$

39. $t^4 - 4t^3 - 5t^2 = 0$ $\quad -1, 0, 5$ **40.** $2t^4 - 8t^3 + 6t^2 = 0$ $\quad 0, 1, 3$

41. $x^3 + 7x^2 - 4x - 28 = 0$ $\quad -7, -2, 2$

42. $x^3 + 5x^2 = 9x + 45$ $\quad -5, -3, 3$

43. $n^3 - 2n^2 - 36n + 72 = 0$ $\quad -6, 2, 6$

44. $n^3 - 10n^2 - 4n + 40 = 0$ $\quad -2, 2, 10$

Exercises 45–52: (Refer to Example 5.) Solve the equation
  (a) symbolically,
  (b) graphically,
  (c) numerically.

45. $x^2 - 2x - 15 = 0$ $\quad -3, 5$ **46.** $x^2 + 7x + 10 = 0$ $\quad -5, -2$

47. $2x^2 - 3x = 2$ $\quad -\frac{1}{2}, 2$ **48.** $4t^2 + 25 = 20t$ $\quad \frac{5}{2}$

49. $3t^2 + 18t + 15 = 0$ $\quad -5, -1$ **50.** $4z^2 = 16$ $\quad -2, 2$

51. $4x^4 + 16x^2 = 16x^3$ $\quad 0, 2$ **52.** $2x^3 + 12x^2 + 18x = 0$ $\quad -3, 0$

EQUATIONS IN QUADRATIC FORM

Exercises 53–62: Solve the equation.

53. $x^4 - 2x^2 - 8 = 0$ $\quad -2, 2$ **54.** $x^4 - 8x^2 - 9 = 0$ $\quad -3, 3$

55. $x^4 - 26x^2 + 25 = 0$ $\quad -5, -1, 1, 5$

56. $x^4 - 21x^2 - 100 = 0$ $\quad -5, 5$

57. $x^4 - 13x^2 + 36 = 0$ $\quad -3, -2, 2, 3$

58. $x^4 - 18x^2 + 81 = 0$ $\quad -3, 3$

59. $4x^4 + 3x^2 = 1$ $\quad -\frac{1}{2}, \frac{1}{2}$

60. $4x^4 = x^2 + 18$ $\quad -\frac{3}{2}, \frac{3}{2}$

61. $9x^4 - 13x^2 + 4 = 0$ $\quad -1, -\frac{2}{3}, \frac{2}{3}, 1$

62. $64x^4 - 180x^2 + 81 = 0$ $\quad -\frac{3}{2}, -\frac{3}{4}, \frac{3}{4}, \frac{3}{2}$

APPLICATIONS

63. *Picture Frame* (Refer to Example 7.) A rectangular frame surrounding a picture is made from boards that are 2 inches wide. The picture inside the frame is 4 inches wider than it is high. If the overall area of the picture and frame is 525 square inches, find the dimensions of the picture. $\quad 17 \times 21$ in.

64. *Picture Frame* The outside measurements of a rectangular frame for a picture are 30 inches by 40

*Answers on page IA-19

inches. The area of the rectangular picture inside the frame is 936 square inches. Find the width of the frame that surrounds the picture.   2 in.

65. *Geometry*   A rectangle is 2 inches longer than it is wide. If each side is increased by 3 inches, the area increases by 183 square inches. Find the dimensions of the rectangle.   28 × 30 in.

66. *Numbers*   If a positive number n is increased by 3, its square equals 121. Find n.   8

67. *Sidewalk Around a Pool*   A 5-foot wide sidewalk around a rectangular swimming pool has a total area of 900 square feet. Find the dimensions of the swimming pool if the pool is 20 feet longer than it is wide.   30 × 50 ft

68. *Height Reached by a Baseball*   The height in feet reached by a batted baseball after t seconds is given by

$$h(t) = -16t^2 + 88t + 4.$$

Determine when the baseball is 100 feet in the air.   1.5 and 4 sec

69. *Height Reached by a Baseball*   The height in feet reached by a batted baseball after t seconds is given by

$$h(t) = -16t^2 + 66t + 2.$$

Determine when the baseball is 70 feet in the air.   2 and $\frac{17}{8}$ sec

70. *Modeling a Hill*   (Refer to Example 3.) The elevation E in feet of a highway x feet along a hill is modeled by

$$E(x) = -0.0001x^2 + 500,$$

where $-2000 \le x \le 2000$. Determine the x-values where the elevation is 400 feet.   −1000, 1000

Exercises 71 and 72: (Refer to Example 8.) On dry, level pavement the stopping distance d in feet for a car traveling at x miles per hour can be estimated by

$$d(x) = \frac{1}{11}x^2 + \frac{11}{3}x.$$

Use this formula to approximate the speed of a car that takes d feet to stop.

71. $d = 220$ feet   33 mph   **72.** $d = 638$ feet   66 mph

73. *Modeling a Highway*   In highway design quadratic polynomials are used not only to model hills but also to model valleys. Valleys or sags in the road are sometimes referred to as *sag curves*. Suppose that the

elevation E in feet of the sag curve x (horizontal) feet along a proposed route is modeled by

$$E(x) = 0.0002x^2 - 0.3x + 500,$$

where $0 \le x \le 1500$. See the accompanying figure. (*Source: F. Mannering.*)

(a) The elevation begins at 500 ft, decreases, and then increases to 500 ft.

(a) Make a table of the elevations for $x = 0$, 300, 600, . . . , 1500 and interpret the values in the table. *

(b) Determine where the elevation is 400 feet.   500 ft and 1000 ft

74. *Biology*   Some types of worms have a remarkable ability to live without moisture. The following table from one study shows the number of worms y surviving after x days.

x (days)	0	20	40
y (worms)	50	48	45

x (days)	80	120	160
y (worms)	36	20	3

Source: D. Brown and P. Rothery, *Models in Biology.*

(a) Plot the data and graph

$$y = -0.00138x^2 - 0.076x + 50.1$$

in the same viewing rectangle. *

(b) Discuss how well the equation models the data.

(c) Estimate the day x when 10 worms remained.

(b) It models the data quite well.   (c) About day 145

WRITING ABOUT MATHEMATICS

75. Explain why the graph of $y = ax^2 + bx + c$ is used to model a dip or valley in a highway rather than the graph of $y = |ax + b|$. Make a sketch to support your reasoning. Assume that $a > 0$.

76. Explain the basic steps that you would use to solve the equation $ax^2 + bx + c = 0$ graphically and numerically. Assume that the equation has two solutions.

*Answers on page IA-19

CHECKING BASIC CONCEPTS ⟨ SECTIONS 5.5 AND 5.6 ⟩

1. Factor each expression.
   (a) $25x^2 - 16$ $(5x - 4)(5x + 4)$
   (b) $x^2 + 12x + 36$ $(x + 6)^2$
   (c) $x^3 - 27$ $(x - 3)(x^2 + 3x + 9)$
   (d) $x^3 - 3x^2 + x - 3$ $(x - 3)(x^2 + 1)$

   (*Hint:* Factor by grouping.)

2. Solve the equation $x^2 - 9 = 0$ graphically. Then solve the equation by factoring. $-3, 3$

3. Use the graph at the top of the next column to solve the equation $x^2 + 4x + 3 = 0$. Then solve the equation symbolically. $-3, -1$

4. If possible, solve each equation.
   (a) $x^2 + 9 = 6x$ 3
   (b) $x^2 + 9 = 0$ No solutions
   (c) $12x^2 + 7x - 10 = 0$ $-\frac{5}{4}, \frac{2}{3}$

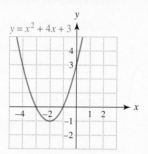

Figure for Exercise 3

5. Solve each equation.
   (a) $x^3 + 5x = 0$ 0
   (b) $x^4 - 81 = 0$ $-3, 3$
   (c) $z^4 + z^2 = 20$ $-2, 2$

5 Summary

Section 5.1   *Polynomial Functions*

Monomials and Polynomials   A monomial is a term with only *nonnegative integer* exponents. A polynomial is either a monomial or a sum of monomials.

Examples: Monomial: $-4x^3y^2$ has degree 5 and coefficient -4

Polynomial: $3x^2 - 4x + 2$ has degree 2 and leading coefficient 3

Addition and Subtraction of Polynomials   To add two polynomials, combine like terms. When subtracting two polynomials, add the first polynomial and the opposite of the second polynomial.

Examples: $(3x^3 - 4x) + (-5x^3 + 7x) = (3 - 5)x^3 + (-4 + 7)x$
$$= -2x^3 + 3x$$

$$(3xy^2 + 4x^2) - (4xy^2 - 6x) = (3xy^2 + 4x^2) + (-4xy^2 + 6x)$$
$$= 3xy^2 - 4xy^2 + 4x^2 + 6x$$
$$= -xy^2 + 4x^2 + 6x$$

Polynomial Functions   If the formula for a function is a polynomial, it is a polynomial function. The following are examples of polynomial functions.

$$f(x) = 2x - 7 \qquad \text{Linear} \qquad \text{Degree 1}$$
$$f(x) = 4x^2 - 5x + 1 \qquad \text{Quadratic} \qquad \text{Degree 2}$$
$$f(x) = 9x^3 + 6x \qquad \text{Cubic} \qquad \text{Degree 3}$$

Example: $f(x) = 4x^3 - 2x^2 + 4$ represents a polynomial function of one variable.
$$f(2) = 4(2)^3 - 2(2)^2 + 4 = 32 - 8 + 4 = 28$$

Section 5.2   *Multiplication of Polynomials*

Product of Two Polynomials   The product of two polynomials may be found by multiplying every term in the first polynomial by every term in the second polynomial.

Example: $(2x + 3)(3x - 4) = 6x^2 - 8x + 9x - 12 = 6x^2 + x - 12$

Special Products
Product of a Sum and Difference $\qquad (a + b)(a - b) = a^2 - b^2$

$\qquad\qquad\qquad\qquad\qquad\qquad$ *Example:* $(x + 3)(x - 3) = x^2 - 9$

Square of a Binomial $\qquad\qquad (a + b)^2 = a^2 + 2ab + b^2$
$\qquad\qquad\qquad\qquad\qquad\qquad (a - b)^2 = a^2 - 2ab + b^2$

$\qquad\qquad\qquad\qquad\qquad\qquad$ *Examples:* $(x + 3)^2 = x^2 + 6x + 9$
$\qquad\qquad\qquad\qquad\qquad\qquad\qquad\qquad (x - 3)^2 = x^2 - 6x + 9$

Section 5.3   *Factoring Polynomials*

Common Factors   When factoring a polynomial, start by factoring out the greatest common factor (GCF).

Examples: $8z^3 - 12z^2 + 16z = 4z(2z^2 - 3z + 4)$
$\qquad\qquad\; 18x^2y^3 - 12x^3y^2 = 6x^2y^2(3y - 2x)$

Zero-Product Property   For all real numbers a and b, if $ab = 0$, then $a = 0$ or $b = 0$ (or both).

Example: $(x - 3)(x + 2) = 0$ implies that either $x - 3 = 0$ or $x + 2 = 0$.

Solving Polynomial Equations by Factoring   Obtain a zero on one side of the equation. Factor the other side of the equation and apply the zero-product property.

Example: $\qquad\qquad x^2 - 7x = 0$
$\qquad\qquad\qquad x(x - 7) = 0 \qquad$ Factor out common factor.
$\qquad\quad x = 0 \quad \text{or} \quad x = 7 \qquad$ Zero-product property

Factoring by Grouping   Grouping can be used to factor cubic expressions with four terms by applying the distributive and associative properties.

Example: $x^3 + x^2 + 5x + 5 = (x^3 + x^2) + (5x + 5)$ Associative property

$$= x^2(x + 1) + 5(x + 1)$$ Distributive property

$$= (x^2 + 5)(x + 1)$$ Distributive property

Section 5.4   *Factoring Trinomials*

Factoring $x^2 + bx + c$ Find integers m and n that satisfy $mn = c$ and $m + n = b$. Then

$$x^2 + bx + c = (x + m)(x + n).$$

Example: $x^2 + 3x + 2 = (x + 1)(x + 2)$ $m = 1, n = 2$

Factoring $ax^2 + bx + c$ Either grouping or FOIL in reverse can be used to factor $ax^2 + bx + c$. The use of FOIL may require some trial and error. Trinomials can also be factored graphically.

Examples: *Grouping*   Find m and n so that $mn = 30$ and $m + n = 17$.

$$6x^2 + 17x + 5 = (6x^2 + 2x) + (15x + 5)$$ $m = 2, n = 15$

$$= 2x(3x + 1) + 5(3x + 1)$$

$$= (2x + 5)(3x + 1)$$

FOIL   Correctly factoring a trinomial requires checking the middle term.

$$2x^2 + 3x - 14 = (2x + 7)\,(x - 2)$$

$$\underset{}{\overset{7x}{\underline{}}}$$

$$\underline{-4x}$$

$$3x$$

It checks. $\longrightarrow$

Graphically   Trinomials can also be factored either graphically or numerically. For example, the x-intercepts on the graph of $f(x) = 2x^2 + x - 1$ are $x = 0.5$ and $x = -1$. Thus $f(x)$ can be factored as

$$2x^2 + x - 1 = 2(x - 0.5)(x + 1)$$

$$= (2x - 1)(x + 1).$$

Section 5.5   *Special Types of Factoring*

Difference of Two Squares

$$a^2 - b^2 = (a - b)(a + b)$$

Example:

$$49x^2 - 36y^2 = (7x)^2 - (6y)^2 = (7x - 6y)(7x + 6y)$$ $a = 7x, b = 6y$

Perfect Square Trinomials

$$a^2 + 2ab + b^2 = (a + b)^2 \quad \text{and}$$
$$a^2 - 2ab + b^2 = (a - b)^2$$

Examples: $x^2 + 2xy + y^2 = (x + y)^2$
$$9r^2 - 12r + 4 = (3r - 2)^2$$

Sum and Difference of Two Cubes

$$a^3 + b^3 = (a + b)(a^2 - ab + b^2) \quad \text{and}$$
$$a^3 - b^3 = (a - b)(a^2 + ab + b^2)$$

Examples: $x^3 + y^3 = (x + y)(x^2 - xy + y^2)$ $a = x, b = y$
$$8t^3 - 27r^6 = (2t - 3r^2)(4t^2 + 6tr^2 + 9r^4) \quad a = 2t, b = 3r^2$$

Section 5.6   *Polynomial Equations*

Solving Polynomial Equations   Follow the strategy presented in Putting It All Together for Section 5.6.

Example:		
	$x^4 = 2x^2 + 8$	Given equation
	$x^4 - 2x^2 - 8 = 0$	Subtract $2x^2 + 8$ from each side.
	$(x^2 - 4)(x^2 + 2) = 0$	Factor trinomial.
	$(x - 2)(x + 2)(x^2 + 2) = 0$	Difference of squares
	$x = 2 \quad \text{or} \quad x = -2$	Zero-product property

CHAPTER

5 Review Exercises

SECTION 5.1

1. Give an example of a binomial and an example of a trinomial. $x + 5; x^2 - 3x + 1$; answers may vary.

2. Write a monomial that represents the volume of 10 identical boxes x inches tall with square bases y inches on a side. What is the total volume of the boxes if $x = 5$ and $y = 8$? $10xy^2$; 3200 in^3

Exercises 3–6: Identify the degree and coefficient of the monomial.

3. $-4x^5$ 5; -4

4. y^3 3; 1

5. $5xy^6$ 7; 5

6. $-9y^{10}$ 10; -9

Exercises 7–10: Combine like terms.

7. $5x - 4x + 10x$ $11x$ **8.** $-3y + 6y$ $3y$

9. $9x^3 - 5x^3 + x^2$ $4x^3 + x^2$

10. $6x^3y - 4x^3 + 8x^3y + 5x^3$ $14x^3y + x^3$

Exercises 11–14: Identify the degree and leading coefficient of the polynomial.

11. $5x^2 - 3x + 5$ $2; 5$ **12.** $-9x^3 - 4x^2 + 6x + 1$ $3; -9$

13. $1 - 5x + 8x^2$ $2; 8$ **14.** $x^3 - 5x + 5 + 2x^4$ $4; 2$

Exercises 15–18: Combine the polynomials.

15. $(3x^2 - x + 7) + (5x^2 + 4x - 8)$ $8x^2 + 3x - 1$

16. $(6z^3 + z) + (17z^3 - 4z^2)$ $23z^3 - 4z^2 + z$

17. $(-4x^2 - 6x + 1) - (-3x^2 - 7x + 1)$ $-x^2 + x$

18. $(3x^3 - 5x + 7) - (8x^3 + x^2 - 2x + 1)$
$-5x^3 - x^2 - 3x + 6$

Exercises 19–22: Evaluate $f(x)$ at the value of x.

19. $f(x) = -4x^3$ $x = 2$ -32

20. $f(x) = 4x - x^2$ $x = -3$ -21

21. $f(x) = 2x^2 - 3x + 2$ $x = -1$ 7

22. $f(x) = 1 - x - 4x^3$ $x = 4$ -259

23. Use the graph to evaluate $f(2)$. -4

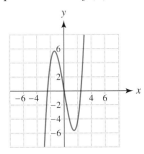

24. Use the table to evaluate $f(x) = 5x - 3x^2$ at $x = 1.5$. 0.75

SECTION 5.2

Exercises 25 and 26: Multiply.

25. $5(3x - 4)$ $15x - 20$ **26.** $-2x(1 + x - 4x^2)$
$-2x - 2x^2 + 8x^3$

Exercises 27–30: Multiply the monomials.

27. $x^3 \cdot x^5$ x^8 **28.** $-2x^3 \cdot 3x$ $-6x^4$

29. $(-7xy^7)(6xy)$ $-42x^2y^8$ **30.** $(12xy^4)(5x^2y)$ $60x^3y^5$

                   $35. \ y^2 - \frac{1}{9}$ $36. \ y^2 - y + \frac{6}{25}$

Exercises 31–44: Multiply the expressions.

31. $(x + 4)(x + 5)$ **32.** $(x - 7)(x - 8)$
    $x^2 + 9x + 20$ $x^2 - 15x + 56$

33. $(6x + 3)(2x - 9)$ **34.** $(2x + 3)(x - 4)$
    $12x^2 - 48x - 27$ $2x^2 - 5x - 12$

35. $\left(y - \frac{1}{3}\right)\left(y + \frac{1}{3}\right)$ **36.** $\left(y - \frac{2}{5}\right)\left(y - \frac{3}{5}\right)$

37. $4x^2(2x^2 - 3x - 1)$ **38.** $-x(4 + 5x - 7x^2)$
    $8x^4 - 12x^3 - 4x^2$ $-4x - 5x^2 + 7x^3$

39. $(4x + y)(4x - y)$ **40.** $(x + 3)^2$
    $16x^2 - y^2$ $x^2 + 6x + 9$

41. $(2y - 5)^2$ **42.** $(a - b)(a^2 + ab + b^2)$
    $4y^2 - 20y + 25$ $a^3 - b^3$

43. $(5m - 2n^4)^2$ $25m^2 - 20mn^4 + 4n^8$

44. $\big((r - 1) + t\big)\big((r - 1) - t\big)$ $r^2 - 2r + 1 - t^2$

SECTION 5.3

Exercises 45–48: Factor out the greatest common factor.

45. $25x^2 - 30x$ **46.** $18x^3 + 6x$ $6x(3x^2 + 1)$
    $5x(5x - 6)$

47. $5y + 15y^2$ **48.** $12x^3 + 8x^2 - 16x$
    $5y(1 + 3y)$ $4x(3x^2 + 2x - 4)$

Exercises 49–54: Use factoring to solve the polynomial equation.

49. $x^2 + 3x = 0$ $-3, 0$ **50.** $10x + 5x^2 = 0$ $-2, 0$

51. $7x^4 = 28x^2$ $-2, 0, 2$ **52.** $10x^4 - 30x^3 = 0$ $0, 3$

53. $2t^2 - 3t + 1 = 0$ $\frac{1}{2}, 1$

54. $4z(z - 3) + 4(z - 3) = 0$ $-1, 3$

Exercises 55 and 56: Use the graph of $y = P(x)$ to do the following.
    (a) *Find the x-intercepts.*
    (b) *Solve the equation $P(x) = 0$.*
    (c) *What are the zeros of $P(x)$?*

55.   (a) $0, 3$ **56.**   (a) $-1, 2$
               (b) $0, 3$ (b) $-1, 2$
               (c) $0, 3$ (c) $-1, 2$

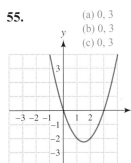

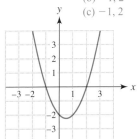

Exercises 57–60: Use grouping to factor the polynomial.

57. $2x^3 + 2x^2 - 3x - 3$ $(x + 1)(2x^2 - 3)$

58. $2x^3 + 3x^2 + 6x + 9$ $(2x + 3)(x^2 + 3)$

59. $z^3 + z^2 + z + 1$ **60.** $ax - bx + ay - by$
$(z + 1)(z^2 + 1)$ $(a - b)(x + y)$

SECTION 5.4

Exercises 61–68: Factor completely.

61. $x^2 + 8x + 12$ **62.** $x^2 - 5x - 50$
$(x + 2)(x + 6)$ $(x - 10)(x + 5)$

63. $9x^2 + 25x - 6$ **64.** $4x^2 - 22x + 10$
$(x + 3)(9x - 2)$ $2(x - 5)(2x - 1)$

65. $x^3 - 4x^2 + 3x$ **66.** $2x^4 + 14x^3 + 20x^2$
$x(x - 3)(x - 1)$ $2x^2(x + 2)(x + 5)$

67. $5x^4 + 15x^3 - 90x^2$ **68.** $10x^3 - 90x^2 + 200x$
$5x^2(x - 3)(x + 6)$ $10x(x - 5)(x - 4)$

Exercises 69 and 70: Use the table to factor the expression. Check your answer by multiplying.

69. $x^2 - 2x - 15$ **70.** $x^2 - 24x + 143$

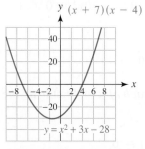

X	Y1
-5	20
-3	0
-1	-12
1	-16
3	-12
5	0
7	20

Y1▤X^2−2X−15

X	Y1
9	8
10	3
11	0
12	-1
13	0
14	3
15	8

Y1▤X^2−24X+143

$(x + 3)(x - 5)$ $(x - 11)(x - 13)$

71. Use the graph to factor $x^2 + 3x - 28$. Check your answer by multiplying.

72. Use the graph to solve $x^2 - 21x + 104 = 0$. Check your solutions.
8, 13

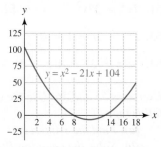

y $(x + 7)(x - 4)$

$-y = x^2 + 3x - 28$

$y = x^2 - 21x + 104$

SECTION 5.5

Exercises 73–88: Factor completely.

73. $t^2 - 49$ **74.** $4y^2 - 9x^2$
$(t - 7)(t + 7)$ $(2y - 3x)(2y + 3x)$

75. $x^2 + 4x + 4$ **76.** $16x^2 - 8x + 1$
$(x + 2)^2$ $(4x - 1)^2$

77. $x^3 - 27$ **78.** $8y^3 + 1$
$(x - 3)(x^2 + 3x + 9)$ $(2y + 1)(4y^2 - 2y + 1)$

79. $125a^3 - 64$ **80.** $64x^3 + 27y^3$
$(5a - 4)(25a^2 + 20a + 16)$ $(4x + 3y)(16x^2 - 12xy + 9y^2)$

81. $10y^3 - 10y$ **82.** $4r^4 - t^6$
$10y(y - 1)(y + 1)$ $(2r^2 - t^3)(2r^2 + t^3)$

83. $m^4 - 16n^4$ **84.** $n^3 - 2n^2 - n + 2$
$(m - 2n)(m + 2n)(m^2 + 4n^2)$ $(n - 2)(n - 1)(n + 1)$

85. $25a^2 - 30ab + 9b^2$ **86.** $2r^3 - 12r^2t + 18rt^2$
$(5a - 3b)^2$ $2r(r - 3t)^2$

87. $a^6 + 27b^3$ **88.** $8p^6 - q^3$
$(a^2 + 3b)(a^4 - 3a^2b + 9b^2)$ $(2p^2 - q)(4p^4 + 2p^2q + q^2)$

SECTION 5.6

Exercises 89 and 90: Solve the equation symbolically and graphically.

89. $x^2 - 16 = 0$ **90.** $x^2 - 2x - 3 = 0$
$-4, 4$ $-1, 3$

Exercises 91–100: Solve the equation.

91. $4x^2 - 28x + 49 = 0$ $\frac{7}{2}$ **92.** $x^2 + 8 = 0$ No solutions

93. $3x^2 = 2x + 5$ $-1, \frac{5}{3}$ **94.** $4x^2 + 5x = 6$ $-2, \frac{3}{4}$

95. $x^3 = x$ $-1, 0, 1$

96. $x^3 - 6x^2 + 11x - 6 = 0$ $1, 2, 3$

97. $x^3 + x^2 - 72x = 0$ **98.** $x^4 - 15x^3 + 56x^2 = 0$
$-9, 0, 8$ $0, 7, 8$

99. $x^4 = 16$ $-2, 2$ **100.** $x^4 + 5x^2 = 36$ $-2, 2$

APPLICATIONS

101. ***Thanksgiving Travel*** The number of people traveling at Thanksgiving in the 1990s increased to a high in 1999. The accompanying graph shows the number of people in millions who traveled 100 miles or more during the Thanksgiving holiday. The function

$$f(x) = -0.061x^2 + 1.52x + 25.2$$

models these data, where $x = 0$ corresponds to 1990, $x = 1$ to 1991, and so on until $x = 9$ corresponds to 1999. (***Source:*** American Automobile Association.)

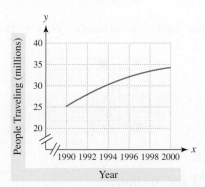

(a) Use $f(x)$ to determine how many people traveled 100 miles or more during the Thanksgiving holiday in 1994. 30.304 million

(b) Use the graph to estimate when the number of travelers reached 32 million. About 1996

 (c) Make a table of $f(x)$ starting at $x = 0$ and incrementing by 1. In what year were there about 28 million travelers?* About 1992

102. *Geometry* Suppose that a triangle has base $x + 2$ and height $x - 3$. Find a polynomial that gives the area of the triangle. $\frac{1}{2}x^2 - \frac{1}{2}x - 3$

103. *High Temperatures* The formula

$$f(x) = -1.466x^2 + 20.25x + 9$$

models the monthly average high temperatures in degrees Fahrenheit at Columbus, Ohio. In this formula $x = 1$ corresponds to January, $x = 2$ to February, and so on. (***Source:*** J. Williams, *The Weather Almanac, 1995*.) 73.6°F

(a) What is the average high temperature in May?

(b) Make a table of $f(x)$, starting at $x = 1$ and incrementing by 1. During what month is the average temperature the greatest?* July

(c) Graph f in $[1, 12, 1]$ by $[30, 90, 10]$ and interpret the graph.* Temperatures increase from January to July and then decrease from July to December.

104. *Probability* Suppose that the likelihood, or chance, that a pitch in softball will be a strike is x percent. Then the likelihood, as a percentage, that two consecutive pitches will not be strikes is given by $100\left(1 - \frac{x}{100}\right)^2$. $100 - 2x + \frac{x^2}{100}$

(a) Multiply this expression.

(b) Let $x = 70$. Use both the given expression and the expression you found in part (a) to obtain the likelihood that two consecutive pitches are not strikes. 9%

105. Write a polynomial that represents the product of three consecutive integers, where x is the largest integer. $(x - 2)(x - 1)(x) = x^3 - 3x^2 + 2x$

106. *Area* Use the area of a rectangle to illustrate that $(x + 2)(x + 7) = x^2 + 9x + 14$.*

107. *Area* Suppose that the area of a small building is 144 square feet and its length is 7 feet longer than its width. Find the dimensions of the building 9 ft by 16 ft

(a) graphically,

(b) numerically, and

(c) symbolically.

108. *Rectangular Pen* A rectangular pen has a perimeter of 50 feet. If x represents its width, write a polynomial that gives the area of the pen in terms of x. $25x - x^2$

109. *Flight of a Golf Ball* If a golf ball is hit upward with a velocity of 66 feet per second (45 mph), its height h in feet above the ground after t seconds can be modeled by

$$h(t) = -16t^2 + 66t.$$ After $\frac{33}{8} = 4.125$ sec

(a) Determine when the ball strikes the ground.

(b) When was the height of the ball 50 feet? After 1 sec and after $\frac{25}{8} = 3.125$ sec

110. *Ticket Prices* If tickets are sold for $50, 600 tickets are expected to be sold. For each $1 reduction in price, an additional 20 tickets will be sold.

(a) Write an expression that gives the revenue from ticket sales when ticket prices are reduced by x dollars. $R(x) = (50 - x)(600 + 20x)$

(b) Determine the ticket price that results in sales of $32,000. $40

111. *Area of a Rectangle* A rectangle has an area of 216 square inches. Its length is 6 inches more than its width. Find the dimensions of the rectangle. 12 in. × 18 in.

112. *Modeling a Hill* The elevation E of a hill x feet along a highway can be modeled by

$$E(x) = -0.0001x^2 + 500,$$

where E is in feet. The crest of the hill corresponds to $x = 0$. Find values of x where E is 400 feet. −1000; 1000

*Answers on page IA-19

CHAPTER

5 Test

Exercises 1 and 2: Simplify the expression by combining like terms.

1. $x^2y^2 - 4x + 9x - 5x^2y^2$ $5x - 4x^2y^2$

2. $(-2x^3 - 6x + 1) - (5x^3 - x^2 + x - 10)$
$-7x^3 + x^2 - 7x + 11$

3. Evaluate $f(x) = 2x^3 - x^2 - 5x + 2$ at $x = -2$. -8

4. Use the graph to evaluate $f(2)$. -2

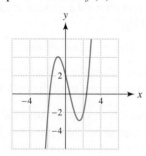

Exercises 5–8: Multiply and simplify.

5. $-\frac{2}{5}x^2(10x - 5)$ **6.** $2xy^7 \cdot 7xy$ $14x^2y^8$
$-4x^3 + 2x^2$

7. $(2x + 1)(5x - 7)$ **8.** $(5 - 3x)^2$ $9x^2 - 30x + 25$
$10x^2 - 9x - 7$

Exercises 9–13: Factor completely.

9. $3x^2 + 7x - 20$ **10.** $5x^4 - 5x^2$
$(x + 4)(3x - 5)$ $5x^2(x - 1)(x + 1)$

11. $2x^3 + x^2 - 10x - 5$
$(2x + 1)(x^2 - 5)$

12. $49x^2 - 14x + 1$ **13.** $x^3 + 8$
$(7x - 1)^2$ $(x + 2)(x^2 - 2x + 4)$

14. Identify the degree and leading coefficient of the polynomial $5 - 4x + x^3$. $3; 1$

15. Multiply $(2m^3 - 4n^2)^2$. $4m^6 - 16m^3n^2 + 16n^4$

16. Use the graph to factor $x^2 + 2x - 48$.
$(x + 8)(x - 6)$

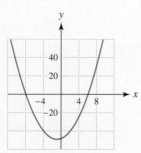

17. *Numbers*   Write a polynomial that represents the product of two consecutive even integers, where x is the smaller integer. $x(x + 2)$

Exercises 18–20: Use factoring to solve the polynomial equation.

18. $5x^2 = 15x$ $0, 3$ **19.** $4t^2 + 19t - 5 = 0$ $-5, \frac{1}{4}$

20. $2z^4 - 8z^2 = 0$ $-2, 0, 2$

21. *Area*   A rectangular picture frame is 4 inches wider than it is high and has an area of 221 square inches.
  (a) Write an equation whose solution gives the height of the picture frame. $x(x + 4) = 221$
  (b) Solve the equation in part (a).
  (c) Find the perimeter of the picture frame.   60 in.
    (b) 13, -17; height is 13 in.

22. *Dew Point*   The formula

$$f(x) = -0.091x^3 + 0.66x^2 + 5.78x + 23.5$$

models the monthly average dew point in degrees Fahrenheit in Birmingham, Alabama. In this formula $x = 1$ corresponds to January, $x = 2$ to February, and so on.   (*Source:* J. Williams, *The Weather Almanac, 1995.*)
  (a) What is the average dew point in May?
  (b) Use the graph of f to discuss how the dew point changes during the year.
(a) About 57.5°F

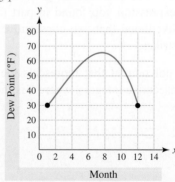

(b) The dew point starts at about 30°F in January and increases to a maximum of about 65°F in July. Then it decreases to 30°F by the end of December.

CHAPTER

5 Extended and Discovery Exercises

INTERPRETING GRAPHS OF REAL-WORLD DATA

Exercises 1 and 2: Many times it is difficult to find formulas that model real-world data accurately. The next two exercises contain data of this type. Instead of formulas, graphs are given. By interpreting these graphs, we can make some interesting observations about nature.

1. *Lynx and Hares* During the years from 1875 through 1905, the Hudson Bay Company in Canada logged trap records of both lynx and snowshoe hares. Line graphs representing these records are shown in the accompanying figures. (*Source:* C. S. Elton and M. Nicholson, "The ten year cycle in numbers of lynx in Canada.") *

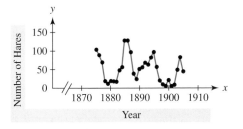

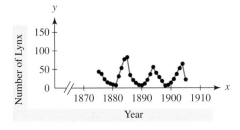

(a) Describe how the numbers of lynx varied during this period.
(b) Describe how the numbers of snowshoe hares varied during this period.
(c) What is the relationship between these graphs? Explain your answer completely.

2. *Blow-Fly Population* A population of blow flies was kept in a laboratory for roughly 20 generations. Adult blow flies need a nutrient found in ground liver in order to lay their eggs. Food and water for the flies were not limited, but the supply of ground liver available was limited. In this experiment both the number of adult flies and the number of eggs laid per day are shown in the accompanying graphs. (*Sources:* A. J. Nicholson, "An Outline of the Dynamics of Animal Populations"; E. Pielou, *Population and Community Ecology: Principles and Methods*.) *

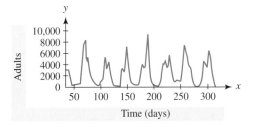

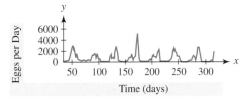

(a) Discuss how the number of adult flies varied during this time period.
(b) Discuss how the number of eggs varied during this time period.
(c) How do the peaks in the graph of the adult flies compare to the peaks in the graph of the eggs?
(d) Explain the relationship between the two graphs.

MODELING NONLINEAR DATA

Exercises 3 and 4: Real-world data often do not lie on a line when they are plotted. Such data are called nonlinear data, and nonlinear functions are used to model this type of data. In the next four exercises you will be asked to find your own functions that model real-world data.

 3. *Planetary Orbits* Johannes Kepler (1571–1630) was the first person to find a formula that models the relationship between a planet's average distance from the sun and the time it takes to orbit the sun. The following table lists a planet's average distance x from the sun and the number of years y it takes to orbit the sun. In this table distances have been normalized so that Earth's distance is exactly 1. For example, Saturn

is 9.54 times farther from the sun than Earth is and requires 29.5 years to orbit the sun.*

Planet	x (distance)	y (period)
Mercury	0.387	0.241
Venus	0.723	0.615
Earth	1.00	1.00
Mars	1.52	1.88
Jupiter	5.20	11.9
Saturn	9.54	29.5

Source: C. Ronan, *The Natural History of the Universe.*

(a) Make a scatterplot of the data. Are the data linear or nonlinear?
(b) Kepler discovered a formula having the form $y = x^k$, which models the data in the table. Graph $y = x^{2.5}$ and the data in the same viewing rectangle. Does y model the data accurately? Explain.
(c) Try to discover a value for k so that $y = x^k$ models the data.
(d) The average distances of Neptune and Pluto from the sun are 30.1 and 39.4, respectively. Estimate how long it takes for each planet to orbit the sun. Check a reference to see whether your answers are accurate.

4. *Women in the Work Force*   The number of women gainfully employed in the work force has changed significantly since 1900. The table lists these numbers in millions at 10-year intervals.*

Year	1900	1910	1920	1930	1940
Work Force	5.3	7.4	8.6	10.8	12.8

Year	1950	1960	1970	1980	1990
Work Force	18.4	23.2	31.5	45.5	56.6

Source: Department of Labor.

(a) Make a scatterplot of the data in [1890, 2000, 20] by [0, 60, 10]. Are the data linear or nonlinear? Explain your answer.
(b) Use trial and error to find a value for k so that $y = k(x - 1900)^2 + 5.3$ models the data.
(c) Use y to predict the number of women that will be in the work force in 2005.

5. *Aging of America*   Americans are living longer. The following table shows the number of Americans expected to be more than 100 years old for various years.*

Year	1994	1996	1998
Number (thousands)	50	56	65

Year	2000	2002	2004
Number (thousands)	75	94	110

Source: Bureau of the Census.

(a) Make a scatterplot of the data. Choose an appropriate viewing rectangle.
(b) Use trial and error to find a value for k so that

$$y = k(x - 1994)^2 + 50$$

models the data.
(c) Use y to predict the number of Americans that will be more than 100 years old in 2006.

6. *Highway Design*   In order to allow enough distance for cars to pass on two-lane highways, engineers calculate minimum sight distances for curves and for hills. See the accompanying figure.*

The following table shows the minimum sight distance y in feet for a car traveling x miles per hour.
(a) Make a scatterplot of the data. As x increases, describe how y changes. Are the data linear or nonlinear?
(b) Find a formula that models the data.
(c) Use your formula to predict the minimum sight distance for a car traveling at 56 miles per hour.

x (mph)	20	30	40	50
y (feet)	810	1090	1480	1840

x (mph)	60	65	70
y (feet)	2140	2310	2490

Source: L. Haefner, *Introduction to Transportation Systems.*

*Answers on page IA-20

7. *Charitable Giving*   In 1998, average charitable giving varied according to income. The average amount given for three different incomes is listed in the table.

Income	$10,000	$40,000	$100,000
Giving	$412	$843	$2550

Source: Gallup for Independent Sector.

(a) Let x be income and y be charitable giving. Set up an augmented matrix whose solution gives values for a, b, and c so that the graph of $y = ax^2 + bx + c$ passes through the points (10000, 412), (40000, 843), and (100000, 2550). (*Hint:* Because the graph passes through the point (10000, 412) the equation

$$412 = a(10{,}000)^2 + b(10{,}000) + c$$

must be satisfied.)

(b) Use a graphing calculator to solve this system of linear equations.

(c) Estimate the average charitable giving for someone earning $20,000. Compare your answer to the actual value of $525.

(a) $\begin{bmatrix} 10{,}000^2 & 10{,}000 & 1 & 412 \\ 40{,}000^2 & 40{,}000 & 1 & 843 \\ 100{,}000^2 & 100{,}000 & 1 & 2550 \end{bmatrix}$

(b) $a \approx 1.56 \times 10^{-7}$, $b \approx 0.007$, and $c \approx 330.9$

(c) $533.30; close to the actual value; note that unrounded values for a, b, and c give $524.37.

Rational Expressions and Functions

Railroads, airports, and highways have been essential in the development of the United States. Without them much of the country's economic and technological growth would have been impossible. Today people are able to travel not only throughout the United States but also throughout the world by airplane, car, train, bus, or boat.

As transportation systems have become more complex, mathematics has played an increasingly important role in their design and operation. Highway designers use mathematics rather than depend on trial and error to find solutions. For example, the following table shows braking distances D for a car traveling downhill on wet pavement at 30 miles per hour for different grades G of the hill. (Grade corresponds to the slope of the road: A larger grade indicates a steeper hill.)

G	0.00	0.05	0.10	0.15	0.20	0.25
D (feet)	86	100	120	150	200	300

In this chapter we show how a rational function can model these data. We also discuss railroad track design, time spent waiting in a line, the ozone layer, skin cancer, probability, population growth, electricity, aerial photography, and memory requirements for storing music on a compact disc.

The future belongs to those who believe in the beauty of their dreams.
—Eleanor Roosevelt

Source: N. Garber and L. Hoel, *Traffic and Highway Engineering.*

TEACHING TIP

Point out that rational functions are used to estimate quantities such as braking distance on a hill.

CHAPTER 6

6.1 INTRODUCTION TO RATIONAL FUNCTIONS AND EQUATIONS

Recognizing and Using Rational Functions · Solving Rational Equations

INTRODUCTION

Suppose that a parking ramp attendant can wait on 5 cars per minute and that cars are randomly leaving the parking ramp at a rate of 4 cars per minute. Is it possible to predict how long the average driver will wait in line? Using rational functions, we can answer this question (see Exercise 75). Rational functions also occur in other types of applications, such as in the design of highways and train tracks. In this section we introduce rational functions and equations.

RECOGNIZING AND USING RATIONAL FUNCTIONS

In Chapter 5 we discussed polynomials. Examples of polynomials include

$$4, \quad x, \quad 2x - 5, \quad 3x^2 - 6x + 1, \quad \text{and} \quad 3x^4 - 7.$$

Rational expressions result when a polynomial is divided by a nonzero polynomial. Three examples of rational expressions are

$$\frac{4}{x}, \quad \frac{x}{2x - 5}, \quad \text{and} \quad \frac{3x^2 - 6x + 1}{3x^4 - 7}.$$

EXAMPLE 1   Recognizing a rational expression

Determine whether each expression is rational.

(a) $\dfrac{4 - x}{5x^2 + 3}$ **(b)** $\dfrac{x^2 - 1}{\sqrt{x} + 2x}$ **(c)** $\dfrac{6}{x - 1}$

Solution **(a)** This expression is rational because both $4 - x$ and $5x^2 + 3$ are polynomials.
(b) This expression is not rational because $\sqrt{x} + 2x$ is not a polynomial.
(c) This expression is rational because both 6 and $x - 1$ are polynomials.

TEACHING TIP

Note that every polynomial is a rational expression but not every rational expression is a polynomial.

Rational expressions are used to define *rational functions*. For example, $\frac{4}{x+1}$ is a rational expression and $f(x) = \frac{4}{x+1}$ represents a rational function.

RATIONAL FUNCTION

Let $p(x)$ and $q(x)$ be polynomials. Then a **rational function** is given by

$$f(x) = \frac{p(x)}{q(x)}.$$

The domain of f includes all x-values such that $q(x) \neq 0$.

EXAMPLE 2   Identifying the domain of rational functions

TEACHING TIP

Review the domain of a function
with the students.

Identify the domain of each function.

(a) $f(x) = \dfrac{1}{x + 2}$ **(b)** $g(x) = \dfrac{2x}{x^2 - 3x + 2}$ **(c)** $h(t) = \dfrac{4}{t^3 - t}$

Solution   **(a)** The domain of f includes all x-values for which the expression $f(x) = \frac{1}{x+2}$ is defined. Thus we must *exclude* values of x for which the denominator equals 0.

$$x + 2 = 0 \qquad \text{Set denominator equal to 0.}$$
$$x = -2 \qquad \text{Subtract 2.}$$

In set-builder notation, $D = \{x \mid x \neq -2\}$.

(b) The domain of g includes values of x except where the denominator equals 0.

$$x^2 - 3x + 2 = 0 \qquad \text{Set denominator equal to 0.}$$
$$(x - 1)(x - 2) = 0 \qquad \text{Factor.}$$
$$x = 1 \quad \text{or} \quad x = 2 \qquad \text{Zero-product property}$$

Thus $D = \{x \mid x \text{ is any real number except 1 and 2}\}$.

(c) The domain of h includes all values of t except where the denominator equals 0.

$$t^3 - t = 0 \qquad \text{Set denominator equal to 0.}$$
$$t(t^2 - 1) = 0 \qquad \text{Factor out } t.$$
$$t(t - 1)(t + 1) = 0 \qquad \text{Difference of squares}$$
$$t = 0 \quad \text{or} \quad t = 1 \quad \text{or} \quad t = -1 \qquad \text{Zero-product property}$$

Thus $D = \{t \mid t \text{ is any real number except 0, 1, and } -1\}$.

Like other functions, rational functions have graphs. To graph a rational function by hand, we usually start by making a table of values, as demonstrated in the next example. Because the graphs of rational functions are typically nonlinear, it is a good idea to plot at least 3 points on each side of an x-value where the formula is undefined.

TEACHING TIP

If you are going to have students
graph rational functions by hand,
do several examples, such as
$f(x) = \frac{1}{x-1}$ and $f(x) = \frac{x}{x+2}$.

EXAMPLE 3   Graphing a rational function

Graph $f(x) = \frac{1}{x}$.

Solution   Make a table of values for $f(x) = \frac{1}{x}$, as shown in Table 6.1. Notice that $x = 0$ is not in the domain of f, and a dash can be used to denote this undefined value. Start by picking three x-values on each side of 0.

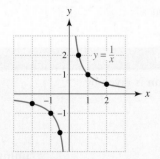

Figure 6.1

TABLE 6.1

x	-2	-1	$-\frac{1}{2}$	0	$\frac{1}{2}$	1	2
$\frac{1}{x}$	$-\frac{1}{2}$	-1	-2	—	2	1	$\frac{1}{2}$

Plot the points shown in Table 6.1 and then connect the points with a smooth curve, as shown in Figure 6.1. Because $f(0)$ is undefined, the graph of $f(x) = \frac{1}{x}$ does not cross the line $x = 0$, the y-axis.

In the next example we evaluate a rational function three different ways.

EXAMPLE 4   Evaluating a rational function

Use Table 6.2, the formula for $f(x)$, and Figure 6.2 to evaluate $f(-1), f(1)$, and $f(2)$.

(a) TABLE 6.2

x	-3	-2	-1	0	1	2	3
$f(x)$	$\frac{3}{2}$	$\frac{4}{3}$	1	0	—	4	3

(b) $f(x) = \dfrac{2x}{x - 1}$ **(c)**

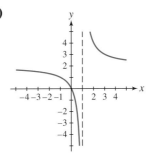

Figure 6.2

Solution   **(a)** *Numerical Evaluation*   Table 6.2 shows that

$$f(-1) = 1, \qquad f(1) \text{ is undefined}, \quad \text{and} \quad f(2) = 4.$$

(b) *Symbolic Evaluation*

$$f(-1) = \frac{2(-1)}{-1 - 1} = 1$$

$$f(1) = \frac{2(1)}{1 - 1} = \frac{2}{0}, \text{ which is undefined. Input 1 is not in the domain of } f.$$

$$f(2) = \frac{2(2)}{2 - 1} = 4$$

(c) *Graphical Evaluation*   To evaluate $f(-1)$ graphically, find $x = -1$ on the x-axis and move upward to the graph of f. The y-value is 1 at the point of intersection, so $f(-1) = 1$, as shown in Figure 6.3(a). In Figure 6.3(b) the vertical line $x = 1$ is called a *vertical asymptote*. Because the graph of f does not intersect this line, $f(1)$ is undefined. Figure 6.3(c) reveals that $f(2) = 4$.

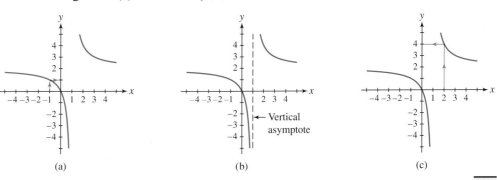

Figure 6.3

A **vertical asymptote** is a vertical line that typically occurs in the graph of a rational function when the denominator of the rational expression is 0 but the numerator is not 0. The graph of a rational function *never* crosses a vertical asymptote. In Figure 6.1, the vertical asymptote is the *y*-axis or $x = 0$.

Technology Note: *Asymptotes, Dot Mode, and Decimal Windows*

When rational functions are graphed on graphing calculators, pseudo-asymptotes often occur because the calculator is simply connecting dots to draw a graph. The accompanying figures show the graph of $y = \frac{2}{x-2}$ in connected mode, dot mode, and with a *decimal*, or *friendly, window*. In dot mode, pixels in the calculator screen are not connected. With dot mode (and sometimes with a decimal window) pseudo-asymptotes do not appear. To learn more about these features consult your owner's manual.

Calculator Help
To set a calculator in dot mode or to set a decimal window, see the Appendix (page AP-10).

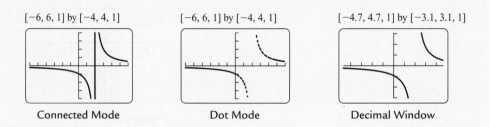

[−6, 6, 1] by [−4, 4, 1]   [−6, 6, 1] by [−4, 4, 1]   [−4.7, 4.7, 1] by [−3.1, 3.1, 1]

Connected Mode   Dot Mode   Decimal Window

Applications involving rational functions are numerous. One instance is in the design of curves for train tracks, which we discuss in the next example.

EXAMPLE 5   Modeling a train track curve

Figure 6.4

When curves are designed for train tracks, sometimes the outer rail is elevated, or banked, so that a locomotive and its cars can safely negotiate the curve at a higher speed than if the tracks were level. Suppose that a circular curve with a radius of *r* feet is being designed for a train traveling 60 miles per hour. Then $f(r) = \frac{2540}{r}$ calculates the proper elevation *y* in inches for the outer rail, where $y = f(r)$. See Figure 6.4.   (*Source:* L. Haefner, *Introduction to Transportation Systems.*)

(a) Evaluate $f(300)$ and interpret the result.
(b) A graph of *f* is shown in Figure 6.5. Discuss how the elevation of the outer rail changes as the radius *r* increases.

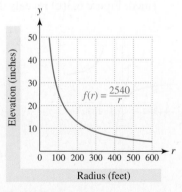

Figure 6.5

Solution   **(a)** $f(300) = \frac{2540}{300} \approx 8.5$. Thus the outer rail on a curve with a radius of 300 feet should be elevated about 8.5 inches for a train to safely travel through it at 60 miles per hour.

(b) As the radius increases (and the curve becomes less sharp), the outer rail needs less elevation.

It becomes less sharp. The elevation becomes less. Yes, because less elevation is needed for curves that are not as sharp. A very large *r* corresponds to tracks that are nearly straight.

Critical Thinking

Refer to Example 5. If the radius of a circular curve becomes large, what happens to the curve? According to $f(x)$, what should happen to the elevation of the outer rail when the radius becomes very large? Does this result agree with your intuition? Explain.

Solving Rational Equations

When working with rational functions, we commonly encounter rational equations. In Example 5, we used $f(r) = \frac{2540}{r}$ to calculate the elevation of the outer rail in a train track curve. Now suppose that the outer rail for a curve is elevated 6 inches. What should be the radius of the curve? To answer this question, we need to solve the **rational equation**

TEACHING TIP

This discussion helps explain how rational equations occur in real life.

$$\frac{2540}{r} = 6.$$

We solve this equation in the next example.

EXAMPLE 6   **Determining the proper radius for a train track curve**

Solve the rational equation $\frac{2540}{r} = 6$ and interpret the result.

Solution   We begin by multiplying both sides of the equation by r.

$$r \cdot \frac{2540}{r} = 6 \cdot r \qquad \text{Multiply by } r.$$

$$2540 = 6r \qquad \text{Simplify.}$$

$$r = \frac{2540}{6} \qquad \text{Divide by 6.}$$

$$r = 423\frac{1}{3} \qquad \text{Rewrite.}$$

A train track curve designed for 60 miles per hour and banked 6 inches should have a radius of about 423 feet.

Multiplication is often used as a first step when solving rational equations. To do so we apply the following property of rational expressions, with $D \neq 0$.

$$D \cdot \frac{C}{D} = C$$

Examples of this property include,

$$5 \cdot \frac{7}{5} = 7 \quad \text{and} \quad (x-1) \cdot \frac{4x}{x-1} = 4x.$$

EXAMPLE 7 Solving rational equations

Solve each rational equation and check your answer.

(a) $\dfrac{3x}{2x-1} = 3$ **(b)** $\dfrac{x+1}{x-2} = \dfrac{3}{x-2}$ **(c)** $\dfrac{6}{x+1} = x$

Solution **(a)** First note that $\frac{1}{2}$ cannot be a solution to this equation because $x = \frac{1}{2}$ results in the left side of the equation being undefined. Begin by multiplying both sides of the equation by $2x - 1$.

$$(2x-1)\cdot\frac{3x}{2x-1} = 3\cdot(2x-1) \qquad \text{Multiply by } (2x-1).$$

$$3x = 3(2x-1) \qquad \text{Simplify.}$$

$$3x = 6x - 3 \qquad \text{Distributive property}$$

$$-3x = -3 \qquad \text{Subtract } 3x.$$

$$x = 1 \qquad \text{Divide by } -3.$$

To check your answer substitute **1** into the given equation for x.

$$\frac{3(1)}{2(1)-1} = 3 \qquad \text{The answer checks.}$$

(b) Each side of the equation is undefined when $x = 2$. Thus 2 cannot be a solution. Begin by multiplying both sides of the equation by $x - 2$.

$$(x-2)\cdot\frac{x+1}{x-2} = \frac{3}{x-2}\cdot(x-2) \qquad \text{Multiply by } x-2.$$

$$x + 1 = 3 \qquad \text{Simplify.}$$

$$x = 2 \qquad \text{Subtract 1.}$$

In this case 2 is not a valid solution. Instead 2 is called an **extraneous solution**, which cannot be used. This result illustrates why it is *important* to check your answers.

(c) The left side of the equation is undefined when $x = -1$. Thus -1 cannot be a solution. To solve this equation start by multiplying both sides by $x + 1$.

$$(x+1)\cdot\frac{6}{x+1} = x\cdot(x+1) \qquad \text{Multiply by } x+1.$$

$$6 = x^2 + x \qquad \text{Simplify.}$$

$$x^2 + x - 6 = 0 \qquad \text{Rewrite the equation.}$$

$$(x+3)(x-2) = 0 \qquad \text{Factor.}$$

$$x = -3 \quad \text{or} \quad x = 2 \qquad \text{Zero-product property}$$

Checking these results confirms that both -3 and 2 are solutions.

The *grade x* of a hill is a measure of its steepness and corresponds to the slope of the road. For example, if a road rises 10 feet for every 100 feet of horizontal distance, it has an uphill grade of $x = \frac{10}{100}$, or 10%, as illustrated in Figure 6.6. The braking distance D in feet for a car traveling 60 miles per hour on a wet, uphill grade is given by

$$D(x) = \frac{3600}{30x+9}.$$

Figure 6.6

In the next example we use this formula to determine the grade associated with a given braking distance.   (**Source:** N. Garber and L. Hoel, *Traffic and Highway Engineering.*)

EXAMPLE 8   Solving a rational equation

The braking distance for a car traveling at 60 miles per hour on a wet, uphill grade is 250 feet. Find the grade of the hill
(a) symbolically,   (b) graphically, and   (c) numerically.

Solution   (a) *Symbolic Solution*   To solve the equation $\frac{3600}{30x+9} = 250$ symbolically, we begin by multiplying both sides by $30x + 9$.

$$\frac{3600}{30x+9} = 250 \qquad \text{Equation to be solved}$$

$$(30x+9) \cdot \frac{3600}{30x+9} = 250 \cdot (30x+9) \qquad \text{Multiply by } (30x+9).$$

$$3600 = 250(30x+9) \qquad \text{Simplify.}$$

$$3600 = 7500x + 2250 \qquad \text{Distributive property}$$

$$1350 = 7500x \qquad \text{Subtract 2250.}$$

$$x = \frac{1350}{7500} \qquad \text{Solve for } x.$$

$$x = 0.18 \qquad \text{Write } x \text{ in decimal form.}$$

Thus the grade is 0.18, or 18%.

(b) *Graphical Solution*   We must find an x-value that satisfies the rational equation

$$\frac{3600}{30x+9} = 250.$$

To solve this equation graphically, we let $Y_1 = 3600/(30X + 9)$ and $Y_2 = 250$. Their graphs intersect at (0.18, 250), as shown in Figure 6.7(a).

Calculator Help
To find a point of intersection, see the Appendix (page AP-7).

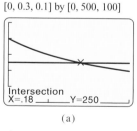

[0, 0.3, 0.1] by [0, 500, 100]

(a)

X	Y₁	Y₂
.15	266.67	250
.16	260.87	250
.17	255.32	250
.18	250	250
.19	244.9	250
.2	240	250
.21	235.29	250

X = .18

(b)

Figure 6.7

(c) *Numerical Solution*   The table shown in Figure 6.7(b) indicates that $y_1 = 250$ when $x = 0.18$.

6.1 PUTTING IT ALL TOGETHER

A rational expression results when a polynomial is divided by a nonzero polynomial. Rational expressions may be used to define rational functions. The following table summarizes basic concepts about rational functions and equations.

Term	Explanation	Example
Rational Function	Let $p(x)$ and $q(x)$ be polynomials with $q(x) \neq 0$. Then a *rational function* is given by $$f(x) = \frac{p(x)}{q(x)}.$$	$$f(x) = \frac{3x}{x + 2}$$ The domain of f includes all real numbers except $x = -2$. A vertical asymptote occurs at $x = -2$ in the graph of f.
Rational Equation	An equation that contains rational expressions is a *rational equation*. When you are solving a rational equation, multiplication is often a good first step.	To solve $\frac{3x}{x + 1} = 6$ begin by multiplying each side by $x + 1$. $$(x + 1) \cdot \frac{3x}{x + 1} = 6 \cdot (x + 1)$$ $$3x = 6x + 6$$ $$-6 = 3x$$ $$x = -2$$ Be sure to check your results.

6.1 EXERCISES

FOR EXTRA HELP

📖 Student's Solutions Manual 📐 InterAct Math *MathXL* MathXL

🚪 MyMathLab ☎ Math Tutor Center 📼 Digital Video Tutor CD 5 Videotape 7

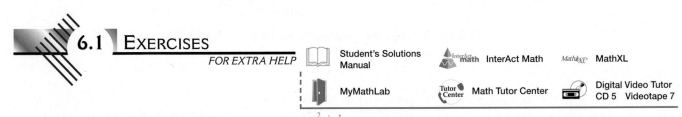

CONCEPTS

1. A polynomial divided by a nonzero polynomial; $\frac{x^2 + 1}{3x}$; answers may vary.

1. What is a rational expression? Give an example.

2. If $f(x) = \frac{6}{x - 4}$, for what input x is $f(x)$ undefined?
$x = 4$

3. What would be a good first step in solving $\frac{3}{x + 7} = x$? Multiply both sides by $x + 7$.

4. Is 5 a solution to the equation $\frac{x + 5}{x - 5} = \frac{10}{x - 5}$? Explain. No; the equation is undefined.

5. Does $x \cdot \frac{5 + x}{x}$ simplify to $5x$? Explain.
No; it simplifies to $5 + x$.

6. If $x \neq 3$, then $\frac{x - 3}{x - 3} =$ _____. 1

7. $\frac{P \cdot R}{Q \cdot R} =$ _____ $\frac{P}{Q}$

8. The domain of $f(x) = \frac{p(x)}{q(x)}$ includes all x-values such that $q(x) \neq$ _____. 0

Exercises 9–14: Determine whether the expression is rational.

9. $\frac{2}{x}$ Yes

10. $\frac{5 - 2x}{x^2}$ Yes

11. $\frac{3x - 5}{2x + 1}$ Yes

12. $|x| + \frac{4}{|x|}$ No

13. $\dfrac{\sqrt{x}}{x^2 - 1}$ No

14. $\dfrac{4x^2 - 3x + 1}{x^3 - 4x}$ Yes

RATIONAL FUNCTIONS

Exercises 15–18: Write a symbolic representation (or formula) for the rational function f described.

15. Divide x by the quantity x plus 1. $f(x) = \dfrac{x}{x + 1}$

16. Add 2 to x and then divide the result by the quantity x plus 5. $f(x) = \dfrac{x + 2}{x + 5}$

17. Divide x squared by the quantity x minus 2. $f(x) = \dfrac{x^2}{x - 2}$

18. Compute the reciprocal of twice x. $f(x) = \dfrac{1}{2x}$

Exercises 19–28: Graph $y = f(x)$. Be sure to include any vertical asymptotes as dashed lines. State the domain of f in set-builder notation.*

19. $\dfrac{1}{x - 1}$ $\{x \mid x \neq 1\}$

20. $\dfrac{1}{x + 3}$ $\{x \mid x \neq -3\}$

21. $\dfrac{1}{2x}$ $\{x \mid x \neq 0\}$

22. $\dfrac{2}{x}$ $\{x \mid x \neq 0\}$

23. $\dfrac{1}{x + 2}$ $\{x \mid x \neq -2\}$

24. $\dfrac{1}{x - 2}$ $\{x \mid x \neq 2\}$

25. $\dfrac{4}{x^2 + 1}$ $\{x \mid -\infty < x < \infty\}$

26. $\dfrac{6}{x^2 + 2}$ $\{x \mid -\infty < x < \infty\}$

27. $\dfrac{3}{2x - 3}$ $\{x \mid x \neq \frac{3}{2}\}$

28. $\dfrac{1}{3x + 2}$ $\{x \mid x \neq -\frac{2}{3}\}$

Exercises 29–34: Evaluate $f(x)$ at the given value of x by hand. State the domain of f in set-builder notation.

29. $f(x) = \dfrac{1}{x - 1}$ $x = -2$ $-\frac{1}{3}; \{x \mid x \neq 1\}$

30. $f(x) = \dfrac{3x}{x^2 - 1}$ $x = 2$
2; $\{x \mid x$ is any real number except -1 and $1.\}$

31. $f(x) = \dfrac{x + 1}{x - 1}$ $x = -3$ $\frac{1}{2}; \{x \mid x \neq 1\}$

32. $f(x) = \dfrac{2x + 1}{3x - 1}$ $x = 0$ $-1; \{x \mid x \neq \frac{1}{3}\}$

33. $f(x) = \dfrac{x^2 - 3x + 5}{x^2 + 1}$ $x = -2$
3; $\{x \mid x$ is any real number.$\}$

34. $f(x) = \dfrac{5}{x^2 - x}$ $x = -1$
$\frac{5}{2}; \{x \mid x$ is any real number except 0 and 1.$\}$

Exercises 35–38: Use the graph to evaluate each expression. Give the equation of any vertical asymptotes.

35. $f(-3)$ and $f(1)$

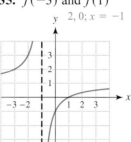
2, 0; $x = -1$

36. $f(-3)$ and $f(2)$

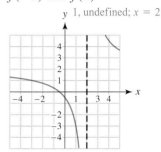
1, undefined; $x = 2$

37. $f(-1)$ and $f(2)$

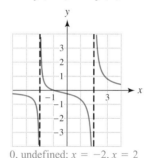
0, undefined; $x = -2, x = 2$

38. $f(-1)$ and $f(1)$

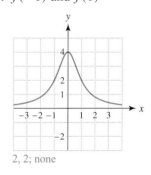
2, 2; none

RATIONAL EQUATIONS

Exercises 39–56: Solve the rational equation. Check your result.

39. $\dfrac{3}{x} = 5$ $\frac{3}{5}$

40. $\dfrac{5}{x} - 2 = 5$ $\frac{5}{7}$

41. $\dfrac{1}{x - 2} = -1$ 1

42. $\dfrac{-5}{x + 4} = -5$ -3

43. $\dfrac{x}{x + 1} - 1 = 1$ -2

44. $\dfrac{3x}{x + 3} = -6$ -2

45. $\dfrac{2x + 1}{3x - 2} = 1$ 3

46. $\dfrac{x + 3}{4x + 1} = \dfrac{3}{5}$ $\frac{12}{7}$

47. $\dfrac{3}{x + 2} = x$ $-3, 1$

48. $\dfrac{6}{2x + 1} = x$ $-2, \frac{3}{2}$

49. $\dfrac{6}{x + 1} = 3x$ $-2, 1$

50. $\dfrac{4}{x - 3} = x$ $-1, 4$

51. $\dfrac{1}{x^2 - 1} = -1$ 0

52. $\dfrac{5x}{x^2 - 5} = \dfrac{x + 2}{x^2 - 5}$ $\frac{1}{2}$

53. $\dfrac{x}{x - 5} = \dfrac{2x - 5}{x - 5}$
No solutions

54. $\dfrac{x}{x + 1} = \dfrac{2x + 1}{x + 1}$
No solutions

*Answers on page IA-20

55. $\dfrac{2x}{x+2} = \dfrac{x-4}{x+2}$ $\quad$ -4

56. $\dfrac{x+3}{x+1} = \dfrac{3x+4}{x+1}$ $\quad$ $-\dfrac{1}{2}$

Exercises 57–62: Solve the rational equation either graphically or numerically. Check your answer.

57. $\dfrac{4+x}{2x} = -0.5$ $\quad$ -2

58. $\dfrac{2x-1}{x-5} = -\dfrac{5}{2}$ $\quad$ 3

59. $\dfrac{2x}{x^2-4} = -\dfrac{2}{3}$ $\quad$ -4, 1

60. $\dfrac{x-1}{x+2} = x$ $\quad$ No solutions

61. $\dfrac{1}{x-1} = x-1$ $\quad$ 0, 2

62. $\dfrac{2}{x+2} = x+1$ $\quad$ -3, 0

USING MORE THAN ONE METHOD

Exercises 63–66: Solve the equation (a) symbolically, (b) graphically, and (c) numerically.

63. $\dfrac{1}{x+2} = 1$ $\quad$ -1

64. $\dfrac{3}{x-1} = 2$ $\quad$ $\dfrac{5}{2}$

65. $\dfrac{x}{2x+1} = \dfrac{2}{5}$ $\quad$ 2

66. $\dfrac{4x-2}{x+1} = \dfrac{3}{2}$ $\quad$ $\dfrac{7}{5}$

APPLICATIONS

Exercises 67–70: Rational Models Match the physical situation with the graph of the rational function that models it best.

67. A population of fish that increases and then levels off $\quad$ c.

68. An insect population that dies out $\quad$ b.

69. The length of a ticket line as the rate at which people arrive in line increases $\quad$ d.

70. The wind speed during a day that is initially calm, becomes windy, and then is calm again $\quad$ a.

a.

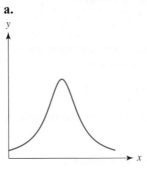

b.

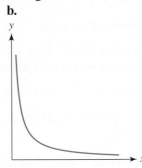

c.

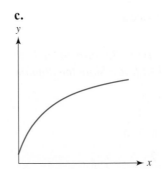

d.

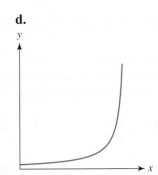

71. *Train Track Curves* (Refer to Example 5.) Let $f(r) = \dfrac{2540}{r}$ compute the elevation of the outer rail in inches for a curve designed for 60 miles per hour with a radius of r feet. (*Source:* L. Haefner.)

(a) Evaluate $f(400)$ and interpret the result.

(b) Construct a table of f, starting at $r = 100$ and incrementing by 50. * $\quad$ It is halved.

(c) From the table, if the radius of the curve doubles, what happens to the elevation of the outer rail?

(d) If the outer rail is elevated 5 inches, what should be the radius of the curve? $\quad$ 508 ft

71. (a) 6.35; a curve with radius of 400 ft will have an outer rail elevation of 6.35 in.

72. *Highway Curves* Engineers need to calculate a minimum safe radius for highway curves. If a curve is too sharp for a given speed, it can be dangerous. To make a sharp curve safer, the road can be banked, or elevated, as illustrated in the accompanying figure. If a curve is designed for a speed of 40 miles per hour and is banked with slope m, then a minimum radius R is computed by

$$R(m) = \dfrac{1600}{15m+2}.$$

(*Source:* N. Garber.)

*Answers on page IA-21

72.(a) About 457; a safe curve with a slope of
        0.1 will have a minimum radius of 457 ft.

where $x < 5$.   (*Source:* N. Garber.)

(a) Evaluate $R(0.1)$ and interpret the result.

(a) Evaluate $T(4)$ and interpret the result.

(b) A graph of R is shown in the figure. Describe what happens to the radius of the curve as the slope of the banking increases.   It decreases.

(b) A graph of T is shown in the figure. Interpret the graph as x increases from 0 to 5. Does this result agree with your intuition?
As more cars try to exit, the waiting time increases; yes.

(a) 1; when cars are leav-
     ing the ramp at a rate
     of 4 vehicles/min, the
     average wait is 1 min.

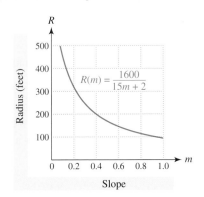

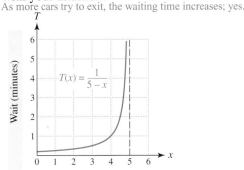

Traffic Rate (vehicles per minute)

(c) If the curve has a radius of 320 feet, what is m?
0.2

(c) Find x if the waiting time is 3 minutes.
4.6 vehicles/min

73. *Uphill Highway Grade*   (Refer to Example 8.) The braking distance for a car traveling 30 miles per hour on a wet *uphill* grade x is given by

$$D(x) = \frac{900}{10.5 + 30x}.$$

76. *People Waiting in Line*   At a post office, workers can wait on 50 people per hour. If people arrive randomly at an average rate of x per hour, then the average number of people N waiting in line is given by

$$N(x) = \frac{x^2}{2500 - 50x},$$

(*Source:* N. Garber.)

(a) Evaluate $D(0.05)$ and interpret the result.

(b) If the braking distance for this car is 60 feet, find the uphill grade x.   0.15

(a) 75; the braking distance is 75 ft when the uphill grade is 0.05.

where $x < 50$.   (*Source:* N. Garber.)

(a) Evaluate $N(30)$ and interpret the result.

74. *Downhill Highway Grade*   (See Exercise 73 and Chapter 6 Introduction.) The braking distance for a car traveling 30 miles per hour on a wet, *downhill* grade x is given by

$$S(x) = \frac{900}{10.5 - 30x}.$$

(b) A graph of N is shown in the figure. Interpret the graph as x increases from 0 to 50. Does this result agree with your intuition?
As people arrive at a faster rate, the length of the line increases; yes.

(a) 100; the braking distance is 100 ft when the downhill grade is 0.05.
(*Source:* N. Garber.)

(a) Evaluate $S(0.05)$ and interpret the result.

(b) Construct a table for $D(x)$ from Exercise 73 and $S(x)$, starting at $x = 0$ and incrementing by 0.05.*

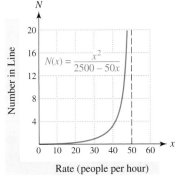

Rate (people per hour)

(c) How do the braking distances for uphill and downhill grades compare? Does this result agree with your driving experience?   The distances for
downhill braking are farther than those for uphill braking; yes

(c) Find x if the average number of people waiting in line is 8.   About 45 people/hr

75. *Time Spent in Line*   If a parking ramp attendant can wait on 5 vehicles per minute and vehicles are leaving the ramp randomly at an average rate of x vehicles per minute, then the average time T in minutes spent waiting in line *and* paying the attendant is given by

77. *Probability*   A jar contains x balls. Each ball has a unique number written on it and only one ball has the winning number. The likelihood, or probability P, of *not* drawing the winning ball is given by

76.(a) 0.9; when people arrive at a rate of 30/hr,
        the line will be about 1 person long.

$$T(x) = \frac{1}{5 - x},$$

$$P(x) = \frac{x - 1}{x},$$ *Answers on page IA-21

where $x > 0$. For example, if $P = 0.99$, then there is a 99% chance of not drawing the winning ball.

(a) Evaluate $P(1)$ and $P(50)$ and interpret the result.
(b) Graph P in $[0, 100, 10]$ by $[0, 1, 0.1]$.*
(c) What happens to the probability of not winning as the number of balls increases? Does this result agree with your intuition? Explain.
(d) How many balls are in the jar if the probability of not winning is 0.975?   40 balls

(c) It increases; yes, there are more balls without winning numbers.

78. *Insect Population*   Suppose that an insect population in thousands per acre is modeled by

$$P(x) = \frac{5x + 2}{x + 1},$$

where $x \geq 0$ is time in months.

77.(a) $P(1) = 0$, $P(50) = 0.98$; when there is only 1 ball, there is no chance of losing; with 50 balls there is a 98% chance of losing.

(a) $4.\overline{72}$; after 10 mo there are about 4727 insects/acre.
(a) Evaluate $P(10)$ and interpret the result.
(b) Graph P in $[0, 50, 10]$ by $[0, 6, 1]$.*
(c) What happens to the insect population after several years?   It stabilizes around 5000 insects/acre.
(d) After how many months is the insect population 4.8 thousand per acre?   After 14 mo

WRITING ABOUT MATHEMATICS

79. Is every polynomial function a rational function? Explain your answer.

80. The domain of a polynomial function includes all real numbers. Does the domain of a rational function include all real numbers? Explain your answer and give an example.

 Group Activity: Working with Real Data

Directions: Form a group of 2 to 4 people. Select someone to record the group's responses for this activity. All members of the group should work cooperatively to answer the questions. If your instructor asks for your results, each member of the group should be prepared to respond.

(a) $x = 0$ (b) It decreases; as the coefficient of friction increases, the road becomes less slippery.

Slippery Roads   If a car is moving on a level highway, its stopping distance depends on road conditions. If the road is slippery, stopping may take longer. A measure of the slipperiness of a road is the coefficient of friction x between the tire and the road, where x satisfies $0 < x \leq 1$. A smaller value for x indicates that the road is slipperier. The stopping distance D in feet for a car traveling at 50 miles per hour on a road with a coefficient of friction x is given by

$$D(x) = \frac{250}{3x}.$$

(a) Graph D. Identify any vertical asymptotes.*
(b) What happens to the stopping distance as x increases to 1? Explain.
(c) What happens to the stopping distance as x decreases to 0? Explain.
(d) In reality, could $x = 0$? Explain. What would happen if a road could have $x = 0$ and a car tried to stop?

(c) It increases; as the coefficient of friction decreases to 0, the road becomes slipperier.
(d) No; there is always some friction because otherwise the car would never stop.

*Answers on page IA-21

6.2 MULTIPLICATION AND DIVISION OF RATIONAL EXPRESSIONS

Simplifying Rational Expressions · Review of Multiplication and Division of Fractions · Multiplication of Rational Expressions · Division of Rational Expressions

INTRODUCTION

In previous chapters we demonstrated how to add, subtract, and multiply polynomials. In this section we show you how to multiply and divide rational expressions, and in the next section we discuss addition and subtraction of rational expressions. We start this section by discussing how to simplify rational expressions.

SIMPLIFYING RATIONAL EXPRESSIONS

When simplifying fractions, we sometimes use the **basic principle of fractions**, which states that

$$\frac{a \cdot c}{b \cdot c} = \frac{a}{b}.$$

This principle holds because $\frac{c}{c} = 1$ and $\frac{a}{b} \cdot 1 = \frac{a}{b}$. It can be used to simplify a fraction.

$$\frac{6}{44} = \frac{3 \cdot 2}{22 \cdot 2} = \frac{3}{22}$$

This same principle can also be used to simplify rational expressions. For example,

$$\frac{(z + 1)(z + 3)}{z(z + 3)} = \frac{z + 1}{z},$$

provided $z \neq -3$.

SIMPLIFYING RATIONAL EXPRESSIONS

The following principle can be used to simplify rational expressions, where A, B, and C are polynomials.

$$\frac{A \cdot C}{B \cdot C} = \frac{A}{B} \qquad B \text{ and } C \text{ not zero}$$

EXAMPLE 1 Simplifying rational expressions

Simplify each expression.

(a) $\dfrac{9x}{3x^2}$ (b) $\dfrac{5y - 10}{10y - 20}$ (c) $\dfrac{2z^2 - 3z - 9}{z^2 + 2z - 15}$ (d) $\dfrac{a^2 - b^2}{a + b}$

Solution (a) First factor out the greatest common factor, $3x$, in the numerator and denominator.

$$\frac{9x}{3x^2} = \frac{3x \cdot 3}{3x \cdot x} = \frac{3}{x}$$

(b) Use the distributive property and then the basic principle of fractions.

$$\frac{5y - 10}{10y - 20} = \frac{5(y - 2)}{10(y - 2)} = \frac{5}{10} = \frac{1}{2}$$

(c) Start by factoring the numerator and denominator.

$$\frac{2z^2 - 3z - 9}{z^2 + 2z - 15} = \frac{(2z + 3)(z - 3)}{(z + 5)(z - 3)} = \frac{2z + 3}{z + 5}$$

(d) Start by factoring the numerator as the difference of squares.

$$\frac{a^2 - b^2}{a + b} = \frac{(a - b)(a + b)}{a + b} = a - b$$

There are a number of ways that a negative sign can be placed in a fraction. For example,

$$-\frac{2}{3} = \frac{-2}{3} = \frac{2}{-3}$$

illustrates three fractions that are equal. This property can also be applied to rational expressions, as demonstrated in the next example.

EXAMPLE 2   Distributing a negative sign

Simplify each expression.

(a) $-\dfrac{1 - z}{z - 1}$ **(b)** $\dfrac{-y - 2}{4y + 8}$ **(c)** $\dfrac{5 - x}{x - 5}$

Solution   **(a)** Start by distributing the negative sign over the numerator.

$$-\frac{1 - z}{z - 1} = \frac{-(1 - z)}{z - 1} = \frac{-1 + z}{z - 1} = \frac{z - 1}{z - 1} = 1$$

Note that the negative sign could also be distributed over the denominator.

(b) Use the distributive property to factor -1 out of the numerator and 4 out of the denominator.

$$\frac{-y - 2}{4y + 8} = \frac{-1(y + 2)}{4(y + 2)} = -\frac{1}{4}$$

(c) Start by factoring -1 out of the numerator.

$$\frac{5 - x}{x - 5} = \frac{-1(-5 + x)}{x - 5} = \frac{-1(x - 5)}{x - 5} = -1$$

≡ MAKING CONNECTIONS ≡

Negative Signs and Rational Expression

In general, $(b - a)$ equals $-1(a - b)$. As a result, if $a \neq b$, then

$$\frac{b - a}{a - b} = -1.$$

See Example 2(c).

REVIEW OF MULTIPLICATION AND DIVISION OF FRACTIONS

TEACHING TIP

Be sure to review how to multiply and divide fractions before starting with rational expressions.

Recall that to multiply two fractions we use the property

$$\frac{a}{b} \cdot \frac{c}{d} = \frac{ac}{bd}.$$

For example,

$$\frac{2}{5} \cdot \frac{3}{7} = \frac{2 \cdot 3}{5 \cdot 7} = \frac{6}{35}.$$

EXAMPLE 3   Multiplying fractions

Multiply and simplify the product.

(a) $\dfrac{4}{9} \cdot \dfrac{3}{8}$ (b) $\dfrac{2}{3} \cdot \dfrac{3}{4} \cdot \dfrac{5}{6}$

Solution   (a) $\dfrac{4}{9} \cdot \dfrac{3}{8} = \dfrac{4 \cdot 3}{8 \cdot 9} = \dfrac{1}{2} \cdot \dfrac{1}{3} = \dfrac{1}{6}$ (b) $\dfrac{2}{3} \cdot \dfrac{3}{4} \cdot \dfrac{5}{6} = \dfrac{6 \cdot 5}{12 \cdot 6} = \dfrac{5}{12}$

Recall that to divide two fractions we "invert and multiply." That is, we change a division problem to a multiplication problem, using the property

$$\frac{a}{b} \div \frac{c}{d} = \frac{a}{b} \cdot \frac{d}{c}.$$

For example,

$$\frac{3}{4} \div \frac{5}{4} = \frac{3}{4} \cdot \frac{4}{5} = \frac{3 \cdot 4}{5 \cdot 4} = \frac{3}{5}.$$

MULTIPLICATION OF RATIONAL EXPRESSIONS

Multiplying rational expressions is similar to multiplying fractions.

PRODUCTS OF RATIONAL EXPRESSIONS

To multiply two rational expressions, multiply numerators and multiply denominators.

$$\frac{A}{B} \cdot \frac{C}{D} = \frac{AC}{BD} \qquad B \text{ and } D \text{ not zero}$$

EXAMPLE 4   Multiplying rational expressions

Multiply.

(a) $\dfrac{1}{x} \cdot \dfrac{x+1}{2x}$ (b) $\dfrac{x-1}{x} \cdot \dfrac{x-1}{x+2}$

Solution   (a) $\dfrac{1}{x} \cdot \dfrac{x+1}{2x} = \dfrac{1 \cdot (x+1)}{x \cdot 2x} = \dfrac{x+1}{2x^2}$

TEACHING TIP

Point out that the denominators do not need to be equal in order to multiply or divide two rational expressions.

(b) $\dfrac{x-1}{x} \cdot \dfrac{x-1}{x+2} = \dfrac{(x-1)(x-1)}{x(x+2)}$

Many times the product of two rational expressions can be reduced. This process is demonstrated in the next two examples.

EXAMPLE 5 Multiplying rational expressions

Multiply and simplify.

(a) $\dfrac{5x}{8} \cdot \dfrac{4}{10x^2}$ (b) $\dfrac{x-2}{2x-1} \cdot \dfrac{x+1}{2x-4}$ (c) $\dfrac{x^2-1}{x^2-4} \cdot \dfrac{x+2}{x-1}$

Solution (a) $\dfrac{5x}{8} \cdot \dfrac{4}{10x^2} = \dfrac{20x}{80x^2}$ Multiply rational expressions.

$= \dfrac{1}{4x}$ Reduce.

(b) $\dfrac{x-2}{2x-1} \cdot \dfrac{x+1}{2x-4} = \dfrac{(x-2)(x+1)}{(2x-1)(2x-4)}$ Multiply rational expressions.

$= \dfrac{(x-2)(x+1)}{(2x-1)2(x-2)}$ Factor $2x-4$.

$= \dfrac{(x+1)(x-2)}{2(2x-1)(x-2)}$ Commutative property

$= \dfrac{x+1}{2(2x-1)}$ Reduce.

(c) $\dfrac{x^2-1}{x^2-4} \cdot \dfrac{x+2}{x-1} = \dfrac{(x^2-1)(x+2)}{(x^2-4)(x-1)}$ Multiply rational expressions.

$= \dfrac{(x-1)(x+1)(x+2)}{(x-2)(x+2)(x-1)}$ Difference of squares

$= \dfrac{(x+1)(x-1)(x+2)}{(x-2)(x-1)(x+2)}$ Commutative property

$= \dfrac{x+1}{x-2}$ Reduce.

EXAMPLE 6 Multiplying rational expressions

Multiply and simplify.

(a) $\dfrac{2x^2y^3}{3xy^2} \cdot \dfrac{(2x^3y)^2}{2(xy)^3}$ (b) $\dfrac{x^3-x}{x-1} \cdot \dfrac{x+1}{x}$

Solution (a) $\dfrac{2x^2y^3}{3xy^2} \cdot \dfrac{(2x^3y)^2}{2(xy)^3} = \dfrac{2x^2y^3 \cdot 4x^6y^2}{3xy^2 \cdot 2x^3y^3}$ Multiply; properties of exponents

$= \dfrac{8x^8y^5}{6x^4y^5}$ Properties of exponents

$= \dfrac{4}{3}x^4$ Reduce.

(b) $\dfrac{x^3 - x}{x - 1} \cdot \dfrac{x + 1}{x} = \dfrac{(x^3 - x)(x + 1)}{x(x - 1)}$ Multiply.

$\qquad\qquad\qquad = \dfrac{x(x^2 - 1)(x + 1)}{x(x - 1)}$ Factor out x.

$\qquad\qquad\qquad = \dfrac{x(x - 1)(x + 1)(x + 1)}{x(x - 1)}$ Difference of squares

$\qquad\qquad\qquad = (x + 1)(x + 1)$ Reduce.

$\qquad\qquad\qquad = (x + 1)^2$ Rewrite.

DIVISION OF RATIONAL EXPRESSIONS

When dividing two rational expressions, *multiply* the first expression by the reciprocal of the second expression. This technique is similar to the division of fractions.

QUOTIENTS OF RATIONAL EXPRESSIONS

To divide two rational expressions, multiply by the reciprocal of the divisor.

$$\frac{A}{B} \div \frac{C}{D} = \frac{A}{B} \cdot \frac{D}{C} \qquad B, C, \text{ and } D \text{ not zero}$$

Note: This technique of multiplying the first rational expression and the reciprocal of the second rational expression is sometimes summarized as "Invert and multiply."

The *reciprocal of a polynomial* $p(x)$ is $\frac{1}{p(x)}$, and the *reciprocal of a rational expression* $\frac{p(x)}{q(x)}$ is $\frac{q(x)}{p(x)}$. The next example demonstrates how to find reciprocals of polynomials and rational expressions.

EXAMPLE 7   Finding reciprocals

Write the reciprocal of each expression.

(a) $3x + 4$ **(b)** $\dfrac{5}{x^2 + 1}$ **(c)** $\dfrac{x - 7}{x + 7}$

Solution **(a)** The reciprocal of $3x + 4$ is $\frac{1}{3x + 4}$.

(b) The reciprocal of $\frac{5}{x^2 + 1}$ is $\frac{x^2 + 1}{5}$.

(c) The reciprocal of $\frac{x - 7}{x + 7}$ is $\frac{x + 7}{x - 7}$.

EXAMPLE 8   Dividing two rational expressions

Divide and simplify.

(a) $\dfrac{2}{x} \div \dfrac{2x - 1}{4x}$ **(b)** $\dfrac{x^2 - 1}{x^2 + x - 6} \div \dfrac{x - 1}{x + 3}$

Solution (a) $\dfrac{2}{x} \div \dfrac{2x-1}{4x} = \dfrac{2}{x} \cdot \dfrac{4x}{2x-1}$ "Invert and multiply."

$$= \dfrac{8x}{x(2x-1)} \quad \text{Multiply.}$$

$$= \dfrac{8}{2x-1} \quad \text{Reduce.}$$

(b) $\dfrac{x^2-1}{x^2+x-6} \div \dfrac{x-1}{x+3} = \dfrac{x^2-1}{x^2+x-6} \cdot \dfrac{x+3}{x-1}$ "Invert and multiply."

$$= \dfrac{(x+1)(x-1)}{(x-2)(x+3)} \cdot \dfrac{x+3}{x-1} \quad \text{Factor.}$$

$$= \dfrac{(x+1)(x-1)(x+3)}{(x-2)(x-1)(x+3)} \quad \text{Commutative property}$$

$$= \dfrac{x+1}{x-2} \quad \text{Reduce.}$$

EXAMPLE 9 Dividing rational expressions

Divide and simplify.

(a) $\dfrac{7a^2}{4b^3} \div \dfrac{21a}{8b^4}$ (b) $\dfrac{2x+2}{x-1} \div (x+1)$ (c) $\dfrac{x^2-25}{x^2+5x+4} \div \dfrac{x^2-10x+25}{2x^2+8x}$

Solution (a) $\dfrac{7a^2}{4b^3} \div \dfrac{21a}{8b^4} = \dfrac{7a^2}{4b^3} \cdot \dfrac{8b^4}{21a}$ "Invert and multiply."

$$= \dfrac{56a^2b^4}{84ab^3} \quad \text{Multiply rational expressions.}$$

$$= \dfrac{2}{3}a^{2-1}b^{4-3} \quad \text{Properties of exponents}$$

$$= \dfrac{2}{3}ab \quad \text{Simplify.}$$

(b) $\dfrac{2x+2}{x-1} \div (x+1) = \dfrac{2x+2}{x-1} \cdot \dfrac{1}{x+1}$ "Invert and multiply."

$$= \dfrac{2(x+1)}{x-1} \cdot \dfrac{1}{x+1} \quad \text{Factor.}$$

$$= \dfrac{2(x+1)}{(x-1)(x+1)} \quad \text{Properties of fractions}$$

$$= \dfrac{2}{x-1} \quad \text{Simplify.}$$

(c) $\dfrac{x^2-25}{x^2+5x+4} \div \dfrac{x^2-10x+25}{2x^2+8x} = \dfrac{x^2-25}{x^2+5x+4} \cdot \dfrac{2x^2+8x}{x^2-10x+25}$

$$= \dfrac{(x-5)(x+5)}{(x+1)(x+4)} \cdot \dfrac{2x(x+4)}{(x-5)^2}$$

$$= \dfrac{2x(x+5)(x-5)(x+4)}{(x+1)(x-5)^2(x+4)}$$

$$= \dfrac{2x(x+5)}{(x+1)(x-5)}$$

In the next example, we find the length of a rectangle when its area and width are expressed as polynomials.

EXAMPLE 10 Finding the dimensions of a rectangle

The area A of a rectangle is $3x^2 + 14x + 15$ and its width W is $x + 3$, as shown in Figure 6.8.
(a) Find the length L of the rectangle.
(b) Find the length if the width is 12 inches.

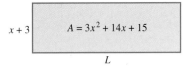

$x + 3$ $A = 3x^2 + 14x + 15$

L

Figure 6.8

Solution (a) Because the area equals length times width, $A = LW$, length equals area divided by width, or $L = \frac{A}{W}$. To determine L, factor the expression for A and then simplify.

$$L = \frac{3x^2 + 14x + 15}{x + 3} = \frac{(3x + 5)(x + 3)}{x + 3} = 3x + 5.$$

The length of the rectangle is $3x + 5$.
(b) If the width is 12 inches, then $x + 3 = 12$ or $x = 9$. The length is

$$L = 3x + 5 = 3(9) + 5 = 32 \text{ inches.}$$

PUTTING IT ALL TOGETHER

The following table summarizes some important concepts found in this section.

Concept	Explanation	Examples
Simplifying Rational Expressions	Use the *basic principle of fractions*. $\dfrac{A \cdot C}{B \cdot C} = \dfrac{A}{B}$ B and C not zero	$\dfrac{5a(a + b)}{7b(a + b)} = \dfrac{5a}{7b}$ and $\dfrac{x^2 - 1}{x - 1} = \dfrac{(x + 1)(x - 1)}{x - 1} = x + 1$
Multiplying Rational Expressions	To multiply two rational expressions, multiply numerators and multiply denominators. $\dfrac{A}{B} \cdot \dfrac{C}{D} = \dfrac{AC}{BD}$ B and D not zero	$\dfrac{5a}{4b^2} \cdot \dfrac{2b^3}{10a^3} = \dfrac{10ab^3}{40a^3b^2} = \dfrac{b}{4a^2}$

continued on next page

continued from previous page

Concept	Explanation	Examples
Dividing Rational Expressions	To divide two rational expressions, multiply by the reciprocal of the divisor. ("Invert and multiply.") $$\frac{A}{B} \div \frac{C}{D} = \frac{A}{B} \cdot \frac{D}{C} \qquad B, C, \text{ and } D \text{ not zero}$$	$$\frac{x}{x+1} \div \frac{x+2}{x+1} = \frac{x}{x+1} \cdot \frac{x+1}{x+2}$$ $$= \frac{x(x+1)}{(x+2)(x+1)}$$ $$= \frac{x}{x+2}$$

6.2 EXERCISES

FOR EXTRA HELP

Student's Solutions Manual   InterAct Math   MathXL

MyMathLab   Math Tutor Center   Digital Video Tutor CD 5   Videotape 7

CONCEPTS

1. Simplify $\frac{2x+3}{2x+3}$.   1

2. Simplify $\frac{x-3}{3-x}$.   −1

3. Is $\frac{x^2-1}{x-1}$ equal to x? Explain.   No; it is equal to $x+1$.

4. Is $\frac{3}{3+x}$ equal to $\frac{1}{x}$? Is it equal to $1+\frac{3}{x}$?   No; no

5. To divide $\frac{2}{3}$ by $\frac{5}{7}$ multiply ____ by ____. $\frac{2}{3}; \frac{7}{5}$

6. $\frac{a}{b} \cdot \frac{c}{d} =$ ____. $\frac{ac}{bd}$ **7.** $\frac{a}{b} \div \frac{c}{d} =$ ____. $\frac{ad}{bc}$

8. $\frac{ac}{bc} =$ ____ $\cdot$ $\frac{a}{b}$

REVIEW OF FRACTIONS

Exercises 9–20: Simplify.

9. $\frac{1}{2} \cdot \frac{4}{5}$ $\frac{2}{5}$

10. $\frac{5}{6} \cdot \frac{3}{10}$ $\frac{1}{4}$

11. $\frac{7}{8} \cdot \frac{4}{3} \cdot (-3)$ $-\frac{7}{2}$

12. $4 \cdot \frac{7}{4} \cdot \frac{1}{2}$ $\frac{7}{2}$

13. $\frac{3}{8} \cdot 2$ $\frac{3}{4}$

14. $-5 \cdot \frac{2}{7}$ $-\frac{10}{7}$

15. $-\frac{7}{11} \div 14$ $-\frac{1}{22}$

16. $6 \div \frac{6}{5}$ 5

17. $\frac{5}{7} \div \frac{15}{14}$ $\frac{2}{3}$

18. $-\frac{2}{3} \div 2$ $-\frac{1}{3}$

19. $6 \div \left(-\frac{1}{3}\right)$ −18

20. $\frac{10}{9} \div \frac{5}{3}$ $\frac{2}{3}$

SIMPLIFYING RATIONAL EXPRESSIONS

Exercises 21–50: Simplify the rational expression.

21. $\frac{5x}{x^2}$ $\frac{5}{x}$

22. $\frac{18t^3}{6t}$ $3t^2$

23. $\frac{3z+6}{z+2}$ 3

24. $\frac{6}{12x+6}$ $\frac{1}{2x+1}$

25. $\frac{2z+2}{3z+3}$ $\frac{2}{3}$

26. $\frac{4x-12}{2x-6}$ 2

27. $\frac{(x-1)(x+1)}{x-1}$ $x+1$

28. $(x+2) \cdot \frac{x-6}{x+2}$ $x-6$

29. $\frac{x^2-4}{x+2}$ $x-2$

30. $\frac{(x+2)(x-5)}{(x+10)(x+2)}$ $\frac{x-5}{x+10}$

31. $\frac{x(x-1)}{(x+1)(x-1)}$ $\frac{x}{x+1}$

32. $\frac{(2x-1)(x-3)}{(x-3)(2x+5)}$ $\frac{2x-1}{2x+5}$

33. $\frac{(3x+1)(x+2)}{(x+2)(5x-2)}$ $\frac{3x+1}{5x-2}$

34. $\frac{(3x+2)(x-7)}{x(x-7)}$ $\frac{3x+2}{x}$

35. $\frac{x+5}{x^2+2x-15}$ $\frac{1}{x-3}$

36. $\frac{x^2-9}{x^2+6x+9} \cdot (x+3)$ $x-3$

37. $\frac{x^2+2x}{x^2+3x+2}$ $\frac{x}{x+1}$

38. $\frac{x^2-3x-10}{x^2-6x+5}$ $\frac{x+2}{x-1}$

39. $\frac{6x^2+7x-5}{2x^2-11x+5}$ $\frac{3x+5}{x-5}$

40. $\frac{30x^2-7x-15}{6x^2+7x-10}$ $\frac{5x+3}{x+2}$

41. $\frac{a^2-b^2}{a-b}$ $a+b$

42. $\frac{a^2+2ab+b^2}{a+b}$ $a+b$

43. $\frac{m^3+n^3}{m+n}$ m^2-mn+n^2

44. $\frac{m^3-n^3}{m-n}$ m^2+mn+n^2

45. $-\dfrac{4-t}{t-4}$ 1

46. $-\dfrac{t-r}{r-t}$ 1

47. $\dfrac{4m-n}{-4m+n}$ -1

48. $\dfrac{2n+10m}{-n-5m}$ -2

49. $\dfrac{5-y}{y-5}$ -1

50. $\dfrac{a-b}{b-a}$ -1

RECIPROCALS

Exercises 51–58: Write the reciprocal of the expression.

51. $4x$ $\frac{1}{4x}$

52. $5x-2$ $\frac{1}{5x-2}$

53. $\dfrac{2a}{5b}$ $\frac{5b}{2a}$

54. $\dfrac{5b^3}{7a^2}$ $\frac{7a^2}{5b^3}$

55. $\dfrac{3-x}{5-x}$ $\frac{5-x}{3-x}$

56. $\dfrac{x^2-4}{3x+1}$ $\frac{3x+1}{x^2-4}$

57. $\dfrac{1}{x^2+1}$ x^2+1

58. $\dfrac{-1}{5-x}$ $x-5$

MULTIPLICATION AND DIVISION OF RATIONAL EXPRESSIONS

Exercises 59–88: Simplify the expression.

59. $\dfrac{1}{2x}\cdot\dfrac{4x}{2}$ 1

60. $\dfrac{5a^2}{7}\cdot\dfrac{7}{10a}$ $\frac{a}{2}$

61. $\dfrac{5a}{4}\cdot\dfrac{12}{5a}$ 3

62. $\dfrac{a^2b}{4c}\cdot\dfrac{8c^2}{3ab^2}$ $\frac{2ac}{3b}$

63. $\dfrac{9x^2y^4}{8xy^6}\cdot\dfrac{(2xy^2)^3}{3(xy)^4}$ 3

64. $\dfrac{(7rt)^2}{8}\cdot\dfrac{8r}{49(rt^2)^3}$ $\frac{1}{t^4}$

65. $\dfrac{x+1}{2x-5}\cdot\dfrac{2x-5}{x}$

66. $\dfrac{x+1}{x}\cdot\dfrac{x}{x+2}$ $\frac{x+1}{x+2}$

67. $\dfrac{(x-5)(x+3)}{3x-1}\cdot\dfrac{x(3x-1)}{(x-5)}$ $x(x+3)$

65. $\frac{x+1}{x}$

68. $\dfrac{b^2+1}{b^2-1}\cdot\dfrac{b-1}{b+1}$ $\frac{b^2+1}{(b+1)^2}$

69. $\dfrac{x^2-2x-35}{2x^3-3x^2}\cdot\dfrac{x^3-x^2}{2x-14}$ $\frac{(x-1)(x+5)}{2(2x-3)}$

70. $\dfrac{2x+4}{x+1}\cdot\dfrac{x^2+3x+2}{4x+2}$ $\frac{(x+2)^2}{2x+1}$

71. $3(n^2-3n+9)$

72. $\frac{5(n+1)}{3}$

71. $\dfrac{3n-9}{n^2-9}\cdot(n^3+27)$

72. $(10n+15)\cdot\dfrac{n+1}{6n+9}$

73. $\dfrac{3n-9}{n^2-9}\cdot\dfrac{n^3+27}{12}$ $\frac{(n^2-3n+9)}{4}$

74. $\dfrac{10n+15}{n^2-1}\cdot\dfrac{n+1}{6n+9}$ $\frac{5}{3(n-1)}$

75. $\dfrac{3x}{2}\div\dfrac{2x}{5}$ $\frac{15}{4}$

76. $\dfrac{x^2+x}{2x+6}\div\dfrac{x}{x+3}$ $\frac{x+1}{2}$

77. $\dfrac{8a^4}{3b}\div\dfrac{a^5}{9b^2}$ $\frac{24b}{a}$

78. $\dfrac{5m^4}{n^2}\div 5m$ $\frac{m^3}{n^2}$

79. $(2n+4)\div\dfrac{n+2}{n-1}$ $2(n-1)$

80. $\dfrac{n+1}{n+3}\div\dfrac{n+1}{n+3}$ 1

81. $\dfrac{6b}{b+2}\div\dfrac{3b^4}{2b+4}$ $\frac{4}{b^3}$

82. $\dfrac{5x^5}{x-2}\div\dfrac{10x^3}{5x-10}$ $\frac{5x^2}{2}$

83. $\dfrac{3a+1}{a^7}\div\dfrac{a+1}{3a^8}$

84. $\dfrac{x^2-16}{x+3}\div\dfrac{x+4}{x^2-9}$ $(x-4)(x-3)$

85. $\dfrac{x+5}{x^3-x}\div\dfrac{x^2-25}{x^3}$ $\frac{x^2}{(x-5)(x^2-1)}$

83. $\frac{3a(3a+1)}{a+1}$

86. $\dfrac{x^2+x-12}{2x^2-9x-5}\div\dfrac{x^2+7x+12}{2x^2-7x-4}$ $\frac{(x-4)(x-3)}{(x-5)(x+3)}$

87. $\dfrac{x^2-3x+2}{x^2+5x+6}\div\dfrac{x^2+x-2}{x^2+2x-3}$ $\frac{(x-2)(x-1)}{(x+2)^2}$

88. $\dfrac{2x^2+x-1}{6x^2+x-2}\div\dfrac{2x^2+5x+3}{6x^2+13x+6}$ 1

GEOMETRY

89. *Area of a Rectangle* The area A of a rectangle is $5x^2+12x+4$ and its width W is $x+2$, as shown in the figure.
(a) Find the length L of the rectangle. $5x+2$
(b) Find the length if the width is 8 feet. 32 ft

$x+2$ $A=5x^2+12x+4$

L

90. *Area of a Rectangle* The area A of a rectangle is x^2-1.
(a) Find its length if its width is $x-1$. $x+1$
(b) Find the dimensions and area of the rectangle when $x=15$. 16 by 14; 224

91. *Volume of a Box* The volume V of a box with a square bottom is $4x^3+4x^2+x$.
(a) If its height is x, find the area of the bottom of the box. $4x^2+4x+1$
(b) Find the dimensions of the box when $x=10$. 21 by 21 by 10

92. *Area of a Triangle* The area A of a triangle is $6x^2-x-15$. Find its height if the base of the triangle is $2x+3$. $2(3x-5)$

WRITING ABOUT MATHEMATICS

93. A student does the following to simplify a rational expression. Is the work correct? Explain any errors and how you would correct them.

$$\frac{3x + x^2}{3x} \overset{?}{=} 1 + x^2$$

94. Explain how to multiply two rational expressions and how to divide two rational expressions.

CHECKING BASIC CONCEPTS   SECTIONS 6.1 AND 6.2

1. Let $f(x) = \frac{x}{x-1}$.

   (a) Evaluate $f(2)$.   2

   (b) Find the domain of f. $\{x \mid x \neq 1\}$

   (c) Graph f. Identify any vertical asymptotes.*

      $x = 1$

2. Solve each equation. Check your answers.

   (a) $\dfrac{6}{2x+3} = 3$ $-\frac{1}{2}$ **(b)** $\dfrac{2}{x-1} = x$ $-1, 2$

3. Simplify $\dfrac{x^2 - 6x - 7}{x^2 - 1}$. $\frac{x-7}{x-1}$

4. Simplify each expression.

   (a) $\dfrac{2x^2}{x^2 - 1} \cdot \dfrac{x+1}{4x}$ $\frac{x}{2(x-1)}$

   (b) $\dfrac{1}{x-2} \div \dfrac{3}{(x-2)(x+3)}$ $\frac{x+3}{3}$

*Answer on page IA-21

6.3   ADDITION AND SUBTRACTION OF RATIONAL EXPRESSIONS

Least Common Multiples · Review of Addition and Subtraction of Fractions · Addition of Rational Expressions · Subtraction of Rational Expressions

INTRODUCTION

In this section we demonstrate how to add and subtract rational expressions. These techniques are similar to techniques used to add and subtract fractions. We begin by discussing least common multiples, which are used to find least common denominators.

LEAST COMMON MULTIPLES

Two friends work part-time at a store. The first person works every fourth day, while the second person works every sixth day. How many days pass before they both work on the same day?

We can answer this question by listing the days that each person works.

First person: 4, 8, **12**, 16, 20, **24**, 28, 32, **36**, 40
Second person: 6, **12**, 18, **24**, 30, **36**, 42

After 12 days, the two friends work on the same day. The next time is after 24 days. The numbers 12 and 24 are *common multiples* of 4 and 6. (Find two more.) However, 12 is the **least common multiple** (LCM) of 4 and 6.

Another way to find the least common multiple for 4 and 6 is first to factor each number into prime numbers:

$$4 = 2 \cdot 2 \quad \text{and} \quad 6 = 2 \cdot 3.$$

To find the least common multiple, list each factor the *greatest* number of times that it occurs in either factorization. Then find the product of these numbers. For our example, the factor 2 occurs two times in the factorization of 4 and only once in the factorization of 6, so list 2 two times. The factor 3 appears only once in the factorization of 6 and not at all in the factorization of 4, so list it once:

$$2, 2, 3.$$

The least common multiple is their product: $2 \cdot 2 \cdot 3 = 12$.

This same procedure can also be used to find the least common multiple for two polynomials.

FINDING THE LEAST COMMON MULTIPLE

The least common multiple (LCM) of two polynomials can be found as follows.

STEP 1 Factor each polynomial completely.

STEP 2 List each factor the greatest number of times that it occurs in either factorization.

STEP 3 Find the product of this list of factors. The result is the LCM.

The next example illustrates how to use this procedure.

EXAMPLE 1   Finding least common multiples

Find the least common multiple for each pair of expressions.
(a) $4x, 5x^3$ **(b)** $x^2 - 2x, (x - 2)^2$
(c) $x + 2, x - 1$ **(d)** $x^2 + 4x + 4, x^2 + 3x + 2$

Solution **(a) STEP 1** Factor each polynomial completely.

$$4x = 2 \cdot 2 \cdot x \quad \text{and} \quad 5x^3 = 5 \cdot x \cdot x \cdot x$$

STEP 2 The factor 2 occurs twice, the factor 5 occurs once, and the factor x occurs at most three times. The list then is 2, 2, 5, x, x, and x.

STEP 3 The LCM is the product $2 \cdot 2 \cdot 5 \cdot x \cdot x \cdot x$, or $20x^3$.

(b) STEP 1 Factor each polynomial completely.

$$x^2 - 2x = x(x - 2) \quad \text{and} \quad (x - 2)^2 = (x - 2)(x - 2)$$

STEP 2 The factor x occurs once, and the factor $(x - 2)$ occurs at most twice. The list of factors is x, $(x - 2)$, and $(x - 2)$.

STEP 3 The LCM is the product: $x(x - 2)^2$, which is left in factored form.

(c) STEP 1 Neither polynomial can be factored.

STEP 2 The list of factors is $(x + 2)$ and $(x - 1)$.

STEP 3 The LCM is the product $(x + 2)(x - 1)$, or $x^2 + x - 2$.

(d) STEP 1 Factor each polynomial as follows.

$$x^2 + 4x + 4 = (x + 2)(x + 2) \quad \text{and} \quad x^2 + 3x + 2 = (x + 1)(x + 2)$$

STEP 2 The factor $(x + 1)$ occurs once and $(x + 2)$ occurs at most twice.

STEP 3 The LCM is the product $(x + 1)(x + 2)^2$, which is left in factored form.

REVIEW OF ADDITION AND SUBTRACTION OF FRACTIONS

Recall that to add two fractions we use the property

$$\frac{a}{c} + \frac{b}{c} = \frac{a + b}{c}.$$

This property requires that the fractions have like denominators. For example,

$$\frac{1}{5} + \frac{3}{5} = \frac{1 + 3}{5} = \frac{4}{5}.$$

When the denominators are not alike, we must find a common denominator. Before adding two fractions, such as $\frac{2}{3}$ and $\frac{1}{4}$, we write them with 12 as their common denominators.

$$\frac{2}{3} = \frac{2}{3} \cdot \frac{4}{4} = \frac{8}{12}$$

$$\frac{1}{4} = \frac{1}{4} \cdot \frac{3}{3} = \frac{3}{12}$$

TEACHING TIP

Review how to add and subtract fractions before adding and subtracting rational expressions.

Once the fractions have a common denominator, we can add them, as in

$$\frac{2}{3} + \frac{1}{4} = \frac{8}{12} + \frac{3}{12} = \frac{11}{12}.$$

Note that a **common denominator** for $\frac{2}{3}$ and $\frac{1}{4}$ is also a *common multiple* of 3 and 4. The **least common denominator** (LCD) for $\frac{2}{3}$ and $\frac{1}{4}$ is equal to the *least common multiple* (LCM) of 3 and 4. Thus the least common denominator is 12.

EXAMPLE 2 Adding fractions

Find the sum.

(a) $\dfrac{3}{4} + \dfrac{1}{8}$ **(b)** $\dfrac{3}{5} + \dfrac{2}{7}$

Solution **(a)** The LCD is 8.

$$\frac{3}{4} + \frac{1}{8} = \frac{3}{4} \cdot \frac{2}{2} + \frac{1}{8} = \frac{6}{8} + \frac{1}{8} = \frac{7}{8}$$

(b) The LCD is 35.

$$\frac{3}{5} + \frac{2}{7} = \frac{3}{5} \cdot \frac{7}{7} + \frac{2}{7} \cdot \frac{5}{5} = \frac{21}{35} + \frac{10}{35} = \frac{31}{35}$$

Recall that subtraction is similar to addition. To subtract two fractions with like denominators we use the property

$$\frac{a}{c} - \frac{b}{c} = \frac{a - b}{c}.$$

For example,

$$\frac{3}{11} - \frac{7}{11} = \frac{3 - 7}{11} = -\frac{4}{11}.$$

EXAMPLE 3 Subtracting fractions

Find the difference.

(a) $\dfrac{3}{10} - \dfrac{2}{15}$ (b) $\dfrac{3}{8} - \dfrac{5}{6}$

Solution (a) The LCD is 30.

$$\frac{3}{10} - \frac{2}{15} = \frac{3}{10} \cdot \frac{3}{3} - \frac{2}{15} \cdot \frac{2}{2} = \frac{9}{30} - \frac{4}{30} = \frac{5}{30} = \frac{1}{6}$$

(b) The LCD is 24.

$$\frac{3}{8} - \frac{5}{6} = \frac{3}{8} \cdot \frac{3}{3} - \frac{5}{6} \cdot \frac{4}{4} = \frac{9}{24} - \frac{20}{24} = -\frac{11}{24}$$

ADDITION OF RATIONAL EXPRESSIONS

Addition of rational expressions is similar to addition of fractions.

SUMS OF RATIONAL EXPRESSIONS

To add two rational expressions with like denominators, add their numerators. The denominator does not change.

$$\frac{A}{C} + \frac{B}{C} = \frac{A + B}{C} \qquad C \text{ not zero}$$

EXAMPLE 4 Adding rational expressions with like denominators

Add and simplify.

(a) $\dfrac{x}{x + 2} + \dfrac{3x - 1}{x + 2}$ (b) $\dfrac{x}{3x^2 + 4x - 4} + \dfrac{2}{3x^2 + 4x - 4}$

Solution (a) The expressions have like denominators, so add the numerators.

$$\frac{x}{x + 2} + \frac{3x - 1}{x + 2} = \frac{x + 3x - 1}{x + 2} \qquad \text{Add numerators.}$$

$$= \frac{4x - 1}{x + 2} \qquad \text{Combine like terms.}$$

(b) The expressions have like denominators, so add the numerators. However, the resulting sum can be reduced by factoring the denominator.

$$\frac{x}{3x^2 + 4x - 4} + \frac{2}{3x^2 + 4x - 4} = \frac{x + 2}{3x^2 + 4x - 4} \qquad \text{Add numerators.}$$

$$= \frac{x + 2}{(3x - 2)(x + 2)} \qquad \text{Factor denominator.}$$

$$= \frac{1}{3x - 2} \qquad \text{Reduce.} \qquad \underline{}$$

To add rational expressions with unlike denominators, we must first write each expression so that it has the same common denominator. For example, the least common denominator for $\frac{1}{x + 2}$ and $\frac{2}{x - 1}$ equals the least common multiple of $x + 2$ and $x - 1$, which was shown to be their product $(x + 2)(x - 1)$ in Example 1(c). To rewrite $\frac{1}{x + 2}$ with the new denominator we multiply it by 1, expressed as $\frac{x - 1}{x - 1}$.

$$\frac{1}{x + 2} \cdot 1 = \frac{1}{x + 2} \cdot \frac{x - 1}{x - 1} = \frac{x - 1}{(x + 2)(x - 1)}$$

Similarly, we multiply $\frac{2}{x - 1}$ by 1, expressed as $\frac{x + 2}{x + 2}$.

$$\frac{2}{x - 1} \cdot 1 = \frac{2}{x - 1} \cdot \frac{x + 2}{x + 2} = \frac{2x + 4}{(x - 1)(x + 2)}$$

Now the two rational expressions have like denominators and can be added.

$$\frac{1}{x + 2} + \frac{2}{x - 1} = \frac{x - 1}{(x + 2)(x - 1)} + \frac{2x + 4}{(x - 1)(x + 2)} \qquad \text{Write with LCD.}$$

$$= \frac{x - 1 + 2x + 4}{(x + 2)(x - 1)} \qquad \text{Add numerators.}$$

$$= \frac{3x + 3}{(x + 2)(x - 1)} \qquad \text{Combine like terms.}$$

TEACHING TIP

Emphasize that to rewrite rational expressions with a common denominator, we multiply each expression by an appropriate form of 1.

EXAMPLE 5   Adding rational expressions with unlike denominators

Add and simplify.

(a) $\dfrac{1}{x} + \dfrac{2}{x^2}$ **(b)** $\dfrac{1}{x^2 - 9} + \dfrac{2}{x + 3}$ **(c)** $\dfrac{a}{a - b} + \dfrac{b}{a + b}$ **(d)** $\dfrac{1}{x - 1} + \dfrac{1}{1 - x}$

Solution   **(a)** The LCD is x^2.

$$\frac{1}{x} \cdot \frac{x}{x} + \frac{2}{x^2} = \frac{x}{x^2} + \frac{2}{x^2} \qquad \text{Write with LCD.}$$

$$= \frac{x + 2}{x^2} \qquad \text{Add numerators.}$$

(b) The LCD is $x^2 - 9 = (x - 3)(x + 3)$.

$$\frac{1}{x^2 - 9} + \frac{2}{x + 3} \cdot \frac{x - 3}{x - 3} = \frac{1}{(x + 3)(x - 3)} + \frac{2x - 6}{(x + 3)(x - 3)} \quad \text{Write with LCD.}$$

$$= \frac{2x - 5}{(x + 3)(x - 3)} \quad \text{Add numerators.}$$

(c) The LCD is $(a - b)(a + b)$.

$$\frac{a}{a - b} \cdot \frac{a + b}{a + b} + \frac{b}{a + b} \cdot \frac{a - b}{a - b} = \frac{a^2 + ab}{(a - b)(a + b)} + \frac{ab - b^2}{(a - b)(a + b)} \quad \text{Write with LCD.}$$

$$= \frac{a^2 + 2ab - b^2}{(a - b)(a + b)} \quad \text{Add numerators.}$$

(d) By multiplying the second expression by $\frac{-1}{-1}$, the LCD can be found.

$$\frac{1}{x - 1} + \frac{1}{1 - x} \cdot \frac{-1}{-1} = \frac{1}{x - 1} + \frac{-1}{(1 - x)(-1)} \quad \text{Write with LCD.}$$

$$= \frac{1}{x - 1} + \frac{-1}{x - 1} \quad \text{Distributive property}$$

$$= \frac{0}{x - 1} \quad \text{Add numerators.}$$

$$= 0 \quad \text{Simplify.}$$

SUBTRACTION OF RATIONAL EXPRESSIONS

Subtraction of rational expressions is similar to subtraction of fractions.

DIFFERENCES OF RATIONAL EXPRESSIONS

To subtract two rational expressions with like denominators, subtract their numerators. The denominator does not change.

$$\frac{A}{C} - \frac{B}{C} = \frac{A - B}{C} \quad C \text{ not zero}$$

When you are subtracting numerators of rational expressions, it is *essential* to apply the distributive property correctly: Subtract every term in the numerator of the second rational expression. For example,

$$\frac{1}{x + 1} - \frac{2x - 1}{x + 1} = \frac{1 - (2x - 1)}{x + 1} = \frac{1 - 2x + 1}{x + 1} = \frac{2 - 2x}{x + 1}.$$

Be sure to place parentheses around the second numerator before subtracting.

TEACHING TIP

Emphasize the distributive property when the second numerator contains more than one term.

EXAMPLE 6 Subtracting rational expressions with like denominators

Subtract and simplify.

(a) $\dfrac{3}{x^2} - \dfrac{x + 3}{x^2}$ **(b)** $\dfrac{2x}{x^2 - 1} - \dfrac{x + 1}{x^2 - 1}$

Solution **(a)** The expressions have like denominators, so subtract the numerators.

$$\frac{3}{x^2} - \frac{x+3}{x^2} = \frac{3 - (x+3)}{x^2} \qquad \text{Subtract numerators.}$$

$$= \frac{3 - x - 3}{x^2} \qquad \text{Distributive property}$$

$$= -\frac{1}{x} \qquad \text{Simplify numerator and reduce.}$$

(b) The expressions have like denominators, so subtract the numerators.

$$\frac{2x}{x^2 - 1} - \frac{x+1}{x^2 - 1} = \frac{2x - (x+1)}{x^2 - 1} \qquad \text{Subtract numerators.}$$

$$= \frac{2x - x - 1}{x^2 - 1} \qquad \text{Distributive property}$$

$$= \frac{x - 1}{(x+1)(x-1)} \qquad \text{Combine like terms; factor.}$$

$$= \frac{1}{x+1} \qquad \text{Reduce.}$$

Technology Note: *Graphical and Numerical Support*

We can give support to our work in Example 6(a) by letting $Y_1 = 3/X^2 - (X + 3)/X^2$, the given expression, and $Y_2 = -1/X$, the simplified expression. In Figures 6.9(a) and 6.9(b) the graphs of y_1 and y_2 appear to be identical. In Figure 6.9(c) numerical support is given, where $y_1 = y_2$ for each value of x.

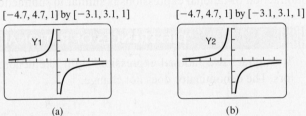

[−4.7, 4.7, 1] by [−3.1, 3.1, 1]   [−4.7, 4.7, 1] by [−3.1, 3.1, 1]

X	Y₁	Y₂
-3	.33333	.33333
-2	.5	.5
-1	1	1
0	ERROR	ERROR
1	-1	-1
2	-.5	-.5
3	-.3333	-.3333
X=-3		

(a)   (b)   (c)

Figure 6.9

EXAMPLE 7   Subtracting rational expressions with unlike denominators

Subtract and simplify.

(a) $\dfrac{5a}{b^2} - \dfrac{4b}{a^2}$ **(b)** $\dfrac{x-1}{x} - \dfrac{5}{x+5}$ **(c)** $\dfrac{1}{x^2 - 3x + 2} - \dfrac{1}{x^2 - x - 2}$

Solution **(a)** The LCD is a^2b^2.

$$\frac{5a}{b^2} \cdot \frac{a^2}{a^2} - \frac{4b}{a^2} \cdot \frac{b^2}{b^2} = \frac{5a^3}{b^2a^2} - \frac{4b^3}{a^2b^2} \qquad \text{Write with LCD.}$$

$$= \frac{5a^3 - 4b^3}{a^2b^2} \qquad \text{Subtract numerators.}$$

(b) The LCD is $x(x + 5)$.

$$\frac{x - 1}{x} \cdot \frac{x + 5}{x + 5} - \frac{5}{x + 5} \cdot \frac{x}{x} \qquad \text{Write with LCD.}$$

$$= \frac{(x - 1)(x + 5)}{x(x + 5)} - \frac{5x}{x(x + 5)} \qquad \text{Multiply.}$$

$$= \frac{(x - 1)(x + 5) - 5x}{x(x + 5)} \qquad \text{Subtract numerators.}$$

$$= \frac{x^2 + 4x - 5 - 5x}{x(x + 5)} \qquad \text{Multiply binomials.}$$

$$= \frac{x^2 - x - 5}{x(x + 5)} \qquad \text{Combine like terms.}$$

(c) Because $x^2 - 3x + 2 = (x - 2)(x - 1)$ and $x^2 - x - 2 = (x - 2)(x + 1)$, the LCD is $(x - 1)(x + 1)(x - 2)$.

$$\frac{1}{(x - 2)(x - 1)} \cdot \frac{(x + 1)}{(x + 1)} - \frac{1}{(x - 2)(x + 1)} \cdot \frac{(x - 1)}{(x - 1)} \qquad \text{Write with LCD.}$$

$$= \frac{(x + 1)}{(x - 2)(x - 1)(x + 1)} - \frac{(x - 1)}{(x - 2)(x + 1)(x - 1)} \qquad \text{Multiply.}$$

$$= \frac{(x + 1) - (x - 1)}{(x - 2)(x - 1)(x + 1)} \qquad \text{Subtract numerators.}$$

$$= \frac{x + 1 - x + 1}{(x - 2)(x - 1)(x + 1)} \qquad \text{Distributive property}$$

$$= \frac{2}{(x - 2)(x - 1)(x + 1)} \qquad \text{Simplify numerator.}$$

The following step-by-step procedure summarizes how to add or subtract rational expressions.

STEPS FOR FINDING SUMS AND DIFFERENCES OF RATIONAL EXPRESSIONS

STEP 1: If the denominators are not common, multiply each expression by 1 written in the appropriate form to obtain the LCD.

STEP 2: Add or subtract the numerators. Combine like terms.

STEP 3: If possible, reduce the final expression by factoring.

AN APPLICATION FROM ELECTRICITY   Sums of rational expressions occur in applications such as electrical circuits. The flow of electricity through a wire can be compared to the flow of water through a hose. Voltage is the force "pushing" the electricity and corresponds to water pressure in a hose. Resistance is the opposition to the flow of electricity, and more resistance results in less flow of electricity. Resistance corresponds to the diameter of a hose; if the diameter is smaller, less water flows. An ordinary light bulb is an example of a resistor in an electrical circuit.

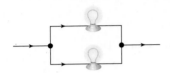

Figure 6.10

Suppose that two light bulbs are wired in parallel so that electricity can flow through either light bulb, as depicted in Figure 6.10. If their resistances are R_1 and R_2, their combined resistance R can be computed by the equation

$$\frac{1}{R} = \frac{1}{R_1} + \frac{1}{R_2}.$$

Resistance is often measured in a unit called *ohms*. A standard 60-watt light bulb might have a resistance of about 200 ohms. (*Source:* R. Weidner and R. Sells, *Elementary Classical Physics, Vol. 2.*)

EXAMPLE 8   Modeling electrical resistance

A 100-watt light bulb with a resistance of $R_1 = 120$ ohms and a 75-watt light bulb with a resistance of $R_2 = 160$ ohms are placed in an electrical circuit, as shown in Figure 6.10. Find their combined resistance.

Solution   Let $R_1 = 120$ and $R_2 = 160$ in the given equation and solve for R.

$$\frac{1}{R} = \frac{1}{R_1} + \frac{1}{R_2}$$ Given equation

$$= \frac{1}{120} + \frac{1}{160}$$ Substitute for R_1 and R_2.

$$= \frac{1}{120} \cdot \frac{4}{4} + \frac{1}{160} \cdot \frac{3}{3}$$ LCD is 480.

$$= \frac{4}{480} + \frac{3}{480}$$ Multiply.

$$= \frac{7}{480}$$ Add.

Because $\frac{1}{R} = \frac{7}{480}$, $R = \frac{480}{7} \approx 69$ ohms.

Critical Thinking

If $\frac{1}{R} = \frac{1}{R_1} + \frac{1}{R_2}$, does $R = R_1 + R_2$? Explain your answer.

No; for example, $\frac{1}{2} = \frac{1}{4} + \frac{1}{4}$, but $2 \neq 4 + 4$.

 PUTTING IT ALL TOGETHER

The following table summarizes some important concepts from this section.

Concept	Explanation	Example
Least Common Multiple (LCM)	To find the LCM, follow the three-step procedure presented on page 397.	To find the LCM of $2x^2 - 2x$ and $8x^2$, factor each expression: $2x^2 - 2x = 2 \cdot x \cdot (x - 1)$ and $8x^2 = 2 \cdot 2 \cdot 2 \cdot x \cdot x.$ The LCM is $2 \cdot 2 \cdot 2 \cdot x \cdot x \cdot (x - 1) = 8x^2(x - 1).$

Concept	Explanation	Example
Least Common Denominator (LCD)	The LCD equals the LCM of the denominators.	The LCD for $\dfrac{3x}{2x^2 - 2x}$ and $\dfrac{5}{8x^2}$ is $8x^2(x - 1)$.
Addition and Subtraction of Rational Expressions	To add (or subtract) two rational expressions with like denominators, add (or subtract) their numerators. The denominator does not change. $$\frac{A}{C} + \frac{B}{C} = \frac{A + B}{C}$$ $$\frac{A}{C} - \frac{B}{C} = \frac{A - B}{C} \quad \text{\small C not zero}$$	$$\frac{x}{x + 1} + \frac{3x}{x + 1} = \frac{4x}{x + 1}$$ If the denominators are not alike, write each term with the LCD first. $$\frac{1}{x} - \frac{2x}{x + 1} = \frac{1}{x} \cdot \frac{x + 1}{x + 1} - \frac{2x}{x + 1} \cdot \frac{x}{x}$$ $$= \frac{x + 1}{x(x + 1)} - \frac{2x^2}{x(x + 1)}$$ $$= \frac{-2x^2 + x + 1}{x(x + 1)}$$

6.3 EXERCISES

FOR EXTRA HELP

CONCEPTS

1. What is the LCM for 6 and 9? 18

2. What is the LCD for $\frac{1}{6}$ and $\frac{1}{9}$? 18

3. What is the LCM for $x^2 - 25$ and $x + 5$? $(x - 5)(x + 5)$

4. What is the LCD for $\frac{1}{x^2 - 25}$ and $\frac{1}{x + 5}$? $(x - 5)(x + 5)$

5. What do you need to find before you can add $\frac{1}{4}$ and $\frac{1}{3}$? A common denominator

6. What do you need to find before you can add $\frac{2}{x}$ and $\frac{1}{2x - 1}$? A common denominator

7. $\dfrac{a}{c} + \dfrac{b}{c} = \underline{\dfrac{a + b}{c}}$.

8. $\dfrac{a}{c} - \dfrac{b}{c} = \underline{\dfrac{a - b}{c}}$.

LEAST COMMON MULTIPLES

Exercises 9–18: Find the least common multiple.

9. 10, 15 30

10. 9, 12 36

11. 34, 51 102

12. 24, 36 72

13. $6a, 9a^2$ $18a^2$

14. $12ab, 6a^2$ $12a^2b$

15. $10x^2, 25(x^2 - x)$ $50x^2(x - 1)$

16. $x^2 - 4, x^2 + 2x$ $x(x - 2)(x + 2)$

17. $x^2 + 2x + 1, x^2 - 4x - 5$ $(x - 5)(x + 1)^2$

18. $4x^2 + 20x + 25, 2x^2 + 5x$ $x(2x + 5)^2$

REVIEW OF FRACTIONS

Exercises 19–26: Simplify.

19. $\frac{1}{7} + \frac{4}{7}$ $\frac{5}{7}$

20. $\frac{2}{5} + \frac{1}{2}$ $\frac{9}{10}$

21. $\frac{2}{3} + \frac{5}{6} + \frac{1}{4}$ $\frac{7}{4}$

22. $\frac{3}{11} + \frac{1}{2} + \frac{1}{6}$ $\frac{31}{33}$

23. $\frac{1}{10} - \frac{3}{10}$ $-\frac{1}{5}$

24. $\frac{2}{9} - \frac{1}{11}$ $\frac{13}{99}$

25. $\frac{3}{2} - \frac{1}{8}$ $\frac{11}{8}$

26. $\frac{3}{12} - \frac{5}{16}$ $-\frac{1}{16}$

ADDITION AND SUBTRACTION OF RATIONAL EXPRESSIONS

Exercises 27–66: Simplify.

27. $\dfrac{1}{x} + \dfrac{3}{x}$ $\dfrac{4}{x}$

28. $\dfrac{2}{x - 1} + \dfrac{x}{x - 1}$ $\dfrac{2 + x}{x - 1}$

29. $\dfrac{2}{x^2 - 4} - \dfrac{x + 1}{x^2 - 4}$ $\dfrac{1 - x}{x^2 - 4}$

30. $\dfrac{2x - 1}{x^2 + 6} - \dfrac{2x + 1}{x^2 + 6}$ $-\dfrac{2}{x^2 + 6}$

31. $\dfrac{2z}{4-z} - \dfrac{3z-4}{4-z}$ 1

32. $\dfrac{z}{z^2-9} - \dfrac{3}{z^2-9}$ $\dfrac{1}{z+3}$

33. $\dfrac{3t}{t^2-t-6} + \dfrac{2-2t}{t^2-t-6}$ $\dfrac{1}{t-3}$

38. $\dfrac{6}{2n-1}$

34. $\dfrac{t}{t^2+5t} + \dfrac{5}{t^2+5t}$ $\dfrac{1}{t}$

35. $\dfrac{5b}{3a} - \dfrac{7b}{5a}$ $\dfrac{4b}{15a}$

40. $\dfrac{5x^2-11x-10}{(x-2)(x+2)}$

36. $\dfrac{a}{ab^2} - \dfrac{b}{a^2b}$ $\dfrac{a^2-b^2}{a^2b^2}$

37. $\dfrac{4}{n-4} + \dfrac{3}{2-n}$ $\dfrac{n+4}{(n-4)(n-2)}$

38. $\dfrac{3}{2n-1} - \dfrac{3}{1-2n}$

39. $\dfrac{x}{x+4} - \dfrac{x+1}{x}$ $\dfrac{-5x-4}{x(x+4)}$

40. $\dfrac{4x}{x+2} + \dfrac{x-5}{x-2}$

41. $\dfrac{2}{x^2} - \dfrac{4x-1}{x}$ $\dfrac{-4x^2+x+2}{x^2}$

42. $\dfrac{2x}{x-5} - \dfrac{x}{x+5}$

43. $\dfrac{x+3}{x-5} + \dfrac{5}{x-3}$ $\dfrac{x^2+5x-34}{(x-5)(x-3)}$

44. $\dfrac{x}{2x-1} + \dfrac{1-x}{3x}$

45. $\dfrac{4n}{n^2-9} - \dfrac{8}{n-3}$ $\dfrac{4(n+6)}{(n-3)(n+3)}$

46. $\dfrac{3n}{(4n-3)^2} - \dfrac{1}{4n-3}$ $\dfrac{3-n}{(4n-3)^2}$

42. $\dfrac{x(x+15)}{(x-5)(x+5)}$

47. $\dfrac{4r}{5t^2} + \dfrac{r}{5t^2}$ $\dfrac{r}{t^2}$

48. $\dfrac{1}{2ab} + \dfrac{1}{2ab}$ $\dfrac{1}{ab}$

44. $\dfrac{x^2+3x-1}{3x(2x-1)}$

49. $\dfrac{x}{x^2-9} + \dfrac{5x}{x-3}$

50. $\dfrac{a^2+1}{a^2-1} + \dfrac{a}{1-a^2}$ $\dfrac{a^2-a+1}{(a-1)(a+1)}$

51. $\dfrac{b}{2b-4} - \dfrac{b-1}{b-2}$ $-\dfrac{1}{2}$

52. $\dfrac{y^2}{2-y} - \dfrac{y}{y^2-4}$ $\dfrac{-y(y+1)^2}{(y-2)(y+2)}$

53. $\dfrac{2x}{x-5} + \dfrac{2x-1}{3x^2-16x+5}$ $\dfrac{6x^2-1}{(x-5)(3x-1)}$

49. $\dfrac{x(5x+16)}{(x-3)(x+3)}$

54. $\dfrac{x+3}{2x-1} + \dfrac{3}{10x^2-5x}$ $\dfrac{5x^2+15x+3}{5x(2x-1)}$

55. $\dfrac{4x^2+4xy-9x+9y}{(x-y)(x+y)}$

55. $\dfrac{4x}{x-y} - \dfrac{9}{x+y}$

56. $\dfrac{1}{a-b} - \dfrac{3a}{a^2-b^2}$ $\dfrac{b-2a}{(a-b)(a+b)}$

57. $\dfrac{3}{x^2-2x+1} + \dfrac{1}{x^2-3x+2}$ $\dfrac{4x-7}{(x-2)(x-1)^2}$

58. $\dfrac{x}{x^2-4} - \dfrac{1}{x^2+4x+4}$ $\dfrac{x^2+x+2}{(x-2)(x+2)^2}$

59. $\dfrac{3x}{x^2+2x-3} + \dfrac{1}{x^2-2x+1}$ $\dfrac{3x^2-2x+3}{(x-1)^2(x+3)}$

60. $\dfrac{3x}{x-y} - \dfrac{3y}{x^2-2xy+y^2}$ $\dfrac{3(x^2-xy-y)}{(x-y)^2}$

61. $\dfrac{-2a^2+3b^2+4c^2}{abc}$

61. $\dfrac{4c}{ab} + \dfrac{3b}{ac} - \dfrac{2a}{bc}$

62. $\dfrac{x^3-x+2}{(x-1)(x+1)}$

62. $x + \dfrac{1}{x-1} - \dfrac{1}{x+1}$

63. $5 - \dfrac{6}{n^2-36} + \dfrac{3}{n-6}$ $\dfrac{5n^2+3n-168}{(n-6)(n+6)}$

64. $\dfrac{6}{t-1} + \dfrac{2}{t-2} + \dfrac{1}{t}$ $\dfrac{9t^2-17t+2}{t(t-2)(t-1)}$

65. $\dfrac{3}{x-5} - \dfrac{1}{x-3} - \dfrac{2x}{x-5}$ $\dfrac{-2(x^2-4x+2)}{(x-5)(x-3)}$

66. $\dfrac{2x+1}{x-1} - \dfrac{3}{x+1} + \dfrac{x}{x-1}$ $\dfrac{3x^2+x+4}{(x-1)(x+1)}$

APPLICATIONS

67. *Electrical Resistance*   (Refer to Example 8.) A 150-watt light bulb with a resistance of 80 ohms and a 40-watt light bulb with a resistance of 300 ohms are wired in parallel. Find the combined resistance of the light bulbs. $\dfrac{1200}{19} \approx 63.2$ ohms

68. *Electrical Resistance*   (Refer to Exercise 67.) Solve the formula $R = \dfrac{R_1 R_2}{R_1 + R_2}$; they are the same.

$$\dfrac{1}{R} = \dfrac{1}{R_1} + \dfrac{1}{R_2}$$

for R. Use your formula to solve Exercise 67. Did you find the same value for R?

69. *Photography*   A lens in a camera has a focal length, which is important in focusing the camera. If an object is at distance D from a lens that has a focal length F, then to be in focus the distance S between the lens and the film should satisfy the equation

$$\dfrac{1}{S} = \dfrac{1}{F} - \dfrac{1}{D}.$$

(See the accompanying figure.) If the focal length is $F = 0.1$ foot and the object is $D = 10$ feet from the camera, find S. $S \approx 0.101$ ft, or about 1.2 in.

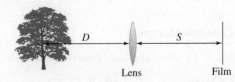

70. *Photography*   (Continuation of Exercise 69.) Suppose that the object is closer to the lens than the focal length of the lens. That is, suppose $D < F$. According to the formula, is it possible to focus the image on the film? Explain your reasoning.

No; if $D < F, \frac{1}{D} > \frac{1}{F}$ and $\frac{1}{F} - \frac{1}{D} < 0$, then S must be negative, which is impossible.

71. *Intensity of a Light Bulb* The intensity of a light bulb at a point varies according to its distance from the light bulb. The expression $\frac{8}{d^2}$ approximates the intensity of a 100-watt light bulb in watts per square meter (W/m^2) at a distance of d meters. Calculate the combined intensity at a point d meters from two 100-watt light bulbs. $\frac{16}{d^2}\,\text{W/m}^2$

72. *Intensity of a Light Bulb* (Refer to the preceding exercise.) Suppose that one 100-watt light bulb is at a distance d and another 100-watt light bulb is at a distance $\frac{1}{2}d$ from a point. Write an expression for the combined intensity of the two light bulbs. $\frac{40}{d^2}\,\text{W/m}^2$

WRITING ABOUT MATHEMATICS

73. A student does the following to add two rational expressions. Explain the error that the student is making and how it can be corrected.
$$\frac{x}{x+1} + \frac{6x}{x} \overset{?}{=} \frac{7x}{2x+1}$$

74. Explain in words how to subtract two rational expressions with like denominators.

6.4 RATIONAL EQUATIONS

Solving Rational Equations · Solving an Equation for a Variable

INTRODUCTION

In Section 6.1 we introduced rational equations. If an equation contains one or more rational expressions, it is often called a *rational equation*. Rational equations occur in applications involving distance and time. For example, if one athlete runs 2 miles per hour faster and finishes 3 minutes sooner than another athlete in a 3-mile race, then the speed of the slower athlete can be found by solving the rational equation
$$\frac{3}{x+2} + \frac{1}{20} = \frac{3}{x}.$$

To better understand why, refer to Example 6. In this section we discuss how to solve different types of rational equations.

SOLVING RATIONAL EQUATIONS

One way to solve a rational equation is to *clear fractions* by multiplying both sides of the equation by the least common denominator (LCD). For example, to solve
$$\frac{1}{2x} + \frac{2}{3} = \frac{5}{2x}$$
multiply each side by the LCD (LCM of 3 and $2x$), which is $6x$.

TEACHING TIP

Clearing fractions is one of the easiest ways for students to solve rational equations.

$$6x\left(\frac{1}{2x} + \frac{2}{3}\right) = 6x\left(\frac{5}{2x}\right) \qquad \text{Multiply each side by } 6x.$$
$$\frac{6x}{2x} + \frac{12x}{3} = \frac{30x}{2x} \qquad \text{Distributive property}$$
$$3 + 4x = 15 \qquad \text{Reduce.}$$
$$4x = 12 \qquad \text{Subtract 3 from each side.}$$
$$x = 3 \qquad \text{Divide each side by 4.}$$

Check this answer to verify that 3 is indeed a solution. (When solving a rational equation, always be sure to check your answer.)

EXAMPLE 1 Solving rational equations

Solve the equation and check your answer.

(a) $\dfrac{x+1}{2x} - \dfrac{x-1}{4x} = \dfrac{1}{3}$ (b) $\dfrac{3}{x-2} + \dfrac{5}{x+2} = \dfrac{12}{x^2-4}$

Solution (a) Note that the left side of the equation is undefined when $x = 0$. Thus 0 cannot be a solution. Start by determining the LCD, which is **$12x$**.

$$12x\left(\dfrac{x+1}{2x} - \dfrac{x-1}{4x}\right) = 12x\left(\dfrac{1}{3}\right) \qquad \text{Multiply each side by } 12x.$$

$$12x\left(\dfrac{x+1}{2x}\right) - 12x\left(\dfrac{x-1}{4x}\right) = \dfrac{12x}{3} \qquad \text{Distributive property}$$

$$6(x+1) - 3(x-1) = 4x \qquad \text{Simplify.}$$

$$6x + 6 - 3x + 3 = 4x \qquad \text{Distributive property}$$

$$3x + 9 = 4x \qquad \text{Combine like terms.}$$

$$x = 9 \qquad \text{Solve for } x.$$

Check:

$$\dfrac{9+1}{2(9)} - \dfrac{9-1}{4(9)} \overset{?}{=} \dfrac{1}{3} \qquad \text{Let } x = 9 \text{ in given equation.}$$

$$\dfrac{10}{18} - \dfrac{8}{36} \overset{?}{=} \dfrac{1}{3} \qquad \text{Simplify fractions.}$$

$$\dfrac{1}{3} = \dfrac{1}{3} \qquad \text{It checks.}$$

(b) Note that both sides of the equation are undefined when $x = 2$ or $x = -2$. Thus neither 2 nor -2 can be a solution. The LCD is $x^2 - 4 = (x-2)(x+2)$.

$$\dfrac{3(x-2)(x+2)}{x-2} + \dfrac{5(x-2)(x+2)}{x+2} = \dfrac{12(x^2-4)}{x^2-4} \qquad \text{Multiply each term by the LCD.}$$

$$3(x+2) + 5(x-2) = 12 \qquad \text{Reduce.}$$

$$3x + 6 + 5x - 10 = 12 \qquad \text{Distributive property}$$

$$8x - 4 = 12 \qquad \text{Combine like terms.}$$

$$8x = 16 \qquad \text{Add 4.}$$

$$x = 2 \qquad \text{Divide by 8.}$$

Check: We already noted that 2 cannot be a solution. Checking this answer gives the following result.

$$\dfrac{3}{2-2} + \dfrac{5}{2+2} \overset{?}{=} \dfrac{12}{2^2-4} \qquad \text{Let } x = 2.$$

$$\dfrac{3}{0} + \dfrac{5}{4} \overset{?}{=} \dfrac{12}{0} \qquad \text{Simplify fractions.}$$

Both sides are undefined because division by 0 is not possible. There are no solutions.

The next example illustrates how to solve a rational equation graphically. Because graphical solutions are only estimates, be sure to check them by substituting observed values in the given equation.

EXAMPLE 2 Solving a rational equation graphically

Solve the equation $\frac{4}{x-1} = 2x$ graphically. Check your results.

Solution Start by graphing $y_1 = \frac{4}{x-1}$ and $y_2 = 2x$. The graph of y_2 is a line with slope 2 passing through the origin. To help graph y_1 make a table of values. The two graphs intersect at $x = -1$ and $x = 2$, as shown in Figure 6.11.

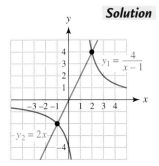

Figure 6.11

Check:

$$\frac{4}{-1-1} \stackrel{?}{=} 2(-1) \qquad \text{Let } x = -1.$$

$$-2 = -2 \qquad \text{It checks.}$$

$$\frac{4}{2-1} \stackrel{?}{=} 2(2) \qquad \text{Let } x = 2.$$

$$4 = 4 \qquad \text{It checks.}$$

The next example illustrates how to solve two rational equations and support the results with a graphing calculator.

EXAMPLE 3 Solving rational equations

Solve each equation. Support your results either graphically or numerically.

(a) $\dfrac{1}{2} + \dfrac{x}{3} = \dfrac{x}{5}$ **(b)** $\dfrac{3}{x-2} = \dfrac{5}{x+2}$

TEACHING TIP

Graphical solutions of rational equations are not emphasized as much as symbolic solutions. However, it is important for students to know that rational equations can also be solved graphically.

$[-9, 9, 1]$ by $[-6, 6, 1]$

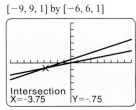

Intersection
X=-3.75   Y=-.75

Figure 6.12

Calculator Help
To find a point of intersection, see the Appendix (page AP-7).

Solution **(a)** The LCD is the product of 2, 3, and 5, which is **30**.

$$30 \cdot \left(\frac{1}{2} + \frac{x}{3}\right) = \frac{x}{5} \cdot 30 \qquad \text{Multiply by the LCD.}$$

$$\frac{30}{2} + \frac{30x}{3} = \frac{30x}{5} \qquad \text{Distributive property}$$

$$15 + 10x = 6x \qquad \text{Reduce.}$$

$$4x = -15 \qquad \text{Subtract } 6x \text{ and } 15.$$

$$x = -\frac{15}{4} \qquad \text{Solve.}$$

This result can be supported graphically by letting $Y_1 = 1/2 + X/3$ and $Y_2 = X/5$. Their graphs intersect at the point $(-3.75, -0.75)$, as shown in Figure 6.12. Therefore the solution to this equation is -3.75, or $-\frac{15}{4}$.

(b) Multiply each side by the LCD, which is $(x-2)(x+2)$.

$$(x-2)(x+2) \cdot \frac{3}{x-2} = \frac{5}{x+2} \cdot (x-2)(x+2) \qquad \text{Multiply by the LCD.}$$

$$\frac{3(x-2)(x+2)}{x-2} = \frac{5(x-2)(x+2)}{x+2} \qquad \text{Multiply expressions.}$$

$$3(x+2) = 5(x-2) \qquad \text{Reduce.}$$

$$3x + 6 = 5x - 10 \qquad \text{Distributive property}$$

$$16 = 2x \qquad \text{Add 10 and subtract } 3x.$$

$$x = 8 \qquad \text{Solve.}$$

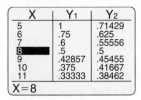

X	Y₁	Y₂
5	1	.71429
6	.75	.625
7	.6	.55556
8	.5	.5
9	.42857	.45455
10	.375	.41667
11	.33333	.38462

X=8

Figure 6.13

Calculator Help
To make a table, see the
Appendix (page AP-3).

To support this result numerically let $Y_1 = 3/(X - 2)$ and $Y_2 = 5/(X + 2)$. The table in Figure 6.13 shows that $y_1 = y_2 = 0.5$ when $x = 8$. The solution is 8.   ____

Technology Note: *Entering Rational Expressions*

When entering a rational expression, use parentheses around the numerator and denominator. The following are examples. Enter

$$y = \frac{3}{x + 2} \quad \text{as} \quad Y_1 = 3/(X + 2).$$

Enter

$$y = \frac{x + 1}{2x - 1} \quad \text{as} \quad Y_1 = (X + 1)/(2X - 1).$$

Sometimes solving a rational equation results in the need to solve a quadratic equation, which is demonstrated in the next example.

EXAMPLE 4   Solving rational equations

Solve the equation.

(a) $\dfrac{1}{x} + \dfrac{1}{x^2} = \dfrac{3}{4}$ **(b)** $\dfrac{2x}{x + 2} + \dfrac{3x}{x - 1} = 7$

Solution   **(a)** The LCD is $4x^2$. Note that 0 cannot be a solution.

$$4x^2 \cdot \left(\frac{1}{x} + \frac{1}{x^2} \right) = \frac{3}{4} \cdot 4x^2 \qquad \text{Multiply by } 4x^2.$$

$$\frac{4x^2}{x} + \frac{4x^2}{x^2} = \frac{12x^2}{4} \qquad \text{Distributive property}$$

$$4x + 4 = 3x^2 \qquad \text{Reduce.}$$

$$0 = 3x^2 - 4x - 4 \qquad \text{Subtract } 4x + 4.$$

$$0 = (3x + 2)(x - 2) \qquad \text{Factor.}$$

$$x = -\frac{2}{3} \quad \text{or} \quad x = 2 \qquad \text{Solve.}$$

Both solutions check.

(b) The LCD is $(x + 2)(x - 1)$. Note that -2 and 1 cannot be solutions.

$$(x + 2)(x - 1)\left(\frac{2x}{x + 2} + \frac{3x}{x - 1} \right) = 7(x + 2)(x - 1) \qquad \text{Multiply by the LCD.}$$

$$\frac{2x(x + 2)(x - 1)}{x + 2} + \frac{3x(x + 2)(x - 1)}{x - 1} = 7(x + 2)(x - 1) \qquad \text{Distributive property.}$$

$$2x(x - 1) + 3x(x + 2) = 7(x + 2)(x - 1) \qquad \text{Reduce.}$$

$$2x^2 - 2x + 3x^2 + 6x = 7(x^2 + x - 2) \qquad \text{Multiply.}$$

$$5x^2 + 4x = 7x^2 + 7x - 14 \qquad \text{Simplify.}$$

$$0 = 2x^2 + 3x - 14 \qquad \text{Subtract } 5x^2 + 4x.$$

$$0 = (2x + 7)(x - 2) \qquad \text{Factor.}$$

Critical Thinking

A bicyclist rides uphill at 6 miles per hour for 1 mile and then rides downhill at 12 miles per hour for 1 mile. What was the average speed of the bicyclist?   8 mph

$$x = -\frac{7}{2} \quad \text{or} \quad x = 2 \qquad \text{Solve.}$$

Both solutions check.

Rational equations occur in applications involving time and rate, as demonstrated in the next example.

EXAMPLE 5   Determining the time required to empty a pool

A pump can empty a swimming pool in 50 hours. To speed up the process a second pump is used that can empty the pool in 80 hours. How long will it take for both pumps working together to empty the pool?

Solution   Because the first pump can empty the entire pool in 50 hours, it can empty $\frac{1}{50}$ of the pool in 1 hour, $\frac{2}{50}$ of the pool in 2 hours, $\frac{3}{50}$ of the pool in 3 hours, and in general, it can empty $\frac{t}{50}$ of the pool in t hours. The second pump can empty the pool in 80 hours, so (using similar reasoning) it can empty $\frac{t}{80}$ of the pool in t hours.

Together the pumps can empty

$$\frac{t}{50} + \frac{t}{80}$$

of the pool in t hours. The job will be complete when the fraction of the pool that is empty equals 1. Thus we must solve the equation

$$\frac{t}{50} + \frac{t}{80} = 1.$$

To solve we can multiply each side by $(50)(80)$.

$$(50)(80)\left(\frac{t}{50} + \frac{t}{80}\right) = 1(50)(80)$$

$$\frac{50 \cdot 80 \cdot t}{50} + \frac{50 \cdot 80 \cdot t}{80} = 4000 \qquad \text{Distributive property}$$

$$80t + 50t = 4000 \qquad \text{Reduce.}$$

$$130t = 4000 \qquad \text{Combine like terms.}$$

$$t = \frac{4000}{130} \approx 30.8 \text{ hours} \qquad \text{Solve.}$$

The two pumps can empty the pool in about 30.8 hours.

If a person drives a car 60 miles per hour for 4 hours, the total distance d traveled is

$$d = 60 \cdot 4 = 240 \text{ miles.}$$

That is, distance equals the product of the rate (speed) and the elapsed time. This may be written as $d = rt$ and expressed verbally as "distance equals rate times time." This formula is used in the next example.

EXAMPLE 6   Solving an application

Suppose that the winner of a 3-mile cross country race finishes 3 minutes ahead of another runner. If the winner runs 2 miles per hour faster than the slower runner, find the average speed of each runner.

Figure 6.14

Solution   Let x be the speed of the slower runner. Then $x + 2$ represents the speed of the winner. See Figure 6.14. To determine the time for each runner to finish the race divide both sides of $d = rt$ by r to obtain

$$t = \frac{d}{r}.$$

The slower runner ran 3 miles at x miles per hour, so the time is $\frac{3}{x}$; the winner ran 3 miles at $x + 2$ miles per hour, so the winning time is $\frac{3}{x + 2}$. If you add 3 minutes (or equivalently $\frac{3}{60} = \frac{1}{20}$ hour) to the winner's time, it equals the slower runner's time, or

$$\frac{3}{x + 2} + \frac{1}{20} = \frac{3}{x}.$$

Note: The runners' speeds are in miles per *hour*, so you need to keep time in hours.

Multiply each side by the LCD, which is $20x(x + 2)$.

$$20x(x + 2)\left(\frac{3}{x + 2} + \frac{1}{20}\right) = 20x(x + 2)\left(\frac{3}{x}\right) \qquad \text{Multiply by the LCD.}$$

$$60x + x(x + 2) = 60(x + 2) \qquad \text{Distributive property}$$

$$60x + x^2 + 2x = 60x + 120 \qquad \text{Distributive property}$$

$$x^2 + 2x - 120 = 0 \qquad \text{Rewrite the equation.}$$

$$(x + 12)(x - 10) = 0 \qquad \text{Factor.}$$

$$x = -12 \quad \text{or} \quad x = 10 \qquad \text{Zero-product property}$$

The only valid solution is 10 because a running speed cannot be negative. Thus the slower runner is running at 10 miles per hour, and the faster runner is running at 12 miles per hour.

SOLVING AN EQUATION FOR A VARIABLE

Sometimes in science and other disciplines, it is necessary to solve a formula for a variable. These formulas are often rational equations. This technique is demonstrated in the next two examples.

EXAMPLE 7   Solving an equation for a variable

Solve the equation $P = \frac{nrT}{V}$ for V. (This formula is used in science to calculate the pressure of a gas.)

Solution Start by multiplying each side of the equation by V.

$$V \cdot P = V\left(\frac{nrT}{V}\right) \qquad \text{Multiply by } V.$$

$$PV = nrT \qquad \text{Simplify.}$$

$$\frac{PV}{P} = \frac{nrT}{P} \qquad \text{Divide each side by } P.$$

$$V = \frac{nrT}{P} \qquad \text{Reduce.}$$

EXAMPLE 8 **Solving an equation from electricity**

Solve the equation $\frac{1}{R} = \frac{1}{R_1} + \frac{1}{R_2}$ for R_2.

Solution Start by multiplying each side of the equation by the LCD: RR_1R_2.

$$(RR_1R_2)\frac{1}{R} = (RR_1R_2)\left(\frac{1}{R_1} + \frac{1}{R_2}\right) \qquad \text{Multiply by the LCD.}$$

$$R_1R_2 = RR_2 + RR_1 \qquad \text{Distributive property}$$

$$R_1R_2 - RR_2 = RR_1 \qquad \text{Subtract } RR_2.$$

$$R_2(R_1 - R) = RR_1 \qquad \text{Factor out } R_2.$$

$$R_2 = \frac{RR_1}{R_1 - R} \qquad \text{Divide each side by } R_1 - R.$$

6.4 PUTTING IT ALL TOGETHER

The following table summarizes the basic steps for solving a rational equation.

Concept	Explanation	Example
Rational Equations	To solve a rational equation first multiply each side of the equation by the LCD. Then solve the resulting polynomial equation. Be sure to check your answer.	Multiply the given equation by $4x^2$. $$\frac{1}{4x} + \frac{2}{x^2} = \frac{1}{x}$$ $$4x^2\left(\frac{1}{4x} + \frac{2}{x^2}\right) = \frac{1}{x} \cdot 4x^2$$ $$\frac{4x^2}{4x} + \frac{8x^2}{x^2} = \frac{4x^2}{x}$$ $$x + 8 = 4x$$ $$8 = 3x$$ $$x = \frac{8}{3}$$

6.4   EXERCISES

FOR EXTRA HELP

Student's Solutions Manual

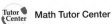 InterAct Math

 MathXL

MyMathLab

 Math Tutor Center

Digital Video Tutor
CD 5   Videotape 7

CONCEPTS

1. When solving the equation $\frac{4}{x + 2} = 2$, what is a good first step?   Multiply each side by $x + 2$.

2. In general, what is a good first step when solving a rational equation?   Multiply each side by the LCD.

3. If $\frac{1}{x} = 2$, then $x =$ _____. $\frac{1}{2}$

4. If $\frac{a}{b} = c$, then $a =$ _____. bc

5. To clear an equation of fractions, multiply each side of the equation by the _____.   LCD

6. To solve a rational equation graphically, graph each side of the equation and determine the point(s) where the graphs _____.   intersect

SOLVING RATIONAL EQUATIONS

Exercises 7–12: Find the LCD.

7. $\frac{1}{x}, \frac{1}{5}$ $5x$

8. $\frac{1}{x - 1}, \frac{1}{x + 5}$
   $(x - 1)(x + 5)$

9. $\frac{1}{x - 1}, \frac{1}{x^2 - 1}$
   $x^2 - 1$

10. $\frac{1}{x^2 - x}, \frac{1}{2x}$ $2x(x - 1)$

11. $\frac{3}{2}, \frac{x}{2x + 1}, \frac{x}{2x - 4}$
    $2(2x + 1)(x - 2)$

12. $\frac{1}{x}, \frac{1}{x^2 - 4x}, \frac{1}{2x}$ $2x(x - 4)$

Exercises 13–34: Solve the rational equation. Check your result.

13. $\frac{x}{3} + \frac{1}{2} = \frac{5}{6}$ 1

14. $\frac{7}{8} - \frac{x}{4} = -\frac{11}{8}$ 9

15. $\frac{2}{x} - \frac{7}{3} = -\frac{29}{15}$ 5

16. $\frac{1}{3x} + \frac{1}{x} = \frac{4}{15}$ 5

17. $\frac{3}{x - 1} = \frac{6}{x + 4}$ 6

18. $\frac{1}{x + 5} = \frac{2}{2x + 1}$
    No solutions

19. $\frac{6}{3z + 4} = \frac{4}{2z - 5}$ No solutions

20. $\frac{2}{z - 1} - \frac{5}{z + 1} = \frac{4}{z^2 - 1}$ No solutions

21. $\frac{5}{t - 1} + \frac{2}{t + 2} = \frac{15}{t^2 + t - 2}$ No solutions

22. $\frac{3}{5t} - \frac{1}{t + 1} = \frac{6}{5t^2 + 5t}$ $-\frac{3}{2}$

23. $\frac{1}{3n} - 2 = \frac{1}{2n}$ $-\frac{1}{12}$

24. $\frac{4}{n} - 3 = \frac{1}{3n}$ $\frac{11}{9}$

25. $\frac{1}{x} + \frac{1}{x^2} = 2$ $1, -\frac{1}{2}$

26. $\frac{1}{x} - \frac{1}{x + 1} = \frac{1}{56}$ $-8, 7$

27. $\frac{x}{x + 2} = \frac{4}{x - 3}$ $-1, 8$

28. $\frac{2x}{1 - x} - \frac{1}{x} = 0$ $-1, \frac{1}{2}$

29. $\frac{2w + 1}{3w} - \frac{4w - 3}{w} = 0$ 1

30. $\frac{1}{2w} - \frac{2}{1 - w} = -\frac{3}{2}$ $-1, \frac{1}{3}$

31. $\frac{3}{2y} + \frac{2y}{y - 4} = -\frac{11}{2}$ $-\frac{4}{15}, 3$

32. $\frac{3}{y - 2} + \frac{6y}{y + 1} = 2$ No solutions

33. $\frac{1}{(x - 1)^2} + \frac{3}{x^2 - 1} = \frac{5}{x^2 - 1}$ 3

34. $\frac{1}{x^2 - 4} + \frac{1}{(x - 2)^2} = \frac{2}{(x + 2)^2}$ $\frac{2}{3}$

Exercises 35–38: Use the graph to solve the rational equation. Then check your answer.

35. $\frac{2}{x} + 1 = 3$ 1

36. $\frac{1}{x - 1} = \frac{2}{x}$ 2

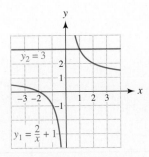

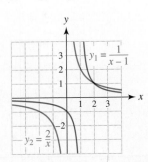

37. $\dfrac{3}{x^2-1} = \dfrac{1}{2}x$ 2

38. $\dfrac{1}{x^2} = -x$ −1

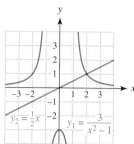

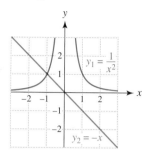

Exercises 39–48: Solve the rational equation graphically. Approximate your answer to the nearest hundredth when appropriate.

39. $\dfrac{1}{x-1} = \dfrac{1}{2}$ 3

40. $\dfrac{1}{x+1} = 2$ $-\dfrac{1}{2}$

41. $\dfrac{3}{x+2} = x$ −3, 1

42. $\dfrac{3}{x-2} = x$ −1, 3

43. $\dfrac{1}{x-2} = 2$ 2.5

44. $\dfrac{2x}{x+1} = 3$ −3

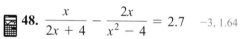 **45.** $\dfrac{1}{x} + \dfrac{1}{x^2} = \dfrac{15}{4}$ −0.4, 0.67

46. $\dfrac{1}{x} + \dfrac{1}{2x} = 2x$ ±0.87

47. $\dfrac{1}{x+2} - \dfrac{1}{x-2} = \dfrac{4}{3}$ ±1

48. $\dfrac{x}{2x+4} - \dfrac{2x}{x^2-4} = 2.7$ −3, 1.64

USING MORE THAN ONE METHOD

Exercises 49–52: Solve the equation (a) symbolically, (b) graphically, and (c) numerically.

49. $\dfrac{1}{x} + \dfrac{2}{3} = 1$ 3

50. $\dfrac{1}{x} - \dfrac{1}{x^2} = -2$ $-1, \dfrac{1}{2}$

51. $\dfrac{1}{x} + \dfrac{1}{x+2} = \dfrac{4}{3}$ $-\dfrac{3}{2}, 1$

52. $\dfrac{1}{x-2} + \dfrac{1}{x+2} = -\dfrac{2}{3}$ −4, 1

SOLVING AN EQUATION FOR A VARIABLE

Exercises 53–66: Solve the equation for the specified variable.

53. $t = \dfrac{d}{r};\quad r$ $r = \dfrac{d}{t}$

54. $r = \dfrac{C}{2\pi};\quad C$ $C = 2\pi r$

55. $h = \dfrac{2A}{b};\quad b$ $b = \dfrac{2A}{h}$

56. $P = VT;\quad T$ $T = \dfrac{P}{V}$

57. $\dfrac{1}{2a} = \dfrac{1}{b};\quad a$ $a = \dfrac{b}{2}$

58. $\dfrac{a}{b} = \dfrac{c}{d};\quad d$ $d = \dfrac{bc}{a}$

59. $\dfrac{1}{R} = \dfrac{1}{R_1} + \dfrac{1}{R_2};\quad R_1$ 59. $R_1 = \dfrac{RR_2}{R_2 - R}$

60. $S = \dfrac{5}{8H};\quad H$ $H = \dfrac{5}{8S}$

61. $T = \dfrac{1}{15-x};\quad x$ 61. $x = 15 - \dfrac{1}{T}$

62. $h = \dfrac{V}{\pi r^2};\quad V$ $V = \pi r^2 h$

63. $\dfrac{1}{r} = \dfrac{1}{t+1};\quad t$ $t = r - 1$

64. $R = \dfrac{R_1 R_2}{R_1 + R_2};\quad R_2$ $R_2 = \dfrac{RR_1}{R_1 - R}$

65. $\dfrac{1}{r} = \dfrac{a}{a+b};\quad b$ $b = a(r-1)$

66. $\dfrac{1}{t+1} = \dfrac{a}{a-b};\quad b$ $b = -at$

APPLICATIONS

67. *Mowing the Lawn*   Suppose that a person with a push mower can mow a large lawn in 5 hours, whereas the lawn can be mowed with a riding mower in 2 hours.

(a) Write an equation whose solution gives the time needed to mow the lawn if both mowers are used at the same time. $\dfrac{x}{5} + \dfrac{x}{2} = 1$

(b) Solve the equation in part (a) symbolically. $\dfrac{10}{7}$ hr

(c) Solve the equation in part (a) either graphically or numerically. $\dfrac{10}{7} \approx 1.43$ hr

68. *Pumping Water*   (Refer to Example 5.) Suppose that a large pump can empty a swimming pool in 40 hours and that a small pump can empty a pool in 70 hours.   68.(a) $\dfrac{x}{40} + \dfrac{x}{70} = 1$

(a) Write an equation whose solution gives the time needed for both pumps to empty the pool.

(b) Solve the equation in part (a) symbolically.

(c) Solve the equation in part (a) either graphically or numerically. $\dfrac{280}{11} = 25.\overline{45}$ hr   (b) $\dfrac{280}{11} = 25.\overline{45}$ hr

69. *Running a Race*   (Refer to Example 6.) The winner of a 5-mile race finishes 7.5 minutes ahead of the second-place runner. On average, the winner ran 2 miles per hour faster than the second-place runner. Find the average running speed for each runner.   Winner: 10 mph; second place runner: 8 mph

70. *Filling a Water Tank*   A large pump can fill a 10,000-gallon tank 5 hours faster than a small pump. The large pump outputs water 100 gallons per hour faster than the small pump. Find the number of gallons pumped in 1 hour by each pump.   Large pump: 500 gal; small pump: 400 gal

71. *Aerial Photographs*   An aerial photograph is being taken of an area of land. The scale S for the photograph is planned to be $S = \frac{1}{10,000}$. (This value for S means that a distance of 10,000 feet on land will be represented by 1 foot in the photograph.) If H represents the height of the airplane above the ground (see the accompanying figure), these quantities are related by the rational equation

$$S = \frac{0.625}{H}.$$

Determine the height at which the plane must fly for the photograph to have the correct scale. (**Source:** N. Garber and L. Hoel, *Traffic and Highway Engineering.*) 6250 ft

72. *Aerial Photographs*   (Continuation of Exercise 71.) Suppose that the scale for the photograph is changed from $\frac{1}{10,000}$ to $\frac{1}{5000}$.
   (a) Should the plane fly higher or lower for this new scale? Explain your reasoning.
   (b) Test your conjecture in part (a) by letting $S = \frac{1}{5000}$ and finding H.   3125 ft

(a) Lower; lower height would show a smaller area, giving a larger scale.

73. *Speed of a Boat*   In still water a tugboat can travel 15 miles per hour. It travels 36 miles upstream and then 36 miles downstream in a total time of 5 hours. Find the speed of the current.   3 mph

74. *Wind Speed*   Without any wind an airplane flies at 200 miles per hour. The plane travels 800 miles into the wind and then returns with the wind in a total time of 8 hours and 20 minutes. Find the average speed of the wind.   40 mph

75. *Speed of an Airplane*   When there is a 50–mile per hour wind, an airplane can fly 675 miles with the wind in the same time that it can fly 450 miles against the wind. Find the speed of the plane when there is no wind.   250 mph

76. *Waiting in Line*   If a ticket agent can wait on 25 people per hour and people are arriving randomly at an average rate of x people per hour, the average time T in hours for people waiting in line *and* paying the agent is

$$T(x) = \frac{1}{25 - x}$$

where $x < 25$.   (**Source:** N. Garber.)

(a),(b) $x = 24.8$; the wait is 5 hr when people arrive at a rate of 24.8/hr.
   (a) Solve the equation $T(x) = 5$ symbolically and interpret the result.
   (b) Solve part (a) either graphically or numerically.

77. *Working Alone*   It takes one employee 3 hours longer to mow a football field than it does a more experienced employee. Together they can mow the grass in 2 hours. How long does it take for each person to mow the football field working alone?   3 hr and 6 hr

78. *Painting a House*   It takes one painter 20 hours longer to paint a house than it does a more experienced painter. Together they can paint the house in 24 hours. How long does it take for each painter to paint the house working alone?   40 hr and 60 hr

79. *Walking Speed*   One person can walk 1 mile per hour faster than another person. The faster person can walk 12 miles in the time it takes the slower person to walk 9 miles. What is the walking speed of each person?   4 mph and 3 mph

80. *Freeway Speed*   A car passes another car on a freeway traveling 5 miles per hour faster than the slower car. The faster car travels 340 miles in the time it takes the slower car to travel 315 miles. What is the speed of each car?   68 mph and 63 mph

81. *Emptying a Pool*   An inlet pipe can fill a pool in 60 hours whereas an outlet pipe can empty the pool in 40 hours. If both pipes are left open, how long will it take to empty the pool if the pool is full initially? 120 hr

82. *Emptying a Boat*   A small leak will fill an empty boat in 5 hours. The boat's bilge pump will empty a full boat in 3 hours. If the boat were half full and leaking, how long would it take the pump to empty the boat?
3 hr 45 min

WRITING ABOUT MATHEMATICS

83. A student does the following to solve a rational equation. Is the work correct? Explain any errors and how you might correct them.

$$\frac{1}{x + 1} + \frac{2}{x - 1} = -1$$
$$(x - 1) + 2(x + 1) \stackrel{?}{=} -1$$
$$3x + 1 \stackrel{?}{=} -1$$
$$x \stackrel{?}{=} -\frac{2}{3}$$

84. Explain the difference between simplifying the expression $\frac{x + 1}{x^2 - 1}$ and solving the equation $\frac{x + 1}{x^2 - 1} = \frac{1}{2}$.

---

1. Simplify each expression.

   (a) $\dfrac{x}{x^2 - 1} + \dfrac{1}{x^2 - 1}$ $\frac{1}{x-1}$

   (b) $\dfrac{1}{x - 2} - \dfrac{3}{x}$ $-\frac{2(x-3)}{x(x-2)}$

   (c) $\dfrac{1}{x(x - 1)} + \dfrac{1}{x^2 - 1} - \dfrac{2}{x(x + 1)}$ $\frac{3}{x(x-1)(x+1)}$

2. Solve each equation.

   (a) $\dfrac{6}{x} - \dfrac{1}{2} = 1$ 4

   (b) $\dfrac{3}{2x - 1} = \dfrac{2}{x + 1}$ 5

(c) $\dfrac{2}{x - 1} + \dfrac{3}{x + 2} = \dfrac{x}{x^2 + x - 2}$ $-\frac{1}{4}$

3. If a gas pump can fill a 200-gallon tank in 12 minutes and a smaller gas pump can fill the same tank in 28 minutes, how long will it take for the pumps to fill the tank together?   8.4 min

4. Solve $\frac{1}{S} = \frac{1}{F} - \frac{1}{D}$ for S. $S = \frac{DF}{D - F}$

6.5 COMPLEX FRACTIONS

Basic Concepts · Simplifying Complex Fractions

INTRODUCTION

If two and a half pizzas are cut into fourths, then there are 10 pieces of pizza. This problem can be written as

$$\frac{2 + \dfrac{1}{2}}{\dfrac{1}{4}} = 10.$$

The expression on the left side of the equation is called a *complex fraction*. Typically, we want to simplify a complex fraction to a fraction with the standard form $\frac{a}{b}$. In this section we discuss how to simplify complex fractions.

BASIC CONCEPTS

A **complex fraction** is a rational expression that contains fractions in its numerator, denominator, or both. Examples of complex fractions include

$$\frac{1 + \dfrac{1}{x}}{1 - \dfrac{1}{x}}, \quad \frac{2x}{\dfrac{4}{x} + \dfrac{3}{x}}, \quad \text{and} \quad \frac{\dfrac{a}{3} + \dfrac{a}{4}}{a - \dfrac{1}{a - 1}}.$$

Working with complex fractions involves division of fractions. When dividing two fractions, we can multiply the first fraction by the reciprocal of the second fraction, which is summarized as follows.

SIMPLIFYING COMPLEX FRACTIONS

For any real numbers a, b, c, and d,

$$\frac{\dfrac{a}{b}}{\dfrac{c}{d}} = \frac{a}{b} \cdot \frac{d}{c},$$

where b, c, and d are not zero.

EXAMPLE 1   Simplifying basic types of complex fractions

Simplify.

(a) $\dfrac{\dfrac{7}{8}}{\dfrac{3}{4}}$ (b) $\dfrac{\dfrac{x}{8}}{\dfrac{3x}{7}}$ (c) $\dfrac{\dfrac{a}{4b}}{\dfrac{a}{6b^2}}$ (d) $\dfrac{2 + \dfrac{1}{2}}{\dfrac{1}{4}}$

Solution   (a) Rather than dividing $\frac{7}{8}$ by $\frac{3}{4}$, multiply $\frac{7}{8}$ by $\frac{4}{3}$.

$$\frac{\dfrac{7}{8}}{\dfrac{3}{4}} = \frac{7}{8} \cdot \frac{4}{3} \qquad \text{"Invert and multiply."}$$

$$= \frac{7}{6} \qquad \text{Multiply and reduce.}$$

(b) Rather than dividing $\frac{x}{8}$ by $\frac{3x}{7}$, multiply $\frac{x}{8}$ by $\frac{7}{3x}$.

$$\frac{\dfrac{x}{8}}{\dfrac{3x}{7}} = \frac{x}{8} \cdot \frac{7}{3x} \qquad \text{"Invert and multiply."}$$

$$= \frac{7}{24} \qquad \text{Multiply and reduce.}$$

(c) Rather than dividing $\frac{a}{4b}$ by $\frac{a}{6b^2}$, multiply $\frac{a}{4b}$ by $\frac{6b^2}{a}$.

$$\frac{\dfrac{a}{4b}}{\dfrac{a}{6b^2}} = \frac{a}{4b} \cdot \frac{6b^2}{a} \qquad \text{"Invert and multiply."}$$

$$= \frac{6ab^2}{4ab} \qquad \text{Multiply fractions.}$$

$$= \frac{3}{2}b \qquad \text{Reduce.}$$

(d) Start by writing $2 + \frac{1}{2}$ as a standard fraction.

$$\frac{2 + \frac{1}{2}}{\frac{1}{4}} = \frac{\frac{5}{2}}{\frac{1}{4}} \qquad \text{Write as improper fractions.}$$

$$= \frac{5}{2} \cdot \frac{4}{1} \qquad \text{"Invert and multiply."}$$

$$= 10 \qquad \text{Simplify.}$$

SIMPLIFYING COMPLEX FRACTIONS

There are two basic strategies for simplifying a complex fraction. The first is to simplify both the numerator and the denominator and then divide the resulting fractions. The second is to multiply the numerator and denominator by the least common denominator of fractions in the numerator and denominator.

SIMPLIFYING THE NUMERATOR AND DENOMINATOR   The next example illustrates the method whereby the numerator and denominator are simplified first.

EXAMPLE 2   **Simplifying complex fractions**

Simplify.

(a) $\dfrac{1 + \dfrac{1}{x}}{1 - \dfrac{1}{x}}$ **(b)** $\dfrac{2t - \dfrac{1}{2t}}{2t + \dfrac{1}{2t}}$ **(c)** $\dfrac{\dfrac{1}{z+1} - \dfrac{1}{z-1}}{\dfrac{2}{z+2} - \dfrac{2}{z-2}}$

Solution   **(a)** First, simplify the numerator by writing it as one term. The LCD is x.

$$1 + \frac{1}{x} = \frac{x}{x} + \frac{1}{x} = \frac{x+1}{x}$$

Second, simplify the denominator by writing it as one term.

$$1 - \frac{1}{x} = \frac{x}{x} - \frac{1}{x} = \frac{x-1}{x}$$

Finally, simplify the complex fraction.

$$\frac{1 + \dfrac{1}{x}}{1 - \dfrac{1}{x}} = \frac{\dfrac{x+1}{x}}{\dfrac{x-1}{x}} \qquad \text{Simplify.}$$

$$= \frac{x+1}{x} \cdot \frac{x}{x-1} \qquad \text{"Invert and multiply."}$$

$$= \frac{x+1}{x-1} \qquad \text{Multiply and reduce.}$$

(b) Combine the terms in the numerator and in the denominator. The LCD is $2t$.

$$\frac{2t - \dfrac{1}{2t}}{2t + \dfrac{1}{2t}} = \frac{\dfrac{4t^2}{2t} - \dfrac{1}{2t}}{\dfrac{4t^2}{2t} + \dfrac{1}{2t}} \qquad \text{Write with the LCD.}$$

$$= \frac{\dfrac{4t^2 - 1}{2t}}{\dfrac{4t^2 + 1}{2t}} \qquad \text{Combine terms.}$$

$$= \frac{4t^2 - 1}{2t} \cdot \frac{2t}{4t^2 + 1} \qquad \text{"Invert and multiply."}$$

$$= \frac{4t^2 - 1}{4t^2 + 1} \qquad \text{Multiply and reduce.}$$

(c) For the numerator the LCD is $(z + 1)(z - 1)$, and for the denominator the LCD is $(z + 2)(z - 2)$.

$$\frac{\dfrac{1}{z + 1} - \dfrac{1}{z - 1}}{\dfrac{2}{z + 2} - \dfrac{2}{z - 2}} = \frac{\dfrac{z - 1}{(z + 1)(z - 1)} - \dfrac{z + 1}{(z + 1)(z - 1)}}{\dfrac{2(z - 2)}{(z + 2)(z - 2)} - \dfrac{2(z + 2)}{(z + 2)(z - 2)}}$$

$$= \frac{\dfrac{-2}{(z + 1)(z - 1)}}{\dfrac{-8}{(z + 2)(z - 1)}}$$

$$= \frac{-2}{(z + 1)(z - 1)} \cdot \frac{(z + 2)(z - 2)}{-8}$$

$$= \frac{(z + 2)(z - 2)}{4(z + 1)(z - 1)}$$

MULTIPLYING BY THE LEAST COMMON DENOMINATOR A second strategy for simplifying a complex fraction is to multiply the numerator and denominator by the LCD of the fractions in the numerator *and* denominator. For example, the LCD for the complex fraction

$$\frac{1 - \dfrac{1}{x}}{1 + \dfrac{1}{2x}}$$

is $2x$. To simplify, multiply the complex fraction by 1, expressed in the form $\frac{2x}{2x}$.

$$\frac{\left(1 - \dfrac{1}{x}\right) \cdot 2x}{\left(1 + \dfrac{1}{2x}\right) \cdot 2x} = \frac{2x - \dfrac{2x}{x}}{2x + \dfrac{2x}{2x}} \qquad \text{Distributive property}$$

$$= \frac{2x - 2}{2x + 1} \qquad \text{Reduce fractions.}$$

In the next example we use this method to simplify other complex fractions.

EXAMPLE 3 Simplifying complex fractions

Simplify.

(a) $\dfrac{\dfrac{1}{x} - \dfrac{1}{y}}{x - y}$ (b) $\dfrac{\dfrac{3}{x-1} - \dfrac{2}{x}}{\dfrac{1}{x-1} + \dfrac{3}{x}}$ (c) $\dfrac{n^{-2} + m^{-2}}{1 + (nm)^{-2}}$

Solution (a) The LCD is xy. Multiply the expression by $\frac{xy}{xy}$.

$$\frac{\left(\dfrac{1}{x} - \dfrac{1}{y}\right) \cdot xy}{(x-y) \cdot xy} = \frac{\dfrac{xy}{x} - \dfrac{xy}{y}}{xy(x-y)}$$ Distributive and commutative properties

$$= \frac{y - x}{xy(x-y)}$$ Reduce fractions in numerator.

$$= \frac{-1(x-y)}{xy(x-y)}$$ Factor out -1.

$$= -\frac{1}{xy}$$ Reduce.

(b) The LCD is $x(x-1)$. Multiply the expression by $\frac{x(x-1)}{x(x-1)}$.

$$\frac{\left(\dfrac{3}{x-1} - \dfrac{2}{x}\right) \cdot x(x-1)}{\left(\dfrac{1}{x-1} + \dfrac{3}{x}\right) \cdot x(x-1)} = \frac{\dfrac{3x(x-1)}{x-1} - \dfrac{2x(x-1)}{x}}{\dfrac{x(x-1)}{x-1} + \dfrac{3x(x-1)}{x}}$$ Distributive property

$$= \frac{3x - 2(x-1)}{x + 3(x-1)}$$ Reduce.

$$= \frac{3x - 2x + 2}{x + 3x - 3}$$ Distributive property

$$= \frac{x + 2}{4x - 3}$$ Combine like terms.

(c) Start by rewriting the ratio with positive exponents.

Critical Thinking

Does the expression $\dfrac{\frac{x}{y}}{2 + \frac{x}{y}}$ equal $\frac{1}{2}$? Explain.

Does the expression $\dfrac{2 + \frac{x}{y}}{\frac{x}{y}}$ equal 3? Explain.

No. It equals $\frac{x}{2y + x}$.

No. It equals $\frac{2y + x}{x}$.

$$\frac{n^{-2} + m^{-2}}{1 + (nm)^{-2}} = \frac{\dfrac{1}{n^2} + \dfrac{1}{m^2}}{1 + \dfrac{1}{n^2 m^2}}$$

The LCD for the numerator *and* the denominator is $n^2 m^2$.

$$\frac{\dfrac{1}{n^2} + \dfrac{1}{m^2}}{1 + \dfrac{1}{n^2 m^2}} = \frac{\left(\dfrac{1}{n^2} + \dfrac{1}{m^2}\right) \cdot n^2 m^2}{\left(1 + \dfrac{1}{n^2 m^2}\right) \cdot n^2 m^2}$$ Multiply by LCD.

$$= \frac{m^2 + n^2}{n^2 m^2 + 1}$$ Distributive property

6.5 PUTTING IT ALL TOGETHER

Important concepts from this section are summarized in the following table.

Concept	Explanation	Examples
Complex Fraction	A rational expression that contains fractions in its numerator, denominator, or both.	$$\dfrac{\dfrac{1}{x}+\dfrac{1}{2x+1}}{1-\dfrac{1}{2x+1}}\text{ and }\dfrac{\dfrac{a}{2b}-\dfrac{b}{2a}}{\dfrac{a}{2b}+\dfrac{b}{2a}}$$
Simplifying Complex Fractions	$$\dfrac{\dfrac{a}{b}}{\dfrac{c}{d}}=\dfrac{a}{b}\cdot\dfrac{d}{c}$$	$$\dfrac{\dfrac{2y}{z}}{\dfrac{y}{z-1}}=\dfrac{2y}{z}\cdot\dfrac{z-1}{y}=\dfrac{2(z-1)}{z}$$
Method I: Simplifying the Numerator and Denominator First	Combine the terms in the numerator, combine the terms in the denominator, and then invert and multiply.	$$\dfrac{\dfrac{1}{2b}+\dfrac{1}{2a}}{\dfrac{1}{2b}-\dfrac{1}{2a}}=\dfrac{\dfrac{a+b}{2ab}}{\dfrac{a-b}{2ab}}$$ $$=\dfrac{a+b}{2ab}\cdot\dfrac{2ab}{a-b}$$ $$=\dfrac{a+b}{a-b}$$
Method II: Multiplying the Numerator and Denominator by the LCD	Start by multiplying the numerator and denominator by the LCD of the numerator *and* the denominator.	$$\dfrac{\dfrac{1}{2b}+\dfrac{1}{2a}}{\dfrac{1}{2b}-\dfrac{1}{2a}}=\dfrac{\left(\dfrac{1}{2b}+\dfrac{1}{2a}\right)\cdot 2ab}{\left(\dfrac{1}{2b}-\dfrac{1}{2a}\right)\cdot 2ab}$$ $$=\dfrac{a+b}{a-b}$$ Note that the LCD is $2ab$.

6.5 EXERCISES

FOR EXTRA HELP

CONCEPTS

1. $\dfrac{\dfrac{5}{7}}{\dfrac{3}{11}}=$

2. $\dfrac{\dfrac{a}{b}}{\dfrac{c}{d}}=$ _____ . $\dfrac{a}{b}\cdot\dfrac{d}{c}$

3. What is a good first step when simplifying

$$\dfrac{2+\dfrac{1}{x-1}}{2-\dfrac{1}{x-1}}?$$

Multiply numerator and denominator by $x-1$. Answers may vary.

4. Explain what a complex fraction is.

A rational expression with fractions in its numerator, denominator, or both.

5. Write the phrase "the quantity z plus three-fourths divided by the quantity z minus three-fourths" as a complex fraction.

6. Write the expression $\frac{a}{b} \div \frac{a-b}{a+b}$ as a complex fraction.

5. $\dfrac{z + \frac{3}{4}}{z - \frac{3}{4}}$ 6. $\dfrac{\frac{a}{b}}{\frac{a-b}{a+b}}$

SIMPLIFYING COMPLEX FRACTIONS

Exercises 7–48: Simplify the complex fraction.

7. $\dfrac{\frac{1}{5}}{\frac{4}{7}}$ $\frac{7}{20}$

8. $\dfrac{\frac{3}{7}}{\frac{2}{9}}$ $\frac{27}{14}$

9. $\dfrac{1+\frac{1}{3}}{1-\frac{1}{3}}$ 2

10. $\dfrac{\frac{1}{2}-3}{\frac{1}{2}+3}$ $-\frac{5}{7}$

11. $\dfrac{2+\frac{2}{3}}{2-\frac{1}{4}}$ $\frac{32}{21}$

12. $\dfrac{\frac{1}{2}+\frac{3}{4}}{\frac{1}{2}-\frac{3}{4}}$ -5

13. $\dfrac{\frac{a}{b}}{\frac{3a}{2b^2}}$ $\frac{2b}{3}$

14. $\dfrac{\frac{7}{y}}{\frac{14}{y}}$ $\frac{1}{2}$

15. $\dfrac{\frac{x}{2y}}{\frac{2x}{3y}}$ $\frac{3}{4}$

16. $\dfrac{\frac{ab^2}{2c}}{\frac{a}{4bc}}$ $2b^3$

17. $\dfrac{\frac{8}{n+1}}{\frac{4}{n-1}}$ $\frac{2(n-1)}{n+1}$

18. $\dfrac{\frac{n}{m-2}}{\frac{3n}{m-2}}$ $\frac{1}{3}$

19. $\dfrac{\frac{2k+3}{k}}{\frac{k-4}{k}}$ $\frac{2k+3}{k-4}$

20. $\dfrac{\frac{2k}{k-7}}{\frac{1}{(k-7)^2}}$ $2k(k-7)$

21. $\dfrac{\frac{3}{z^2-4}}{\frac{z}{z^2-4}}$ $\frac{3}{z}$

22. $\dfrac{\frac{z}{(z-2)^2}}{\frac{2z}{z^2-4}}$ $\frac{z+2}{2(z-2)}$

23. $\dfrac{\frac{x}{x^2-16}}{\frac{1}{x-4}}$ $\frac{x}{x+4}$

24. $\dfrac{\frac{4y}{x-y}}{\frac{1}{x^2-y^2}}$ $4y(x+y)$

25. $\dfrac{1+\frac{1}{x}}{x+1}$ $\frac{1}{x}$

26. $\dfrac{2-x}{\frac{1}{x}-\frac{1}{2}}$ $2x$

27. $\dfrac{\frac{1}{x-3}}{\frac{1}{x}-\frac{3}{x-3}}$ $-\frac{x}{2x+3}$

28. $\dfrac{5+\frac{1}{x-1}}{\frac{1}{x-1}-\frac{1}{4}}$ $-\frac{4(5x-4)}{x-5}$

29. $\dfrac{\frac{1}{x}+\frac{2}{x^2}}{\frac{3}{x}-\frac{1}{x^2}}$ $\frac{x+2}{3x-1}$

30. $\dfrac{\frac{1}{x-1}+\frac{2}{x}}{2-\frac{1}{x}}$ $\frac{3x-2}{(x-1)(2x-1)}$

31. $\dfrac{\frac{1}{x+3}+\frac{2}{x-3}}{2-\frac{1}{x-3}}$

31. $\frac{3(x+1)}{(x+3)(2x-7)}$

32. $\dfrac{\frac{1}{x}+\frac{2}{x}}{\frac{1}{x-1}+\frac{x}{2}}$ $\frac{6(x-1)}{x(x^2-x+2)}$

33. $\dfrac{\frac{4}{x-5}}{\frac{1}{x+5}+\frac{1}{x}}$

33. $\frac{4x(x+5)}{(x-5)(2x+5)}$

34. $\dfrac{\frac{1}{x-4}+\frac{1}{x-4}}{1-\frac{1}{x+4}}$ $\frac{2(x+4)}{(x-4)(x+3)}$

35. $\dfrac{\frac{1}{p^2q}+\frac{1}{pq^2}}{\frac{1}{p^2q}-\frac{1}{pq^2}}$ $\frac{p+q}{q-p}$

36. $\dfrac{\frac{1}{p-1}}{\frac{1}{p-1}+2}$ $\frac{1}{2p-1}$

37. $\dfrac{\frac{1}{a}+\frac{1}{b}}{\frac{1}{b}-\frac{1}{a}}$ $\frac{a+b}{a-b}$

38. $\dfrac{\frac{1}{a}+\frac{1}{b}+\frac{1}{c}}{\frac{1}{ab}+\frac{1}{bc}}$ $\frac{bc+ac+ab}{c+a}$

39. $\dfrac{\frac{1}{x}+\frac{1}{x+1}}{\frac{2}{x+1}-\frac{1}{x+1}}$

39. $\frac{2x+1}{x}$

40. $\dfrac{\frac{2}{x-1}-4}{\frac{1}{x-1}+\frac{1}{x-2}}$ $-2(x-2)$

41. $\dfrac{3^{-1}-4^{-1}}{5^{-1}+4^{-1}}$ $\frac{5}{27}$

42. $\dfrac{1+2^{-3}}{2^{-3}-1}$ $-\frac{9}{7}$

43. $\dfrac{m^{-1}-2n^{-2}}{1+(mn)^{-2}}$

$\frac{mn^2-2m}{m^2n^2+1}$

44. $\dfrac{1+p^{-2}}{1-p^{-2}}$ $\frac{p^2+1}{p^2-1}$

45. $\dfrac{1 - (2n + 1)^{-1}}{1 + (2n + 1)^{-1}}$ $\dfrac{n}{n+1}$ **46.** $\dfrac{(a + b)^{-1} - (a - b)^{-1}}{1 + (a - b)^{-1}}$ $-\dfrac{2b}{a^2 - b^2 + a + b}$

47. $\dfrac{\dfrac{x}{x^2 - 4} - \dfrac{1}{x^2 - 4}}{\dfrac{1}{x + 4}}$ $\dfrac{(x - 1)(x + 4)}{x^2 - 4}$

48. $\dfrac{\dfrac{1}{x^2 + 2x + 1} - \dfrac{1}{x^2 - 2x + 1}}{(x + 1)(x - 1)}$ $-\dfrac{4x}{(x + 1)^3(x - 1)^3}$

APPLICATIONS

49. *Annuity*   If P dollars are deposited every month in an account paying an annual interest rate r expressed as a decimal, then the amount A in the account after 2 years can be approximated by

$$\left(P\left(1 + \frac{r}{12}\right)^{24} - P \right) \div \frac{r}{12}.$$

$\dfrac{P\left(1 + \dfrac{r}{12}\right)^{24} - P}{\dfrac{r}{12}}$

Write this expression as a complex fraction.

50. *Annuity*   (Continuation of the preceding exercise.) Use a calculator to evaluate the expression when $r = 0.06$ (6%) and $P = \$250$. Interpret the result.

51. *Resistance in Electricity*   Light bulbs are often wired so that electricity can flow through either bulb as illustrated in the accompanying figure.

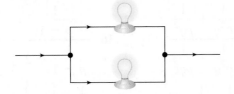

In this way, if one bulb burns out, the other bulb still works. If two light bulbs have resistances R_1 and R_2, then their combined resistance R is given by the complex fraction

$$R = \cfrac{1}{\dfrac{1}{R_1} + \dfrac{1}{R_2}}.$$

Simplify this formula. $R = \dfrac{R_1 R_2}{R_1 + R_2}$

52. *Resistance in Electricity*   (Refer to the preceding exercise.) Evaluate the formula

$$R = \cfrac{1}{\dfrac{1}{R_1} + \dfrac{1}{R_2}}$$

when $R_1 = 75$ ohms and $R_2 = 100$ ohms.
About 42.9 ohms

WRITING ABOUT MATHEMATICS

53. A student simplifies a complex fraction as follows. Explain what the student's mistake is and how to work it correctly.

$$\dfrac{\dfrac{1}{x} + \dfrac{1}{y}}{\dfrac{1}{x} + \dfrac{1}{y}} \overset{?}{=} \dfrac{\dfrac{1}{x}}{\dfrac{1}{x}} + \dfrac{\dfrac{1}{y}}{\dfrac{1}{y}} \overset{?}{=} 1 + 1 = 2$$

54. Describe one method for simplifying a complex fraction.

50. $6357.99; depositing $250 each month into an account paying 6% annual interest will result in a total amount of $6357.99 after 2 years.

6.6   MODELING WITH PROPORTIONS AND VARIATION

Proportions · Direct Variation · Inverse Variation · Joint Variation

INTRODUCTION

Proportions are used frequently to solve problems in everyday life. The following are examples.

- If someone earns $100 per day, that person can earn $500 in 5 days.
- If a car goes 210 miles on 10 gallons of gas, the car can go 420 miles on 20 gallons of gas.
- If a person walks a mile in 16 minutes, that person can walk a half mile in 8 minutes.

Many applications involve proportions or variation. In this section we discuss some of them.

PROPORTIONS

A 650-megabyte compact disc (CD) can store about 74 minutes of music. Suppose that we have already recorded some music on the CD and 256 megabytes are still available. Using proportions we can determine how many more minutes of music could be recorded. A **proportion** is a statement that two ratios (fractions) are equal.   (*Source:* Maxell Corporation.)

Let x be the number of minutes available on the CD. Then 74 minutes are to 650 megabytes as x minutes are to 256 megabytes, which can be written as the proportion

$$\frac{74}{650} = \frac{x}{256}.$$

Solving this equation for x gives

$$x = \frac{74 \cdot 256}{650} \approx 29.1 \text{ minutes.}$$

About 29 minutes are still available on the CD.

MAKING CONNECTIONS

Proportions and Fractional Parts

We could have solved the preceding problem by noting that the fraction of the CD still available for recording music is $\frac{256}{650}$. So $\frac{256}{650}$ of 74 minutes equals

$$\frac{256}{650} \cdot 74 \approx 29.1 \text{ minutes.}$$

The following property is a convenient way to solve proportions:

$$\frac{a}{b} = \frac{c}{d} \quad \text{is equivalent to} \quad ad = bc,$$

provided $b \neq 0$ and $d \neq 0$. This is a result of multiplying each side of the equation by a common denominator bd, and is sometimes referred to as *clearing fractions*.

$$bd \cdot \frac{a}{b} = \frac{c}{d} \cdot bd \qquad \text{Multiply by } bd.$$

$$\frac{bda}{b} = \frac{cbd}{d} \qquad \text{Property of multiplying fractions}$$

$$ad = bc \qquad \text{Reduce.}$$

For example, the proportion

$$\frac{6}{5} = \frac{8}{x}$$

TEACHING TIP

You may want to refer to clearing fractions as cross multiplying when you discuss simplifying proportions.

is equivalent to

$$6x = 40 \quad \text{or} \quad x = \frac{40}{6} = \frac{20}{3}.$$

EXAMPLE 1   Calculating the water content in snow

Six inches of light, fluffy snow are equivalent to about half an inch of rain in terms of water content. If 21 inches of snow fall, estimate the water content.

Solution   Let x be the equivalent amount of rain. Then 6 inches of snow is to $\frac{1}{2}$ inch of rain as 21 inches of snow is to x inches of rain, which can be written as the proportion

$$\frac{6}{\frac{1}{2}} = \frac{21}{x}.$$

Solving this equation gives

$$6x = \frac{21}{2} \quad \text{or} \quad x = \frac{21}{12} = 1.75.$$

Thus 21 inches of light, fluffy snow is equivalent to about 1.75 inches of rain.

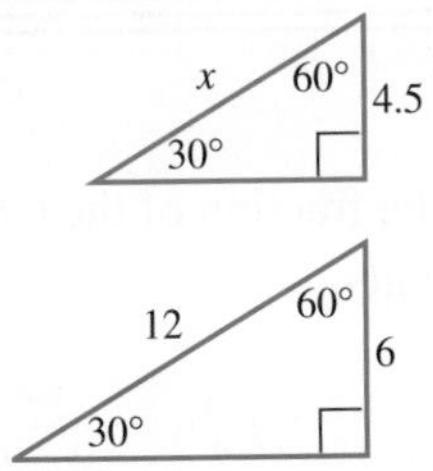

Proportions frequently occur in geometry when we work with similar figures. Two triangles are similar if the measures of their corresponding angles are equal. Corresponding sides of similar triangles are proportional. Figure 6.15 shows two right triangles that are similar because each has angles of 30°, 60°, and 90°.

We can find the length of side x by using proportions. Side x is to 12 as 4.5 is to 6, which can be written as the proportion

$$\frac{x}{12} = \frac{4.5}{6}. \qquad \frac{\text{Hypotenuse}}{\text{Hypotenuse}} = \frac{\text{Shorter leg}}{\text{Shorter leg}}$$

Figure 6.15

Solving yields the equation

$$6x = 4.5(12) \qquad \text{Clear fractions.}$$
$$x = 9. \qquad \text{Divide by 6.}$$

EXAMPLE 2   Calculating the height of a tree

A 6–foot tall person casts a 4–foot long shadow. If a nearby tree casts a 44–foot long shadow, estimate the height of the tree. See Figure 6.16.

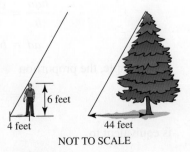

NOT TO SCALE

Figure 6.16

Solution   The triangles shown in Figure 6.17 are similar because the measures of the corresponding angles are equal. Therefore their sides are proportional. Let h be the height of the tree.

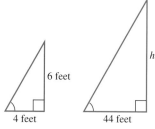

Figure 6.17

$$\frac{h}{6} = \frac{44}{4} \qquad \frac{\text{Height}}{\text{Height}} = \frac{\text{Shadow length}}{\text{Shadow length}}$$

$$4h = 6(44) \qquad \text{Clear fractions.}$$

$$h = \frac{6(44)}{4} \qquad \text{Divide by 4.}$$

$$h = 66 \qquad \text{Simplify.}$$

The tree is 66 feet tall.

DIRECT VARIATION

If your wage is \$9 per hour, the amount you earn is proportional to the number of hours that you work. If you worked H hours, your total pay P satisfies the equation

$$\frac{P}{H} = \frac{9}{1}, \qquad \frac{\text{Pay}}{\text{Hours}}$$

or, equivalently,

$$P = 9H.$$

We say that your pay P is *directly proportional* to the number of hours H worked. The constant of proportionality is 9.

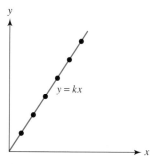

Figure 6.18 Direct Variation, $k > 0$

DIRECT VARIATION

Let x and y denote two quantities. Then y is **directly proportional** to x, or y **varies directly** with x, if there is a nonzero number k such that

$$y = kx.$$

The number k is called the **constant of proportionality**, or the **constant of variation**.

The graph of $y = kx$ is a line passing through the origin, as illustrated in Figure 6.18. Sometimes data in a scatterplot indicate that two quantities are directly proportional. The constant of proportionality k corresponds to the slope of the graph.

EXAMPLE 3   Modeling college tuition

Table 6.3 lists the tuition for taking various numbers of credits.

TABLE 6.3

Credits	3	5	8	11	17
Tuition	\$189	\$315	\$504	\$693	\$1071

(a) A scatterplot of the data is shown in Figure 6.19. Could the data be modeled using a line?

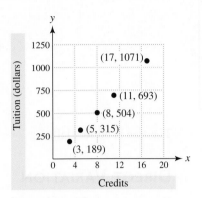

Figure 6.19

(b) Explain why tuition is directly proportional to the number of credits taken.
(c) Find the constant of proportionality. Interpret your result.
(d) Predict the cost of taking 15 credits.

Solution **(a)** The data are linear and suggest a line passing through the origin.
(b) Because the data can be modeled by a line passing through the origin, tuition is directly proportional to the number of credits taken. Hence doubling the credits will double the tuition and tripling the credits will triple the tuition.
(c) The slope of the line equals the constant of proportionality k. If we use the first and last data points (3, 189) and (17, 1071), the slope is

$$k = \frac{1071 - 189}{17 - 3} = 63.$$

That is, tuition is $63 per credit. If we graph the line $y = 63x$, it models the data as shown in Figure 6.20. This graph can also be created with a graphing calculator.
(d) If y represents tuition and x represents the credits taken, 15 credits would cost

$$y = 63(15) = \$945.$$

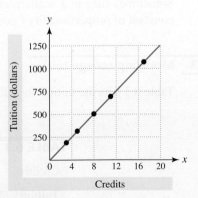

Figure 6.20

========================= MAKING CONNECTIONS =========================

Ratios and the Constant of Proportionality

The constant of proportionality in Example 3 can also be found by calculating the ratios $\frac{y}{x}$, where y is the tuition and x is the credits taken. Note that each ratio in the table equals 63 because the equation $y = 63x$ is equivalent to the equation $\frac{y}{x} = 63$.

x	3	5	8	11	17
y	189	315	504	693	1071
$\frac{y}{x}$	63	63	63	63	63

INVERSE VARIATION

When two quantities vary inversely, an increase in one quantity results in a decrease in the second quantity. For example, at 25 miles per hour a car travels 100 miles in 4 hours, whereas at 50 miles per hour the car travels 100 miles in 2 hours. Doubling the speed (or rate) decreases the travel time by half. Distance equals rate times time, so $d = rt$. Thus

$$100 = rt, \quad \text{or equivalently,} \quad t = \frac{100}{r}.$$

TEACHING TIP

Emphasize that if data vary inversely, then data points (x, y) lie on a curve, where the products xy always equal the constant k.

We say that the time t to travel 100 miles is *inversely proportional* to the speed or rate r. The constant of proportionality or constant of variation is 100.

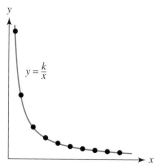

Figure 6.21 Inverse Variation, $k > 0$

▌▌▌▌▌ **INVERSE VARIATION**

Let x and y denote two quantities. Then y is **inversely proportional** to x, or y **varies inversely** with x, if there is a nonzero number k such that

$$y = \frac{k}{x}.$$

▌▌▌▌▌

Note: We assume that the constant k is positive.

The data shown in Figure 6.21 represent inverse variation and are modeled by $y = \frac{k}{x}$. Note that, as x increases, y decreases.

A wrench is commonly used to loosen a nut on a bolt. See Figure 6.22. If the nut is difficult to loosen, a wrench with a longer handle is often helpful.

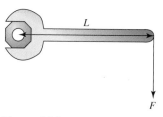

Figure 6.22

EXAMPLE 4   Loosening a nut on a bolt

Table 6.4 lists the force F necessary to loosen a particular nut with wrenches of different lengths L.
(a) Make a scatterplot of the data and discuss the graph. Are the data linear?
(b) Explain why the force F is inversely proportional to the handle length L. Find k so that $F = \frac{k}{L}$ models the data.
(c) Predict the force needed to loosen the nut with an 8-inch wrench.

TABLE 6.4

L (inches)	6	10	12	15	20
F (pounds)	10	6	5	4	3

Solution   (a) The scatterplot shown in Figure 6.23 reveals that the data are nonlinear. As the length L of the wrench increases, the force F necessary to loosen the nut decreases.

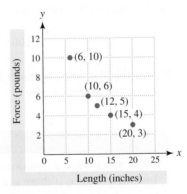

Figure 6.23

(b) If F is inversely proportional to L, then $F = \frac{k}{L}$, or $FL = k$. That is, the product of F and L equals the constant of proportionality k. In Table 6.4, the product of F and L always equals 60 for each data point. Thus F is inversely proportional to L with constant of proportionality $k = 60$.
(c) If $L = 8$, then $F = \frac{60}{8} = 7.5$. A wrench with an 8-inch handle requires a force of 7.5 pounds to loosen the nut.

EXAMPLE 5   Analyzing data

Determine whether the data in each table represent direct variation, inverse variation, or neither.

(a)
x	4	5	10	20
y	50	40	20	10

(b)
x	2	5	9	11
y	14	35	63	77

(c)
x	2	4	6	8
y	10	16	24	48

Solution (a) As x increases, y decreases. Because $xy = 200$ for each data point, the equation $y = \frac{200}{x}$ models the data. The data represent inverse variation. The data and equation are graphed in Figure 6.24(a).

(b) As $\frac{y}{x} = 7$ for each data point in the table, the equation $y = 7x$ models the data. These data represent direct variation. The data and equation are graphed in Figure 6.24(b).

(c) Neither the product xy nor the ratio $\frac{y}{x}$ are constant for the data in the table. Therefore these data represent neither direct variation nor inverse variation. The data are plotted in Figure 6.24(c). Note that the data values increase and are nonlinear.

Technology Note:
Scatterplots and Graphs

A graphing calculator can be used to create scatterplots and graphs. A scatterplot of the data in Table 6.4 is shown in the first figure. In the second figure the data and the equation $y = \frac{60}{x}$ are graphed.

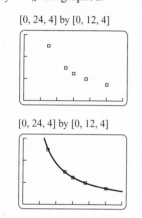

[0, 24, 4] by [0, 12, 4]

[0, 24, 4] by [0, 12, 4]

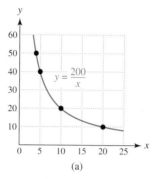

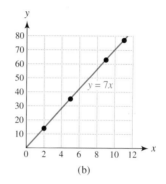

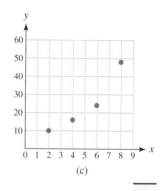

(a)   (b)   (c)

Figure 6.24

Calculator Help
To make a scatterplot see the Appendix (page AP-4).

JOINT VARIATION

In many applications a quantity depends on more than one variable. In **joint variation** a quantity varies as the product of more than one variable. For example, the formula for the area A of a rectangle is given by

$$A = WL,$$

where W and L are the width and length, respectively. Thus the area of a rectangle varies jointly with the width and length.

JOINT VARIATION

Let x, y, and z denote three quantities. Then z varies jointly as x and y if there is a nonzero number k such that

$$z = kxy.$$

Sometimes joint variation can involve a power of a variable. For example, the volume V of a cylinder is given by $V = \pi r^2 h$, where r is its radius and h is its height, as illustrated in Figure 6.25. In this case we say that the volume varies jointly with the height and the *square* of the radius. The constant of variation is $k = \pi$.

Figure 6.25

EXAMPLE 6   Strength of a rectangular beam

The strength S of a rectangular beam varies jointly as its width w and the square of its thickness t. See Figure 6.26. If a beam 3 inches wide and 5 inches thick supports 750 pounds, how much can a similar beam 2 inches wide and 6 inches thick support?

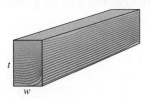

Solution   The strength of a beam is modeled by $S = kwt^2$, where k is a constant of variation. We can find k by substituting $S = 750$, $w = 3$, and $t = 5$ in the formula.

$$750 = k \cdot 3 \cdot 5^2 \qquad \text{Substitute into } S = kwt^2.$$

$$k = \frac{750}{3 \cdot 5^2} \qquad \text{Solve for } k.$$

$$= 10 \qquad \text{Simplify.}$$

t

w

Figure 6.26

Thus $S = 10wt^2$ models the strength of this type of beam. When $w = 2$ and $t = 6$, the beam can support

$$S = 10 \cdot 2 \cdot 6^2 = 720 \text{ pounds.}$$

If the width doubles the strength doubles, whereas if the thickness doubles the strength quadruples. If both triple, the strength increases by 27 times.

Critical Thinking

Compare the increased strength of a beam if the width doubles and if the thickness doubles. What happens to the strength of a beam if both the width and thickness triple?

6.6   PUTTING IT ALL TOGETHER

In this section we introduced some basic concepts of proportion and variation. They are summarized in the following table.

Concept	Explanation	Examples
Proportion	A statement that two ratios are equal	$\dfrac{10}{13} = \dfrac{32}{x}$ and $\dfrac{x}{7} = \dfrac{2}{5}$
Direct Variation	Two quantities x and y vary according to the equation $y = kx$, where k is a nonzero constant. The constant of proportionality (or variation) is k.	$y = 3x$ or $\dfrac{y}{x} = 3$ $\begin{array}{c\|ccc} x & 1 & 2 & 4 \\ \hline y & 3 & 6 & 12 \end{array}$ Note that, if x doubles, then y also doubles.
Inverse Variation	Two quantities x and y vary according to the equation $y = \frac{k}{x}$, where k is a nonzero constant. The constant of proportionality (or variation) is k.	$y = \dfrac{2}{x}$ or $xy = 2$ $\begin{array}{c\|ccc} x & 1 & 2 & 4 \\ \hline y & 2 & 1 & \frac{1}{2} \end{array}$ Note that, if x doubles, then y decreases by half.

Concept	Explanation	Examples
Joint Variation	Three quantities x, y, and z vary according to the equation $z = kxy$, where k is a constant.	The area A of a triangle varies jointly as b and h according to the equation $A = \frac{1}{2}bh$, where b is its base and h is its height. The constant of variation is $k = \frac{1}{2}$.

6.6 EXERCISES

FOR EXTRA HELP

 Student's Solutions Manual   InterAct Math   MathXL

MyMathLab   Math Tutor Center   Digital Video Tutor CD 6   Videotape 7

CONCEPTS

1. What is a proportion?
   A statement that two ratios are equal.

2. If 5 is to 6 as x is to 7, write a proportion that allows you to find x. $\frac{5}{6} = \frac{x}{7}$

3. Suppose that y is directly proportional to x. If x doubles, what happens to y?   It doubles.

4. Suppose that y is inversely proportional to x. If x doubles, what happens to y?   It is reduced by half.

5. If y varies inversely with x, then xy equals a _____.
   constant

6. If y varies directly with x, then $\frac{y}{x}$ equals a _____.
   constant

7. If z varies jointly with x and y, then $z =$ _____. kxy

8. If z varies jointly with the square of x and the cube of y, then $z =$ _____. kx^2y^3

9. Would a food bill B generally vary directly or inversely with the number of people N being fed? Explain your reasoning.
   Directly; if the number of people doubled, the food bill would double.

10. Would the time T needed to paint a building vary directly or inversely with the number of painters N working on the job? Explain your reasoning.
    Inversely; increasing the number of painters would decrease the time needed to paint the building.

PROPORTIONS

Exercises 11–18: Solve the proportion.

11. $\frac{x}{14} = \frac{5}{7}$ 10

12. $\frac{x}{5} = \frac{4}{9}$ $\frac{20}{9}$

13. $\frac{8}{x} = \frac{2}{3}$ 12

14. $\frac{5}{11} = \frac{9}{x}$ $\frac{99}{5}$

15. $\frac{6}{13} = \frac{h}{156}$ 72

16. $\frac{25}{a} = \frac{15}{8}$ $\frac{40}{3}$

17. $\frac{3}{2} = \frac{2x}{9}$ $\frac{27}{4}$

18. $\frac{7}{4z} = \frac{5}{3}$ $\frac{21}{20}$

Exercises 19–26: Complete the following.

   (a) *Write a proportion that models the situation.*
   (b) *Solve the proportion for x.*

19. 7 is to 9, as 10 is to x (a) $\frac{7}{9} = \frac{10}{x}$ (b) $x = \frac{90}{7}$

20. x is to 11, as 9 is to 2   (a) $\frac{x}{11} = \frac{9}{2}$ (b) $x = \frac{99}{2}$

21. A triangle has sides of 3, 4, and 6. In a similar triangle the shortest side is 5 and the longest side is x.
    (a) $\frac{5}{3} = \frac{x}{6}$ (b) $x = 10$

22. A rectangle has sides of 9 and 14. In a similar rectangle the longer side is 8 and the shorter side is x.
    (a) $\frac{8}{14} = \frac{x}{9}$ (b) $x = \frac{36}{7}$

23. If you earn $78 in 6 hours, you can earn x dollars in 8 hours.   (a) $\frac{78}{6} = \frac{x}{8}$ (b) $x = \$104$

24. If 12 gallons of gasoline contain 1.2 gallons of ethanol, 18 gallons of gasoline contain x gallons of ethanol.   (a) $\frac{12}{1.2} = \frac{18}{x}$ (b) $x = 1.8$ gal

25. If 2 cassette tapes can record 90 minutes of music, 5 cassette tapes can record x minutes.   (a) $\frac{2}{90} = \frac{5}{x}$
    (b) $x = 225$ min

26. If a gas pump fills a 30-gallon tank in 8 minutes, it can fill a 17-gallon tank in x minutes.
    26.(a) $\frac{30}{8} = \frac{17}{x}$
    26.(b) $x = \frac{68}{15} \approx 4.53$ min

VARIATION

Exercises 27–32: *Let y be directly proportional to x.*
(a) *Use the given information to find the constant of proportionality k.*
(b) *Find y when x = 7.*

27. $y = 6$ when $x = 3$ **28.** $y = 7$ when $x = 14$
(a) $k = 2$ (b) $y = 14$ (a) $k = 0.5$ (b) $y = 3.5$

29. $y = 5$ when $x = 2$ (a) $k = 2.5$ (b) $y = 17.5$

30. $y = 11$ when $x = 22$ (a) $k = 0.5$ (b) $y = 3.5$

31. $y = -120$ when $x = 16$ (a) $k = -7.5$ (b) $y = -52.5$

32. $y = -34$ when $x = 17$ (a) $k = -2$ (b) $y = -14$

Exercises 33–38: *Let y be inversely proportional to x.*
(a) *Use the given information to find the constant of proportionality k.*
(b) *Find y when x = 10.*

33. $y = 5$ when $x = 4$ (a) $k = 20$ (b) $y = 2$

34. $y = 2$ when $x = 30$ (a) $k = 60$ (b) $y = 6$

35. $y = 100$ when $x = \frac{1}{2}$ (a) $k = 50$ (b) $y = 5$

36. $y = \frac{1}{4}$ when $x = 40$ (a) $k = 10$ (b) $y = 1$

37. $y = 20$ when $x = 20$ (a) $k = 400$ (b) $y = 40$

38. $y = \frac{45}{4}$ when $x = 8$ (a) $k = 90$ (b) $y = 9$

Exercises 39–44: *Let z vary jointly with x and y.*
(a) *Use the given information to find the constant of variation k.*
(b) *Find z when x = 5 and y = 7.*

39. $z = 6$ when $x = 3$ and $y = 8$
(a) $k = 0.25$ (b) $z = 8.75$

40. $z = 135$ when $x = 2.5$ and $y = 9$
(a) $k = 6$ (b) $z = 210$

41. $z = 5775$ when $x = 25$ and $y = 21$
(a) $k = 11$ (b) $z = 385$

42. $z = 1530$ when $x = 22.5$ and $y = 4$
(a) $k = 17$ (b) $z = 595$

43. $z = 25$ when $x = \frac{1}{2}$ and $y = 5$
(a) $k = 10$ (b) $y = 350$

44. $z = 12$ when $x = \frac{1}{4}$ and $y = 12$
(a) $k = 4$ (b) $y = 140$

Exercises 45–50: *(Refer to Example 5.)*
(a) *Determine whether the data represent direct variation, inverse variation, or neither.*
(b) *If the data represent either direct or inverse variation, find an equation that models the data.*
(c) *Graph the equation and the data.* *

45.

x	2	3	4	5
y	3	4.5	6	7.5

(a) Direct   (b) $y = 1.5x$

46.

x	3	6	9	12
y	12	6	4	3

(a) Inverse   (b) $y = \dfrac{36}{x}$

47.

x	10	20	30	40
y	12	6	5	4

(a) Neither
(b) N/A
(c) N/A

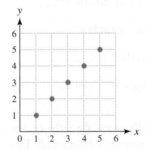

48.

x	2	6	10	14
y	105	35	21	15

(a) Inverse
(b) $y = \dfrac{210}{x}$

49.

x	4	6	12	20
y	10	20	30	40

(a) Neither
(b) N/A
(c) N/A

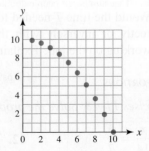

50.

x	1	5	9	15
y	6	30	54	90

(a) Direct
(b) $y = 6x$

Exercises 51–56: *Use the graph to determine whether the data represent direct variation, inverse variation, or neither. Find the constant of variation whenever possible.*

51. Direct; $k = 1$

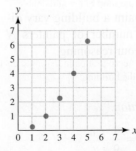

52. Inverse; $k = 6$

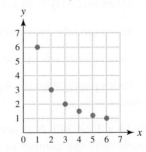

53. Neither

54. Neither

*Answers on page IA-21

55. Direct; $k = 2$ **56.** Inverse; $k = 8$

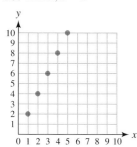

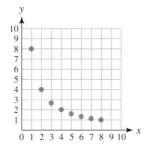

APPLICATIONS

57. *Recording Music*   A 600-megabyte CD can record 68 minutes of music. How many minutes can be recorded on 360 megabytes?   40.8 min

58. *Height of a Tree*   (Refer to Example 2.) A 6-foot person casts a 7-foot shadow, and a nearby tree casts a 27-foot shadow. Estimate the height of the tree.
About 23.1 ft

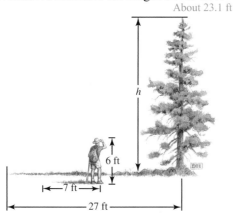

59. *Water Content in Snow*   (Refer to Example 1.) Eight inches of heavy, wet snow are equivalent to an inch of rain. Estimate the water content in 11 inches of heavy, wet snow.   1.375 in.

60. *Wages*   If a person working for an hourly wage earns $143 in 11 hours, how much will that person earn in 17 hours? $221

61. *Rolling Resistance of Cars*   If you were to try and push a car, you would experience *rolling resistance*. This resistance equals the force necessary to keep the car moving slowly in neutral gear. The following table shows the rolling resistance R for passenger cars of different gross weights W. (***Source:*** N. Garber and L. Hoel, *Traffic and Highway Engineering.*)

W (pounds)	2000	2500	3000	3500
R (pounds)	24	30	36	42

(a) Do the data represent direct or inverse variation? Explain.   Direct; the ratios $\frac{R}{W}$ always equal 0.012.

(b) Find an equation that models the data. Graph the equation with the data. * $R = 0.012W$

(c) Estimate the rolling resistance of a 3200-pound car.   38.4 lb

62. *Transportation Costs*   The use of a particular toll bridge varies inversely according to the toll. When the toll is $0.75, 6000 vehicles are using the bridge. Estimate the number of users if the toll is $0.40.   (***Source:*** N. Garber.)   11,250 users

63. *Flow of Water*   The gallons of water G flowing in 1 minute through a hose with a cross-sectional area A are shown in the table.

A (square inch)	0.2	0.3	0.4	0.5
G (gallons)	5.4	8.1	10.8	13.5

(a) Do the data represent direct or inverse variation? Explain.   Direct; the ratios $\frac{G}{A}$ always equal 27.

(b) Find an equation that models the data. Graph the equation with the data. * $G = 27A$

(c) Interpret the constant of variation k.   For each square-inch increase in the cross-sectional area of the hose, the flow increases by 27 gal/min.

64. *Hooke's Law*   The accompanying table shows the distance D that a spring stretches when a weight W is hung on it.

W (pounds)	2	6	9	15
D (inches)	1.5	4.5	6.75	11.25

(a) Do the data represent direct or inverse variation? Explain.   Direct; the ratios $\frac{D}{W}$ always equal 0.75.

(b) Find an equation that models the data. $D = 0.75W$

(c) How far will the spring stretch if an 11-pound weight is hung on it, as depicted in the accompanying figure?   8.25 in.

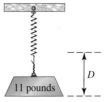

*Answers on page IA-21

65. *Tightening Lug Nuts*   (Refer to Example 4.) When a tire is mounted on a car, the lug nuts should not be over-tightened. The following table shows the maximum force used with wrenches of different lengths.

L (inches)	8	10	16
F (pounds)	150	120	75

(a) $F = \dfrac{1200}{L}$

Source: Tires Plus.

(a) Model the data, using the equation $F = \frac{k}{L}$.

(b) How much force should be used with a wrench 20 inches long?   60 lb

66. *Cost of Tuition*   (Refer to Example 3.) The cost of tuition is directly proportional to the number of credits taken. If 6 credits cost $435, find the cost of 11 credits. What does the constant of proportionality represent? $797.50; k represents the cost per credit.

67. *Air Temperature and Altitude*   In the first 6 miles of Earth's atmosphere, air cools as the altitude increases. The following graph shows the temperature change y in degrees Fahrenheit at an altitude of x miles.
(*Source:* A. Miller and R. Anthes, *Meteorology.*)

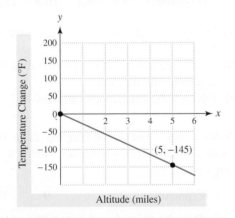

(a) Does this graph represent direct variation or inverse variation?   Direct

(b) Find an equation that models the data in the graph. $y = -29x$

(c) Is the constant of proportionality k positive or negative? Interpret k.

(d) Estimate the change in air temperature 3.5 miles high.   101.5°F decrease

68. *Ozone and UV Radiation*   Ozone in the upper atmosphere filters out approximately 90% of the harmful ultraviolet (UV) rays from the sun. Depletion of the ozone layer has caused an increase in the amount

67.(c) Negative; for each 1-mile increase in altitude the temperature decreases by 29°F.

of UV radiation reaching Earth's surface. An increase in UV radiation is associated with skin cancer. The following graph shows the percentage increase y in UV radiation for a decrease in the ozone layer of x percent.   (*Source:* R. Turner, D. Pearce, and I. Bateman, *Environmental Economics.*)

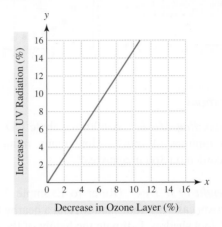

(a) Does this graph represent direct variation or inverse variation?   Direct

(b) Find an equation that models the data in the graph. $y = 1.5x$

(c) Estimate the percentage increase in UV radiation if the ozone layer decreases by 7%.   10.5%

69. *Electrical Resistance*   The electrical resistance of a wire is directly proportional to its length. If a 35-foot-long wire has a resistance of 2 ohms, find the resistance of a 25-foot-long wire.   About 1.43 ohms

70. *Resistance and Current*   The current that flows through an electrical circuit is inversely proportional to the resistance. When the resistance R is 150 ohms, the current I is 0.8 amp. Find the current when the resistance is 40 ohms.   3 amps

71. *Joint Variation*   The variable z varies jointly as the second power of x and the third power of y. Write a formula for z if $z = 31.9$ when $x = 2$ and $y = 2.5$. $z = 0.5104x^2y^3$

72. *Wind Power*   The electrical power generated by a windmill varies jointly with the square of the diameter of the area swept out by the blades and the cube of the wind velocity. If a windmill with an 8-foot diameter and a 10-mile-per-hour wind generates 2405 watts, how much power would be generated if the blades swept out an area 12 feet in diameter and the wind speed was 15 miles per hour?   About 18,263 watts

73. *Strength of a Beam*   (Refer to Example 6.) If a beam 5 inches wide and 3 inches thick supports 300 pounds, how much can a similar beam 5 inches wide and 2 inches thick support?   About 133 lb

74. *Carpeting*   The cost of carpet for a rectangular room varies jointly as its width and length. If a room 11 feet wide and 14 feet long costs $539 to carpet, find the cost to carpet a room 17 feet by 19 feet. Interpret the constant of variation *k*.
$1130.50; *k* represents a $3.50/ft² cost.

75. *Weight on the Moon*   The weight of a person on the moon is directly proportional to the weight of the person on Earth. If a 175-pound person weighs 28 pounds on the moon, how much will a 220-pound person weigh on the moon?   About 35.2 lb

76. *Weight Near Earth*   The weight *W* of a person near Earth is inversely proportional to the square of the person's distance *d* from the *center* of Earth. If a person weighs 200 pounds when $d = 4000$ miles, how much does the same person weigh when $d = 7000$ miles? (*Note:* The radius of Earth is about 4000 miles.)
About 65.3 lb

77. *Ohm's Law*   The voltage *V* in an electrical circuit varies jointly with the amperage *I* and resistance *R*. If $V = 220$ when $I = 10$ and $R = 22$, find *V* when $I = 15$ and $R = 50$.   750

78. *Revenue*   The revenue *R* from selling *x* items at price *p* varies jointly with *x* and *p*. If $R = \$24,000$ when $x = 3000$ and $p = \$8$, find *x* when $R = \$30,000$ and $p = \$6$.   5000

WRITING ABOUT MATHEMATICS

79. Explain in words what it means for a quantity *y* to be directly proportional to a quantity *x*.

80. Explain in words what it means for a quantity *y* to be inversely proportional to a quantity *x*.

CHECKING BASIC CONCEPTS   SECTIONS 6.5 AND 6.6

1. Simplify each complex fraction.

(a) $\dfrac{3 - \dfrac{1}{x^2}}{3 + \dfrac{1}{x^2}}$ (b) $\dfrac{\dfrac{2}{x-1} - \dfrac{2}{x+1}}{\dfrac{4}{x^2-1}}$

(a) $\dfrac{3x^2 - 1}{3x^2 + 1}$ (b) 1

2. Suppose that *y* is directly proportional to *x* and that $y = 6$ when $x = 8$.
   (a) Find the constant of proportionality *k*. $k = 0.75$
   (b) Find *y* when $x = 11$. $y = 8.25$

3. Determine whether the data represent direct variation or inverse variation. Find an equation that models the data.

(a)
x	10	15	25	40
y	4	6	10	16

Direct; $y = 0.4x$

(b)
x	5	10	15	20
y	24	12	8	6

Inverse; $y = \dfrac{120}{x}$

6.7 DIVISION OF POLYNOMIALS

Division by a Monomial · Division by a Polynomial · Synthetic Division

INTRODUCTION

The study of polynomials has occupied the minds of mathematicians for centuries. During the sixteenth century, Italian mathematicians discovered how to solve higher degree polynomial equations. In this section we demonstrate symbolic methods for dividing polynomials. Division is often needed to factor higher degree polynomials and to solve polynomial equations. (*Source:* H. Eves, *An Introduction to the History of Mathematics.*)

DIVISION BY A MONOMIAL

TEACHING TIP

Point out that these two properties are addition and subtraction of fractions in "reverse."

To divide a polynomial by a monomial we use the two properties

$$\frac{a + b}{c} = \frac{a}{c} + \frac{b}{c} \quad \text{and} \quad \frac{a - b}{c} = \frac{a}{c} - \frac{b}{c}.$$

For example,

$$\frac{3x^2 + x}{x} = \frac{3x^2}{x} + \frac{x}{x}$$
$$= 3x + 1. \qquad \text{Divide each term by } x, \text{ where } x \neq 0.$$

Recall that we can check our work by using multiplication when dividing natural numbers. Because

$$\frac{6}{2} = 3,$$

$2 \cdot 3 = 6$. Similarly, to check whether

$$\frac{3x^2 + x}{x} = 3x + 1,$$

we multiply x and $3x + 1$.

$$x(3x + 1) = x \cdot 3x + x \cdot 1 \qquad \text{Distributive property}$$
$$= 3x^2 + x \qquad \text{It checks.}$$

Graphical support is shown in Figures 6.27(a) and 6.27(b), where the graphs of $Y_1 = (3X^2 + X)/X$ and $Y_2 = 3X + 1$ appear to be identical. In Figure 6.27(c) numerical support is given, where $y_1 = y_2$ for all x-values except 0. Note that we assumed that $x \neq 0$ in $\frac{3x^2 + x}{x}$ because 0 would result in this expression being undefined.

[−4.7, 4.7, 1] by [−3.1, 3.1, 1]   [−4.7, 4.7, 1] by [−3.1, 3.1, 1]

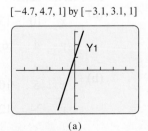

(a)

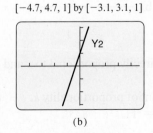

(b)

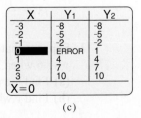

(c)

Figure 6.27

EXAMPLE 1 Dividing by a monomial

Divide and check.

(a) $\dfrac{5x^3 - 15x^2}{15x}$ (b) $\dfrac{4x^2 + 8x - 12}{4x^2}$ (c) $\dfrac{5x^2y + 10xy^2}{5xy}$

Solution (a) $\dfrac{5x^3 - 15x^2}{15x} = \dfrac{5x^3}{15x} - \dfrac{15x^2}{15x} = \dfrac{x^2}{3} - x$

Check: $15x\left(\dfrac{x^2}{3} - x\right) = \dfrac{15x \cdot x^2}{3} - 15x \cdot x$

$$= 5x^3 - 15x^2$$

(b) $\dfrac{4x^2 + 8x - 12}{4x^2} = \dfrac{4x^2}{4x^2} + \dfrac{8x}{4x^2} - \dfrac{12}{4x^2} = 1 + \dfrac{2}{x} - \dfrac{3}{x^2}$

Check: $4x^2\left(1 + \dfrac{2}{x} - \dfrac{3}{x^2}\right) = 4x^2 \cdot 1 + \dfrac{4x^2 \cdot 2}{x} - \dfrac{4x^2 \cdot 3}{x^2}$

$$= 4x^2 + 8x - 12$$

(c) $\dfrac{5x^2y + 10xy^2}{5xy} = \dfrac{5x^2y}{5xy} + \dfrac{10xy^2}{5xy} = x + 2y$

Check: $5xy(x + 2y) = 5xy \cdot x + 5xy \cdot 2y$

$$= 5x^2y + 10xy^2$$

========= MAKING CONNECTIONS =========

Division and Canceling Incorrectly

When dividing expressions, students commonly "cancel" incorrectly. For example,

$$\frac{x + 3x^2}{x} \neq 1 + 3x^2 \quad \text{and} \quad \frac{x + 3x^2}{x} \neq 3x^2.$$

Rather,

$$\frac{x + 3x^2}{x} = \frac{x}{x} + \frac{3x^2}{x} = 1 + 3x.$$

Dividing the monomial into *every* term in the numerator is important.

DIVISION BY A POLYNOMIAL

First, we briefly review division of natural numbers.

$$
\begin{array}{r}
\text{Quotient} \rightarrow \quad 58 \text{ R } 1 \quad \leftarrow \text{Remainder}\\
\text{Divisor} \rightarrow \quad 3\overline{)175} \quad \leftarrow \text{Dividend}\\
\underline{15}\\
25\\
\underline{24}\\
1
\end{array}
$$

Because $3 \cdot 58 + 1 = 175$, the answer checks. The quotient and remainder also can be expressed as $58\frac{1}{3}$. Division of polynomials is similar to long division of natural numbers.

EXAMPLE 2 Dividing polynomials

Divide $4x^2 - 2x + 1$ by $2x + 1$ and check.

Solution Begin by dividing $2x$ into $4x^2$.

$$
\begin{array}{r}
2x \\
2x + 1 \overline{)4x^2 - 2x + 1} \\
\underline{4x^2 + 2x} \\
-4x + 1
\end{array}
\qquad
\begin{array}{l}
\dfrac{4x^2}{2x} = 2x \\[4pt]
2x(2x + 1) = 4x^2 + 2x \\
\text{Subtract } -2x - 2x = -4x. \\
\text{Bring down the 1.}
\end{array}
$$

Next, divide $2x$ into $-4x$.

$$
\begin{array}{r}
2x \ - \ 2 \\
2x + 1 \overline{)4x^2 - 2x + 1} \\
\underline{4x^2 + 2x} \\
-4x + 1 \\
\underline{-4x - 2} \\
3
\end{array}
\qquad
\begin{array}{l}
\dfrac{-4x}{2x} = -2 \\[10pt]
-2(2x + 1) = -4x - 2 \\
\text{Subtract } 1 - (-2) = 3. \\
\text{Remainder is 3.}
\end{array}
$$

The quotient is $2x - 2$ with remainder 3, which can also be written as

$$
2x - 2 + \frac{3}{2x + 1}, \qquad \text{Quotient} + \frac{\text{Remainder}}{\text{Divisor}}
$$

in the same manner as 58 R 1 was expressed as $58\frac{1}{3}$. Polynomial division is checked by multiplying the divisor and the quotient and adding the remainder.

$$
(2x + 1)(2x - 2) + 3 = 4x^2 - 4x + 2x - 2 + 3
$$

$$
\underset{\text{Divisor}}{\uparrow} \quad \underset{\text{Quotient}}{\uparrow} \quad \underset{\text{Remainder}}{\uparrow} \quad = 4x^2 - 2x + 1 \leftarrow \text{Given polynomial}
$$

EXAMPLE 3 Dividing polynomials

Divide $2x^3 - 5x^2 + 4x - 1$ by $x - 1$.

Solution Begin by dividing x into $2x^3$.

$$
\begin{array}{r}
2x^2 \\
x - 1 \overline{)2x^3 - 5x^2 + 4x - 1} \\
\underline{2x^3 - 2x^2} \\
-3x^2 + 4x
\end{array}
\qquad
\begin{array}{l}
\dfrac{2x^3}{x} = 2x^2 \\[6pt]
2x^2(x - 1) = 2x^3 - 2x^2 \\
\text{Subtract } -5x^2 - (-2x^2) = -3x^2. \\
\text{Bring down } 4x.
\end{array}
$$

Next, divide x into $-3x^2$.

$$
\begin{array}{r}
2x^2 - 3x \\
x - 1 \overline{)2x^3 - 5x^2 + 4x - 1} \\
\underline{2x^3 - 2x^2} \\
-3x^2 + 4x \\
\underline{-3x^2 + 3x} \\
x - 1
\end{array}
\qquad
\begin{array}{l}
\dfrac{-3x^2}{x} = -3x \\[16pt]
-3x(x - 1) = -3x^2 + 3x \\
\text{Subtract } 4x - 3x = x. \\
\text{Bring down } -1.
\end{array}
$$

Finally, divide x into x.

$$
\begin{array}{r}
2x^2 - 3x + 1 \\
x - 1\overline{)2x^3 - 5x^2 + 4x - 1} \\
\underline{2x^3 - 2x^2} \\
-3x^2 + 4x \\
\underline{-3x^2 + 3x} \\
x - 1 \\
\underline{x - 1} \\
0
\end{array}
$$

$\dfrac{x}{x} = 1$

$1(x - 1) = x - 1$

Subtract. Remainder is 0.

The quotient is $2x^2 - 3x + 1$, and the remainder is 0.

EXAMPLE 4   Dividing by a quadratic divisor

Divide $3x^3 - 2x^2 - 4x + 4$ by $x^2 - 1$.

Solution   Begin by writing $x^2 - 1$ as $x^2 + 0x - 1$. Then

$$
\begin{array}{r}
3x - 2 \\
x^2 + 0x - 1\overline{)3x^3 - 2x^2 - 4x + 4} \\
\underline{3x^3 + 0x^2 - 3x} \\
-2x^2 - x + 4 \\
\underline{-2x^2 - 0x + 2} \\
-x + 2
\end{array}
$$

The quotient is $3x - 2$, and the remainder is $-x + 2$, or $2 - x$, which can also be written as

$$
3x - 2 + \frac{2 - x}{x^2 - 1}.
$$

EXAMPLE 5   Dividing into a polynomial with missing terms

Divide $2x^3 - 3$ by $x + 1$.

Solution   Begin by writing $2x^3 - 3$ as $2x^3 + 0x^2 + 0x - 3$. Then

$$
\begin{array}{r}
2x^2 - 2x + 2 \\
x + 1\overline{)2x^3 + 0x^2 + 0x - 3} \\
\underline{2x^3 + 2x^2} \\
-2x^2 + 0x \\
\underline{-2x^2 - 2x} \\
2x - 3 \\
\underline{2x + 2} \\
-5
\end{array}
$$

The quotient is $2x^2 - 2x + 2$ with remainder -5, which can be written as

$$
2x^2 - 2x + 2 - \frac{5}{x + 1}.
$$

SYNTHETIC DIVISION

A shortcut called **synthetic division** can be used to divide $x - k$, where k is a number, into a polynomial. For example, to divide $x - 2$ into $3x^3 - 8x^2 + 7x - 6$, we do the following (with the equivalent long division shown at the right).

Synthetic Division

$$\begin{array}{r|rrrr} 2 & 3 & -8 & 7 & -6 \\ & & 6 & -4 & 6 \\ \hline & 3 & -2 & 3 & 0 \end{array}$$

Long Division of Polynomials

$$\begin{array}{r} 3x^2 - 2x + 3 \\ x - 2\overline{)3x^3 - 8x^2 + 7x - 6} \\ \underline{3x^3 - 6x^2} \\ -2x^2 + 7x \\ \underline{-2x^2 + 4x} \\ 3x - 6 \\ \underline{3x - 6} \\ 0 \end{array}$$

Note how the highlighted numbers in the expression for long division correspond to the third row in synthetic division. The remainder is 0, which is the last number in the third row. The quotient is $3x^2 - 2x + 3$. Its coefficients are 3, -2, and 3 and are located in the third row. To divide $x - 2$ into $3x^3 - 8x + 7x - 6$ with synthetic division use the following steps.

STEP 1. In the top row write 2 (the value of k) on the left and then write the coefficients of the dividend $3x^3 - 8x^2 + 7x - 6$.

STEP 2. **(a)** Copy the leading coefficient 3 of $3x^3 - 8x + 7x - 6$ in the third row and multiply it by 2 (the value of k). Write the result 6 in the second row below -8. Add -8 and 6 in the second column to obtain the -2 in the third row.

(b) Repeat the process by multiplying -2 by 2 and place the result -4 below 7. Then add 7 and -4 to obtain 3.

(c) Multiply 3 by 2 and place the result 6 below the -6. Adding 6 and -6 gives 0.

STEP 3. The last number in the third row is 0, which is the remainder. The other numbers in the third row are the coefficients of the quotient, which is $3x^2 - 2x + 3$.

EXAMPLE 6   Performing synthetic division

Use synthetic division to divide $x^4 - 5x^3 + 9x^2 - 10x + 3$ by $x - 3$.

Solution   Because the divisor is $x - 3$, the value of k is 3.

$$\begin{array}{r|rrrrr} 3 & 1 & -5 & 9 & -10 & 3 \\ & & 3 & -6 & 9 & -3 \\ \hline & 1 & -2 & 3 & -1 & 0 \end{array}$$

The quotient is $x^3 - 2x^2 + 3x - 1$ and the remainder is 0. This result is also expressed by

$$\frac{x^4 - 5x^3 + 9x^2 - 10x + 3}{x - 3} = x^3 - 2x^2 + 3x - 1 + \frac{0}{x - 3}, \quad \text{or}$$

$$\frac{x^4 - 5x^3 + 9x^2 - 10x + 3}{x - 3} = x^3 - 2x^2 + 3x - 1.$$

≡≡≡ MAKING CONNECTIONS ≡≡≡

Factors and Remainders

Multiplying the last equation in the solution to Example 6 by $x - 3$ gives

$$x^4 - 5x^3 + 9x^2 - 10x + 3 = (x - 3)(x^3 - 2x^2 + 3x - 1).$$

That is, $x - 3$ is a *factor* of $x^4 - 5x^3 + 9x^2 - 10x + 3$ because the remainder is 0.

This concept is true in general: If a polynomial $p(x)$ is divided by $x - k$ and the remainder is 0, then $x - k$ is a factor of $p(x)$.

TEACHING TIP

Point out that to perform synthetic division the divisor should be written as $x - k$ for some real number k.

EXAMPLE 7   Performing synthetic division

Use synthetic division to divide $2x^3 - x + 5$ by $x + 1$.

Solution   Write $2x^3 - x + 5$ as $2x^3 + 0x^2 - x + 5$. The divisor $x + 1$ can be written as

$$x + 1 = x - (-1),$$

so we let $k = -1$.

$$\begin{array}{r|rrrr} -1 & 2 & 0 & -1 & 5 \\ & & -2 & 2 & -1 \\ \hline & 2 & -2 & 1 & 4 \end{array}$$

Critical Thinking

Suppose that $p(x)$ is a polynomial and that $(x - k)$ divides into $p(x)$ with remainder 0.

1. Evaluate $p(k)$.   0
2. Give one x-intercept on the graph of $p(x)$. k

The remainder is 4, and the quotient is $2x^2 - 2x + 1$. This result can also be expressed as

$$\frac{2x^3 - x + 5}{x + 1} = 2x^2 - 2x + 1 + \frac{4}{x + 1}.$$

6.7   PUTTING IT ALL TOGETHER

The following table summarizes division of polynomials.

Type of Division	Explanation	Example
By a Monomial	Use the property $\frac{a \pm b}{c} = \frac{a}{c} \pm \frac{b}{c}$ to divide a polynomial by a monomial. Be sure to divide the denominator into every term of the numerator.	$\dfrac{8a^3 - 4a^2}{2a} = \dfrac{8a^3}{2a} - \dfrac{4a^2}{2a} = 4a^2 - 2a$
By a Polynomial	Division by a polynomial may be done in a manner similar to long division of natural numbers. See Examples 2–5.	When $2x^2 - 7x + 4$ is divided by $2x - 1$, the quotient is $x - 3$ and the remainder is 1. This result may be expressed as $$\dfrac{2x^2 - 7x + 4}{2x - 1} = x - 3 + \dfrac{1}{2x - 1}.$$

continued on next page

continued from previous page

Type of Division	Explanation	Example
Synthetic	Synthetic division is a fast way to divide a polynomial by a divisor in the form $x - k$.	Divide $4x^2 + 7x - 14$ by $x + 3$. $\begin{array}{r} -3\rlap{\vert} \quad 4 \quad\;\; 7 \quad -14 \\ \underline{\quad\quad\; -12 \quad\;\; 15} \\ 4 \quad -5 \quad\;\; 1 \end{array}$ The quotient is $4x - 5$ with remainder 1.

6.7 EXERCISES

FOR EXTRA HELP

📖 Student's Solutions Manual

🚪 MyMathLab

InterAct Math

Tutor Center Math Tutor Center

MathXL

Digital Video Tutor
CD 6   Videotape 7

CONCEPTS

1. To divide a monomial into a polynomial, divide the monomial into every _____ in the numerator. term

2. $\dfrac{a + b}{c} =$ _____. $\dfrac{a}{c} + \dfrac{b}{c}$

3. Because $\frac{21}{5} = 4$ with remainder 1, it follows that $21 =$ _____ · _____ + _____. 5; 4; 1

4. Because $\dfrac{3x^2 - 11x + 8}{3x - 5} = x - 2$ with remainder -2, $3x^2 - 11x + 8 = ($_____$) \cdot ($_____$) + ($_____$)$.
   $3x - 5; x - 2; -2$

5. Is it possible to use synthetic division to divide $3x^3 - 2x^2 + x - 3$ by $x^2 - 2x$? Explain.
   No; the divisor is not in the form $x - k$.

6. Where is the remainder located when you finish with synthetic division? The last number in the third row

DIVISION BY A MONOMIAL

Exercises 7–12: Divide and check. Give graphical or numerical support for your result.

7. $\dfrac{4x - 6}{2}$ $2x - 3$

8. $\dfrac{4x^2 - 8x + 12}{4}$ $x^2 - 2x + 3$

9. $\dfrac{6x^3 - 9x}{3x}$ $2x^2 - 3$

10. $\dfrac{3x^4 + x^2}{6x^2}$ $\frac{1}{2}x^2 + \frac{1}{6}$

11. $(4x^2 - x + 1) \div 2x^2$ $2 - \dfrac{1}{2x} + \dfrac{1}{2x^2}$

12. $(5x^3 - 4x + 2) \div 20x$ $\frac{1}{4}x^2 - \frac{1}{5} + \frac{1}{10x}$

Exercises 13–22: Divide.

13. $\dfrac{9x^2 - 12x - 3}{3}$ $3x^2 - 4x - 1$

14. $\dfrac{10x^3 - 15x^2 + 5x}{5}$ $2x^3 - 3x^2 + x$

15. $\dfrac{12a^3 - 18a}{6a}$ $2a^2 - 3$

16. $\dfrac{50x^4 + 25x^2 + 100x}{25x}$ $2x^3 + x + 4$

17. $(16x^3 - 24x) \div (12x)$ $\frac{4}{3}x^2 - 2$

18. $(2y^4 - 4y^2 + 16) \div (2y^2)$ $y^2 - 2 + \dfrac{8}{y^2}$

19. $(a^2b^2 - 4ab + ab^2) \div (ab)$ $ab - 4 + b$

20. $(10x^3y^2 + 5x^2y^3) \div (5x^2y^2)$ $2x + y$

21. $\dfrac{6m^4n^4 + 3m^2n^2 - 12}{3m^2n^2}$
    $2m^2n^2 + 1 - \dfrac{4}{m^2n^2}$

22. $\dfrac{6p^2q^4 - 9p^6q^2}{-3pq}$
    $-2pq^3 + 3p^5q$

DIVISION BY A POLYNOMIAL

26. $2x^2 - 3x - 6 - \dfrac{4}{x - 2}$

Exercises 23–28: Divide and check.

23. $\dfrac{3x^2 - 16x + 21}{x - 3}$ $3x - 7$

24. $\dfrac{4x^2 - x - 18}{x + 2}$ $4x - 9$

25. $\dfrac{2x^3 + 3x^2 - 2x - 2}{2x + 3}$ $x^2 - 1 + \dfrac{1}{2x + 3}$

26. $\dfrac{2x^3 - 7x^2 + 8}{x - 2}$

27. $(6x^2 - 11x + 4) \div (2x - 3)$ $3x - 1 + \dfrac{1}{2x - 3}$

28. $(10x^2 - 5) \div (x - 1)$ $10x + 10 + \dfrac{5}{x - 1}$

31. $x^2 - 4x + 19 - \dfrac{80}{x + 4}$ 32. $2x^2 + 3x + 6 + \dfrac{17}{x - 2}$

Exercises 29–42: Divide.

29. $\dfrac{4x^3 + 8x^2 - x - 2}{x + 2}$ $4x^2 - 1$

30. $\dfrac{3x^3 - 4x^2 + 3x - 2}{x - 1}$ $3x^2 - x + 2$

31. $\dfrac{x^3 + 3x - 4}{x + 4}$

32. $\dfrac{2x^3 - x^2 + 5}{x - 2}$

33. $(3x^3 + 8x^2 - 21x + 7) \div (3x - 1)$ $x^2 + 3x - 6 + \dfrac{1}{3x - 1}$

34. $(14x^3 + 3x^2 - 9x + 3) \div (7x - 2)$ $2x^2 + x - 1 + \dfrac{1}{7x - 2}$

35. $(2a^4 + 5a^3 - 2a^2 - 5a) \div (2a + 5)$ $a^3 - a$

36. $(4b^4 + 10b^3 - 2b^2 - 3b + 5) \div (2b + 1)$
    36. $2b^3 + 4b^2 - 3b + \dfrac{5}{2b + 1}$

37. $\dfrac{3x^3 + 4x^2 - 12x - 16}{x^2 - 4}$ $3x + 4$

    39. $x + 1 + \dfrac{1}{x^2 - 1}$

38. $\dfrac{2x^4 - x^3 - 5x^2 + 4x - 12}{2x^2 - x + 3}$ $x^2 - 4$

39. $\dfrac{x^3 + x^2 - x}{x^2 - 1}$

40. $\dfrac{x^3 + x^2 - 6x}{x^2 - 2x}$ $x + 3$

41. $(2a^4 - 3a^3 + 14a^2 - 8a + 10) \div (a^2 - a + 5)$

42. $(2z^3 + 3z^2 - 9z - 12) \div (z^2 - 1)$

41. $2a^2 - a + 3 - \dfrac{5}{a^2 - a + 5}$ 42. $2z + 3 - \dfrac{7z + 9}{z^2 - 1}$

SYNTHETIC DIVISION

    43. $x + 4 + \dfrac{3}{x - 1}$

Exercises 43–54: Use synthetic division to divide.

43. $\dfrac{x^2 + 3x - 1}{x - 1}$

44. $\dfrac{2x^2 + x - 1}{x - 3}$ $2x + 7 + \dfrac{20}{x - 3}$

45. $(3x^2 - 22x + 7) \div (x - 7)$ $3x - 1$

46. $(5x^2 + 29x - 6) \div (x + 6)$ $5x - 1$

47. $\dfrac{x^3 + 7x^2 + 14x + 8}{x + 4}$ $x^2 + 3x + 2$

48. $\dfrac{2x^3 + 3x^2 + 2x + 4}{x + 1}$ $2x^2 + x + 1 + \dfrac{3}{x + 1}$

49. $\dfrac{2x^3 + x^2 - 1}{x - 2}$ $2x^2 + 5x + 10 + \dfrac{19}{x - 2}$

50. $\dfrac{x^3 + x - 2}{x + 3}$ $x^2 - 3x + 10 - \dfrac{32}{x + 3}$

51. $(x^3 - 2x^2 - 2x + 4) \div (x - 4)$ $x^2 + 2x + 6 + \dfrac{28}{x - 4}$

52. $(2x^4 + 3x^2 - 4) \div (x + 2)$ $2x^3 - 4x^2 + 11x - 22 + \dfrac{40}{x + 2}$

53. $(b^4 - 1) \div (b - 1)$ $b^3 + b^2 + b + 1$

54. $(a^2 + a) \div (a + 2.5)$ $a - 1.5 + \dfrac{3.75}{a + 2.5}$

GEOMETRY

    60. If $\dfrac{p(x)}{x - k}$ has remainder r, then $p(k) = r$.

55. *Area of a Rectangle* Use the figure to find the length L of the rectangle from its width and area A.

Determine the length when $x = 8$ feet. $3x + 5$; 29 ft

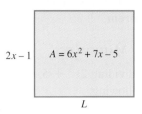

56. *Area of a Rectangle* Use the figure to find the width W of the rectangle from its length and area A. Determine the width when $x = 20$ inches.

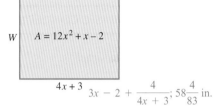

$3x - 2 + \dfrac{4}{4x + 3}$; $58\dfrac{4}{83}$ in.

57. *Volume of a Box* The volume of a rectangular box is $x^3 + 7x^2 + 14x + 8$. If the width of the box is $x + 1$ and its length is $x + 4$, find the height of the box. $x + 2$

58. *Area of a Triangle* The area A of a triangle is $12x^2 - 5x - 3$. If the height of the triangle is $3x + 1$, find the length of its base. $8x - 6$

THEOREMS ABOUT POLYNOMIALS

59. *Remainder Theorem* Divide $p(x)$ by $x - k$ and determine the remainder. Then evaluate $p(k)$.
    (a) $p(x) = x^2 - 3x + 2$ $k = 1$ 0; 0
    (b) $p(x) = 3x^2 + 5x - 2$ $k = -2$ 0; 0
    (c) $p(x) = 3x^3 - 4x^2 - 5x + 3$ $k = 2$ 1; 1
    (d) $p(x) = x^3 - 2x^2 - x + 2$ $k = -1$ 0; 0
    (e) $p(x) = x^4 - 5x^2 - 1$ $k = 3$ 35; 35

60. *Remainder Theorem* Try to generalize the results from Exercise 59. It can be done, and the result is called the **remainder theorem**.

61. *Factor Theorem* Evaluate $p(k)$. Then determine whether $x - k$ is a factor of $p(x)$.
    (a) $p(x) = x^2 + x - 6$ $k = 2$ 0; Yes
    (b) $p(x) = x^2 + 4x - 5$ $k = 1$ 0; Yes
    (c) $p(x) = x^2 + 8x + 11$ $k = -2$ -1; No
    (d) $p(x) = x^3 + x^2 + x + 1$ $k = -1$ 0; Yes
    (e) $p(x) = x^3 - 3x^2 - x - 3$ $k = 2$ -9; No

62. *Factor Theorem*   Try to generalize the results from Exercise 61. It can be done and the result is called the **factor theorem.**   If $p(k) = 0$, then $x - k$ is a factor of $p(x)$.

WRITING ABOUT MATHEMATICS

63. A student dividing $2x^3 + 5x^2 - 13x + 5$ by $2x - 1$ does the following.

$$\begin{array}{r|rrrr} 1 & 2 & 5 & -13 & 5 \\ & & 2 & 7 & -6 \\ \hline & 2 & 7 & -6 & -1 \end{array}$$

What would you tell the student?

64. If you add, subtract, or multiply two polynomials is the result a polynomial? If you divide two polynomials is the result always a polynomial? Explain.

CHECKING BASIC CONCEPTS   ⟨   SECTION 6.7   ⟩

1. Divide and simplify.

3. (a) $2x^2 - 3x - 3 - \dfrac{4}{x - 1}$

(a) $\dfrac{2x - x^2}{x^2}$ $\dfrac{2}{x} - 1$ **(b)** $\dfrac{6a^2 - 9a + 15}{3a}$ $2a - 3 + \dfrac{5}{a}$

2. Divide

$$\dfrac{10x^2 - x + 4}{2x + 1}.$$ $5x - 3 + \dfrac{7}{2x + 1}$

3. Use synthetic division to divide

$$2x^3 - 5x^2 - 1$$

by each expression.   (b) $2x^2 - 9x + 18 - \dfrac{37}{x + 2}$

(a) $x - 1$ **(b)** $x + 2$

CHAPTER

Summary

Section 6.1   *Introduction to Rational Functions and Equations*

Rational Functions   A rational function is given by $f(x) = \dfrac{p(x)}{q(x)}$, where $p(x)$ and $q(x)$ are polynomials. The domain of f includes all x-values such that $q(x) \neq 0$.

Example: $f(x) = \dfrac{4}{x - 2}$ defines a rational function with domain $\{x \mid x \neq 2\}$.

Graphs of Rational Functions   Graphs of rational functions are not lines but curves. A vertical asymptote typically occurs at x-values where the denominator equals zero, but the numerator does not. The graph of a rational function never crosses a vertical asymptote. Graphing a rational function by hand may require plotting several points on each side of a vertical asymptote.

Example: $f(x) = \dfrac{2x}{x - 2}$

A vertical asymptote occurs at $x = 2$. Note that the graph does not cross this vertical asymptote.

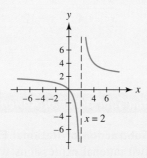

Rational Equations   A rational equation contains one or more rational expressions. To solve a rational equation in the form $\frac{A}{B} = C$, start by multiplying each side of the equation by B to obtain $A = BC$. This step clears fractions from the equation.

Example: To solve $\frac{2x}{x-3} = 8$, start by multiplying both sides by $x - 3$.

$$(x - 3)\frac{2x}{x-3} = (x - 3)8$$
$$2x = 8x - 24$$
$$x = 4$$

Check your answer.

Section 6.2   *Multiplication and Division of Rational Expressions*

Simplifying a Rational Expression   To simplify a rational expression, factor the numerator and the denominator. Then apply the following property where P, Q, and R are polynomials.

$$\frac{PR}{QR} = \frac{P}{Q}$$

Example: $\dfrac{x^2 - 1}{x^2 + 2x + 1} = \dfrac{(x - 1)(x + 1)}{(x + 1)(x + 1)} = \dfrac{x - 1}{x + 1}$

Multiplying Rational Expressions   To multiply two rational expressions, multiply numerators and multiply denominators. Simplify the result, if possible.

$$\frac{A}{B} \cdot \frac{C}{D} = \frac{AC}{BD} \qquad \text{B and D not zero}$$

Example: $\dfrac{3}{x - 1} \cdot \dfrac{x - 1}{x + 1} = \dfrac{3(x - 1)}{(x - 1)(x + 1)} = \dfrac{3}{x + 1}$

Dividing Rational Expressions   To divide two rational expressions, multiply by the reciprocal of the divisor. Simplify the result, if possible.

$$\frac{A}{B} \div \frac{C}{D} = \frac{A}{B} \cdot \frac{D}{C} = \frac{AD}{BC} \qquad \text{B, C, and D not zero}$$

Example:

$$\frac{x+1}{x^2-4} \div \frac{x+1}{x-2} = \frac{x+1}{(x-2)(x+2)} \cdot \frac{x-2}{x+1}$$

$$= \frac{(x+1)(x-2)}{(x-2)(x+2)(x+1)} = \frac{1}{x+2}$$

Section 6.3   *Addition and Subtraction of Rational Expressions*

Addition and Subtraction of Rational Expressions with Like Denominators   To add (subtract) two rational expressions with like denominators, add (subtract) their numerators. The denominator does not change.

$$\frac{A}{C} + \frac{B}{C} = \frac{A+B}{C} \quad \text{and} \quad \frac{A}{C} - \frac{B}{C} = \frac{A-B}{C}$$

Examples: $\dfrac{2x}{2x+1} + \dfrac{3x}{2x+1} = \dfrac{5x}{2x+1}$ and

$$\frac{x}{x^2-1} - \frac{1}{x^2-1} = \frac{x-1}{x^2-1} = \frac{x-1}{(x-1)(x+1)} = \frac{1}{x+1}$$

Finding the Least Common Denominator   The least common denominator (LCD) is the least common multiple (LCM) of the denominators.

Example: The LCD for $\frac{1}{x(x+1)}$ and $\frac{1}{x^2}$ is $x^2(x+1)$.

Addition and Subtraction of Rational Expressions with Unlike Denominators First write each rational expression with the LCD. Then add or subtract the rational expressions.

Example: $\dfrac{2}{x+1} - \dfrac{1}{x} = \dfrac{2x}{x(x+1)} - \dfrac{x+1}{x(x+1)} = \dfrac{2x-(x+1)}{x(x+1)} = \dfrac{x-1}{x(x+1)}$

Note that the LCD is $x(x+1)$.

Section 6.4   *Rational Equations*

Solving Rational Equations   A first step in solving a rational equation is to multiply each side by the LCD of the rational expressions to clear fractions from the equation. *Be sure to check all answers.*

Example: The LCD for the equation $\frac{2}{x} + 1 = \frac{4-x}{x}$ is x.

$$\frac{2}{x} + 1 = \frac{4-x}{x} \qquad \text{Given equation}$$

$$x\left(\frac{2}{x} + 1\right) = \left(\frac{4-x}{x}\right)x \qquad \text{Multiply by } x.$$

$$2 + x = 4 - x \qquad \text{Clear fractions.}$$

$$2x = 2 \qquad \text{Add } x \text{ and subtract 2.}$$

$$x = 1 \qquad \text{Divide by 2.}$$

Section 6.5 Complex Fractions

Complex Fractions A complex fraction is a rational expression that contains fractions in its numerator, denominator, or both. The following equation can be used to simplify a complex fraction.

$$\frac{\dfrac{a}{b}}{\dfrac{c}{d}} = \frac{a}{b} \cdot \frac{d}{c}$$

Example:
$$\frac{\dfrac{1-x}{2}}{\dfrac{4}{1+x}} = \frac{1-x}{2} \cdot \frac{1+x}{4} = \frac{(1-x)(1+x)}{(2)(4)} = \frac{1-x^2}{8}$$

Simplifying Complex Fractions

Method I: Combine terms in the numerator, combine terms in the denominator, and simplify the resulting expression.

Method II: Multiply the numerator and denominator by the LCD for both and simplify the resulting expression.

Example: *Method I:*
$$\frac{2 - \dfrac{1}{b}}{2 + \dfrac{1}{b}} = \frac{\dfrac{2b-1}{b}}{\dfrac{2b+1}{b}} = \frac{2b-1}{b} \cdot \frac{b}{2b+1} = \frac{2b-1}{2b+1}$$

Method II: The LCD is b.

$$\frac{\left(2 - \dfrac{1}{b}\right)b}{\left(2 + \dfrac{1}{b}\right)b} = \frac{2b - \dfrac{b}{b}}{2b + \dfrac{b}{b}} = \frac{2b-1}{2b+1}$$

Section 6.6 Modeling with Proportions and Variation

Proportions A proportion is a statement that two ratios are equal.

Example: $\frac{5}{x} = \frac{4}{7}$ (in words, 5 is to x as 4 is to 7.)

Similar Triangles Two triangles are similar if the measures of their corresponding angles are equal. Corresponding sides of similar triangles are proportional.

Example: A right triangle has legs with lengths 3 and 4. A similar right triangle has a shorter leg with length 6. Its longer leg can be found by solving the proportion $\frac{3}{6} = \frac{4}{x}$, or $x = 8$.

Direct Variation A quantity y is *directly proportional* to a quantity x, or y *varies directly* with x, if there is a nonzero constant k such that $y = kx$. The number k is called the *constant of proportionality* or the *constant of variation*.

Example: If y varies directly with x, then the ratios $\frac{y}{x} = k$. The following data satisfy $\frac{y}{x} = 4$, so the constant of variation is 4.

x	1	2	3	4
y	4	8	12	16

Inverse Variation   A quantity y is *inversely proportional* to a quantity x, or y *varies inversely* with x, if there is a nonzero constant k such that $y = \frac{k}{x}$.

Example: If y varies inversely with x, then $xy = k$. The following data satisfy $xy = 12$, so the constant of variation is 12.

x	1	2	4	6
y	12	6	3	2

Joint Variation   The quantity z *varies jointly* as x and y if $z = kxy$, $k \neq 0$.

Example: The area A of a rectangle varies jointly, as the width W and length L because $A = LW$. Note that $k = 1$ in this example.

Section 6.7   *Division of Polynomials*

Division of a Polynomial by a Monomial   Divide the monomial into *every* term of the polynomial.

Example: $\dfrac{4x^4 - 8x^3 + 16x^2}{8x^2} = \dfrac{4x^4}{8x^2} - \dfrac{8x^3}{8x^2} + \dfrac{16x^2}{8x^2} = \dfrac{x^2}{2} - x + 2$

Division of a Polynomial by a Polynomial   Division of polynomials is similar to long division of natural numbers.

Example: Divide $2x^3 - 3x + 3$ by $x - 1$. (Be sure to include $0x^2$.)

$$
\begin{array}{r}
2x^2 + 2x - 1 \\
x - 1\overline{)2x^3 + 0x^2 - 3x + 3} \\
\underline{2x^3 - 2x^2} \\
2x^2 - 3x \\
\underline{2x^2 - 2x} \\
-x + 3 \\
\underline{-x + 1} \\
2
\end{array}
$$

The quotient is $2x^2 + 2x - 1$ with remainder 2, which can be written as

$$2x^2 + 2x - 1 + \frac{2}{x - 1}.$$

Synthetic Division   Synthetic division is a fast way to divide a polynomial by an expression in the form $x - k$, where k is a constant.

Example: Divide $3x^3 + 4x^2 - 7x - 1$ by $x + 2$.

$$\begin{array}{r|rrrr} -2 & 3 & 4 & -7 & -1 \\ & & -6 & 4 & 6 \\ \hline & 3 & -2 & -3 & 5 \end{array}$$

The quotient is $3x^2 - 2x - 3$ with remainder 5, which can be written as

$$3x^2 - 2x - 3 + \frac{5}{x + 2}.$$

CHAPTER 6 Review Exercises

SECTION 6.1

Exercises 1 and 2: Write a symbolic representation (or formula) for the rational function f described.

1. Divide 1 by the quantity x minus 1. $f(x) = \frac{1}{x-1}$

2. Subtract 3 from x and then divide the result by x. $f(x) = \frac{x-3}{x}$

3. Sketch a graph of $f(x) = \frac{1}{2x+4}$. Show any vertical asymptotes as dashed lines. State the domain of f in set-builder notation.* $\{x \mid x \neq -2\}$

4. Evaluate $f(x) = \frac{1}{x^2-1}$ at $x = 3$. Find any x-values that are not in the domain of f. $\frac{1}{8}; x = \pm 1$

Exercises 5 and 6: Use the graph to evaluate the expressions. Give the equation of any vertical asymptotes.

5. $f(0)$ and $f(2)$ 6. $f(-3)$ and $f(-2)$

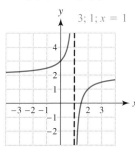
3; 1; x = 1

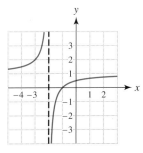
2; undefined; x = -2

Exercises 7 and 8: If possible, evaluate f(x) at the given values of x.

7. $f(x) = \frac{3}{x+2}$ $x = -3, x = 2$ $-3; 0.75$

8. $f(x) = \frac{2x}{x^2-4}$ $x = -2, x = 3$ Undefined; 1.2

Exercises 9–12: Solve the rational equation. Check your answer.

9. $\frac{3-x}{x} = 2$ 1

10. $\frac{1}{x+3} = \frac{1}{5}$ 2

11. $\frac{x}{x-2} = \frac{2x-2}{x-2}$ No solutions

12. $\frac{4}{2-3x} = -1$ 2

SECTION 6.2

Exercises 13–18: Simplify the expression.

13. $\frac{4a}{6a^4}$ $\frac{2}{3a^3}$

14. $\frac{(x-3)(x+2)}{(x+1)(x-3)}$ $\frac{x+2}{x+1}$

15. $\frac{x^2-4}{x-2}$ $x+2$

16. $\frac{x^2-6x-7}{2x^2-x-3}$ $\frac{x-7}{2x-3}$

17. $\frac{8-x}{x-8}$ -1

18. $-\frac{3-2x}{2x-3}$ 1

Exercises 19–26: Simplify the expression.

19. $\dfrac{1}{2y} \cdot \dfrac{4y^2}{8}$ $\dfrac{y}{4}$

20. $\dfrac{x+2}{x-5} \cdot \dfrac{x-5}{x+1}$ $\dfrac{x+2}{x+1}$

21. $\dfrac{x^2+1}{x^2-1} \cdot \dfrac{x-1}{x+1}$ $\dfrac{x^2+1}{(x+1)^2}$

22. $\dfrac{x^2+2x+1}{x^2-9} \cdot \dfrac{x+3}{x+1}$ $\dfrac{x+1}{x-3}$

23. $\dfrac{1}{3y} \div \dfrac{1}{9y^4}$ $3y^3$

24. $\dfrac{2x+2}{3x-3} \div \dfrac{x+1}{x-1}$ $\dfrac{2}{3}$

25. $\dfrac{x^2+2x}{x^2-25} \div \dfrac{x+2}{x+5}$ $\dfrac{x}{x-5}$

26. $\dfrac{x^2+2x-15}{x^2+4x+3} \div \dfrac{x-3}{x+1}$ $\dfrac{x+5}{x+3}$

SECTION 6.3

Exercises 27–32: Find the least common multiple.

27. $36, 24, 16$ 144

28. $4ab, a^2b$ $4a^2b$

29. $9x^2y, 6xy^3$ $18x^2y^3$

30. $(x-1), (x+2)$ $(x-1)(x+2)$

31. $x^2-9, x(x+3)$ $x(x-3)(x+3)$

32. $x^2, x-3, x^2-6x+9$ $x^2(x-3)^2$

Exercises 33–42: Simplify.

33. $\dfrac{1}{x+4}+\dfrac{3}{x+4}$ $\dfrac{4}{x+4}$

34. $\dfrac{2}{x}+\dfrac{x-3}{x^2}$ $\dfrac{3(x-1)}{x^2}$

35. $\dfrac{1}{x+1}-\dfrac{x}{(x+1)^2}$

36. $\dfrac{2x}{x^2-4}-\dfrac{2}{x-2}$ $\dfrac{-4}{(x-2)(x+2)}$

37. $\dfrac{4}{1-t}+\dfrac{t}{t-1}$ $\dfrac{t-4}{t-1}$ **35.** $\dfrac{1}{(x+1)^2}$

38. $\dfrac{2}{y-2}-\dfrac{2}{y+2}+\dfrac{y}{y^2-4}$ $\dfrac{y+8}{(y-2)(y+2)}$

39. $\dfrac{4b}{a^2c}-\dfrac{3a}{b^2c}$ $\dfrac{4b^3-3a^3}{a^2b^2c}$

40. $\dfrac{r}{5t^2}+\dfrac{t}{5r^2}$ $\dfrac{r^3+t^3}{5r^2t^2}$

41. $\dfrac{4}{a^2-b^2}-\dfrac{2}{a+b}$ $\dfrac{2(a-b-2)}{(a-b)(a+b)}$

42. $\dfrac{a}{a-b}+\dfrac{b}{a+b}$ $\dfrac{a^2+2ab-b^2}{(a-b)(a+b)}$

SECTION 6.4

Exercises 43–50: Solve the rational equation. Check your result.

43. $\dfrac{4}{x}-\dfrac{5}{2x}=\dfrac{1}{2}$ 3

44. $\dfrac{1}{x-4}=\dfrac{3}{2x-1}$ 11

45. $\dfrac{2}{x^2}-\dfrac{1}{x}=1$ $-2, 1$

46. $\dfrac{1}{x+4}-\dfrac{1}{x}=1$ -2

47. $\dfrac{1}{x^2-1}-\dfrac{1}{x-1}=\dfrac{2}{3}$ $-2, \dfrac{1}{2}$

48. $\dfrac{1}{x-3}+\dfrac{1}{x+3}=\dfrac{-5}{x^2-9}$ $-\dfrac{5}{2}$

49. $\dfrac{1}{(x-2)^2}-\dfrac{1}{x^2-4}=\dfrac{2}{(x-2)^2}$ 0

50. $\dfrac{1}{x^2+3x+2}+\dfrac{x}{x+2}=\dfrac{1}{2}$ $0, 1$

Exercises 51–52: Use the graph to solve the rational equation. Then check your answer.

51. $\dfrac{1}{x}=\dfrac{2}{x+2}$ 2 **52.** $\dfrac{3}{x-1}=\dfrac{1}{2}x$ $-2, 3$

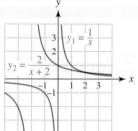

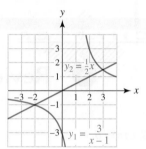

Exercises 53–56: Solve the equation for the specified variable.

53. $m=\dfrac{y_2-y_1}{x_2-x_1}; y_2$
$y_2=m(x_2-x_1)+y_1$

54. $T=\dfrac{a}{b+2}; a$
$a=T(b+2)$

55. $\dfrac{1}{f}=\dfrac{1}{p}+\dfrac{1}{q}; p$
$p=\dfrac{fq}{q-f}$

56. $I=\dfrac{2a+3b}{ab}; b$ $b=\dfrac{2a}{aI-3}$

SECTION 6.5

Exercises 57–64: Simplify the complex fraction.

57. $\dfrac{\frac{3}{5}}{\frac{10}{13}}$ $\dfrac{39}{50}$

58. $\dfrac{\frac{4}{ab}}{\frac{2}{bc}}$ $\dfrac{2c}{a}$

59. $\dfrac{\frac{2n-1}{n}}{\frac{3n}{2n+1}}$ $\dfrac{4n^2-1}{3n^2}$

60. $\dfrac{\frac{1}{x-y}}{\frac{1}{x^2-y^2}}$ $x+y$

61. $\dfrac{2+\frac{3}{x}}{2-\frac{3}{x}}$ $\dfrac{2x+3}{2x-3}$

62. $\dfrac{\frac{1}{x}+\frac{1}{2}}{\frac{1}{4}-\frac{2}{x}}$ $\dfrac{2(x+2)}{x-8}$

63. $\dfrac{\dfrac{4}{x}+\dfrac{1}{x-1}}{\dfrac{1}{x}-\dfrac{2}{x-1}}$ $\dfrac{4-5x}{x+1}$

64. $\dfrac{\dfrac{1}{x+3}-\dfrac{1}{x-3}}{\dfrac{4}{x+3}-\dfrac{2}{x-3}}$ $\dfrac{-3}{x-9}$

SECTION 6.6

Exercises 65–68: Solve the proportion.

65. $\dfrac{x}{6}=\dfrac{6}{20}$ $\dfrac{9}{5}$

66. $\dfrac{11}{x}=\dfrac{5}{7}$ $\dfrac{77}{5}$

67. $\dfrac{x+1}{5}=\dfrac{x}{3}$ $\dfrac{3}{2}$

68. $\dfrac{3}{7}=\dfrac{4}{x-1}$ $\dfrac{31}{3}$

69. If $x+1$ is to 5 as 10 is to 15, use a proportion to find the value of x. $\dfrac{7}{3}$

70. A rectangle has sides with lengths 7 and 8. Find the longer side of a similar rectangle whose shorter side has length 11. $\dfrac{88}{7}\approx 12.6$

71. Suppose that y varies directly as x. If $y=8$ when $x=2$, find y when $x=7$. $y=28$

72. Suppose that y varies inversely as x. If $y=5$ when $x=10$, find y when $x=25$. $y=2$

73. Suppose that z varies jointly with x and y. If $z=483$ when $x=23$ and $y=7$, find the constant of variation k. $k=3$

74. Suppose that z varies jointly with x and the square of y. If $z=891$ when $x=22$ and $y=3$, find z when $x=10$ and $y=4$. $z=720$

Exercises 75 and 76: Use the table to determine whether the data represent direct or inverse variation. Find an equation that models the data.

75.

x	2	4	5	8
y	100	50	40	25

Inverse; $y=\dfrac{200}{x}$

76.

x	3	7	8	11
y	9	21	24	33

Direct; $y=3x$

Exercises 77 and 78: Determine whether the graph represents direct or inverse variation. Find the constant of variation k.

77. Direct; $k=\frac{1}{2}$

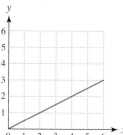

78. Inverse; $k=6$

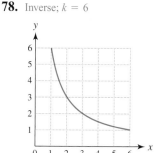

SECTION 6.7

Exercises 79–86: Divide.

79. $\dfrac{10x+15}{5}$ $2x+3$

80. $\dfrac{2x^2+x}{x}$ $2x+1$

81. $(4x^3-x^2+2x)\div(2x^2)$ $2x-\dfrac{1}{2}+\dfrac{1}{x}$

82. $(4a^3b-6ab^2)\div(2a^2b^2)$ $\dfrac{2a}{b}-\dfrac{3}{a}$

83. $\dfrac{2x^2-x-2}{x+1}$ $2x-3+\dfrac{1}{x+1}$

84. $(x^3+x-1)\div(x+1)$ $x^2-x+2-\dfrac{3}{x+1}$

85. $(6x^3-7x^2+5x-1)\div(3x-2)$ $2x^2-x+1+\dfrac{1}{3x-2}$

86. $\dfrac{2x^3-9x^2+21x-21}{x^2-2}$ $2x-9+\dfrac{25x-39}{x^2-2}$

Exercises 87 and 88: Use synthetic division to divide.

87. $\dfrac{2x^2-11x+13}{x-3}$ $2x-5-\dfrac{2}{x-3}$

88. $(3x^3+10x^2-4x+19)\div(x+4)$

$3x^2-2x+4+\dfrac{3}{x+4}$

APPLICATIONS

89. *Downhill Highway Grade*   The braking distance D in feet for a car traveling downhill at 40 miles per hour on a wet grade x is given by

$$D(x)=\dfrac{1600}{9.6-30x}.$$

(*Source:* N. Garber.)

(a) In this formula a level road is represented by $x=0$ and a 10% downhill grade is represented by $x=0.1$. Evaluate $D(0)$ and $D(0.1)$. How

$D(0)=166.\overline{6}$ ft, $D(0.1)=242.\overline{42}$ ft; about 75.8 ft

much does the downhill grade add to the braking distance compared to a level road?

(b) If the braking distance is 200 feet, estimate the downhill grade x. $x = 0.05\overline{3}$ or $5.\overline{3}\%$

90. *Time Spent in Line* Suppose that amusement park attendants can wait on 10 vehicles per minute and vehicles are arriving at the park randomly at an average rate of x vehicles per minute. Then the average time T in minutes spent waiting in line and paying the attendant is given by

$$T(x) = \frac{1}{10 - x},$$

where $x < 10$.   (*Source:* N. Garber and L. Hoel, *Traffic and Highway Engineering.*)

(a) Construct a table of T, starting at $x = 9$ and incrementing by 0.1. *

(b) What happens to the waiting time as x approaches 10? Interpret this result.
It increases; as vehicles arrive at a faster rate, the wait in line increases.

91. *Number of Cars Waiting* A car wash can clean 15 cars per hour. If cars are arriving randomly at an average rate of x per hour, the average number N of cars waiting in line is given by

$$N(x) = \frac{x^2}{225 - 15x},$$

where $x < 15$.   (*Source:* N. Garber.)

(a) Estimate the average length of a line when 14 cars per hour are arriving.   About 13 cars

(b) A graph of $y = N(x)$ is shown in the figure. Interpret the graph as x increases. Does it agree with your intuition?
As x increases, the number of cars in line increases; yes.

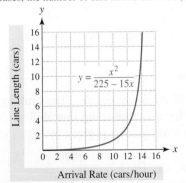

92. *Fish Population* Suppose that a fish population P in thousands found in a lake is modeled by

$$P(x) = \frac{5}{x^2 + 1},$$

where $x \geq 0$ is time in years.

(a) $P(0) = 5$; initially there were 5000 fish in the lake.

(a) Evaluate $P(0)$ and interpret the result.

(b) Graph P in [0, 6, 1] by [0, 6, 1]. *

(c) What happens to the population over this 6-year period?   It decreases.

(d) When was the population 1000?   After 2 yr

93. *Working Together* Suppose that two students are working collaboratively to solve a large number of quadratic equations. The first student can solve all the problems in 2 hours, whereas the second student can solve them in 3 hours.

(a) Write an equation whose solution gives the time needed to solve all the problems if the two students split the problems up and share answers.

(b) Solve the equation in part (a) symbolically.

(c) Solve the equation in part (a) either graphically or numerically.   (b),(c) $\frac{6}{5} = 1.2$ hr   (a) $\frac{x}{2} + \frac{x}{3} = 1$

94. *Speed of a Boat* In still water a riverboat can travel 12 miles per hour. It travels 48 miles upstream and then 48 miles downstream in a total time of 9 hours. Find the speed of the current.   4 mph

95. *Recording Music* A 650-megabyte CD can record 74 minutes of music. Estimate the number of minutes that can be recorded on 387 megabytes.   About 44 min

96. *Height of a Building* A 5-foot-tall person casts a 3-foot-long shadow, while a nearby building casts a 26-foot-long shadow, as illustrated in the accompanying figure. Find the height of the building.   About 43.3 ft

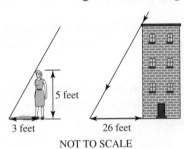

NOT TO SCALE

97. *Light Bulbs* The approximate resistances R for light bulbs of wattage W are measured and recorded in the following table.   (*Source:* D. Horn, *Basic Electronics Theory.*)

W (watts)	50	100	200	250
R (ohms)	242	121	60.5	48.4

(a) Make a scatterplot of the data. Do the data represent direct or inverse variation? *   Inverse

97.(b) $R = \dfrac{12{,}100}{W}$; $k = 12{,}100$

(b) Find an equation that models the data. What is the constant of proportionality k?

(c) Find R for a 55-watt light bulb. $R = 220$ ohms

98. *Scales*   The distance D that the spring in a produce scale stretches is directly proportional to the weight W of the fruits and vegetables placed in the pan.

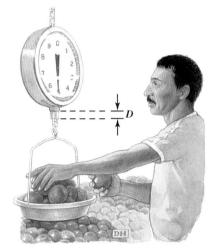

(a) If 5 pounds of apples stretch the spring 0.3 inch, find an equation that relates D and W. What is the constant of proportionality k?

(b) How far will 7 pounds of oranges stretch the spring?   0.42 in.

(a) $D = 0.06W$; $k = 0.06$

99. *Air Temperature and Altitude*   In the first 30,000 feet of Earth's atmosphere the *change* in air temperature is directly proportional to the altitude. If the temperature is $80°F$ on the ground and $62°F$ 4000 feet above the ground, find the air temperature at 6000 feet.   (**Source:** L. Battan, *Weather in Your Life.*) $53°F$

100. *Skin Cancer and UV Radiation*   Depletion of the ozone layer has caused an increase in the amount of UV radiation reaching Earth's surface. The following table shows the estimated percentage increase in skin cancer y for an x percent increase in the amount of UV radiation reaching Earth's surface.   (**Source:** R. Turner, D. Pearce, and I. Bateman, *Environmental Economics.*)

x (%)	0	1	2	3	4
y (%)	0	3.5	7	10.5	14

(a) Do these data represent direct variation, inverse variation, or neither?   Direct

(b) Find an equation that models the data in the table. $y = 3.5x$

(c) Estimate the percentage increase in skin cancer if UV radiation increases by 2.3%.   8.05%

CHAPTER

6 Test

1. Write a symbolic representation (formula) for $f(x)$ that divides x by the quantity x plus 2. $f(x) = \dfrac{x}{x + 2}$

2. Let $f(x) = \dfrac{1}{4x^2 - 1}$.

(a) Evaluate $f(-2)$. $\frac{1}{15}$

(b) Write the domain of f in set-builder notation. $\left\{ x \mid x \neq \pm\frac{1}{2} \right\}$

3. Graph $y = \dfrac{x}{x + 1}$. Show any vertical asymptotes as dashed lines.*

4. Use factoring to simplify $\dfrac{x^2 - 2x - 15}{2x^2 - x - 21}$. $\dfrac{x - 5}{2x - 7}$

Exercises 5–8: Simplify.

5. $\dfrac{x^2 + 4}{x^2 - 4} \cdot \dfrac{x - 2}{x + 2}$ $\dfrac{x^2 + 4}{(x + 2)^2}$

6. $\dfrac{1}{4y^2} \div \dfrac{1}{8y^4}$ $2y^2$

7. $\dfrac{1}{z + 4} - \dfrac{z}{(z + 4)^2}$ $\dfrac{4}{(z + 4)^2}$

8. $\dfrac{\dfrac{1}{x - 2} + \dfrac{x}{x - 2}}{\dfrac{1}{3} - \dfrac{5}{x - 2}}$ $\dfrac{3x + 3}{x - 17}$

Exercises 9 and 10: Solve the rational equation.

9. $\dfrac{t}{5t + 1} = \dfrac{2}{7}$ $-\frac{2}{3}$

10. $\dfrac{1}{x^2 - 4} - \dfrac{1}{x - 2} = \dfrac{1}{x + 2}$ $\frac{1}{2}$

11. A triangle has sides with lengths 12, 15, and 20. Find the longest side of a similar triangle with a shortest side of length 7. $\frac{35}{3}$

*Answer on page IA-22

12. Suppose that y varies directly as x. If $y = 8$ when $x = 23$, find y when $x = 10$. $\frac{80}{23}$

13. Use the table to determine whether the data represent direct or inverse variation. Find an equation that models the data.

x	2	4	5	10
y	50	25	20	10

Inverse; $y = \dfrac{100}{x}$

14. Determine whether the data represent direct or inverse variation. Find an equation that models the data.

Direct; $y = 1.5x$

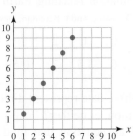

Exercises 15 and 16: Divide.

15. $\dfrac{4a^3 + 10a}{2a}$ $2a^2 + 5$ **16.** $\dfrac{3x^3 + 5x^2 - 2}{x + 2}$ $3x^2 - x + 2 - \dfrac{6}{x + 2}$

17. *Height of a Building*   A person 73 inches tall casts a shadow 50 inches long while a nearby building casts a shadow 15 feet long. Find the height of the building.   21.9 ft

18. *Time Spent in Line*   Suppose that parking lot attendants can wait on 25 vehicles per minute and vehicles are arriving at the lot randomly at an average rate of x vehicles per minute. Then the average time T in minutes spent waiting in line and paying the attendant is given by

$$T(x) = \frac{1}{25 - x},$$

where $x < 25$.   (*Source:* N. Garber and L. Hoel, *Traffic and Highway Engineering.*)

(a) Graph T in $[0, 25, 5]$ by $[0, 2, 0.5]$. Identify any vertical asymptotes. * $x = 25$

(b) If the wait is 1 minute, how many vehicles are arriving on average?   24 vehicles/min

19. *Working Together*   Suppose that one pump can empty a pool in 24 hours, and a second pump can empty the pool in 30 hours.

(a) Write an equation whose solution gives the time needed for the pumps working together to empty the pool. $\dfrac{x}{24} + \dfrac{x}{30} = 1$

(b) Solve the equation in part (a). $\dfrac{40}{3} \approx 13.3$ hr

20. *Dew Point and Altitude*   In the first 30,000 feet of Earth's atmosphere the change in the dew point is directly proportional to the altitude. If the dew point is $50°F$ on the ground and $39°F$ 10,000 feet above the ground, find the dew point at 7500 feet.   (*Source:* L. Battan, *Weather in Your Life.*) $41.75°F$

CHAPTER

6 Extended and Discovery Exercises

RATIONAL APPROXIMATIONS

1. Rational expressions are used to approximate other types of expressions in computer software. Graph each expression on the left for $1 \le x \le 15$ and try to match it with the graph of the rational expression on the right that approximates it best.

(a) $\sqrt{x}$ iii

(b) $\sqrt{4x + 1}$ ii

i. $\dfrac{2 - 2x^2}{3x^2 + 10x + 3}$

ii. $\dfrac{15x^2 + 75x + 33}{x^2 + 23x + 31}$

(c) $\sqrt[3]{x}$ iv

(d) $\dfrac{1 - \sqrt{x}}{1 + \sqrt{x}}$ i

iii. $\dfrac{10x^2 + 80x + 32}{x^2 + 40x + 80}$

iv. $\dfrac{7x^3 + 42x^2 + 30x + 2}{2x^3 + 30x^2 + 42x + 7}$

OTHER TYPES OF DIRECT VARIATION

Exercises 2–6: Sometimes a quantity y varies directly as a power of x. For example, the area A of a circle varies directly as the second power of the radius r, since $A = \pi r^2$ and π is a constant. Let x and y denote two quantities and

*Answer on page IA-22

n be a positive number. Then y is directly proportional to the nth power of x, or y varies directly as the nth power of x, if there exists a nonzero number k such that

$$y = kx^n.$$

2. Let y be directly proportional to the second power of x. If x doubles, what happens to y?   It quadruples.

3. Let y be directly proportional to the $\frac{1}{2}$ power of x. If x quadruples, what happens to y?   It doubles.

4. *Modeling a Pendulum*   The time T required for a pendulum to swing back and forth once is called its period. See the accompanying figure. The length L of a pendulum is directly proportional to the nth power of T for some positive integer n. The accompanying table lists the period T for various lengths L.

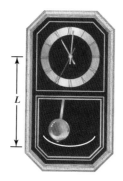

T (seconds)	1.11	1.36	1.57	1.76
L (feet)	1.0	1.5	2.0	2.5

T (seconds)	1.92	2.08	2.22
L (feet)	3.0	3.5	4.0

(a) Find the constant of proportionality k and the value of n. (*Hint:* If $L = kT^n$ for constants k and n, the ratio $\frac{L}{T^n} = k$.) $k \approx 0.811, n = 2$

(b) Predict T for a pendulum having a length of 2.2 feet.   About 1.65 sec

5. *Allometric Growth*   If x is the weight of a fiddler crab and y is the weight of its claws, then y is directly proportional to the 1.25 power of x; that is, $y = kx^{1.25}$. Suppose that a typical crab with a body weight of 2.1 grams has claws weighing 1.125 grams.

(*Source:* D. Brown and P. Rothery, *Models in Biology: Mathematics, Statistics, and Computing.*)

(a) Find the constant of proportionality k. Round your answer to the nearest thousandth. $k \approx 0.445$

(b) Estimate the weight of a fiddler crab with claws weighing 0.8 gram.   About 1.60 g

6. *Volume*   The volume V of a cylinder is directly proportional to the square of its radius r. If a cylinder with a radius of 5 inches has a volume of 150 cubic inches, what is the volume of a cylinder with the same height and a radius of 7 inches?   294 in^3.

OTHER TYPES OF INVERSE VARIATION

Exercises 7–10: Sometimes a quantity varies inversely to a power of x. Let x and y denote two quantities and n be a positive number. Then y is inversely proportional to the nth power of x, or y varies inversely as the nth power of x, if there exists a nonzero number k such that

$$y = \frac{k}{x^n}.$$

7. Let y be inversely proportional to the second power of x. If x doubles, what happens to y?   It is reduced to $\frac{1}{4}$ of its value.

8. Let y be inversely proportional to the third power of x. If x doubles, what happens to y?   It is reduced to $\frac{1}{8}$ of its value.

9. *Earth's Gravity*   The weight W of an object can be modeled by $W = \frac{k}{d^2}$, where d is the distance that the object is from Earth's center and k is a constant. Earth's radius is about 4000 miles.

(a) Find k for a person who weighs 200 pounds on Earth's surface. $k = 3.2 \times 10^9$

(b) Graph W in a convenient viewing rectangle. At what distance from Earth's center is this person's weight 50 pounds?*   8000 mi

(c) How far from the center of Earth would an object be if its weight were 1% of its weight on the surface of Earth?   40,000 mi

10. *Modeling Brightness*   Inverse variation occurs when the intensity of a light is measured. If you increase your distance from a light bulb, the intensity of the light decreases. Intensity I is inversely proportional to the second power of the distance d. The equation $I = \frac{k}{d^2}$ models this phenomenon. The following table gives the intensity of a 100-watt light bulb at various distances. (*Source:* R. Weidner and R. Sells, *Elementary Classical Physics, Vol. 2.*)

d (meters)	0.5	2	3	4
I (watts/square meter)	31.68	1.98	0.88	0.495

(a) Find the constant of proportionality k. $k = 7.92$

(b) Graph I in $[0, 5, 1]$ by $[0, 30, 5]$. What happens to the intensity as the distances increase?*   It decreases.

(c) If the distance from the light bulb doubles, what happens to the intensity?   It is reduced to $\frac{1}{4}$ of its value.

(d) Determine d when $I = 1$ watt per square meter.   About 2.81 m

*Answers on page IA-22

CHAPTERS

1-6   Cumulative Review Exercises

3. Natural: 1; whole: 0, 1; integer: $-\frac{12}{4}$, 0, 1; rational: $-\frac{12}{4}$, 0, 1, 2.$\overline{11}$, $\frac{13}{2}$; irrational: $\sqrt{3}$

Exercises 1 and 2: Evaluate the formula for the given value of the variable.

1. $y = \sqrt{74 + t}$ $t = 7$ 9

2. $r = 16 - w^2$ $w = -4$ 0

3. Classify each real number as one or more of the following: natural number, whole number, integer, rational number, or irrational number.

$$-\frac{12}{4}, 0, \sqrt{3}, 1, 2.\overline{11}, \frac{13}{2}$$

4. Select the formula that best models the data.
   (i) $y = 2x - 5$ **(ii)** $y = x - 7$ **(iii)** $y = 2x + 3$

   (i)

x	-2	-1	0	1	2
y	-9	-7	-5	-3	-1

Exercises 5 and 6: Simplify the expression. Write the result using positive exponents.

5. $\dfrac{18x^{-2}y^3}{3x^2y^{-3}}$ $\dfrac{6y^6}{x^4}$

6. $\left(\dfrac{2c^2}{3d^3}\right)^{-2}$ $\dfrac{9d^6}{4c^4}$

7. Write 67,300,000,000 in scientific notation. 6.73×10^{10}

8. Identify the domain and range of the relation $S = \{(-3, 5), (0, 1), (-1, -2), (4, 0)\}$. $D = \{-3, -1, 0, 4\}$ $R = \{-2, 0, 1, 5\}$

Exercises 9 and 10: Evaluate the given formula for $x = -2, -1, 0, 1$ and 2. Plot the resulting ordered pairs. *

$(-2, -7), (-1, -4), (0, -1), (1, 2), (2, 5)$

9. $y = 3x - 1$

10. $y = \dfrac{4 - x^2}{2}$ $(-2, 0), (-1, \frac{3}{2}),$ $(0, 2), (1, \frac{3}{2}), (2, 0)$

11. Sketch the graph of $f(x) = x^2 + 2$ by hand.*

12. Find the domain of $f(x) = \dfrac{5}{x - 1}$. $\{x \mid x \neq 1\}$

13. Use the table to write the formula for $f(x) = ax + b$.

x	-2	-1	0	1	2
$f(x)$	-5	-3	-1	1	3

$f(x) = 2x - 1$

14. Sketch a graph of $f(x) = -2$.*

15. Find the slope and the y-intercept of the graph of $f(x) = -3x + 2$. $-3; 2$

16. Calculate the slope of the line passing through the points $(6, -3)$ and $(2, 9)$. -3

17. Sketch the graph of a line passing through the point $(3, -1)$ with slope $m = -2$.*

18. Use the graph to express the equation of the line in slope–intercept form. $y = -\frac{1}{2}x + 2$

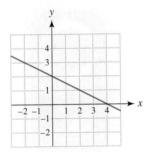

Exercises 19 and 20: Write the slope–intercept form for a line satisfying the given conditions.

19. Parallel to $y = 2x + 3$, passing through $(1, 4)$
    $y = 2x + 2$

20. Perpendicular to $y = \frac{2}{3}x - 2$, passing through $(2, 1)$
    $y = -\frac{3}{2}x + 4$

Exercises 21 and 22: Solve the equation.

21. $\dfrac{2}{5}(x + 1) - 6 = -4$ 4

22. $\dfrac{1}{4}\left(\dfrac{t - 5}{3}\right) - 6 = \dfrac{2}{3}t - (3t + 7)$ $-\dfrac{7}{29}$

23. Use the graph to solve the equation $y_1 = y_2$.   3

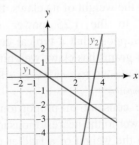

Exercises 24 and 25: Solve the inequality symbolically. Write the solution set in interval notation.

24. $\dfrac{2x + 3}{4} \le \dfrac{1}{3}$ $\left(-\infty, -\frac{5}{6}\right]$

25. $\dfrac{1}{2}z - 5 > \dfrac{3}{4}z - (2z + 5)$ $(0, \infty)$

Exercises 26 and 27: Solve the compound inequality. Graph the solution set on a number line.*

26. $-6 \le -\dfrac{2}{3}x - 4 < -2$ $(-3, 3]$

27. $3x - 1 \le 5$ or $2x + 5 > 13$ $(-\infty, 2] \cup (4, \infty)$

28. Solve the absolute value equation $\left|\frac{1}{3}x + 6\right| = 4$.
$-30, -6$

Exercises 29 and 30: Solve the absolute value inequality. Write the solution set in interval notation.

29. $\left|2x - 3\right| < 11$ **30.** $-3\left|t - 5\right| \le -18$
$(-4, 7)$ $(-\infty, -1] \cup [11, \infty)$

31. Determine which pair is a solution to the system of equations.
$(2, -6), (-8, -1)$ $(-8, -1)$
$$x + 2y = -10$$
$$3x - 10y = -14$$

32. Shade the solution set in the xy-plane.*
$$x + y < 4$$
$$x - 2y \ge 1$$

Exercises 33 and 34: Solve the system of equations.

33. $2x - 8y = 5$ **34.** $2x - 3y = 12$
  $4x + 2y = 1$ $\left(\frac{1}{2}, -\frac{1}{2}\right)$ $-x + 2y = -6$ $(6, 0)$

35. Maximize the objective function R subject to the given constraints.
$$R = 2x + 3y$$
$$2x + y \le 6$$
$$x + 2y \le 6$$
$$x \ge 0, y \ge 0 \quad R = 10$$

36. Use elimination and substitution to solve the system of linear equations.
$$2x + 3y - z = 3$$
$$3x - y + 4z = 10$$
$$2x + y - 2z = -1 \quad (1, 1, 2)$$

37. Write the system of linear equations as an augmented matrix. Then use Gaussian elimination to solve the system. Write the solution as an ordered triple.
$$\begin{array}{rcl} x + y - z &=& 4 \\ -x - y - z &=& 0 \\ x - 2y + z &=& -9 \end{array} \quad \left[\begin{array}{rrr|r} 1 & 1 & -1 & 4 \\ -1 & -1 & -1 & 0 \\ 1 & -2 & 1 & -9 \end{array}\right]; (-1, 3, -2)$$

38. Evaluate $\det A$.
$$A = \begin{bmatrix} 4 & -2 \\ 1 & 3 \end{bmatrix} \quad 14$$

39. Find the area of the triangle by using a determinant. Assume that the units are inches. 8 in^2

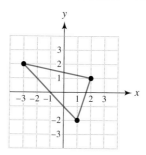

40. Use Cramer's rule to solve the system of equations.
$$6x + 7y = 8$$
$$-8x + 5y = 18 \quad (-1, 2)$$

Exercises 41 and 42: Multiply the expressions.

41. $3x^2(x^3 + 5x - 2)$ **42.** $(2x - 5)(x + 3)$
$3x^5 + 15x^3 - 6x^2$ $2x^2 + x - 15$

43. Use factoring to solve the polynomial equation.
$6x + 3x^2 = 0$ $-2, 0$

44. Use grouping to factor the polynomial.
$3a^3 - a^2 + 15a - 5$ $(3a - 1)(a^2 + 5)$

Exercises 45–48: Factor completely.

45. $4x^2 + 5x - 6$ **46.** $6x^3 - 9x^2 - 6x$
$(4x - 3)(x + 2)$ $3x(x - 2)(2x + 1)$

47. $9a^2 - 4b^2$ **48.** $64t^3 + 27$
$(3a - 2b)(3a + 2b)$ $(4t + 3)(16t^2 - 12t + 9)$

Exercises 49 and 50: Solve the equation.

49. $3x^2 - 11x = 4$ **50.** $x^4 - x^3 - 30x^2 = 0$
$-\frac{1}{3}, 4$ $-5, 0, 6$

Exercises 51–54: Simplify the expressions.

51. $\dfrac{x^2 + 3x - 10}{x^2 - 4} \cdot \dfrac{x - 2}{x + 5}$ $\frac{x - 2}{x + 2}$

52. $\dfrac{x^2 + 2x - 24}{x^2 + 3x - 18} \div \dfrac{x + 3}{x^2 - 9}$ $x - 4$

53. $\dfrac{2}{t + 2} - \dfrac{t}{t^2 - 4}$ **54.** $\dfrac{4a}{3ab^2} + \dfrac{b}{a^2c}$ $\dfrac{4a^2c + 3b^3}{3a^2b^2c}$

$\dfrac{t - 4}{t^2 - 4}$

Exercises 55 and 56: Solve the rational equation. Check your result.

55. $\dfrac{1}{x + 4} + \dfrac{1}{x - 4} = \dfrac{-7}{x^2 - 16}$ $-\dfrac{7}{2}$

56. $\dfrac{1}{y^2 + 3y - 4} - \dfrac{y}{y - 1} = -1$ -3

57. Solve the equation for z.
$$J = \dfrac{y + z}{z}$$ $z = \dfrac{y}{J - 1}$

58. Simplify the complex fraction.
$$\dfrac{\dfrac{4}{x^2} + \dfrac{1}{x}}{\dfrac{4}{x^2} - \dfrac{1}{x}}$$ $\dfrac{4 + x}{4 - x}$

59. Suppose that y varies inversely as x. If $y = 2$ when $x = 4$, find y when x is 16. $\dfrac{1}{2}$

60. Divide.
$$(x^3 + 2x + 11) \div (x + 2)$$ $x^2 - 2x + 6 - \dfrac{1}{x + 2}$

APPLICATIONS

61. *Temperature Scales* The table shows equivalent temperatures in degrees Fahrenheit and degrees Celsius.

°F	−40	32	59	95	212
°C	−40	0	15	35	100

  (a) Plot the data. Let the x-axis correspond to the Fahrenheit temperature and the y-axis correspond to the Celsius temperature. What type of relation exists between the data?* Linear
  (b) Find $f(x) = m(x - h) + k$ so that f receives the Fahrenheit temperature as input and outputs the corresponding Celsius temperature. $f(x) = \frac{5}{9}(x - 32)$

  (c) If the temperature is 104° F, what is the equivalent temperature in degrees Celsius? 40° C

62. *Geometry* An isosceles triangle has two shorter sides of the same length and a longer side that is 7 inches longer than half of the length of either of the shorter sides. If the perimeter of the triangle is 22 inches, what are the lengths of the three sides? 6, 6, and 10 in.

63. *Burning Calories* During strenuous exercise, an athlete burns 690 calories per hour on a stair climber and 540 calories per hour on a stationary bicycle. During a 90-minute workout the athlete burns 885 calories. How much time (in hours) was spent on each type of exercise equipment? (*Source: Runner's World.*)
Stair climber: $\frac{1}{2}$ hr; stationary bicycle: 1 hr

64. *Tickets* The price of admission to a county fair is $2 for children and $5 for adults. If a group of 30 people pays $78 to enter the fairgrounds, find the number of children and the number of adults in the group.
24 children, 6 adults

65. *Area of a Rectangle* A rectangle has an area of 165 square feet. Its length is 4 feet more than its width. Find the dimensions of the rectangle. 11 ft by 15 ft

66. *Flight of a Ball* If a ball is thrown upward with a velocity of 44 feet per second (30 miles per hour), its height h in feet above the ground can be modeled by
$$h(t) = -16t^2 + 44t,$$
where t is in seconds. (a) After 2.75 sec
  (a) Determine when the ball strikes the ground.
  (b) When did the ball reach a height of 18 feet?
  After 0.5 and 2.25 sec

67. *Working Together* An amateur painter can paint a room in 15 hours. A professional painter can paint the same room in 10 hours.
  (a) Write an equation whose solution gives the time needed to paint the room if the two painters work together. $\dfrac{x}{15} + \dfrac{x}{10} = 1$
  (b) Solve the equation in part (a). 6 hr

68. *Height of a Tree* A 6-foot-tall person casts a 4-foot-long shadow while a nearby tree casts a 32-foot-long shadow. Find the height of the tree. 48 ft

CHAPTER

7

Radical Expressions and Functions

Throughout history, people have created new numbers. Often these new numbers were met with resistance and regarded as being imaginary or unreal. The number 0 was not invented at the same time as the natural numbers. There was no Roman numeral for 0, which is one reason why our calendar started with A.D. 1 and, as a result, the twenty-first century began in 2001. No doubt there were skeptics during the time of the Roman Empire who questioned why anyone needed a number to represent nothing. Negative numbers also met strong resistance. After all, how could anyone possibly have −6 apples?

In this chapter we describe a new number system called *complex numbers*, which involve square roots of negative numbers. The Italian mathematician Cardano (1501–1576) was one of the first mathematicians to work with complex numbers and called them useless. René Descartes (1596–1650) originated the term *imaginary number*, which is associated with complex numbers. However, today complex numbers are used in many applications, such as electricity, fiber optics, and the design of airplanes. We are privileged to study in a period of days what took people centuries to discover.

> Bear in mind that the wonderful things
> you learn in schools are the work of many
> generations, produced by enthusiastic effort
> and infinite labor in every country.
> —Albert Einstein

Source: *Historical Topics for the Mathematics Classroom, Thirty-first Yearbook*, NCTM.

TEACHING TIP

Students often do not see any reason to learn complex numbers. This introduction will help students understand that they are like any other set of numbers and that they are used frequently to solve equations.

461

7.1 RADICAL EXPRESSIONS AND RATIONAL EXPONENTS

Radical Notation · Rational Exponents · Properties of Rational Exponents

INTRODUCTION

Cellular phone technology has become a part of everyday life. In order to have cellular phone coverage, transmission towers, or cellular sites, are spread throughout a region. To estimate the minimum broadcasting distance for each cellular site, radical expressions are needed. (See Example 3.) In this section we discuss radical expressions and rational exponents and show how to manipulate them symbolically.   (*Source:* C. Smith, *Practical Cellular & PCS Design.*)

RADICAL NOTATION

Recall the definition of the square root of a number a.

SQUARE ROOT
The number b is a *square root* of a if $b^2 = a$.

EXAMPLE 1   Finding square roots

Find the square roots of 100.

Solution   The square roots of 100 are 10 *and* -10 because $10^2 = 100$ and $(-10)^2 = 100$.

Every positive number a has two square roots, one positive and one negative. Recall that the *positive* square root is called the *principal square root* and is denoted $\sqrt{a}$. The *negative* square root is denoted $-\sqrt{a}$. To identify both square roots we write $\pm\sqrt{a}$. The symbol $\pm$ is read "plus or minus." The symbol $\sqrt{}$ is called the **radical sign**. The expression under the radical sign is called the **radicand**, and an expression containing a radical sign is called a **radical expression**. Examples of radical expressions include

$$\sqrt{6}, \quad 5 + \sqrt{x + 1}, \quad \text{and} \quad \sqrt{\frac{3x}{2x - 1}}.$$

In the next example we show how to find the principal square root of an expression.

EXAMPLE 2   Finding principal square roots

Find the principal square root of each expression.
(a) 25   **(b)** 17   **(c)** 0.49   **(d)** $\frac{4}{9}$ **(e)** $c^2, c > 0$

Solution   **(a)** Because $5 \cdot 5 = 25$, the principal, or positive, square root of 25 is $\sqrt{25} = 5$.
(b) The principal square root of 17 is $\sqrt{17}$. This value is not an integer, but we can approximate it. Figure 7.1 shows that $\sqrt{17} \approx 4.12$, rounded to the nearest hundredth.

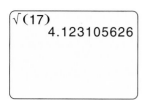

Figure 7.1

Note that calculators do not give exact answers when approximating many radical expressions; they give decimal approximations.

(c) Because $(0.7)(0.7) = 0.49$, the principal square root of 0.49 is $\sqrt{0.49} = 0.7$.

(d) Because $\frac{2}{3} \cdot \frac{2}{3} = \frac{4}{9}$, the principal square root of $\frac{4}{9}$ is $\sqrt{\frac{4}{9}} = \frac{2}{3}$.

(e) The principal square root of c^2 is $\sqrt{c^2} = c$, as c is positive.

In the next example we use the principal square root to estimate the minimum transmission distance for a cellular site.

EXAMPLE 3   Estimating cellular phone transmission distance

If the ground is level, a cellular transmission tower will broadcast its signal in roughly a circular pattern, whose radius can be altered by changing the strength of its signal. See Figure 7.2. Suppose that a city has an area of 50 square miles and that there are 10 identical transmission towers spread evenly throughout the city. Estimate a *minimum* transmission radius R for each tower. (Note that a larger distance would probably be necessary to adequately cover the city.)   (*Source:* C. Smith.)

Solution   The circular area A covered by one transmission tower is $A = \pi R^2$. The total area covered by 10 towers is $10\pi R^2$, which must equal *at least* 50 square miles.

Figure 7.2

$$10\pi R^2 = 50$$
$$\pi R^2 = 5 \qquad \text{Divide by 10.}$$
$$R^2 = \frac{5}{\pi} \qquad \text{Divide by } \pi.$$
$$R = \sqrt{\frac{5}{\pi}} \approx 1.26 \qquad \text{Take principal square root.}$$

Each transmission tower must broadcast with a minimum radius of approximately 1.26 miles.

Another common radical expression is the cube root of a number a, denoted $\sqrt[3]{a}$.

CUBE ROOT

The number b is a *cube root* of a if $b^3 = a$.

Although the square root of a negative number is not a real number, the cube root of a negative number is a negative real number. *Every real number has one real cube root.*

We demonstrate how to find cube roots in the next example.

EXAMPLE 4   Finding cube roots

Find the cube root of each expression.
(a) 8 (b) -27 (c) 16 (d) $\frac{1}{64}$ (e) d^6

Solution   **(a)** $\sqrt[3]{8} = 2$ because $2^3 = 2 \cdot 2 \cdot 2 = 8$.

(b) $\sqrt[3]{-27} = -3$ because $(-3)^3 = (-3)(-3)(-3) = -27$.

(c) $\sqrt[3]{16}$ is not an integer. Figure 7.3 shows that $\sqrt[3]{16} \approx 2.52$.

(d) $\sqrt[3]{\frac{1}{64}} = \frac{1}{4}$ because $\left(\frac{1}{4}\right)^3 = \frac{1}{4} \cdot \frac{1}{4} \cdot \frac{1}{4} = \frac{1}{64}$.

(e) $\sqrt[3]{d^6} = d^2$ because $(d^2)^3 = d^2 \cdot d^2 \cdot d^2 = d^{2+2+2} = d^6$.

$\sqrt[3]{(16)}$
            2.5198421

Figure 7.3

Calculator Help
To calculate a cube root, see
the Appendix (page AP-1).

We can generalize square roots and cube roots to include the *n*th root of a number *a*. The number *b* is an ***n*th root** of *a* if $b^n = a$, where *n* is a positive integer, and the principal *n*th root is denoted $\sqrt[n]{a}$. The number *n* is called the **index**. For the square root the index is 2, although we usually write $\sqrt{a}$ rather than $\sqrt[2]{a}$. When *n* is odd, we are finding an **odd root**, and when *n* is even, we are finding an **even root**. The square root $\sqrt{a}$ is an example of an even root, and the cube root $\sqrt[3]{a}$ is an example of an odd root.

Note: An odd root of a negative number is a negative number, but the even root of a negative number is *not* a real number.

We find *n*th roots in the next example.

EXAMPLE 5   Finding nth roots

Find each root, if possible.

(a) $\sqrt[4]{16}$ **(b)** $\sqrt[5]{-32}$ **(c)** $\sqrt[4]{-81}$

Solution   **(a)** $\sqrt[4]{16} = 2$ because $2^4 = 2 \cdot 2 \cdot 2 \cdot 2 = 16$.

TEACHING TIP

Emphasize that odd roots are defined for negative numbers but that
the even roots are not defined for
negative numbers unless complex
numbers are allowed.

(b) $\sqrt[5]{-32} = -2$ because $(-2)^5 = (-2)(-2)(-2)(-2)(-2) = -32$.

(c) The even root of a negative number is not a real number.

Consider the calculations

$$\sqrt{3^2} = \sqrt{9} = 3, \quad \sqrt{(-4)^2} = \sqrt{16} = 4, \quad \text{and} \quad \sqrt{(-6)^2} = \sqrt{36} = 6.$$

In general, the expression $\sqrt{x^2}$ equals $|x|$. Graphical support is shown in Figure 7.4, where the graphs of $Y_1 = \sqrt{(X^2)}$ and $Y_2 = abs(X)$ appear to be identical.

$[-6, 6, 1]$ by $[-4, 4, 1]$ $[-6, 6, 1]$ by $[-4, 4, 1]$

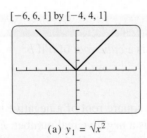
(a) $y_1 = \sqrt{x^2}$

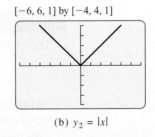
(b) $y_2 = |x|$

Figure 7.4

THE EXPRESSION $\sqrt{x^2}$

For every real number *x*, $\sqrt{x^2} = |x|$.

EXAMPLE 6 Simplifying expressions

Write each expression in terms of an absolute value.

(a) $\sqrt{(-3)^2}$ **(b)** $\sqrt{(x+1)^2}$ **(c)** $\sqrt{z^2-4z+4}$

Solution **(a)** $\sqrt{x^2}=|x|$, so $\sqrt{(-3)^2}=|-3|=3$

(b) $\sqrt{(x+1)^2}=|x+1|$

(c) $\sqrt{z^2-4z+4}=\sqrt{(z-2)^2}=|z-2|$

RATIONAL EXPONENTS

When m and n are integers, the product rule states that $a^m a^n = a^{m+n}$. This rule can be extended to include exponents that are fractions. For example,

$$4^{1/2} \cdot 4^{1/2} = 4^{1/2+1/2} = 4^1 = 4.$$

That is, if we multiply $4^{1/2}$ by itself, the result is 4. Because we also know that $\sqrt{4} \cdot \sqrt{4} = 4$, this discussion suggests that $4^{1/2} = \sqrt{4}$ and motivates the following definition.

THE EXPRESSION $a^{1/n}$

If n is an integer greater than 1, then

$$a^{1/n} = \sqrt[n]{a}.$$

Note: If $a < 0$ and n is an even positive integer, then $a^{1/n}$ is not a real number.

In the next two examples, we show how to interpret rational exponents.

EXAMPLE 7 Interpreting rational exponents

Write each expression in radical notation. Then evaluate the expression to the nearest hundredth when appropriate.

(a) $36^{1/2}$ **(b)** $23^{1/5}$ **(c)** $x^{1/3}$ **(d)** $(5x)^{1/2}$

Solution **(a)** The exponent $\frac{1}{2}$ indicates a square root. Thus $36^{1/2} = \sqrt{36}$, which evaluates to 6.

```
23^(1/5)
       1.872171231
5ˣ√(23)
       1.872171231
```

Figure 7.5

(b) The exponent $\frac{1}{5}$ indicates a fifth root. Thus $23^{1/5} = \sqrt[5]{23}$, which is not an integer. Figure 7.5 shows this expression approximated in both exponential and radical notation. In either case $23^{1/5} \approx 1.87$.

(c) The exponent $\frac{1}{3}$ indicates a cube root, so $x^{1/3} = \sqrt[3]{x}$.

(d) The exponent $\frac{1}{2}$ indicates a square root, so $(5x)^{1/2} = \sqrt{5x}$.

Calculator Help
To calculate other roots, see the Appendix (page AP-1).

Suppose that we want to define the expression $8^{2/3}$. On the one hand, using properties of exponents we have

$$8^{1/3} \cdot 8^{1/3} = 8^{1/3+1/3} = 8^{2/3}.$$

On the other hand, we have

$$8^{1/3} \cdot 8^{1/3} = \sqrt[3]{8} \cdot \sqrt[3]{8} = 2 \cdot 2 = 4.$$

Thus $8^{2/3} = 4$, and that value is obtained whether we interpret $8^{2/3}$ as either

$$8^{2/3} = (8^{1/3})^2 = (\sqrt[3]{8})^2 = 2^2 = 4$$

or

$$8^{2/3} = (8^2)^{1/3} = \sqrt[3]{8^2} = \sqrt[3]{64} = 4.$$

This result suggests the following definition.

THE EXPRESSION $a^{m/n}$

If m and n are positive integers with $\frac{m}{n}$ in lowest terms, then

$$a^{m/n} = \sqrt[n]{a^m} = (\sqrt[n]{a})^m.$$

Note: If $a < 0$ and n is an even integer, then $a^{m/n}$ is not a real number.

EXAMPLE 8   Interpreting rational exponents

Write each expression in radical notation. Then evaluate the expression when the result is an integer.

(a) $(-27)^{2/3}$ **(b)** $12^{3/5}$

Solution   **(a)** The exponent $\frac{2}{3}$ indicates that we either take the cube root of -27 and then square it or that we square -27 and then take the cube root. In either case the result will be the same. Thus

$$(-27)^{2/3} = (\sqrt[3]{-27})^2 = (-3)^2 = 9$$

or

$$(-27)^{2/3} = \sqrt[3]{(-27)^2} = \sqrt[3]{729} = 9.$$

(b) The exponent $\frac{3}{5}$ indicates that we either take the fifth root of 12 and then cube it or that we cube 12 and then take the fifth root. Thus

$$12^{3/5} = (\sqrt[5]{12})^3 \quad \text{or} \quad 12^{3/5} = \sqrt[5]{12^3}.$$

This result is not an integer.

Technology Note: *Rational Exponents*

When evaluating expressions with rational (fractional) exponents, be sure to put parentheses around the fraction. For example, most calculators will evaluate 8^(2/3) and 8^2/3 differently. The accompanying figure shows evaluation of $8^{2/3}$ input correctly, 8^(2/3), as 4 but shows evaluation of $8^{2/3}$ input incorrectly, 8^2/3, as $\frac{8^2}{3} = 21.\overline{3}$.

Correct →   8^(2/3)
                                    4
Incorrect →   8^2/3
                          21.33333333

From properties of exponents we know that $a^{-n} = \frac{1}{a^n}$, where n is a positive integer. We now define this property for negative rational exponents.

THE EXPRESSION $a^{-m/n}$

If m and n are positive integers with $\frac{m}{n}$ in lowest terms, then

$$a^{-m/n} = \frac{1}{a^{m/n}}, \qquad a \neq 0.$$

EXAMPLE 9   Interpreting negative rational exponents

Write each expression in radical notation and then evaluate.

  (a) $(64)^{-1/3}$ **(b)** $(81)^{-3/4}$

Solution   **(a)** $(64)^{-1/3} = \dfrac{1}{64^{1/3}} = \dfrac{1}{\sqrt[3]{64}} = \dfrac{1}{4}.$

           (b) $(81)^{-3/4} = \dfrac{1}{81^{3/4}} = \dfrac{1}{(\sqrt[4]{81})^3} = \dfrac{1}{3^3} = \dfrac{1}{27}.$

PROPERTIES OF RATIONAL EXPONENTS

Any rational number can be written as a ratio of two integers. That is, if p is a rational number, then $p = \frac{m}{n}$, where m and n are integers. Properties for integer exponents also apply to rational exponents—with one exception. If n is even in the expression $a^{m/n}$ and $\frac{m}{n}$ is written in lowest terms, then a must be nonnegative (not negative) for the result to be a real number.

PROPERTIES OF EXPONENTS

Let p and q be rational numbers written in lowest terms. For all real numbers a and b for which the expressions are real numbers the following properties hold.

1. $a^p \cdot a^q = a^{p+q}$ Product rule for exponents

2. $a^{-p} = \dfrac{1}{a^p}, \quad \dfrac{1}{a^{-p}} = a^p$ Negative exponents

3. $\left(\dfrac{a}{b}\right)^{-p} = \left(\dfrac{b}{a}\right)^p$ Negative exponents for quotients

4. $\dfrac{a^p}{a^q} = a^{p-q}$ Quotient rule for exponents

5. $(a^p)^q = a^{pq}$ Power rule for exponents

6. $(ab)^p = a^p b^p$ Power rule for products

7. $\left(\dfrac{a}{b}\right)^p = \dfrac{a^p}{b^p}$ Power rule for quotients

---

In the next two examples, we apply these properties.

EXAMPLE 10 Applying properties of exponents

Write each expression using rational exponents and simplify. Write the answer with a positive exponent. Assume that all variables are positive numbers.

(a) $\sqrt{x} \cdot \sqrt[3]{x}$ **(b)** $\sqrt[3]{27x^2}$ **(c)** $\dfrac{\sqrt[4]{16x}}{\sqrt[3]{x}}$ **(d)** $\left(\dfrac{x^2}{81}\right)^{-1/2}$

Solution **(a)** $\sqrt{x} \cdot \sqrt[3]{x} = x^{1/2} \cdot x^{1/3}$ Use rational exponents.

$$= x^{1/2+1/3}$$ Product rule for exponents

$$= x^{5/6}$$ Simplify.

(b) $\sqrt[3]{27x^2} = (27x^2)^{1/3}$ Use rational exponents.

$$= 27^{1/3}(x^2)^{1/3}$$ Power rule for products

$$= 3x^{2/3}$$ Power rule for exponents

(c) $\dfrac{\sqrt[4]{16x}}{\sqrt[3]{x}} = \dfrac{(16x)^{1/4}}{x^{1/3}}$ Use rational exponents.

$$= \dfrac{16^{1/4}x^{1/4}}{x^{1/3}}$$ Power rule for products

$$= 16^{1/4}x^{1/4-1/3}$$ Quotient rule for exponents

$$= 2x^{-1/12}$$ Simplify.

$$= \dfrac{2}{x^{1/12}}$$ Negative exponents

(d) $\left(\dfrac{x^2}{81}\right)^{-1/2} = \left(\dfrac{81}{x^2}\right)^{1/2}$ Negative exponents for quotients

$$= \dfrac{(81)^{1/2}}{(x^2)^{1/2}}$$ Power rule for quotients

$$= \dfrac{9}{x}$$ Power rule for exponents; simplify.

EXAMPLE 11 Applying properties of exponents

Write each expression with positive rational exponents and simplify, if possible.

(a) $\sqrt[3]{4} \cdot \sqrt[6]{4}$ **(b)** $\sqrt[3]{\sqrt{x+1}}$ **(c)** $\sqrt[5]{c^{15}}$ **(d)** $\dfrac{y^{-1/2}}{x^{-1/3}}$ **(e)** $\sqrt{x}(\sqrt{x}-1)$

Solution **(a)** $\sqrt[3]{4} \cdot \sqrt[6]{4} = 4^{1/3} \cdot 4^{1/6} = 4^{1/3+1/6} = 4^{1/2} = \sqrt{4} = 2$

(b) $\sqrt[3]{\sqrt{x+1}} = \left((x+1)^{1/2}\right)^{1/3} = (x+1)^{1/6}$

(c) $\sqrt[5]{c^{15}} = (c^{15})^{1/5} = c^{15/5} = c^3$

(d) $\dfrac{y^{-1/2}}{x^{-1/3}} = \dfrac{x^{1/3}}{y^{1/2}}$

(e) $\sqrt{x}(\sqrt{x}-1) = x^{1/2}(x^{1/2}-1) = x^{1/2}x^{1/2} - x^{1/2} = x - x^{1/2}$

7.1 PUTTING IT ALL TOGETHER

Properties of radicals and rational exponents are summarized in the following table.

Concept	Explanation	Examples
nth Root of a Real Number	The nth root of a real number a is b if $b^n = a$ and the principal nth root is denoted $\sqrt[n]{a}$. If $a < 0$ and n is even, $\sqrt[n]{a}$ is not a real number.	The square roots of 25 are 5 and -5. The principal square root is $\sqrt{25} = 5$. $\sqrt[3]{-125} = -5$ because $$(-5)^3 = (-5)(-5)(-5) = -125.$$
Rational Exponents	If m and n are positive integers with $\frac{m}{n}$ in lowest terms, $$a^{m/n} = \sqrt[n]{a^m} = \left(\sqrt[n]{a}\right)^m.$$ If $a < 0$ and n is even, $a^{m/n}$ is not a real number.	$8^{4/3} = \left(\sqrt[3]{8}\right)^4 = 2^4 = 16$ and $(-27)^{3/4} = (\sqrt[4]{-27})^3$ is *not* a real number.
Properties of Exponents	Let p and q be rational numbers. For all real numbers a and b for which the expressions are real numbers the following properties hold. 1. $a^p \cdot a^q = a^{p+q}$ 2. $a^{-p} = \dfrac{1}{a^p}, \dfrac{1}{a^{-p}} = a^p$ 3. $\left(\dfrac{a}{b}\right)^{-p} = \left(\dfrac{b}{a}\right)^p$ 4. $\dfrac{a^p}{a^q} = a^{p-q}$ 5. $(a^p)^q = a^{pq}$ 6. $(ab)^p = a^p b^p$ 7. $\left(\dfrac{a}{b}\right)^p = \dfrac{a^p}{b^p}$	$2^{1/3} \cdot 2^{2/3} = 2^{1/3+2/3} = 2^1 = 2$ $2^{-1/2} = \dfrac{1}{2^{1/2}}, \dfrac{1}{3^{-1/4}} = 3^{1/4}$ $\left(\dfrac{3}{4}\right)^{-4/5} = \left(\dfrac{4}{3}\right)^{4/5}$ $\dfrac{7^{2/3}}{7^{1/3}} = 7^{2/3-1/3} = 7^{1/3}$ $(8^{2/3})^{1/2} = 8^{2/6} = 8^{1/3} = 2$ $(2x)^{1/3} = 2^{1/3} x^{1/3}$ $\left(\dfrac{x}{y}\right)^{1/6} = \dfrac{x^{1/6}}{y^{1/6}}$

7.1 EXERCISES

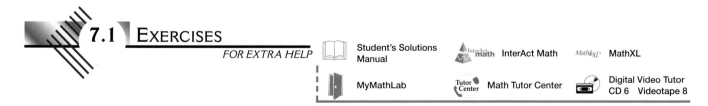

FOR EXTRA HELP

Student's Solutions Manual

MyMathLab

InterAct Math

Math Tutor Center

MathXL

Digital Video Tutor
CD 6   Videotape 8

CONCEPTS

1. What are the square roots of 9? ± 3

2. What is the principal square root of 9?   3

3. What is the cube root of 8?   2

4. Does every real number have a cube root?   Yes

5. If $b^n = a$ and $b > 0$, then $\sqrt[n]{a} =$ _____. b

6. Write $a^{1/n}$ in radical notation. $\sqrt[n]{a}$

7. Write $a^{m/n}$ in radical notation. $(\sqrt[n]{a})^m$ or $\sqrt[n]{a^m}$

8. Does $(a^{1/3})^2 = a^{2/3}$? Yes

RADICAL EXPRESSIONS

Exercises 9–28: If possible, evaluate the expression by hand. If you cannot, approximate the answer to the nearest hundredth. Variables represent any real number.

9. $\sqrt{9}$ 3

10. $\sqrt{121}$ 11

11. $-\sqrt{5}$ -2.24

12. $\sqrt{11}$ 3.32

13. $\sqrt{z^2}$ $|z|$

14. $-\sqrt{(x+2)^2}$ $-|x+2|$

15. $\sqrt[3]{27}$ 3

16. $\sqrt[3]{64}$ 4

17. $\sqrt[3]{-64}$ -4

18. $-\sqrt[3]{-1}$ 1

19. $\sqrt[3]{5}$ 1.71

20. $\sqrt[3]{-13}$ -2.35

21. $-\sqrt[3]{x^9}$ $-x^3$

22. $\sqrt[3]{(x+1)^6}$ $(x+1)^2$

23. $\sqrt[3]{(2x)^6}$ $4x^2$

24. $\sqrt[3]{9x^3}$ $2.08x$

25. $\sqrt[4]{81}$ 3

26. $\sqrt[5]{-1}$ -1

27. $\sqrt[5]{-7}$ -1.48

28. $\sqrt[4]{6}$ 1.57

RATIONAL EXPONENTS

Exercises 29–34: Write the expression in radical notation.

29. $6^{1/2}$ $\sqrt{6}$

30. $7^{1/3}$ $\sqrt[3]{7}$

31. $(xy)^{1/2}$ $\sqrt{xy}$

32. $x^{2/3}y^{1/5}$ $\sqrt[3]{x^2} \cdot \sqrt[5]{y}$

33. $y^{-1/5}$ $\frac{1}{\sqrt[5]{y}}$

34. $\left(\frac{x}{y}\right)^{-2/7}$ $\sqrt[7]{\left(\frac{y}{x}\right)^2} = \sqrt[7]{\frac{y^2}{x^2}}$

Exercises 35–56: If possible, evaluate the expression by hand. If you cannot, approximate the answer to the nearest hundredth.

35. $16^{1/2}$ 4

36. $8^{1/3}$ 2

37. $256^{1/4}$ 4

38. $4^{3/2}$ 8

39. $32^{1/5}$ 2

40. $(-32)^{1/5}$ -2

41. $(-8)^{4/3}$ 16

42. $(-1)^{3/5}$ -1

43. $2^{1/2} \cdot 2^{2/3}$ 2.24

44. $5^{3/5} \cdot 5^{1/10}$ 3.09

45. $\left(\frac{4}{9}\right)^{1/2}$ $\frac{2}{3}$

46. $\left(\frac{27}{64}\right)^{1/3}$ $\frac{3}{4}$

47. $\frac{4^{2/3}}{4^{1/2}}$ 1.26

48. $\frac{6^{1/5} \cdot 6^{3/5}}{6^{2/5}}$ 2.05

49. $4^{-1/2}$ $\frac{1}{2}$

50. $9^{-3/2}$ $\frac{1}{27}$

51. $(-8)^{-1/3}$ $-\frac{1}{2}$

52. $(49)^{-1/2}$ $\frac{1}{7}$

53. $\left(\frac{1}{16}\right)^{-1/4}$ 2

54. $\left(\frac{16}{25}\right)^{-3/2}$ $\frac{125}{64}$

55. $(2^{1/2})^3$ 2.83

56. $(5^{6/5})^{-1/2}$ 0.38

Exercises 57–86: Simplify the expression. Assume that all variables are positive.

57. $(x^2)^{3/2}$ x^3

58. $(y^4)^{1/2}$ y^2

59. $(x^2y^8)^{1/2}$ xy^4

60. $(y^{10}z^4)^{1/4}$ $y^{5/2}z$

61. $\sqrt[3]{x^3y^6}$ xy^2

62. $\sqrt{16x^4}$ $4x^2$

63. $\sqrt{\frac{y^4}{x^2}}$ $\frac{y^2}{x}$

64. $\sqrt[3]{\frac{x^{12}}{z^6}}$ $\frac{x^4}{z^2}$

65. $\sqrt{y^3} \cdot \sqrt[3]{y^2}$ $y^{13/6}$

66. $\left(\frac{x^6}{81}\right)^{1/4}$ $\frac{x^{3/2}}{3}$

67. $\left(\frac{x^6}{27}\right)^{2/3}$ $\frac{x^4}{9}$

68. $\left(\frac{1}{x^8}\right)^{-1/4}$ x^2

69. $\left(\frac{x^2}{y^6}\right)^{-1/2}$ $\frac{y^3}{x}$

70. $\frac{\sqrt{x}}{\sqrt[3]{27x^6}}$ $\frac{1}{3x^{3/2}}$

71. $\sqrt{\sqrt{y}}$ $y^{1/4}$

72. $\sqrt{\sqrt[3]{(3x)^2}}$ $(3x)^{1/3}$

73. $(a^{-1/2})^{4/3}$ $\frac{1}{a^{2/3}}$

74. $(x^{-3/2})^{2/3}$ $\frac{1}{x}$

75. $(a^3b^6)^{1/3}$ ab^2

76. $(64x^3y^{18})^{1/6}$ $2x^{1/2}y^3$

77. $\frac{(k^{1/2})^{-3}}{(k^2)^{1/4}}$ $\frac{1}{k^2}$

78. $\frac{(b^{3/4})^4}{(b^{4/5})^{-5}}$ b^7

79. $\sqrt{b} \cdot \sqrt[4]{b}$ $b^{3/4}$

80. $\sqrt[3]{t} \cdot \sqrt[5]{t}$ $t^{8/15}$

81. $\sqrt{z} \cdot \sqrt[3]{z^2} \cdot \sqrt[4]{z^3}$ $z^{23/12}$

82. $\sqrt{b} \cdot \sqrt[3]{b} \cdot \sqrt[5]{b}$ $b^{31/30}$

83. $p^{1/2}(p^{3/2} + p^{1/2})$ $p^2 + p$

84. $d^{3/4}(d^{1/4} - d^{-1/4})$ $d - d^{1/2}$

85. $\sqrt[3]{x}(\sqrt{x} - \sqrt[3]{x^2})$ $x^{5/6} - x$

86. $\frac{1}{2}\sqrt{x}(\sqrt{x} + \sqrt[4]{x^2})$ x

Exercises 87–102: Simplify the expression. Assume that all variables are real numbers.

87. $\sqrt{(-4)^2}$ 4

88. $\sqrt{9^2}$ 9

89. $\sqrt{y^2}$ $|y|$

90. $\sqrt{z^4}$ z^2

91. $\sqrt{(a+3)^2}$ $|a+3|$

92. $\sqrt{(a-b)^2}$ $|a-b|$

93. $\sqrt{(x-5)^2}$ $|x-5|$

94. $\sqrt{(2x-1)^2}$ $|2x-1|$

95. $\sqrt{x^2 - 2x + 1}$ $|x - 1|$

96. $\sqrt{4x^2 + 4x + 1}$ $|2x + 1|$

97. $\sqrt[4]{y^4}$ $|y|$

98. $\sqrt[4]{x^8 z^4}$ $x^2|z|$

99. $\sqrt[4]{x^{12}}$ $|x^3|$

100. $\sqrt[6]{x^6}$ $|x|$

101. $\sqrt[5]{x^5 y^{10}}$ xy^2

102. $\sqrt[5]{32(x + 4)^5}$ $2(x + 4)$

APPLICATIONS

103. *Cellular Phone Technology*   (Refer to Example 3.) Suppose that a city has an area of 65 square miles and 15 cellular transmission towers spread evenly throughout it. Estimate a minimum radius R for each tower. $R \approx 1.17$ mi

104. *Musical Tones*   One octave on a piano contains 12 keys (including both the black and white keys). The frequency of each successive key increases by a factor of $2^{1/12}$. For example, middle C is two keys below the first D above it. Therefore the frequency of this D is

$$2^{1/12} \cdot 2^{1/12} = 2^{1/6} \approx 1.12$$

times greater than middle C.

(a) If two tones are one octave apart, how do their frequencies compare?   The higher tone has twice the frequency.

(b) The A tone below middle C has a frequency of 220 cycles per second. Middle C is 3 keys above this A note. Estimate the frequency of middle C.   About 261.6 cycles/sec

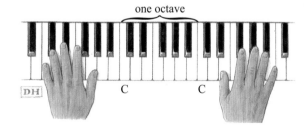

one octave

Exercises 105 and 106: Heron's Formula   Suppose the lengths of the sides of a triangle are a, b, and c as illustrated in the figure.

If the **semiperimeter** *of the triangle is* $s = \frac{1}{2}(a + b + c)$, *then the area of the triangle is*

$$A = \sqrt{s(s - a)(s - b)(s - c)}.$$

Find the area of the triangle with the given sides.

105. $a = 3, b = 4, c = 5$ **106.** $a = 5, b = 9, c = 10$
     $A = 6$ $A = \sqrt{504} \approx 22.45$

WRITING ABOUT MATHEMATICS

107. Try to calculate $\sqrt{-7}$, $\sqrt[4]{-56}$, and $\sqrt[6]{-10}$ with a calculator. Describe what happens when you evaluate an even root of a negative number. Does the same difficulty occur when you evaluate an odd root of a negative number? Try to evaluate $\sqrt[3]{-7}$, $\sqrt[5]{-56}$, and $\sqrt[7]{-10}$. Explain.

108. Explain the difference between a root and a power of a number. Give examples.

7.2 SIMPLIFYING RADICAL EXPRESSIONS

Product Rule for Radical Expressions · Quotient Rule for Radical Expressions · Rationalizing Denominators Having Square Roots

INTRODUCTION

In this section we discuss performing arithmetic operations with radical expressions. We demonstrate use of these skills to solve equations that contain radical expressions.

PRODUCT RULE FOR RADICAL EXPRESSIONS

Consider the following examples of multiplying radical expressions.

$$\sqrt{4} \cdot \sqrt{25} = 2 \cdot 5 = 10 \quad \text{and} \quad \sqrt{4 \cdot 25} = \sqrt{100} = 10$$

implies that

$$\sqrt{4} \cdot \sqrt{25} = \sqrt{4 \cdot 25} \quad \text{(see Figure 7.6(a))}.$$

Similarly,

$$\sqrt[3]{8} \cdot \sqrt[3]{27} = 2 \cdot 3 = 6 \quad \text{and} \quad \sqrt[3]{8 \cdot 27} = \sqrt[3]{216} = 6$$

implies that

$$\sqrt[3]{8} \cdot \sqrt[3]{27} = \sqrt[3]{8 \cdot 27} \quad \text{(see Figure 7.6(b))}.$$

TEACHING TIP

It is not necessary to show students how to use a calculator. These calculator screens, like others in the text, are optional.

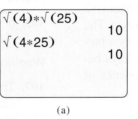

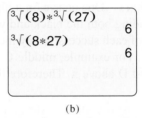

(a)   (b)

Figure 7.6

These examples suggest that the product of two (like) roots is equal to the root of their product.

PRODUCT RULE FOR RADICAL EXPRESSIONS

Let a and b be real numbers, where $\sqrt[n]{a}$ and $\sqrt[n]{b}$ are both defined. Then

$$\sqrt[n]{a} \cdot \sqrt[n]{b} = \sqrt[n]{a \cdot b}.$$

Note: The product rule only works when the radicals have the *same* index. For example, the product $\sqrt{2} \cdot \sqrt[3]{4}$ cannot be simplified because the indexes are 2 and 3. However, by using rational exponents, we can simplify this product. See Example 5.

We apply the product rule in the next two examples.

EXAMPLE 1   Multiplying radical expressions

Multiply each pair of radical expressions.
(a) $\sqrt{5} \cdot \sqrt{20}$ (b) $\sqrt[3]{-3} \cdot \sqrt[3]{9}$ (c) $\sqrt[3]{-5} \cdot \sqrt[3]{7}$ (d) $\sqrt[4]{\frac{1}{3}} \cdot \sqrt[4]{\frac{1}{9}} \cdot \sqrt[4]{\frac{1}{3}}$

Solution   (a) $\sqrt{5} \cdot \sqrt{20} = \sqrt{5 \cdot 20} = \sqrt{100} = 10$
(b) $\sqrt[3]{-3} \cdot \sqrt[3]{9} = \sqrt[3]{-3 \cdot 9} = \sqrt[3]{-27} = -3$
(c) $\sqrt[3]{-5} \cdot \sqrt[3]{7} = \sqrt[3]{-5 \cdot 7} = \sqrt[3]{-35}$

(d) The product rule can also be applied to three or more factors. Thus

$$\sqrt[4]{\frac{1}{3}} \cdot \sqrt[4]{\frac{1}{9}} \cdot \sqrt[4]{\frac{1}{3}} = \sqrt[4]{\frac{1}{3} \cdot \frac{1}{9} \cdot \frac{1}{3}} = \sqrt[4]{\frac{1}{81}} = \frac{1}{3}$$

because $\frac{1}{3} \cdot \frac{1}{3} \cdot \frac{1}{3} \cdot \frac{1}{3} = \frac{1}{81}$.

EXAMPLE 2 Multiplying radical expressions containing variables

Multiply each pair of radical expressions. Assume that all variables are positive.

(a) $\sqrt{x} \cdot \sqrt{x^3}$ **(b)** $\sqrt[3]{2a} \cdot \sqrt[3]{5a}$ **(c)** $\sqrt{11} \cdot \sqrt{xy}$ **(d)** $\sqrt[5]{\frac{2x}{y}} \cdot \sqrt[5]{\frac{16y}{x}}$

Solution   **(a)** $\sqrt{x} \cdot \sqrt{x^3} = \sqrt{x \cdot x^3} = \sqrt{x^4} = x^2$
     (b) $\sqrt[3]{2a} \cdot \sqrt[3]{5a} = \sqrt[3]{2a \cdot 5a} = \sqrt[3]{10a^2}$
     (c) $\sqrt{11} \cdot \sqrt{xy} = \sqrt{11xy}$
     (d) $\sqrt[5]{\frac{2x}{y}} \cdot \sqrt[5]{\frac{16y}{x}} = \sqrt[5]{\frac{2x}{y} \cdot \frac{16y}{x}}$ Product rule

$$= \sqrt[5]{\frac{32xy}{xy}}$$ Multiply fractions.

$$= \sqrt[5]{32}$$ Reduce.

$$= 2$$ $2^5 = 32$

An integer a is a **perfect nth power** if there exists an integer b such that $b^n = a$. Thus 36 is a **perfect square** because $6^2 = 36$, 8 is a **perfect cube** because $2^3 = 8$, and 81 is a *perfect fourth power* because $3^4 = 81$.

The product rule for radicals can be used to simplify radical expressions. For example, because the largest perfect square factor of 50 is 25, the expression $\sqrt{50}$ can be simplified as

$$\sqrt{50} = \sqrt{25} \cdot \sqrt{2} = 5\sqrt{2}.$$

This procedure is generalized as follows.

SIMPLIFYING RADICALS (nth ROOTS)

1. Determine the largest perfect nth power factor of the radicand.
2. Use the product rule to factor out and simplify this perfect nth power.

EXAMPLE 3 Simplifying radical expressions

Simplify each expression.
(a) $\sqrt{300}$ **(b)** $\sqrt[3]{16}$ **(c)** $\sqrt{54}$ **(d)** $\sqrt[4]{512}$

Solution   **(a)** First note that $300 = 100 \cdot 3$ and that 100 is the largest perfect square factor of 300. Thus

$$\sqrt{300} = \sqrt{100} \cdot \sqrt{3} = 10\sqrt{3}.$$

(b) The largest perfect cube factor of 16 is 8. Thus $\sqrt[3]{16} = \sqrt[3]{8} \cdot \sqrt[3]{2} = 2\sqrt[3]{2}$.

(c) $\sqrt{54} = \sqrt{9} \cdot \sqrt{6} = 3\sqrt{6}$

(d) $\sqrt[4]{512} = \sqrt[4]{256} \cdot \sqrt[4]{2} = 4\sqrt[4]{2}$ because $4^4 = 256$.

Note: To simplify a cube root of a negative number we factor out the negative of the largest perfect cube factor. For example, $-16 = -8 \cdot 2$, so $\sqrt[3]{-16} = \sqrt[3]{-8} \cdot \sqrt[3]{2} = -2\sqrt[3]{2}$. This procedure can be used with any negative odd root of a number.

EXAMPLE 4 Simplifying radical expressions

Simplify each expression. Assume that all variables are positive.

(a) $\sqrt{25x^4}$ **(b)** $\sqrt{32n^3}$ **(c)** $\sqrt[3]{-16x^3y^5}$ **(d)** $\sqrt[3]{2a} \cdot \sqrt[3]{4a^2b}$

Solution
(a) $\sqrt{25x^4} = 5x^2$

(b) $\sqrt{32n^3} = \sqrt{(16n^2)2n}$ $16n^2$ is the largest perfect square factor.

$\qquad\qquad = \sqrt{16n^2} \cdot \sqrt{2n}$ Product rule

$\qquad\qquad = 4n\sqrt{2n}$ $(4n)^2 = 16n^2$

(c) $\sqrt[3]{-16x^3y^5} = \sqrt[3]{(-8x^3y^3)2y^2}$ $8x^3y^3$ is the largest perfect cube factor.

$\qquad\qquad = \sqrt[3]{-8x^3y^3} \cdot \sqrt[3]{2y^2}$ Product rule

$\qquad\qquad = -2xy\sqrt[3]{2y^2}$ $(-2xy)^3 = -8x^3y^3$

(d) $\sqrt[3]{2a} \cdot \sqrt[3]{4a^2b} = \sqrt[3]{(2a)(4a^2b)}$ Product rule

$\qquad\qquad = \sqrt[3]{(8a^3)b}$ $8a^3$ is the largest perfect cube factor.

$\qquad\qquad = \sqrt[3]{8a^3} \cdot \sqrt[3]{b}$ Product rule

$\qquad\qquad = 2a\sqrt[3]{b}$ $(2a)^3 = 8a^3$

The product rule for radical expressions cannot be used if the radicals do not have the same indexes. In this case we use rational exponents, as illustrated in the next example.

EXAMPLE 5 Multiplying radicals with different indexes

Simplify each expression. Write your answer in radical notation.

(a) $\sqrt{5} \cdot \sqrt[4]{5}$ **(b)** $\sqrt{2} \cdot \sqrt[3]{4}$ **(c)** $\sqrt[3]{x} \cdot \sqrt[4]{x}$

Solution
(a) Because $\sqrt{5} = 5^{1/2}$ and $\sqrt[4]{5} = 5^{1/4}$,

$$\sqrt{5} \cdot \sqrt[4]{5} = 5^{1/2} \cdot 5^{1/4} = 5^{1/2+1/4} = 5^{3/4}.$$

In radical notation, $5^{3/4} = \sqrt[4]{5^3} = \sqrt[4]{125}$.

(b) First note that $\sqrt[3]{4} = \sqrt[3]{2^2} = 2^{2/3}$. Thus

$$\sqrt{2} \cdot \sqrt[3]{4} = 2^{1/2} \cdot 2^{2/3} = 2^{1/2+2/3} = 2^{7/6}.$$

In radical notation, $2^{7/6} = \sqrt[6]{2^7} = \sqrt[6]{2^6 \cdot 2^1} = \sqrt[6]{2^6} \cdot \sqrt[6]{2} = 2\sqrt[6]{2}$.

(c) $\sqrt[3]{x} \cdot \sqrt[4]{x} = x^{1/3} \cdot x^{1/4} = x^{7/12} = \sqrt[12]{x^7}$

QUOTIENT RULE FOR RADICAL EXPRESSIONS

Consider the following examples of dividing radical expressions.

$$\sqrt{\frac{4}{9}} = \sqrt{\frac{2}{3} \cdot \frac{2}{3}} = \frac{2}{3} \quad \text{and} \quad \frac{\sqrt{4}}{\sqrt{9}} = \frac{2}{3}$$

implies that

$$\sqrt{\frac{4}{9}} = \frac{\sqrt{4}}{\sqrt{9}}. \quad \text{See Figure 7.7.}$$

```
√(4/9)▶Frac
              2/3
√(4)/√(9)▶Frac
              2/3
```

Figure 7.7

Calculator Help
To use the Frac feature, see the Appendix (page AP-2).

These examples suggest that the root of a quotient is equal to the quotient of the roots.

QUOTIENT RULE FOR RADICAL EXPRESSIONS

Let a and b be real numbers, where $\sqrt[n]{a}$ and $\sqrt[n]{b}$ are both defined and $b \neq 0$. Then

$$\sqrt[n]{\frac{a}{b}} = \frac{\sqrt[n]{a}}{\sqrt[n]{b}}.$$

EXAMPLE 6   Simplifying quotients

Simplify each radical expression. Assume that all variables are positive.

(a) $\sqrt[3]{\dfrac{5}{8}}$ **(b)** $\sqrt[4]{\dfrac{x}{16}}$ **(c)** $\sqrt{\dfrac{16}{y^2}}$

Solution   **(a)** $\sqrt[3]{\dfrac{5}{8}} = \dfrac{\sqrt[3]{5}}{\sqrt[3]{8}} = \dfrac{\sqrt[3]{5}}{2}$

(b) $\sqrt[4]{\dfrac{x}{16}} = \dfrac{\sqrt[4]{x}}{\sqrt[4]{16}} = \dfrac{\sqrt[4]{x}}{2}$

(c) $\sqrt{\dfrac{16}{y^2}} = \dfrac{\sqrt{16}}{\sqrt{y^2}} = \dfrac{4}{y}$ because $y > 0$.

═══ MAKING CONNECTIONS ═══

Rules for Radical Expressions and Rational Exponents

The rules for radical expressions are a result of the properties of rational exponents.

$$\sqrt[n]{a \cdot b} = \sqrt[n]{a} \cdot \sqrt[n]{b} \quad \text{is equivalent to} \quad (a \cdot b)^{1/n} = a^{1/n} \cdot b^{1/n}.$$

$$\sqrt[n]{\frac{a}{b}} = \frac{\sqrt[n]{a}}{\sqrt[n]{b}} \quad \text{is equivalent to} \quad \left(\frac{a}{b}\right)^{1/n} = \frac{a^{1/n}}{b^{1/n}}.$$

TEACHING TIP

You may want to discuss Making Connections earlier to justify the product rule for radical expressions.

EXAMPLE 7   Simplifying radical expressions

Simplify each radical expression. Assume that all variables are positive.

(a) $\dfrac{\sqrt{40}}{\sqrt{10}}$ **(b)** $\sqrt[4]{\dfrac{16x^3}{y^4}}$ **(c)** $\sqrt{\dfrac{5a^2}{8}} \cdot \sqrt{\dfrac{5a^3}{2}}$

Solution (a) $\dfrac{\sqrt{40}}{\sqrt{10}} = \sqrt{\dfrac{40}{10}} = \sqrt{4} = 2$

(b) $\sqrt[4]{\dfrac{16x^3}{y^4}} = \dfrac{\sqrt[4]{16x^3}}{\sqrt[4]{y^4}} = \dfrac{\sqrt[4]{16} \cdot \sqrt[4]{x^3}}{\sqrt[4]{y^4}} = \dfrac{2\sqrt[4]{x^3}}{y}$

(c) To simplify this expression, we use both the product and quotient rules.

$$\sqrt{\dfrac{5a^2}{8}} \cdot \sqrt{\dfrac{5a^3}{2}} = \sqrt{\dfrac{25a^5}{16}} \qquad \text{Product rule}$$

$$= \dfrac{\sqrt{25a^5}}{\sqrt{16}} \qquad \text{Quotient rule}$$

$$= \dfrac{\sqrt{(25a^4)} \cdot \sqrt{a}}{\sqrt{16}} \qquad \text{Factor out largest perfect square.}$$

$$= \dfrac{5a^2\sqrt{a}}{4} \qquad (5a^2)^2 = 25a^4.$$

RATIONALIZING DENOMINATORS HAVING SQUARE ROOTS

Quotients containing radical expressions can appear to be different but actually be equal. For example, $\dfrac{1}{\sqrt{3}}$ and $\dfrac{\sqrt{3}}{3}$ represent the same real number even though they look like they are unequal. To show that they are equal, we multiply the first quotient by 1 in the form $\dfrac{\sqrt{3}}{\sqrt{3}}$:

$$\dfrac{1}{\sqrt{3}} \cdot \dfrac{\sqrt{3}}{\sqrt{3}} = \dfrac{1 \cdot \sqrt{3}}{\sqrt{3} \cdot \sqrt{3}} = \dfrac{\sqrt{3}}{3}.$$

Note: $\sqrt{b} \cdot \sqrt{b} = \sqrt{b^2} = b$ for any *positive* number b.

One way to standardize radical expressions is to remove any radical expressions from the denominator. This process is called **rationalizing the denominator**. Exercise 105 suggests one reason why people rationalized denominators before calculators were invented. The next example demonstrates how to rationalize the denominator of several quotients.

EXAMPLE 8 Rationalizing the denominator

Rationalize each denominator. Assume that all variables are positive.

(a) $\dfrac{1}{\sqrt{2}}$ (b) $\dfrac{3}{5\sqrt{3}}$ (c) $\sqrt{\dfrac{x}{24}}$ (d) $\dfrac{xy}{\sqrt{y^3}}$

Solution (a) We start by multiplying this expression by 1 in the form $\dfrac{\sqrt{2}}{\sqrt{2}}$:

$$\dfrac{1}{\sqrt{2}} \cdot \dfrac{\sqrt{2}}{\sqrt{2}} = \dfrac{\sqrt{2}}{\sqrt{4}} = \dfrac{\sqrt{2}}{2}.$$

Note that the expression $\dfrac{\sqrt{2}}{2}$ does not have a radical in the denominator.

(b) We multiply this expression by 1 in the form $\frac{\sqrt{3}}{\sqrt{3}}$:

$$\frac{3}{5\sqrt{3}} \cdot \frac{\sqrt{3}}{\sqrt{3}} = \frac{3\sqrt{3}}{5\sqrt{9}} = \frac{3\sqrt{3}}{5 \cdot 3} = \frac{\sqrt{3}}{5}.$$

(c) Because $\sqrt{24} = \sqrt{4} \cdot \sqrt{6} = 2\sqrt{6}$, we start by simplifying the expression.

$$\sqrt{\frac{x}{24}} = \frac{\sqrt{x}}{\sqrt{24}} = \frac{\sqrt{x}}{2\sqrt{6}}$$

To rationalize the denominator we multiply this expression by 1 in the form $\frac{\sqrt{6}}{\sqrt{6}}$:

$$\frac{\sqrt{x}}{2\sqrt{6}} = \frac{\sqrt{x}}{2\sqrt{6}} \cdot \frac{\sqrt{6}}{\sqrt{6}} = \frac{\sqrt{6x}}{12}.$$

(d) Because $\sqrt{y^3} = \sqrt{y^2} \cdot \sqrt{y} = y\sqrt{y}$ and $y > 0$, we start by simplifying the expression.

$$\frac{xy}{\sqrt{y^3}} = \frac{xy}{y\sqrt{y}} = \frac{x}{\sqrt{y}}$$

To rationalize the denominator we multiply by 1 in the form $\frac{\sqrt{y}}{\sqrt{y}}$:

$$\frac{x}{\sqrt{y}} \cdot \frac{\sqrt{y}}{\sqrt{y}} = \frac{x\sqrt{y}}{y}.$$

7.2 PUTTING IT ALL TOGETHER

In this section we discussed how to simplify radical expressions. Results are summarized in the following table.

Procedure	Explanation	Examples
Product Rule for Radical Expressions	Let a and b be real numbers, where $\sqrt[n]{a}$ and $\sqrt[n]{b}$ are both defined. Then $$\sqrt[n]{a} \cdot \sqrt[n]{b} = \sqrt[n]{a \cdot b}.$$	$$\sqrt{2} \cdot \sqrt{32} = \sqrt{64} = 8$$
Quotient Rule for Radical Expressions	Let a and b be real numbers, where $\sqrt[n]{a}$ and $\sqrt[n]{b}$ are both defined and $b \neq 0$. Then $$\sqrt[n]{\frac{a}{b}} = \frac{\sqrt[n]{a}}{\sqrt[n]{b}}.$$	$$\frac{\sqrt{60}}{\sqrt{15}} = \sqrt{\frac{60}{15}} = \sqrt{4} = 2 \quad \text{and}$$ $$\sqrt[3]{\frac{x^2}{-27}} = \frac{\sqrt[3]{x^2}}{\sqrt[3]{-27}} = \frac{\sqrt[3]{x^2}}{-3} = \frac{-\sqrt[3]{x^2}}{3}$$
Rationalizing the Denominator	Write the quotient without a radical expression in the denominator.	To rationalize $\frac{5}{\sqrt{7}}$ multiply the expression by 1 in the form $\frac{\sqrt{7}}{\sqrt{7}}$: $$\frac{5}{\sqrt{7}} \cdot \frac{\sqrt{7}}{\sqrt{7}} = \frac{5\sqrt{7}}{\sqrt{49}} = \frac{5\sqrt{7}}{7}.$$

7.2 EXERCISES

FOR EXTRA HELP

Student's Solutions Manual

 InterAct math　InterAct Math

 MathXL

MyMathLab

 Tutor Center　Math Tutor Center

 Digital Video Tutor
CD 6　Videotape 8

CONCEPTS

1. Does $\sqrt{2} \cdot \sqrt{3}$ equal $\sqrt{6}$?　Yes

2. Does $\sqrt{5} \cdot \sqrt[3]{5}$ equal 5?　No

3. $\sqrt[3]{a} \cdot \sqrt[3]{b} =$ _____　$\sqrt[3]{ab}$

4. $\dfrac{\sqrt{a}}{\sqrt{b}} = \sqrt{?}$　$\dfrac{a}{b}$

5. $\dfrac{\sqrt[n]{a}}{\sqrt[n]{b}} = \sqrt[n]{?}$　$\dfrac{a}{b}$

6. To rationalize the denominator for $\dfrac{1}{\sqrt{3}}$, multiply by 1 in the form _____.　$\dfrac{\sqrt{3}}{\sqrt{3}}$

7. Is $\sqrt[3]{3}$ equal to 1? Explain.　No; $1^3 \ne 3$

8. Is 64 a perfect cube? Explain.　Yes; $4^3 = 64$

MULTIPLYING AND DIVIDING

Exercises 9–50: Simplify the expression. Assume that all variables are positive.

9. $\sqrt{3} \cdot \sqrt{3}$　3

10. $\sqrt{2} \cdot \sqrt{18}$　6

11. $\sqrt{2} \cdot \sqrt{50}$　10

12. $\sqrt[3]{-2} \cdot \sqrt[3]{-4}$　2

13. $\sqrt[3]{4} \cdot \sqrt[3]{16}$　4

14. $\sqrt[3]{x} \cdot \sqrt[3]{x^2}$　x

15. $\sqrt{\dfrac{9}{25}}$　$\dfrac{3}{5}$

16. $\sqrt[3]{\dfrac{x}{8}}$　$\dfrac{\sqrt[3]{x}}{2}$

17. $\sqrt{\dfrac{1}{2}} \cdot \sqrt{\dfrac{1}{8}}$　$\dfrac{1}{4}$

18. $\sqrt{\dfrac{5}{3}} \cdot \sqrt{\dfrac{1}{3}}$　$\dfrac{\sqrt{5}}{3}$

19. $\sqrt{\dfrac{x}{2}} \cdot \sqrt{\dfrac{x}{8}}$　$\dfrac{x}{4}$

20. $\sqrt{\dfrac{4}{y}} \cdot \sqrt{\dfrac{y}{5}}$　$\dfrac{2}{\sqrt{5}}$, or $\dfrac{2\sqrt{5}}{5}$

21. $\dfrac{\sqrt{45}}{\sqrt{5}}$　3

22. $\dfrac{\sqrt{7}}{\sqrt{28}}$　$\dfrac{1}{2}$

23. $\sqrt[3]{-4} \cdot \sqrt[3]{-16}$　4

24. $\sqrt[3]{9} \cdot \sqrt[3]{3}$　3

25. $\sqrt[4]{9} \cdot \sqrt[4]{9}$　3

26. $\sqrt[5]{16} \cdot \sqrt[5]{-2}$　-2

27. $\dfrac{\sqrt[5]{64}}{\sqrt[5]{-2}}$　-2

28. $\dfrac{\sqrt[4]{324}}{\sqrt[4]{4}}$　3

29. $\dfrac{\sqrt{a^2 b}}{\sqrt{b}}$　a

30. $\dfrac{\sqrt{4xy^2}}{\sqrt{x}}$　$2y$

31. $\dfrac{\sqrt[3]{54}}{\sqrt[3]{2}}$　3

32. $\dfrac{\sqrt[3]{x^3 y^7}}{\sqrt[3]{y^4}}$　xy

33. $\sqrt{4x^4}$　$2x^2$

34. $\sqrt[3]{-8y^3}$　$-2y$

35. $\sqrt[3]{-5a^6}$　$-a^2\sqrt[3]{5}$

36. $\sqrt{9x^2 y}$　$3x\sqrt{y}$

37. $\sqrt[4]{16x^4 y}$　$2x\sqrt[4]{y}$

38. $\sqrt[3]{8xy^3}$　$2y\sqrt[3]{x}$

39. $\sqrt{3x} \cdot \sqrt{12x}$　$6x$

40. $\sqrt{6x^5} \cdot \sqrt{6x}$　$6x^3$

41. $\sqrt[3]{8x^6 y^3 z^9}$　$2x^2 yz^3$

42. $\sqrt{16x^4 y^6}$　$4x^2 y^3$

43. $\sqrt[4]{\dfrac{3}{4}} \cdot \sqrt[4]{\dfrac{27}{4}}$　$\dfrac{3}{2}$

44. $\sqrt[5]{\dfrac{4}{-9}} \cdot \sqrt[5]{\dfrac{8}{-27}}$　$\dfrac{2}{3}$

45. $\sqrt[3]{12} \cdot \sqrt[3]{ab}$　$\sqrt[3]{12ab}$

46. $\sqrt{5x} \cdot \sqrt{5z}$　$5\sqrt{xz}$

47. $\sqrt[4]{25z} \cdot \sqrt[4]{25z}$　$5\sqrt{z}$

48. $\sqrt[5]{3z^2} \cdot \sqrt[5]{7z}$　$\sqrt[5]{21z^3}$

49. $\sqrt[5]{\dfrac{7a}{b^2}} \cdot \sqrt[5]{\dfrac{b^2}{7a^6}}$　$\dfrac{1}{a}$

50. $\sqrt[3]{\dfrac{8m}{n}} \cdot \sqrt[3]{\dfrac{n^4}{m^2}}$　$\dfrac{2n}{\sqrt[3]{m}}$

Exercises 51–56: Use properties of polynomials to simplify the expression. Assume all radicands are positive.

51. $\sqrt{x + 4} \cdot \sqrt{x - 4}$　$\sqrt{x^2 - 16}$

52. $\sqrt[3]{x - 1} \cdot \sqrt[3]{x^2 + x + 1}$　$\sqrt[3]{x^3 - 1}$

53. $\sqrt[3]{a + 1} \cdot \sqrt[3]{a^2 - a + 1}$　$\sqrt[3]{a^3 + 1}$

54. $\sqrt{b - 1} \cdot \sqrt{b + 1}$　$\sqrt{b^2 - 1}$

55. $\dfrac{\sqrt{x^2 + 2x + 1}}{\sqrt{x + 1}}$　$\sqrt{x + 1}$

56. $\dfrac{\sqrt{x^2 - 4x + 4}}{\sqrt{x - 2}}$　$\sqrt{x - 2}$

Exercises 57–62: Complete the equation.

57. $\sqrt{500} =$ _____ $\sqrt{5}$　10

58. $\sqrt{28} =$ _____ $\sqrt{7}$　2

59. $\sqrt{8} =$ _____ $\sqrt{2}$　2

60. $\sqrt{99} =$ _____ $\sqrt{11}$　3

61. $\sqrt{45} =$ _____ $\sqrt{5}$　3

62. $\sqrt{243} =$ _____ $\sqrt{3}$　9

Exercises 63–82: Simplify the radical expression by factoring out the largest perfect nth power. Assume that all variables are positive.

63. $\sqrt{200}$ $10\sqrt{2}$

64. $\sqrt{72}$ $6\sqrt{2}$

65. $\sqrt[3]{81}$ $3\sqrt[3]{3}$

66. $\sqrt[3]{256}$ $4\sqrt[3]{4}$

67. $\sqrt[4]{64}$ $2\sqrt{2}$

68. $\sqrt[5]{27 \cdot 81}$ $3\sqrt[5]{9}$

69. $\sqrt[5]{-64}$ $-2\sqrt[5]{2}$

70. $\sqrt[3]{-81}$ $-3\sqrt[3]{3}$

71. $\sqrt{b^5}$ $b^2\sqrt{b}$

72. $\sqrt{t^3}$ $t\sqrt{t}$

73. $\sqrt{8n^3}$ $2n\sqrt{2n}$

74. $\sqrt{32a^2}$ $4a\sqrt{2}$

75. $\sqrt{12a^2b^5}$ $2ab^2\sqrt{3b}$

76. $\sqrt{20a^3b^2}$ $2ab\sqrt{5a}$

77. $\sqrt[3]{125x^4y^5}$ $5xy\sqrt[3]{xy^2}$

78. $\sqrt[3]{81a^5b^2}$ $3a\sqrt[3]{3a^2b^2}$

79. $\sqrt[3]{5t} \cdot \sqrt[3]{125t}$ $5\sqrt[3]{5t^2}$

80. $\sqrt[4]{4bc^3} \cdot \sqrt[4]{64ab^3c^2}$ $4bc\sqrt[4]{ac}$

81. $\sqrt[4]{\dfrac{9t^5}{r^8}} \cdot \sqrt[4]{\dfrac{9r}{5t}}$ $\dfrac{3t}{r}\sqrt[4]{5r^3}$

82. $\sqrt[5]{\dfrac{4t^6}{r}} \cdot \sqrt[5]{\dfrac{8t}{r^6}}$ $\dfrac{2t}{r}\sqrt[5]{\dfrac{t^2}{r^2}}$

Exercises 83–92: Simplify the expression. Assume that all variables are positive and write your answer in radical notation.   **87.** $3\sqrt[12]{3^{11}}$

83. $\sqrt{3} \cdot \sqrt[3]{3}$ $\sqrt[6]{3^5}$

84. $\sqrt{5} \cdot \sqrt[3]{5}$ $\sqrt[6]{5^5}$

85. $\sqrt[4]{8} \cdot \sqrt[3]{4}$ $2\sqrt[12]{2^5}$

86. $\sqrt[5]{16} \cdot \sqrt{2}$ $2\sqrt[10]{2^3}$

87. $\sqrt[4]{27} \cdot \sqrt[3]{9} \cdot \sqrt{3}$

88. $\sqrt[5]{16} \cdot \sqrt[3]{16}$ $4\sqrt[15]{2^2}$

89. $\sqrt[4]{x^3} \cdot \sqrt[3]{x}$ $x\sqrt[12]{x}$

90. $\sqrt[4]{x^3} \cdot \sqrt{x}$ $x\sqrt[4]{x}$

91. $\sqrt[4]{rt} \cdot \sqrt[3]{r^2t}$ $\sqrt[12]{r^{11}t^7}$

92. $\sqrt[3]{a^3b^2} \cdot \sqrt{a^2b}$ $a^2b\sqrt[6]{b}$

Exercises 93–102: Rationalize the denominator.

93. $\dfrac{1}{\sqrt{7}}$ $\dfrac{\sqrt{7}}{7}$

94. $\dfrac{1}{\sqrt{23}}$ $\dfrac{\sqrt{23}}{23}$

95. $\dfrac{4}{\sqrt{3}}$ $\dfrac{4\sqrt{3}}{3}$

96. $\dfrac{8}{\sqrt{2}}$ $4\sqrt{2}$

97. $\dfrac{5}{3\sqrt{5}}$ $\dfrac{\sqrt{5}}{3}$

98. $\dfrac{6}{11\sqrt{3}}$ $\dfrac{2\sqrt{3}}{11}$

99. $\sqrt{\dfrac{b}{12}}$ $\dfrac{\sqrt{3b}}{6}$

100. $\sqrt{\dfrac{5b}{72}}$ $\dfrac{\sqrt{10b}}{12}$

101. $\dfrac{rt}{2\sqrt{r^3}}$ $\dfrac{t\sqrt{r}}{2r}$

102. $\dfrac{m^2n}{2\sqrt{m^5}}$ $\dfrac{n\sqrt{m}}{2m}$

APPLICATIONS

103. *Bird Wings* Heavier birds tend to have larger wings than lighter birds do. For some birds the relationship between the surface area A of the bird's wings in square inches and its weight W in pounds can be modeled by $A = 100\sqrt[3]{W^2}$. (*Source:* C. Pennycuick, *Newton Rules Biology.*)

    (a) Find the area of the wings when the weight is 8 pounds. $400\ \text{in}^2$

    (b) Write this formula with rational exponents.
        $A = 100W^{2/3}$

104. *Orbits and Distance* Johannes Kepler (1571–1630) discovered a relationship between a planet's distance D from the sun and the time T it takes to orbit the sun. This formula is given by $T = \sqrt{D^3}$, where T is in Earth years and $D = 1$ corresponds to the distance between Earth and the sun, or $93{,}000{,}000$ miles.   (a) About 164.3 yr

    (a) Neptune is 30 times farther from the sun than Earth ($D = 30$). Estimate the number of years required for Neptune to orbit the sun.

    (b) Write this formula with rational exponents.
        $T = D^{3/2}$

WRITING ABOUT MATHEMATICS

105. Suppose that a student knows that $\sqrt{3} \approx 1.73205$ and does not have a calculator. Which of the following expressions would be easier to evaluate by hand? Why?

$$\frac{1}{\sqrt{3}} \quad \text{or} \quad \frac{\sqrt{3}}{3}$$

106. Explain how the product and quotient rules for radical expressions are the result of properties of rational exponents.

1. Find the following.
   (a) The square roots of 49 ± 7
   (b) The principal square root of 49 7
   (c) The solutions to $x^2 = 49$ ± 7

2. Evaluate.
   (a) $\sqrt[3]{-8}$ -2 **(b)** $-\sqrt[4]{81}$ -3

3. Write the expression in radical notation.
   (a) $x^{3/2}$ **(b)** $x^{2/3}$ **(c)** $x^{-2/5}$

   (a) $\sqrt{x^3}$ or $(\sqrt{x})^3$ (b) $\sqrt[3]{x^2}$ or $(\sqrt[3]{x})^2$
   (c) $\dfrac{1}{\sqrt[5]{x^2}}$ or $\dfrac{1}{(\sqrt[5]{x})^2}$

4. Simplify $\sqrt{(x-1)^2}$ for any real number x. $|x-1|$

5. Simplify each expression. Assume that all variables are positive.
   (a) $(64^{-3/2})^{1/3}$ $\frac{1}{8}$ **(b)** $\sqrt{5} \cdot \sqrt{20}$ 10
   (c) $\sqrt[3]{-8x^4y}$ **(d)** $\sqrt{\dfrac{4b}{5}} \cdot \sqrt{\dfrac{4b^3}{5}}$ $\frac{4b^2}{5}$

6. Simplify $\sqrt[3]{7} \cdot \sqrt{7}$. $\sqrt[6]{7^5}$ 5.(c) $-2x\sqrt[3]{xy}$

7. Rationalize the denominator for $\dfrac{6}{2\sqrt{6}}$. $\frac{\sqrt{6}}{2}$

7.3 OPERATIONS ON RADICAL EXPRESSIONS

Addition and Subtraction · Multiplication · Rationalizing the Denominator

INTRODUCTION

So far we have discussed how to add, subtract, multiply, and divide numbers and variables. In this section we extend these operations to radical expressions. In doing so, we use many of the techniques discussed in Sections 7.1 and 7.2.

ADDITION AND SUBTRACTION

We can add $2x^2$ and $5x^2$ to obtain $7x^2$ because they are *like* terms. That is,

TEACHING TIP

Compare adding like radical expressions to adding like terms.

$$2x^2 + 5x^2 = (2 + 5)x^2 = 7x^2.$$

We can add and subtract **like radicals**, which have the same index and the same radicand. For example, we can add $3\sqrt{2}$ and $5\sqrt{2}$ because they are like radicals.

$$3\sqrt{2} + 5\sqrt{2} = (3 + 5)\sqrt{2} = 8\sqrt{2}$$

Sometimes two radical expressions that are not alike can be added by changing them to like radicals. For example, $\sqrt{20}$ and $\sqrt{5}$ are unlike radicals. However,

$$\sqrt{20} = \sqrt{4 \cdot 5} = \sqrt{4} \cdot \sqrt{5} = 2\sqrt{5},$$

so

$$\sqrt{20} + \sqrt{5} = 2\sqrt{5} + \sqrt{5} = 3\sqrt{5}.$$

We cannot combine $x + x^2$ because they are unlike terms. Similarly, we cannot combine $\sqrt{2} + \sqrt{5}$ because they are unlike radicals. When combining radicals, the first step is to see if we can write pairs of terms as like radicals, as demonstrated in the next example.

EXAMPLE 1   Finding like radicals

Write each pair of terms as like radicals, if possible.
(a) $\sqrt{45},\ \sqrt{20}$ **(b)** $\sqrt{27},\ \sqrt{5}$ **(c)** $5\sqrt[3]{16},\ 4\sqrt[3]{54}$

Solution   **(a)** The expressions $\sqrt{45}$ and $\sqrt{20}$ are unlike radicals. However, they can be changed to like radicals as follows.

$$\sqrt{45} = \sqrt{9 \cdot 5} = \sqrt{9} \cdot \sqrt{5} = 3\sqrt{5} \quad \text{and}$$

$$\sqrt{20} = \sqrt{4 \cdot 5} = \sqrt{4} \cdot \sqrt{5} = 2\sqrt{5}$$

The expressions $3\sqrt{5}$ and $2\sqrt{5}$ are like radicals.

(b) The expressions $\sqrt{27} = 3\sqrt{3}$ and $\sqrt{5}$ are unlike radicals and cannot be written as like radicals.

(c) $5\sqrt[3]{16} = 5\sqrt[3]{8 \cdot 2} = 5\sqrt[3]{8} \cdot \sqrt[3]{2} = 5 \cdot 2 \cdot \sqrt[3]{2} = 10\sqrt[3]{2}$ and

$4\sqrt[3]{54} = 4\sqrt[3]{27 \cdot 2} = 4\sqrt[3]{27} \cdot \sqrt[3]{2} = 4 \cdot 3 \cdot \sqrt[3]{2} = 12\sqrt[3]{2}$

The expressions $10\sqrt[3]{2}$ and $12\sqrt[3]{2}$ are like radicals.

We use these techniques to add radical expressions in the next two examples.

EXAMPLE 2   Adding radical expressions

Add the expressions and simplify.
(a) $10\sqrt{11} + 4\sqrt{11}$ **(b)** $5\sqrt[3]{6} + \sqrt[3]{6}$
(c) $\sqrt{12} + 7\sqrt{3}$ **(d)** $3\sqrt{2} + \sqrt{8} + \sqrt{18}$

Solution   **(a)** $10\sqrt{11} + 4\sqrt{11} = (10 + 4)\sqrt{11} = 14\sqrt{11}$

(b) $5\sqrt[3]{6} + \sqrt[3]{6} = (5 + 1)\sqrt[3]{6} = 6\sqrt[3]{6}$

(c) $\sqrt{12} + 7\sqrt{3} = \sqrt{4 \cdot 3} + 7\sqrt{3}$
$\qquad\qquad\quad = \sqrt{4} \cdot \sqrt{3} + 7\sqrt{3}$
$\qquad\qquad\quad = 2\sqrt{3} + 7\sqrt{3}$
$\qquad\qquad\quad = 9\sqrt{3}$

(d) $3\sqrt{2} + \sqrt{8} + \sqrt{18} = 3\sqrt{2} + \sqrt{4 \cdot 2} + \sqrt{9 \cdot 2}$
$\qquad\qquad\qquad\qquad\quad = 3\sqrt{2} + \sqrt{4} \cdot \sqrt{2} + \sqrt{9} \cdot \sqrt{2}$
$\qquad\qquad\qquad\qquad\quad = 3\sqrt{2} + 2\sqrt{2} + 3\sqrt{2}$
$\qquad\qquad\qquad\qquad\quad = 8\sqrt{2}$

Caution: $\sqrt{9 + 4} \neq \sqrt{9} + \sqrt{4} = 3 + 2 = 5$. Rather, $\sqrt{9 + 4} = \sqrt{13} \approx 3.61$.

Critical Thinking

$\sqrt{a} = c\sqrt{d}$ and $b = e\sqrt{d}$.
That is, $a = c^2 d$ and $b = e^2 d$.

Suppose that $a \neq b$. What must be true about a and b for us to be able to simplify $\sqrt{a} + \sqrt{b}$ using the methods that we have discussed in this section?

EXAMPLE 3 Adding radical expressions

Add the expressions and simplify. Assume that all variables are positive.

(a) $\sqrt[4]{32} + 3\sqrt[4]{2}$ **(b)** $-2\sqrt{4x} + \sqrt{x}$ **(c)** $3\sqrt{3k} + 5\sqrt{12k} + 9\sqrt{48k}$

Solution **(a)** Because $\sqrt[4]{32} = \sqrt[4]{16 \cdot 2} = \sqrt[4]{16} \cdot \sqrt[4]{2} = 2\sqrt[4]{2}$, we can add and simplify as follows.

$$\sqrt[4]{32} + 3\sqrt[4]{2} = 2\sqrt[4]{2} + 3\sqrt[4]{2} = 5\sqrt[4]{2}$$

(b) Note that $\sqrt{4x} = \sqrt{4} \cdot \sqrt{x} = 2\sqrt{x}$.

$$-2\sqrt{4x} + \sqrt{x} = -2(2\sqrt{x}) + \sqrt{x} = -4\sqrt{x} + \sqrt{x} = -3\sqrt{x}$$

(c) Note that $\sqrt{12k} = \sqrt{4} \cdot \sqrt{3k} = 2\sqrt{3k}$ and that $\sqrt{48k} = \sqrt{16} \cdot \sqrt{3k} = 4\sqrt{3k}$.

$$\begin{aligned}
3\sqrt{3k} + 5\sqrt{12k} + 9\sqrt{48k} &= 3\sqrt{3k} + 5(2\sqrt{3k}) + 9(4\sqrt{3k}) \\
&= (3 + 10 + 36)\sqrt{3k} \\
&= 49\sqrt{3k}
\end{aligned}$$

Subtraction of radical expressions is similar to addition, as illustrated in the next example.

EXAMPLE 4 Subtracting radical expressions

Subtract and simplify. Assume that all variables are positive.

(a) $5\sqrt{7} - 3\sqrt{7}$ **(b)** $3\sqrt[3]{xy^2} - 2\sqrt[3]{xy^2}$

(c) $\sqrt{16x^3} - \sqrt{x^3}$ **(d)** $\sqrt[3]{\dfrac{5x}{27}} - \dfrac{\sqrt[3]{5x}}{6}$

Solution **(a)** $5\sqrt{7} - 3\sqrt{7} = (5 - 3)\sqrt{7} = 2\sqrt{7}$

(b) $3\sqrt[3]{xy^2} - 2\sqrt[3]{xy^2} = (3 - 2)\sqrt[3]{xy^2} = \sqrt[3]{xy^2}$

(c) $\begin{aligned}[t]
\sqrt{16x^3} - \sqrt{x^3} &= \sqrt{16} \cdot \sqrt{x^3} - \sqrt{x^3} \\
&= 4\sqrt{x^3} - \sqrt{x^3} \\
&= 3\sqrt{x^3} \\
&= 3x\sqrt{x}
\end{aligned}$

(d) $\sqrt[3]{\dfrac{5x}{27}} - \dfrac{\sqrt[3]{5x}}{6} = \dfrac{\sqrt[3]{5x}}{\sqrt[3]{27}} - \dfrac{\sqrt[3]{5x}}{6}$ Quotient rule for radical expressions

$$= \dfrac{\sqrt[3]{5x}}{3} - \dfrac{\sqrt[3]{5x}}{6}$$ Evaluate $\sqrt[3]{27} = 3$.

$$= \dfrac{2\sqrt[3]{5x}}{6} - \dfrac{\sqrt[3]{5x}}{6}$$ Find a common denominator.

$$= \dfrac{2\sqrt[3]{5x} - \sqrt[3]{5x}}{6}$$ Subtract numerators.

$$= \dfrac{\sqrt[3]{5x}}{6}$$ Simplify.

EXAMPLE 5   Subtracting radical expressions

Subtract and simplify. Assume that all variables are positive.

(a) $\dfrac{5\sqrt{2}}{3} - \dfrac{2\sqrt{2}}{4}$ **(b)** $\sqrt[4]{81a^5b^6} - \sqrt[4]{16ab^2}$ **(c)** $3\sqrt[3]{\dfrac{n^5}{27}} - 2\sqrt[3]{n^2}$

Solution   **(a)** $\dfrac{5\sqrt{2}}{3} - \dfrac{2\sqrt{2}}{4} = \dfrac{5\sqrt{2}}{3} \cdot \dfrac{4}{4} - \dfrac{2\sqrt{2}}{4} \cdot \dfrac{3}{3}$ LCD is 12.

$= \dfrac{20\sqrt{2}}{12} - \dfrac{6\sqrt{2}}{12}$ Multiply fractions.

$= \dfrac{14\sqrt{2}}{12}$ Subtract numerators.

$= \dfrac{7\sqrt{2}}{6}$ Reduce.

(b) $\sqrt[4]{81a^5b^6} - \sqrt[4]{16ab^2} = \sqrt[4]{81a^4b^4} \cdot \sqrt[4]{ab^2} - \sqrt[4]{16} \cdot \sqrt[4]{ab^2}$ Factor out perfect powers.

$= 3ab\sqrt[4]{ab^2} - 2\sqrt[4]{ab^2}$ Simplify.

$= (3ab - 2)\sqrt[4]{ab^2}$ Distributive property

(c) $3\sqrt[3]{\dfrac{n^5}{27}} - 2\sqrt[3]{n^2} = 3\sqrt[3]{\dfrac{n^3}{27}} \cdot \sqrt[3]{n^2} - 2\sqrt[3]{n^2}$ Factor out perfect cube.

$= \dfrac{3\sqrt[3]{n^3}}{\sqrt[3]{27}} \cdot \sqrt[3]{n^2} - 2\sqrt[3]{n^2}$ Quotient rule

$= n\sqrt[3]{n^2} - 2\sqrt[3]{n^2}$ Simplify.

$= (n - 2)\sqrt[3]{n^2}$ Distributive property

Radicals often occur in geometry. In the next example, we find the perimeter of a triangle by adding radical expressions.

EXAMPLE 6   Finding the perimeter of a triangle

Find the *exact* perimeter of the right triangle shown in Figure 7.8. Then approximate your answer to the nearest hundredth of a foot.

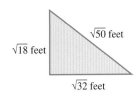

Figure 7.8

Solution   The sum of the lengths of the sides of the triangle is

$$\sqrt{18} + \sqrt{32} + \sqrt{50} = 3\sqrt{2} + 4\sqrt{2} + 5\sqrt{2} = 12\sqrt{2}.$$

The perimeter is $12\sqrt{2} \approx 16.97$ feet.

MULTIPLICATION

Some types of radical expressions can be multiplied like binomials. For example, because $(a - b)(a + b) = a^2 - b^2$ we have

$$(\sqrt{x} - 2)(\sqrt{x} + 2) = (\sqrt{x})^2 - (2)^2 = x - 4,$$

provided x is not negative. The next example demonstrates this technique.

EXAMPLE 7   Multiplying radical expressions

Multiply and simplify.

(a) $(4 + \sqrt{3})(4 - \sqrt{3})$ **(b)** $(\sqrt{b} - 4)(\sqrt{b} + 5)$

Solution   **(a)** This expression is in the form $(a + b)(a - b)$, which equals $a^2 - b^2$.

$$(4 + \sqrt{3})(4 - \sqrt{3}) = (4)^2 - (\sqrt{3})^2$$
$$= 16 - 3$$
$$= 13$$

(b) This expression can be multiplied and then simplified.

$$(\sqrt{b} - 4)(\sqrt{b} + 5) = \sqrt{b} \cdot \sqrt{b} + 5\sqrt{b} - 4\sqrt{b} - 4 \cdot 5$$
$$= b + \sqrt{b} - 20$$

Compare this product with $(b - 4)(b + 5) = b^2 + b - 20$.

RATIONALIZING THE DENOMINATOR

In mathematics it is common to write expressions without radicals in the denominator. When the denominator is either a sum or difference containing a square root, we multiply the numerator and denominator by the *conjugate* of the denominator.

$$\frac{1}{1 + \sqrt{2}} = \frac{1}{1 + \sqrt{2}} \cdot \frac{1 - \sqrt{2}}{1 - \sqrt{2}} \qquad \text{Multiply numerator and denominator by the conjugate.}$$

$$= \frac{1 - \sqrt{2}}{(1)^2 - (\sqrt{2})^2} \qquad \text{Sum and difference}$$

$$= \frac{1 - \sqrt{2}}{1 - 2} \qquad \text{Simplify.}$$

$$= \frac{1 - \sqrt{2}}{-1} \qquad \text{Subtract.}$$

$$= -1 + \sqrt{2} \qquad \text{Simplify.}$$

If the denominator consists of two terms, at least one of which contains a radical expression, then the **conjugate** of the denominator is found by changing a $+$ sign to a $-$ sign or vice versa. For example, the conjugate of $\sqrt{2} + \sqrt{3}$ is $\sqrt{2} - \sqrt{3}$ and the conjugate of $\sqrt{3} - 1$ is $\sqrt{3} + 1$. In the next example, we use this method to rationalize the denominator of fractions that contain radicals.

_____

EXAMPLE 8   Rationalizing the denominator

Rationalize the denominator.

(a) $\dfrac{3 + \sqrt{5}}{2 - \sqrt{5}}$ (b) $\dfrac{\sqrt{x}}{\sqrt{x} - 2}$

Solution   (a) The conjugate of the denominator is $2 + \sqrt{5}$.

$$\frac{3 + \sqrt{5}}{2 - \sqrt{5}} = \frac{(3 + \sqrt{5})}{(2 - \sqrt{5})} \cdot \frac{(2 + \sqrt{5})}{(2 + \sqrt{5})}$$ Multiply by 1.

$$= \frac{6 + 3\sqrt{5} + 2\sqrt{5} + (\sqrt{5})^2}{(2)^2 - (\sqrt{5})^2}$$ Multiply.

$$= \frac{11 + 5\sqrt{5}}{4 - 5}$$ Combine terms.

$$= -11 - 5\sqrt{5}$$ Simplify.

(b) The conjugate of the denominator is $\sqrt{x} + 2$.

$$\frac{\sqrt{x}}{\sqrt{x} - 2} = \frac{\sqrt{x}}{(\sqrt{x} - 2)} \cdot \frac{(\sqrt{x} + 2)}{(\sqrt{x} + 2)}$$ Multiply by 1.

$$= \frac{x + 2\sqrt{x}}{x - 4}$$ Multiply.

_____

7.3   PUTTING IT ALL TOGETHER

In this section we discussed how to add, subtract, and multiply radical expressions. Rationalization of the denominator is a technique that can sometimes be helpful when dividing rational expressions. The following table summarizes important topics in this section.

Concept	Explanation	Examples
Adding and Subtracting Radical Expressions	Combine like radicals when adding or subtracting.	$6\sqrt{13} + \sqrt{13} = (6 + 1)\sqrt{13} = 7\sqrt{13}$
	We cannot combine unlike radicals such as $\sqrt{2}$ and $\sqrt{5}$. But sometimes we can rewrite radicals and then combine.	$\sqrt{40} - \sqrt{10} = \sqrt{4} \cdot \sqrt{10} - \sqrt{10}$ $= 2\sqrt{10} - \sqrt{10}$ $= \sqrt{10}$
Like Radicals	Like radicals have the same index and the same radicand.	$7\sqrt{5}$ and $3\sqrt{5}$ are like radicals. $5\sqrt[3]{ab}$ and $\sqrt[3]{ab}$ are like radicals. $\sqrt[3]{5}$ and $\sqrt[3]{4}$ are unlike radicals. $\sqrt[3]{7}$ and $\sqrt{7}$ are unlike radicals.

continued on next page

continued from previous page

Concept	Explanation	Examples
Multiplying Radical Expressions	Radical expressions can sometimes be multiplied like binomials.	$(\sqrt{a} - 5)(\sqrt{a} + 5) = a - 25$ and $(\sqrt{x} - 3)(\sqrt{x} + 1) = x - 2\sqrt{x} - 3$
Conjugate	The conjugate is found by changing a $+$ sign to a $-$ sign or vice versa.	*Expression* *Conjugate* $\sqrt{x} + 7$ $\sqrt{x} - 7$ $\sqrt{a} - 2\sqrt{b}$ $\sqrt{a} + 2\sqrt{b}$
Rationalizing the Denominator	Multiply the numerator and denominator by the conjugate of the denominator.	$\dfrac{1}{1 - \sqrt{3}} = \dfrac{1}{1 - \sqrt{3}} \cdot \dfrac{(1 + \sqrt{3})}{(1 + \sqrt{3})}$ $= \dfrac{1 + \sqrt{3}}{1 - 3}$ $= -\dfrac{1}{2} - \dfrac{1}{2}\sqrt{3}$

7.3   EXERCISES

FOR EXTRA HELP

📖 Student's Solutions Manual

🚪 MyMathLab

InterAct math InterAct Math

Tutor Center Math Tutor Center

MathXL MathXL

📼 Digital Video Tutor CD 6   Videotape 8

CONCEPTS

1. $\sqrt{a} + \sqrt{a} =$ _____ $2\sqrt{a}$

2. $\sqrt[3]{b} + \sqrt[3]{b} + \sqrt[3]{b} =$ _____ $3\sqrt[3]{b}$

3. You cannot simplify $\sqrt[3]{4} + \sqrt[3]{7}$ because they are not _____ radicals. like   **4.** Yes; $4\sqrt{15} - 3\sqrt{15} = \sqrt{15}$

4. Can you simplify $4\sqrt{15} - 3\sqrt{15}$? Explain.

5. What is the conjugate of $\sqrt{t} - 5$? $\sqrt{t} + 5$

6. To rationalize the denominator of $\dfrac{1}{5 - \sqrt{2}}$, multiply this expression by _____. $\frac{5 + \sqrt{2}}{5 + \sqrt{2}}$

LIKE RADICALS

Exercises 7–16: (Refer to Example 1.) Write the pair of terms as like radicals, if possible. Assume that all variables are positive. 9. $\sqrt{7}, 2\sqrt{7}, 3\sqrt{7}$

7. $\sqrt{12}, \sqrt{24}$ Not possible   **8.** $\sqrt{18}, \sqrt{27}$ Not possible

9. $\sqrt{7}, \sqrt{28}, \sqrt{63}$ **10.** $\sqrt{200}, \sqrt{300}, \sqrt{500}$ Not possible

11. $\sqrt[3]{16}, \sqrt[3]{-54}$ **12.** $\sqrt[3]{80}, \sqrt[3]{10}$ $2\sqrt[3]{10}, \sqrt[3]{10}$
 $2\sqrt[3]{2}, -3\sqrt[3]{2}$

Not possible
 13. $\sqrt{x^2 y}, \sqrt{4y^2}$ **14.** $\sqrt{x^5 y^3}, \sqrt{9xy}$  $x^2 y\sqrt{xy}, 3\sqrt{xy}$

15. $\sqrt[3]{8xy}, \sqrt[3]{x^4 y^4}$ **16.** $\sqrt[3]{64x^4}, \sqrt[3]{-8x}$
 $2\sqrt[3]{xy}, xy\sqrt[3]{xy}$ $4x\sqrt[3]{x}, -2x\sqrt[3]{x}$

Exercises 17–52: Simplify the expression. Assume that all variables are positive.   19. $8\sqrt{5} + \sqrt{2}$

17. $2\sqrt{3} + 7\sqrt{3}$ $9\sqrt{3}$ **18.** $8\sqrt{7} + 2\sqrt{7}$ $10\sqrt{7}$

19. $9\sqrt{5} + \sqrt{2} - \sqrt{5}$ **20.** $11\sqrt{11} - 5\sqrt{11}$ $6\sqrt{11}$

21. $\sqrt{x} + \sqrt{x} - \sqrt{y}$ **22.** $\sqrt{xy^2} - \sqrt{x}$ $(y - 1)\sqrt{x}$
 $2\sqrt{x} - \sqrt{y}$

23. $\sqrt[3]{z} + \sqrt[3]{z}$ $2\sqrt[3]{z}$ **24.** $\sqrt[3]{y} - \sqrt[3]{y}$ 0

25. $2\sqrt[3]{6} - 7\sqrt[3]{6}$ $-5\sqrt[3]{6}$ **26.** $18\sqrt[3]{3} + 3\sqrt[3]{3}$ $21\sqrt[3]{3}$

27. $\sqrt[3]{y^6} - \sqrt[3]{y^3}$ $y^2 - y$ **28.** $2\sqrt{20} + 7\sqrt{5} + 3\sqrt{2}$

29. $3\sqrt{28} + 3\sqrt{7}$ $9\sqrt{7}$ **30.** $9\sqrt{18} - 2\sqrt{8}$ $23\sqrt{2}$

31. $\sqrt{44} - 4\sqrt{11}$ **32.** $\sqrt[4]{5} + 2\sqrt[4]{5}$ $3\sqrt[4]{5}$
 $-2\sqrt{11}$

33. $2\sqrt[3]{16} + \sqrt[3]{2} - \sqrt{2}$ $5\sqrt[3]{2} - \sqrt{2}$

28. $11\sqrt{5} + 3\sqrt{2}$

34. $5\sqrt[3]{x} - 3\sqrt[3]{x}$ $2\sqrt[3]{x}$ **35.** $\sqrt[3]{xy} - 2\sqrt[3]{xy}$ $-\sqrt[3]{xy}$

36. $3\sqrt{x^3} - \sqrt{x}$ $(3x-1)\sqrt{x}$ **37.** $\sqrt{4x+8} + \sqrt{x+2}$ $3\sqrt{x+2}$

38. $\sqrt{2a+1} + \sqrt{8a+4}$ $3\sqrt{2a+1}$

39. $\dfrac{4\sqrt{3}}{3} + \dfrac{\sqrt{3}}{6}$ $\dfrac{3\sqrt{3}}{2}$ **40.** $\dfrac{8\sqrt{5}}{7} + \dfrac{4\sqrt{5}}{2}$ $\dfrac{22\sqrt{5}}{7}$

41. $\dfrac{15\sqrt{8}}{4} - \dfrac{2\sqrt{2}}{5}$ $\dfrac{71\sqrt{2}}{10}$ **42.** $\dfrac{23\sqrt{11}}{2} - \dfrac{\sqrt{44}}{8}$ $\dfrac{45\sqrt{11}}{4}$

43. $2\sqrt[4]{64} - \sqrt[4]{324} + \sqrt[4]{4}$ $2\sqrt{2}$

44. $2\sqrt[3]{16} - 5\sqrt[3]{54} + 10\sqrt[3]{2}$ $-\sqrt[3]{2}$

45. $5\sqrt[4]{x^5} - \sqrt[4]{x}$ $(5x-1)\sqrt[4]{x}$ **46.** $20\sqrt[3]{b^4} - 4\sqrt[3]{b}$ $4\sqrt[3]{b}(5b-1)$

47. $\sqrt{64x^3} - \sqrt{x} + 3\sqrt{x}$ $(8x+2)\sqrt{x}$ or $2\sqrt{x}(4x+1)$

48. $2\sqrt{3z} + 3\sqrt{12z} + 3\sqrt{48z}$ $20\sqrt{3z}$

49. $\sqrt[4]{81a^5b^5} - \sqrt[4]{ab}$ $(3ab-1)\sqrt[4]{ab}$ **50.** $\sqrt[4]{xy^5} - \sqrt[4]{x^5y}$ $(y-x)\sqrt[4]{xy}$

51. $5\sqrt[3]{\dfrac{n^4}{125}} - 2\sqrt[3]{n}$ $(n-2)\sqrt[3]{n}$ **52.** $\sqrt[3]{\dfrac{8x}{27}} - \dfrac{2\sqrt[3]{x}}{3}$ 0

Exercises 53–62: Multiply and simplify.

53. $(3+\sqrt{7})(3-\sqrt{7})$ 2 **54.** $(5-\sqrt{5})(5+\sqrt{5})$ 20

55. $(11-\sqrt{2})(11+\sqrt{2})$ 119

56. $(6+\sqrt{3})(6-\sqrt{3})$ 33

57. $(\sqrt{x}+8)(\sqrt{x}-8)$ $x-64$

58. $(\sqrt{ab}-3)(\sqrt{ab}+3)$ $ab-9$

59. $(\sqrt{ab}-\sqrt{c})(\sqrt{ab}+\sqrt{c})$ $ab-c$

60. $(\sqrt{2x}+\sqrt{3y})(\sqrt{2x}-\sqrt{3y})$ $2x-3y$

61. $(\sqrt{x}-7)(\sqrt{x}+8)$ $x+\sqrt{x}-56$

62. $(\sqrt{ab}-1)(\sqrt{ab}-2)$ $ab-3\sqrt{ab}+2$

Exercises 63–76: Rationalize the denominator.

63. $\dfrac{1}{3-\sqrt{2}}$ $\dfrac{3+\sqrt{2}}{7}$ **64.** $\dfrac{1}{\sqrt{3}-2}$ $-\sqrt{3}-2$

65. $\dfrac{\sqrt{2}}{\sqrt{5}+2}$ $\sqrt{10}-2\sqrt{2}$ **66.** $\dfrac{\sqrt{3}}{\sqrt{3}+2}$ $2\sqrt{3}-3$

67. $\dfrac{\sqrt{7}-2}{\sqrt{7}+2}$ $\dfrac{11-4\sqrt{7}}{3}$ **68.** $\dfrac{\sqrt{3}-1}{\sqrt{3}+1}$ $2-\sqrt{3}$

69. $\dfrac{1}{\sqrt{7}-\sqrt{6}}$ $\sqrt{7}+\sqrt{6}$ **70.** $\dfrac{1}{\sqrt{8}-\sqrt{7}}$ $\sqrt{8}+\sqrt{7}$

71. $\dfrac{\sqrt{z}}{\sqrt{z}-3}$ $\dfrac{z+3\sqrt{z}}{z-9}$ **72.** $\dfrac{2\sqrt{z}}{2-\sqrt{z}}$ $\dfrac{4\sqrt{z}+2z}{4-z}$

73. $\dfrac{\sqrt{a}+\sqrt{b}}{\sqrt{a}-\sqrt{b}}$ **74.** $\dfrac{\sqrt{x}-2\sqrt{y}}{\sqrt{x}+2\sqrt{y}}$

75. $\dfrac{1}{\sqrt{x+1}-\sqrt{x}}$ $\sqrt{x+1}+\sqrt{x}$ **76.** $\dfrac{1}{\sqrt{a+1}+\sqrt{a}}$ $\sqrt{a+1}-\sqrt{a}$

GEOMETRY

77. *Perimeter* (Refer to Example 6.) Find the exact perimeter of the right triangle. Then approximate your answer. $12\sqrt{3} \approx 20.8$ cm

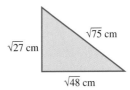

$\sqrt{75}$ cm

$\sqrt{27}$ cm

$\sqrt{48}$ cm

78. *Perimeter* Find the exact perimeter of the rectangle. Then approximate your answer. $10\sqrt{2} \approx 14.1$ cm

73. $\dfrac{a+2\sqrt{ab}+b}{a-b}$

74. $\dfrac{x-4\sqrt{xy}+4y}{x-4y}$

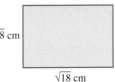

$\sqrt{8}$ cm

$\sqrt{18}$ cm

WRITING ABOUT MATHEMATICS

79. What are like radicals? Give examples.

80. A student simplifies an expression *incorrectly:*

$$\sqrt{8} + \sqrt[3]{16} \stackrel{?}{=} \sqrt{4\cdot 2} + \sqrt[3]{8\cdot 2}$$
$$\stackrel{?}{=} \sqrt{4}\cdot\sqrt{2} + \sqrt[3]{8}\cdot\sqrt[3]{2}$$
$$\stackrel{?}{=} 2\sqrt{2} + 2\sqrt[3]{2}$$
$$\stackrel{?}{=} 4\sqrt{4}$$
$$\stackrel{?}{=} 8.$$

Explain the error that the student made. What would you do differently?

Group Activity: Working with Real Data

Directions: Form a group of 2 to 4 people. Select someone to record the group's responses for this activity. All members of the group should work cooperatively to answer the questions. If your instructor asks for your results, each member of the group should be prepared to respond.

Designing a Paper Cup   A paper drinking cup is being designed in the shape shown in the accompanying figure. The amount of paper needed to manufacture the cup is determined by the surface area S of the cup, which is given by

$$S = \pi r \sqrt{r^2 + h^2},$$

where r is the radius and h is the height.

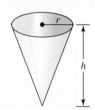

(b) No, the answers are 20.13 and 25.92. The square root of a sum does not equal the sum of the square roots.

(a) Approximate S to the nearest hundredth when $r = 1.5$ inches and $h = 4$ inches.   20.13 in²

(b) Could the formula for S be simplified as follows?

$$\pi r \sqrt{r^2 + h^2} \stackrel{?}{=} \pi r (\sqrt{r^2} + \sqrt{h^2})$$
$$\stackrel{?}{=} \pi r (r + h)$$

Try evaluating this formula with $r = 1.5$ inches and $h = 4$ inches. Is your answer the same as in part (a)? Explain.

(c) Discuss why evaluating real-world formulas correctly is important.   Answers may vary.

(d) In general, does $\sqrt{a + b}$ equal $\sqrt{a} + \sqrt{b}$? Justify your answer by completing the following table. Approximate answers to the nearest hundredth when appropriate.   No

a	b	$\sqrt{a + b}$	$\sqrt{a} + \sqrt{b}$
0	4	2	2
4	0	2	2
5	4	3	4.24
9	7	4	5.65
4	16	4.47	6
25	100	11.18	15

7.4   RADICAL FUNCTIONS

The Square Root Function · The Square Root Property · The Cube Root Function · Power Functions · Modeling with Power Functions (Optional)

INTRODUCTION

A good punter can kick a football so that it has a long *hang time*. Hang time is the length of time that the football is in the air. Long hang time gives the kicking team time to run down the field and stop the punt return. Using square roots, we can derive a function that calculates hang time.

THE SQUARE ROOT FUNCTION

50 feet

To derive a function that calculates the hang time of a football we need two facts from physics. First, when a ball is kicked into the air, half the hang time of the ball is spent going up and the other half is spent coming down. Second, the time t in seconds required for a ball to fall from a height of h feet is modeled by the equation

$$16t^2 = h.$$

Solving this equation for t gives half the hang time.

$16t^2 = h$	Given equation
$t^2 = \dfrac{h}{16}$	Divide by 16.
$\sqrt{t^2} = \sqrt{\dfrac{h}{16}}$	Take the square root of each side.
$\|t\| = \sqrt{\dfrac{h}{16}}$	$\sqrt{a^2} = \|a\|$
$t = \dfrac{\sqrt{h}}{4}$	Assume that $t \geq 0$ and simplify.

Half the hang time is $\frac{\sqrt{h}}{4}$, so the total hang time T in seconds is given by

$$T(h) = \frac{\sqrt{h}}{2},$$

where h is the maximum height of the ball.

In the next example, we use this formula to calculate hang time.

EXAMPLE 1   Calculating hang time

If a football is kicked 50 feet into the air, estimate the hang time. Does the hang time double for a football kicked 100 feet into the air?

Solution   A football kicked 50 feet into the air has a hang time of

$$T(50) = \frac{\sqrt{50}}{2} \approx 3.5 \text{ seconds}.$$

If the football is kicked 100 feet into the air, the hang time is

$$T(100) = \frac{\sqrt{100}}{2} = 5 \text{ seconds}.$$

The hang time does not double.

Critical Thinking

How high would a football have to be kicked to have twice the hang time of a football kicked 50 feet into the air? 200 ft

---

The square root function is given by $f(x) = \sqrt{x}$. The domain of the square root function is all nonnegative real numbers because we have not defined the square root of a negative number. Table 7.1 lists three points that lie on the graph of $f(x) = \sqrt{x}$. In Figure 7.9 theses points are plotted and the graph of $y = \sqrt{x}$ has been sketched. Note that the graph does not appear to the left of the origin because the square root function is undefined for negative inputs.

TABLE 7.1

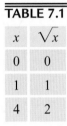

x	$\sqrt{x}$
0	0
1	1
4	2

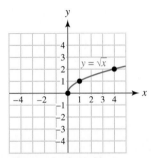

Figure 7.9   Square Root Function

Technology Note: *Square Roots of Negative Numbers*

If a table of values for $y_1 = \sqrt{x}$ includes both negative and positive values for x, then many calculators give error messages when x is negative, as shown in the accompanying figure.

X	Y1
-9	ERROR
-4	ERROR
-1	ERROR
0	0
1	1
4	2
9	3

Y1⬛√(X)

EXAMPLE 2   Finding the domain of a function

Let $f(x) = \sqrt{x - 1}$.

(a) Find the domain of f. Write your answer in interval notation.
(b) Graph $y = f(x)$ and compare it to the graph of $y = \sqrt{x}$.

Solution   **(a)** For $f(x)$ to be defined, $x - 1$ cannot be negative. Thus valid inputs for x must satisfy

$$x - 1 \geq 0 \quad \text{or} \quad x \geq 1.$$

The domain is $[1, \infty)$.

(b) Table 7.2 provides points for the graph of $y = \sqrt{x - 1}$. Note in Figure 7.10 that the graph appears only when $x \geq 1$. This graph is similar to $y = \sqrt{x}$ (see Figure 7.9) except that it is shifted one unit to the right.

TABLE 7.2

x	$\sqrt{x - 1}$
1	0
2	1
5	2

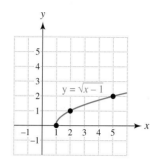

Figure 7.10

EXAMPLE 3   Finding the domain of a function

Find the domain of each function. Write your answer in interval notation.
(a) $f(x) = \sqrt{4 - 2x}$ **(b)** $g(x) = \sqrt{x^2 + 1}$

Solution   **(a)** To determine when $f(x)$ is defined, we must solve the inequality $4 - 2x \geq 0$.

$$4 - 2x \geq 0 \qquad \text{Inequality to be solved}$$
$$4 \geq 2x \qquad \text{Add } 2x \text{ to each side.}$$
$$2 \geq x \qquad \text{Divide each side by 2.}$$

The domain is $(-\infty, 2]$.
(b) Regardless of the value of x, the expression $x^2 + 1$ is always positive because $x^2 \geq 0$. Thus $g(x)$ is defined for all real numbers, and its domain is $(-\infty, \infty)$.

THE SQUARE ROOT PROPERTY

Square roots can be used to solve the equation $x^2 = k$ for x, whenever $k \geq 0$.

$$x^2 = k \qquad \text{Given equation}$$
$$\sqrt{x^2} = \sqrt{k} \qquad \text{Take the square root of each side.}$$
$$|x| = \sqrt{k} \qquad \sqrt{x^2} = |x| \text{ for all } x.$$
$$x = \pm\sqrt{k} \qquad |x| = b \text{ implies } x = \pm b$$

The fact that $x^2 = k$ is equivalent to $x = \pm\sqrt{k}$ is sometimes called the **square root property**. Note that, if $k < 0$, the equation $x^2 = k$ has no real solutions.

SQUARE ROOT PROPERTY

Let k be a nonnegative number. Then the solutions to the equation

$$x^2 = k$$

are given by $x = \pm\sqrt{k}$.

Note: Recall that the symbol $\pm$ indicates "plus or minus." Thus "±2" is equivalent to "2 or -2."

EXAMPLE 4 | **Applying the square root property**

Solve each equation.
(a) $x^2 = 4$ **(b)** $n^2 = 7$ **(c)** $(t + 2)^2 = 25$

Solution   **(a)** Apply the square root property.

$$x^2 = 4 \qquad \text{Given equation}$$
$$x = \pm\sqrt{4} \qquad \text{Square root property}$$
$$x = \pm2 \qquad \text{Simplify.}$$

(b) Apply the square root property.

$$n^2 = 7 \qquad \text{Given equation}$$
$$n = \pm\sqrt{7} \qquad \text{Square root property}$$

(c) After applying the square root property, solve for t.

$$(t + 2)^2 = 25 \qquad \text{Given equation}$$
$$t + 2 = \pm\sqrt{25} \qquad \text{Square root property}$$
$$t + 2 = \pm5 \qquad \text{Simplify.}$$
$$t = -2 \pm 5 \qquad \text{Add } -2 \text{ to each side.}$$

There are two solutions: $-2 + 5 = 3$ and $-2 - 5 = -7$.

═══ MAKING CONNECTIONS ═══

The Square Root Property and Graphical Solutions

Graphically the equation $x^2 = 4$ has two solutions, as shown in the accompanying figures. In the left-hand figure, the graphs of $y_1 = x^2$ and $y_2 = 4$ intersect when $x = \pm2$. However, the equation $x^2 = -2$ has no solutions because the graphs of $y_1 = x^2$ and $y_2 = -2$ in the right-hand figure have no points of intersection.

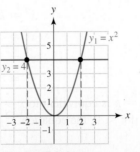

Two Solutions

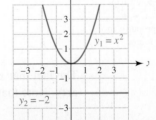

No Solutions

THE CUBE ROOT FUNCTION

The cube root function is given by $f(x) = \sqrt[3]{x}$. Cube roots are defined for both positive and negative numbers, so the domain of the cube root function includes all real numbers.

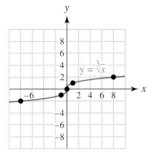

Figure 7.11 Cube Root Function

Table 7.3 lists points that lie on the graph of the cube root function. Figure 7.11 shows a graph of $y = \sqrt[3]{x}$.

TABLE 7.3 Cube Root Function

x	−27	−8	−1	0	1	8	27
$\sqrt[3]{x}$	−3	−2	−1	0	1	2	3

In some parts of the United States, wind power is used to generate electricity. Suppose that the diameter of the circular path created by the blades for a wind-powered generator is 8 feet. Then the wattage W generated by a wind velocity of v miles per hour is modeled by

$$W(v) = 2.4v^3.$$

If the wind blows at 10 miles per hour, the generator can produce about

$$W(10) = 2.4 \cdot 10^3 = 2400 \text{ watts.}$$

(*Source: Conquering the Sciences,* Sharp Electronics.)

In the next example, we use this formula to model a windmill.

EXAMPLE 5 Modeling a windmill

The formula $W(v) = 2.4v^3$ is used to calculate the watts generated when there is a wind velocity of v miles per hour.
(a) Find a function f that calculates the wind velocity when W watts are being produced.
(b) If the wattage doubles, has the wind velocity also doubled? Explain.

Solution **(a)** Solve $W = 2.4v^3$ for v.

$W = 2.4v^3$	Given formula
$\dfrac{W}{2.4} = v^3$	Divide by 2.4.
$\sqrt[3]{\dfrac{W}{2.4}} = \sqrt[3]{v^3}$	Take the cube root of each side.
$v = \sqrt[3]{\dfrac{W}{2.4}}$	Simplify and rewrite equation.

Thus $f(W) = \sqrt[3]{\dfrac{W}{2.4}}$.

(b) Table 7.4 shows that, when the power doubles from 1000 watts to 2000 watts, the wind velocity increases only from about 7.5 to 9.4 miles per hour. For the wattage to double, the wind velocity does not need to double.

TABLE 7.4 Wind Speed $f(W) = \sqrt[3]{\dfrac{W}{2.4}}$

W (watts)	0	1000	2000	4000
Wind Speed (mph)	0	7.5	9.4	11.9

Critical Thinking

In Example 5, if the wind speed v doubles, by what factor does the wattage $W = 2.4v^3$ increase?

Conversely, if the wattage W doubles, by what factor does the wind speed $v = \sqrt[3]{\frac{W}{2.4}}$ increase?   8; $\sqrt[3]{2}$

In Example 5 we used the fact that $\sqrt[3]{a^3} = a$ to solve the equation for v. Because $\sqrt[3]{a} = a^{1/3}$, from the properties of exponents we have

$$\sqrt[3]{a^3} = (a^3)^{1/3} = a^1 = a$$

for any real number a. We use this fact again in the next example to solve two equations.

EXAMPLE 6   **Using cube roots to solve equations**

Solve each equation.
(a) $x^3 = 64$ **(b)** $2(z - 1)^3 = 16$

Solution   **(a)** Take the cube root of each side.

$$
\begin{array}{ll}
x^3 = 64 & \text{Given equation} \\
\sqrt[3]{x^3} = \sqrt[3]{64} & \text{Take the cube root of each side.} \\
x = 4 & \text{Simplify.}
\end{array}
$$

(b) Start by dividing each side by 2.

$$
\begin{array}{ll}
2(z - 1)^3 = 16 & \text{Given equation} \\
(z - 1)^3 = 8 & \text{Divide by 2.} \\
\sqrt[3]{(z - 1)^3} = \sqrt[3]{8} & \text{Take the cube root of each side.} \\
z - 1 = 2 & \text{Simplify.} \\
z = 3 & \text{Add 1 to each side.}
\end{array}
$$

POWER FUNCTIONS

Power functions are a generalization of root functions. Examples of power functions include

$$f(x) = x^{1/2}, \quad g(x) = x^{2/3}, \quad \text{and} \quad h(x) = x^{-3/5}.$$

The exponents for power functions can be rational numbers. Any rational number can be written in lowest terms as $\frac{m}{n}$, where m and n are integers.

TEACHING TIP

Power functions are used extensively in calculus. They are also used in biology and economics.

POWER FUNCTION

If a function can be represented by

$$f(x) = x^p,$$

where p is a rational number, then it is a **power function**. If $p = \frac{1}{n}$, where $n \geq 2$ is an integer, then f is also a **root function**, which is given by

$$f(x) = \sqrt[n]{x}.$$

EXAMPLE 7   Evaluating power functions

If possible, evaluate $f(x)$ at the given value of x.
(a) $f(x) = x^{0.75}$ at $x = 16$ **(b)** $f(x) = x^{1/4}$ at $x = -81$

Solution   **(a)** $0.75 = \frac{3}{4}$, so $f(x) = x^{3/4}$. Thus

$$f(16) = 16^{3/4} = (16^{1/4})^3 = 2^3 = 8$$

because $16^{1/4} = \sqrt[4]{16} = 2$.
(b) $f(-81) = (-81)^{1/4} = \sqrt[4]{-81}$, which is undefined. There is no real number a such that $a^4 = -81$ because a^4 is never negative.

In the next example, we investigate the graph of $y = x^p$ for different values of p.

EXAMPLE 8   Graphing power functions

The graphs of three power functions,

$$f(x) = x^{1/3}, \quad g(x) = x^{0.75}, \quad \text{and} \quad h(x) = x^{1.4}$$

are shown in Figure 7.12. Discuss how the value of p affects the graph of $y = x^p$ when $x > 1$ and when $0 < x < 1$.

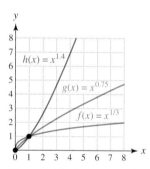

Figure 7.12   Power Functions

Solution   First note that $g(x)$ and $h(x)$ can be written as $g(x) = x^{3/4}$ and $h(x) = x^{7/5}$. When $x > 1$, $h(x) > g(x) > f(x)$ and the graphs increase (rise) faster for larger values of p. When $0 < x < 1$, $h(x) < g(x) < f(x)$. Thus smaller values of p result in larger y-values when $0 < x < 1$. All three graphs appear to intersect at the points $(0, 0)$ and $(1, 1)$.

MODELING WITH POWER FUNCTIONS (OPTIONAL)

Allometry is the study of the relative sizes of different characteristics of an organism. For example, the weight of a bird is related to the surface area of its wings: Heavier birds tend to have larger wings. Allometric relations are often modeled with $f(x) = kx^p$, where k and p are constants.   (*Source:* C. Pennycuick, *Newton Rules Biology.*)

The next example illustrates the use of modeling with power functions.

___

EXAMPLE 9   **Modeling surface area of wings**

The surface area A of a bird's wings with weight w is shown in Table 7.5.

TABLE 7.5

w (kilograms)	0.5	2.0	3.5	5.0
$A(x)$ (square meters)	0.069	0.175	0.254	0.325

Calculator Help

To make a scatterplot, see the Appendix (page AP-4).

(a) Make a scatterplot of the data. Discuss any trends in the data.
(b) Biologists modeled the data with $A(w) = kw^{2/3}$, where k is a constant. Find k.
(c) Graph A and the data in the same viewing rectangle.
(d) Estimate the area of the wings of a 3-kilogram bird.

Solution   **(a)** A scatterplot of the data is shown in Figure 7.13(a). As the weight of a bird increases so does the surface area of its wings.

[0, 6, 1] by [0, 0.4, 0.1]

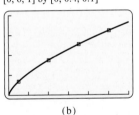

(a)

[0, 6, 1] by [0, 0.4, 0.1]

(b)

Figure 7.13

(b) To determine k, substitute one of the data points into $A(w)$.

$$A(w) = kw^{2/3} \qquad \text{Given formula}$$

$$0.175 = k(2)^{2/3} \qquad \begin{array}{l} \text{Let } w = 2 \text{ and } A(w) = 0.175 \\ \text{(any data point could be used).} \end{array}$$

$$k = \frac{0.175}{2^{2/3}} \qquad \text{Solve for } k.$$

$$k \approx 0.11 \qquad \text{Approximate } k.$$

Thus $A(w) = 0.11w^{2/3}$.

(c) The data and graph of $Y_1 = 0.11X^{(2/3)}$ are shown in Figure 7.13(b). Note that the graph appears to pass through each data point.

(d) $A(3) = 0.11(3)^{2/3} \approx 0.23$ square meter

7.4 ▶ PUTTING IT ALL TOGETHER

In this section we discussed some new functions involving radicals and rational exponents. Properties of these functions are summarized in the following table.

Function	Explanation
Square Root and Cube Root	The square root and cube root functions are given by $$f(x) = \sqrt{x} \quad \text{and} \quad g(x) = \sqrt[3]{x},$$ respectively. The cube root function is defined for all inputs, whereas the square root function is defined only for nonnegative inputs. Their graphs are shown in the accompanying figures.

Function	Explanation
Square Root and Cube Root (*continued*)	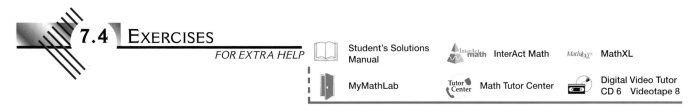 Square Root Function Cube Root Function
Power	If a function f can be defined by $f(x) = x^p$, where p is a rational number, then it is a power function. If $p = \frac{1}{n}$, where $n \geq 2$ is an integer, f is also a root function that can be represented by $f(x) = \sqrt[n]{x}$. ***Example:*** $f(x) = x^{5/3}$ Power function $g(x) = x^{1/4}$ or Both a root and power function $g(x) = \sqrt[4]{x}$

The following table summarizes how to use square roots and cube roots to solve certain types of equations.

Concept	Explanation	Examples
Square Root Property	If $k \geq 0$, the solutions to the equation $x^2 = k$ are given by $x = \pm\sqrt{k}$.	$x^2 = 81$ is equivalent to $x = \pm 9$ and $x^2 = 5$ is equivalent to $x = \pm\sqrt{5}$
Solve Equations with Cube Roots	The solution to the equation $x^3 = k$ is given by $x = \sqrt[3]{k}$.	$x^3 = 8$ is equivalent to $x = 2$ and $x^3 = 11$ is equivalent to $x = \sqrt[3]{11}$

7.4 EXERCISES

FOR EXTRA HELP

📖 Student's Solutions Manual   🔺 InterAct Math   MathXL

🚪 MyMathLab   📞 Math Tutor Center   Digital Video Tutor CD 6   Videotape 8

CONCEPTS

1. Sketch a graph of the square root function.*

2. Sketch a graph of the cube root function.*

3. What is the domain of the square root function?
$\{x \mid x \geq 0\}$

4. What is the domain of the cube root function?
All real numbers

5. Give a symbolic representation for a power function.
$f(x) = x^p$, p is rational

6. Give a symbolic representation for a root function.
$f(x) = \sqrt[n]{x}$

7. What is the domain of $f(x) = \sqrt[4]{x}$? $\{x \mid x \geq 0\}$

8. Let $f(x) = x^p$ and $g(x) = x^q$ with $p > q$. When $x > 1$, is $x^p > x^q$ or $x^p < x^q$? $x^p > x^q$

*Answers on page IA-22

ROOT FUNCTIONS

Exercises 9–12: Evaluate the function at the given value of the variable.

9. $T(h) = \dfrac{\sqrt{h}}{2}$ $\qquad$ $h = 100$ $\quad$ 5

10. $L(k) = 2\sqrt{k} + 2$ $\qquad$ $k = 23$ $\quad$ 10

11. $f(x) = \sqrt{x + 5} + \sqrt{x}$ $\qquad$ $x = 4$ $\quad$ 5

12. $f(x) = \dfrac{\sqrt{x - 5} - \sqrt{x}}{2}$ $\qquad$ $x = 9$ $\quad$ $-\frac{1}{2}$

Exercises 13–24: (Refer to Example 2.) Find the domain of f. Write your answer in interval notation.

13. $f(x) = \sqrt{x + 1}$ $\qquad$ **14.** $f(x) = \sqrt{x - 2}$
$[-1, \infty)$ $\qquad\qquad\qquad$ $[2, \infty)$

15. $f(x) = \sqrt{2x - 4}$ $\qquad$ **16.** $f(x) = \sqrt{4x + 2}$
$[2, \infty)$ $\qquad\qquad\qquad$ $[-\frac{1}{2}, \infty)$

17. $f(x) = \sqrt{1 - x}$ $\qquad$ **18.** $f(x) = \sqrt{6 - 3x}$
$(-\infty, 1]$ $\qquad\qquad\qquad$ $(-\infty, 2]$

19. $f(x) = \sqrt{8 - 5x}$ $\qquad$ **20.** $f(x) = \sqrt{3 - 2x}$

21. $f(x) = \sqrt{3x^2 + 4}$ $\qquad$ **22.** $f(x) = \sqrt{1 + 2x^2}$
$(-\infty, \infty)$ $\qquad\qquad\qquad$ $(-\infty, \infty)$

23. $f(x) = \dfrac{1}{\sqrt{2x + 1}}$ $\qquad$ **24.** $f(x) = \dfrac{1}{\sqrt{x - 1}}$ $\quad$ $(1, \infty)$

$(-\frac{1}{2}, \infty)$ $\qquad\qquad$ 19. $(-\infty, \frac{8}{5}]$ $\quad$ 20. $(-\infty, \frac{3}{2}]$

EQUATIONS AND GRAPHS

Exercises 25–40: Solve the equation.

25. $x^2 = 49$ $\quad$ ± 7 $\qquad$ **26.** $x^2 = 9$ $\quad$ ± 3

27. $2z^2 = 200$ $\quad$ ± 10 $\qquad$ **28.** $3z^2 = 48$ $\quad$ ± 4

29. $(t + 1)^2 = 16$ $\quad$ $-5, 3$ $\qquad$ **30.** $(t - 5)^2 = 81$ $\quad$ $-4, 14$

31. $(4 - 2x)^2 = 100$ $\qquad$ **32.** $(3x - 6)^2 = 25$ $\quad$ $\frac{1}{3}, \frac{11}{3}$
$-3, 7$

33. $b^3 = 64$ $\quad$ 4 $\qquad$ **34.** $a^3 = 1000$ $\quad$ 10

35. $2t^3 = -128$ $\quad$ -4 $\qquad$ **36.** $3t^3 = -81$ $\quad$ -3

37. $(x + 1)^3 = 8$ $\quad$ 1 $\qquad$ **38.** $(4 - x)^3 = -1$ $\quad$ 5

39. $(2 - 5z)^3 = -125$ $\quad$ $\frac{7}{5}$ **40.** $(2x + 4)^3 = 125$ $\quad$ $\frac{1}{2}$

Exercises 41–46: Graph the equation. Compare the graph to either $y = \sqrt{x}$ or $y = \sqrt[3]{x}$.*

41. $y = \sqrt{x} + 2$ $\qquad$ **42.** $y = \sqrt{x} - 1$
Shifted 2 units left $\qquad$ Shifted 1 unit right

43. $y = \sqrt{x + 2}$ $\qquad$ **44.** $y = \sqrt[3]{x} + 2$
Shifted 2 units upward $\qquad$ Shifted 2 units upward

45. $y = \sqrt[3]{x + 2}$ $\qquad$ **46.** $y = \sqrt[3]{x} - 1$
Shifted 2 units left $\qquad$ Shifted 1 unit downward

POWER FUNCTIONS

Exercises 47–54: If possible, evaluate f(x) at the given value of x. When appropriate, approximate the answer to the nearest hundredth.

47. $f(x) = x^{5/2}$ $\qquad$ $x = 4, x = 5$ $\quad$ 32; 55.90

48. $f(x) = x^{-3/4}$ $\qquad$ $x = 1, x = 3$ $\quad$ 1; 0.44

49. $f(x) = x^{-7/5}$ $\qquad$ $x = -32, x = 10$ $\quad$ $-\frac{1}{128} \approx -0.01$; 0.04

50. $f(x) = x^{4/3}$ $\qquad$ $x = -8, x = 27$ $\quad$ 16; 81

51. $f(x) = x^{1/4}$ $\qquad$ $x = 256, x = -10$ $\quad$ 4; Not possible

52. $f(x) = x^{3/4}$ $\qquad$ $x = 16, x = -1$ $\quad$ 8; Not possible

53. $f(x) = x^{2/5}$ $\qquad$ $x = 32, x = -32$ $\quad$ 4; 4

54. $f(x) = x^{5/6}$ $\qquad$ $x = -5, x = 64$ $\quad$ Not possible; 32

Exercises 55–58: Graph f and g in the window $[0, 6, 1]$ by $[0, 6, 1]$. Which function is greater when $x > 1$?*

55. $f(x) = x^{1/5}, g(x) = x^{1/3}$ $\quad$ $g(x)$

56. $f(x) = x^{4/5}, g(x) = x^{5/4}$ $\quad$ $g(x)$

57. $f(x) = x^{1.2}, g(x) = x^{0.45}$ $\quad$ $f(x)$

58. $f(x) = x^{-1.4}, g(x) = x^{1.4}$ $\quad$ $g(x)$

APPLICATIONS

59. *Jumping* (Refer to Example 1.) If a person jumps 4 feet off the ground, estimate how long the person is in the air. $\quad$ 1 sec

60. *Hang Time* (Refer to Example 1.) Find the hang time for a golf ball hit 80 feet into the air. $\quad$ About 4.5 sec

61. *Aging More Slowly* Albert Einstein in his theory of relativity showed that, if a person travels at nearly the speed of light, then time slows down significantly. Suppose that there are twins; one remains on Earth and the other leaves in a very fast spaceship having velocity v. If the twin on Earth ages T_0 years, then according to Einstein the twin in the spaceship ages T years, where

$$T(v) = T_0\sqrt{1 - (v/c)^2}.$$

In this formula c represents the speed of light, which is 186,000 miles per second.
(a) Evaluate T when $v = 0.8c$ (eight-tenths the speed of light) and $T_0 = 10$ years. (*Hint:* Simplify $\frac{v}{c}$ without using 186,000 miles per second.) $\quad$ 6 yr
(b) Interpret your result. $\quad$ The twin in the spaceship will be 4 yr younger than the twin on Earth. $\quad$ *Answers on pages IA-22–IA-23

62. *Increasing Your Weight* (Refer to Exercise 61.) Albert Einstein also showed that the weight (mass) of an object increases when traveling near the speed of light. If a person's weight on Earth is W_0, then the same person's weight W in a spaceship traveling at velocity v is

$$W(v) = \frac{W_0}{\sqrt{1 - (v/c)^2}}.$$

  (a) Evaluate W when $v = 0.6c$ (six-tenths the speed of light) and $W_0 = 220$ pounds (100 kilograms).
  (b) Interpret your result.   275 lb
  A 220-lb person traveling at 60% of the speed of light weighs 275 lb.

63. *Wind Power* (Refer to Example 5.) If a wind-powered generator has blades that create a circular path with a diameter of 10 feet, then the wattage W generated by a wind velocity of v miles per hour is modeled by $W(v) = 3.8v^3$.
  (a) If the wind velocity doubles, what happens to the wattage generated?   It increases by a factor of 8.
  (b) Solve $W = 3.8v^3$ for v. $v = \sqrt[3]{W/3.8}$
  (c) If the wind generator is producing 30,400 watts, find the wind speed.   20 mph

64. *Modeling Wing Span* (Refer to Example 9.) Biologists have found that the weight W of a bird and the length L of its wing span are related by $L = kW^{1/3}$, where k is a constant. The following table lists L and W for one species of bird.   (***Source:*** C. Pennycuick.)

W (kilograms)	0.1	0.4	0.8	1.1
L (meters)	0.422	0.670	0.844	0.938

$k \approx 0.91$
  (a) Use the data to approximate the value of k.
  (b) Graph L and the data in the same viewing rectangle. What happens to L as W increases? *It increases.
  (c) Estimate the wing span of a bird weighing 0.7 kilogram.   About 0.808 m
  (d) Find L when $W = 0.65$, and interpret the result.
  About 0.788; a bird weighing 0.65 kg has a wing span of about 0.788 m.

65. *Pulse Rate in Animals* The following table lists typical pulse rates R in beats per minute (bpm) for animals with various weights W in pounds.
(***Source:*** C. Pennycuick.)

W (pounds)	20	150	500	1500
R (beats per minute)	198	72	40	23

  (a) Describe what happens to the pulse rate as the size of the animal increases.   It decreases.
  (b) Plot the data in [0, 1600, 400] by [0, 220, 20].*
  (c) These data can be modeled by $R = kW^{-1/2}$. Find k. $k \approx 885$
  (d) Find R when $W = 700$, and interpret the result.
  $R \approx 33$; a 700-lb animal will have a pulse rate of about 33 bpm.

66. *Design of Open Channels* To protect cities from flooding during heavy rains, open channels are sometimes constructed to handle runoff. The rate R at which water flows through the channel is modeled by $R = k\sqrt{m}$, where m is the slope of the channel and k is a constant determined by the shape of the channel.
(***Source:*** N. Garber and L. Hoel, *Traffic and Highway Design.*)
  (a) Suppose that a channel has a slope of $m = 0.01$ (or 1%) and a runoff rate of $R = 340$ cubic feet per second (cfs). Find k. $k = 3400$
  (b) If the slope of the channel increases to $m = 0.04$ (or 4%), what happens to R? Be specific.
           It doubles to 680 cfs

WRITING ABOUT MATHEMATICS

67. Explain why a root function is an example of a power function.

68. Discuss the shape of the graph of $y = x^p$ as p increases. Assume that p is a positive rational number and that x is a positive real number.

CHECKING BASIC CONCEPTS ⟨ SECTIONS 7.3 AND 7.4 ⟩

---

1. Simplify each expression.
   (a) $\sqrt{3} \cdot \sqrt{12}$ 6
   (b) $\dfrac{\sqrt[3]{81}}{\sqrt[3]{3}}$ 3
   (c) $\sqrt{36x^6}, x > 0$ $6x^3$

2. Simplify each expression.
   (a) $5\sqrt{6} + 2\sqrt{6} + \sqrt{7}$ $7\sqrt{6} + \sqrt{7}$
   (b) $8\sqrt[3]{x} - 3\sqrt[3]{x}$ $5\sqrt[3]{x}$
   (c) $\sqrt{9x} - \sqrt{4x}$ $\sqrt{x}$

3. Simplify each expression.
   (a) $\sqrt[3]{xy^4} - \sqrt[3]{x^4y}$ $(y - x)\sqrt[3]{xy}$
   (b) $(4 - \sqrt{2})(4 + \sqrt{2})$ 14

4. Rationalize the denominator of $\dfrac{2}{\sqrt{5} - 1}$. $\frac{\sqrt{5} + 1}{2}$

5. Sketch a graph of each function and then evaluate $f(-1)$, if possible.*
   (a) $f(x) = \sqrt{x}$ $f(-1)$ is undefined.
   (b) $f(x) = \sqrt[3]{x}$ $f(-1) = -1$
   (c) $f(x) = \sqrt{x^2}$ $f(-1) = 1$

6. Evaluate $f(x) = 0.2x^{2/3}$ when $x = 64$.   3.2

7. Find the domain of $f(x) = \sqrt{x - 4}$. Write your answer in interval notation. $[4, \infty)$

8. Solve the equation $(x + 1)^2 = 16$ for x. $-5, 3$

*Answers on page IA-23

7.5   EQUATIONS INVOLVING RADICAL EXPRESSIONS

Solving Radical Equations · The Distance Formula

INTRODUCTION

In Section 7.4 we showed that for some types of birds there is a relationship between their weight and the size of their wings—heavier birds tend to have larger wings. This relationship can sometimes be modeled by $A = 100\sqrt[3]{W^2}$, where W is weight in pounds and A is area in square inches. Suppose that we want to estimate the weight of a bird whose wings have an area of 600 square inches. To do so we would need to solve the equation

$$600 = 100\sqrt[3]{W^2}$$

TEACHING TIP

Use the introduction to explain how equations involving radicals occur in real life.

for W. This equation contains a radical expression. In this section we explain how to solve this type of equation. (***Source:*** C. Pennycuick, *Newton Rules Biology.*)

SOLVING RADICAL EQUATIONS

Many times, equations contain either radical expressions or rational exponents. Examples include

$$\sqrt{x} = 6, \quad 5x^{1/2} = 1, \quad \text{and} \quad \sqrt[3]{x - 1} = 3.$$

One strategy for solving an equation containing a square root is to isolate the square root and then square each side of the equation. This technique is an example of the *power rule for solving equations.*

	POWER RULE FOR SOLVING EQUATIONS

If each side of an equation is raised to the same integer power, then any solutions to the given equation are among the solutions to the new equation. That is, the solutions to the equation $a = b$ are among the solutions to $a^n = b^n$.

We must check our solutions when applying the power rule. For example, consider the equation $2x = 6$. If we square each side, we obtain $4x^2 = 36$. Solving this new equation gives $x^2 = 9$, or $x = \pm 3$. Here, 3 is a solution to both equations, but -3 is an **extraneous solution** that satisfies the second equation but not the given equation.

We illustrate this method in the next example.

EXAMPLE 1   Solving a radical equation symbolically

Solve $\sqrt{2x - 1} = 3$. Check your solution.

Solution   Begin by squaring each side of the equation.

$$\sqrt{2x - 1} = 3 \qquad \text{Given equation}$$
$$(\sqrt{2x - 1})^2 = 3^2 \qquad \text{Square each side.}$$
$$2x - 1 = 9 \qquad \text{Simplify.}$$
$$2x = 10 \qquad \text{Add 1.}$$
$$x = 5 \qquad \text{Divide by 2.}$$

To check our work we substitute $x = 5$ in the given equation.

$$\sqrt{2(5) - 1} \stackrel{?}{=} 3$$
$$3 = 3 \qquad \text{It checks.}$$

Note: To solve the equation in Example 1, we used the fact that

$$\left(\sqrt{a}\right)^2 = \sqrt{a} \cdot \sqrt{a} = a.$$

The following steps are used to solve a radical equation.

TEACHING TIP

Emphasize the importance of checking any answers after applying the power rule.

	SOLVING A RADICAL EQUATION

STEP 1: Isolate a radical term on one side of the equation.

STEP 2: Apply the power rule by raising each side of the equation to the power equal to the index of the isolated radical term.

STEP 3: Solve the equation. If it still contains a radical, repeat Steps 1 and 2.

STEP 4: Check your answers by substituting each result in the *given* equation.

In the next example, we apply these steps to a radical equation.

EXAMPLE 2   Isolating the radical term

Solve $\sqrt{4 - x} + 5 = 8$.

Solution   **STEP 1:** To isolate the radical term, we subtract 5 from each side of the equation.

$$\sqrt{4 - x} + 5 = 8 \qquad \text{Given equation}$$
$$\sqrt{4 - x} = 3 \qquad \text{Subtract 5.}$$

STEP 2: The isolated term involves a square root, so we must square each side.

$$(\sqrt{4 - x})^2 = (3)^2 \qquad \text{Square each side.}$$

STEP 3: Next we solve the resulting equation. (It is not necessary to repeat Steps 1 and 2 because the resulting equation does not contain any radical expressions.)

$$4 - x = 9 \qquad \text{Simplify.}$$
$$-x = 5 \qquad \text{Subtract 4.}$$
$$x = -5 \qquad \text{Multiply by } -1.$$

STEP 4: To check our work we substitute $x = -5$ in the given equation.

$$\sqrt{4 - (-5)} + 5 \stackrel{?}{=} 8$$
$$\sqrt{9} + 5 \stackrel{?}{=} 8$$
$$8 = 8 \qquad \text{It checks.}$$

Example 3 shows why we must check our answers when squaring each side of an equation.

EXAMPLE 3   Solving a radical equation

Solve $\sqrt{3x + 3} = 2x - 1$. Check your results and then solve the equation graphically.

Solution   *Symbolic Solution*   Begin by squaring each side of the equation.

$$\sqrt{3x + 3} = 2x - 1 \qquad \text{Given equation}$$
$$(\sqrt{3x + 3})^2 = (2x - 1)^2 \qquad \text{Square each side.}$$
$$3x + 3 = 4x^2 - 4x + 1 \qquad \text{Expand.}$$
$$0 = 4x^2 - 7x - 2 \qquad \text{Subtract } 3x + 3.$$
$$0 = (4x + 1)(x - 2) \qquad \text{Factor.}$$
$$x = -\frac{1}{4} \quad \text{or} \quad x = 2 \qquad \text{Solve for } x.$$

To check these values substitute $x = -\frac{1}{4}$ and $x = 2$ in the given equation.

$$\sqrt{3\left(-\frac{1}{4}\right) + 3} \stackrel{?}{=} 2\left(-\frac{1}{4}\right) - 1$$
$$\sqrt{2.25} \stackrel{?}{=} -1.5$$
$$1.5 \neq -1.5 \qquad \text{It does not check.}$$

Thus $-\frac{1}{4}$ is an *extraneous solution*. Next substitute $x = 2$ in the given equation.

TEACHING TIP

Extraneous solutions occur with symbolic solutions but not with graphical solutions.

$$\sqrt{3 \cdot 2 + 3} \stackrel{?}{=} 2 \cdot 2 - 1$$
$$\sqrt{9} \stackrel{?}{=} 3$$
$$3 = 3 \qquad \text{It checks.}$$

The only solution is 2.

Graphical Solution   The solution 2 is supported graphically in Figure 7.14, where the graphs of $Y_1 = \sqrt{(3X + 3)}$ and $Y_2 = 2X - 1$ intersect at the point $(2, 3)$. Note that the graphical solution does not give an extraneous solution.

Calculator Help

To find a point of intersection, see the Appendix (page AP-7).

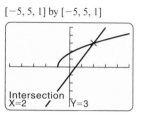

$[-5, 5, 1]$ by $[-5, 5, 1]$

Intersection
X=2   Y=3

Figure 7.14

Example 3 demonstrates that checking solutions is essential when you are squaring each side of an equation. Squaring may introduce extraneous solutions, which are solutions to the new equation but are not solutions to the given equation.

When an equation contains two or more terms with square roots, it may be necessary to square each side of the equation more than once. In these situations, isolate one of the square roots and then square each side of the equation. If a radical term remains after simplifying, repeat these steps. We apply this technique in the next example.

EXAMPLE 4   Squaring twice

Solve $\sqrt{2x} - 1 = \sqrt{x + 1}$.

Solution   Begin by squaring each side of the equation.

$\sqrt{2x} - 1 = \sqrt{x + 1}$	Given equation
$(\sqrt{2x} - 1)^2 = (\sqrt{x + 1})^2$	Square each side.
$(\sqrt{2x})^2 - 2(\sqrt{2x})(1) + 1^2 = x + 1$	$(a - b)^2 = a^2 - 2ab + b^2$
$2x - 2\sqrt{2x} + 1 = x + 1$	Simplify.
$2x - 2\sqrt{2x} = x$	Subtract 1.
$x = 2\sqrt{2x}$	Subtract x and add $2\sqrt{2x}$.
$x^2 = 4(2x)$	Square each side again.
$x^2 - 8x = 0$	Subtract $8x$.
$x(x - 8) = 0$	Factor.
$x = 0 \quad \text{or} \quad x = 8$	Solve.

To check your solutions substitute $x = 0$ in the given equation.

$$\sqrt{2 \cdot 0} - 1 \overset{?}{=} \sqrt{0 + 1}$$

$$-1 \neq 1 \qquad \text{It does not check.}$$

Now substitute $x = 8$.

$$\sqrt{2 \cdot 8} - 1 \overset{?}{=} \sqrt{8 + 1}$$

$$3 = 3 \qquad \text{It checks.}$$

The only solution is 8.

In the next example we apply the power rule to an equation that contains a cube root.

EXAMPLE 5   Solving an equation containing an isolated cube root

Solve $\sqrt[3]{4x - 7} = 4$.

Solution   **STEP 1:** The radical term is already isolated on the left side of the equation, so we proceed to Step 2.

STEP 2: Because the index is 3, we cube each side of the equation.

$$\sqrt[3]{4x - 7} = 4 \qquad \text{Given equation}$$

$$(\sqrt[3]{4x - 7})^3 = (4)^3 \qquad \text{Cube each side.}$$

STEP 3: We solve the resulting equation.

$$4x - 7 = 64 \qquad \text{Simplify.}$$

$$4x = 71 \qquad \text{Add 7 to each side.}$$

$$x = \frac{71}{4} \qquad \text{Divide each side by 4.}$$

STEP 4: To check our work we substitute $x = \frac{71}{4}$ in the given equation.

$$\sqrt[3]{4\left(\frac{71}{4}\right) - 7} \stackrel{?}{=} 4$$

$$\sqrt[3]{64} \stackrel{?}{=} 4$$

$$4 = 4 \qquad \text{It checks.}$$

In the next example we solve the equation presented in the introduction to this section.

EXAMPLE 6   Finding the weight of a bird

Solve the equation $600 = 100\sqrt[3]{W^2}$ to determine the weight in pounds of a bird having wings with an area of 600 square inches.

Solution   Begin by dividing each side of the equation by 100.

$$\frac{600}{100} = \sqrt[3]{W^2} \qquad \text{Divide each side by 100.}$$

$$(6)^3 = (\sqrt[3]{W^2})^3 \qquad \text{Cube each side.}$$

$$216 = W^2 \qquad \text{Simplify.}$$

$$W = \sqrt{216} \qquad \text{Take principal square root, } W > 0.$$

$$W \approx 14.7 \qquad \text{Approximate.}$$

The weight of the bird is approximately 14.7 pounds.

Technology Note: *Graphing Radical Expressions*

The equation in Example 6 can be solved graphically. Sometimes it is more convenient to use rational exponents than radical notation. Thus $y = 100 \sqrt[3]{W^2}$ can be entered as $Y_1 = 100X^{\wedge}(2/3)$. (Be sure to include parentheses around the 2/3.) The accompanying figure shows y_1 intersecting the line $y_2 = 600$ near the point $(14.7, 600)$, which supports our symbolic result.

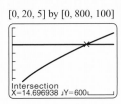

[0, 20, 5] by [0, 800, 100]

In the next example we solve an equation containing different powers of x. This equation would be difficult to solve symbolically, but an *approximate* solution can be found graphically.

EXAMPLE 7   **Solving an equation with a rational exponent**

Solve $x^{2/3} = 3 - x^2$ graphically.

Solution   Graph $Y_1 = X^{\wedge}(2/3)$ and $Y_2 = 3 - X^{\wedge}2$. Their graphs intersect near $(-1.34, 1.21)$ and $(1.34, 1.21)$, as shown in Figure 7.15. Thus the solutions are given by $x \approx \pm 1.34$.

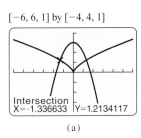

[−6, 6, 1] by [−4, 4, 1]

(a)

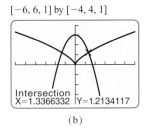

[−6, 6, 1] by [−4, 4, 1]

(b)

Figure 7.15

THE DISTANCE FORMULA

One of the most famous theorems in mathematics is the **Pythagorean theorem**. It states that, if a right triangle has legs a and b with hypotenuse c (see Figure 7.16), then

$$a^2 + b^2 = c^2.$$

For example, if the legs of a right triangle are $a = 3$ and $b = 4$, the hypotenuse is $c = 5$ because $3^2 + 4^2 = 5^2$.

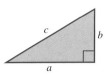

Figure 7.16
$a^2 + b^2 = c^2$

EXAMPLE 8   Applying the Pythagorean theorem

A rectangular television screen has a width of 20 inches and a height of 15 inches. Find the diagonal of the television. Why is it called a 25-inch television?

Solution   In Figure 7.17, let $a = 20$ and $b = 15$. Then the diagonal of the television corresponds to the hypotenuse of a right triangle with legs of 20 inches and 15 inches.

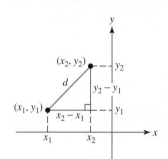

Figure 7.17

$$
\begin{aligned}
c^2 &= a^2 + b^2 && \text{Pythagorean theorem} \\
c &= \sqrt{a^2 + b^2} && \text{Take the principal square root, } c > 0. \\
c &= \sqrt{20^2 + 15^2} && \text{Substitute } a = 20 \text{ and } b = 15. \\
c &= 25 && \text{Simplify.}
\end{aligned}
$$

A 25-inch television has a diagonal of 25 inches.

The Pythagorean theorem can be used to determine the distance between two points. Suppose that a line segment has endpoints (x_1, y_1) and (x_2, y_2), as illustrated in Figure 7.18. The lengths of the legs of the right triangle are $x_2 - x_1$ and $y_2 - y_1$. The distance d is the hypotenuse of a right triangle. Applying the Pythagorean theorem, we have

$$
d^2 = (x_2 - x_1)^2 + (y_2 - y_1)^2.
$$

Distance is nonnegative, so we let d be the principal square root and obtain

$$
d = \sqrt{(x_2 - x_1)^2 + (y_2 - y_1)^2}.
$$

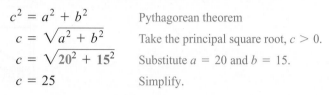

Figure 7.18

DISTANCE FORMULA

The **distance** d between the points (x_1, y_1) and (x_2, y_2) in the xy-plane is

$$
d = \sqrt{(x_2 - x_1)^2 + (y_2 - y_1)^2}.
$$

EXAMPLE 9   Finding distance between points

Find the distance between the points $(-2, 3)$ and $(1, -4)$.

Solution   Start by letting $(x_1, y_1) = (-2, 3)$ and $(x_2, y_2) = (1, -4)$. Then substitute these values into the distance formula.

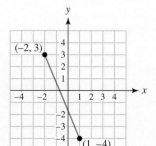

Figure 7.19

$$
\begin{aligned}
d &= \sqrt{(x_2 - x_1)^2 + (y_2 - y_1)^2} && \text{Distance formula} \\
&= \sqrt{(1 - (-2))^2 + (-4 - 3)^2} && \text{Substitute.} \\
&= \sqrt{9 + 49} && \text{Simplify.} \\
&= \sqrt{58} && \text{Take the square root.} \\
&\approx 7.62 && \text{Approximate.}
\end{aligned}
$$

The distance between the points, as shown in Figure 7.19, is exactly $\sqrt{58}$ units, or about 7.62 units. Note that we would obtain the same result if we let $(x_1, y_1) = (1, -4)$ and $(x_2, y_2) = (-2, 3)$.

EXAMPLE 10 Designing a highway curve

Figure 7.20 shows a circular highway curve joining a straight section of road. A surveyor is trying to locate the *x*-coordinate of the *point of curvature PC* where the two sections of the highway meet. The distance between the surveyor and *PC* should be 400 feet. Estimate the *x*-coordinate of *PC* if *x* is positive.

Solution In Figure 7.20, the distance between the points $(0, 75)$ and $(x, 300)$ is 400 feet. We can apply the distance formula and solve for *x*.

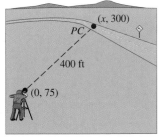

$$d = \sqrt{(x_2 - x_1)^2 + (y_2 - y_1)^2} \qquad \text{Distance formula}$$
$$400 = \sqrt{(x - 0)^2 + (300 - 75)^2} \qquad \text{Substitute.}$$
$$400^2 = (x - 0)^2 + (300 - 75)^2 \qquad \text{Square each side.}$$
$$160{,}000 = x^2 + 50{,}625 \qquad \text{Simplify.}$$
$$x^2 = 109{,}375 \qquad \text{Solve for } x^2.$$
$$x = \sqrt{109{,}375} \qquad \text{Take the principal square root, } x > 0.$$
$$x \approx 330.7 \qquad \text{Approximate.}$$

Figure 7.20

The *x*-coordinate is about 330.7.

PUTTING IT ALL TOGETHER

In this section we focused on equations that contain either radical expressions or rational exponents. A good strategy for solving an equation containing radical expressions *symbolically* is to raise each side of the equation to the same integer power. However, checking answers is important to eliminate any extraneous solutions. Note that these extraneous solutions do not occur when an equation is being solved graphically.

Concept	Description	Example
Power Rule for Solving Equations	If each side of an equation is raised to the same integer power, any solutions to the given equation are among the solutions to the new equation.	$\sqrt{2x} = x$ $2x = x^2 \qquad$ Square each side. $x^2 - 2x = 0 \qquad$ Rewrite equation. $x = 0 \quad \text{or} \quad x = 2 \qquad$ Factor and solve. Be sure to check any solutions.
Pythagorean Theorem	If *c* is the hypotenuse of a right triangle and *a* and *b* are its legs, then $a^2 + b^2 = c^2$.	If the sides of the right triangle are $a = 5$, $b = 12$, and $c = 13$, then they satisfy $a^2 + b^2 = c^2$ or $5^2 + 12^2 = 13^2$. ![triangle with sides 13, 5, 12]

continued on next page

continued from previous page

Concept	Description	Example
Distance Formula	The distance d between the points (x_1, y_1) and (x_2, y_2) is $$d = \sqrt{(x_2 - x_1)^2 + (y_2 - y_1)^2}.$$	The distance between $(2, 3)$ and $(-3, 4)$ is $$d = \sqrt{(-3 - 2)^2 + (4 - 3)^2}$$ $$= \sqrt{(-5)^2 + (1)^2} = \sqrt{26}.$$

7.5 EXERCISES

FOR EXTRA HELP

Student's Solutions Manual   InterAct Math   MathXL

MyMathLab   Math Tutor Center   Digital Video Tutor CD 7 Videotape 8

CONCEPTS

1. What is a good first step for solving $\sqrt{4x - 1} = 5$?
Square each side.

2. What is a good first step for solving $\sqrt[3]{x + 1} = 6$?
Cube each side.

3. Can an equation involving rational exponents have more than one solution?   Yes

4. When you square each side of an equation to solve for an unknown, what must you do with any answers?
Check them.

5. What is the Pythagorean theorem used for?
Finding an unknown side of a right triangle.

6. If the legs of a right triangle are 3 and 4, what is the length of the hypotenuse?   5

7. What formula can you use to find the distance d between two points? $d = \sqrt{(x_2 - x_1)^2 + (y_2 - y_1)^2}$

8. Write the equation $\sqrt{x} + \sqrt[4]{x^3} = 2$ with rational exponents. $x^{1/2} + x^{3/4} = 2$

SYMBOLIC SOLUTIONS

Exercises 9–34: Solve the equation symbolically. Check your results.

9. $\sqrt{x} = 8$ 64

10. $\sqrt{3z} = 6$ 12

11. $\sqrt[4]{x} = 3$ 81

12. $\sqrt[3]{x - 4} = 2$ 12

13. $\sqrt{2t + 4} = 4$ 6

14. $\sqrt{y + 4} = 3$ 5

15. $\sqrt{x + 6} = x$ 3

16. $\sqrt{z + 6} = z$ 9

17. $\sqrt[3]{x} = 3$ 27

18. $\sqrt[3]{x + 10} = 4$ 54

19. $\sqrt[3]{2z - 4} = -2$ -2

20. $\sqrt[3]{z - 1} = -3$ -26

21. $\sqrt[4]{t + 1} = 2$ 15

22. $\sqrt[4]{5t} = 5$ 125

23. $\sqrt{5z - 1} = \sqrt{z + 1}$ $\frac{1}{2}$

24. $y = \sqrt{y + 1} + 1$ 3

25. $\sqrt{1 - x} = 1 - x$ $0, 1$

26. $\sqrt[3]{4x} = x$ $-2, 0, 2$

27. $\sqrt{b^2 - 4} = b - 2$ 2

28. $\sqrt{b^2 - 2b + 1} = b$ $\frac{1}{2}$

29. $\sqrt{1 - 2x} = x + 7$ -4

30. $\sqrt{4 - y} = y - 2$ 3

31. $\sqrt{x} = \sqrt{x - 5} + 1$ 9

32. $\sqrt{x - 1} = \sqrt{x + 4} - 1$ 5

33. $\sqrt{2t - 2} + \sqrt{t} = 7$ 9

34. $\sqrt{x + 1} - \sqrt{x - 6} = 1$ 15

Exercises 35–44: Solve the equation graphically. Approximate solutions to the nearest hundredth when appropriate.

35. $\sqrt[3]{x + 5} = 2$ 3   **36.** $\sqrt[3]{x} + \sqrt{x} = 3.43$ 3.60

37. $\sqrt{2x - 3} = \sqrt{x} - \dfrac{1}{2}$ 1.88

38. $x^{4/3} - 1 = 2$ ±2.28

39. $x^{5/3} = 2 - 3x^2$ **40.** $x^{3/2} = \sqrt{x + 2} - 2$ No solutions
−1, 0.70

41. $z^{1/3} - 1 = 2 - z$ 1.79   **42.** $z^{3/2} - 2z^{1/2} - 1 = 0$ 2.62

43. $\sqrt{y + 2} + \sqrt{3y + 2} = 2$ −0.47

44. $\sqrt{x + 1} - \sqrt{x - 1} = 4$ No solutions

USING MORE THAN ONE METHOD

Exercises 45–48: Solve the equation
    (a) symbolically,
    (b) graphically, and
    (c) numerically.

45. $2\sqrt{x} = 8$ 16   **46.** $\sqrt[3]{5 - x} = 2$ −3

47. $\sqrt{6z - 2} = 8$ 11   **48.** $\sqrt{y + 4} = \dfrac{y}{3}$ 12

SOLVING AN EQUATION FOR A VARIABLE

Exercises 49–52: Solve the equation for the indicated variable.

49. $T = 2\pi\sqrt{\dfrac{L}{32}}$ for L $L = \dfrac{8T^2}{\pi^2}$

50. $Z = \sqrt{L^2 + R^2}$ for R $R = \pm\sqrt{Z^2 - L^2}$

51. $r = \sqrt{\dfrac{A}{\pi}}$ for A $A = \pi r^2$

52. $F = \dfrac{1}{2\pi\sqrt{LC}}$ for C $C = \dfrac{1}{4\pi^2 LF^2}$

PYTHAGOREAN THEOREM

Exercises 53–60: If the sides of a triangle are a, b, and c and they satisfy $a^2 + b^2 = c^2$, the triangle is a right triangle. Determine whether the triangle with the given sides is a right triangle.

53. $a = 6$ $b = 8$ $c = 10$ Yes

54. $a = 5$ $b = 12$ $c = 13$ Yes

55. $a = \sqrt{5}$ $b = \sqrt{9}$ $c = \sqrt{14}$ Yes

56. $a = 4$ $b = 5$ $c = 7$ No

57. $a = 7$ $b = 24$ $c = 25$ Yes

58. $a = 1$ $b = \sqrt{3}$ $c = 2$ Yes

59. $a = 8$ $b = 8$ $c = 16$ No

60. $a = 11$ $b = 60$ $c = 61$ Yes

Exercises 61–64: Find the length of the missing side in the right triangle.

61. $\sqrt{32} = 4\sqrt{2}$ **62.** 8

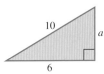

63. 7   **64.** $\sqrt{48} = 4\sqrt{3}$

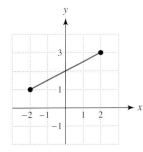
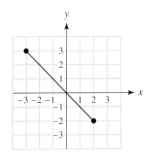

Exercises 65–70: A right triangle has legs a and b with hypotenuse c. Find the length of the missing side.

65. $a = 3, b = 4$ $c = 5$ **66.** $a = 4, b = 7$ $c = \sqrt{65}$

67. $a = \sqrt{3}, c = 8$ **68.** $a = \sqrt{6}, c = \sqrt{10}$ $b = 2$
$b = \sqrt{61}$

69. $b = 48, c = 50$ **70.** $b = 10, c = 26$ $a = 24$
$a = 14$

DISTANCE FORMULA

Exercises 71–74: Find the length of the line segment in the figure.

71. $\sqrt{20} = 2\sqrt{5}$ **72.** $\sqrt{50} = 5\sqrt{2}$

73. $\sqrt{4000} = 20\sqrt{10}$ **74.** $\sqrt{23,125} = 25\sqrt{37}$

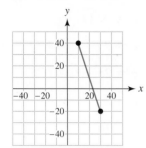

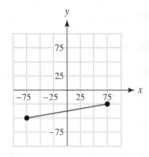

Exercises 75–78: Find the distance between the points.

75. $(-1, 2), (4, 10)$ $\sqrt{89}$ **76.** $(5, -40), (-6, 20)$ 61

77. $(0, -3), (4, 0)$ 5   **78.** $(3, 9), (-4, 2)$ $\sqrt{98} = 7\sqrt{2}$

Exercises 79–82: (Refer to Example 10.) Find x if the distance between the given points is d. Assume that x is positive.

79. $(x, 3), (0, 6)$ $d = 5$ 4

80. $(x, -1), (6, 11)$ $d = 13$ 1, 11

81. $(x, -5), (62, 6)$ $d = 61$ 2, 122

82. $(x, 3), (12, -4)$ $d = 25$ 36

APPLICATIONS

*Exercises 83 and 84: **Weight of a Bird** (Refer to Example 6.) Estimate the weight of a bird having wings of area A.*

83. $A = 400$ square inches $W = 8$ lb

84. $A = 1000$ square inches $W = \sqrt{1000} \approx 31.6$ lb

*Exercises 85–88: **Distance to the Horizon** Because of Earth's curvature, a person can see a limited distance to the horizon. The higher the location of the person, the farther that person can see. The distance D in miles to the horizon can be estimated by $D(h) = 1.22\sqrt{h}$, where h is the height of the person above the ground in feet.*

85. Find D for a 6-foot-tall person standing on level ground.   About 3 mi

86. Find D for a person on top of Mount Everest with a height of 29,028 feet.   About 208 mi

87. How high does a person need to be to see 20 miles?
       About 269 ft

88. How high does a plane need to fly for the pilot to be able to see 100 miles?   About 6719 ft

89. ***Diagonal of a Television***   (Refer to Example 8.) A rectangular television screen is 11.4 inches by 15.2 inches. Find the diagonal of the television set.   19 in.

90. ***Dimensions of a Television***   The height of a television with a 13-inch diagonal is $\frac{3}{4}$ of its width. Find the width and height of the television set.   10.4 in. by 7.8 in.

91. ***DVD and Picture Dimensions***   If the picture shown on a television set is h units high and w units wide, the *aspect ratio* of the picture is $\frac{w}{h}$ (see the accompanying figure). Digital video discs support the newer aspect ratio of $\frac{16}{9}$ rather than the older ratio of $\frac{4}{3}$. If the width of a picture with an aspect ratio of $\frac{16}{9}$ is 29 inches, approximate the height and diagonal of the rectangular picture. (***Source:*** J. Taylor, *DVD Demystified*.) $h \approx 16.3$ in., $d = 33.3$ in.

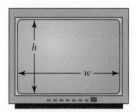

92. ***Flood Control***   The spillway capacity of a dam is important in flood control. Spillway capacity Q in cubic feet of water per second flowing over the spillway depends on the width W and the depth D of the spillway, as illustrated in the accompanying figure. If W and D are measured in feet, capacity can be modeled by $Q = 3.32WD^{3/2}$.   (***Source:*** D. Callas, Project Director, *Snapshots of Applications in Mathematics*.)   (b) About 9 ft

   (a) Find the capacity of a spillway with $W = 20$ feet and $D = 5$ feet.   About 742 ft³/sec

   (b) A spillway with a width of 30 feet is to have a capacity of $Q = 2690$ cubic feet per second. Estimate the appropriate depth of the spillway.

93. ***Sky Diving***   When sky divers initially fall from an airplane, their velocity v in miles per hour after free falling d feet can be approximated by $v = \frac{60}{11}\sqrt{d}$. (Because of air resistance, they will eventually reach a terminal velocity and the formula will no longer be valid.) How far do sky divers need to fall to attain the following velocities? (These values for d represent minimum distances.)

(a) 60 miles per hour   **(b)** 100 miles per hour
121 ft   About 336 ft

94. *Guy Wire*   A guy wire attached to the top of a 30-foot-long pole is anchored 10 feet from the base of the pole, as illustrated in the accompanying figure. Find the length of the guy wire to the nearest tenth of a foot.   About 31.6 ft

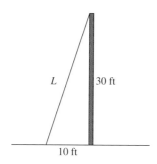

95. *Skid Marks*   Vehicles involved in accidents often leave skid marks, which can be used to determine how fast a vehicle was traveling. To determine this speed, officials often use a test vehicle to compare skid marks on the same section of road. Suppose that a vehicle in a crash left skid marks D feet long and that a test vehicle traveling at v miles per hour leaves skid marks d feet long. Then the speed V of the vehicle involved in the crash is given by

$$V = v\sqrt{\frac{D}{d}}.$$

(a) About 38 mph; the vehicle involved in the accident was traveling about 38 mph.

(*Source:* N. Garber and L. Hoel, *Traffic and Highway Engineering.*)

(a) Find V if $v = 30$ mph, $D = 285$ feet, and $d = 178$ feet. Interpret your result.

(b) A test vehicle traveling at 45 mph leaves skid marks 255 feet long. How long would the skid marks be for a vehicle traveling 60 miles per hour?   About 453 ft

96. *Highway Curves*   If a circular curve without any banking has a radius of R feet, the speed limit L in miles per hour for the curve is $L = 1.5\sqrt{R}$. (*Source:* N. Garber.)

(a) Find the speed limit for a curve having a radius of 400 feet.   30 mph

(b) If the radius of a curve doubles, what happens to the speed limit?   It increases by a factor of $\sqrt{2} \approx 1.4$.

(c) A curve with a 40-mile-per-hour speed limit is being designed. What should be its radius?   About 711 ft

97. *45°–45° Right Triangle*   Suppose that the legs of a right triangle with angles of 45° and 45° both have length a, as depicted in the accompanying figure. Find the length of the hypotenuse. $a\sqrt{2}$

98. *30°–60° Right Triangle*   In a right triangle with angles of 30° and 60°, the shortest side is half the length of the hypotenuse (see the accompanying figure). If the hypotenuse has length c, find the length of the other two sides in terms of c. $a = \frac{1}{2}c, b = \frac{\sqrt{3}}{2}c$

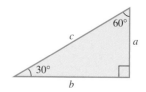

WRITING ABOUT MATHEMATICS

99. A student solves an equation *incorrectly* as follows.

$$\sqrt{3 - x} = \sqrt{x} - 1$$
$$(\sqrt{3 - x})^2 \overset{?}{=} (\sqrt{x})^2 - (1)^2$$
$$3 - x \overset{?}{=} x + 1$$
$$-2x \overset{?}{=} -2$$
$$x \overset{?}{=} 1$$

(a) How could you convince the student that the answer is wrong?

(b) Discuss where the error was made.

100. When each side of an equation is squared, you must check your results. Explain why.

Group Activity: Working with Real Data

Directions: Form a group of 2 to 4 people. Select someone to record the group's responses for this activity. All members of the group should work cooperatively to answer the questions. If your instructor asks for your results, each member of the group should be prepared to respond.

Simple Pendulum   Gravity is responsible for an object falling toward Earth. The farther the object falls, the faster it is moving when it hits the ground. For each second that an object falls, its speed increases by a constant amount, called the *acceleration due to gravity*, denoted g. One way to calculate the value of g is to use a simple pendulum. See the accompanying figure.

The time T for a pendulum to swing back and forth once is called its *period* and is given by

$$T = 2\pi\sqrt{\frac{L}{g}},$$

where L equals the length of the pendulum. The accompanying table lists the periods of pendulums with different lengths.

L (feet)	0.5	1.0	1.5
T (seconds)	0.78	1.11	1.36

(a) Solve the formula for g. $g = \dfrac{4\pi^2 L}{T^2}$

(b) Use the table to determine the value of g. (*Note:* The units for g are feet per second per second.) 32

(c) Interpret your result.
For each second that an object falls, its speed increases by 32 ft/sec.

7.6 COMPLEX NUMBERS

Basic Concepts · **Addition, Subtraction, and Multiplication** · **Powers of *i*** · **Complex Conjugates and Division**

INTRODUCTION

Mathematics is both applied and theoretical. A common misconception is that abstract or theoretical mathematics is unimportant in today's world. Many new ideas with great practical importance were first developed as abstract concepts with no particular application in mind. For example, complex numbers, which are related to square roots of negative numbers, started as an abstract concept to solve equations. Today complex numbers are used in many sophisticated applications, such as the design of electrical circuits, ships, and airplanes. Even the *fractal image* shown in Figure 7.21 would not have been discovered without complex numbers.   (*Source:* D. Kincaid and W. Cheney, *Numerical Analysis.*)

Figure 7.21 A Fractal: *The Cube Roots of Unity*

BASIC CONCEPTS

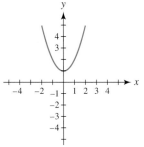

Figure 7.22

A graph of $y = x^2 + 1$ is shown in Figure 7.22. There are no x-intercepts, so the equation $x^2 + 1 = 0$ has no real number solutions.

If we try to solve $x^2 + 1 = 0$ by subtracting 1 from each side, the result is $x^2 = -1$. Because $x^2 \geq 0$ for any real number x, there are no real solutions. However, mathematicians have invented solutions.

$$x^2 = -1$$
$$x = \pm \sqrt{-1} \qquad \text{Square root property}$$

We now define a number called the **imaginary unit**, denoted i.

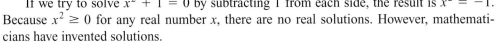

PROPERTIES OF THE IMAGINARY UNIT i

$$i = \sqrt{-1} \quad \text{and} \quad i^2 = -1$$

By creating the number i, the solutions to the equation $x^2 + 1 = 0$ are i and $-i$. Using the real numbers and the imaginary unit i, we can define a new set of numbers called the *complex numbers*. A **complex number** can be written in **standard form**, as $a + bi$, where a and b are real numbers. The **real part** is a and the **imaginary part** is b. Every real number a is also a complex number because it can be written $a + 0i$. A complex number $a + bi$ with $b \neq 0$ is an **imaginary number**. Table 7.6 lists several complex numbers with their real and imaginary parts.

TABLE 7.6

Complex Number: $a + bi$	$-3 + 2i$	5	$-3i$	$-1 + 7i$	$-5 - 2i$	$4 + 6i$
Real Part: a	-3	5	0	-1	-5	4
Imaginary Part: b	2	0	-3	7	-2	6

Figure 7.23 shows how different sets of numbers are related. Note that *the set of complex numbers contains the set of real numbers*.

TEACHING TIP

Use Figure 7.23 to help students visualize how different sets of numbers are related.

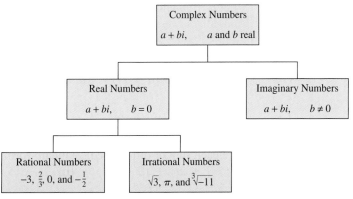

Figure 7.23

Using the imaginary unit i, we may write the square root of a negative number as a complex number. For example, $\sqrt{-2} = i\sqrt{2}$, and $\sqrt{-4} = i\sqrt{4} = 2i$. This method is summarized as follows.

Calculator Help
To set your calculator in $a + bi$ mode, see the Appendix (page AP-11).

THE EXPRESSION $\sqrt{-a}$

If $a > 0$, then $\sqrt{-a} = i\sqrt{a}$.

EXAMPLE 1 Writing the square root of a negative number

Write each square root using the imaginary unit i.

(a) $\sqrt{-25}$ (b) $\sqrt{-7}$ (c) $\sqrt{-20}$

Solution (a) $\sqrt{-25} = i\sqrt{25} = 5i$ (b) $\sqrt{-7} = i\sqrt{7}$

(c) $\sqrt{-20} = i\sqrt{20} = i\sqrt{4}\sqrt{5} = 2i\sqrt{5}$

TEACHING TIP

Compare addition, subtraction, and multiplication of complex numbers to addition, subtraction, and multiplication of binomials.

ADDITION, SUBTRACTION, AND MULTIPLICATION

Arithmetic operations can be defined for complex numbers.

ADDITION AND SUBTRACTION To add the complex numbers $(-3 + 2i)$ and $(2 - i)$ add the real parts and then add the imaginary parts.

$$(-3 + 2i) + (2 - i) = (-3 + 2) + (2i - i)$$
$$= (-3 + 2) + (2 - 1)i$$
$$= -1 + i$$

This same process works for subtraction.

$$(6 - 3i) - (2 + 5i) = (6 - 2) + (-3i - 5i)$$
$$= (6 - 2) + (-3 - 5)i$$
$$= 4 - 8i$$

This method is summarized as follows.

SUM OR DIFFERENCE OF COMPLEX NUMBERS

Let $a + bi$ and $c + di$ be two complex numbers. Then

$$(a + bi) + (c + di) = (a + c) + (b + d)i \qquad \text{Sum}$$

and

$$(a + bi) - (c + di) = (a - c) + (b - d)i. \qquad \text{Difference}$$

EXAMPLE 2 Adding and subtracting complex numbers

Write each sum or difference in standard form.
(a) $(-7 + 2i) + (3 - 4i)$ (b) $3i - (5 - i)$

Solution (a) $(-7 + 2i) + (3 - 4i) = (-7 + 3) + (2 - 4)i = -4 - 2i$

(b) $3i - (5 - i) = 3i - 5 + i = -5 + (3 + 1)i = -5 + 4i$

Technology Note: *Complex Numbers*

Many calculators can perform arithmetic with complex numbers. The figure shows a calculator display for the results in Example 2.

Calculator Help

To access the imaginary unit i, see the Appendix (page AP-11).

```
(-7+2i)+(3-4i)
              -4-2i
3i-(5-i)
              -5+4i
```

MULTIPLICATION   We multiply two complex numbers in the same way that we multiply binomials and then we apply the property $i^2 = -1$.

EXAMPLE 3   Multiplying complex numbers

Write each product in standard form.
(a) $(2 - 3i)(1 + 4i)$ **(b)** $(5 - 2i)(5 + 2i)$

Solution   **(a)** Multiply the complex numbers like binomials.

$$(2 - 3i)(1 + 4i) = (2)(1) + (2)(4i) - (3i)(1) - (3i)(4i)$$
$$= 2 + 8i - 3i - 12i^2$$
$$= 2 + 5i - 12(-1)$$
$$= 14 + 5i$$

(b) Multiply these complex numbers in the same way.

$$(5 - 2i)(5 + 2i) = (5)(5) + (5)(2i) - (2i)(5) - (2i)(2i)$$
$$= 25 + 10i - 10i - 4i^2$$
$$= 25 - 4(-1)$$
$$= 29$$

```
(2-3i)(1+4i)
            14+5i
(5-2i)(5+2i)
               29
```

Figure 7.24

These results are supported in Figure 7.24.

POWERS OF i

An interesting pattern appears when powers of i are calculated.

$$i^1 = i$$
$$i^2 = -1$$
$$i^3 = i^2 \cdot i = -1 \cdot i = -i$$
$$i^4 = i^2 \cdot i^2 = (-1)(-1) = 1$$
$$i^5 = i^4 \cdot i = (1)i = i$$
$$i^6 = i^4 \cdot i^2 = (1)(-1) = -1$$
$$i^7 = i^4 \cdot i^3 = (1)(-i) = -i$$
$$i^8 = i^4 \cdot i^4 = (1)(1) = 1$$

The powers of i cycle with the pattern i, -1, $-i$, and 1. These examples suggest the following method for calculating powers of i.

> ### POWERS OF i
>
> The value of i^n can be found by dividing n by 4. If the remainder is r, then
>
> $$i^n = i^r.$$
>
> Note that $i^0 = 1$, $i^1 = i$, $i^2 = -1$, and $i^3 = -i$.

EXAMPLE 4   Calculating powers of i

Evaluate each expression.
(a) i^9 **(b)** i^{19} **(c)** i^{40}

Solution   **(a)** When 9 is divided by 4, the result is 2 with remainder 1. Thus $i^9 = i^1 = i$.
(b) When 19 is divided by 4, the result is 4 with remainder 3. Thus $i^{19} = i^3 = -i$.
(c) When 40 is divided by 4, the result is 10 with remainder 0. Thus $i^{40} = i^0 = 1$.

COMPLEX CONJUGATES AND DIVISION

The **complex conjugate** of $a + bi$ is $a - bi$. To find the conjugate, we change the sign of the imaginary part b. Table 7.7 contains examples of complex numbers and their conjugates.

TABLE 7.7   Complex Conjugates

Number	$2 + 5i$	$6 - 3i$	$-2 + 7i$	$-1 - i$	5	$-4i$
Conjugate	$2 - 5i$	$6 + 3i$	$-2 - 7i$	$-1 + i$	5	$4i$

The product of two complex conjugates is a real number, as we demonstrated in Example 3(b). This property is used to divide two complex numbers. To convert the quotient $\frac{2 + 3i}{3 - i}$ into standard form $a + bi$, we multiply the numerator and the denominator by the complex conjugate of the denominator, which is $3 + i$. The next example illustrates this method.

EXAMPLE 5   Dividing complex numbers

Write each quotient in standard form.
(a) $\dfrac{2 + 3i}{3 - i}$ **(b)** $\dfrac{4}{2i}$

Solution   **(a)** Multiply the numerator and denominator by $3 + i$.

$$\frac{2 + 3i}{3 - i} = \frac{(2 + 3i)(3 + i)}{(3 - i)(3 + i)} \qquad \text{Multiply by 1.}$$

$$= \frac{2(3) + (2)(i) + (3i)(3) + (3i)(i)}{(3)(3) + (3)(i) - (i)(3) - (i)(i)} \qquad \text{Expand.}$$

$$= \frac{6 + 2i + 9i + 3i^2}{9 + 3i - 3i - i^2} \qquad \text{Simplify.}$$

$$= \frac{6 + 11i + 3(-1)}{9 - (-1)} \qquad i^2 = -1$$

$$= \frac{3 + 11i}{10} \qquad \text{Simplify.}$$

$$= \frac{3}{10} + \frac{11}{10}i \qquad \frac{a + bi}{c} = \frac{a}{c} + \frac{b}{c}i$$

(b) Multiply the numerator and denominator by $-2i$.

$$\frac{4}{2i} = \frac{(4)(-2i)}{(2i)(-2i)} \qquad \text{Multiply by 1.}$$

$$= \frac{-8i}{-4i^2} \qquad \text{Simplify.}$$

$$= \frac{-8i}{-4(-1)} \qquad i^2 = -1$$

$$= \frac{-8i}{4} \qquad \text{Simplify.}$$

$$= -2i \qquad \text{Divide.}$$

These results are supported in Figure 7.25.

```
(2+3i)/(3-i)►Fra
c
        3/10+11/10i
4/(2i)
              -2i
```

Figure 7.25

7.6 PUTTING IT ALL TOGETHER

In this section we discussed complex numbers and how to perform arithmetic operations with them. Complex numbers allow us to solve equations that could not be solved only with real numbers. The following table summarizes the important concepts in the section.

Concept	Explanation	Examples
Complex Numbers	A complex number can be expressed as $a + bi$, where a and b are real numbers. The imaginary unit i satisfies $i = \sqrt{-1}$ and $i^2 = -1$. As a result, we can write $\sqrt{-a} = i\sqrt{a}$ if $a > 0$.	$\sqrt{-13} = i\sqrt{13}$ and $\sqrt{-9} = 3i$
Addition, Subtraction, and Multiplication	To add (subtract) complex numbers, add (subtract) the real parts and then add (subtract) the imaginary parts. Multiply complex numbers in a similar manner to how *FOIL* is used to multiply binomials. Then apply the property $i^2 = -1$.	$(3 + 6i) + (-1 + 2i)$ Sum $= (3 + -1) + (6 + 2)i$ $= 2 + 8i$ $(2 - 5i) - (1 + 4i)$ Difference $= (2 - 1) + (-5 - 4)i$ $= 1 - 9i$ $(-1 + 2i)(3 + i)$ Product $= (-1)(3) + (-1)(i) + (2i)(3) + (2i)(i)$ $= -3 - i + 6i + 2i^2$ $= -3 + 5i + 2(-1)$ $= -5 + 5i$

continued on next page

continued from previous page

Concept	Explanation	Examples
Complex Conjugates	The conjugate of $a + bi$ is $a - bi$.	The conjugate of $3 - 5i$ is $3 + 5i$.
Division	To simplify a quotient, multiply the numerator and denominator by the complex conjugate of the denominator. Then simplify the expression and write it in standard form as $a + bi$.	$\dfrac{10}{1 + 2i} = \dfrac{10(1 - 2i)}{(1 + 2i)(1 - 2i)}$ $= \dfrac{10 - 20i}{5}$ $= 2 - 4i$

7.6 EXERCISES

FOR EXTRA HELP

Student's Solutions Manual

MyMathLab

 InterAct Math

 Math Tutor Center

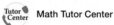 MathXL

Digital Video Tutor
CD 7   Videotape 8

CONCEPTS

1. Give an example of a complex number that is not a real number. $2 + 3i$; answers may vary.

2. Can you give an example of a real number that is not a complex number? Explain.   No; any real number a can be written as $a + 0i$.

3. $\sqrt{-1} = $ _____ i

4. $i^2 = $ _____ -1

5. $\sqrt{-a} = $ _____, if $a > 0$. $i\sqrt{a}$

6. The complex conjugate of $10 + 7i$ is _____. $10 - 7i$

7. The standard form for a complex number is _____. $a + bi$

8. Write $\dfrac{2 + 4i}{2}$ in standard form. $1 + 2i$

9. The real part of $4 - 5i$ is _____. 4

10. The imaginary part of $4 - 5i$ is _____. -5

COMPLEX NUMBERS

Exercises 11–20: Use the imaginary unit to write the expression.

11. $\sqrt{-5}$ $i\sqrt{5}$

12. $\sqrt{-21}$ $i\sqrt{21}$

13. $\sqrt{-100}$ $10i$

14. $\sqrt{-49}$ $7i$

15. $\sqrt{-144}$ $12i$

16. $\sqrt{-64}$ $8i$

17. $\sqrt{-12}$ $2i\sqrt{3}$

18. $\sqrt{-8}$ $2i\sqrt{2}$

19. $\sqrt{-18}$ $3i\sqrt{2}$

20. $\sqrt{-48}$ $4i\sqrt{3}$

Exercises 21–42: Write the expression in standard form.

21. $(5 + 3i) + (-2 - 3i)$ 3

22. $(1 - i) + (5 - 7i)$ $6 - 8i$

23. $(2i) + (-8 + 5i)$ $-8 + 7i$

24. $(-3i) + (5i)$ $2i$

25. $(2 - 7i) - (1 + 2i)$ $1 - 9i$

26. $(1 + 8i) - (3 + 9i)$ $-2 - i$

27. $(5i) - (10 - 2i)$ $-10 + 7i$

28. $(1 + i) - (1 - i)$ $2i$

29. $4(5 - 3i)$ $20 - 12i$

30. $(1 + 2i)(-6 - i)$ $-4 - 13i$

31. $(-3 - 4i)(5 - 4i)$ $-31 - 8i$

32. $(3 + 5i)(3 - 5i)$ 34

33. $(-4i)(5i)$ 20

34. $(-6i)(-4i)$ -24

35. $3i + (2 - 3i) - (1 - 5i)$ $1 + 5i$

36. $4 - (5 - 7i) + (3 + 7i)$ $2 + 14i$

37. $(2 + i)^2$ $3 + 4i$

38. $(-1 + 2i)^2$ $-3 - 4i$

39. $2i(-3 + i)$ $-2 - 6i$

40. $5i(1 - 9i)$ $45 + 5i$

41. $i(1 + i)^2$ -2

42. $2i(1 - i)^2$ 4

Exercises 43–50: (Refer to Example 4.) Simplify the power of i.

43. i^{11} $-i$

44. i^{50} -1

45. i^{21} i

46. i^{103} $-i$

47. i^{58} -1

48. i^{61} i

49. i^{64} 1

50. i^{28} 1

Exercises 51–58: Write the complex conjugate.

51. $3 + 4i$ $3 - 4i$ **52.** $1 - 4i$ $1 + 4i$

53. $-6i$ $6i$ **54.** -10 -10

55. $5 - 4i$ $5 + 4i$ **56.** $7 + 2i$ $7 - 2i$

57. -1 -1 **58.** $19i$ $-19i$

Exercises 59–72: Write the expression in standard form.

59. $\dfrac{2}{1 + i}$ $1 - i$ **60.** $\dfrac{-6}{2 - i}$ $-\dfrac{12}{5} - \dfrac{6}{5}i$

61. $\dfrac{3i}{5 - 2i}$ $-\dfrac{6}{29} + \dfrac{15}{29}i$ **62.** $\dfrac{-8}{2i}$ $4i$

63. $\dfrac{8 + 9i}{5 + 2i}$ $2 + i$ **64.** $\dfrac{3 - 2i}{1 + 4i}$ $-\dfrac{5}{17} - \dfrac{14}{17}i$

65. $\dfrac{5 + 7i}{1 - i}$ $-1 + 6i$ **66.** $\dfrac{-7 + 4i}{3 - 2i}$ $-\dfrac{29}{13} - \dfrac{2}{13}i$

67. $\dfrac{2 - i}{i}$ $-1 - 2i$ **68.** $\dfrac{3 + 2i}{-i}$ $-2 + 3i$

69. $\dfrac{1}{i} + \dfrac{1}{2i}$ $-\dfrac{3}{2}i$ **70.** $\dfrac{3}{4i} + \dfrac{2}{i}$ $-\dfrac{11}{4}i$

71. $\dfrac{1}{-1 + i} - \dfrac{2}{i}$ $-\dfrac{1}{2} + \dfrac{3}{2}i$ **72.** $-\dfrac{3}{2i} - \dfrac{2}{1 + i}$ $-1 + \dfrac{5}{2}i$

APPLICATIONS

Exercises 73 and 74: **Corrosion in Airplanes** *Corrosion in the metal surface of an airplane can be difficult to detect visually. One test used to locate it involves passing an alternating current through a small area on the plane's surface. If the current varies from one region to another, it may indicate that corrosion is occurring. The impedance Z (or opposition to the flow of electricity) of the metal is related to the voltage V and current I by the equation $Z = \frac{V}{I}$, where Z, V, and I are complex numbers. Calculate Z for the given values of V and I.* (**Source:** Society for Industrial and Applied Mathematics.)

73. $V = 40 + 70i, I = 2 + 3i$ $\frac{290}{13} + \frac{20}{13}i$

74. $V = 10 + 20i, I = 3 + 7i$ $\frac{85}{29} - \frac{5}{29}i$

WRITING ABOUT MATHEMATICS

75. A student multiplies $(2 + 3i)(4 - 5i)$ *incorrectly* to obtain $8 - 15i$. What was the student's mistake?

76. A student divides $\frac{6 - 10i}{3 + 2i}$ *incorrectly* to obtain $2 - 5i$. What was the student's mistake?

CHECKING BASIC CONCEPTS   SECTIONS 7.5 AND 7.6

1. Solve each equation. Check your answers.
  (a) $\sqrt{2x - 4} = 2$ 4 **(b)** $\sqrt[3]{x - 1} = 3$ 28
  (c) $\sqrt{3x} = 1 + \sqrt{x + 1}$ 3

2. Find the distance between the points $(-3, 5)$ and $(2, -7)$. 13

3. A 16-inch diagonal television set has a rectangular picture with a width of 12.8 inches. Find the height of the picture.   9.6 in.

4. Use the imaginary unit i to write each expression.
  (a) $\sqrt{-64}$ $8i$
  (b) $\sqrt{-17}$ $i\sqrt{17}$

5. Simplify each expression.
  (a) $(2 - 3i) + (1 - i)$ $3 - 4i$
  (b) $4i - (2 + i)$ $-2 + 3i$
  (c) $(3 - 2i)(1 + i)$ $5 + i$
  (d) $\dfrac{3}{2 - 2i}$ $\dfrac{3}{4} + \dfrac{3}{4}i$

Summary

Radicals and Radical Notation

Square Root
b is a square root of a if $b^2 = a$.

Principal Square Root
$\sqrt{a} = b$ if $b^2 = a$ and $b \geq 0$.

Examples: $\sqrt{16} = 4$, $-\sqrt{9} = -3$,
and $\pm\sqrt{36} = \pm 6$

Cube Root
b is the cube root of a if $b^3 = a$.

Examples: $\sqrt[3]{27} = 3$, $\sqrt[3]{-8} = -2$

nth root
b is the nth root of a if $b^n = a$.

Example: $\sqrt[4]{16} = 2$ because $2^4 = 16$.

Note: An *even* root of a *negative* number is not a real number. Also, $\sqrt[n]{a}$ denotes the *principal* nth root.

Absolute Value
The expressions $|x|$ and $\sqrt{x^2}$ are equivalent.

Example: $\sqrt{(x + y)^2} = |x + y|$

The Expression $a^{1/n}$
$a^{1/n} = \sqrt[n]{a}$ if n is an integer greater than 1.

Examples: $5^{1/2} = \sqrt{5}$ and $64^{1/3} = \sqrt[3]{64} = 4$

The Expression $a^{m/n}$
$a^{m/n} = \sqrt[n]{a^m}$ or $a^{m/n} = (\sqrt[n]{a})^m$

Examples: $8^{2/3} = \sqrt[3]{8^2} = \sqrt[3]{64} = 4$ and
$8^{2/3} = (\sqrt[3]{8})^2 = (2)^2 = 4$

Properties of Exponents

Product Rule
$a^p a^q = a^{p+q}$

Negative Exponents
$a^{-p} = \dfrac{1}{a^p}, \dfrac{1}{a^{-p}} = a^p$

Negative Exponents for Quotients
$\left(\dfrac{a}{b}\right)^{-p} = \left(\dfrac{b}{a}\right)^p$

Quotient Rule for Exponents
$\dfrac{a^p}{a^q} = a^{p-q}$

Power Rule for Exponents
$(a^p)^q = a^{pq}$

Power Rule for Products
$(ab)^p = a^p b^p$

Power Rule for Quotients
$\left(\dfrac{a}{b}\right)^p = \dfrac{a^p}{b^p}$

Section 7.2 *Simplifying Radical Expressions*

Product Rule for Radical Expressions

$$\sqrt[n]{a} \cdot \sqrt[n]{b} = \sqrt[n]{a \cdot b},$$

provided each expression is defined.

Example: $\sqrt[3]{3} \cdot \sqrt[3]{9} = \sqrt[3]{27} = 3$

Perfect *n*th Power An integer a is a perfect nth power if $b^n = a$ for some integer b.

Examples: 25 is a perfect square, 8 is a perfect cube, and 16 is a perfect fourth power.

Quotient Rule for Radical Expressions

$$\sqrt[n]{\frac{a}{b}} = \frac{\sqrt[n]{a}}{\sqrt[n]{b}},$$

provided each expression is defined.

Example: $\dfrac{\sqrt[3]{24}}{\sqrt[3]{3}} = \sqrt[3]{\dfrac{24}{3}} = \sqrt[3]{8} = 2$

Section 7.3 *Operations on Radical Expressions*

Addition and Subtraction To add or subtract radical expressions, combine like radicals.

Examples: $2\sqrt[3]{4} + 3\sqrt[3]{4} = 5\sqrt[3]{4}$ and $\sqrt{5} - 2\sqrt{5} = -\sqrt{5}$

Multiplication Sometimes radical expressions can be multiplied like binomials.

Example: $(5 - \sqrt{3})(5 + \sqrt{3}) = (5)^2 - (\sqrt{3})^2 = 25 - 3 = 22$ because
$(a - b)(a + b) = a^2 - b^2$.

Rationalizing the Denominator Multiply the numerator and denominator by the conjugate of the denominator.

Example: $\dfrac{1}{4 + \sqrt{2}} = \dfrac{1}{(4 + \sqrt{2})} \cdot \dfrac{(4 - \sqrt{2})}{(4 - \sqrt{2})} = \dfrac{4 - \sqrt{2}}{(4)^2 - (\sqrt{2})^2} = \dfrac{4 - \sqrt{2}}{14}$

Section 7.4 *Radical Functions*

The Square Root Function The square root function is denoted $f(x) = \sqrt{x}$. Its domain is $\{x \mid x \geq 0\}$ and its graph is shown in the figure.

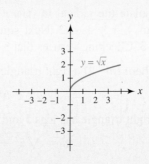

The Square Root Property Let k be a nonnegative number. Then the solutions to $x^2 = k$ are given by $x = \pm\sqrt{k}$.

Example: $x^2 = 100$ is equivalent to $x = \pm\sqrt{100} = \pm 10$.

The Cube Root Function

The cube root function is denoted $f(x) = \sqrt[3]{x}$. Its domain is all real numbers and its graph is shown in the figure.

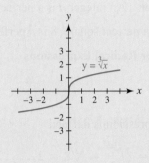

Power Functions If a function can be defined by $f(x) = x^p$, where p is a rational number, then it is a power function.

Examples: $f(x) = x^{4/5}$ and $g(x) = x^{2.3}$

Section 7.5 *Equations Involving Radical Expressions*

Power Rule for Solving Radical Equations The solutions to $a = b$ are among the solutions to $a^n = b^n$, where n is an integer.

Example: The solutions to $\sqrt{3x + 3} = 2x - 1$ are among the solutions to $3x + 3 = (2x - 1)^2$.

Solving Radical Equations

STEP 1: Isolate a radical term on one side of the equation.

STEP 2: Apply the power rule by raising each side of the equation to the power equal to the index of the isolated radical term.

STEP 3: Solve the equation. If it still contains a radical, repeat Steps 1 and 2.

STEP 4: Check your answers by substituting each result in the *given* equation.

Example: To isolate the radical in $\sqrt{x + 1} + 4 = 6$ subtract 4 from each side to obtain $\sqrt{x + 1} = 2$. Next square each side, which gives $x + 1 = 4$ or $x = 3$. Checking verifies that 3 is a solution.

Pythagorean Theorem If a right triangle has legs a and b with hypotenuse c, then
$$a^2 + b^2 = c^2.$$

Example: If a right triangle has legs 5 and 12, then the hypotenuse equals
$$c = \sqrt{5^2 + 12^2} = \sqrt{169} = 13.$$

The Distance Formula The distance d between (x_1, y_1) and (x_2, y_2) is
$$d = \sqrt{(x_2 - x_1)^2 + (y_2 - y_1)^2}.$$

Example: The distance between $(-1, 3)$ and $(4, 5)$ is
$$d = \sqrt{(4 - (-1))^2 + (5 - 3)^2} = \sqrt{25 + 4} = \sqrt{29}.$$

Section 7.6   *Complex Numbers*

Complex Numbers

Imaginary Unit	$i = \sqrt{-1}$ and $i^2 = -1$
Standard Form	$a + bi$, where a and b are real numbers
	Examples: $4 + 3i$, $5 - 6i$, 8, and $-2i$
Real Part	The real part of $a + bi$ is a.
	Example: The real part of $3 - 2i$ is 3.
Imaginary Part	The imaginary part of $a + bi$ is b.
	Example: The imaginary part of $2 - i$ is -1.
Arithmetic Operations	Arithmetic operations are similar to arithmetic operations on binomials.

Examples: $(2 + 2i) + (3 - i) = 5 + i$,
$(1 - i) - (1 - 2i) = i$,
$(1 - i)(1 + i) = 1^2 - i^2 = 1 - (-1) = 2$,   and

$$\frac{2}{1 - i} = \frac{2}{1 - i} \cdot \frac{1 + i}{1 + i} = \frac{2 + 2i}{2} = 1 + i$$

Powers of i   The value of i^n equals i^r, where r is the remainder when n is divided by 4.

Example: $i^{21} = i^1 = i$ because when 21 is divided by 4 the remainder is 1.

CHAPTER 7 Review Exercises

SECTION 7.1

Exercises 1–12: Simplify the expression.

1. $\sqrt{4}$ 2

2. $\sqrt{36}$ 6

3. $\sqrt{9x^2}$ $3|x|$

4. $\sqrt{(x - 1)^2}$ $|x - 1|$

5. $\sqrt[3]{-64}$ -4

6. $\sqrt[3]{-125}$ -5

7. $\sqrt[3]{x^6}$ x^2

8. $\sqrt[3]{27x^3}$ $3x$

9. $\sqrt[4]{16}$ 2

10. $\sqrt[5]{-1}$ -1

11. $\sqrt[4]{x^8}$ $\;x^2$

12. $\sqrt[5]{(x+1)^5}$ $\;x+1$

Exercises 13–16: Write the expression in radical notation.

13. $14^{1/2}$ $\;\sqrt{14}$

14. $(-5)^{1/3}$ $\;\sqrt[3]{-5}$

15. $\left(\dfrac{x}{y}\right)^{3/2}$ $\;\left(\sqrt{\dfrac{x}{y}}\right)^3$ or $\sqrt{\left(\dfrac{x}{y}\right)^3}$

16. $(xy)^{-2/3}$ $\;\dfrac{1}{\sqrt[3]{(xy)^2}}$ or $\dfrac{1}{(\sqrt[3]{xy})^2}$

Exercises 17–20: Evaluate the expression.

17. $(-27)^{2/3}$ $\;9$

18. $16^{1/4}$ $\;2$

19. $16^{3/2}$ $\;64$

20. $81^{3/4}$ $\;27$

Exercises 21–24: Simplify the expression. Assume that all variables are positive.

21. $(z^3)^{2/3}$ $\;z^2$

22. $(x^2y^4)^{1/2}$ $\;xy^2$

23. $\left(\dfrac{x^2}{y^6}\right)^{3/2}$ $\;\dfrac{x^3}{y^9}$

24. $\left(\dfrac{x^3}{y^6}\right)^{-1/3}$ $\;\dfrac{y^2}{x}$

SECTION 7.2

Exercises 25–40: Simplify the expression. Assume that all variables are positive.

25. $\sqrt{2}\cdot\sqrt{32}$ $\;8$

26. $\sqrt[3]{-4}\cdot\sqrt[3]{2}$ $\;-2$

27. $\sqrt[3]{x^4}\cdot\sqrt[3]{x^2}$ $\;x^2$

28. $\dfrac{\sqrt{80}}{\sqrt{20}}$ $\;2$

29. $\sqrt[3]{-\dfrac{x}{8}}$ $\;-\dfrac{\sqrt[3]{x}}{2}$

30. $\sqrt{\dfrac{1}{3}}\cdot\sqrt{\dfrac{1}{3}}$ $\;\dfrac{1}{3}$

31. $\sqrt{48}$ $\;4\sqrt{3}$

32. $\sqrt{54}$ $\;3\sqrt{6}$

33. $\sqrt[3]{\dfrac{3}{x}}\cdot\sqrt[3]{\dfrac{9}{x^2}}$ $\;\dfrac{3}{x}$

34. $\sqrt{32a^3b^2}$ $\;4ab\sqrt{2a}$

35. $\sqrt{3xy}\cdot\sqrt{27xy}$ $\;9xy$

36. $\sqrt[3]{-25z^2}\cdot\sqrt[3]{-5z^2}$ $\;5z\sqrt[3]{z}$

37. $\sqrt{x^2+2x+1}$ $\;x+1$

38. $\sqrt[4]{\dfrac{2a^2}{b}}\cdot\sqrt[4]{\dfrac{8a^3}{b^3}}$ $\;\dfrac{2a\sqrt[4]{a}}{b}$

39. $2\sqrt{x}\cdot\sqrt[3]{x}$ $\;2\sqrt[6]{x^5}$

40. $\sqrt[3]{rt}\cdot\sqrt[4]{r^2t^4}$ $\;\sqrt[6]{r^5t^8}$ or $t\sqrt[6]{r^5t^2}$

Exercises 41 and 42: Rationalize the denominator.

41. $\dfrac{4}{\sqrt{5}}$ $\;\dfrac{4\sqrt{5}}{5}$

42. $\dfrac{r}{2\sqrt{t}}$ $\;\dfrac{r\sqrt{t}}{2t}$

SECTION 7.3

Exercises 43–52: Simplify the expression. Assume that all variables are positive.

43. $3\sqrt{3}+\sqrt{3}$ $\;4\sqrt{3}$

44. $\sqrt[3]{x}+2\sqrt[3]{x}$ $\;3\sqrt[3]{x}$

45. $3\sqrt[3]{5}-6\sqrt[3]{5}$ $\;-3\sqrt[3]{5}$

46. $\sqrt[4]{y}-2\sqrt[4]{y}$ $\;-\sqrt[4]{y}$

47. $2\sqrt{12}+7\sqrt{3}$ $\;11\sqrt{3}$

48. $3\sqrt{18}-2\sqrt{2}$ $\;7\sqrt{2}$

49. $7\sqrt[3]{16}-\sqrt[3]{2}$ $\;13\sqrt[3]{2}$

50. $\sqrt{4x+4}+\sqrt{x+1}$ $\;3\sqrt{x+1}$

51. $\sqrt{4x^3}-\sqrt{x}$ $\;(2x-1)\sqrt{x}$

52. $\sqrt[3]{ab^4}+2\sqrt[3]{a^4b}$ $\;(b+2a)\sqrt[3]{ab}$

Exercises 53–56: Multiply and simplify.

53. $(3+\sqrt{6})(3-\sqrt{6})$ $\;3$

54. $(10-\sqrt{5})(10+\sqrt{5})$ $\;95$

55. $(\sqrt{a}+\sqrt{2b})(\sqrt{a}-\sqrt{2b})$ $\;a-2b$

56. $(\sqrt{xy}-1)(\sqrt{xy}+2)$ $\;xy+\sqrt{xy}-2$

Exercises 57–60: Rationalize the denominator.

57. $\dfrac{1}{\sqrt{2}+3}$ $\;\dfrac{3-\sqrt{2}}{7}$

58. $\dfrac{2}{5-\sqrt{7}}$ $\;\dfrac{5+\sqrt{7}}{9}$

59. $\dfrac{1}{\sqrt{8}-\sqrt{7}}$ $\;\sqrt{8}+\sqrt{7}$

60. $\dfrac{\sqrt{a}-\sqrt{b}}{\sqrt{a}+\sqrt{b}}$ $\;\dfrac{a-2\sqrt{ab}+b}{a-b}$

SECTION 7.4

Exercises 61 and 62: Graph the equation.*

61. $y=\sqrt{x}$

62. $y=\sqrt[3]{x}$

Exercises 63 and 64: Graph the equation. Compare the graph to either $y=\sqrt{x}$ or $y=\sqrt[3]{x}$.*

63. $y=\sqrt{x}-2$
  Shifted 2 units downward

64. $y=\sqrt[3]{x-1}$
  Shifted 1 unit to the right

Exercises 65–68: Find the domain of f. Write your answer in interval notation.

65. $f(x)=\sqrt{x-1}$
  $[1,\infty)$

66. $f(x)=\sqrt{6-2x}$
  $(-\infty,3]$

67. $f(x)=\sqrt{x^2+1}$
  $(-\infty,\infty)$

68. $f(x)=\dfrac{1}{\sqrt{x+2}}$
  $(-2,\infty)$

Exercises 69–74: Solve.

69. $x^2=121$ $\;\pm11$

70. $2z^2=32$ $\;\pm4$

71. $(x-1)^2=16$ $\;-3,5$

72. $x^3=64$ $\;4$

73. $(x-1)^3=8$ $\;3$

74. $(2x-1)^3=27$ $\;2$

SECTION 7.5

Exercises 75–80: Solve. Check your answer.

75. $\sqrt{x+2}=x$ $\;2$

76. $\sqrt{2x-1}=\sqrt{x+3}$ $\;4$

77. $\sqrt[3]{x-1}=2$ $\;9$

78. $\sqrt[3]{3x}=3$ $\;9$

79. $\sqrt{2x} = x - 4$ 8   **80.** $\sqrt{x} + 1 = \sqrt{x + 2}$ $\frac{1}{4}$

 Exercises 81 and 82: Solve the equation graphically. Approximate solutions to the nearest hundredth when appropriate.

81. $\sqrt[3]{2x - 1} = 2$ 4.5   **82.** $x^{2/3} = 3 - x$ 1.62

Exercises 83 and 84: A right triangle has legs a and b with hypotenuse c. Find the length of the missing side.

83. $a = 4, b = 7$ **84.** $a = 5, c = 8$ $b = \sqrt{39}$
$c = \sqrt{65}$

Exercises 85 and 86: Find the distance between the points.

85. $(-2, 3), (2, -2)$ **86.** $(2, -3), (-4, 1)$
$\sqrt{41}$ $\sqrt{52} = 2\sqrt{13}$

SECTION 7.6

Exercises 87–92: Write the complex expression in standard form.

87. $(1 - 2i) + (-3 + 2i)$ -2

88. $(1 + 3i) - (3 - i)$ $-2 + 4i$
      89. $5 + i$

89. $(1 - i)(2 + 3i)$ **90.** $\dfrac{3 + i}{1 - i}$ $1 + 2i$

91. $\dfrac{i(4 + i)}{2 - 3i}$ $-\dfrac{14}{13} + \dfrac{5}{13}i$ **92.** $(1 - i)^2(1 + i)$ $2 - 2i$

APPLICATIONS

93. *Hang Time* (Refer to Example 1, Section 7.4.) A football is punted and has a hang time of 4.6 seconds. Estimate the height that it was kicked to the nearest foot. About 85 ft

94. *Baseball Diamond* The four bases of a baseball diamond form a square 90 feet on a side. Find the distance from home plate to second base. $\sqrt{16,200} \approx 127.3$ ft

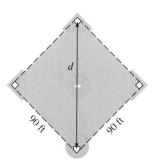

95. *Falling Time* The time T in seconds for an object to fall from a height of h feet is given by $T = \frac{1}{4}\sqrt{h}$. If a person steps off a 10-foot-high board into a swimming pool, how long is the person in the air? About 0.79 sec

96. *Highway Curves* If a circular highway curve is banked with a slope of $m = \frac{1}{10}$ (see the accompanying figure) and has a radius of R feet, then the speed limit L in miles per hour for the curve is given by

$$L = \sqrt{3.75R}.$$

(***Source:*** N. Garber and L. Hoel, *Traffic and Highway Engineering.*)
   (a) Find the speed limit if the curve has a radius of 500 feet. About 43 mph
   (b) With no banking, the speed limit is given by $L = 1.5\sqrt{R}$. Find the speed limit for a curve with no banking and a radius of 500 feet. How does banking affect the speed limit? Does this result agree with your intuition?
   About 34 mph; a steeper bank allows for a higher speed limit; yes.

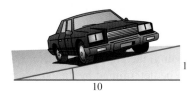

97. *Geometry* Find the length of a side of a square if the square has an area of 7 square feet. $\sqrt{7} \approx 2.65$ ft

98. *Geometry* A cube has sides of length $\sqrt{5}$.
   (a) Find the area of one side of the cube. 5 units^2
   (b) Find the volume of the cube. $5\sqrt{5}$ units^3
   (c) Find the length of the diagonal of one of the sides. $\sqrt{10}$ units
   (d) Find the distance from A to B in the figure.
   $\sqrt{15}$ units

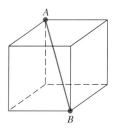

99. *Pendulum* The time required for a pendulum to swing back and forth is called its *period* (see the figure on the next page). The period T of a pendulum does not depend on its weight, only on its length L and gravity. It is given by $T = 2\pi\sqrt{\frac{L}{32.2}}$, where T is

in seconds and L is in feet. Estimate the length of a pendulum with a period of 1 second. About 0.82 ft

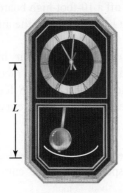

L

100. *Pendulum* (Refer to Exercise 99.) If a pendulum were on the moon, its period could be calculated by $T = 2\pi\sqrt{\frac{L}{5.1}}$. Estimate the length of a pendulum with a period of 1 second on the moon. Compare your answer to that for Exercise 99. About 0.13 ft; it is shorter.

101. *Population Growth* In 1790 the population of the United States was 4 million, and by 2000 it had grown to 281 million. The average annual percentage growth in the population r (expressed as a decimal) can be determined by the polynomial equation

$r = \sqrt[210]{\frac{281}{4}} - 1 \approx 0.02$; from 1790 to 2000 the average annual percentage growth rate was about 2%.

$281 = 4(1 + r)^{210}$. Solve this equation for r and interpret the result.

102. *Surface Area of a Cone* The surface area of a cone having radius r and height h is given by $S = \pi r \sqrt{r^2 + h^2}$. See the accompanying figure. Estimate the surface area if $r = 11$ inches and $h = 60$ inches. About 2108 in²

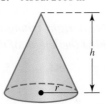

h

r

103. *Radioactive Carbon Dating* Living plants and animals have a constant amount of radioactive carbon in their cells, which comes from the carbon dioxide they breathe. When a plant or animal dies, the exchange of oxygen and carbon dioxide halts and the amount of radioactive carbon starts to decrease. The fraction of radioactive carbon remaining t years after death is given by $2^{-t/5700}$. Find the fraction left after each time period.

(a) 5700 years $0.5 = \frac{1}{2}$ **(b)** 20,000 years
About 0.09, or $\frac{9}{100}$

CHAPTER

7 Test

Exercises 1–4: Simplify the expression.

1. $\sqrt{25x^4}$ $5x^2$

2. $\sqrt[3]{8z^6}$ $2z^2$

3. $\sqrt[4]{16x^4y^5}$ $2xy\sqrt[4]{y}$

4. $(\sqrt{3} - \sqrt{2})(\sqrt{3} + \sqrt{2})$
1

Exercises 5 and 6: Write the expression in radical notation.

5. $7^{2/5}$ $\sqrt[5]{7^2}$ or $(\sqrt[5]{7})^2$

6. $\left(\frac{x}{y}\right)^{-2/3}$ $\sqrt[3]{\left(\frac{y}{x}\right)^2}$ or $\left(\sqrt[3]{\frac{y}{x}}\right)^2$

Exercises 7 and 8: Evaluate the expression without a calculator.

7. $(-8)^{4/3}$ 16

8. $36^{-3/2}$ $\frac{1}{216}$

9. Find the domain of $f(x) = \sqrt{4 - x}$. Write your answer in interval notation. $(-\infty, 4]$

10. Sketch a graph of $y = \sqrt{x + 3}$. *

Exercises 11–16: Simplify the expression. Assume that all variables are positive.

11. $(2z^{1/2})^3$ $8z^{3/2}$

12. $\left(\frac{y^2}{z^3}\right)^{-1/3}$ $\frac{z}{y^{2/3}}$

13. $\sqrt{3} \cdot \sqrt{27}$ 9

14. $\frac{\sqrt{y^3}}{\sqrt{4y}}$ $\frac{y}{2}$

*Answer on page IA-23

15. $7\sqrt{7} - 3\sqrt{7} + \sqrt{5}$ $4\sqrt{7} + \sqrt{5}$ 16. $7\sqrt[3]{x} - \sqrt[3]{x}$ $6\sqrt[3]{x}$

17. Solve the equation $\sqrt{2x + 2} = x - 11$.   17

18. Rationalize the denominator of $\dfrac{1}{\sqrt{14} - \sqrt{13}}$. $\sqrt{14} + \sqrt{13}$

19. One leg of a right triangle has length 7 and the hypotenuse has length 13. Find the length of the third side. $\sqrt{120} \approx 10.95$

20. Find the distance between the points $(-3, 5)$ and $(-1, 7)$. $\sqrt{8} = 2\sqrt{2}$

Exercises 21–24: Write the complex expression in standard form.

21. $(-5 + i) + (7 - 20i)$ $2 - 19i$

22. $(3i) - (6 - 5i)$ $-6 + 8i$

23. $\left(\dfrac{1}{2} - i\right)\left(\dfrac{1}{2} + i\right)$ $\frac{5}{4}$ 24. $\dfrac{2i}{5 + 2i}$ $\frac{4}{29} + \frac{10}{29}i$

25. **Volume of a Sphere**   The volume V of a sphere is given by $V = \frac{4}{3}\pi r^3$, where r is its radius. $r = \sqrt[3]{\dfrac{3V}{4\pi}}$
    (a) Solve the equation for r.
    (b) Find the radius of a sphere with a volume of 50 cubic inches.   About 2.29 in.

26. **Wing Span of a Bird**   The wing span L of a bird with weight W can sometimes be modeled by $L = 27.4W^{1/3}$, where L is in inches and W is in pounds. Use this formula to estimate the weight of a bird that has a wing span of 30 inches. (**Source:** C. Pennycuick, *Newton Rules Biology*.)   1.31 lb

7 Extended and Discovery Exercises

 1. *Moons of Jupiter*   The accompanying table lists the orbital distances and periods of several moons of Jupiter. Let x be the distance and y be the period. These data can be modeled by a power function of the form $f(x) = 0.0002x^{m/n}$. Use trial and error to find the value of the fraction $\frac{m}{n}$. Graph f and the data in the same viewing rectangle. * $\dfrac{m}{n} = \dfrac{3}{2}$

Moon	Distance (10^3 kilometers)	Period (days)
Metis	128	0.29
Almathea	181	0.50
Thebe	222	0.67
Io	422	1.77
Europa	671	3.55
Ganymede	1070	7.16
Callisto	1883	16.69

Source: M. Zeilik, Introductory Astronomy and Astrophysics.

2. *Modeling Wood in a Tree*   In forestry the volume of timber in a given area of forest is often estimated. To make such estimates, scientists have developed formulas to find the amount of wood contained in a tree with height h in feet and diameter d in inches. One study concluded that the volume V of wood in a tree could be modeled by the equation $V = kh^{1.12}d^{1.98}$, where k is a constant. Note that the diameter is measured 4.5 feet above the ground. (**Source:** B. Ryan, B. Joiner, and T. Ryan, *Minitab Handbook*.)
    (a) A tree with an 11-inch diameter and a 47-foot height has a volume of 11.4 cubic feet. Approximate the constant k. $k \approx 0.001325$
    (b) Estimate the volume of wood in the same type of tree with $d = 20$ inches and $h = 105$ feet.   About 91.6 ft^3

3. *Area of Skin*   The surface area of the skin covering the human body is a function of more than one variable. Both height and weight influence the surface area of a person's body. Hence a taller person tends to have a larger surface area, as does a heavier person.

*Answer on page IA-23

3.(b) It increases by a factor of $2^{0.425} \approx 1.34$.

A formula to determine the area of a person's skin in square inches is $S = 15.7(w^{0.425})(h^{0.725})$, where w is weight in pounds and h is height in inches.   (**Source:** H. Lancaster, *Quantitative Methods in Biological and Medical Sciences*.)

(a) About 2754 in.^{2}

(a) Use S to estimate the area of a person's skin who is 65 inches tall and weighs 154 pounds.

(b) If a person's weight doubles, what happens to the area of the person's skin? Explain.

(c) If a person's height doubles, what happens to the area of the person's skin? Explain.

It increases by a factor of $2^{0.725} \approx 1.65$.

4. *Minimizing Cost*   A natural gas line running along a river is to be connected from point A to a cabin on the other bank located at point D, as illustrated in the accompanying figure. The width of the river is 500 feet, and the distance from point A to point C is 1000 feet. The cost of running the pipe along the shoreline is \$30 per foot, and the cost of running it underwater is \$50 per foot. The cost of connecting the gas line from A to D is to be minimized.

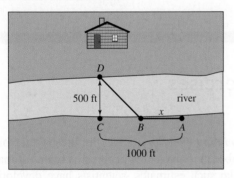

(a) Write an expression that gives the cost of running the line from A to B if the distance between these points is x feet. $30x$

(b) Find the distance from B to D in terms of x.

(c) Write an expression that gives the cost of running the line from B to D. $50\sqrt{(1000 - x)^2 + 500^2}$

(d) Use your answer from parts (a) and (c) to write an expression that gives the cost of running the line from A to B to D.

 (e) Graph your expression from part (d) in the window $[0, 1000, 100]$ by $[40000, 60000, 5000]$ to determine the value of x that minimizes the cost of the line going from A to D. What is the minimum cost? * $x = 625$ ft; \$50,000

(b) $d = \sqrt{(1000 - x)^2 + 500^2}$

(d) $30x + 50\sqrt{(1000 - x)^2 + 500^2}$

*Answer on page IA-23

Quadratic Functions and Equations

Technology brings with it unforeseen consequences. The powerful insecticide DDT was a miracle of science that promised an adequate food supply for the world. But in a matter of a few decades its environmental impact became a worldwide disaster that had the potential to threaten human beings as a species. Medical technology in the twentieth century has increased the average life span from 47 years to 77 years, but it has also forced societies to cope with the possibilities created by genetic engineering.

Technology is sometimes used to help teach important concepts in mathematics and to solve applications. Without technology many modern inventions would be impossible. However, technology is not a replacement for mathematical understanding and judgment because mathematical concepts change little over time. On the one hand, the human mind is capable of mathematical insight and decision making, but it is not particularly proficient at performing long, tedious calculations. On the other hand, computers and calculators are incapable of possessing genuine mathematical insight, but they are excellent at performing arithmetic and other routine computation. In this way, technology can complement the human mind in the study and application of mathematics.

> **People are still the most extraordinary computers of all.**
> —John F. Kennedy

Source: F. Allen, "Technology at the End of the Century," *Invention and Technology*, Winter 2000.

TEACHING TIP

Point out that technology cannot replace human intelligence and understanding.

8.1 QUADRATIC FUNCTIONS AND THEIR GRAPHS

Graphs of Quadratic Functions · Basic Transformations of Graphs · Min–Max Applications

INTRODUCTION

Suppose that a hotel is considering giving a group discount on room rates. The regular price is \$80, but for each room rented the price decreases by \$2. On the one hand, if the hotel rents one room it makes only \$78. On the other hand, if the hotel rents 40 rooms, the rooms are all free and the hotel makes nothing. Is there an optimal number of rooms between 1 and 40 that should be rented to maximize the revenue? In this section we use quadratic functions and their graphs to answer this question. Quadratic functions are used not only in business, but they are used also in a wide variety of fields, such as road construction and medicine. In fact, quadratic functions are an important concept throughout mathematics.

GRAPHS OF QUADRATIC FUNCTIONS

In Chapter 5 we discussed how a quadratic function could be represented by a polynomial of degree 2. We now give an alternative definition of a quadratic function.

QUADRATIC FUNCTION

A quadratic function can be written in the form

$$f(x) = ax^2 + bx + c,$$

where a, b, and c are real numbers with $a \neq 0$.

The graph of *any* quadratic function is a *parabola*. Recall that a parabola is a ∪-shaped graph that either opens upward or downward. The graph of the simple quadratic function $y = x^2$ is a parabola that opens upward, with its *vertex* located at the origin, as shown in Figure 8.1(a). The **vertex** is the *lowest* point on the graph of a parabola that opens upward and the *highest* point on the graph of a parabola that opens downward. A parabola opening downward is shown in Figure 8.1(b). Its vertex is the point $(0, 2)$ and is the highest point on a graph. If we were to fold either graph along the y-axis, the left and right sides of the graph would match. That is, both parts of the graph are symmetric with respect to the y-axis. In this case the y-axis is the **axis of symmetry** for the graph. Figure 8.1(c) shows a parabola that opens upward with vertex $(2, -1)$ and axis of symmetry $x = 2$.

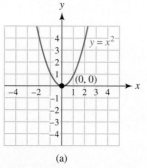

(a)

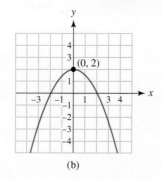

(b)

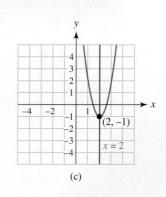

(c)

Figure 8.1

Suppose that the graph of $y = x^2$ shown in Figure 8.1(a) represents a valley. If we walk from *left to right*, the valley "goes down" and then "goes up." Mathematically, we say that the graph of $y = x^2$ is *decreasing* when $x \leq 0$ and *increasing* when $x \geq 0$. The vertex represents the point at which the graph switches from decreasing to increasing. In Figure 8.1(b), the graph increases when $x \leq 0$ and decreases when $x \geq 0$, and in Figure 8.1(c) the graph decreases when $x \leq 2$ and increases when $x \geq 2$.

Note: When determining where a graph is increasing and where it is decreasing, we must "walk" along the graph *from left to right*. (We read English from left to right, which might help you remember.)

EXAMPLE 1   Graphing quadratic functions

Graph each quadratic function. Identify the vertex and the axis of symmetry. Then state where the graph is increasing and where it is decreasing.
(a) $f(x) = x^2 - 1$ **(b)** $f(x) = -(x + 1)^2$ **(c)** $x^2 + 4x + 3$

Solution   **(a)** Begin by making a convenient table of values (see Table 8.1). Then plot the points and sketch a smooth ∪-shaped curve that opens upward, as shown in Figure 8.2. The lowest point on this graph is $(0, -1)$, which is the vertex. The axis of symmetry is the vertical line $x = 0$, which passes through the vertex and coincides with the y-axis. Note also the symmetry of the y-values in Table 8.1 about the point $(0, -1)$. This graph is decreasing when $x \leq 0$ and increasing when $x \geq 0$.

TABLE 8.1

x	$y = x^2 - 1$	
-2	3	
-1	0	
Vertex → 0	-1	Equal
1	0	
2	3	

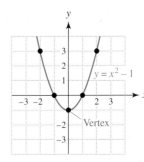

Figure 8.2

(b) Make a table of values (see Table 8.2). Plot the points and sketch a smooth ∩-shaped curve opening downward, as shown in Figure 8.3. The highest point on this graph is $(-1, 0)$, which is the vertex. The axis of symmetry is the vertical line $x = -1$, which passes through the vertex. This graph is increasing when $x \leq -1$ and decreasing when $x \geq -1$.

TABLE 8.2

x	$y = -(x + 1)^2$	
-3	-4	
-2	-1	
Vertex → -1	0	Equal
0	-1	
1	-4	

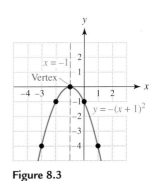

Figure 8.3

(c) Make a table of values (see Table 8.3). Plot the points and sketch a smooth U-shaped graph opening upward, as shown in Figure 8.4. The lowest point on this graph is $(-2, -1)$, which is the vertex. The axis of symmetry is the vertical line $x = -2$, which passes through the vertex. The graph is decreasing when $x \leq -2$ and increasing when $x \geq -2$.

TABLE 8.3

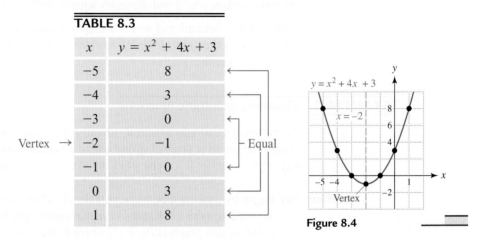

x	$y = x^2 + 4x + 3$
-5	8
-4	3
-3	0
-2	-1
-1	0
0	3
1	8

Vertex →

Equal

Figure 8.4

Rather than graphing a quadratic function to find its vertex, we can use the following formula. This formula can be derived by completing the square, a technique discussed in the next section.

VERTEX FORMULA

The x-coordinate of the vertex of the graph of $y = ax^2 + bx + c$, $a \neq 0$, is given by

$$x = -\frac{b}{2a}.$$

To find the y-coordinate of the vertex, substitute this x-value into the equation.

Note: The equation of the axis of symmetry for $f(x) = ax^2 + bx + c$ is $x = -\frac{b}{2a}$, and the vertex is $\left(-\frac{b}{2a}, f\left(-\frac{b}{2a}\right)\right)$.

We apply this formula in the next example.

EXAMPLE 2 Finding the vertex of a parabola

Find the vertex for the graph of $f(x) = 2x^2 - 4x + 1$. Support your answer graphically.

Solution For $f(x) = 2x^2 - 4x + 1$, $a = 2$ and $b = -4$. The x-value of the vertex is

$$x = -\frac{b}{2a} = -\frac{(-4)}{2(2)} = 1.$$

To find the y-value of the vertex, substitute $x = 1$ in the given formula.

$$f(1) = 2(1)^2 - 4(1) + 1 = -1.$$

Thus the vertex is located at $(1, -1)$, which is supported by Figure 8.5.

[−4.7, 4.7, 1] by [−3.1, 3.1, 1]

Y1=2X^2−4X+1

X=1   Y=−1

Figure 8.5

BASIC TRANSFORMATIONS OF GRAPHS

In this subsection we discuss the graph of $y = ax^2$, where $a \neq 0$. First, we consider the case where $a > 0$ by graphing $y_1 = \frac{1}{2}x^2$, $y_2 = x^2$, and $y_3 = 2x^2$, as shown in Figure 8.6(a). Note that $a = \frac{1}{2}$, $a = 1$, and $a = 2$ and that as a increases, the resulting parabola becomes narrower. The graph of $y_1 = \frac{1}{2}x^2$ is wider than the graph of $y_2 = x^2$, and the graph of $y_3 = 2x^2$ is narrower than the graph of $y_2 = x^2$. In general, the graph of $y = ax^2$ is wider than the graph of $y = x^2$ when $0 < a < 1$ and narrower than the graph of $y = x^2$ when $a > 1$. When $a > 0$, the graph of $y = ax^2$ never lies below the x-axis.

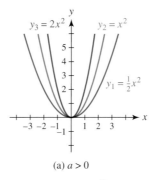

(a) $a > 0$

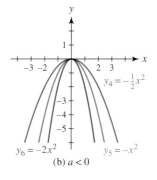

(b) $a < 0$

Figure 8.6 $y = ax^2$

When $a < 0$, the graph of $y = ax^2$ never lies above the x-axis because, for any input x, the product $ax^2 \leq 0$. The graphs of $y_4 = -\frac{1}{2}x$, $y_5 = -x^2$, and $y_6 = -2x^2$ are shown in Figure 8.6(b). The graph of $y_4 = -\frac{1}{2}x^2$ is wider than the graph of $y_5 = -x^2$ and the graph of $y_6 = -2x^2$ is narrower than the graph of $y_5 = -x^2$.

Note that the graph of $y_1 = \frac{1}{2}x^2$ can be *transformed* into the graph of $y_4 = -\frac{1}{2}x^2$ by *reflecting* it across the x-axis. The graph of y_4 is a **reflection** of the graph of y_1 across the x-axis. That is, if the point (x, y) is on the graph of y_1, then the point $(x, -y)$ is on the graph of y_4. Similarly, the graphs of $y_2 = x^2$ and $y_3 = 2x^2$ can be transformed into the graphs of $y_5 = -x^2$ and $y_6 = -2x^2$, respectively, by reflecting them across the x-axis.

THE GRAPH OF $y = ax^2$

The graph of $y = ax^2$ is a parabola that opens upward when $a > 0$ and opens downward when $a < 0$. As the value of $|a|$ increases, the graph of $y = ax^2$ becomes narrower. The vertex is $(0, 0)$, and the axis of symmetry is the y-axis.

EXAMPLE 3   Graphing $y = ax^2$

Compare the graph of $g(x) = -3x^2$ to the graph of $f(x) = x^2$. Then graph both functions on the same coordinate axes.

Solution   Both graphs are parabolas. However, the graph of g opens downward and is narrower than the graph of f. Their graphs are shown in Figure 8.7 (on the following page).

Critical Thinking

Suppose that the graph of y_1 is a reflection of the graph of y_2 across the y-axis. If the point (x, y) lies on the graph of y_1, what point must lie on the graph of y_2?

The point $(-x, y)$

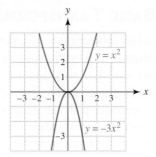

Figure 8.7

MIN–MAX APPLICATIONS

Sometimes when a quadratic function f is used to model real-world data, the vertex provides important information. The reason is that the y-coordinate of the vertex gives either the maximum value of $f(x)$ or the minimum value of $f(x)$. For example, Figure 8.8(a) shows a parabola that opens upward. The minimum y-value on this graph is 1 and occurs at the vertex $(2, 1)$. Similarly, Figure 8.8(b) shows a parabola that opens downward. The maximum y-value on this graph is 3 and occurs at the vertex $(-1, 3)$.

TEACHING TIP

You may want to emphasize that a minimum or maximum is a y-value *not* a point on the graph.

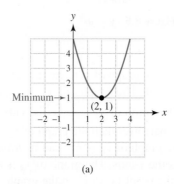

(a)

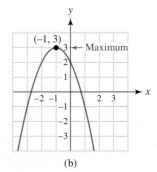

(b)

Figure 8.8

In the next example, we demonstrate finding a maximum value.

EXAMPLE 4 Finding maximum height

A baseball is hit into the air and its height h in feet after t seconds can be calculated by $h(t) = -16t^2 + 96t + 3$.
(a) What is the height of the baseball when it is hit?
(b) Determine the maximum height of the baseball.

Solution **(a)** The baseball is hit when $t = 0$, so $h(0) = -16(0)^2 + 96(0) + 3 = 3$ feet.
(b) The graph of h opens downward because $a = -16 < 0$. Thus the maximum height of the baseball occurs at the vertex. To find the vertex, we apply the vertex formula with $a = -16$ and $b = 96$.

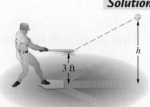

$$t = -\frac{b}{2a} = -\frac{96}{2(-16)} = 3 \text{ seconds}$$

The maximum height of the baseball occurs at $t = 3$ seconds and is

$$h(3) = -16(3)^2 + 96(3) + 3 = 147 \text{ feet.}$$

In the next example, we answer the question presented in the introduction to this section.

EXAMPLE 5   Maximizing revenue

A hotel is considering giving the following group discount on room rates. The regular price for a room is $80, but for each room rented the price decreases by $2.
(a) A graph of the revenue received from renting x rooms is shown in Figure 8.9. Interpret the graph.

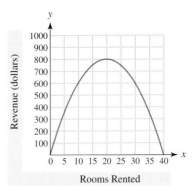

Figure 8.9

(b) What is the maximum revenue? How many rooms should be rented to receive the maximum revenue?
(c) Write a formula for $y = f(x)$ whose graph is shown in Figure 8.9.
(d) Use $f(x)$ to determine symbolically the maximum revenue and the number of rooms that should be rented.

Solution **(a)** The revenue increases at first, reaches a maximum, which corresponds to the vertex, and then decreases.
(b) In Figure 8.9 the vertex is (20, 800). Thus the maximum revenue of $800 occurs when 20 rooms are rented.
(c) If x rooms are rented, the price for each room is $80 - 2x$. The revenue equals the number of rooms rented times the price of each room. Thus $f(x) = x(80 - 2x)$.
(d) First, multiply $x(80 - 2x)$ to obtain $80x - 2x^2$ and then let $f(x) = -2x^2 + 80x$. The x-coordinate of the vertex is

$$x = -\frac{b}{2a} = -\frac{80}{2(-2)} = 20.$$

The y-coordinate is

$$f(20) = -2(20)^2 + 80(20) = 800.$$

These calculations verify our results in part (b).

Technology Note: *Locating a Vertex*

Some graphing calculators can locate a vertex on a parabola with either the MAXIMUM or MINIMUM utility. The maximum for the graph in Example 5 is found in the accompanying figure. This utility is typically more accurate than the TRACE utility.

Calculator Help

To find a minimum or maximum, see the Appendix (page AP-12).

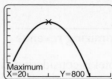

[0, 50, 10] by [0, 1000, 100]

Maximum
X=20   Y=800

In the next example, we minimize a quadratic function that models percentages of births by cesarean section (C-section).

EXAMPLE 6   Analyzing births by cesarean section

The percentage P of births performed by cesarean section between 1991 and 2001 is modeled by

$$P(t) = 0.105t^2 - 1.08t + 23.6,$$

where t is the year, and $t = 1$ corresponds to 1991, $t = 2$ to 1992, and so on.   (*Source:* The National Center for Health Statistics.)

(a) Estimate the year when the percentage of births by cesarean section was minimum.

(b) What is this minimum percentage?

Solution   **(a)** The graph of P is a parabola that opens upward because $a = 0.105 > 0$. Therefore the t-coordinate of the vertex represents the year when the percentage of births done by cesarean section was minimum, or

$$t = -\frac{b}{2a} = -\frac{-1.08}{2(0.105)} \approx 5.1.$$

Because $t = 5$ corresponds to 1995, the minimum percentage occurred during 1995.

(b) In 1995, this percentage was about $P(5) = 0.105(5)^2 - 1.08(5) + 23.6 \approx 20.8\%$.

PUTTING IT ALL TOGETHER

The following table summarizes some of the important topics in this section.

Concept	Explanation	Examples
Quadratic Function	Can be written as $$f(x) = ax^2 + bx + c, a \neq 0$$	$f(x) = x^2 + x - 2$ and $g(x) = -2x^2 + 4$ $(b = 0)$

Concept	Explanation	Examples
Graph of a Quadratic Function	Its graph is a parabola that opens upward if $a > 0$ and downward if $a < 0$. The value of $\lvert a \rvert$ affects the width of the parabola. The vertex can be used to determine the maximum or minimum output of a quadratic function.	The graph of $y = -\frac{1}{4}x^2$ opens downward, and is wider than the graph of $y = x^2$ as shown in the figure. Each graph has its vertex at $(0, 0)$.
Vertex of a Parabola	The x-coordinate of the vertex for the function $f(x) = ax^2 + bx + c$ with $a \neq 0$ is given by $$x = -\frac{b}{2a}.$$ The y-coordinate of the vertex is found by substituting this x-value in the equation. Hence the vertex is $\left(-\frac{b}{2a}, f\left(-\frac{b}{2a}\right)\right)$.	If $f(x) = -2x^2 + 8x - 7$, then $$x = -\frac{8}{2(-2)} = 2$$ and $$f(2) = -2(2)^2 + 8(2) - 7 = 1.$$ The vertex is $(2, 1)$. The graph of f opens downward because $a < 0$.

8.1 EXERCISES

FOR EXTRA HELP

📖 Student's Solutions Manual

🚪 MyMathLab

 InterAct Math

 Math Tutor Center

 MathXL

📼 Digital Video Tutor
CD 7   Videotape 9

CONCEPTS

1. The graph of a quadratic function is called a _____.
   parabola

2. If a parabola opens upward, what is the lowest point on the parabola called?   The vertex

3. If a parabola is symmetric with respect to the y-axis, the y-axis is called the _____.   axis of symmetry

4. The vertex of $y = x^2$ is _____. $(0, 0)$

5. Sketch a parabola that opens downward with a vertex of $(1, 2)$.*

6. If $y = ax^2 + bx + c$, the x-coordinate of the vertex is given by $x =$ _____. $-\frac{b}{2a}$

7. Compared to the graph of $y = x^2$, the graph of $y = 2x^2$ is (wider/narrower).   narrower

8. The graph of $y = -x^2$ is similar to the graph of $y = x^2$ except that it is _____ across the x-axis.   reflected

9. Any quadratic function can be written in the form $f(x) =$ _____. $ax^2 + bx + c$ with $a \neq 0$

10. If a parabola opens downward, the point with the largest y-value is called the _____.   vertex

*Answer on page IA-24

Exercises 11–14: Use the graph of f to evaluate the expressions.

11. $f(-2)$ and $f(0)$ $0, -4$ **12.** $f(-2)$ and $f(2)$ $4, -4$

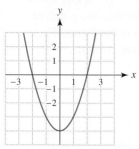
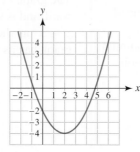

13. $f(-3)$ and $f(1)$ $-2, -2$ **14.** $f(-1)$ and $f(2)$ $-2, 1$

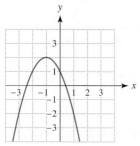
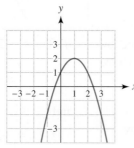

15. $(1, -2)$; $x = 1$; upward; increasing: $x \geq 1$; decreasing: $x \leq 1$

GRAPHS OF QUADRATIC FUNCTIONS

Exercises 15–18: Identify the vertex, axis of symmetry, and whether the parabola opens upward or downward. State where the graph is increasing and where it is decreasing.

15.

16. $(0, 4)$; $x = 0$; downward; increasing: $x \leq 0$; decreasing: $x \geq 0$

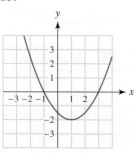
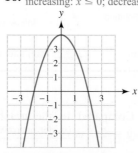

17.

18. $(3, -5)$; $x = 3$; upward; increasing: $x \geq 3$; decreasing: $x \leq 3$

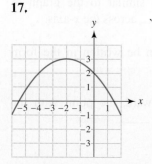
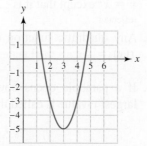

$(-2, 3)$; $x = -2$; downward; increasing: $x \leq -2$; decreasing: $x \geq -2$

Exercises 19–34: Do the following for the given f(x). *
(a) Graph $y = f(x)$.
(b) Use the graph to identify the vertex and axis of symmetry.
(c) Evaluate $f(-2)$ and $f(3)$.

19. $f(x) = x^2 - 2$ **20.** $f(x) = x^2 - 1$

21. $f(x) = -3x^2 + 1$ **22.** $f(x) = \frac{1}{2}x^2 + 2$

23. $f(x) = (x - 1)^2$ **24.** $f(x) = (x + 2)^2$

25. $f(x) = x^2 + x - 2$ **26.** $f(x) = x^2 - 2x + 2$

27. $f(x) = 2x^2 - 3$ **28.** $f(x) = 1 - 2x^2$

29. $f(x) = 2x - x^2$ **30.** $f(x) = x^2 + 2x - 8$

31. $f(x) = -2x^2 + 4x - 1$

32. $f(x) = -\frac{1}{2}x^2 + 2x - 3$

33. $f(x) = \frac{1}{4}x^2 - x + 5$ **34.** $f(x) = 3 - 6x - 4x^2$

Exercises 35–42: Find the vertex of the parabola.

35. $f(x) = x^2 - 4x - 2$ $(2, -6)$

36. $f(x) = 2x^2 + 6x - 3$ $\left(-\frac{3}{2}, -\frac{15}{2}\right)$

37. $f(x) = -\frac{1}{3}x^2 - 2x + 1$ $(-3, 4)$ 38. $(2, 1)$

38. $f(x) = 5 - 4x + x^2$ **39.** $f(x) = 3 - 2x^2$ $(0, 3)$

40. $f(x) = \frac{1}{4}x^2 - 3x - 2$ $(6, -11)$

41. $f(x) = -0.3x^2 + 0.6x + 1.1$ $(1, 1.4)$

42. $f(x) = 25 - 10x + 20x^2$ $\left(\frac{1}{4}, \frac{95}{4}\right)$

Exercises 43–50: Graph f(x). Compare the graph to $y = x^2$. *

43. $f(x) = -x^2$ **44.** $f(x) = -2x^2$
   Reflected across the x-axis   Reflected across the x-axis and narrower

45. $f(x) = 2x^2$ Narrower   **46.** $f(x) = 3x^2$ Narrower

47. $f(x) = \frac{1}{4}x^2$ Wider   **48.** $f(x) = \frac{1}{2}x^2$ Wider

49. $f(x) = -\frac{1}{2}x^2$ **50.** $f(x) = -\frac{3}{2}x^2$
   Reflected across the x-axis and wider   Reflected across the x-axis and narrower

Exercises 51–56: Find the minimum y-value on the graph of $y = f(x)$. Then state where the graph of f is increasing and where it is decreasing.

51. $f(x) = x^2 + 2x - 1$ **52.** $f(x) = x^2 + 6x + 2$
   -2; increasing: $x \geq -1$; -7; increasing: $x \geq -3$;
   decreasing: $x \leq -1$ decreasing: $x \leq -3$

*Answers on pages IA-24–IA-25

56. $\frac{25}{4}$; increasing: $x \geq \frac{1}{2}$; decreasing: $x \leq \frac{1}{2}$

53. $-\frac{25}{4}$; increasing: $x \geq \frac{5}{2}$; decreasing: $x \leq \frac{5}{2}$ 54. $-\frac{9}{4}$; increasing: $x \geq \frac{3}{2}$; decreasing: $x \leq \frac{3}{2}$

53. $f(x) = x^2 - 5x$ **54.** $f(x) = x^2 - 3x$

55. $f(x) = 2x^2 + 2x - 3$ **56.** $f(x) = 3x^2 - 3x + 7$

55. $-\frac{7}{2}$; increasing: $x \geq -\frac{1}{2}$; decreasing: $x \leq -\frac{1}{2}$

Exercises 57–62: Find the maximum y-value on the graph of $y = f(x)$. Then state where the graph of f is increasing and where it is decreasing.

57. $f(x) = -x^2 + 2x + 5$ 6; increasing: $x \leq 1$; decreasing: $x \geq 1$

58. $f(x) = -x^2 + 4x - 3$ 1; increasing: $x \leq 2$; decreasing: $x \geq 2$

59. $f(x) = 4x - x^2$ **60.** $f(x) = 6x - x^2$

9; increasing: $x \leq 3$; decreasing: $x \geq 3$

61. $f(x) = -2x^2 + x - 5$ $-\frac{39}{8}$; increasing: $x \leq \frac{1}{4}$; decreasing: $x \geq \frac{1}{4}$

62. $f(x) = -5x^2 + 15x - 2$ $\frac{37}{4}$; increasing: $x \leq \frac{3}{2}$; decreasing: $x \geq \frac{3}{2}$

APPLICATIONS   59. 4; increasing: $x \leq 2$; decreasing: $x \geq 2$

*Exercises 63–66: **Quadratic Models**   Match the physical situation with the graph (a.–d.) that models it best.*

63. The height y of a stone thrown from ground level after x seconds.   d.

64. The number of people attending a popular movie x weeks after its opening.   b.

65. The temperature after x hours in a house when the furnace quits and a repair person fixes it.   a.

66. The population of the United States from 1800 to the present.   c.

a.

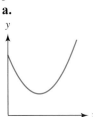

b.

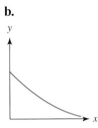

c.

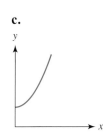

d.

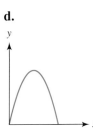

67. *Height Reached by a Baseball*   (Refer to Example 4.) A baseball is hit into the air, and its height h in feet after t seconds is given by $h(t) = -16t^2 + 64t + 2$.
  (a) What is the height of the baseball when it is hit?
    2 ft

(b) After how many seconds did the baseball reach its maximum height?   2 sec
(c) Determine the maximum height of the baseball.
    66 ft

68. *Height Reached by a Golf Ball*   A golf ball is hit into the air, and its height h in feet after t seconds is given by $h(t) = -16t^2 + 128t$.   0 ft
  (a) What is the height of the golf ball when it is hit?
  (b) After how many seconds did the golf ball reach its maximum height?   4 sec
  (c) Determine the maximum height of the golf ball.
    256 ft

69. *Height Reached by a Baseball*   Suppose that a baseball is thrown upward with an initial velocity of 66 feet per second (45 miles per hour) and it is released 6 feet above the ground. Its height h after t seconds is given by $\frac{66}{32} \approx 2$ sec; about 74 ft

$$h(t) = -16t^2 + 66t + 6.$$

After how many seconds does the baseball reach a maximum height? Estimate this height.

70. *Throwing a Baseball on the Moon*   (Refer to Exercise 69.) If the same baseball were thrown the same way on the moon, its height h above the moon's surface after t seconds would be   Moon; about 359 ft

$$h(t) = -2.55t^2 + 66t + 6.$$

Does the baseball go higher on the moon or on Earth? What is the difference in these two heights?

71. *Concert Tickets*   (Refer to Example 5.) An agency is promoting concert tickets by offering a group-discount rate. The regular price is $100 and for each ticket bought the price decreases by $1. (One ticket costs $99, two tickets cost $98 each, and so on.)
  (a) A graph of the revenue received from selling x tickets is shown in the figure. When is revenue increasing and when is it decreasing?

The revenue increases when $x \leq 50$, and it decreases when $x \geq 50$.

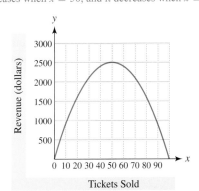

Tickets Sold

(b) What is the maximum revenue? How many tickets should be sold to a group to maximize revenue? $2500; 50

(c) Write a formula for $y = f(x)$ whose graph is shown in the figure. $f(x) = x(100 - x)$

(d) Use $f(x)$ to determine symbolically the maximum revenue and the number of tickets that should be sold. $2500; 50

72. *Maximizing Revenue* The regular price for a round-trip ticket to Las Vegas, Nevada, charged by an airline charter company is $300. For a group rate the company will reduce the price of each ticket by $1.50 for every passenger on the flight.

(a) Write a formula $f(x)$ that gives the revenue from selling x tickets. $f(x) = x(300 - 1.5x)$

(b) Determine how many tickets should be sold to maximize the revenue. What is the maximum revenue?
  100 tickets; $15,000

73. *Maximizing Area* A rectangular pen being constructed for a pet requires 60 feet of fence.

(a) Write a formula $f(x)$ that gives the area of the pen if one side of the pen has length x.

(b) Find the dimensions of the pen that give the largest area. What is the largest area?
  (a) $f(x) = x(30 - x)$ (b) 15 ft by 15 ft; 225 ft^2

74. *Maximizing Area* A farmer is fencing a rectangular area for cattle using a straight portion of a river as one side of the rectangle as illustrated in the figure. Note that there is no fence along the river. If the farmer has 1200 feet of fence, find the dimensions for the rectangular area that gives a maximum area for the cattle.
  300×600 ft

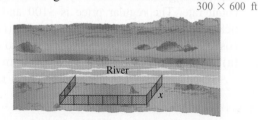

75. *Seedling Growth* The effect of temperature on the growth of melon seedlings was studied. In this study the seedlings were grown at different temperatures, and their heights were measured after a fixed period of time. The findings of this study can be modeled by

$$f(x) = -0.095x^2 + 5.4x - 52.2,$$

where x is the temperature in degrees Celsius and the output $f(x)$ gives the resulting average height in centimeters. (*Source:* R. Pearl, "The growth of *Cucumis melo* seedlings at different temperatures.")

(a) Graph f in [20, 40, 5] by [0, 30, 5].*

(b) Estimate graphically the temperature that resulted in the greatest height for the melon seedlings.

(c) Solve part (b) symbolically. (b) About 28.4°C

76. *Game Length* The quadratic function defined by

$$L(x) = -2x^2 + 8000x - 7,999,820$$

approximates the length of the average major league baseball game in minutes during year x, where $1998 \le x \le 2002$. (*Source:* Elias Sports Bureau.)

(a) Determine the year when games were the longest.

(b) How long did the average game last during that year? (a) 2000 (b) 180 min

WRITING ABOUT MATHEMATICS

77. If a quadratic function is represented by

$$f(x) = ax^2 + bx + c,$$

explain how the values of a and c affect the graph of f.

78. Suppose that a quantity Q is modeled by the formula $Q(x) = ax^2 + bx + c$ with $a < 0$. Explain how to find the x-value that maximizes $Q(x)$. How do you find the maximum value of $Q(x)$?

*Answer on page IA-25

8.2 PARABOLAS AND MODELING

**Vertical and Horizontal Translations · Vertex Form ·
Modeling with Quadratic Functions (Optional)**

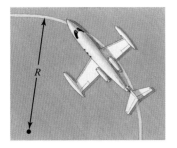

INTRODUCTION

A taxiway used by an airplane to exit a runway often contains curves. A curve that is too sharp for the speed of the plane is a safety hazard. The scatterplot shown in Figure 8.10 gives an appropriate radius R of a curve designed for an airplane taxiing x miles per hour. The data are nonlinear because they do not lie on a line. In this section we explain how a quadratic function may be used to model such data. First, we discuss translations of parabolas.

TEACHING TIP

Explain that the data in Figure 8.10 are nonlinear because each 10-unit increase in x results in varying increases in R.

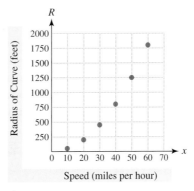

Figure 8.10

VERTICAL AND HORIZONTAL TRANSLATIONS

The graph of $y = x^2$ is a parabola opening upward with vertex $(0, 0)$. Suppose that we graph $y_1 = x^2$, $y_2 = x^2 + 1$, and $y_3 = x^2 - 2$ in the same xy-plane, as calculated for Table 8.4 and shown in Figure 8.11. All three graphs have the same shape. However, compared to the graph of $y_1 = x^2$, the graph of $y_2 = x^2 + 1$ is shifted *upward* 1 unit and the graph of $y_3 = x^2 - 2$ is shifted *downward* 2 units. Such shifts are called **translations** because they do not change the shape of a graph—only its position.

TABLE 8.4

x	$y_1 = x^2$	$y_2 = x^2 + 1$	$y_3 = x^2 - 2$
-2	4	5	2
-1	1	2	-1
0	0	1	-2
1	1	2	-1
2	4	5	2

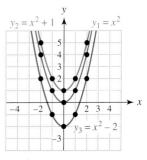

Figure 8.11

Next, suppose that we graph $y_1 = x^2$ and $y_2 = (x - 1)^2$ in the same xy-plane. Compare Tables 8.5 and 8.6. Note that the y-values are equal when the x-value for y_2 is 1 unit *larger* than the x-value for y_1. For example, $y_1 = 4$ when $x = -2$ and $y_2 = 4$ when $x = -1$. Thus the graph of $y_2 = (x - 1)^2$ has the same shape as the graph of $y_1 = x^2$, except that it is translated *horizontally to the right* 1 unit, as illustrated in Figure 8.12.

TABLE 8.5

x	$y_1 = x^2$
-2	4
-1	1
0	0
1	1
2	4

TABLE 8.6

x	$y_2 = (x - 1)^2$
-1	4
0	1
1	0
2	1
3	4

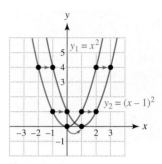

Figure 8.12

The graphs $y_1 = x^2$ and $y_2 = (x + 2)^2$ are shown in Figure 8.13. Note that Tables 8.7 and 8.8 show their y-values to be equal when the x-value for y_2 is 2 units *smaller* than the x-value for y_1. As a result, the graph of $y_2 = (x + 2)^2$ has the same shape as the graph of $y_1 = x^2$ except that it is translated *horizontally to the left* 2 units.

TABLE 8.7

x	$y_1 = x^2$
-2	4
-1	1
0	0
1	1
2	4

TABLE 8.8

x	$y_2 = (x + 2)^2$
-4	4
-3	1
-2	0
-1	1
0	4

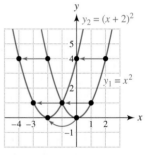

Figure 8.13

These results are summarized as follows.

||||||| VERTICAL AND HORIZONTAL TRANSLATIONS OF PARABOLAS

Let h and k be positive numbers.

If students understand the method presented in the box, they will have an easier time understanding the discussion of vertex form.

To graph	*shift the graph of $y = x^2$ by k units*
$y = x^2 + k$	upward.
$y = x^2 - k$	downward.

To graph	*shift the graph of $y = x^2$ by h units*
$y = (x - h)^2$	right.
$y = (x + h)^2$	left.

TEACHING TIP

The next example demonstrates this method.

EXAMPLE 1   Translating the graph $y = x^2$

Sketch the graph of the equation and identify the vertex.
(a) $y = x^2 + 2$ **(b)** $y = (x + 3)^2$ **(c)** $y = (x - 2)^2 - 3$

Solution   **(a)** The graph of $y = x^2 + 2$ is similar to the graph of $y = x^2$ except that it has been translated upward 2 units, as shown in Figure 8.14(a). The vertex is $(0, 2)$.
(b) The graph of $y = (x + 3)^2$ is similar to the graph of $y = x^2$ except that it has been translated *left* 3 units, as shown in Figure 8.14(b). The vertex is $(-3, 0)$.

   Note: If you are thinking that the graph should be shifted right (instead of left) 3 units, try graphing $y = (x + 3)^2$ on a graphing calculator.

(c) The graph of $y = (x - 2)^2 - 3$ is similar to the graph of $y = x^2$ except that it has been translated downward 3 units *and* right 2 units, as shown in Figure 8.14(c). The vertex is $(2, -3)$.

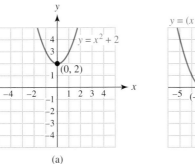
(a)

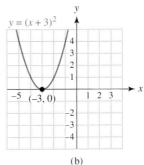
(b)

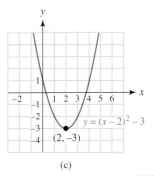
(c)

Figure 8.14

VERTEX FORM

Suppose that a parabola has the equation $y = ax^2 + bx + c$ with vertex (h, k). We can write this equation in a different form called the *vertex form* by transforming the graph of $y = x^2$. The vertex for $y = x^2$ is $(0, 0)$ so we need to translate it h units horizontally and k units vertically. Thus $y = (x - h)^2 + k$ has vertex (h, k). For the graph of our new equation to open correctly and have the same shape as $y = ax^2 + bx + c$, we must be sure that their leading coefficients are identical. That is, the graph of $y = a(x - h)^2 + k$ is identical to $y = ax^2 + bx + c$, provided that the vertex for the second equation is (h, k). This discussion is summarized as follows.

VERTEX FORM OF A PARABOLA

The **vertex form of a parabola** with vertex (h, k) is

$$y = a(x - h)^2 + k,$$

where $a \neq 0$ is a constant. If $a > 0$, the parabola opens upward; if $a < 0$, the parabola opens downward.

In the next three examples, we demonstrate the graphing of parabolas in vertex form, finding their equations, and writing vertex forms of equations.

EXAMPLE 2   Graphing parabolas in vertex form

Compare the graph of $y = f(x)$ to the graph of $y = x^2$. Then sketch a graph of $y = f(x)$ and $y = x^2$ in the same xy-plane.
(a) $f(x) = \frac{1}{2}(x - 5)^2 + 2$ **(b)** $f(x) = -3(x + 5)^2 - 1$

Solution **(a)** Both graphs are parabolas. However, compared to the graph of $y = x^2$, the graph of $y = f(x)$ is translated 5 units right and 2 units upward. The vertex for $f(x)$ is $(5, 2)$, whereas the vertex of $y = x^2$ is $(0, 0)$. Because $a = \frac{1}{2}$, the graph of $y = f(x)$ opens wider than the graph of $y = x^2$. These graphs are shown in Figure 8.15(a).

(b) Compared to the graph of $y = x^2$, the graph of $y = f(x)$ is translated 5 units left and 1 unit downward. The vertex for $f(x)$ is $(-5, -1)$. Because $a = -3$, the graph of $y = f(x)$ opens downward and is narrower than the graph of $y = x^2$. These graphs are shown in Figure 8.15(b).

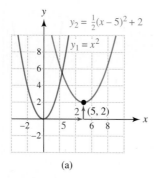
(a)

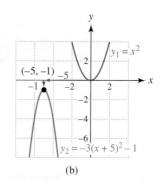
(b)

Figure 8.15

EXAMPLE 3   Finding equations of parabolas

Write the vertex form of a parabola with $a = 2$ and vertex $(-2, 1)$. Then express this equation in the form $y = ax^2 + bx + c$.

Solution The vertex form of a parabola is

$$y = a(x - h)^2 + k,$$

where the vertex is (h, k). For $a = 2$, $h = -2$, and $k = 1$, the equation becomes

$$y = 2(x - (-2))^2 + 1 \quad \text{or} \quad y = 2(x + 2)^2 + 1.$$

To write this equation in the form $y = ax^2 + bx + c$, do the following.

$$
\begin{aligned}
y &= 2(x^2 + 4x + 4) + 1 &&\text{Multiply } (x + 2)^2. \\
  &= (2x^2 + 8x + 8) + 1 &&\text{Distributive property} \\
  &= 2x^2 + 8x + 9 &&\text{Add.}
\end{aligned}
$$

The equivalent equation is $y = 2x^2 + 8x + 9$.

If we are given the equation $y = x^2 + 4x + 2$, can we write it in vertex form? The answer is *yes*, and in this process we use the **completing the square method**. Because

$$\left(x + \frac{b}{2}\right)^2 = x^2 + 2x\left(\frac{b}{2}\right) + \left(\frac{b}{2}\right)^2$$

$$= x^2 + bx + \left(\frac{b}{2}\right)^2,$$

we can complete the square for $y = x^2 + bx + c$ by adding and subtracting $\left(\frac{b}{2}\right)^2$. For $y = x^2 + 8x + 2$, we have $b = 8$, and must add *and* subtract $\left(\frac{b}{2}\right)^2 = \left(\frac{8}{2}\right)^2 = 16$ on the right side of the equation to complete the square.

$$
\begin{aligned}
y &= x^2 + 8x + 2 && \text{Given equation} \\
&= (x^2 + 8x + 16) - 16 + 2 && \text{Add and subtract 16.} \\
&= (x + 4)^2 - 14 && \text{Perfect square trinomial}
\end{aligned}
$$

Thus $y = x^2 + 8x + 2$ and $y = (x + 4)^2 - 14$ are equivalent equations. The vertex for this parabola is $(-4, -14)$. Note that we added *and* subtracted 16, so the right side of the equation did not change in value.

EXAMPLE 4 Writing vertex form

Write each equation in vertex form. Identify the vertex.
(a) $y = x^2 - 6x - 1$ **(b)** $y = x^2 + 3x + 4$ **(c)** $y = 2x^2 + 4x - 1$

Solution **(a)** Because $\left(\frac{b}{2}\right)^2 = \left(\frac{-6}{2}\right)^2 = 9$, add and subtract 9 on the right side.

$$
\begin{aligned}
y &= x^2 - 6x - 1 && \text{Given equation} \\
&= (x^2 - 6x + 9) - 9 - 1 && \text{Add and subtract 9.} \\
&= (x - 3)^2 - 10 && \text{Perfect square trinomial}
\end{aligned}
$$

The vertex is $(3, -10)$.
(b) Because $\left(\frac{b}{2}\right)^2 = \left(\frac{3}{2}\right)^2 = \frac{9}{4}$, add and subtract $\frac{9}{4}$ on the right side.

$$
\begin{aligned}
y &= x^2 + 3x + 4 && \text{Given equation} \\
&= \left(x^2 + 3x + \frac{9}{4}\right) - \frac{9}{4} + 4 && \text{Add and subtract } \tfrac{9}{4}. \\
&= \left(x + \frac{3}{2}\right)^2 + \frac{7}{4} && \text{Perfect square trinomial}
\end{aligned}
$$

The vertex is $\left(-\frac{3}{2}, \frac{7}{4}\right)$.
(c) This equation is slightly different because the leading coefficient is 2 rather than 1. Start by factoring 2 from the first two terms on the right side.

$$
\begin{aligned}
y &= 2x^2 + 4x - 1 && \text{Given equation} \\
&= 2(x^2 + 2x) - 1 && \text{Factor out 2.} \\
&= 2(x^2 + 2x + 1 - 1) - 1 && \left(\tfrac{b}{2}\right)^2 = \left(\tfrac{2}{2}\right)^2 = 1 \\
&= 2(x^2 + 2x + 1) - 2 - 1 && \text{Distributive property} \\
&= 2(x + 1)^2 - 3 && \text{Perfect square trinomial}
\end{aligned}
$$

The vertex is $(-1, -3)$.

Critical Thinking

What does c represent on the graph of $y = ax^2 + bx + c$?

The y-intercept

Note: If $h = -\frac{b}{2a}$ and $k = f\left(-\frac{b}{2a}\right)$, then the formulas $f(x) = ax^2 + bx + c$ and $f(x) = a(x - h)^2 + k$ represent the same quadratic function.

MODELING WITH QUADRATIC FUNCTIONS (OPTIONAL)

In the introduction to this section we discussed airport taxiway curves designed for airplanes. The data previously shown in Figure 8.10 are listed in Table 8.9.

A second scatterplot of the data is shown in Figure 8.16. The data may be modeled by $R(x) = ax^2$ for some value a. To illustrate this relation graph R for different values of a. In Figures 8.17–8.19, R has been graphed for $a = 2$, -1, and $\frac{1}{2}$, respectively. When $a > 0$ the parabola opens upward and when $a < 0$ the parabola opens downward. Larger values of $|a|$ make a parabola narrower, whereas smaller values of $|a|$ make the parabola wider. Through trial and error, $a = \frac{1}{2}$ gives a good fit to the data, so $R(x) = \frac{1}{2}x^2$ models the data.

TABLE 8.9

x (mph)	R (ft)
10	50
20	200
30	450
40	800
50	1250
60	1800

Source: Federal Aviation Administration.

TEACHING TIP

This subsection helps students understand how the parameters a, h, and k affect the graph of a quadratic function. However, it is *optional*.

Calculator Help

To make a scatterplot, see the Appendix (page AP-4).

$[-70, 70, 10]$ by $[-2000, 2000, 500]$

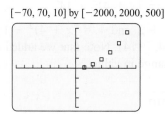

Figure 8.16

$[-70, 70, 10]$ by $[-2000, 2000, 500]$

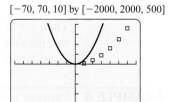

Figure 8.17 $a = 2$

$[-70, 70, 10]$ by $[-2000, 2000, 500]$

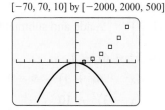

Figure 8.18 $a = -1$

$[-70, 70, 10]$ by $[-2000, 2000, 500]$

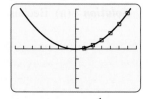

Figure 8.19 $a = \frac{1}{2}$

We can also find this value of a symbolically, as demonstrated in the next example.

EXAMPLE 5   Modeling safe taxiway speed

Find a value for the constant a symbolically so that $R(x) = ax^2$ models the data in Table 8.9. Check your result by making a table of values for $R(x)$.

Solution   Table 8.9 shows that, when $x = 10$ miles per hour, the curve radius is $R(x) = 50$ feet. Therefore

$$R(10) = 50 \quad \text{or} \quad a(10)^2 = 50.$$

Solving for a gives

$$a = \frac{50}{10^2} = \frac{1}{2}.$$

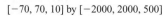

X	Y1
0	0
10	50
20	200
30	450
40	800
50	1250
60	1800

Y1 = .5X²

Figure 8.20

To be sure that $R(x) = \frac{1}{2}x^2$ is correct, construct a table, as shown in Figure 8.20. Its values agree with those in Table 8.9.

Critical Thinking

If the speed of a taxiing airplane doubles, what should happen to the radius of a safe taxiway curve?

It should increase by a factor of 4.

In 1981, the first cases of AIDS were reported in the United States. Since then, AIDS has become one of the most devastating diseases of recent times. Table 8.10 lists the *cumulative* number of AIDS cases in the United States for various years. For example, between 1981 and 1990, a total of 199,608 AIDS cases were reported.

A scatterplot of these data is shown in Figure 8.21. To model these nonlinear data, we want to find (the right half of) a parabola with the shape illustrated in Figure 8.22. We do so in the next example.

TABLE 8.10

Years	AIDS Cases
1981	425
1984	11,106
1987	71,414
1990	199,608
1993	417,835
1996	609,933

Source: Department of Health and Human Services.

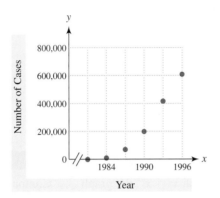

Figure 8.21 AIDS Cases

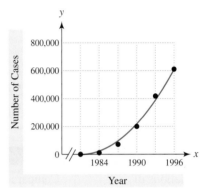

Figure 8.22 Modeling AIDS Cases

EXAMPLE 6   Modeling AIDS cases

Use the data in Table 8.10 to complete the following.

(a) Make a scatterplot of the data in [1980, 1997, 2] by [−10000, 800000, 100000].

(b) The lowest data point in Table 8.10 is (1981, 425). Let this point be the vertex of a parabola that opens upward. Graph $y = a(x - 1981)^2 + 425$ together with the data by first letting $a = 1000$.

(c) Use trial and error to adjust the value of a until the graph models the data.

(d) Use your final equation to estimate the number of AIDS cases in 1992. Compare it to the known value of 338,786.

Solution   **(a)** A scatterplot of the data is shown in Figure 8.23.

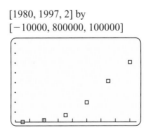

[1980, 1997, 2] by
[−10000, 800000, 100000]

Figure 8.23

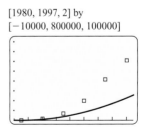

[1980, 1997, 2] by
[−10000, 800000, 100000]

Figure 8.24 $a = 1000$

(b) A graph of $y = 1000(x - 1981)^2 + 425$ is shown in Figure 8.24. To have a better fit of the data, a larger value for a is needed.

[1980, 1997, 2] by
[−10000, 800000, 100000]

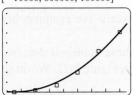

Figure 8.25 $a = 2700$

(c) Figure 8.25 shows the effect of adjusting the value of a to 2700. This value provides a reasonably good fit. (Note that you may decide on a slightly different value for a.)
(d) If $a = 2700$, the modeling equation becomes

$$y = 2700(x - 1981)^2 + 425.$$

To estimate the number of AIDS cases in 1992, substitute $x = 1992$ to obtain

$$y = 2700(1992 - 1981)^2 + 425 = 327{,}125.$$

This number is about 12,000 less than the known value of 338,786.   ⎯⎯⎯

8.2   PUTTING IT ALL TOGETHER

The following table summarizes some of the important topics in this section.

Concept	Explanation	Examples
Translations of Parabolas	Compared to the graph $y = x^2$, the graph of $y = x^2 + k$ is shifted vertically k units and the graph of $y = (x - h)^2$ is shifted horizontally h units.	Compared to the graph of $y = x^2$, the graph of $y = x^2 - 4$ is shifted downward 4 units. Compared to the graph of $y = x^2$, the graph of $y = (x - 4)^2$ is shifted right 4 units and the graph of $y = (x + 4)^2$ is shifted left 4 units.
Vertex Form of a Parabola	The vertex form of a parabola with vertex (h, k) is $$y = a(x - h)^2 + k,$$ where $a \neq 0$ is a constant. If $a > 0$, the parabola opens upward; if $a < 0$, the parabola opens downward.	The graph of $y = 3(x + 2)^2 - 7$ has a vertex of $(-2, -7)$ and opens upward because $a > 0$.
Completing the Square Method	To complete the square to obtain the vertex form, add and subtract $\left(\frac{b}{2}\right)^2$ on the right side of $y = x^2 + bx + c$. Then factor the perfect square trinomial.	If $y = x^2 + 10x - 3$, then add and subtract $\left(\frac{b}{2}\right)^2 = \left(\frac{10}{2}\right)^2 = 25$ on the right side of this equation. $$y = (x^2 + 10x + 25) - 25 - 3$$ $$= (x + 5)^2 - 28$$ The vertex is $(-5, -28)$.

8.2 EXERCISES

FOR EXTRA HELP

 Student's Solutions Manual

 InterAct Math

 MathXL

MyMathLab

Math Tutor Center

Digital Video Tutor CD 7 Videotape 9

CONCEPTS

1. Compared to the graph of $y = x^2$, the graph of $y =$ _____ is shifted upward 2 units. $x^2 + 2$

2. Compared to the graph of $y = x^2$, the graph of $y =$ _____ is shifted to the right 2 units. $(x - 2)^2$

3. The vertex of $y = (x - 1)^2 + 2$ is _____. $(1, 2)$

4. The vertex of $y = (x + 1)^2 - 2$ is _____. $(-1, -2)$

5. A quadratic function may be written either in the form _____ or _____.
$f(x) = ax^2 + bx + c; f(x) = a(x - h)^2 + k$

6. The vertex form of a parabola is given by _____ and its vertex is _____. $y = a(x - h)^2 + k; (h, k)$

7. The graph of $y = -x^2$ is a parabola that opens _____. downward

8. The x-coordinate of the vertex of $y = ax^2 + bx + c$ is $x =$ _____. $-\frac{b}{2a}$

GRAPHS OF PARABOLAS

Exercises 9–28: Do the following.
(a) Sketch a graph of the equation.
(b) Identify the vertex.
(c) Compare the graph to the graph of $y = x^2$. (State the transformations used.)

9. $f(x) = x^2 - 4$

10. $f(x) = x^2 - 1$

11. $f(x) = 2x^2 + 1$

12. $f(x) = \frac{1}{2}x^2 + 1$

13. $f(x) = (x - 3)^2$

14. $f(x) = (x + 1)^2$

15. $f(x) = -x^2$

16. $f(x) = -(x + 2)^2$

17. $f(x) = 2 - x^2$

18. $f(x) = (x - 1)^2$

19. $f(x) = (x + 2)^2$

20. $f(x) = (x - 2)^2 - 3$

21. $f(x) = (x + 1)^2 - 2$

22. $f(x) = (x - 3)^2 + 1$

23. $f(x) = (x - 1)^2 + 2$

24. $f(x) = \frac{1}{2}(x + 3)^2 - 3$

25. $f(x) = 2(x - 5)^2 - 4$

26. $f(x) = -3(x + 4)^2 + 5$

27. $f(x) = -\frac{1}{2}(x + 3)^2 + 1$

28. $f(x) = 2(x - 5)^2 + 10$

VERTEX FORM

Exercises 29–32: (Refer to Example 3.) Write the vertex form of a parabola that satisfies the conditions given. Then write the equation in the form $y = ax^2 + bx + c$.

29. Vertex $(3, 4)$ and $a = 3$ $y = 3(x - 3)^2 + 4;$ $y = 3x^2 - 18x + 31$

30. Vertex $(-1, 3)$ and $a = -5$ $y = -5(x + 1)^2 + 3;$ $y = -5x^2 - 10x - 2$

31. Vertex $(5, -2)$ and $a = -\frac{1}{2}$ $y = -\frac{1}{2}(x - 5)^2 - 2;$ $y = -\frac{1}{2}x^2 + 5x - \frac{29}{2}$

32. Vertex $(-2, -6)$ and $a = \frac{3}{4}$ $y = \frac{3}{4}(x + 2)^2 - 6; y = \frac{3}{4}x^2 + 3x - 3$

Exercises 33–36: Write the vertex form of a parabola that satisfies the conditions given. Assume that $a = \pm 1$.

33. Opens upward, vertex $(1, 2)$ $y = (x - 1)^2 + 2$

34. Opens downward, vertex $(-1, -2)$ $y = -(x + 1)^2 - 2$

35. Opens downward, vertex $(0, -3)$ $y = -(x - 0)^2 - 3$

36. Opens upward, vertex $(5, -4)$ $y = (x - 5)^2 - 4$

Exercises 37–40: Write the vertex form of the parabola shown in the graph. Assume that $a = \pm 1$.

37. $y = (x - 0)^2 - 3$

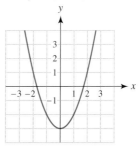

38. $y = (x - 2)^2 - 3$

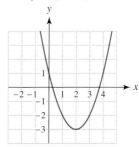

*Answers on pages IA-25–IA-26

39. $y = -(x + 1)^2 + 2$ **40.** $y = -(x + 3)^2 - 1$

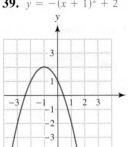
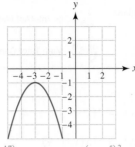

45. $y = \left(x + \frac{3}{2}\right)^2 - \frac{17}{4};\ \left(-\frac{3}{2}, -\frac{17}{4}\right)$ **46.** $y = \left(x + \frac{5}{2}\right)^2 - \frac{41}{4};\ \left(-\frac{5}{2}, -\frac{41}{4}\right)$

Exercises 41–54: (Refer to Example 4.) Write the equation in vertex form. Identify the vertex.

41. $y = x^2 + 2x - 3$ **42.** $y = x^2 + 4x + 1$
$y = (x + 1)^2 - 4;\ (-1, -4)$ $y = (x + 2)^2 - 3;\ (-2, -3)$

43. $y = x^2 - 4x + 5$ **44.** $y = x^2 - 8x + 10$
$y = (x - 2)^2 + 1;\ (2, 1)$ $y = (x - 4)^2 - 6;\ (4, -6)$

45. $y = x^2 + 3x - 2$ **46.** $y = x^2 + 5x - 4$

47. $y = x^2 - 7x + 1$ **48.** $y = x^2 - 3x + 5$

49. $y = 3x^2 + 6x - 1$ **50.** $y = 2x^2 + 4x - 9$
$y = 2(x + 1)^2 - 11;\ (-1, -11)$

51. $y = 2x^2 - 3x$ **52.** $y = 3x^2 - 7x$

53. $y = -2x^2 - 8x + 5$ **54.** $y = -3x^2 + 6x + 1$
$y = -2(x + 2)^2 + 13;\ (-2, 13)$ $y = -3(x - 1)^2 + 4;\ (1, 4)$

MODELING DATA

Exercises 55–58: Find a value for the constant a so that $f(x) = ax^2$ models the data. If you are uncertain about your value for a, check it by making a table of values.

55.
x	1	2	3
y	2	8	18

$a = 2$

56.
x	-2	0	2
y	6	0	6

$a = \frac{3}{2}$

57.
x	2	4	6	8
y	1.2	4.8	10.8	19.2

$a = 0.3$

58.
x	5	10	15	20
y	17.5	70	157.5	280

$a = 0.7$

*Exercises 59–62: **Modeling Quadratic Data** (Refer to Example 6.) Find a quadratic function expressed in vertex form that models the data in the given table.*

59.
x	1	2	3	4
y	-3	-1	5	15

$y = 2(x - 1)^2 - 3$

60.
x	-2	-1	0	1	2
y	5	2	-7	-22	-43

$y = -3(x + 2)^2 + 5$

61.
x	1980	1990	2000	2010
y	6	55	210	450

$y = 0.5(x - 1980)^2 + 6$

62.
x	1990	1995	2000	2005
y	10	60	205	470

$y = 2(x - 1990)^2 + 10$

63. *Braking Distance* The table lists approximate stopping distances D in feet for cars traveling at x miles per hour on dry, level pavement.

x	12	24	36	48
D	12	48	108	192

(a) Make a scatterplot of the data.*
(b) Find a function given by $D(x) = ax^2$ that models these data. $D(x) = \frac{1}{12}x^2$

64. *Health Care Costs* The table lists *approximate* percentage increases in the cost of health insurance premiums between 1992 and 2000.

Year	1992	1994	1996	1998	2000
Increase	11%	4%	1%	4%	11%

Source: Kaiser Family Foundation.

(a) Make a scatterplot of the data.*
(b) Find a function given by $C(x) = a(x - h)^2 + k$ that models these data. (Answers may vary.)
$C(x) = 0.65(x - 1996)^2 + 1$

WRITING ABOUT MATHEMATICS

65. Explain how to find the vertex of $y = x^2 + bx + c$ by completing the square.

66. If $f(x) = a(x - h)^2 + k$, explain how the values of a, h, and k affect the graph of $y = f(x)$.

47. $y = \left(x - \frac{7}{2}\right)^2 - \frac{45}{4};\ \left(\frac{7}{2}, -\frac{45}{4}\right)$ **48.** $y = \left(x - \frac{3}{2}\right)^2 + \frac{11}{4};\ \left(\frac{3}{2}, \frac{11}{4}\right)$ **49.** $y = 3(x + 1)^2 - 4;\ (-1, -4)$

51. $y = 2\left(x - \frac{3}{4}\right)^2 - \frac{9}{8};\ \left(\frac{3}{4}, -\frac{9}{8}\right)$ **52.** $y = 3\left(x - \frac{7}{6}\right)^2 - \frac{49}{12};\ \left(\frac{7}{6}, -\frac{49}{12}\right)$

*Answers on page IA-26

CHECKING BASIC CONCEPTS   SECTIONS 8.1 AND 8.2

1. Graph each quadratic function. Identify the vertex and axis of symmetry.*
   (a) $f(x) = x^2 - 2$ $(0, -2); x = 0$
   (b) $f(x) = x^2 - 2x - 2$ $(1, -3); x = 1$

2. Compare the graph of $y_1 = 2x^2$ to the graph of $y_2 = -\frac{1}{2}x^2$. y_1 opens upward, whereas y_2 opens downward; y_1 is narrower than y_2

3. Find the maximum y-value on the graph of $y = -3x^2 + 12x - 5$. State where the graph is increasing and where it is decreasing.
   7; increasing: $x \leq 2$; decreasing: $x \geq 2$

4. Sketch a graph of $y = f(x)$. Compare the graph of f to the graph of $y = x^2$.*
   (a) $f(x) = (x - 1)^2 + 2$ 1 unit right, 2 units up
   (b) $f(x) = -(x + 3)^2$
   Reflected across the x-axis, 3 units left

5. Write the vertex form for each equation.
   (a) $y = x^2 + 14x - 7$ $y = (x + 7)^2 - 56$
   (b) $y = 4x^2 + 8x - 2$ $y = 4(x + 1)^2 - 6$

*Answers on page IA-27

8.3   QUADRATIC EQUATIONS

Basics of Quadratic Equations · The Square Root Property · Completing the Square · Solving an Equation for a Variable · Applications of Quadratic Equations

INTRODUCTION

In Section 8.2 we modeled curves on airport taxiways by using $R(x) = \frac{1}{2}x^2$. In this formula x represented the airplane's speed in miles per hour, and R represented the radius of the curve in feet. This formula may be used to determine the speed limit for a curve with a radius of 650 feet by solving the *quadratic equation*

$$\frac{1}{2}x^2 = 650.$$

TEACHING TIP

Use the introduction to explain how a quadratic equation can occur in applications.

In this section we demonstrate techniques for solving this and other quadratic equations.

BASICS OF QUADRATIC EQUATIONS

Any quadratic function f can be represented by $f(x) = ax^2 + bx + c$ with $a \neq 0$. Examples of quadratic functions include

$$f(x) = 2x^2 - 1, \quad g(x) = -\frac{1}{3}x^2 + 2x, \quad \text{and} \quad h(x) = x^2 + 2x - 1.$$

TEACHING TIP

Point out that a quadratic function can be written as $f(x) = ax^2 + bx + c$ and that a quadratic equation can be written as $ax^2 + bx + c = 0$.

Quadratic functions can be used to write quadratic equations. Examples of quadratic equations include

$$2x^2 - 1 = 0, \quad -\frac{1}{3}x^2 + 2x = 0, \quad \text{and} \quad x^2 + 2x - 1 = 3.$$

┃┃┃┃┃┃┃┃┃┃   **QUADRATIC EQUATION**

A **quadratic equation** is an equation that can be written as

$$ax^2 + bx + c = 0,$$

where a, b, and c are real numbers with $a \neq 0$.   ┃┃┃┃┃┃┃┃┃

Solutions to the quadratic equation $ax^2 + bx + c = 0$ correspond to x-intercepts of the graph of $y = ax^2 + bx + c$. Because the graph of a quadratic function is either ∪-shaped or ∩-shaped, it can intersect the x-axis zero, one, or two times, as illustrated in Figure 8.26. Hence a quadratic equation can have zero, one, or two real solutions.

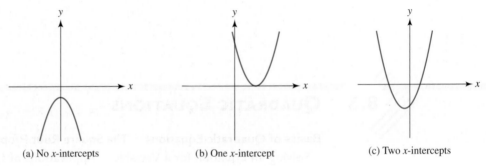

(a) No x-intercepts   (b) One x-intercept   (c) Two x-intercepts

Figure 8.26

We have already solved quadratic equations by factoring, graphing, and constructing tables. In the next example we apply these three techniques to quadratic equations that have zero, one, and two real solutions.

EXAMPLE 1   **Solving quadratic equations**

Solve each quadratic equation. Support your results numerically and graphically.

(a) $2x^2 + 1 = 0$ (No real solutions)
(b) $x^2 + 4 = 4x$ (One real solution)
(c) $x^2 - 6x + 8 = 0$ (Two real solutions)

Solution   **(a)** *Symbolic Solution*

$$2x^2 + 1 = 0 \qquad \text{Given equation}$$
$$2x^2 = -1 \qquad \text{Subtract 1.}$$
$$x^2 = -\frac{1}{2} \qquad \text{Divide by 2.}$$

This equation has no real-number solutions because $x^2 \geq 0$ for all real numbers x. Note that the graph of $y = 2x^2 + 1$ has no x-intercepts.

Numerical and Graphical Solution The points in Table 8.11 for $y = 2x^2 + 1$ are plotted in Figure 8.27 and connected with a parabolic graph. The graph of $y = 2x^2 + 1$ has no x-intercepts, indicating that there are no real solutions. Note that the y-values in Table 8.11 are always positive.

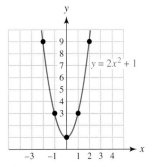

TABLE 8.11

x	y
-2	9
-1	3
0	1
1	3
2	9

Figure 8.27 No Solutions

(b) *Symbolic Solution*

$x^2 + 4 = 4x$	Given equation
$x^2 - 4x + 4 = 0$	Subtract $4x$ from both sides.
$(x - 2)(x - 2) = 0$	Factor.
$x - 2 = 0 \quad \text{or} \quad x - 2 = 0$	Zero-product property
$x = 2$	There is one solution.

Numerical and Graphical Solution Because the given equation is equivalent to $x^2 - 4x + 4 = 0$, we let $y = x^2 - 4x + 4$. The points in Table 8.12 are plotted in Figure 8.28 and connected with a parabolic graph. The graph of $y = x^2 - 4x + 4$ has one x-intercept, 2. Note that in Table 8.12, $y = 0$ when $x = 2$, indicating that the equation has one solution.

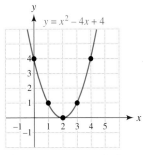

TABLE 8.12

x	y
0	4
1	1
2	0
3	1
2	4

Figure 8.28 One Solution

(c) *Symbolic Solution*

$x^2 - 6x + 8 = 0$	Given equation
$(x - 2)(x - 4) = 0$	Factor.
$x - 2 = 0 \quad \text{or} \quad x - 4 = 0$	Zero-product property
$x = 2 \quad \text{or} \quad x = 4$	There are two solutions.

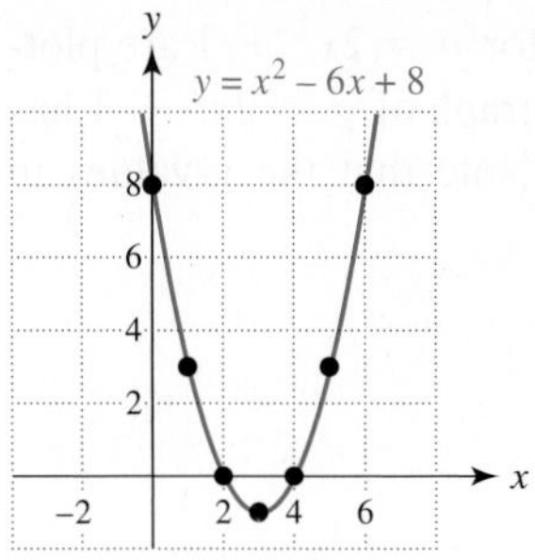

$y = x^2 - 6x + 8$

Figure 8.29 Two Solutions

Numerical and Graphical Solution   The points in Table 8.13 for $y = x^2 - 6x + 8$ are plotted in Figure 8.29 and connected with a parabolic graph. The graph of $y = x^2 - 6x + 8$ has two x-intercepts, 2 and 4, indicating two solutions. Note that in Table 8.13 $y = 0$ when $x = 2$ or $x = 4$.

TABLE 8.13

x	0	1	2	3	4	5	6
y	8	3	0	-1	0	3	8

TEACHING TIP

If you covered the square root property in Section 7.4, you may skip this subsection. However, if you are teaching Chapter 8 before Chapter 7, it is important to cover the square root property now.

THE SQUARE ROOT PROPERTY

The *square root property* is a symbolic method used to solve quadratic equations that are missing x-terms. The following is an example of the square root property.

$$x^2 = 25 \quad \text{is equivalent to} \quad x = \pm 5$$

The expression $x = \pm 5$ (read "x equals plus or minus 5") indicates that either $x = 5$ or $x = -5$. Each value is a solution because $(5)^2 = 25$ and $(-5)^2 = 25$.

SQUARE ROOT PROPERTY

Let k be a nonnegative number. Then the solutions to the equation

$$x^2 = k$$

are given by $x = \pm \sqrt{k}$. If $k < 0$, then this equation has no real solutions.

Before applying the square root property in the next two examples, we review a quotient property of square roots. If a and b are positive numbers, then

$$\sqrt{\frac{a}{b}} = \frac{\sqrt{a}}{\sqrt{b}}.$$

For example,

$$\sqrt{\frac{25}{36}} = \frac{\sqrt{25}}{\sqrt{36}} = \frac{5}{6}.$$

EXAMPLE 2   Using the square root property

Solve each equation.
(a) $x^2 = 7$ **(b)** $16x^2 - 9 = 0$ **(c)** $(x - 4)^2 = 25$

Solution **(a)** $x^2 = 7$ is equivalent to $x = \pm \sqrt{7}$ by the square root property. The solutions are $\sqrt{7}$ and $-\sqrt{7}$.

TEACHING TIP

The square root property can be used to solve a quadratic equation when there is no x- term.

(b)

$$16x^2 - 9 = 0 \qquad \text{Given equation}$$
$$16x^2 = 9 \qquad \text{Add 9.}$$
$$x^2 = \frac{9}{16} \qquad \text{Divide by 16.}$$
$$x = \pm\sqrt{\frac{9}{16}} \qquad \text{Square root property}$$
$$x = \pm\frac{3}{4} \qquad \text{Simplify.}$$

The solutions are $\frac{3}{4}$ and $-\frac{3}{4}$.

(c)

$$(x - 4)^2 = 25 \qquad \text{Given equation.}$$
$$(x - 4) = \pm\sqrt{25} \qquad \text{Square root property}$$
$$x - 4 = \pm 5 \qquad \text{Simplify.}$$
$$x = 4 \pm 5 \qquad \text{Add 4.}$$
$$x = 9 \quad \text{or} \quad x = -1 \qquad \text{Evaluate } 4 + 5 \text{ and } 4 - 5.$$

The solutions are 9 and -1.

If an object is dropped from a height of h feet, its distance d above the ground after t seconds is given by

$$d(t) = h - 16t^2.$$

This formula can be used to estimate the time it takes for a falling object to hit the ground.

EXAMPLE 3   Modeling a falling object

A toy falls from a window 30 feet above the ground. How long does the toy take to hit the ground?

Solution   The height of the window above the ground is 30 feet so let $d(t) = 30 - 16t^2$. The toy strikes the ground when the distance d above the ground equals 0.

$$30 - 16t^2 = 0 \qquad \text{Equation to solve}$$
$$-16t^2 = -30 \qquad \text{Subtract 30.}$$
$$t^2 = \frac{30}{16} \qquad \text{Divide by } -16.$$
$$t = \pm\sqrt{\frac{30}{16}} \qquad \text{Square root property}$$
$$t = \pm\frac{\sqrt{30}}{4} \qquad \text{Simplify.}$$

Time cannot be negative in this problem, so the appropriate solution is $t = \frac{\sqrt{30}}{4} \approx 1.4$. The toy hits the ground after about 1.4 seconds.

COMPLETING THE SQUARE

In Section 8.2, we used the *method of completing the square* to find the vertex of a parabola. This method can also be used to solve quadratic equations. Because

$$x^2 + bx + \left(\frac{b}{2}\right)^2 = \left(x + \frac{b}{2}\right)^2,$$

we can solve a quadratic equation in the form $x^2 + bx = d$, where b and d are constants, by adding $\left(\frac{b}{2}\right)^2$ to each side and then factoring the resulting perfect square trinomial.

In the equation $x^2 + 6x = 7$ we have $b = 6$, so we add $\left(\frac{6}{2}\right)^2 = 9$ to each side.

$x^2 + 6x = 7$	Given equation
$x^2 + 6x + 9 = 7 + 9$	Add 9 to each side.
$(x + 3)^2 = 16$	Perfect square trinomial
$x + 3 = \pm 4$	Square root property
$x = -3 \pm 4$	Add -3 to each side.
$x = 1 \quad \text{or} \quad x = -7$	Simplify $-3 + 4$ and $-3 - 4$.

The solutions are 1 and -7.

Note that the left side of the equation becomes a perfect square trinomial. We show how to create one in the next example.

EXAMPLE 4 Creating a perfect square trinomial

Find the term that should be added to $x^2 - 10x$ to form a perfect square trinomial.

Solution The coefficient of the x-term is -10, so we let $b = -10$. To complete the square we divide b by 2 and then square the result.

$$\left(\frac{b}{2}\right)^2 = \left(\frac{-10}{2}\right)^2 = 25$$

If we add 25, a perfect square trinomial is formed.

$$x^2 - 10x + 25 = (x - 5)^2 \qquad \underline{\hspace{1cm}}$$

Completing the square can be used to solve quadratic equations when a trinomial does not factor easily, as illustrated in the next two examples.

EXAMPLE 5 Completing the square when the leading coefficient is 1

Solve the equation $x^2 - 4x + 2 = 0$.

Solution Start by writing the equation in the form $x^2 + bx = d$.

$x^2 - 4x + 2 = 0$	Given equation
$x^2 - 4x = -2$	Subtract 2.
$x^2 - 4x + 4 = -2 + 4$	Add $\left(\frac{b}{2}\right)^2 = \left(\frac{-4}{2}\right)^2 = 4$.
$(x - 2)^2 = 2$	Perfect square trinomial
$x - 2 = \pm\sqrt{2}$	Square root property
$x = 2 \pm \sqrt{2}$	Solve.

The solutions are $2 + \sqrt{2} \approx 3.41$ and $2 - \sqrt{2} \approx 0.59$. $\underline{\hspace{1cm}}$

EXAMPLE 6   Completing the square when the leading coefficient is not 1

Solve the equation $2x^2 + 7x - 5 = 0$.

Solution   Start by writing the equation in the form $x^2 + bx = d$. That is, add 5 to each side and then divide the equation by 2 so that the leading coefficient of the x^2-term becomes 1.

$$2x^2 + 7x - 5 = 0 \qquad \text{Given equation}$$

$$2x^2 + 7x = 5 \qquad \text{Add 5.}$$

$$x^2 + \frac{7}{2}x = \frac{5}{2} \qquad \text{Divide by 2.}$$

$$x^2 + \frac{7}{2}x + \frac{49}{16} = \frac{5}{2} + \frac{49}{16} \qquad \text{Add } \left(\frac{b}{2}\right)^2 = \left(\frac{7}{4}\right)^2 = \frac{49}{16}.$$

$$\left(x + \frac{7}{4}\right)^2 = \frac{89}{16} \qquad \text{Perfect square trinomial}$$

$$x + \frac{7}{4} = \pm\frac{\sqrt{89}}{4} \qquad \text{Square root property}$$

$$x = \frac{-7 \pm \sqrt{89}}{4} \qquad \text{Add } -\frac{7}{4}.$$

The solutions are $\dfrac{-7 + \sqrt{89}}{4} \approx 0.61$ and $\dfrac{-7 - \sqrt{89}}{4} \approx -4.1$.

Critical Thinking

What happens if you try to solve

$$2x^2 - 13 = 1$$

by completing the square? What method should you use to solve this problem?

Because $b = 0$, you would add 0 to each side; the square root property.

SOLVING AN EQUATION FOR A VARIABLE

We often need to solve an equation or formula for a variable. For example, the formula $V = \frac{1}{3}\pi r^2 h$ calculates the volume of the cone shown in Figure 8.30. Let's say that we know the volume V is 120 cubic inches and the height h is 15 inches. We can then find the radius of the cone by solving the equation for r.

$$V = \frac{1}{3}\pi r^2 h \qquad \text{Given equation}$$

$$3V = \pi r^2 h \qquad \text{Multiply by 3.}$$

$$\frac{3V}{\pi} = r^2 h \qquad \text{Divide by } \pi.$$

$$\frac{3V}{\pi h} = r^2 \qquad \text{Divide by } h.$$

$$r = \pm\sqrt{\frac{3V}{\pi h}} \qquad \text{Square root property; rewrite.}$$

Figure 8.30

Because $r \geq 0$, we use the positive or *principal square root*. Thus for $V = 120$ cubic inches and $h = 15$ inches,

$$r = \sqrt{\frac{3(120)}{\pi(15)}} = \sqrt{\frac{24}{\pi}} \approx 2.8 \text{ inches.}$$

EXAMPLE 7 Solving equations for variables

Solve each equation for the specified variable.
(a) $s = -\frac{1}{2}gt^2 + h$, for t **(b)** $d^2 = x^2 + y^2$, for y

Solution **(a)** Begin by subtracting h from each side of the equation.

$$s = -\frac{1}{2}gt^2 + h \qquad \text{Given equation}$$

$$s - h = -\frac{1}{2}gt^2 \qquad \text{Subtract } h.$$

$$-2(s - h) = gt^2 \qquad \text{Multiply by } -2.$$

$$\frac{2h - 2s}{g} = t^2 \qquad \text{Divide by } g; \text{ simplify.}$$

$$t = \pm\sqrt{\frac{2h - 2s}{g}} \qquad \text{Square root property}$$

(b) Begin by subtracting x^2 from each side of the equation.

$$d^2 = x^2 + y^2 \qquad \text{Given equation}$$

$$d^2 - x^2 = y^2 \qquad \text{Subtract } x^2.$$

$$y = \pm\sqrt{d^2 - x^2} \qquad \text{Square root property}$$

APPLICATIONS OF QUADRATIC EQUATIONS

In the introduction to this section we discussed how the solution to the equation

$$\frac{1}{2}x^2 = 650$$

would give a safe speed limit for a curve with a radius of 650 feet on an airport taxiway. We solve this problem in the next example.

EXAMPLE 8 Finding a safe speed limit

Solve the equation $\frac{1}{2}x^2 = 650$ and interpret any solutions.

Solution Use the square root property to solve this problem.

$$\frac{1}{2}x^2 = 650 \qquad \text{Given equation}$$

$$x^2 = 1300 \qquad \text{Multiply by 2.}$$

$$x = \pm\sqrt{1300} \qquad \text{Square root property}$$

The solutions are $\sqrt{1300} \approx 36$ and $-\sqrt{1300} \approx -36$. The solution of $x \approx 36$ indicates that a safe speed limit for a curve with a radius of 650 feet should be 36 miles per hour. (The negative solution has no physical meaning in this problem.)

In applications, solving a quadratic equation either graphically or numerically is often easier than solving it symbolically. We do so in the next example.

EXAMPLE 9   Modeling Internet users

Use of the Internet in Western Europe has increased dramatically. Figure 8.31 shows a scatterplot of online users in Western Europe, together with a graph of a function f that models the data. The function f is given by

$$f(x) = 0.976x^2 - 4.643x + 0.238,$$

where the output is in millions of users. In this formula $x = 6$ corresponds to 1996, $x = 7$ to 1997, and so on, until $x = 12$ represents 2002.   (**Source:** Nortel Networks.)

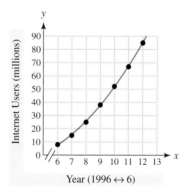

Figure 8.31 Internet Usage in Western Europe

(a) Evaluate $f(10)$ and interpret the result.
(b) Graph f and estimate the year when the number of Internet users reached 85 million. Compare your result with Figure 8.31.
(c) Solve part (b) numerically.

Solution (a) Substituting $x = 10$ into the formula yields

$$f(10) = 0.976(10)^2 - 4.643(10) + 0.238 \approx 51.4.$$

Because $x = 10$ corresponds to 2000, there were about 51.4 million Internet users in Western Europe in 2000.
(b) Graph $Y_1 = .976X^2 - 4.643X + .238$ and $Y_2 = 85$, as shown in Figure 8.32. Their graphs intersect near $x = 12$, which corresponds to 2002 and agrees with Figure 8.31.
(c) Construct the table for y_1, as shown in Figure 8.33, which reveals $y_1 \approx 85$ when $x = 12$.

Calculator Help
To find a point of intersection, see the Appendix (page AP-7).

[5, 13, 1] by [0, 100, 10]

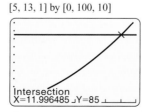

Intersection
X=11.996485 Y=85

Figure 8.32

X	Y₁	Y₂
9	37.507	85
10	51.408	85
11	67.261	85
12	85.066	85
13	104.82	85
14	126.53	85
15	150.19	85

X=12

Figure 8.33

8.3 PUTTING IT ALL TOGETHER

Quadratic equations can be expressed in the form $ax^2 + bx + c = 0$, $a \neq 0$. They can have zero, one, or two real solutions and may be solved symbolically, graphically, and numerically. Symbolic techniques for solving quadratic equations include factoring, the square root property, and completing the square. We discussed factoring extensively in Chapter 5, so the following table summarizes only the square root property and the method of completing the square.

Technique	Description	Examples
Square Root Property	If $k \geq 0$, the solutions to the equation $x^2 = k$ are $\pm\sqrt{k}$.	$x^2 = 100$ is equivalent to $x = \pm 10$ and $x^2 = 13$ is equivalent to $x = \pm\sqrt{13}$
Method of Completing the Square	To solve an equation in the form $x^2 + bx = d$, add $\left(\frac{b}{2}\right)^2$ to each side of the equation. Factor the resulting perfect square trinomial and solve for x by applying the square root property.	To solve $x^2 + 8x - 3 = 0$, begin by adding 3 to each side to obtain $x^2 + 8x = 3$. Because $b = 8$, add $\left(\frac{8}{2}\right)^2 = 16$ to each side. $\begin{aligned} x^2 + 8x + 16 &= 3 + 16 &&\text{Add 16 to each side.} \\ (x+4)^2 &= 19 &&\text{Perfect square trinomial} \\ x + 4 &= \pm\sqrt{19} &&\text{Square root property} \\ x &= -4 \pm\sqrt{19} &&\text{Add } -4. \\ x &\approx 0.36, -8.36 &&\text{Approximate.} \end{aligned}$

8.3 EXERCISES

FOR EXTRA HELP

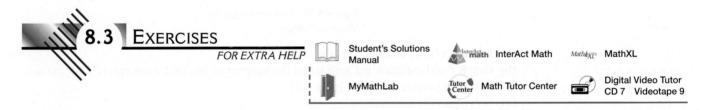

Student's Solutions Manual   InterAct Math   MathXL
MyMathLab   Math Tutor Center   Digital Video Tutor CD 7 Videotape 9

CONCEPTS

1. Give an example of a quadratic equation. How many real solutions can a quadratic equation have?
   $x^2 + 3x - 2 = 0$ (answers may vary); 0, 1, or 2 solutions

2. Is a quadratic equation a linear equation or a nonlinear equation?   Nonlinear

3. Name three symbolic methods that can be used to solve a quadratic equation.
   Factoring, square root property, and completing the square

4. Sketch a graph of a quadratic function that has two x-intercepts and opens downward.*

5. Sketch a graph of a quadratic function that has no x-intercepts and opens upward.*

6. If the graph of $y = ax^2 + bx + c$ intersects the x-axis twice, how many solutions does the equation $ax^2 + bx + c = 0$ have? Explain.
   Two; the solutions are the x-intercepts.

7. Solve $x^2 = 64$. What property did you use?
   $x = \pm 8$; the square root property

8. To solve $x^2 + bx = 6$ by completing the square, what value should be added to each side of the equation? $\left(\frac{b}{2}\right)^2$

Exercises 9–16: Determine whether the given equation is quadratic.

9. $x^2 - 3x + 1 = 0$ Yes

10. $2x^2 - 3 = 0$ Yes

*Answers on page IA-27

11. $3x + 1 = 0$ No   **12.** $x^3 - 3x^2 + x = 0$ No

13. $-3x^2 + x = 16$ Yes **14.** $x^2 - 1 = 4x$ Yes

15. $x^2 = \sqrt{x} + 1$ No **16.** $\dfrac{1}{x-1} = 5$ No

SOLVING QUADRATIC EQUATIONS

Exercises 17–20: A graph of $y = ax^2 + bx + c$ is given. Use this graph to solve $ax^2 + bx + c = 0$, if possible.

17. $-2, 1$

18. -2

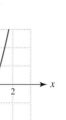
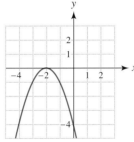

19. No real solutions

20. $-3, 0$

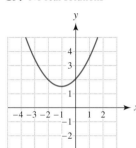
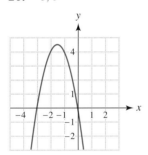

Exercises 21–24: A table of $y = ax^2 + bx + c$ is given. Use this table to solve $ax^2 + bx + c = 0$.

21. $-2, 3$

X	Y1
-3	6
-2	0
-1	-4
0	-6
1	-6
2	-4
3	0

Y1◼X^2−X−6

22. $-6, 4$

X	Y1
-6	0
-4	-16
-2	-24
0	-24
2	-16
4	0
6	24

Y1◼X^2+2X−24

23. -0.5

X	Y1
-2	9
-1.5	4
-1	1
-.5	0
.5	1
1	4
	9

Y1◼4X^2+4X+1

24. $-3, 1$

X	Y1
-4	-2.5
-3	0
-2	1.5
-1	2
0	1.5
1	0
2	-2.5

Y1◼−X^2/2−X+3/2

Exercises 25–32: Solve the quadratic equation. Support your results numerically and graphically.

25. $x^2 - 4x - 5 = 0$ $-1, 5$ **26.** $x^2 - x - 6 = 0$ $-2, 3$

27. $x^2 + 2x = 3$ $-3, 1$ **28.** $x^2 + 4x = 5$ $-5, 1$

29. $x^2 = 9$ $-3, 3$ **30.** $x^2 = 4$ $-2, 2$

31. $4x^2 - 4x - 3 = 0$ $-\frac{1}{2}, \frac{3}{2}$ **32.** $2x^2 + x = 1$ $-1, \frac{1}{2}$

Exercises 33–40: Solve by factoring.

33. $x^2 + 2x - 35 = 0$ $-7, 5$ **34.** $2x^2 - 7x + 3 = 0$ $\frac{1}{2}, 3$

35. $6x^2 - x - 1 = 0$ **36.** $x^2 + 4x + 6 = -3x$ $-6, -1$

37. $2x^2 + x + 3 = 6x$ **38.** $6x^2 - x = 15$ $-\frac{3}{2}, \frac{5}{3}$

39. $2(5x^2 + 9) = 27x$ **40.** $15(3x^2 + x) = 10$ $-\frac{2}{3}, \frac{1}{3}$
$\frac{6}{5}, \frac{3}{2}$

35. $-\frac{1}{3}, \frac{1}{2}$ 37. $1, \frac{3}{2}$

Exercises 41–50: Use the square root property to solve the equation.

41. $x^2 = 144$ ± 12 **42.** $4x^2 - 5 = 0$ $\pm \frac{\sqrt{5}}{2}$

43. $5x^2 - 64 = 0$ $\pm \frac{8}{\sqrt{5}}$ **44.** $3x^2 = 7$ $\pm \sqrt{\frac{7}{3}}$

45. $(x + 1)^2 = 25$ $-6, 4$ **46.** $(x + 4)^2 = 9$ $-7, -1$

47. $(x - 1)^2 = 64$ $-7, 9$ **48.** $(x - 3)^2 = 0$ 3

49. $(2x - 1)^2 = 5$ **50.** $(5x + 3)^2 = 7$
$\frac{1 \pm \sqrt{5}}{2}$ $\frac{-3 \pm \sqrt{7}}{5}$

COMPLETING THE SQUARE

Exercises 51–54: To solve the equation by completing the square, what value should you add to each side of the equation?

51. $x^2 + 4x = -3$ 4 **52.** $x^2 - 6x = 4$ 9

53. $x^2 - 5x = 4$ $\frac{25}{4}$ **54.** $x^2 + 3x = 1$ $\frac{9}{4}$

Exercises 55–58: (Refer to Example 4.) Find the term that should be added to the expression to form a perfect square trinomial. Write the resulting perfect square trinomial in factored form.

55. $x^2 - 8x$ $16; (x - 4)^2$ **56.** $x^2 - 5x$ $\frac{25}{4}; \left(x - \frac{5}{2}\right)^2$

57. $x^2 + 9x$ $\frac{81}{4}; \left(x + \frac{9}{2}\right)^2$ **58.** $x^2 + x$ $\frac{1}{4}; \left(x + \frac{1}{2}\right)^2$

Exercises 59–74: Solve the equation by completing the square.

59. $x^2 - 2x = 24$
-4, 6

60. $x^2 - 2x + \frac{1}{2} = 0$ $1 \pm \frac{1}{\sqrt{2}}$

61. $x^2 + 6x - 2 = 0$
$-3 \pm \sqrt{11}$

62. $x^2 - 16x = 5$ $8 \pm \sqrt{69}$

63. $x^2 - 3x = 5$ $\frac{3 \pm \sqrt{29}}{2}$

64. $x^2 + 5x = 2$ $\frac{-5 \pm \sqrt{33}}{2}$

65. $x^2 - 5x + 1 = 0$ $\frac{5 \pm \sqrt{21}}{2}$

66. $x^2 - 9x + 7 = 0$ $\frac{9 \pm \sqrt{53}}{2}$

67. $x^2 - 4 = 2x$ $1 \pm \sqrt{5}$

68. $x^2 + 1 = 7x$ $\frac{7 \pm 3\sqrt{5}}{2}$

69. $2x^2 - 3x = 4$ $\frac{3 \pm \sqrt{41}}{4}$

70. $3x^2 + 6x - 5 = 0$ $\frac{-3 \pm 2\sqrt{6}}{3}$

71. $4x^2 - 8x - 7 = 0$

72. $25x^2 - 20x - 1 = 0$ $\frac{2 \pm \sqrt{5}}{5}$

73. $36x^2 + 18x + 1 = 0$ $\frac{-3 \pm \sqrt{5}}{12}$ 71. $\frac{2 \pm \sqrt{11}}{2}$

74. $12x^2 + 8x - 2 = 0$ $\frac{-2 \pm \sqrt{10}}{6}$

Solving Equations by More Than One Method

Exercises 75–80: Solve the quadratic equation
    (a) *symbolically,*
    (b) *graphically, and*
    (c) *numerically.*

75. $x^2 - 3x - 18 = 0$
-3, 6

76. $\frac{1}{2}x^2 + 2x - 6 = 0$ -6, 2

77. $x^2 - 8x + 15 = 0$
3, 5

78. $2x^2 + 3 = 7x$ $\frac{1}{2}, 3$

79. $4(x^2 + 35) = 48x$
5, 7

80. $4x(2 - x) = -5$ $-\frac{1}{2}, \frac{5}{2}$

Solving an Equation for a Variable

Exercises 81–88: Solve the equation for the specified variable.

81. $x = y^2 - 1$ for y $y = \pm\sqrt{x + 1}$

82. $x = 9y^2$ for y $y = \pm\frac{\sqrt{x}}{3}$

83. $K = \frac{1}{2}mv^2$ for v $v = \pm\sqrt{\frac{2K}{m}}$

84. $c^2 = a^2 + b^2$ for b $b = \pm\sqrt{c^2 - a^2}$

85. $E = \frac{k}{r^2}$ for r $r = \pm\sqrt{\frac{k}{E}}$

86. $W = I^2 R$ for I $I = \pm\sqrt{\frac{W}{R}}$

87. $LC = \frac{1}{(2\pi f)^2}$ for f $f = \pm\frac{1}{2\pi\sqrt{LC}}$

88. $F = \frac{KmM}{r^2}$ for r $r = \pm\sqrt{\frac{KmM}{F}}$

Applications

89. *Safe Curve Speed* (Refer to Example 8.) Find a safe speed limit x for an airport taxiway curve with the given radius R.
    (a) $R = 450$ feet 30 mph **(b)** $R = 800$ feet 40 mph

90. *Braking Distance* The braking distance y in feet that it takes for a car to stop on wet, level pavement can be estimated by $y = \frac{1}{9}x^2$, where x is the speed of the car in miles per hour. Find the speed associated

with each braking distance. (*Source:* L. Haefner, *Introduction to Transportation Systems.*)
    (a) 25 feet **(b)** 361 feet **(c)** 784 feet
        15 mph   57 mph   84 mph

91. *Falling Object* If a toy to hit the ground if it is dropped out of a window 60 feet above the ground? Does it take twice as long as it takes to fall from a window 30 feet above the ground? About 1.9 sec; no

92. *Falling Object* If a metal ball is thrown *downward* with an initial velocity of 22 feet per second (15 mph) from a 100-foot water tower, its height h in feet above the ground after t seconds is modeled by

$$h(t) = -16t^2 - 22t + 100.$$

    (a) Determine symbolically when the height of the ball is 62 feet. 1 sec after being thrown
    (b) Support your result either graphically or numerically.
    (c) If the ball is thrown *upward* at 22 feet per second, then its height is given by

$$h(t) = -16t^2 + 22t + 100.$$

    Determine when the height of the ball is 80 feet.

2 sec after being thrown

93. *Distance* Two athletes start jogging at the same time. One jogs north at 6 miles per hour while the second jogs east at 8 miles per hour. After how long are the two athletes 20 miles apart? 2 hr

94. *Geometry* A triangle has an area of 35 square inches, and its base is 3 inches more than its height. Find the base and height of the triangle.
Base: 10 in.; height: 7 in.

95. *Construction* A rectangular plot of land has an area of 520 square feet and is 6 feet longer than it is wide.
    (a) Write a quadratic equation in the form $ax^2 + bx + c = 0$, whose solution gives the width of the plot of land. $x^2 + 6x - 520 = 0$
    (b) Solve the equation. $x = -26, 20$; 20 ft

96. *Modeling Motion* The height h of a tennis ball above the ground after t seconds is shown in the graph. Estimate when the ball was 25 feet above the ground.   0.5 and 2.5 sec

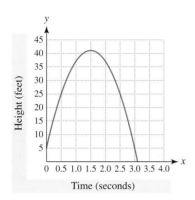

Time (seconds)

97. *Seedling Growth* (Refer to Exercise 75, Section 8.1.) The heights of melon seedlings grown at different temperatures are shown in the following graph. At what temperatures were the heights of the seedlings about 22 centimeters? (***Source:*** R. Pearl, "The growth of *Cucumis melo* seedlings at different temperatures.")
About 23°C and 34°C

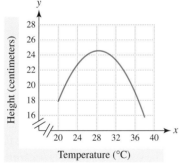

Temperature (°C)

98. *Modeling Internet Users* (Refer to Example 9.) Estimate either graphically or numerically when the number of Internet users in Western Europe is expected to reach 150 million.   2005

99. *U.S. Population* The table shows the population of the United States in millions from 1800 through 2000 at 20-year intervals.

Year	1800	1820	1840	1860
Population	5	10	17	31

Year	1880	1900	1920	1940
Population	50	76	106	132

Year	1960	1980	2000
Population	179	226	269

Source: Bureau of the Census.

The rate of increase for each 20-year period is not constant.

(a) Without plotting the data, how do you know that the data are nonlinear?

(b) These data are modeled by

$$f(x) = 0.0066(x - 1800)^2 + 5.$$

Find the vertex of the graph of f and interpret the result.   (1800, 5); in 1800 the population was 5 million.

(c) Estimate when the U.S. population reached 85 million.   1910

100. *Trade Deficit* The U.S. trade deficit in billions of dollars for the years 1997, 1998, and 1999 can be computed by   1998

$$f(x) = 16x^2 - 63,861x + 63,722,378,$$

where x is the year. In which year was the trade deficit \$164 billion? (***Source:*** Department of Commerce.)

WRITING ABOUT MATHEMATICS

101. Suppose that you are asked to solve

$$ax^2 + bx + c = 0.$$

Explain how the graph of $y = ax^2 + bx + c$ can be used to find any solutions to the equation.

102. Explain why a quadratic equation could not have more than two solutions. (*Hint:* Consider the graph of $y = ax^2 + bx + c$.)

Group Activity: Working with Real Data

Directions: Form a group of 2 to 4 people. Select someone to record the group's responses for this activity. All members of the group should work cooperatively to answer the questions. If your instructor asks for the results, each member of the group should be prepared to respond.

Minimum Wage   The table shows the minimum wage for three different years.

Year	1940	1968	1997
Wage	$0.25	$1.60	$5.45

Source: Bureau of Labor Statistics.

   (a) Make a scatterplot of the data in the viewing rectangle [1930, 2010, 10] by [0, 6, 1]. *

(b) $f(x) = 0.0016(x - 1940)^2 + 0.25$;   answers may vary
(b) Find a quadratic function given by
$$f(x) = a(x - h)^2 + k$$
that models the data.

(c) Estimate the minimum wage in 1976 and compare it to the actual value of $2.30. $2.32; it is very close.

(d) Estimate the year when the minimum wage was $1.00.   1961

(e) If current trends continue, predict the minimum wage in 2005.   About $7

*Answer on page IA-27

8.4   THE QUADRATIC FORMULA

**Solving Quadratic Equations · The Discriminant ·
Quadratic Equations Having Complex Solutions**

INTRODUCTION

To model the stopping distance of a car, highway engineers compute two quantities. The first quantity is the *reaction distance*, which is the distance a car travels from the time a driver first recognizes a hazard until the brakes are applied. The second quantity is *braking distance*, which is the distance a car travels after a driver applies the brakes. *Stopping distance* equals the sum of the reaction distance and the braking distance. If a car is traveling x miles per hour, highway engineers estimate the reaction distance in feet as $\frac{11}{3}x$ and the braking distance in feet as $\frac{1}{9}x^2$. To estimate the total stopping distance d in feet, they add the two expressions to obtain

$$d(x) = \frac{1}{9}x^2 + \frac{11}{3}x.$$

If a car's headlights don't illuminate the road beyond **500** feet, a safe nighttime speed limit x for the car can be determined by solving the quadratic equation

$$\frac{1}{9}x^2 + \frac{11}{3}x = 500.$$

(*Source:* L. Haefner, *Introduction to Transportation Systems*.)
    In this section we learn how to solve this equation with the quadratic formula.

SOLVING QUADRATIC EQUATIONS

Recall that any quadratic equation can be written in the form

$$ax^2 + bx + c = 0.$$

If we solve this equation for x in terms of a, b, and c by completing the square, we obtain the **quadratic formula**. We assume that $a > 0$ and derive it as follows.

$ax^2 + bx + c = 0$	Quadratic equation
$ax^2 + bx = -c$	Subtract c.
$x^2 + \dfrac{b}{a}x = -\dfrac{c}{a}$	Divide by a.
$x^2 + \dfrac{b}{a}x + \dfrac{b^2}{4a^2} = -\dfrac{c}{a} + \dfrac{b^2}{4a^2}$	Add $\left(\dfrac{b/a}{2}\right)^2 = \dfrac{b^2}{4a^2}$.
$\left(x + \dfrac{b}{2a}\right)^2 = -\dfrac{c}{a} + \dfrac{b^2}{4a^2}$	Perfect square trinomial
$\left(x + \dfrac{b}{2a}\right)^2 = -\dfrac{c \cdot 4a}{a \cdot 4a} + \dfrac{b^2}{4a^2}$	Multiply $-\dfrac{c}{a}$ by $\dfrac{4a}{4a}$.
$\left(x + \dfrac{b}{2a}\right)^2 = -\dfrac{4ac}{4a^2} + \dfrac{b^2}{4a^2}$	Simplify.
$\left(x + \dfrac{b}{2a}\right)^2 = \dfrac{-4ac + b^2}{4a^2}$	Add fractions.
$\left(x + \dfrac{b}{2a}\right)^2 = \dfrac{b^2 - 4ac}{4a^2}$	Rewrite.
$x + \dfrac{b}{2a} = \pm\sqrt{\dfrac{b^2 - 4ac}{4a^2}}$	Square root property
$x = -\dfrac{b}{2a} \pm \sqrt{\dfrac{b^2 - 4ac}{4a^2}}$	Add $-\dfrac{b}{2a}$.
$x = -\dfrac{b}{2a} \pm \dfrac{\sqrt{b^2 - 4ac}}{2a}$	Property of square roots
$x = \dfrac{-b \pm \sqrt{b^2 - 4ac}}{2a}$	Combine fractions.

QUADRATIC FORMULA

The solutions to $ax^2 + bx + c = 0$ with $a \neq 0$ are given by

$$x = \frac{-b \pm \sqrt{b^2 - 4ac}}{2a}.$$

Note: The quadratic formula provides the solutions to *any* quadratic equation. It always "works."

═══════════════ MAKING CONNECTIONS ═══════════════

Completing the Square and the Quadratic Formula

The quadratic formula results from completing the square for the equation $ax^2 + bx + c = 0$. When you use the quadratic formula, the work of completing the square has already been done for you.

The next three examples illustrate how to solve quadratic equations symbolically and graphically.

EXAMPLE 1   Solving a quadratic equation having two solutions

Solve the equation $2x^2 - 3x - 1 = 0$. Support your results graphically.

Solution   **Symbolic Solution**   Let $a = 2$, $b = -3$, and $c = -1$.

$$x = \frac{-b \pm \sqrt{b^2 - 4ac}}{2a} \qquad \text{Quadratic formula}$$

$$x = \frac{-(-3) \pm \sqrt{(-3)^2 - 4(2)(-1)}}{2(2)} \qquad \text{Substitute for } a, b, \text{ and } c.$$

$$x = \frac{3 \pm \sqrt{17}}{4} \qquad \text{Simplify.}$$

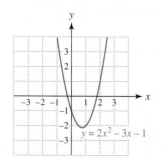

Figure 8.34   Two x-intercepts

The solutions are $\frac{3 + \sqrt{17}}{4} \approx 1.78$ and $\frac{3 - \sqrt{17}}{4} \approx -0.28$.

Graphical Solution   The graph of $y = 2x^2 - 3x - 1$ is shown in Figure 8.34. Note that the two x-intercepts correspond to the two solutions to $2x^2 - 3x - 1 = 0$. Estimating from this graph, we see that the solutions are approximately -0.25 and 1.75, which supports our symbolic solution.

Critical Thinking

Use the results of Example 1 to evaluate each expression mentally.

$$2\left(\frac{3 + \sqrt{17}}{4}\right)^2 - 3\left(\frac{3 + \sqrt{17}}{4}\right) - 1$$

$$2\left(\frac{3 - \sqrt{17}}{4}\right)^2 - 3\left(\frac{3 - \sqrt{17}}{4}\right) - 1$$

Both equal 0

EXAMPLE 2   Solving a quadratic equation having one solution

Solve the equation $25x^2 + 20x + 4 = 0$. Support your result graphically.

Solution **Symbolic Solution** Let $a = 25$, $b = 20$, and $c = 4$.

$$x = \frac{-b \pm \sqrt{b^2 - 4ac}}{2a} \qquad \text{Quadratic formula}$$

$$= \frac{-20 \pm \sqrt{20^2 - 4(25)(4)}}{2(25)} \qquad \text{Substitute for } a, b, \text{ and } c.$$

$$= \frac{-20 \pm \sqrt{0}}{50} \qquad \text{Simplify.}$$

$$= \frac{-20}{50} = -0.4 \qquad \sqrt{0} = 0$$

There is one solution, -0.4.

Graphical Solution The graph of $y = 25x^2 + 20x + 4$ is shown in Figure 8.35. Note that the one x-intercept, -0.4, corresponds to the solution to $25x^2 + 20x + 4 = 0$.

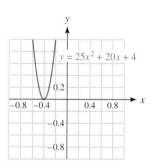

Figure 8.35 One x-intercept

EXAMPLE 3 **Recognizing a quadratic equation having no real solutions**

Solve the equation $5x^2 - x + 3 = 0$. Support your result graphically.

Solution **Symbolic Solution** Let $a = 5$, $b = -1$, and $c = 3$.

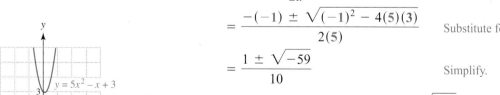

Figure 8.36 No x-intercepts

$$x = \frac{-b \pm \sqrt{b^2 - 4ac}}{2a} \qquad \text{Quadratic formula}$$

$$= \frac{-(-1) \pm \sqrt{(-1)^2 - 4(5)(3)}}{2(5)} \qquad \text{Substitute for } a, b, \text{ and } c.$$

$$= \frac{1 \pm \sqrt{-59}}{10} \qquad \text{Simplify.}$$

There are no real solutions to this equation because $\sqrt{-59}$ is not a real number. (Later in this section we discuss how to find complex solutions to quadratic equations such as this one.)

Graphical Solution The graph of $y = 5x^2 - x + 3$ is shown in Figure 8.36. Note that there are no x-intercepts, indicating that the equation $5x^2 - x + 3 = 0$ has no real solutions.

Earlier in this section we discussed how engineers estimate safe stopping distances for automobiles. In the next example we solve the equation presented in the introduction.

EXAMPLE 4 **Modeling stopping distance**

If a car's headlights do not illuminate the road beyond 500 feet, estimate a safe nighttime speed limit x for the car by solving $\frac{1}{9}x^2 + \frac{11}{3}x = 500$.

Solution Begin by subtracting 500 from each side of the equation.

$$\frac{1}{9}x^2 + \frac{11}{3}x - 500 = 0.$$

To eliminate fractions multiply each side by the LCD, which is 9. (This step is not necessary, but it makes the problem easier to work.)

$$x^2 + 33x - 4500 = 0.$$

Now let $a = 1$, $b = 33$, and $c = -4500$ in the quadratic formula.

$$x = \frac{-b \pm \sqrt{b^2 - 4ac}}{2a} \qquad \text{Quadratic formula}$$

$$= \frac{-33 \pm \sqrt{(33)^2 - 4(1)(-4500)}}{2(1)} \qquad \text{Substitute for } a, b, \text{ and } c.$$

$$= \frac{-33 \pm \sqrt{19{,}089}}{2} \qquad \text{Simplify.}$$

The solutions are

$$\frac{-33 + \sqrt{19{,}089}}{2} \approx 52.6 \quad \text{and} \quad \frac{-33 - \sqrt{19{,}089}}{2} \approx -85.6.$$

The negative solution has no physical meaning because negative speeds are not possible. The other solution is 52.6, so an appropriate speed limit might be 50 miles per hour. ____

THE DISCRIMINANT

The expression $b^2 - 4ac$ in the quadratic formula is called the **discriminant**. It provides information about the number of solutions to a quadratic equation.

THE DISCRIMINANT AND QUADRATIC EQUATIONS

To determine the number of solutions to the quadratic equation $ax^2 + bx + c = 0$, evaluate the discriminant $b^2 - 4ac$.

1. If $b^2 - 4ac > 0$, there are two real solutions.
2. If $b^2 - 4ac = 0$, there is one real solution.
3. If $b^2 - 4ac < 0$, there are no real solutions; there are two complex solutions.

EXAMPLE 5   Using the discriminant

Use the discriminant to determine the number of solutions to $4x^2 + 25 = 20x$. Then solve the equation, using the quadratic formula.

Solution   Write the equation as $4x^2 - 20x + 25 = 0$ so that $a = 4$, $b = -20$, and $c = 25$. The discriminant evaluates to

$$b^2 - 4ac = (-20)^2 - 4(4)(25) = 0.$$

Thus there is one real solution.

$$x = \frac{-b \pm \sqrt{b^2 - 4ac}}{2a} \qquad \text{Quadratic formula}$$

$$= \frac{-(-20) \pm \sqrt{0}}{2(4)} \qquad \text{Substitute.}$$

$$= \frac{20}{8} = 2.5 \qquad \text{Simplify.}$$

The only solution is 2.5.

We also need to be able to analyze graphs of quadratic functions, which we demonstrate in the next example.

EXAMPLE 6   Analyzing graphs of quadratic functions

TEACHING TIP

Emphasize that to find the *x*-intercepts on the graph of a parabola, we can solve the quadratic equation $ax^2 + bx + c = 0$ using any of the techniques learned so far.

A graph of $f(x) = ax^2 + bx + c$ is shown in Figure 8.37.
(a) State whether $a > 0$ or $a < 0$.
(b) Solve the equation $ax^2 + bx + c = 0$.
(c) Determine whether the discriminant is positive, negative, or zero.

Solution   **(a)** The parabola opens downward, so $a < 0$.
(b) The solutions correspond to the x-intercepts, -3 and 2.
(c) There are two solutions, so the discriminant is positive.

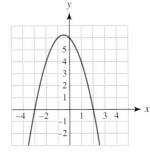

Figure 8.37

TEACHING TIP

If you teach Chapter 8 before Chapter 7, delay this subsection until you have covered Section 7.6.

QUADRATIC EQUATIONS HAVING COMPLEX SOLUTIONS

The quadratic equation $ax^2 + bx + c = 0$ has no real solutions if the discriminant, $b^2 - 4ac$, is negative. For example, the quadratic equation $x^2 + 4 = 0$ has $a = 1$, $b = 0$, and $c = 1$. Its discriminant is

$$b^2 - 4ac = 0^2 - 4(1)(4) = -16 < 0,$$

so this equation has no real solutions. However, if we use complex numbers, we can solve this equation as follows.

$$x^2 + 4 = 0 \qquad \text{Given equation}$$
$$x^2 = -4 \qquad \text{Subtract 4.}$$
$$x = \pm\sqrt{-4} \qquad \text{Square root property}$$
$$x = \sqrt{-4} \quad \text{or} \quad x = -\sqrt{-4} \qquad \text{Meaning of } \pm$$
$$x = 2i \quad \text{or} \quad x = -2i \qquad \text{The expression } \sqrt{-a}$$

The solutions are $\pm 2i$. We check each solution to $x^2 + 4 = 0$ as follows.

$$(2i)^2 + 4 = (2)^2 i^2 + 4 = 4(-1) + 4 = 0 \qquad \text{It checks.}$$
$$(-2i)^2 + 4 = (-2)^2 i^2 + 4 = 4(-1) + 4 = 0 \qquad \text{It checks.}$$

This result can be generalized as follows.

TEACHING TIP

When a quadratic equation has no x-term, have students use the square root property rather than the quadratic formula.

THE EQUATION $x^2 + k = 0$

If $k > 0$, the solutions to $x^2 + k = 0$ are given by $x = \pm i \sqrt{k}$.

EXAMPLE 7 Solving a quadratic equation having complex solutions

Solve $x^2 + 5 = 0$.

Solution The solutions are $\pm i \sqrt{5}$. That is, $x = i \sqrt{5}$ or $x = -i \sqrt{5}$.

When $b \neq 0$, the preceding method cannot be used. Consider the quadratic equation $2x^2 + x + 3 = 0$, which has $a = 2$, $b = 1$, and $c = 3$. Its discriminant is

$$b^2 - 4ac = 1^2 - 4(2)(3) = -23 < 0.$$

This equation has two complex solutions as demonstrated in the next example.

EXAMPLE 8 Solving a quadratic equation having complex solutions

Solve $2x^2 + x + 3 = 0$. Write your answer in standard form: $a + bi$.

Solution Let $a = 2$, $b = 1$, and $c = 3$.

Calculator Help
To set your calculator in $a + bi$ mode or to access the imaginary unit i, see the Appendix (page AP-11).

$$x = \frac{-b \pm \sqrt{b^2 - 4ac}}{2a} \qquad \text{Quadratic formula}$$

$$= \frac{-1 \pm \sqrt{1^2 - 4(2)(3)}}{2(2)} \qquad \text{Substitute for } a, b, \text{ and } c.$$

$$= \frac{-1 \pm \sqrt{-23}}{4} \qquad \text{Simplify.}$$

$$= \frac{-1 \pm i \sqrt{23}}{4} \qquad \sqrt{-23} = i \sqrt{23}$$

$$= -\frac{1}{4} \pm i \frac{\sqrt{23}}{4} \qquad \text{Divide each term by 4.}$$

The solutions are $-\frac{1}{4} + i \frac{\sqrt{23}}{4}$ and $-\frac{1}{4} - i \frac{\sqrt{23}}{4}$.

Critical Thinking

Use the results of Example 8 to evaluate each expression mentally.

$$2\left(-\frac{1}{4} + i\frac{\sqrt{23}}{4}\right)^2 + \left(-\frac{1}{4} + i\frac{\sqrt{23}}{4}\right) + 3 \quad \text{and} \quad 2\left(-\frac{1}{4} - i\frac{\sqrt{23}}{4}\right)^2 + \left(-\frac{1}{4} - i\frac{\sqrt{23}}{4}\right) + 3$$

Both expressions equal 0.

Sometimes we can use properties of radicals to simplify a solution to a quadratic equation, as demonstrated in the next example.

EXAMPLE 9   Solving a quadratic equation having complex solutions

Solve $\frac{3}{4}x^2 + 1 = x$. Write your answer in standard form: $a + bi$.

Solution   Begin by subtracting x from each side of the equation and then multiply by 4 to clear fractions. The resulting equation is $3x^2 - 4x + 4 = 0$. Substitute $a = 3$, $b = -4$, and $c = 4$ in the quadratic formula.

$$x = \frac{-b \pm \sqrt{b^2 - 4ac}}{2a} \qquad \text{Quadratic formula}$$

$$= \frac{-(-4) \pm \sqrt{(-4)^2 - 4(3)(4)}}{2(3)} \qquad \text{Substitute.}$$

$$= \frac{4 \pm \sqrt{-32}}{6} \qquad \text{Simplify.}$$

$$= \frac{4 \pm 4i\sqrt{2}}{6} \qquad \sqrt{-32} = i\sqrt{32} = i\sqrt{16}\sqrt{2} = 4i\sqrt{2}$$

$$= \frac{2}{3} \pm \frac{2}{3}i\sqrt{2} \qquad \text{Divide 6 into each term and reduce.}$$

PUTTING IT ALL TOGETHER

Quadratic equations can be solved symbolically by using factoring, the square root property, completing the square, and the quadratic formula. Graphical and numerical methods can also be used to solve quadratic equations. In this section we discussed the quadratic formula and its discriminant, which we summarize in the following table.

Concept	Explanation	Examples
Quadratic Formula	The quadratic formula can be used to solve *any* quadratic equation written as $ax^2 + bx + c = 0$. The solutions are given by $$x = \frac{-b \pm \sqrt{b^2 - 4ac}}{2a}.$$	For the equation $$2x^2 - 3x + 1 = 0$$ with $a = 2$, $b = -3$, and $c = 1$, the solutions are $$\frac{-(-3) \pm \sqrt{(-3)^2 - 4(2)(1)}}{2(2)} = \frac{3 \pm \sqrt{1}}{4} = 1, \frac{1}{2}.$$

continued on next page

continued from previous page

Concept	Explanation	Examples
The Discriminant	The expression $b^2 - 4ac$ is called the discriminant. The discriminant may be used to determine the number of solutions to $ax^2 + bx + c = 0$. 1. $b^2 - 4ac > 0$ indicates two real solutions. 2. $b^2 - 4ac = 0$ indicates one real solution. 3. $b^2 - 4ac < 0$ indicates no real solutions; rather, there are two complex solutions.	For the equation $$x^2 + 4x - 1 = 0$$ with $a = 1$, $b = 4$, and $c = -1$, the discriminant is $$b^2 - 4ac = 4^2 - 4(1)(-1) = 20 > 0,$$ indicating two real solutions.
Quadratic Formula and Complex Solutions	If the discriminant is negative $(b^2 - 4ac < 0)$, the solutions to a quadratic equation are complex numbers. If $k > 0$, the solutions to $x^2 + k = 0$ are given by $x = \pm i \sqrt{k}$.	$$2x^2 - x + 3 = 0$$ $$x = \frac{1 \pm \sqrt{(-1)^2 - 4(2)(3)}}{2(2)}$$ $$= \frac{1 \pm \sqrt{-23}}{4} = \frac{1}{4} \pm i \frac{\sqrt{23}}{4}$$ $x^2 + 9 = 0$ is equivalent to $x = \pm 3i$ and $x^2 + 7 = 0$ is equivalent to $x = \pm i \sqrt{7}$.

8.4 EXERCISES

FOR EXTRA HELP

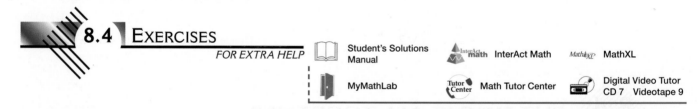

Student's Solutions Manual   InterAct Math   MathXL
MyMathLab   Math Tutor Center   Digital Video Tutor CD 7   Videotape 9

CONCEPTS

1. What is the quadratic formula used for?
   To solve quadratic equations of the form $ax^2 + bx + c = 0$

2. What basic algebraic technique is used to derive the quadratic formula?   Completing the square

3. What is the discriminant? $b^2 - 4ac$

4. If the discriminant evaluates to 0, what does that indicate about the quadratic equation?   One solution

5. Name four symbolic techniques for solving a quadratic equation.   Factoring, square root property, completing the square, and the quadratic formula

6. Does every quadratic equation have at least one real solution? Explain.   No; not when $b^2 - 4ac < 0$

THE QUADRATIC FORMULA

Exercises 7–10: Use the quadratic formula to solve the equation. Support your result graphically and numerically. If there are no real solutions, say so.

7. $2x^2 + 11x - 6 = 0$ $-6, \frac{1}{2}$
8. $x^2 + 2x - 24 = 0$ $-6, 4$
9. $-x^2 + 2x - 1 = 0$ 1
10. $3x^2 - x + 1 = 0$ No real solutions

Exercises 11–28: Solve by using the quadratic formula. If there are no real solutions, say so.

11. $x^2 - 6x - 16 = 0$ $-2, 8$
12. $2x^2 - 9x + 7 = 0$ $1, \frac{7}{2}$
13. $4x^2 - x - 1 = 0$ $\frac{1 \pm \sqrt{17}}{8}$
14. $-x^2 + 2x + 1 = 0$ $1 \pm \sqrt{2}$
15. $-3x^2 + 2x - 1 = 0$ No real solutions
16. $x^2 + x + 3 = 0$ No real solutions

67. $\frac{1}{2} \pm i \frac{\sqrt{7}}{2}$ 69. $-\frac{3}{4} \pm i \frac{\sqrt{23}}{4}$ 73. $-\frac{1}{2} \pm i \frac{\sqrt{7}}{2}$ 75. $-\frac{1}{5} \pm i \frac{\sqrt{19}}{5}$ 76. $\frac{1}{7} \pm \frac{3}{7} i \sqrt{3}$ 77. $-\frac{3}{4} \pm i \frac{\sqrt{23}}{4}$ 78. $\frac{3}{2} \pm i \frac{\sqrt{15}}{2}$

17. $36x^2 - 36x + 9 = 0$ $\frac{1}{2}$

18. $4x^2 - 5.6x + 1.96 = 0$ 0.7

19. $2x(x - 3) = 2$ $\frac{3 \pm \sqrt{13}}{2}$ **20.** $x(x + 1) + x = 5$ $-1 \pm \sqrt{6}$

21. $(x - 1)(x + 1) + 2 = 4x$ $2 \pm \sqrt{3}$

22. $\frac{1}{2}(x - 6) = x^2 + 1$ **23.** $\frac{1}{2}x(x + 1) = 2x^2 - \frac{3}{2}$

24. $\frac{1}{2}x^2 - \frac{1}{4}x + \frac{1}{2} = x$ $\frac{1}{2}, 2$ **25.** $2x(x - 1) = 7$ $\frac{1 \pm \sqrt{15}}{2}$

26. $3x(x - 4) = 4$ $\frac{6 \pm 4\sqrt{3}}{3}$ **27.** $-3x^2 + 10x - 5 = 0$ $\frac{5 \pm \sqrt{10}}{3}$

28. $-2x^2 + 4x - 1 = 0$ $\frac{2 \pm \sqrt{2}}{2}$

22. No real solutions

THE DISCRIMINANT

Exercises 29–34: A graph of $y = ax^2 + bx + c$ is shown.
   (a) *State whether $a > 0$ or $a < 0$.*
   (b) *Solve $ax^2 + bx + c = 0$, if possible.*
   (c) *Determine whether the discriminant is positive, negative, or zero.*

29.   (a) $a > 0$ (b) $-1, 2$
   (c) Positive

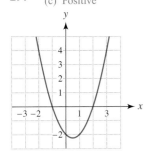

30.   (a) $a > 0$ (b) -1
   (c) Zero

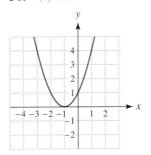

31.   (a) $a > 0$ (b) No real solutions
   (c) Negative

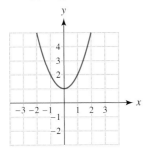

32.   (a) $a < 0$ (b) No real solutions
   (c) Negative

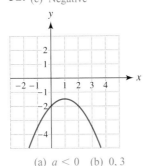

33.   (a) $a < 0$ (b) 2
   (c) Zero

34.   (a) $a < 0$ (b) 0, 3
   (c) Positive

Exercises 35–42: Do the following for the given equation.
   (a) *Evaluate the discriminant.*
   (b) *How many real solutions are there?*
   (c) *Support your answer for part (b) by using graphing.*

35. $3x^2 + x - 2 = 0$ **36.** $5x^2 - 13x + 6 = 0$
   (a) 25   (b) 2   (a) 49   (b) 2

37. $x^2 - 4x + 4 = 0$ **38.** $\frac{1}{4}x^2 + 4 = 2x$ (a) 0   (b) 1
   (a) 0   (b) 1

39. $\frac{1}{2}x^2 + \frac{3}{2}x + 2 = 0$ **40.** $x - 3 = 2x^2$ (a) -23 (b) 0
   (a) $-\frac{7}{4}$ (b) 0

41. $x(x + 3) = 3$ **42.** $(4x - 1)(x - 3) = -25$
   (a) 21   (b) 2   (a) -279 (b) 0

Exercises 43–52: Use the quadratic formula to find any x-intercepts on the graph of the equation.

43. $y = x^2 - 2x - 1$ **44.** $y = x^2 + 3x + 1$ $\frac{-3 \pm \sqrt{5}}{2}$
   $1 \pm \sqrt{2}$

45. $y = -2x^2 - x + 3$ **46.** $y = -3x^2 - x + 4$ $-\frac{4}{3}, 1$
   $-\frac{3}{2}, 1$

47. $y = x^2 + x + 5$ **48.** $y = 3x^2 - 2x + 5$ None
   None

49. $y = x^2 + 9$ None   **50.** $y = x^2 + 11$ None

51. $y = 3x^2 + 4x - 2$ **52.** $y = 4x^2 - 2x - 3$
   $\frac{-2 \pm \sqrt{10}}{3}$ $\frac{1 \pm \sqrt{13}}{4}$

COMPLEX SOLUTIONS

Exercises 53–84: Solve the equation. Write complex solutions in standard form.

53. $x^2 + 9 = 0$ $\pm 3i$ **54.** $x^2 + 16 = 0$ $\pm 4i$

55. $x^2 + 80 = 0$ $\pm 4i\sqrt{5}$ **56.** $x^2 + 20 = 0$ $\pm 2i\sqrt{5}$

57. $x^2 + \frac{1}{4} = 0$ $\pm \frac{1}{2}i$ **58.** $x^2 + \frac{9}{4} = 0$ $\pm \frac{3}{2}i$

59. $16x^2 + 9 = 0$ $\pm \frac{3}{4}i$ **60.** $25x^2 + 36 = 0$ $\pm \frac{6}{5}i$

61. $x^2 = -6$ $\pm i\sqrt{6}$ **62.** $x^2 = -75$ $\pm 5i\sqrt{3}$

63. $x^2 - 3 = 0$ $\pm \sqrt{3}$ **64.** $x^2 - 8 = 0$ $\pm 2\sqrt{2}$

65. $x^2 + 2 = 0$ $\pm i\sqrt{2}$ **66.** $x^2 + 4 = 0$ $\pm 2i$

67. $x^2 - x + 2 = 0$ **68.** $x^2 + 2x + 3 = 0$ $-1 \pm i\sqrt{2}$

69. $2x^2 + 3x + 4 = 0$ **70.** $3x^2 - x = 1$ $\frac{1 \pm \sqrt{13}}{6}$

71. $x^2 + 1 = 4x$ $2 \pm \sqrt{3}$ **72.** $3x^2 + 2 = x$ $\frac{1}{6} \pm i\frac{\sqrt{23}}{6}$

73. $x^2 + x = -2$ **74.** $x(x - 4) = -8$ $2 \pm 2i$

75. $5x^2 + 2x + 4 = 0$ **76.** $7x^2 - 2x + 4 = 0$

77. $\frac{1}{2}x^2 + \frac{3}{4}x + 1 = 0$ **78.** $-\frac{1}{3}x^2 + x - 2 = 0$

79. $x(x + 2) = x - 4$ **80.** $x - 5 = 2x(2x + 1)$
   $-\frac{1}{2} \pm i\frac{\sqrt{15}}{2}$ $-\frac{1}{8} \pm i\frac{\sqrt{79}}{8}$

81. $\frac{1 \pm \sqrt{3}}{2}$

81. $x(2x - 1) = 1 + x$ **82.** $2x = x(3 - 4x)$ $0, \frac{1}{4}$

83. $x^2 = x(1 - x) - 2$ **84.** $2x^2 = 2x(5 - x) - 8$

$\frac{1}{4} \pm i\frac{\sqrt{15}}{4}$ $\frac{5}{4} \pm i\frac{\sqrt{7}}{4}$

YOU DECIDE THE METHOD

Exercises 85–92: Find exact solutions to the quadratic equation, using a method of your choice. Explain why you chose the method you did.

-1; answers may vary.

85. $x^2 - 3x + 2 = 0$ **86.** $x^2 + 2x + 1 = 0$

1, 2; answers may vary.

87. $0.5x^2 - 1.75x - 1 = 0$ **88.** $\frac{3}{5}x^2 + \frac{9}{10}x - \frac{3}{5} = 0$

$-\frac{1}{2}, 4$; answers may vary.

89. $x^2 - 5x + 2 = 0$ **90.** $2x^2 - x - 4 = 0$

91. $2x^2 + x = -8$ **92.** $4x^2 = 2x - 3$

$-\frac{1}{4} \pm \frac{3}{4}i\sqrt{7}$; quadratic formula $\frac{1}{4} \pm i\frac{\sqrt{11}}{4}$;
quadratic formula

APPLICATIONS

Exercises 93–96: Modeling Stopping Distance   (Refer to Example 4.) Use $d = \frac{1}{9}x^2 + \frac{11}{3}x$ to find a safe speed x for the following stopping distances d.

93. 42 feet 9 mph   **94.** 152 feet 24 mph

95. 390 feet 45 mph   **96.** 726 feet 66 mph

97. *Modeling U.S. AIDS Deaths*   The cumulative numbers in thousands of AIDS deaths from 1984 through 1994 may be modeled by

$$f(x) = 2.39x^2 + 5.04x + 5.1,$$

where $x = 0$ corresponds to 1984, $x = 1$ to 1985, and so on until $x = 10$ corresponds to 1994. See the accompanying graph. Use the formula for $f(x)$ to estimate the year when the total number of AIDS deaths reached 200 thousand. Compare your result with that shown in the graph.
$x \approx 8.04$, or about 1992; this agrees with the graph.

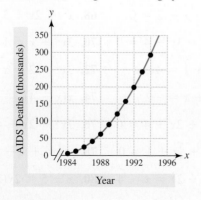

98. *Screen Dimensions*   The width of a rectangular computer screen is 3 inches more than its height. If the area of the screen is 154 square inches, find its dimensions
  (a) graphically,
  (b) numerically, and
  (c) symbolically.   11 in. by 14 in.

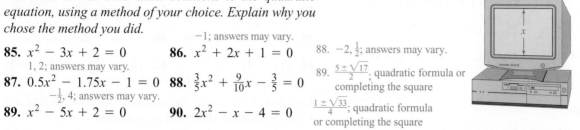

88. $-2, \frac{1}{2}$; answers may vary.

89. $\frac{5 \pm \sqrt{17}}{2}$, quadratic formula or
  completing the square

$\frac{1 \pm \sqrt{33}}{4}$; quadratic formula
or completing the square

99. *Canoeing*   A camper paddles a canoe 2 miles downstream in a river that has a 2-mile-per-hour current. To return to camp, the canoeist travels upstream on a different branch of the river. It is 4 miles long and has a 1-mile-per-hour current. The total trip (both ways) takes 3 hours. Find the average speed of the canoe in still water. (*Hint:* Time equals distance divided by rate.)
$\frac{1 \pm \sqrt{17}}{2} \approx 2.6$ mph

100. *Airplane Speed*   A pilot flies 500 miles against a 20-mile-per-hour wind. On the next day, the pilot flies back home with a 10-mile-per-hour tail wind. The total trip (both ways) takes 4 hours. Find the speed of the airplane without a wind.
$130 \pm 5\sqrt{634} \approx 256$ mph

101. *Modeling Water Flow*   When water runs out of a hole in a cylindrical container, the height of the water in the container can often be modeled by a quadratic function. The data in the table show the height y in centimeters of water at 30-second intervals in a metal can that had a small hole in it.

Time	0	30	60	90
Height	16	11.9	8.4	5.3

Time	120	150	180
Height	3.1	1.4	0.5

These data are modeled by

$$f(x) = 0.0004x^2 - 0.15x + 16.$$

  (a) The rate of change is not constant
  (b) 75 sec; answers may vary.

  (a) Explain why a linear function would not be appropriate for modeling this data.
  (b) Use the table to estimate the time at which the height was 7 centimeters.
  (c) Use $f(x)$ and the quadratic formula to solve part (b).   75 sec

102. *Hospitals* The general trend in the number of hospitals in the United States from 1945 through 2000 is modeled by

$$f(x) = -1.38x^2 + 84x + 5865,$$

where $x = 5$ corresponds to 1945, $x = 10$ to 1950, and so on until $x = 60$ represents 2000. See the scatterplot and accompanying graph.

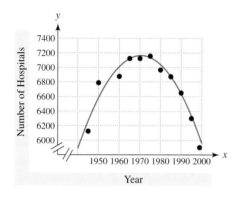

Number of Hospitals

Year

(a) Increased from 1945 to 1970 and then decreased from 1970 to 2000.

(a) Describe any trends in the numbers of hospitals from 1945 to 2000.

(b) What information does the vertex of the graph of f give?   (c) 7143; about the same.

(c) Use the formula for $f(x)$ to estimate the number of hospitals in 1970 ($x = 30$). Compare your result with that shown in the graph.

(d) Use the formula for $f(x)$ to estimate the year (or years) when there were 6300 hospitals. Compare your result with that shown in the graph.   About 1946 and 1995; agrees with graph.

WRITING ABOUT MATHEMATICS

103. Explain how the discriminant can be used to determine the number of solutions to a quadratic equation.

104. Let $f(x) = ax^2 + bx + c$. If you know the value of $b^2 - 4ac$, what information does this give you about the graph of f? Explain your answer.

102.(b) An estimate of the maximum number of hospitals and the year it took place.

CHECKING BASIC CONCEPTS   SECTIONS 8.3 AND 8.4

1. Solve the quadratic equation $2x^2 - 7x + 3 = 0$ symbolically and graphically. $\frac{1}{2}, 3$

2. Use the square root property to solve $x^2 = 5$. $\pm\sqrt{5}$

3. Complete the square to solve $x^2 - 4x + 1 = 0$. $2 \pm \sqrt{3}$

4. Solve the equation $x^2 + y^2 = 1$ for y. $y = \pm\sqrt{1 - x^2}$

5. Use the quadratic formula to solve each equation.
   (a) $2x^2 = 3x + 1$ $\frac{3 \pm \sqrt{17}}{4}$

   (b) $9x^2 - 24x + 16 = 0$ $\frac{4}{3}$
   (c) $x^2 + x + 2 = 0$ $-\frac{1}{2} \pm i\frac{\sqrt{7}}{2}$

6. Calculate the discriminant for each equation and give the number of real solutions.
   (a) $x^2 - 5x + 5 = 0$ 5; 2 real solutions
   (b) $2x^2 - 5x + 4 = 0$ -7; no real solutions
   (c) $49x^2 - 56x + 16 = 0$ 0; 1 real solution

8.5 QUADRATIC INEQUALITIES

Basic Concepts · Graphical and Numerical Solutions · Symbolic Solutions

INTRODUCTION

Quadratic inequalities are nonlinear inequalities. These inequalities are often simple enough to be solved by hand. In this section we discuss how to solve them graphically, numerically, and symbolically.

BASIC CONCEPTS

If the equals sign in a quadratic equation is replaced with $>$, $\geq$, $<$, or $\leq$, a **quadratic inequality** results. Examples of quadratic inequalities include

$$x^2 + 4x - 3 < 0, \quad 5x^2 \geq 5, \quad \text{and} \quad 1 - z \leq z^2.$$

Any quadratic equation can be written as

$$ax^2 + bx + c = 0, \qquad a \neq 0,$$

so any quadratic inequality can be written as

$$ax^2 + bx + c > 0, \qquad a \neq 0,$$

where $>$ may be replaced with $\geq$, $<$, or $\leq$.

The next example demonstrates how to identify a quadratic inequality.

EXAMPLE 1 Identifying a quadratic inequality

Determine whether the inequality is quadratic.
(a) $5x + x^2 - x^3 \leq 0$ **(b)** $4 + 5x^2 > 4x^2 + x$

Solution **(a)** This inequality is not quadratic because x^3 occurs in the inequality.
(b) Write the inequality as follows.

$$
\begin{array}{ll}
4 + 5x^2 > 4x^2 + x & \text{Given inequality} \\
4 + 5x^2 - 4x^2 - x > 0 & \text{Subtract } 4x^2 \text{ and } x. \\
4 + x^2 - x > 0 & \text{Combine like terms.} \\
x^2 - x + 4 > 0 & \text{Rewrite the expression.}
\end{array}
$$

Because the inequality can be written in the form $ax^2 + bx + c > 0$ with $a = 1$, $b = -1$, and $c = 4$, it is a quadratic inequality.

GRAPHICAL AND NUMERICAL SOLUTIONS

Equality often is the boundary between *greater than* and *less than*, so a first step in solving an inequality is to determine the x-values where equality occurs. We begin by using this concept with graphical and numerical techniques.

A graph of $y = x^2 - x - 2$ with x-intercepts -1 and 2 is shown in Figure 8.38. The solutions to $x^2 - x - 2 = 0$ are given by $x = -1$ or $x = 2$. Between the x-intercepts the graph dips below the x-axis and the y-values are negative. Thus the solutions to $x^2 - x - 2 < 0$ satisfy $-1 < x < 2$. To check this result we select a **test value**. For example, 0 lies between -1 and 2. If we substitute $x = 0$ in the inequality, it results in a true statement.

$$0^2 - 0 - 2 < 0 \qquad \text{True}$$

When $x < -1$ or $x > 2$, the graph lies above the x-axis and the y-values are positive. Thus the solutions to $x^2 - x - 2 > 0$ satisfy $x < -1$ or $x > 2$. For example, 3 is greater than 2 and -3 is less than -1. Therefore both 3 and -3 are solutions. We can verify this result by substituting 3 and -3 as test values in the inequality.

$$3^2 - 3 - 2 > 0 \qquad \text{True}$$
$$(-3)^2 - (-3) - 2 > 0 \qquad \text{True}$$

In the next two examples, we use graphical and numerical methods to solve quadratic inequalities.

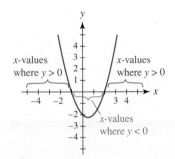

Figure 8.38

EXAMPLE 2 Solving a quadratic inequality

Make a table of values for $y = x^2 - 3x - 4$ and then sketch the graph. Use the table and graph to solve $x^2 - 3x - 4 \leq 0$. Write your answer in interval notation.

Solution The points calculated for Table 8.14 are plotted in Figure 8.39 and connected with a smooth ∪-shaped graph.

Numerical Solution Table 8.14 shows that $x^2 - 3x - 4$ equals 0 when $x = -1$ or $x = 4$. Between these values, $x^2 - 3x - 4$ is negative so the solution set to $x^2 - 3x - 4 \leq 0$ is $-1 \leq x \leq 4$ or in interval notation, $[-1, 4]$.

Graphical Solution In Figure 8.39 the graph of $y = x^2 - 3x - 4$ shows that the x-intercepts are -1 and 4. Between these values, the graph dips *below* the x-axis. Thus the solution set is $[-1, 4]$.

TABLE 8.14

x	$y = x^2 - 3x - 4$
-2	6
-1	0
0	-4
1	-6
2	-6
3	-4
4	0
5	6

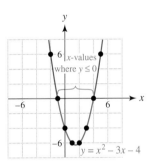

Figure 8.39

EXAMPLE 3 Solving a quadratic inequality

Solve $x^2 > 1$. Write your answer in interval notation.

Solution First, rewrite $x^2 > 1$ as $x^2 - 1 > 0$. The graph $y = x^2 - 1$ is shown in Figure 8.40 with x-intercepts -1 and 1. The graph lies *above* the x-axis and is shaded red to the left of $x = -1$ and to the right of $x = 1$. Thus the solution set is $x < -1$ or $x > 1$, which can be written in interval notation as $(-\infty, -1) \cup (1, \infty)$.

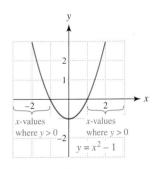

Figure 8.40

Critical Thinking

i. $(-3, 4)$
ii. $(-\infty, -3) \cup (4, \infty)$

The graph of $y = -x^2 + x + 12$ is a parabola opening downward with x-intercepts of -3 and 4. Solve each inequality.

i. $-x^2 + x + 12 > 0$ **ii.** $-x^2 + x + 12 < 0$

In the next example we show how quadratic inequalities are used in highway design.

EXAMPLE 4   Determining elevations on a sag curve

Parabolas are frequently used in highway design to model hills and sags (valleys) along a proposed route. Suppose that the elevation E in feet of a sag, or *sag curve*, is given by

$$E(x) = 0.00004x^2 - 0.4x + 2000,$$

where x is the horizontal distance in feet along the sag curve and $0 \le x \le 10{,}000$. See Figure 8.41. Estimate graphically the x-values for elevations of 1500 feet or less.   (*Source:* F. Mannering and W.Kilareski, *Principles of Highway Engineering and Traffic Analysis.*)

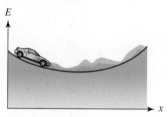

Figure 8.41

Solution   *Graphical Solution*   We must solve the quadratic inequality

$$0.00004x^2 - 0.4x + 2000 \le 1500.$$

TEACHING TIP

If students wonder where quadratic functions and equations are used in applications, tell them that they occur frequently in highway design. See Example 4.

To do so, we let $Y_1 = .00004X^2 - .4X + 2000$ represent the sag or valley in the road and $Y_2 = 1500$ represent a horizontal line with an elevation of 1500 feet. Their graphs intersect at $x \approx 1464$ and $x \approx 8536$, as shown in Figure 8.42. The elevation of the proposed route is less than 1500 feet between these x-values. Therefore the elevation of the road is 1500 feet or less when $1464 \le x \le 8536$ (approximately).

Calculator Help

To find a point of intersection, see the Appendix (page AP-7).

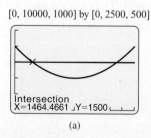

[0, 10000, 1000] by [0, 2500, 500]

Intersection
X=1464.4661 Y=1500

(a)

[0, 10000, 1000] by [0, 2500, 500]

Intersection
X=8535.5339 Y=1500

(b)

Figure 8.42

SYMBOLIC SOLUTIONS

To solve a quadratic inequality we first solve the corresponding equality. We can then write the solution to the inequality, using the following method.

SOLUTIONS TO QUADRATIC INEQUALITIES

Let $ax^2 + bx + c = 0$, $a > 0$, have two real solutions p and q, where $p < q$.

$ax^2 + bx + c < 0$ is equivalent to $p < x < q$ (see left-hand figure).

$ax^2 + bx + c > 0$ is equivalent to $x < p$ or $x > q$ (see right-hand figure).

Quadratic inequalities involving $\le$ or $\ge$ can be solved similarly.

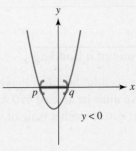

Solutions lie between p and q.

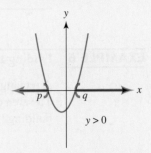

Solutions lie "outside" p and q.

We demonstrate this method in the next two examples.

EXAMPLE 5   Solving quadratic inequalities

Solve each inequality symbolically. Write your answer in interval notation.
(a) $6x^2 - 7x - 5 \ge 0$ **(b)** $x(3 - x) > -18$

Solution   **(a)** Begin by solving $6x^2 - 7x - 5 = 0$.

$$6x^2 - 7x - 5 = 0$$

$$(2x + 1)(3x - 5) = 0 \qquad \text{Factor.}$$

$$2x + 1 = 0 \quad \text{or} \quad 3x - 5 = 0 \qquad \text{Zero-product property}$$

$$x = -\frac{1}{2} \quad \text{or} \quad x = \frac{5}{3} \qquad \text{Solve.}$$

Therefore the solutions to $6x^2 - 7x - 5 \ge 0$ lie "outside" these two values and satisfy $x \le -\frac{1}{2}$ or $x \ge \frac{5}{3}$. In interval notation the solution set is $\left(-\infty, -\frac{1}{2}\right] \cup \left[\frac{5}{3}, \infty\right)$.

(b) First, rewrite the inequality as follows.

$$x(3 - x) > -18 \qquad \text{Given inequality}$$

$$3x - x^2 > -18 \qquad \text{Distributive property}$$

$$3x - x^2 + 18 > 0 \qquad \text{Add 18.}$$

$$-x^2 + 3x + 18 > 0 \qquad \text{Rewrite.}$$

$$x^2 - 3x - 18 < 0 \qquad \text{Multiply by } -1; \text{ reverse the inequality symbol.}$$

Next, solve $x^2 - 3x - 18 = 0$.

$$(x + 3)(x - 6) = 0 \qquad \text{Factor.}$$

$$x = -3 \quad \text{or} \quad x = 6 \qquad \text{Solve.}$$

Solutions to $x^2 - 3x - 18 < 0$ lie between these two values and satisfy $-3 < x < 6$. In interval notation the solution set is $(-3, 6)$.

TEACHING TIP

Be sure to discuss this Critical
Thinking exercise because it addresses some special cases.

Critical Thinking

Graph $y = x^2 + 1$ and solve the following inequalities.

    i. $x^2 + 1 > 0$ **ii.** $x^2 + 1 < 0$

Now graph $y = (x - 1)^2$ and solve the following inequalities.

    iii. $(x - 1)^2 \geq 0$ **iv.** $(x - 1)^2 \leq 0$

   i. All real numbers
  ii. No solutions
 iii. All real numbers
 iv. 1

EXAMPLE 6   Finding the dimensions of a building

A rectangular building needs to be 7 feet longer than it is wide, as illustrated in Figure 8.43. The area of the building must be at least 450 square feet. What widths x are possible for this building? Support your results with a table of values.

Figure 8.43

Solution   *Symbolic Solution*   If x is the width of the building, $x + 7$ is the length of the building and its area is $x(x + 7)$. The area must be at least 450 square feet, so the inequality $x(x + 7) \geq 450$ must be satisfied. First solve the following quadratic equation.

$x(x + 7) = 450$	Quadratic equation
$x^2 + 7x = 450$	Distributive property
$x^2 + 7x - 450 = 0$	Subtract 450.
$x = \dfrac{-7 \pm \sqrt{7^2 - 4(1)(-450)}}{2(1)}$	Quadratic formula; $a = 1$, $b = 7$, and $c = -450$
$= \dfrac{-7 \pm \sqrt{1849}}{2}$	Simplify.
$= \dfrac{-7 \pm 43}{2}$	$\sqrt{1849} = 43$
$= 18, -25$	Evaluate.

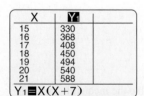

Figure 8.44

Thus the solutions to $x(x + 7) \geq 450$ are $x \leq -25$ or $x \geq 18$. The width is positive, so the building width must be 18 feet or more.

Numerical Solution   A table of values is shown in Figure 8.44, where $Y_1 = X(X + 7)$ equals 450 when $x = 18$. For $x \geq 18$ the area is *at least* 450 square feet.

8.5 PUTTING IT ALL TOGETHER

The following table summarizes solutions of quadratic inequalities containing the symbols $<$ or $>$. Cases involving $\leq$ or $\geq$ are solved similarly.

Method	Explanation
Solving a Quadratic Inequality Symbolically	Let $ax^2 + bx + c = 0$, $a > 0$, have two real solutions p and q, where $p < q$. $ax^2 + bx + c < 0$ is equivalent to $p < x < q$ $ax^2 + bx + c > 0$ is equivalent to $x < p$ or $x > q$ *Examples:* The solutions to $x^2 - 3x + 2 = 0$ are given by $x = 1$ or $x = 2$. The solutions to $x^2 - 3x + 2 < 0$ are given by $1 < x < 2$. The solutions to $x^2 - 3x + 2 > 0$ are given by $x < 1$ or $x > 2$.
Solving a Quadratic Inequality Graphically	Given $ax^2 + bx + c < 0$ with $a > 0$, graph $y = ax^2 + bx + c$ and locate any x-intercepts. If there are two x-intercepts, then solutions correspond to x-values between the x-intercepts. Solutions to $ax^2 + bx + c > 0$ correspond to x-values "outside" the x-intercepts.
Solving a Quadratic Inequality Numerically	If a quadratic inequality is expressed as $$ax^2 + bx + c < 0 \text{ with } a > 0,$$ solve $$y = ax^2 + bx + c = 0$$ with a table. If there are two solutions, then the solutions to the given inequality lie between these values. Solutions to $ax^2 + bx + c > 0$ lie "outside" these values.

8.5 EXERCISES

FOR EXTRA HELP

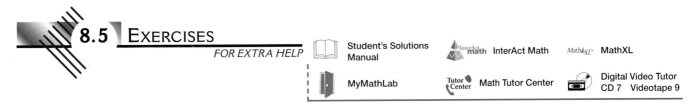

Student's Solutions Manual   InterAct Math   MathXL
MyMathLab   Math Tutor Center   Digital Video Tutor CD 7 Videotape 9

CONCEPTS

1. How is a quadratic inequality different from a quadratic equation?
It has an inequality symbol rather than an equals sign.

2. Do quadratic inequalities typically have two solutions? Explain.   No, they often have infinitely many.

3. Is 3 a solution to $x^2 < 7$?   No

4. Is 5 a solution to $x^2 \geq 25$?   Yes

5. The solutions to $x^2 - 2x - 8 = 0$ are -2 and 4. What are the solutions to $x^2 - 2x - 8 < 0$?
$-2 < x < 4$

6. The solutions to $x^2 + 2x - 3 = 0$ are -3 and 1. What are the solutions to $x^2 + 2x - 3 > 0$?
$x < -3$ or $x > 1$

Exercises 7–12: Determine whether the inequality is quadratic.

7. $x^2 + 4x + 5 < 0$ Yes **8.** $x > x^3 - 5$ No

9. $x^2 > 19$ Yes

10. $x(x - 1) - 2 \geq 0$ Yes

11. $4x > 1 - x$ No

12. $2x(x^2 + 3) < 0$ No

Exercises 13–18: Determine whether the given value of x is a solution.

13. $2x^2 + x - 1 > 0$ $x = 3$ Yes

14. $x^2 - 3x + 2 \leq 0$ $x = 2$ Yes

15. $x^2 + 2 \leq 0$ $x = 0$ No

16. $2x(x - 3) \geq 0$ $x = 1$ No

17. $x^2 - 3x \leq 1$ $x = -3$ No

18. $4x^2 - 5x + 1 > 30$ $x = -2$ No

SOLVING QUADRATIC INEQUALITIES

Exercises 19–24: Use the graph of

$$y = ax^2 + bx + c$$

to solve each quadratic equation or inequality.
 (a) $ax^2 + bx + c = 0$
 (b) $ax^2 + bx + c < 0$
 (c) $ax^2 + bx + c > 0$

19.
(a) $-3, 2$
(b) $-3 < x < 2$
(c) $x < -3$ or $x > 2$

20.
(a) $-2, 0$
(b) $-2 < x < 0$
(c) $x < -2$ or $x > 0$

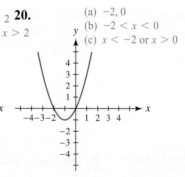

21.

22.
(a) No real solutions
(b) No real solutions
(c) All real numbers

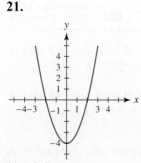

(a) $-2, 2$
(b) $-2 < x < 2$
(c) $x < -2$ or $x > 2$

23.
(a) $-10, 5$
(b) $x < -10$ or $x > 5$
(c) $-10 < x < 5$

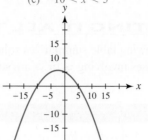

24.
(a) $-8, 4$
(b) $x < -8$ or $x > 4$
(c) $-8 < x < 4$

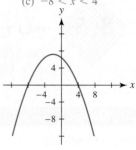

Exercises 25–28: Use the table for

$$y = ax^2 + bx + c$$

to solve each quadratic equation or inequality.
 (a) $ax^2 + bx + c = 0$
 (b) $ax^2 + bx + c < 0$
 (c) $ax^2 + bx + c > 0$

25. $y = x^2 - 4$

x	-3	-2	-1	0	1	2	3
y	5	0	-3	-4	-3	0	5

(a) $-2, 2$ (b) $-2 < x < 2$ (c) $x < -2$ or $x > 2$

26. $y = x^2 - x - 2$

x	-3	-2	-1	0	1	2	3
y	10	4	0	-2	-2	0	4

(a) $-1, 2$ (b) $-1 < x < 2$ (c) $x < -1$ or $x > 2$

27. $y = x^2 + 4x$

x	-5	-4	-3	-2	-1	0	1
y	5	0	-3	-4	-3	0	5

(a) $-4, 0$ (b) $-4 < x < 0$ (c) $x < -4$ or $x > 0$

28. $y = -2x^2 - 2x + 1.5$

x	-2	-1.5	-1	-0.5	0	0.5	1
y	-2.5	0	1.5	2	1.5	0	-2.5

(a) $-1.5, 0.5$ (b) $x < -1.5$ or $x > 0.5$ (c) $-1.5 < x < 0.5$

Exercises 29–38: Solve the quadratic inequality by any method. Write your answer in interval notation.

29. $x^2 + 4x + 3 < 0$
$(-3, -1)$

30. $x^2 + x - 2 \leq 0$ $[-2, 1]$

31. $2x^2 - x - 15 \geq 0$
$(-\infty, -2.5] \cup [3, \infty)$

32. $3x^2 - 3x - 6 > 0$
$(-\infty, -1) \cup (2, \infty)$

33. $2x^2 \leq 8$ $[-2, 2]$

34. $x^2 < 9$ $(-3, 3)$

35. $x^2 > -5$ $(-\infty, \infty)$

36. $-x^2 \geq 1$ No solutions

37. $-x^2 + 3x > 0$ $(0, 3)$

38. $-8x^2 - 2x + 1 \leq 0$
$(-\infty, -0.5] \cup [0.25, \infty)$

39. (a) $-2, 2$ (b) $-2 < x < 2$ (c) $x < -2$ or $x > 2$

40. (a) $\pm\sqrt{5}$ (b) $-\sqrt{5} \le x \le \sqrt{5}$ (c) $x \le -\sqrt{5}$ or $x \ge \sqrt{5}$

Exercises 39–42: Solve the quadratic equation in part (a) symbolically. Use the results to solve the inequalities in parts (b) and (c).

39. (a) $x^2 - 4 = 0$ **40. (a)** $x^2 - 5 = 0$
    (b) $x^2 - 4 < 0$ **(b)** $x^2 - 5 \le 0$
    (c) $x^2 - 4 > 0$ **(c)** $x^2 - 5 \ge 0$

41. (a) $x^2 + x - 1 = 0$ $\frac{-1 \pm \sqrt{5}}{2}$
    (b) $x^2 + x - 1 < 0$ $\frac{-1-\sqrt{5}}{2} < x < \frac{-1+\sqrt{5}}{2}$
    (c) $x^2 + x - 1 > 0$ $x < \frac{-1-\sqrt{5}}{2}$ or $x > \frac{-1+\sqrt{5}}{2}$

42. (a) $x^2 + 4x - 5 = 0$ $-5, 1$
    (b) $x^2 + 4x - 5 \le 0$ $-5 \le x \le 1$
    (c) $x^2 + 4x - 5 \ge 0$ $x \le -5$ or $x \ge 1$

Exercises 43–52: Solve the quadratic inequality symbolically. Write your answer in interval notation.

43. $x^2 + 10x + 21 \le 0$ **44.** $x^2 - 7x - 18 < 0$
  $[-7, -3]$ $(-2, 9)$

45. $3x^2 - 9x + 6 > 0$ **46.** $7x^2 + 34x - 5 \ge 0$
  $(-\infty, 1) \cup (2, \infty)$ $(-\infty, -5] \cup \left[\frac{1}{7}, \infty\right)$

47. $x^2 < 10$ **48.** $x^2 \ge 64$
  $(-\sqrt{10}, \sqrt{10})$ $(-\infty, -8] \cup [8, \infty)$

49. $x(x - 6) > 0$ **50.** $1 - x^2 \le 0$
  $(-\infty, 0) \cup (6, \infty)$ $(-\infty, -1] \cup [1, \infty)$

51. $x(4 - x) \le 2$ **52.** $2x(1 - x) \ge 2$
  $(-\infty, 2 - \sqrt{2}] \cup [2 + \sqrt{2}, \infty)$ No solutions

APPLICATIONS

53. *Highway Design* (Refer to Example 4 and Figure 8.41.) The elevation E of a sag curve in feet is given by

$$E(x) = 0.0000375x^2 - 0.175x + 1000,$$

where $0 \le x \le 4000$.
    (a) Estimate graphically the x-values for which the elevation is 850 feet or less. (*Hint:* Use $[0, 4000, 1000]$ by $[500, 1200, 100]$ as a viewing rectangle.) From 1131 ft to 3535 ft (approximately)
    (b) For what x-values is the elevation 850 feet or more? Before 1131 ft or after 3535 ft (approximately)

54. *Early Cellular Phone Use* Our society is in transition from an industrial to an informational society. Cellular communication has played an increasingly large role in this transition. The number of cellular subscribers in the United States in thousands from 1985 to 1991 can be modeled by

$$f(x) = 163x^2 - 146x + 205,$$

where x is the year and $x = 0$ corresponds to 1985, $x = 1$ to 1986, and so on. (*Source:* M. Paetsch, *Mobile Communication in the U.S. and Europe.*)

    (a) Write a quadratic inequality whose solution set represents the years when there were 2 million subscribers or more. $163x^2 - 146x + 205 \ge 2000$
    (b) Solve this inequality.   About 1989 or after

55. *Heart Disease Death Rates* From 1960 to 1995, age-adjusted heart disease rates decreased dramatically. The number of deaths per 100,000 people can be modeled by

$$f(x) = -0.014777x^2 + 54.14x - 49,060,$$

where x is the year, as illustrated in the accompanying figure. (*Source:* Department of Health and Human Services.)

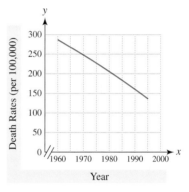

    About 183; they agree (approx.)
    (a) Evaluate $f(1985)$, using both the formula and the graph. How do your results compare?
    (b) Use the graph to estimate the years when this death rate was 250 or less.   About 1970 or after
    (c) Solve part (b) by using the quadratic formula.
                 About 1969 or after

56. *Accidental Deaths* From 1910 to 1996 the number of accidental deaths per 100,000 people generally decreased and can be modeled by

$$f(x) = -0.001918x^2 + 6.93x - 6156,$$

where x is the year, as shown in the accompanying figure. (*Source:* Department of Health and Human Services.)

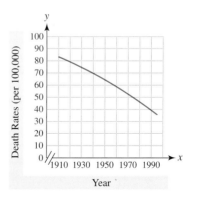

(a) About 61.5, which agrees with the graph (approx.)

(a) Evaluate $f(1955)$, using both the formula and the graph. How do your results compare?

(b) Use the graph to estimate when this death rate was 60 or more. About 1958 or earlier

(c) Solve part (b) by using the quadratic formula.
About 1958 or earlier

57. *Dimensions of a Pen* A rectangular pen for a pet is 5 feet longer than it is wide. Give possible values for the width w of the pen if its area must be between 176 and 500 square feet, inclusively.
From 11 ft to 20 ft

58. *Dimensions of a Cylinder* The volume of a cylindrical can is given by $V = \pi r^2 h$, where r is its radius and h is its height. See the accompanying figure. If $h = 6$ inches and the volume of the can must be 50 cubic inches or more, estimate to the nearest tenth of an inch possible values for r. 1.6 in. or more

59. Consider the inequality $x^2 < 0$. Discuss the solutions to this inequality and explain your reasoning.

60. Explain how the graph of $y = ax^2 + bx + c$ can be used to solve the inequality

$$ax^2 + bx + c > 0$$

when $a < 0$. Assume that the x-intercepts of the graph are p and q with $p < q$.

8.6 EQUATIONS IN QUADRATIC FORM

Higher Degree Polynomial Equations · Equations Having Rational Exponents

INTRODUCTION

Although many equations are *not* quadratic equations, they can sometimes be put into quadratic form. These equations are *reducible to quadratic form*. To express such an equation in quadratic form we often use substitution. In this section we discuss this process.

HIGHER DEGREE POLYNOMIAL EQUATIONS

Sometimes a fourth degree polynomial can be factored like a quadratic trinomial, provided it does not have an x-term or an x^3-term. Let's consider the equation $x^4 - 5x^2 + 4 = 0$.

$x^4 - 5x^2 + 4 = 0$	Given equation
$(x^2)^2 - 5(x^2) + 4 = 0$	Properties of exponents

We use the substitution $u = x^2$.

$u^2 - 5u + 4 = 0$	Let $u = x^2$.
$(u - 4)(u - 1) = 0$	Factor.
$u - 4 = 0 \quad$ or $\quad u - 1 = 0$	Zero-product property
$u = 4 \quad$ or $\quad u = 1$	Solve each equation.

Because the given equation uses the variable x, we must give the solutions in terms of x. We substitute x^2 for u and then solve to obtain the following four solutions.

$$x^2 = 4 \quad \text{or} \quad x^2 = 1 \qquad \text{Substitute } x^2 \text{ for } u.$$

$$x = \pm 2 \quad \text{or} \quad x = \pm 1 \qquad \text{Square root property}$$

The solutions are $-2, -1, 1,$ and 2.

In the next example we solve a sixth degree polynomial equation.

EXAMPLE 1   Solving equations by substitution

Solve $2x^6 + x^3 = 1$.

Solution   Start by subtracting 1 from each side.

$$2x^6 + x^3 - 1 = 0 \qquad \text{Subtract 1.}$$

$$2(x^3)^2 + (x^3) - 1 = 0 \qquad \text{Properties of exponents}$$

$$2u^2 + u - 1 = 0 \qquad \text{Let } u = x^3.$$

$$(2u - 1)(u + 1) = 0 \qquad \text{Factor.}$$

$$2u - 1 = 0 \quad \text{or} \quad u + 1 = 0 \qquad \text{Zero-product property}$$

$$u = \frac{1}{2} \quad \text{or} \quad u = -1 \qquad \text{Solve.}$$

Now substitute x^3 for u, and solve for x to obtain the following two solutions.

$$x^3 = \frac{1}{2} \quad \text{or} \quad x^3 = -1 \qquad \text{Substitute } x^3 \text{ for } u.$$

$$x = \sqrt[3]{\frac{1}{2}} \quad \text{or} \quad x = -1 \qquad \text{Take cube root of each side.}$$

EQUATIONS HAVING RATIONAL EXPONENTS

Equations that have rational exponents are sometimes reducible to quadratic form. Consider the following example, in which two solutions are presented.

EXAMPLE 2   Solving an equation having negative exponents

Solve $-6m^{-2} + 13m^{-1} + 5 = 0$.

Solution   **Solution I**   Use the substitution $u = m^{-1} = \frac{1}{m}$ and $u^2 = m^{-2} = \frac{1}{m^2}$.

$$-6m^{-2} + 13m^{-1} + 5 = 0 \qquad \text{Given equation}$$

$$-6u^2 + 13u + 5 = 0 \qquad \text{Let } u = m^{-1} \text{ and } u^2 = m^{-2}.$$

$$6u^2 - 13u - 5 = 0 \qquad \text{Multiply by } -1.$$

$$(2u - 5)(3u + 1) = 0 \qquad \text{Factor.}$$

$$2u - 5 = 0 \quad \text{or} \quad 3u + 1 = 0 \qquad \text{Zero-product property}$$

$$u = \frac{5}{2} \quad \text{or} \quad u = -\frac{1}{3} \qquad \text{Solve for } u.$$

Because $u = \frac{1}{m}$, $m = \frac{1}{u}$. Thus $m = \frac{2}{5}$ or $m = -3$.

Solution II   Another way to solve this equation is to multiply each side by the LCD, m^2.

$$-6m^{-2} + 13m^{-1} + 5 = 0 \qquad \text{Given equation}$$

$$m^2(-6m^{-2} + 13m^{-1} + 5) = m^2 \cdot 0 \qquad \text{Multiply by } m^2.$$

$$-6m^2 m^{-2} + 13m^2 m^{-1} + 5m^2 = 0 \qquad \text{Distributive property}$$

$$-6 + 13m + 5m^2 = 0 \qquad \text{Add exponents.}$$

$$5m^2 + 13m - 6 = 0 \qquad \text{Rewrite the equation.}$$

$$(5m - 2)(m + 3) = 0 \qquad \text{Factor.}$$

$$5m - 2 = 0 \quad \text{or} \quad m + 3 = 0 \qquad \text{Zero-product property}$$

$$m = \frac{2}{5} \quad \text{or} \quad m = -3 \qquad \text{Solve.}$$

In the next example we solve an equation having fractional exponents.

EXAMPLE 3   Solving an equation having rational exponents

Solve $x^{2/3} - 2x^{1/3} - 8 = 0$.

Solution   Use the substitution $u = x^{1/3}$.

$$x^{2/3} - 2x^{1/3} - 8 = 0 \qquad \text{Given equation}$$

$$(x^{1/3})^2 - 2(x^{1/3}) - 8 = 0 \qquad \text{Rewrite the equation.}$$

$$u^2 - 2u - 8 = 0 \qquad \text{Let } u = x^{1/3}.$$

$$(u - 4)(u + 2) = 0 \qquad \text{Factor.}$$

$$u - 4 = 0 \quad \text{or} \quad u + 2 = 0 \qquad \text{Zero-product property}$$

$$u = 4 \quad \text{or} \quad u = -2 \qquad \text{Solve.}$$

Because $u = x^{1/3}$, $u^3 = (x^{1/3})^3 = x$. Thus $x = 4^3 = 64$ or $x = (-2)^3 = -8$.

8.6 PUTTING IT ALL TOGETHER

The following table demonstrates how to reduce some types of equations to quadratic form.

Equation	Substitution	Examples
Higher Degree Polynomial	Let $u = x^n$ for some integer n.	To solve $x^4 - 3x^2 - 4 = 0$, let $u = x^2$. This equation becomes $$u^2 - 3u - 4 = 0.$$
Rational Exponents	Pick a substitution that reduces the equation to quadratic form.	To solve $n^{-2} + 6n^{-1} + 9 = 0$, let $u = n^{-1}$. This equation becomes $$u^2 + 6u + 9 = 0.$$ To solve $6x^{2/5} - 5x^{1/5} - 4 = 0$, let $u = x^{1/5}$. This equation becomes $$6u^2 - 5u - 4 = 0.$$

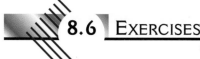

8.6 EXERCISES

FOR EXTRA HELP

 Student's Solutions Manual

 MyMathLab

 InterAct Math

 Math Tutor Center

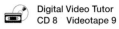 MathXL

Digital Video Tutor
CD 8   Videotape 9

Exercises 1–6: Use the given substitution to solve the equation.

1. $x^4 - 7x^2 + 6 = 0$ $u = x^2$ $\pm 1, \pm\sqrt{6}$

2. $2k^4 - 7k^2 + 6 = 0$ $u = k^2$ $\pm\frac{\sqrt{6}}{2}, \pm\sqrt{2}$

3. $3z^6 + z^3 - 10 = 0$ $u = z^3$ $-\sqrt[3]{2}, \sqrt[3]{\frac{5}{3}}$

4. $2x^6 + 17x^3 + 8 = 0$ $u = x^3$ $-\sqrt[3]{\frac{1}{2}}, -2$

5. $4n^{-2} + 17n^{-1} + 15 = 0$ $u = n^{-1}$ $-\frac{4}{5}, -\frac{1}{3}$

6. $m^{-2} + 24 = 10m^{-1}$ $u = m^{-1}$ $\frac{1}{6}, \frac{1}{4}$

Exercises 7–24: Solve the equation. Find all real solutions.   **9.** $-\sqrt[3]{\frac{1}{3}}, \sqrt[3]{2}$ **10.** $-\sqrt[3]{\frac{4}{3}}, -\sqrt[3]{\frac{1}{2}}$ **11.** $-\frac{1}{8}, \frac{2}{5}$

7. $x^4 = 8x^2 + 9$ $-3, 3$ **8.** $3x^4 = 10x^2 + 8$ $-2, 2$

9. $3x^6 - 5x^3 - 2 = 0$ **10.** $6x^6 + 11x^3 + 4 = 0$

11. $2z^{-2} + 11z^{-1} = 40$ **12.** $z^{-2} - 10z^{-1} + 25 = 0$ $\frac{1}{5}$

13. $x^{2/3} - 2x^{1/3} + 1 = 0$ 1 **14.** $3x^{2/3} + 18x^{1/3} = 48$ $-512, 8$

15. $x^{2/5} - 33x^{1/5} + 32 = 0$ $1, 32^5 = 33,554,432$

16. $x^{2/5} - 80x^{1/5} - 81 = 0$ $-1, 81^5 = 3,486,784,401$

17. $x - 13\sqrt{x} + 36 = 0$ $16, 81$

18. $x - 17\sqrt{x} + 16 = 0$ $1, 256$

19. $z^{1/2} - 2z^{1/4} + 1 = 0$ 1

20. $z^{1/2} - 4z^{1/4} + 4 = 0$ 16

21. $(x + 1)^2 - 5(x + 1) - 14 = 0$ $-3, 6$

22. $2(x - 5)^2 + 5(x - 5) + 3 = 0$ $\frac{7}{2}, 4$

23. $(x^2 - 1)^2 - 4 = 0$ $-\sqrt{3}, \sqrt{3}$

24. $(x^2 - 9)^2 - 8(x^2 - 9) + 16 = 0$ $-\sqrt{13}, \sqrt{13}$

WRITING ABOUT MATHEMATICS

25. Explain how to solve $ax^4 - bx^2 + c = 0$. Assume that the left side of the equation factors.

26. Explain what it means for an equation to be reducible to quadratic form.

CHECKING BASIC CONCEPTS   SECTIONS 8.5 AND 8.6

1. Solve the quadratic inequality $(-\infty, -2) \cup (3, \infty)$

$$x^2 - x - 6 > 0.$$

Write your answer in interval notation.

2. Solve the quadratic inequality $\left[-1, -\frac{2}{3}\right]$

$$3x^2 + 5x + 2 \le 0.$$

Write your answer in interval notation.

3. Solve $x^6 + 6x^3 - 16 = 0.$ $-2, \sqrt[3]{2}$

4. Solve $x^{2/3} - 7x^{1/3} - 8 = 0.$ $-1, 8^3 = 512$

Summary

Quadratic Function   Any quadratic function f can be written as

$$f(x) = ax^2 + bx + c \quad (a \neq 0).$$

Graph of a Quadratic Function   Its graph is $\cup$-shaped and called a parabola. If $a > 0$, the parabola opens upward; if $a < 0$, the parabola opens downward. The vertex of a parabola is either the lowest point on a parabola that opens upward or the highest point on a parabola that opens downward. The x-coordinate of the vertex is given by $x = -\frac{b}{2a}$.

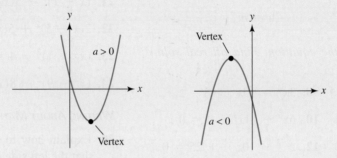

Axis of Symmetry   The axis of symmetry is a vertical line that passes through the vertex of the graph of a quadratic function. If the vertex is (h, k), then the axis of symmetry is $x = h$. The parabola is symmetric with respect to this line.

Vertical and Horizontal Translations   Let h and k be positive numbers.

To graph	*shift the graph of $y = x^2$ by k units*
$y = x^2 + k$	upward.
$y = x^2 - k$	downward.

To graph	*shift the graph of $y = x^2$ by h units*
$y = (x - h)^2$	right.
$y = (x + h)^2$	left.

Example: Compared to $y = x^2$, the graph of $y = (x - 1)^2 + 2$ is translated right 1 unit and upward 2 units.

Vertex Form   Any quadratic function can be expressed in vertex form as

$$f(x) = a(x - h)^2 + k.$$

In this form the point (h, k) is the vertex. A quadratic function can be put in this form by completing the square.

Example: $\quad y = x^2 + 10x - 4 \qquad\qquad$ Given equation
$$= (x^2 + 10x + 25) - 25 - 4 \qquad \left(\tfrac{b}{2}\right)^2 = \left(\tfrac{10}{2}\right)^2 = 25$$
$$= (x + 5)^2 - 29$$

The vertex is $(-5, -29)$.

Section 8.3   *Quadratic Equations*

Quadratic Equations   Any quadratic equation can be written as $ax^2 + bx + c = 0$ and can have zero, one, or two real solutions. These solutions correspond to the x-intercepts on the graph of $y = ax^2 + bx + c$. These equations can be solved by factoring or by completing the square.

Example: $\qquad x^2 + x - 2 = 0$
$$(x + 2)(x - 1) = 0$$
$$x = -2 \quad \text{or} \quad x = 1$$

The x-intercepts for $y = x^2 + x - 2$
are -2 and 1.

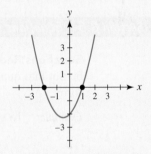

Completing the Square   To solve $x^2 + bx = d$ by completing the square add $\left(\tfrac{b}{2}\right)^2$ to each side of the equation.

Section 8.4   *The Quadratic Formula*

The Quadratic Formula   The solutions to $ax^2 + bx + c = 0$ $(a \neq 0)$ are given by
$$x = \frac{-b \pm \sqrt{b^2 - 4ac}}{2a}.$$

Example: Solve $2x^2 + 3x - 1 = 0$ by letting $a = 2$, $b = 3$, and $c = -1$.
$$x = \frac{-3 \pm \sqrt{3^2 - 4(2)(-1)}}{2(2)} = \frac{-3 \pm \sqrt{17}}{4} \approx 0.28, -1.78$$

The Discriminant   The expression $b^2 - 4ac$ evaluates to a real number and is called the discriminant. If $b^2 - 4ac > 0$, there are two real solutions; if $b^2 - 4ac = 0$, there is one real solution; and if $b^2 - 4ac < 0$, there are no real solutions, rather there are two complex solutions.

Example: For $2x^2 + 3x - 1 = 0$, the discriminant is
$$b^2 - 4ac = 3^2 - 4(2)(-1) = 17 > 0.$$

There are two real solutions to this quadratic equation.

Quadratic Inequalities When the equals sign in a quadratic equation is replaced with $<$, $>$, $\leq$, or $\geq$, a quadratic inequality results. For example,

$$3x^2 - x + 1 = 0$$

is a quadratic equation and

$$3x^2 - x + 1 > 0$$

is a quadratic inequality. Like quadratic equations, quadratic inequalities can be solved symbolically, graphically, and numerically. An important first step in solving a quadratic inequality is to solve the corresponding quadratic equation.

Examples: The solutions to $x^2 - 5x - 6 = 0$ are $x = -1, 6$.

The solutions to $x^2 - 5x - 6 < 0$ satisfy $-1 < x < 6$.

The solutions to $x^2 - 5x - 6 > 0$ satisfy $x < -1$ or $x > 6$.

Equations Reducible to Quadratic Form An equation that is not quadratic, but can be put into quadratic form by using a substitution is said to be reducible to quadratic form.

Example: To solve $x^{2/3} - 2x^{1/3} - 15 = 0$ let $u = x^{1/3}$. This equation becomes

$$u^2 - 2u - 15 = 0.$$

Factoring results in $(u + 3)(u - 5) = 0$, or $u = -3$ or 5. Because $u = x^{1/3}$, $x = u^3$ and $x = (-3)^3 = -27$ or $x = (5)^3 = 125$.

CHAPTER

8 Review Exercises

1. $(-3, 4)$; $x = -3$; downward; increasing: $x \leq -3$; decreasing: $x \geq -3$ 2. $(1, 0)$; $x = 1$; upward; increasing: $x \geq 1$; decreasing: $x \leq 1$

SECTION 8.1

Exercises 1 and 2: Identify the vertex, axis of symmetry, and whether the parabola opens upward or downward. State where the graph is increasing and where it is decreasing.

1.

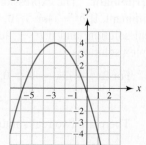

2.

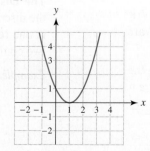

Exercises 3–6: Do the following.
  (a) *Graph f. **
  (b) *Use the graph to identify the vertex and axis of symmetry.*
  (c) *Evaluate f(x) at the given value of x.*

3. $f(x) = x^2 - 2$, $x = -1$
  (b) $(0, -2); x = 0$ (c) -1
4. $f(x) = -x^2 + 4x - 3$, $x = 3$
  (b) $(2, 1); x = 2$ (c) 0
5. $f(x) = -\frac{1}{2}x^2 + x + \frac{3}{2}$, $x = -2$
  (b) $(1, 2); x = 1$ (c) -2.5
6. $f(x) = 2x^2 + 8x + 5$, $x = -3$
  (b) $(-2, -3); x = -2$ (c) -1
7. Find the minimum y-value located on the graph of $y = 2x^2 - 6x + 1$. $-\frac{7}{2}$

8. Find the maximum y-value located on the graph of $y = -3x^2 + 2x - 5$. $-\frac{14}{3}$

Exercises 9–12: Find the vertex of the parabola.

9. $f(x) = x^2 - 4x - 2$ $(2, -6)$

10. $f(x) = 5 - x^2$ $(0, 5)$

11. $f(x) = -\frac{1}{4}x^2 + x + 1$ $(2, 2)$

12. $f(x) = 2 + 2x + x^2$ $(-1, 1)$

Section 8.2

Exercises 13–18: Do the following.

  (a) *Graph f. **
  (b) *Compare the graph of f with the graph of $y = x^2$.*

13. $f(x) = x^2 + 2$ **14.** $f(x) = 3x^2$ (b) Narrower
  (b) Shifted up 2 units
15. $f(x) = (x - 2)^2$ **16.** $f(x) = (x + 1)^2 - 3$
  (b) Shifted right 2 units   (b) Shifted left 1 unit and down 3 units
17. $f(x) = \frac{1}{2}(x + 1)^2 + 2$ (b) Wider, shifted left 1 unit and up 2 units

18. $f(x) = 2(x - 1)^2 - 3$ (b) Narrower, shifted right 1 unit and down 3 units

19. Write the vertex form of a parabola with $a = -4$ and vertex $(2, -5)$. $y = -4(x - 2)^2 - 5$

20. Write the vertex form of a parabola that opens downward with vertex $(-4, 6)$. Assume that $a = \pm 1$.
  $y = -(x + 4)^2 + 6$

Exercises 21–24: Write the equation in vertex form. Identify the vertex.
  $y = \left(x - \frac{7}{2}\right)^2 - \frac{45}{4}; \left(\frac{7}{2}, -\frac{45}{4}\right)$
21. $y = x^2 + 4x - 7$ **22.** $y = x^2 - 7x + 1$
  $y = (x + 2)^2 - 11; (-2, -11)$
23. $y = 2x^2 - 3x - 8$ **24.** $y = 3x^2 + 6x - 2$
  $y = 2\left(x - \frac{3}{4}\right)^2 - \frac{73}{8}; \left(\frac{3}{4}, -\frac{73}{8}\right)$ $y = 3(x + 1)^2 - 5; (-1, -5)$

Exercises 25 and 26: Find a value for the constant a so that $f(x) = ax^2 - 1$ models the data.

25.

x	1	2	3
$f(x)$	2	11	26

   $a = 3$

26.

x	-1	0	1
$f(x)$	$-\frac{3}{4}$	-1	$-\frac{3}{4}$

   $a = \frac{1}{4}$

Section 8.3

Exercises 27–30: Use the graph of

$$y = ax^2 + bx + c$$

to solve $ax^2 + bx + c = 0$.

27. $-2, 3$ **28.** -1

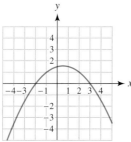 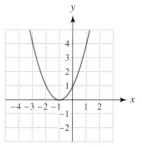

29. No real solutions   **30.** $-4, 6$

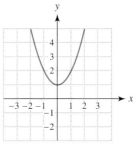 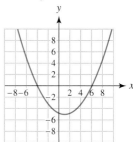

Exercises 31 and 32: Use the table of

$$y = ax^2 + bx + c$$

to solve $ax^2 + bx + c = 0$.

31. $-10, 5$ **32.** $-0.5, 0.25$

X	Y1	
-20	250	
-15	100	
-10	0	
-5	-50	
0	-50	
5	0	
10	100	
Y1■X^2+5X−50		

X	Y1	
-.75	2	
-.5	0	
-.25	-1	
0	-1	
.25	0	
.5	2	
.75	5	
Y1■8X^2+2X−1		

*Answers on page IA-27

📱 *Exercises 33–36: Solve the quadratic equation*

    (a) *graphically and*

    (b) *numerically.*

33. $x^2 - 5x - 50 = 0$ **34.** $\frac{1}{2}x^2 + x - \frac{3}{2} = 0$
$-5, 10$ $-3, 1$

35. $\frac{1}{4}x^2 + \frac{1}{2}x = 2$ $-4, 2$ **36.** $\frac{1}{2}x + \frac{3}{4} = \frac{1}{4}x^2$ $-1, 3$

Exercises 37–40: Solve the equation by factoring.

37. $x^2 + x - 20 = 0$ **38.** $x^2 + 11x + 24 = 0$
$-5, 4$ $-8, -3$

39. $15x^2 - 4x - 4 = 0$ **40.** $7x^2 - 25x + 12 = 0$
$-\frac{2}{5}, \frac{2}{3}$ $\frac{4}{7}, 3$

Exercises 41–44: Use the square root property to solve the equation.

41. $x^2 = 100$ ± 10 **42.** $3x^2 = \frac{1}{3}$ $\pm\frac{1}{3}$

43. $4x^2 - 6 = 0$ $\pm\frac{\sqrt{6}}{2}$ **44.** $5x^2 = x^2 - 4$
                                No real solutions

Exercises 45–48: Solve the equation by completing the square.

45. $x^2 + 6x = -2$ **46.** $x^2 - 4x = 6$ $2 \pm \sqrt{10}$
$-3 \pm \sqrt{7}$

47. $x^2 - 2x - 5 = 0$ **48.** $2x^2 + 6x - 1 = 0$
$1 \pm \sqrt{6}$ $\frac{-3 \pm \sqrt{11}}{2}$

Exercises 49 and 50: Solve the equation for the specified variable.

49. $F = \dfrac{k}{(R + r)^2}$ for R **50.** $2x^2 + 3y^2 = 12$ for y
$R = -r \pm \sqrt{\frac{k}{F}}$ $y = \pm\sqrt{\frac{12 - 2x^2}{3}}$

SECTION 8.4

Exercises 51–56: Solve the equation, using the quadratic formula.

51. $x^2 - 9x + 18 = 0$ **52.** $x^2 - 24x + 143 = 0$
$3, 6$ $11, 13$

53. $6x^2 + x = 1$ $-\frac{1}{2}, \frac{1}{3}$ **54.** $5x^2 + 1 = 5x$ $\frac{5 \pm \sqrt{5}}{10}$

55. $x(x - 8) = 5$ **56.** $2x(2 - x) = 3 - 2x$
$4 \pm \sqrt{21}$ $\frac{3 \pm \sqrt{3}}{2}$

Exercises 57–60: A graph of $y = ax^2 + bx + c$ is shown.

    (a) *State whether $a > 0$ or $a < 0$.*

    (b) *Solve $ax^2 + bx + c = 0$.*

    (c) *Determine whether the discriminant is positive, negative, or zero.*

57. (a) $a > 0$ (b) $-2, 3$ (c) Positive

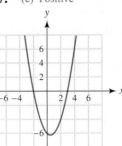

58. (a) $a > 0$ (b) 2 (c) Zero

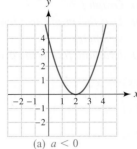

59. (a) $a < 0$ (b) No real solutions (c) Negative

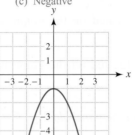

60. (a) $a < 0$ (b) $-4, 2$ (c) Positive

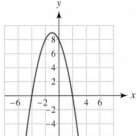

Exercises 61–64: Complete the following for the given equation.

    (a) *Evaluate the discriminant.*

    (b) *How many real solutions are there?*

📱   *(c)* *Support your answer for part (b) graphically.*

61. $2x^2 - 3x + 1 = 0$ **62.** $7x^2 + 2x - 5 = 0$
(a) 1   (b) 2   (a) 144   (b) 2

63. $3x^2 + x + 2 = 0$ (a) -23 (b) 0

64. $4.41x^2 - 12.6x + 9 = 0$ (a) 0   (b) 1

Exercises 65–68: Solve the equation. Write complex solutions in standard form.

65. $x^2 + x + 5 = 0$ **66.** $2x^2 + 8 = 0$ $\pm 2i$
$-\frac{1}{2} \pm i\frac{\sqrt{19}}{2}$

67. $2x^2 = x - 1$ **68.** $7x^2 = 2x - 5$ $\frac{1}{7} \pm i\frac{\sqrt{34}}{7}$
$\frac{1}{4} \pm i\frac{\sqrt{7}}{4}$

SECTION 8.5

Exercises 69 and 70: Use the graph of

$$y = ax^2 + bx + c$$

to solve each quadratic equation or inequality.

    (a) $ax^2 + bx + c = 0$

    (b) $ax^2 + bx + c < 0$

    (c) $ax^2 + bx + c > 0$

(a) $-2, 6$
(b) $-2 < x < 6$
69. (c) $x < -2$ or $x > 6$

(a) $-2, 0$
(b) $x < -2$ or $x > 0$
70. (c) $-2 < x < 0$

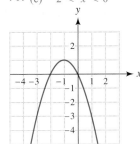

Exercises 71 and 72: Use the table of

$$y = ax^2 + bx + c$$

to solve each quadratic equation or inequality.
(a) $ax^2 + bx + c = 0$
(b) $ax^2 + bx + c < 0$
(c) $ax^2 + bx + c > 0$

71. $y = x^2 - 16$ 　　(a) $-4, 4$　(b) $-4 < x < 4$
　　　　　　　　　　(c) $x < -4$ or $x > 4$

x	-6	-4	-2	0	2	4	6
y	20	0	-12	-16	-12	0	20

72. $y = x^2 + x - 2$

x	-3	-2	-1	0	1	2	3
y	4	0	-2	-2	0	4	10

(a) $-2, 1$　(b) $-2 < x < 1$
(c) $x < -2$ or $x > 1$

Exercises 73 and 74: Solve the quadratic equation in part (a) symbolically. Use the results to solve the inequalities in parts (b) and (c).

73. (a) $x^2 - 2x - 3 = 0$　$-1, 3$
　　(b) $x^2 - 2x - 3 < 0$　$-1 < x < 3$
　　(c) $x^2 - 2x - 3 > 0$　$x < -1$ or $x > 3$

74. (a) $2x^2 - 7x - 15 = 0$　$-\frac{3}{2}, 5$
　　(b) $2x^2 - 7x - 15 \leq 0$　$-\frac{3}{2} \leq x \leq 5$
　　(c) $2x^2 - 7x - 15 \geq 0$　$x \leq -\frac{3}{2}$ or $x \geq 5$

Exercises 75–78: Solve the quadratic inequality. Write your answer in interval notation.

75. $x^2 + 4x + 3 \leq 0$　$[-3, -1]$

76. $5x^2 - 16x + 3 < 0$　$\left(\frac{1}{5}, 3\right)$

77. $6x^2 - 13x + 2 > 0$　$\left(-\infty, \frac{1}{6}\right) \cup (2, \infty)$

78. $x^2 \geq 5$　$(-\infty, -\sqrt{5}] \cup [\sqrt{5}, \infty)$

SECTION 8.6

Exercises 79–82: Solve the equation.

79. $x^4 - 14x^2 + 45 = 0$　$\pm\sqrt{5}, \pm 3$

80. $2z^{-2} + z^{-1} - 28 = 0$　$-\frac{1}{4}, \frac{2}{7}$

81. $x^{2/3} - 9x^{1/3} + 8 = 0$　$1, 512$

82. $(x - 1)^2 + 2(x - 1) + 1 = 0$　0

APPLICATIONS

83. *Construction* A rain gutter is being fabricated from a flat sheet of metal so that the cross section of the gutter is a rectangle, as shown in the accompanying figure. The width of the metal sheet is 12 inches.

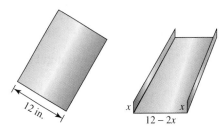

(a) Write a formula $f(x)$ that gives the area of the cross section.　$f(x) = x(12 - 2x)$
(b) To hold the greatest amount of rainwater, the cross section should have maximum area. Find the dimensions that result in this maximum.
　　　　　　　　　　　　　　　　6 in. by 3 in.

84. *Height of a Stone* Suppose that a stone is thrown upward with an initial velocity of 44 feet per second (30 miles per hour) and is released 4 feet above the ground. Its height h in feet after t seconds is given by

$$h(t) = -16t^2 + 44t + 4.$$
　　　　　　　　　　　　1 sec and 1.75 sec
(a) When does the stone reach a height of 32 feet?
(b) After how many seconds does the stone reach maximum height? Estimate this height.
　　1.375 sec; 34.25 ft

85. *Maximizing Revenue* Hotel rooms normally cost $90 per night. However, for a group rate the management is considering reducing the cost of a room by $3 for every room rented.　$f(x) = x(90 - 3x)$
(a) Write a formula $f(x)$ that gives the revenue from renting x rooms at the group rate.
(b) Graph f in $[0, 30, 5]$ by $[0, 800, 100]$.*
(c) How many rooms should be rented to yield revenue of $600?　10 or 20 rooms
(d) How many rooms should be rented to maximize revenue?　15 rooms

*Answer on page IA-27

86. *Airline Complaints*   In 2000, major U.S. airlines promised better customer service. From 1997 through 1999, the number of complaints per 100,000 passengers can be modeled by

$$f(x) = 0.4(x - 1997)^2 + 0.8,$$

where x represents the year.   (*Source:* Department of Transportation.)

(a) Evaluate $f(1999)$. Interpret the result.

(b) Graph f in [1997, 1999, 1] by [0.5, 3, 0.5]. Discuss how complaints changed over this time period.*   Complaints increased.

(a) 2.4; in 1999 there were 2.4 complaints per 100,000 passengers

87. *Braking Distance*   On dry pavement a safe braking distance d in feet for a car traveling x miles per hour is $d = \frac{x^2}{12}$. For each distance d, find x.   (F. Mannering, *Principles of Highway Engineering and Traffic Control.*)

(a) $d = 144$ feet   **(b)** $d = 300$ feet   60 mph

$\sqrt{1728} \approx 41.6$ mph

88. *Numbers*   The product of two numbers is 143. One number is 2 more than the other.

(a) Write an equation whose solution gives the smaller number x. $x(x + 2) = 143$

(b) Solve the equation.

$x = -13$ or $x = 11$; the numbers are -13 and -11 or 11 and 13.

89. *Educational Attainment*   From 1940 through 1991, the percentage of people with a high school diploma increased dramatically, as shown in the table.

Year	1940	1950	1960
H.S. Diploma (%)	25	34	44

Year	1970	1980	1991
H.S. Diploma (%)	55	69	78

Source: Bureau of the Census.

(a) Plot the data. *

(b) Would it be reasonable to model these data with a linear function rather than a quadratic function? Explain your reasoning.   Yes, the data are nearly linear.

(c) Find a function that models the data.

$f(x) = 1.04(x - 1940) + 25$; answers may vary.

90. *U. S. Energy Consumption*   From 1950 to 1970 per capita consumption of energy in millions of Btu can be modeled by

$$f(x) = \frac{1}{4}(x - 1950)^2 + 220,$$

where x is the year.   (*Source:* Department of Energy.)

90. (c) $f(1996) = 749$; no; the trend represented by this model did not continue after 1970.

(a) (1950, 220); in 1950 the per capita consumption was at a low of 220 million Btu.

(a) Find and interpret the vertex.

(b) Graph f in [1950, 1970, 5] by [200, 350, 25]. What happened to energy consumption during this time period?*   It increased.

(c) Use f to predict the consumption in 1996. Actual consumption was 354 million Btu. Did f provide a good model for 1996? Explain.

91. *Screen Dimensions*   A square computer screen has an area of 123 square inches. Approximate its dimensions.   About 11.1 in. by 11.1 in.

92. *Flying a Kite*   A kite is being flown, as illustrated in the accompanying figure. If 130 feet of string have been let out, find the value of x.   50 ft

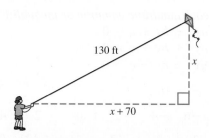

93. *Area*   A uniform strip of grass is to be planted around a rectangular swimming pool, as illustrated in the accompanying figure. The swimming pool is 30 feet wide and 50 feet long. If there is only enough grass seed to cover 250 square feet, estimate the width x that the strip of grass should be.   About 1.5 ft

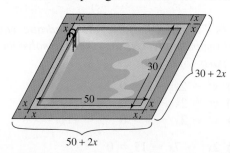

94. *Dimensions of a Cone*   The volume V of a cone is given by $V = \frac{1}{3}\pi r^2 h$, where r is its base radius and h is its height. See the accompanying figure. If $h = 20$ inches and the volume of the cone must be between 750 and 1700 cubic inches, inclusively, estimate to the nearest tenth of an inch possible values for r.

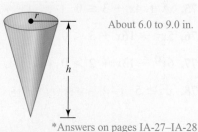

About 6.0 to 9.0 in.

*Answers on pages IA-27–IA-28

Test

1. Find the vertex and axis of symmetry for the graph of
   $f(x) = -\frac{1}{2}x^2 + x + 1.$ $\left(1, \frac{3}{2}\right); x = 1$

2. Find the minimum y-value located on the graph of
   $y = x^2 + 3x - 5.$ $-\frac{29}{4}$

3. Find the exact value for the constant a so that
   $f(x) = ax^2 + 2$ models the data in the table.

x	2	0	2	4
$f(x)$	0	2	0	-6

   $a = -\frac{1}{2}$

4. Graph $f(x) = \frac{1}{2}(x - 3)^2 + 2$ and compare the graph of f to the graph of $y = x^2.$*
   It is wider, translated right 3 units, and translated upward 2 units.

5. Write $y = x^2 - 6x + 2$ in vertex form. Identify the vertex. $y = (x - 3)^2 - 7; (3, -7)$

6. Use the graph of
   $$y = ax^2 + bx + c$$
   to solve $ax^2 + bx + c = 0.$ $-1, 2$

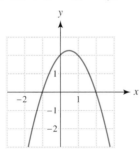

Exercises 7 and 8: Solve the quadratic equation.

7. $3x^2 + 11x - 4 = 0$ $-4, \frac{1}{3}$ 8. $2x^2 = 2 - 6x^2$ $-\frac{1}{2}, \frac{1}{2}$

9. Solve $x^2 - 8x = 1$ by completing the square. $4 \pm \sqrt{17}$

10. Solve $x(-2x + 3) = -1$, using the quadratic formula. $\frac{3 \pm \sqrt{17}}{4}$

11. A graph of $y = ax^2 + bx + c$ is shown at the top of the next column.
    (a) State whether $a > 0$ or $a < 0.$ $a < 0$
    (b) Solve $ax^2 + bx + c = 0.$ $-3, 1$
    (c) Determine whether the discriminant is positive, negative, or zero. Positive

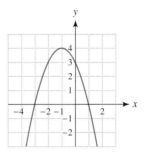

12. Complete the following for $-3x^2 + 4x - 5 = 0.$
    (a) Evaluate the discriminant. -44
    (b) How many real solutions are there? No real solutions
    (c) Support your answer for part (b) graphically.
    The graph of $y = -3x^2 + 4x - 5$ does not intersect the x-axis

Exercises 13 and 14: Use the graph of
$$y = ax^2 + bx + c$$
to solve each equation or inequality.
   (a) $ax^2 + bx + c = 0$
   (b) $ax^2 + bx + c < 0$
   (c) $ax^2 + bx + c > 0$

13.
(a) $-1, 1$
(b) $-1 < x < 1$
(c) $x < -1$ or $x > 1$

14.
(a) $-10, 20$
(b) $x < -10$ or $x > 20$
(c) $-10 < x < 20$

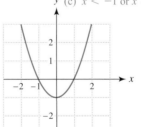
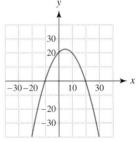

15. Solve the quadratic equation in part (a) symbolically. Use the result to solve the inequalities in parts (b) and (c) and write your answer in interval notation.
    (a) $8x^2 - 2x - 3 = 0$ $-\frac{1}{2}, \frac{3}{4}$
    (b) $8x^2 - 2x - 3 \leq 0$ $\left[-\frac{1}{2}, \frac{3}{4}\right]$
    (c) $8x^2 - 2x - 3 \geq 0$ $\left(-\infty, -\frac{1}{2}\right] \cup \left[\frac{3}{4}, \infty\right)$

16. Solve $x^6 - 3x^3 + 2 = 0.$ Find all real solutions. $1, \sqrt[3]{2}$

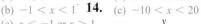

*Answer on page IA-28

17. *Braking Distance*   On wet pavement a safe braking distance d in feet for a car traveling x miles per hour is $d = \frac{x^2}{9}$. What speed corresponds to a braking distance of 250 feet?   (F. Mannering, *Principles of Highway Engineering and Traffic Control.*) $\sqrt{2250} \approx 47.4$ mph

18. *Construction*   A fence is being constructed along a 20-foot building, as shown in the accompanying figure. No fencing is used along the building.
(a) If 200 feet of fence are available, find a formula $f(x)$ that gives the area enclosed by the fence and building. $f(x) = (x + 20)(90 - x)$
(b) What value of x gives the greatest area?   35

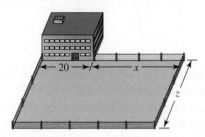

19. *Height of a Stone*   Suppose that a stone is thrown upward with an initial velocity of 88 feet per second (60 miles per hour) and is released 8 feet above the ground. Its height h in feet after t seconds is given by

$$h(t) = -16t^2 + 88t + 8.$$

(a) Graph h in [0, 6, 1] by [0, 150, 50]. *
(b) When does the stone strike the ground?
(c) After how many seconds does the stone reach maximum height? Estimate this height.   2.75 sec; 129 ft
(b)   After about 5.6 sec

CHAPTER 8 Extended and Discovery Exercises

MODELING DATA WITH A QUADRATIC FUNCTION

1. *Survival Rate of Birds*   The survival rate of sparrowhawks varies according to their age. The following table summarizes the results of one study by listing the age in years and the percentage of birds that survived the previous year. For example, 52% of sparrowhawks that reached age 6 lived to be 7 years old.
(*Source:* D. Brown and P. Rothery, *Models in Biology: Mathematics, Statistics and Computing.*)

Age	1	2	3	4	5
Percent (%)	45	60	71	67	67

Age	6	7	8	9
Percent (%)	61	52	30	25

(a) Try to explain the relationship between age and the likelihood of surviving the next year. *
(b) Make a scatterplot of the data. What type of function might model the data? Explain your reasoning. *

(c) Graph each function. Which of the following functions models the data better? *

$$f_1(x) = -3.57x + 71.1$$
$$f_2(x) = -2.07x^2 + 17.1x + 33$$

(d) Use one of these functions to estimate the likelihood of a 5.5-year-old sparrowhawk surviving for 1 more year. *

2. *Photosynthesis and Temperature*   Photosynthesis is the process by which plants turn sunlight into energy. At very cold temperatures photosynthesis may halt even though the sun is shining. In one study the efficiency of photosynthesis for an Antarctic species of grass was investigated. The following table lists results for various temperatures. The temperature x is in degrees Celsius, and the efficiency y is given as a percent. The purpose of the research was to determine the temperature at which photosynthesis is most efficient.   (*Source:* D. Brown.)

*Answers on page IA-28

2.(b) Quadratic; the data seem to form a parabola opening downward.
(c) $f(x) = -0.25(x - 12)^2 + 95$; answers may vary.

x (°C)	−1.5	0	2.5	5	7	10	12
y (%)	33	46	55	80	87	93	95

x (°C)	15	17	20	22	25	27	30
y (%)	91	89	77	72	54	46	34

(a) Plot the data.*
(b) What type of function might model these data? Explain your reasoning.
(c) Find a function f that models the data.
(d) Use f to estimate the temperature at which photosynthesis is most efficient in this type of grass.
About 12°C; answers may vary.

TRANSLATIONS OF PARABOLAS IN COMPUTER GRAPHICS

Exercises 3 and 4: In video games with two-dimensional graphics, the background is often translated to give the illusion that a character in the game is moving. The simple scene on the left shows a mountain and an airplane. To make it appear that the airplane is flying, the mountain can be translated to the left, as shown in the figure on the right. (**Reference:** C. Pokorny and C. Gerald, *Computer Graphics.*)

 3. *Video Games*   Suppose that the mountain in the figure on the left is modeled by $f(x) = -0.4x^2 + 4$ and that the airplane is located at the point $(1, 5)$.
(a) Graph f in $[-4, 4, 1]$ by $[0, 6, 1]$, where the units are kilometers. Plot the point $(1, 5)$ to show the location of the airplane.*
(b) Assume that the airplane is moving horizontally to the right at 0.2 kilometer per second. To give a video game player the illusion that the airplane is moving, graph the image of the mountain and the position of the airplane after 10 seconds.*

 4. *Video Games*   (Refer to Exercise 3.) Discuss how you could create the illusion of the airplane moving to the left and gaining altitude as it passes over the mountain. Try to perform a translation of this type. Explain your reasoning.   Translate the mountain to the right and down. One example might be $f(x) = -0.4(x - 2)^2 + 4 - 2$.

5. Discriminant: $121 = 11^2$. It will factor; $(2x + 1)(5x - 3)$

*Exercises 5–8:   **Factoring and the Discriminant**   If the discriminant of the trinomial $ax^2 + bx + c$ with integer coefficients is a perfect square, then it can be factored. For example, on the one hand, the discriminant of $6x^2 + x - 2$ is*

$$1^2 - 4(6)(-2) = 49,$$

which is a perfect square ($7^2 = 49$), so we can factor the trinomial as

$$6x^2 + x - 2 = (2x - 1)(3x + 2).$$

On the other hand, the discriminant for $x^2 + x - 1$ is

$$1^2 - 4(1)(-1) = 5,$$

which is not a perfect square, so we cannot factor this trinomial by using integers as coefficients. Similarly, if the discriminant is negative, the trinomial cannot be factored by using integer coefficients. Use the discriminant to predict whether the trinomial can be factored. Then test your prediction.

5. $10x^2 - x - 3$ **6.** $4x^2 - 3x - 6$
                                          Discriminant: 105. It will not factor.
7. $3x^2 + 2x - 2$ **8.** $2x^2 + x + 3$
Discriminant: 28. It will not factor.   Discriminant: −23. It will not factor.

*Exercises 9–14: **Polynomial Inequalities**   The solution set for a polynomial inequality can be found by first determining the boundary numbers. For example, to solve $f(x) = x^3 - 4x > 0$ begin by solving $x^3 - 4x = 0$. The solutions (boundary numbers) are $-2, 0,$ and 2. The function $f(x) = x^3 - 4x$ is either only positive or only negative on intervals between consecutive zeros. To determine the solution set, we can evaluate test values for each interval as shown on the left below.*

Interval	Test Value	$f(x) = x^3 - 4x$
$(-\infty, -2)$	$x = -3$	$f(-3) = -15 < 0$
$(-2, 0)$	$x = -1$	$f(-1) = 3 > 0$
$(0, 2)$	$x = 1$	$f(1) = -3 < 0$
$(2, \infty)$	$x = 3$	$f(3) = 15 > 0$

$[-6, 6, 1]$ by $[-4, 4, 1]$

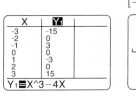 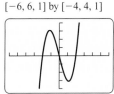

We can see that $f(x) > 0$ for $(-2, 0) \cup (2, \infty)$. These results also are supported graphically in the figure on the right above, where the graph of f is above the x-axis when $-2 < x < 0$ or when $x > 2$.

*Answers on page IA-28

Use these concepts to solve the polynomial inequality.

9. $x^3 - x^2 - 6x > 0$ $(-2, 0) \cup (3, \infty)$

10. $x^3 - 3x^2 + 2x < 0$ $(-\infty, 0) \cup (1, 2)$

11. $x^3 - 7x^2 + 14x \le 8$ $(-\infty, 1] \cup [2, 4]$

12. $9x - x^3 \ge 0$ $(-\infty, -3] \cup [0, 3]$

13. $x^4 - 5x^2 + 4 > 0$ $(-\infty, -2) \cup (-1, 1) \cup (2, \infty)$

14. $1 < x^4$ $(-\infty, -1) \cup (1, \infty)$

Exercises 15–20: **Rational Inequalities** *Rational inequalities can be solved using many of the same techniques that are used to solve other types of inequalities. However, there is one important difference. For a rational inequality, the boundary between greater than and less than can either be an x-value where equality occurs or an x-value where a rational expression is undefined. For example, consider the inequality* $f(x) = \frac{2-x}{2x} > 0$. *The solution to the equation* $\frac{2-x}{2x} = 0$ *is 2. The rational expression* $\frac{2-x}{2x}$ *is undefined when* $x = 0$. *Therefore we select test values on the intervals* $(-\infty, 0)$, $(0, 2)$, *and* $(2, \infty)$. *The table reveals that* $f(x) > 0$ *for* $(0, 2)$.

Interval	Test Value	$f(x) = \dfrac{2-x}{2x}$
$(-\infty, 0)$	$x = -0.5$	$f(-0.5) = -2.5 < 0$
$(0, 2)$	$x = 1$	$f(1) = 0.5 > 0$
$(2, \infty)$	$x = 2.5$	$f(2.5) = -0.1 < 0$

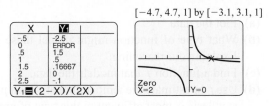

Note that $f(x)$ *changes from negative to positive at* $x = 0$, *where* $f(x)$ *is undefined. These results are supported graphically in the figure on the right above.*

Solve the rational inequality.

15. $\frac{3-x}{3x} \ge 0$ $(0, 3]$ **16.** $\frac{x-2}{x+2} > 0$ $(-\infty, -2) \cup (2, \infty)$

17. $\frac{3-2x}{1+x} < 3$ **18.** $\frac{x+1}{4-2x} \ge 1$ $[1, 2)$

19. $\frac{5}{x^2 - 4} < 0$ $(-2, 2)$ **20.** $\frac{x}{x^2 - 1} \ge 0$

    17. $(-\infty, -1) \cup (0, \infty)$ $(-1, 0] \cup (1, \infty)$

9

Exponential and Logarithmic Functions

In 1900, the Swedish scientist Svante Arrhenius first predicted a greenhouse effect resulting from emissions of carbon dioxide by industrialized countries. His classic calculation made use of logarithms and predicted that a doubling of the carbon dioxide concentration in the atmosphere would raise the average global temperature by 7°F to 11°F. An increase in world population has resulted in higher emissions of greenhouse gases, such as carbon dioxide, and these emissions have the potential to alter Earth's climate and destroy portions of the ozone layer.

In this chapter we use exponential and logarithmic functions to model a wide variety of phenomena, such as greenhouse gases, acid rain, the decline of the bluefin tuna, the demand for liver transplants, diversity of bird species, hurricanes, and earthquakes. Mathematics plays a key role in understanding, controlling, and predicting natural phenomena and people's effect on them.

**Human history becomes more and more a race
between education and catastrophe.**
—H. G. Wells

Source: M. Kraljic, *The Greenhouse Effect.*

9.1 COMPOSITE AND INVERSE FUNCTIONS

Composition of Functions · **One-to-One Functions** · **Inverse Functions** · **Tables and Graphs of Inverse Functions**

INTRODUCTION

Suppose that you walk into a classroom, turn on the lights, and sit down at your desk. How could you undo or reverse these actions? You might stand up from the desk, turn off the lights, and walk out of the classroom. Note that you must not only perform the "inverse" of each action, but you also must do them in the *reverse order*. In mathematics, we undo an arithmetic operation by performing its inverse operation. For example, the inverse operation of addition is subtraction, and the inverse operation of multiplication is division. In this section, we explore these concepts further by discussing inverse functions.

COMPOSITION OF FUNCTIONS

Many tasks in life are performed in *sequence*, such as putting on your socks and then your shoes. These types of situations also occur in mathematics. For example, suppose that we want to calculate the number of ounces in 3 tons. Because there are 2000 pounds in one ton, we might first multiply 3 by 2000 to obtain 6000 pounds. There are 16 ounces in a pound, so we could multiply 6000 by 16 to obtain 96,000 ounces. This particular calculation involves a *sequence* of calculations that can be represented by the diagram shown in Figure 9.1.

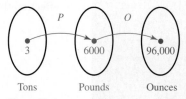

Tons   Pounds   Ounces

Figure 9.1

The results shown in Figure 9.1 can be calculated by using functions. Suppose that we let $P(x) = 2000x$ convert x tons to P pounds and also let $O(x) = 16x$ convert x pounds to O ounces. We can calculate the number of ounces in 3 tons by performing the *composition of O and P*. This method can be expressed symbolically as

$$(O \circ P)(3) = O\big(P(3)\big) \qquad \text{First compute } P(3).$$
$$= O(2000 \cdot 3) \qquad P(x) = 2000x$$
$$= O(6000) \qquad \text{Simplify.}$$
$$= 16(6000) \qquad O(x) = 16x$$
$$= 96,000. \qquad \text{Multiply.}$$

Note that the output for function P—namely, $P(3)$—becomes the input for function O. That is, we evaluate $O\big(P(3)\big)$ by calculating $P(3)$ first and then substituting the result of 6000 in function O.

COMPOSITION OF FUNCTIONS

If f and g are functions, then the **composite function** $g \circ f$, or **composition** of g and f, is defined by

$$(g \circ f)(x) = g\big(f(x)\big).$$

Note: We read $g\big(f(x)\big)$ as "g of f of x."

The compositions $g \circ f$ and $f \circ g$ represent evaluating functions f and g in a different order. When evaluating $g \circ f$, function f is performed first followed by function g, whereas for $f \circ g$ function g is performed first followed by function f. Note that in general $(g \circ f)(x) \neq (f \circ g)(x)$. That is, the order in which functions are applied makes a difference, the same way that putting on your socks and then your shoes is quite different from putting on your shoes and then your socks.

EXAMPLE 1   **Finding composite functions**

Evaluate $(g \circ f)(2)$ and then find a formula for $(g \circ f)(x)$.

(a) $f(x) = x^3, g(x) = 3x - 2$ **(b)** $f(x) = 5x, g(x) = x^2 - 3x + 1$

(c) $f(x) = \sqrt{2x}, g(x) = \dfrac{1}{x-1}$

Solution **(a)** $(g \circ f)(2) = g\big(f(2)\big)$ Composition of functions

$\qquad\qquad = g(8)$ $f(2) = 2^3 = 8$

$\qquad\qquad = 22$ $g(8) = 3(8) - 2 = 22$

Note that the output from f—namely, $f(2)$—becomes the input for g.

$(g \circ f)(x) = g\big(f(x)\big)$ Composition of functions

$\qquad\quad = g(x^3)$ $f(x) = x^3$

$\qquad\quad = 3x^3 - 2$ $g(x) = 3x - 2$

(b) $(g \circ f)(2) = g\big(f(2)\big)$ Composition of functions

$\qquad\qquad = g(10)$ $f(2) = 5(2) = 10$

$\qquad\qquad = 71$ $g(10) = 10^2 - 3(10) + 1 = 71$

$(g \circ f)(x) = g\big(f(x)\big)$ Composition of functions

$\qquad\quad = g(5x)$ $f(x) = 5x$

$\qquad\quad = (5x)^2 - 3(5x) + 1$ $g(x) = x^2 - 3x + 1$

$\qquad\quad = 25x^2 - 15x + 1$ Simplify.

(c) $(g \circ f)(2) = g\big(f(2)\big)$ Composition of functions

$\qquad\qquad = g(2)$ $f(2) = \sqrt{2(2)} = 2$

$\qquad\qquad = 1$ $g(2) = \dfrac{1}{2-1} = 1$

$(g \circ f)(x) = g\big(f(x)\big)$ Composition of functions

$\qquad\quad = g(\sqrt{2x})$ $f(x) = \sqrt{2x}$

$\qquad\quad = \dfrac{1}{\sqrt{2x} - 1}$ $g(x) = \dfrac{1}{x-1}$

Composite functions can be evaluated both numerically and graphically, as demonstrated in the next two examples.

EXAMPLE 2   Evaluating composite functions with tables

Use Tables 9.1 and 9.2 to evaluate each expression.
(a) $(f \circ g)(2)$ **(b)** $(g \circ f)(3)$ **(c)** $(f \circ f)(0)$

TABLE 9.1

x	0	1	2	3
$f(x)$	3	2	0	1

TABLE 9.2

x	0	1	2	3
$g(x)$	1	3	2	0

Solution   **(a)** $(f \circ g)(2) = f\big(g(2)\big)$ Composition of functions
$\qquad\qquad\quad = f(2)$ $g(2) = 2$
$\qquad\qquad\quad = 0$ $f(2) = 0$

(b) $(g \circ f)(3) = g\big(f(3)\big)$ Composition of functions
$\qquad\qquad\quad = g(1)$ $f(3) = 1$
$\qquad\qquad\quad = 3$ $g(1) = 3$

(c) $(f \circ f)(0) = f\big(f(0)\big)$ Composition of functions
$\qquad\qquad\quad = f(3)$ $f(0) = 3$
$\qquad\qquad\quad = 1$ $f(3) = 1$

EXAMPLE 3   Evaluating composite functions graphically

Use Figure 9.2 to evaluate $(g \circ f)(2)$.

TEACHING TIP

Numerical and graphical composition of functions gives students a better understanding of what composition is.

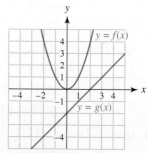

Figure 9.2

Solution   Because $(g \circ f)(2) = g\big(f(2)\big)$, start by using Figure 9.2 to evaluate $f(2)$. Figure 9.3(a) shows that $f(2) = 4$, which becomes the input for g. Figure 9.3(b) reveals that $g(4) = 2$. Thus

$$(g \circ f)(2) = g\big(f(2)\big) = g(4) = 2.$$

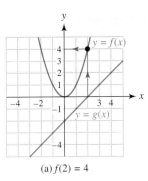

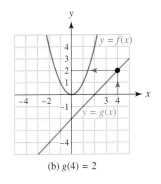

(a) $f(2) = 4$　　　　　　(b) $g(4) = 2$

Figure 9.3

ONE-TO-ONE FUNCTIONS

If we change the input for a function, does the output also change? Do *different inputs* always result in *different outputs* for every function? The answer is no. For example, if $f(x) = x^2 + 1$, then the inputs –2 and 2 result in the *same* output, 5. That is, $f(-2) = 5$ and $f(2) = 5$. However, for $g(x) = 2x$, *different inputs* always result in *different outputs*. Thus we say that g is a *one-to-one function*, whereas f is not.

ONE-TO-ONE FUNCTION
A function f is **one-to-one** if, for any c and d in the domain of f, $$c \neq d \quad \text{implies that} \quad f(c) \neq f(d).$$ That is, different inputs always result in different outputs.

One way to determine whether a function f is one-to-one is to look at its graph. Suppose that a function has two different inputs that result in the same output. Then there must be two points on its graph that have the same y-value but different x-values. For example, if $f(x) = 2x^2$, then $f(-1) = 2$ and $f(1) = 2$. Thus the points $(-1, 2)$ and $(1, 2)$ both lie on the graph of f, as shown in Figure 9.4(a). Two points with different x-values and the same y-value determine a horizontal line, as shown in Figure 9.4(b). This horizontal line intersects the graph of f more than once, indicating that different inputs do *not* always have different outputs. Thus $f(x) = 2x^2$ is *not* one-to-one.

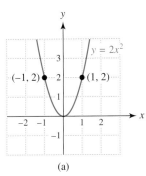

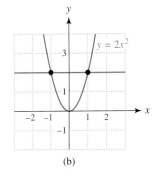

(a)　　　　　　(b)

Figure 9.4

This discussion motivates the **horizontal line test**.

TEACHING TIP

Review the difference between the vertical line test and the horizontal line test.

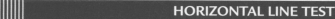

HORIZONTAL LINE TEST

If every horizontal line intersects the graph of a function f at most once, then f is a one-to-one function.

We apply the horizontal line test in the next example.

EXAMPLE 4   Using the horizontal line test

Determine whether each graph in Figure 9.5 represents a one-to-one function.

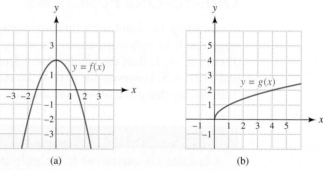

(a)   (b)

Figure 9.5

Solution   Figure 9.6(a) shows one of many horizontal lines that intersect the graph of $y = f(x)$ twice. Therefore function f is *not* one-to-one.

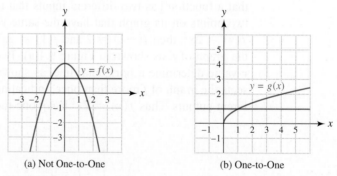

(a) Not One-to-One   (b) One-to-One

Figure 9.6

Figure 9.6(b) suggests that every horizontal line will intersect the graph of $y = g(x)$ *at most* once. Therefore function g is one-to-one.

INVERSE FUNCTIONS

Turning on a light and turning off a light are inverse operations from ordinary life. Inverse operations undo each other. In mathematics, adding **5** to x, and subtracting **5** from x are inverse operations because

$$x + 5 - 5 = x.$$

Similarly, multiplying x by **5** and dividing x by **5** are inverse operations because

$$\frac{5x}{5} = x.$$

In general, addition and subtraction are inverse operations and multiplication and division are inverse operations.

EXAMPLE 5   **Finding inverse operations**

State the inverse operations for each statement. Then write a function f for the given statement and a function g for its inverse operations.
(a) Divide x by 3.
(b) Cube x and then add 1 to the result.

Solution   **(a)** The inverse of dividing x by 3 is to *multiply x by 3*. Thus

$$f(x) = \frac{x}{3} \quad \text{and} \quad g(x) = 3x.$$

(b) When there is more than one operation, we must perform the inverse operations in *reverse order*. The inverse operations in reverse order are to subtract 1 from x and take the cube root of the result. Thus

$$f(x) = x^3 + 1 \quad \text{and} \quad g(x) = \sqrt[3]{x} - 1.$$

Functions f and g in Example 5 are examples of *inverse functions*. Note that, if $f(x) = \frac{x}{3}$ and $g(x) = 3x$, then

$$f(15) = 5 \quad \text{and} \quad g(5) = 15.$$

In general, if f and g are inverse functions, then $f(a) = b$ implies $g(b) = a$. Thus

$$(g \circ f)(a) = g(f(a)) = g(b) = a$$

for any a in the domain of f, whenever g and f are inverse functions. The composition of a function with its inverse leaves the input unchanged.

INVERSE FUNCTIONS

Let f be a one-to-one function. Then f^{-1} is the **inverse function** of f, if

$$(f^{-1} \circ f)(x) = f^{-1}(f(x)) = x, \quad \text{for every } x \text{ in the domain of } f, \quad \text{and}$$
$$(f \circ f^{-1})(x) = f(f^{-1}(x)) = x, \quad \text{for every } x \text{ in the domain of } f^{-1}.$$

Note: In the expression $f^{-1}(x)$, the -1 is *not* an exponent. That is, $f^{-1}(x) \neq \frac{1}{f(x)}$. Rather, if $f(x) = \frac{x}{3}$, then $f^{-1}(x) = 3x$ and, if $f(x) = x^3 + 1$, then $f^{-1}(x) = \sqrt[3]{x} - 1$.

EXAMPLE 6 Verifying inverses

Verify that $f^{-1}(x) = 3x$ if $f(x) = \frac{x}{3}$.

Solution We must show that $(f^{-1} \circ f)(x) = x$ and that $(f \circ f^{-1})(x) = x$.

$$(f^{-1} \circ f)(x) = f^{-1}\big(f(x)\big) \qquad \text{Composition of functions}$$

$$= f^{-1}\left(\frac{x}{3}\right) \qquad f(x) = \frac{x}{3}$$

$$= 3\left(\frac{x}{3}\right) \qquad f^{-1}(x) = 3x$$

$$= x \qquad \text{Simplify.}$$

$$(f \circ f^{-1})(x) = f\big(f^{-1}(x)\big) \qquad \text{Composition of functions}$$

$$= f(3x) \qquad f^{-1}(x) = 3x$$

$$= \frac{3x}{3} \qquad f(x) = \frac{x}{3}$$

$$= x \qquad \text{Simplify.}$$

The definition of inverse functions states that f must be a one-to-one function. To understand why, consider Figure 9.7. In Figure 9.7(a) a one-to-one function f is represented by a diagram. To find f^{-1} the arrows are reversed. For example, $f(1) = 3$ implies that $f^{-1}(3) = 1$, the arrow from 1 to 3 for f must be redrawn from 3 to 1 for f^{-1}.

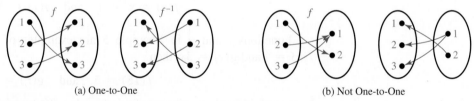

(a) One-to-One   (b) Not One-to-One

Figure 9.7

To be a *function* each input must correspond to exactly one output, which is the case in Figure 9.7(a). However, a different function f that is *not* a one-to-one function because inputs 2 and 3 both result in output 1 is shown is Figure 9.7(b). If the arrows for f are reversed to represent its inverse, then input 1 has two outputs, 2 and 3. Because no inverse *function* can satisfy both $f^{-1}(1) = 2$ and $f^{-1}(1) = 3$ at once, f^{-1} does not exist here.

The following steps can be used to find the inverse of a function symbolically.

FINDING AN INVERSE FUNCTION

To find f^{-1} for a one-to-one function f perform the following steps.

STEP 1: Let $y = f(x)$.

STEP 2: Interchange x and y.

STEP 3: Solve the formula for y. The resulting formula is $y = f^{-1}(x)$.

We apply these steps in the next example.

EXAMPLE 7   Finding an inverse function

Find the inverse of each one-to-one function.
(a) $f(x) = 3x - 7$ (b) $g(x) = (x + 2)^3$

Solution (a) **STEP 1:** Let $y = 3x - 7$.

STEP 2: Write the formula as $x = 3y - 7$.

STEP 3: To solve for y start by adding 7 to each side.

$$x + 7 = 3y \qquad \text{Add 7 to each side.}$$

$$\frac{x + 7}{3} = y \qquad \text{Divide each side by 3.}$$

Thus $f^{-1}(x) = \frac{x + 7}{3}$ or $f^{-1}(x) = \frac{1}{3}x + \frac{7}{3}$.

(b) **STEP 1:** Let $y = (x + 2)^3$.

STEP 2: Write the formula as $x = (y + 2)^3$.

STEP 3: To solve for y start by taking the cube root of each side.

$$\sqrt[3]{x} = y + 2 \qquad \text{Take cube root of each side.}$$

$$\sqrt[3]{x} - 2 = y \qquad \text{Subtract 2 from each side.}$$

Thus $g^{-1}(x) = \sqrt[3]{x} - 2$.

TABLES AND GRAPHS OF INVERSE FUNCTIONS

Inverse functions can be represented with tables and graphs. Table 9.3 shows a table of values for a function f.

TABLE 9.3

x	1	2	3	4	5
$f(x)$	3	6	9	12	15

Because $f(1) = 3$, $f^{-1}(3) = 1$. Similarly, $f(2) = 6$ implies that $f^{-1}(6) = 2$ and so on. Table 9.4 lists values for $f^{-1}(x)$.

TABLE 9.4

x	3	6	9	12	15
$f^{-1}(x)$	1	2	3	4	5

Note that the domain of f is $\{1, 2, 3, 4, 5\}$ and that the range of f is $\{3, 6, 9, 12, 15\}$, whereas the domain of f^{-1} is $\{3, 6, 9, 12, 15\}$ and the range of f^{-1} is $\{1, 2, 3, 4, 5\}$. *The domain of f is the range of f^{-1}, and the range of f is the domain of f^{-1}.* This statement is true in general for a function and its inverse.

If $f(a) = b$, then the point (a, b) lies on the graph of f. This statement also means that $f^{-1}(b) = a$ and that the point (b, a) lies on the graph of f^{-1}. These points are shown in Figure 9.8(a) with a blue line segment connecting them. The line $y = x$ is a perpendicular bisector of this line segment. As a result, the graph of f^{-1} can be obtained from the graph of f by reflecting the graph of f across the line $y = x$. For example, the graph of a function f and its inverse is shown in Figure 9.8(b).

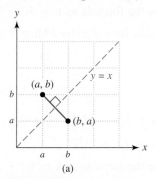

(a)

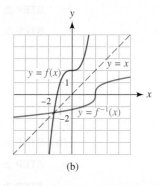

(b)

Figure 9.8

GRAPHS OF FUNCTIONS AND THEIR INVERSES

The graph of f^{-1} is a reflection of the graph of f across the line $y = x$.

EXAMPLE 8   Graphing an inverse function

The graph of $y = f(x)$ is shown in Figure 9.9.
(a) Sketch a graph of $y = f^{-1}(x)$.
(b) If $f(x) = 2x - 1$, find $f^{-1}(x)$ symbolically. Does this result agree with your graph?

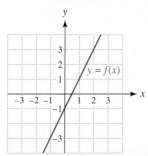

Figure 9.9

Solution   **(a)** The graph of $y = f^{-1}(x)$ is the reflection of the graph of $y = f(x)$ across the line $y = x$ and is shown in Figure 9.10.

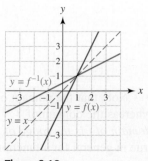

Figure 9.10

(b) Let $y = 2x - 1$ and interchange x and y to obtain $x = 2y - 1$. Solving for y gives $y = \frac{1}{2}x + \frac{1}{2}$. Thus $f^{-1}(x) = \frac{1}{2}x + \frac{1}{2}$, and its graph is a line with slope $\frac{1}{2}$ and y-intercept $\frac{1}{2}$. This result agrees with the graph of $y = f^{-1}(x)$ shown in Figure 9.10. ═════

9.1 PUTTING IT ALL TOGETHER

The following table summarizes some of the basic concepts about composite and inverse functions.

Concept	Explanation	Examples
Composite Functions	The composite of g and f is given by $$(g \circ f)(x) = g(f(x)),$$ and represents a *new* function whose name is $g \circ f$.	If $f(x) = 1 - 4x$ and $g(x) = x^3$, then $$(g \circ f)(x) = g(f(x))$$ $$= g(1 - 4x)$$ $$= (1 - 4x)^3.$$
One-to-One Functions	Function f is one-to-one if different inputs always give different outputs.	$f(x) = x^2$ is not one-to-one because $f(-4) = f(4) = 16$, whereas $g(x) = x + 1$ is one-to-one because, if two inputs differ, then adding 1 does not change this difference.
Horizontal Line Test	Used to determine whether a function is one-to-one from its graph	$f(x) = x^2$ is not one-to-one because a horizontal line can intersect its graph more than once.
Inverse Functions	f^{-1} will undo the operations performed by f. That is, $$(f^{-1} \circ f)(x) = x \quad \text{and}$$ $$(f \circ f^{-1})(x) = x.$$	If $f(x) = x^3$, then $f^{-1}(x) = \sqrt[3]{x}$ because cubing a number x and then taking its cube root results in the number x.

20.(a) −2
(b) 8
(c) $(g \circ f)(x) = (x + 3)^{3/2} - 3$
(d) $(f \circ g)(x) = \sqrt{x^3}$

9.1 EXERCISES

FOR EXTRA HELP

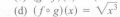

Student's Solutions Manual

 InterAct Math

 MathXL

 MyMathLab

Tutor Center   Math Tutor Center

Digital Video Tutor
CD 8   Videotape 10

19.(a) $\frac{11}{2}$
(b) $-\frac{1}{17}$
(c) $(g \circ f)(x) = 3 - \frac{5}{x}$
(d) $(f \circ g)(x) = \frac{1}{3 - 5x}$

CONCEPTS

1. $(g \circ f)(7) =$ _____ $g(f(7))$

2. $(f \circ g)(x) =$ _____ $f(g(x))$

3. Does $(f \circ g)(x)$ always equal $(g \circ f)(x)$? No

4. If a function f is one-to-one, then different _____ always result in different _____. inputs; outputs

5. If $f(3) = 5$ and $f(7) = 5$, then could f be one-to-one? No

6. If every horizontal line intersects the graph of f at most once, then f is _____. one-to-one

7. The inverse operation of subtracting 10 is _____. adding 10

8. $(f^{-1} \circ f)(7) =$ _____ 7

9. If $f(6) = 8$, then $f^{-1}(\underline{\quad}) =$ _____. 8; 6

10. If $f^{-1}(y) = x$, then $f(\underline{\quad}) =$ _____. x; y

11. For f to have an inverse function, f must be _____. one-to-one

12. The graph of f^{-1} is a _____ of the graph of f across the line _____. reflection; y = x

COMPOSITE FUNCTIONS

Exercises 13–22: For the given $f(x)$ and $g(x)$, find the following.

(a) $(g \circ f)(-2)$ *(b)* $(f \circ g)(4)$
(c) $(g \circ f)(x)$ *(d)* $(f \circ g)(x)$

13.(a) 7
(b) 49
(c) $(g \circ f)(x) = x^2 + 3$
(d) $(f \circ g)(x) = (x + 3)^2$

13. $f(x) = x^2$ $g(x) = x + 3$

14. $f(x) = 4x^2$ $g(x) = 5x$

14.(a) 80
(b) 1600
(c) $(g \circ f)(x) = 20x^2$
(d) $(f \circ g)(x) = 100x^2$

15. $f(x) = 2x$ $g(x) = x^3 - 1$

15.(a) −65
(b) 126
(c) $(g \circ f)(x) = 8x^3 - 1$
(d) $(f \circ g)(x) = 2x^3 - 2$

16. $f(x) = 3x + 1$ $g(x) = x^2 + 4x$

17. $f(x) = \frac{1}{2}x$ $g(x) = |x - 2|$

17.(a) 3   (b) 1
(c) $(g \circ f)(x) = \left|\frac{1}{2}x - 2\right|$
(d) $(f \circ g)(x) = \frac{1}{2}|x - 2|$

18. $f(x) = 6x$ $g(x) = \frac{2}{x - 5}$

16.(a) 5   (b) 97
(c) $(g \circ f)(x) = 9x^2 + 18x + 5$
(d) $(f \circ g)(x) = 3x^2 + 12x + 1$

19. $f(x) = \frac{1}{x}$ $g(x) = 3 - 5x$

22.(a) $-\frac{107}{18}$
(b) $\frac{47}{4}$
(c) $(g \circ f)(x) = 3x - \frac{1}{9x}$
(d) $(f \circ g)(x) = 3x - \frac{1}{x}$

20. $f(x) = \sqrt{x + 3}$ $g(x) = x^3 - 3$

21. $f(x) = 2x$ $g(x) = 4x^2 - 2x + 5$

22. $f(x) = 9x - \frac{1}{3x}$ $g(x) = \frac{x}{3}$

21.(a) 77   (b) 122
(c) $(g \circ f)(x) = 16x^2 - 4x + 5$
(d) $(f \circ g)(x) = 8x^2 - 4x + 10$

Exercises 23–28: Use the tables to evaluate the given expression.

x	−2	−1	0	1	2
$f(x)$	2	1	0	−1	−2

x	−2	−1	0	1	2
$g(x)$	0	1	−1	2	−2

23. (a) $(f \circ g)(0)$ 1   **(b)** $(g \circ f)(-1)$ 2

24. (a) $(f \circ g)(1)$ −2   **(b)** $(g \circ f)(-2)$ −2

25. (a) $(f \circ f)(-1)$ −1   **(b)** $(g \circ g)(0)$ 1

26. (a) $(g \circ g)(2)$ 0   **(b)** $(f \circ f)(1)$ 1

27. (a) $(f^{-1} \circ g)(-2)$ 0   **(b)** $(g^{-1} \circ f)(2)$ 2

28. (a) $(f \circ g^{-1})(1)$ 1   **(b)** $(g \circ f^{-1})(-2)$ −2

Exercises 29–30: Use the graph to evaluate each expression.

29. (a) $(f \circ g)(0)$ 2
(b) $(g \circ f)(1)$ −3
(c) $(f \circ f)(-1)$ −1

18.(a) $-\frac{2}{17}$
(b) −12
(c) $(g \circ f)(x) = \frac{2}{6x - 5}$
(d) $(f \circ g)(x) = \frac{12}{x - 5}$

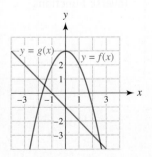

30. (a) $(f \circ g)(1)$ 4
(b) $(g \circ f)(-2)$ −3
(c) $(g \circ g)(-2)$ 0

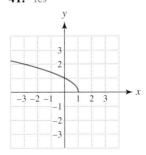

41. Yes

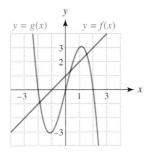

42. No

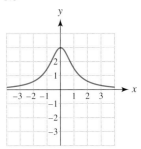

Exercises 31–36: Show that f is not one-to-one by finding two inputs that result in the same output. Answers may vary.

31. $f(x) = 5x^2$
$f(1) = f(-1) = 5$

32. $f(x) = 4 - x^2$
$f(2) = f(-2) = 0$

33. $f(x) = x^4 + 100$
$f(1) = f(-1) = 101$

34. $f(x) = \dfrac{x^2}{x^2 + 1}$
$f(3) = f(-3) = \frac{9}{10}$

35. $f(x) = x^4 - 3x^2$
$f(2) = f(-2) = 4$

36. $f(x) = \sqrt{x^2 - 1}$
$f(1) = f(-1) = 0$

Exercises 37–42: Use the horizontal line test to determine whether the graph represents a one-to-one function.

37. Yes

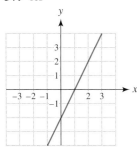

38. Yes

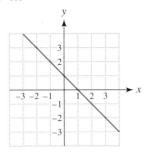

39. No

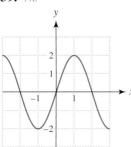

40. No

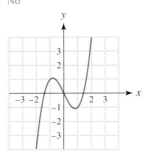

Exercises 43–50: (Refer to Example 5.) Give the inverse operation for the statement. Then write a function f for the given statement and a function g for its inverse.

43. Multiply x by 7.   Divide x by 7; $f(x) = 7x$; $g(x) = \dfrac{x}{7}$

44. Subtract 10 from x.   Add 10 to x; $f(x) = x - 10$; $g(x) = x + 10$

45. Add 5 to x and then divide the result by 2.

46. Multiply x by 6 and then add 8 to the result.

47. Multiply x by $\frac{1}{2}$ and then subtract 3 from the result.
Add 3 to x and multiply the result by 2; $f(x) = \frac{1}{2}x - 3$; $g(x) = 2(x + 3)$

48. Divide x by 10 and then add 20 to the result.

49. Cube the sum of x and 5.
Take the cube root of x and subtract 5; $f(x) = (x + 5)^3$; $g(x) = \sqrt[3]{x} - 5$

50. Take the cube root of x and then subtract 2.
Cube the sum of x and 2; $f(x) = \sqrt[3]{x} - 2$; $g(x) = (x + 2)^3$

Exercises 51–58: (Refer to Example 6.) Verify that $f(x)$ and $f^{-1}(x)$ are indeed inverse functions. *

51. $f(x) = 4x$ $f^{-1}(x) = \dfrac{x}{4}$

52. $f(x) = \dfrac{2x}{3}$ $f^{-1}(x) = \dfrac{3x}{2}$

53. $f(x) = 3x + 5$ $f^{-1}(x) = \dfrac{x - 5}{3}$

54. $f(x) = x + 7$ $f^{-1}(x) = x - 7$

55. $f(x) = x^3$ $f^{-1}(x) = \sqrt[3]{x}$

56. $f(x) = \sqrt[3]{x - 4}$ $f^{-1}(x) = x^3 + 4$

57. $f(x) = \dfrac{1}{x}$ $f^{-1}(x) = \dfrac{1}{x}$

58. $f(x) = \dfrac{x + 7}{7}$ $f^{-1}(x) = 7x - 7$

45. Multiply x by 2 then subtract 5;
$f(x) = \dfrac{x + 5}{2}$; $g(x) = 2x - 5$

46. Subtract 8 from x and divide the result by 6;
$f(x) = 6x + 8$; $g(x) = \dfrac{x - 8}{6}$

48. Subtract 20 from x and multiply the result by 10;
$f(x) = \dfrac{x}{10} + 20$; $g(x) = 10(x - 20)$

*Answers on page IA-28

59. $f^{-1}(x) = \dfrac{x}{12}$ 63. $f^{-1}(x) = \dfrac{x+2}{5}$ 64. $f^{-1}(x) = \dfrac{x-4}{3}$

Exercises 59–74: (Refer to Example 7.) Find $f^{-1}(x)$.

59. $f(x) = 12x$

60. $f(x) = \frac{3}{4}x$ $f^{-1}(x) = \frac{4}{3}x$

61. $f(x) = x + 8$
$f^{-1}(x) = x - 8$

62. $f(x) = x - 3$
$f^{-1}(x) = x + 3$

63. $f(x) = 5x - 2$

64. $f(x) = 3x + 4$

65. $f(x) = -\frac{1}{2}x + 1$
$f^{-1}(x) = -2(x - 1)$

66. $f(x) = \frac{3}{4}x - \frac{1}{4}$
$f^{-1}(x) = \frac{4}{3}\left(x + \frac{1}{4}\right)$

67. $f(x) = 8 - x$
$f^{-1}(x) = 8 - x$

68. $f(x) = 5 - x$
$f^{-1}(x) = 5 - x$

69. $f(x) = \dfrac{x + 1}{2}$
$f^{-1}(x) = 2x - 1$

70. $f(x) = \dfrac{3 - x}{5}$
$f^{-1}(x) = 3 - 5x$

71. $f(x) = \sqrt[3]{2x}$
$f^{-1}(x) = \dfrac{x^3}{2}$

72. $f(x) = \sqrt[3]{x + 4}$
$f^{-1}(x) = x^3 - 4$

73. $f(x) = x^3 - 8$
$f^{-1}(x) = \sqrt[3]{x + 8}$

74. $f(x) = (x - 5)^3$
$f^{-1}(x) = \sqrt[3]{x} + 5$

Exercises 75–78: Use the table to make a table of values for $f^{-1}(x)$.* State the domain and range for f and for f^{-1}.

75.

x	0	1	2	3	4
$f(x)$	0	5	10	15	20

76.

x	−4	−2	0	2	4
$f(x)$	1	2	3	4	5

77.

x	−5	0	5	10	15
$f(x)$	4	2	0	−2	−4

78.

x	0	2	4	6	8
$f(x)$	8	6	4	2	0

Exercises 79–82: (Refer to Example 8.) Use the graph of $y = f(x)$ to sketch a graph of $f^{-1}(x)$. Include the graph of f and the line $y = x$ in your graph.*

79.

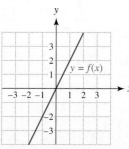

80.

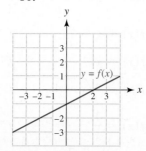

81.

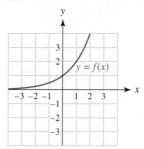

82.

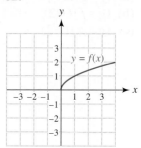

77. Domain of f = range of f^{-1} = $\{-5, 0, 5, 10, 15\}$
Range of f = domain of f^{-1} = $\{-4, -2, 0, 2, 4\}$

78. Domain of f = range of f^{-1} = $\{0, 2, 4, 6, 8\}$
Range of f = domain of f^{-1} = $\{0, 2, 4, 6, 8\}$

APPLICATIONS

83. *Circular Wave*   A stone is dropped in a lake, creating a circular wave. The radius r of the wave in feet after t seconds is $r(t) = 2t$.
   (a) Its circumference C is given by $C(r) = 2\pi r$. Evaluate $(C \circ r)(5)$ and interpret your result.
   (b) Find $(C \circ r)(t)$. $(C \circ r)(t) = 4\pi t$

(a) 20π; after 5 sec, the wave has a circumference of $20\pi \approx 62.8$ ft.

84. *Volume of a Balloon*   The volume V of a spherical balloon with radius r is given by $V(r) = \frac{4}{3}\pi r^3$. Suppose that the balloon is being inflated so that the radius in inches after t seconds is $r(t) = \sqrt[3]{t}$.
   (a) Evaluate $(V \circ r)(3)$ and interpret your result.
   (b) Find $(V \circ r)(t)$. $(V \circ r)(t) = \frac{4}{3}\pi t$

(a) 4π; after 3 sec, the balloon has a volume of $4\pi \approx 12.6$ in^3.

85. *Temperature and Mosquitoes*   Temperature can affect the number of mosquitoes observed on a summer night. Graphs of two functions, T and M, are shown. Function T calculates the temperature on a summer evening h hours past midnight, and M calculates the number of mosquitoes observed per 100 square feet when the outside temperature is T.

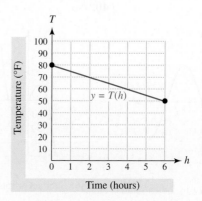

75. Domain of f = range of f^{-1} = $\{0, 1, 2, 3, 4\}$
Range of f = domain of f^{-1} = $\{0, 5, 10, 15, 20\}$

76. Domain of f = range of f^{-1} = $\{-4, -2, 0, 2, 4\}$
Range of f = domain of f^{-1} = $\{1, 2, 3, 4, 5\}$

*Answers on page IA-28

85.(b) 150; 1 hr after midnight there are 150 mosquitoes per 100 sq ft.
  (c) The number of mosquitoes per 100 sq ft, *h* hr after midnight

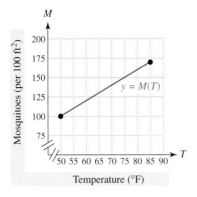

(a) Find $T(1)$ and $M(75)$. 75°; 150
(b) Evaluate $(M \circ T)(1)$ and interpret your result.
(c) What does $(M \circ T)(h)$ calculate?
(d) Find equations for the lines in each graph.
(e) Use your answers from part (d) to write a formula for $(M \circ T)(h)$. $(M \circ T)(h) = -10h + 160$
   (d) $T(h) = -5h + 80$; $M(T) = 2T$

86. Skin Cancer and Ozone Ozone in the stratosphere filters out most of the harmful ultraviolet (UV) rays from the sun. However, depletion of the ozone layer is affecting this protection. The formula $U(x) = 1.5x$ calculates the percent increase in UV radiation for an *x* percent decrease in the thickness of the ozone layer. The formula $C(x) = 3.5x$ calculates the percent increase in skin cancer cases when the UV radiation increases by *x* percent. (**Source:** R. Turner, D. Pierce, and I. Bateman, *Environmental Economics*.) *
(a) Evaluate $U(2)$ and $C(3)$ and interpret each result.
(b) Find $(C \circ U)(2)$ and interpret the result.
(c) Find $(C \circ U)(x)$. What does this formula calculate?

87. College Degree The table lists the percentage *P* of people 25 or older completing 4 or more years of college during year *x*.

x	1960	1980	2000
P(x)	8	16	27

Source: Bureau of the Census.

(a) Evaluate $P(1980)$ and interpret the results.
(b) Make a table for $P^{-1}(x)$. *
(c) Evaluate $P^{-1}(16)$. 1980

87.(a) 16; in 1980, 16% of people 25 or older completed 4 or more years of college.

89.(b) $f^{-1}(x) = \frac{9}{5}(x - 32)$ converts *x* degrees Fahrenheit to an equivalent temperature in degrees Celsius.

88. High School Grades The table lists the percentage of college freshmen with a high school grade average of A or A– during year *x*.

x	1970	1980	1990	2000
P(x)	20	26	29	43

Source: Department of Education.

(a) Evaluate $P(1970)$ and interpret the results.
(b) Make a table for $P^{-1}(x)$. * (a) 20; in 1970, 20% of college freshmen had a high school grade average of A or A–.
(c) Evaluate $P^{-1}(43)$. 2000

89. Temperature The function given by $f(x) = \frac{5}{9}x + 32$ converts *x* degrees Celsius to an equivalent temperature in degrees Fahrenheit.
(a) Is *f* a one-to-one function? Why or why not?
(b) Find a formula for f^{-1} and interpret what it calculates. 89. (a) Yes; different inputs result in different outputs.

90.(a) Yes; different inputs result in different outputs.
90. Feet and Yards The function given by $f(x) = 3x$ converts *x* yards to feet.
(a) Is *f* a one-to-one function? Why or why not?
(b) Find a formula for f^{-1} and interpret what it calculates. $f^{-1}(x) = \frac{x}{3}$ converts *x* ft to yd.

91. Quarts and Gallons Write a function *f* that converts *x* gallons to quarts. Then find a formula for $f^{-1}(x)$ and interpret what it computes.
   $f(x) = 4x$; $f^{-1}(x) = \frac{x}{4}$ converts *x* qt to gal.
92. One-to-One Function The table lists monthly average wind speeds at Hilo, Hawaii, in miles per hour from July through December, where *x* is the month.

x	July	Aug	Sept	Oct	Nov	Dec
f(x)	7	7	7	7	7	7

92.(a) No; different inputs have the same outputs.
(a) Is function *f* one-to-one? Explain.
(b) Does f^{-1} exist? No
(c) What happens if you try to make a table for f^{-1}?
(d) Could *f* be one-to-one if it were computed at a different location? What would have to be true about the monthly average wind speeds?
(c) Input 7 has several different outputs.

(d) Yes; the wind speed each month would have to be unique.
WRITING ABOUT MATHEMATICS

93. Explain the difference between $(g \circ f)(2)$ and $(f \circ g)(2)$. Are they always equal? If *f* and *g* are inverse functions, what are the values of $(g \circ f)(2)$ and $(f \circ g)(2)$?

94. Explain what it means for a function to be one-to-one.

*Answers on page IA-29

9.2 EXPONENTIAL FUNCTIONS

Basic Concepts · Graphs of Exponential Functions ·
Models Involving Exponential Functions · The Natural Exponential Function

INTRODUCTION

Many times the growth of a quantity depends on the amount or number present. The more money deposited in an account, the more interest the account earns; that is, the interest earned is proportional to the amount of money in an account. For example, if a person has $100 in an account and receives 10% annual interest, the interest accrued the first year will be $10, and the balance in the account will be $110 at the end of 1 year. Similarly, if a person begins with $1000 in a similar account, the balance in the account will be $1100 at the end of 1 year. This type of growth is called *exponential growth* and can be modeled by an *exponential function*.

BASIC CONCEPTS

Suppose that an insect population doubles each week. Table 9.5 shows the populations after *x* weeks. Note that, as the population of insects becomes larger, the *increase* in population each week becomes greater. The population is increasing by 100%, or doubling numerically, each week. When a quantity increases by a constant percentage (or constant factor) at regular intervals, its growth is exponential.

TABLE 9.5

Week	0	1	2	3	4	5
Population	100	200	400	800	1600	3200

We can model the data in Table 9.5 by using the exponential function

$$f(x) = 100(2)^x.$$

For example,

$$f(0) = 100(2)^0 = 100 \cdot 1 = 100,$$
$$f(1) = 100(2)^1 = 100 \cdot 2 = 200,$$
$$f(2) = 100(2)^2 = 100 \cdot 4 = 400,$$

and so on. Note that the exponential function *f* has a *variable as an exponent*.

EXPONENTIAL FUNCTION

A function represented by

$$f(x) = Ca^x, \quad a > 0 \quad \text{and} \quad a \neq 1,$$

is an **exponential function with base *a* and coefficient *C*.** (Unless stated otherwise, assume that $C > 0$.)

In the formula $f(x) = Ca^x$, a is called the **growth factor** when $a > 1$ and the **decay factor** when $0 < a < 1$. For an exponential function, each time x increases by 1 unit $f(x)$ increases by a *factor* of a when $a > 1$ and decreases by a factor of a when $0 < a < 1$. Moreover, as

$$f(0) = Ca^0 = C(1) = C,$$

the value of C equals the value of $f(x)$ when $x = 0$. If x represents time, C represents the initial value of f when time equals 0. Figure 9.11 illustrates **exponential growth** and **exponential decay** for $x > 0$.

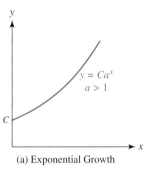

(a) Exponential Growth   (b) Exponential Decay

Figure 9.11

The set of valid inputs (domain) for an exponential function includes all real numbers. The set of corresponding outputs (range) includes all positive real numbers.

In the next example we evaluate some exponential functions. When evaluating an exponential function, we evaluate a^x before multiplying by C. This standard order of precedence is much like doing multiplication before addition. For example, $2(3)^2$ should be evaluated as

$$2(9) = 18 \quad not \text{ as} \quad (6)^2 = 36.$$

EXAMPLE 1   Evaluating exponential functions

Evaluate $f(x)$ for the given value of x.

(a) $f(x) = 10(3)^x \qquad x = 2$ **(b)** $f(x) = 5\left(\frac{1}{2}\right)^x \qquad x = 3$

(c) $f(x) = \frac{1}{3}(2)^x \qquad x = -1$

Solution **(a)** $f(2) = 10(3)^2 = 10 \cdot 9 = 90$

(b) $f(3) = 5\left(\frac{1}{2}\right)^3 = 5 \cdot \frac{1}{8} = \frac{5}{8}$

(c) $f(-1) = \frac{1}{3}(2)^{-1} = \frac{1}{3} \cdot \frac{1}{2} = \frac{1}{6}$

═══════════════════════ MAKING CONNECTIONS ═══════════════════════

The Expressions a^{-x} and $\left(\frac{1}{a}\right)^x$

Using properties of exponents, we can write 2^{-x} as

$$2^{-x} = \frac{1}{2^x} = \left(\frac{1}{2}\right)^x.$$

In general, the expressions a^{-x} and $\left(\frac{1}{a}\right)^x$ are equal.

In the next example, we determine whether a function is linear or exponential.

EXAMPLE 2   Finding linear and exponential functions

Use each table to determine whether f is a linear or an exponential function. Find a formula for f.

(a)

x	0	1	2	3	4
$f(x)$	16	8	4	2	1

(b)

x	0	1	2	3	4
$f(x)$	5	7	9	11	13

(c)

x	0	1	2	3	4
$f(x)$	1	3	9	27	81

Solution
(a) Each time x increases by 1 unit, $f(x)$ decreases by a factor of $\frac{1}{2}$. Therefore f is an exponential function with a decay factor of $\frac{1}{2}$. Because $f(0) = 16$, $C = 16$ and so $f(x) = 16\left(\frac{1}{2}\right)^x$. This expression can also be written as $f(x) = 16(2)^{-x}$.

(b) Each time x increases by 1 unit, $f(x)$ increases by 2 units. Therefore f is a linear function, and the slope of its graph equals 2. The y-intercept is 5, so $f(x) = 2x + 5$.

(c) Each time x increases by 1 unit, $f(x)$ increases by a factor of 3. Therefore f is an exponential function with a growth factor of 3. Because $f(0) = 1$, $C = 1$ and so $f(x) = 1(3)^x$, or $f(x) = 3^x$.

═══ MAKING CONNECTIONS ═══

Linear and Exponential Functions

For a *linear function*, given by $f(x) = ax + b$, each time x increases by 1 unit y increases (or decreases) by a units, where a equals the slope of the graph of f.

For an *exponential function*, given by $f(x) = Ca^x$, each time x increases by 1 unit y increases by a factor of a when $a > 1$ and decreases by a factor of a when $0 < a < 1$. The constant a equals either the growth factor or the decay factor.

If $100 are deposited in a savings account paying 10% annual interest, the interest earned after 1 year equals $100 \times 0.10 = 10. The total amount of money in the account after 1 year is $100(1 + 0.10) = 110. Each year the money in the account increases by a factor of 1.10, so after x years there will be $100(1.10)^x$ dollars in the account. Thus compound interest is an example of exponential growth.

▌▌▌▌   COMPOUND INTEREST

If C dollars are deposited in an account and if interest is paid at the end of each year with an annual rate of interest r, expressed in decimal form, then after x years the account will contain A dollars, where

$$A = C(1 + r)^x.$$

The growth factor is $(1 + r)$.

Note: The compound interest formula takes the form of an exponential function with

$$a = 1 + r.$$

EXAMPLE 3 | Calculating compound interest

A 20-year-old worker deposits $2000 in a retirement account that pays 13% annual interest at the end of each year. How much money will be in the account when the worker is 65 years old? What is the growth factor?

Solution Here, $C = 2000$, $r = 0.13$, and $x = 45$. The amount in the account after 45 years is

$$A = 2000(1 + 0.13)^{45} \approx \$489{,}282.80,$$

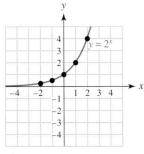

```
2000(1+.13)^45
          489282.8038
```

Figure 9.12

which is supported by Figure 9.12. In this dramatic example of exponential growth, $2000 grows to nearly half a million dollars in 45 years. Each year the amount of money on deposit is multiplied by a factor of $(1 + 0.13)$, so the growth factor is 1.13.

GRAPHS OF EXPONENTIAL FUNCTIONS

We can graph $f(x) = 2^x$ by first plotting some points, as in Table 9.6.

TABLE 9.6

x	-2	-1	0	1	2
2^x	$\frac{1}{4}$	$\frac{1}{2}$	1	2	4

Figure 9.13

If we plot these points and sketch the graph, we obtain Figure 9.13. Note that, for negative values of x, $0 < 2^x < 1$ and that, for positive values of x, $2^x > 1$. The graph of $y = 2^x$ passes through the point $(0, 1)$, never intersects the x-axis, and always lies above the x-axis.

We can investigate the graphs of exponential functions further by graphing $y = 1.3^x$, $y = 1.7^x$, and $y = 2.5^x$ (see Figure 9.14). For $a > 1$ the graph of $y = a^x$ *increases* at a faster rate for larger values of a. We now graph $y = 0.7^x$, $y = 0.5^x$, and $y = 0.15^x$ (see Figure 9.15). Note that, if $0 < a < 1$, the graph of $y = a^x$ *decreases* more rapidly for smaller values of a. The graph of $y = a^x$ is *increasing* when $a > 1$ and *decreasing* when $0 < a < 1$ (from left to right).

Critical Thinking

Every graph of $y = a^x$ passes through what point? Why?

The point $(0, 1)$ because any nonzero base raised to the power 0 equals 1.

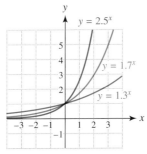

Figure 9.14

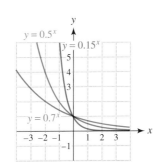

Figure 9.15

In the next example we show the dramatic difference between the outputs of linear and exponential functions.

EXAMPLE 4   **Comparing exponential and linear functions**

Compare $f(x) = 3^x$ and $g(x) = 3x$ graphically and numerically for $x \geq 0$.

Solution   *Graphical Comparison*   The graphs of $Y_1 = 3^X$ and $Y_2 = 3X$ are shown in Figure 9.16. The graph of the exponential function y_1 increases much faster than the graph of the linear function y_2.

Numerical Comparison   The tables of $Y_1 = 3^X$ and $Y_2 = 3X$ are shown in Figure 9.17. The values for y_1 increase much faster than the values for y_2.

[0, 5, 1] by [0, 120, 20]

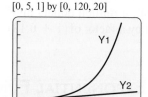

Figure 9.16

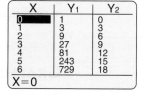

Figure 9.17

The results of Example 4 are true in general: For large enough inputs, exponential functions with $a > 1$ grow far faster than any linear function.

═══ MAKING CONNECTIONS ═══

Exponential and Polynomial Functions

The function $f(x) = 2^x$ is an exponential function. The base 2 is a constant and the exponent x is a variable, so $f(3) = 2^3 = 8$.

The function $g(x) = x^2$ is a polynomial function. The base x is a variable and the exponent 2 is a constant, so $g(3) = 3^2 = 9$.

The table clearly shows that the exponential function grows much faster than the polynomial function for larger values of x.

x	0	2	4	6	8	10	12
2^x	1	4	16	64	256	1024	4096
x^2	0	4	16	36	64	100	144

MODELS INVOLVING EXPONENTIAL FUNCTIONS

Traffic flow on highways can be modeled by exponential functions whenever traffic patterns occur randomly. In the next example we model traffic at an intersection by using an exponential function.

EXAMPLE 5   **Modeling traffic flow**

On average, a particular intersection has 360 vehicles arriving randomly each hour. Highway engineers use $f(x) = (0.905)^x$ to estimate the likelihood, or probability, that no

vehicle will enter the intersection within a period of x seconds.   (***Source:*** F. Mannering and
W. Kilareski, *Principles of Highway Engineering and Traffic Analysis.*)
(a) Compute $f(5)$ and interpret the results.
(b) A graph of $y = f(x)$ is shown in Figure 9.18. Discuss this graph.

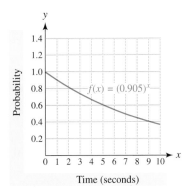

Figure 9.18

(c) Is this function an example of exponential growth or decay?

Solution   **(a)** The result $f(5) = (0.905)^5 \approx 0.61$ indicates that there is a 61% chance that no vehicle
will enter the intersection during any particular 5-second interval.
(b) As the number of seconds increases, there is less chance that no car will enter the intersection.
(c) Because the graph is decreasing and $a = 0.905 < 1$, this function is an example of
exponential decay.

In the next example, we use an exponential function to model how trees grow in a forest.

EXAMPLE 6   Modeling tree density in a forest

Ecologists studied the spacing of individual trees in a British Columbia forest. This pine forest was 40 to 50 years old and contained approximately 1600 randomly spaced trees per
acre. The probability or likelihood that no tree is located within a circle of radius x feet can
be estimated by $P(x) = (0.892)^x$. For example, $P(4) \approx 0.63$ means that, if a person picks a
point at random in the forest, there is a 63% chance that no tree will be located within 4 feet
of the person.   (***Source:*** E. Pielou, *Populations and Community Ecology.*)
(a) Evaluate $P(8)$ and interpret the result.
(b) Graph P in [0, 20, 5] by [0, 1, 0.1] and discuss the graph.

Solution   **(a)** The probability $P(8) = (0.892)^8 \approx 0.40$ means that there is a 40% chance that no tree
is growing within a circle of radius 8 feet.
(b) The graph of $Y_1 = 0.892^\wedge X$, as shown in Figure 9.19, indicates that the larger the circle, the less the likelihood is of no tree being inside the circle.

[0, 20, 5] by [0, 1, 0.1]

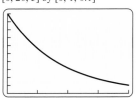

Figure 9.19

The Natural Exponential Function

A special type of exponential function is called the *natural exponential function*, $f(x) = e^x$. The base e is a special number in mathematics similar to π. The number π is approximately 3.14, whereas the number e is approximately 2.72. The number e is named for the great Swiss mathematician, Leonhard Euler (1707–1783). Most calculators have a special key that can be used to compute the natural exponential function.

TEACHING TIP

You may want to discuss how to evaluate the natural exponential function with a calculator.

NATURAL EXPONENTIAL FUNCTION

The function represented by

$$f(x) = e^x$$

is the **natural exponential function**, where $e \approx 2.71828$.

This function is frequently used to model **continuous growth**. For example, the fact that births and deaths occur throughout the year, not just at one time during the year, must be recognized when population growth is being modeled. If a population P is growing continuously at r percent per year, expressed as a decimal, we can model this population after x years by

$$P = Ce^{rx},$$

where C is the initial population. To evaluate natural exponential functions, we use a calculator, as in the next example.

EXAMPLE 7   Modeling population

In 1994 Florida's population was 14 million people and was growing at a continuous rate of 1.53%. This population in millions x years after 1994 could be modeled by

$$f(x) = 14e^{0.0153x}.$$

Estimate the population in 2002.

Calculator Help
To evaluate the natural exponential function, see the Appendix (page AP-1).

Solution   As 2002 is 8 years after 1994, we evaluate $f(8)$ and obtain

$$f(8) = 14e^{0.0153(8)} \approx 15.8,$$

which is supported by Figure 9.20. (Be sure to include parentheses around the exponent of e.) This model estimates that the population of Florida was about 15.8 million in 2002.

```
14e^(.0153*8)
      15.82288531
```

Figure 9.20

Critical Thinking

Sketch a graph of $y = 2^x$ and $y = 3^x$ in the same xy-plane. Then use these two graphs to sketch a graph of $y = e^x$. How do these graphs compare?

The graph of $y = e^x$ lies between the graphs of $y = 2^x$ and $y = 3^x$. It is closer to the graph of $y = 3^x$.

PUTTING IT ALL TOGETHER

The following table summarizes some important concepts of exponential functions and compound interest.

Topic	Explanation	Example
Exponential Function	An exponential function can be written as $f(x) = Ca^x$, where $a > 0$ and $a \neq 1$. If $a > 1$, the function models exponential growth, and if $0 < a < 1$, the function models exponential decay. The natural exponential function has $C = 1$ and $a = e \approx 2.71828$; that is, $f(x) = e^x$.	$f(x) = 3(2)^x$ models exponential growth and $g(x) = 2\left(\frac{1}{3}\right)^x$ models exponential decay.
Compound Interest	If C dollars are deposited in an account and if interest is paid at the end of each year with an annual rate of interest r, expressed as a decimal, then after x years the account will contain A dollars, where $$A = C(1 + r)^x.$$ The growth factor is $(1 + r)$.	If $1000 are deposited in an account paying 5% annual interest, then after 6 years the amount A in the account is $$A = 1000(1 + 0.05)^6 \approx \$1340.10.$$

9.2 EXERCISES

FOR EXTRA HELP

Student's Solutions Manual

MyMathLab

InterAct Math

Math Tutor Center

MathXL

Digital Video Tutor
CD 8   Videotape 10

CONCEPTS

1. Give a general formula for an exponential function f.
   $f(x) = Ca^x$

2. Sketch a graph of an exponential function that illustrates exponential decay.*   Answers may vary.

3. Does the graph of $f(x) = a^x$, $a > 1$, illustrate exponential growth or decay?   Growth

4. Evaluate the expressions 2^x and x^2 for $x = 5$.   32; 25

5. Give an approximate value for e to the nearest thousandth.   2.718

6. Evaluate e^2 and π^2 using your calculator.
   7.389; 9.870 (approximately)

7. If a quantity y grows exponentially, then for each unit increase in x, y increases by a constant _____.   factor

8. If $f(x) = 1.5^x$ what is the growth factor?   1.5

EVALUATING AND GRAPHING EXPONENTIAL FUNCTIONS

Exercises 9–20: Evaluate the exponential function for the given values of x by hand when possible. Approximate answers to the nearest hundredth when appropriate.

9. $f(x) = 3^x$ $x = -2, x = 2$ $\frac{1}{9}$; 9

10. $f(x) = 5^x$ $x = -1, x = 3$ $\frac{1}{5}$; 125

*Answer on page IA-29

11. $f(x) = 5(2^x)$ $\qquad x = 0, x = 5$ 5; 160

12. $f(x) = 3(7^x)$ $\qquad x = -2, x = 0$ $\frac{3}{49}$; 3

13. $f(x) = \left(\frac{1}{2}\right)^x$ $\qquad x = -2, x = 3$ 4; $\frac{1}{8}$

14. $f(x) = \left(\frac{1}{4}\right)^x$ $\qquad x = 0, x = 2$ 1; $\frac{1}{16}$

15. $f(x) = 5(3)^{-x}$ $\qquad x = -1, x = 2$ 15; $\frac{5}{9}$

16. $f(x) = 4\left(\frac{3}{7}\right)^x$ $\qquad x = 1, x = 4$ $\frac{12}{7}$; $\frac{324}{2401}$

17. $f(x) = 1.8^x$ $\qquad x = -3, x = 1.5$ 0.17; 2.41

18. $f(x) = 0.91^x$ $\qquad x = 5.1, x = 10$ 0.62; 0.39

19. $f(x) = 3(0.6)^x$ $\qquad x = -1, x = 2$ 5; 1.08

20. $f(x) = 5(4.5)^{-x}$ $\qquad x = -2.1, x = 5.9$
117.68; 7.00×10^{-4}

Exercises 21–26: (Refer to Example 2.) A table for a function f is given.
  (a) *Determine whether f represents exponential growth, exponential decay, or linear growth.*
  (b) *Find a formula for f.*

21.

x	0	1	2	3	4
$f(x)$	64	16	4	1	$\frac{1}{4}$

(a) Exponential decay
(b) $f(x) = 64\left(\frac{1}{4}\right)^x$

22.

x	0	1	2	3	4
$f(x)$	$\frac{1}{2}$	1	2	4	8

(a) Exponential growth
(b) $f(x) = \frac{1}{2}(2)^x$

23.

x	0	1	2	3	4
$f(x)$	8	11	14	17	20

(a) Linear growth
(b) $f(x) = 3x + 8$

24.

x	-2	-1	0	1	2
$f(x)$	4	2	1	$\frac{1}{2}$	$\frac{1}{4}$

(a) Exponential decay
(b) $f(x) = \left(\frac{1}{2}\right)^x$

25.

x	-2	-1	0	1	2
$f(x)$	2.56	3.2	4	5	6.25

(a) Exponential growth
(b) $f(x) = 4(1.25)^x$

26.

x	-2	-1	0	1	2
$f(x)$	-6	-2	2	6	10

(a) Linear growth
(b) $f(x) = 4x + 2$

Exercises 27–30: Use the graph of $y = Ca^x$ to determine C and a.

27. $C = 1, a = 2$

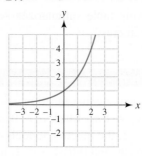

28. $C = 1, a = \frac{1}{2}$

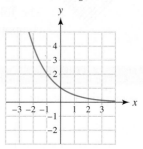

29. $C = 4, a = \frac{1}{4}$

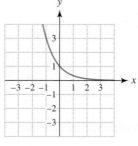

30. $C = 2, a = \frac{3}{2}$

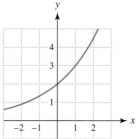

Exercises 31–34: Match the formula with its graph (a.–d.). Do not use a calculator.

31. $f(x) = 1.5^x$ c.

32. $f(x) = \frac{1}{4}(2^x)$ b.

33. $f(x) = 4\left(\frac{1}{2}\right)^x$ d.

34. $f(x) = \left(\frac{1}{3}\right)^x$ a.

a.

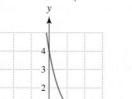

b.

c.

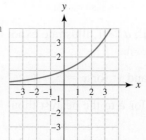

d.

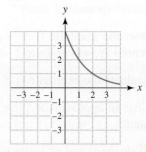

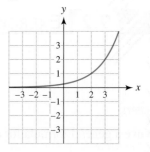

64. No; at 5% the interest earned is $314.45, and at 10% it is $796.87, which is more than twice as much.

Exercises 35–46: Graph y = f(x). State whether the graph illustrates exponential growth or exponential decay. *

35. $f(x) = 2^x$ Growth   **36.** $f(x) = 3^x$ Growth

37. $f(x) = \left(\frac{1}{4}\right)^x$ Decay   **38.** $f(x) = \left(\frac{1}{2}\right)^x$ Decay

39. $f(x) = 2^{-x}$ Decay   **40.** $f(x) = 3^{-x}$ Decay

41. $f(x) = 3^x - 1$ Growth **42.** $f(x) = 2^x + 1$ Growth

43. $f(x) = 2^{x-1}$ Growth **44.** $f(x) = 2^{x+1}$ Growth

45. $f(x) = 4\left(\frac{1}{3}\right)^x$ Decay   **46.** $f(x) = 3\left(\frac{1}{2}\right)^x$ Decay

*Exercises 47–56: **Exponents** Use properties of exponents to simplify the expression.*

47. $e^2 e^5$ e^7 **48.** $a^2 \cdot a^{-4}$ $\frac{1}{a^2}$

49. $\dfrac{a^4 a^{-2}}{a^3}$ $\frac{1}{a}$ **50.** $\dfrac{e^2 e^{-1}}{e}$ 1

51. $e^x e^{y-x}$ e^y **52.** $a^{1-x} a^{x-1}$ 1

53. $\dfrac{2^{x+3}}{2^x}$ $2^3 = 8$ **54.** $\dfrac{e^{2x}}{e^x}$ e^x

55. $5^{-y} \cdot 5^{3y}$ $5^{2y} = 25^y$ **56.** $4^{-x} \cdot 4^{2x} \cdot 4^x$ $4^{2x} = 16^x$

COMPOUND INTEREST

Exercises 57–62: (Refer to Example 3.) If C dollars are deposited in an account paying r percent annual interest, approximate the amount in the account after x years.

57. $C = \$1500$ $r = 9\%$ $x = 10$ years $3551.05

58. $C = \$1500$ $r = 15\%$ $x = 10$ years $6068.34

59. $C = \$200$ $r = 20\%$ $x = 50$ years $1,820,087.63

60. $C = \$5000$ $r = 8.4\%$ $x = 7$ years $8793.77

61. $C = \$560$ $r = 1.4\%$ $x = 25$ years $792.75

62. $C = \$750$ $r = 10\%$ $x = 13$ years $2589.20

63. *Interest* Suppose that $1000 are deposited in an account paying 8% interest for 10 years. If $2000 had been deposited instead of $1000, would there be twice the money in the account after 10 years? Explain. Yes; this is equivalent to having two accounts, each containing $1000 initially.

64. *Interest* Suppose that $500 are deposited in an account paying 5% interest for 10 years. If the interest rate had been 10% instead of 5%, would the total interest earned after 10 years be twice as much? Explain.

65. *Federal Debt* In 2003 the federal budget deficit was about $300 billion. At the same time, 30-year treasury bonds were paying 4.95% interest. Suppose that U.S. citizens loaned $300 billion to the federal government at 4.95%. If the federal government waited 30 years to pay the entire amount back, including the interest, how much would it be? (*Source:* U.S. Treasury Department.)   About $1.28 trillion

66. *Federal Debt* Repeat Exercise 65 but suppose that the interest rate is 2% higher. How much would the federal government owe after 30 years? Is the national debt sensitive to interest rates? About $2.25 trillion; yes

THE NATURAL EXPONENTIAL FUNCTION

Exercises 67–70: Evaluate f(x) for the given value of x. Approximate answers to the nearest hundredth.

67. $f(x) = e^x$ $x = 1.2$ 3.32

68. $f(x) = 2e^x$ $x = 2$ 14.78

69. $f(x) = 1 - e^x$ $x = -2$ 0.86

70. $f(x) = 4e^{-x}$ $x = 1.5$ 0.89

 Exercises 71–74: Graph f(x) in [−4, 4, 1] by [0, 8, 1]. State whether the graph illustrates exponential growth or exponential decay. *

71. $f(x) = e^{0.5x}$ Growth **72.** $f(x) = e^x + 1$ Growth

73. $f(x) = 1.5e^{-0.32x}$ **74.** $f(x) = 2e^{-x} + 1$ Decay
   Decay

APPLICATIONS

75. *Modeling Population* (Refer to Example 7.) In 1997 the population of Arizona was 4.56 million and growing continuously at a rate of 3.1%.
   (a) Write a function f that models Arizona's population in millions x years after 1997.
   (b) Graph f in [0, 10, 1] by [4, 7, 1]. * $f(x) = 4.56e^{0.031x}$
   (c) Estimate the population of Arizona in 2003. About 5.49 million

76. *Dating Artifacts* Radioactive carbon-14 is found in all living things and is used to date objects containing organic material. Suppose that an object initially contains C grams of carbon-14. After x years it will contain A grams, where

$$A = C(0.99988)^x.$$

 (a) Let $C = 10$ and graph A over a 20,000-year period. Is this function an example of exponential growth or decay? * Decay   (b) About 5 g; $\frac{1}{2}$
   (b) How many grams are left after 5700 years? What fraction of the carbon-14 is left?

*Answers on pages IA-29–IA-30

77. *E. coli Bacteria* A strain of bacteria that inhabits the intestines of animals is named *Escherichia coli* (*E. coli*). These bacteria are capable of rapid growth and can be dangerous to humans—particularly children. The table shows the results of one study of the growth of *E. coli* bacteria, where concentrations are listed in thousands of bacteria per milliliter.

t (minutes)	0	50	100
Concentration	500	1000	2000

t (minutes)	150	200
Concentration	4000	8000

Source: G. S. Stent, *Molecular Biology of Bacterial Viruses.*

(a) Find C and a so that $f(t) = Ca^{t/50}$ models the data. $C = 500, a = 2$
(b) Use $f(t)$ to estimate the concentration of bacteria after 170 minutes. About 5278 thousand/mL
(c) Discuss the growth of this strain of bacteria over a 300-minute time period. The growth is exponential.

78. *Internet Use* Internet use in Western Europe has grown rapidly. The table shows the number of Internet users y in millions during year x, where $x = 0$ corresponds to 2000, $x = 1$ to 2001, and $x = 2$ to 2002.

x (year)	0	1	2
y (millions)	52	67	85

Source: Nortel Networks.

(a) Approximate C and a so that $f(x) = Ca^x$ models the data. (*Hint:* To find a, estimate the factor by which y increases each year.) $C = 52, a \approx 1.28$
(b) Use $f(x)$ to estimate the number of users in 2004 $(x = 4)$. About 140 million
(c) How long is this type of growth likely to continue?
For a short period of time because the growth factor is relatively large
79. *Cellular Phone Use* In 1985, there were about 203,000 cellular phone subscribers in the United States. This number increased to about 84 million users in 2000, as illustrated in the figure at the top of the next column. The rapid growth in cellular phone subscribers in millions can be modeled by $f(x) = 0.0272(1.495)^{x-1980}$, where x is the year. (*Source:* Cellular Telecommunications Industry Association.)
(a) Evaluate $f(1995)$ and interpret the result.
(b) What is the growth factor for $f(x)$? Explain what the growth factor indicates about cellular phone subscribers from 1985 to 2000.

(a) About 11.3; in 1995 there were about 11.3 million cellular phone subscribers.

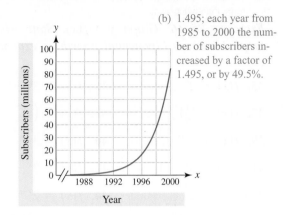

(b) 1.495; each year from 1985 to 2000 the number of subscribers increased by a factor of 1.495, or by 49.5%.

81.(a) 1; the probability that no vehicle will enter the intersection during a period of 0 seconds is 1 or 100%.

80. *Swimming Pool Maintenance* Chlorine is frequently used to disinfect swimming pools. The chlorine concentration should remain between 1.5 and 2.5 parts per million (ppm). After a warm, sunny day only 80% of the chlorine may remain in the water, with the other 20% dissipating into the air or combining with other chemicals in the water. (*Source:* D. Thomas, *Swimming Pool Operator's Handbook.*)
(a) Let $f(x) = 3(0.8)^x$ model the concentration of chlorine in parts per million after x days. What is the initial concentration of chlorine in the pool? 3 ppm
(b) If no more chlorine is added, estimate when the chlorine level drops below 1.5 parts per million. During day 3

81. *Modeling Traffic Flow* (Refer to Example 5.) Construct a table of $f(x) = (0.905)^x$, starting at $x = 0$ and incrementing by 10, until $x = 50$.*
(a) Evaluate $f(0)$ and interpret the result.
(b) After how many seconds is there only a 5% chance that no cars have entered the intersection? About 30 sec

82. *Modeling Tree Density* (Refer to Example 6.)
(a) Evaluate $P(10)$, $P(20)$, and $P(30)$. Interpret the results.*
(b) What happens to $P(x)$ as x becomes large? Explain how this probability relates to the spacing of trees in a forest.*

WRITING ABOUT MATHEMATICS

83. A student evaluates $f(x) = 4(2)^x$ at $x = 3$ and obtains 512. Did the student evaluate the function correctly? What was the student's error?

84. For a set of data, how can you distinguish between linear growth and exponential growth? Give an example of each type of data.

*Answers on page IA-30

CHECKING BASIC CONCEPTS SECTIONS 9.1 AND 9.2

1. If $f(x) = 2x^2 + 5x - 1$ and $g(x) = x + 1$, find each expression.
   (a) $(g \circ f)(1)$ 7   (b) $(f \circ g)(x)$
   $(f \circ g)(x) = 2x^2 + 9x + 6$

2. Sketch a graph of $f(x) = x^2 - 1$.*
   (a) Is f a one-to-one function? Explain.
   (b) Does f have an inverse function? No
   (a) No; it does not pass the horizontal line test.

3. If $f(x) = 4x - 3$, find $f^{-1}(x)$. $f^{-1}(x) = \dfrac{x+3}{4}$

4. Evaluate $f(-2)$ if $f(x) = 3(2^x)$. $\frac{3}{4}$

5. Sketch a graph of $f(x) = \left(\frac{1}{3}\right)^x$.*

6. Use the graph of $y = Ca^x$ to determine the constants C and a. $C = 2, a = \frac{1}{2}$

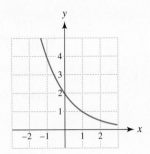

*Answers on page IA-30

9.3 LOGARITHMIC FUNCTIONS

The Common Logarithmic Function · The Inverse of the Common Logarithmic Function · Logarithms with Other Bases

INTRODUCTION

Logarithmic functions are used in many applications. For example, if one airplane weighs twice as much as another, does the heavier airplane typically need a runway that is twice as long? Using a logarithmic function, we can answer this question. Logarithmic functions are also used to measure the intensity of sound. In this section we discuss logarithmic functions and several of their applications.

THE COMMON LOGARITHMIC FUNCTION

In applications, measurements can vary greatly in size. Table 9.7 lists some examples of objects, with the approximate distances in meters across each.

TABLE 9.7

Object	Distance (meters)
Atom	10^{-9}
Protozoan	10^{-4}
Small Asteroid	10^2
Earth	10^7
Universe	10^{26}

Source: C. Ronan, *The Natural History of the Universe.*

Each distance is listed in the form 10^k for some k. The value of k distinguishes one measurement from another. The *common logarithmic function* or *base-10 logarithmic function*, denoted *log* or log_{10}, outputs k if the input x can be expressed as 10^k for some real number k. For example, $\log 10^{-9} = -9$, $\log 10^2 = 2$, and $\log 10^{1.43} = 1.43$. For any real number k, $\log 10^k = k$. Some values for $f(x) = \log x$ are given in Table 9.8.

TEACHING TIP

Emphasize that $\log 10^k = k$. The logarithm of a number is an exponent.

TABLE 9.8

x	10^{-4}	10^{-3}	10^{-2}	10^{-1}	10^0	10^1	10^2	10^3	10^4
$\log x$	-4	-3	-2	-1	0	1	2	3	4

We use this information to define the common logarithm.

COMMON LOGARITHM

The **common logarithm of a positive number x**, denoted $\log x$, is calculated as follows. If x is written as $x = 10^k$, then

$$\log x = k,$$

where k is a real number. That is, $\log 10^k = k$.
The function given by

$$f(x) = \log x$$

is called the **common logarithmic function**.

The common logarithmic function outputs an exponent k, which may be positive, negative, or zero. However, a valid input must be positive because 10^k is always positive. *The expression log x equals the exponent k on base* 10 *that gives the number x.* For example, $\log 1000 = 3$ because $1000 = 10^3$.

Note: Previously, we have always used one letter, such as f or g, to *name* a function. The common logarithm is the first function for which we use three letters, *log*, to name it. Thus $f(x)$, $g(x)$, and $\log(x)$ all represent functions. Generally, $\log(x)$ is written without parentheses as $\log x$. We can also define a function f to be the common logarithmic function by writing $f(x) = \log x$.

EXAMPLE 1   **Evaluating common logarithms**

Simplify each common logarithm.
(a) $\log 100$ **(b)** $\log \frac{1}{10}$ **(c)** $\log \sqrt{1000}$ **(d)** $\log 45$

Solution   **(a)** $100 = 10^2$, so $\log 100 = \log 10^2 = 2$

(b) $\log \frac{1}{10} = \log 10^{-1} = -1$

(c) $\log \sqrt{1000} = \log (10^3)^{1/2} = \log 10^{3/2} = \frac{3}{2}$

(d) How to write 45 as a power of 10 is not obvious. However, we can use a calculator to determine that log 45 ≈ 1.6532. Thus 10^(1.6532) ≈ 45. Figure 9.21 supports these answers.

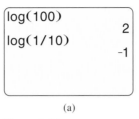

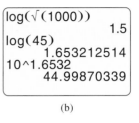

(a)   (b)

Figure 9.21

The points $(10^{-1}, -1)$, $(10^0, 0)$, $(10^{0.5}, 0.5)$, and $(10^1, 1)$ are on the graph of $y = \log x$. Plotting these points, as shown in Figure 9.22(a), and sketching the graph of $y = \log x$ results in Figure 9.22(b). Note some important features of this graph.

- The graph of the common logarithm increases very slowly for large values of x. For example, x must be 100 for log x to reach 2 and x must be 1000 for log x to reach 3.
- The graph passes through the point $(1, 0)$. Thus log 1 = 0.
- The graph does not exist for negative values of x. The domain of log x includes only positive numbers. The range of log x includes all real numbers.
- When $0 < x < 1$, log x outputs negative values. The y-axis is a vertical asymptote, so as x approaches 0, log x approaches $-\infty$.

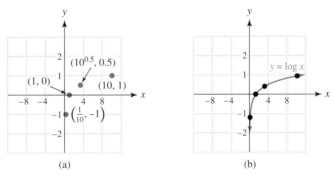

(a)   (b)

Figure 9.22

═══ MAKING CONNECTIONS ═══

The Common Logarithmic Function and the Square Root Function

Much like the square root function, the common logarithmic function does not have an easy-to-evaluate formula. For example, we can calculate $\sqrt{4} = 2$ and $\sqrt{100} = 10$ mentally, but for $\sqrt{2}$ we usually rely on a calculator. Similarly, we can mentally calculate log 1000 = log 10^3 = 3, whereas we can use a calculator to approximate log 45. The notation log x is implied to be $\log_{10} x$ much like $\sqrt{x}$ equals $\sqrt[2]{x}$. Another similarity between the square root function and the common logarithmic function is that their domains do not include negative numbers. If only real numbers are allowed as outputs, both $\sqrt{-3}$ and log (-3) are undefined expressions.

The Inverse of the Common Logarithmic Function

The graph of $y = \log x$ just shown in Figure 9.22(b) is a one-to-one function because it passes the horizontal line test. Different inputs always result in different outputs. Thus the common logarithmic function has an inverse function. To determine this inverse function for $\log x$, consider Tables 9.9 and 9.10.

TABLE 9.9

x	-2	-1	0	1	2
10^x	10^{-2}	10^{-1}	10^0	10^1	10^2

TABLE 9.10

x	10^{-2}	10^{-1}	10^0	10^1	10^2
$\log x$	-2	-1	0	1	2

If we start with the number 2, compute 10^2, and then calculate $\log 10^2$, the result is 2. That is,

$$\log(10^2) = 2.$$

In general, $\log 10^x = x$ for any real number x. Now suppose that we perform the calculations in reverse order by taking the common logarithm and then computing a power of 10. For example, suppose that we start with the number 100. The result is

$$10^{\log 100} = 10^2 = 100.$$

In general, $10^{\log x} = x$ for any positive number x.

The *inverse function* of $f(x) = \log x$ is $f^{-1}(x) = 10^x$. That is, if $\log x = y$, then $10^y = x$. Note that composition of these two functions satisfies the definition of an inverse function.

$$(f \circ f^{-1})(x) = f\left(f^{-1}(x)\right) \quad \text{and} \quad (f^{-1} \circ f)(x) = f^{-1}\left(f(x)\right)$$
$$= f(10^x) \qquad\qquad\qquad = f^{-1}(\log x)$$
$$= \log 10^x \qquad\qquad\qquad = 10^{\log x}$$
$$= x \qquad\qquad\qquad\qquad = x$$

In general, the graph of $y = f^{-1}(x)$ is a reflection of the graph of $y = f(x)$ across the line $y = x$. The graphs of $y = \log x$ and $y = 10^x$ are shown in Figure 9.23. Note that the graph of $y = 10^x$ is a reflection of the graph of $y = \log x$ across the line $y = x$.

These inverse properties are summarized as follows.

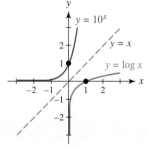

Figure 9.23

INVERSE PROPERTIES OF THE COMMON LOGARITHM

The following properties hold for common logarithms.

$$\log 10^x = x, \qquad \text{for any real number } x$$
$$10^{\log x} = x, \qquad \text{for any positive real number } x$$

EXAMPLE 2   Applying inverse properties

Use inverse properties to simplify each expression.
(a) $\log 10^{\pi}$ **(b)** $\log 10^{x^2+1}$ **(c)** $10^{\log 7}$ **(d)** $10^{\log 3x}, x > 0$

Solution   **(a)** Because $\log 10^x = x$ for any real number x, $\log 10^{\pi} = \pi$.
(b) $\log 10^{x^2+1} = x^2 + 1$
(c) Because $10^{\log x} = x$ for any positive real number x, $10^{\log 7} = 7$.
(d) $10^{\log 3x} = 3x$, provided x is a positive number.

We can also graph logarithmic functions, as demonstrated in the next example.

EXAMPLE 3   Graphing the logarithmic functions

Graph f and compare the graph to $y = \log x$.
(a) $f(x) = \log(x - 2)$ **(b)** $f(x) = \log(x) + 1$

Solution   **(a)** We can use our knowledge of translations to sketch the graph of $y = \log(x - 2)$. For example, the graph of $y = (x - 2)^2$ is similar to the graph of $y = x^2$, except that it is translated 2 units to the *right*. Thus the graph of $y = \log(x - 2)$ is similar to the graph of $y = \log x$, except that it is translated 2 units to the right, as shown in Figure 9.24. The graph of $y = \log x$ passes through $(1, 0)$, so the graph of $y = \log(x - 2)$ passes through $(3, 0)$. Also, instead of the y-axis being a vertical asymptote, the line $x = 2$ is the vertical asymptote.

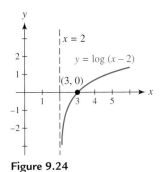

Figure 9.24   Figure 9.25

(b) The graph of $y = \log(x) + 1$ is similar to the graph of $y = \log x$, except that it is translated 1 unit *upward*. This graph is shown in Figure 9.25. Note that the graph of $y = \log(x) + 1$ passes through the point $(1, 1)$.

Note: The graph of $y = \log x$ has a vertical asympotote when $x = 0$ and is undefined when $x < 0$. Thus the graph of $\log(x - 2)$ has a vertical asymptote when $x - 2 = 0$, or $x = 2$. It is undefined when $x - 2 < 0$ or $x < 2$.

Logarithms are used to model quantities that vary greatly in intensity. For example, the human ear is extremely sensitive and able to detect intensities on the eardrum ranging from 10^{-16} watts per square centimeter (w/cm^2) to 10^{-4} w/cm^2, which usually is painful. The next example illustrates modeling sound with logarithms.

EXAMPLE 4 Modeling sound levels

Sound levels in decibels (dB) can be computed by $f(x) = 160 + 10 \log x$, where x is the intensity of the sound in watts per square centimeter. Ordinary conversation has an intensity of 10^{-10} w/cm^2. What decibel level is this? (**Source:** R. Weidner and R. Sells, *Elementary Classical Physics, Vol. 2.*)

Solution To find the decibel level for ordinary conversation, evaluate $f(10^{-10})$.

$$f(10^{-10}) = 160 + 10 \log(10^{-10}) \qquad \text{Substitute } x = 10^{-10}.$$
$$= 160 + 10(-10) \qquad \text{Evaluate } \log(10^{-10}).$$
$$= 60 \qquad \text{Simplify.}$$

Ordinary conversation corresponds to 60 dB.

Critical Thinking

If the sound level increases by 10 dB by what factor does the intensity x increase?

A factor of 10

LOGARITHMS WITH OTHER BASES

Common logarithms are base-10 logarithms, but we can define logarithms having other bases. For example, base-2 logarithms are frequently used in computer science. Some values for the base-2 logarithmic function, denoted $f(x) = \log_2 x$, are shown in Table 9.11. If x can be expressed as $x = 2^k$ for some real number k, then $\log_2 x = \log_2 2^k = k$.

TABLE 9.11

x	2^{-3}	2^{-2}	2^{-1}	2^0	2^1	2^2	2^3
$\log_2 x$	-3	-2	-1	0	1	2	3

Logarithms with other bases are evaluated in the next three examples.

EXAMPLE 5 Evaluating base-2 logarithms

Simplify each logarithm.
(a) $\log_2 8$ **(b)** $\log_2 \frac{1}{4}$

Solution **(a)** The expression $\log_2 8$ represents the exponent on base 2 that gives 8. Because $8 = 2^3$, $\log_2 8 = \log_2 2^3 = 3$.

(b) Because $\frac{1}{4} = \frac{1}{2^2} = 2^{-2}$, $\log_2 \frac{1}{4} = \log_2 2^{-2} = -2$

TEACHING TIP

Be sure that students understand common logarithms before presenting logarithms with other bases. Logarithms with other bases can be developed just like common logarithms.

Some values of base-e logarithms are shown in Table 9.12. A base-e logarithm is referred to as a **natural logarithm** and denoted either $\log_e x$ or $\ln x$. Natural logarithms are used in mathematics, science, economics, electronics, and communications.

Calculator Help

To evaluate the natural logarithmic function, see the Appendix (page AP-1).

TABLE 9.12

x	e^{-3}	e^{-2}	e^{-1}	e^0	e^1	e^2	e^3
$\ln x$	-3	-2	-1	0	1	2	3

To evaluate natural logarithms we usually use a calculator.

EXAMPLE 6   Evaluating natural logarithms

Approximate to the nearest hundredth.
(a) ln 10   **(b)** ln $\frac{1}{2}$

Solution   **(a)** Figure 9.26 shows that ln 10 ≈ 2.30.
(b) Figure 9.26 shows that ln $\frac{1}{2}$ ≈ −0.69.

We now define base-*a* logarithms.

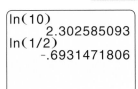

```
ln(10)
       2.302585093
ln(1/2)
       -.6931471806
```

Figure 9.26

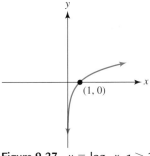

Figure 9.27 $y = \log_a x, a > 1$

BASE-*a* LOGARITHMS

The **logarithm with base *a* of a positive number *x***, denoted $\log_a x$, is calculated as follows. If *x* is written as $x = a^k$, then

$$\log_a x = k,$$

where $a > 0$, $a \neq 1$, and k is a real number. That is, $\log_a a^k = k$.
The function given by

$$f(x) = \log_a x$$

is called the **logarithmic function with base *a***.

Remember that *a logarithm is an exponent.* The expression $\log_a x$ equals the exponent k such that $a^k = x$. The graph of $y = \log_a x$ with $a > 1$ is shown in Figure 9.27. Note that the graph passes through the point $(1, 0)$. Thus $\log_a 1 = 0$.

Critical Thinking

Explain why $\log_a 1 = 0$ for any positive base a, $a \neq 1$.   Because $a^0 = 1$ for any positive base a.

Note: The natural logarithm, ln *x*, is a base-*a* logarithm with base *e*. That is, $\ln x = \log_e x$.

EXAMPLE 7   Evaluating base-*a* logarithms

Simplify each logarithm.
(a) $\log_5 25$ **(b)** $\log_4 \frac{1}{64}$ **(c)** $\log_7 1$ **(d)** $\log_3 9^{-1}$

Solution   **(a)** $25 = 5^2$, so $\log_5 25 = \log_5 5^2 = \mathbf{2}$.
(b) $\frac{1}{64} = \frac{1}{4^3} = 4^{-3}$, so $\log_4 \frac{1}{64} = \log_4 4^{-3} = \mathbf{-3}$.
(c) $1 = 7^0$, so $\log_7 1 = \log_7 7^0 = \mathbf{0}$. (Note that the logarithm of 1 is always 0, regardless of the base.)
(d) $9^{-1} = (3^2)^{-1} = 3^{-2}$, so $\log_3 9^{-1} = \log_3 3^{-2} = \mathbf{-2}$.

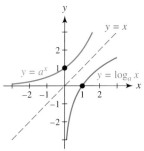

Figure 9.28 $a > 1$

The graph of $y = \log_a x$ in Figure 9.27 passes the horizontal line test, so it is a one-to-one function and it has an inverse. If we let $f(x) = \log_a x$, then $f^{-1}(x) = a^x$. This statement is a generalization of the fact that $\log x$ and 10^x represent inverse functions. The graphs of $y = \log_a x$ and $y = a^x$ with $a > 1$ are shown in Figure 9.28. Note that the graph of $y = a^x$ is a reflection of the graph of $y = \log_a x$ across the line $y = x$.

These inverse properties for logarithmic and exponential functions are summarized by the following.

TEACHING TIP

Students must understand inverse properties before they attempt to solve exponential and logarithmic equations in Section 9.5.

INVERSE PROPERTIES

The following properties hold for logarithms with base *a*.

$$\log_a a^x = x, \qquad \text{for any real number } x$$
$$a^{\log_a x} = x, \qquad \text{for any positive number } x$$

EXAMPLE 8   Applying inverse properties

Simplify each expression.
(a) $\ln e^{0.5x}$ **(b)** $e^{\ln 4}$ **(c)** $2^{\log_2 7x}$ **(d)** $10^{\log(9x-3)}$

Solution   **(a)** $\ln e^{0.5x} = 0.5x$ because $\ln e^k = k$ for all k.
(b) $e^{\ln 4} = 4$ because $e^{\ln k} = k$ for all positive k.
(c) $2^{\log_2 7x} = 7x$ for $x > 0$ because $a^{\log_a k} = k$ for all positive k.
(d) $10^{\log(9x-3)} = 9x - 3$ for $x > \frac{1}{3}$ because $10^{\log k} = k$ for all positive k.

Logarithms occur in many applications. One application is runway length for airplanes, which we discuss in the next example.

EXAMPLE 9   Calculating runway length

There is a mathematical relationship between an airplane's weight x and the runway length required at takeoff. For certain types of airplanes, the minimum runway length L in thousands of feet may be modeled by $L(x) = 1.3 \ln x$, where x is in thousands of pounds.
(*Source:* L. Haefner, *Introduction to Transportation Systems.*)
(a) Estimate the runway length needed for an airplane weighing 10,000 pounds.
(b) Does a 20,000-pound airplane need twice the runway length that a 10,000-pound airplane needs? Explain.

Solution   **(a)** Because $L(10) = 1.3 \ln(10) \approx 3$, an airplane weighing 10,000 pounds requires a runway 3000 feet long.
(b) Because $L(20) = 1.3 \ln(20) \approx 3.9$, a 20,000-pound airplane does not need twice the runway length needed by a 10,000-pound airplane. Rather the heavier airplane needs roughly 3900 feet of runway, or only an extra 900 feet.

PUTTING IT ALL TOGETHER

Common logarithms are base-10 logarithms. If a positive number x is written as $x = 10^k$, then $\log x = k$. The value of $\log x$ represents the exponent on the base 10 that gives x. We can define logarithms having other bases. For example, the natural logarithm is a base-e logarithm that is usually evaluated using a calculator. The following table summarizes some important concepts related to base-a logarithms.

Concept	Description	Examples
Base-a Logarithms	Logarithms can be defined for any base a, where $a > 0$ and $a \neq 1$. Thus $\log_a x = k$ means $x = a^k$. In other words, if we can write x as $x = a^k$, then $$\log_a x = \log_a a^k = k.$$ When $a = 10$, we write $\log x$, which indicates a common logarithm. When $a = e$, we write $\ln x$, which indicates a natural logarithm. The domain of $f(x) = \log_a x$ is all positive numbers, and its range is all real numbers. The graph of $y = \log_a x$ with $a > 1$ is shown in the figure at the right. Note that the graph passes through the point $(1, 0)$.	$\log 1000 = \log 10^3 = 3,$ $\log_2 16 = \log_2 2^4 = 4,$ and $\log_3 \dfrac{1}{81} = \log_3 3^{-4} = -4$
Inverse Properties	The following properties hold for logarithms with base a. $$\log_a a^x = x, \quad \text{for any real number } x$$ $$a^{\log_a x} = x, \quad \text{for any positive number } x$$	$\log 10^{7.48} = 7.48$ and $2^{\log_2 63} = 63$

9.3 EXERCISES

FOR EXTRA HELP

📖 Student's Solutions Manual

🚪 MyMathLab

🔺 InterAct Math

Tutor Center   Math Tutor Center

MathXL

Digital Video Tutor
CD 8   Videotape 10

CONCEPTS

1. What is the base of the common logarithm?   10

2. What is the base of the natural logarithm? e

3. What are the domain and range of $\log x$?
   $D = \{x \mid x > 0\}$; R: all real numbers

4. What are the domain and range of $\log_a x$?
   $D = \{x \mid x > 0\}$; R: all real numbers

5. $\log 10^k = $ _____ k

6. $\ln e^k = $ _____ k

7. If $\log x = k$, then $10^k = $ _____. x

8. $10^{\log x} = $ _____ x

9. What does k equal if $10^k = 5$? $\log 5$

10. What does k equal if $2^k = 5$? $\log_2 5$

EVALUATING AND GRAPHING LOGARITHMIC FUNCTIONS

Exercises 11–52: Simplify the expression.

11. $\log 10^5$ 5

12. $\log 10$ 1

13. $\log 10^{-4}$ -4

14. $\log 10^{-1}$ -1

15. $\log 1$ 0

16. $\log \sqrt[3]{100}$ $\frac{2}{3}$

17. $\log \frac{1}{100}$ -2

18. $\log \frac{1}{10}$ -1

19. $\log 10^{4.7}$ 4.7

20. $\log 10^{2x+4}$ $2x + 4$

21. $\log_5 5^{6x}$ $6x$

22. $\log_3 3^3$ 3

23. $\log \sqrt{\dfrac{1}{1000}}$ $-\frac{3}{2}$

24. $\log_2 2^6$ 6

25. $\log_2 4$ 2

26. $\log_2 \frac{1}{32}$ -5

27. $\log_2 \frac{1}{16}$ -4

28. $\log_3 27$ 3

29. $\log_3 \frac{1}{9}$ −2   **30.** $\log_4 16$ 2

31. $\ln 1$ 0   **32.** $\ln e^2$ 2

33. $\log 0.001$ −3   **34.** $\log 0.0001$ −4

35. $\log_5 \frac{1}{25}$ −2   **36.** $\log_8 64$ 2

37. $10^{\log 2}$ 2   **38.** $10^{\log 7.5}$ 7.5

39. $10^{\log x^2}$ x^2 **40.** $10^{\log|x|}$ $|x|$

41. $5^{\log_5 17}$ 17   **42.** $9^{\log_9 73}$ 73

43. $4^{\log_4 (2x)^2}$ $(2x)^2$ **44.** $b^{\log_b (x-1)}$ $x-1$

45. $10^{\log 5}$ 5   **46.** $\ln e^{3/4}$ $\frac{3}{4}$

47. $\ln e^{-5x}$ −5x   **48.** $e^{\ln 2x}$ 2x

49. $\log 10^{(2x-7)}$ 2x − 7   **50.** $\log 10^{(8-4x)}$ 8 − 4x

51. $5^{\log_5 0.6z}$ 0.6z   **52.** $7^{\log_7 (x-9)}$ x − 9

Exercises 53–60: Evaluate the logarithm, using a calculator. Round values to the nearest thousandth.

53. $\log 25$ 1.398   **54.** $\log 0.501$ −0.300

55. $\log 1.45$ 0.161   **56.** $\log \frac{1}{35}$ −1.544

57. $\ln 7$ 1.946   **58.** $\ln 126$ 4.836

59. $\ln \frac{4}{7}$ −0.560   **60.** $\ln 0.67$ −0.400

Exercises 61–64: Graph f in $[-4, 4, 1]$ by $[-4, 4, 1]$. Compare this graph to the graph of $y = \ln x$.* Identify the domain of f.

61. $f(x) = \ln|x|$ **62.** $f(x) = \ln(x) - 2$
Shifted 2 units downward; $D = \{x|x > 0\}$

63. $f(x) = \ln(x + 2)$ **64.** $f(x) = 2\ln x$
Shifted 2 units to the left; $D = \{x|x > -2\}$ Increases faster; $D = \{x|x > 0\}$

Exercises 65–68: Without using a calculator match $f(x)$ with its graph (a.–d.).

65. $f(x) = \log x$ d.   **66.** $f(x) = \log_3 x$ b.

67. $f(x) = \log_3(x) + 2$ **68.** $f(x) = \log(x + 1)$ c.
a.   a.   **b.**

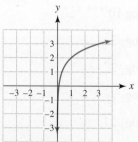   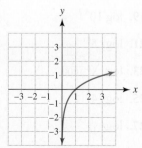

61. This is a reflection across the y-axis together with the graph of $y = \ln x$; $D = \{x|x \neq 0\}$

c.   **d.**

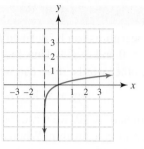   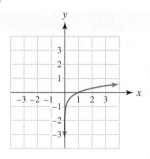

Exercises 69–76: Graph $y = f(x)$. Compare the graph to the graph of $y = \log x$.*

69. $f(x) = \log(x) - 1$ **70.** $f(x) = \log(x) + 2$
1 unit downward   2 units upward

71. $f(x) = \log(x + 1)$ **72.** $f(x) = \log(x + 2)$
1 unit to the left   2 units to the left

73. $f(x) = \log(x - 1)$ **74.** $f(x) = \log(x - 3)$
1 unit to the right   3 units to the right

75. $f(x) = 2\log x$ **76.** $f(x) = -\log x$
Increases faster   Reflected across the x-axis

Exercises 77 and 78: Complete the table.

77.

x	$\frac{1}{4}$	$\frac{1}{2}$	1	$\sqrt{2}$	64
$\log_2 x$	−2	−1	0	$\frac{1}{2}$	6

78.

x	$\frac{1}{7}$	1	$\sqrt{7}$	7	49
$\log_7 x$	−1	0	$\frac{1}{2}$	1	2

APPLICATIONS

79. *Modeling Sound* (Refer to Example 4.) At professional football games in domed stadiums the decibel level may reach 110. The eardrum usually experiences pain when the intensity of the sound reaches 10^{-4} watts per square centimeter. How many decibels does this quantity represent? Is the noise at a football game likely to hurt some people's eardrums? 120 dB; yes

80. *Runway Length* (Refer to Example 9.)
  (a) A graph of $L(x) = 1.3\ln x$ is shown in the accompanying figure. As the weight of the plane increases, what can be said about the length of the runway required? It increases, but it doesn't double when the weight of the plane doubles.

*Answers on page IA-30

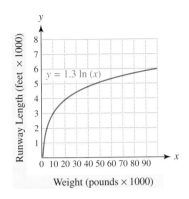

$y = 1.3 \ln(x)$

Runway Length (feet × 1000)

Weight (pounds × 1000)

(b) Evaluate $L(50)$ and interpret the result.
About 5.086; a 50,000-pound airplane needs a runway at least 5086 feet long.

81. *Hurricanes* Some of the largest storms on Earth are hurricanes, which have diameters that can exceed 300 miles. The barometric air pressure P in inches of mercury at a distance of d miles from the eye of a severe hurricane can sometimes be modeled by the formula $P(d) = 0.48 \ln(d + 1) + 27$. Average air pressure is about 30 inches of mercury. (*Source:* A. Miller and R. Anthes, *Meteorology.*)

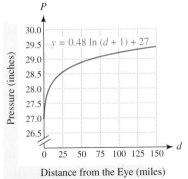

(a) Evaluate $P(0)$ and $P(50)$. Interpret the results.
(b) A graph of $y = P(d)$ is shown in the figure. Describe how the air pressure changes as the distance from the eye of the hurricane increases.
It increases rapidly at first and then more slowly.

$y = 0.48 \ln(d + 1) + 27$

Pressure (inches)

Distance from the Eye (miles)

81.(a) $P(0) = 27$; the air pressure at the eye of the hurricane is 27 inches of mercury. $P(50) \approx 28.9$; the air pressure 50 miles from the eye is about 28.9 inches of mercury.

(c) Is the eye of the hurricane a low pressure area or a high pressure area? Low

82. *Predicting Wind Speed* Wind speed typically varies in the first 20 meters above the ground. Close to the ground, wind speed is often less than it is at 20 meters above the ground. For this reason wind speeds are usually measured at heights from 5 to 10 meters by the U.S. Weather Service. For a particular day, let

$$W(x) = 2.76 \log(h + 1) + 2.3$$

compute the wind speed W in meters per second at a height h meters above the ground. (*Source:* A. Miller.)
(a) Find the wind speed at a height of 10 meters.
5.17 m/sec
(b) A graph of $y = W(h)$ is shown in the accompanying figure. Interpret the graph.
Wind speed increases with height rapidly at first and then more slowly.

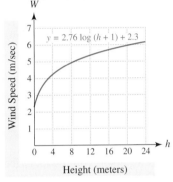

$y = 2.76 \log(h + 1) + 2.3$

Wind Speed (m/sec)

Height (meters)

83. *Earthquakes* The Richter scale is used to determine the intensity of earthquakes, which corresponds to the amount of energy released. If an earthquake has an intensity of x, its *magnitude*, as computed by the Richter scale, is given by $R(x) = \log \frac{x}{I_0}$, where I_0 is the intensity of a small, measurable earthquake.
(a) On July 26, 1963, an earthquake in Yugoslavia had a magnitude of 6.0 on the Richter scale, and on August 19, 1977, an earthquake in Indonesia measured 8.0. Find the intensity x for each of these earthquakes if $I_0 = 1$. 10^6; 10^8
(b) How many times more intense was the Indonesian earthquake than the Yugoslavian earthquake?
100 times

84. *Growth in Salary* Suppose that a person's salary is initially \$40,000 and could be determined by either $f(x)$ or $g(x)$, where x represents the number of years of experience.
i. $f(x) = 40,000(1.1)^x$
ii. $g(x) = 40,000 \log(10 + x)$
Would most people prefer that their salaries increase exponentially or logarithmically? Explain your answer. Exponentially because it grows faster over time.

85. *Calories Consumed and Land Ownership* In developing countries there is a relationship between the amount of land a person owns and the average daily calories consumed. This relationship is modeled by

$$C(x) = 645 \log (x + 1) + 1925,$$

where x is the amount of land owned in acres and $0 \le x \le 4$.   (*Source:* D. Grigg, *The World Food Problem.*)

(a) Find the average daily caloric intake for a person who owns 1 acre of land.   About 2119 calories

(b) A graph of $y = C(x)$ is shown in the figure. How is the number of calories consumed each day affected by the amount of land owned?
Caloric intake increases as the amount of land increases.

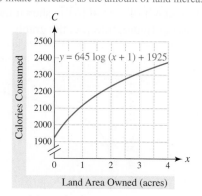

(c) Does a person who owns twice as much land as another person consume twice the calories? Explain.   No; the growth levels off and is not linear.

86. *Magnitude of a Star* The first stellar brightness scale was developed 2000 years ago by two Greek astronomers, Hipparchus and Ptolemy. The brightest star in the sky was given a magnitude of 1, and the faintest star was given a magnitude of 6. In 1856 this scale was described mathematically by the formula

$$M = 6 - 2.5 \log \frac{I}{I_0},$$

where M is the magnitude of a star with an intensity of I and I_0 is the intensity of the faintest star seen in the sky.

Note: The intensity of a star can be measured with instruments in watts per square centimeter.   (*Source:* M. Zeilik, *Introductory Astronomy and Astrophysics.*)

(a) Find M if $I = 10$ and $I_0 = 1$.   3.5

(b) What is the magnitude of a star that is 100 times more intense than the faintest star?   1

(c) If the intensity of a star increases by a factor of 10, what happens to its magnitude?
It decreases by 2.5.

87. *Population of Urban Regions* Although less industrialized urban regions of the world are experiencing exponential population growth, industrialized urban regions are experiencing logarithmic population growth. Population in less industrialized urban regions can be modeled by

$$f(x) = 0.338(1.035)^x,$$

whereas the population in industrialized urban regions can be modeled by

$$g(x) = 0.36 + 0.15 \ln (x + 1).$$

In these formulas the output is in billions of people and x is the year, where $x = 0$ corresponds to 1950, $x = 10$ to 1960, and so on until $x = 80$ corresponds to 2030.   (*Source:* D. Meadows, *Beyond The Limits.*)

(a) Evaluate $f(50)$ and $g(50)$. Interpret the results. *

(b) Graph f and g in [0, 80, 10] by [0, 5, 1]. Compare the two graphs. *

88. *Path Loss for Cellular Phones* For cellular phones to work throughout a country, large numbers of cellular towers are necessary. How well the signal is propagated throughout a region depends on the location of these towers. One quick way to estimate the strength of a signal at a distance of x kilometers is to use the formula

$$D(x) = -121 - 36 \log x.$$

This formula computes the decrease in the signal, using decibels, so it is always negative. For example, $D(1) = -121$ means that at a distance of 1 kilometer the signal has decreased in strength by 121 decibels.   (*Source:* C. Smith, *Practical Cellular & PCS Design.*)

*Answers on page IA-30

(a) Evaluate $D(3)$ and interpret the result.

 (b) Graph D in $[1, 10, 1]$ by $[-160, -120, 10]$. *

(c) What happens to the signal as the distance increases?   It decreases in strength.

(a) About -138; at a distance of 3 km the signal has decreased by 138 dB.

WRITING ABOUT MATHEMATICS

89. Explain in words what $\log_a x$ means and give an example.

90. How would you explain to a student that $\log_a 1 \neq 1$?

Group Activity: Working with Real Data

Directions: Form a group of 2 to 4 people. Select someone to record the group's responses for this activity. All members of the group should work cooperatively to answer the questions. If your instructor asks for your results, each member of the group should be prepared to respond.

 Greenhouse Gases   Carbon dioxide (CO_2) is a greenhouse gas in the atmosphere that may raise average temperatures on Earth. The burning of fossil fuels could be responsible for the increased levels of carbon dioxide in the atmosphere. If current trends continue, future concentrations of atmospheric carbon dioxide in parts per million (ppm) are expected to reach the levels shown in the accompanying table. The CO_2 concentration in the year 2000 was greater than it had been at any time in the previous 160,000 years.

Year	2000	2050	2100	2150	2200
CO_2 (ppm)	364	467	600	769	987

Source: R. Turner, *Environmental Economics.*

(a) Let x represent the year, where $x = 0$ corresponds to 2000, $x = 1$ to 2001, and so on. Find values for C and a so that $f(x) = Ca^x$ models the data. $C = 364, a \approx 1.005$

(b) Graph f and the data together in the same viewing rectangle. *

(c) Use $f(x)$ to estimate graphically the year when the carbon dioxide concentration will be double the preindustrial level of 280 ppm.   In 2086

*Answers on page IA-31

9.4 PROPERTIES OF LOGARITHMS

Basic Properties · Change of Base Formula

INTRODUCTION

The discovery of logarithms by John Napier (1550–1617) played an important role in the history of science. Logarithms were instrumental in allowing Johannes Kepler (1571–1630) to calculate the positions of the planet Mars, which led to his discovery of the laws of planetary motion. Kepler's laws were used by Isaac Newton (1642–1727) to discover the universal laws of gravity. Although calculators and computers have made tables of logarithms obsolete, applications involving logarithms still play an important role in modern day computation. One reason for their continued importance is that logarithms possess several important properties.

BASIC PROPERTIES

In this subsection we discuss three important properties of logarithms. The first property is the product rule for logarithms.

PRODUCT RULE FOR LOGARITHMS

For positive numbers m, n, and $a \neq 1$,

$$\log_a mn = \log_a m + \log_a n.$$

This property may be verified by using properties of exponents and the fact that $\log_a a^k = k$ for any real number k. Here, we verify the product property for logarithms. Other properties presented can be verified in a similar manner.

If m and n are positive numbers, we can write $m = a^c$ and $n = a^d$ for some real numbers c and d.

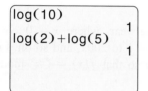

$$\log_a mn = \log_a(a^c a^d) = \log_a(a^{c+d}) = c + d \quad \text{and}$$
$$\log_a m + \log_a n = \log_a a^c + \log_a a^d = c + d$$

Figure 9.29

Thus $\log_a mn = \log_a m + \log_a n$.

This property is illustrated in Figure 9.29, which shows that

$$\log 10 = \log(2 \cdot 5) = \log 2 + \log 5.$$

In the next two examples, we demonstrate various operations involving logarithms.

EXAMPLE 1   Writing logarithms as sums

Write each expression as a sum of logarithms. Assume that x is positive.
(a) $\log 21$ **(b)** $\ln 5x$ **(c)** $\log_2 x^3$

Solution   **(a)** $\log 21 = \log(3 \cdot 7) = \log 3 + \log 7$
            (b) $\ln 5x = \ln(5 \cdot x) = \ln 5 + \ln x$
            (c) $\log_2 x^3 = \log_2(x \cdot x \cdot x) = \log_2 x + \log_2 x + \log_2 x$

EXAMPLE 2   Combining logarithms

Write each expression as one logarithm. Assume that x and y are positive.
(a) $\log 5 + \log 6$ **(b)** $\ln x + \ln xy$ **(c)** $\log_3 2x + \log_3 5x$

Solution   **(a)** $\log 5 + \log 6 = \log(5 \cdot 6) = \log 30$
            (b) $\ln x + \ln xy = \ln(x \cdot xy) = \ln x^2 y$
            (c) $\log_3 2x + \log_3 5x = \log_3(2x \cdot 5x) = \log_3 10x^2$

The second property is the quotient rule for logarithms.

QUOTIENT RULE FOR LOGARITHMS

For positive numbers m, n, and $a \neq 1$,

$$\log_a \frac{m}{n} = \log_a m - \log_a n.$$

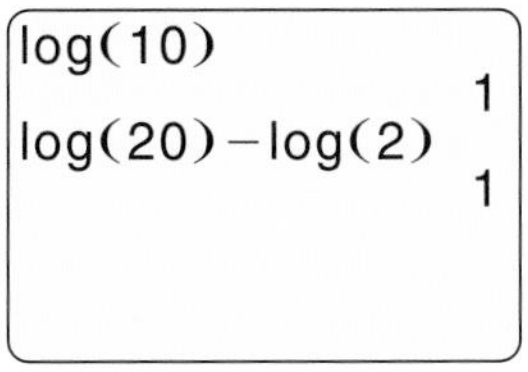

```
log(10)
                    1
log(20)−log(2)
                    1
```

Figure 9.30

This property is illustrated in Figure 9.30, which shows that

$$\log 10 = \log \frac{20}{2} = \log 20 - \log 2.$$

EXAMPLE 3 Writing logarithms as differences

Write each expression as a difference of two logarithms. Assume that all variables are positive.

(a) $\log \dfrac{3}{2}$ **(b)** $\ln \dfrac{3x}{y}$ **(c)** $\log_5 \dfrac{x}{z^4}$

Solution **(a)** $\log \dfrac{3}{2} = \log 3 - \log 2$ **(b)** $\ln \dfrac{3x}{y} = \ln 3x - \ln y$

(c) $\log_5 \dfrac{x}{z^4} = \log_5 x - \log_5 z^4$

TEACHING TIP

Emphasize the note. It identifies four common mistakes.

Note: $\log_a (m + n) \neq \log_a m + \log_a n;$ $\log_a (m - n) \neq \log_a m - \log_a n;$

$$\log_a (mn) \neq \log_a m \cdot \log_a n; \quad \log_a \left(\frac{m}{n} \right) \neq \frac{\log_a m}{\log_a n}$$

EXAMPLE 4 Combining logarithms

Write each expression as one term. Assume that x is positive.

(a) $\log 50 - \log 25$ **(b)** $\ln x^3 - \ln x$ **(c)** $\log_4 15x - \log_4 5x$

Solution **(a)** $\log 50 - \log 25 = \log \dfrac{50}{25} = \log 2$

(b) $\ln x^3 - \ln x = \ln \dfrac{x^3}{x} = \ln x^2$

(c) $\log_4 15x - \log_4 5x = \log_4 \dfrac{15x}{5x} = \log_4 3$

The third property is the power rule for logarithms. To illustrate this rule we use

$$\log x^3 = \log (x \cdot x \cdot x) = \log x + \log x + \log x = 3 \log x.$$

Thus $\log x^3 = 3 \log x$. This example is generalized in the following rule.

POWER RULE FOR LOGARITHMS

For positive numbers m and $a \neq 1$ and any real number r,

$$\log_a (m^r) = r \log_a m.$$

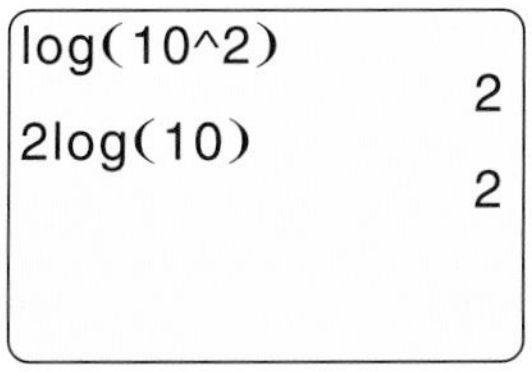

```
log(10^2)
                    2
2log(10)
                    2
```

Figure 9.31

We use a calculator and the equation

$$\log 10^2 = 2 \log 10$$

to illustrate this property. Figure 9.31 shows the result.

We apply the power rule in the next example.

EXAMPLE 5   Applying the power rule

Rewrite each expression, using the power rule.
(a) $\log 5^6$ (b) $\ln (0.55)^{x-1}$ (c) $\log_5 8^{kx}$

Solution   (a) $\log 5^6 = 6 \log 5$
(b) $\ln (0.55)^{x-1} = (x - 1) \ln (0.55)$
(c) $\log_5 8^{kx} = kx \log_5 8$

Sometimes we use more than one property to simplify an expression. We assume that all variables are positive in the next two examples.

EXAMPLE 6   Combining logarithms

Write each expression as one logarithm.
(a) $3 \log x + \log x^2$ (b) $2 \ln x - \ln \sqrt{x}$

Solution   (a) $3 \log x + \log x^2 = \log x^3 + \log x^2$ Power rule

$$= \log (x^3 \cdot x^2)$$ Product rule

$$= \log x^5$$ Properties of exponents

(b) $2 \ln x - \ln \sqrt{x} = 2 \ln x - \ln x^{1/2}$ $\sqrt{x} = x^{1/2}$

$$= \ln x^2 - \ln x^{1/2}$$ Power rule

$$= \ln \frac{x^2}{x^{1/2}}$$ Quotient rule

$$= \ln x^{3/2}$$ Properties of exponents

EXAMPLE 7   Expanding logarithms

Write each expression in terms of logarithms of x, y, and z.
(a) $\log \dfrac{x^2 y^3}{\sqrt{z}}$ (b) $\ln \sqrt[3]{\dfrac{xy}{z}}$

Solution   (a) $\log \dfrac{x^2 y^3}{\sqrt{z}} = \log x^2 y^3 - \log \sqrt{z}$ Quotient rule

$$= \log x^2 + \log y^3 - \log z^{1/2}$$ Product rule

$$= 2 \log x + 3 \log y - \tfrac{1}{2} \log z$$ Power rule

(b) $\ln \sqrt[3]{\dfrac{xy}{z}} = \ln \left(\dfrac{xy}{z} \right)^{1/3}$ $\sqrt[3]{m} = m^{1/3}$

$$= \tfrac{1}{3} \ln \frac{xy}{z}$$ Power rule

$$= \tfrac{1}{3} (\ln xy - \ln z)$$ Quotient rule

$$= \tfrac{1}{3} (\ln x + \ln y - \ln z)$$ Product rule

$$= \tfrac{1}{3} \ln x + \tfrac{1}{3} \ln y - \tfrac{1}{3} \ln z$$ Distributive property

---

EXAMPLE 8 Applying properties of logarithms

Using only properties of logarithms and the approximations $\ln 2 \approx 0.7$, $\ln 3 \approx 1.1$, and $\ln 5 \approx 1.6$, find an approximation for each expression.

(a) $\ln 8$ **(b)** $\ln 15$ **(c)** $\ln \dfrac{10}{3}$

Solution **(a)** $\ln 8 = \ln 2^3 = 3 \ln 2 \approx 3(0.7) = 2.1$

(b) $\ln 15 = \ln(3 \cdot 5) = \ln 3 + \ln 5 \approx 1.1 + 1.6 = 2.7$

(c) $\ln \dfrac{10}{3} = \ln\left(\dfrac{2 \cdot 5}{3}\right) = \ln 2 + \ln 5 - \ln 3 \approx 0.7 + 1.6 - 1.1 = 1.2$

CHANGE OF BASE FORMULA

Most calculators only have keys to evaluate common and natural logarithms. Occasionally, it is necessary to evaluate a logarithmic function with a base other than 10 or e. In these situations we use the following change of base formula, which we illustrate in the next example.

CHANGE OF BASE FORMULA

Let x and $a \neq 1$ be positive real numbers. Then

$$\log_a x = \frac{\log x}{\log a} \quad \text{or} \quad \log_a x = \frac{\ln x}{\ln a}.$$

EXAMPLE 9 Change of base formula

Approximate $\log_2 14$ to the nearest thousandth.

Solution Use the change of base formula,

$$\log_2 14 = \frac{\log 14}{\log 2} \approx 3.807 \quad \text{or} \quad \log_2 14 = \frac{\ln 14}{\ln 2} \approx 3.807.$$

Figure 9.32 supports these results.

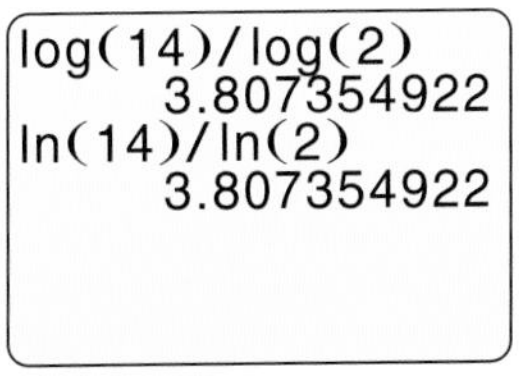

```
log(14)/log(2)
        3.807354922
ln(14)/ln(2)
        3.807354922
```

Figure 9.32

9.4 PUTTING IT ALL TOGETHER

The following table summarizes some important properties for base-a logarithms. Common and natural logarithms satisfy the same properties.

Type of Property	Description	Examples
Logarithmic	The following properties hold for positive numbers m, n, and $a \neq 1$ and for any real number r. **1.** $\log_a mn = \log_a m + \log_a n$ **2.** $\log_a \frac{m}{n} = \log_a m - \log_a n$ **3.** $\log_a (m^r) = r \log_a m$	**1.** $\log 20 = \log 10 + \log 2$ **2.** $\log \frac{45}{6} = \log 45 - \log 6$ **3.** $\ln x^6 = 6 \ln x$
Change of Base	Let x and $a \neq 1$ be positive real numbers. Then $$\log_a x = \frac{\log x}{\log a} \quad \text{and} \quad \log_a x = \frac{\ln x}{\ln a}.$$	The expression $\log_3 6$ is equivalent to either $$\frac{\log 6}{\log 3} \quad \text{or} \quad \frac{\ln 6}{\ln 3}.$$

9.4 EXERCISES

FOR EXTRA HELP

📖 Student's Solutions Manual   InterAct Math   MathXL MathXL

🚪 MyMathLab   Tutor Center Math Tutor Center   Digital Video Tutor CD 8   Videotape 10

CONCEPTS

1. $\log 12 = \log 3 + \log (\underline{\hspace{1cm}})$ 4

2. $\ln 5 = \ln 20 - \ln (\underline{\hspace{1cm}})$ 4

3. $\log 8 = (\underline{\hspace{1cm}}) \log 2$ 3

4. $\log mn = \underline{\hspace{1cm}}$ $\log m + \log n$

5. $\log \dfrac{m}{n} = \underline{\hspace{1cm}}$ $\log m - \log n$

6. $\log (m^r) = \underline{\hspace{1cm}}$ $r \log m$

7. Does $\log x + \log y$ equal $\log (x + y)$ for all positive numbers x and y? No

8. Does $\log x - \log y$ equal $\log \left(\frac{x}{y}\right)$ for all positive numbers x and y? Yes

9. Give the change of base formula. $\log_a x = \dfrac{\log x}{\log a}$ or $\log_a x = \dfrac{\ln x}{\ln a}$

10. $\log_a 1 = \underline{\hspace{1cm}}$ and $\log_a a = \underline{\hspace{1cm}}$. 0; 1

BASIC PROPERTIES OF LOGARITHMS

Exercises 11–16: Write the expression as a sum of two or more logarithms.

11. $\ln (3 \cdot 5)$ $\ln 3 + \ln 5$

12. $\log (7 \cdot 11)$ $\log 7 + \log 11$

13. $\log_3 xy$ $\log_3 x + \log_3 y$

14. $\log_5 y^2$ $\log_5 y + \log_5 y$

15. $\ln 10z$ $\ln 2 + \ln 5 + \ln z$

16. $\log x^2 y$ $\log x + \log x + \log y$

Exercises 17–22: Write the expression as a difference of two logarithms.

17. $\log \frac{7}{3}$ $\log 7 - \log 3$

18. $\ln \frac{11}{13}$ $\ln 11 - \ln 13$

19. $\ln \dfrac{x}{y}$ $\ln x - \ln y$

20. $\log \dfrac{2x}{z}$ $\log 2x - \log z$

21. $\log_2 \dfrac{45}{x}$ $\log_2 45 - \log_2 x$

22. $\log_7 \dfrac{5x}{4z}$ $\log_7 5x - \log_7 4z$

Exercises 23–30: Write the expression as one logarithm.

23. $\log 45 + \log 5$ $\log 225$ **24.** $\log 30 - \log 10$ $\log 3$

25. $\ln x + \ln y$ $\ln xy$ **26.** $\ln m + \ln n - \ln n$ $\ln m$

27. $\ln 7x^2 + \ln 2x$ $\ln 14x^3$ **28.** $\ln x + \ln y - \ln z$ $\ln \frac{xy}{z}$

29. $\ln x + \ln y^2 - \ln y$ $\ln xy$ **30.** $\ln \sqrt{z} - \ln z^3 + \ln y^3$ $\ln \frac{y^3}{z^{5/2}}$

Exercises 31–40: Rewrite the expression, using the power rule.

31. $\log 3^6$ $6 \log 3$ **32.** $\log x^8$ $8 \log x$

33. $\ln 2^x$ $x \ln 2$ **34.** $\ln (0.77)^{x+1}$ $(x + 1) \ln 0.77$

35. $\log_2 5^{1/4}$ $\frac{1}{4} \log_2 5$ **36.** $\log_3 \sqrt{x}$ $\frac{1}{2} \log_3 x$

37. $\log_4 \sqrt[3]{z}$ $\frac{1}{3} \log_4 z$ **38.** $\log_7 3^\pi$ $\pi \log_7 3$

39. $\log x^{y-1}$ $(y - 1) \log x$ **40.** $\ln a^{2b}$ $2b \ln a$

Exercises 41–52: Use properties of logarithms to write the expression as one logarithm.

41. $4 \log z - \log z^3$ $\log z$ **42.** $2 \log_5 y + \log_5 x$ $\log_5 xy^2$

43. $\log x + 2 \log x + 2 \log y$ $\log x^3 y^2$

44. $\log x^2 + 3 \log z - 5 \log y$ $\log \frac{x^2 z^3}{y^5}$

45. $\log x - 2 \log \sqrt{x}$ 0 **46.** $\ln y^2 - 6 \ln \sqrt[3]{y}$ 0

47. $\ln 2^{x+1} - \ln 2$ $\ln 2^x$ **48.** $\ln 8^{1/2} + \ln 2^{1/2}$ $\ln 4$

49. $2 \log_3 \sqrt{x} - 3 \log_3 x$ **50.** $\ln \sqrt[3]{x} + \ln \sqrt{x}$ $\ln x^{5/6}$

51. $2 \log_a (x + 1) - \log_a (x^2 - 1)$ $\log_a \frac{x + 1}{x - 1}$

    49. $\log_3 \frac{1}{x^2}$

52. $\log_b (x^2 - 9) - \log_b (x - 3)$ $\log_b (x + 3)$

Exercises 53–64: Use properties of logarithms to write the expression in terms of logarithms of x, y, and z.

53. $\log xy^2$ $\log x + 2 \log y$ **54.** $\log \frac{x^2}{y^3}$ $2 \log x - 3 \log y$

55. $\ln \frac{x^4 y}{z}$ $4 \ln x + \ln y - \ln z$ **56.** $\ln \frac{\sqrt{x}}{y}$ $\frac{1}{2} \ln x - \ln y$

57. $\log_4 \frac{\sqrt[3]{z}}{\sqrt{y}}$ $\frac{1}{3} \log_4 z - \frac{1}{2} \log_4 y$ **58.** $\log_2 \sqrt{\frac{x}{y}}$ $\frac{1}{2} \log_2 x - \frac{1}{2} \log_2 y$

59. $\log (x^4 y^3)$ $4 \log x + 3 \log y$ **60.** $\log (x^2 y^4 z^3)$ $2 \log x + 4 \log y + 3 \log z$

61. $\ln \frac{1}{y} - \ln \frac{1}{x}$ $\ln x - \ln y$ **62.** $\ln \frac{1}{xy}$ $-\ln x - \ln y$

63. $\log_4 \sqrt{\frac{x^3 y}{z^2}}$ **64.** $\log_3 \left(\frac{x^2 \sqrt{z}}{y^3} \right)$

$\frac{3}{2} \log_4 x + \frac{1}{2} \log_4 y - \log_4 z$ $2 \log_3 x + \frac{1}{2} \log_3 z - 3 \log_3 y$

Exercises 65–68: Graph f and g in the window $[-6, 6, 1]$ by $[-4, 4, 1]$. If the two graphs appear to be identical, prove that they are, using properties of logarithms. *

65. $f(x) = \log x^3, g(x) = 3 \log x$
By the power rule, $\log x^3 = 3 \log x$
66. $f(x) = \ln x + \ln 3, g(x) = \ln 3x$
By the product rule, $\ln x + \ln 3 = \ln 3x$
67. $f(x) = \ln (x + 5), g(x) = \ln x + \ln 5$
Not the same
68. $f(x) = \log (x - 2), g(x) = \log x - \log 2$
Not the same

Exercises 69–78: (Refer to Example 8.) Using only properties of logarithms and the approximations $\log 2 \approx 0.3$, $\log 5 \approx 0.7$, and $\log 13 \approx 1.1$, find an approximation for the expression.

69. $\log 16$ 1.2 **70.** $\log 125$ 2.1

71. $\log 65$ 1.8 **72.** $\log 26$ 1.4

73. $\log 130$ 2.1 **74.** $\log 100$ 2

75. $\log \frac{5}{2}$ 0.4 **76.** $\log \frac{26}{5}$ 0.7

77. $\log \frac{1}{13}$ -1.1 **78.** $\log \frac{1}{65}$ -1.8

Exercises 79–84: Use the change of base formula to approximate each expression to the nearest hundredth.

79. $\log_3 5$ 1.46 **80.** $\log_5 12$ 1.54

81. $\log_2 25$ 4.64 **82.** $\log_7 8$ 1.07

83. $\log_9 102$ 2.10 **84.** $\log_6 293$ 3.17

85. $10 \log (10^{16} x) = 10 (\log 10^{16} + \log x)$
$= 10 (16 + \log x)$
$= 160 + 10 \log x$

APPLICATIONS

85. *Modeling Sound* (Refer to Example 4, Section 9.3.) The formula $f(x) = 10 \log (10^{16} x)$ can be used to calculate the decibel level of a sound with an intensity x. Use properties of logarithms to simplify this formula to

$$f(x) = 160 + 10 \log x.$$

*Answers on page IA-31

86. *Cellular Phone Technology* A formula used to calculate the strength of a signal for a cellular phone is

$$L = 110.7 - 19.1 \log h + 55 \log d,$$

where h is the height of the cellular phone tower and d is the distance the phone is from the tower. Use properties of logarithms to write an expression for L that contains only one logarithm. (***Source:*** C. Smith, *Practical Cellular & PCS Design.*) $110.7 + \log \dfrac{d^{55}}{h^{19.1}}$

87. State the three basic properties of logarithms and give an example of each.

88. A student insists that $\log(x - y)$ is equal to $\log x - \log y$. How could you convince the student otherwise?

CHECKING BASIC CONCEPTS   SECTIONS 9.3 AND 9.4

1. Simplify each expression without using a calculator.
 (a) $\log 10^4$ 4
 (b) $\ln e^x$ x
 (c) $\log_2 \frac{1}{8}$ -3
 (d) $\log_5 \sqrt{5}$ $\frac{1}{2}$

2. Sketch a graph of $f(x) = \log x.$*
 (a) What are the domain and range of f?
 (b) Evaluate $f(1)$.   0
 (c) Can the common logarithm of a positive number be negative? Explain.   Yes; for example, $\log \frac{1}{10} = -1$
 (d) Can the common logarithm of a negative number be positive? Explain.
   No; negative numbers are not in the domain of $\log x$.

 (a) $D = \{x \mid x > 0\}$; R: all real numbers

3. Write the expression in terms of logarithms of x, y, and z.
 (a) $\log xy$ $\log x + \log y$
 (b) $\ln \dfrac{x}{yz}$ $\ln x - \ln y - \ln z$
 (c) $\ln x^2$ $2 \ln x$
 (d) $\log \dfrac{x^2 y^3}{\sqrt{z}}$ $2 \log x + 3 \log y - \frac{1}{2} \log z$

4. Write the expression as one logarithm.
 (a) $\log x + \log y$ $\log xy$
 (b) $\ln 2x - 3 \ln y$ $\ln \dfrac{2x}{y^3}$
 (c) $2 \log_2 x + 3 \log_2 y - \log_2 z$ $\log_2 \dfrac{x^2 y^3}{z}$

*Answers on page IA-31

9.5 EXPONENTIAL AND LOGARITHMIC EQUATIONS

Exponential Equations and Models · Logarithmic Equations and Models

INTRODUCTION

Although we have solved many equations throughout this course, one equation that we have not solved *symbolically* is $a^x = k$. This exponential equation occurs frequently in applications and is used to model either exponential growth or decay. Logarithmic equations contain logarithms and are also used in modeling real-world data. To solve exponential equations we use logarithms, and to solve logarithmic equations we use exponential expressions.

EXPONENTIAL EQUATIONS AND MODELS

To solve the equation

$$10 + x = 100$$

we subtract 10 from each side because addition and subtraction are inverse operations.

$$10 + x - 10 = 100 - 10$$
$$x = 90$$

To solve the equation

$$10x = 100$$

we divide each side by 10 because multiplication and division are inverse operations.

$$\frac{10x}{10} = \frac{100}{10}$$
$$x = 10$$

Now suppose that we want to solve the exponential equation

$$10^x = 100.$$

What is new about this type of equation is that the variable x is an *exponent*. The inverse operation of 10^x is log x. Rather than subtracting 10 from each side or dividing each side by 10, we take the base-10 logarithm of each side. Doing so results in

$$\log 10^x = \log 100.$$

Because $\log 10^x = x$ for all real numbers x, the equation becomes

$$x = \log 100, \quad \text{or equivalently,} \quad x = 2.$$

These concepts are applied in the next example.

EXAMPLE 1   **Solving exponential equations**

Solve.
(a) $10^x = 150$ **(b)** $e^x = 40$ **(c)** $2^x = 50$ **(d)** $0.9^x = 0.5$

Solution **(a)**

TEACHING TIP

Emphasize that, to solve an exponential equation, students will need to take a logarithm of each side of the equation.

$10^x = 150$	Given equation
$\log 10^x = \log 150$	Take the common logarithm of each side.
$x = \log 150 \approx 2.18$	Inverse property: $\log 10^x = x$ for all x

(b) The inverse operation of e^x is ln x, so we take the natural logarithm of each side.

$e^x = 40$	Given equation
$\ln e^x = \ln 40$	Take the natural logarithm of each side.
$x = \ln 40 \approx 3.69$	Inverse property: $\ln e^x = x$ for all x

(c) The inverse operation of 2^x is $\log_2 x$. Calculators do not usually have a base-2 logarithm key, so we take the common logarithm of each side and then apply the power rule.

$2^x = 50$	Given equation
$\log 2^x = \log 50$	Take the common logarithm of each side.
$x \log 2 = \log 50$	Power rule: $\log (m^r) = r \log m$
$x = \dfrac{\log 50}{\log 2} \approx 5.64$	Divide by log 2 and approximate.

(d) This time we begin by taking the natural logarithm of each side.

$$0.9^x = 0.5 \qquad \text{Given equation}$$

$$\ln 0.9^x = \ln 0.5 \qquad \text{Take the natural logarithm of each side.}$$

$$x \ln 0.9 = \ln 0.5 \qquad \text{Power rule: } \ln (m^r) = r \ln m$$

$$x = \frac{\ln 0.5}{\ln 0.9} \approx 6.58 \qquad \text{Divide by } \ln 0.9 \text{ and approximate.}$$

═══════════════════ MAKING CONNECTIONS ═══════════════════

Logarithms of Quotients and Quotients of Logarithms

The solution in Example 1(c) is $\frac{\log 50}{\log 2}$. Note that

$$\frac{\log 50}{\log 2} \neq \log 50 - \log 2.$$

However, $\log 50 - \log 2 = \log \frac{50}{2} = \log 25$ by the quotient rule for logarithms, as shown in the figure.

```
log(50)/log(2)
          5.64385619
log(50)−log(2)
          1.397940009
log(25)
          1.397940009
```

The next two examples illustrate methods for solving exponential equations.

EXAMPLE 2   Solving exponential equations

Solve each equation.
(a) $2e^x - 1 = 5$ **(b)** $3^{x-5} = 15$ **(c)** $e^{2x} = e^{x+5}$ **(d)** $3^{2x} = 2^{x+3}$

Solution   **(a)** Begin by solving for e^x.

$$2e^x - 1 = 5 \qquad \text{Given equation}$$

$$2e^x = 6 \qquad \text{Add 1 to each side.}$$

$$e^x = 3 \qquad \text{Divide each side by 2.}$$

$$\ln e^x = \ln 3 \qquad \text{Take the natural logarithm.}$$

$$x = \ln 3 \approx 1.10 \qquad \text{Inverse property: } \ln e^k = k$$

(b) Start by taking the common logarithm of each side.

$$3^{x-5} = 15 \qquad \text{Given equation}$$

$$\log 3^{x-5} = \log 15 \qquad \text{Take the common logarithm of each side.}$$

$$(x - 5) \log 3 = \log 15 \qquad \text{Power rule for logarithms}$$

$$x - 5 = \frac{\log 15}{\log 3} \qquad \text{Divide by } \log 3.$$

$$x = \frac{\log 15}{\log 3} + 5 \approx 7.46 \qquad \text{Add 5 to each side and approximate.}$$

(c) Because the bases are equal, the exponents must also be equal. To verify this assertion, take the natural logarithm of each side.

$$e^{2x} = e^{x+5}$$ Given equation

$$\ln e^{2x} = \ln e^{x+5}$$ Take the natural logarithm.

$$2x = x + 5$$ Inverse property: $\ln e^k = k$

$$x = 5$$ Subtract x.

(d) In this equation, the bases are not equal. However, we can still solve the equation by taking a common logarithm of each side. A logarithm of any base could be used.

$$3^{2x} = 2^{x+3}$$ Given equation

$$\log 3^{2x} = \log 2^{x+3}$$ Take the common logarithm.

$$2x \log 3 = (x + 3) \log 2$$ Power rule for logarithms

$$2x \log 3 = x \log 2 + 3 \log 2$$ Distributive property

$$2x \log 3 - x \log 2 = 3 \log 2$$ Subtract $x \log 2$.

$$x(2 \log 3 - \log 2) = 3 \log 2$$ Factor out x.

$$x = \frac{3 \log 2}{2 \log 3 - \log 2}$$ Divide by $2 \log 3 - \log 2$.

$$x \approx 1.38$$ Approximate.

EXAMPLE 3 Solving an exponential equation

Graphs for $f(x) = 0.2e^x$ and $g(x) = 4$ are shown in Figure 9.33.
(a) Use the graphs to estimate the solution to the equation $f(x) = g(x)$.
(b) Check your estimate by solving the equation symbolically.

Solution **(a)** The graphs intersect near the point $(3, 4)$. Therefore the solution is given by $x \approx 3$.
(b) We must solve the equation $0.2(e^x) = 4$.

$$0.2(e^x) = 4$$ Given equation

$$e^x = 20$$ Divide each side by 0.2.

$$\ln e^x = \ln 20$$ Take the natural logarithm of each side.

$$x = \ln 20$$ Inverse property: $\ln e^k = k$

$$x \approx 2.996$$ Approximate.

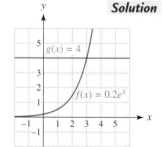

Figure 9.33

Note: The graphical estimate did not give the *exact* solution of $\ln 20$.

In Section 9.2 we showed that, if $1000 are deposited in a savings account paying 10% annual interest at the end of each year, the amount A in the account after x years is given by

$$A(x) = 1000(1.1)^x.$$

After 10 years there will be

$$A(10) = 1000(1.1)^{10} \approx \$2593.74$$

in the account. To calculate how long it will take for $4000 to accrue in the account, we need to solve the exponential equation

$$1000(1.1)^x = 4000.$$

We do so in the next example.

EXAMPLE 4   **Solving exponential equations**

Solve $1000(1.1)^x = 4000$ symbolically. Give graphical support for your answer.

Solution   ***Symbolic Solution***   Begin by dividing each side of the equation by 1000.

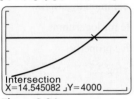

$[0, 20, 5]$ by $[0, 6000, 1000]$

Intersection
X=14.545082 Y=4000

Figure 9.34

$1000(1.1)^x = 4000$	Given equation
$1.1^x = 4$	Divide by 1000.
$\log 1.1^x = \log 4$	Take the common logarithm of each side.
$x \log 1.1 = \log 4$	Power rule for logarithms
$x = \dfrac{\log 4}{\log 1.1} \approx 14.5$	Divide by log 1.1 and approximate.

Interest is paid at the end of the year, so it will take 15 years for \$1000 earning 10% annual interest to grow to \$4000.

Graphical Solution   Graphical support is shown in Figure 9.34, where the graphs of $Y_1 = 1000*1.1^\wedge X$ and $Y_2 = 4000$ intersect when $x \approx 14.5$.

In the next example, we model the life span of a robin with an exponential function.

EXAMPLE 5   **Modeling the life span of robins**

The life span of 129 robins was monitored over a 4-year period in one study. The formula $f(x) = 10^{-0.42x}$ can be used to calculate the percentage of robins remaining after x years. For example, $f(1) \approx 0.38$ means that after 1 year 38% of the robins were still alive.
(***Source:*** D. Lack, *The Life Span of a Robin.*)
(a) Evaluate $f(2)$ and interpret the result.
(b) Determine when 5% of the robins remained.

Solution   **(a)** $f(2) = 10^{-0.42(2)} \approx 0.145$. After 2 years about 14.5% of the robins were still alive.
(b) Use $5\% = 0.05$ and solve the following equation.

$10^{-0.42x} = 0.05$	Equation to solve
$\log 10^{-0.42x} = \log 0.05$	Take the common logarithm of each side.
$-0.42x = \log 0.05$	Inverse property: $\log 10^k = k$
$x = \dfrac{\log 0.05}{-0.42} \approx 3.1$	Divide by -0.42.

After about 3 years only 5% of the robins were still alive.

LOGARITHMIC EQUATIONS AND MODELS

To solve an exponential equation we use logarithms. To solve a logarithmic equation we *exponentiate* each side of the equation. To do so we use the fact that if $x = y$, then $a^x = a^y$ for any positive base a. For example, to solve

$$\log x = 3$$

we exponentiate each side of the equation, using base 10.

$$10^{\log x} = 10^3$$

Because $10^{\log x} = x$ for all positive x,

$$x = 10^3 = 1000.$$

To solve logarithmic equations we frequently use the inverse property

$$a^{\log_a x} = x.$$

Examples of this inverse property include

$$e^{\ln 2k} = 2k, \quad 2^{\log_2 x} = x, \quad \text{and} \quad 10^{\log (x+5)} = x + 5.$$

The next two examples show how to solve logarithmic equations, followed by two applications of these methods.

EXAMPLE 6   Solving logarithmic equations

Solve and approximate solutions to the nearest hundredth when appropriate.
(a) $2 \log x = 4$ **(b)** $\ln 3x = 5.5$ **(c)** $\log_2 (x + 4) = 7$

Solution **(a)**

$2 \log x = 4$	Given equation
$\log x = 2$	Divide each side by 2.
$10^{\log x} = 10^2$	Exponentiate each side, using base 10.
$x = 100$	Inverse property: $10^{\log k} = k$

(b)

$\ln 3x = 5.5$	Given equation
$e^{\ln 3x} = e^{5.5}$	Exponentiate each side, using base e.
$3x = e^{5.5}$	Inverse property: $e^{\ln k} = k$
$x = \dfrac{e^{5.5}}{3} \approx 81.56$	Divide each side by 3 and approximate.

(c)

$\log_2 (x + 4) = 7$	Given equation
$2^{\log_2 (x+4)} = 2^7$	Exponentiate each side, using base 2.
$x + 4 = 2^7$	Inverse property: $2^{\log_2 k} = k$
$x = 2^7 - 4$	Subtract 4 from each side.
$x = 124$	Simplify.

TEACHING TIP

Emphasize that, to solve a logarithmic equation, students will need to exponentiate each side of the equation.

Because the domain of any logarithmic function includes only positive numbers, it is important to check answers, as emphasized in the next example.

EXAMPLE 7   Solving a logarithmic equation

Solve $\log (x + 2) + \log (x - 2) = \log 5$. Check the answers.

Solution   Start by applying the product rule for logarithms.

$\log (x + 2) + \log (x - 2) = \log 5$	Given equation
$\log ((x + 2)(x - 2)) = \log 5$	Product rule
$\log (x^2 - 4) = \log 5$	Multiply.
$10^{\log (x^2 - 4)} = 10^{\log 5}$	Exponentiate using base 10.
$x^2 - 4 = 5$	Inverse properties
$x^2 = 9$	Add 4.
$x = \pm 3$	Square root property.

Check each answer.

$$\log (3 + 2) + \log (3 - 2) \overset{?}{=} \log 5 \qquad \log (-3 + 2) + \log (-3 - 2) \overset{?}{=} \log 5$$
$$\log 5 + \log 1 \overset{?}{=} \log 5 \qquad\qquad \log (-1) + \log (-5) \neq \log 5$$
$$\log 5 + 0 \overset{?}{=} \log 5$$
$$\log 5 = \log 5$$

Although 3 is a solution, -3 is not, because both $\log (-1)$ and $\log (-5)$ are undefined expressions.

EXAMPLE 8   Modeling runway length

For some types of airplanes with weight x, the minimum runway length L required at takeoff is modeled by

$$L(x) = 3 \log x.$$

In this equation L is measured in thousands of feet and x is measured in thousands of pounds. Estimate the weight of the heaviest airplane that can take off from a runway 5100 feet long.   (**Source:** L. Haefner, *Introduction to Transportation Systems.*)

Solution   Runway length is measured in thousands of feet, so we must solve the equation $L(x) = 5.1$.

$$\begin{array}{ll}
3 \log x = 5.1 & L(x) = 5.1 \\
\log x = 1.7 & \text{Divide each side by 3.} \\
10^{\log x} = 10^{1.7} & \text{Exponentiate each side, using base 10.} \\
x = 10^{1.7} & \text{Inverse property: } 10^{\log k} = k \\
x \approx 50.1 & \text{Approximate.}
\end{array}$$

The largest airplane that can take off from this runway weighs about 50,000 pounds.

Critical Thinking

In Example 9, Section 9.3, we used the formula $L(x) = 1.3 \ln x$ to model runway length. Are $L(x) = 1.3 \ln x$ and $L(x) = 3 \log x$ equivalent formulas? Explain.

Yes; they are approximately the same because

$$3 \log x = 3 \left(\frac{\ln x}{\ln 10} \right) = \frac{3}{\ln 10} \cdot \ln x \approx 1.3 \ln x.$$

EXAMPLE 9   Modeling bird populations

Near New Guinea there is a relationship between the number of different species of birds and the size of an island. Larger islands tend to have a greater variety of birds. Table 9.13 lists the number of species of birds y found on islands with an area of x square kilometers.

TABLE 9.13

x (km^2)	0.1	1	10	100	1000
y (species)	10	15	20	25	30

Source: B. Freedman, *Environmental Ecology.*

(a) Find values for the constants a and b so that $y = a + b \log x$ models the data.

(b) Predict the number of bird species on an island of 15,000 square kilometers.

Solution (a) Because $\log 1 = 0$, substitute $x = 1$ and $y = 15$ in the equation to find a.

$$15 = a + b \log 1$$
$$15 = a + b \cdot 0$$
$$15 = a$$

Thus $y = 15 + b \log x$. To find b substitute $x = 10$ and $y = 20$.

$$20 = 15 + b \log 10$$
$$20 = 15 + b \cdot 1$$
$$5 = b$$

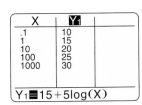

Figure 9.35

The data in Table 9.13 are modeled by $y = 15 + 5 \log x$. This result is supported by Figure 9.35.

(b) To predict the number of species on an island of 15,000 square kilometers, let $x = 15,000$ and find y.

$$y = 15 + 5 \log 15,000 \approx 36$$

The model estimates about 36 different species of birds on this island.

9.5 PUTTING IT ALL TOGETHER

Exponential and logarithmic equations occur in many applications. When solving exponential equations, we usually take the logarithm of each side. Similarly, when solving logarithmic equations, we usually *exponentiate* each side of the equation. That is, if $x = y$, then $a^x = a^y$ for any positive base a. We do so because a^x and $\log_a x$ represent inverse operations, much like adding and subtracting or multiplying and dividing. Basic steps for solving exponential and logarithmic equations are summarized in the following table.

Type of Equation	Procedure	Example	
Exponential	Begin by solving for the exponential expression a^x. Then take a logarithm of each side.	$4e^x + 1 = 9$	Given equation
		$e^x = 2$	Solve for e^x.
		$\ln e^x = \ln 2$	Take the natural logarithm.
		$x = \ln 2$	Inverse property: $\ln e^k = k$
Logarithmic	Begin by solving for the logarithm in the equation. Then exponentiate each side of the equation, using the same base as the logarithm.	$\dfrac{1}{3} \log 2x = 1$	Given equation
		$\log 2x = 3$	Multiply by 3.
		$10^{\log 2x} = 10^3$	Exponentiate using base 10.
		$2x = 1000$	Inverse property: $10^{\log k} = k$
		$x = 500$	Divide by 2.

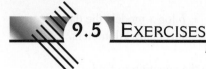

9.5 EXERCISES

FOR EXTRA HELP

 Student's Solutions Manual

 MyMathLab

 InterAct Math

 Math Tutor Center

MathXL

 Digital Video Tutor
CD 8   Videotape 10

CONCEPTS

1. To solve $x - 5 = 50$, what should be done?
Add 5 to each side.

2. To solve $5x = 50$, what should be done?
Divide each side by 5.

3. To solve $10^x = 50$, what should be done?
Take the common logarithm of each side.

4. To solve $\log x = 5$, what should be done?
Exponentiate each side using base 10.

5. $\log 10^x =$ _____ x **6.** $10^{\log x} =$ _____ x

7. $\ln e^{2x} =$ _____ $2x$ **8.** $e^{\ln (x+7)} =$ _____
$x + 7$

9. Does $\dfrac{\log 5}{\log 4}$ equal $\log \frac{5}{4}$? Explain.
No; $\log \frac{5}{4} = \log 5 - \log 4$

10. Does $\dfrac{\log 5}{\log 4}$ equal $\log 5 - \log 4$? Explain.
No; $\log 5 - \log 4 = \log \frac{5}{4}$

11. How many solutions are there to the equation $\log x = k$, where k is any real number? 1

12. How many solutions are there to the equation $10^x = k$, where k is a positive number? 1

EXPONENTIAL EQUATIONS

Exercises 13–40: Solve the equation. Approximate answers to the nearest hundredth when appropriate.

13. $10^x = 1000$ 3   **14.** $10^x = 0.01$ -2

15. $2^x = 64$ 6   **16.** $3^x = 27$ 3

17. $2^{x-3} = 8$ 6   **18.** $3^{2x} = 81$ 2

19. $4^x + 3 = 259$ 4   **20.** $3(5^{2x}) = 300$ $\frac{\log 100}{2 \log 5} \approx 1.43$

21. $10^{0.4x} = 124$ **22.** $0.75^x = 0.25$ $\frac{\log 0.25}{\log 0.75} \approx 4.82$
$\frac{\log 124}{0.4} \approx 5.23$

23. $e^{-x} = 1$ 0   **24.** $0.5^{-5x} = 5$ $\frac{\log 5}{-5 \log 0.5} \approx 0.46$

25. $e^x - 1 = 6$ $\ln 7 \approx 1.95$ **26.** $2e^{4x} = 15$ $\frac{\ln 7.5}{4} \approx 0.50$

27. $2(10)^{x+2} = 35$ **28.** $10^{3x} + 10 = 1500$ $\frac{\log 1490}{3} \approx 1.06$

29. $3.1^{2x} - 4 = 16$ **30.** $5.4^{x-1} = 85$ $\frac{\log 85}{\log 5.4} + 1 \approx 3.63$

31. $e^{3x} = e^{2x-1}$ -1 **32.** $e^{x^2} = e^{3x-2}$ 1, 2

33. $5^{4x} = 5^{x^2-5}$ $-1, 5$ **34.** $2^{4x} = 2^{x+3}$ 1

35. $e^{2x} \cdot e^x = 10$ $\frac{\ln 10}{3} \approx 0.77$ **36.** $10^{x-2} \cdot 10^x = 1000$ 2.5

27. $\log \frac{35}{2} - 2 \approx -0.76$ 29. $\frac{\log 20}{2 \log 3.1} \approx 1.32$

37. $e^x = 2^{x+2}$ $\frac{2 \ln 2}{1 - \ln 2} \approx 4.52$

38. $2^{2x} = 3^{x-1}$ $\frac{\log 3}{\log 3 - 2 \log 2} \approx -3.82$

39. $4^{0.5x} = 5^{x+2}$ $\frac{2 \log 5}{0.5 \log 4 - \log 5} \approx -3.51$

40. $3^{2x} = 7^{x+1}$ $\frac{\log 7}{2 \log 3 - \log 7} \approx 7.74$

Exercises 41–44: (Refer to Example 3.) The symbolic and graphical representations of f and g are given.

(a) Use the graph to solve $f(x) = g(x)$.

(b) Solve $f(x) = g(x)$ symbolically.

41. $f(x) = 0.2(10^x)$,
$g(x) = 2$ (a) 1
      (b) 1

42. $f(x) = e^x$,
$g(x) = 7.4$
      (a) 2
      (b) $\ln 7.4 \approx 2.001$

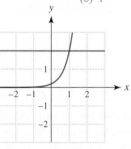

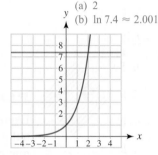

43. $f(x) = 2^{-x}$,
$g(x) = 4$ (a) -2
      (b) -2

44. $f(x) = 0.1(3^x)$,
$g(x) = 0.9$ (a) 2
      (b) 2

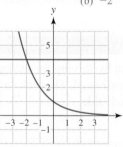

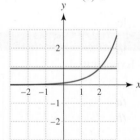

Exercises 45–52: Solve the equation symbolically. Give graphical or numerical support. Approximate answers to the nearest hundredth when appropriate.

45. $10^x = 0.1$ -1 **46.** $2(10^x) = 2000$ 3

47. $4e^x + 5 = 9$ 0   **48.** $e^x + 6 = 36$ $\ln 30 \approx 3.40$

49. $4^x = 1024$ 5   **50.** $3^x = 729$ 6

51. $(0.55)^x + 0.55 = 2$ **52.** $5(0.9)^x = 3$
$\frac{\log 1.45}{\log 0.55} \approx -0.62$ $\frac{\log 0.6}{\log 0.9} \approx 4.85$

Exercises 53–56: The given equation cannot be solved symbolically. Find any solutions either graphically or numerically to the nearest hundredth.

53. $e^x - x = 2$ −1.84, 1.15 **54.** $x \log x = 1$ 2.51

55. $\ln x = e^{-x}$ 1.31   **56.** $10^x - 2 = \log (x + 2)$
−1.99, 0.38

LOGARITHMIC EQUATIONS   65. $\frac{2^{2.3}}{5} \approx 0.98$

Exercises 57–78: Solve the equation. Approximate answers to the nearest hundredth when appropriate.

57. $\log x = 2$ 100   **58.** $\log x = 0.01$ $10^{0.01} \approx 1.02$

59. $\ln x = 5$ $e^5 \approx 148.41$ **60.** $2 \ln x = 4$ $e^2 \approx 7.39$

61. $\log 2x = 7$ 5,000,000 **62.** $6 \ln 4x = 12$ $\frac{e^2}{4} \approx 1.85$

63. $\log_2 x = 4$ 16   **64.** $\log_2 x = 32$
$2^{32} = 4,294,967,296$

65. $\log_2 5x = 2.3$ **66.** $2 \log_3 4x = 10$ 60.75

67. $2 \log x + 5 = 7.8$ **68.** $\ln (x - 1) = 3.3$
$10^{1.4} \approx 25.12$ $e^{3.3} + 1 \approx 28.11$
69. $5 \ln (2x + 1) = 55$ **70.** $5 - \log (x + 3) = 2.6$
$10^{2.4} - 3 \approx 248.19$
71. $\log x^2 = \log x$ 1   **72.** $\ln x^2 = \ln (3x - 2)$ 1, 2

73. $\ln x + \ln (x + 1) = \ln 30$ 5 69. $\frac{e^{11} - 1}{2} \approx 29,936.57$

74. $\log (x - 1) + \log (2x + 1) = \log 14$ 3

75. $\log_3 3x - \log_3 (x + 2) = \log_3 2$ 4

76. $\log_4 (x^2 - 1) - \log_4 (x - 1) = \log_4 6$ 5

77. $\log_2 (x - 1) + \log_2 (x + 1) = 3$ 3   91.(a) About 8503; in 1994 about 8503 people were waiting for liver transplants.

78. $\log_4 (x^2 + 2x + 1) - \log_4 (x + 1) = 2$ 15

Exercises 79–82: Two functions, f and g, are given.
(a) *Use the graph to solve* $f(x) = g(x)$.
(b) *Solve* $f(x) = g(x)$ *symbolically.*

79. $f(x) = \ln x$,   **80.** $f(x) = \log_2 x$,
$g(x) = 0.7$ $g(x) = 1.6$
(a) 2   (a) 3
(b) $e^{0.7} \approx 2.01$ (b) $2^{1.6} \approx 3.03$

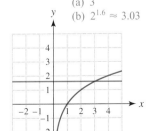

81. $f(x) = 5 \log 2x$,   **82.** $f(x) = 2 \ln (x) - 3$,
$g(x) = 3$ (a) 2 $g(x) = 0.9$ (a) 7
(b) $\frac{1}{2}(10^{0.6}) \approx 1.99$ (b) $e^{1.95} \approx 7.03$

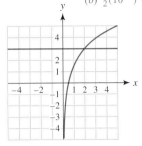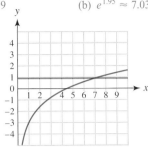

Exercises 83–88: Solve the equation symbolically. Give graphical or numerical support. Approximate answers to the nearest hundredth.

83. $\log x = 1.6$ **84.** $\ln x = 2$ $e^2 \approx 7.39$
$10^{1.6} \approx 39.81$
85. $\ln (x + 1) = 1$ **86.** $2 \log (2x + 3) = 8$ 4998.5
$e - 1 \approx 1.72$
87. $17 - 6 \log_3 x = 5$ 9 **88.** $4 \log_2 x + 7 = 12$
$2^{1.25} \approx 2.38$

APPLICATIONS

89. *Growth of a Mutual Fund*   (Refer to Example 4.) An investor deposits \$2000 in a mutual fund that returned 15% at the end of 1 year. Determine the length of time required for the investment to triple its value if the annual rate of return remains the same. 8 yr

90. *Savings Account*   (Refer to Example 4.) If a savings account pays 6% annual interest at the end of each year, how many years will it take for the account to double in value? 12 yr

91. *Liver Transplants*   In the United States the gap between available organs for liver transplants and people who need them has widened. The number of individuals waiting for liver transplants can be modeled by

$$f(x) = 2339(1.24)^{x-1988},$$

where x is the year.   (*Source:* United Network for Organ Sharing.)
(a) Evaluate $f(1994)$ and interpret the result.
(b) Determine when the number of individuals waiting for liver transplants was 20,000.
In about 1998

92. *Life Span of a Robin*   (Refer to Example 5.) Determine when 50% of the robins in the study were still alive.   After 0.72 yr

93. *Runway Length*   (Refer to Example 8.) Determine the weight of the heaviest airplane that can take off from a runway having a length of $\frac{3}{4}$ mile. (*Hint:* 1 mile = 5280 feet.)   About 20,893 lb

94. Runway Length (Refer to Example 8.)

(a) Suppose that an airplane is 10 times heavier than a second airplane. How much longer should the runway be for the heavier airplane than for the lighter airplane? (*Hint:* Let the heavier airplane have weight $10x$.) 3000 ft

(b) If the runway length is increased by 3000 feet, by what factor can the weight of an airplane that uses the runway be increased? 10

95. The Decline of Bluefin Tuna Bluefin tuna are large fish that can weigh 1500 pounds and swim at a speed of 55 miles per hour. They are used for sushi, and a prime fish can be worth more than $30,000. As a result, the number of western Atlantic bluefin tuna has declined dramatically. Their numbers in thousands between 1974 and 1991 can be modeled by $f(x) = 230(10^{-0.055x})$, where x is the number of years after 1974. See the accompanying graph. (*Source:* B. Freedman.)

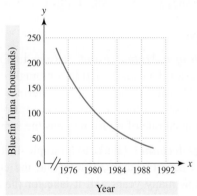

Year

(a) Evaluate $f(1)$ and interpret the result.

(b) Use the graph to estimate the year in which bluefin tuna numbered 115 thousand. In 1979

(c) Solve part (b) symbolically.
   (a) About 203; in 1975 there were about 203 thousand bluefin tuna.

96. Insect Populations (Refer to Example 9.) The table lists numbers of species of insects y found on islands having areas of x square miles.

x (square miles)	1	2	4
y (species)	1000	1500	2000

x (square miles)	8	16
y (species)	2500	3000

(a) Find values for constants a and b so that $y = a + b \log_2 x$ models the data. $a = 1000, b = 500$

(b) Construct a table for y and verify that your equation models the data.*

(c) Estimate the number of species of insects on an island having an area of 12 square miles. About 2792

Exercises 97 and 98: (Refer to Example 9.) Find values for a and b so that $y = a + b \log x$ models the data in the table.

97.

x	0.1	1	10	100
y	22	25	28	31

$a = 25, b = 3$

98.

x	0.01	1	100	1000
y	−10	−2	6	10

$a = -2, b = 4$

99. Calories Consumed and Land Ownership In developing countries there is a relationship between the amount of land a person owns and the average number of calories consumed daily. This relationship is modeled by

$$f(x) = 645 \log(x + 1) + 1925,$$

where x is the amount of land owned in acres and $0 \le x \le 4$. (*Source:* D. Grigg, *The World Food Problem.*)

(a) Estimate graphically the number of acres owned by a typical person consuming 2200 calories per day. About 1.67 acres

(b) Solve part (a) symbolically.

100. Population of Industrialized Urban Regions The number of people living in industrialized urban regions throughout the world has not grown exponentially. Instead it has grown logarithmically and is modeled by

$$f(x) = 0.36 + 0.15 \ln(x - 1949).$$

In this formula the output is billions of people and the input x is the year, where

$$1950 \le x \le 2030.$$

(*Source:* D. Meadows, *Beyond The Limits.*)

(a) Determine either graphically or numerically when this population may reach 1 billion. In 2020

(b) Solve part (a) symbolically.

101. Fertilizer Use Between 1950 and 1980, the use of chemical fertilizers increased worldwide. The table lists worldwide average use y in kilograms per acre

*Answers on page IA-31

101.(b) Each year the amount of fertilizer increased by a factor of 1.06, or by 6%.

of cropland during year x. (**Source:** D. Grigg, *The World Food Problem.*)

x	1950	1963	1972	1979
y	5.0	11.3	22.0	31.2

(a) Are the data linear or nonlinear? Explain.

(b) The equation $y = 5(1.06)^{(x-1950)}$ may be used to model the data. The growth factor is 1.06. What does this growth factor indicate about fertilizer use during this time period?

(c) Estimate the year when fertilizer use was 15 kilograms per acre of cropland.   In 1968

(a) Nonlinear; they do not increase at a constant rate.

102. *Greenhouse Gases*   If current trends continue, future concentrations of atmospheric carbon dioxide (CO_2) in parts per million (ppm) are expected to increase. This increase in concentration of CO_2 has been accelerated by burning fossil fuels and deforestation. The exponential equation $y = 364(1.005)^x$ may be used to model CO_2 in parts per million, where $x = 0$ corresponds to 2000, $x = 1$ to 2001, and so on.   (**Source:** R. Turner, *Environmental Economics.*) Estimate the year when the CO_2 concentration could be double the preindustrial level of 280 parts per million.

In 2086

103. *Modeling Sound*   The formula

$$f(x) = 160 + 10 \log x$$

is used to calculate the decibel level of a sound with intensity x measured in watts per square centimeter. The noise level at a basketball game can reach 100 decibels. Find the intensity x of this sound. 10^{-6} w/cm^2

104. *Loudness of a Sound*   (Refer to Exercise 103.)

(a) Show that, if the intensity of a sound increases by a factor of 10 from x to $10x$, the decibel level increases by 10 decibels. (*Hint:* Show that

$$160 + 10 \log 10x = 170 + 10 \log x.)*$$

(b) Find the increase in decibels if the intensity x increases by a factor of 1000.   30 dB

(c) Find the increase in the intensity x if the decibel level increases by 20.   100 times

105. *Hurricanes*   (Refer to Exercise 81, Section 9.3.) The barometric air pressure in inches of mercury at a distance of x miles from the eye of a severe hurricane is given by

$$f(x) = 0.48 \ln (x + 1) + 27.$$

(**Source:** A. Miller and R. Anthes, *Meteorology.*)
Determine how far from the eye the pressure is 28 inches of mercury.   About 7 miles

106. *Earthquakes*   The Richter scale is used to determine the intensity of earthquakes, which corresponds to the amount of energy released. If an earthquake has an intensity of x, its magnitude, as computed by the Richter scale, is given by $R(x) = \log \frac{x}{I_0}$, where I_0 is the intensity of a small, measurable earthquake.

(a) If x is 1000 times greater than I_0, how large is this increase on the Richter scale?   3 units

(b) If the Richter scale increases from 5 to 8, by what factor did the intensity x increase?   1000

WRITING ABOUT MATHEMATICS

107. Explain in words the basic steps for solving the equation $a(10^x) - b = c$ and then write the solution.

108. Explain in words the basic steps for solving the equation $a \log 3x = b$ and then write the solution.

CHECKING BASIC CONCEPTS   SECTION 9.5

1. Solve the equation. Approximate answers to the nearest hundredth when appropriate.

(a) $2(10^x) = 40$ **(b)** $2^{3x} + 3 = 150$

(c) $\ln x = 4.1$ **(d)** $4 \log 2x = 12$ 500
   $e^{4.1} \approx 60.34$

2. Solve $\log (x + 4) + \log (x - 4) = \log 48$. Check the answers.   8

1. (a) $\log 20 \approx 1.30$

1. (b) $\dfrac{\log 147}{3 \log 2} \approx 2.40$

3. If $500 are deposited in a savings account that pays 3% annual interest at the end of each year, the amount of money A in the account after x years is given by $A = 500(1.03)^x$. Estimate the number of years required for this amount to reach $900.
20 yr

*Answer on page IA-31

Summary

Section 9.1   *Composite and Inverse Functions*

Composition of Functions   If f and g are functions, then the composite function $g \circ f$, or composition of g and f, is defined by $(g \circ f)(x) = g\big(f(x)\big)$.

Example: If $f(x) = x - 5$ and $g(x) = 2x^2 + 4x - 6$, then $(g \circ f)(x)$ is

$$g\big(f(x)\big) = g(x - 5)$$
$$= 2(x - 5)^2 + 4(x - 5) - 6.$$

One-to-One Function   A function f is one-to-one if, for any c and d in the domain of f,

$$c \neq d \quad \text{implies that} \quad f(c) \neq f(d).$$

That is, different inputs always result in different outputs.

Example: $f(x) = x^2 + 4$ is *not* one-to-one; $-3 \neq 3$, but $f(-3) = f(3) = 13$.

Horizontal Line Test   If every horizontal line intersects the graph of a function f at most once, then f is a one-to-one function.

Examples:

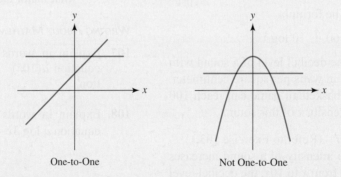

One-to-One   Not One-to-One

Inverse Functions   If f is one-to-one, then f has an inverse function, denoted f^{-1}, that satisfies

$$(f^{-1} \circ f)(x) = x \quad \text{and} \quad (f \circ f^{-1})(x) = x.$$

Example: $f(x) = 7x$ and $f^{-1}(x) = \frac{x}{7}$ are inverse functions.

Section 9.2   *Exponential Functions*

Exponential Function   An exponential function is defined by $f(x) = Ca^x$, where $a > 0$, $C > 0$, and $a \neq 1$. Its domain (set of valid inputs) is all real numbers and its range (outputs) is all positive real numbers.

Example: $f(x) = e^x$ is the natural exponential function and $e \approx 2.71828$.

Exponential Growth and Decay   When $a > 1$, the graph of $f(x) = Ca^x$ models exponential growth, and when $0 < a < 1$, it models exponential decay. The base a either represents the growth factor or the decay factor. The constant C equals $f(0)$.

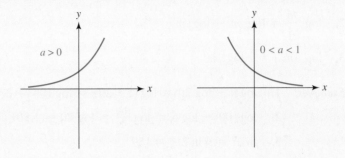

Example: $f(x) = 1.5(2)^x$ is an exponential function with $a = 2$ and $C = 1.5$. It models exponential growth because $a > 1$. The growth factor is 2 because for each unit increase in x, the output from $f(x)$ increases by a factor of 2.

Section 9.3   *Logarithmic Functions*

Base-a Logarithms   The logarithm with base a of a positive number x is denoted $\log_a x$. If $\log_a x = b$, then $x = a^b$. That is, $\log_a x$ represents the exponent on base a that results in x.

Example: $\log_2 16 = 4$ because $16 = 2^4$.

Domain and Range of Logarithmic Functions   The domain (set of valid inputs) of a logarithmic function is the set of all positive real numbers and the range (outputs) is the set of real numbers.

Graph of a Logarithmic Function   The graph of a logarithmic function passes through the point $(1, 0)$, as illustrated in the following graph. As x becomes large, $\log_a x$ with $a > 1$ grows very slowly.

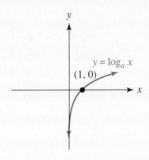

Section 9.4   *Properties of Logarithms*

Basic Properties   Logarithms have several important properties. For positive numbers m, n, and $a \neq 1$ and any real number r,

1. $\log_a mn = \log_a m + \log_a n$.

2. $\log_a \dfrac{m}{n} = \log_a m - \log_a n$.

3. $\log_a (m^r) = r \log_a m$.

Examples: **1.** $\log 5 + \log 20 = \log (5 \cdot 20) = \log 100 = 2$

2. $\log 100 - \log 5 = \log \frac{100}{5} = \log 20 \approx 1.301$

3. $\ln 2^6 = 6 \ln 2 \approx 4.159$

Note: $\log_a 1 = 0$ for any valid base a. Thus $\log 1 = 0$ and $\log_2 1 = 0$.

Inverse Properties   The following inverse properties are important for solving exponential and logarithmic equations.

1. $\log_a a^x = x$,   for any real number x

2. $a^{\log_a x} = x$,   for any positive number x

Examples: **1.** $\log_2 2^\pi = \pi$

2. $10^{\log 2.5} = 2.5$

Section 9.5   *Exponential and Logarithmic Equations*

Solving Equations   The calculations a^x and $\log_a x$ are inverse operations, much like addition and subtraction or multiplication and division. When solving an exponential equation, we usually take a logarithm of each side. When solving a logarithmic equation, we usually exponentiate each side.

Examples:

$2(5)^x = 22$	Exponential equation
$5^x = 11$	Divide by 2.
$\log 5^x = \log 11$	Take the common logarithm.
$x \log 5 = \log 11$	Power rule
$x = \dfrac{\log 11}{\log 5}$	Divide by $\log 5$.
$\log 2x = 2$	Logarithmic equation
$10^{\log 2x} = 10^2$	Exponentiate each side.
$2x = 100$	Inverse properties
$x = 50$	Divide by 2.

CHAPTER

9 Review Exercises

9. $(f \circ f^{-1})(x) = 2\left(\dfrac{x+9}{2}\right) - 9 = x$

$(f^{-1} \circ f)(x) = \dfrac{(2x-9)+9}{2} = x$

10. $(f \circ f^{-1})(x) = (\sqrt[3]{x-1})^3 + 1 = x$

$(f^{-1} \circ f)(x) = \sqrt[3]{(x^3+1)-1} = x$

SECTION 9.1

Exercises 1 and 2: For the given f(x) and g(x), find the following.

  (a) $(g \circ f)(-2)$ **(b)** $(f \circ g)(x)$

1. $f(x) = 2x^2 - 4x,$ $g(x) = 5x + 1$ (a) 81
(b) $(f \circ g)(x) = 50x^2 - 2$

2. $f(x) = \sqrt[3]{x-6},$ $g(x) = 4x^3$ (a) -32
(b) $(f \circ g)(x) = \sqrt[3]{4x^3 - 6}$

3. Use the tables to evaluate each expression.
  (a) $(f \circ g)(2)$ 0 **(b)** $(g \circ f)(1)$ 3

x	0	1	2	3
$f(x)$	3	2	1	0

x	0	1	2	3
$g(x)$	1	2	3	0

4. Use the graph to evaluate each expression.
  (a) $(f \circ g)(-1)$ 3
  (b) $(g \circ f)(2)$ -2
  (c) $(f \circ f)(1)$ -1

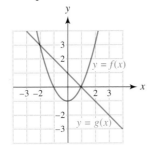

Exercises 5 and 6: Show that f is not one-to-one by finding two inputs that result in the same output. Answers may vary.

5. $f(x) = \dfrac{4}{1 + x^2}$ **6.** $f(x) = x^2 - 2x + 1$
  $f(1) = f(-1) = 2$ $f(0) = f(2) = 1$

Exercises 7 and 8: Use the horizontal line test to determine whether the graph represents a one-to-one function.

7.   No   **8.**   Yes

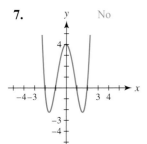   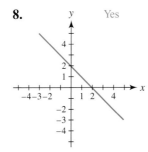

Exercises 9 and 10: Verify that f(x) and $f^{-1}(x)$ are indeed inverse functions.

  9. $f(x) = 2x - 9$ $f^{-1}(x) = \dfrac{x+9}{2}$

  10. $f(x) = x^3 + 1$ $f^{-1}(x) = \sqrt[3]{x-1}$

Exercises 11–14: Find $f^{-1}(x)$ for the one-to-one function f.

11. $f(x) = 5x$ $f^{-1}(x) = \dfrac{x}{5}$ **12.** $f(x) = x - 11$
                                   $f^{-1}(x) = x + 11$

13. $f(x) = 2x + 7$ **14.** $f(x) = \dfrac{4}{x}$ $f^{-1}(x) = \dfrac{4}{x}$
  $f^{-1}(x) = \dfrac{x-7}{2}$

15. Use the table to make a table of values for $f^{-1}(x)$.*
  What are the domain and range for f^{-1}?

x	0	1	2	3
$f(x)$	10	8	7	3

$D = \{3, 7, 8, 10\}; R = \{0, 1, 2, 3\}$

16. Use the graph of $y = f(x)$ to sketch a graph of $y = f^{-1}(x)$. Include the graph of f and the line $y = x$ in your graph.*

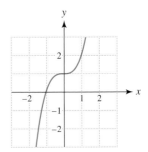

SECTIONS 9.2 AND 9.3

Exercises 17–20: Evaluate the exponential function for the given values of x.

17. $f(x) = 6^x$ $x = -1,$ $x = 2$ $\frac{1}{6}; 36$

18. $f(x) = 5(2^{-x})$ $x = 0,$ $x = 3$ $5; \frac{5}{8}$

19. $f(x) = \left(\frac{1}{3}\right)^x$ $x = -1,$ $x = 4$ $3; \dfrac{1}{81}$

20. $f(x) = 3\left(\frac{1}{6}\right)^x$ $x = 0,$ $x = 1$ $3; \dfrac{1}{2}$

*Answers on page IA-31

Exercises 21–24: Graph f. State whether the graph illustrates exponential growth, exponential decay, or logarithmic growth. *

22. Exponential decay

21. $f(x) = 2^x$
Exponential growth

22. $f(x) = \left(\frac{1}{2}\right)^x$

23. $f(x) = \ln(x + 1)$
Logarithmic growth

24. $f(x) = 3^{-x}$
Exponential decay

Exercises 25 and 26: A table for a function f is given.
  (a) *Determine whether f represents linear or exponential growth.*
  (b) *Find a formula for f.*

25.

x	0	1	2	3	4
$f(x)$	5	10	20	40	80

(a) Exponential growth   (b) $f(x) = 5(2)^x$

26.

x	0	1	2	3	4
$f(x)$	5	10	15	20	25

(a) Linear growth   (b) $f(x) = 5x + 5$

27. Use the graph of $y = Ca^x$ to find C and a.

$C = \frac{1}{2}, a = 2$

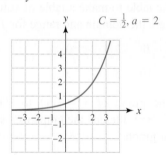

28. Use the graph of $y = k \log_2 x$ to find k. $k = 2$

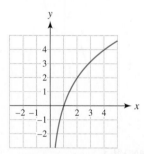

Exercises 29 and 30: If C dollars are deposited in an account that pays r percent annual interest at the end of each year, approximate the amount in the account after x years.

29. $C = \$1200$ $r = 10\%$ $x = 9$ years $\$2829.54$

30. $C = \$900$ $r = 18\%$ $x = 40$ years $\$675,340.51$

Exercises 31–34: Evaluate f(x) for the given value of x. Approximate answers to the nearest hundredth.

31. $f(x) = 2e^x - 1$ $x = 5.3$ 399.67

32. $f(x) = 0.85^x$ $x = 2.1$ 0.71

33. $f(x) = 2 \log x$ $x = 55$ 3.48

34. $f(x) = \ln(2x + 3)$ $x = 23$ 3.89

Exercises 35–38: Evaluate the logarithm by hand.

35. $\log 0.001$ -3

36. $\log \sqrt{10,000}$ 2

37. $\ln e^{-4}$ -4

38. $\log_4 16$ 2

Exercises 39–42: Approximate the logarithm to the nearest thousandth.

39. $\log 65$ 1.813

40. $\ln 0.85$ -0.163

41. $\ln 120$ 4.787

42. $\log_2 \frac{2}{5}$ -1.322

Exercises 43–46: Simplify, using inverse properties of logarithms.

43. $10^{\log 7}$ 7

44. $\log_2 2^{5/9}$ $\frac{5}{9}$

45. $\ln e^{6-x}$ $6 - x$

46. $e^{2 \ln x}$ x^2

Section 9.4

Exercises 47–52: Write the expression by using sums and differences of logarithms of x, y, and z.

47. $\ln xy$ $\ln x + \ln y$

48. $\log \dfrac{x}{y}$ $\log x - \log y$

49. $\ln\left(x^2 y^3\right)$ $2 \ln x + 3 \ln y$

50. $\log \dfrac{\sqrt{x}}{z^3}$ $\frac{1}{2} \log x - 3 \log z$

51. $\log_2 \dfrac{x^2 y}{z}$

$2 \log_2 x + \log_2 y - \log_2 z$

52. $\log_3 \sqrt[3]{\dfrac{x}{y}}$ $\frac{1}{3} \log_3 x - \frac{1}{3} \log_3 y$

Exercises 53–56: Write the expression as one logarithm.

53. $\log 45 + \log 5 - \log 3$ $\log 75$

54. $\log_4 2x + \log_4 5x$ $\log_4 (10x^2)$

55. $2 \ln x - 3 \ln y$ $\ln \dfrac{x^2}{y^3}$

56. $\log x^4 - \log x^3 + \log y$ $\log xy$

*Answers on page IA-31

Exercises 57–60: Rewrite the expression, using the power rule.

57. $\log 6^3$ $3 \log 6$

58. $\ln x^2$ $2 \ln x$

59. $\log_2 5^{2x}$ $(2x) \log_2 5$

60. $\log_4 (0.6)^{x+1}$
   $(x + 1) \log_4 0.6$

SECTION 9.5

Exercises 61–70: Solve the equation. Approximate answers to the nearest hundredth when appropriate.

61. $10^x = 100$ 2

62. $2^{2x} = 256$ 4

63. $3e^x + 1 = 28$ $\ln 9 \approx 2.20$

64. $0.85^x = 0.2$ $\frac{\log (0.2)}{\log (0.85)} \approx 9.90$

65. $5 \ln x = 4$ $e^{0.8} \approx 2.23$

66. $\ln 2x = 5$ $\frac{1}{2}e^5 \approx 74.21$

67. $2 \log x = 80$ 10^{40}

68. $3 \log x - 5 = 1$ 100

69. $2^{x+4} = 3^x$ $\frac{4 \log 2}{\log 3 - \log 2} \approx 6.84$

70. $\ln (2x + 1) + \ln (x - 5) = \ln 13$ 6

Exercises 71 and 72: Graphs and formulas for f and g are given.
    (a) Solve $f(x) = g(x)$ graphically.
    (b) Solve $f(x) = g(x)$ symbolically.

71. $f(x) = \frac{1}{2}(2^x)$,
$g(x) = 4$
   (a) 3
   (b) 3

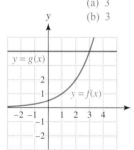

72. $f(x) = \log_2 2x$,
$g(x) = 3$
   (a) 4
   (b) 4

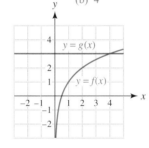

73.(a) 64π; after 8 sec, the balloon has a surface area of $64\pi \approx 201$ in^2.

APPLICATIONS

73. *Surface Area of a Balloon* The surface area S of a spherical balloon with radius r is given by $S(r) = 4\pi r^2$. Suppose that the balloon is being inflated so that its radius in inches after t seconds is $r(t) = \sqrt{2t}$.
   (a) Evaluate $(S \circ r)(8)$ and interpret your result.
   (b) Find $(S \circ r)(t)$. $(S \circ r)(t) = 8\pi t$

74. *Sales Tax* Suppose that $f(x) = 0.08x$ calculates the sales tax in dollars on an item that costs x dollars.
   (a) Is f a one-to-one function? Why?
     Yes; different inputs result in different outputs.

   (b) Find a formula for f^{-1} and interpret what it calculates. $f^{-1}(x) = \frac{x}{0.08}$ calculates the cost of an item whose sales tax is x dollars.

75. *Growth of a Mutual Fund* An investor deposits $1500 in a mutual fund that returns 12% annually. Determine the time required for the investment to double in value.   7 yr

76. *Modeling Data* Find values for the constants a and b so that $y = a + b \log x$ models these data. $a = 100, b = 50$

x	0.1	1	10	100	1000
y	50	100	150	200	250

77. *Modeling Data* Find values for the constants C and a so that $y = Ca^x$ models these data. $C = 3, a = 2$

x	0	1	2	3	4
y	3	6	12	24	48

78. *Earthquakes* The Richter scale, used to determine the magnitude of earthquakes, is based on the formula $R(x) = \log \frac{x}{I_0}$, where x is the measured intensity. Let $I_0 = 1$. Find the intensity x for an earthquake with $R = 7$. 10^7

79. *Modeling Population* In 1997 the population of Nevada was 1.68 million and growing continuously at an annual rate of 4.8%. The population of Nevada in millions x years after 1997 can be modeled by
$$f(x) = 1.68e^{0.048x}.$$ (b) About 2.24 million
   (a) Graph f in [0, 10, 2] by [0, 4, 1]. Does this function represent exponential growth or decay? *   Growth
   (b) Predict the population of Nevada in 2003.
   (c) Estimate the year when the population might reach 3 million.   2009

80. (a) 1000; there were 1000 bacteria/mL initially.

80. *Modeling Bacteria* A colony of bacteria can be modeled by $N(t) = 1000e^{0.0014t}$, where N is measured in bacteria per milliliter and t is in minutes.
   (a) Evaluate $N(0)$ and interpret the result.
   (b) Estimate how long it takes for N to double.
     About 495.11 min

81. *Modeling Wind Speed* Wind speeds are usually measured at heights from 5 to 10 meters above the ground. For a particular day, $f(x) = 1.2 \ln (x) + 5$ computes the wind speed in meters per second x meters above the ground, where $x \geq 1$. (*Source:* A. Miller and R. Anthes, *Meteorology*.)   (a) About 6.93 m/sec
   (a) Find the wind speed at a height of 5 meters.
   (b) Estimate the height at which the wind speed is 8 meters per second.   12.18 m   *Answers on page IA-31

9 Test

1. If $f(x) = 4x^3 - 5x$ and $g(x) = x + 7$, then evaluate $(g \circ f)(1)$ and $(f \circ g)(x)$.
   $6; (f \circ g)(x) = 4(x + 7)^3 - 5(x + 7)$

2. Use the graph to evaluate each expression.
   (a) $(f \circ g)(-1)$　3
   (b) $(g \circ f)(1)$　3

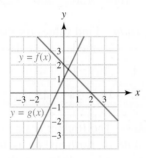

3. Explain why $f(x) = x^2 - 25$ is not a one-to-one function.　$-5 \neq 5$, but $f(-5) = f(5) = 0$

4. If $f(x) = 5 - 2x$, find $f^{-1}(x)$.　$f^{-1}(x) = \dfrac{5 - x}{2}$

5. Use the graph of $y = f(x)$ to sketch a graph of $y = f^{-1}(x)$. Include the graph of f and the line $y = x$ in your graph. *

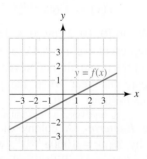

6. Use the table to write a table of values for $f^{-1}(x)$. * What are the domain and range of f^{-1}?

x	1	2	3	4
$f(x)$	8	6	4	2

   $D = \{2, 4, 6, 8\}; R = \{1, 2, 3, 4\}$

7. Evaluate $f(x) = 3\left(\frac{1}{4}\right)^x$ at $x = 2$.　$\frac{3}{16}$

8. Graph $f(x) = 1.5^{-x}$. State whether the graph illustrates exponential growth, exponential decay, or logarithmic growth. *　Exponential decay

Exercises 9 and 10: A table for a function f is given.
   (a) *Determine whether f represents linear or exponential growth.*
   (b) *Find a formula for $f(x)$.*

9.
x	-2	-1	0	1	2
$f(x)$	0.75	1.5	3	6	12

   (a) Exponential　(b) $f(x) = 3(2)^x$

10.
x	-2	-1	0	1	2
$f(x)$	-4	-2.5	-1	0.5	2

   (a) Linear　(b) $f(x) = 1.5x - 1$

11. Use the graph of $y = Ca^x$ to find C and a.

$C = 1, a = \frac{1}{2}$

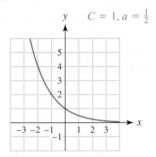

12. If \$750 are deposited in an account paying 7% annual interest at the end of each year, approximate the amount in the account after 5 years.　\$1051.91

13. Let $f(x) = 1.5 \ln(x - 5)$. Approximate $f(21)$ to the nearest hundredth.　4.16

14. Evaluate $\log \sqrt{10}$ by hand.　$\frac{1}{2}$

15. Approximate $\log_2 43$ to the nearest thousandth.　5.426

16. Graph $f(x) = \log(x - 2)$. Compare this graph to the graph of $y = \log x$. *　Shifted to the right 2 units

17. Write $\log \dfrac{x^3 y^2}{\sqrt{z}}$, using sums and differences of logarithms of x, y, and z.　$3 \log x + 2 \log y - \frac{1}{2} \log z$

18. Write $4 \ln x - 5 \ln y + \ln z$ as one logarithm.　$\ln \dfrac{x^4 z}{y^5}$

19. Rewrite $\log 7^{2x}$, using the power rule.　$2x \log 7$

20. Simplify $\ln e^{1-3x}$, using inverse properties of logarithms.　$1 - 3x$

*Answers on page IA-32

Exercises 21–24: Solve the equation. Approximate answers to the nearest hundredth when appropriate.

21. $2e^x = 50$
ln 25 ≈ 3.22

22. $3(10)^x - 7 = 143$
log 50 ≈ 1.70

23. $5 \log x = 9$
$10^{1.8} ≈ 63.10$

24. $3 \ln 5x = 27$
$\frac{1}{5}e^9 ≈ 1620.62$

25. *Modeling Data* Find values for constants a and b so that $y = a + b \log x$ models the data. $a = 5; b = 3$

x	0.01	0.1	1	10	100
y	−1	2	5	8	11

26. *Modeling Bacteria Growth* A sample of bacteria is growing continuously at a rate of 9% per hour and can be modeled by

$$f(x) = 4e^{0.09x},$$

where the input x represents elapsed time in hours and the output $f(x)$ is in millions of bacteria.

(a) What was the initial number of bacteria in the sample? 4 million

(b) Evaluate $f(5)$ and interpret the result.

(c) Does this function represent exponential growth or decay? Growth

(d) Determine the elapsed time when there were 6 million bacteria. After 4.51 hr

(b) $4e^{0.45} ≈ 6.27$; after 5 hr there were about 6.27 million bacteria.

CHAPTER 9 Extended and Discovery Exercises

Exercises 1–4: Radioactive Carbon Dating While an animal is alive, it breathes both carbon dioxide and oxygen. Because a small portion of normal atmospheric carbon dioxide is made up of radioactive carbon-14, a fixed percentage of the animal's body is composed of carbon-14. When the animal dies, it quits breathing and the carbon-14 disintegrates without being replaced. One method used to determine when an animal died is to estimate the percentage of carbon-14 remaining in its bones. The **half-life** of carbon-14 is 5730 years. That is, half the original amount of carbon-14 in bones of a fossil will remain after 5730 years. The percentage P, in decimal form, of carbon-14 remaining after x years is modeled by $P(x) = a^x$.

1. Find the value of a. (*Hint:* $P(5730) = 0.5$.)
$a ≈ 0.999879$

2. Calculate the percentage of carbon-14 remaining after 10,000 years. About 29.8%

3. Estimate the age of a fossil with $P = 0.9$.
About 871 yr

4. Estimate the age of a fossil with $P = 0.01$.
About 38,100 yr

 *Exercises 5–8: Modeling Blood Flow in Animals* For medical reasons, dyes may be injected into the bloodstream to determine the health of internal organs. In one study in-

volving animals, the dye BSP was injected to assess blood flow in the liver. The results are listed in the accompanying table, where x represents the elapsed time in minutes and y is the concentration of the dye in the bloodstream in milligrams per milliliter (mg/mL). Scientists modeled the data with $f(x) = 0.133(0.878(0.73^x) + 0.122(0.92^x))$.

x (minutes)	1	2	3	4
y (mg/mL)	0.102	0.077	0.057	0.045

x (minutes)	5	7	9	13
y (mg/mL)	0.036	0.023	0.015	0.008

x (minutes)	16	19	22
y (mg/mL)	0.005	0.004	0.003

Source: F. Harrison, "The measurement of liver blood flow in conscious calves."

5. Graph f together with the data. Comment on the fit. *
The fit is quite good.

6. Determine the y-intercept and interpret the result.
0.133; the initial concentration is 0.133 mg/mL.

7. What happens to the concentration of the dye after a long period of time? Explain.

It decreases to 0 as the animal's body eliminates the dye from the bloodstream. *Answer on page IA-32

8. Estimate graphically the time at which the concentration of the dye reached 40% of its initial amount. Would you want to solve this problem symbolically? Explain.   After 3.33 min; no, doing so would be very difficult.

Exercises 9 and 10: Acid Rain   *Air pollutants frequently cause acid rain. A measure of acidity is pH, which measures the concentration of the hydrogen ions in a solution, and ranges from 1 to 14. Pure water is neutral and has a pH of 7, acid solutions have a pH less than 7, and alkaline solutions have a pH greater than 7. The pH of a substance can be computed by $f(x) = -\log x$, where x represents the hydrogen ion concentration in moles per liter. Pure water exposed to normal carbon dioxide in the atmosphere has a pH of 5.6. If the pH of a lake drops below this level, it is indicative of an acid lake.*   (*Source:* G. Howells, *Acid Rain and Acid Water.*)

9. In rural areas of Europe, rainwater typically has a hydrogen ion concentration of $x = 10^{-4.7}$. Find its pH. What effect might this rain have on a lake with a pH of 5.6?   4.7; this rain could cause the pH to drop below 5.6.

10. Seawater has a pH of 8.2. Compared to seawater, how many times greater is the hydrogen ion concentration in rainwater from rural Europe?   About 3162 times greater

Exercises 11 and 12: Investment Account   *If x dollars are deposited every 2 weeks (26 times per year) in an account paying an annual interest rate r, expressed in decimal form, the amount A in the account after n years can be approximated by the formula*

$$A = x\left[\frac{(1 + r/26)^{26n} - 1}{(r/26)}\right].$$

11. If $100 are deposited every 2 weeks in an account paying 9% interest, approximate the amount in the account after 10 years.   About $42,055.97

12. Suppose that your retirement account pays 12% annual interest. Determine how much you should de-posit in this account every 2 weeks, in order to have one million dollars at age 65.   For a 19-year-old student the amount is $18.80.

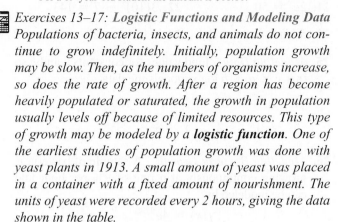

Exercises 13–17: Logistic Functions and Modeling Data   *Populations of bacteria, insects, and animals do not continue to grow indefinitely. Initially, population growth may be slow. Then, as the numbers of organisms increase, so does the rate of growth. After a region has become heavily populated or saturated, the growth in population usually levels off because of limited resources. This type of growth may be modeled by a **logistic function**. One of the earliest studies of population growth was done with yeast plants in 1913. A small amount of yeast was placed in a container with a fixed amount of nourishment. The units of yeast were recorded every 2 hours, giving the data shown in the table.*

Time (hours)	0	2	4	6
Yeast (units)	9.6	29.0	71.1	174.6

Time (hours)	8	10	12
Yeast (units)	350.7	513.3	594.8

Time (hours)	14	16	18
Yeast (units)	640.8	655.9	661.8

Source: D. Brown, *Models in Biology.*

13. Make a scatterplot of the data. *

14. Describe the growth of yeast and explain the graph.
Slowly at first, then rapidly, and then levels off.

15. The data are modeled by the logistic function given by

$$Y(t) = \frac{663}{(1 + 71.6(0.579)^t)}.$$

Graph Y and the data in the same viewing rectangle. *

16. Determine graphically when the amount of yeast equals 400 units.   After 8.6 hr

17. Solve Exercise 16 symbolically.   After 8.6 hr

2. Natural: none; whole: 0; integer: $-3, 0$;
rational: $-\frac{11}{7}, -3, 0, 5.\overline{18}$; irrational: $\sqrt{6}, \pi$

CHAPTERS 1–9   Cumulative Review Exercises   **665**

1–9 Cumulative Review Exercises

1. Write the number 0.000429 in scientific notation.
4.29×10^{-4}

2. Classify each real number as one or more of the following: natural number, whole number, integer, rational number, or irrational number.
$$-\frac{11}{7}, -3, 0, \sqrt{6}, \pi, 5.\overline{18}$$

3. Select the formula that best models the data in the table. (iii)

x	-2	-1	0	1	2
y	-7	-5	-3	-1	1

   (i) $y = 3x + 1$ **(ii)** $y = x - 3$ **(iii)** $y = 2x - 3$

4. State whether the equation illustrates an identity, commutative, associative, or distributive property.
Commutative
$$(5 - y) + 9 = 9 + (5 - y)$$

Exercises 5–8: Simplify the expression. Write the result with positive exponents.

5. $\left(\dfrac{1}{d^2}\right)^{-2}$ d^4

6. $\left(\dfrac{8a^2}{2b^3}\right)^{-3}$ $\dfrac{b^9}{64a^6}$

7. $\dfrac{(2x^{-2}y^3)^2}{xy^{-2}}$ $\dfrac{4y^8}{x^5}$

8. $\dfrac{x^{-3}y}{4x^2y^{-3}}$ $\dfrac{y^4}{4x^5}$

9. Use the graph to express the equation of the line in slope–intercept form. $y = \frac{5}{4}x + 1$

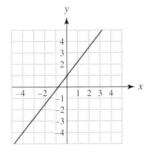

10. Find the domain of $f(x) = \dfrac{10}{x + 3}$. $\{x \mid x \neq -3\}$

11. Use the table to write the formula for $f(x) = ax + b$.

x	-2	-1	0	1	2
$f(x)$	-11	-7	-3	1	5

$f(x) = 4x - 3$

12. Write the equation of the vertical line passing through the point $(4, 7)$. $x = 4$

13. Calculate the slope of the line passing through the points $(4, -1)$ and $(2, -3)$.   1

14. Sketch the graph of a line passing through the point $(-1, -2)$ with slope $m = 3$. *

Exercises 15 and 16: Write the slope–intercept form for a line satisfying the given conditions.

15. Perpendicular to $y = -\frac{1}{7}x - 8$, passing through $(1, 1)$
$y = 7x - 6$

16. Parallel to $y = 3x - 1$, passing through $(0, 5)$
$y = 3x + 5$

17. Use the graph to solve the equation $y_1 = y_2$. -1

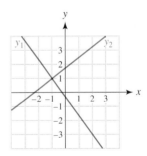

18. Use the table to solve $y < -4$, where y represents a linear function. Write the solution set as an inequality.

x	-2	-1	0	1	2
y	-24	-14	-4	6	16

$x < 0$

Exercises 19–24: Solve the equation or inequality. Write the solutions to the inequalities in interval notation.

19. $\frac{2}{3}(x - 3) + 8 = -6$ -18

*Answer on page IA-32

20. $\frac{1}{3}z + 6 < \frac{1}{4}z - (5z - 6)$ $(-\infty, 0)$

21. $\left(\dfrac{t + 2}{3}\right) - 10 = \frac{1}{3}t - (5t + 8)$ $\frac{4}{15}$

22. $-10 \le -\frac{3}{5}x - 4 < -1$ $(-5, 10]$

23. $-2|t - 4| \ge -12$ **24.** $\left|\frac{1}{2}x - 5\right| = 3$ $4, 16$
 $[-2, 10]$

25. Shade the solution set in the xy-plane.*

$$x + y > 3$$
$$2x - y \ge 3$$

26. Evaluate $det\ A$. 2

$$A = \begin{bmatrix} -1 & -2 \\ 3 & 4 \end{bmatrix}$$

Exercises 27–30: Solve the system of equations, if possible. Write the solution as an ordered pair or ordered triple where appropriate.

27. $4x - 3y = 1$ $(1, 1)$
$5x + 2y = 7$

28. $2x - 3y = -2$
      $-6x + 9y = 5$
      No solutions

29. $2x - y + 3z = -2$ **30.** $x + y - z = -1$
    $x + 5y - 2z = -8$ $-x - y - z = -1$
   $-3x - y - 3z = 6$ $x - 2y + z = 1$
   $(-4, 0, 2)$ $(0, 0, 1)$

31. Maximize the objective function R, subject to the given constraints. $R = 21$

$$R = 2x + 5y$$
$$3x + y \le 12$$
$$x + 3y \le 12$$
$$x \ge 0, y \ge 0$$

32. Find the area of the triangle by using a determinant. Assume that units are inches. $8\ in^2$

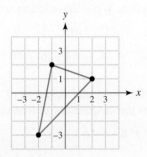

Exercises 33–36: Factor completely.

33. $2x^3 - 4x^2 + 2x$
 $2x(x - 1)^2$

34. $4a^2 - 25b^2$
 $(2a - 5b)(2a + 5b)$

35. $8t^3 - 27$
 $(2t - 3)(4t^2 + 6t + 9)$

36. $4a^3 - 2a^2 + 10a - 5$
 $(2a^2 + 5)(2a - 1)$

Exercises 37–40: Solve the equation.

37. $6x^2 - 7x - 10 = 0$ **38.** $9x^2 = 4$ $-\frac{2}{3}, \frac{2}{3}$

39. $x^4 - 2x^3 = 15x^2$ **40.** $5x - 10x^2 = 0$ $0, \frac{1}{2}$
 $-3, 0, 5$
                                         37. $-\frac{5}{6}, 2$

Exercises 41 and 42: Simplify the expression.

41. $\dfrac{x^2 + 5x + 6}{x^2 - 9} \cdot \dfrac{x - 3}{x + 2}$ 1

42. $\dfrac{x^2 - 2x - 8}{x^2 + x - 12} \div \dfrac{(x - 4)^2}{x^2 - 16}$ $\dfrac{x + 2}{x - 3}$

Exercises 43 and 44: Solve the rational equation. Check your result.

43. $\dfrac{2}{x + 2} - \dfrac{1}{x - 2} = \dfrac{-3}{x^2 - 4}$ 3

44. $\dfrac{3y}{y^2 + y - 2} = \dfrac{1}{y - 1} - 2$ -3

45. Solve the equation for J. $J = \dfrac{2z}{P - 1}$

$$P = \dfrac{J + 2z}{J}$$

46. Simplify the complex fraction. $\dfrac{x^3 + 3}{x^3 - 3}$

$$\dfrac{\dfrac{3}{x^2} + x}{x - \dfrac{3}{x^2}}$$

47. Suppose that y varies as x. If $y = 15$ when $x = 3$, find y when x is 8. 40

48. Divide. $3x^2 + 6x + 10 + \dfrac{5}{x - 2}$
$$(3x^3 - 2x - 15) \div (x - 2)$$

Exercises 49–54: Simplify the expression. Assume that all variables are positive.

49. $\left(\dfrac{x^6}{y^9}\right)^{2/3}$ $\dfrac{x^4}{y^6}$ **50.** $\sqrt[3]{-x^4} \cdot \sqrt[3]{-x^5}$ x^3

51. $\sqrt{5ab} \cdot \sqrt{20ab}$ $10ab$ **52.** $2\sqrt{24} - \sqrt{54}$ $\sqrt{6}$

53. $\sqrt[3]{a^5b^4} + 3\sqrt[3]{a^5b}$ **54.** $(5 + \sqrt{5})(5 - \sqrt{5})$ 20
 $(b + 3)a\sqrt[3]{a^2b}$

55. Rationalize the denominator. $\dfrac{5 + \sqrt{3}}{11}$

$$P = \dfrac{2}{5 - \sqrt{3}}$$

*Answer on page IA-32

56. Find the domain of f. Write your answer in interval notation. $(4, \infty)$

$$f(x) = \frac{3}{\sqrt{x - 4}}$$

Exercises 57 and 58: Solve. Check your answer.

57. $2(x + 1)^2 = 50$ **58.** $\sqrt{x + 6} = x$ 3
$-6, 4$

Exercises 59 and 60: Write the complex expression in standard form.

59. $(-2 + 3i) - (-5 - 2i)$ $3 + 5i$

60. $\dfrac{3 - i}{1 + 3i}$ $-i$

61. Find the vertex of the parabola determined by $f(x) = 3x^2 - 12x + 13$. $(2, 1)$

62. Find the maximum y-value on the parabola determined by $y = -2x^2 + 6x - 1$. $\frac{7}{2}$

63. Compare the graph of $f(x) = (x - 3)^2 + 2$ to the graph of $y = x^2$. Shifted to the right 3 units and up 2 units

64. Write the equation $y = x^2 + 6x - 2$ in vertex form and identify the vertex. $y = (x + 3)^2 - 11; (-3, -11)$

Exercises 65–68: Solve the quadratic equation by using the method of your choice.

65. $x^2 - 13x + 40 = 0$ **66.** $2d^2 - 5 = d$ $\frac{1 \pm \sqrt{41}}{4}$
$5, 8$

67. $z^2 - 4z = -2$ **68.** $x^4 - 10x^2 + 24 = 0$
$2 \pm \sqrt{2}$ $\pm 2, \pm \sqrt{6}$

69. A graph of $y = ax^2 + bx + c$ is shown.
   (a) Solve $ax^2 + bx + c = 0$.
   (b) State whether $a > 0$ or $a < 0$.
   (c) Determine whether the discriminant is positive, negative, or zero.

(a) $-1, 3$
(b) $a < 0$
(c) Positive

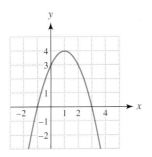

70. Solve the quadratic inequality. Write your answer in interval notation. $(-\infty, -7] \cup [2, \infty)$

$$x^2 + 5x - 14 \geq 0$$

71. For $f(x) = x^2 - 2$ and $g(x) = 2x + 1$, find the following.
   (a) $(f \circ g)(1)$ 7
   (b) $(g \circ f)(x)$ $(g \circ f)(x) = 2x^2 - 3$

72. Show that f is not one-to-one by finding two inputs that result in the same output. Answers may vary.

$$f(x) = x^2 + x - 6$$ $f(-4) = f(3) = 6$

73. Find $f^{-1}(x)$ for the one-to-one function $f(x) = \frac{3}{x}$.
$f^{-1}(x) = \frac{3}{x}$

74. If \$800 are deposited in an account that pays 7.5% annual interest at the end of each year, approximate the amount in the account after 15 years. \$2367.10

Exercises 75 and 76: Evaluate without a calculator.

75. $\log_3 81$ 4 **76.** $e^{\ln (2x)}$ $2x$

77. Write the expression by using sums and differences of logarithms of x and y. Assume x and y are positive.

$$\log \frac{\sqrt{x}}{y^2}$$ $\frac{1}{2} \log x - 2 \log y$

78. Write the expression as one logarithm. $\ln (5x^3)$

$$2 \ln x + \ln 5x$$

Exercises 79 and 80: Solve the equation. Approximate answers to the nearest hundredth.

79. $6 \log x - 2 = 9$ 68.13

80. $2^{3x} = 17$ 1.36

APPLICATIONS

81. *Population Growth* The population P of a community with an annual percentage growth rate r (expressed as a decimal) after t years is given by $P = P_0(1 + r)^t$, where P_0 represents the initial population of the community. If a community having an initial population of $P_0 = 12,000$ grew to a population of $P = 14,600$ in $t = 5$ years, find the annual percentage growth rate for this community. 4%

82. *Wing Span of a Bird* The wing span L of a bird with weight W can sometimes be modeled by $L = 27.4 \sqrt[3]{W}$, where L is in inches and W is in pounds. Use this formula to estimate the weight of a bird that has a wing span of 36 inches. (*Source:* C. Pennycuick, *Newton Rules Biology.*) 2.27 lb

83. *U.S. Energy Consumption*   From 1950 to 1970, per capita consumption of energy in millions of Btu can be modeled by $f(x) = 0.25x^2 - 975x + 950{,}845$, where x is the year.   (*Source:* Department of Energy.)

(a) During what year was per capita energy consumption at its lowest?   1950

(b) What was the minimum value for per capita energy consumption?   220 million Btu

84. *Braking Distance*   On dry, level pavement a safe braking distance d in feet for a car traveling x miles per hour is $d = \frac{x^2}{12}$. What speed corresponds to a braking distance of 350 feet?   (*Source:* F. Mannering, *Principles of Highway Engineering and Traffic Control.*)

$\sqrt{4200} \approx 64.8$ mph

85. *Investing for Retirement*   A college student invests $8000 in an account that pays interest annually. If the student would like this investment to be worth $1,000,000 in 45 years, what annual interest rate would the account need to pay?   About 11.3 %

86. *Modeling Wind Speed*   Wind speeds are usually measured at heights from 5 to 10 meters above the ground. For a particular day, $f(x) = 1.4 \ln(x) + 7$ computes the wind speed in meters per second x meters above the ground, where $x \geq 1$.   (*Source:* A. Miller and R. Anthes, *Meteorology.*)

(a) Find the wind speed at a height of 8 meters.

(b) Estimate the height at which the wind speed is 10 meters per second.   (a) 9.91 m/sec
(b) 8.52 m

10

Conic Sections

Throughout history people have been fascinated with the universe around them and compelled to understand its mysteries. Conic sections, which include parabolas, circles, ellipses, and hyperbolas, have played an important role in gaining this understanding. Although conic sections were described and named by the Greek astronomer Apollonius in 200 B.C., not until much later were they used to model motion in the universe. In the sixteenth century Tycho Brahe, the greatest observational astronomer of the age, recorded precise data on planetary movement in the sky. Using Brahe's data in 1619, Johannes Kepler determined that planets move in elliptical orbits around the sun. In 1686 Newton used Kepler's work to show that elliptical orbits are the result of his famous theory of gravitation. We now know that all celestial objects—including planets, comets, asteroids, and satellites—travel in paths described by conic sections. Today scientists search the sky for information about the universe with enormous radio telescopes in the shape of parabolic dishes.

Conic sections have had a profound influence on people's understanding of their world and the cosmos. In this chapter we introduce you to these age-old curves.

The art of asking the right questions in mathematics is more important than the art of solving them.
—Georg Cantor

Source: Historical Topics for the Mathematics Classroom, Thirty-first Yearbook, NCTM.

TEACHING TIP

Both celestial objects and atomic particles travel in trajectories that can be modeled by conic sections.

10.1   PARABOLAS AND CIRCLES

Types of Conic Sections · **Graphs of Parabolas with Horizontal Axes of Symmetry** ·
Equations of Circles

INTRODUCTION

In this section we discuss two types of conic sections: parabolas and circles. Recall that we discussed parabolas with vertical axes of symmetry in Chapter 8. In this section we discuss parabolas with horizontal axes of symmetry, but first we introduce the three basic types of conic sections.

TYPES OF CONIC SECTIONS

Conic sections are named after the different ways that a plane can intersect a cone. The three basic curves are parabolas, ellipses, and hyperbolas. A circle is a special case of an ellipse. Figure 10.1 shows the three types of conic sections along with an example of the graph associated with each.

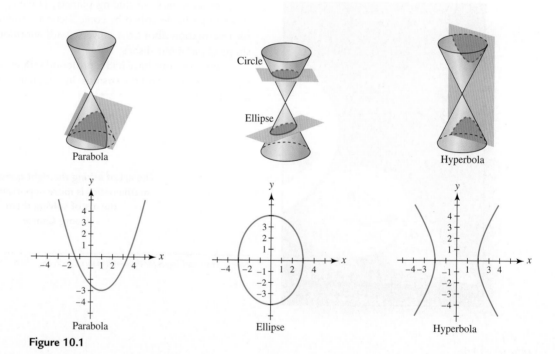

Figure 10.1

GRAPHS OF PARABOLAS WITH HORIZONTAL AXES OF SYMMETRY

Recall that the *vertex form of a parabola* with a vertical axis of symmetry is

$$y = a(x - h)^2 + k,$$

where (h, k) is the vertex. If $a > 0$, the parabola opens upward; if $a < 0$, the parabola opens downward, as shown in Figure 10.2. The preceding equation can also be expressed in the form

$$y = ax^2 + bx + c.$$

In this form the x-coordinate of the vertex is $x = -\frac{b}{2a}$.

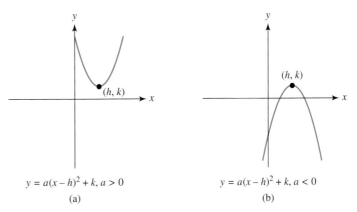

$$y = a(x - h)^2 + k, a > 0$$

(a)

$$y = a(x - h)^2 + k, a < 0$$

(b)

Figure 10.2 Vertical Axes of Symmetry

Interchanging the roles of x and y gives equations for parabolas that open to the right or the left. In this case, their axes of symmetry are horizontal.

PARABOLAS WITH HORIZONTAL AXES OF SYMMETRY

The graph of $x = a(y - k)^2 + h$ is a parabola that opens to the right if $a > 0$ and to the left if $a < 0$. The vertex of the parabola is located at (h, k).

The graph of $x = ay^2 + by + c$ is a parabola opening to the right if $a > 0$ and to the left if $a < 0$. The y-coordinate of its vertex is $y = -\frac{b}{2a}$.

These parabolas are illustrated in Figure 10.3.

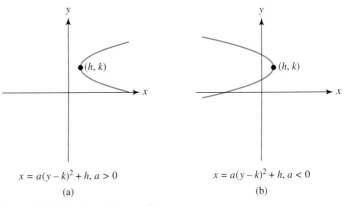

$$x = a(y - k)^2 + h, a > 0$$

(a)

$$x = a(y - k)^2 + h, a < 0$$

(b)

Figure 10.3 Horizontal Axes of Symmetry

EXAMPLE 1　Graphing a parabola

Graph $x = -\frac{1}{2}y^2$. Find its vertex and axis of symmetry.

Solution　The equation can be written in vertex form because $x = -\frac{1}{2}(y - 0)^2 + 0$. The vertex is $(0, 0)$, and because $a = -\frac{1}{2} < 0$, the parabola opens to the left. We can make a table of values, as shown in Table 10.1, and plot a few points to help determine the location and shape of the graph. To obtain Table 10.1, we first choose a y-value and then calculate an x-value. The resulting graph is shown in Figure 10.4. Its axis of symmetry is the x-axis, or $y = 0$.

TABLE 10.1

y	x
-2	-2
-1	$-\frac{1}{2}$
0	0
1	$-\frac{1}{2}$
2	-2

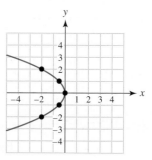

Figure 10.4

EXAMPLE 2　Graphing a parabola

Graph $x = (y - 3)^2 + 2$. Find its vertex and axis of symmetry.

Solution　As $h = 2$ and $k = 3$ in the equation $x = a(y - k)^2 + h$, the vertex is $(2, 3)$, and because $a = 1 > 0$, the parabola opens to the right. This parabola has the same shape as $y = x^2$, except that it opens to the right rather than upward. To graph this parabola we can make a table of values and plot a few points. Table 10.2 can be obtained by first choosing y-values and then calculating corresponding x-values using $x = (y - 3)^2 + 2$.

Sometimes, finding the x- and y-intercepts of the parabola is helpful when you are graphing. To find the x-intercept let $y = 0$ in $x = (y - 3)^2 + 2$. The x-intercept is $x = (0 - 3)^2 + 2 = 11$. To find any y-intercepts let $x = 0$ in $x = (y - 3)^2 + 2$. Here $0 = (y - 3)^2 + 2$ means that $(y - 3)^2 = -2$, which has no real solution, and that this parabola has no y-intercepts.

Both the graph of the parabola and the points from Table 10.2 are shown in Figure 10.5. Note that there are no y-intercepts and that the x-intercept is correct. The axis of symmetry is $y = 3$ because, if we fold the graph on the horizontal line $y = 3$, the two sides match.

TABLE 10.2

y	x
1	6
2	3
3	2
4	3
5	6

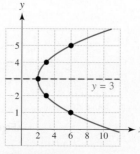

Figure 10.5

EXAMPLE 3   Graphing a parabola and finding its vertex

Identify the vertex and then graph each parabola.
(a) $x = -y^2 + 1$ **(b)** $x = y^2 - 2y - 1$

Solution   **(a)** If we rewrite $x = -y^2 + 1$ as $x = -(y - 0)^2 + 1$, then $h = 1$ and $k = 0$, so the vertex is $(1, 0)$. By letting $y = 0$ in $x = -y^2 + 1$ we find that the x-intercept is $x = -0^2 + 1 = 1$. Similarly, we let $x = 0$ in $x = -y^2 + 1$ to find the y-intercepts. The equation $0 = -y^2 + 1$ has solutions -1 and 1.

The parabola opens to the left because $a = -1 < 0$. Additional points given in Table 10.3 will help in graphing the parabola shown in Figure 10.6.

TABLE 10.3

y	x
-2	-3
-1	0
0	1
1	0
2	-3

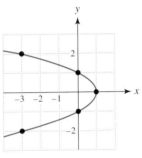

Figure 10.6

(b) The y-coordinate of the vertex is given by

$$y = -\frac{b}{2a} = -\frac{-2}{2(1)} = 1.$$

To find the x-coordinate of the vertex, substitute $y = 1$ into the given equation.

$$x = (1)^2 - 2(1) - 1 = -2$$

The vertex is $(-2, 1)$. The parabola opens to the right because $a = 1 > 0$. The additional points given in Table 10.4 help in graphing the parabola shown in Figure 10.7. Note that the y-intercepts do not have integer values and that the quadratic formula would be needed to find an approximation for these values.

TABLE 10.4

y	x
-1	2
0	-1
1	-2
2	-1
3	2

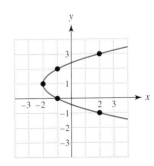

Figure 10.7

EQUATIONS OF CIRCLES

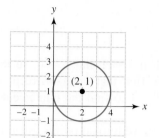

Figure 10.8

A **circle** consists of the set of points in a plane that are the same distance from a fixed point. The fixed distance is called the **radius**, and the fixed point is called the **center.** In Figure 10.8 all points lying on the circle are a distance of 2 units from the center $(2, 1)$. Therefore the radius of the circle equals 2.

We can find the equation of the circle shown in Figure 10.8 by using the distance formula. If a point (x, y) lies on the graph of a circle, its distance from the center $(2, 1)$ is 2 and

$$\sqrt{(x - 2)^2 + (y - 1)^2} = 2.$$

Squaring both sides gives

$$(x - 2)^2 + (y - 1)^2 = 2^2.$$

This equation represents the standard equation for a circle with center $(2, 1)$ and radius 2.

STANDARD EQUATION OF A CIRCLE

The **standard equation of a circle** with center (h, k) and radius r is

$$(x - h)^2 + (y - k)^2 = r^2.$$

EXAMPLE 4   Graphing a circle

Graph $x^2 + y^2 = 9$. Find the radius and center.

Solution   The equation $x^2 + y^2 = 9$ can be written in standard form as

$$(x - 0)^2 + (y - 0)^2 = 3^2.$$

Therefore the center is $(0, 0)$ and the radius is 3. Its graph is shown in Figure 10.9.

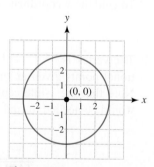

Figure 10.9

EXAMPLE 5   Graphing a circle

Graph $(x + 1)^2 + (y - 3)^2 = 4$. Find the radius and center.

Solution   Write the equation as

$$(x - (-1))^2 + (y - 3)^2 = 2^2.$$

The center is $(-1, 3)$, and the radius is 2. Its graph is shown in Figure 10.10.

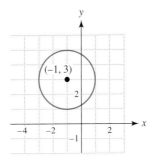

Figure 10.10

In the next example we use the *method of completing the square* to find the center and radius of a circle. (To review completing the square, refer to Sections 8.2 and 8.3.)

EXAMPLE 6   **Finding the center of a circle**

Find the center and radius of the circle given by $x^2 + 4x + y^2 - 6y = 5$.

Solution   Begin by writing the equation as

$$(x^2 + 4x + \underline{\hphantom{xx}}) + (y^2 - 6y + \underline{\hphantom{xx}}) = 5.$$

To complete the square, add $\left(\frac{4}{2}\right)^2 = 4$ and $\left(\frac{-6}{2}\right)^2 = 9$ to each side of the equation.

$$(x^2 + 4x + 4) + (y^2 - 6y + 9) = 5 + 4 + 9$$

Factoring the perfect square trinomials yields

$$(x + 2)^2 + (y - 3)^2 = 18.$$

The center is $(-2, 3)$, and because $18 = \left(\sqrt{18}\right)^2$, the radius is $\sqrt{18}$.

TEACHING TIP

You may need to review completing the square with students before working Example 6.

Critical Thinking

Does the following equation represent a circle? If so, give its center and radius.

$$x^2 + y^2 + 10y = -32$$

No. The circle is undefined because the radius is $\sqrt{-7}$.

Technology Note: *Graphing Circles in a Square Viewing Rectangle*

The graph of a circle does not represent a function. One way to graph a circle with a graphing calculator is to solve the equation for y and obtain two equations. One equation gives the upper half of the circle, and the other equation gives the lower half.

For example, to graph $x^2 + y^2 = 4$ in the viewing rectangle $[-4.7, 4.7, 1]$ by $[-3.1, 3.1, 1]$ begin by solving for y.

$$x^2 + y^2 = 4 \qquad \text{Given equation}$$
$$y^2 = 4 - x^2 \qquad \text{Subtract } x^2$$
$$y = \pm\sqrt{4 - x^2} \qquad \text{Square root property}$$

Then graph $Y_1 = \sqrt{(4 - X^2)}$ and $Y_2 = -\sqrt{(4 - X^2)}$. The graph of y_1 generates the upper half of the circle, and the graph of y_2 generates the lower half of the circle, as shown in Figure 10.11.

$[-4.7, 4.7, 1]$ by $[-3.1, 3.1, 1]$ $[-4.7, 4.7, 1]$ by $[-3.1, 3.1, 1]$ $[-4.7, 4.7, 1]$ by $[-3.1, 3.1, 1]$

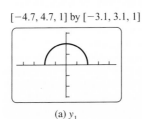

(a) y_1

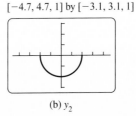

(b) y_2

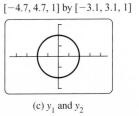

(c) y_1 and y_2

Figure 10.11

(continued)

Calculator Help

To set a square viewing rectangle, see the Appendix (page AP-6).

If a circle is not graphed in a *square viewing rectangle*, it will appear to be an oval rather than a circle. In a square viewing rectangle a circle will appear circular. Figure 10.12 shows the circle graphed in a viewing rectangle that is not square. Consult your owner's manual to learn more about square viewing rectangles for your calculator.

$[-4, 4, 1]$ by $[-5, 5, 1]$

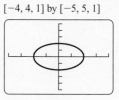

Figure 10.12

 PUTTING IT ALL TOGETHER

The following table summarizes some basic concepts about parabolas and circles.

Concept	Explanation	Example
Parabola with Horizontal Axis	Vertex form: $x = a(y - k)^2 + h$. If $a > 0$, it opens to the right; if $a < 0$, it opens to the left. The vertex is (h, k).	$x = 2(y - 1)^2 + 4$ opens to the right and its vertex is $(4, 1)$.
Standard Equation of a Circle	Standard equation: $(x - h)^2 + (y - k)^2 = r^2$. The radius is r and the center is (h, k).	$(x + 2)^2 + (y - 1)^2 = 16$ has center $(-2, 1)$ and radius 4.

These parabolas may also be expressed as $x = ay^2 + by + c$, where the y-coordinate of the vertex is $y = -\frac{b}{2a}$.

 **10.1 EXERCISES**

FOR EXTRA HELP

Student's Solutions Manual   InterAct Math   MathXL

MyMathLab   Math Tutor Center   Digital Video Tutor CD 8   Videotape 11

2. The first parabola has a vertical axis of symmetry, and the second has a horizontal axis of symmetry.

CONCEPTS

1. Name the three general types of conic sections.
   Parabola, ellipse, hyperbola
2. What is the difference between the graphs of $y = ax^2 + bx + c$ and $x = ay^2 + by + c$?

3. If a parabola has a horizontal axis of symmetry, does it represent a function?   No

4. Sketch a graph of a parabola with a horizontal axis of symmetry. *

5. If a parabola has two y-intercepts, does it represent a function? Why or why not?
   No; it does not pass the vertical line test.

6. If $x = a(y - k)^2 + h$, what is the vertex? (h, k)

7. The graph of $x = -y^2$ opens to the _____.   left

8. The graph of $x = 2y^2 + y - 1$ opens to the _____.   right

9. The graph of $(x - h)^2 + (y - k)^2 = r^2$ is a _____ with center _____.   circle; (h, k)

10. The graph of $x^2 + y^2 = r^2$ is a circle with center _____ and radius _____. $(0, 0); r$

PARABOLAS

Exercises 11–30: Graph the parabola. Find the vertex and axis of symmetry. *

11. $x = y^2$ $(0, 0); y = 0$ 12. $x = -y^2$ $(0, 0); y = 0$

13. $x = y^2 + 1$ $(1, 0); y = 0$ 14. $x = y^2 - 1$ $(-1, 0); y = 0$

15. $x = 2y^2$ $(0, 0); y = 0$ 16. $x = \frac{1}{4}y^2$ $(0, 0); y = 0$

17. $x = (y - 1)^2 + 2$ $(2, 1); y = 1$ 18. $x = (y - 2)^2 + 1$ $(1, 2); y = 2$

19. $y = (x + 2)^2 + 1$ $(-2, 1); x = -2$ 20. $y = (x - 4)^2 + 5$ $(4, 5); x = 4$

21. $x = \frac{1}{2}(y + 1)^2 - 3$ $(-3, -1); y = -1$ 22. $x = -2(y + 3)^2 + 1$ $(1, -3); y = -3$

23. $x = -3(y - 1)^2$ $(0, 1); y = 1$ 24. $x = \frac{1}{4}(y + 2)^2 - 3$ $(-3, -2); y = -2$ 30. $\left(\frac{5}{3}, -\frac{2}{3}\right); y = -\frac{2}{3}$

25. $y = 2x^2 - x + 1$ 26. $y = -x^2 + 2x + 2$ $(1, 3); x = 1$

27. $x = \frac{1}{2}y^2 + y - 1$ 28. $x = -2y^2 + 3y + 2$ $\left(\frac{25}{8}, \frac{3}{4}\right); y = \frac{3}{4}$

29. $x = 3y^2 + y$ 30. $x = -\frac{3}{2}y^2 - 2y + 1$

25. $\left(\frac{1}{4}, \frac{7}{8}\right); x = \frac{1}{4}$ 27. $\left(-\frac{3}{2}, -1\right); y = -1$ 29. $\left(-\frac{1}{12}, -\frac{1}{6}\right); y = -\frac{1}{6}$

Exercises 31–34: Use the graph to determine the equation of the parabola. (Hint: Either $a = 1$ or $a = -1$.)

31. $y = x^2$
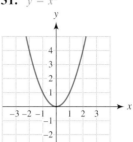

32. $x = -y^2$
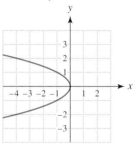

33. $x = (y + 1)^2 - 2$
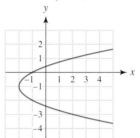

34. $y = -(x - 1)^2 + 3$
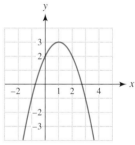

Exercises 35–38: Determine the direction that the parabola opens if it satisfies the given conditions.

35. Passing through $(2, 0)$, $(-2, 0)$, and $(0, -2)$ Upward

36. Passing through $(0, -3)$, $(0, 2)$, and $(1, 1)$ To the left

37. Vertex $(1, 2)$ passing through $(-1, -2)$ with a vertical axis   Downward

38. Vertex $(-1, 3)$ passing through $(0, 0)$ with a horizontal axis   To the right

39. What x-values are possible for the graph of $x = 2y^2$? $x \geq 0$

40. What y-values are possible for the graph of $x = 2y^2$?   All real numbers

41. How many y-intercepts does a parabola
   $$x = a(y - k)^2 + h$$
   have if $a > 0$ and $h < 0$?   Two

42. Does the graph of $x = ay^2 + by + c$ always have a y-intercept? Explain.
   No; for example, it could have vertex $(1, 10)$ and open to the right.

*Answers on pages IA-32–IA-33

43. What is the *x*-intercept for the graph of   1
$$x = 3y^2 - y + 1?$$

44. What are the *y*-intercepts for the graph of   1 and 2
$$x = y^2 - 3y + 2?$$

CIRCLES

Exercises 45–50: Write the standard equation of the circle with the given radius r and center C.

45. $r = 1$ $C = (0, 0)$ $x^2 + y^2 = 1$

46. $r = 4$ $C = (2, 3)$ $(x - 2)^2 + (y - 3)^2 = 16$

47. $r = 3$ $C = (-1, 5)$ $(x + 1)^2 + (y - 5)^2 = 9$

48. $r = 5$ $C = (5, -3)$ $(x - 5)^2 + (y + 3)^2 = 25$

49. $r = \sqrt{2}$ $C = (-4, -6)$ $(x + 4)^2 + (y + 6)^2 = 2$

50. $r = \sqrt{6}$ $C = (0, 4)$ $x^2 + (y - 4)^2 = 6$

Exercises 51–54: Use the graph to find the standard equation of the circle.

51. $x^2 + y^2 = 16$

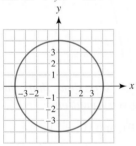

52. $(x - 1)^2 + (y + 1)^2 = 9$

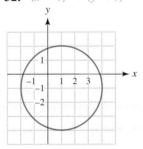

53. $(x + 3)^2 + (y - 2)^2 = 1$

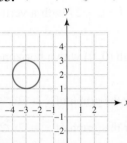

54. $x^2 + (y + 3)^2 = 4$

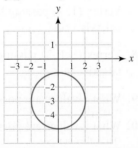

Exercises 55–64: Find the radius and center of the circle. Then graph the circle. *

55. $x^2 + y^2 = 9$ 3; (0, 0)   **56.** $x^2 + y^2 = 1$ 1; (0, 0)

57. $(x - 1)^2 + (y - 3)^2 = 9$ 3; (1, 3)

58. $(x + 2)^2 + (y + 1)^2 = 4$ 2; (-2, -1)

59. $(x + 5)^2 + (y - 5)^2 = 25$ 5; (-5, 5)

60. $(x - 4)^2 + (y + 3)^2 = 16$ 4; (4, -3)

61. $x^2 + 6x + y^2 - 2y = -1$ 3; (-3, 1)

62. $x^2 + y^2 + 12y + 32 = 0$ 2; (0, -6)

63. $x^2 + 6x + y^2 - 2y + 3 = 0$ $\sqrt{7}$; (-3, 1)

64. $x^2 - 4x + y^2 + 4y = -3$ $\sqrt{5}$; (2, -2)

APPLICATIONS

65. *Radio Telescopes*   The Parks radio telescope has the shape of a parabolic dish, as depicted in the accompanying figure. A cross section of this telescope can be modeled by $x = \frac{32}{11,025}y^2$, where $-105 \leq y \leq 105$; the units are feet.

(a) Graph the cross-sectional shape of the dish in $[-40, 40, 10]$ by $[-120, 120, 20]$. *

(b) Find the depth *d* of the dish.   32 ft

66. *Train Tracks*   To make a curve safer for trains, parabolic curves are sometimes used instead of circular curves. See the accompanying figure on the next page.   (*Source:* F. Mannering and W. Kilareski, *Principles of Highway Engineering and Traffic Analysis.*)

(a) Suppose that a curve must pass through the points $(-1, 0)$, $(0, 2)$, and $(0, -2)$, where the units are kilometers. Find an equation for the train tracks in the form $x = \frac{1}{4}(y - 0)^2 - 1$
$$x = a(y - h)^2 + k.$$

*Answers on pages IA-33–IA-34

(b) Find another point that lies on the train tracks.
(3, 4); answers may vary.

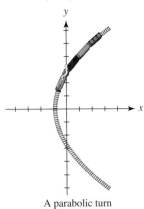

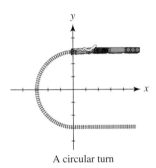

A parabolic turn

A circular turn

67. *Trajectories of Comets* Under certain circumstances, a comet can pass by the sun once and never return. In this situation the comet may travel in a parabolic path, as illustrated in the accompanying figure. Suppose that a comet's path is given by $x = -2.5y^2$, where the sun is located at $(-0.1, 0)$ and the units are astronomical units (A.U.). One astronomical unit equals 93 million miles. (*Source:* W. Thomson, *Introduction to Space Dynamics.*)

(a) Plot a point for the sun's location and then graph the path of the comet. *

(b) Find the distance from the sun to the comet when the comet is located at $(-2.5, 1)$.
2.6 A.U., or 241,800,000 mi

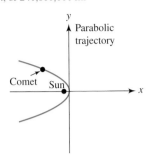

68.(a) As the comet travels farther from the sun, its velocity slows.

68. *Speed of a Comet* (Continuation of Exercise 67.) The velocity V in meters per second of a comet traveling in a parabolic trajectory about the sun is given by $V = \frac{k}{\sqrt{D}}$, where D is the distance from the sun in meters and $k = 1.15 \times 10^{10}$.

(a) How does the velocity of the comet change as its distance from the sun changes?

(b) Calculate the velocity of the comet when it is closest to the sun. (*Hint:* 1 mile $\approx$ 1609 meters.)
About 94,000 m/sec

WRITING ABOUT MATHEMATICS

69. Suppose that you are given the equation
$$x = a(y - k)^2 + h.$$

(a) Explain how you can determine the direction that the parabola opens.

(b) Explain how to find the axis of symmetry and the vertex.

(c) If the points $(0, 4)$ and $(0, -2)$ lie on the graph of x, what is the axis of symmetry?

(d) Generalize part (c) if $(0, y_1)$ and $(0, y_2)$ lie on the graph of x.

70. Suppose that you are given the vertex of a parabola. Can you determine the axis of symmetry? Explain.

Group Activity: Working with Real Data

Directions: Form a group of 2 to 4 people. Select someone to record the group's responses for this activity. All members of the group should work cooperatively to answer the questions. If your instructor asks for your results, each member of the group should be prepared to respond.

Radio Telescope The U.S. Naval Research Laboratory designed a giant radio telescope weighing 3450 tons. Its parabolic dish has a diameter of 300 feet and a depth of 44 feet, as shown in the accompanying figure. (*Source:* J. Mar, *Structure Technology for Large Radio and Radar Telescope Systems.*)

(a) Determine an equation of the form $x = ay^2$, $a > 0$, that models a cross section of the dish. $x = \frac{11}{5625}y^2$

 (b) Graph your equation in an appropriate viewing rectangle. *

*Answer on page IA-34

10.2 ELLIPSES AND HYPERBOLAS

Equations of Ellipses · Equations of Hyperbolas

INTRODUCTION

Celestial objects travel in paths or trajectories determined by conic sections. For this reason, conic sections have been studied for centuries. In modern times physicists have learned that subatomic particles can also travel in trajectories determined by conic sections. Recall that the three main types of conic sections are parabolas, ellipses, and hyperbolas and that circles are a special type of ellipse. In Section 8.2 and Section 10.1, we discussed parabolas and circles. In this section we focus on ellipses and hyperbolas and some of their applications.

EQUATIONS OF ELLIPSES

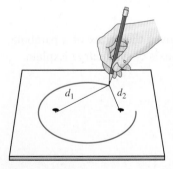

Figure 10.13

One method used to sketch an ellipse is to tie the ends of a string to two nails driven into a flat board. If a pencil is placed against the string anywhere between the nails, as shown in Figure 10.13, and is used to draw a curve, the resulting curve is an ellipse. The sum of the distances d_1 and d_2 between the pencil and each of the nails is always fixed by the length of the string. The location of the nails corresponds to the foci of the ellipse. An **ellipse** is the set of points in a plane, the sum of whose distances from two fixed points is constant. Each fixed point is called a **focus** (plural *foci*) of the ellipse.

Critical Thinking

What happens to the shape of the ellipse shown in Figure 10.13 as the nails are moved farther apart? What happens to its shape as the nails are moved closer together? When would a circle be formed?

In Figure 10.14 the **major axis** and the **minor axis** are labeled for each ellipse. The major axis is the longer of the two axes. Figure 10.14(a) shows an ellipse with a *horizontal* major axis, and Figure 10.14(b) shows an ellipse with a *vertical* major axis. The **vertices**, V_1 and V_2, of each ellipse are located at the endpoints of the major axis, and the **center** of the ellipse is the midpoint of the major axis (or the intersection of the major and minor axes).

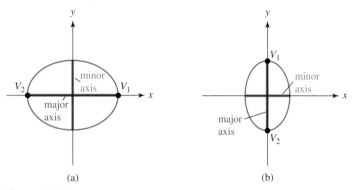

Figure 10.14

A vertical line can intersect the graph of an ellipse more than once, so an ellipse cannot be modeled by a function. However, some ellipses can be represented by the following equations.

IIIIIIII   **STANDARD EQUATIONS FOR ELLIPSES CENTERED AT (0, 0)**

The ellipse with center at the origin, *horizontal* major axis, and equation

$$\frac{x^2}{a^2} + \frac{y^2}{b^2} = 1, \qquad a > b > 0,$$

has vertices $(\pm a, 0)$ and endpoints of the minor axis $(0, \pm b)$.

The ellipse with center at the origin, *vertical* major axis, and equation

$$\frac{x^2}{b^2} + \frac{y^2}{a^2} = 1, \qquad a > b > 0,$$

has vertices $(0, \pm a)$ and endpoints of the minor axis $(\pm b, 0)$.

IIIIIIII

Figure 10.15(a) shows an ellipse having a horizontal major axis; Figure 10.15(b) shows one having a vertical major axis. The coordinates of the vertices V_1 and V_2 and endpoints of the minor axis U_1 and U_2 are labeled.

TEACHING TIP

When graphing an ellipse by hand, the student should first plot the vertices and the endpoints of the minor axis. Then the student can use these four points to sketch the ellipse.

Critical Thinking

Suppose that $a = b$ for an ellipse centered at (0, 0). What can be said about the ellipse? Explain.

It is a circle with radius a.

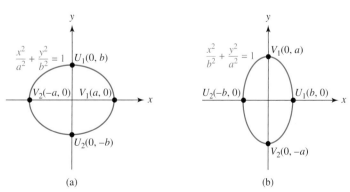

Figure 10.15

In the next example we show how to sketch graphs of ellipses.

EXAMPLE 1   Sketching graphs of ellipses

Sketch a graph of each ellipse. Label the vertices and endpoints of the minor axes.

(a) $\dfrac{x^2}{25} + \dfrac{y^2}{4} = 1$ (b) $9x^2 + 4y^2 = 36$

Solution (a) The equation $\dfrac{x^2}{25} + \dfrac{y^2}{4} = 1$ describes an ellipse with $a^2 = 25$ and $b^2 = 4$. (When you are deciding whether 25 or 4 represents a^2, let a^2 be the larger of the two numbers.) Thus $a = 5$ and $b = 2$, so the ellipse has a horizontal major axis with vertices $(\pm 5, 0)$ and the endpoints of the minor axis are $(0, \pm 2)$. Plot these four points and then sketch the ellipse, as shown in Figure 10.16(a).

(b) The equation $9x^2 + 4y^2 = 36$ can be put into standard form by dividing each side by 36.

$$9x^2 + 4y^2 = 36 \qquad \text{Given equation}$$

$$\frac{9x^2}{36} + \frac{4y^2}{36} = \frac{36}{36} \qquad \text{Divide by 36.}$$

$$\frac{x^2}{4} + \frac{y^2}{9} = 1 \qquad \text{Simplify.}$$

This ellipse has a vertical major axis with $a = 3$ and $b = 2$. The vertices are $(0, \pm 3)$, and the endpoints of the minor axis are $(\pm 2, 0)$, as shown in Figure 10.16(b).

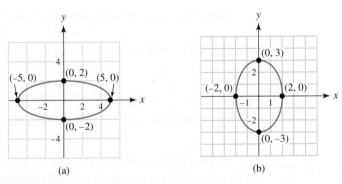

(a)   (b)

Figure 10.16

Planets travel around the sun in elliptical orbits. Astronomers have measured the values of a and b for each planet. Utilizing this information, we can find the equation of a planet's orbit, as illustrated in the next example.

EXAMPLE 2   Modeling the orbit of Mercury

Except for Pluto, the planet Mercury has the least circular orbit of the nine planets. For Mercury $a = 0.387$ and $b = 0.379$. The units are astronomical units (A.U.), where 1 A.U. equals 93 million miles—the distance between Earth and the sun. Graph $\dfrac{x^2}{a^2} + \dfrac{y^2}{b^2} = 1$ to model the orbit of Mercury in $[-0.6, 0.6, 0.1]$ by $[-0.4, 0.4, 0.1]$. Then plot the sun at the point $(0.08, 0)$.   (**Source:** M. Zeilik, *Introductory Astronomy and Astrophysics.*)

Solution The orbit of Mercury is given by

$$\frac{x^2}{0.387^2} + \frac{y^2}{0.379^2} = 1.$$

To graph an ellipse with some graphing calculators, we must solve the equation for y. Doing so results in two equations.

$$\frac{x^2}{0.387^2} + \frac{y^2}{0.379^2} = 1$$

$$\frac{y^2}{0.379^2} = 1 - \frac{x^2}{0.387^2}$$

$$\frac{y}{0.379} = \pm\sqrt{1 - \frac{x^2}{0.387^2}}$$

$$y = \pm 0.379\sqrt{1 - \frac{x^2}{0.387^2}}$$

The orbit of Mercury results from graphing these two equations. See Figures 10.17(a) and (b). The point $(0.08, 0)$ represents the position of the sun in Figure 10.17(b).

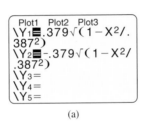

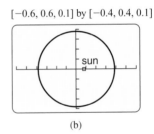

$[-0.6, 0.6, 0.1]$ by $[-0.4, 0.4, 0.1]$

(a)   (b)

Figure 10.17

Critical Thinking

Use Figure 10.17 and the information in Example 2 to estimate the minimum and maximum distances that Mercury is from the sun.   Minimum: about 0.307 A.U., or 28,551,000 mi
Maximum: about 0.467 A.U., or 43,431,000 mi

EQUATIONS OF HYPERBOLAS

The third type of conic section is the **hyperbola**, which is the set of points in a plane, the difference of whose distances from two fixed points is constant. Each fixed point is called a **focus** of the hyperbola. Figure 10.18 shows a hyperbola whose equation is

$$\frac{x^2}{4} - \frac{y^2}{9} = 1.$$

This hyperbola is centered at the origin and has two **branches**, a *left branch* and a *right branch*. The **vertices** are $(-2, 0)$ and $(2, 0)$, and the line segment connecting the vertices is called the **transverse axis**.

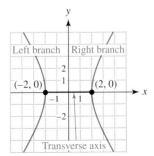

Figure 10.18

By the vertical line test, a hyperbola cannot be represented by a function, but many hyperbolas can be described by the following equations.

STANDARD EQUATIONS FOR HYPERBOLAS CENTERED AT (0, 0)

The hyperbola with center at the origin, *horizontal* transverse axis, and equation

$$\frac{x^2}{a^2} - \frac{y^2}{b^2} = 1$$

has vertices $(\pm a, 0)$.

The hyperbola with center at the origin, *vertical* transverse axis, and equation

$$\frac{y^2}{a^2} - \frac{x^2}{b^2} = 1$$

has vertices $(0, \pm a)$.

Hyperbolas, along with the coordinates of their vertices, are shown in Figure 10.19. The two parts of the hyperbola in Figure 10.19(a) are the *left branch* and *right branch*, whereas in Figure 10.19(b) the hyperbola has an *upper branch* and a *lower branch*. The dashed rectangle in each figure is called the **fundamental rectangle**, and its four vertices are determined by either $(\pm a, \pm b)$ or $(\pm b, \pm a)$. If its diagonals are extended, they correspond to the asymptotes of the hyperbola. The lines $y = \pm\frac{b}{a}x$ and $y = \pm\frac{a}{b}x$ are **asymptotes** for the hyperbolas, respectively, and may be used as an aid to graphing them.

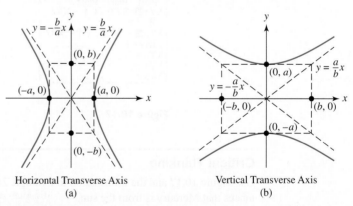

Horizontal Transverse Axis   Vertical Transverse Axis
(a)   (b)

Figure 10.19

Note: A hyperbola consists of two solid curves, or branches. The dashed lines and rectangles are not part of the actual graph but are used as an aid for sketching the graph.

One interpretation of an asymptote of a hyperbola can be based on trajectories of comets as they approach the sun. Comets travel in parabolic, elliptic, or hyperbolic trajectories. If the speed of a comet is too slow, the gravitational pull of the sun captures the comet in an elliptic orbit (see Figure 10.20(a) on the next page). If the speed of the comet is too fast, the sun's gravity is too weak to capture the comet and the comet passes by it in a hyperbolic trajectory. Near the sun the gravitational pull is stronger, and the comet's trajectory is curved. Farther from the sun, the gravitational pull becomes weaker, and the comet eventually returns to a straight-line trajectory determined by the *asymptote* of the hyperbola (see Figure 10.20(b)). Finally, if the speed is neither too slow nor too fast, the comet will travel in a parabolic path (see Figure 10.20(c)).

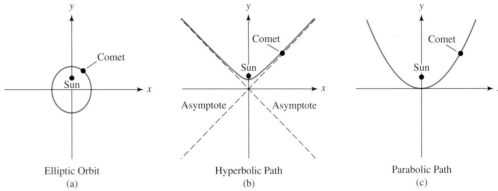

Figure 10.20

Critical Thinking

If a comet is observed at regular intervals, which type of conic section describes its path?   Elliptic

---

EXAMPLE 3   **Sketching the graph of a hyperbola**

Sketch a graph of $\frac{y^2}{4} - \frac{x^2}{9} = 1$. Label the vertices and show the asymptotes.

Solution   The equation is in standard form with $a^2 = 4$ and $b^2 = 9$, so $a = 2$ and $b = 3$. It has a vertical transverse axis with vertices $(0, -2)$ and $(0, 2)$. The vertices of the fundamental rectangle are $(\pm 3, \pm 2)$, that is, $(3, 2)$, $(3, -2)$, $(-3, 2)$, and $(-3, -2)$. The asymptotes are the diagonals of this rectangle and are given by $y = \pm \frac{a}{b}x$, or $y = \pm \frac{2}{3}x$. Figure 10.21 shows all these features.

TEACHING TIP

When graphing a hyperbola by hand, the student should first sketch the fundamental rectangle. Next the student should sketch the asymptotes, which correspond to the extended diagonals of the fundamental rectangle. Finally, the student can use these features to sketch the hyperbola.

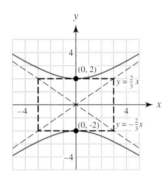

Figure 10.21

EXAMPLE 4   **Determining the equation of a hyperbola from its graph**

Use the graph shown in Figure 10.22 to determine an equation of the hyperbola.

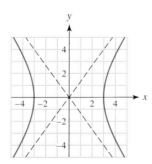

Figure 10.22

Solution The hyperbola has a horizontal transverse axis, so the x^2 term must come first in the equation. The vertices of the hyperbola are $(\pm 3, 0)$, which indicates that $a = 3$ and so $a^2 = 9$. The value of b can be found by noting that one of the asymptotes passes through the point $(3, 4)$. This asymptote has the equation $y = \frac{b}{a}x$ or $y = \frac{4}{3}x$, so let $b = 4$ and $b^2 = 16$. The equation of the hyperbola is $\frac{x^2}{9} - \frac{y^2}{16} = 1$.

Technology Note: *Graphing a Hyperbola with a Graphing Calculator*

The graph of a hyperbola does not represent a function. One way to graph a hyperbola with a graphing calculator is to solve the equation for y and obtain two equations. One equation gives the upper half of the hyperbola and the other equation gives the lower half. For example, to graph $\frac{y^2}{4} - \frac{x^2}{8} = 1$ in the viewing rectangle $[-6, 6, 1]$ by $[-4, 4, 1]$ begin by solving for y.

$$\frac{y^2}{4} = 1 + \frac{x^2}{8} \qquad \text{Add } \frac{x^2}{8}.$$

$$y^2 = 4\left(1 + \frac{x^2}{8}\right) \qquad \text{Multiply by 4.}$$

$$y = \pm\, 2\sqrt{1 + \frac{x^2}{8}} \qquad \text{Square root property}$$

Graph $Y_1 = 2\sqrt{(1 + X^2/8)}$ and $Y_2 = -2\sqrt{(1 + X^2/8)}$. The results are shown in Figure 10.23.

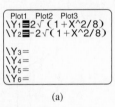

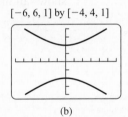

$[-6, 6, 1]$ by $[-4, 4, 1]$

(a)

(b)

Figure 10.23

10.2 PUTTING IT ALL TOGETHER

The following table summarizes some basic concepts about ellipses and hyperbolas.

Concept	Description	
Ellipses Centered at $(0, 0)$ with $a > b > 0$	*Horizontal Major Axis* Vertices: $(a, 0)$ and $(-a, 0)$ Endpoints of minor axis: $(0, b)$ and $(0, -b)$ $$\frac{x^2}{a^2} + \frac{y^2}{b^2} = 1$$	*Vertical Major Axis* Vertices: $(0, a)$ and $(0, -a)$ Endpoints of minor axis: $(-b, 0)$ and $(b, 0)$ $$\frac{x^2}{b^2} + \frac{y^2}{a^2} = 1$$

Concept	Description
Ellipses Centered at (0, 0) with $a > b > 0$ (*continued*)	

	Horizontal Transverse Axis	Vertical Transverse Axis
Hyperbolas Centered at (0, 0) with $a > 0$ and $b > 0$	Vertices: $(a, 0)$ and $(-a, 0)$ Asymptotes: $y = \pm\dfrac{b}{a}x$ $\dfrac{x^2}{a^2} - \dfrac{y^2}{b^2} = 1$	Vertices: $(0, a)$ and $(0, -a)$ Asymptotes: $y = \pm\dfrac{a}{b}x$ $\dfrac{y^2}{a^2} - \dfrac{x^2}{b^2} = 1$

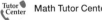

10.2 EXERCISES

FOR EXTRA HELP

📖 Student's Solutions Manual

🚪 MyMathLab

InterAct math InterAct Math

Tutor Center Math Tutor Center

MathXL MathXL

📼 Digital Video Tutor CD 9   Videotape 11

CONCEPTS

1. Sketch an ellipse with a horizontal major axis.*

2. Sketch a hyperbola with a vertical transverse axis.*

3. The ellipse whose standard equation is $\dfrac{x^2}{a^2} + \dfrac{y^2}{b^2} = 1$, $a > b > 0$, has a _____ major axis.   horizontal

4. The ellipse whose standard equation is $\dfrac{y^2}{a^2} + \dfrac{x^2}{b^2} = 1$, $a > b > 0$, has a _____ major axis.   vertical

5. What is the maximum number of times that a line can intersect an ellipse?   2

6. What is the maximum number of times that a parabola can intersect an ellipse?   4

7. The hyperbola whose equation is $\dfrac{x^2}{a^2} - \dfrac{y^2}{b^2} = 1$ has _____ and _____ branches.   left; right

8. The hyperbola whose equation is $\dfrac{y^2}{a^2} - \dfrac{x^2}{b^2} = 1$ has _____ and _____ branches.   lower; upper

9. How are the asymptotes of a hyperbola related to the fundamental rectangle?   They are the diagonals extended.

*Answers on page IA-34

10. Could an ellipse be centered at the origin and have vertices $(4, 0)$ and $(0, -5)$?   No

ELLIPSES

Exercises 11–22: Graph the ellipse. Label the vertices and endpoints of the minor axis. *

11. $\dfrac{x^2}{9} + \dfrac{y^2}{25} = 1$ **12.** $\dfrac{y^2}{9} + \dfrac{x^2}{25} = 1$

13. $\dfrac{x^2}{9} + \dfrac{y^2}{4} = 1$ **14.** $\dfrac{x^2}{3} + \dfrac{y^2}{9} = 1$

15. $x^2 + \dfrac{y^2}{4} = 1$ **16.** $\dfrac{x^2}{9} + y^2 = 1$

17. $\dfrac{y^2}{5} + \dfrac{x^2}{7} = 1$ **18.** $\dfrac{y^2}{11} + \dfrac{x^2}{6} = 1$

19. $36x^2 + 4y^2 = 144$ **20.** $25x^2 + 16y^2 = 400$

21. $6y^2 + 7x^2 = 42$ **22.** $9x^2 + 5y^2 = 45$

Exercises 23–26: Use the graph to determine the equation of the ellipse.

23. $\dfrac{x^2}{9} + \dfrac{y^2}{4} = 1$

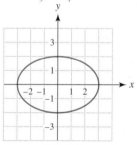

24. $\dfrac{y^2}{9} + \dfrac{x^2}{4} = 1$

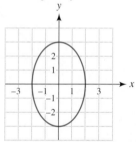

25. $\dfrac{y^2}{25} + \dfrac{x^2}{16} = 1$

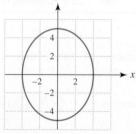

26. $\dfrac{x^2}{25} + \dfrac{y^2}{16} = 1$

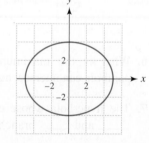

HYPERBOLAS

Exercises 27–38: Graph the hyperbola. Show the asymptotes and vertices. *

27. $\dfrac{x^2}{4} - \dfrac{y^2}{9} = 1$ **28.** $\dfrac{y^2}{4} - \dfrac{x^2}{9} = 1$

29. $\dfrac{x^2}{25} - \dfrac{y^2}{16} = 1$ **30.** $\dfrac{y^2}{25} - \dfrac{x^2}{16} = 1$

31. $x^2 - y^2 = 1$ **32.** $y^2 - x^2 = 1$

33. $\dfrac{x^2}{3} - \dfrac{y^2}{4} = 1$ **34.** $\dfrac{y^2}{5} - \dfrac{x^2}{8} = 1$

35. $9y^2 - 4x^2 = 36$ **36.** $36x^2 - 25y^2 = 900$

37. $16x^2 - 4y^2 = 64$ **38.** $y^2 - 9x^2 = 9$

Exercises 39–42: Use the graph to determine an equation of the hyperbola.

39. $x^2 - y^2 = 1$

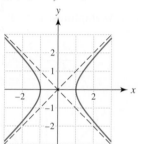

40. $\dfrac{x^2}{4} - \dfrac{y^2}{9} = 1$

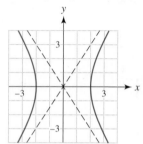

41. $\dfrac{y^2}{4} - \dfrac{x^2}{9} = 1$

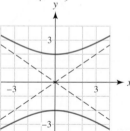

42. $\dfrac{y^2}{16} - \dfrac{x^2}{4} = 1$

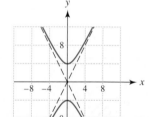

APPLICATIONS

43. *Geometry of an Ellipse*   The area inside an ellipse is given by $A = \pi ab$, and its perimeter can be approximated by

$$P = 2\pi\sqrt{\dfrac{a^2 + b^2}{2}}.$$

Approximate A and P to the nearest hundredth for each ellipse.

(a) $\dfrac{x^2}{16} + \dfrac{y^2}{25} = 1$ **(b)** $\dfrac{x^2}{7} + \dfrac{y^2}{2} = 1$

    $A \approx 62.83; P \approx 28.45$ $A \approx 11.75; P \approx 13.33$

44. *Geometry of an Ellipse*   (Refer to Exercise 43.) If $a = b$ in the equation for an ellipse, the ellipse is a circle. Let $a = b$ in the formulas for the area and

*Answers on pages IA-34–IA-35

44. Yes; $A = \pi a^2$, $P = 2\pi a$; as a is the radius of the circle, each formula is correct.

perimeter of an ellipse. Do the equations simplify to the area and perimeter for a circle? Explain.

45. *Planet Orbit* (Refer to Example 2.) The planet Pluto has the least circular orbit of any planet. For Pluto $a = 39.44$ and $b = 38.20$.

   (a) Graph the elliptic orbit of Pluto in the window $[-60, 60, 10]$ by $[-40, 40, 10]$. Plot the point $(9.82, 0)$ to show the position of the sun. Assume that the major axis is horizontal. *
   (b) Use the information in Exercise 43 to determine how far Pluto travels in one orbit around the sun and approximate the area inside its orbit.

46. *Halley's Comet* (Refer to Example 2.) One of the most famous comets is Halley's comet. It travels in an elliptical orbit with $a = 17.95$ and $b = 4.44$ and passes by Earth roughly every 76 years. The most recent pass by Earth was in February 1986. (*Source:* M. Zeilik.)

   (a) Graph the orbit of Halley's comet in $[-21, 21, 5]$ by $[-14, 14, 5]$. Assume that the major axis is horizontal and that all units are in astronomical units. Plot a point at $(17.36, 0)$ to represent the position of the sun. *
   (b) Use the formula in Exercise 43 to estimate how many miles Halley's comet travels in one orbit around the sun. $P \approx 82.2$ A.U., or about 7.64×10^9 mi
   (c) Estimate the average speed of Halley's comet in miles per hour. About 11,500 mph

47. *Satellite Orbit* The orbit of Explorer VII and the outline of Earth's surface are shown in the accompanying figure. This orbit is described by

$$\frac{x^2}{4464^2} + \frac{y^2}{4462^2} = 1,$$

and the surface of Earth is described by

$$\frac{(x - 164)^2}{3960^2} + \frac{y^2}{3960^2} = 1.$$

Find the maximum and minimum heights of the satellite above Earth's surface if all units are miles. (*Source:* W. Thomson, *Introduction to Space Dynamics.*)

Maximum: 668 mi; minimum: 340 mi

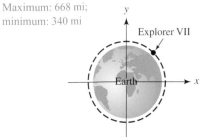

48. *Weight Machines* Elliptic shapes are used rather than circular shapes in modern weight machines. Suppose that the ellipse shown in the accompanying figure is represented by the equation $r_1 = 4$ in.; $r_2 = 10$ in.

$$\frac{x^2}{16} + \frac{y^2}{100} = 1,$$

where the units are inches. Find r_1 and r_2.

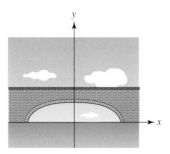

49. *Arch Bridge* The arch under a bridge is designed as the upper half of an ellipse as illustrated in the accompanying figure. Its equation is modeled by

$$400x^2 + 10,000y^2 = 4,000,000,$$

where the units are feet. Find the height and width of the arch. Height: 20 ft; width: 200 ft

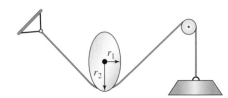

50. *Population Growth* Suppose that the population y of a country can be modeled by the upper right branch of the hyperbola Its growth becomes nearly linear.

$$\frac{x^2}{a^2} - \frac{y^2}{b^2} = 1,$$

where x represents time in years. What happens to the population after a long period of time?

WRITING ABOUT MATHEMATICS

51. Explain how the values of a and b affect the graph of $\frac{x^2}{a^2} + \frac{y^2}{b^2} = 1$. Assume that $a > b > 0$.

52. Explain how the values of a and b affect the graph of $\frac{x^2}{a^2} - \frac{y^2}{b^2} = 1$. Assume that a and b are positive.

45.(b) $P \approx 243.9$ A.U., or about 2.27×10^{10} mi; $A \approx 4733$ sq A.U., or about 4.09×10^{19} sq mi

*Answers on page IA-35

CHECKING BASIC CONCEPTS   ⟨ SECTIONS 10.1 AND 10.2 ⟩

---

1. Graph the parabola $x = (y - 2)^2 + 1$.* Find the vertex and axis of symmetry. $(1, 2); y = 2$

2. Find the equation of the circle with center $(1, -2)$ and radius 2. Graph the circle.*
   $(x - 1)^2 + (y + 2)^2 = 4$

3. Find the x- and y-intercepts on the graph of
   $$\frac{x^2}{4} + \frac{y^2}{9} = 1.$$
   x-intercept: ± 2; y-intercept: ± 3

4. Graph the following. Label any vertices and state the type of conic section that it represents. *

   (a) $x = y^2$ Parabola   **(b)** $\dfrac{x^2}{16} + \dfrac{y^2}{25} = 1$ Ellipse

   (c) $\dfrac{x^2}{4} - \dfrac{y^2}{9} = 1$ Hyperbola

   (d) $(x - 1)^2 + (y + 2)^2 = 9$ Circle (and ellipse)

   *Answers on page IA-35

10.3   NONLINEAR SYSTEMS OF EQUATIONS AND INEQUALITIES

Basic Concepts · **Solving Nonlinear Systems of Equations** · **Solving Nonlinear Systems of Inequalities**

INTRODUCTION

$V = \pi r^2 h$

$A = 2\pi rh$

Figure 10.24 Cylindrical Container

To describe characteristics of curved objects we often need *nonlinear equations*. The equations of the conic sections discussed in this chapter are but a few examples of nonlinear equations. For instance, cylinders have a curved shape, as illustrated in Figure 10.24. If the radius of a cylinder is denoted r and its height h, then its volume V is given by the nonlinear equation

$$V = \pi r^2 h$$

and its side area A is given by the nonlinear equation

$$A = 2\pi rh.$$

If we want to manufacture a cylindrical container that holds 35 cubic inches and whose side area is 50 square inches, we need to solve the following **system of nonlinear equations**. (This system is solved in Example 4.)

$$\pi r^2 h = 35$$
$$2\pi rh = 50$$

In this section we solve systems of nonlinear equations and inequalities.

BASIC CONCEPTS

One way to locate the points at which the line $y = 2x$ intersects the circle $x^2 + y^2 = 5$, is to graph both equations (see Figure 10.25).

The equation describing the circle is nonlinear. Another way to locate the points of intersection is symbolically, by solving the nonlinear system of equations.

$$y = 2x$$
$$x^2 + y^2 = 5$$

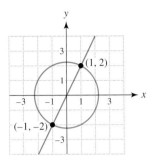

Figure 10.25

Linear systems of equations can have zero, one, or infinitely many solutions. It is possible for a system of nonlinear equations to have *any number* of solutions. Figure 10.25 shows that this nonlinear system of equations has two solutions: $(-1, -2)$ and $(1, 2)$.

SOLVING NONLINEAR SYSTEMS OF EQUATIONS

Nonlinear systems of equations can sometimes be solved graphically, numerically, and symbolically. One symbolic technique is the **method of substitution**, which we demonstrate in the next example.

EXAMPLE 1   Solving a nonlinear system of equations symbolically

Solve

$$y = 2x$$
$$x^2 + y^2 = 5$$

symbolically. Check any solutions.

Solution   Substitute $2x$ for y in the second equation and solve for x.

$$x^2 + (2x)^2 = 5 \qquad \text{Let } y = 2x \text{ in the second equation.}$$
$$x^2 + 4x^2 = 5 \qquad \text{Properties of exponents}$$
$$5x^2 = 5 \qquad \text{Combine like terms.}$$
$$x^2 = 1 \qquad \text{Divide by 5.}$$
$$x = \pm 1 \qquad \text{Square root property}$$

To determine corresponding y-values, substitute $x = \pm 1$ into $y = 2x$; the solutions are $(1, 2)$ and $(-1, -2)$. To check $(1, 2)$, substitute $x = 1$ and $y = 2$ into the given equations.

$$2 \overset{?}{=} 2(1) \qquad \text{True}$$
$$(1)^2 + (2)^2 \overset{?}{=} 5 \qquad \text{True}$$

To check $(-1, -2)$, substitute $x = -1$ and $y = -2$ into the given equations.

$$-2 \overset{?}{=} 2(-1) \qquad \text{True}$$
$$(-1)^2 + (-2)^2 \overset{?}{=} 5 \qquad \text{True}$$

In the next example we solve a nonlinear system of equations graphically and symbolically.

EXAMPLE 2   Solving a nonlinear system of equations

Solve the nonlinear system of equations graphically and symbolically.

$$x^2 - y = 2$$
$$x^2 + y = 4$$

Solution   *Graphical Solution*   Begin by solving each equation for y.

$$y = x^2 - 2$$
$$y = 4 - x^2$$

Graph $Y_1 = X^2 - 2$ and $Y_2 = 4 - X^2$. The solutions are approximately $(-1.73, 1)$ and $(1.73, 1)$, as shown in Figure 10.26. The graphs consist of two parabolas intersecting at two points.

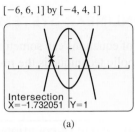

$[-6, 6, 1]$ by $[-4, 4, 1]$

Intersection
X=-1.732051 Y=1

(a)

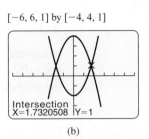

$[-6, 6, 1]$ by $[-4, 4, 1]$

Intersection
X=1.7320508 Y=1

(b)

Figure 10.26

Symbolic Solution   Solving the first equation for y gives $y = x^2 - 2$. Substitute this expression for y in the second equation and solve for x.

$x^2 + y = 4$	Second equation
$x^2 + (x^2 - 2) = 4$	Substitute $y = x^2 - 2$.
$2x^2 = 6$	Combine like terms; add 2.
$x^2 = 3$	Divide by 2.
$x = \pm\sqrt{3}$	Square root property

To determine y, substitute $x = \pm\sqrt{3}$ in $y = x^2 - 2$.

$$y = (\sqrt{3})^2 - 2 = 3 - 2 = 1$$
$$y = (-\sqrt{3})^2 - 2 = 3 - 2 = 1$$

The *exact* solutions are $(\sqrt{3}, 1)$ and $(-\sqrt{3}, 1)$.

EXAMPLE 3   **Solving a nonlinear system of equations**

TEACHING TIP

Point out that nonlinear systems of equations can sometimes be solved by using either substitution or elimination.

Solve the nonlinear system of equations symbolically and graphically.

$$x^2 - y^2 = 3$$
$$x^2 + y^2 = 5$$

Solution   ***Symbolic Solution***   Instead of using substitution on this nonlinear system of equations, we use elimination. Note that, if we add the two equations, the y-variable will be eliminated.

$$\begin{aligned} x^2 - y^2 &= 3 \\ x^2 + y^2 &= 5 \\ \hline 2x^2 \qquad &= 8 \end{aligned}$$ Add equations.

Solving gives $x^2 = 4$, or $x = \pm 2$. To determine y, substitute 4 for x^2 in $x^2 + y^2 = 5$.

$$4 + y^2 = 5 \quad \text{or} \quad y^2 = 1$$

Because $y^2 = 1$, $y = \pm 1$. Thus there are four solutions: $(2, 1)$, $(2, -1)$, $(-2, 1)$, and $(-2, -1)$.

Graphical Solution   The graph of the first equation is a hyperbola, and the graph of the second is a circle with radius $\sqrt{5}$. The four points of intersection are $(\pm 2, \pm 1)$, as shown in Figure 10.27 on the next page.

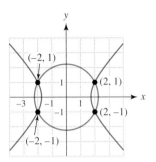

Figure 10.27

In the next example we solve the system of equations presented in the introduction.

EXAMPLE 4   Modeling the dimensions of a can

Find the dimensions of a can having a volume V of 35 cubic inches and a side area A of 50 square inches by solving the following system of nonlinear equations symbolically.

$$\pi r^2 h = 35$$
$$2\pi r h = 50$$

Solution   We can find r by solving the following equation.

$$\frac{50}{2\pi r} = \frac{35}{\pi r^2} \qquad h = \frac{50}{2\pi r} \quad \text{and} \quad h = \frac{35}{\pi r^2}$$

$$50\pi r^2 = 70\pi r \qquad \text{Clear fractions.}$$

$$50\pi r^2 - 70\pi r = 0 \qquad \text{Subtract } 70\pi r.$$

$$10\pi r(5r - 7) = 0 \qquad \text{Factor out } 10\pi r.$$

$$10\pi r = 0 \quad \text{or} \quad 5r - 7 = 0 \qquad \text{Zero-product property}$$

$$r = 0 \quad \text{or} \quad r = \frac{7}{5} = 1.4 \qquad \text{Solve.}$$

Because $h = \frac{50}{2\pi r}$, $r = 0$ is not possible, but we can find h by substituting **1.4** for r in the formula.

$$h = \frac{50}{2\pi(\mathbf{1.4})} \approx 5.68$$

A can having a volume of 35 cubic inches and a side area of 50 square inches has a radius of 1.4 inches and a height of about 5.68 inches.

SOLVING NONLINEAR SYSTEMS OF INEQUALITIES

In Section 4.3 we solved systems of linear inequalities. A **system of nonlinear inequalities** can be solved similarly by using graphical techniques. For example, consider the system of nonlinear inequalities

$$y \geq x^2 - 2$$
$$y \leq 4 - x^2.$$

The graph of $y = x^2 - 2$ is a parabola opening upward. The solution set to $y \geq x^2 - 2$ includes all points lying on or above this parabola. See Figure 10.28(a). Similarly, the graph of $y = 4 - x^2$ is a parabola opening downward. The solution set to $y \leq 4 - x^2$ includes all points lying on or below this parabola. See Figure 10.28(b).

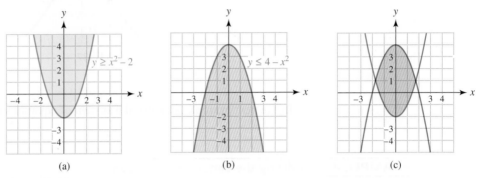

Figure 10.28

The solution set for this *system* of nonlinear inequalities includes all points (x, y) in *both* shaded regions. The *intersection* of the shaded regions is shown in Figure 10.28(c).

EXAMPLE 5   Solving a system of nonlinear inequalities graphically

Shade the solution set for the system of inequalities.

$$\frac{x^2}{4} + \frac{y^2}{9} < 1$$

$$y > 1$$

Solution   The solutions to $\frac{x^2}{4} + \frac{y^2}{9} < 1$ lie inside the ellipse $\frac{x^2}{4} + \frac{y^2}{9} = 1$. See Figure 10.29(a). Solutions to $y > 1$ lie above the line $y = 1$, as shown in Figure 10.29(b). The intersection of these two regions is shown in Figure 10.29(c). Note that a dashed curve and line are used when equality is not involved.

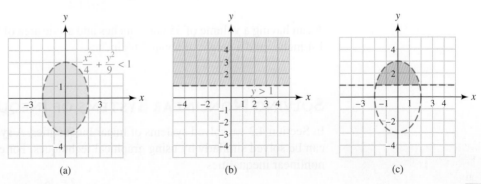

Figure 10.29

EXAMPLE 6   Solving a system of nonlinear inequalities graphically

Shade the solution set for the following system of inequalities.

$$x^2 + y \leq 4$$
$$-x + y \geq 2$$

Solution   The solutions to $x^2 + y \leq 4$ lie below the parabola $y = -x^2 + 4$, and the solutions to $-x + y \geq 2$ lie above the line $y = x + 2$. The appropriate shaded region is shown in Figure 10.30. Both the parabola and the line are solid because equality is included in both inequalities.

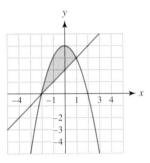

Figure 10.30

In the next example we use a graphing calculator to shade a region that lies above both graphs, using the "$Y_1=$" menu. This feature allows us to shade either above or below the graph of a function.

EXAMPLE 7   Solving a system of inequalities with a graphing calculator

Shade the solution set for the following system of inequalities.

$$y \geq x^2 - 2$$
$$y \geq -1 - x$$

Solution   Enter $Y_1 = X^2 - 2$ and $Y_2 = -1 - X$, as shown in Figure 10.31(a). Note that the option to shade above the graphs of Y_1 and Y_2 was selected to the left of Y_1 and Y_2. Then the two equations were graphed in Figure 10.31(b). The solution set corresponds to where there are both vertical and horizontal lines.

Calculator Help

To shade the solution set to a system of inequalities, see the Appendix (page AP-7).

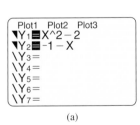

Figure 10.31

10.3 PUTTING IT ALL TOGETHER

In this section we discussed nonlinear systems of equations in two variables. Unlike a linear system of equations, a nonlinear system of equations can have any number of solutions. Systems of nonlinear equations can be solved symbolically and graphically. Systems of nonlinear inequalities involving two variables usually have infinitely many solutions, which can be represented by a shaded region in the xy-plane. The following table summarizes these concepts.

Concept	Explanation
Nonlinear Systems of Equations	To solve the following system of equations symbolically, using *substitution*, solve the first equation for y. $$x + y = 5 \quad \text{or} \quad y = 5 - x$$ $$x^2 - y = 1$$ Substitute $5 - x$ for y in the second equation and solve the resulting quadratic equation. (*Elimination* can also be used on this system.) $$x^2 - (5 - x) = 1 \quad \text{or} \quad x^2 + x - 6 = 0$$ implies that $$x = -3 \quad \text{or} \quad x = 2.$$ Then $y = 5 - (-3) = 8$ or $y = 5 - 2 = 3$. The solutions are $(-3, 8)$ and $(2, 3)$. Graphical support is shown in the accompanying figure. $(-3, 8)$ $y = x^2 - 1$ $(2, 3)$ $y = 5 - x$
Nonlinear Systems of Inequalities	To solve the following system of inequalities graphically, solve each equation for y. $$x + y \le 5 \quad \text{or} \quad y \le 5 - x$$ $$x^2 - y \le 1 \quad \text{or} \quad y \ge x^2 - 1$$ The solutions lie above the parabola and below the line, as shown in the following figure. $y = x^2 - 1$ $y = 5 - x$

10.3 EXERCISES

FOR EXTRA HELP

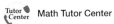
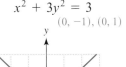

CONCEPTS

1. How many solutions can a system of nonlinear equations have?   Any number

2. If a system of nonlinear equations has two equations, how many equations does a solution have to satisfy?   2

3. Determine mentally the number of solutions to the following system of equations. Explain your reasoning.

$$y = x$$
$$x^2 + y^2 = 4$$

Two; the line intersects the circle twice.

4. Describe the solution set to $x^2 + y^2 \leq 1$.
All points inside and including a circle of radius 1 centered at the origin.

5. Does $(-2, -1)$ satisfy $5x^2 - 2y^2 > 18$?   No

6. Does $(3, 4)$ satisfy $x^2 - 2y \geq 4$?   No

7. Sketch a parabola and ellipse with four points of intersection. *   Answers may vary.

8. Sketch a line and a hyperbola with two points of intersection. *   Answers may vary.

NONLINEAR SYSTEMS OF EQUATIONS

Exercises 9–12: Use the graph to estimate all solutions to the system of equations. Check each solution.

9. $x^2 + y^2 = 10$

$$y = 3x$$

(1, 3), (−1, −3)

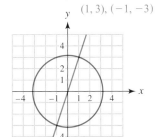

10. $x^2 + 3y^2 = 16$

$$y = -x$$

(−2, 2), (2, −2)

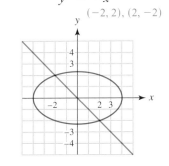

11. $y^2 - x^2 = 1$

$$x^2 + 3y^2 = 3$$

(0, −1), (0, 1)

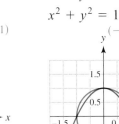

12. $y = 1 - x^2$

$$x^2 + y^2 = 1$$

(−1, 0), (0, 1), (1, 0)

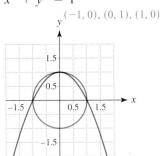

Exercises 13–18: Solve the system of equations symbolically. Check your solutions.

13. $y = 2x$

$$x^2 + y^2 = 45$$

(3, 6), (−3, −6)

14. $y = x$

$$y^2 = 3 - 2x^2$$

(1, 1), (−1, −1)

15. $x + y = 1$

$$x^2 - y^2 = 3$$ (2, −1)

16. $y - x = -1$

$$y = 2x^2$$

No real solutions

17. $y - x^2 = 0$

$$x^2 + y^2 = 6$$

$(-\sqrt{2}, 2), (\sqrt{2}, 2)$

18. $x^2 - y^2 = 4$

$$x^2 + y^2 = 4$$

(2, 0), (−2, 0)

Exercises 19–22: Solve the system of equations graphically. Check your solutions.

19. $y = x^2 - 3$

$$2x^2 - y = 1 - 3x$$

(−1, −2), (−2, 1)

20. $x + y = 2$

$$x - y^2 = 3$$ No real solutions

21. $y - x = -4$

$$x - y^2 = -2$$

(7, 3), (2, −2)

22. $xy = 1$

$$y = x$$ (−1, −1), (1, 1)

Exercises 23–26: Solve the system of equations

 (a) *symbolically,*
 (b) *graphically, and*
 (c) *numerically.*

23. $y = -2x$

$$x^2 + y = 3$$

(−1, 2), (3, −6)

24. $4x - y = 0$

$$x^3 - y = 0$$

(−2, −8), (0, 0), (2, 8)

25. $xy = 1$

$$x - y = 0$$

(−1, −1), (1, 1)

26. $x^2 + y^2 = 4$

$$y - x = 2$$

(−2, 0), (0, 2)

*Answers on page IA-36

NONLINEAR SYSTEMS OF INEQUALITIES

Exercises 27–30: Shade the solution set in the xy-plane. *

27. $y \geq x^2$

28. $y \leq x^2 - 1$

29. $\dfrac{x^2}{4} + \dfrac{y^2}{9} > 1$

30. $x^2 + y^2 \leq 1$

Exercises 31–38: Shade the solution set in the xy-plane. Then use the graph to select one solution. *

31. $y > x^2 + 1$
$y < 3$
(0, 2); answers may vary.

32. $y > x^2$
$y < x + 2$
(0, 1); answers may vary.

33. $x^2 + y^2 \leq 1$
$y < x$
$\left(\frac{1}{2}, -\frac{1}{2}\right)$; answers may vary.

34. $y > x^2 - 2$
$y \leq 2 - x^2$
(0, 0); answers may vary.

35. $x^2 + y^2 \leq 1$
$(x - 2)^2 + y^2 \leq 1$
(1, 0)

36. $x^2 - y \geq 2$
$(x + 1)^2 + y^2 \leq 4$
(−2, 0); answers may vary.

37. $x^2 - y^2 \leq 4$
$x^2 + y^2 \leq 9$
(0, 0); answers may vary.

38. $3x + 2y < 6$
$x^2 + y^2 \leq 16$
(0, 0); answers may vary.

Exercises 39 and 40: Match the inequality or system of inequalities with its graph (a. or b.).

39. $y \leq \dfrac{1}{2}x^2$ a.

40. $y \geq x^2 + 1$
$y \leq 5$ b.

a.

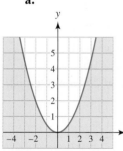

b.

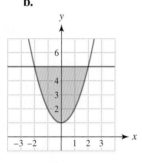

Exercises 41 and 42: Use the graph to write the inequality or system of inequalities.

41. $y \geq x^2$, $y < 4 - x$

42. $x^2 + y^2 \leq 9$

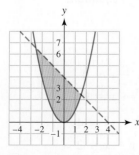

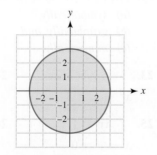

APPLICATIONS

43. *Dimensions of a Can*   (Refer to Example 4.) Find the dimensions of a cylindrical container with a volume of 40 cubic inches and a side area of 50 square inches **(a)** graphically and **(b)** symbolically.
$r = 1.6$ in., $h \approx 4.97$ in.

44. *Dimensions of a Can*   (Refer to Example 4.) Is it possible to design an aluminum can with volume of 60 cubic inches and side area of 60 square inches? If so, find the dimensions of the can.
Yes; $r = 2$ in. and $h \approx 4.77$ in.

45. *Dimensions of a Cone*   The volume V of a cone is given by $V = \frac{1}{3}\pi r^2 h$, and the surface area S of its side is given by $S = \pi r \sqrt{r^2 + h^2}$, where h is the height and r is the radius of the base (see the accompanying figure). (b) $r \approx 2.02$ ft, $h \approx 7.92$ ft;
$r \approx 3.76$ ft, $h \approx 2.30$ ft

(a) Solve each equation for h.

(b) Estimate r and h graphically for a cone with volume V of 34 cubic feet and surface area S of 52 square feet. (a) $h = \dfrac{3V}{\pi r^2}$; $h = \sqrt{\left(\dfrac{S}{\pi r}\right)^2 - r^2}$

46. *Area and Perimeter*   The area of a room is 143 feet, and its perimeter is 48 feet. Let x be the width and y be the length of the room. See the accompanying figure.
(a) Write a system of equations that models this situation. $xy = 143$, $2x + 2y = 48$
(b) Solve the system. $x = 11$ ft, $y = 13$ ft

*Answers on page IA-36

WRITING ABOUT MATHEMATICS

47. A student *incorrectly* changes the system of inequalities

$$x^2 - y \geq 6 \qquad \text{to} \qquad y \geq x^2 - 6$$
$$2x - y \leq -3 \qquad\qquad y \leq 2x + 3.$$

The student discovers that the point $(1, 2)$ satisfies the second system but not the first. Explain the student's error.

48. Explain graphically how systems of nonlinear equations can have any number of solutions. Sketch graphs of different systems with 0, 1, 2, and 3 solutions.

CHECKING BASIC CONCEPTS ⬭ **SECTION 10.3**

1. Solve the following system of equations symbolically and graphically. $(1, -1), (3, 3)$

$$x^2 - y = 2x$$
$$2x - y = 3$$

2. Determine mentally the number of solutions to the following system of equations.   2

$$y = x^2 - 4$$
$$y = x$$

3. The solution set for a system of inequalities is shown in the accompanying figure.
(a) Find one ordered pair (x, y) that is a solution and one that is not. $(0, 3), (4, 4)$; answers may vary.

(b) Write the system of inequalities represented by the graph.

$$y \geq 2 - x$$
$$y \leq 4 - x^2$$

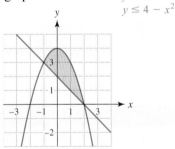

4. Shade the solution set for the following system of inequalities. *

$$x^2 + y^2 \leq 4$$
$$y < 1$$

*Answer on page IA-36

Summary

Section 10.1   *Parabolas and Circles*

There are three basic types of conic sections: parabolas, ellipses, and hyperbolas. A parabola can have a vertical or a horizontal axis. Two forms of an equation for a parabola with a vertical axis are

$$y = ax^2 + bx + c \quad \text{and} \quad y = a(x - h)^2 + k.$$

If $a > 0$ the parabola opens upward, and if $a < 0$ it opens downward (see the figure on the left). The vertex is located at (h, k). Two forms of an equation for a parabola with a horizontal axis are

$$x = ay^2 + by + c \quad \text{and} \quad x = a(y - k)^2 + h.$$

If $a > 0$ the parabola opens to the right, and if $a < 0$ it opens to the left (see the figure on the right). The vertex is located at (h, k).

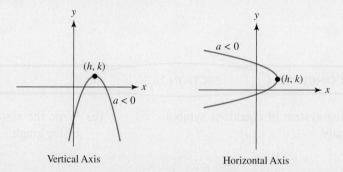

Vertical Axis   Horizontal Axis

The standard equation for a circle with center (h, k) and radius r is

$$(x - h)^2 + (y - k)^2 = r^2.$$

Section 10.2 *Ellipses and Hyperbolas*

Ellipses   The standard equation for an ellipse centered at the origin with a horizontal major axis is $\frac{x^2}{a^2} + \frac{y^2}{b^2} = 1$, $a > b > 0$, and the vertices are $(\pm a, 0)$, as shown in the figure on the left. The standard equation for an ellipse centered at the origin with a vertical major axis is $\frac{x^2}{b^2} + \frac{y^2}{a^2} = 1$, $a > b > 0$, and the vertices are $(0, \pm a)$, as shown in the figure on the right. Circles are a special type of ellipse, with the major and minor axes having equal lengths.

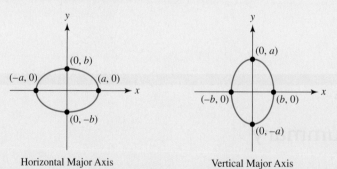

Horizontal Major Axis   Vertical Major Axis

Hyperbolas   The standard equation for a hyperbola centered at the origin with a horizontal transverse axis is $\frac{x^2}{a^2} - \frac{y^2}{b^2} = 1$, the asymptotes are given by $y = \pm \frac{b}{a}x$, and the vertices are $(\pm a, 0)$, as shown in the figure on the left. The standard equation for a hyperbola centered at the origin with a vertical transverse axis is $\frac{y^2}{a^2} - \frac{x^2}{b^2} = 1$, the asymptotes are $y = \pm \frac{a}{b}x$, and the vertices are $(0, \pm a)$, as shown in the figure on the right.

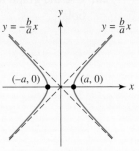

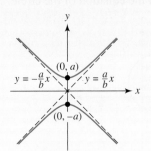

Horizontal Transverse Axis   Vertical Transverse Axis

Section 10.3   *Nonlinear Systems of Equations and Inequalities*

Systems of nonlinear equations can have any number of solutions. The methods of substitution or elimination can often be used to solve a system of nonlinear equations symbolically. Nonlinear systems can also be solved graphically. The solution set for a system of two nonlinear inequalities with two variables is typically a region in the *xy*-plane. A solution is an ordered pair (x, y) that satisfies both inequalities. The solution set for $y \geq x^2 - 2$ and $y \leq 4 - \frac{1}{2}x^2$ is shaded in the accompanying figure.

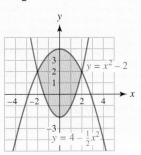

CHAPTER
10 Review Exercises

SECTION 10.1

Exercises 1–6: Graph the parabola. Find the vertex and axis of symmetry.*

1. $x = 2y^2$ $(0, 0); y = 0$ **2.** $x = -(y + 1)^2$
                                   $(0, -1); y = -1$

3. $x = -2(y - 2)^2$ **4.** $x = (y + 2)^2 - 1$
   $(0, 2); y = 2$ $(-1, -2); y = -2$

5. $x = -3y^2 + 1$ **6.** $x = \frac{1}{2}y^2 + y - 3$
   $(1, 0); y = 0$
                        $\left(-\frac{7}{2}, -1\right); y = -1$

7. Use the graph to determine the equation of the parabola.

$x = y^2$

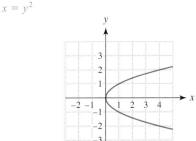

*Answers on pages IA-36–IA-37

8. Use the graph to find the equation of the circle.

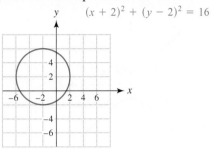

$(x + 2)^2 + (y - 2)^2 = 16$

9. Write the equation of the circle with radius 1 and center $(0, 0)$. $x^2 + y^2 = 1$

10. Write the equation of the circle with radius 4 and center $(2, -3)$. $(x - 2)^2 + (y + 3)^2 = 16$

Exercises 11–14: Find the radius and center of the circle. Then graph the circle. *

11. $x^2 + y^2 = 25$ $5; (0, 0)$

12. $(x - 2)^2 + y^2 = 9$ $3; (2, 0)$

13. $(x + 3)^2 + (y - 1)^2 = 5$ $\sqrt{5}; (-3, 1)$

14. $x^2 - 2x + y^2 + 2y = 7$ $3; (1, -1)$

SECTION 10.2

Exercises 15–18: Graph the ellipse. Label the vertices and endpoints of the minor axis. *

15. $\dfrac{x^2}{4} + \dfrac{y^2}{25} = 1$

16. $x^2 + \dfrac{y^2}{4} = 1$

17. $25x^2 + 20y^2 = 500$

18. $4x^2 + 9y^2 = 36$

19. Use the graph to determine the equation of the ellipse.

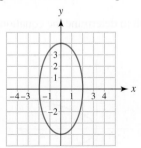

$\dfrac{y^2}{16} + \dfrac{x^2}{4} = 1$

20. Use the graph to determine the equation of the hyperbola.

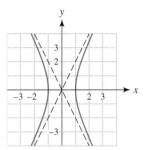

$x^2 - \dfrac{y^2}{4} = 1$

Exercises 21–24: Graph the hyperbola. Show the asymptotes. *

21. $\dfrac{x^2}{9} - \dfrac{y^2}{4} = 1$

22. $\dfrac{y^2}{25} - \dfrac{x^2}{16} = 1$

23. $y^2 - x^2 = 1$

24. $25x^2 - 16y^2 = 400$

SECTION 10.3

Exercises 25–28: Use the graph to estimate all solutions to the system of equations. Check each solution.

25. $x^2 + y^2 = 9$
$x + y = 3$
$(0, 3), (3, 0)$

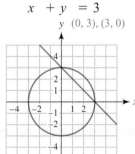

26. $xy = 2$
$y = 2x$
$(-1, -2), (1, 2)$

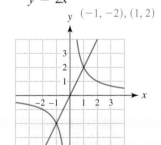

27. $x^2 - y = x$
$y = x$ $(0, 0), (2, 2)$

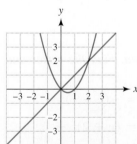

28. $x^2 + y^2 = 5$
$x^2 - y^2 = 3$

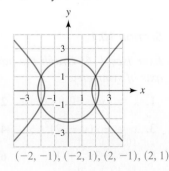

$(-2, -1), (-2, 1), (2, -1), (2, 1)$

*Answers on page IA-37

Exercises 29–32: Solve the system of equations. Check your solutions.

29. $y = x$
$x^2 + y^2 = 32$
$(-4, -4), (4, 4)$

30. $x - y = 4$
$x^2 + y^2 = 16$
$(0, -4), (4, 0)$

31. $y = x^2$
$2x^2 + y = 3$
$(-1, 1), (1, 1)$

32. $y = x^2 + 1$
$2x^2 - y = 3x - 3$
$(1, 2), (2, 5)$

Exercises 33 and 34: Solve the system of equations graphically.

33. $2x - y = 4$
$x^2 + y = 4$
$(-4, -12), (2, 0)$

34. $x^2 + y = 0$
$x^2 + y^2 = 2$
$(-1, -1), (1, -1)$

Exercises 35 and 36: Solve the system of equations
(a) *symbolically,*
(b) *graphically, and*
(c) *numerically.*

35. $y = x$
$x^2 + 2y = 8$
$(2, 2), (-4, -4)$

36. $y = x^3$
$x^2 - y = 0$ $(1, 1), (0, 0)$

Exercises 37–44: Shade the solution set in the xy-plane. *

37. $y \geq 2x^2$

38. $y < 2x - 3$

39. $y < -x^2$

40. $\dfrac{x^2}{9} + \dfrac{y^2}{16} \leq 1$

41. $y - x^2 \geq 1$
$y \leq 2$

42. $x^2 + y \leq 4$
$3x + 2y \geq 6$

43. $y > x^2$
$y < 4 - x^2$

44. $\dfrac{x^2}{4} + \dfrac{y^2}{9} > 1$
$x^2 + y^2 < 16$

Exercises 45 and 46: Use the graph to write the system of inequalities.

45. $y \geq x^2 - 2$
$y \leq 2 - x$

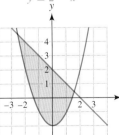

46. $y \geq x$
$x^2 + y^2 \leq 4$

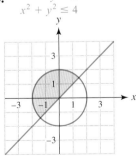

APPLICATIONS

47. *Area and Perimeter* The area of a desktop is 1000 square inches, and its perimeter is 130 inches. Let x be the width and y be the length of the desktop.
(a) Write a system of equations that models this situation. $xy = 1000$, $2x + 2y = 130$
(b) Solve the system graphically.
(c) Solve the system symbolically.
(b), (c) $x = 25$ in., $y = 40$ in.

48. *Numbers* The product of two positive numbers is 60, and their difference is 7. Let x be the smaller number and y be the larger number.
(a) Write a system of equations whose solution gives the two numbers. $xy = 60$, $y - x = 7$
(b) Solve the system graphically. (b), (c) $x = 5, y = 12$
(c) Solve the system symbolically.

49. *Dimensions of a Container* The volume of a cylindrical container is $V = \pi r^2 h$, and its surface area, *excluding* the top and bottom, is $A = 2\pi rh$. Find the dimensions of a container with $A = 100$ square feet and $V = 50$ cubic feet. Is your answer unique? $r = 1$ ft, $h \approx 15.92$ ft; yes

50. *Dimensions of a Container* The volume of a cylindrical container is $V = \pi r^2 h$, and its surface area, *including* the top and bottom, is $A = 2\pi rh + 2\pi r^2$. Graphically find the dimensions of a can with $A = 80$ square inches and $V = 35$ cubic inches. Is your answer unique?
Either $r \approx 0.94$ in., $h \approx 12.60$ in. or $r \approx 3.00$ in., $h \approx 1.23$ in.; no

51. *Geometry of an Ellipse* The area inside an ellipse is given by $A = \pi ab$, and its perimeter P can be approximated by
$$P = 2\pi\sqrt{\dfrac{a^2 + b^2}{2}}.$$
(a) Graph $\dfrac{x^2}{5} + \dfrac{y^2}{12} = 1$. *
(b) Estimate its area and perimeter.
$A \approx 24.33, P \approx 18.32$

*Answers on pages IA-37–IA-38

52. *Orbit of Mars*   Mars has an elliptical orbit that is nearly circular, with $a = 1.524$ and $b = 1.517$, where the units are astronomical units (1 A.U. = 93 million miles).   (*Source:* M. Zeilik.)

(b) $P \approx 9.55$ A.U., or about 8.9×10^8 mi
$A \approx 7.26$ square A.U., or about 6.3×10^{16} mi^2

 (a) Graph the orbit of Mars in $[-3, 3, 1]$ by $[-2, 2, 1]$. Plot the point (0.14, 0) to show the position of the sun. Assume that the major axis is horizontal. *

(b) Use the information in Exercise 51 to estimate how far Mars travels in one orbit around the sun. Approximate the area inside its orbit.

CHAPTER

 **10** Test

1. Graph the parabola $x = (y - 4)^2 - 2$. Find the vertex and axis of symmetry. * $(-2, 4); y = 4$

2. Use the graph to determine the equation of the parabola. $x = -y^2 + 1$

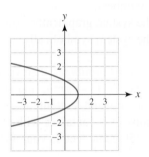

3. Use the graph to find the equation of the circle. $(x - 2)^2 + (y + 4)^2 = 4$

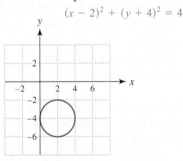

4. Write the equation of the circle with radius 10 and center $(-5, 2)$. $(x + 5)^2 + (y - 2)^2 = 100$

5. Find the radius and center of the circle given by

$$x^2 + 4x + y^2 - 6y = 3.$$

Then graph the circle. * $r = 4$, center $= (-2, 3)$

6. Graph the ellipse $\frac{x^2}{16} + \frac{y^2}{49} = 1$. Label the vertices and endpoints of the minor axis. *

7. Use the graph to determine the equation of the ellipse. $\frac{x^2}{100} + \frac{y^2}{64} = 1$

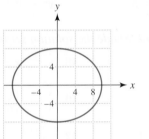

8. Graph the hyperbola $4x^2 - 9y^2 = 36$. Show the asymptotes. *

9. Use the graph to estimate all solutions to the system of equations. Check each solution by substitution in the system of equations. $(0, -4), (4, 0)$

$$x^2 + y^2 = 16 \quad \text{and} \quad x - y = 4$$

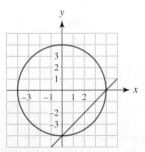

10. Solve the system of equations symbolically.

$$x - y = 3 \quad \text{and} \quad x^2 + y^2 = 17 \quad (-1, -4), (4, 1)$$

*Answers on page IA-38

11. Solve the system of equations graphically.

$$2x^2 - y = 4 \quad \text{and} \quad x^2 + y = 8 \quad (-2, 4), (2, 4)$$

12. Shade the solution set in the *xy*-plane.*

$$3x + y > 6 \quad \text{and} \quad x^2 + y^2 < 25$$

13. Use the graph to write the system of inequalities.

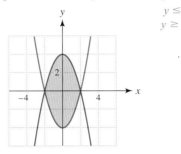

$$y \leq 4 - x^2$$
$$y \geq x^2 - 4$$

14. *Area and Perimeter*   The area of a rectangular swimming pool is 5000 square feet, and its perimeter is 300 feet. Let *x* be the width and *y* be the length of the pool.
   (a) Write a system of equations that models this situation. $xy = 5000, \quad 2x + 2y = 300$
   (b) Solve the system.   50 ft by 100 ft

15. *Dimensions of a Box*   The volume of a rectangular box with a square bottom and open top is $V = x^2 y$, and its surface area is $A = x^2 + 4xy$, where *x* represents its width and length and *y* represents its height. Estimate graphically the dimensions of a box with $V = 1183$ cubic inches and $A = 702$ square inches. Is your answer unique? (*Hint:* Substitute appropriate values for *V* and *A*, and then solve each equation for *y*.)
Either $x \approx 22.08$ in., $y \approx 2.43$ in. or $x \approx 7.29$ in., $y \approx 22.24$ in.; no.

16. *Orbit of Uranus*   The planet Uranus has an elliptical orbit that is nearly circular, with $a = 19.18$ and $b = 19.16$, where units are astronomical units (1 A.U. = 93 million miles).   (*Source:* M. Zeilik.)

   (a) Graph the orbit of Uranus in $[-30, 30, 10]$ by $[-20, 20, 10]$. Plot the point $(0.9, 0)$ to show the position of the sun. Assume that the major axis is horizontal.*
   (b) Find the minimum distance between Uranus and the sun.   18.28 A.U., or about 1,700,040,000 mi

*Answers on page IA-38

Extended and Discovery Exercises

Exercises 1–2: Foci of Parabolas   The focus of a parabola is a point that has special significance. When a parabola is rotated about its axis, it sweeps out a shape called a **paraboloid**, as illustrated in the top figure on the following page. Paraboloids have an important reflective property. When incoming rays of light from the sun or distant stars strike the surface of a paraboloid, each ray is reflected toward the focus, as shown in the figure labeled "Reflective Property." If the rays are sunlight, intense heat is produced, which can be used to generate solar heat. Radio signals from distant space also concentrate at the focus, and scientists can measure these signals by placing a receiver there.

   The same reflective property of a paraboloid can be used in reverse. If a light source is placed at the focus, the light is reflected straight ahead, as depicted in the figure labeled "Headlight." Searchlights, flashlights, and car headlights make use of this reflective property.

   The focus is always located inside a parabola, on its axis of symmetry. If the distance between the vertex and the focus is $|p|$, the following equations can be used to locate the focus. Note that the value of *p* may be either positive or negative.

EQUATION OF A PARABOLA WITH VERTEX (0, 0)

Vertical Axis

The parabola with a focus at $(0, p)$ has the equation $x^2 = 4py$.

Horizontal Axis

The parabola with a focus at $(p, 0)$ has the equation $y^2 = 4px$.

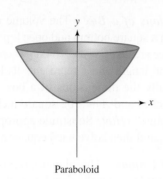

Paraboloid

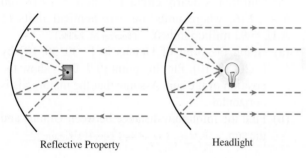

Reflective Property   Headlight

1. Sketch a graph of each parabola. Label the vertex and focus.*
   (a) $x^2 = 4y$ (b) $y^2 = -8x$ (c) $x = 2y^2$

2. The reflective property of paraboloids is used in satellite dishes and radio telescopes. The U.S. Naval Research Laboratory designed a giant radio telescope weighing 3450 tons. Its parabolic dish has a diameter of 300 feet and a depth of 44 feet, as shown in the accompanying figures. (*Source:* J. Mar, *Structure Technology for Large Radio and Radar Telescope Systems.*)
   (a) Find an equation in the form $y = ax^2$ that describes a cross section of this dish. $y = \frac{11}{5625}x^2$
   (b) If the receiver is located at the focus, how far should it be from the vertex? $\frac{5625}{44} \approx 127.8$ ft

focus

300 ft
44 ft

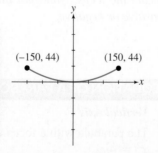

$(-150, 44)$ $(150, 44)$

Radio Telescope

Exercises 3 and 4: **Translations of Ellipses and Hyperbolas** *Ellipses and hyperbolas can be translated so that they are centered at a point (h, k), rather than at the origin. These techniques are the same as those used for parabolas and circles. To translate a conic section so that it is centered at (h, k) rather than $(0, 0)$, replace x with $(x - h)$ and replace y with $(y - k)$. For example, to center $\frac{x^2}{9} + \frac{y^2}{4} = 1$ at $(-1, 2)$, change its equation to $\frac{(x + 1)^2}{9} + \frac{(y - 2)^2}{4} = 1$. See the accompanying figures.*

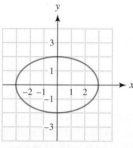

Ellipse Centered at $(0, 0)$

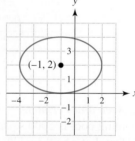

$(-1, 2)$

Ellipse Centered at $(-1, 2)$

3. Graph each conic section. For hyperbolas give the equations of the asymptotes.*
   (a) $\dfrac{(x - 3)^2}{25} + \dfrac{(y - 1)^2}{9} = 1$
   (b) $\dfrac{(x + 1)^2}{4} + \dfrac{(y + 2)^2}{16} = 1$
   (c) $\dfrac{(x + 1)^2}{4} - \dfrac{(y - 3)^2}{9} = 1$ $y = \pm\frac{3}{2}(x + 1) + 3$
   (d) $\dfrac{(y - 4)^2}{16} - \dfrac{(x + 1)^2}{4} = 1$ $y = \pm 2(x + 1) + 4$

4. Write the equation of an ellipse having the following properties.
   (a) Horizontal major axis of length 8, minor axis of length 4, and centered at $(-3, 5)$.
   (b) Vertical major axis of length 10, minor axis of length 6, and centered at $(2, -3)$.

5. Determine the center of the conic section by completing the square.
   (a) $9x^2 - 18x + 4y^2 + 24y + 9 = 0$ $(1, -3)$
   (b) $25x^2 + 150x - 16y^2 + 32y - 191 = 0$ $(-3, 1)$

4. (a) $\dfrac{(x + 3)^2}{16} + \dfrac{(y - 5)^2}{4} = 1$ (b) $\dfrac{(y + 3)^2}{25} + \dfrac{(x - 2)^2}{9} = 1$

*Answers on page IA-38

CHAPTER 11

Sequences and Series

In this final chapter we present sequences and series, which are essential topics because they are used to model and approximate important quantities. For example, complicated population growth can be modeled with sequences, and accurate approximations for numbers such as π and e are made with series. Series also are essential to the solution of many modern applied mathematics problems.

Although you may not always recognize the impact of mathematics on everyday life, its influence is nonetheless profound. Mathematics is the *language of technology*—it allows experiences to be quantified. In the preceding chapters we showed numerous examples of mathematics being used to model the real world. Computers, CD players, highway design, weather, hurricanes, electricity, government data, cellular phones, medicine, ecology, business, sports, and psychology represent only some of the applications of mathematics. In fact, if a subject is studied in enough detail, mathematics usually appears in one form or another. Although predicting what the future may bring is difficult, one thing *is* certain—mathematics will continue to play an important role in both theoretical research and the real world.

The gains of education are never really lost.
—Franklin Roosevelt

11.1   SEQUENCES

Basic Concepts · Representations of Sequences · Models and Applications

INTRODUCTION

Sequences are ordered lists. For example, names listed alphabetically represent a sequence. Figure 11.1 shows an insect population in thousands per acre over a 6-year period. Listing populations by year is another example of a sequence. In mathematics a sequence is a function, for which valid inputs must be natural numbers. For example, we can use a function f to define this sequence by letting $f(1)$ represent the insect population after 1 year, $f(2)$ represent the insect population after 2 years, and in general let $f(n)$ represent the population after n years. In this section we discuss sequences and how they can be represented.

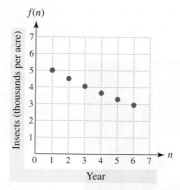

Figure 11.1 An Insect Population

BASIC CONCEPTS

Suppose that an individual's starting salary is $40,000 per year and that the person's salary is increased by 10% each year. This situation is modeled by

$$f(n) = 40,000(1.10)^n.$$

We do not allow the input n to be any real number, but rather limit n to a natural number because the individual's salary is constant throughout a particular year. The first 5 terms of the sequence are

$$f(1), f(2), f(3), f(4), f(5).$$

They can be computed as follows.

$$f(1) = 40,000(1.10)^1 = 44,000$$
$$f(2) = 40,000(1.10)^2 = 48,400$$
$$f(3) = 40,000(1.10)^3 = 53,240$$
$$f(4) = 40,000(1.10)^4 = 58,564$$
$$f(5) = 40,000(1.10)^5 \approx 64,420$$

This sequence is represented numerically in Table 11.1.

TABLE 11.1

n	1	2	3	4	5
$f(n)$	44,000	48,400	53,240	58,564	64,420

A graphical representation results when each data point in Table 11.1 is plotted in the xy-plane, as illustrated in Figure 11.2. Note that graphs of sequences are scatterplots.

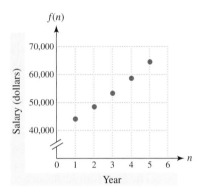

Figure 11.2

TEACHING TIP

Point out that the graph of a sequence is a scatterplot.

The preceding sequence is an example of a *finite sequence* of numbers. The even natural numbers,

$$2, 4, 6, 8, 10, 12, 14, \ldots$$

are an example of an *infinite sequence* represented by $f(n) = 2n$, when n is a natural number. The three dots, or periods (called an *ellipsis*), indicate that the pattern continues indefinitely.

SEQUENCES

A **finite sequence** is a function whose domain is $D = \{1, 2, 3, \ldots, n\}$ for some fixed natural number n.

An **infinite sequence** is a function whose domain is the set of natural numbers.

Because sequences are functions, many of the concepts discussed in previous chapters apply to sequences. Instead of letting y represent the output, however, the convention is to write $a_n = f(n)$, where n is a natural number in the domain of the sequence. The *terms* of a sequence are

$$a_1, a_2, a_3, \ldots, a_n, \ldots.$$

The first term is $a_1 = f(1)$, the second term is $a_2 = f(2)$, and so on. The **nth term**, or **general term**, of a sequence is $a_n = f(n)$.

EXAMPLE 1 Computing terms of a sequence

Write the first four terms of each sequence for $n = 1, 2, 3$, and 4.

(a) $f(n) = 2n - 1$ **(b)** $f(n) = 3(-2)^n$ **(c)** $f(n) = \dfrac{n}{n + 1}$

Solution **(a)** For $a_n = f(n) = 2n - 1$, we write

TEACHING TIP

Do some examples like Example 1.

$$a_1 = f(1) = 2(1) - 1 = 1;$$
$$a_2 = f(2) = 2(2) - 1 = 3;$$
$$a_3 = f(3) = 2(3) - 1 = 5;$$
$$a_4 = f(4) = 2(4) - 1 = 7.$$

The first four terms are 1, 3, 5, and 7.

(b) For $a_n = f(n) = 3(-2)^n$, we write

$$a_1 = f(1) = 3(-2)^1 = -6;$$
$$a_2 = f(2) = 3(-2)^2 = 12;$$
$$a_3 = f(3) = 3(-2)^3 = -24;$$
$$a_4 = f(4) = 3(-2)^4 = 48.$$

The first four terms are -6, 12, -24, and 48.

(c) For $a_n = f(n) = \dfrac{n}{n + 1}$, we write

$$a_1 = f(1) = \frac{1}{1 + 1} = \frac{1}{2};$$
$$a_2 = f(2) = \frac{2}{2 + 1} = \frac{2}{3};$$
$$a_3 = f(3) = \frac{3}{3 + 1} = \frac{3}{4};$$
$$a_4 = f(4) = \frac{4}{4 + 1} = \frac{4}{5}.$$

The first four terms are $\frac{1}{2}, \frac{2}{3}, \frac{3}{4}$, and $\frac{4}{5}$. Note that, although the input to a sequence is a natural number, the output need not be a natural number.

Technology Note: *Generating Sequences*

Many graphing calculators can generate sequences if you change the MODE from function (Func) to sequence (Seq). In Figure 11.3 the sequences from Example 1 are generated. On some calculators the sequence utility is found in the LIST OPS menus. The expression

$$\text{seq}(2n - 1, n, 1, 4)$$

represents terms 1 through 4 of the sequence $a_n = 2n - 1$ with the variable n.

TEACHING TIP

Students can successfully complete this section without having to use a graphing calculator.

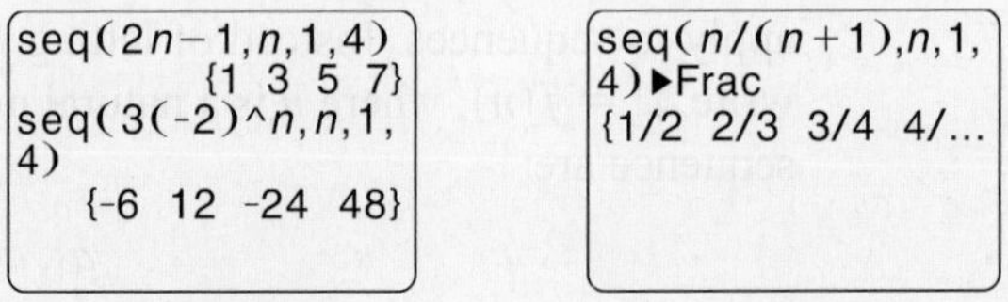

```
seq(2n-1,n,1,4)
        {1 3 5 7}
seq(3(-2)^n,n,1,
4)
    {-6 12 -24 48}
```
(a)

```
seq(n/(n+1),n,1,
4)▶Frac
{1/2 2/3 3/4 4/...
```
(b)

Figure 11.3

REPRESENTATIONS OF SEQUENCES

Because sequences are functions, they can be represented symbolically, graphically, and numerically. The next two examples illustrate such representations.

EXAMPLE 2 Using a graphical representation

Use Figure 11.4 to write the terms of the sequence.

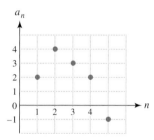

Figure 11.4

Solution The points $(1, 2)$, $(2, 4)$, $(3, 3)$, $(4, 2)$, $(5, -1)$ are shown in the graph. The terms of the sequence are $a_1 = 2$, $a_2 = 4$, $a_3 = 3$, $a_4 = 2$, and $a_5 = -1$.

EXAMPLE 3 Representing a sequence

The average person in the United States uses 100 gallons of water each day. Give symbolic, numerical, and graphical representations for a sequence that models the total amount of water used over a 7-day period.

Solution **Symbolic Representation** Let $a_n = 100n$ for $n = 1, 2, 3, \ldots, 7$.

Numerical Representation Table 11.2 contains the sequence.

TABLE 11.2

n	a_n
1	100
2	200
3	300
4	400
5	500
6	600
7	700

Graphical Representation Plot the points $(1, 100)$, $(2, 200)$, $(3, 300)$, $(4, 400)$, $(5, 500)$, $(6, 600)$, and $(7, 700)$, as shown in Figure 11.5.

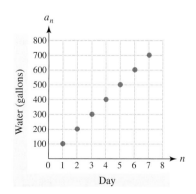

Figure 11.5 Water Usage

TEACHING TIP

Show symbolic, numerical, and graphical representations of at least one sequence. Emphasize that a sequence is a function.

MODELS AND APPLICATIONS

A population model for a species of insect with a life span of 1 year can be described with a sequence. Suppose that each adult female insect produces, on average, r female offspring that survive to reproduce the following year. Let a_n represent the female insect population at the beginning of year n. Then the number of female insects is given by

$$a_n = Cr^{n-1},$$

where C is the initial population of female insects.   (*Source:* D. Brown and P. Rothery, *Models in Biology.*)

EXAMPLE 4   Modeling numbers of insects

Suppose that the initial population of adult female insects is 500 per acre and that $r = 1.04$. Then the average number of female insects per acre at the beginning of year n is described by

$$a_n = 500(1.04)^{n-1}.$$

Represent the female insect population numerically and graphically. Discuss the results. By what percent is the population increasing each year?

Solution   *Numerical Representation*   Table 11.3 contains approximations for the first 7 terms of the sequence. The insect population increases from 500 to about 633 insects per acre during this time period.

TABLE 11.3

n	1	2	3	4	5	6	7
a_n	500	520	540.8	562.43	584.93	608.33	632.66

Graphical Representation   Plot the points (1, 500), (2, 520), (3, 540.8), (4, 562.43), (5, 584.93), (6, 608.33), and (7, 632.66), as shown in Figure 11.6. These results indicate that the insect population gradually increases. Because the growth factor is 1.04, the population is increasing by 4% each year.

Critical Thinking

Explain how the value of r in Example 4 affects the population of female insects over time. Assume that $r > 0$.

Each year there are r times as many female insects as there were the previous year. The annual growth factor is 1.04.

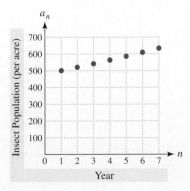

Figure 11.6

Technology Note: *Graphs and Tables of Sequences*

In the sequence mode, many graphing calculators are capable of representing sequences graphically and numerically.

Figure 11.7(a) shows how to enter the sequence from Example 4 to produce the table of values shown in Figure 11.7(b).

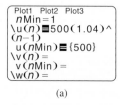

(a)

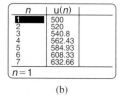

(b)

Figure 11.7

Figures 11.8(a) and (b) show the set-up for graphing the sequence from Example 4 to produce the graph shown in Figure 11.8(c).

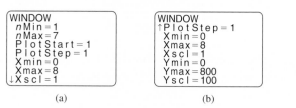

(a)

(b)

[0, 8, 1] by [0, 800, 100]

(c)

Figure 11.8

EXAMPLE 5   Interpreting a model

Figure 11.9 shows growth in a sample of bacteria over a 15-hour period when the food supply is limited. Interpret the graph.

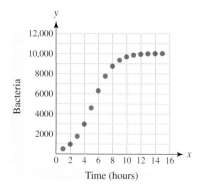

Figure 11.9

Solution   The sample of bacteria grows slowly at first and then more rapidly. Because of the limited food supply, the number of bacteria levels off near 10,000 after several hours.

11.1   PUTTING IT ALL TOGETHER

An infinite sequence is a function whose domain is the set of natural numbers. A finite sequence has the domain $D = \{1, 2, 3, \ldots, n\}$ for some fixed natural number n. Graphs of sequences are scatterplots, *not* continuous lines and curves.

Sequences are functions that may be represented symbolically, numerically, and graphically. Examples of representations of sequences are shown in the following table.

Representation	Example
Symbolic	$a_n = n - 3$ represents a sequence. The first four terms of the sequence are $-2, -1, 0$, and 1 because $$a_1 = 1 - 3 = -2, a_2 = 2 - 3 = -1,$$ $$a_3 = 3 - 3 = 0, \text{ and } a_4 = 4 - 3 = 1.$$
Numerical	A numerical representation for $a_n = n - 3$ with $n = 1, 2, 3$, and 4 is shown in the table. | n	1	2	3	4
---	---	---	---	---
a_n	-2	-1	0	1	
Graphical	For a graphical representation of the first four terms of $a_n = n - 3$, the points $(1, -2), (2, -1), (3, 0)$, and $(4, 1)$ are plotted.

11.1   EXERCISES

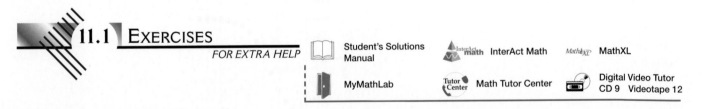

CONCEPTS

1. Give an example of a finite sequence.   1, 2, 3, 4

2. Give an example of an infinite sequence.   1, 3, 5, 7, . . .

3. An infinite sequence is a _____ whose domain is _____.   function; the set of natural numbers

4. An ordered list is a _____.   sequence

5. The third term in the sequence $4, -5, 6, -7, 8$ is _____.   6

6. The graph of a sequence is not a continuous graph but rather a _____.   scatterplot

7. If $f(n)$ represents a sequence, the second term of the sequence is given by _____. $f(2)$

8. If a_n represents a sequence, the fourth term of the sequence is given by_____. a_4

EVALUATING AND REPRESENTING SEQUENCES

Exercises 9–16: Write the first four terms of the sequence for $n = 1, 2, 3,$ and 4.

9. $f(n) = n^2$ $1, 4, 9, 16$

10. $f(n) = 3n + 4$ $7, 10, 13, 16$

11. $f(n) = \dfrac{1}{n + 5}$ $\frac{1}{6}, \frac{1}{7}, \frac{1}{8}, \frac{1}{9}$

12. $f(n) = 3^n$ $3, 9, 27, 81$

13. $f(n) = 5\left(\frac{1}{2}\right)^n$ $\frac{5}{2}, \frac{5}{4}, \frac{5}{8}, \frac{5}{16}$

14. $f(n) = n^2 + 2n$ $3, 8, 15, 24$

15. $f(n) = 9$ $9, 9, 9, 9$

16. $f(n) = (-1)^n$ $-1, 1, -1, 1$

Exercises 17–24: Write the first three terms of the sequence for $n = 1, 2,$ and 3.

17. $a_n = n^3$ $1, 8, 27$

18. $a_n = 5 - n$ $4, 3, 2$

19. $a_n = \dfrac{4n}{3 + n}$ $1, \frac{8}{5}, 2$

20. $a_n = 3^{-n}$ $\frac{1}{3}, \frac{1}{9}, \frac{1}{27}$

21. $a_n = 2n^2 + n - 1$ $2, 9, 20$

22. $a_n = n^4 - 1$ $0, 15, 80$

23. $a_n = -2$ $-2, -2, -2$

24. $a_n = n^n$ $1, 4, 27$

Exercises 25 and 26: Use the numerical representation to evaluate $\frac{1}{2}(a_1 + a_4)$.

25.

n	1	2	3	4	5	7
a_n	10	8	6	4	2	

26.

n	1	2	3	4	5	12.5
a_n	-5	0	10	30	60	

Exercises 27–30: Use the graph to write the terms of the sequence.

27. $3, 4, 5, 3, 1$

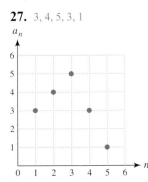

28. $1, 2, 4, 8, 6$

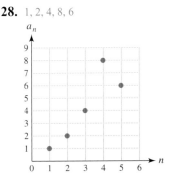

29. $6, 5, 4, 3, 2, 1$

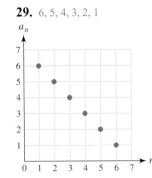

30. $4, 1, 0, 1, 2$

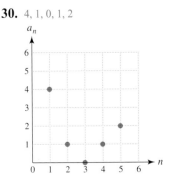

Exercises 31–36: Represent the first seven terms of the sequence numerically and graphically.

31. $a_n = n + 1$

32. $a_n = \frac{1}{2}n - \frac{1}{2}$

33. $a_n = n^2 - n$

34. $a_n = \frac{1}{2}n^2$

35. $a_n = 2^n$

36. $a_n = 2(0.5)^n$

APPLICATIONS

37. *Solid Waste* On average, each U.S. resident in 1995 generated 30 pounds of solid waste per week. Give symbolic, graphical, and numerical representations for a sequence that models the total amount of waste produced over a 7-week period. (*Source:* Environmental Protection Agency.)* $a_n = 30n$, for $n = 1, 2, 3, \ldots, 7$

38. *Carbon Dioxide Emitters* Because people burn fossil fuels, the United States emits more carbon dioxide than any other country in the world, or about 5.8 billion metric tons per year. (A metric ton is about 2200 pounds.) Give symbolic, graphical, and numerical representations for a sequence that models the total amount of carbon dioxide emitted in the United States in a 5-year period. (*Source:* Energy Information Administration.)* $a_n = 5.8n$, for $n = 1, 2, 3, 4, 5$

39. *Geometry* The lengths of the sides of a sequence of squares are given by 1, 2, 3, and 4, as shown in the following figure. Write sequences that give
(a) the areas of the squares, and $1, 4, 9, 16$
(b) the perimeters of the squares. $4, 8, 12, 16$

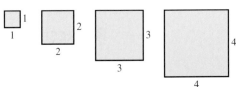

*Answers on page IA-39

40. *Salaries*   An individual's starting salary is $50,000, and the individual receives an increase of 8% per year. Give symbolic, numerical, and graphical representations for this person's salary over 5 years.*
$a_n = 50,000(1.08)^{n-1}$, for $n = 1, 2, 3, 4, 5$

41. *Depreciation*   Automobiles usually depreciate in value over time. Often, a newer automobile may be worth only 80% of its previous year's value. Suppose that a car is worth $25,000 new.   (a) $20,000; $16,000

   (a) How much is it worth after 1 year? After 2 years?

   (b) Write a formula for a sequence that gives the car's value after n years. $a_n = 25,000(0.8)^n$

   (c) Make a table that shows how much the car was worth each year during the first 7 years.*

42. *Falling Object*   The distance d that an object falls during *consecutive* seconds is shown in the table. For example, during the third second (from $n = 2$ to $n = 3$) an object falls a distance of 80 feet.

n (seconds)	1	2	3	4	5
d (feet)	16	48	80	112	144

   (a) Find values for c and b so that $d = cn + b$ models these data. $c = 32, b = -16$

   (b) How far does an object fall during the sixth second?   176 ft

43. *Auditorium Seating*   An auditorium has 50 seats in the first row, 55 seats in the second row, 60 seats in the third row, and so on.

   (a) Make a table that shows the number of seats in the first seven rows.*

   (b) Write a formula that gives the number of seats in row n. $a_n = 50 + 5(n - 1)$, or $a_n = 45 + 5n$

   (c) How many seats are there in row 23?   160 seats

   (d) Graph the number of seats in each row for $n = 1, 2, 3, \ldots, 10$.*

44. *Modeling Insect Populations*   (Refer to Example 4.) Suppose that the initial population of insects is 2048 per acre and that $r = 0.5$. Use a sequence to represent the insect population over a 7-year period

   (a) symbolically,

   (b) numerically, and*

   (c) graphically.*
     (a) $a_n = 2048(0.5)^{n-1}$, for $n = 1, 2, 3, \ldots, 7$

WRITING ABOUT MATHEMATICS

45. Compare the graph of $f(x) = 2x + 1$, where x is a real number, with the graph of the sequence $f(n) = 2n + 1$, where n is a natural number.

46. Explain what a sequence is. Describe the difference between a finite and an infinite sequence.
                          *Answers on page IA-40

11.2   ARITHMETIC AND GEOMETRIC SEQUENCES

Representations of Arithmetic Sequences · Representations of Geometric Sequences · Applications and Models

INTRODUCTION

Indoor air pollution has become more hazardous as people spend 80% to 90% of their time in tightly sealed, energy-efficient buildings, which often lack proper ventilation. Many contaminants such as tobacco smoke, formaldehyde, radon, lead, and carbon monoxide are often allowed to increase to unsafe levels. One way to alleviate this problem is to use efficient ventilation systems. Mathematics plays an important role in determining the proper amount of ventilation. In this section we use sequences to model ventilation in classrooms. Before implementing this model, however, we discuss the basic concepts relating to two special types of sequences.

REPRESENTATIONS OF ARITHMETIC SEQUENCES

If a sequence is defined by a linear function, it is an *arithmetic sequence.* For example,

$$f(n) = 2n - 3$$

represents an arithmetic sequence because $f(x) = 2x - 3$ defines a linear function. The first five terms of this sequence are shown in Table 11.4.

Each time n increases by 1, the next term is 2 more than the previous term. We say that the *common difference* of this arithmetic sequence is $d = 2$. That is, the difference between successive terms equals 2. When these terms are graphed, they lie on the line $y = 2x - 3$, as illustrated in Figure 11.10. Arithmetic sequences are represented by linear functions and so their graphical representations consist of collinear points (points that lie on a line). The slope m of the line equals the common difference d.

TABLE 11.4

n	$f(n)$
1	-1
2	1
3	3
4	5
5	7

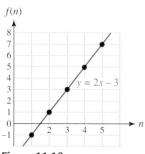

Figure 11.10

ARITHMETIC SEQUENCE

An **arithmetic sequence** is a linear function given by $a_n = dn + c$ whose domain is the set of natural numbers. The value of d is called the **common difference**.

EXAMPLE 1   Recognizing arithmetic sequences

Determine whether f is an arithmetic sequence. If it is, identify the common difference d.
(a) $f(n) = 2 - 3n$.

(b)

n	$f(n)$
1	10
2	5
3	0
4	-5
5	-10

(c) A graph of f is shown in Figure 11.11.

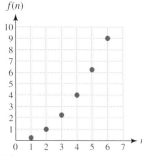

Figure 11.11

Solution **(a)** This sequence is arithmetic because $f(x) = -3x + 2$ defines a linear function. The common difference is $d = -3$.
(b) The table reveals that each term is found by adding -5 to the previous term. This represents an arithmetic sequence with common difference $d = -5$.
(c) The sequence shown in Figure 11.11 is not an arithmetic sequence because the points are not collinear. That is, there is no common difference.

$$\equiv \text{MAKING CONNECTIONS} \equiv$$

Common Difference and Slope

The common difference d of an arithmetic sequence equals the slope of the line passing through the collinear points. For example, if $a_n = -2n + 4$, the common difference is -2, and the slope of the line passing through the points on the graph of a_n is also -2 (see Figure 11.12).

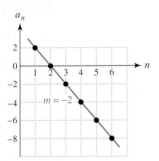

Figure 11.12

EXAMPLE 2   **Finding symbolic representations**

Find the general term a_n for each arithmetic sequence.
(a) $a_1 = 3$ and $d = 4$ **(b)** $a_1 = 3$ and $a_4 = 12$

Solution **(a)** Let $a_n = dn + c$. For $d = 4$, we write $a_n = 4n + c$, and to find c we use $a_1 = 3$.

$$a_1 = 4(1) + c = 3 \quad \text{or} \quad c = -1$$

Thus $a_n = 4n - 1$.

(b) Because $a_1 = 3$ and $a_4 = 12$, the common difference d equals the slope of the line passing through the points $(1, 3)$ and $(4, 12)$, or

$$d = \frac{12 - 3}{4 - 1} = 3.$$

Therefore $a_n = 3n + c$. To find c we use $a_1 = 3$ and obtain

$$a_1 = 3(1) + c = 3 \quad \text{or} \quad c = 0.$$

Thus $a_n = 3n$.

Consider the arithmetic sequence

$$1, 5, 9, 13, 17, 21, 25, 29, \ldots.$$

The common difference is $d = 4$, and the first term is $a_1 = 1$. To find the second term we add d to the first term. To find the third term we add $2d$ to the first term, and to find the fourth term we add $3d$ to the first term a_1. That is,

$$a_1 = 1,$$
$$a_2 = a_1 + 1d = 1 + 1 \cdot 4 = 5,$$
$$a_3 = a_1 + 2d = 1 + 2 \cdot 4 = 9,$$
$$a_4 = a_1 + 3d = 1 + 3 \cdot 4 = 13,$$

and, in general, a_n is determined by

$$a_n = a_1 + (n - 1)d = 1 + (n - 1)4.$$

This result suggests the following formula.

GENERAL TERM OF AN ARITHMETIC SEQUENCE

The nth term a_n of an arithmetic sequence is given by

$$a_n = a_1 + (n - 1)d,$$

where a_1 is the first term and d is the common difference.

EXAMPLE 3 Finding terms of an arithmetic sequence

If $a_1 = 5$ and $d = 3$, find a_{54}.

Solution To find a_{54}, apply the formula $a_n = a_1 + (n - 1)d$.

$$a_{54} = 5 + (54 - 1)3 = 164$$

REPRESENTATIONS OF GEOMETRIC SEQUENCES

If a sequence is defined by an exponential function, it is a *geometric sequence*. For example,

$$f(n) = 3(2)^{n-1}$$

represents a geometric sequence because $f(x) = 3(2)^{x-1}$ defines an exponential function. The first five terms of this sequence are shown in Table 11.5.

TABLE 11.5

n	1	2	3	4	5
$f(n)$	3	6	12	24	48

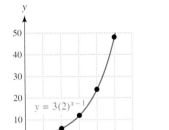

Figure 11.13

Successive terms are found by multiplying the previous term by 2. We say that the *common ratio* of this geometric sequence equals 2. Note that the ratios of successive terms are $\frac{6}{3}, \frac{12}{6}, \frac{24}{12}$, and $\frac{48}{24}$ and that they all equal the common ratio 2. When the terms in Table 11.5 are graphed, they do *not* lie on a line. Rather they lie on the exponential curve $y = 3(2)^{x-1}$, as shown in Figure 11.13. A geometric sequence with a positive common ratio is an exponential function, and its terms reflect either *exponential growth* or *exponential decay*.

GEOMETRIC SEQUENCE

A **geometric sequence** is given by $a_n = a_1(r)^{n-1}$, where n is a natural number and $r \neq 0$ or 1. The value of r is called the **common ratio**, and a_1 is the first term of the sequence.

TEACHING TIP

An arithmetic sequence is a linear function, and a geometric sequence with a positive r is an exponential function.

EXAMPLE 4   **Recognizing geometric sequences**

Determine whether f is a geometric sequence. If it is, identify the common ratio.

(a) $f(n) = 2(0.9)^{n-1}$

(b)

n	1	2	3	4	5
$f(n)$	8	4	2	1	$\frac{1}{2}$

(c) A graph of f is shown in Figure 11.14.

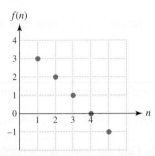

Figure 11.14

Solution   **(a)** This sequence is geometric because $f(n) = 2(0.9)^{n-1}$ is an exponential function. The common ratio is $r = 0.9$.

(b) The table shows that each successive term is half the previous term. This progression represents a geometric sequence with a common ratio of $r = \frac{1}{2}$.

(c) The sequence shown in Figure 11.14 is not a geometric sequence because the points are collinear. There is no common ratio.

═══════════════════════ MAKING CONNECTIONS ═══════════════════════

Common Ratios and Growth or Decay Factors

If the common ratio r of a geometric sequence is positive, then r equals either the growth factor or the decay factor for an exponential function.

EXAMPLE 5   **Finding symbolic representations**

Find a general term a_n for each geometric sequence.

(a) $a_1 = \frac{1}{2}$ and $r = 5$ **(b)** $a_1 = 2$, $a_3 = 18$, and $r < 0$.

Solution   **(a)** Let $a_n = a_1(r)^{n-1}$. Because $a_1 = \frac{1}{2}$ and $r = 5$, we can write $a_n = \frac{1}{2}(5)^{n-1}$.

(b) $a_1 = 2$ and $a_3 = 18$, so

$$\frac{a_3}{a_1} = \frac{18}{2} = 9.$$

Now $a_3 = a_1 \cdot r^2$ because a_3 is obtained from multiplying a_1 by r twice. Thus

$$r^2 = 9 \quad \text{or} \quad r = \pm 3.$$

It is specified that $r < 0$, so $r = -3$ and $a_n = 2(-3)^{n-1}$.

No; $r = \pm \sqrt[4]{\frac{a_5}{a_1}}$; we cannot determine the sign of r.

Critical Thinking

If we are given a_1 and a_5, can we determine the common ratio of a geometric series? Explain.

EXAMPLE 6 **Finding a term of a geometric sequence**

If $a_1 = 5$ and $r = 3$, find a_{10}.

Solution To find a_{10}, apply the formula $a_n = a_1(r)^{n-1}$ with $a_1 = 5$, $r = 3$, and $n = 10$.

$$a_{10} = 5(3)^{10-1} = 5(3)^9 = 98,415$$

Applications and Models

Sequences are frequently used to describe a variety of situations. In the next example, we use a sequence to model classroom ventilation.

EXAMPLE 7 Modeling classroom ventilation

Ventilation is an effective means for removing indoor air pollutants. According to the American Society of Heating, Refrigerating, and Air-Conditioning Engineers (ASHRAE), a classroom should have a ventilation rate of 900 cubic feet per hour per person.
(a) Write a sequence that gives the hourly ventilation necessary for 1, 2, 3, 4, and 5 people in a classroom. Is this sequence arithmetic, geometric, or neither?
(b) Write the general term for this sequence. Why is it reasonable to limit the domain to natural numbers?
(c) Find a_{30} and interpret the result.

Solution **(a)** One person requires 900 cubic feet of air circulated per hour, two people require 1800, three people 2700, and so on. The first five terms of this sequence are

900, 1800, 2700, 3600, 4500.

This sequence is arithmetic, with a common difference of 900.
(b) The nth term equals $900n$, so we let $a_n = 900n$. Because we cannot have a fraction of a person, limiting the domain to the natural numbers is reasonable.
(c) The result $a_{30} = 900(30) = 27,000$ indicates that a classroom with 30 people should have a ventilation rate of 27,000 cubic feet per hour.

Chlorine is frequently added to the water to disinfect swimming pools. The chlorine concentration should remain between 1.5 and 2.5 parts per million (ppm). On a warm, sunny day 30% of the chlorine may dissipate from the water. In the next example we use a sequence to model the amount of chlorine in a pool at the beginning of each day. (**Source:** D. Thomas, *Swimming Pool Operator's Handbook.*)

EXAMPLE 8   Modeling chlorine in a swimming pool

A swimming pool on a warm, sunny day begins with a high chlorine content of 4 parts per million.

(a) Write a sequence that models the amount of chlorine in the pool at the beginning of the first 3 days, assuming that no additional chlorine is added and that the days are warm and sunny. Is this sequence arithmetic, geometric, or neither?

(b) Write the general term for this sequence.

(c) At the beginning of what day does the chlorine first drop below 1.5 parts per million?

Solution **(a)** Because 30% of the chlorine dissipates, 70% remains in the water at the beginning of the next day. If the concentration at the beginning of the first day is 4 parts per million, then at the beginning of the second day it is

$$4 \cdot 0.70 = 2.8 \text{ parts per million,}$$

and at the start of the third day it is

$$2.8 \cdot 0.70 = 1.96 \text{ parts per million.}$$

The first three terms are

$$4, 2.8, 1.96.$$

Successive terms are found by multiplying the previous term by 0.7. Thus the sequence is geometric, with common ratio 0.7.

(b) The initial amount is $a_1 = 4$ and the common ratio is $r = 0.7$, so the sequence can be represented by $a_n = 4(0.7)^{n-1}$.

(c) The table shown in Figure 11.15 reveals that $a_4 = 4(0.7)^{4-1} \approx 1.372 < 1.5$. Thus, at the beginning of the fourth day, the chlorine level in the swimming pool drops below the recommended minimum of 1.5 parts per million.

n	$u(n)$
1	4
2	2.8
3	1.96
4	1.372
5	.9604
6	.67228
7	.4706

$u(n) \blacksquare 4(.7)^{\wedge}(n-1)$

Figure 11.15

PUTTING IT ALL TOGETHER

In this section we discussed two types of sequences: arithmetic and geometric. Arithmetic sequences are linear functions, and geometric sequences with positive r are exponential functions. The inputs for both are limited to the natural numbers. Each successive term in an arithmetic sequence is found by adding the common difference d to the previous term. For a geometric sequence each successive term is found by multiplying the previous term by the common ratio r. The graph of an arithmetic sequence consists of points that lie on a line, whereas the graph of a geometric sequence (with a positive r) consists of points that lie on an exponential curve. Examples are shown in the following table.

Sequence	Formula	Example
Arithmetic	$a_n = dn + c$ or $a_n = a_1 + (n - 1)d$, where d is the common difference and a_1 is the first term.	If $a_n = 5n + 2$, then the common difference is $d = 5$ and the terms of the sequence are $$7, 12, 17, 22, 27, 32, 37, \ldots .$$ Each term is found by adding 5 to the previous term. The general term can be written as $$a_n = 7 + 5(n - 1).$$
Geometric	$a_n = a_1(r)^{n-1}$, where r is the common ratio and a_1 is the first term.	If $a_n = 4(-2)^{n-1}$, then the common ratio is $r = -2$ and the first term is $a_1 = 4$. The terms of the sequence are $$4, -8, 16, -32, 64, -128, 256, \ldots .$$ Each term is found by multiplying the previous term by -2.

11.2 EXERCISES

FOR EXTRA HELP

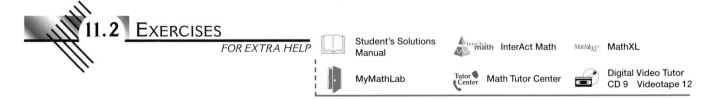

CONCEPTS

1. An arithmetic sequence is a(n) <u>linear/exponential</u> function.
  linear

2. A geometric sequence with $r > 0$ is a(n) <u>linear/exponential</u> function.   exponential

3. Give an example of an arithmetic sequence. State the common difference. $a_n = 3n + 1$; 3

4. Give an example of a geometric sequence. State the common ratio. $a_n = 5(2)^{n-1}$; 2

5. To find successive terms in an arithmetic sequence, _____ the common difference to the _____ term.
  add; previous

6. To find successive terms in a geometric sequence, _____ the previous term by the _____.
  multiply; common ratio

7. Find the next term in the arithmetic sequence 3, 7, 11, 15. What is the common difference?   19; 4

8. Find the next term in the geometric sequence 2, −4, 8, −16. What is the common ratio? 32; −2

9. Write the general term a_n for a geometric sequence, using a_1 and r. $a_n = a_1(r)^{n-1}$

10. Write the general term a_n for an arithmetic sequence using a_1 and d. $a_n = a_1 + (n-1)d$

ARITHMETIC SEQUENCES

Exercises 11–28: (Refer to Example 1.) Determine whether f is an arithmetic sequence. Identify the common difference when possible.

11. $f(n) = 10n - 5$ **12.** $f(n) = -3n - 5$ Yes; −3
Yes; 10

13. $f(n) = 6 - n$ **14.** $f(n) = 6 + \frac{1}{2}n$ Yes; $\frac{1}{2}$
Yes; −1

15. $f(n) = n^3 + 1$ No   **16.** $f(n) = 5\left(\frac{1}{3}\right)^{n-1}$ No

17.

n	1	2	3	4
$f(n)$	3	6	9	12

Yes; 3

18.

n	1	2	3	4
$f(n)$	−7	−5	−3	−1

Yes; 2

19.

n	1	2	3	4
$f(n)$	10	7	4	1

Yes; −3

20.

n	1	2	3	4
$f(n)$	1	2	4	8

No

21.

n	1	2	3	4
$f(n)$	−4	0	8	12

No

22.

n	1	2	3	4
$f(n)$	1	2.5	4	5.5

Yes; 1.5

23. Yes; 1   **24.** Yes; −1

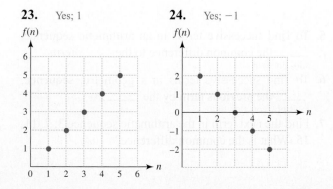

25. No   **26.** No

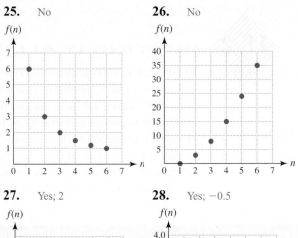

27. Yes; 2   **28.** Yes; −0.5

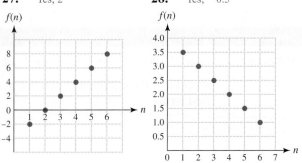

Exercises 29–34: (Refer to Example 2.) Find the general term a_n for the arithmetic sequence.

29. $a_1 = 7$ and $d = -2$ **30.** $a_1 = 5$ and $a_2 = 9$
$a_n = -2n + 9$ $a_n = 4n + 1$

31. $a_1 = -2$ and $a_3 = 6$ $a_n = 4n - 6$

32. $a_2 = 7$ and $a_3 = 10$ $a_n = 3n + 1$

33. $a_8 = 16$ and $a_{12} = 8$ $a_n = -2n + 32$

34. $a_3 = 7$ and $d = -5$ $a_n = -5n + 22$

Exercises 35–38: (Refer to Example 3.)

35. If $a_1 = -3$ and $d = 2$, find a_{32}.   59

36. If $a_1 = 2$ and $d = -3$, find a_{19}.   −52

37. If $a_1 = -3$ and $a_2 = 0$, find a_9.   21

38. If $a_3 = -3$ and $d = 4$, find a_{62}.   233

GEOMETRIC SEQUENCES

Exercises 39–54: (Refer to Example 4.) Determine whether f is a geometric sequence. Identify the common ratio when possible.

39. $f(n) = 3^n$ Yes; 3   **40.** $f(n) = 2(4)^n$ Yes; 4

41. $f(n) = \frac{2}{3}(0.8)^{n-1}$ **42.** $f(n) = 7 - 3n$ No
Yes; 0.8

43. $f(n) = 2(n-1)^2$ No   **44.** $f(n) = 2\left(-\frac{3}{4}\right)^{n-1}$ Yes; $-\frac{3}{4}$

45.   Yes; 2

n	1	2	3	4
$f(n)$	2	4	8	16

46.   Yes; $-\frac{1}{2}$

n	1	2	3	4
$f(n)$	-6	3	-1.5	0.75

47.   No

n	1	2	3	4
$f(n)$	1	4	9	16

48.   No

n	1	2	3	4
$f(n)$	7	4	-1	-8

49.   Yes; 4

n	1	2	3	4
$f(n)$	2	8	32	128

50.   Yes; $\frac{1}{2}$

n	1	2	3	4
$f(n)$	1	$\frac{1}{2}$	$\frac{1}{4}$	$\frac{1}{8}$

51. Yes; 2   **52.** No

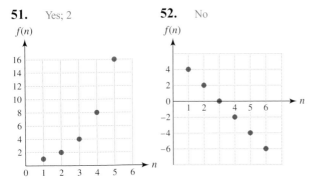

53. No   **54.** Yes; $\frac{1}{2}$

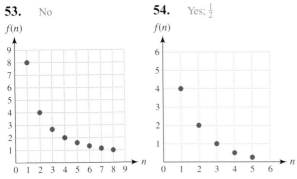

Exercises 55–60: (Refer to Example 5.) Find the general term a_n for the geometric sequence.

55. $a_1 = 1.5$ and $r = 4$ **56.** $a_1 = 3$ and $r = \frac{1}{4}$ $a_n = 3\left(\frac{1}{4}\right)^{n-1}$

   $a_n = 1.5(4)^{n-1}$

57. $a_1 = -3$ and $a_2 = 6$ $a_n = -3(-2)^{n-1}$

58. $a_1 = 2$ and $a_4 = 54$ $a_n = 2(3)^{n-1}$

59. $a_1 = 1$, $a_3 = 16$, and $r > 0$ $a_n = 1(4)^{n-1}$

60. $a_2 = 3$, $a_4 = 12$, and $r < 0$ $a_n = -1.5(-2)^{n-1}$

Exercises 61–64: (Refer to Example 6.)

61. If $a_1 = 2$ and $r = 3$, find a_8.   4374

62. If $a_1 = 4$ and $a_2 = 2$, find a_9. $\frac{1}{64}$

63. If $a_1 = -1$ and $a_2 = 3$, find a_6.   243

64. If $a_3 = 5$ and $r = -3$, find a_7.   405

65.(c) 60,000; when there are 20 people, the ventilation rate should be 60,000 cubic feet per hour.

APPLICATIONS

65. *Room Ventilation* (Refer to Example 7.) In areas such as bars and lounges that allow smoking, the ventilation rate should be 3000 cubic feet per hour per person. (*Source:* ASHRAE.)
  (a) Write a sequence that gives the hourly ventilation necessary for 1, 2, 3, 4, and 5 people in a barroom. Is this sequence arithmetic, geometric, or neither?   3000, 6000, 9000, 12,000, 15,000; arithmetic
  (b) Write the general term for this sequence. $a_n = 3000n$
  (c) Find a_{20} and interpret the result.
  (d) Give a graphical representation for this sequence, using $n = 1, 2, 3, \ldots, 8$. Are the points collinear?*   Yes

66. *Chlorine in Swimming Pools* (Refer to Example 8.) Suppose that the water in a swimming pool initially has a chlorine content of 3 parts per million and that 20% of the chlorine dissipates each day.
  (a) If no additional chlorine is added, write the general term for a sequence that gives the chlorine concentration at the beginning of each day.
  (b) Give a graphical representation for this sequence, using $n = 1, 2, 3, \ldots, 8$. Are the points collinear? Is this sequence arithmetic, geometric, or neither?*   No; geometric   (a) $a_n = 3(0.8)^{n-1}$

67. *Salary* Suppose that an employee receives a \$2000 raise each year and that the sequence a_n models the employee's salary after n years. Is this sequence arithmetic, geometric, or neither? Explain.
Arithmetic; the common difference is 2000.

68. *Salary* Suppose that an employee receives a 7% increase in salary each year and that the sequence a_n models the employee's salary after n years. Is this sequence arithmetic, geometric, or neither? Explain.
Geometric; the common ratio is 1.07.   *Answers on page IA-40

69.(c) $a_7 \approx 231{,}306$; at the beginning of the 7th
year, it will be worth about $231,306.

69. *Appreciation of Lake Property*   A certain type of lake property in northern Minnesota is increasing in value by 15% per year. Let the sequence a_n give the value of this type of lake property at the beginning of year n.

(a) Is a_n arithmetic, geometric, or neither? Explain your reasoning.   Geometric; the common ratio is 1.15.

(b) Write the general term for this sequence if $a_1 = \$100{,}000$. $a_n = 100{,}000\,(1.15)^{n-1}$

(c) Find a_7 and interpret the result.

(d) Give a graph for a_n, where $n = 1, 2, 3, \ldots, 10.$*

70. *Falling Object*   The total distance D_n that an object falls in n seconds is shown in the table. Is the sequence arithmetic, geometric, or neither? Explain your reasoning.

n (seconds)	1	2	3	4	5
D_n (feet)	16	64	144	256	400

Neither; there is neither a common difference nor a common ratio.

71. *Theater Seating*   A theater has 40 seats in the first row, 42 seats in the second row, 44 seats in the third row, and so on.

(a) Can the number of seats in each row be modeled by an arithmetic or geometric sequence? Explain.

(b) Write the general term for a sequence a_n that gives the number of seats in row n.

(a) Arithmetic; the common difference is 2.

(b) $a_n = 40 + 2(n - 1)$

(c) How many seats are there in row 20?   78

72.(b) Geometric; the common ratio is 0.85.

72. *Bouncing Ball*   A tennis ball bounces back to 85% of the height from which it was dropped and then to 85% of the height of each successive bounce.

(a) Write the general term for a sequence a_n that gives the maximum height of the ball on the nth bounce. Let $a_1 = 5$ feet. $a_n = 5(0.85)^{n-1}$

(b) Is the sequence arithmetic or geometric? Explain.

(c) Find a_8 and interpret the result.

About 1.6; on the 8th bounce the ball reaches a maximum height of about 1.6 ft.

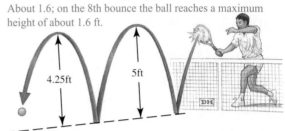

4.25ft   5ft

DH

WRITING ABOUT MATHEMATICS

73. If you have a table of values for a sequence, how can you determine whether it is geometric? Give an example.

74. If you have a graph of a sequence, how can you determine whether it is arithmetic? Give an example.

CHECKING BASIC CONCEPTS   SECTIONS 11.1 AND 11.2

1. Write the first four terms of the sequence defined by $a_n = \dfrac{n}{n+4}$ $\frac{1}{5}, \frac{1}{3}, \frac{3}{7}, \frac{1}{2}$

2. Represent the sequence $a_n = n + 1$ graphically and numerically for $n = 1, 2, 3, 4, 5.$*

3. Use the table to determine whether the sequence is arithmetic or geometric. Write the general term for the sequence.

(a)

n	1	2	3	4	5
a_n	−2	1	4	7	10

Arithmetic; $a_n = 3n - 5$

Geometric; $a_n = 3(-2)^{n-1}$

(b)

n	1	2	3	4	5
a_n	3	−6	12	−24	48

4. Find the general term a_n for an arithmetic sequence with $a_1 = 5$ and $d = 2$. $a_n = 2n + 3$

5. Find the general term a_n for a geometric sequence with $a_1 = 5$ and $r = 2$. $a_n = 5(2)^{n-1}$

*Answers on page IA-40

11.3   SERIES

Basic Concepts · Arithmetic Series · Geometric Series · Summation Notation

INTRODUCTION

Although the terms *sequence* and *series* are sometimes used interchangeably in everyday life, they represent different mathematical concepts. In mathematics a sequence is a function whose domain is the set of natural numbers, whereas a series is a summation of the terms in a sequence. Series have played a central role in the development of modern mathematics. Today series are often used to approximate functions that are too complicated to have formulas. Series are also used to calculate accurate approximations for numbers such as π and e.

BASIC CONCEPTS

Suppose that a person has a starting salary of $30,000 per year and receives a $2000 raise each year. Then the *sequence*

$$30{,}000, \ 32{,}000, \ 34{,}000, \ 36{,}000, \ 38{,}000$$

lists these salaries over a 5-year period. The total amount earned is given by the *series*

$$30{,}000 \ + \ 32{,}000 \ + \ 34{,}000 \ + \ 36{,}000 \ + \ 38{,}000,$$

whose sum is $170,000. We now define the concept of a series.

FINITE SERIES

A **finite series** is an expression of the form

$$a_1 + a_2 + a_3 + \cdots + a_n.$$

EXAMPLE 1   Computing total reported AIDS cases

Table 11.6 presents a sequence a_n that computes the number of AIDS cases diagnosed each year from 1991 through 1997, where $n = 1$ corresponds to 1991.

TABLE 11.6

n	1	2	3	4	5	6	7
a_n	60,124	79,054	79,049	71,209	66,233	54,656	31,153

Source: Department of Health and Human Services.

(a) Write a series whose sum represents the total number of AIDS cases diagnosed from 1991 to 1997. Find its sum.
(b) Interpret the sum $a_1 + a_2 + a_3 + \cdots + a_{10}$.

Solution   **(a)** A series that represents the total number of AIDS cases diagnosed from 1991 through 1997 is

$$60{,}124 + 79{,}054 + 79{,}049 + 71{,}209 + 66{,}233 + 54{,}656 + 31{,}153 = 441{,}478.$$

Thus 441,478 AIDS cases were diagnosed from 1991 through 1997.

(b) The series $a_1 + a_2 + a_3 + \cdots + a_{10}$ represents the total number of AIDS cases diagnosed from 1991 through 2000.

ARITHMETIC SERIES

Summing the terms of an arithmetic sequence results in an **arithmetic series**. For example, $a_n = 2n - 1$ for $n = 1, 2, 3, \ldots, 7$ defines the arithmetic sequence

$$1, 3, 5, 7, 9, 11, 13.$$

The corresponding arithmetic *series* is

$$1 + 3 + 5 + 7 + 9 + 11 + 13,$$

whose sum is 49. The following formula gives the sum of the first n terms of an arithmetic sequence.

SUM OF THE FIRST n TERMS OF AN ARITHMETIC SEQUENCE

The **sum of the first n terms of an arithmetic sequence**, denoted S_n, is found by averaging the first and nth terms and then multiplying by n. That is,

$$S_n = a_1 + a_2 + a_3 + \cdots + a_n = n\left(\frac{a_1 + a_n}{2}\right).$$

The series $1 + 3 + 5 + 7 + 9 + 11 + 13$ consists of 7 terms, where the first term is **1** and the last term is **13**. Substituting in the formula gives

$$S_7 = 7\left(\frac{1 + 13}{2}\right) = 49,$$

which agrees with the sum obtained by adding the 7 terms.

Because $a_n = a_1 + (n - 1)d$ for an arithmetic sequence, S_n can also be written

$$S_n = n\left(\frac{a_1 + a_n}{2}\right)$$

$$= \frac{n}{2}(a_1 + a_n)$$

$$= \frac{n}{2}(a_1 + a_1 + (n - 1)d)$$

$$= \frac{n}{2}(2a_1 + (n - 1)d).$$

TEACHING TIP

The advantage of the second formula for the sum of an arithmetic sequence is that determining a_n is not necessary.

EXAMPLE 2 Finding the sum of a finite arithmetic series

Suppose that a person has a starting annual salary of $30,000 and receives a $1500 raise each year. Calculate the total amount earned after 10 years.

Solution The sequence describing the salaries during year n is given by

$$a_n = 30,000 + 1500(n - 1).$$

One way to calculate the sum of the first 10 terms, denoted S_{10}, is to find a_1 and a_{10}, or

$$a_1 = 30,000 + 1500(1 - 1) = 30,000$$
$$a_{10} = 30,000 + 1500(10 - 1) = 43,500.$$

Thus the total amount earned during this 10-year period is

$$S_{10} = 10\left(\frac{a_1 + a_{10}}{2}\right)$$
$$= 10\left(\frac{30,000 + 43,500}{2}\right)$$
$$= \$367,500.$$

This sum can also be found with the second formula by letting $d = 1500$.

$$S_n = \frac{n}{2}(2a_1 + (n - 1)d)$$

$$= \frac{10}{2}(2 \cdot 30,000 + (10 - 1)1500)$$

$$= 5(60,000 + 9 \cdot 1500)$$
$$= \$367,500.$$

EXAMPLE 3 Finding the sum of an arithmetic series

Find the sum of the following series.

$$2 + 4 + 6 + \cdots + 100$$

Solution The first term of this series is $a_1 = 2$, and the common difference is $d = 2$. This series represents the even numbers from 2 to **100**, so the number of terms is $n = $ **50.** Using the formula

$$S_n = n\left(\frac{a_1 + a_n}{2}\right)$$

for the sum of an arithmetic series, we obtain

$$S_{50} = 50\left(\frac{2 + 100}{2}\right)$$

$$= 2550.$$

Technology Note: *Sum of a Series*

The "seq(" utility, found on some calculators under the LIST OPS menus, generates a sequence. The "sum(" utility found on some calculators under the LIST MATH menus, calculates the sum of the sequence inside the parentheses. To verify the result in Example 2, let $a_n = 30{,}000 + 1500(n - 1)$. The value 367,500 for S_{10} is shown in Figure 11.16(a). The result found in Example 3 is shown in Figure 11.16(b).

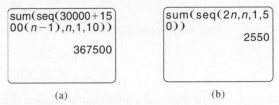

(a)   (b)

Figure 11.16

GEOMETRIC SERIES

A **geometric series** is the sum of the terms of a geometric sequence. For example,

$$1, 2, 4, 8, 16, 32$$

is a geometric sequence with $a_1 = 1$ and $r = 2$. Then

$$1 + 2 + 4 + 8 + 16 + 32$$

is a geometric series. We can use the following formula to sum a finite geometric series.

SUM OF THE FIRST *n* TERMS OF A GEOMETRIC SEQUENCE

If its first term is a_1 and its common ratio is r, then the **sum of the first *n* terms of a geometric sequence** is given by

$$S_n = a_1\left(\frac{1 - r^n}{1 - r}\right),$$

provided $r \neq 1$.

EXAMPLE 4   Finding the sum of finite geometric series

Find the sum of each series.
(a) $1 + 2 + 4 + 8 + 16 + 32 + 64 + 128 + 256$
(b) $\frac{1}{2} - \frac{1}{4} + \frac{1}{8} - \frac{1}{16} + \frac{1}{32}$

Solution **(a)** This series is geometric, with $n = 9$, $a_1 = 1$, and $r = 2$, so

$$S_9 = 1\left(\frac{1 - 2^9}{1 - 2}\right) = 511.$$

(b) This series is geometric, with $n = 5$, $a_1 = \frac{1}{2} = 0.5$, and $r = -\frac{1}{2} = -0.5$, so

$$S_5 = 0.5\left(\frac{1 - (-0.5)^5}{1 - (-0.5)}\right) = \frac{11}{32} = 0.34375.$$

ANNUITIES   A sum of money from which regular payments are made is called an **annuity**. An annuity may be purchased with a lump sum deposit or by deposits made at various intervals. Suppose that $1000 are deposited at the end of each year in an annuity account that pays an annual interest rate I expressed as a decimal. At the end of the first year the account contains $1000. At the end of the second year $1000 are deposited again. In addition, the first deposit of $1000 would have received interest during the second year. Therefore the value of the annuity after 2 years is

$$1000 + 1000(1 + I).$$

After 3 years the balance is

$$1000 + 1000(1 + I) + 1000(1 + I)^2,$$

and after n years this amount is given by

$$1000 + 1000(1 + I) + 1000(1 + I)^2 + \cdots + 1000(1 + I)^{n-1}.$$

This series is a geometric series with its first term $a_1 = 1000$ and the common ratio $r = (1 + I)$. The sum of the first n terms is given by

$$S_n = a_1\left(\frac{1 - (1 + I)^n}{1 - (1 + I)}\right) = a_1\left(\frac{(1 + I)^n - 1}{I}\right).$$

EXAMPLE 5   Finding the future value of an annuity

Suppose that a 20-year-old worker deposits $1000 into an annuity account at the end of each year. If the interest rate is 12%, find the future value of the annuity when the worker is 65 years old.

Solution   Let $a_1 = 1000$, $I = 0.12$, and $n = 45$. The future value of the annuity is

$$S_n = a_1\left(\frac{(1 + I)^n - 1}{I}\right)$$

$$= 1000\left(\frac{(1 + 0.12)^{45} - 1}{0.12}\right)$$

$$\approx \$1{,}358{,}230.$$

SUMMATION NOTATION

Summation notation is used to write series efficiently. The symbol Σ, the uppercase Greek letter *sigma*, is used to indicate a sum.

SUMMATION NOTATION

$$\sum_{k=1}^{n} a_k = a_1 + a_2 + a_3 + \cdots + a_n$$

The letter k is called the **index of summation**. The numbers 1 and n represent the subscripts of the first and last terms in the series. They are called the **lower limit** and **upper limit** of the summation, respectively.

EXAMPLE 6   Using summation notation

Evaluate each series.

(a) $\displaystyle\sum_{k=1}^{5} k^2$ (b) $\displaystyle\sum_{k=1}^{4} 5$ (c) $\displaystyle\sum_{k=3}^{6} (2k - 5)$

Solution   (a) $\displaystyle\sum_{k=1}^{5} k^2 = 1^2 + 2^2 + 3^2 + 4^2 + 5^2 = 55$

TEACHING TIP

Do several examples like Example 6. Students may need some practice before they understand summation notation.

(b) $\displaystyle\sum_{k=1}^{4} 5 = 5 + 5 + 5 + 5 = 20$

(c) $\displaystyle\sum_{k=3}^{6} (2k - 5) = \underset{k=3}{(2(3) - 5)} + \underset{k=4}{(2(4) - 5)} + \underset{k=5}{(2(5) - 5)} + \underset{k=6}{(2(6) - 5)}$

$$= 1 + 3 + 5 + 7 = 16$$

Summation notation is used frequently in statistics. The next example demonstrates how averages can be expressed in summation notation.

EXAMPLE 7   Applying summation notation

Express the average of the n numbers $x_1, x_2, x_3, \ldots, x_n$ in summation notation.

Solution   The average of n numbers can be written as

$$\frac{x_1 + x_2 + x_3 + \cdots + x_n}{n}.$$

This expression is equivalent to $\frac{1}{n}\left(\sum_{k=1}^{n} x_k\right)$.

Series play an essential role in various applications, as illustrated by the next example.

EXAMPLE 8   Modeling air filtration

Suppose that an air filter removes 90% of the impurities entering it.
(a) Find a series that represents the amount of impurities removed by a sequence of n air filters. Express this answer in summation notation.
(b) How many air filters would be necessary to remove 99.99% of the impurities?

Solution   (a) The first filter removes 90% of the impurities, so 10%, or 0.1, passes through it. Of the 0.1 that passes through the first filter, 90% is removed by the second filter, while 10% of 10%, or 0.01, passes through. Then, 10% of 0.01, or 0.001, passes through the third filter. Figure 11.17 depicts these results, from which we can establish a pattern. If we let 100%, or 1, represent the amount of impurities entering the first air filter, the amount removed by n filters equals

$$(0.9)(1) + (0.9)(0.1) + (0.9)(0.01) + (0.9)(0.001) + \cdots + (0.9)(0.1)^{n-1}.$$

In summation notation we write this series as $\sum_{k=1}^{n} 0.9(0.1)^{k-1}$.

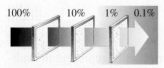

100%   10%   1%   0.1%

Figure 11.17 Impurities Passing Through Air Filters

(b) To remove 99.99%, or 0.9999, of the impurities requires 4 air filters, because

$$\sum_{k=1}^{4} 0.9(0.1)^{k-1} = (0.9)(1) + (0.9)(0.1) + (0.9)(0.01) + (0.9)(0.001)$$
$$= 0.9 + 0.09 + 0.009 + 0.0009$$
$$= 0.9999.$$

11.3 PUTTING IT ALL TOGETHER

A sequence is an ordered list such as

$$a_1, a_2, a_3, a_4, a_5, \ldots, a_n.$$

A series is the summation of the terms of a sequence and can be expressed as

$$a_1 + a_2 + a_3 + a_4 + a_5 + \cdots + a_n.$$

The following table summarizes concepts related to arithmetic and geometric series.

Series	Description	Example
Finite Arithmetic	$a_1 + a_2 + a_3 + \cdots + a_n,$ where $a_n = dn + c \quad$ or $\quad a_n = a_1 + (n-1)d.$ The sum of the first n terms is $$S_n = n\left(\frac{a_1 + a_n}{2}\right) \quad \text{or}$$ $$S_n = \frac{n}{2}(2a_1 + (n-1)d),$$ where a_1 is the first term and d is the common difference.	The series $$4 + 7 + 10 + 13 + 16 + 19 + 22$$ is defined by $$a_n = 3n + 1 \quad \text{or} \quad a_n = 4 + 3(n-1).$$ Its sum is $$S_7 = 7\left(\frac{4 + 22}{2}\right) = 91 \quad \text{or}$$ $$S_7 = \frac{7}{2}(2 \cdot 4 + (7-1)3) = 91.$$
Finite Geometric	$a_1 + a_2 + a_3 + \cdots + a_n,$ where $a_n = a_1(r)^{n-1}$ for nonzero constants a_1 and r. The sum of the first n terms is $$S_n = a_1\left(\frac{1 - r^n}{1 - r}\right),$$ where a_1 is the first term and r is the common ratio.	The series $$3 + 6 + 12 + 24 + 48 + 96$$ has $a_1 = 3$ and $r = 2$. Its sum is $$S_6 = 3\left(\frac{1 - 2^6}{1 - 2}\right) = 189.$$

11.3 EXERCISES

FOR EXTRA HELP

 Student's Solutions Manual

 InterAct Math    MathXL

MyMathLab   Math Tutor Center   Digital Video Tutor CD 9   Videotape 12

CONCEPTS

1. The summation of the terms of a sequence is called a(n) _____.   series

2. Find the sum of the series $1 + 2 + 3 + 4$.   10

3. The series $1 + 3 + 5 + 7 + 9$ is an example of a(n) _____ series.   arithmetic

4. The series $1 + 3 + 9 + 27 + 81$ is an example of a(n) _____ series.   geometric

5. If $a_1 + a_2 + a_3 + \cdots + a_n$ is an arithmetic series, its sum is $S_n =$ _____. $n\left(\dfrac{a_1 + a_n}{2}\right)$ or $\dfrac{n}{2}(2a_1 + (n-1)d)$

6. If $a_1 + a_2 + a_3 + \cdots + a_n$ is a geometric series with the common ratio r, its sum is $S_n =$ _____. $a_1\left(\dfrac{1 - r^n}{1 - r}\right)$

7. The symbol $\sum$ is used to indicate a _____.   sum

8. Write $\sum_{k=1}^{4} a_k$ as a sum. $a_1 + a_2 + a_3 + a_4$

9. $\sum_{n=1}^{5} a_1 + (n-1)d$ is an example of a(n) _____ series.   arithmetic

10. $\sum_{n=1}^{4} a_1 r^{n-1}$ is an example of a(n) _____ series.   geometric

SUMS OF SERIES

Exercises 11–16: Find the sum of the arithmetic series by using a formula.

11. $3 + 5 + 7 + 9 + 11 + 13$ 48

12. $7.5 + 6 + 4.5 + 3 + 1.5 + 0 + (-1.5)$ 21

13. $1 + 2 + 3 + 4 + \cdots + 40$ 820

14. $1 + 3 + 5 + 7 + \cdots + 99$ 2500

15. $-7 + (-4) + (-1) + 2 + 5$ -5

16. $89 + 84 + 79 + 74 + 69 + 64 + 59 + 54$ 572

Exercises 17–22: Find the sum of the geometric series by using a formula.

17. $3 + 9 + 27 + 81 + 243 + 729 + 2187$ 3279

18. $2 - 1 + \frac{1}{2} - \frac{1}{4} + \frac{1}{8} - \frac{1}{16} + \frac{1}{32}$ $\frac{43}{32}$

19. $1 - 2 + 4 - 8 + 16 - 32 + 64 - 128$ -85

20. $2 + \frac{1}{2} + \frac{1}{8} + \frac{1}{32} + \frac{1}{128} + \frac{1}{512}$ $\frac{1365}{512}$

21. $0.5 + 1.5 + 4.5 + 13.5 + 40.5 + 121.5$ 182

22. $0.6 + 0.3 + 0.15 + 0.075 + 0.0375$ 1.1625

*Exercises 23–26: **Annuities** (Refer to Example 5.) Find the future value of the annuity.*

23. $a_1 = \$2000$ $I = 0.08$ $n = 20$ $91,523.93

24. $a_1 = \$500$ $I = 0.15$ $n = 10$ $10,151.86

25. $a_1 = \$10,000$ $I = 0.11$ $n = 5$ $62,278.01

26. $a_1 = \$3000$ $I = 0.19$ $n = 45$ $39,610,272.68

SUMMATION NOTATION

Exercises 27–34: Write the terms of the series and find their sum.

27. $\sum_{k=1}^{4} 2k$ $2 + 4 + 6 + 8;\ 20$

28. $\sum_{k=1}^{6} (k - 1)$ $0 + 1 + 2 + 3 + 4 + 5;\ 15$

29. $\sum_{k=1}^{8} 4$ $4 + 4 + 4 + 4 + 4 + 4 + 4 + 4;\ 32$

30. $\sum_{k=2}^{6} (5 - 2k)$ $1 + (-1) + (-3) + (-5) + (-7);\ -15$

31. $\sum_{k=1}^{7} k^2$ $1 + 4 + 9 + 16 + 25 + 36 + 49;\ 140$

32. $\sum_{k=1}^{4} 5(2)^{k-1}$ $5 + 10 + 20 + 40;\ 75$

33. $\sum_{k=4}^{5} (k^2 - k)$ $12 + 20;\ 32$

34. $\sum_{k=1}^{4} \log k$ $\log 1 + \log 2 + \log 3 + \log 4;\ \log 24$

Exercises 35–38: Write each series in summation notation.

35. $1^4 + 2^4 + 3^4 + 4^4 + 5^4 + 6^4$ $\sum_{k=1}^{6} k^4$

36. $1 + \frac{1}{5^1} + \frac{1}{5^2} + \frac{1}{5^3} + \frac{1}{5^4}$ $\sum_{k=1}^{5} \frac{1}{5^{k-1}}$

37. $1 + \frac{1}{2^2} + \frac{1}{3^2} + \frac{1}{4^2} + \frac{1}{5^2}$ 37. $\sum_{k=1}^{5} \frac{1}{k^2}$

38. $1 + \frac{1}{10} + \frac{1}{100} + \frac{1}{1000} + \frac{1}{10,000}$ $\sum_{k=1}^{5} \frac{1}{10^{k-1}}$

39. Verify that $\sum_{k=1}^{n} k = \frac{n(n+1)}{2}$ by using a formula for the sum of the first n terms of an arithmetic series. *

40. Use Exercise 39 to find the sum of the series $\sum_{k=1}^{200} k$.
20,100

APPLICATIONS

41. *Prison Escapees* The table lists the number of escapees from state prisons each year.

Year	1990	1991	1992
Escapees	8518	9921	10,706

Year	1993	1994	1995
Escapees	14,035	14,307	12,249

Source: Bureau of Justice Statistics.

(a) Write a series whose sum is the total number of escapees from 1990 to 1995.
(b) Find its sum.   69,736
(a) 8518 + 9921 + 10,706 + 14,035 + 14,307 + 12,249

42. *Captured Prison Escapees* (Refer to Exercise 41.) The table lists the number of escapees from state prisons who were captured, including inmates who may have escaped during a previous year.

Year	1990	1991	1992
Captured	9324	9586	10,031

Year	1993	1994	1995
Captured	12,872	13,346	12,166

Source: Bureau of Justice Statistics.

(a) Write a series whose sum is the total number of escapees captured from 1990 to 1995.
(b) Find its sum.   67,325
(c) Compare the number of escapees to the number captured during this time period.
Some escapees were not captured.

43. *Area* A sequence of smaller squares is formed by connecting the midpoints of the sides of a larger square as shown in the figure.

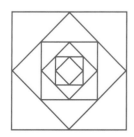

42.(a) 9324 + 9586 + 10,031 + 12,872 + 13,346 + 12,166

(a) If the area of the largest square is 1 square unit, give the first five terms of a sequence that describes the area of each successive square.
(b) Use a formula to sum the areas of the first 10 squares. $\frac{1023}{512}$ (a) $1, \frac{1}{2}, \frac{1}{4}, \frac{1}{8}, \frac{1}{16}$

44. *Perimeter* (Refer to Exercise 43.) Use a formula to find the sum of the perimeters of the first 10 squares.
About 13.23

45. *Stacking Logs* A stack of logs is made in layers, with one log less in each layer, as shown in the accompanying figure. If the top layer has 6 logs and the bottom row has 14 logs, what is the total number of logs in the pile? Use a formula to find this sum.   90 logs

46. *Stacking Logs* (Refer to Exercise 45.) Suppose that a stack of logs has 15 logs in the top layer and a total of 10 layers. How many logs are in the stack?   195 logs

47. *Salaries* Suppose that an individual's starting salary is $35,000 per year and that the individual receives a $2000 raise each year. Find the total amount earned over 20 years. $1,080,000

48. *Salaries* Suppose that an individual's starting salary is $35,000 per year and that the individual receives a 10% raise each year. Find the total amount earned over 20 years. $2,004,624.98

49. *Bouncing Ball* A tennis ball first bounces to 75% of the height from which it was dropped and then to 75% of the height of each successive bounce. If it is dropped from a height of 10 feet, find the distance it *falls* between the fourth and fifth bounce.   About 3.16 ft

50. *Bouncing Ball* A tennis ball first bounces to 75% of the height from which it was dropped and then to 75% of the height of each successive bounce. If it is dropped from a height of 10 feet, find the *total* distance it travels before it reaches its fifth bounce. (*Hint:* Make a sketch.)   About 51.02 ft

*Answers on page IA-40

51. Discuss the difference between a sequence and a series. Give an example of each.

52. Suppose that an arithmetic series has $a_1 = 1$ and a common difference of $d = 2$, whereas a geometric

series has $a_1 = 1$ and a common ratio of $r = 2$. Discuss how their sums compare as the number of terms n becomes large. (*Hint:* Calculate each sum for $n = 10, 20,$ and 30.)

Group Activity: ▶ Working with Real Data

Directions: Form a group of 2 to 4 people. Select someone to record the group's responses for this activity. All members of the group should work cooperatively to answer the questions. If your instructor asks for your results, each member of the group should be prepared to respond.

Depreciation For tax purposes, businesses frequently depreciate equipment. Two different methods of depreciation are called *straight-line depreciation* and *sum-of-the-years'-digits*. Suppose that a college student buys a $3000 computer to start a business that provides Internet services. This student estimates the life of the computer at 4 years, after which its value will be $200. The difference between $3000 and $200, or $2800, may be deducted from the student's taxable income over a 4-year period.

In straight-line depreciation, equal portions of $2800 are deducted each year over the 4 years. The sum-of-the-years'-digits method calculates depreciation differently. For a computer having a useful life of 4 years, the sum of the years is computed by

$$1 + 2 + 3 + 4 = 10.$$

With this method, $\frac{4}{10}$ of $2800 is deducted the first year, $\frac{3}{10}$ the second year, and so on, until $\frac{1}{10}$ is deducted the fourth year. Both depreciation methods yield a total deduction of $2800 over the 4 years.   (*Source:* Sharp Electronics Corporation, *Conquering the Sciences.*)

(a) Find an arithmetic sequence that gives the amount depreciated each year by each method.

(b) Write a series whose sum is the amount depreciated over 4 years by each method.

(a) Straight-line: 700, 700, 700, 700
     Sum-of-years'-digits: 1120, 840, 560, 280

(b) Straight-line: 700 + 700 + 700 + 700
     Sum-of-years'-digits: 1120 + 840 + 560 + 280

11.4   THE BINOMIAL THEOREM

Pascal's Triangle · Factorial Notation and Binomial Coefficients ·
Using the Binomial Theorem

INTRODUCTION

In this section we demonstrate how to expand expressions of the form $(a + b)^n$, where n is a natural number. These expressions occur in statistics, finite mathematics, computer science, and calculus. The two methods that we discuss are Pascal's triangle and the binomial theorem.

PASCAL'S TRIANGLE

TEACHING TIP

Pascal's triangle provides a simple way to find the coefficients for expanding a binomial.

Expanding $(a + b)^n$ for increasing values of n gives the following results.

$$(a + b)^0 = \qquad\qquad 1$$
$$(a + b)^1 = \qquad\qquad 1a + 1b$$
$$(a + b)^2 = \qquad\qquad 1a^2 + 2ab + 1b^2$$
$$(a + b)^3 = \qquad\qquad 1a^3 + 3a^2b + 3ab^2 + 1b^3$$
$$(a + b)^4 = \qquad\qquad 1a^4 + 4a^3b + 6a^2b^2 + 4ab^3 + 1b^4$$
$$(a + b)^5 = \qquad 1a^5 + 5a^4b + 10a^3b^2 + 10a^2b^3 + 5ab^4 + 1b^5$$

Note that $(a + b)^1$ has two terms, starting with a and ending with b; $(a + b)^2$ has three terms, starting with a^2 and ending with b^2; and in general, $(a + b)^n$ has $n + 1$ terms, starting with a^n and ending with b^n. The exponent on a decreases by 1 each successive term, and the exponent on b increases by 1 each successive term.

```
        1
      1   1
    1   2   1
  1   3   3   1
1   4   6   4   1
1  5  10  10  5   1
```

Figure 11.18 Pascal's Triangle

The triangle formed by the highlighted numbers is called **Pascal's triangle**. This triangle consists of 1s along the sides, and each element inside the triangle is the sum of the two numbers above it, as shown in Figure 11.18. Pascal's triangle is usually written without variables and can be extended to include as many rows as needed.

We can use this triangle to expand $(a + b)^n$, where n is a natural number. For example, the expression $(m + n)^4$ consists of five terms written as

$$(m + n)^4 = \_m^4 + \_m^3n^1 + \_m^2n^2 + \_m^1n^3 + \_n^4.$$

Because there are five terms, the coefficients can be found in the fifth row of Pascal's triangle, which is

$$1 \quad 4 \quad 6 \quad 4 \quad 1.$$

Thus

$$(m + n)^4 = \underline{1}\,m^4 + \underline{4}\,m^3n^1 + \underline{6}\,m^2n^2 + \underline{4}\,m^1n^3 + \underline{1}\,n^4$$
$$= m^4 + 4m^3n + 6m^2n^2 + 4mn^3 + n^4.$$

EXAMPLE 1   Expanding a binomial

Expand each binomial, using Pascal's triangle.
(a) $(x + 2)^5$ **(b)** $(2m - n)^3$

Solution   **(a)** To find the coefficients, use the sixth row in Pascal's triangle.

$$(x + 2)^5 = \underline{1}\,x^5 + \underline{5}\,x^4 \cdot 2^1 + \underline{10}\,x^3 \cdot 2^2 + \underline{10}\,x^2 \cdot 2^3 + \underline{5}\,x^1 \cdot 2^4 + \underline{1}\,(2^5)$$
$$= x^5 + 10x^4 + 40x^3 + 80x^2 + 80x + 32$$

(b) To find the coefficients, use the fourth row in Pascal's triangle.

$$(2m - n)^3 = \underline{1}\,(2m)^3 + \underline{3}\,(2m)^2(-n)^1 + \underline{3}\,(2m)^1(-n)^2 + \underline{1}\,(-n)^3$$
$$= 8m^3 - 12m^2n + 6mn^2 - n^3$$

FACTORIAL NOTATION AND BINOMIAL COEFFICIENTS

An alternative to Pascal's triangle is the binomial theorem, which makes use of **factorial notation**.

n FACTORIAL (*n*!)

For any positive integer,

$$n! = 1 \cdot 2 \cdot 3 \cdot \cdots \cdot n.$$

We also define $0! = 1$.

Note: Because multiplication is commutative, *n* factorial can also be defined as

$$n! = n \cdot (n - 1) \cdot (n - 2) \cdot \cdots \cdot 2 \cdot 1.$$

Examples include the following.

$$0! = 1$$
$$1! = 1$$
$$2! = 1 \cdot 2 = 2$$
$$3! = 1 \cdot 2 \cdot 3 = 6$$
$$4! = 1 \cdot 2 \cdot 3 \cdot 4 = 24$$
$$5! = 1 \cdot 2 \cdot 3 \cdot 4 \cdot 5 = 120$$

Figure 11.19 supports these results. On some calculators, factorial (!) can be accessed in the MATH PRB menus.

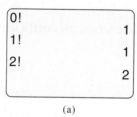
(a)

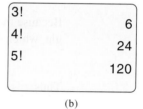
(b)

Figure 11.19

EXAMPLE 2   Evaluating factorial expressions

Simplify the expression.

(a) $\frac{5!}{3!2!}$ **(b)** $\frac{4!}{4!0!}$

Solution   **(a)** $\frac{5!}{3!2!} = \frac{1 \cdot 2 \cdot 3 \cdot 4 \cdot 5}{(1 \cdot 2 \cdot 3)(1 \cdot 2)} = \frac{120}{6 \cdot 2} = 10$

(b) $0! = 1$, so $\frac{4!}{4!0!} = \frac{4!}{4!(1)} = \frac{4!}{4!} = 1$

The expression $_nC_r$ represents a *binomial coefficient* that can be used to calculate the numbers in Pascal's triangle.

BINOMIAL COEFFICIENT $_nC_r$

For *n* and *r* nonnegative integers, $n \geq r$,

$$_nC_r = \frac{n!}{(n - r)!r!}$$

is a **binomial coefficient.**

Values of $_nC_r$ for $r = 0, 1, 2, \ldots, n$ correspond to the $n + 1$ numbers in row $n + 1$ of Pascal's triangle.

EXAMPLE 3   Calculating $_nC_r$

Calculate $_3C_r$ for $r = 0, 1, 2, 3$ by hand. Check your results on a calculator. Compare these numbers with the fourth row in Pascal's triangle.

Solution

$$_3C_0 = \frac{3!}{(3 - 0)!\,0!} = \frac{6}{6 \cdot 1} = 1$$

$$_3C_1 = \frac{3!}{(3 - 1)!\,1!} = \frac{6}{2 \cdot 1} = 3$$

$$_3C_2 = \frac{3!}{(3 - 2)!\,2!} = \frac{6}{1 \cdot 2} = 3$$

$$_3C_3 = \frac{3!}{(3 - 3)!\,3!} = \frac{6}{1 \cdot 6} = 1$$

These results are supported in Figure 11.20. The fourth row of Pascal's triangle is

$$1 \quad 3 \quad 3 \quad 1,$$

which agrees with the calculated values for $_3C_r$. On some calculators, the MATH PRB menus are used to calculate $_nC_r$.

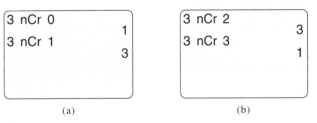

(a)   (b)

Figure 11.20

USING THE BINOMIAL THEOREM

The binomial coefficients can be used to expand expressions of the form $(a + b)^n$. To do so, we use the **binomial theorem**.

BINOMIAL THEOREM

For any positive integer n and any numbers a and b,

$$(a + b)^n = {}_nC_0 a^n + {}_nC_1 a^{n-1}b^1 + \cdots + {}_nC_{n-1} a^1 b^{n-1} + {}_nC_n b^n.$$

Using the results of Example 3, we write

$$(a + b)^3 = {}_3C_0 a^3 + {}_3C_1 a^2 b^1 + {}_3C_2 a^1 b^2 + {}_3C_3 b^3$$
$$= 1a^3 + 3a^2 b + 3ab^2 + 1b^3$$
$$= a^3 + 3a^2 b + 3ab^2 + b^3.$$

EXAMPLE 4   Expanding a binomial

Use the binomial theorem to expand each expression.
(a) $(x + y)^5$ **(b)** $(3 - 2x)^4$

Solution   **(a)** The coefficients are calculated as follows.

$$_5C_0 = \frac{5!}{(5 - 0)!\,0!} = 1, \qquad _5C_1 = \frac{5!}{(5 - 1)!\,1!} = 5, \qquad _5C_2 = \frac{5!}{(5 - 2)!\,2!} = 10$$

$$_5C_3 = \frac{5!}{(5 - 3)!\,3!} = 10, \qquad _5C_4 = \frac{5!}{(5 - 4)!\,4!} = 5, \qquad _5C_5 = \frac{5!}{(5 - 5)!\,5!} = 1$$

Using the binomial theorem, we arrive at the following result.

$$(x + y)^5 = {}_5C_0 x^5 + {}_5C_1 x^4 y^1 + {}_5C_2 x^3 y^2 + {}_5C_3 x^2 y^3 + {}_5C_4 x^1 y^4 + {}_5C_5 y^5$$
$$= 1x^5 + 5x^4 y + 10x^3 y^2 + 10x^2 y^3 + 5xy^4 + 1y^5$$
$$= x^5 + 5x^4 y + 10x^3 y^2 + 10x^2 y^3 + 5xy^4 + y^5$$

(b) The coefficients are calculated as follows.

$$_4C_0 = \frac{4!}{(4 - 0)!\,0!} = 1, \qquad _4C_1 = \frac{4!}{(4 - 1)!\,1!} = 4, \qquad _4C_2 = \frac{4!}{(4 - 2)!\,2!} = 6,$$

$$_4C_3 = \frac{4!}{(4 - 3)!\,3!} = 4, \qquad _4C_4 = \frac{4!}{(4 - 4)!\,4!} = 1$$

Using the binomial theorem with $a = 3$ and $b = (-2x)$, we arrive at the following result.

$$(3 - 2x)^4 = {}_4C_0 (3)^4 + {}_4C_1 (3)^3 (-2x) + {}_4C_2 (3)^2 (-2x)^2$$
$$+ {}_4C_3 (3)(-2x)^3 + {}_4C_4 (-2x)^4$$
$$= 1(81) + 4(27)(-2x) + 6(9)(4x^2) + 4(3)(-8x^3) + 1(16x^4)$$
$$= 81 - 216x + 216x^2 - 96x^3 + 16x^4$$

The binomial theorem gives *all* of the terms of $(a + b)^n$. However, we can find any individual term by noting that the $(r + 1)$st term in the binomial expansion for $(a + b)^n$ is given by the formula $_nC_r a^{n-r} b^r$, for $0 \le r \le n$. The next example shows how to use this formula to find the $(r + 1)$st term of $(a + b)^n$.

EXAMPLE 5   Finding the *k*th term in a binomial expansion

Find the third term of $(x - y)^5$.

Solution   In this example the $(r + 1)$st term is the *third* term in the expansion of $(x - y)^5$. That is, $r + 1 = 3$, or $r = 2$. Also, the exponent in the expression is $n = 5$. To get this binomial into the form $(a + b)^n$, we note that the first term in the binomial is $a = x$ and that the second term in the binomial is $b = -y$. Substituting the values for r, n, a, and b in the formula for the $(r + 1)$st term yields

$$_5C_2 (x)^{5-2} (-y)^2 = 10x^3 y^2.$$

The third term in the binomial expansion of $(x - y)^5$ is $10x^3 y^2$.

11.4 PUTTING IT ALL TOGETHER

In this section we showed how to expand the expression $(a + b)^n$ by using Pascal's triangle and the binomial theorem. The following table outlines important topics from this section.

Topic	Explanation	Example
Pascal's Triangle	$$\begin{array}{ccccccc} & & & 1 & & & \\ & & 1 & & 1 & & \\ & 1 & & 2 & & 1 & \\ 1 & & 3 & & 3 & & 1 \\ \end{array}$$ $$\begin{array}{ccccccccc} 1 & & 4 & & 6 & & 4 & & 1 \\ 1 & & 5 & & 10 & & 10 & & 5 & & 1 \end{array}$$ To expand $(a + b)^n$, use row $n + 1$ in the triangle.	$(a + b)^3 = 1a^3 + 3a^2b + 3ab^2 + 1b^3$ (Row 4)
Factorial Notation	The expression $n!$ equals $$1 \cdot 2 \cdot 3 \cdot \cdots \cdot n.$$	$5! = 1 \cdot 2 \cdot 3 \cdot 4 \cdot 5 = 120$
Binomial Coefficient ${}_nC_r$	$${}_nC_r = \frac{n!}{(n-r)!\,r!}$$	$${}_6C_4 = \frac{6!}{(6-4)!\,4!} = \frac{6!}{2!\,4!} = \frac{720}{2 \cdot 24} = 15$$
Binomial Theorem	$(a + b)^n = {}_nC_0 a^n + {}_nC_1 a^{n-1}b^1 + \cdots$ $\qquad + {}_nC_{n-1} a^1 b^{n-1} + {}_nC_n b^n$	$(a + b)^4 = {}_4C_0 a^4 + {}_4C_1 a^3b + {}_4C_2 a^2b^2$ $\qquad + {}_4C_3 ab^3 + {}_4C_4 b^4$ $\quad = 1a^4 + 4a^3b + 6a^2b^2 + 4ab^3 + 1b^4$ $\quad = a^4 + 4a^3b + 6a^2b^2 + 4ab^3 + b^4$

11.4 EXERCISES

FOR EXTRA HELP

📖 Student's Solutions Manual   InterAct Math   *MathXL* MathXL

🚪 MyMathLab   Tutor Center Math Tutor Center   Digital Video Tutor CD 9 Videotape 12

CONCEPTS

1. How many terms result from expanding $(a + b)^4$? 5

2. How many terms result from expanding $(a + b)^n$?
$n + 1$

3. To find the coefficients for the expansion of $(a + b)^3$, what row of Pascal's triangle do you use? 4

4. Write down the first 5 rows of Pascal's triangle.*

5. $4! = $ _____ 24

6. $1 \cdot 2 \cdot 3 \cdot 4 \cdot 5 \cdot 6 = $ _____ $6! = 720$

7. ${}_nC_r = $ _____   **8.** $(a + b)^2 = $ _____

USING PASCAL'S TRIANGLE

Exercises 9–16: Use Pascal's triangle to expand the expression.

9. $(x + y)^3$
$x^3 + 3x^2y + 3xy^2 + y^3$

10. $(x + y)^4$
$x^4 + 4x^3y + 6x^2y^2 + 4xy^3 + y^4$

*Answers on page IA-40

13. $a^5 - 5a^4b + 10a^3b^2 - 10a^2b^3 + 5ab^4 - b^5$ 14. $27x^3 + 54x^2y + 36xy^2 + 8y^3$

11. $(2x + 1)^4$ **12.** $(2x - 1)^4$
$16x^4 + 32x^3 + 24x^2 + 8x + 1$ $16x^4 - 32x^3 + 24x^2 - 8x + 1$

13. $(a - b)^5$ **14.** $(3x + 2y)^3$

15. $(x^2 + 1)^3$ **16.** $\left(\frac{1}{2} - x^2\right)^5$
$x^6 + 3x^4 + 3x^2 + 1$ $\frac{1}{32} - \frac{5}{16}x^2 + \frac{5}{4}x^4 - \frac{5}{2}x^6 + \frac{5}{2}x^8 - x^{10}$

FACTORIALS AND BINOMIAL COEFFICIENTS

Exercises 17–30: Evaluate the expression.

17. $3!$ 6   **18.** $6!$ 720

19. $\frac{4!}{3!}$ 4   **20.** $\frac{6!}{3!}$ 120

21. $\frac{2!}{0!}$ 2   **22.** $\frac{5!}{1!}$ 120

23. $\frac{5!}{2!3!}$ 10   **24.** $\frac{6!}{4!2!}$ 15

25. $_5C_4$ 5   **26.** $_3C_1$ 3

27. $_6C_5$ 6   **28.** $_2C_2$ 1

29. $_4C_0$ 1   **30.** $_4C_3$ 4

Exercises 31–36: Evaluate the binomial coefficient with a calculator.

31. $_{12}C_7$ 792   **32.** $_{13}C_8$ 1287

33. $_9C_5$ 126   **34.** $_{25}C_{14}$ 4,457,400

35. $_{19}C_{11}$ 75,582   **36.** $_{10}C_6$ 210

THE BINOMIAL THEOREM

Exercises 37–48: Use the binomial theorem to expand the expression.

37. $(m + n)^3$ **38.** $(m + n)^5$
$m^3 + 3m^2n + 3mn^2 + n^3$ $m^5 + 5m^4n + 10m^3n^2 + 10m^2n^3 + 5mn^4 + n^5$

$1 - 12x + 54x^2 - 108x^3 + 81x^4$

39. $(x - y)^4$ **40.** $(1 - 3x)^4$
$x^4 - 4x^3y + 6x^2y^2 - 4xy^3 + y^4$

41. $(2a + 1)^3$ **42.** $(x^2 - 1)^3$
$8a^3 + 12a^2 + 6a + 1$ $x^6 - 3x^4 + 3x^2 - 1$

43. $(x + 2)^5$ **44.** $(a - 3)^5$
$x^5 + 10x^4 + 40x^3 + 80x^2 + 80x + 32$

45. $(3 + 2m)^4$ **46.** $(m - 3n)^3$
$81 + 216m + 216m^2 + 96m^3 + 16m^4$

47. $(2x - y)^3$ **48.** $(2a + 3b)^4$
$8x^3 - 12x^2y + 6xy^2 - y^3$

Exercises 49–54: The $(r + 1)$st term of the expression $(a + b)^n$, $0 \le r \le n$, is given by $_nC_ra^{n-r}b^r$. Find the specified term. Refer to Example 5.

49. The first term of $(a + b)^8$ a^8

50. The second term of $(a - b)^{10}$ $-10a^9b$

51. The fourth term of $(x + y)^7$ $35x^4y^3$

52. The sixth term of $(a + b)^9$ $126a^4b^5$

53. The first term of $(2m + n)^9$ $512m^9$

54. The eighth term of $(2a - b)^8$ $-16ab^7$

WRITING ABOUT MATHEMATICS

55. Explain how to find the numbers in Pascal's triangle.

56. Compare the expansion of $(a + b)^n$ to the expansion of $(a - b)^n$. Give an example.

44. $a^5 - 15a^4 + 90a^3 - 270a^2 + 405a - 243$

46. $m^3 - 9m^2n + 27mn^2 - 27n^3$

48. $16a^4 + 96a^3b + 216a^2b^2 + 216ab^3 + 81b^4$

CHECKING BASIC CONCEPTS   SECTIONS 11.3 AND 11.4

1. Determine whether the series is arithmetic or geometric.
  (a) $\frac{1}{2} + \frac{1}{4} + \frac{1}{8} + \cdots + \frac{1}{256}$ Geometric
  (b) $\frac{1}{2} + \frac{5}{2} + \frac{9}{2} + \frac{13}{2} + \frac{17}{2}$ Arithmetic

2. Use a formula to find the sum of the arithmetic series   312
$$4 + 8 + 12 + \cdots + 48.$$

3. Use a formula to find the sum of the geometric series -341
$$1 - 2 + 4 - 8 + 16 - 32 + 64 - 128$$
$$+ 256 - 512.$$

4. Use Pascal's triangle to expand $(x - y)^4$.
$x^4 - 4x^3y + 6x^2y^2 - 4xy^3 + y^4$

5. Use the binomial theorem to expand $(x + 2)^3$.
$x^3 + 6x^2 + 12x + 8$

CHAPTER
11 Summary

Section 11.1   *Sequences*

An infinite sequence is a function whose domain is the natural numbers. A finite sequence is a function whose domain is $D = \{1, 2, 3, \ldots, n\}$ for some natural number n. Because sequences are functions, they have symbolic, graphical, and numerical representations.

Example: $a_n = 2n$ is a symbolic representation of the even natural numbers. The first six terms of this sequence are represented numerically and graphically in the table and figure.

n	1	2	3	4	5	6
a_n	2	4	6	8	10	12

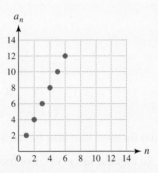

Section 11.2   *Arithmetic and Geometric Sequences*

Two common types of sequences are arithmetic and geometric.

Arithmetic Sequence   An arithmetic sequence is determined by a linear function of the form $f(n) = dn + c$ or $f(n) = a_1 + (n-1)d$. Successive terms in an arithmetic sequence are found by adding the common difference d to the previous term. The sequence $1, 3, 5, 7, 9, 11, \ldots$ is an arithmetic sequence with its first term $a_1 = 1$, common difference $d = 2$, and general term $a_n = 2n - 1$.

Geometric Sequence   The general term for a geometric sequence is given by $f(n) = a_1 r^{n-1}$. Successive terms in a geometric sequence are found by multiplying the previous term by the common ratio r. The sequence $3, 6, 12, 24, 48, \ldots$ is a geometric sequence with its first term $a_1 = 3$, common ratio $r = 2$, and general term $a_n = 3(2)^{n-1}$.

Section 11.3   *Series*

Series   A series results when the terms of a sequence are summed. The series associated with the sequence 2, 4, 6, 8, 10 is

$$2 + 4 + 6 + 8 + 10,$$

and its sum equals 30. An arithmetic series results when the terms of an arithmetic sequence are summed, and a geometric series results when the terms of a geometric sequence are summed. In this chapter, we discussed formulas for finding sums of arithmetic and geometric series. See Putting It All Together for Section 11.3.

Summation Notation   Summation notation can be used to write series efficiently. For example,

$$1^2 + 2^2 + 3^2 + 4^2 + 5^2 = \sum_{k=1}^{5} k^2.$$

Section 11.4   *The Binomial Theorem*

Pascal's triangle may be used to find the coefficients for the expansion of $(a + b)^n$, where n is a natural number.

$$
\begin{array}{ccccccccccc}
 & & & & & 1 & & & & & \\
 & & & & 1 & & 1 & & & & \\
 & & & 1 & & 2 & & 1 & & & \\
 & & 1 & & 3 & & 3 & & 1 & & \\
 & 1 & & 4 & & 6 & & 4 & & 1 & \\
1 & & 5 & & 10 & & 10 & & 5 & & 1
\end{array}
$$

The binomial theorem can also be used to expand powers of binomials.

Example: To expand $(x + y)^4$, use the fifth row of Pascal's triangle.

$$(x + y)^4 = 1x^4 + 4x^3y + 6x^2y^2 + 4xy^3 + 1y^4$$
$$= x^4 + 4x^3y + 6x^2y^2 + 4xy^3 + y^4$$

CHAPTER

11 Review Exercises

SECTION 11.1

Exercises 1–4: Write the first four terms of the sequence for n = 1, 2, 3, and 4.

1. $f(n) = n^3$ $1, 8, 27, 64$

2. $f(n) = 5 - 2n$ $3, 1, -1, -3$

3. $f(n) = \dfrac{2n}{n^2 + 1}$ $1, \frac{4}{5}, \frac{3}{5}, \frac{8}{17}$

4. $f(n) = (-2)^n$ $-2, 4, -8, 16$

Exercises 5–6: Use the graph to write the terms of the sequence.

5. $-2, 0, 4, 2$

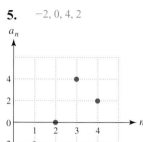

6. $5, 3, 2, 1$

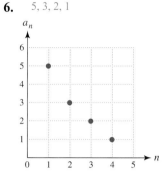

Exercises 7–10: Represent the first seven terms of the sequence with $n = 1, 2, \ldots, 7$ numerically and graphically.*

7. $a_n = 2n$

8. $a_n = n^2 - 4$

9. $a_n = 4\left(\frac{1}{2}\right)^n$

10. $a_n = \sqrt{n}$

Section 11.2

Exercises 11–18: Determine whether f is an arithmetic sequence. Identify the common difference when possible.

11. $f(n) = 5n - 1$ Yes; 5 **12.** $f(n) = 4 - n^2$ No

13. $f(n) = 2^n$ No   **14.** $f(n) = 4 - \frac{1}{3}n$ Yes; $-\frac{1}{3}$

15.

n	1	2	3	4
$f(n)$	20	17	14	11

Yes; -3

16.

n	1	2	3	4
$f(n)$	-3	0	6	12

No

17. Yes; -1

18. No

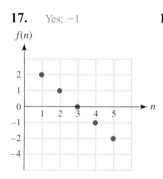

Exercises 19 and 20: Find the general term a_n for the arithmetic sequence.

19. $a_1 = -3$ and $d = 4$ **20.** $a_1 = 2$ and $a_2 = -3$
$a_n = 4n - 7$ $a_n = -5n + 7$

Exercises 21–28: Determine whether f is a geometric sequence. Identify the common ratio when possible.

21. $f(n) = 2(4)^n$ Yes; 4   **22.** $f(n) = 2n^4$ No

23. $f(n) = 1 - 2n$ No   **24.** $f(n) = 5(0.7)^n$ Yes; 0.7

25. No

n	1	2	3	4
$f(n)$	5	4	3	1

26. Yes; $-\frac{1}{3}$

n	1	2	3	4
$f(n)$	27	-9	3	-1

27. No   **28.** Yes; 2

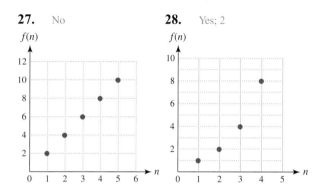

Exercises 29 and 30: Find the general term a_n for the geometric sequence.

29. $a_1 = 5$ and $r = 0.9$ **30.** $a_1 = 2$ and $a_2 = 8$
$a_n = 5(0.9)^{n-1}$ $a_n = 2(4)^{n-1}$

Section 11.3

Exercises 31–34: Find the sum, using a formula.

31. $4 + 9 + 14 + 19 + 24 + 29 + 34 + 39 + 44$ 216

32. $4.5 + 3.0 + 1.5 + 0 - 1.5$ 7.5

33. $1 - 4 + 16 - 64 + \cdots + 4096$ 3277

34. $1 + \frac{1}{2} + \frac{1}{4} + \frac{1}{8} + \frac{1}{16} + \cdots + \frac{1}{256}$ $\frac{511}{256}$

Exercises 35–38: Write the terms of the series.

35. $\displaystyle\sum_{k=1}^{5} 2k + 1$ **36.** $\displaystyle\sum_{k=1}^{4} \frac{1}{k + 1}$ $\frac{1}{2} + \frac{1}{3} + \frac{1}{4} + \frac{1}{5}$
$3 + 5 + 7 + 9 + 11$

37. $\displaystyle\sum_{k=1}^{4} k^3$ **38.** $\displaystyle\sum_{k=2}^{7} (1 - k)$
$1 + 8 + 27 + 64$ $-1 + (-2) + (-3) + (-4) + (-5) + (-6)$

Exercises 39–42: Write the series in summation notation.

39. $1 + 2 + 3 + \cdots + 20$ $\displaystyle\sum_{k=1}^{20} k$

*Answers on page IA-41

40. $1 + \frac{1}{2} + \frac{1}{3} + \cdots + \frac{1}{20}$ $\sum\limits_{k=1}^{20} \frac{1}{k}$ 41. $\sum\limits_{k=1}^{9} \frac{k}{k+1}$

41. $\frac{1}{2} + \frac{2}{3} + \frac{3}{4} + \cdots + \frac{9}{10}$

42. $1^2 + 2^2 + 3^2 + 4^2 + 5^2 + 6^2 + 7^2$ $\sum\limits_{k=1}^{7} k^2$

Section 11.4

Exercises 43–46: Use Pascal's triangle to expand the expression.

43. $(x + 4)^3$
$x^3 + 12x^2 + 48x + 64$

44. $(2x + 1)^4$
$16x^4 + 32x^3 + 24x^2 + 8x + 1$

45. $(x - y)^5$ $x^5 - 5x^4y + 10x^3y^2 - 10x^2y^3 + 5xy^4 - y^5$

46. $(a - 1)^6$ $a^6 - 6a^5 + 15a^4 - 20a^3 + 15a^2 - 6a + 1$

Exercises 47–50: Evaluate the expression.

47. $3!$ 6

48. $\frac{5!}{3!2!}$ 10

49. $_6C_3$ 20

50. $_4C_3$ 4

Exercises 51–54: Use the binomial theorem to expand the expression. $a^5 + 5a^4b + 10a^3b^2 + 10a^2b^3 + 5ab^4 + b^5$

51. $(m + 2)^4$

52. $(a + b)^5$

$m^4 + 8m^3 + 24m^2 + 32m + 16$

53. $(x - 3y)^4$

54. $(3x - 2)^3$ $27x^3 - 54x^2 + 36x - 8$

$x^4 - 12x^3y + 54x^2y^2 - 108xy^3 + 81y^4$

Applications

55. *Salaries*   An individual's starting salary is $45,000, and the individual receives a 10% raise each year. Give symbolic, numerical, and graphical representa-

tions for this person's salary over 7 years. What type of sequence is it? *
$a_n = 45{,}000(1.1)^{n-1}$, for $n = 1, 2, 3, \ldots, 7$; geometric

56. *Salaries*   An individual's starting salary is $45,000, and the individual receives an increase of $5000 each year. Give symbolic, numerical, and graphical representations for this person's salary over 7 years. What type of sequence is it? *
$a_n = 45{,}000 + 5000(n - 1)$, for $n = 1, 2, 3, \ldots, 7$; arithmetic

57. *Rain Forests*   Rain forests are defined as forests that grow in regions that receive more than 70 inches of rain each year. The world is losing an estimated 49 million acres of rain forests annually. Give symbolic, graphical, and numerical representations for a sequence that models the total number of acres (in millions) lost over a 7-year period.   (*Source: New York Times Almanac*, 1999.) * $a_n = 49n$, for $n = 1, 2, 3, \ldots, 7$

58. *Home Mortgage Payments*   The average home mortgage payment in 1996 was $1087 per month. Since then, mortgage payments have risen, on average, by 2.5% per year. $a_n = 1087(1.025)^{n-1}$

(a) Write a sequence a_n that models the average mortgage payment in year n, where $n = 1$ corresponds to 1996, $n = 2$ to 1997, and so on.

(b) Is a_n arithmetic, geometric, or neither? Explain your reasoning.   Geometric; the common ratio is 1.025.

(c) Find a_5 and interpret the result.

(d) Give a graphical representation for a_n, where $n = 1, 2, 3, \ldots, 10$. *

(c) About 1200; the average mortgage payment in 2000 was about $1200 per month.

11 Test

1. Write the first four terms of the sequence for $n = 1, 2, 3,$ and 4. $\frac{1}{2}, \frac{4}{3}, \frac{9}{4}, \frac{16}{5}$

$$f(n) = \frac{n^2}{n + 1}.$$

2. Use the graph to write the terms of the sequence.
$-3, 2, 1, -2, 3$ a_n

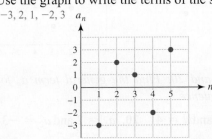

3. List the first seven terms of $a_n = n^2 - n$ in a table. Let $n = 1, 2, \ldots, 7$.*

4. Expand the expression $(2x - 1)^4$.
$16x^4 - 32x^3 + 24x^2 - 8x + 1$

Exercises 5 and 6: Determine whether the sequence is arithmetic or geometric. Identify either the common difference or the common ratio.

5. $f(n) = 7 - 3n$ Arithmetic; -3

6.

n	1	2	3	4
$f(n)$	-2	4	-8	16

Geometric; -2

7. Find the general term a_n for the arithmetic sequence if $a_1 = 2$ and $d = -3$.
$a_n = 2 - 3(n - 1)$, or $a_n = 5 - 3n$

8. Find the general term a_n for the geometric sequence if $a_1 = 2$ and $a_3 = 4.5$. $a_n = 2(1.5)^{n-1}$

Exercises 9 and 10: Determine whether f is a geometric sequence. Identify the common ratio when possible.

9. $f(n) = -3(2.5)^n$ Yes; 2.5

10.   No

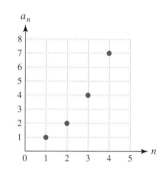

Exercises 11–12: Find the sum, using a formula.

11. $-1 + 2 + 5 + 8 + 11 + 14 + 17 + 20 + 23$ 99

12. $1 - \frac{2}{3} + \frac{4}{9} - \frac{8}{27} + \frac{16}{81} - \frac{32}{243} + \frac{64}{729}$ $\frac{463}{729}$

13. Write the terms of the series $\sum_{k=2}^{7} 3k$.
$6 + 9 + 12 + 15 + 18 + 21$

14. Write the series $1^3 + 2^3 + 3^3 + \cdots + 60^3$ in summation notation. $\sum_{k=1}^{60} k^3$

15. Evaluate $\frac{7!}{4!3!}$.   35   16. Evaluate $_5C_3$.   10

17. *Auditorium Seating*   An auditorium has 50 seats in the first row, 57 seats in the second row, 64 seats in the third row, and so on. Use a formula to find the total number of seats in the first 45 rows.   9180

18. *Median Home Price*   In 1997 the median price of a single-family home was \$159,700 and was increasing at a rate of 4% per year. Give symbolic, numerical, and graphical representations for the median home price over a 7-year period, starting in 1997. What type of sequence is it?*
$a_n = 159{,}700(1.04)^{n-1}$ for $n = 1, 2, 3, \ldots, 7$; geometric

19. *Tent Worms*   Large numbers of tent worms can defoliate trees and ruin crops. After they mature, they spin a cocoon and develop into moths that lay eggs. Suppose that an initial population of 2000 tent worms doubles every 5 days. $a_n = 2000(2)^{n-1}$
   (a) Write a formula for a_n that models the number of tent worms after $n - 1$ five-day time periods. (*Hint:* $a_1 = 2000$, $a_2 = 4000$, and $a_3 = 8000$.)
   (b) Is a_n arithmetic, geometric, or neither? Explain your reasoning.   Geometric; common ratio is 2.
   (c) Find a_6 and interpret the result.
   (d) Give a graph for a_n, where $n = 1, 2, 3, 4, 5, 6$.*

   (c) 64,000; after 30 days there are 64,000 worms.

*Answers on page IA-42

Extended and Discovery Exercises

SEQUENCES AND SERIES

*Exercises 1 and 2: Recursive Sequences   Some sequences are not defined by a formula for a_n. Instead they are defined recursively. With a **recursive formula** you*

must find terms a_1 through a_{n-1} before you can find a_n. For example, let

$$a_1 = 2$$
$$a_n = a_{n-1} + 3, \qquad \text{for } n \geq 2.$$

To find a_2, a_3, and a_4, we let $n = 2, 3, 4$.

$$a_2 = a_1 + 3 = 2 + 3 = 5$$
$$a_3 = a_2 + 3 = 5 + 3 = 8$$
$$a_4 = a_3 + 3 = 8 + 3 = 11$$

The first four terms of the sequence are 2, 5, 8, 11.

1. **Fibonacci Sequence** The Fibonacci sequence dates back to 1202 and is one of the most famous sequences in mathematics. It can be defined recursively as follows.

$$a_1 = 1, \qquad a_2 = 1$$
$$a_n = a_{n-1} + a_{n-2}, \qquad \text{for } n \geq 3$$

Find the first 12 terms of this sequence.
1, 1, 2, 3, 5, 8, 13, 21, 34, 55, 89, 144

2. **Insect Populations** Frequently the population of a particular insect does not continue to grow indefinitely. Instead, its population grows rapidly at first and then levels off because of competition for limited resources. In one study, the behavior of the winter moth was modeled with a sequence similar to the following, where a_n gives the population density in thousands per acre during year n.

$$a_1 = 1$$
$$a_n = 2.85a_{n-1} - 0.19a_{n-1}^2, \qquad n \geq 2$$

(**Source:** G. Varley and G. Gradwell, "Population models for the winter moth.")

(a) Make a table for $n = 1, 2, 3, \ldots, 7$. Describe what happens to the population density of the winter moth.*

Note: Many graphing calculators are capable of generating tables and graphs for a recursive sequence.

(b) Graph the sequence for $n = 1, 2, 3, \ldots, 20$. Discuss the graph.*

3. **Bode's Law** The average distances of the planets from the sun display a pattern first described by Johann Bode in 1772. This relationship is called Bode's law and was proposed before Uranus, Neptune, and Pluto were discovered. It is a sequence defined by

$$a_1 = 0.4$$
$$a_n = 0.3(2)^{n-2} + 0.4, \qquad \text{for } n = 2, 3, 4, \ldots, 10.$$

In this sequence, a distance of 1 unit corresponds to the average Earth–sun distance of 93 million miles. The number n represents the nth planet. The actual distances of the planets, including an average dis-

tance for the asteroids, are listed in the accompanying table. (**Source:** M. Zeilik, *Introductory Astronomy and Astrophysics.*)

(a) Find a_4 and interpret the result.
(b) Calculate the terms of Bode's sequence. Compare them with the values in the table.
(c) If there is another planet beyond Pluto, use Bode's law to predict its distance from the sun.

(a) 1.6; the average distance between Mars and the sun is 1.6 units, or 148.8 million miles.
(b) 0.4, 0.7, 1, 1.6, 2.8, 5.2, 10, 19.6, 38.8, 77.2; does not account for Neptune.
(c) If we assume that 38.8 corresponds to Pluto, the next planet should be at 77.2.

Planet	Distance
Mercury	0.39
Venus	0.72
Earth	1.00
Mars	1.52
Asteroids	2.8
Jupiter	5.20
Saturn	9.54
Uranus	19.2
Neptune	30.1
Pluto	39.5

4. **Calculating π** The quest for an accurate estimation for π is a fascinating story covering thousands of years. Because π is an irrational number, it cannot be represented exactly by a fraction. Its decimal expansion neither repeats nor has a pattern. The ability to compute π was essential to the development of societies because π appears in formulas used in construction, surveying, and geometry. In early historical records, π was given the value of 3. Later the Egyptians used a value of

$$\frac{256}{81} \approx 3.1605.$$

Not until the discovery of series was an exceedingly accurate decimal approximation of π possible. In 1989, π was computed to 1,073,740,000 digits, which required 100 hours of supercomputer time. Why would anyone want to compute π to so many decimal places? One practical reason is to test electrical circuits in new computers. If a computer has a small defect in its hardware, there is a good chance that an error will appear after it has performed trillions of arithmetic calculations during the computation of π. (**Source:** P. Beckmann, *A History of Pi.*) The series given by

$$\frac{\pi^4}{90} \approx \frac{1}{1^4} + \frac{1}{2^4} + \frac{1}{3^4} + \frac{1}{4^4} + \frac{1}{5^4} + \cdots + \frac{1}{n^4}$$

*Answers on page IA-42

can be used to estimate π, where larger values of n give better approximations.

(a) Approximate π by finding the sum of the first four terms.   About 3.138997889

 (b) Use a calculator to approximate π by summing the first 50 terms. Compare the result to the actual value of π.
3.141590776; it is correct to 5 decimal places.

5. *Infinite Series*   The sum S of an infinite geometric series can be found if its common ratio r satisfies $|r| < 1$. It is given by

$$S = \frac{a_1}{1 - r}.$$

If $|r| \geq 1$, this sum does not exist. For example, the infinite geometric series

$$1 + \frac{1}{2} + \frac{1}{4} + \frac{1}{8} + \frac{1}{16} + \cdots$$

has $a_1 = 1$ and $r = \frac{1}{2}$.   Therefore its sum S equals

$$S = \frac{1}{1 - \frac{1}{2}} = 2.$$

You might want to add terms of this series to see how increasing the number of terms results in a number closer to 2. Find the sum of each infinite geometric series.

(a) $2 - 1 + \frac{1}{2} - \frac{1}{4} + \frac{1}{8} - \frac{1}{16} + \cdots$ $\frac{4}{3}$

(b) $1 + \frac{1}{3} + \frac{1}{9} + \frac{1}{27} + \frac{1}{81} + \cdots$ $\frac{3}{2}$

(c) $0.1 + 0.01 + 0.001 + 0.0001 + \cdots$ $0.\overline{1} = \frac{1}{9}$

(d) $0.12 + 0.0012 + 0.000012$
   $+ 0.00000012 + \cdots$ $0.\overline{12} = \frac{4}{33}$

CHAPTERS 1-11 Cumulative Review Exercises

1. State whether the equation illustrates an identity, commutative, associative, or distributive property.
Distributive
$$29(102) = 29(100) + 29(2)$$

2. Identify the domain and range of the relation $S = \{(-6, 5), (-2, 1), (0, 3), (2, 0)\}$. $D = \{-6, -2, 0, 2\}$ $R = \{0, 1, 3, 5\}$

Exercises 3–6: Simplify the expression. Write the result using positive exponents.

3. $\dfrac{x^{-2}y^3}{(3xy^{-2})^3}$ $\dfrac{y^9}{27x^5}$

4. $\left(\dfrac{3b}{6a^2}\right)^{-4}$ $\dfrac{16a^8}{b^4}$

5. $\left(\dfrac{1}{z^2}\right)^{-5}$ z^{10}

6. $\dfrac{8x^{-3}y^2}{4x^3y^{-1}}$ $\dfrac{2y^3}{x^6}$

7. Find the domain of
$$f(x) = \frac{-5}{x - 8}.$$ $D = \{x \mid x \neq 8\}$

8. Use the table to write the formula for $f(x) = ax + b$.

x	-2	-1	0	1	2
$f(x)$	5	3	1	-1	-3

$f(x) = -2x + 1$

9. Write the equation of the horizontal line that passes through the point $(2, 3)$. $y = 3$

10. Find the slope and the y-intercept of the graph of $f(x) = -3x + 5$. $-3; 5$

Exercises 11 and 12: Write the slope-intercept form for a line satisfying the given conditions.

11. Perpendicular to $y = -\frac{2}{3}x - 4$, passing through $(1, 4)$ $y = \frac{3}{2}x + \frac{5}{2}$

12. Parallel to $y = 2x - 7$, passing through $(5, 2)$
   $y = 2x - 8$

Exercises 13–18: Solve the equation or inequality. Write the solutions to inequalities in interval notation.

13. $\frac{2}{5}(x - 4) = -12$ -26

14. $\frac{2}{5}z + \frac{1}{4}z > 2 - (z - 1)$ $\left(\frac{20}{11}, \infty\right)$

15. $-3|t - 5| \leq -18$ $(-\infty, -1] \cup [11, \infty)$

16. $\left|4 + \frac{2}{3}x\right| = 6$ $-15, 3$

17. $\frac{1}{4}t - (2t + 5) + 6 = \frac{t + 3}{4}$ $\frac{1}{8}$

18. $-3 \le \frac{2}{3}x + 5 < 11$ $[-12, 9)$

19. Determine which of the following is a solution to the given system of equations. $(3, -2)$

$$(3, -2), (-1, 3)$$
$$3x + y = 7$$
$$-2x - 3y = 0$$

20. Shade the solution set in the xy-plane.*

$$x - y < 4$$
$$x + 2y \ge 7$$

Exercises 21 and 22: Solve the system of equations. Write the solution as an ordered pair or ordered triple where appropriate.

21. $x - 2y = 1$ **22.** $x + y + z = 5$
$-2x + 7y = 4$ $-2x - y + z = -10$
   $(5, 2)$ $x + 2y + 8z = 1$
                                        $(3, 3, -1)$

23. Maximize the objective function R subject to the given constraints. $R = 22$

$$R = 3x + 8y$$
$$x + 4y \le 10$$
$$4x + y \le 10$$
$$x \ge 0, y \ge 0$$

24. Evaluate det A.   17

$$A = \begin{bmatrix} 4 & -3 \\ 3 & 2 \end{bmatrix}$$

Exercises 25 and 26: Multiply the expressions.

25. $2x^3(4x^4 - 3x^3 + 5)$ **26.** $(2z - 7)(3z + 4)$
   $8x^7 - 6x^6 + 10x^3$ $6z^2 - 13z - 28$

Exercises 27 and 28: Factor completely.

27. $4x^2 - 9y^2$ **28.** $2a^3 - a^2 + 8a - 4$
   $(2x - 3y)(2x + 3y)$ $(a^2 + 4)(2a - 1)$

Exercises 29 and 30: Solve the equation.

29. $4x^2 - x - 3 = 0$ **30.** $x^4 - 10x^3 = -24x^2$
   $-\frac{3}{4}, 1$ $0, 4, 6$

Exercises 31 and 32: Simplify the expression.

31. $\dfrac{x^2 - 7x + 10}{x^2 - 25} \cdot \dfrac{x + 5}{x + 1}$ $\dfrac{x - 2}{x + 1}$

32. $\dfrac{x^2 + 7x + 12}{x^2 - 9} \div \dfrac{x^2 - 5x + 6}{(x - 3)^2}$ $\dfrac{x + 4}{x - 2}$

Exercises 33 and 34: Solve the rational equation. Check your result.

33. $\dfrac{2}{x + 5} = \dfrac{-3}{x^2 - 25} + \dfrac{1}{x - 5}$ 12

34. $\dfrac{2y}{y^2 - 3y + 2} = \dfrac{1}{y - 2} + 2$ $\frac{1}{2}, 3$

35. Solve the equation for W. $W = \dfrac{3C - 5R}{2}$

$$R = \dfrac{3C - 2W}{5}$$

36. Simplify the complex fraction. $\dfrac{1 + 2x}{1 - 4x}$

$$\dfrac{\dfrac{1}{x^2} + \dfrac{2}{x}}{\dfrac{1}{x^2} - \dfrac{4}{x}}$$

Exercises 37 and 38: Simplify the expression. Assume that all variables are positive.

37. $\sqrt[3]{x^4y^4} - 2\sqrt[3]{xy}$ **38.** $(4 + \sqrt{2})(4 - \sqrt{2})$
   $(xy - 2)\sqrt[3]{xy}$ 14

Exercises 39 and 40: Solve. Check your answer.

39. $8(x - 3)^2 = 200$ **40.** $3\sqrt{2x + 6} = 6x$ $\frac{3}{2}$
   $-2, 8$

Exercises 41 and 42: Write the complex expression in standard form.

41. $(-3 + i)(-4 - 2i)$ **42.** $\dfrac{2 - 6i}{1 + 2i}$ $-2 - 2i$
   $14 + 2i$

43. Find the minimum y-value located on the graph of $y = 3x^2 + 8x + 5$. $-\frac{1}{3}$

44. Write the equation $y = 2x^2 + 8x + 17$ in vertex form and identify the vertex.
   $y = 2(x + 2)^2 + 9; (-2, 9)$

Exercises 45 and 46: Solve the quadratic equation using the method of your choice. Write any complex solutions in standard form.

45. $x^2 - 4x + 13 = 0$ $2 \pm 3i$

46. $z^2 - 4z = 32$ $-4, 8$

*Answers on page IA-42

47. A graph of $y = ax^2 + bx + c$ is shown.
 (a) Solve $ax^2 + bx + c = 0$. $-3, 1$
 (b) State whether $a > 0$ or $a < 0$. $a > 0$
 (c) Determine whether the discriminant is positive, negative, or zero. positive

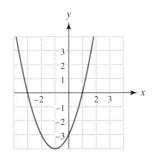

48. Solve the quadratic inequality. Write your answer in interval notation. $(-\infty, \infty)$

$$x^2 + 2x + 3 > 0$$

49. For $f(x) = x^2 + 1$ and $g(x) = 3x - 2$, find the following.
 (a) $(f \circ g)(-2)$ 65
 (b) $(g \circ f)(x)$ $(g \circ f)(x) = 3x^2 + 1$

50. Find $f^{-1}(x)$ for the one-to-one function

$$f(x) = \frac{3x + 1}{2}.$$ $f^{-1}(x) = \frac{2x - 1}{3}$

51. Write the following expression by using sums and differences of logarithms of x and y. $3 \ln x + \frac{1}{2} \ln y$

$$\ln \left(x^3 \sqrt{y} \right)$$

52. Write the following expression as one logarithm. Assume x and y are positive.

$$2 \log x - \log 4xy$$ $\log \frac{x}{4y}$

Exercises 53 and 54: Solve the equation. Approximate answers to the nearest hundredth.

53. $8 \log x + 3 = 17$ **54.** $4^{2x} = 5$ 0.58
56.23
55. Graph the parabola $x = (y - 3)^2 + 1$. Find the vertex and the axis of symmetry.* $(1, 3); y = 3$

56. Find the center and the radius of the circle $x^2 - 6x + y^2 + 2y = -6$. $(3, -1); 2$

Exercises 57 and 58: Graph the ellipse or hyperbola. Label the vertices and the endpoints of the minor axis on the ellipse. Show the asymptotes on the hyperbola.*

57. $\dfrac{x^2}{4} + \dfrac{y^2}{9} = 1$ **58.** $\dfrac{x^2}{16} - \dfrac{y^2}{4} = 1$

Exercises 59 and 60: Use the graph to determine the equation of the ellipse or hyperbola.

59. $\dfrac{y^2}{4} - \dfrac{x^2}{16} = 1$ **60.** $\dfrac{x^2}{16} + \dfrac{y^2}{4} = 1$

59.
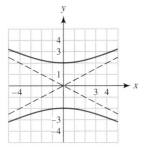

60.
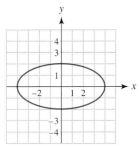

61. Solve the system of nonlinear equations. Check your solutions. $(1, 2), (-1, 2)$

$$y = x^2 + 1$$
$$x^2 + 2y = 5$$

62. Shade the solution set in the xy-plane.*

$$y \geq x^2 - 2$$
$$y \leq -x$$

Exercises 63–66: Determine whether f is an arithmetic or a geometric sequence. If it is arithmetic, find the common difference. If it is geometric, find the common ratio.

63. $f(n) = 5 - 2n$ **64.** $f(n) = 3(0.2)^n$
  Arithmetic; -2 Geometric; 0.2
65. $f(n) = 7(4)^n$ **66.** $f(n) = 6n + 1$
  Geometric; 4 Arithmetic; 6
67. Find the general term a_n for the arithmetic sequence where $a_1 = 2$ and $a_2 = 5$. $a_n = 3n - 1$

68. Find the general term a_n for the geometric sequence where $a_1 = 4$ and $a_2 = 12$. $a_n = 4(3)^{n-1}$

Exercises 69 and 70: Find the sum using a formula.

69. $3 + 7 + 11 + 15 + 19 + \cdots + 35$ 171

70. $1 - 2 + 4 - 8 + 16 - \cdots + 1024$ 683

*Answers on page IA-42

72. $8a^3 - 60a^2b + 150ab^2 - 125b^3$

Exercises 71 and 72: Expand the binomial expression.

71. $(2x + 3)^4$ **72.** $(2a - 5b)^3$

$16x^4 + 96x^3 + 216x^2 + 216x + 81$

APPLICATIONS

73. *Radius of a Circle* If a circle has an area of A square units, its radius r is given by $r = \sqrt{\frac{A}{\pi}}$. Find the radius of a circle with an area of 14 square inches. Approximate this radius to the nearest hundredth of an inch. $\sqrt{\frac{14}{\pi}} \approx 2.11$ in.

74. *Distance from Work* Starting at a warehouse, a delivery truck driver travels down a straight highway for 3 hours at 40 miles per hour, stops and unloads the truck for 1 hour, and then returns to the warehouse at 60 miles per hour. Sketch a graph that shows the distance between the truck and the warehouse over this period of time.*

75. *Exercise and Fluid Consumption* When a person exercises, the total amount of fluid he or she will need that day increases depending on the person's weight and the duration of the exercise. To determine the number of ounces of fluid needed, divide the person's weight by 2 and then add 0.4 ounces for every minute of exercise. (*Source: Runner's World.*)

(a) Write a function that gives the fluid requirements for a person weighing 170 pounds who exercises for x minutes a day.

(b) If an athlete who exercises for 90 minutes requires 130 ounces of fluid, determine the athlete's weight.

(a) $f(x) = 0.4x + 85$

(b) 188 lb

76. *Airplane Speed* An airplane travels 1080 miles into the wind in 3 hours. The return trip with the wind takes 2.7 hours. Find the average speed of the airplane and the average wind speed.

Airplane: 380 mph, wind: 20 mph

77. *Size of a Tent* The length of a rectangular tent floor is 6 feet shorter than twice the width. If the area of the tent floor is 108 square feet, what are the dimensions of the tent?   9 by 12 ft

78. *Working Together* Suppose that one person can weed a garden in 60 minutes and a second person can weed the same garden in 90 minutes. How long would it take these two people to weed the garden if they worked together?   36 min

79. *Numbers* The product of two positive numbers is 96. If the larger number is subtracted from 3 times the smaller number, the result is 12. Let x be the smaller number and let y be the larger number.

(a) Write a system of equations for this situation.

(b) What are the two numbers?   8 and 12

(a) $xy = 96$; $3x - y = 12$

80. *Marching Band* A band is marching in a triangular formation so that 1 person is in the first row, 3 people are in the second row, 5 people are in the third row, and so on. Use a formula to find the total number of musicians in the marching band if the last row contains 23 people.   144

*Answers on page IA-42

Appendix

Using the Graphing Calculator

OVERVIEW OF THE APPENDIX

The intent of this appendix is to provide instruction for the TI-83, TI-83 Plus, and TI-84 Plus graphing calculators that may be used in conjunction with this textbook. It includes specific keystrokes needed to work several examples from the text. Students are also advised to consult the *Graphing Calculator Guidebook* provided by the manufacturer.

ENTERING MATHEMATICAL EXPRESSIONS

EVALUATING π: To evaluate π use the following keystrokes, as shown in the first and second lines of Figure A.1. (Do *not* use 3.14 or $\frac{22}{7}$ for π.)

$$\boxed{\text{2nd}}\ \boxed{\wedge[\pi]}\ \boxed{\text{ENTER}}$$

```
π
          3.141592654
√(200)
          14.14213562
10^4
                  10000
```
Figure A.1

EVALUATING A SQUARE ROOT: To evaluate a square root, such as $\sqrt{200}$, use the following keystrokes, as shown in the third and fourth lines of Figure A.1.

$$\boxed{\text{2nd}}\ \boxed{x^2[\sqrt{\ }\ ]}\ \boxed{2}\ \boxed{0}\ \boxed{0}\ \boxed{)}\ \boxed{\text{ENTER}}$$

EVALUATING AN EXPONENTIAL EXPRESSION: To evaluate an exponential expression, such as 10^4, use the following keystrokes, as shown in the last two lines of Figure A.1.

$$\boxed{1}\ \boxed{0}\ \boxed{\wedge}\ \boxed{4}\ \boxed{\text{ENTER}}$$

EVALUATING A CUBE ROOT: To evaluate a cube root, such as $\sqrt[3]{64}$, use the following keystrokes, as shown in the first and second lines of Figure A.2.

$$\boxed{\text{MATH}}\ \boxed{4}\ \boxed{6}\ \boxed{4}\ \boxed{)}\ \boxed{\text{ENTER}}$$

```
³√(64)
                      4
5ˣ√23
          1.872171231
```
Figure A.2

EVALUATING OTHER ROOTS: To evaluate a fifth root, such as $\sqrt[5]{23}$, use the following keystrokes, as shown in the third and fourth lines of Figure A.2.

$$\boxed{5}\ \boxed{\text{MATH}}\ \boxed{5}\ \boxed{2}\ \boxed{3}\ \boxed{\text{ENTER}}$$

EVALUATING THE NATURAL EXPONENTIAL FUNCTION: To evaluate $14e^{0.0153(8)}$, use the following keystrokes, as shown in the first and second lines of Figure A.3.

$$\boxed{1}\ \boxed{4}\ \boxed{\text{2nd}}\ \boxed{\text{LN }[e^x]}\ \boxed{.}\ \boxed{0}\ \boxed{1}\ \boxed{5}\ \boxed{3}\ \boxed{\times}\ \boxed{8}\ \boxed{)}\ \boxed{\text{ENTER}}$$

```
14e^(.0153*8)
          15.82288531
log(100)
                      2
ln(10)
          2.302585093
```
Figure A.3

EVALUATING THE COMMON LOGARITHMIC FUNCTION: To evaluate $\log(100)$, use the following keystrokes, as shown in the third and fourth lines of Figure A.3.

$$\boxed{\text{LOG}}\ \boxed{1}\ \boxed{0}\ \boxed{0}\ \boxed{)}\ \boxed{\text{ENTER}}$$

EVALUATING THE NATURAL LOGARITHMIC FUNCTION: To evaluate $\ln(10)$, use the following keystrokes, as shown in the last two lines of Figure A.3.

$$\boxed{\text{LN}}\ \boxed{1}\ \boxed{0}\ \boxed{)}\ \boxed{\text{ENTER}}$$

SUMMARY: ENTERING MATHEMATICAL EXPRESSIONS

To access the *number* π, use [2nd] [^[π]].

To evaluate a *square root*, use [2nd] [x²[√]].

To evaluate an *exponential expression*, use the [^] key. To square a number, the [x²] key can also be used.

To evaluate a *cube root*, use [MATH] [4].

To evaluate a *kth root*, use [k] [MATH] [5].

To access the *natural exponential function*, use [2nd] [LN [eˣ]].

To access the *common logarithmic function*, use [LOG].

To access the *natural logarithmic function*, use [LN].

EXPRESSING ANSWERS AS FRACTIONS

To evaluate $\frac{1}{3} + \frac{2}{5} - \frac{4}{9}$ in fraction form, use the following keystrokes, as shown in the last three lines of Figure 1.7 on page 17.

[(] [1] [÷] [3] [)] [+] [(] [2] [÷] [5] [)] [−] [(] [4] [÷] [9] [)] [MATH] [1] [ENTER]

SUMMARY: EXPRESSING ANSWERS AS FRACTIONS

Enter the arithmetic expression. To access the "Frac" feature, use the keystrokes [MATH] [1]. Then press [ENTER].

DISPLAYING NUMBERS IN SCIENTIFIC NOTATION

```
Normal  Sci  Eng
Float      0123456789
Radian     Degree
Func Par Pol Seq
Connected  Dot
Sequential    Simul
Real   a+bi  re^θi
Full    Horiz  G-T
```

Figure A.4

To display numbers in scientific notation, set the graphing calculator in scientific mode (Sci), by using the following keystrokes. See Figure A.4. (These keystrokes assume that the calculator is in normal mode.)

[MODE] [▷] [ENTER] [2nd] [MODE [QUIT]]

In scientific mode we can display the numbers 5432 and 0.00001234 in scientific notation, as shown in Figure A.5.

```
5432
           5.432E3
.00001234
           1.234E-5
```

Figure A.5

SUMMARY: SETTING SCIENTIFIC MODE

If your calculator is in normal mode, it can be set in scientific mode by pressing

[MODE] [▷] [ENTER] [2nd] [MODE [QUIT]].

These keystrokes return the graphing calculator to the home screen.

Entering Numbers in Scientific Notation

Numbers can be entered in scientific notation. For example, to enter 4.2×10^{-3} in scientific notation, use the following keystrokes. (Be sure to use the negation key $(-)$ rather than the subtraction key.)

[4] [.] [2] [2nd] [,[EE]] [(−)] [3]

This number can also be entered using the following keystrokes. See Figure A.6.

[4] [.] [2] [×] [1] [0] [^] [(] [(−)] [3] [)]

```
4.2E-3
                .0042
4.2*10^(-3)
                .0042
```

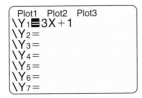

Figure A.6

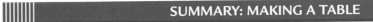

SUMMARY: ENTERING NUMBERS IN SCIENTIFIC NOTATION

One way to enter a number in scientific notation is to use the keystrokes

[2nd] [,[EE]]

to access an exponent (EE) of 10.

Making a Table

To make a table of values for $y = 3x + 1$ starting at $x = 4$ and incrementing by 2, begin by pressing [Y =] and then entering the formula $Y_1 = 3X + 1$, as shown in Figure A.7. To set the table parameters, press the following keys. See Figure A.8.

[2nd] [WINDOW [TBLSET]] [4] [ENTER] [2]

```
Plot1  Plot2  Plot3
\Y1■3X+1
\Y2=
\Y3=
\Y4=
\Y5=
\Y6=
\Y7=
```

Figure A.7

These keystrokes specify a table that starts at $x = 4$ and increments the x-values by 2. Therefore, the values of Y_1 at $x = 4, 6, 8, \ldots$ appear in the table. To create this table, press the following keys.

[2nd] [GRAPH [TABLE]]

```
TABLE SETUP
 TblStart=4
 ΔTbl=2
Indpnt:  Auto  Ask
Depend:  Auto  Ask
```

Figure A.8

We can scroll through x- and y-values by using the arrow keys. See Figure A.9. Note that there is no first or last x-value in the table.

X	Y1
4	13
6	19
8	25
10	31
12	37
14	43
16	49

Y1■3X+1

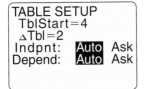

Figure A.9

SUMMARY: MAKING A TABLE

1. Enter the formula for the equation using [Y =].
2. Press [2nd] [WINDOW [TBLSET]] to set the starting x-value and the increment between x-values appearing in the table.
3. Create the table by pressing [2nd] [GRAPH [TABLE]].

SETTING THE VIEWING RECTANGLE (WINDOW)

```
ZOOM MEMORY
1:ZBox
2:Zoom In
3:Zoom Out
4:ZDecimal
5:ZSquare
6:ZStandard
7↓ZTrig
```
Figure A.10

There are at least two ways to set the standard viewing rectangle of $[-10, 10, 1]$ by $[-10, 10, 1]$. The first involves pressing (ZOOM) followed by (6). See Figure A.10. The second method for setting the standard viewing rectangle is to press (WINDOW), and enter the following keystrokes. See Figure A.11.

(−) 1 0 ENTER 1 0 ENTER 1 ENTER

(−) 1 0 ENTER 1 0 ENTER 1 ENTER

```
WINDOW
 Xmin=-10
 Xmax=10
 Xscl=1
 Ymin=-10
 Ymax=10
 Yscl=1
 Xres=1
```
Figure A.11

(Be sure to use the negation key (−) rather than the subtraction key.) Other viewing rectangles can be set in a similar manner by pressing (WINDOW) and entering the appropriate values. To see the viewing rectangle, press (GRAPH). An example is shown in Figure 1.32 on page 57.

| ‖‖‖‖ | SUMMARY: SETTING THE VIEWING RECTANGLE |

To set the standard viewing rectangle, press (ZOOM)(6). To set any viewing rectangle, press (WINDOW) and enter the necessary values. To see the viewing rectangle, press (GRAPH).

Note: You do not need to change "Xres" from 1.

MAKING A SCATTERPLOT OR A LINE GRAPH

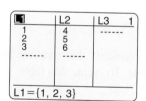

Figure A.12

To make a scatterplot with the points $(-5, -5)$, $(-2, 3)$, $(1, -7)$, and $(4, 8)$ begin by following these steps.

1. Press (STAT) followed by (1).

2. If list L1 is not empty, use the arrow keys to place the cursor on L1, as shown in Figure A.12. Then press (CLEAR) followed by (ENTER). This deletes all elements in the list. Similarly, if L2 is not empty, clear the list.

3. Input each x-value into list L1 followed by (ENTER). Input each y-value into list L2 followed by (ENTER). See Figure A.13.

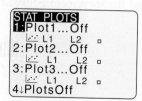

Figure A.13

It is essential that both lists have the same number of values—otherwise an error message appears when a scatterplot is attempted. Before these four points can be plotted, "STAT-PLOT" must be turned on. It is accessed by pressing

(2nd)(Y = [STAT PLOT]),

as shown in Figure A.14.

```
STAT PLOTS
1:Plot1...Off
   ⋯ L1   L2   □
2:Plot2...Off
   ⋯ L1   L2   □
3:Plot3...Off
   ⋯ L1   L2   □
4↓PlotsOff
```
Figure A.14

There are three possible "STATPLOTS", numbered 1, 2, and 3. Any one of the three can be selected. The first plot can be selected by pressing (1). Next, place the cursor over "On" and press (ENTER) to turn "Plot1" on. There are six types of plots that can be selected. The first type is a *scatterplot* and the second type is a *line graph*, so place the cursor over the first type of plot and press (ENTER) to select a scatterplot. (To make the line graph, place the cursor over the second type of plot and press (ENTER).) The x-values are stored in list L1, so select L1 for "Xlist" by pressing (2nd)(1). Similarly, press (2nd)(2) for the "Ylist," since the y-values are stored in list L2. Finally, there are three styles of marks that can be used to show data points in the graph. We will usually use the first, because it is largest and shows

Figure A.15

$[-10, 10, 1]$ by $[-10, 10, 1]$

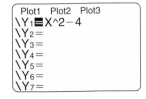

Figure A.16

up the best. Make the screen appear as in Figure A.15. Before plotting the four data points, be sure to set an appropriate viewing rectangle. Then press (GRAPH). The data points appear as in Figure A.16.

Remark 1: A fast way to set the viewing rectangle for any scatterplot is to select the "ZOOMSTAT" feature by pressing (ZOOM)(9). This feature automatically scales the viewing rectangle so that all data points are shown.

Remark 2: If an equation has been entered into the (Y =) menu and selected, it will be graphed with the data. This feature is used frequently to model data.

||||||| SUMMARY: MAKING A SCATTERPLOT OR A LINE GRAPH

The following are basic steps necessary to make either a scatterplot or a line graph.

1. Use (STAT)(1) to access lists L1 and L2.
2. If list L1 is not empty, place the cursor on L1 and press (CLEAR)(ENTER). Repeat for list L2, if it is not empty.
3. Enter the x-values into list L1 and the y-values into list L2.
4. Use (2nd)(Y = [STAT PLOT]) to select appropriate parameters for the scatterplot or line graph.
5. Set an appropriate viewing rectangle. Press (GRAPH). Otherwise, press (ZOOM)(9). This feature automatically sets the viewing rectangle and plots the data.

Note: (ZOOM)(9) *cannot* be used to set a viewing rectangle for the graph of a function.

|||||||

ENTERING A FORMULA

Figure A.17

To enter a formula, press (Y =). For example, use the following keystrokes after "$Y_1 = $" to enter $y = x^2 - 4$. See Figure A.17.

(Y =)(CLEAR)(X, T, θ, n)(^)(2)(−)(4)

Note that there is a built-in key to enter the variable X. If "$Y_1 = $" does not appear after pressing (Y =), press (MODE) and make sure the calculator is set in *function mode,* denoted "Func". See Figure A.18.

||||||| SUMMARY: ENTERING A FORMULA

To enter a formula, press (Y =). To delete an existing formula, press (CLEAR).

|||||||

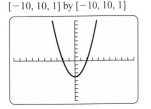

Figure A.18

$[-10, 10, 1]$ by $[-10, 10, 1]$

Figure A.19

GRAPHING A FUNCTION

To graph a function, such as $y = x^2 - 4$, start by pressing (Y =) and enter $Y_1 = X^2 - 4$. If there is an equation already entered, remove it by pressing (CLEAR). The equals signs in "$Y_1 = $" should be in reverse video (a dark rectangle surrounding a white equals sign), which indicates that the equation will be graphed. If the equals sign is not in reverse video, place the cursor over it and press (ENTER). Set an appropriate viewing rectangle and then press (GRAPH). The graph of f will appear in the specified viewing rectangle. See Figures A.17 and A.19.

SUMMARY: GRAPHING A FUNCTION

1. Use the Y = menu to enter the formula for the function.
2. Use the WINDOW menu to set an appropriate viewing rectangle.
3. Press GRAPH.

GRAPHING A VERTICAL LINE

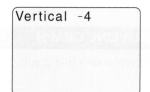

Vertical -4

Figure A.20

[−6, 6, 1] by [−6, 6, 1]

Figure A.21

Set an appropriate window (or viewing rectangle). Then return to the home screen by pressing

2nd MODE [QUIT].

To graph a vertical line, such as $x = -4$, press

2nd PRGM [DRAW] 4 (−) 4.

See Figure A.20. Pressing ENTER will make the vertical line appear, as shown in Figure A.21.

SUMMARY: GRAPHING THE VERTICAL LINE $x = h$

1. Set an appropriate window by pressing WINDOW.
2. Return to the home screen by pressing 2nd MODE [QUIT].
3. Draw a vertical line by pressing 2nd PRGM [DRAW] 4 *h* ENTER.

SQUARING A VIEWING RECTANGLE

ZOOM MEMORY
1:ZBox
2:Zoom In
3:Zoom Out
4:ZDecimal
5:ZSquare
6:ZStandard
7↓ZTrig

Figure A.22

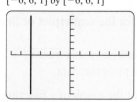

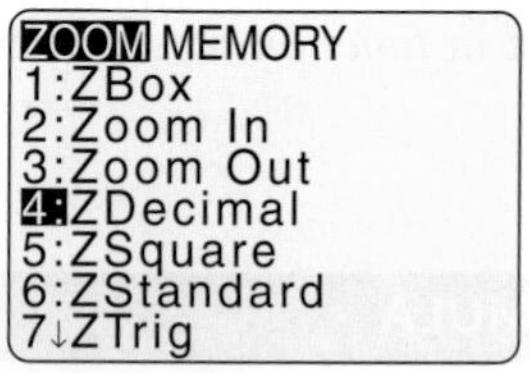

In a square viewing rectangle the graph of $y = x$ is a line that makes a 45° angle with the positive x-axis, a circle appears circular, and all sides of a square have the same length. An approximate square viewing rectangle can be set if the distance along the x-axis is 1.5 times the distance along the y-axis. Examples of viewing rectangles that are (approximately) square include

$$[-6, 6, 1] \text{ by } [-4, 4, 1] \quad \text{and} \quad [-9, 9, 1] \text{ by } [-6, 6, 1].$$

Square viewing rectangles can be set automatically by pressing either

ZOOM 4 or ZOOM 5.

ZOOM 4 provides a *decimal window*, which is discussed later. See Figure A.22.

SUMMARY: SQUARING A VIEWING RECTANGLE

Either ZOOM 4 or ZOOM 5 may be used to produce a square viewing rectangle. An (approximately) square viewing rectangle has the form

$$[-1.5k, 1.5k, 1] \text{ by } [-k, k, 1],$$

where k is a positive number.

LOCATING A POINT OF INTERSECTION

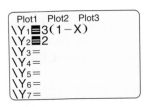

Figure A.23

In Example 7, Section 3.1 on page 151, we find the point of intersection for two lines. To find the point of intersection for the graphs of

$$y_1 = 3(1 - x) \quad \text{and} \quad y_2 = 2,$$

start by entering Y_1 and Y_2, as shown in Figure A.23. Set the window, and graph both equations. Then press the following keys to find the intersection point.

(2nd) (TRACE [CALC]) (5)

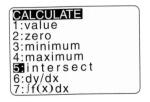

Figure A.24

See Figure A.24, where the "intersect" utility is being selected. The calculator prompts for the first curve, as shown in Figure A.25. Use the arrow keys to locate the cursor near the point of intersection and press (ENTER). Repeat these steps for the second curve. Finally we are prompted for a guess. For each of the three prompts, place the free-moving cursor near the point of intersection and press (ENTER). The approximate coordinates of the point of intersection are shown in Figure 3.5 on page 151.

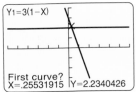

Figure A.25

SUMMARY: FINDING A POINT OF INTERSECTION

1. Graph the two equations in an appropriate viewing rectangle.
2. Press (2nd) (TRACE [CALC]) (5).
3. Use the arrow keys to select an approximate location for the point of intersection. Press (ENTER) to make the three selections for "First curve?", "Second curve?", and "Guess?". (Note that if the cursor is near the point of intersection, you usually do not need to move the cursor for each selection. Just press (ENTER) three times.)

ACCESSING THE ABSOLUTE VALUE

Figure A.26

In Example 8, Section 3.5 on page 197, the absolute value is used to graph $y_1 = |x - 50|$. To graph y_1, begin by entering $Y_1 = \text{abs}(X - 50)$. The absolute value (abs) is accessed by pressing

(MATH) (▷) (1).

See Figure A.26.

SUMMARY: ACCESSING THE ABSOLUTE VALUE

1. Press (MATH).
2. Position the cursor over "NUM".
3. Press (1) to select the absolute value.

SHADING A SYSTEM OF INEQUALITIES

In Example 6, Section 4.3 on page 247, we are asked to shade the solution set for the system of linear inequalities $2x + y \le 5$, $-2x + y \ge 1$. Begin by solving each inequality for y to obtain $y \le 5 - 2x$ and $y \ge 2x + 1$. Then let $Y_1 = 5 - 2X$ and $Y_2 = 2X + 1$, as shown in

Figure 4.18(b). Position the cursor to the left of Y_1, and press (ENTER) three times. The triangle that appears indicates that the calculator will shade the region below the graph of Y_1. Next locate the cursor to the left of Y_2 and press (ENTER) twice. This triangle indicates that the calculator will shade the region above the graph of Y_2. After setting the viewing rectangle to $[-15, 15, 5]$ by $[-10, 10, 5]$ press (GRAPH). The result is shown in Figure 4.18(c).

||||||| **SUMMARY: SHADING A SYSTEM OF INEQUALITIES**

1. Solve each inequality for y.
2. Enter each formula as Y_1 and Y_2 in the (Y =) menu.
3. Locate the cursor to the left of Y_1 and press (ENTER) two or three times, to shade either above or below the graph of Y_1. Repeat for Y_2.
4. Set an appropriate viewing rectangle.
5. Press (GRAPH).

Note: The "Shade" utility in the DRAW menu can also be used to shade the region *between* two graphs.

|||||||

ENTERING THE ELEMENTS OF A MATRIX

In Example 6(b), Section 4.6 on page 276, the elements of a matrix are entered. The augmented matrix A is given by

$$A = \begin{bmatrix} 1 & 1 & 2 & | & 1 \\ -1 & 0 & 1 & | & -2 \\ 2 & 1 & 5 & | & -1 \end{bmatrix}.$$

Use the following keystrokes on the TI-83 Plus or TI-84 Plus to define a matrix A with dimension 3×4. (*Note:* On the TI-83 the matrix menu is found by pressing (MATRIX).)

(2nd) (x^{-1} [MATRIX]) (▷) (▷) (1) (3) (ENTER) (4) (ENTER)

See Figure 4.25(a).

Then input the 12 elements of the matrix A, row by row. Finish each entry by pressing (ENTER). After these elements have been entered, press

(2nd) (MODE [QUIT])

to return to the home screen. To display the matrix A, press

(2nd) (x^{-1} [MATRIX]) (1) (ENTER).

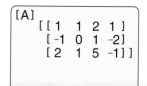

Figure A.27

See Figure A.27.

||||||| **SUMMARY: ENTERING THE ELEMENTS OF A MATRIX A**

1. Begin by accessing the matrix A by pressing (2nd) (x^{-1} [MATRIX]) (▷) (▷) (1).
2. Enter the dimension of A by pressing (m) (ENTER) (n) (ENTER), where the dimension of the matrix is $m \times n$.
3. Input each element of the matrix, row by row. Finish each entry by pressing (ENTER). Use (2nd) (MODE [QUIT]) to return to the home screen.

Note: On the TI-83, replace the keystrokes (2nd) (x^{-1} [MATRIX]) with (MATRIX).

|||||||

REDUCED ROW-ECHELON FORM

In Example 6(b), Section 4.6 on page 276, the reduced row-echelon form of a matrix is found. To find this reduced row-echelon form, use the following keystrokes from the home screen on the TI-83 Plus or TI-84 Plus.

$$\boxed{\text{2nd}}\ \boxed{x^{-1}\ [\text{MATRIX}]}\ \boxed{\triangleright}\ \boxed{\text{ALPHA}}\ \boxed{\text{APPS [B]}}\ \boxed{\text{2nd}}\ \boxed{x^{-1}\ [\text{MATRIX}]}\ \boxed{1}\ \boxed{)}\ \boxed{\text{ENTER}}$$

The resulting matrix is shown in Figure 4.25(b). On the TI-83 graphing calculator use the following keystrokes to find the reduced row-echelon form.

$$\boxed{\text{MATRIX}}\ \boxed{\triangleright}\ \boxed{\text{ALPHA}}\ \boxed{\text{MATRIX [B]}}\ \boxed{\text{MATRIX}}\ \boxed{1}\ \boxed{)}\ \boxed{\text{ENTER}}$$

▌▌▌▌▌ SUMMARY: FINDING REDUCED ROW-ECHELON FORM OF A MATRIX

1. To make rref([A]) appear on the home screen, use the following keystrokes for the TI-83 Plus or TI-84 Plus graphing calculator.

$$\boxed{\text{2nd}}\ \boxed{x^{-1}\ [\text{MATRIX}]}\ \boxed{\triangleright}\ \boxed{\text{ALPHA}}\ \boxed{\text{APPS [B]}}\ \boxed{\text{2nd}}\ \boxed{x^{-1}\ [\text{MATRIX}]}\ \boxed{1}\ \boxed{)}$$

2. Press $\boxed{\text{ENTER}}$ to calculate the reduced row-echelon form.
3. Use arrow keys to access elements that do not appear on the screen.

Note: On the TI-83, replace the keystrokes $\boxed{\text{2nd}}\boxed{x^{-1}[\text{MATRIX}]}$ with $\boxed{\text{MATRIX}}$ and $\boxed{\text{APPS [B]}}$ with $\boxed{\text{MATRIX [B]}}$.   ▌▌▌▌▌▌▌

EVALUATING A DETERMINANT

In Example 3(a), Section 4.7 on page 283, a graphing calculator is used to evaluate a determinant of a matrix. Start by entering the 9 elements of the 3×3 matrix A, as shown in Figure 4.27(a). To compute det A, perform the following keystrokes from the home screen.

$$\boxed{\text{2nd}}\ \boxed{x^{-1}\ [\text{MATRIX}]}\ \boxed{\triangleright}\ \boxed{1}\ \boxed{\text{2nd}}\ \boxed{x^{-1}\ [\text{MATRIX}]}\ \boxed{1}\ \boxed{)}\ \boxed{\text{ENTER}}$$

The results are shown in the last two lines of Figure 4.27(b).

▌▌▌▌▌ SUMMARY: EVALUATING A DETERMINANT OF A MATRIX

1. Enter the dimension and elements of the matrix A.
2. Return to the home screen by pressing

$$\boxed{\text{2nd}}\ \boxed{\text{MODE [QUIT]}}.$$

3. On the TI-83 Plus or TI-84 Plus, perform the following keystrokes.

$$\boxed{\text{2nd}}\ \boxed{x^{-1}\ [\text{MATRIX}]}\ \boxed{\triangleright}\ \boxed{1}\ \boxed{\text{2nd}}\ \boxed{x^{-1}\ [\text{MATRIX}]}\ \boxed{1}\ \boxed{)}\ \boxed{\text{ENTER}}$$

Note: On the TI-83, replace the keystrokes $\boxed{\text{2nd}}\ \boxed{x^{-1}[\text{MATRIX}]}$ with $\boxed{\text{MATRIX}}$.   ▌▌▌▌▌▌▌

LOCATING AN X-INTERCEPT OR ZERO

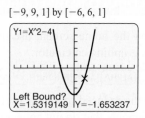

Figure A.28

In Section 5.3 on page 330, we locate an x-intercept or *zero* of $f(x) = x^2 - 4$. Start by entering $Y_1 = X^2 - 4$ into the $\boxed{Y =}$ menu. Set the viewing rectangle to $[-9, 9, 1]$ by $[-6, 6, 1]$ and graph Y_1. Afterwards, press the following keys to invoke the zero finder. See Figure A.28.

$$\boxed{\text{2nd}}\ \boxed{\text{TRACE [CALC]}}\ \boxed{2}$$

The graphing calculator prompts for a left bound. Use the arrow keys to set the cursor to the left of the x-intercept and press $\boxed{\text{ENTER}}$. The graphing calculator then prompts for a right bound. Set the cursor to the right of the x-intercept and press $\boxed{\text{ENTER}}$. Finally the graphing calculator prompts for a guess. Set the cursor roughly at the x-intercept and press $\boxed{\text{ENTER}}$. See Figures A.29–A.31. The calculator then approximates the x-intercept or zero automatically, as shown in the Technology Note on page 330. The zero of -2 can be found similarly.

$[-9, 9, 1]$ by $[-6, 6, 1]$

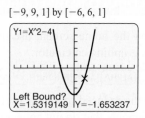

Figure A.29

$[-9, 9, 1]$ by $[-6, 6, 1]$

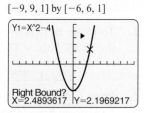

Figure A.30

$[-9, 9, 1]$ by $[-6, 6, 1]$

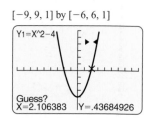

Figure A.31

SUMMARY: LOCATING AN x-INTERCEPT OR ZERO

1. Graph the function in an appropriate viewing rectangle.
2. Press $\boxed{\text{2nd}}\ \boxed{\text{TRACE [CALC]}}\ \boxed{2}$.
3. Select the left and right bounds, followed by a guess. Press $\boxed{\text{ENTER}}$ after each selection. The calculator then approximates the x-intercept or zero.

SETTING CONNECTED AND DOT MODE

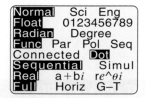

Figure A.32

To set your graphing calculator in dot mode, press $\boxed{\text{MODE}}$, position the cursor over "Dot", and press $\boxed{\text{ENTER}}$. See Figure A.32. Graphs will now appear in dot mode rather than connected mode.

SUMMARY: SETTING CONNECTED OR DOT MODE

1. Press $\boxed{\text{MODE}}$.
2. Position the cursor over "Connected" or "Dot". Press $\boxed{\text{ENTER}}$.

SETTING A DECIMAL WINDOW

With a decimal window, the cursor stops on convenient x-values. In the decimal window $[-9.4, 9.4, 1]$ by $[-6.2, 6.2, 1]$ the cursor stops on x-values that are multiples of 0.2. If we reduce the viewing rectangle to $[-4.7, 4.7, 1]$ by $[-3.1, 3.1, 1]$, the cursor stops on x-values

Figure A.33

that are multiples of 0.1. To set this smaller window automatically, press (ZOOM)(4). See Figure A.33. Decimal windows are also useful when graphing rational functions with asymptotes in connected mode.

SUMMARY: SETTING A DECIMAL WINDOW

1. Press (ZOOM)(4) to set the viewing rectangle $[-4.7, 4.7, 1]$ by $[-3.1, 3.1, 1]$.
2. A larger decimal window is $[-9.4, 9.4, 1]$ by $[-6.2, 6.2, 1]$.

SETTING $a + bi$ MODE

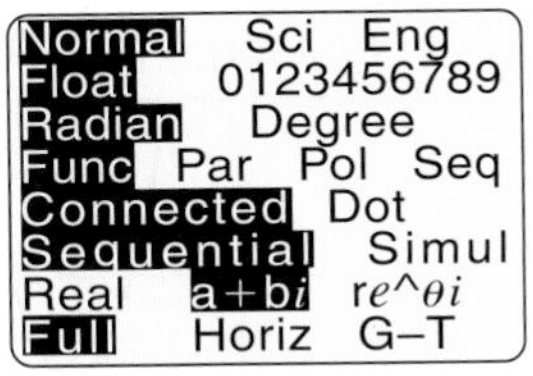

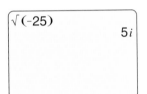

Figure A.34

In Example 1, Section 7.6 on page 514, the expression $\sqrt{-25}$ is evaluated. To evaluate expressions containing square roots of negative numbers, set your calculator in $a + bi$ mode by using the following keystrokes.

(MODE)(▽)(▽)(▽)(▽)(▽)(▽)(▷)(ENTER)(2nd)(MODE [QUIT])

See Figures A.34 and A.35.

SUMMARY: SETTING $a + bi$ MODE

1. Press (MODE).
2. Move the cursor to the seventh line and highlight $a + bi$.
3. Press (2nd)(MODE [QUIT]) and return to the home screen.

$\sqrt{(-25)}$

$5i$

Figure A.35

EVALUATING COMPLEX ARITHMETIC

Complex arithmetic can be performed much like other arithmetic expressions. This is done by entering

(2nd)(. [i])

to obtain the imaginary unit i from the home screen. For example, to find the sum $(-2 + 3i) + (4 - 6i)$, perform the following keystrokes on the home screen.

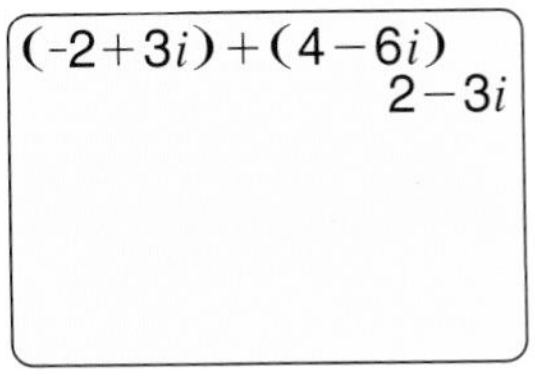

$(-2+3i)+(4-6i)$

$2-3i$

Figure A.36

(()((-))(2)(+)(3)(2nd)(. [i])( ))(+)(( )(4)(-)(6)(2nd)(. [i])( ))(ENTER)

The result is shown in Figure A.36. Other complex arithmetic operations are done similarly.

SUMMARY: EVALUATING COMPLEX ARITHMETIC

Enter a complex expression in the same way as you would any arithmetic expression. To obtain the complex number i, use (2nd)(. [i]).

FINDING MAXIMUM AND MINIMUM VALUES

Figure A.37

To find a minimum y-value y (or vertex) on the graph of $f(x) = 1.5x^2 - 6x + 4$, start by entering $Y_1 = 1.5X^2 - 6X + 4$ from the (Y=) menu. Set the viewing rectangle and then perform the following keystrokes to find the minimum y-value.

$$\boxed{\text{2nd}}\ \boxed{\text{TRACE [CALC]}}\ \boxed{3}$$

See Figure A.37.

The calculator prompts for a left bound. Use the arrow keys to position the cursor left of the vertex and press (ENTER). Similarly, position the cursor to the right of the vertex for the right bound and press (ENTER). Finally, the graphing calculator asks for a guess between the left and right bounds. Place the cursor near the vertex and press (ENTER). See Figures A.38–A.40. The minimum value is shown in Figure A.41.

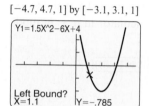

Figure A.38

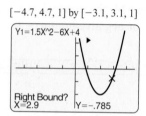

Figure A.39

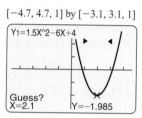

Figure A.40

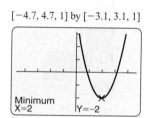

Figure A.41

A maximum of the function f on an interval can be found in a similar manner, except enter

$$\boxed{\text{2nd}}\ \boxed{\text{TRACE [CALC]}}\ \boxed{4}\ .$$

The calculator prompts for left and right bounds, followed by a guess. Press (ENTER) after the cursor has been located appropriately for each prompt. The graphing calculator will display the maximum y-value. For example, see the Technology Note on page 536.

SUMMARY: FINDING MAXIMUM AND MINIMUM VALUES

1. Graph the function in an appropriate viewing rectangle.
2. Press (2nd) (TRACE [CALC]) (3) to find a minimum y-value.
3. Press (2nd) (TRACE [CALC]) (4) to find a maximum y-value.
4. Use the arrow keys to locate the left and right x-bounds, followed by a guess. Press (ENTER) to select each position of the cursor.

CHAPTER 1: REAL NUMBERS AND ALGEBRA

Section 1.1

19. Natural: 6; Whole: 6; Integer: -5, 6;

Rational: $-5, 6, \dfrac{1}{7}, 0.2$; Irrational: $\sqrt{7}$

20. Natural: $\sqrt{9}$; Whole: $\sqrt{9}$; Integer: -3, $\sqrt{9}$;

Rational: $-3, \dfrac{2}{9}, \sqrt{9}, -1.37$; Irrational: none

21. Natural: $\dfrac{3}{1}$; Whole: $\dfrac{3}{1}$; Integer: $\dfrac{3}{1}$;

Rational: $\dfrac{3}{1}, -\dfrac{5}{8}, \sqrt{9}, 0.\overline{45}$; Irrational: $\sqrt{5}$, π

22. Natural: $\dfrac{50}{10}$; Whole: $0, \dfrac{50}{10}$; Integer: $0, \dfrac{50}{10}$;

Rational: $0, \dfrac{50}{10}, -\dfrac{23}{27}, 0.\overline{6}$; Irrational: $-\sqrt{3}$

23. Natural: $\sqrt{9}$; Whole: $\sqrt{9}$; Integer: -2, $\sqrt{9}$;

Rational: $-2, \dfrac{1}{2}, \sqrt{9}, 0.\overline{26}$; Irrational: none

24. Natural: $\sqrt{4}, \dfrac{4}{2}$; Whole: $\sqrt{4}, \dfrac{4}{2}$; Integer: $\sqrt{4}, \dfrac{4}{2}$;

Rational: $\sqrt{4}, \dfrac{4}{2}, 0.26$; Irrational: $\sqrt{6}$

Section 1.2

9. ![number line −5 to 5 with points]

10. ![number line −25 to 25]

11. ![number line −500 to 500]

12. ![number line −0.5 to 0.5]

13. ![number line −5 to 5]

14. ![number line −5 to 5]

Section 1.3

139.

Country	1996	2025
China	1.2551×10^{9}	1.48×10^{9}
Germany	8.24×10^{7}	8.09×10^{7}
India	9.758×10^{8}	1.3302×10^{9}
Mexico	9.58×10^{7}	1.302×10^{8}
U.S.	2.65×10^{8}	3.325×10^{8}

Section 1.4

54.

Speed (mph)	10	20	30	40	50	60	70
Braking Distance (ft)	8.3	33.3	75	133.3	208.3	300	408.3

Checking Basic Concepts 1.3 & 1.4

5.

People	10	20	30	40
Ventilation (ft³/hr)	9000	18,000	27,000	36,000

Section 1.5

3.

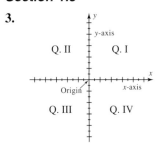

4. Scatterplot   Line Graph

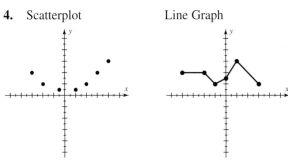

11. $S = \{(1, 3), (3, 7), (5, 11), (7, 15), (9, 19)\}$
$D = \{1, 3, 5, 7, 9\}; R = \{3, 7, 11, 15, 19\}$

12. $S = \{(-2.1, 9.6), (-1.5, 7.4), (0.7, 3.3),$
$(1.3, -2.0), (2.9, -8.8)\}$
$D = \{-2.1, -1.5, 0.7, 1.3, 2.9\}$
$R = \{-8.8, -2.0, 3.3, 7.4, 9.6\}$

13. $S = \{(1996, 5.5), (1997, 4.9), (1998, 4.5),$
$(1999, 4.2), (2000, 4.0), (2001, 4.2)\}$
$D = \{1996, 1997, 1998, 1999, 2000, 2001\}$
$R = \{4.0, 4.2, 4.5, 4.9, 5.5\}$

14. $S = \{(1800, 5), (1840, 17), (1880, 50), (1920, 106),$
$(1960, 179), (2000, 281)\}$
$D = \{1800, 1840, 1880, 1920, 1960, 2000\}$
$R = \{5, 17, 50, 106, 179, 281\}$

15. $S = \{(-3, 2), (-2, 1), (2, -3), (3, 3)\}$
$D = \{-3, -2, 2, 3\}; R = \{-3, 1, 2, 3\}$

16. $S = \{(-3, -3), (-2, 1), (0, 2), (3, 0)\}$
$D = \{-3, -2, 0, 3\}; R = \{-3, 0, 1, 2\}$

17. $S = \{(-4, 4), (-3, 2), (-2, 0), (0, -3), (2, 4), (4, 4)\}$
$D = \{-4, -3, -2, 0, 2, 4\}; R = \{-3, 0, 2, 4\}$

18. $S = \{(-8, -8), (-8, 4), (-4, 8), (4, -4), (4, 4), (8, 8)\}$
$D = \{-8, -4, 4, 8\}; R = \{-8, -4, 4, 8\}$

19. $S = \{(1970, 29), (1980, 41), (1990, 79), (2000, 64)\}$
$D = \{1970, 1980, 1990, 2000\}; R = \{29, 41, 64, 79\}$

20. $S = \{(1950, 485), (1960, 375), (1970, 150),$
$(1980, 95), (1990, 70)\}$
$D = \{1950, 1960, 1970, 1980, 1990\}$
$R = \{70, 95, 150, 375, 485\}$

21. (1, 2): QI
(−3, 0): *x*-axis
(0, −2): *y*-axis
(−1, 3): QII

22. (2, 6): QI
(−4, −4): QIII
(−2, 0): *x*-axis
(0, −5): *y*-axis

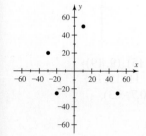

23. (10, 50): QI
(−30, 20): QII
(−20, −25): QIII
(50, −25): QIV

24. (0.2, 3): QI
(0.4, 1): QI
(0.6, −1): QIV
(0.8, −3): QIV

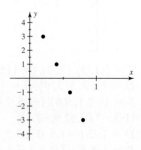

25. (0, 0), (1, 4), (2, 8), (3, 12)
26. (0, 5), (1, 8), (2, 11), (3, 14)
27. (0, 4), (1, 3), (2, 0), (3, −5)
28. (0, 0), (1, 3), (2, 12), (3, 27)
29. $(0, 1), \left(1, \dfrac{1}{2}\right), \left(2, \dfrac{1}{5}\right), \left(3, \dfrac{1}{10}\right)$
30. $\left(0, \dfrac{2}{5}\right), \left(1, \dfrac{1}{2}\right), \left(2, \dfrac{2}{3}\right), (3, 1)$

31. (a) $D = \{-3, -2, 0, 1\}$
$R = \{-4, -3, 0, 2, 4\}$
(b) Xmin: −3, Xmax: 1
Ymin: −4, Ymax: 4
(d)

32. (a) $D = \{-4, 0, 1, 3, 5\}$
$R = \{-4, -2, 0, 1, 3\}$
(b) Xmin: −4, Xmax: 5
Ymin: −4, Ymax: 3
(d)

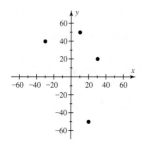

33. (a) $D = \{-30, 10, 20, 30\}; R = \{-50, 20, 40, 50\}$
(b) Xmin: −30, Xmax: 30, Ymin: −50, Ymax: 50
(d)

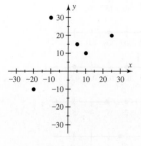

34. (a) $D = \{-20, -10, 5, 10, 25\}; R = \{-10, 10, 15, 20, 30\}$
(b) Xmin: −20, Xmax: 25, Ymin: −10, Ymax: 30
(d)

35.

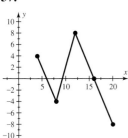

36.

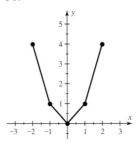

37.

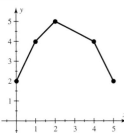

38.

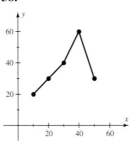

39.

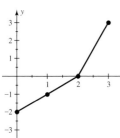

40.

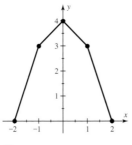

41.

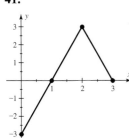

42.

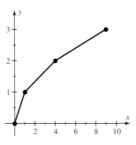

43. $(-2, -6)$, $(-1, -3)$, $(0, 0)$, $(1, 3)$, $(2, 6)$

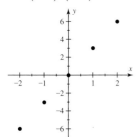

44. $(-2, 4)$, $(-1, 2)$, $(0, 0)$, $(1, -2)$, $(2, -4)$

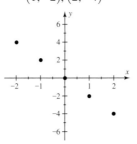

45. $(-2, 4)$, $(-1, 3)$, $(0, 2)$, $(1, 1)$, $(2, 0)$

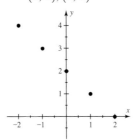

46. $(-2, 0)$, $(-1, 2)$, $(0, 4)$, $(1, 6)$, $(2, 8)$

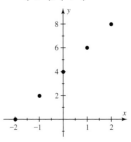

47. $(-2, 3)$, $(-1, 0)$, $(0, -1)$, $(1, 0)$, $(2, 3)$

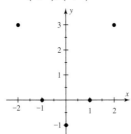

48. $(-2, 2)$, $(-1, 0.5)$, $(0, 0)$, $(1, 0.5)$, $(2, 2)$

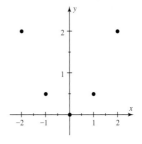

49. $[-10, 10, 1]$ by $[-10, 10, 1]$

50. $[-12, 12, 2]$ by $[-8, 8, 2]$

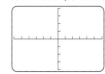

51. $[0, 100, 10]$ by $[-50, 50, 10]$

52. $[-30, 30, 5]$ by $[-20, 20, 5]$

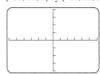

53. $[1980, 1995, 1]$ by $[12000, 16000, 1000]$

54. $[1900, 1990, 10]$ by $[1700, 2800, 100]$

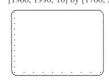

59. $[-6, 6, 1]$ by $[-6, 6, 1]$

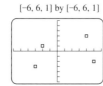

60. $[-6, 6, 1]$ by $[-10, 10, 1]$

61. [−30, 30, 5] by [−50, 50, 5]

62. [−20, 20, 2] by [−20, 20, 2]

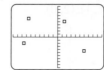

63. [−200, 200, 50] by [−250, 250, 50]

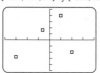

64. [−200, 200, 50] by [−100, 100, 25]

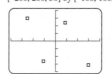

65. (a)

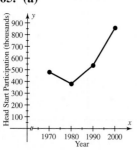

(b) Head Start participation decreased then increased.

66. (a)

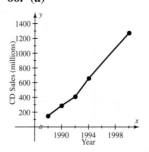

(b) CD Sales increased.

67. (a)

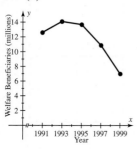

(b) The number of welfare beneficiaries increased, then decreased.

68. (a)

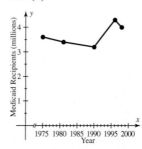

(b) The number of medicaid recipients decreased, then increased, and then decreased again.

69. (a)

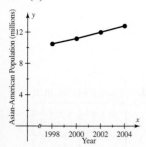

(b) Asian-American population increased.

70. (a)

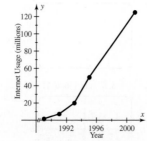

(b) Internet usage increased dramatically.

Checking Basic Concepts 1.5

2. $(1, 4)$: QI; $(0, -3)$: y-axis; $(2, -2)$: QIV; $(-2, 3)$: QII

3. $(-2, -2), (-1, 1), (0, 2),$ $(1, 1), (2, -2)$

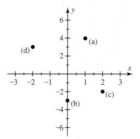

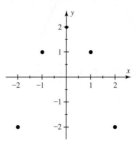

4.

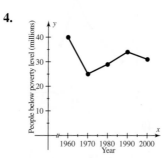

The number of people below the poverty level decreased, started to increase, and then decreased again.

Chapter 1 Review Exercises

1. Natural: 9; Whole: 9; Integer: −2, 9;

Rational: $-2, 9, \dfrac{2}{5}, 2.68$; Irrational: $\sqrt{11}, \pi$

2. Natural: $\dfrac{6}{2}$; Whole: $\dfrac{6}{2}, \dfrac{0}{4}$; Integer: $\dfrac{6}{2}, \dfrac{0}{4}$;

Rational: $\dfrac{6}{2}, -\dfrac{2}{7}, 0.\overline{3}, \dfrac{0}{4}$; Irrational: $\sqrt{6}$

21.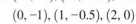

77. $(-2, 6), (-1, 3), (0, 0),$ $(1, -3), (2, -6)$

78. $(-2, -2), (-1, -1.5),$ $(0, -1), (1, -0.5), (2, 0)$

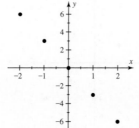

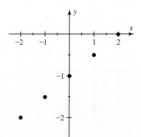

79. $(-2, 4), (-1, 1), (0, 0),$
$(1, 1), (2, 4)$

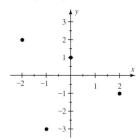

80. $(-2, 1), (-1, 2.5), (0, 5),$
$(1, 2.5), (2, 1)$

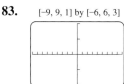

81. $(-2, 2)$: QII
$(-1, -3)$: QIII
$(0, 1)$: y-axis
$(2, -1)$: QIV

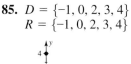

82. $(-15, -5)$: QIII
$(-5, 0)$: x-axis
$(10, 20)$: QI
$(20, -10)$: QIV

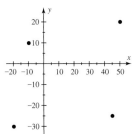

83. $[-9, 9, 1]$ by $[-6, 6, 3]$

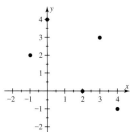

84. $[-20, 20, 5]$ by $[-12, 12, 4]$

85. $D = \{-1, 0, 2, 3, 4\}$
$R = \{-1, 0, 2, 3, 4\}$

86. $D = \{-20, -10, 45, 50\}$
$R = \{-30, -25, 10, 20\}$

92.

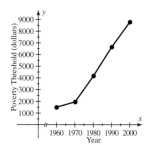

The poverty threshold has increased.

Chapter 1 Test

4.

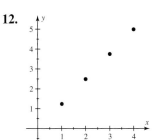

12.

13. $[-20, 20, 5]$ by $[-5, 40, 5]$

Chapter 1 Extended and Discovery Exercises

2. (a)

The injury rate has decreased.

CHAPTER 2: LINEAR FUNCTIONS AND MODELS

Section 2.1

31.

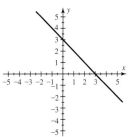

32.

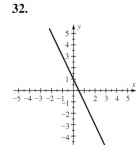

33.

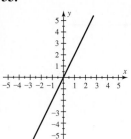

34.

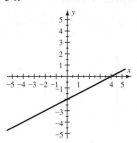

35.

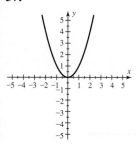

36.

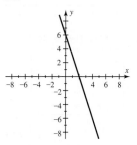

37.

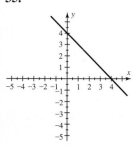

38.

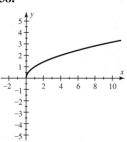

39.

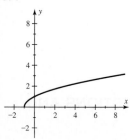

40.

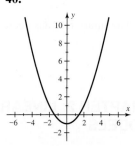

51.

x	−3	−2	−1	0	1	2	3
y = f(x)	2	3	4	5	6	7	8

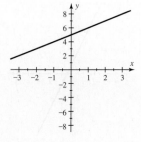

52.

x	−3	−2	−1	0	1	2	3
y = f(x)	9	4	1	0	1	4	9

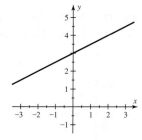

53.

x	−3	−2	−1	0	1	2	3
y = f(x)	−17	−12	−7	−2	3	8	13

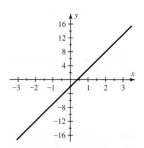

54.

x	−3	−2	−1	0	1	2	3
y = f(x)	1.5	2	2.5	3	3.5	4	4.5

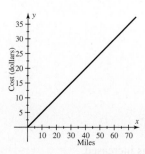

59.

Miles	10	20	30	40	50	60	70
Cost	$5	$10	$15	$20	$25	$30	$35

60.

Income	$1000	$2000	$3000	$4000	$5000	$6000	$7000
Tax	$150	$300	$450	$600	$750	$900	$1050

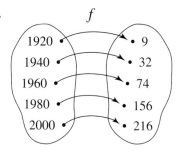

88.

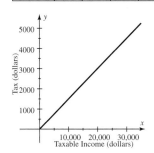

Section 2.2

47.

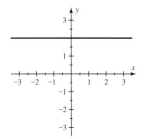

48.

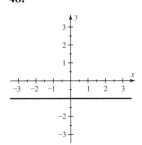

49.

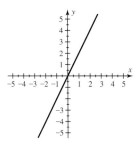

50.

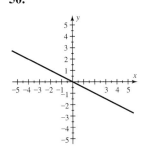

51.

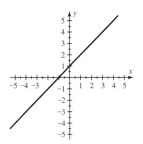

52.

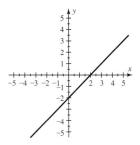

53.

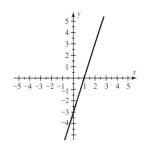

54.

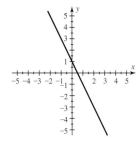

55.

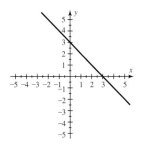

56.

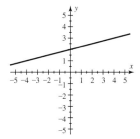

67. (a)

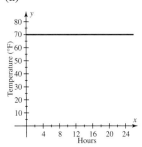

(b)

Hours	0	4	8	12	16	20	24
Temp. (°F)	70	70	70	70	70	70	70

68. (a)

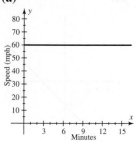

(b)

Minutes (x)	0	1	2	3	4	5	6
Speed (f)	60	60	60	60	60	60	60

70. (a)

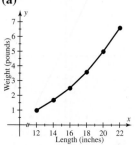

73. (a) [1820, 1995, 20] by [0, 40, 10]

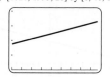

(b)

Year (x)	1820	1840	1860	1880	1900	1920	1940
Median Age	16.7	18.5	20.3	22.1	23.9	25.7	27.5

80. (a) $N(0) = 333,200$; There were 333,200 private sector doctors in 1970.
$N(30) = 791,000$; There were 791,000 private sector doctors in 2000.

(b) 15,260 represents the increase in number of private sector doctors each year.
333,200 represents the initial number of private sector doctors in 1970.

Checking Basic Concepts 2.1 & 2.2

1.

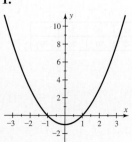

4.

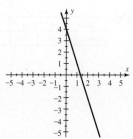

6. (a) 32.98; In 1990 the median age was about 33 years.
(b) 0.264: The median age is increasing by 0.264 years each year.
27.7: In 1970 the median age was 27.7 years.

Section 2.3

21.

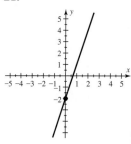

22.

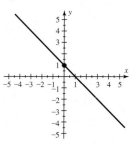

23.

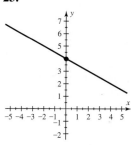

24.

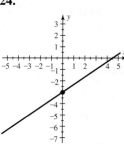

25.

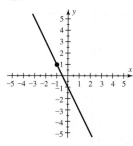

26.

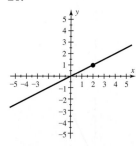

27.

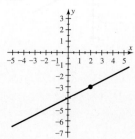

28.

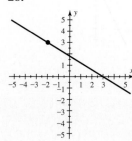

29. (b)

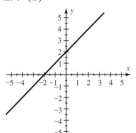

30. (b)

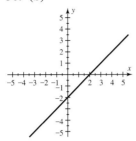

31. (b)

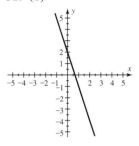

32. (b)

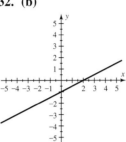

33. (b)

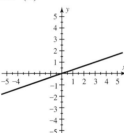

34. (b)

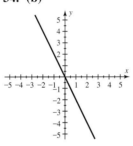

35. (b)

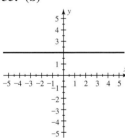

36. (b)

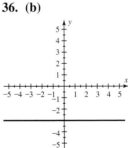

37. (b)

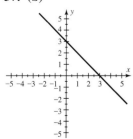

38. (b)

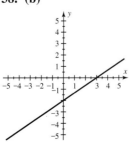

61. (a) $m_1 = 50$, $m_2 = 0$, $m_3 = 150$

(b) m_1: The pump added water at the rate of 50 gallons per hour.

m_2: The pump neither added nor removed water.

m_3: The pump added water at the rate of 150 gallons per hour.

(c) Initially the pool contained 100 gallons of water. The pump added 200 gallons of water over the first 4 hours at a rate of 50 gallons per hour. Then the pump was turned off for 2 hours. Finally, the pump added 300 gallons of water over the last 2 hours at a rate of 150 gallons per hour.

62. (a) $m_1 = 125$, $m_2 = 0$, $m_3 = -125$

(b) m_1: The pump added water at the rate of 125 gallons per hour.

m_2: The pump neither added nor removed water.

m_3: The pump removed water at the rate of 125 gallons per hour.

(c) Initially the pool is empty. The pump added 500 gallons of water over the first 4 hours at a rate of 125 gallons per hour. Then the pump was turned off for 4 hours. Finally, the pump removed 500 gallons of water over the last 4 hours at a rate of 125 gallons per hour so that the pool was empty.

63. (a) $m_1 = 100$, $m_2 = 25$, $m_3 = -100$

(b) m_1: The pump added water at the rate of 100 gallons per hour.

m_2: The pump added water at the rate of 25 gallons per hour.

m_3: The pump removed water at the rate of 100 gallons per hour.

(c) Initially the pool contained 100 gallons of water. The pump added 200 gallons of water over the first 2 hours at a rate of 100 gallons per hour. Then the pump added 100 gallons of water over the next 4 hours at a rate of 25 gallons per hour. Finally, the pump removed 200 gallons of water over the last 2 hours at a rate of 100 gallons per hour.

64. (a) $m_1 = -100$, $m_2 = -50$, $m_3 = -25$

(b) m_1: The pump removed water at the rate of 100 gallons per hour.

m_2: The pump removed water at the rate of 50 gallons per hour.

m_3: The pump removed water at the rate of 25 gallons per hour.

(c) Initially the pool contained 500 gallons of water. The pump removed 200 gallons of water over the first 2 hours at a rate of 100 gallons per hour. Then the pump removed 100 gallons of water over the next 2 hours at a rate of 50 gallons per hour. Finally, the pump removed 50 gallons of water over the last 2 hours at a rate of 25 gallons per hour.

65. (a) $m_1 = 50$, $m_2 = 0$, $m_3 = -20$, $m_4 = 0$

(b) m_1: The driver is traveling away from home at a rate of 50 miles per hour.

m_2: The car is not moving.

m_3: The driver is traveling toward home at a rate of 20 miles per hour.

m_4: The car is not moving.

(c) The car started at home and moved away from home at 50 mph for 1 hour to a location 50 miles from home. The car was then parked for 1 hour. Next the car moved toward home at 20 mph for 2 hours to a location 10 miles from home. Finally, the car was parked for 1 hour.

66. (a) $m_1 = 50$, $m_2 = -50$, $m_3 = 50$

(b) m_1: The driver is traveling away from home at a rate of 50 miles per hour.

m_2: The driver is traveling toward home at a rate of 50 miles per hour.

m_3: The driver is traveling away from home at a rate of 50 miles per hour.

(c) The car started at home and moved away from home at 50 mph for 1 hour to a location 50 miles from home. The car then returned home in 1 hour at 50 mph. Finally, the car moved away from home at 50 mph for 2 hours to a location 100 miles from home.

67. (a) $m_1 = -50$, $m_2 = 0$, $m_3 = -50$

(b) m_1: The driver is traveling toward home at a rate of 50 miles per hour.

m_2: The car is not moving.

m_3: The driver is traveling toward home at a rate of 50 miles per hour.

(c) The car started 300 miles from home and moved toward home at 50 mph for 2 hours to a location 200 miles from home. The car was then parked for 1 hour. Finally, the car moved toward home at 50 mph for 4 hours at which point it was home.

68. (a) $m_1 = -50$, $m_2 = 0$, $m_3 = 50$, $m_4 = 0$

(b) m_1: The driver is traveling toward home at a rate of 50 miles per hour.

m_2: The car is not moving.

m_3: The driver is traveling away from home at a rate of 50 miles per hour.

m_4: The car is not moving.

(c) The car started 100 miles from home and went home at 50 mph for 2 hours. The car was then parked for 1 hour. Next the car moved away from home at 50 mph for 1 hour to a location 50 miles from home. Finally, the car was parked for 2 hours.

69.

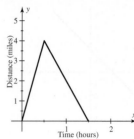

70.

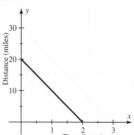

71.

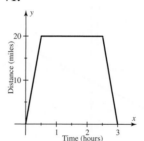

72.

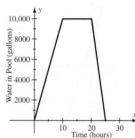

73. (b)

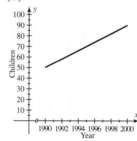

75. (b) -416; The number of federally insured banks decreased by 416 each year.

(c) $13,723$; Initially, there were 13,723 federally insured banks in 1987.

76. (b) 0.581; The population density increased by 0.581 per year.

(c) 21.5; Initially, the population density was 21.5 people per square mile in 1900.

81. (b)

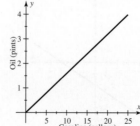

82. (b)

Group Activity After Section 2.3

(a)
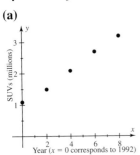

Section 2.4

53. (b)
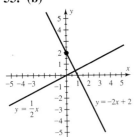

54. (b)
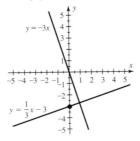

55. (b)
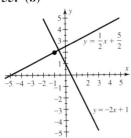

56. (b)
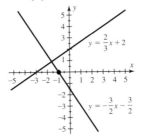

57. (b)
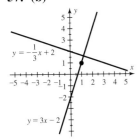

58. (b)
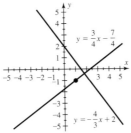

95. (b)
[1988, 1995, 1] by [600, 1200, 100]
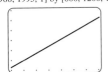

96. (b)
[1960, 1995, 5] by [60, 220, 20]
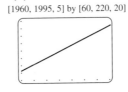

97. (a)
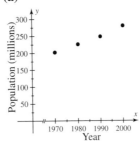

Chapter 2 Review Exercises

9.
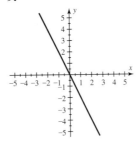

10.
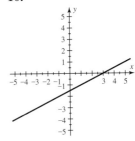

11.
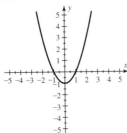

12.
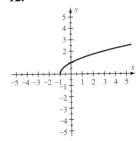

16.

x	−3	−2	−1	0	1	2	3
$y = f(x)$	−11	−8	−5	−2	1	4	7

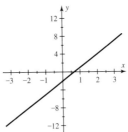

37.

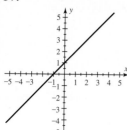

38.

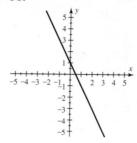

39.

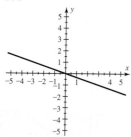

40.

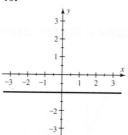

49.

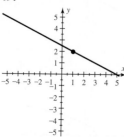

50.

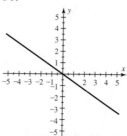

54. (a) $m_1 = 250$, $m_2 = 500$, $m_3 = 0$, $m_4 = -750$

 (b) m_1: Water is being added to the pool at a rate of 250 gallons per hour.

 m_2: Water is being added to the pool at a rate of 500 gallons per hour.

 m_3: No water is being added or removed.

 m_4: Water is being removed from the pool at a rate of 750 gallons per hour.

 (c) Initially the pool contains 500 gallons of water. For the first 2 hours water is added to the pool at a rate of 250 gallons per hour until there are 1000 gallons in the pool. Then water is added at a rate of 500 gallons per hour for 1 hour until there are 1500 gallons in the pool. For the next hour, no water is added or removed. Finally, water is removed from the pool at a rate of 750 gallons per hour for 1 hour until it contains 750 gallons.

55.

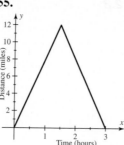

56. (b)

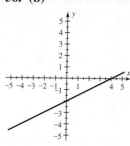

71. (a) $m_1 = 1.3$, $m_2 = 2.35$, $m_3 = 2.4$, $m_4 = 2.7$

 (b) m_1: From 1920 to 1940 the population increased on average by 1.3 million per year. The other slopes may be interpreted similarly.

72. For the first 2 minutes the inlet pipe is open. For the next 3 minutes both pipes are open. For the next 2 minutes only the outlet pipe is open. Finally, for the last 3 minutes both pipes are closed.

73. (b) [1885, 1965, 10] by [22, 26, 1]

76. (a)

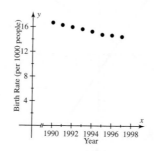

77. (a) 113; In 1995 there were 113 unhealthy days.

 (b) $D = \{1995, 1996, 1997, 1998, 1999\}$

 $R = \{27, 56, 60, 94, 113\}$

78. (a)

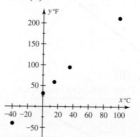

79.

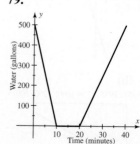

Chapter 2 Test

2. **(a)**

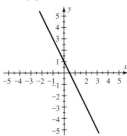

(b)

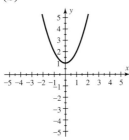

4.

x	−3	−2	−1	0	1	2	3
$y = f(x)$	4	−1	−4	−5	−4	−1	4

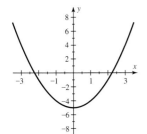

13.

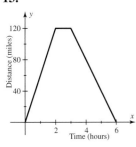

14. **(a)**

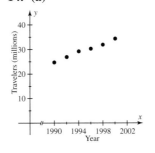

Chapter 2 Extended and Discovery Exercises

1. **(a)**

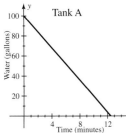

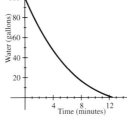

The graph for tank A is linear because the pump takes out water at a constant rate. The graph for tank B is nonlinear because the rate at which water flows out of the tank varies.

2. **(a)**

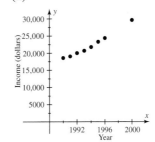

4. $y_1 = x, y_2 = x + 2$
$y_3 = -x, y_4 = -x + 4$

5. $y_1 = 1, y_2 = 5$
$x_1 = 1, x_2 = 5$

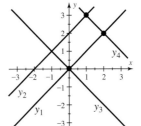

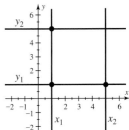

6. $y_1 = x - 4, y_2 = x + 4$
$y_3 = -x - 4, y_4 = -x + 4$

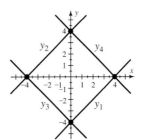

7. **(a)**

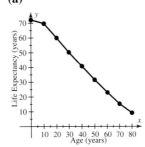

(b) $m_1 = -0.24, m_2 = -0.98, m_3 = -0.97,$
$m_4 = -0.95, m_5 = -0.93, m_6 = -0.85,$
$m_7 = -0.76, m_8 = -0.63$
Each slope represents the decrease in remaining life expectancy for each year a person lives.

CHAPTER 3: LINEAR EQUATIONS AND INEQUALITIES

Group Activity After Section 3.1

(a)

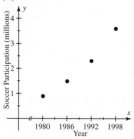

Section 3.3

80. (a) [1984, 1991, 1] by [0, 350, 50]

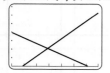

Section 3.4

33.

34.

35.

36.

37.

38.

39.

40.

97. (a)

x	4	5	6	7	8	9	10
$f(x) = 70x + 50$	330	400	470	540	610	680	750

Section 3.5

98. (a)

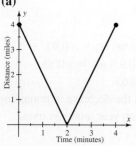

Chapter 3 Review

41.

42.

43.

44.

Chapter 3 Test

8.

Chapter 3 Extended and Discovery Exercises

3.   (a)   **(d)**

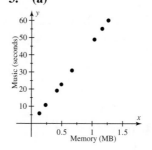 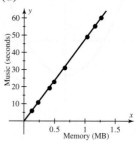

4.   (b)

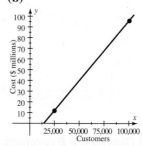

Chapters 1–3 Cumulative Review Exercises

7.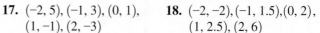

17. $(-2, 5), (-1, 3), (0, 1),$
$(1, -1), (2, -3)$

18. $(-2, -2), (-1, 1.5), (0, 2),$
$(1, 2.5), (2, 6)$

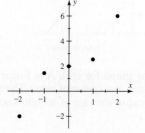

19.

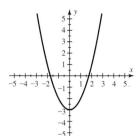

26.

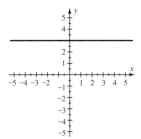

9.

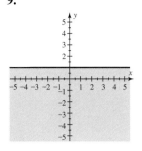

10.

29.

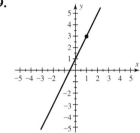

11.

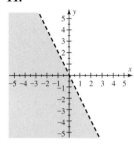

12.

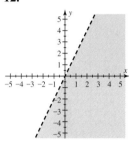

43.

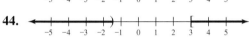

44.

54.

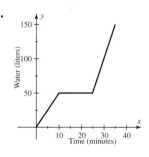

13.

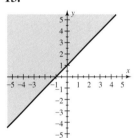

14.

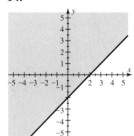

CHAPTER 4: SYSTEMS OF LINEAR EQUATIONS

Section 4.3

7.

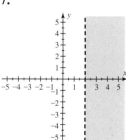

8.

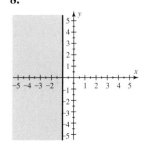

15.

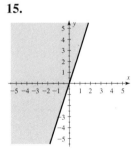

16.

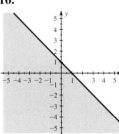

17.

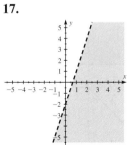

18.

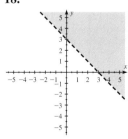

19.

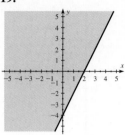

20.

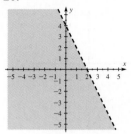

29.

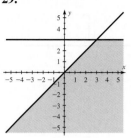

30.

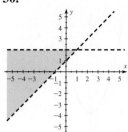

21.

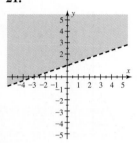

22.

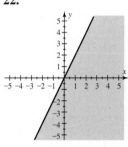

31.

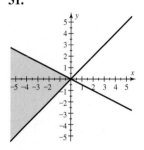

32.

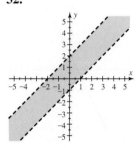

23.

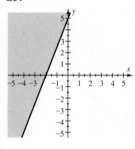

24.

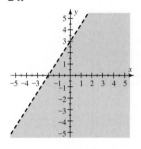

33.

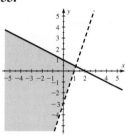

34.

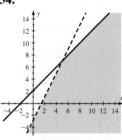

25.

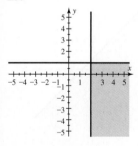

26.

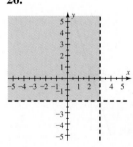

35.

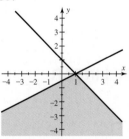

36.

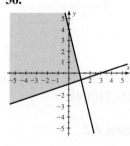

27.

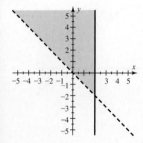

28.

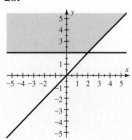

37.

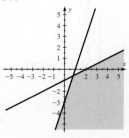

38.

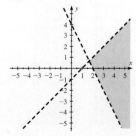

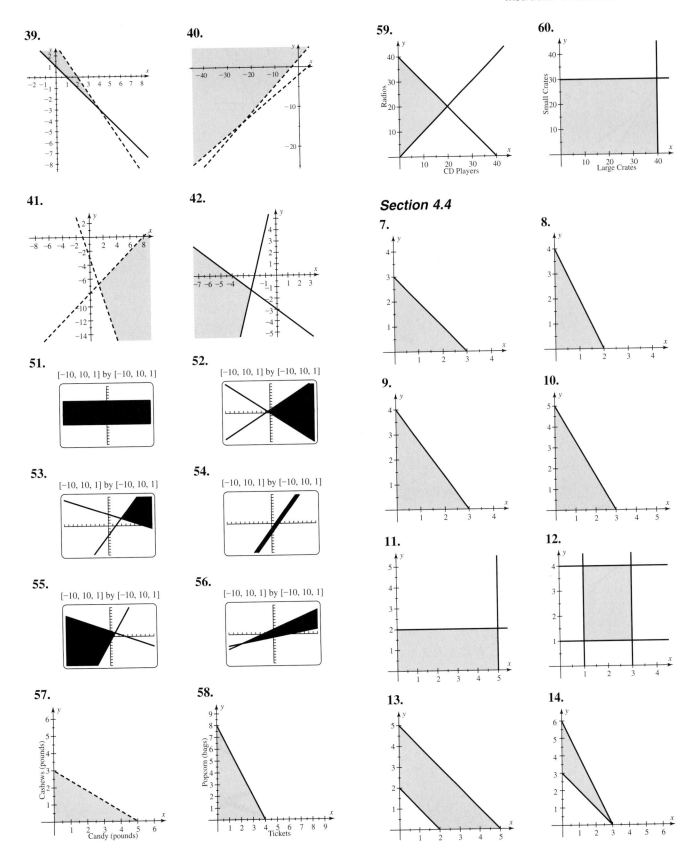

39.

40.

41.

42.

51. [−10, 10, 1] by [−10, 10, 1]

52. [−10, 10, 1] by [−10, 10, 1]

53. [−10, 10, 1] by [−10, 10, 1]

54. [−10, 10, 1] by [−10, 10, 1]

55. [−10, 10, 1] by [−10, 10, 1]

56. [−10, 10, 1] by [−10, 10, 1]

57.

58.

59.

60.

Section 4.4

7.

8.

9.

10.

11.

12.

13.

14.

15.
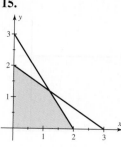

16.
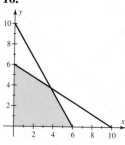

23.
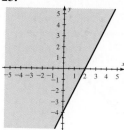

24.
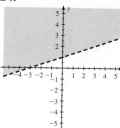

17.
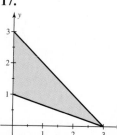

18.
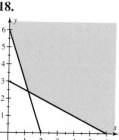

25.
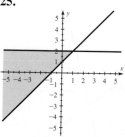

26.
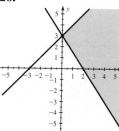

19.
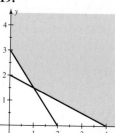

20.
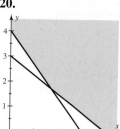

27.
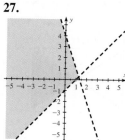

28.
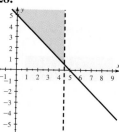

Checking Basic Concepts 4.3 & 4.4

2.
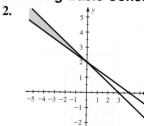

Chapter 4 Test

5.
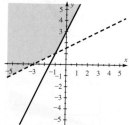

Chapter 4 Review Exercises

21.
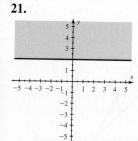

22.
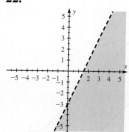

Chapter 4 Extended and Discovery Exercises

15.
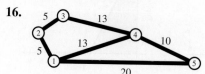

16.
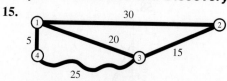

CHAPTER 5: POLYNOMIAL EXPRESSIONS AND FUNCTIONS

Section 5.1

107.

t	3	4	5	6	7	8	9
$y = f(t)$	126.875	110	96.875	87.5	81.875	80	81.875

Group Activity After Section 5.1

(b)

Checking Basic Concepts 5.1 & 5.2

6.

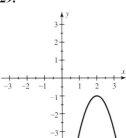

Section 5.3

93. (c)

t	3	4	5	6	7	8
$y = h(t)$	240	256	240	192	112	0

97. (a)

t	20	30	40	50	60	70	80
$y = f(t)$	4520	10,080	17,840	27,800	39,960	54,320	70,880

Section 5.6

29.   **30.**

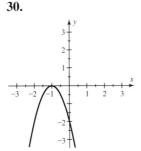

31.

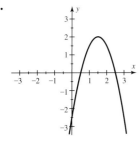

73. (a)

x	0	300	600	900	1200	1500
$y = E(x)$	500	428	392	392	428	500

74. (a) $[-10, 170, 10]$ by $[0, 55, 5]$

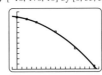

Chapter 5 Review Exercises

101. (c)

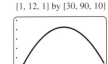

(table for 101(c))

X	Y₁
0	25.2
1	26.659
2	27.996
3	29.211
4	30.304
5	31.275
6	32.124

X=2

103. (b)

X	Y₁
1	27.784
2	43.636
3	56.556
4	66.544
5	73.6
6	77.724
7	78.916

X=7

(c)

$[1, 12, 1]$ by $[30, 90, 10]$

106.

(area model: 2 | 2x | 14, x | x² | 7x, bottom x | 7)

Chapter 5 Extended and Discovery Exercises

1.   (a) The population of lynx oscillated during the recorded time period at nearly 10-year intervals. **(b)** The population of snowshoe hares oscillated during the recorded time period at nearly 10-year intervals. **(c)** As the number of snowshoe hares increased, the lynx would have more plentiful prey and hence the lynx population would begin to increase. As the lynx population increased, the snowshoe hares would be killed in increasing numbers causing their population to decrease. With a limited number of snowshoe hares available for food, the lynx population would decline. Now with fewer predators, the snowshoe hare population could begin to rise again. This cycle repeated itself three times during the recorded time period.

2. **(a)** The number of adult flies oscillated during the recorded time period at fairly regular intervals. **(b)** The number of eggs oscillated during the recorded time period at roughly the same intervals as the adult flies. **(c)** The peaks of the graph of the adult flies correspond to the low points on the graph of the eggs. **(d)** When the population of adult flies became large, fewer eggs were laid because there was not enough liver. Fewer eggs meant fewer adults. When there were fewer adults, there was plenty of liver and a lot of eggs were laid. Numerous flies hatched and the adult population grew dramatically. This process repeats itself.

3. **(a)**   **(b)**

[0, 10, 1] by [0, 30, 3]   [0, 10, 1] by [0, 30, 3]

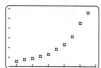   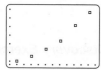

These data are nonlinear.   This model is accurate for only the first three planets.

(c) The model $y = x^{1.5}$ fits the data quite well. **(d)** The orbit for Neptune is approximately 165.1 years. The orbit for Pluto is approximately 247.3 years.

4. **(a)** [1890, 2000, 20] by [0, 60, 10]

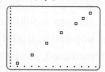

These data are nonlinear. **(b)** $k \approx 0.006$ **(c)** In 2005, the number of women in the work force will be about 71.5 million.

5. **(a)** [1993, 2005, 1] by [45, 115, 10]

These data are nonlinear shown in graph.

(b) $k \approx 0.7$ **(c)** In 2006, about 150.8 thousand Americans will be older than 100.

6. **(a)** [15, 75, 5] by [700, 2600, 100]

As x increases, y increases. These are roughly linear data.
(b) $y = 33.6(x - 20) + 810$ (*answers may vary*)
(c) The minimum sight distance for a car traveling 56 mph is about 2020 feet.

CHAPTER 6: RATIONAL EXPRESSIONS AND FUNCTIONS

Section 6.1

19.   **20.**

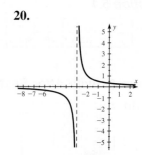

21.   **22.**

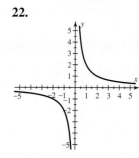

23.   **24.**

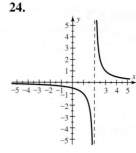

25.   **26.**

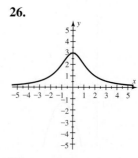

27.   **28.**

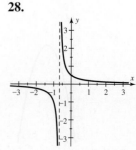

71. (b)

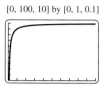

X	Y1
100	25.4
150	16.933
200	12.7
250	10.16
300	8.4667
350	7.2571
400	6.35

Y1■2540/X

74. (b)

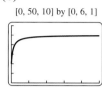

X	Y1	Y2
0	85.714	85.714
.05	75	100
.1	66.667	120
.15	60	150
.2	54.545	200
.25	50	300
.3	46.154	600

X=0

48. (c)

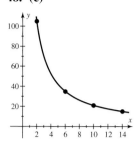

50. (c)

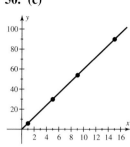

77. (b)

[0, 100, 10] by [0, 1, 0.1]

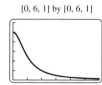

78. (b)

[0, 50, 10] by [0, 6, 1]

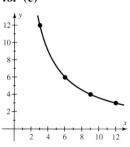

61. (b)

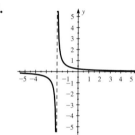

63. (b)

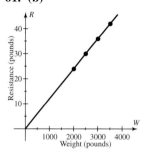

Group Activity After Section 6.1

(a)

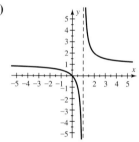

Chapter 6 Review Exercises

3.

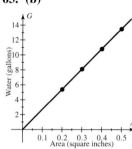

Checking Basic Concepts 6.1 & 6.2

1.   (c)

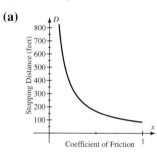

90. (a)

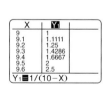

X	Y1
9	1
9.1	1.1111
9.2	1.25
9.3	1.4286
9.4	1.6667
9.5	2
9.6	2.5

Y1■1/(10−X)

92. (b)

[0, 6, 1] by [0, 6, 1]

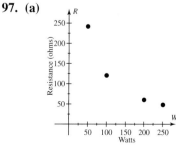

Section 6.6

45. (c)

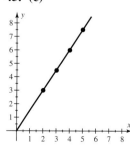

46. (c)

97. (a)

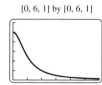

Chapter 6 Test

3.

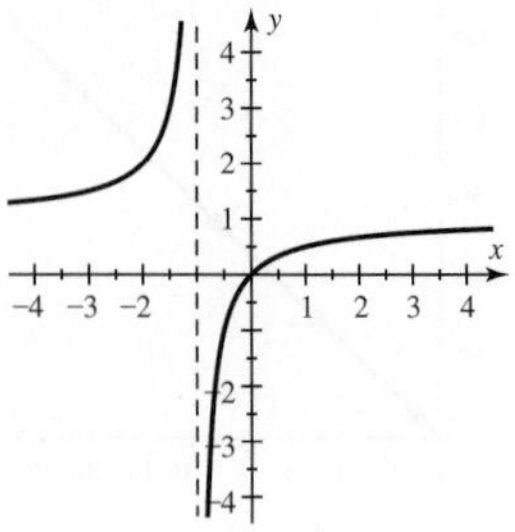

18. (a) [0, 25, 5] by [0, 2, 0.5]

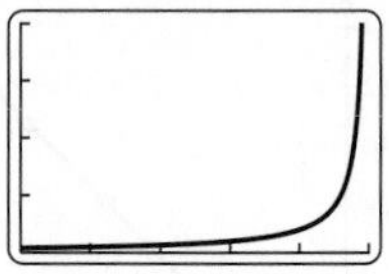

17.

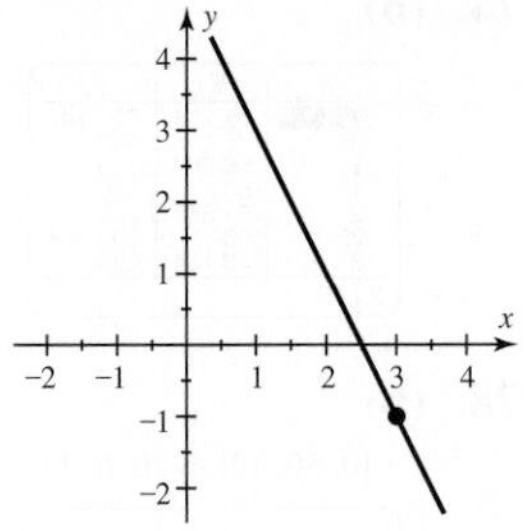

26.

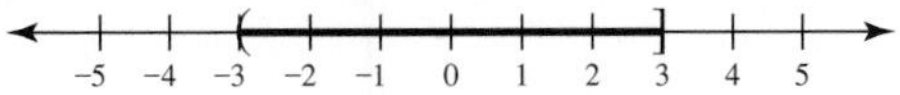

27.

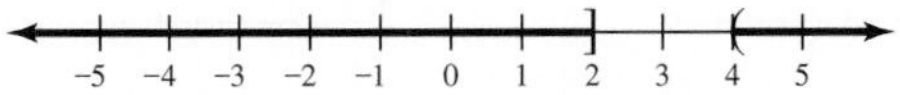

32.

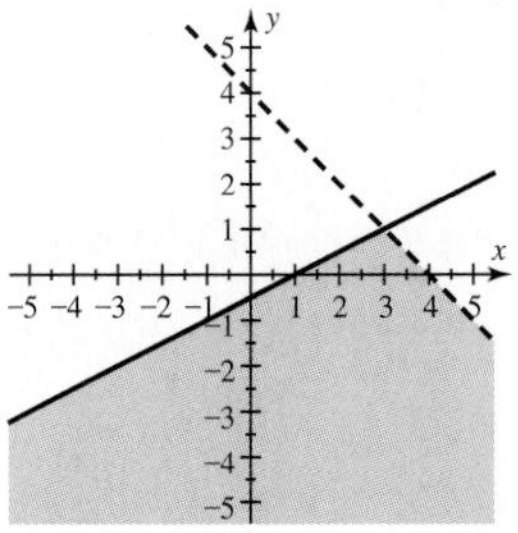

61. (a)

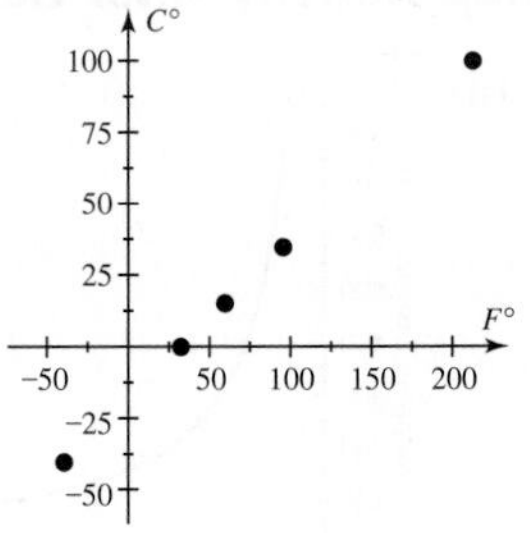

Chapter 6 Extended and Discovery Exercises

9. (b) [0, 10000, 1000] by [0, 200, 50]

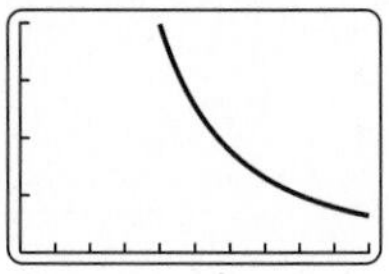

10. (b) [0, 5, 1] by [0, 30, 5]

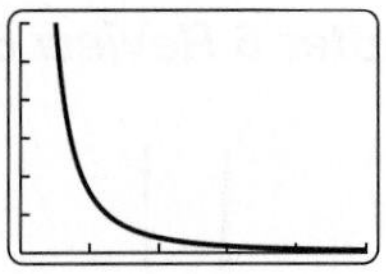

Chapters 1–6 Cumulative Review Exercises

9.

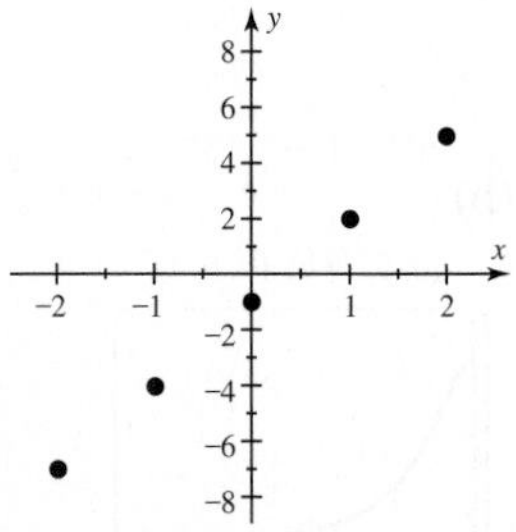

10.

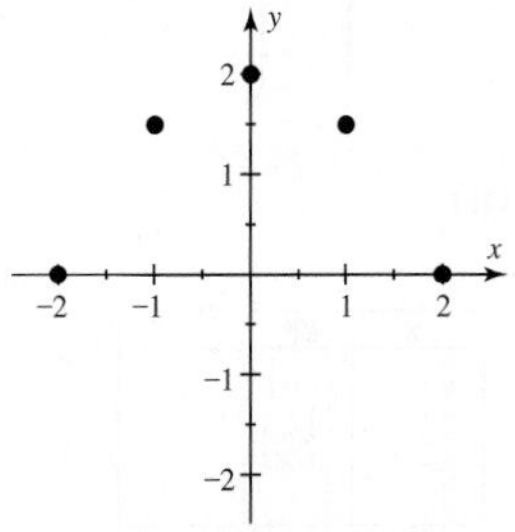

11.

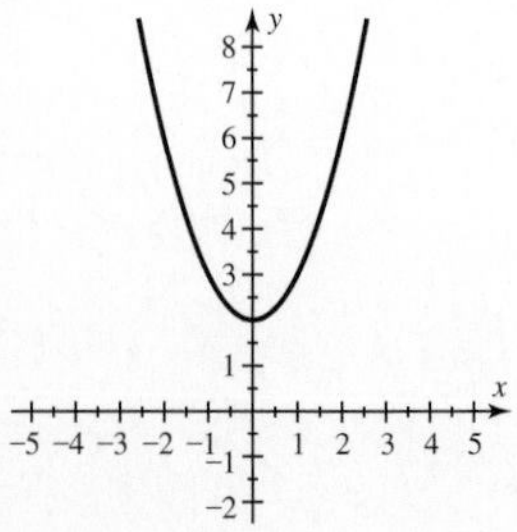

14.

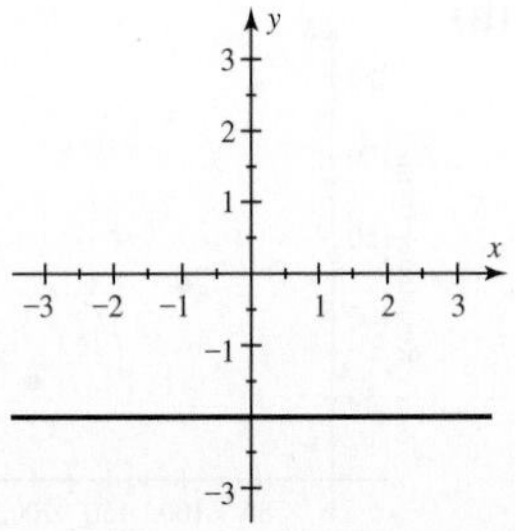

CHAPTER 7: RADICAL EXPRESSIONS AND FUNCTIONS

Section 7.4

1.

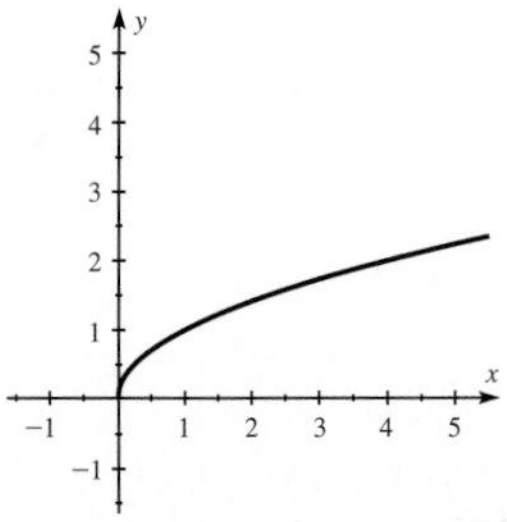

2.

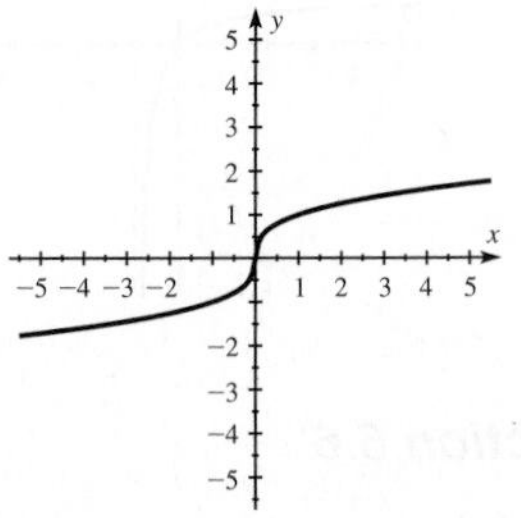

41.

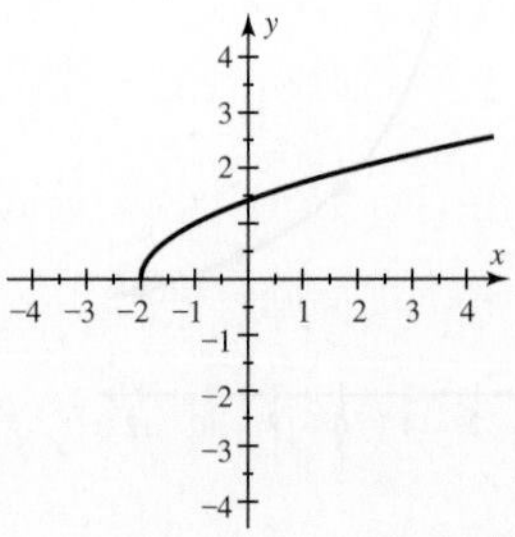

42.

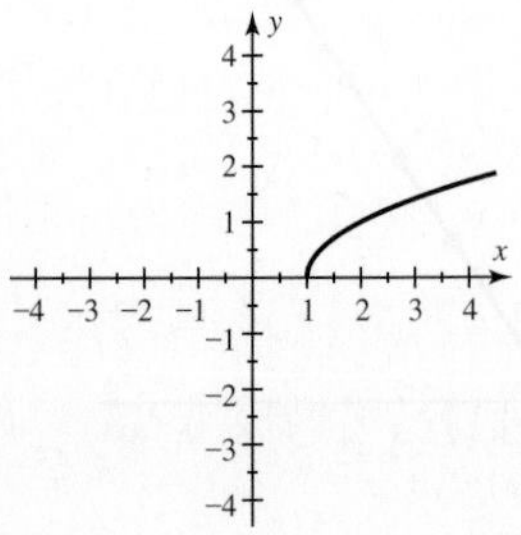

43.

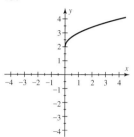

44.

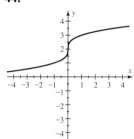

(c)

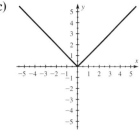

45.

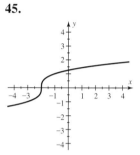

46.

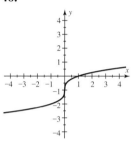

Chapter 7 Review Exercises

61.

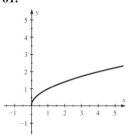

62.

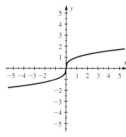

55.

[0, 6, 1] by [0, 6, 1]

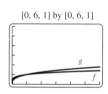

56.

[0, 6, 1] by [0, 6, 1]

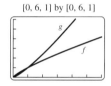

63.

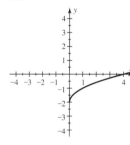

64.

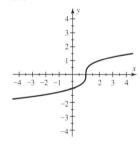

57.

[0, 6, 1] by [0, 6, 1]

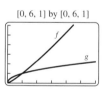

58.

[0, 6, 1] by [0, 6, 1]

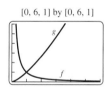

Chapter 7 Test

10.

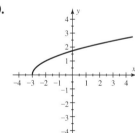

64. (b)

[0, 1.5, 0.1] by [0, 1, 0.1]

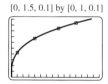

65. (b)

[0, 1600, 400] by [0, 220, 20]

Checking Basic Concepts 7.3 & 7.4

5. (a)

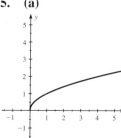

(b)

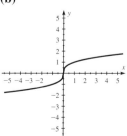

Chapter 7 Extended and Discovery Exercises

1.

[0, 2000, 500] by [0, 20, 2]

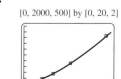

4. (e)

[0, 1000, 100] by [40000, 60000, 5000]

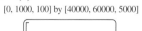

CHAPTER 8: QUADRATIC FUNCTIONS AND EQUATIONS

Section 8.1

5.

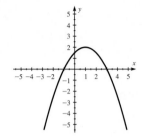

19. (a)

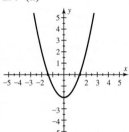

(b) $(0, -2); x = 0$
(c) $2; 7$

20. (a)

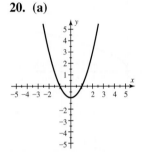

(b) $(0, -1); x = 0$
(c) $3; 8$

21. (a)

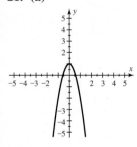

(b) $(0, 1); x = 0$
(c) $-11; -26$

22. (a)

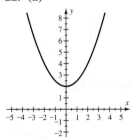

(b) $(0, 2); x = 0$
(c) $4; 6.5$

23. (a)

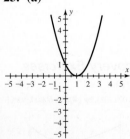

(b) $(1, 0); x = 1$
(c) $9; 4$

24. (a)

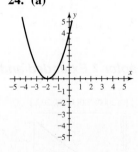

(b) $(-2, 0); x = -2$
(c) $0; 25$

25. (a)

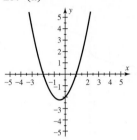

(b) $(-0.5, -2.25); x = -0.5$
(c) $0; 10$

26. (a)

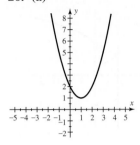

(b) $(1, 1); x = 1$
(c) $10; 5$

27. (a)

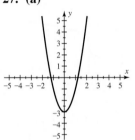

(b) $(0, -3); x = 0$
(c) $5; 15$

28. (a)

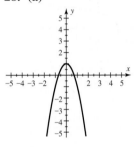

(b) $(0, 1); x = 0$
(c) $-7; -17$

29. (a)

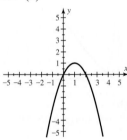

(b) $(1, 1); x = 1$
(c) $-8; -3$

30. (a)

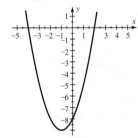

(b) $(-1, -9); x = -1$
(c) $-8; 7$

31. (a)

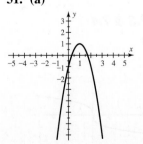

(b) $(1, 1); x = 1$
(c) $-17; -7$

32. (a)

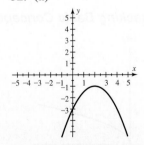

(b) $(2, -1); x = 2$
(c) $-9; -1.5$

33. (a)

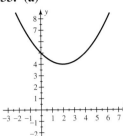

34. (a)

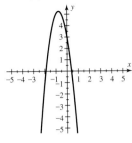

75. (a)

[20, 40, 5] by [0, 30, 5]

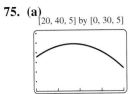

(b) $(2, 4)$; $x = 2$

(c) 8; 4.25

(b) $(-0.75, 5.25)$; $x = -0.75$

(c) -1; -51

Section 8.2

43.

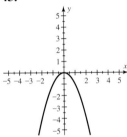

44.

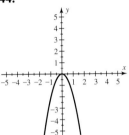

9. (a)

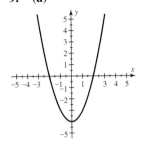

10. (a)

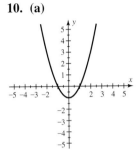

(b) $(0, -4)$

(c) Down 4 units

(b) $(0, -1)$

(c) Down 1 unit

45.

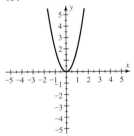

46.

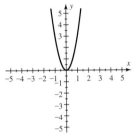

11. (a)

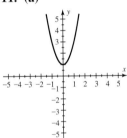

12. (a)

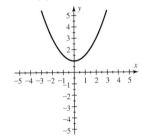

(b) $(0, 1)$

(c) Narrower and up 1 unit

(b) $(0, 1)$

(c) Wider and up 1 unit

47.

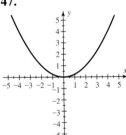

48.

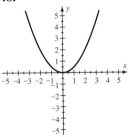

13. (a)

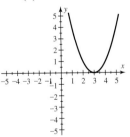

14. (a)

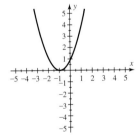

49.

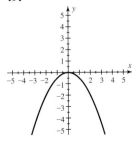

50.

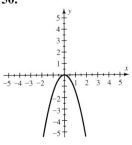

(b) $(3, 0)$

(c) Right 3 units

(b) $(-1, 0)$

(c) Left 1 unit

15. (a)

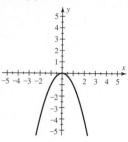

(b) $(0, 0)$
(c) Reflected across the x-axis

16. (a)

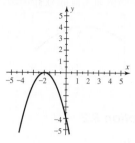

(b) $(-2, 0)$
(c) Reflected across the x-axis and left 2 units

23. (a)

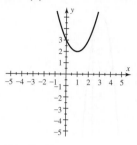

(b) $(1, 2)$
(c) Right 1 unit and up 2 units

24. (a)

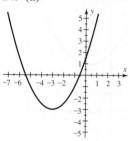

(b) $(-3, -3)$
(c) Wider, left 3 units and down 3 units

17. (a)

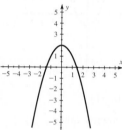

(b) $(0, 2)$
(c) Reflected across the x-axis and up 2 units

18. (a)

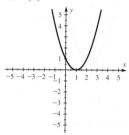

(b) $(1, 0)$
(c) Right 1 unit

25. (a)

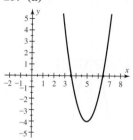

(b) $(5, -4)$
(c) Narrower, right 5 units and down 4 units

26. (a)

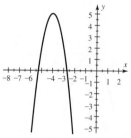

(b) $(-4, 5)$
(c) Narrower, reflected across the x-axis, left 4 units and up 5 units

19. (a)

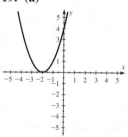

(b) $(-2, 0)$
(c) Left 2 units

20. (a)

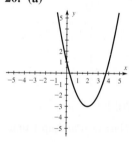

(b) $(2, -3)$
(c) Right 2 units and down 3 units

27. (a)

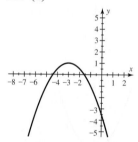

(b) $(-3, 1)$
(c) Wider, reflected across the x-axis, left 3 units and up 1 unit

28. (a)

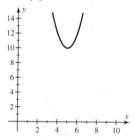

(b) $(5, 10)$
(c) Narrower, right 5 units and up 10 units

21. (a)

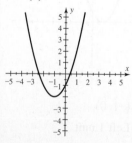

(b) $(-1, -2)$
(c) Left 1 unit and down 2 units

22. (a)

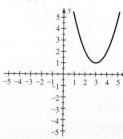

(b) $(3, 1)$
(c) Right 3 units and up 1 unit

63. (a)

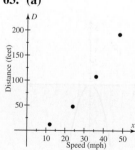

64. (a)

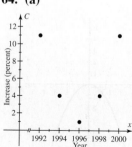

Checking Basic Concepts 8.1 & 8.2

1. (a)

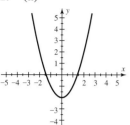

(b)

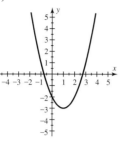

4. (a)

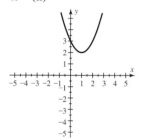

(b)

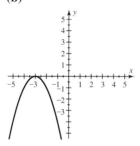

Section 8.3

4.

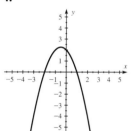

5.

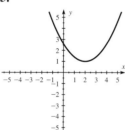

Group Activity After Section 8.3

(a) [1930, 2010, 10] by [0, 6, 1]

Chapter 8 Review Exercises

3. (a)

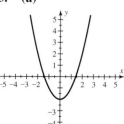

4. (a)

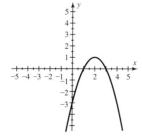

5. (a)

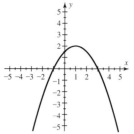

6. (a)

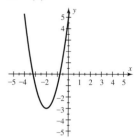

13. (a)

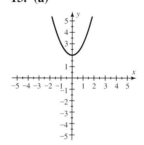

14. (a)

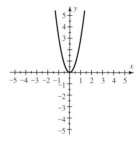

15. (a)

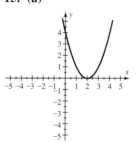

16. (a)

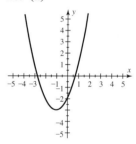

17. (a)

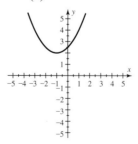

18. (a)

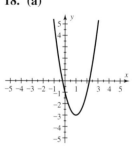

85. (b)

[0, 30, 5] by [0, 800, 100]

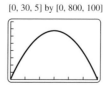

86. (b)

[1997, 1999, 1] by [0.5, 3, 0.5]

89. (a)

[1935, 1995, 10] by [0, 100, 10]

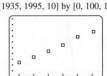

90. (b)

[1950, 1970, 5] by [200, 350, 25]

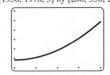

3. (a)

[−4, 4, 1] by [0, 6, 1]

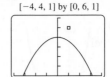

(b)

[−4, 4, 1] by [0, 6, 1]

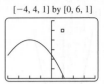

Chapter 8 Test

4.

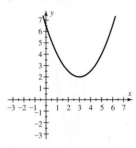

19. (a)   [0, 6, 1] by [0, 150, 50]

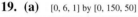

Chapter 8 Extended and Discovery Exercises

1. (a) For the first 3 years of life, the likelihood of survival increases with age. After 3 years of life, it decreases with age.

(b) A quadratic function could model the data since the data points resemble a parabolic shape.

[0, 10, 1] by [0, 75, 5]

(c) f_2 models the data better.

[0, 10, 1] by [0, 75, 5]   [0, 10, 1] by [0, 75, 5]

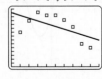

(d) $f_2(6.5) \approx 56.7\%$

2. (a) [−5, 35, 5] by [0, 100, 10]

CHAPTER 9: EXPONENTIAL AND LOGARITHMIC FUNCTIONS

Section 9.1

51. $(f \circ f^{-1})(x) = 4\left(\dfrac{x}{4}\right) = x; \ (f^{-1} \circ f)(x) = \dfrac{4x}{4} = x$

52.–58. Show $(f \circ f^{-1})(x) = (f^{-1} \circ f)(x) = x$.
See the answer to Exercise 51 above.

75.

x	0	5	10	15	20
$f^{-1}(x)$	0	1	2	3	4

76.

x	1	2	3	4	5
$f^{-1}(x)$	−4	−2	0	2	4

77.

x	4	2	0	−2	−4
$f^{-1}(x)$	−5	0	5	10	15

78.

x	8	6	4	2	0
$f^{-1}(x)$	0	2	4	6	8

79.

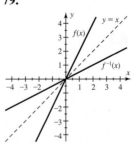

80.

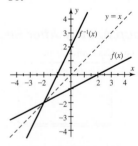

81.

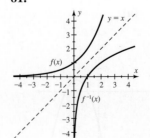

82.

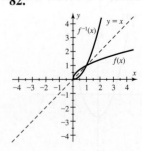

86. (a) $U(2) = 3$; there is a 3% increase in UV radiation when there is a 2% decrease in the thickness of the ozone layer. $C(3) = 10.5$; there is a 10.5% increase in skin cancer cases when the UV radiation level increases by 3%.
(b) $(C \circ U)(2) = 10.5$; there is a 10.5% increase in skin cancer cases when there is a 2% decrease in the thickness of the ozone layer.
(c) $(C \circ U)(x) = 5.25x$; it calculates the percent increase in skin cancer cases when the thickness of the ozone layer decreases by x percent.

87. (b)

x	8	16	27
$P^{-1}(x)$	1960	1980	2000

88. (b)

x	20	26	29	43
$P^{-1}(x)$	1970	1980	1990	2000

Section 9.2

2.
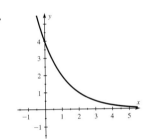

35.
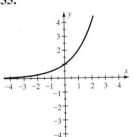

36.
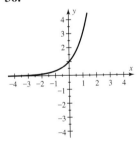

37.
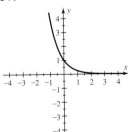

38.
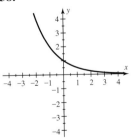

39.
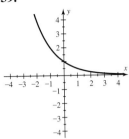

40.
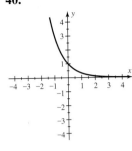

41.
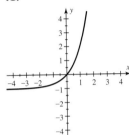

42.
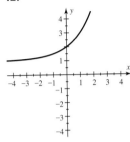

43.
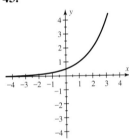

44.
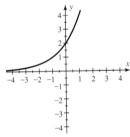

45.
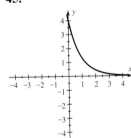

46.
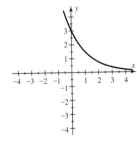

71. $[-4, 4, 1]$ by $[0, 8, 1]$
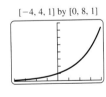

72. $[-4, 4, 1]$ by $[0, 8, 1]$
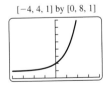

73. $[-4, 4, 1]$ by $[0, 8, 1]$
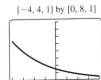

74. $[-4, 4, 1]$ by $[0, 8, 1]$
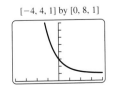

75. (b)

[0, 10, 1] by [4, 7, 1]

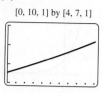

76. (a)

[0, 20000, 5000] by [0, 12, 1]

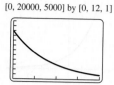

81.

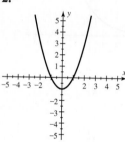

X	Y₁
0	1
10	.36854
20	.13582
30	.05006
40	.01845
50	.0068
60	.00251

Y₁ ■(0.905)^X

82. (a) $P(10) \approx 0.32$; there is a 32% chance that a randomly chosen point in the forest will not have a tree within 10 feet; $P(20) \approx 0.10$ and $P(30) \approx 0.03$ may be interpreted similarly.
(b) The probability decreases; trees are generally closely spaced in a forest; finding a large area in the forest that contains no trees is unlikely.

Checking Basic Concepts 9.1 & 9.2

2.

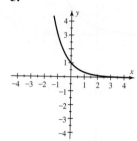

5.

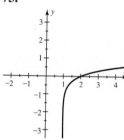

Section 9.3

61. [−4, 4, 1] by [−4, 4, 1]

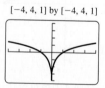

62. [−4, 4, 1] by [−4, 4, 1]

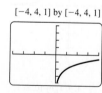

63. [−4, 4, 1] by [−4, 4, 1]

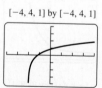

64. [−4, 4, 1] by [−4, 4, 1]

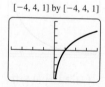

69.

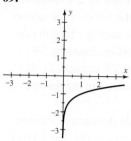

70.

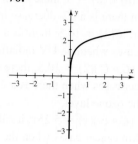

71.

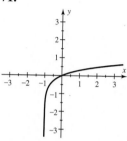

72.

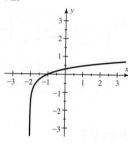

73.

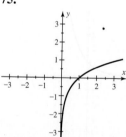

74.

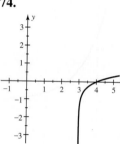

75.

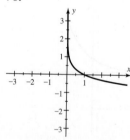

76.

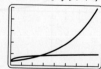

87. (a) $f(50) \approx 1.89$; in 2000 the population of less industrialized urban regions was 1.89 billion. $g(50) \approx 0.95$; in 2000 the population of industrialized urban regions was 0.95 billion.

(b) [0, 80, 10] by [0, 5, 1]

The population of less industrialized urban regions grew faster than the population of industrialized urban regions.

88. (b) [1, 10, 1] by [−160, −120, 10]

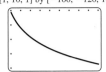

Group Activity After Section 9.3

(b) [0, 250, 50] by [0, 1000, 100]

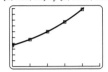

Section 9.4

65. [−6, 6, 1] by [−4, 4, 1]   [−6, 6, 1] by [−4, 4, 1]

66. [−6, 6, 1] by [−4, 4, 1]   [−6, 6, 1] by [−4, 4, 1]

67. [−6, 6, 1] by [−4, 4, 1]   [−6, 6, 1] by [−4, 4, 1]

68. [−6, 6, 1] by [−4, 4, 1]   [−6, 6, 1] by [−4, 4, 1]

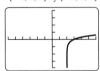 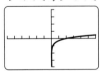

Checking Basic Concepts 9.3 & 9.4

2.

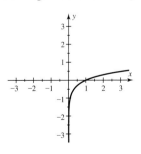

Section 9.5

96. (b)

x	1	2	4	8	16
$y = 1000 + 500\log_2 x$	1000	1500	2000	2500	3000

104. (a)
$$160 + 10\log 10x = 160 + 10(\log 10 + \log x)$$
$$= 160 + 10(1 + \log x)$$
$$= 160 + 10 + 10\log x)$$
$$= 170 + 10\log x$$

Chapter 9 Review Exercises

15.

x	10	8	7	3
$f^{-1}(x)$	0	1	2	3

16.

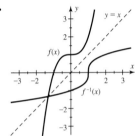

21.

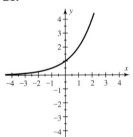

22.

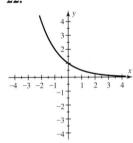

23.

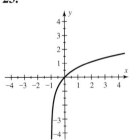

24.

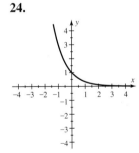

79. (a) [0, 10, 2] by [0, 4, 1]

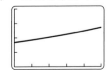

Chapter 9 Test

5.

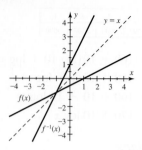

6.

x	8	6	4	2
$f^{-1}(x)$	1	2	3	4

8.

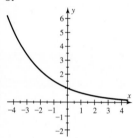

16.

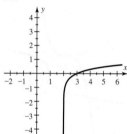

Chapter 9 Extended and Discovery Exercises

5.   [0, 25, 5] by [0, 0.11, 0.01]

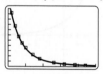
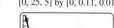
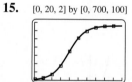

13.   [0, 20, 2] by [0, 700, 100]

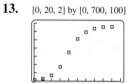

15.   [0, 20, 2] by [0, 700, 100]

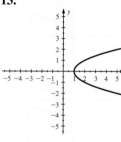

Chapters 1–9 Cumulative Review Exercises

14.

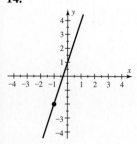

25.

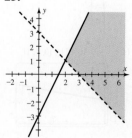

CHAPTER 10: CONIC SECTIONS

Section 10.1

4.

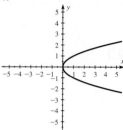

11.

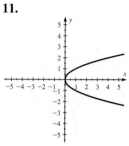

12.

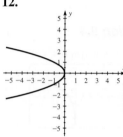

13.

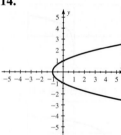

14.

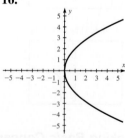

15.

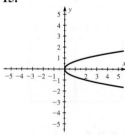

16.

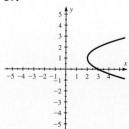

17.

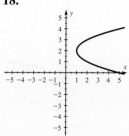

18.

19.

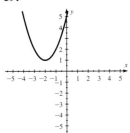

20.

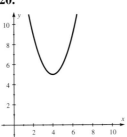

29.

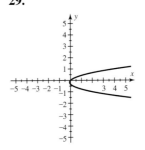

30.

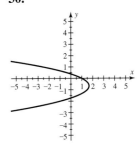

21.

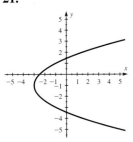

22.

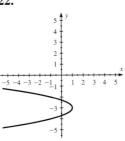

55.

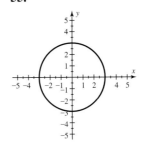

56.

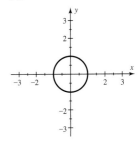

23.

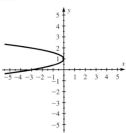

24.

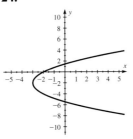

57.

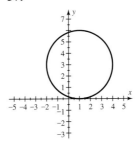

58.

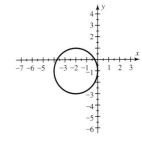

25.

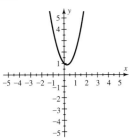

26.

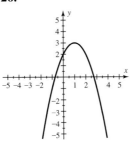

59.

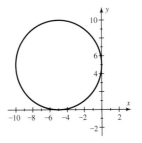

60.

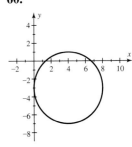

27.

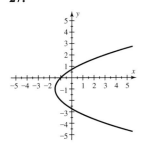

28.

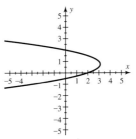

61.

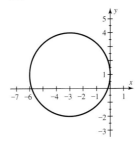

62.

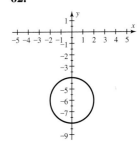

63.

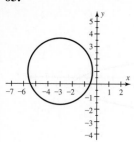

64.

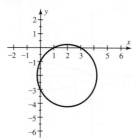

13.

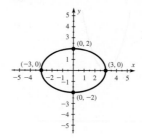

14.

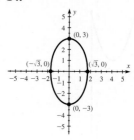

65. (a)

[−40, 40, 10] by [−120, 120, 20]

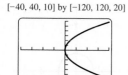

67. (a)

[−1.5, 1.5, 0.5] by [−1, 1, 0.5]

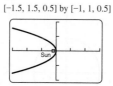

15.

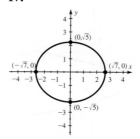

16.

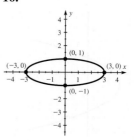

Group Activity After Section 10.1

(b)

[−50, 50, 10] by [−180, 180, 20]

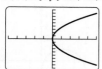

17.

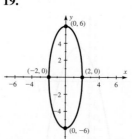

18.

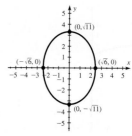

Section 10.2

1.

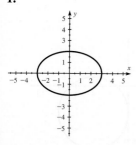

2.

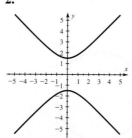

19.

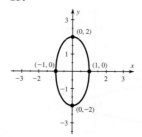

20.

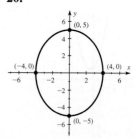

11.

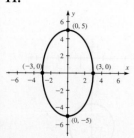

12.

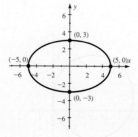

21.

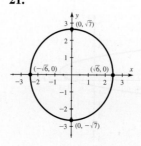

22.

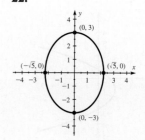

27.

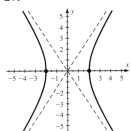

28.

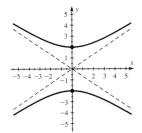

37.

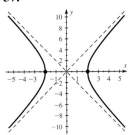

38.

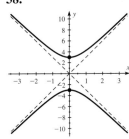

29.

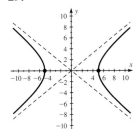

30.

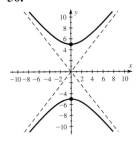

45. (a)

[−60, 60, 10] by [−40, 40, 10]

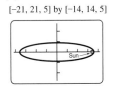

46. (a)

[−21, 21, 5] by [−14, 14, 5]

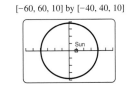

Checking Basic Concepts 10.1 & 10.2

31.

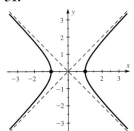

32.

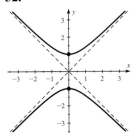

1.

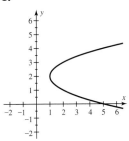

2.

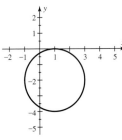

33.

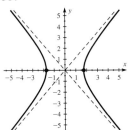

34.

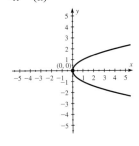

4. (a)

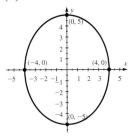

(b)

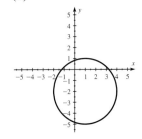

35.

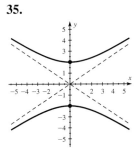

36.

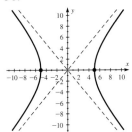

(c)

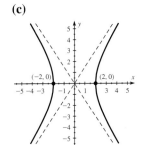

(d)

Section 10.3

7.

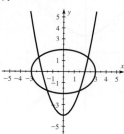

8.

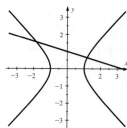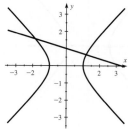

27.

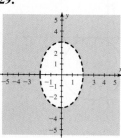

28.

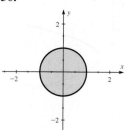

29.

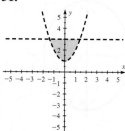

30.

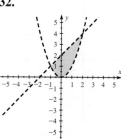

31.

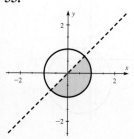

32.

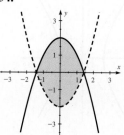

33.

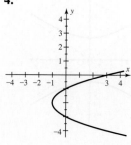

34.

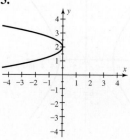

35.

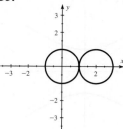

36.

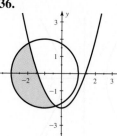

37.

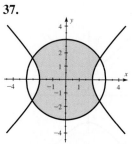

38.

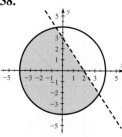

Checking Basic Concepts 10.3

4.

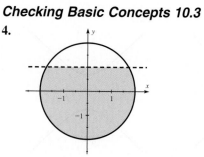

Chapter 10 Review Exercises

1.

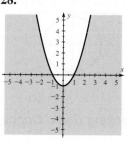

2.

3.

4.

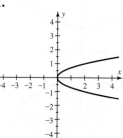
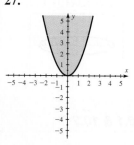
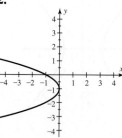

5.

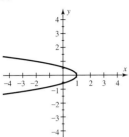

6.

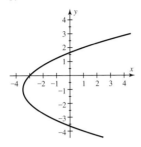

21.

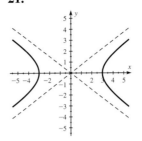

22.

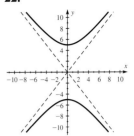

11.

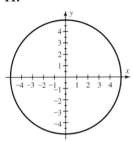

12.

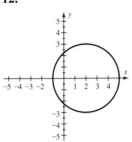

23.

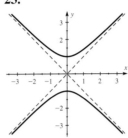

24.

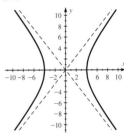

13.

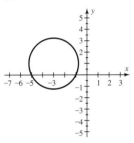

14.

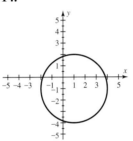

37.

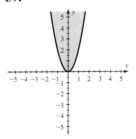

38.

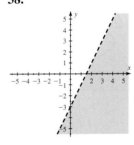

15.

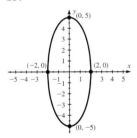

16.

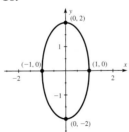

39.

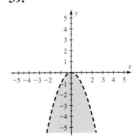

40.

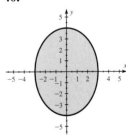

17.

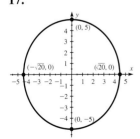

18.

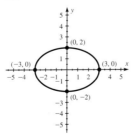

41.

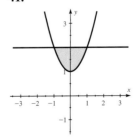

42.

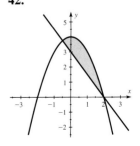

43.

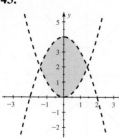

44.

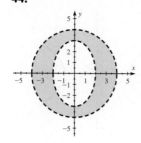

51. (a) [−7.5, 7.5, 1] by [−5, 5, 1]

52. (a) [−3, 3, 1] by [−2, 2, 1]

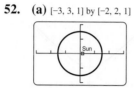

Chapter 10 Test

1.

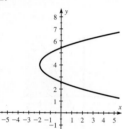

5.

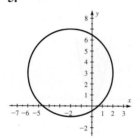

6.

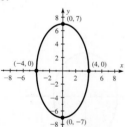

8.

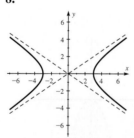

12.

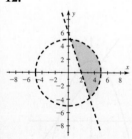

16. (a) [−30, 30, 10] by [−20, 20, 10]

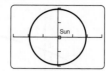

Chapter 10 Extended and Discovery Exercises

1. (a)

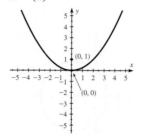

(b)

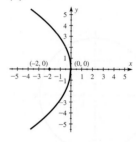

(c)

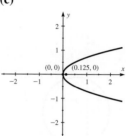

3. (a)

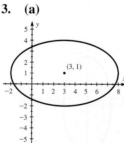

(b)

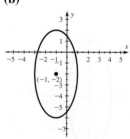

(c)

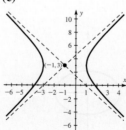

(d)

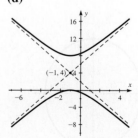

CHAPTER 11: SEQUENCES AND SERIES

Section 11.1

31.

n	1	2	3	4	5	6	7
a_n	2	3	4	5	6	7	8

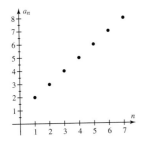

32.

n	1	2	3	4	5	6	7
a_n	0	0.5	1	1.5	2	2.5	3

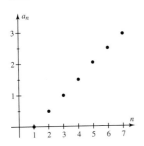

33.

n	1	2	3	4	5	6	7
a_n	0	2	6	12	20	30	42

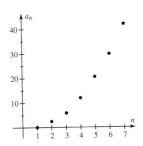

34.

n	1	2	3	4	5	6	7
a_n	0.5	2	4.5	8	12.5	18	24.5

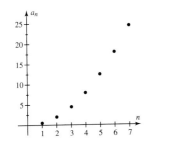

35.

n	1	2	3	4	5	6	7
a_n	2	4	8	16	32	64	128

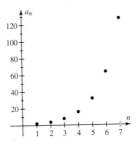

36.

n	1	2	3	4	5	6	7
a_n	1	0.5	0.25	0.125	0.0625	0.0313	0.0156

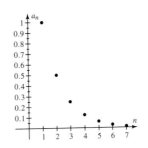

37.

n	1	2	3	4	5	6	7
a_n	30	60	90	120	150	180	210

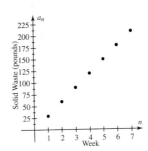

38.

n	1	2	3	4	5
a_n	5.8	11.6	17.4	23.2	29

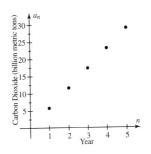

40.

n	1	2	3	4	5
a_n	50,000	54,000	58,320	62,986	68,024

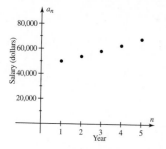

41. (c)

n	1	2	3	4	5	6	7
a_n	20,000	16,000	12,800	10,240	8192	6553.6	5242.9

43. (a)

n	1	2	3	4	5	6	7
a_n	50	55	60	65	70	75	80

(d)

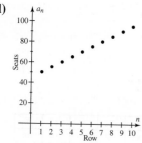

44. (b)

n	1	2	3	4	5	6	7
a_n	2048	1024	512	256	128	64	32

(c)

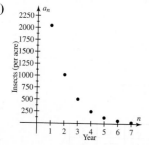

Section 11.2

65. (d)

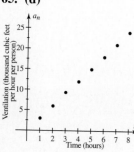

66. (b)

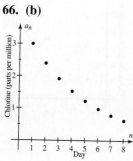

69. (d)

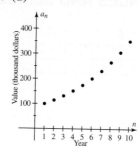

Checking Basic Concepts 11.1 & 11.2

2.

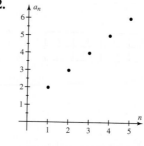

n	1	2	3	4	5
a_n	2	3	4	5	6

Section 11.3

39. $\displaystyle\sum_{k=1}^{n} k = 1 + 2 + 3 + \cdots + n$

$$= n\left(\frac{a_1 + a_n}{2}\right)$$

$$= n\left(\frac{1 + n}{2}\right)$$

$$= \frac{n(n+1)}{2}$$

Section 11.4

4.

```
            1
         1     1
      1     2     1
   1     3     3     1
1     4     6     4     1
```

Chapter 11 Review Exercises

7.

n	1	2	3	4	5	6	7
a_n	2	4	6	8	10	12	14

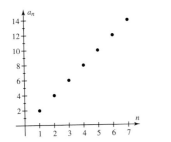

8.

n	1	2	3	4	5	6	7
a_n	−3	0	5	12	21	32	45

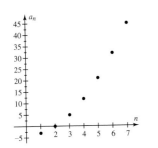

9.

n	1	2	3	4	5	6	7
a_n	2	1	0.5	0.25	0.125	0.0625	0.0313

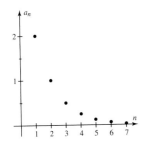

10.

n	1	2	3	4	5	6	7
a_n	1	1.4142	1.7321	2	2.2361	2.4495	2.6458

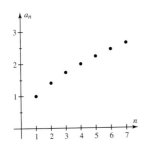

55.

n	1	2	3	4	5	6	7
a_n	45,000	49,500	54,450	59,895	65,885	72,473	79,720

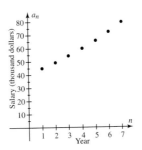

56.

n	1	2	3	4	5	6	7
a_n	45,000	50,000	55,000	60,000	65,000	70,000	75,000

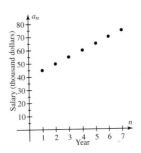

57.

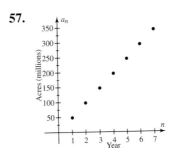

n	1	2	3	4	5	6	7
a_n	49	98	147	196	245	294	343

58.

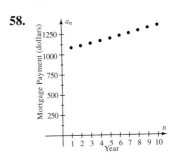

Chapter 11 Test

3.

n	1	2	3	4	5	6	7
a_n	0	2	6	12	20	30	42

18.

n	1	2	3	4	5	6	7
a_n	159,700	166,088	172,732	179,641	186,826	194,299	202,071

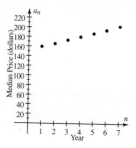

19. (d)

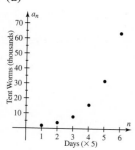

Chapter 11 Extended and Discovery Exercises

2. (a)

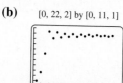

The population density of the winter moth increases and then begins to oscillate. Eventually it approaches a constant number of about 9.74 thousand per acre.

(b) [0, 22, 2] by [0, 11, 1]

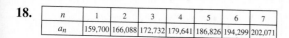

The moth population increases at first and then oscillates until it approaches a constant number of about 9.74 thousand per acre.

Chapters 1–11 Cumulative Review Exercises

20.

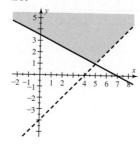

55.

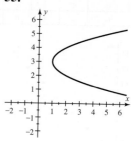

57.

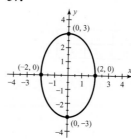

58.

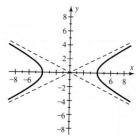

62.

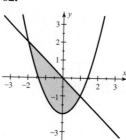

74.

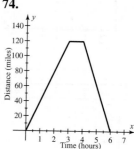

Bibliography

Baase, S. *Computer Algorithms: Introduction to Design and Analysis.* 2nd ed. Reading, Mass.: Addison-Wesley Publishing Company, 1988.

Battan, L. *Weather in Your Life.* San Francisco: W. H. Freeman, 1983.

Beckmann, P. *A History of PI.* New York: Barnes and Noble, Inc., 1993.

Brown, D., and P. Rothery. *Models in Biology: Mathematics, Statistics and Computing.* West Sussex, England: John Wiley and Sons Ltd, 1993.

Callas, D. *Snapshots of Applications in Mathematics.* Deli, New York: State University College of Technology, 1994.

Carr, G. *Mechanics of Sport.* Champaign, Ill.: Human Kinetics, 1997.

Conquering the Sciences. Sharp Electronics Corporation, 1986.

Elton, C. S., and M. Nicholson. "The ten year cycle in numbers of lynx in Canada." *J. Anim. Ecol.* 11 (1942): 215–244.

Eves, H. *An Introduction to the History of Mathematics,* 5th ed. Philadelphia: Saunders College Publishing, 1983.

Freedman, B. *Environmental Ecology: The Ecological Effects of Pollution, Disturbance, and Other Stresses.* 2nd ed. San Diego: Academic Press, 1995.

Friedhoff, M., and W. Benzon. *The Second Computer Revolution: Visualization.* New York: W. H. Freeman, 1991.

Garber, N., and L. Hoel. *Traffic and Highway Engineering.* Boston, Mass.: PWS Publishing Co., 1997.

Goldstein, M., and J. Larson. *Jackie Joyner-Kersee: Superwoman.* Minneapolis: Lerner Publications Company, 1994.

Grigg, D. *The World Food Problem.* Oxford: Blackwell Publishers, 1993.

Haefner, L. *Introduction to Transportation Systems.* New York: Holt, Rinehart and Winston, 1986.

Harrison, F., F. Hills, J. Paterson, and R. Saunders. "The measurement of liver blood flow in conscious calves." *Quarterly Journal of Experimental Physiology* 71: 235–247.

Historical Topics for the Mathematics Classroom, Thirty-first Yearbook. National Council of Teachers of Mathematics, 1969.

Horn, D. *Basic Electronics Theory.* Blue Ridge Summit, Penn.: TAB Books, 1989.

Howells, G. *Acid Rain and Acid Waters.* 2nd ed. New York: Ellis Horwood, 1995.

Karttunen, H., P. Kroger, H. Oja, M. Poutanen, K. Donner, eds. *Fundamental Astronomy.* 2nd ed. New York: Springer-Verlag, 1994.

Kincaid, D., and W. Cheney. *Numerical Analysis.* Pacific Grove, Calif.: Brooks/Cole Publishing Company, 1991.

Kraljic, M. *The Greenhouse Effect.* New York: The H. W. Wilson Company, 1992.

Lack, D. *The Life of a Robin.* London: Collins, 1965.

Lancaster, H. *Quantitative Methods in Biological and Medical Sciences: A Historical Essay.* New York: Springer-Verlag, 1994.

Mannering, F., and W. Kilareski. *Principles of Highway Engineering and Traffic Analysis.* New York: John Wiley and Sons, 1990.

Mar, J., and H. Liebowitz. *Structure Technology for Large Radio and Radar Telescope Systems.* Cambridge, Mass.: The MIT Press, 1969.

Meadows, D. *Beyond the Limits.* Post Mills, Vermont: Chelsea Green Publishing Co., 1992.

Miller, A., and J. Thompson. *Elements of Meteorology.* 2nd ed. Columbus, Ohio: Charles E. Merrill Publishing Company, 1975.

Miller, A., and R. Anthes. *Meteorology.* 5th ed. Columbus, Ohio: Charles E. Merrill Publishing Company, 1985.

Monroe, J. *Steffi Graf.* Mankato, Minn.: Crestwood House, 1988.

Motz, L., and J. Weaver. *The Story of Mathematics.* New York: Plenum Press, 1993.

Nemerow, N., and A. Dasgupta. *Industrial and Hazardous Waste Treatment.* New York: Van Nostrand Reinhold, 1991.

Nicholson, A. J. "An Outline of the dynamics of animal populations." *Austr. J. Zool.* 2 (1935): 9–65.

Nielson, G., and B. Shriver, eds. *Visualization in Scientific Computing.* Los Alamitos, Calif.: IEEE Computer Society Press, 1990.

Nilsson, A. *Greenhouse Earth.* New York: John Wiley and Sons, 1992.

Paetsch, M. *Mobile Communications in the U.S. and Europe: Regulation, Technology, and Markets.* Norwood, Mass.: Artech House, Inc., 1993.

Pearl, R., T. Edwards, and J. Miner. "The growth of *Cucumis melo* seedlings at different temperatures." *J. Gen. Physiol.* 17: 687–700.

Pennycuick, C. *Newton Rules Biology.* New York: Oxford University Press, 1992.

Pielou, E. *Population and Community Ecology: Principles and Methods.* New York: Gordon and Breach Science Publishers, 1974.

Pokorny, C., and C. Gerald. *Computer Graphics: The Principles behind the Art and Science.* Irvine, Calif.: Franklin, Beedle, and Associates, 1989.

Ronan, C. *The Natural History of the Universe.* New York: MacMillan Publishing Company, 1991.

Sharov, A., and I. Novikov. *Edwin Hubble, The Discoverer of the Big Bang Universe.* New York: Cambridge University Press, 1993.

Smith, C. *Practical Cellular and PCS Design.* New York: McGraw-Hill, 1998.

Stent, G. S. *Molecular Biology of Bacterial Viruses.* San Francisco: W. H. Freeman, 1963.

Taylor, J. *DVD Demystified.* New York: McGraw-Hill, 1998.

Taylor, W. *The Geometry of Computer Graphics.* Pacific Grove, Calif.: Wadsworth and Brooks/Cole, 1992.

Thomas, D. *Swimming Pool Operators Handbook.* National Swimming Pool Foundation of Washington, D.C., 1972.

Thomas, V. *Science and Sport.* London: Faber and Faber, 1970.

Thomson, W. *Introduction to Space Dynamics.* New York: John Wiley and Sons, 1961.

Toffler, A., and H. Toffler. *Creating a New Civilization: The Politics of the Third Wave.* Kansas City, Mo.: Turner Publications, 1995.

Triola, M. *Elementary Statistics.* 7th ed. Reading, Mass.: Addison-Wesley Publishing Company, 1998.

Tucker, A., A. Bernat, W. Bradley, R. Cupper, and G. Scragg. *Fundamentals of Computing I Logic: Problem Solving, Programs, and Computers.* New York: McGraw-Hill, 1995.

Turner, R. K., D. Pierce, and I. Bateman. *Environmental Economics, An Elementary Approach.* Baltimore: The Johns Hopkins University Press, 1993.

Varley, G., and G. Gradwell. "Population models for the winter moth." *Symposium of the Royal Entomological Society of London* 4: 132–142.

Wang, T. *ASHRAE Trans.* 81, Part 1 (1975): 32.

Weidner, R., and R. Sells. *Elementary Classical Physics,* Vol. 2. Boston: Allyn and Bacon, Inc., 1965.

Williams, J. *The Weather Almanac 1995.* New York: Vintage Books, 1994.

Wright, J. *The New York Times Almanac 1999.* New York: Penguin Group, 1998.

Zeilik, M., S. Gregory, and D. Smith. *Introductory Astronomy and Astrophysics.* 3rd ed. Philadelphia: Saunders College Publishers, 1992.

Index

Videotape and CD Index

Section	Exercise Numbers	Example Numbers	Section	Exercise Numbers	Example Numbers
1.1	21, 45, 47, 53, 55, 61, 63, 65, 69, 91	—	7.1	65	—
1.2	67, 105	—	7.2	11, 25, 35, 39, 77, 81, 97, 101	—
1.3	27, 37a, 51a, 53a, 93	—	7.3	1, 9, 31, 47, 49, 57, 61, 65, 75	—
1.4	5, 6, 7, 13, 17, 23, 25, 27, 29, 43, 61	—	7.4	15, 47	—
1.5	—	—	7.5	31	—
			7.6	21, 25, 29, 31, 33	1, 4, 5
2.1	19	—			
2.2	7, 9, 11, 25, 33, 39, 42, 53, 55, 73	—	8.1	19, 25, 47, 69	2, 3, 6
2.3	31	—	8.2	21, 43, 49, 57, 59	1, 3
2.4	31, 49	—	8.3	43, 47, 61, 90a	—
			8.4	9, 15, 33, 55, 67	1
3.1	15, 17, 35, 65, 79	3, 5, 9	8.5	53	—
3.2	5, 7, 27, 29	3, 6, 8	8.6	2, 11, 15, 19, 21	1
3.3	17	—			
3.4	37, 39	—	9.1	23, 45, 69, 77	1, 4, 7, 8
3.5	7, 15, 21, 29, 39, 53, 91	—	9.2	9, 11, 13, 17, 21, 23, 57, 75	—
			9.3	29	—
4.1	—	—	9.4	11, 13, 17, 19, 31, 33, 41, 43	7, 8, 9
4.2	9, 17, 35, 43, 45	3, 6, 11	9.5	15, 23, 47, 57, 67, 87, 95, 99	—
4.3	17, 19, 33, 37, 51, 53	—			
4.4	29, 37	1, 2	10.1	13, 17, 47, 59, 61	—
4.5	23	—	10.2	—	—
4.6	13	—	10.3	15	—
4.7	3, 9, 11, 19, 23, 31	—			
			11.1	33	—
5.1	23, 29, 49, 63, 79, 85	1, 7, 10, 12	11.2	35, 57, 71	—
5.2	11, 19, 31, 35, 47, 61, 77, 87	—	11.3	11, 15, 19, 23, 27, 33, 37, 47	—
5.3	81	—	11.4	47	—
5.4	35	—			
5.5	11, 19, 49, 53, 67, 73	1, 4, 6			
5.6	7, 11, 15, 33, 55	5, 7			
6.1	45	—			
6.2	9, 17, 51, 55, 77, 85	1, 6, 10			
6.3	21, 25, 29, 41, 43	1, 5, 6			
6.4	9, 13, 17, 21, 45, 59, 67a,b	—			
6.5	17, 25, 29, 33, 35, 43	—			
6.6	27, 29, 71	—			
6.7	17, 23, 31, 33, 37, 47, 53	—			

Library of Functions
Basic Functions

Several important functions are used in algebra. The following provides symbolic, numerical, and graphical representations for several of these basic functions.

Absolute Value Function: $f(x) = |x|$

x	-2	-1	0	1	2
$|x|$	2	1	0	1	2

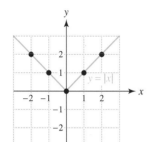

Domain: $(-\infty, \infty)$
Range: $[0, \infty)$

Square Function: $f(x) = x^2$

x	-2	-1	0	1	2
x^2	4	1	0	1	4

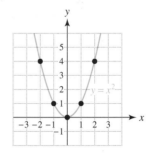

Domain: $(-\infty, \infty)$
Range: $[0, \infty)$

Cube Function: $f(x) = x^3$

x	-2	-1	0	1	2
x^3	-8	-1	0	1	8

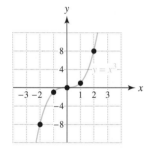

Domain: $(-\infty, \infty)$
Range: $(-\infty, \infty)$

Square Root Function: $f(x) = \sqrt{x}$

x	0	1	4	9
$\sqrt{x}$	0	1	2	3

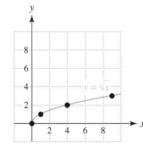

Domain: $[0, \infty)$
Range: $[0, \infty)$

Cube Root Function: $f(x) = \sqrt[3]{x}$

x	-8	-1	0	1	8
$\sqrt[3]{x}$	-2	-1	0	1	2

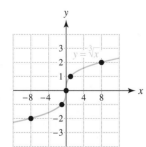

Domain: $(-\infty, \infty)$
Range: $(-\infty, \infty)$

Reciprocal Function: $f(x) = \dfrac{1}{x}$

x	-2	-1	0	1	2
$\dfrac{1}{x}$	$-\dfrac{1}{2}$	-1	—	1	$\dfrac{1}{2}$

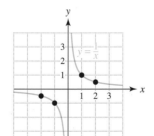

Domain: $(-\infty, 0) \cup (0, \infty)$
Range: $(-\infty, 0) \cup (0, \infty)$